Part III: Production and Cost

Chapter 7: Production Economics

Chapter 8: Cost Analysis

Chapter 9: Applications of Cost Theory

Part IV: Pricing and Output Decisions: Strategy and Tactics

Chapter 10: Prices, Output, and Strategy: Pure and Monopolistic Competition

11th Edition

Managerial Economics

Applications, Strategy, and Tactics

James R. McGuigan

JRM Investments

R. Charles Moyer

University of Louisville

Frederick H. deB. Harris

Babcock Graduate School of Management

Wake Forest University

THOMSON

SOUTH-WESTERN

Australia · Brazil · Canada · Mexico · Singapore · Spain · United Kingdom · United States

THOMSON
SOUTH-WESTERN

Managerial Economics: Applications, Strategy, and Tactics, 11th Edition
James R. McGuigan, R. Charles Moyer, and Frederick H. deB. Harris

VP/Editorial Director
Jack W. Calhoun

Editor-in-Chief
Alex von Rosenberg

Senior Acquisitions Editor
Steven Scoble

Developmental Editor
Amy Ray

Associate Marketing Manager
Jennifer Garamy

Content Project Manager
Kelly Hoard

Technology Project Manager
Dana Cowden

Marketing Coordinator
Courtney Wolstoncraft

Senior Frontlist Buyer
Sandee Milewski

Art Director
Michelle Kunkler

Internal and Cover Designer
Beckmeyer Design
Cincinnati, Ohio

Cover Images
© ImageDJ/Alamy

Production House:
LEAP Publishing Services, Inc.

Compositor
ICC Macmillan Inc.

Printer
Transcontinental
Louiseville, Canada

Printed in Canada
1 2 3 4 5 10 09 08 07

Student Edition ISBN 13:
978-0-324-42160-6

Student Edition ISBN 10:
0-324-42160-5

Library of Congress Control Number:
2007901208

For more information about our products, contact us at:

Thomson Learning Academic Resource Center

1-800-423-0563

Thomson Higher Education
5191 Natorp Boulevard
Mason, OH 45040
USA

To my family
J.R.M.

To Sally, Laura, and Craig
R.C.M.

To my family, Roger Sherman, and Ken Elzinga
F.H.B.H.

BRIEF CONTENTS

CONTENTS

CONTENTS

CONTENTS

CONTENTS

CONTENTS

CONTENTS

PREFACE

Organization of the Text

Responding to user feedback, the succinct new 11th edition has been shortened and streamlined. The book thoroughly covers key topics, while less-used material is now found on the textbook's Web site to give the instructors optimal flexibility in their course coverage. Part I of the book provides an overview of managerial economics, establishes shareholder wealth as an objective, and introduces the fundamental economic concepts of demand and supply, marginal analysis, net present value, risk and decision analysis. Part II examines the areas of demand analysis and forecasting techniques in domestic and export markets. A unique feature of the book is an extensive chapter on international business economics, import/export trade, and an introduction to international finance. In this edition, we have added new material on China, India, and the global marketplace so students get an understanding of the global economic environment and what they must do as managers to maximize efficiency and shareholder wealth in this new competitive landscape.

Part III deals with production and cost analysis, including linear programming concepts for the production process choices that characterize real-world operations management. Part IV focuses on price determination and capacity choice in theory and practice. The strategic framework of Michael Porter and the new tactical insights from sequential business games are highlighted. The unique features here include more extensive material on applied game theory than in other managerial economics books and an extensive treatment of revenue management in the chapter on pricing. Part V includes coverage of corporate governance, auction design, information economics, choice of organization form, and economic regulation including an extensive discussion of externalities and optimal abatement of externalities. A final chapter addresses the techniques of capital budgeting from the theory of corporate finance.

Although the primary focus of the book is on private sector management, we recognize that many students of economics and business management pursue careers in the public and not-for-profit sectors of the economy. Consequently, we have included a discussion of the philosophy of public involvement in the economy, the objective of public and not-for-profit organizations, and coverage of specific analytical tools that are of use in these sectors.

Student Preparation

The text is designed for use by upper-level undergraduates and first-level graduate students in business schools, departments of economics, graduate schools of management, public administration, and information technology. Students are presumed to have a background in the basic principles of economics. Prior course work in statistics and quantitative methods is desirable but not essential because all of the concepts employed in the text or Web appendices are fully developed within the text. The book makes occasional use of elementary concepts of differential calculus after a review of these basic concepts. However, in all cases where calculus is employed, one or more alternative approaches, such as graphical, algebraic, or tabular analysis, are also presented. Spreadsheet applications have become so prominent in the practice of managerial economics that we now explain many concepts of optimization in this context.

PREFACE

PEDAGOGICAL FEATURES OF THE 11TH EDITION

The eleventh edition of *Managerial Economics* makes extensive use of pedagogical learning aids to enhance student learning. The key features of the book are:

1. **Part Openers.** Each major section of the book opens with a brief discussion of the material contained in the following chapters. The relationship of the material in the section to the goal of shareholder wealth maximization and efficient resource allocation is illustrated with a schematic diagram appearing on the first page of each part opener.
2. **Managerial Challenges.** Each chapter opens with a Managerial Challenge illustrating a real-life economic analysis problem faced by managers that is related to the material to be covered in the chapter. Many of these challenges have been updated with more contemporary illustrations.
3. **What Went Right/What Went Wrong.** Most chapters contain one (or more) What Went Right/What Went Wrong features that allow students to relate real-world business decisions to what they have learned, and to show how management decisions can have positive and negative outcomes.
4. **Chapter Glossaries.** In the margins of the text, new terms are defined as they are introduced. The placement of the glossary terms next to the location where the term is first used reinforces the importance of these new concepts and aids in later studying.
5. **Chapter Preview.** Each chapter begins with a Chapter Preview that briefly summarizes the major issues that are covered in the chapter.
6. **International Perspectives.** Throughout the book, special International Perspectives sections are provided that illustrate the application of managerial economics concepts to problems faced by managers in an increasingly global economy.
7. **Extensive Use of Examples.** More than 300 real-world applications and examples derived from actual practice are provided and highlighted throughout the text. These examples help the tools and concepts to come alive and thereby enhance student learning. They are listed on the inside front and back covers to highlight the prominence of this feature of the book.
8. **Point-by-Point Summaries.** Each chapter ends with a detailed, point-by-point summary of important concepts from the chapter.
9. **Diversity of Presentation Approaches.** Important analytical concepts are presented in several different ways, including tabular analysis, graphical analysis, and algebraic analysis. Again, when elementary differential calculus is used, at least one alternative mode of analysis also is presented for the student.
10. **Exercises.** Each chapter contains a large problem analysis set. Check answers to selected problems color-coded in blue, boldface type are provided at the end of the text. Problems that can be solved using Excel are highlighted with an Excel icon.
11. **Short Case Exercises.** Many chapters include short case problems that extend the concepts and tools developed in the text.

Ancillary Materials

A complete set of ancillary materials is available to adopters to supplement the text, including the following:

Instructor's Manual and Test Bank

Prepared by the authors, the instructor's manual and test bank that accompanies the book contains suggested answers to the end-of-chapter exercises and cases. The authors have taken great care to provide an error-free manual for instructors to use. The manual is available both in a hard copy form and on the book's Web site (www.thomsonedu.com/economics/mcguigan) in MS Word to make it easy for instructors to provide portions of these solutions to students, if they desire. The Test Bank, containing a large collection of true-false, multiple-choice, and numerical problems, is available to adopters. The Test Bank is also available on the Web site.

ExamView

Simplifying the preparation of quizzes and exams, this easy-to-use test creation software includes all of the questions in the printed test bank and is compatible with Microsoft Windows. Instructors select questions by previewing them on the screen, choosing them randomly, or picking them by number. And they can easily add or edit questions, instructions, and answers. Quizzes can also be created and administered online, whether over the Internet, a local area network (LAN), or a wide area network (WAN).

Textbook Support Web Site

When you adopt *Managerial Economics: Applications, Strategy, and Tactics,* 11e, you and your students will have access to a rich array of teaching and learning resources that you won't find anywhere else. Located at www.thomsonedu.com/economics/mcguigan, this outstanding site features six additional Web Appendices including appendices on indifference curve analysis, international parity conditions, linear programming applications, a capacity planning case study, joint product pricing and transfer prices, and decision making under uncertainty. It also provides links to additional instructor and student resources, as well as a "Talk-to-the-Author" link.

PowerPoint Presentation

Available on the product companion Web site, this comprehensive package provides an excellent lecture aid for instructors. Prepared by Richard D. Marcus at the University of Wisconsin-Milwaukee, these slides cover many of the most important topics from the text, and they can be customized by instructors to meet specific course needs.

ThomsonNOW

Timesaving and efficient, ThomsonNOW customizes the learning curve for students and makes the path from assignment through grading and reporting quick and easy for instructors. Student-personalized learning plans lead them efficiently through textbook material, focusing on what each student still needs to learn—making every minute of study pay off. Students using ThomsonNOW overwhelmingly report that it helps them understand their course content better and score better on tests. Instructors love the effect assigning ThomsonNOW has on classroom participation and performance.

Economic Applications

Located at http://econapps.swlearning.com, this site includes South-Western's dynamic Web features: EconNews, EconDebate, and EconData Online. Organized by pertinent economic topics and searchable by topic or feature, these Web features are easy to integrate into the classroom. EconNews, EconDebate, and EconData all deepen your understanding of theoretical concepts through hands-on exploration and analysis for the latest economic news stories, policy debates, and data. These features are updated on a regular basis.

InfoTrac® College Edition

InfoTrac is a fully searchable online university library containing complete articles and their images. The database allows access to hundreds of scholarly and popular publications—all reliable sources—including magazines, journals, encyclopedias, and newsletters. If an access card came with this book, students can start using many of these resources right away by following the directions on the card.

Acknowledgments

A number of reviewers, users, and colleagues have been particularly helpful in providing us with many worthwhile comments and suggestions at various stages in the development of this and earlier editions of the book. Included among these individuals are:

William Beranek, J. Walter Elliott, William J. Kretlow, William Gunther, J. William Hanlon, Robert Knapp, Robert S. Main, Edward Sussna, Bruce T. Allen, Allen Moran, Edward Oppermann, Dwight Porter, Robert L. Conn, Allen Parkman, Daniel Slate, Richard L. Pfister, J. P. Magaddino, Richard A. Stanford, Donald Bumpass, Barry P. Keating, John Wittman, Sisay Asefa, James R. Ashley, David Bunting, Amy H. Dalton, Richard D. Evans, Gordon V. Karels, Richard S. Bower, Massoud M. Saghafi, John C. Callahan, Frank Falero, Ramon Rabinovitch, D. Steinnes, Jay Damon Hobson, Clifford Fry, John Crockett, Marvin Frankel, James T. Peach, Paul Kozlowski, Dennis Fixler, Steven Crane, Scott L. Smith, Edward Miller, Fred Kolb, Bill Carson, Jack W. Thornton, Changhee Chae, Robert B. Dallin, Christopher J. Zappe, Anthony V. Popp, Phillip M. Sisneros, George Brower, Carlos Sevilla, Dean Baim, Charles Callahan, Phillip Robins, Bruce Jaffee, Alwyn du Plessis, Darly Winn, Gary Shoesmith, Richard J. Ward, William H. Hoyt, Irvin Grossack, William Simeone, Satyajit Ghosh, David Levy, Audie Brewton, Simon Hakim, Patricia Sanderson, David P. Ely, Albert A. O'Kunade, Doug Sharp, Arne Dag Sti, Walker Davidson, David Buschena, George M. Radakovic, Harpal S. Grewal, Stephen J. Silver, Michael J. O'Hara, Luke M. Froeb, Dean Waters, Jake Vogelsang, Lynda Y. de la Viña, Audie R. Brewton, Paul M. Hayashi, Richard D. Marcus, Lawrence B. Pulley, Tim Mages, Paul M. Hayashi, Robert Brooker, Richard D. Evans, Carl Emomoto, William Simeone, Charles Leathers, Marshall Medoff, Gary Brester, Stephan Gohmann, L. Joe Moffitt, Satyajit Ghosh, Christopher Erickson, Antoine El Khoury, and Steven Rock.

PREFACE

People who were especially helpful in the preparation of the eleventh edition include Rajeev K. Goel, Lee S. Redding, Paul J. Hoyt, Bijan Vasigh, Cheryl A. Casper, Semoon Chang, Kwang Soo Cheong, Barbara M. Fischer, John A. Karikari, Richard D. Marcus, Francis D. Mummery, Lucjan T. Orlowski, Dennis Proffitt, and Steven S. Shwiff.

We are also indebted to Richard D. Marcus, Bob Hebert, Sarah E. Harris, Wake Forest University, and the University of Louisville for the support they provided and owe thanks to our faculty colleagues for the encouragement and assistance provided on a continuing basis during the preparation of the manuscript. We wish to express our appreciation to the members of the South-Western/Thomson Learning staff—particularly, Jenny Garamy, Amy Ray, Kelly Hoard, Steve Scoble, and Steve Momper—for their help in the preparation and promotion of this book. We are grateful to the Literary Executor of the late Sir Ronald A. Fisher, F.R.S.; to Dr. Frank Yates, F.R.S.; and to Longman Group, Ltd., London, for permission to reprint Table III from their book *Statistical Tables for Biological, Agricultural, and Medical Research* (6th ed., 1974).

James R. McGuigan
R. Charles Moyer
Frederick H. deB. Harris

ABOUT THE AUTHORS

JAMES R. MCGUIGAN

James R. McGuigan owns and operates his own numismatic investment firm. Prior to this activity, he was Associate Professor of Finance and Business Economics in the School of Business Administration at Wayne State University. He also taught at the University of Pittsburgh.

McGuigan received his undergraduate degree from Carnegie-Mellon University. He earned an M.B.A. at the Graduate School of Business at the University of Chicago and his Ph.D. from the University of Pittsburgh.

In addition to his interests in economics, he has co-authored books in financial management, including *Contemporary Financial Management,* with R. Charles Moyer. His research articles on options have been published in the *Journal of Financial and Quantitative Analysis.*

R. CHARLES MOYER

R. Charles Moyer is the dean of The College of Business at the University of Louisville. Previously, he held the GMAC Insurance Chair in Finance at the Babcock Graduate School of Management, Wake Forest University and was Professor of Finance and Chairman of the Department of Finance at Texas Tech University. Professor Moyer has also taught at the University of Houston, Lehigh University, and the University of New Mexico, and spent a year at the Federal Reserve Bank of Cleveland. Moyer earned his B.A. in Economics from Howard University and his M.B.A. and Ph.D. in Finance and Managerial Economics from the University of Pittsburgh. In addition to this text, Moyer has also co-authored *Contemporary Financial Management, Fundamentals of Contemporary Financial Management,* and *Financial Management with Lotus 1-2-3.* He has been published in many leading journals, including *Financial Management, Journal of Financial and Quantitative Analysis, Journal of Finance, Financial Review, Journal of Financial Research,* and *International Journal of Forecasting.*

FREDERICK H. deB. HARRIS

Frederick H. deB. Harris is the John B. McKinnon Professor of Managerial Economics and Finance at the Babcock Graduate School of Management, Wake Forest University. His specialties are pricing tactics and capacity planning. Professor Harris has taught managerial economics courses in three business schools in the United States and Europe. He holds a B.A. in Economics from Dartmouth College and a Ph.D. in Financial Economics from the University of Virginia.

Professor Harris has published widely in financial and economics journals including the *Review of Economics and Statistics, Journal of Financial and Quantitative Analysis, Journal of Financial Markets, Journal of Operations Management,* and *Journal of Industrial Economics.* From 1988 to 1993, he served on the Board of Associate Editors of the *Journal of Industrial Economics.* In addition, Professor Harris often benchmarks the revenue management functions of large companies and writes about his findings in management practice journals like *Marketing Management, Journal of Pricing,* and the *International Journal of Revenue Management.*

Awards and recognitions include two awards for "Best Academic Publication of the Year," Babcock School Professor of the Year, and Most Popular Courses designations. Additionally, *Inc.* magazine (2000) and *BusinessWeek's Guide to the Best Business Schools* (1997–2003) identify Professor Harris as among Outstanding Faculty.

PART I

Introduction

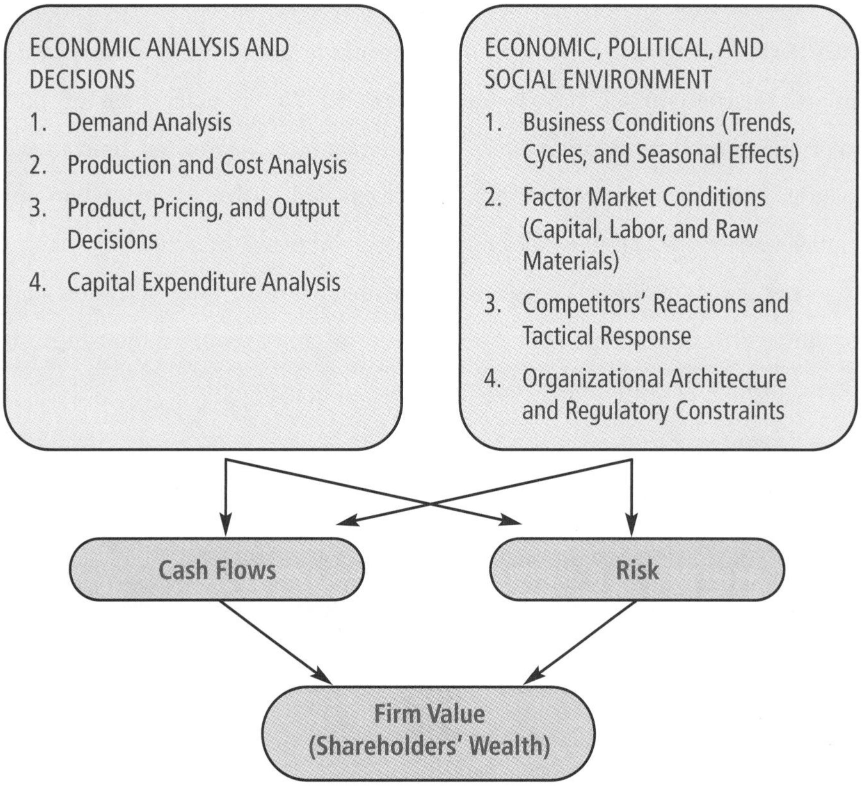

Part I (Introduction) presents an overview of managerial economics analysis and introduces some key economic concepts and tools. In the first chapter, the goals of the firm, the decision-making process, and the philosophy of optimization are introduced. The role of profit is explained, and the relationship between owner-principals and manager-agents is discussed. Chapter 2 reviews fundamental economic concepts, including marginal analysis, comparative statics of demand and supply, net present value, risk-return analysis, and the measurement of risk. Appendix 2A provides a self-contained introduction to optimization and constrained optimization techniques, including applications of basic calculus. Linear programming applications appear later to support the discussion of production and cost.

CHAPTER

1

INTRODUCTION AND GOALS OF THE FIRM

CHAPTER PREVIEW Managerial economics is the application of microeconomic theory and methodology to problems faced by decision makers in the private, public, and not-for-profit sectors. Managerial economics assists managers in efficiently allocating scarce resources, planning corporate strategy, and executing effective tactics. This chapter defines economic profit and examines the role of profits in allocating resources in a free enterprise system. The primary goal of the firm, namely, shareholder wealth maximization, is developed along with a discussion of how managerial decisions influence shareholder wealth. The problems associated with the separation of ownership and control and agency relationships in large corporations are explored.

MANAGERIAL CHALLENGE

Executive Performance Bonus Plan: General Electric[1]

Separation of ownership (shareholders) and control (management) in large corporations permits managers to pursue goals, such as maximization of their own personal welfare, that are not always in the long-term interests of shareholders. As a result of pressure from large institutional shareholders such as Fidelity Funds, statutes (Sarbanes-Oxley) that mandate stronger corporate governance, and federal tax laws that severely limit the deductibility of executive pay, a growing number of corporations seek to assure that a larger proportion of the manager's pay occurs in the form of performance-based bonuses. They are doing so by (1) tying executive bonuses to the performance of comparably situated competitor companies, (2) raising the performance hurdles that trigger executive bonuses, and (3) eliminating severance packages that provide windfalls for executives whose poor performance leads to a takeover or their own dismissal.

In 2005, CEOs of the 350 largest U.S. corporations were paid $6 million in median total direct compensation.[2] The 10 companies with the highest shareholder returns the last five years paid $10.6 million in salary, bonus, and long-term incentives. The 10 companies with the lowest shareholder returns the last five years paid $1.6 million. Figure 1.1 shows that across these 350 companies since 1999, the managerial incentive pay mirrored corporate profitability, spiking when profits grow and collapsing when profits decline.

General Electric CEO Jeff Immelt had a 2005 salary of $3.2 million, a cash bonus of $5.9 million, and gains on long-term incentives that converted to stock options of $3.8 million. GE distributes stock options to 45,000 of its 300,000 employees, but decided that half of CEO Jeff Immelt's 250,000 "performance share units" should only convert to stock options if GE cash flow grew

MANAGERIAL CHALLENGE

Figure 1.1 CEO Pay Trends

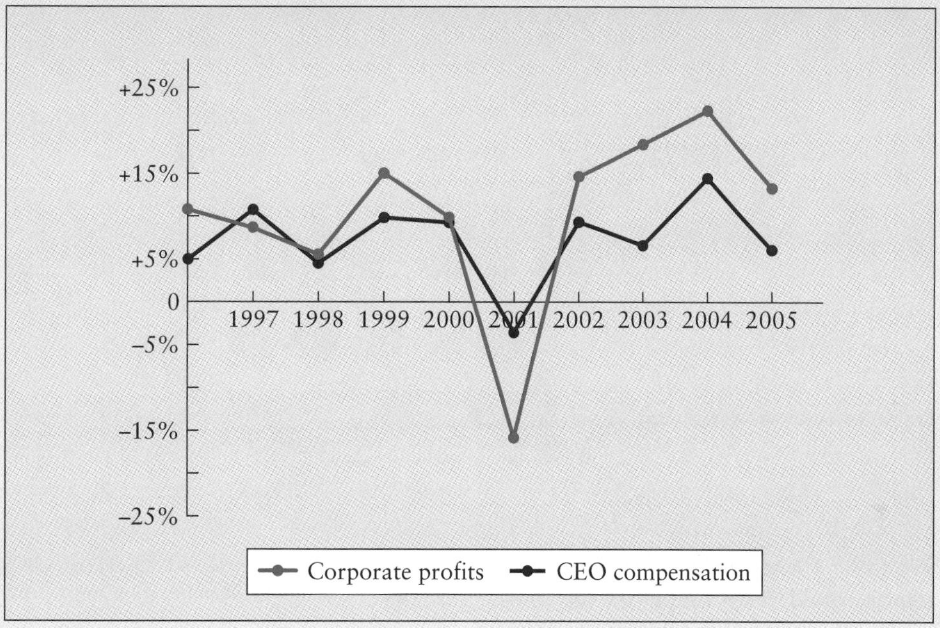

Source: Mercer Human Resource Consulting

at an average of 10 percent or more for five years, and the other half should convert only if GE shareholder return exceeded the five-year cumulative total return on the S&P 500 index.

In another performance-based executive contract, Salomon Brothers (the investment banking predecessor of Smith Barney) paid their chairperson, Deryck C. Maughan, an annual base salary of $1 million plus an annual performance bonus of up to $24 million. This bonus was based on Salomon's overall rate of return on equity and its rate of return *relative* to the firm's five major competitors.[3] The table at the top of the next page shows the possible performance bonuses that the chairperson could earn. For example, if Salomon's annual return on equity was 5 percent, and was not different from the average rate of return of the five rival investment banking firms, then the Salomon chairperson would earn no performance bonus. On the other hand, the payment of the maximum

$24 million bonus would require the firm to have an extraordinary year—Salomon's return on equity

MANAGERIAL CHALLENGE

Annual bonus, in millions of dollars

Salomon Brothers' return on equity minus the average of five competitors	5%	10%	15%	20%	25%	30%
+10	$1	$2.5	$7	$12	$17	$24
+5	$0.5	$2	$6	$9	$12	$17
0	$0	$1.5	$5	$7	$9	$12
-5	$0	$1	$4	$6	$8	$10
-10	$0	$0.5	$3	$4	$5	$7

Salomon Brothers' return on equity

Source: Salomon Brothers Inc. proxy statements, U.S. Securities and Exchange Commission

would have to be 30 percent (or more), and this rate of return would have to be 10 (or more) percentage points above the average of its five major competitors.

The objective of the firm and how to motivate managers to pursue this objective is the primary topic discussed in this chapter.

[1] Based on Mercer Human Resource Consulting, CEO Pay Survey, *The Wall Street Journal* (April 10, 2006), p. B7.

[2] Based on Jiann Lublin, "Goodbye to Pay for No Performance," *The Wall Street Journal* (April 11, 2005), p. R1. Kathryn Kranhold, "Sign of the Times: GE Chief Immelt," *The Wall Street Journal* (September 18, 2003), p. B1.

[3] These competitors are Merrill Lynch, Morgan Stanley, Bear Sterns, J. P. Morgan, and Bankers Trust.

WHAT IS MANAGERIAL ECONOMICS?

Managerial economics extracts from microeconomic theory those concepts and techniques that enable managers to select strategic direction, to allocate efficiently the resources available, and to respond effectively to tactical issues. All managerial decision making seeks to do the following:

> To identify the alternative means of achieving given objective(s), and then to select an alternative that accomplishes the objective(s) in the most resource-efficient manner, taking into account the constraints and the likely actions and reactions of rival decision makers.

For example, consider the following stylized decision problem:

EXAMPLE

CAPACITY EXPANSION AT HONDA, N.A., AND TOYOTA MOTORS, N.A.

Honda and Toyota are attempting to expand their already substantial assembly operations in North America. Both companies face increasing demand for their U.S.-manufactured vehicles, especially Toyota Camrys and Honda Accords. Camrys and Accords rate extremely high in consumer reports on durability and reliability. The demand for used Accords is so strong that they depreciate only 45 percent in their first four years. Other competing vehicles may depreciate as much as 65 percent in the same period. Toyota and Honda have identified two possible strategies (S1 and S2) to meet the growing demand for Camrys and Accords. Strategy S1 involves an internal expansion of capacity at Toyota's $700 million Princeton, Indiana, plant and Honda's Marysville, Ohio, plant. Strategy S2 involves the purchase and renovation of assembly plants now owned by General Motors. The new plants will likely receive substantial public subsidies through reduced property taxes. The older plants already possess an enormous infrastructure of local suppliers and regulatory relief.

The objective of Toyota's managers is to maximize the value today (present value) of the expected future returns (profit) from the expansion. This problem can be summarized as follows:

Objective function:	Maximize the present value (PV) of profit (S1, S2)
Decision rule:	Choose strategy S1 if PV(Profit S1) > PV(Profit S2)
	Choose strategy S2 if PV(Profit S1) < PV(Profit S2)

This simple illustration shows how resource-allocation decisions of managers attempt to maximize the value of their firms across forward-looking dynamic strategies for growth while respecting all ethical, legal, and regulatory constraints.

The Decision-Making Model

The ability to make good decisions is the key to successful managerial performance. All decision making shares several common elements. First, the decision maker must *establish the objectives of the organization*. Next, the decision maker must *identify the problem* requiring a solution. For example, the CEO of electronics retailer Circuit City may note that the profit margin on sales has been decreasing. This decrease could be caused by pricing errors, declining labor productivity, or the use of outdated retailing concepts. Once the source or sources of the problem are identified, the manager can move to an *examination of potential solutions*. The choice between these alternatives depends on an *analysis of the relative costs and benefits,* as well as other organizational and societal constraints that may make one alternative preferable to another.

The final step in the decision-making process, after all alternatives have been evaluated, is to analyze the best available alternative under a variety of changes in the assumptions before making a recommendation. This crucial final step is referred to as a *sensitivity analysis*. Knowing the limitations of the planned course of action as the decision environment changes, the manager can then proceed to an *implementation of the decision,* monitoring carefully any unintended consequences or unanticipated changes in the market. This six-step decision-making process is illustrated in Figure 1.2.

The Role of Profits

Economic Profit
The difference between total revenue and total economic cost. Economic cost includes a "normal" rate of return on the capital contributions of the firm's partners.

Economic profit is the difference between total revenue and total economic cost. *Total revenue* is measured as the sales receipts of a firm, that is, price times quantity sold. The *economic cost* of any activity may be thought of as the highest valued

Figure 1.2 The Decision-Making Process

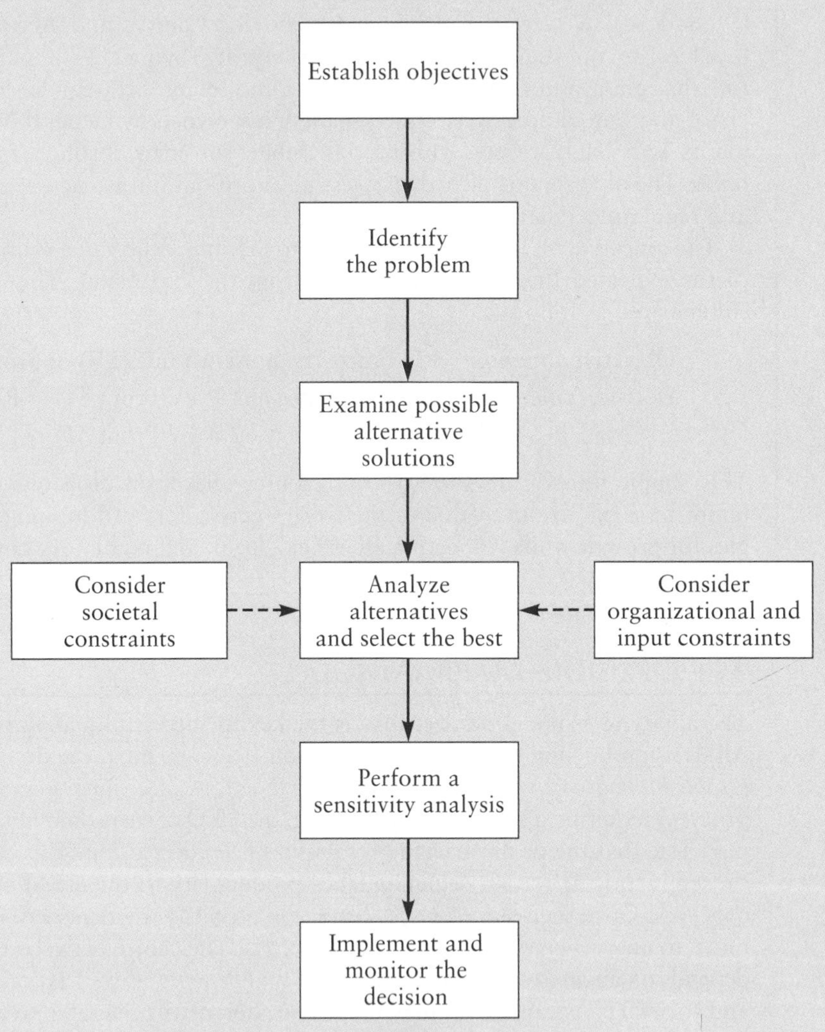

alternative opportunity that is forgone. To attract labor, capital, intellectual property, land, and materials, the firm must offer to pay a price that is sufficient to convince the owners of these resources to sacrifice other alternative activities and commit their resources to this use. Thus, economic costs may be thought of as *opportunity costs,* or the costs of attracting a resource from its next best alternative use. Accordingly, the term *economic cost* in this book refers to all costs, both explicit and implicit, including a normal return (profit) for owners of the resources. In a general sense, economic profit may be defined as the *difference between total revenue and total economic cost.* When we refer to profit maximization in this book, we mean an objective of maximizing this concept of economic profit of the firm.

WHY ARE PROFITS NECESSARY?

In a free enterprise system, economic profits play an important role in guiding the decisions made by the thousands of competing independent resource owners. The existence of profits determines the type and quantity of goods and services that are produced and sold, as well as the resulting derived demand for resources. Because of this important role played by profits, we will review several theories of profit.

RISK-BEARING THEORY OF PROFIT Some economists have argued that economic profits above a competitive rate of return are necessary to compensate the owners of the firm for the risk they assume when making their investments. Because a firm's shareholders are not entitled to a fixed rate of return on their investment—that is, they are claimants to the firm's residual cash flows after all contractual payments have been made—they need to be compensated for this risk in the form of a higher rate of return.

EXAMPLE

RISK AND PROFITABILITY: HARRAH'S

The relationship between risk and profit levels can be seen in the case of Harrah's, the hotel and casino operator. During 2002, Harrah's earned a return on net worth of 22.9 percent, compared with a mean return on net worth of 11 percent for all firms in the hotel and gaming industry, 2001–2005. Hotel and casino firms are subject to severe competitive pressures. MGM Mirage earned 11.2 percent on net worth in 2002, and Hilton earned 9.6 percent. The hotel and gaming industry also experiences substantial swings in profitability over time. The 22.9 percent return on net worth of Harrah's fell to 8.4 percent in 2005 while MGM Mirage's return rose to 14.8 percent. Firms that operate in a high-risk environment require the potential for high profits exhibited by Harrah's in 2002 in order to attract investment capital.

The risk-bearing theory of profits is explained in the context of normal profits, where *normal* is defined in terms of the relative risk of alternative investments. Normal profits for a high-risk firm, such as a casino operator, should be higher than normal profits for firms of lesser risk, such as water utilities. Indeed, the industry average return on net worth for the hotel and gaming industry was 12.6 percent in 2005, compared with 9 percent for the water utility industry.

TEMPORARY DISEQUILIBRIUM THEORY OF PROFIT According to the temporary disequilibrium theory of profit, all firms should tend to earn a long-run equilibrium normal rate of profit (adjusted for risk). At any point in time, however, an individual firm or the firms in a specific industry might earn a rate of return above or below this long-run normal return level. Higher or lower returns can occur because of temporary dislocations (shocks) in various sectors of the economy. For example, U.S. firms that produced oil and natural gas experienced a dramatic increase in profits in response to supply shortages following the invasion of Kuwait by Iraq in 1990 and during the general strike in Venezuela in 2002. Rates of return rose substantially. However, those high returns declined shortly after the war and strike ended, when market conditions led to excess supplies.

Similarly, if a new, inexpensive, and readily available energy source were to be discovered, oil prices would decline substantially. Over time, some producers would leave this increasingly unprofitable market until a normal rate of profit was restored for the remaining firms. The inability of our economic system to adjust instantaneously to changes in market conditions may result in short-term profits above or below normal levels.

Monopoly Theory of Profit In some industries, one firm is effectively able to dominate the market and potentially earn above-normal rates of return for a long period of time. This ability to dominate the market may arise from economies of scale (a situation in which one large firm can produce additional units of output at a lower cost than can smaller firms), control of essential natural resources, control of critical patents, or governmental restrictions that prohibit competition. The conditions under which a monopolist can earn above-normal profits are discussed in greater depth in Chapter 11.

Innovation Theory of Profit The innovation theory of profit suggests that above-normal profits are the reward for successful innovations. Firms that develop high-quality products (such as Porsche) or firms that successfully identify unique market opportunities (such as Microsoft) are rewarded with the potential for above-normal profits. Indeed, the U.S. patent system is designed to ensure that these above-normal return opportunities furnish strong incentives for continued innovation.

Managerial Efficiency Theory of Profit Closely related to the innovation theory is the managerial efficiency theory of profit. This theory maintains that above-normal profits can arise because of the exceptional managerial skills of well-managed firms. The ability to earn above-normal profits by exercising high-quality managerial skills is a continuing incentive for greater efficiency in any economic system.

No single theory of profit can explain the observed profit rates in each industry, nor are these theories necessarily mutually exclusive. Profit performance is invariably the result of many factors, including differential risk, innovation, managerial skills, the existence of monopoly power, and chance occurrences. The important thing to remember is that profit and profit opportunities play a major role in determining the efficient allocation of resources in any economy. Without the market signals that profits give, it would be necessary to develop alternative schemes on which to base resource-allocation decisions. These alternatives are often highly bureaucratic and frequently lack the responsiveness to changing market conditions that a free enterprise system provides.

Objective of the Firm

Managerial economic analysis focuses on the maximizing decisions of consumers and business firms. Economics assumes consumers deliberate over numerous possible purchases in order to secure their maximum total use value from constrained household budgets. Similarly, business firms are assumed to deliberate over numerous possible product offerings, manufacturing processes, pricing policies, and distribution channels in order to secure their maximum long-term profitability from constrained assets. Although these constrained optimization models yield many insights, they ignore spontaneous, impulsive consumer decisions that are more appropriately the subject of marketing and consumer psychology. In the same way, the simple profit-maximization model ignores the timing and risk of profit streams so prominent in the field of finance. Shareholder wealth-maximization as an objective of the firm overcomes both these limitations.

THE SHAREHOLDER WEALTH-MAXIMIZATION MODEL OF THE FIRM

Shareholder Wealth

A measure of the value of a firm. Shareholder wealth is equal to the value of a firm's common stock, which, in turn, is equal to the present value of all future cash returns expected to be generated by the firm for the benefit of its owners.

To maximize the value of the firm, managers should maximize shareholder wealth. **Shareholder wealth** is measured by the market value of a firm's common stock, which is equal to the present value of all expected future cash flows to equity owners (assumed for now to be equal to profits) discounted at the shareholders' required rate of return:

$$V_0 \cdot (\text{Shares Outstanding}) = \frac{\pi_1}{(1+k_e)^1} + \frac{\pi_2}{(1+k_e)^2} + \frac{\pi_3}{(1+k_e)^3} + \ldots + \frac{\pi_\infty}{(1+k_e)^\infty}$$

$$V_0 \cdot (\text{Shares Outstanding}) = \sum_{t=1}^{\infty} \frac{\pi_t}{(1+k_e)^t} \qquad [1.1]$$

where V_0 is the current value of a share of stock (the stock price), π_t represents the economic profits expected in each of the future periods (from period 1 to ∞), and k_e equals the required rate of return. A number of different factors (e.g., interest rates and economy-wide business cycles) influence the firm's stock price in ways that are beyond the manager's control, but many factors (e.g., innovation and cost control) are not.

Note that Equation 1.1 does take into account the timing of future profits. By discounting all future profits at the required rate of return, k_e, Equation 1.1 shows that a dollar received in the future is worth less than a dollar received immediately. (The techniques of discounting to present value are explained in more detail in Chapter 2 and Appendix A.) Equation 1.1 also provides a way to evaluate different levels of risk when k_e is increased to account for greater risk. Thus, the greater the risk associated with receiving a future cash flow stream, the higher the required rate of return used to discount those cash flows, and the lower the present value. In short, shareholder value is determined by the amount, timing, and risk of the firm's expected profits.

EXAMPLE

SHAREHOLDER WEALTH MAXIMIZATION: BERKSHIRE HATHAWAY[4]

Warren E. Buffett, former chairperson and CEO of Berkshire Hathaway, Inc., described the long-term economic goal of Berkshire Hathaway as follows: "to maximize the average annual rate of gain in intrinsic business value on a per-share basis." Berkshire's book value per share increased from $19.46 in 1964, when he acquired the firm, to $91,485 at the end of 2005, a compound annual rate of growth of 21.5 percent. The Standard and Poor's 500 companies experienced 10.3 percent growth over this same time period.

[4] *Annual Report,* Berkshire Hathaway, Inc. (2005).

Berkshire's directors are all major stockholders. In addition, at least four of the directors have more than 50 percent of their family's net worth invested in Berkshire. Insiders own more than 47 percent of the firm's stock. As a result, Buffett's firm has always placed a high premium on the goal of maximizing shareholder wealth.

Additional insight regarding the achievement of the shareholder wealth-maximization goal can be gained by decomposing the profit concept, π, into its important elements. Profit in period t, π_t, is equal to total revenue (TR_t) minus total costs (TC_t), or

$$\pi_t = TR_t - TC_t \tag{1.2}$$

Similarly, total revenue in period t equals price per unit (P_t) times quantity sold (Q_t), or

$$TR_t = P_t \cdot Q_t \tag{1.3}$$

Total cost in period t equals variable cost per unit (V_t) times the number of units of output (Q_t) plus fixed costs in period t, F_t, or

$$TC_t = V_t \cdot Q_t + F_t \tag{1.4}$$

By combining Equations 1.2, 1.3, and 1.4 with Equation 1.1, we get

$$V_0 \cdot (\text{Shares Outstanding}) = \sum_{t=1}^{\infty} \frac{P_t \cdot Q_t - V_t \cdot Q_t - F_t}{(1 + k_e)^t} \tag{1.5}$$

The integrative nature of the shareholder wealth-maximization model is illustrated in Figure 1.3. The term $P_t \cdot Q_t$ represents the total revenue generated by the firm. From a decision-making perspective, this value is dependent on the firm's demand function (discussed in Chapters 3–6) and the firm's pricing decisions (see Chapters 10–14). The firm's costs, both fixed (F_t) and variable (V_t) are discussed in Chapters 8 and 9. A firm that chooses a capital-intensive production technology (discussed in Chapter 7) will tend to have a higher proportion of fixed costs than will a firm that chooses a more labor-intensive technology.

EXAMPLE

Resource Allocation Decisions and Shareholder Wealth: Apple Computer[5]

In distributing its stylish iMac personal computers and high-tech iPods, Apple considered three distribution channels. On the one hand, copying Dell's direct-to-the-consumer approach would entail buying components from Motorola, AMD, and Intel, and then hiring third-party manufacturers to assemble what each customer ordered just-in-time to fulfill Internet or telephone sales. Inventories and capital equipment costs would be low, making almost all costs variable. Alternatively, Apple could

[5] Based on Nick Wingfield, "How Apple's Store Strategy Beat the Odds," *The Wall Street Journal* (May 17, 2006), p. B1.

enter into distribution agreements with an independent electronics retailer such as Computer Tree. Finally, Apple could retail its own products in Apple Stores. This third approach entails enormous capital investment and a lower proportion of variable cost especially if the retail chain sought high visibility locations and needed lots of space.

Recently Apple opened its 147th retail store on Fifth Avenue in New York City. The location left little doubt as to the allocation of company resources to this new distribution strategy. Apple occupies a sprawling subterranean space topped by a glass cube, designed by Steve Jobs himself, across from Central Park and the famed Plaza Hotel. Apple's profits in this most heavily trafficked tourist and retail corridor will rely on several initiatives; (1) in-store theaters for workshop training on iMac programs to record music or edit home movies, (2) numerous technical experts available for troubleshooting with no waiting time, and (3) continuing investment in one of the world's most valuable brands. In 2005, Apple made $151 million in operating profits on $2.35 billion in sales at Apple Stores, a 6.4 percent margin relative to approximately 2 percent company-wide.

Figure 1.3 The Determinants of Firm Value

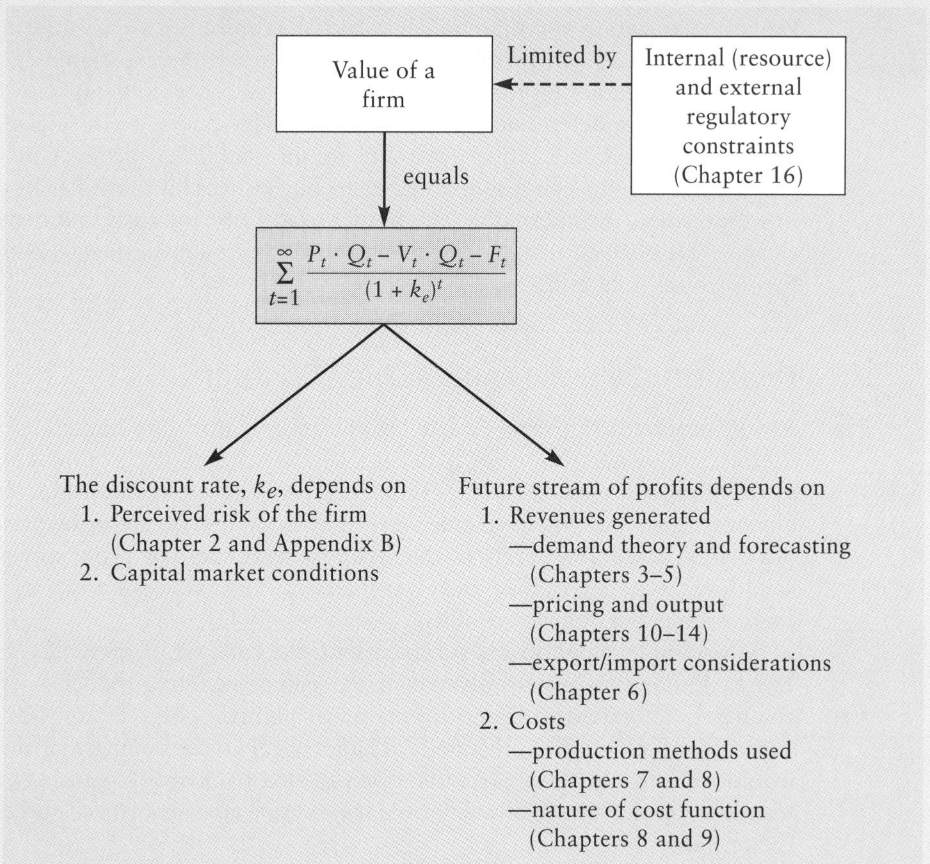

Economic Profits, Accounting Profits, and Cash Flows

The economic profit concept we use is *not* the same as the accounting definition of earnings, or net income, for several reasons. First, accounting profits can be ambiguous because generally accepted accounting principles allow a great deal of latitude when it comes to reporting profits. In addition, accounting profits do not take into account the opportunity cost of the capital invested by a firm's owners. Finally, accounting profits might not reflect actual *cash flows* because of the arbitrary statement of depreciation and the frequent misstatement of the value of inventories.

In practice, managers who seek to maximize shareholder wealth focus on maximizing the present value of the cash flows available to the equity owners of the firm. The definition of cash flow available to a firm's equity owners is unambiguous and consistent with the objective of maximizing the present value of expected future economic profits. Throughout this text, when the term *profit* is used, it means economic, not accounting-defined profits. When used in this way, the profit concept is consistent with the cash flow concept and will lead to shareholder wealth-maximizing decisions by managers.

Separation of Ownership and Control: The Principal-Agent Problem

Profit maximization and shareholder wealth maximization are useful concepts when alternative choices can be easily identified and when the associated costs and revenues can be readily estimated. Examples include scheduling capacity for optimal production runs, determining an optimal inventory policy given sales patterns and available production facilities, introducing an established product in a new geographic market, and choosing whether to buy or lease a machine. In other cases, however, where the alternatives are harder to identify, the costs and benefits are less clear, or the goals of owners and managers are not aligned, managers often pursue their own self-interests.

Divergent Objectives and Agency Conflict

Agency Relationship
A basis for delegating decision-making authority from principals to agents.

As sole proprietorships and closely held businesses grow into limited liability corporations, the owners (the principals) frequently delegate decision-making authority to professional managers (the agents) in an **agency relationship**. Because the manager-agents usually have much less to lose than the owner-principals, the agents often seek acceptable levels (rather than a maximum) of profit and shareholder wealth while pursuing their own self-interests. This issue is known as a principal-agent problem or "agency conflict."

For example, as oil prices subsided with the collapse of the OPEC cartel in the 1990s, Exxon's managers diversified the company into product lines, including computer software development, which was an area where Exxon had little or no expertise or competitive advantage. The managers were hoping that diversification would smooth out their executive bonuses tied to quarterly earnings, and it did. However, the decision to diversify ended up causing an extended decline in the value of Exxon's stock.

Pursuing their own self-interests can also lead managers to focus on their own long-term job security. In some instances it can motivate them to limit the amount of risk taken by the firm because an unfavorable outcome resulting from the risk could lead to their dismissal. But failing to take risks can be deadly in and of itself. Kodak is a good example. In the early 2000s, Kodak's executives didn't want to risk developing early digital photography products. When the demand for digital products subsequently soared, Kodak was left with too few markets for its traditional film products. Like Exxon, its stock value seriously declined.

Finally, the cash flow to owners erodes when the firm's resources are diverted from their most productive uses to perks for managers. In 1988 RJR Nabisco was a firm that had become bloated with corporate retreats in Florida, an extensive fleet of corporate airplanes and hangars, and an executive fixation on an awful tasting new product (the "smokeless" cigarette Premier). These management choices left RJR Nabisco with substantially less value in the marketplace than would have been possible with better resource allocation decisions. Recognizing the value enhancement potential, Kohlberg Kravis Roberts & Co. (KKR) initiated a hostile takeover bid and acquired RJR Nabisco for $25 billion in early 1989. The purchase price offered to common stockholders by KKR was $109 per share, much better than the $50 to $55 pre-takeover price. The new owners moved quickly to sell many of RJR's poorly performing assets, slash operating expenses, and cancel the Premier project. Although the deal was heavily leveraged with a large amount of debt loaned at high interest rates, a much improved cash flow allowed KKR to pay down the debt within seven years, substantially ahead of schedule.

To forge a closer alliance between the interests of shareholders and managers, some companies structure a larger proportion of the manager's compensation in the form of performance-based payments. For example, in 2002 Walt Disney's Michael Eisner received more than $20.2 million in long-term compensation (in addition to his $750,000 salary) as a reward for increasing Walt Disney's market value tenfold from $2 billion to $23 billion during his 10 years as CEO.[6] Other firms such as Hershey Foods, CSX, Union Carbide, General Motors, and Xerox require senior managers and directors to own a substantial amount of company stock as a condition of employment. The idea behind this stipulation is to align the pocketbook interests of managers directly with those of stockholders. In sum, how motivated a manager will be to act in the interests of the firm's stockholders depends on the structure of his or her compensation package, the threat of dismissal, and the threat of takeover by a new group of owners.

EXAMPLE

AGENCY COSTS AND CORPORATE RESTRUCTURING: O.M. SCOTT & SONS

The existence of high agency costs sometimes prompts firms to financially restructure themselves to achieve higher operating efficiencies. For example, the lawn products firm O.M. Scott & Sons, previously a subsidiary of ITT, was purchased by the Scott managers in a highly leveraged buyout (LBO). Faced with heavy interest and principal payments from the debt-financed LBO transaction and having the potential to profit directly from more efficient operation of the firm, the new owner-managers quickly put in place accounting controls and operating procedures designed to improve Scott's performance. By monitoring inventory levels more

[6] "That Eye-Popping Executive Pay," *BusinessWeek* (April 25, 1994), pp. 52–58.

closely and negotiating more aggressively with suppliers, the firm was able to reduce its average monthly working capital investment from an initial level of $75 million to $35 million. At the same time, incentive pay for the sales force caused revenue to increase from $160 million to a record $200 million.[7]

Agency Problems

Two common factors that give rise to all principal-agent problems are the inherent unobservable nature of managerial effort and the presence of random disturbances in team production. The job performance of piecework garment workers is easily monitored, but the work effort of salespeople and manufacturer's trade representatives may not be observable at less-than-prohibitive cost. Directly observing managerial input is even more problematic because managers contribute what one might call "creative ingenuity." Creative ingenuity in anticipating problems before they arise is inherently unobservable. Owners know it when they see it, but often do not recognize when it is missing. As a result, in explaining fluctuations in company performance, the manager's creative ingenuity is often inseparable from good and bad luck. Owners therefore find it difficult to know when to reward managers for upturns and when to blame them for poor performance.

Agency Costs

Costs associated with resolving conflicts of interest among shareholders, managers, and lenders. Agency costs include the cost of monitoring and bonding performance, the cost of constructing contracts designed to minimize agency conflicts, and the loss in efficiency resulting from unresolved agent-principal conflicts.

In an attempt to mitigate these agency problems, firms incur several **agency costs,** which include the following:

1. Payroll expenditures to structure executive compensation in a way that aligns the incentives for management with shareholder interests, such as grants of restricted stock or deferred stock options, discussed as a mechanism design issue in Chapter 15.
2. Internal audits and accounting oversight boards to monitor management's actions. In addition, many large creditors, especially banks, now monitor financial ratios and investment decisions of large debtor companies on a monthly or even biweekly basis. These initiatives strengthen the firm's *corporate governance.* See Table 1.1 for implementation mechanisms of corporate governance.

Table 1.1 Implementation Mechanisms of Corporate Governance

- Internal monitoring by independent board of director subcommittees
- Internal/external monitoring by large creditors
- Internal/external monitoring by owners of large blocks of stock
- Auditing and variance analysis
- Internal benchmarking
- Corporate culture of ethical duties
- High employee morale supportive of whistle blowers

3. Bonding expenditures and fraud liability insurance to protect the shareholders from managerial dishonesty.
4. Lost profits arising from complex organizational structures designed to limit managerial discretion, but which prevent timely responses to opportunities.

[7] A more complete discussion of the Scott experience can be found in Brett Duval Fromson, "Life After Debt: How LBOs Do It," *Fortune* (March 13, 1989), pp. 91–92.

WHAT WENT RIGHT • WHAT WENT WRONG

SATURN CORPORATION[8]

When General Motors rolled out their "different kind of car company" in 1991, J.D. Powers rated product quality 8 percent ahead of Honda, and customers liked the no-haggle selling process. Saturn achieved the 200,000 unit sales enjoyed by the Honda Civic and the Toyota Corolla in two short years and caught the 285,000 volume of the Ford Escort by 1995. Making interpersonal aspects of customer service the number-one priority and possessing superior inventory and MIS systems, Saturn dealerships proved profitable and quickly developed a reputation for high customer loyalty in the industry.

However, with pricing of the base Saturn model $1,200 below the $12,050 rival Japanese compact cars, the GM parent earned only a $400 gross profit margin per vehicle. In a typical year it meant GM was recovering only about $100 million of its $3 billion capital investment, a paltry 3 percent return. Netting out GM's 11 percent cost of capital, each Saturn was losing approximately $1,000. These figures compare to a $3,300 gross profit margin per vehicle in some of GM's other divisions. Consequently, cash flow was not reinvested in the Saturn division, products were not updated, and the models stagnated. By 1997, sales were slumping at −9 percent and in 1998 they fell an additional 20 percent.

Two problems appear responsible for Saturn's midlife crisis. First, GM failed to adopt a change-management view of what would be required to transfer the first-time Saturn owners to more profitable GM divisions. The corporate strategy was that price-conscious young Saturn buyers would eventually trade up to Buick and Oldsmobile. Instead, middle-aged loyal Saturn owners sought to trade up within Saturn, and finding no sporty larger models available, they switched to larger Japanese imports like the Honda Accord and Toyota Camry. Second, yen-dollar exchange rates fluctuated sharply between 1995 and 2005 from 94 to 130 yen per U.S. dollar. This shifting exchange rate made it possible at times for Honda and Toyota to discount the dollar prices of Civics, Accords, Corollas, and Camrys without reducing the yen revenue from these exports.

Saturn has now learned that companies whose products are exposed to competition from foreign producers must plan product introductions and marketing campaigns to account for this global competitive environment. Recent product introductions included a sport wagon, a fuel-efficient SUV, and a high-profile sports coupe. The new Saturn gasoline-electric hybrid is likely to underprice Toyota's much heralded hybrid while retaining all the loyalty-building features of Saturn quality.

[8] Based on M. Cohen, "Saturn's Supply-Chain Innovation," *Sloan Management Review,* Summer 2000, pp. 93–96; "Small Car Sales Are Back" *BusinessWeek* (September 22, 1997), pp. 40–42; and "Why Didn't GM Do More for Saturn?" *BusinessWeek* (March 16, 1998), p. 62.

IMPLICATIONS OF SHAREHOLDER WEALTH MAXIMIZATION

Critics of those who want to align the interests of managers with equity owners often allege that maximizing shareholder wealth focuses on short-term payoffs—sometimes to the detriment of long-term profits. However, the evidence suggests just the opposite. Short-term cash flows reflect only a small fraction of the firm's share price; the first five years of expected dividend payouts explain only 18 percent and the first

WHAT WENT RIGHT WHAT WENT WRONG

ELI LILLY DEPRESSED BY LOSS OF PROZAC PATENT[9]

Pharmaceutical giants such as GlaxoSmithKline, Merck, Pfizer, and Eli Lilly expend an average of $802 million to develop a new drug. It takes 12.3 years to research and test for efficacy and side effects, conduct clinical trials, and then produce and market a new drug. Only 4 in 100 candidate molecules or screening compounds lead to investigational new drugs (INDs). Only 5 in 200 INDs display sufficient efficacy in animal testing to warrant human trials. Clinical failure occurs in 6 of 10 human trials, and only half of the FDA-proposed drugs are ultimately approved. In sum, the joint probability of successful drug discovery and development is just $0.04 \times 0.025 \times 0.4 \times 0.5 = 0.0002$, two hundredths of 1 percent. Those few patented drugs that do make it to the pharmacy shelves, especially the blockbusters with several billion dollars in sales, must contribute enough operating profit to recover the cost of all these R&D failures.

In 2000, one of the key extension patents for Eli Lilly's blockbuster drug for the treatment of depression, Prozac, was overturned by a regulator and a U.S. federal judge. Within one month, Eli Lilly lost 70 percent of Prozac's sales to the generic equivalents. Although this company has several other blockbusters, Eli Lilly's share price plummeted 32 percent. CEO Sidney Taurel said he had made a mistake in not rolling out Prozac's successor replacement drug when the patent extension for Prozac was first challenged. Taurel then moved quickly to establish a new management concept throughout the company. Now, each new Eli Lilly drug is assigned a team of scientists, marketers, and regulatory experts who oversee the entire life cycle of the product from research inception to patent expiration. The key function of these cross-functionally integrated teams is contingency analysis and scenario planning to deal with the unexpected.

[9] C. Kennedy, F. Harris, and M. Lord, "Integrating Public Policy and Public Affairs into Pharmaceutical Marketing: Differential Pricing and the AIDS Pandemic," *Journal of Public Policy and Marketing* (Fall 2004), pp. 1–23; and "Eli Lilly: Bloom and Blight," *The Economist* (October 26, 2002), p. 60.

ten years only 35 percent of the share prices of NYSE stocks.[10] The goal of shareholder wealth maximization requires a long-term focus.

Admittedly, value-maximizing managers must manage change—sometimes radical changes in competition (airlines), technology (Internet sales), and regulation (cigarettes)—but they must do so with an eye to the long-run sustainable profitability of the business. In short, value-maximizing managers must anticipate change and make contingency plans.

Shareholder wealth maximization also reflects changes in the information available to the public about a company's expected future cash flows and foreseeable risks. As such, it reflects the strategic investment opportunities a management team develops, not only the firm's preexisting positive net present value investments. Amgen, a biotechnology company, had shareholder value of $42 million in 1983

[10] J. R. Woolridge, "Competitive Decline: Is a Myopic Stock Market to Blame?" *Journal of Applied Corporate Finance* (Spring 1988), pp. 26–36.

despite no sales, no cash flow, no capital assets, no patents, and poorly protected trade secrets. By 2003, Amgen had sales of more than $7.9 billion and cash flow of $2 billion annually. Over the intervening 20 years, Amgen had developed and exercised enormously valuable strategic opportunities in biotechnology.

In general, only about 85 percent of shareholder value can be explained by even 30 years of cash flows.[11] The remainder reflects the capitalized value of strategic options to expand some profitable lines of business, to abandon others, and to retain but delay investment in still others until more information becomes available.

Value-maximizing behavior on the part of managers is also distinguishable from satisficing behavior. Satisficers strive to "hit their targets" (e.g., achieve sales growth, return on investment, or safety rating targets). Not value maximizers. Rather than trying to meet a standard like 97 percent, 99 percent, or 99.9 percent error-free takeoffs and landings, or to deliver a 9, 11, or 12.1 percent return on shareholders' equity, the value-maximizing manager will commit himself or herself to continuous incremental improvements. Any time the marginal benefits of an action exceed its marginal costs, the value-maximizing manager will just do it.

Caveats to Maximizing Shareholder Value

Managers should concentrate on maximizing shareholder value alone only if three conditions are met. These conditions require (1) complete markets, (2) no significant asymmetric information, and (3) known recontracting costs. We now discuss how a violation of these conditions necessitates a much larger view of management's role in firm decision making.

Complete Markets For all the effects of management decisions to directly influence a company's cash flows, forward or futures markets as well as spot markets must be available for the firm's inputs, output, and by-products. For example, forward and futures markets for crude oil and coffee bean inputs allow Texaco and Starbucks Coffee to plan their costs with more accurate cash flow projections. For a small 3–5 percent fee known in advance, value-maximizing managers can use forward or futures markets to lock in their input expense and avoid unexpected cost increases. This completeness of the markets allows a reduction in the cost-covering prices of gasoline and cappuccino.

EXAMPLE

Tradable Pollution Permits at Duke Power[12]

Similarly, completing the market by establishing a market system for tradable air pollution permits has set a price on the sulfur dioxide (SO_2) by-product from burning high-sulfur coal. SO_2 emissions from coal-fired power plants have raised the acidity of rain and mist in eastern forests from Maine to Georgia to levels almost 100 times higher than the natural acidity of rainfall in the Grand Tetons in the far northwestern United States. Dead trees, peeling paint, increased asthma, and stone decomposition on buildings and monuments have been the result. To elicit

[11] Woolridge, op. cit.

[12] Based on "Cornering the Market," *The Wall Street Journal* (June 5, 1995), p. B1; and *Economic Report of the President, February 2000* (Washington, DC: U.S.G.P.O., 2000), pp. 240–264.

substantial pollution abatement at the least cost, the Clean Air Act of 1990 created a market for the rights to emit SO_2.

The Environmental Protection Agency issued tradable pollution allowances (TPAs) to 467 known SO_2 polluters for approximately 70 percent of the previous year's emissions. The utility companies doing the polluting then began to trade the allowances. Companies that were able to abate their emissions at a low cost (perhaps because they had smokestack scrubbing equipment) sold their allowances to plants that couldn't abate their emissions as cost-effectively. In other words, the low-cost abaters were able to cut their emissions cheaply and then sell the permits they didn't need to high-cost abaters. The result was that the nation's air got 30 percent cleaner at the least possible cost.

As a result of the growing completeness of this market, electric utilities such as Duke Power now know what expense line to incorporate in their cash flow projections for the SO_2 by-products of operating with high-sulfur coal. TPAs can sell for more than $100 per ton, and a single utility plant operation may require 15,000 tons of permits or more. The continuous trade-off between installing multimillion dollar pollution abatement equipment, utilizing higher-cost alternative fuels such as low-sulfur coal and natural gas, or paying the current market price of these EPA-issued pollution permits can now be explicitly analyzed and the least cost solutions found.

No Asymmetric Information Monitoring and coordination problems within the corporation and contracting problems between sellers and buyers often arise because of asymmetric information. Line managers and employees can misunderstand what senior executives intend and miscommunicate these intentions to customers. A Food Lion memo challenging employees to find a thousand different ways to save 1 percent of their own costs elicited undesirable shortcuts in food preparation and storage. TV newswoman Dianne Sawyer then secretly recorded seafood counter employees spraying old fish with a light concentration of ammonia to restore the red appearance of fresh salmon. Clearly, this behavior was not what the senior executives intended Food Lion customers to believe overzealous cost-cutters would regularly do to their seafood.

Building a good reputation with customers, workers, and the surrounding tax jurisdiction is one way companies deal with the problem of asymmetric information, and managers must attend to these reputation effects on shareholder value. We discuss the implications of asymmetric information on cost-covering equilibrium prices in competitive markets in Chapter 10.

Known Recontracting Costs Finally, to focus exclusively on the discounted present value of future cash flows necessitates that managers obtain not only sales revenue and expense estimates but also forecasts of future *recontracting costs* for pivotal inputs. Owners of professional sports teams are acutely aware of how unknown recontracting costs with star players can affect the value of their franchises. A pivotal player can often "hold up" the firm's owners when the time comes for contract renewals. In another instance, Westinghouse entered into long-term supply contracts to provide fuel rods to nuclear power plants across the country. Thereafter, when the market price of uranium quadrupled, Westinghouse refused to deliver the promised fuel rods and the utility companies then sued for damages. Value-maximizing managers must anticipate and mitigate these recontracting problems.

EXAMPLE

LOW EARTH ORBIT SPACE JUNK: MOTOROLA AND TELEDESIC[13]

Satellite orbital paths are becoming congested with space junk. The U.S. Air Force's Space Command tracks 8,500 objects that are 10 centimeters or larger in low earth orbit (6–125 miles up) and 1 meter or larger in geosynchronous orbit (20,000 miles up). However, a collision with an object as small as one-half a centimeter will depressurize the space shuttle resulting in "mission loss." In July 1996, Cerise, a French satellite, tumbled out of orbit after colliding with small pieces of an exploded Arienne 4 French rocket. The vastness of interstellar space is just that—vast—but geosynchronous and low earth orbits are becoming congested. About 70 to 100 new commercial and military satellites are launched per year worldwide at a cost of about $8,000 to $25,000 per pound. Lockheed Martin is testing an X-33 rocket that will reduce this cost to $1,000 per pound. As companies such as Aeroastro and Kelly Space develop still cheaper launch systems that can achieve escape velocity, the congestion will surely worsen.

The problem is that satellite orbital paths are common property resources like deep sea fisheries. No company or nation has an incentive to economize on their use in order to achieve maximum sustainable yield because no one can appropriate the benefits of doing so. No private property rights are specified, assigned, or enforced. As a result, each producer has an incentive to overuse the resource. When congestion occurs, the costs are widespread, but the catastrophic accident costs fall upon individual parties. Who owes what to whom when a future Cerise plows into a Motorola satellite has not been determined. This lack of private property rights and the consequentially incomplete market prevents all but the most vague analysis of projected cash flows.

When Motorola contracted with Teledesic to launch a swarm of 924 new communication satellites into low earth orbit, Teledesic began to lobby for the privatization of the common property resources associated with satellite orbital paths. More complete markets could then emerge to price the paths, and that would enable meaningful recontracting cost analysis of the projected cash flow expense for replacing a satellite.

To the extent markets are incomplete, information is asymmetric, or recontracting costs are unknown, managers must attend to these matters in order to maximize shareholder wealth rather than simply focusing myopically on maximizing the net present value of expected future cash flows.

RESIDUAL CLAIMANTS

A growing consensus believes that the primary duty of management and the board of directors of a company is to the shareholders themselves. Shareholders have a residual claim on the firm's net cash flows after all expected contractual returns have been paid. All the other stakeholders (employees, customers, bondholders, banks, suppliers, the surrounding tax jurisdictions, the community in which plants are located, etc.) have *contractual* expected returns. If expectations created by those contracts are not met, any of these stakeholders has access to the full force of the contract law in securing whatever they are due. Shareholders have contractual rights too, but

[13] Based on "To Boldly Dump," *The Economist* (March 29, 1997), p. 87; and "They're Going Crazy in Space," *BusinessWeek* (July 28, 1997), p. 89.

those rights simply entitle them to whatever is left over, that is, to the residual. As a consequence, when shareholder owners hire a CEO and a board, they impose a fiduciary duty to allocate the company's resources in such a way as to maximize the net present value of these residual claims, which constitutes the objective of shareholder wealth maximization.

Be clear, however, that the value of any company's stock is quite dependent on reputation effects. Underfunding a pension plan or polluting the environment results in massive losses of capitalized value because the financial markets anticipate (correctly) that such a company will have reduced future cash flows. Labor costs to attract new employees will rise; tax jurisdictions will reduce the tax preferences offered in new plant locations; customers may boycott; and the public relations, lobbying, and legal costs of such a company will surely rise. All these factors imply that wealth-maximizing managers must be carefully attuned to stakeholder interests precisely because it is in their shareholders' best interests to do so.

Goals in the Public Sector and Not-for-Profit Enterprises[14]

The value-maximization objective developed for private sector firms is not an appropriate objective in the public sector or in not-for-profit (NFP) organizations. These organizations pursue a different set of objectives because of the nature of the goods and services they supply and the manner in which they are funded.

Three characteristics of NFP organizations distinguish them from for-profit enterprises and influence decision making in the enterprise. First, no one possesses a right to receive profit or surpluses in an NFP enterprise. The absence of a profit motive can have a serious impact on the incentive to be efficient. Second, NFP enterprises are exempt from taxes on corporate income. Finally, many NFP enterprises benefit from the fact that donations to them are tax deductible. These tax benefits give NFP enterprises an advantage when competing with for-profit enterprises.

Not-for-profit organizations include performing arts groups, museums, libraries, hospitals, churches, volunteer organizations, cooperatives, credit unions, labor unions, professional societies, foundations, and fraternal organizations. Some of these organizations offer services to a group of clients, such as the patients of a hospital. Others provide services primarily to their members. Country clubs and credit unions are examples. Finally, some NFP organizations produce products to benefit the general public. Local symphony and theater companies are examples.

The most important feature that distinguishes NFP organizations from private sector and public (government) sector organizations is their sources of financial support. NFP organizations receive a large percentage of their externally generated funds from voluntary contributions. The greater the proportion of external funds from contributions as a percentage of total revenue, the closer the organization is to being a pure NFP organization. In contrast, the lower the percentage of contributions to total revenue, the closer the organization is to being a business firm or government agency. For example, by this criterion a credit union would be expected to have organizational objectives that are similar to those of banks, whereas the American Economic Association, a professional association of economists, is more nearly like an NFP organization.

[14] This section draws heavily on Burton A. Weisbrod, *The Nonprofit Economy* (Cambridge, MA: Harvard University Press, 1988).

Public sector (government) agencies tend to provide services that have significant public-good characteristics. In contrast to private goods, such as a bite-sized candy bar, for example, a **public good** can be consumed by more than one person. Moreover, excluding those who do not pay for the good from consuming it can only be done at a prohibitively high cost. Examples of public goods include national defense and flood control. If an antiballistic missile system or a flood control levy is constructed, those behind the shield cannot be excluded from its protection even if they refuse to contribute to the cost. Even if one could exclude the nonpayers, the indivisibility of consumption from flood control makes the incremental cost (and therefore the efficient price) of adding another participant quite low.

Public Goods

Goods that may be consumed by more than one person at the same time with little or no extra cost, and for which it is expensive or impossible to exclude those who do not pay.

Some goods, such as recreational facilities and the performing arts, have both private-good and public-good characteristics. For example, concerts and parks may be shared (within limits) and are partially nonexcludable in the sense that they convey prestige and quality-of-life benefits to the entire community.[15] The more costly the exclusion, the more likely the good or service will be provided by the public sector rather than the private sector. Portrait artists and personal fitness trainers offer pay-as-you-go private fee arrangements. Chamber music fans and tennis court users often organize in consumption-sharing and cost-sharing clubs. On the other hand, open-air symphony concerts and large parks usually necessitate some public financing.

NOT-FOR-PROFIT OBJECTIVES

Several organizational objectives have been suggested for the NFP enterprise. They include the following:

1. Maximizing the quantity and quality of output subject to a break-even budget constraint
2. Maximizing the utility of the NFP's administrators
3. Maximizing cash flows
4. Maximizing the utility (satisfaction) of contributors

For NFP organizations that rely heavily on external contributions, the overriding objective is to satisfy current and prospective contributors. This focus does not mean that the other objectives are mutually exclusive. It is common to find an NFP organization that seeks to satisfy its contributors by (1) efficiently managing its resources, (2) increasing its capacity to supply high-quality goods or services, and (3) providing a rewarding work environment for its administrators. As reliance on outside contributors lessens, the other objectives gain importance to the organization.

THE EFFICIENCY OBJECTIVE IN NOT-FOR-PROFIT ORGANIZATIONS

Although both public sector agencies and NFP organizations pursue many objectives, economists focus on the efficiency dimension of those objectives. Whatever set of objectives the organization decides to pursue, these objectives should be pursued in the most resource-efficient fashion.

Cost-Benefit Analysis

A resource-allocation model that can be used by public sector and not-for-profit organizations to evaluate programs or investments on the basis of the magnitude of the discounted costs and benefits.

Cost-benefit analysis has been developed to determine how efficient the allocation of public and NFP resources among competing uses are. This model is the counterpart

[15] William J. Baumol and W. G. Bowen, *Performing Arts: The Economic Dilemma* (Brookfield, VT: Ashgate Publishing Co., 1993).

of the capital budgeting model in the private sector. The benefits and costs associated with investments are estimated, and the projects are evaluated on the basis of which one yields the "biggest bang for the buck." Because government and NFP spending is normally constrained by a budget ceiling, the goals actually used to evaluate expenditures for any public purpose can be any one of the following:

1. Maximize the benefits for given costs
2. Minimize the costs while achieving a fixed level of benefits
3. Maximize the net benefits (benefits minus costs)

Cost-benefit analysis is only one factor in the final decision. It does furnish decision makers with the results of a careful analysis of the costs and returns associated with alternative actions. It does not, however, incorporate many of the more subjective considerations or less easily quantifiable objectives into the analysis, like how fair it might be. For example, a cost-benefit analysis typically does not consider the effect of a proposed project on the income distribution of the people within the community where the project is being proposed. Concern for these matters must be introduced at another stage in the analysis, generally through the political process.

NFP institutions are often faced with decision-making problems not unlike those of a public agency. Not-for-profits exist to supply some good (or service) in the most efficient manner. An NFP hospital, for example, might provide a certain quantity and quality of medical service to the citizens of a community, given a resource or budget constraint. Decisions about what programs to fund should be based on an analysis of benefits and costs generated by the competing programs.

SUMMARY

- *Economic profit* is defined as the difference between *total revenues* and *total economic costs.* Economic costs include a normal rate of return on the capital contributed by the firm's owners. Economic profits exist to compensate investors for the risk they assume, because of temporary disequilibrium conditions that may occur in a market, because of the existence of monopoly power, and as a reward to firms that are especially innovative or highly efficient.
- As an overall objective of the firm, the *shareholder wealth-maximization* model is appealing. It is flexible enough to account for differential levels of risk and timing differences in the receipt of benefits and the incurring of future costs. Because shareholder wealth is defined in terms of the value of the stock, this goal provides a precise performance measure that is free from the problems associated with using various accounting measures.
- Managers may not always behave in a manner consistent with the shareholder wealth-maximization objective. The agency costs associated with preventing or at least mitigating these deviations from the owner-principal's objective are substantial.
- Changes in the firm's performance, perhaps unrelated to a manager's effort, combined with the unobservable nature of their creative ingenuity, presents a difficult *principal-agent problem* to resolve. This combination makes it difficult for owner-principals to know when to blame manager-agents for weak performances versus giving them credit for strong performances.
- *Governance mechanisms* (including internal monitoring by subcommittees appointed by boards of directors and large creditors, internal/external monitoring by large-block shareholders, auditing, and variance analysis) can be used to mitigate agency problems by limiting managerial discretion.
- Shareholder wealth maximization implies a firm should be forward-looking, dynamic, and have a long-term outlook; anticipate and manage change; acquire strategic investment opportunities; and maximize the present value of expected cash flows to owners within the boundaries of the statutory law, administrative law, and ethical standards of conduct.
- Shareholder wealth maximization will be difficult to achieve when firms suffer from problems related to

incomplete markets, asymmetric information, and unknown recontracting costs. In the absence of these complications, managers should maximize the present value of the discounted future net cash flows to residual claimants—namely, equity owners. If any of the complicating factors are present, managers must first attend to those issues before attempting to maximize shareholder wealth.

- Not-for-profit enterprises exist to supply a good or service desired by their primary contributors.
- Public sector organizations often provide services having significant public-good characteristics. Public goods are goods that can be consumed by more than one person at a time with little additional cost, and for which excluding those who do not pay for the goods is exceptionally difficult or prohibitively expensive.
- Regardless of their specific objectives, both public and private institutions should seek to furnish their goods or services in the most efficient way, that is, at the least cost possible.

Exercises

Answers to the exercises in blue can be found in Appendix C at the back of the book.

1. Explain several dimensions of the shareholder-principal conflict with manager-agents known as the principal-agent problem. To mitigate agency problems between senior executives and shareholders, should the compensation committee of the board devote more to executive salary and bonus (cash compensation) or more to long-term incentives? Why? What role does each type of pay play in motivating managers?
2. If long-term profitability has been mired at 4 percent operating margins or less for the last five years, what percentage would you use to trigger executive bonuses? Why? What issues would arise with hiring and retaining the best managers?
3. In the period leading up to the war in Iraq, oil prices increased significantly, as did the profits earned by many oil companies. Some politicians argued that these profits were undeserved, and they called for price rollbacks or increased taxes. Discuss the pros and cons of these proposals in the context of the various theories of profit.
4. In 2000, firms in the drug industry earned an average return on net worth of 25 percent, compared with an average return of 15 percent earned by more than 1,400 firms followed by *Value Line*. Which theory or theories of profit do you think best explain(s) the performance of the drug industry?
5. In the context of the shareholder wealth-maximization model of a firm, what is the expected impact of each of the following events on the value of the firm? Explain why.
   a. New foreign competitors enter the market.
   b. Strict pollution control requirements are implemented by the government.
   c. A previously nonunion workforce votes to unionize.
   d. The rate of inflation increases substantially.
   e. A major technological breakthrough is achieved by the firm, reducing its costs of production.
6. After Iraq's oil supply was disrupted in the second Gulf War, the price of jet fuel used by airlines increased dramatically. As the CEO of US Airways, you have been presented with the following options to deal with this problem:
   a. Raise airfares to reflect the expense reduction.
   b. Decrease the number of flights per day in some markets.
   c. Enter into forward contracts to buy jet fuel at a fixed price for the next two years and set airfares to a level that will cover these costs of being hedged.

   Evaluate these options in the context of the decision-making model presented in the text.
7. How would each of the following actions be expected to affect shareholder wealth?
   a. RJR Nabisco sells its Del Monte division for more than $1 billion.
   b. Ford Motor Company pays $2.5 billion for Jaguar.
   c. General Motors offers large rebates to stimulate sales of its automobiles.

d. **Rising interest rates cause the required returns of shareholders to increase.**
e. **Import restrictions are placed on the French competitors of Napa wineries.**
f. **A sudden drop occurs in the expected future rate of inflation.**
g. **A new labor-saving machine is purchased by Wonder Bread and results in the layoff of 300 employees.**

CASE EXERCISES

DESIGNING A MANAGERIAL INCENTIVES CONTRACT

Specific Electric Co. asks you to implement a pay-for-performance incentive contract for its new CEO. The CEO can either work hard with a personal opportunity cost of $200,000 or reduce her effort, thereby avoiding the personal cost. The CEO faces three possible outcomes: the probability of her company experiencing good luck is 30 percent, medium luck, 40 percent, and bad luck, 30 percent. Although the management team can distinguish the three "states" of luck as the quarter unfolds, the Compensation Subcommittee of the Board of Directors (and the shareholders) cannot do so. Sometime thereafter, the CEO decides to expend high or low work effort, and one of the following observable shareholder values then results.

	Shareholder Value (in $millions)		
	Good Luck (30%)	Medium Luck (40%)	Bad Luck (30%)
High CEO Effort	$1,000	$800	$500
Low CEO Effort	$ 800	$500	$300

Assume the company has 10 million shares outstanding offered at a $65 initial share price, implying a $650 million initial shareholder value. Because the CEO's effort and the company's luck are unobservable to the owners and company directors, it is not possible when the company's share price falls to $50 and the company's value to $500 million to distinguish whether the company experienced low CEO effort and medium luck, or high CEO effort and bad luck. Similarly, it is not possible to distinguish low CEO effort and good luck from high CEO effort and medium luck.

Answer the following questions from the perspective of a member of the Compensation Committee of the Board of Directors who is aligned with shareholders' interests and is deciding on bonus plans for the CEO.

QUESTIONS

1. What is the maximum amount it would be worth to shareholders to elicit high CEO effort all the time rather than low CEO effort all the time?
2. If you decide to pay 1 percent of this amount (in Question 1) as a cash bonus, what performance level (what share price or shareholder value) in the table should trigger the bonus? Suppose you decide to elicit high CEO effort when, and if, medium luck occurs by paying a bonus should the company's value rise to $800 million. What criticism of this incentive contract plan can you see?
3. Suppose you decide to elicit high CEO effort when, and if, good luck occurs by paying a bonus only for an increase in the company's value to $1 billion. What criticism of this incentive contract plan can you see?

4. Suppose you decide to elicit high CEO effort when, and if, bad luck occurs by paying the bonus when the company's value falls to $500,000. What criticism of this incentive contract plan can you see?

5. In an effort to identify the share price that should trigger a bonus payment for the CEO and maximize shareholder value, how much would you, the Compensation Committee, be willing to pay an auditor to examine the expense and revenue flows in real time and deliver perfect forecasting information about the "luck" the firm is experiencing? Compare shareholder value with this perfect information relative to the best choice among the incentive contract plans in Questions 2, 3, and 4.

6. Design a stock option-based incentive plan to elicit high effort. Show that this incentive contract improves shareholder value relative to the best of the cash-based incentive plans in Questions 2, 3, or 4.

7. Design an incentive plan that seeks to elicit high effort by granting restricted stock. Show that this incentive contract improves shareholder value relative to all prior alternatives.

8. Financial audits are basically sampling procedures to verify with a predetermined accuracy the sources and uses of the company receipts and expenditures; the larger the sample, the higher is the accuracy. What's the maximum amount the Compensation Committee of the Board will be willing to pay for a perfect forecast if it were possible for the auditors to distinguish good from medium luck? What about medium from bad luck?

REDUCING GREENHOUSE GASES[16]

The U.N. Kyoto Protocol of December 1997 would have obligated the United States to reduce by approximately 25 percent the emission of carbon dioxide and other greenhouse gases between 2000 and 2010. Brazil, China, India, and Mexico were all exempted from the agreement. Kyoto's regulatory quota system was rejected by the United States but adopted by the Europeans. Britain set up a tradable permit system in 2002; the EU followed in 2005. The cost to produce one kilowatt hour of coal-fired electricity is now priced higher (at $34.90) than the cost of the requisite coal itself.

QUESTION

1. Assuming an efficient reduction in greenhouse gases is desirable, how will a tradable permit system accomplish that goal?

[16] Based on "Letting the Free Market Clear the Air," *BusinessWeek* (November 6, 2000), pp. 200–204; and "Carbon Trading: Revving Up," *The Economist* (July 9, 2005), p. 65.

CHAPTER

2

Fundamental Economic Concepts

CHAPTER PREVIEW A few fundamental microeconomic concepts provide cornerstones for all of the analysis in managerial economics. Five of the most important are demand and supply, marginal analysis, net present value, the meaning and measurement of risk, and the trade-offs that must be made between risk and return. We will review how the determinants of demand and supply establish a market equilibrium price. Marginal analysis tools are central when a decision-maker is seeking to optimize some objective, such as profits or shareholder wealth. Appendix 2A develops the relationship between marginal analysis and differential calculus. The net present value concept provides the linkage between the long-term decisions made by a firm and the shareholder wealth-maximization objective. Because most economic decisions involve an element of risk, the meaning and measurement of risk is an important concept for managers. Risk-return analysis is important to an understanding of the many trade-offs that managers must make as they plan new products, expand capacity, or change prices.

MANAGERIAL CHALLENGE

Revenue Management at American Airlines[1]

Airlines face highly cyclical demand; American Airlines reported net losses for 2000–2005 but expects to report renewed profitability in the continuing expansion of 2005–2006. Demand also fluctuates day to day. One of the ways American copes with random demand is through marginal analysis using revenue management techniques. Revenue or "yield" management (RM) is an integrated demand-management, order-booking, and capacity-planning process.

Winning orders in a service industry *without slashing prices* requires that companies create perceived value for segmented classes of differentiated customers. Business travelers on airlines, for example, will pay substantial premiums for last-minute responsiveness to their flight change requests. Other business travelers demand exceptional delivery reliability and on-time performance. In contrast, most vacation excursion travelers want commodity-like service at rock-bottom prices. Although only 15–20 percent of most airlines' seats are in the business segment, 65–75 percent of the profit contribution on a typical flight comes from this group. The problem is that airline capacity must be planned and allocated well in advance of customer arrivals, often before demand is fully known, yet unsold inventory perishes at the moment of departure. This same management challenge faces hospitals, management consulting firms, TV stations, and printing businesses, all of whom must acquire and schedule capacity before the demands for elective surgeries, a crisis management team, Thursday's TV ads, or the next week's press run are fully known.

MANAGERIAL CHALLENGE

© DIGITAL VISION/GETTY IMAGES

One approach to minimizing unsold inventory and yet capturing all last-minute high-profit business is to auction off capacity to the highest bidder. The auction for free-wheeling electricity works just that way: Power companies bid at 15 minutes before the hour for excess supplies that other utilities agree to deliver on the hour. However, in airlines (like many other service businesses) prices cannot be adjusted quickly as the moment of departure approaches. Instead, revenue managers employ large historical databases to predict segmented customer demand in light of current arrivals on the reservation system. They then compare the expected marginal profit from holding in reserve another seat in business class in anticipation of "last-minute" demand to the alternative expected marginal profit from accepting one more advance reservation request at a discount.

Suppose on the 9:00 A.M. Dallas to Chicago flight next Monday, 63 of American's 170 seats have been protected for first class, business class, and full coach fares but only 50 have been sold; the remaining 107 seats have been authorized for sale at a discount. Three days before departure, another advance reservation request arrives in the discount class which is presently full. Should American reallocate capacity and take on the new discount passenger? The answer depends on the marginal profit from each class and the predicted probability of excess demand (beyond 63 seats) next Monday in the business classes.

If the \$721 full coach fare has a \$500 marginal profit and the \$155 discount fare has a \$100 marginal profit, the seat in question should not be reallocated from business to discount customers unless the probability of "stocking out" in business is less than 0.20 (accounting for the likely incidence of cancellations and no-shows). For example, if the probability is 0.25, the expected marginal profit from holding an empty seat for another potential business customer is \$125, whereas the marginal profit from selling that seat to the discount customer is only \$100. Even an advance-payment no-refund seat request from the discount class should be refused. Every company has some viable orders that should be refused because additional capacity held in reserve for the anticipated arrival of higher profit customers is not "idle capacity" but rather a predictable revenue opportunity waiting to happen.

In this chapter, we develop the marginal analysis technique pivotal to solving American's seat allocation decision problem. Chapter 14 discusses the price discrimination analysis that underlies revenue management applications.

[1] Based on Robert Cross, *Revenue Management* (New York: Broadway Books, 1995); and Frederick Harris and Peter Peacock, "Hold My Place Please: Yield Management Improves Capacity Allocation Guesswork," *Marketing Management* (Fall 1995), pp. 34–46.

DEMAND AND SUPPLY: A QUICK REVIEW

THE EQUILIBRIUM MARKET PRICE

Demand and supply simultaneously determine the equilibrium market price (P_{eq}). That is, P_{eq} sets the desired rate of purchase (Q_d/t) in Figure 2.1 equal to the planned rate of sale (Q_s/t). But what ultimately determines this metric of "value" in a marketplace? Among the earliest answers can be found in the Aristotelian concept of intrinsic use value. Because diamonds secure marriage covenants and peace pacts between nations,

Figure 2.1 Demand and Supply Determine the Equilibrium Market Price

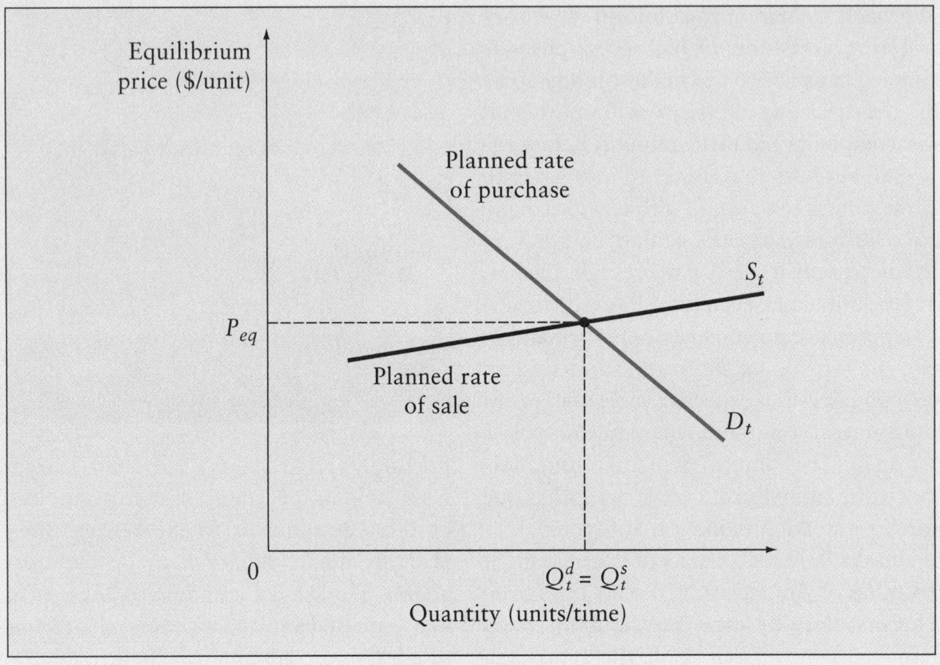

they provide enormous use value and should therefore exhibit high market value. The problem with this theory of value arises when one considers cubic zirconia diamonds. No one other than a jewel merchant can distinguish the artificial cubic zirconia from the real thing, and therefore the intrinsic uses are identical. Yet, cubic zirconia diamonds sell for many times less than natural stones of like grade and color. Why? One clue arose at the end of the Middle Ages, when the Catholic monasteries produced hand-copied Bibles and sold them for huge sums (i.e., $21,000 in 2006 dollars) to other monasteries and the nobility. Yet, Guttenberg came along with a beautiful "mass produced" printed facsimile that could be put to exactly the same intrinsic use, and yet, the market value fell almost one hundred fold to $250 in 2006 dollars. Why?

Equilibrium market price results from the interaction of demanders and suppliers involved in an exchange. In addition to the use value demanders anticipate from a product, a supplier's cost will also influence the market price observed. Ultimately, therefore, what minimum asking price suppliers require to cover their costs is just as pivotal in determining value in exchange as what maximum offer price buyers are willing to pay. Guttenberg Bibles and cubic zirconia diamonds exchange at lower "value" not because they are intrinsically less useful but simply because the bargain struck between buyers and sellers of these products will likely be negotiated down to a level that just covers their lower cost plus a small profit. Otherwise, new competitors are likely to enter the market and win the business by asking less.

Even when the cost of production is nearly identical and intrinsic use value is nearly identical, equilibrium market prices can still differ markedly. One additional determinant of value helps to explain why. Market value depends upon relative scarcity. Hardwoods are scarce in Japan but plentiful in Sweden. Even though timber cutting and sawmill planing cost the same in both locations, the hardwood forest has scarcity value as raw material in Japan that it does not have in Sweden. To take another example, whale oil for use in lamps all around the world stayed at a nearly constant price for several centuries until whale species began to be harvested at rates beyond their sustainable yield. As whale resources became scarcer, the whalers who expended no additional cost on better equipment or longer voyages came home with less oil from reduced catches. With less raw material on the market, the input price of whale oil rose. Consequently, despite unchanged other costs of production, the scarcer input led to a higher final product price. Similar results occur in the commodity market for coffee beans or orange juice when climate changes or insect infestations in the tropics cause crop projections to decline and scarcity value to rise.

EXAMPLE

Discovery of Jojoba Bean Causes a Collapse of Whale Oil Lubricant Prices[2]

Until the last decade of the twentieth century, the best known lubricant for high friction machinery with repeated temperature extremes such as fan blades in aircraft jet engines, contact surfaces in metal-cutting tools, and gearboxes in auto transmissions was a naturally occurring substance—sperm whale oil. In the early 1970s, the United States placed sperm whales on the endangered species list and banned their harvest. With the increasing scarcity of whales, the world market price of whale oil lubricant approached $200 per quart. Research and development for synthetic oil substitutes tried again and again but failed to find a replacement. Finally, a California scientist suggested the extract of the jojoba bean as a natural, environmentally friendly lubricant. The jojoba bean grows like a weed throughout the desert Southwest in the United States on wild trees that can be domesticated and cultivated to yield beans for up to 150 years. After production ramped up from 150 tons in 1986 to 700 tons in 1995, solvent-extracted jojoba sold for $10 per quart. When tested in the laboratory, jojoba bean extract exhibits some lubrication properties that exceed those of sperm whale oil (e.g., thermal stability over 400°). Although 85–90 percent of jojoba bean output is used in the production of cosmetics, the confirmation of this plentiful substitute for high friction lubricants caused a collapse in whale lubricant prices. Sperm whale lubricant has the same cost of production and the same use value as before the discovery of jojoba beans, but the scarcity value of the raw material input declined tenfold. Consequently, a quart of sperm whale lubricant now sells for less than $20 per quart.

The Diamond-Water Paradox and the Marginal Revolution

So equilibrium price in a marketplace is related to intrinsic use value, production cost, and input scarcity. In addition, however, most products and services have more than one use. And often these differences relate to how much or how often the product has already been consumed. For example, the initial access to e-mail servers or the Internet for several hours per day is often essential to maintaining good communication with colleagues and business associates. Additional access makes it possible to employ search engines such as Netscape or Yahoo! for information related to a work assignment. Even more access affords an opportunity to meet friends in a chat room. Finally, some households might purchase still more hours of access on the chance that a desire to surf the Web would arise unexpectedly. Each of these uses has its own distinct value along a continuum starting with necessities and ending with frivolous nonessentials. Accordingly, what a customer will pay for

[2] Based on "Jojoba Producers Form a Marketing Coop," *Chemical Marketing Reporter* (January 8, 1995), p. 10.

another hour of Internet access depends on the incremental hour in question. The greater the utilization already, the lower the use value remaining.

Marginal Use Value

The additional value of the consumption of one more unit; the greater the utilization already, the lower the use value remaining.

This concept of a **marginal use value** that declines as the rate of consumption increases leads to a powerful insight about consumer behavior. The question was posed, "Why should something as essential to human life as water sell for low market prices while something as frivolous as cosmetic diamonds sell for high market prices?" The initial answer was that water is inexpensive to produce in most parts of the world while diamonds require difficult search and discovery, expensive mining, and extensive transportation and security expenses. In other words, diamonds cost more than water, so minimum asking prices of suppliers dictate the higher market value observed for diamonds. However, recall that supply is only one of what Alfred Marshall famously called "two blades of the scissors" representing demand and supply. You can stab with one blade but you can't cut paper, and using supply alone you can't fully explain equilibrium market price.

The diamond-water paradox was therefore restated more narrowly, "Why should consumers bid low offer prices for something as essential as water while bidding high offer prices for something as frivolous as diamonds?" The resolution of the paradox hinges on distinguishing marginal use value (marginal utility) from total use value (total utility). Clearly, in some circumstances and locales, the use value of water is enormous. At an oasis in the desert, water does prevent thirsting to death. And even in the typical city, the first couple of ounces of some liquid each day serve this same function, but that's the first couple of ounces. The next couple of dozen gallons per day remain at high use value for drinking, flushing indoor plumbing, cooking, body washing, etc. Thereafter, water is used for clothes washing, landscape watering, car washing, and sundry lesser purposes. Indeed, if one asks the typical American household (which consumes 80–100 gallons per person per day) to identify its least valuable use of water each day, the answer may come back truly frivolous—perhaps something like the water that runs down the sink drain while brushing teeth. In other words, the marginal use value of water in most developed countries is the water that saves the consumer the inconvenience of turning the water taps (on and off) twice rather than once. And it is this marginal use value at the relevant margin, not the total utility across all uses, that determines a typical consumer's meager willingness to pay.

Marginal Utility and Marginal Cost Simultaneously Determine Equilibrium Market Price

Marginal Utility

The use value obtained from the last unit consumed.

Marginal Cost

The incremental variable cost of the next unit supplied.

Alfred Marshall had it right; demand and supply do simultaneously determine market equilibrium price "like two blades of a pair of scissors." On the one hand, **marginal utility** determines the maximum offer price consumers are willing to pay for each additional unit of consumption on the demand side of the market. And on the other, again a marginal concept—**marginal cost**—determines the minimum asking price producers are willing to accept for each additional unit supplied. Water is both cheaper to produce and more frivolous than diamonds *at the relevant margin*, and hence water's market equilibrium price is lower than that of diamonds. Figure 2.2 illustrates this concept of marginal use value for water varying from the essential first few ounces to the water left running while brushing one's teeth.

At the same time, the marginal cost of producing water remains low throughout the 900-gallon range of a typical household's consumption. In contrast, diamonds exhibit steeply rising marginal cost even at relatively small volume, and customers continue to employ cosmetic diamonds for highly valuable uses even out to the relevant margin where typical households find their purchases occurring. Therefore, diamonds should trade for equilibrium market prices that exceed the equilibrium market price of water.

Figure 2.2 The Diamond–Water Paradox Resolved

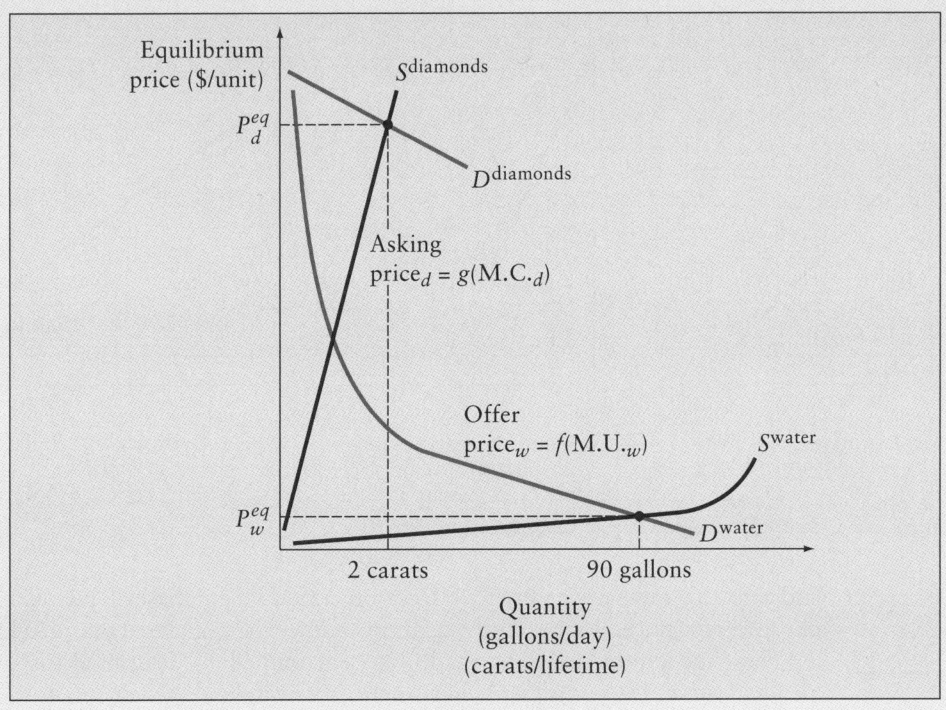

INDIVIDUAL AND MARKET DEMAND CURVES

We have seen that the market-clearing price (P_{eq}), which sets the desired rate of purchase (Q_d/t) equal to the planned rate of sale (Q_s/t), is simultaneously both the maximum offer price demanders are willing to pay (the "offer") and the minimum asking price sellers are willing to accept (the "ask"). But what determines Q_d/t and Q_s/t? The demand schedule is the simplest form of the demand relationship. It is merely a list of prices and corresponding quantities of a commodity that would be demanded by some individual or group of individuals at uniform prices. Table 2.1 shows the demand schedule for regular-size pizzas at a Pizza Hut restaurant. This demand schedule

Table 2.1 Simplified Demand Schedule: Pizza Hut Restaurant

Price of Pizza ($/Unit)	Quantity of Pizzas Sold (Units Per Time Period)
10	50
9	60
8	70
7	80
6	90
5	100

Figure 2.3 Individual and Market Demand Curves

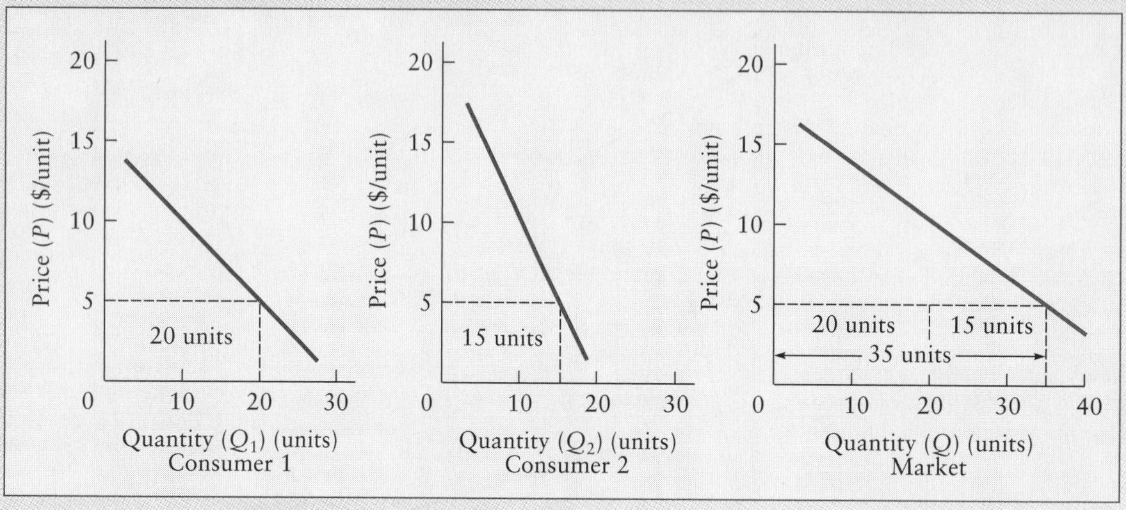

indicates that *if* the price were $9.00, customers would purchase 60 per night. Note that the lower the price, the greater the quantity that will be demanded than at a higher price.

Demand Curve
A relationship between price and quantity demanded, holding other determinants of demand constant.

The expenditure decisions made by each individual determine his or her own **demand curve.** The consumer behavior underlying individual demand is often the basis for making advertising and promotion decisions. The market demand curve is equal to the sum of the individual demands. As shown in Figure 2.3, for two individuals, the market demand curve is obtained through the horizontal summation of the quantities demanded at each price.[3] For example, at a price of $5.00 per unit, consumers 1 and 2 would purchase 20 and 15 units, respectively, yielding a market demand of 35 units. Other points on the market demand curve are obtained in a similar manner. Market demand serves as a basis for making many pricing and output decisions.

THE DEMAND FUNCTION

The demand schedule (or curve) specifies the relationship between prices and quantity demanded, *holding constant the influence of all other factors.* A demand function specifies all these other factors that management will often consider, including the design and packaging of products, the amount and distribution of the firm's advertising budget, the size of the sales force, promotional expenditures, the time period of adjustment for any price changes, and taxes or subsidies. As detailed in Table 2.2, the **demand function** for domestic autos can be represented as

Demand Function
A relationship between quantity demanded and all the determinants of demand.

$$Q_D = f(P, P_S, P_C, Y, A, A_C, N, C_P, P_E, T_A, T/S \ldots) \quad [2.1]$$

where Q_D = quantity demanded of (e.g., General Motors Malibu auto)
P = price of the good or service (the auto)
P_S = price of substitute goods or services (e.g., Honda Accord)

[3] For goods that can be shared, such as pools, concerts, and flood control projects, market demand is the vertical summation of the willingness to pay of the individual demanders.

Table 2.2 Partial List of Factors Affecting Demand

Demand Factor	Expected Effect
Increase (decrease) in price of substitute goods[a] (P_S)	Increase (decrease) in demand (Q_D)
Increase (decrease) in price of complementary goods[b] (P_C)	Decrease (increase) in Q_D
Increase (decrease) in consumer income levels[c] (Y)	Increase (decrease) in Q_D
Increase (decrease) in the amount of advertising and marketing expenditures (A)	Increase (decrease) in Q_D
Increase (decrease) in level of advertising and marketing by competitors (A_C)	Decrease (increase) in Q_D
Increase (decrease) in population (N)	Increase (decrease) in Q_D
Increase (decrease) in consumer preferences for the good or service (C_P)	Increase (decrease) in Q_D
Expected future price increases (decreases) for the good (P_E)	Increase (decrease) in Q_D
Time period of adjustment increases (decreases) (T_A)	Increase (decrease) in Q_D
Taxes (subsidies) on the good increase (decrease) (T/S)	Decrease (increase) in Q_D

[a] Two goods are substitutes if an increase (decrease) in the price of Good 1 results in an increase (decrease) in the quantity demanded of Good 2, holding other factors constant, such as the price of Good 2, other prices, income, and so on, or vice versa. For example, margarine may be viewed as a rather good substitute for butter. As the price of butter increases, more people will decrease their consumption of butter and increase their consumption of margarine.

[b] Goods that are used in conjunction with each other, either in production or consumption, are called *complementary goods*. For example, DVDs are used in conjunction with DVD players. An increase in the price of DVD players would have the effect of decreasing the demand for DVDs, *ceteris paribus*. In other words, two goods are complementary if a decrease in the price of Good 1 results in an increase in the quantity demanded of Good 2, *ceteris paribus*. Similarly, two goods are complements if an increase in the price of Good 1 results in a decrease in the quantity demanded of Good 2.

[c] The case of inferior goods—that is, those goods that are purchased in smaller total quantities as income levels rise—will be discussed in Chapter 3.

P_C = price of complementary goods or services (gasoline, tires)
Y = income of consumers
A = advertising and promotion expenditures
A_C = competitors' advertising and promotion expenditures
N = size of the potential target market (demographic factors)
C_P = consumer tastes and preferences for the good or service
P_E = expected future price appreciation or depreciation
T_A = adjustment time period
T/S = taxes or subsidies

The demand schedule or demand curve merely deals with the price-quantity relationship itself. *Changes in the price (P) of the good or service will result only in movement along the demand curve, whereas changes in any of the other demand determinants in the demand function (P_S, P_C, Y, A, A_C, N, C_P, P_E, and so on) will shift the curve.* This distinction is illustrated graphically in Figure 2.4. The initial demand relationship is line DD'. If the original price were P_1, quantity Q_1 would be demanded. If the price declined to P_2, the quantity demanded would increase to Q_2. If, however, changes occurred in the other determinants of demand, we would expect to have a shift in the entire demand curve. If, for example, a general tax reduction were enacted and, as a result, consumer disposable income increased, the new demand curve might become $D_1D'_1$. At any price, P_1, along $D_1D'_1$, a greater quantity, Q_3, will be demanded than at the same price on the original curve DD'. Similarly, if the prices of substitute products were to decline, the demand curve would shift downward and to the left. At any price, P_1, along the new curve

Figure 2.4 Shifts in Demand

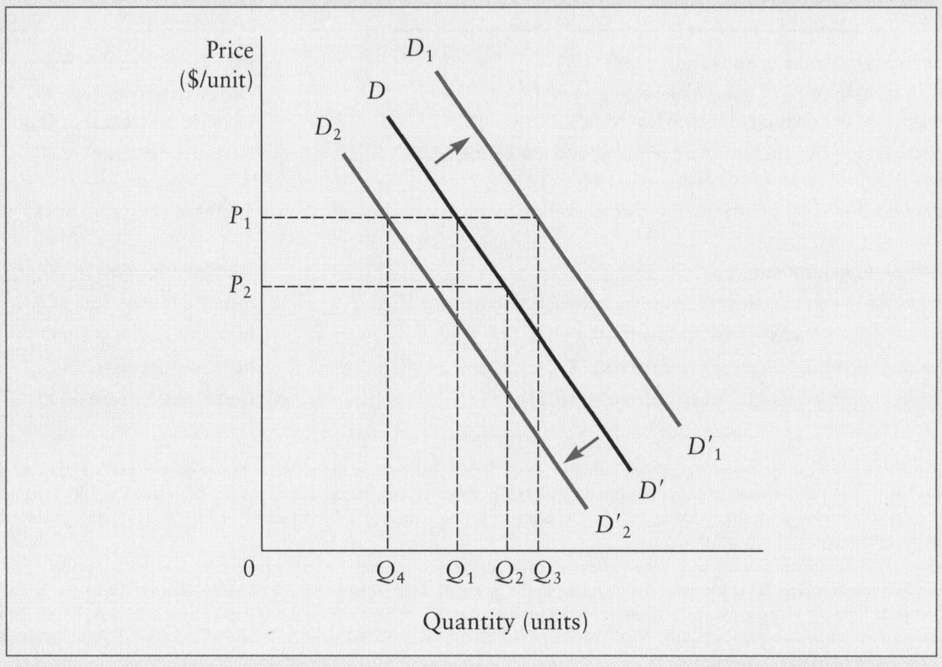

$D_2D'_2$, a smaller quantity, Q_4, would be demanded than at the same price on either DD' or $D_1D'_1$.

In summary, movement *along* a demand curve is often referred to as *a change in the quantity demanded,* while holding constant the effects of factors other than price that affect demand. In contrast, a shift of the entire demand curve is often referred to as *a change in demand* and is always caused by some demand determinant other than price.

EXAMPLE

Complement Strategy at General Motors and GMAC[4]

Identifying, developing, and managing effectively the relationships with suppliers of complementary products in order to increase the demand for one's own product has become a key element of corporate strategy. The other five forces of competition (threat of substitutes, intensity of rivalry, threat of entry, power of buyers, and power of suppliers) are much more difficult to influence. To eliminate the competition from substitute products requires a never-ending upstaging of new imitators and can seldom provide sustainable competitive advantage. To cooperate effectively with rivals often constitutes a violation of the antitrust laws of the United States or the tougher antitrust laws of the European Union. To erect permanent barriers to entry requires the best product differentiation ad campaigns and relationship marketing. Finally, the power of buyers and suppliers is often beyond a firm's control. Consequently,

[4] Adam Brandenberg and Barry Nalebuff explain this role of complementary products in *Co-Opetition* (New York: Bantam Books, 1996). Michael Porter's five forces of competition model is described in Chapter 10 (see Figure 10.2).

many companies today seek to develop complementary products to drive demand for their primary products.

To meet this challenge, General Motors (GM) expanded its operations to include high-end auto loans and specialty auto insurance products (General Motors Acceptance Corporation, GMAC). GM didn't go this direction because the loan and insurance markets are particularly profitable businesses in their own right, but rather because these offerings reduce the time and inconvenience involved with arranging loans and insurance when people buy automobiles. Offering these services makes it easier to sell profitable Suburbans, Cadillacs, and other luxury cars and trucks.

Similarly, Intel engineers responsible for designing computer chips now regularly outpace the demands of current PC applications for speed and computation capacity. So, Intel entered into a joint venture with ProShare to accelerate the development of inexpensive interactive video, desktop video conferencing, and video telephone products. These new complementary technologies will require much larger and faster computer chips. Other examples that illustrate a company's astute use of complements to increase the demand for their primary products are Michelin tires and travel guides, Borders books and in-store coffee bars, inexpensive reading glasses displayed alongside Hallmark greeting cards, as well as convenience stores and fast-food franchises in gas stations.

Traded Goods In addition to the determinants of demand already mentioned, the demand for goods traded in foreign markets is also influenced by external factors such as exchange rate fluctuations. When Microsoft sells computer software overseas, it prefers to be paid in U.S. dollars. The reason behind this preference is that a company such as Microsoft incurs few offshore expenses beyond advertising and therefore cannot simply match payables and receivables in a foreign currency. To accept euros, Japanese Yen, or Australian dollars in payment for software purchase orders would introduce an exchange rate risk exposure for which Microsoft would want to be compensated in the form of higher prices on its software. Consequently, the foreign exports of Microsoft are typically transacted in U.S. dollars and are therefore tied inextricably to the price of the dollar against other currencies. As the value of the dollar rises, offshore buyers must pay a larger amount of their own currency to obtain the U.S. dollars required to complete a purchase order for Microsoft's software, and this exchange value decreases the export demand. Similarly, a lower value of the dollar reduces the euro or yen price of the product, raising the export demand for Microsoft software. Even in a large domestic market such as the United States, companies often find that these export demand considerations are key determinants of their overall demand.

EXAMPLE

EXCHANGE RATE IMPACTS ON DEMAND: CUMMINS ENGINE COMPANY

Cummins Engine Company of Columbus, Indiana, is the largest independent manufacturer of new and replacement diesel engines for heavy trucks and for construction, mining, and agricultural machinery. GMC, Ford, and Daimler-Benz are their major competitors, and 38 percent of sales occur offshore. The Cummins and Daimler-Benz large diesel truck engines sell for approximately $40,000 and €32,000, respectively. In the 2002 recession, Cummins suffered substantial declines in cash flow. One reason was obvious; diesel replacement engines are not needed when fewer goods are being delivered and therefore fewer diesels are wearing out.

In addition, however, between 1999 and 2002, the value of the U.S. dollar (€ per $) increased by 30 percent from €.85/$ to €1.15/$. This change in the exchange value meant that a $40,000 Cummins diesel engine that had sold for €34,000 in Munich in 1999 became €46,000, whereas the €32,000 Mercedes diesel alternative that had been selling for $37,647 in Detroit declined to $27,826 because of the stronger U.S. dollar. Cummins faced two unattractive options, either of which would reduce its cash flow. It could either cut its profit margins and maintain unit sales, or maintain margins but have both offshore and domestic sales collapse. The company chose to cut margins and maintain sales. By 2005, the dollar's value had eroded, returning to €.85/$, and Cummins' sales performance markedly improved. In the interim, demand for Cummins engines was adversely affected by the temporary appreciation of the U.S. dollar.

Individual and Market Supply Curves

What determines Q_s/t? Like the demand schedule, the supply schedule is a list of prices and corresponding quantities that an individual or group of sellers desire to sell at uniform prices, *holding constant the influence of all other factors*. A number of these other determinants of supply that management will often need to consider are detailed in Table 2.3. The **supply function** can be represented as

Supply Function

A relationship between quantity supplied and all the determinants of supply.

$$Q_s = f(P, P_I, P_{UI}, T, EE, F, RC, P_E, T_A, T/S \ldots) \qquad [2.2]$$

where Q_s = quantity supplied (e.g., of domestic autos)
P = price of the autos
P_I = price of inputs (e.g., sheet metal)
P_{UI} = price of unused substitute inputs (e.g., fiberglass)
T = technological improvements (e.g., robotic welding)
EE = entry or exit of other auto sellers
F = accidental supply interruptions from fires, floods, etc.
RC = costs of regulatory compliance
P_E = expected (future) changes in price
T_A = adjustment time period
T/S = taxes or subsidies

Table 2.3 Partial List of Factors Affecting Supply

Supply Factor	Expected Effect at Every Price
Increase (decrease) in the price of inputs (P_I)	Decrease (increase) in supply
Increase (decrease) in the price of unused substitute inputs (P_{UI})	Decrease (increase) in supply
Technological improvements (T)	Increase in supply
Entry (Exit) of other sellers (EE)	Increase (decrease) in supply
Supply disruptions (F)	Decrease in supply
Increase (decrease) in regulatory costs (RC)	Decrease (increase) in supply
Expected future price increases (decreases) (P_E)	Decrease (increase) in supply
Time period of adjustment lengthens (shortens) (T_A)	Increase (decrease) in supply
Taxes (subsidies) (T/S)	Decrease (increase) in supply

Supply Curve
A relationship between price and quantity supplied, holding other determinants of supply constant.

Again, changes in the price (P) of the good or service will result only in movement along the given **supply curve**, whereas changes in any of the other independent variables (P_I, P_{UI}, T, EE, F, RC, P_E, and so on) in the function shift the supply curve. As with demand, a movement *along* a supply curve is referred to as *a change in the quantity supplied,* while holding constant other determinants of supply. A shift of the entire supply curve is often referred to as *a change in supply* and is always caused by some supply determinant other than price.

EXAMPLE

NAFTA and the Reduced Labor Costs of Ford Assembly Plants in Detroit

The North American Free Trade Agreement (NAFTA) made it possible to buy subassemblies such as axles and engine blocks from Mexican suppliers, including Cifunsa, SA, without paying any import tariff when the parts arrived in the United States. Because UAW labor in Detroit auto assembly plants also makes axle subassemblies, the Mexican labor input can be thought of as an unused substitute input from the point of view of Ford Motor Company. NAFTA in effect lowered the input cost of substitute inputs for Ford. This factor means fewer employers would pursue labor contracts with United Auto Workers (UAW) in Detroit and instead shift some of their production south across the Mexican border. Less demand implies lower equilibrium wages will be offered and accepted by UAW assembly line labor. Hence, the indirect effect of NAFTA was a reduction in input costs for UAW labor that the Ford Motor Co. did utilize. As usual, lower input cost implies a shift of the supply curve down and to the right, an increase in supply.

Marginal Analysis

Marginal Analysis
A basis for making various economic decisions, which analyzes the additional (marginal) benefits derived from a particular decision and compares them with the additional (marginal) costs incurred.

Marginal analysis is one of the most useful concepts in microeconomics. Resource-allocation decisions typically are expressed in terms of the marginal equilibrium conditions that must be satisfied to attain an optimal solution. The familiar profit-maximization rule for the firm of setting output at the point where "marginal cost equals marginal revenue" is one such example. Long-term investment decisions (capital expenditures) also are made using marginal analysis decision rules. Only if the expected return from an investment project (i.e., the *marginal return* to the firm) exceeds the cost of funds that must be acquired to finance the project (the *marginal cost* of capital), should the project be undertaken. Following this important marginal decision rule leads to the maximization of shareholder wealth.

EXAMPLE

Tenneco Shipyard Marginal Analysis

Resource-allocation decisions should be made by comparing the marginal (or incremental) benefits of a change in the level of an activity with the marginal (or incremental) costs of the change. *Marginal benefit* is defined as the change in total benefits that are derived from undertaking some economic activity, such as additional shipbuilding at Tenneco Shipyards. For example, the marginal revenue (a benefit) derived from producing and selling one more supertanker is equal to the difference between total revenue, assuming the additional unit is not sold, and total revenue including the additional sale.

Similarly, *marginal cost* is defined as the change in total costs that occurs from undertaking some economic activity, such as the production of an additional ship design including the opportunity costs, and therefore may not necessarily always be equal to the cash outlays alone. Perhaps the Tenneco design team has an opportunity for higher net profit as subcontractors on Boeing projects. If so, Tenneco's routine ship-design work should be contracted out to other shipbuilding design firms who can become trusted subcontractors to Tenneco.

More generally, a change in the level of an economic activity is desirable if the marginal benefits exceed the marginal costs, which is equivalent to saying that the increase in total revenues exceeds the increase in total costs. Therefore, in decisions involving the expansion of an economic activity, the optimal level occurs at the point where the marginal benefits are equal to the marginal costs. If we define *net marginal return* as the *difference* between marginal benefits and marginal costs, then an equivalent optimality condition is that the level of the activity should be increased to the point where the net marginal return is zero.

EXAMPLE

Marginal Analysis and Capital Budgeting Decisions: Sara Lee Corporation

The capital budgeting decision problem facing a typical firm, such as Sara Lee Corporation, can be used to illustrate the application of marginal analysis decision rules. Sara Lee has the following schedule of potential investment projects (all assumed to be of equal risk) available to it:

Project	Investment Required ($ millions)	Expected Rate of Return	Cumulative Investment ($ millions)
A	$25.0	27.0%	$ 25.0
B	15.0	24.0	40.0
C	40.0	21.0	80.0
D	35.0	18.0	115.0
E	12.0	15.0	127.0
F	20.0	14.0	147.0
G	18.0	13.0	165.0
H	13.0	11.0	178.0
I	7.0	8.0	185.0

Sara Lee estimates the cost of acquiring the funds needed to finance these investment projects as follows:

Block of Funds ($ millions)	Cost of Capital	Cumulative Funds Raised ($ millions)
First $50.0	10.0%	$ 50.0
Next $25.0	10.5	75.0
Next $40.0	11.0	115.0
Next $50.0	12.2	165.0
Next $20.0	14.5	185.0

The expected rate of return on these projects can be thought of as the marginal (or incremental) return available to Sara Lee as it undertakes each additional investment project. Similarly, the cost-of-capital schedule may be thought of as the marginal cost of acquiring the needed funds. Following the marginal analysis rules means that Sara Lee should invest in additional projects as long as the expected rate of return on the project exceeds the marginal cost of capital funds needed to finance the project.

Project A, which offers an expected return of 27 percent and requires an outlay of \$25 million, is acceptable because the marginal return exceeds the marginal cost of capital (10.0 percent for the first \$50 million of funds raised by Sara Lee). In fact, an examination of the tables indicates that projects A through G all meet the marginal analysis test because the marginal return from each of these projects exceeds the marginal cost of capital funds needed to finance these projects. In contrast, projects H and I should not be undertaken because they offer returns of 11 and 8 percent, respectively, compared with a marginal cost of capital of 14.5 percent for the \$20 million in funds needed to finance these projects.

In summary, marginal analysis instructs decision makers to determine the additional (marginal) costs and additional (marginal) benefits associated with a proposed action. *Only if the marginal benefits exceed the marginal costs* (i.e., if net marginal benefits are positive) should the action be taken.

TOTAL, MARGINAL, AND AVERAGE RELATIONSHIPS

Economic relationships can be presented using tabular, graphic, and algebraic frameworks. Let us first use a tabular presentation. Suppose that the total profit π_T of a firm is a function of the number of units of output produced Q, as shown in columns 1 and 2 of Table 2.4.

Table 2.4 Total, Marginal, and Average Profit Relationships

(1) Number of Units of Output Per Unit of Time Q	(2) Total Profit $\pi_T(Q)$ (\$)	(3) Marginal Profit $\Delta\pi(Q) = \pi_T(Q) - \pi_T(Q-1)$ (\$/Unit)	(4) Average Profit $\pi_A(Q) = \pi_T(Q)/Q$ (\$/Unit)
0	−200	0	—
1	−150	50	−150.00
2	−25	125	−12.50
3	200	225	66.67
4	475	275	118.75
5	775	300	155.00
6	1,075	300	179.17
7	1,325	250	189.29
8	1,475	150	184.38
9	1,500	25	166.67
10	1,350	−150	135.00

Marginal profit, which represents the change in total profit resulting from a one-unit increase in output, is shown in column 3 of the table. (A Δ is used to represent a "change" in some variable.) The marginal profit $\Delta\pi(Q)$ of any level of output Q is calculated by taking the difference between the total profit at this level $\pi_T(Q)$ and at one unit below this level $\pi_T(Q-1)$.[5] In comparing the marginal and total profit functions, we note that for increasing output levels, the marginal profit values remain positive as long as the total profit function is increasing. Only when the total profit function begins decreasing—that is, at $Q =$ 10 units—does the marginal profit become negative. The average profit function values $\pi_A(Q)$, shown in column 4 of Table 2.4, are obtained by dividing the total profit figure $\pi_T(Q)$ by the output level Q. In comparing the marginal and the average profit function values, we see that the average profit function $\pi_A(Q)$ is increasing as long as the marginal profit is greater than the average profit—that is, up to $Q = 7$ units. Beyond an output level of $Q = 7$ units, the marginal profit is less than the average profit and the average profit function values are decreasing.

By examining the total profit function $\pi_T(Q)$ in Table 2.4, we see that profit is maximized at an output level of $Q = 9$ units. Given that the objective is to maximize total profit, then the optimal output decision would be to produce and sell 9 units. If the marginal analysis decision rule discussed earlier in this section is used, the same (optimal) decision is obtained. Applying the rule to this problem, the firm would expand production as long as the *net* marginal return—that is, marginal revenue minus marginal cost (marginal profit)—is positive. From column 3 of Table 2.4, we can see that the marginal profit is positive for output levels up to $Q = 9$. Therefore, the marginal profit decision rule would indicate that 9 units should be produced, which is the same decision that was obtained from the total profit function.

The relationships among the total, marginal, and average profit functions and the optimal output decision also can be represented graphically. A set of *continuous* profit functions, analogous to those presented in Table 2.4 for discrete integer values of output (Q), is shown in Figure 2.5. At the break-even output level Q_1, both total profits and average profits are zero. The marginal profit function, which equals the *slope* of the total profit function, takes on its maximum value at an output of Q_2 units. This point corresponds to the *inflection point*. Below the inflection point, total profits are increasing at an increasing rate, and hence marginal profits are increasing. Above the inflection point, up to an output level Q_4, total profits are increasing at a decreasing rate and consequently marginal profits are decreasing. The average profit function, which represents the slope of a straight line drawn from the origin 0 to each point on the total profit function, takes on its maximum value at an output of Q_3 units. The average profit necessarily equals the marginal profit at this point, because the slope of the $0A$ line, which defines the average profit, is also equal to the slope of the total profit function at point A, which defines the marginal profit. Finally, total profit is maximized at an output of Q_4 units where marginal profit equals 0. Beyond Q_4 the total profit function is decreasing, and consequently the marginal profit function takes on negative values.

---

[5] Web Appendix A expands upon the idea that the total profit function can be maximized by identifying the level of activity at which the marginal profit function goes to zero.

Figure 2.5 Total, Average, and Marginal Profit Functions

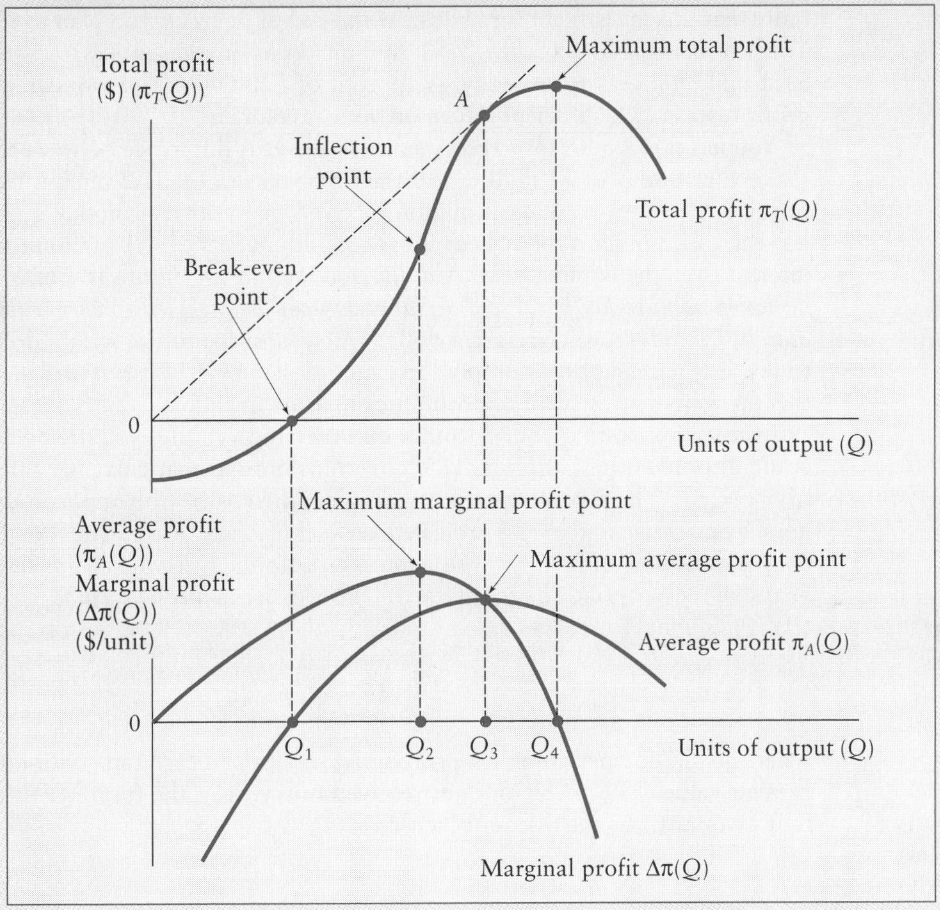

THE NET PRESENT VALUE CONCEPT

The MR = MC rule, just discussed, is best suited for situations when the costs and benefits occur at approximately the same time. Many economic decisions require that costs be incurred immediately but result in a stream of benefits over several future time periods. In these cases, the *net present value* (NPV) *rule* provides appropriate guidance for decision makers.

The NPV of an investment made by a firm represents the contribution of that investment to the value of the firm and, accordingly, to the wealth of shareholders. The net present value concept is used to evaluate the cash flows generated from the firm's activities. Hence, the NPV concept plays a central role in the achievement of shareholder wealth maximization.

DETERMINING THE NET PRESENT VALUE OF AN INVESTMENT

To understand the NPV rule, consider the following situation: You just inherited $1 million. Your financial advisor suggests that you use these funds to purchase a piece of land near a proposed new highway interchange. Your advisor, who is also a state road commissioner, is certain that the interchange will be built and that in one year the value of this land will increase to \$1.2 million. Hence, you believe initially that this investment is riskless. At the end of one year you plan to sell the land. You are being asked to invest \$1 million today in the anticipation of receiving \$1.2 million a year from today, or a profit of \$200,000. You wonder whether this profit represents a sufficient return on your investment.

You feel it is important to recognize the one-year difference between the time you make your outlay of \$1 million and the time you receive \$1.2 million from the sale of the land. A return of \$1.2 million received one year from today must be worth less than \$1.2 million today because you could invest your \$1 million today to earn interest over the coming year. *A dollar received in the future is worth less than a dollar in hand today because a dollar today can be invested to earn a return immediately.* Therefore, to compare a dollar received in the future with a dollar in hand today, it is necessary to multiply the future dollar by a *discount factor* that reflects the alternative investment opportunities that are available.

Instead of investing your \$1 million in the land venture, you are aware that you could also invest in a one-year U.S. government bond that currently offers a return of 5 percent. The 5 percent return represents the return (the opportunity cost) forgone by investing in the land project. The 5 percent rate also can be thought of as the compensation to an investor who agrees to postpone receiving a cash return for one year. The appropriate discount factor, also called a *present value interest factor* (*PVIF*), is equal to

$$PVIF = \frac{1}{1+i}$$

Present Value

The value today of a future amount of money or a series of future payments evaluated at the appropriate discount rate.

where i is the compensation for postponing receipt of a cash return for one year. The **present value** (PV_0) of an amount received one year in the future (FV_1) is equal to that amount times the discount factor, or

$$PV_0 = FV_1 \times (PVIF) \qquad [2.3]$$

In the case of the land project, the present value of the promised \$1.2 million expected to be received in one year is equal to

$$PV_0 = \$1.2 \text{ million} \left(\frac{1}{1+0.05}\right) = \$1{,}142{,}857$$

If you invested \$1,142,857 today to earn 5 percent for the coming year, you would have \$1.2 million at the end of the year. You are clearly better off with the proposed land investment (assuming that it really is riskless like the U.S. government bond investment). How much better off are you?

The answer to this question is at the heart of NPV calculations. The land investment project is worth \$1,142,857 today to an investor who demands a 5 percent return on this type of investment. You, however, have been able to acquire this investment for only \$1 million. Thus your present wealth has increased by undertaking this investment by \$142,857 (\$1,142,857 present value of the projected investment opportunity payoffs minus the required initial investment of \$1 million). The NPV of this investment is \$142,857. In general, the NPV of an investment is equal to

$$\text{NPV} = \text{Present value of future returns} - \text{Initial outlay} \qquad [2.4]$$

This example was simplified by assuming that the returns from the investment were received exactly one year from the date of the initial outlay. The NPV rule can be generalized to cover returns received over any number of future time periods. In Appendix A the present value concept is developed in more detail so that it can be applied in more complex investment settings.

SOURCES OF POSITIVE NET PRESENT VALUE PROJECTS

What causes some projects to have a positive NPV and others to have a negative NPV? When product and factor markets are other than perfectly competitive, it is possible for a firm to earn above-normal profits (economic rents) that result in positive net present value projects. The reasons why these above-normal profits may be available arise from conditions that define each type of product and factor market and distinguish it from a perfectly competitive market. These reasons include the following barriers to entry and other factors:

1. Buyer preferences for established brand names
2. Ownership or control of favored distribution systems (such as exclusive auto dealerships or airline hubs)
3. Patent control of superior product designs or production techniques
4. Exclusive ownership of superior natural resource deposits
5. Inability of new firms to acquire necessary factors of production (management, labor, equipment)
6. Superior access to financial resources at lower costs (economies of scale in attracting capital)
7. Economies of large-scale production and distribution arising from
   a. Capital-intensive production processes
   b. High initial start-up costs

These factors can permit a firm to identify positive net present value projects for internal investment. If the barriers to entry are sufficiently high (such as a patent on key technology) so as to prevent any new competition or if the start-up period for competitive ventures is sufficiently long, then it is possible that a project may have a positive net present value. However, in assessing the viability of such a project, the manager or analyst must consider the likely period of time when above-normal returns can be earned before new competitors emerge and force cash flows back to a more normal level. It is generally unrealistic to expect to be able to earn above-normal returns over the entire life of an investment project.

RISK AND THE NPV RULE

The preceding land investment example assumed that the investment was riskless. Therefore, the rate of return used to compute the discount factor and the net present value was the riskless rate of return available on a U.S. government bond having a one-year maturity. What if you do not believe your investment advisor who says that the construction of the new interchange is a certainty, or you are not confident about your advisor's estimate of the value of the land in one year? To compensate for the perceived risk of this investment, you decide that you require a 15 percent rate of return on your investment. Using a 15 percent required rate of return in calculating the discount factor, the present value of the expected $1.2 million sales price of the land is $1,008,696 [$1.2 million × (1/1.15)]. Thus, the NPV of this investment declines to $8,696. The increase in the perceived risk of the investment results in a dramatic decline in its NPV.

A primary problem facing managers is the difficulty of evaluating the risk associated with investments and then translating that risk into a discount rate that reflects an adequate level of risk compensation. In the next section of this chapter we discuss the risk concept and the factors that affect investment risk and influence the required rate of return on an investment.

Meaning and Measurement of Risk

We begin the discussion of risk analysis by defining several key terms and concepts. Although the examples presented here deal primarily with investment decisions, the ideas are applicable to all other types of economic decisions, such as those of pricing and production.

The Meaning of Risk-Free and Risky Investments

Risk implies a chance for some unfavorable outcome to occur. From the perspective of security analysis or the analysis of an investment project, risk is the *possibility that actual cash flows (returns) will be less than forecasted cash flows (returns)*. More generally, **risk** refers to the chance that you will encounter an outcome that differs from the expected outcome. When a range of potential outcomes is associated with a decision and the decision maker is able to assign probabilities to each of these possible outcomes, risk is said to exist.

Risk
A decision-making situation that involves variability in the possible outcomes whose probabilities can be specified by the decision maker.

An investment decision is said to be *risk-free* if the outcome (dollar returns) from the initial investment is known with certainty. A good example of a risk-free investment is U.S. Treasury securities. There is virtually no chance that the Treasury will fail to redeem these securities at maturity or that the Treasury will default on any interest payments owed.[6]

In contrast, US Airways bonds constitute a *risky* investment opportunity because it is possible that US Airways will default on one or more interest payments and will lack sufficient funds at maturity to redeem the bonds at face value.

In summary, *risk* refers to the potential variability of outcomes from a decision. The more variable these outcomes are, the greater the risk.

Probability Distributions

Probability
The percentage chance that a particular outcome will occur.

The **probability** that a particular outcome will occur is defined as the relative frequency or *percentage chance* of its occurrence. Probabilities may be either objectively or subjectively determined. An objective determination is based on past outcomes of similar events, whereas a subjective determination is merely an opinion made by an

[6] Note that this discussion of risk deals with *dollar returns* and ignores such other considerations as potential losses in purchasing power. In addition, it assumes that securities are held until maturity, which is not always the case. Sometimes a security must be sold before maturity and at such times the seller may suffer a capital loss (selling for less than face value) because of changes in the level of interest rates.

individual about the likelihood that a given event will occur. In the case of decisions that are frequently repeated, such as the drilling of developmental oil wells in an established oil field, reasonably good objective estimates can be made about the success of a new well. In contrast, for totally new decisions or one-of-a-kind investments, subjective estimates about the likelihood of various outcomes are necessary. The fact that many probability estimates in business are at least partially subjective does not diminish their usefulness.

EXAMPLE

PROBABILITY DISTRIBUTIONS AND RISK: US AIRWAYS BONDS

Consider an investor who is contemplating the purchase of US Airways bonds. That investor might assign the probabilities associated with the three possible outcomes from this investment, as shown in Table 2.5. These probabilities are interpreted to mean that a 30 percent chance exists that the bonds will not be in default over their life and will be redeemed at maturity, a 65 percent chance of interest default during the life of the bonds, and a 5 percent chance that the bonds will not be redeemed at maturity. In this example, no other outcomes are deemed possible.

Table 2.5 Possible Outcomes from Investing in US Airways Bonds

Outcome	Probability
No default, bonds redeemed at maturity	0.30
Default on interest for one or more periods	0.65
No interest default, but bonds not redeemed at maturity	0.05
	1.00

Using either objective or subjective methods, the decision maker can develop a probability distribution for the possible outcomes. Table 2.6 shows the probability distribution of net cash flows for two sample investments. The lowest estimated annual net cash flow (NCF) for each investment—$200 for Investment I and $100 for Investment II—represents pessimistic forecasts about the investments' performance; the middle values ($300 and $300) could be considered normal performance levels; and the highest values ($400 and $500) are optimistic estimates.

Table 2.6 Probability Distributions of the Annual Net Cash Flows (NCF) from Two Investments

Investment I		Investment II	
Possible NCF	Probability	Possible NCF	Probability
$200	0.2	$100	0.2
300	0.6	300	0.6
400	0.2	500	0.2
	1.0		1.0

EXPECTED VALUES

Expected Value
The weighted average of the possible outcomes where the weights are the probabilities of the respective outcomes.

From this information, the expected value of each decision alternative can be calculated. The **expected value** is defined as the weighted average of the possible outcomes. It is the value that is expected to occur on average if the decision (such as an investment) were repeated a large number of times.

Algebraically, the expected value may be defined as

$$\bar{r} = \sum_{j=1}^{n} r_j p_j \qquad [2.5]$$

where $\bar{r}$ is the expected value; r_j is the outcome for the jth case, among n possible outcomes; and p_j is the probability that the jth outcome will occur. The expected cash flows for Investments I and II are calculated in Table 2.7 using Equation 2.5. In this example both investments have expected values of annual net cash flows equaling $300.

Table 2.7 Computation of the Expected Returns from Two Investments

Investment I			Investment II		
r_j	p_j	$r_j \times p_j$	r_j	p_j	$r_j \times p_j$
$200	0.2	$ 40	$100	0.2	$ 20
300	0.6	180	300	0.6	180
400	0.2	80	500	0.2	100
	Expected value: $\bar{r}_I$ = $300				$\bar{r}_{II}$ = $300

STANDARD DEVIATION: AN ABSOLUTE MEASURE OF RISK

Standard Deviation
A statistical measure of the dispersion or variability of possible outcomes.

The **standard deviation** is a statistical measure of the dispersion of a variable about its mean. It is defined as the square root of the weighted average squared deviations of individual outcomes from the mean:

$$\sigma = \sqrt{\sum_{j=1}^{n} (r_j - \bar{r}_j)^2 p_j} \qquad [2.6]$$

where σ is the standard deviation.

The standard deviation can be used to measure the variability of a decision alternative. As such, it gives an indication of the risk involved in the alternative. The larger the standard deviation, the more variable the possible outcomes and the riskier the decision alternative. A standard deviation of zero indicates no variability and thus no risk.

Table 2.8 shows the calculation of the standard deviations for Investments I and II. These calculations show that Investment II appears to be *riskier* than Investment I because the expected cash flows from Investment II are *more variable.*

This example dealt with a *discrete* probability distribution of outcomes (net cash flows) for each investment; that is, a *limited* number of possible outcomes were identified and probabilities were assigned to them. In reality, however, many different outcomes are possible for each investment decision, ranging from losses each year to annual net cash flows in excess of the optimistic estimates of $400 and $500. To indicate the probability of *all* possible outcomes, it is necessary to construct a

Table 2.8 Computation of the Standard Deviations for Two Investments

	j	r_j	$\bar{r}$	$r_j - \bar{r}$	$(r_j - \bar{r})^2$	p_j	$(r_j - \bar{r})^2 p_j$
Investment I	1	$200	$300	$−100	$10,000	0.2	$2,000
	2	300	300	0	0	0.6	0
	3	400	300	100	10,000	0.2	2,000

$$\sum_{j=1}^{3} (r_j - \bar{r})^2 p_j = \$4{,}000$$

$$\sigma = \sqrt{\sum_{j=1}^{n} (r_j - \bar{r})^2 p_j} = \sqrt{4{,}000} = \$63.25$$

	j	r_j	$\bar{r}$	$r_j - \bar{r}$	$(r_j - \bar{r})^2$	p_j	$(r_j - \bar{r})^2 p_j$
Investment II	1	$100	$300	$−200	$40,000	0.2	$8,000
	2	300	300	0	0	0.6	0
	3	500	300	200	40,000	0.2	8,000

$$\sum_{j=1}^{3} (r_j - \bar{r})^2 p_j = \$16{,}000$$

$$\sigma = \sqrt{\sum_{j=1}^{n} (r_j - \bar{r})^2 p_j} = \sqrt{16{,}000} = \$126.49$$

Figure 2.6 Continuous Probability Distributions for Two Investments

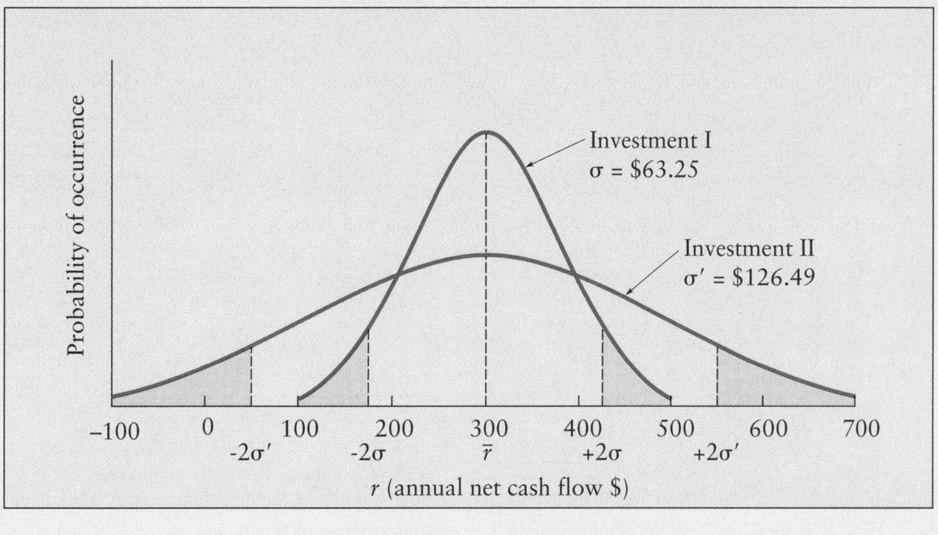

continuous probability distribution. Conceptually, this task involves assigning probabilities to each possible outcome such that the sum of the probabilities over possible outcomes totals 1.0 (see Figure 2.6). This figure shows that Investment I has a tighter probability distribution and smaller standard deviation, indicating a lower variability of returns, and Investment II has a flatter distribution and larger standard deviation, indicating higher variability and, by extension, more risk.

Normal Probability Distribution

The outcomes from many decisions can be estimated by assuming that they follow the *normal* probability distribution. This assumption is often correct or nearly correct, and it greatly simplifies the analysis. The normal probability distribution is characterized by a symmetrical, bell-like curve. If the expected continuous probability distribution for the possible outcomes is approximately normal, a table of the *standard normal probability distribution function* (Table 1 in Appendix B at the end of this book) can be used to compute the probability of occurrence of any particular outcome. From this table, for example, it is apparent that the actual outcome should be between plus and minus 1 standard deviation from the expected value 68.26 percent of the time,[7] between plus and minus 2 standard deviations 95.44 percent of the time, and between plus and minus 3 standard deviations 99.74 percent of the time (see Figure 2.7). So a "3 sigma event" occurs less than 1 percent of the time with a relative frequency 0.0026 (i.e., 1.0 − 0.9974), and a "9 sigma event" occurs almost never, with a relative frequency less than 0.0001. Nevertheless, extraordinary events can and do happen (see *What Went Right . . .* box on LTCM).

The number of standard deviations z that a particular value of r is from the mean $\bar{r}$ can be computed as

$$z = \frac{r - \bar{r}}{\sigma} \quad [2.7]$$

Figure 2.7 A Sample Illustration of Areas Under the Normal Probability Distribution Curve

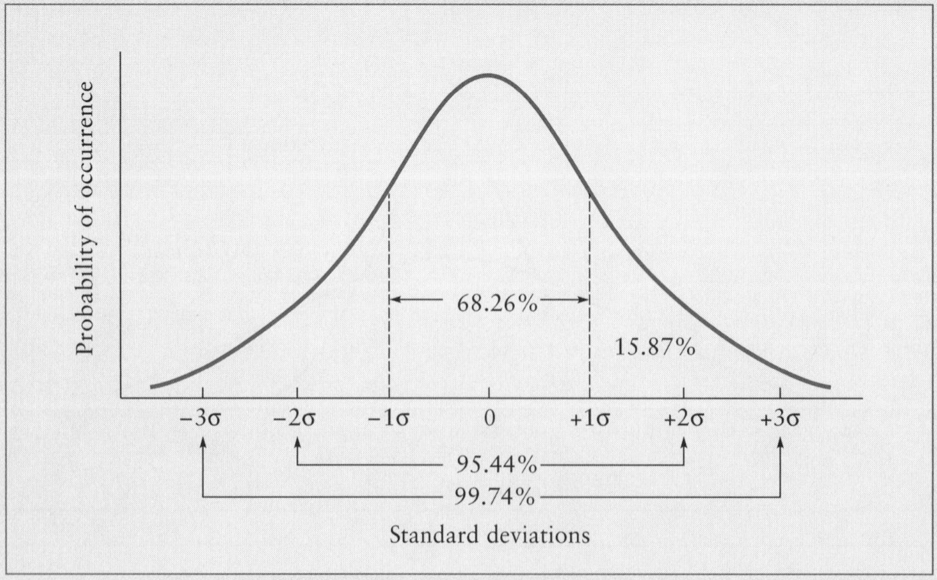

[7] For example, Table 1 indicates a probability of 0.1587 of a value occurring that is greater than $+1\sigma$ from the mean *and* a probability of 0.1587 of a value occurring that is less than -1σ from the mean. Hence the probability of a value *between* $+1\sigma$ and -1σ is 68.26 percent; that is, 1.00 − (2 × 0.1587).

WHAT WENT RIGHT • WHAT WENT WRONG

LONG-TERM CAPITAL MANAGEMENT (LTCM)[8]

LTCM operated from June 1993 to September 1998 as a hedge fund that invested highly leveraged private capital in arbitrage trading strategies on the financial derivative markets. LTCM's principal activity was examining interest rate derivative contracts throughout the world for evidence of minor mispricing and then betting enormous sums on the subsequent convergence of those contracts to predictable equilibrium prices. The mispricing might be only several cents per thousand dollars invested, which meant LTCM often risked millions or even billions on one bet. With sometimes as many as 100 independent bets spread across dozens of different government bond markets, LTCM appeared globally diversified. In a typical month, 60 such convergence strategies with positions in several thousand counterparty contracts would make money and another 40 strategies with a similar number of counterparties would lose money. Steadily, the profits mounted. From approximately $1 billion net asset value (equity) in February 1994, LTCM reached $7 billion of net asset value in January 1998. LTCM then paid out $2.4 billion in a one-time distribution to nonpartners which equaled a 40 percent annual compound return on their investment (ROI). Shortly thereafter, in August 1998 the remaining $4.6 billion equity shrank by 45 percent, and then 1 month later shrank by another 82 percent to less than $500 million. In September 1998, the hedge fund was taken over by 14 Wall Street banks that inserted $3.6 billion to cover the firm's debts and assumed 90 percent of the ownership. What went wrong?

One potential explanation is that such events are fully expected in an enterprise so risky that it returns a 40 percent ROI. Anticipated risk and expected return *are* highly positively correlated. However, LTCM's annual return had a standard deviation from June 1993 to June 1998 of only 11.5 percent per year as compared to 10 percent for the S&P 500 stocks. In this respect, LTCM's return volatility was quite ordinary. Another potential explanation is that LTCM's $129 billion on the June 1998 balance sheet was overwhelmed by excessive off-balance sheet assets and liabilities. Although the absolute size of the numbers is staggering (e.g., $1.2 trillion in interest rate swaps, $28 billion in foreign exchange derivatives, and $36 billion in equity derivatives), LTCM's 9 percent ratio of on-balance sheet to off-balance sheet assets was similar to that of a typical securities firm (about 12 percent) or bank (about 15 percent). Even LTCM's high financial leverage ($129 billion assets to $4.7 billion equity = 26 to 1) was customary practice for derivatives traders.

What appears to have gone wrong for LTCM was that the default of the Russian government debt in August 1998 set in motion a truly extraordinary sequence of events. Investors around the globe took a "flight to quality" and quickly bid up the price of U.S. Treasury securities, which set off general turmoil in the bond markets across the world. Within one month, interest rate volatility stood at a standard deviation of 36 percent per year when 3 percent would have been typical. LTCM was caught on the wrong side of many interest rate derivative positions as the contract prices adjusted to this extraordinary volatility. Liquidity dried up altogether in some contracts, and no trade was available at any price. LTCM had "stress tested" their trading positions against so-called "3 sigma events" (a one-day loss of $35 million) that occur with less than 1 percent frequency in normal probability distributions, but this August–September 1998 volatility proved to be a 9 sigma event (i.e., a one-day loss of $553 million). With massive investments highly leveraged and exposed to a 9 sigma event, LTCM was unable to sell off many of its money-losing positions at any positive price and hemorrhaged $2 billion in one month.

[8] R. Lowenstein, *When Genius Failed* (New York: Random House, 2000); remarks by Dave Modest, NBER Conference, May 1999; and "Case Study: LTCM," *eRisk* (2000).

Table 1 in Appendix B and Equation 2.7 can be used to compute the probability of an annual net cash flow for Investment I being less than some value r: for example, \$205. First, the number of standard deviations that \$205 is from the mean must be calculated. Substituting the mean and the standard deviation from Tables 2.7 and 2.8 into Equation 2.7 yields

$$z = \frac{\$205 - \$300}{\$63.25}$$
$$= -1.50$$

In other words, the annual cash flow value of \$205 is 1.5 standard deviations *below* the mean. Reading from the negative 1.5 row in Table 1 gives a value of 0.0668, or 6.68 percent. Thus a 6.68 percent probability exists that Investment I will have annual net cash flows less than \$205. Conversely, the probability is 93.32 percent (1 − 0.0668) that the investment will have a cash flow greater than \$205.

A Practical Approach for Estimating Standard Deviations

Most business decisions have outcomes best represented by a continuous probability distribution of possible outcomes, not the discrete distribution of outcomes, such as those shown in Tables 2.5 and 2.6. Under these circumstances, a simple technique can be used to derive the standard deviation of possible outcomes. Assuming that the distribution of possible outcomes is approximately normally distributed, information can be developed in a form useful for making the necessary computations.

For example, the individual responsible for making estimates of the expected return and risk from a decision, such as an investment project or the pricing of a new product, could be asked to supply the following information:

1. Estimate the most optimistic outcome. The most optimistic outcome is defined to be an outcome that would not be exceeded more than 5 percent (or any other prespecified percentage) of the time.
2. Estimate the most pessimistic outcome. The most pessimistic outcome is defined to be an outcome that you would not expect to do worse more than 5 percent of the time.
3. With a normal distribution, the expected value will be midway between the most optimistic and the most pessimistic estimate.
4. Calculate the value of one standard deviation from Appendix B, Table 1.

EXAMPLE

Estimation of the Standard Deviation: Procter & Gamble

When pricing a new product, the product manager of Procter & Gamble estimates that the most optimistic (not expected to be exceeded more than 5 percent of the time) price the firm can charge is \$5.00 per unit. The most pessimistic (not expected to be less than this amount more than 5 percent of the time) estimate of the price that can be charged is \$3.50. Assuming normality, the expected price is \$4.25. From Table 1 in Appendix B, the z-value that leaves 5 percent in either tail of the normal distribution is approximately 1.645 standard deviations (σ) to the right or left of the expected value. This z-value corresponds to the distance between the expected value and either the most optimistic or the most pessimistic estimate of price. Hence, the probability of a price of at least \$5.00 is equal to the probability of a z-value *greater* than +1.645. To calculate the standard deviation (σ) of this distribution, use the most optimistic outcome (\$5.00), the expected outcome (\$4.25), and the z-value:

$$z = 1.645 = \frac{(\$5.00 - \$4.25)}{\sigma}$$

$$\sigma = \frac{\$0.75}{1.645}$$

$$= \$0.46$$

In this case the expected value is \$4.25 with a standard deviation of \$0.46.

COEFFICIENT OF VARIATION: A RELATIVE MEASURE OF RISK

Coefficient of Variation
The ratio of the standard deviation to the expected value; a relative measure of risk.

The standard deviation is an appropriate measure of risk when the decision alternatives being compared are approximately equal in size (that is, have similar expected values of the outcomes) and the outcomes are estimated to have symmetrical probability distributions. Because the standard deviation is an *absolute* measure of variability, however, it is generally not suitable for comparing alternatives of differing size. In these cases the **coefficient of variation** provides a better measure of risk.

The coefficient of variation (v) considers relative variation and thus is well suited for use when a comparison is being made between two unequally sized decision alternatives. It is defined as the ratio of the standard deviation σ to the expected value $\bar{r}$, or

$$v = \frac{\sigma}{\bar{r}} \qquad [2.8]$$

In general, when comparing two equally sized decision alternatives, the standard deviation is an appropriate measure of risk. When comparing two unequally sized alternatives, the coefficient of variation is the more appropriate measure of risk.

EXAMPLE

RELATIVE RISK MEASUREMENT: ARROW TOOL COMPANY

Arrow Tool Company is considering two investments, T and S. Investment T has expected annual net cash flows of \$100,000 and a standard deviation of \$20,000, whereas Investment S has expected annual net cash flows of \$4,000 and a \$2,000 standard deviation. Intuition tells us that Investment T is less risky because its *relative* variation is smaller. As the coefficient of variation increases, so does the relative risk of the decision alternative. The coefficients of variation for Investments T and S are computed as

Investment T:

$$v = \frac{\sigma}{\bar{r}}$$
$$= \frac{\$20,000}{\$100,000}$$
$$= 0.20$$

Investment S:

$$v = \frac{\sigma}{\bar{r}}$$
$$= \frac{\$2,000}{\$4,000}$$
$$= 0.5$$

Cash flows of Investment S have a larger coefficient of variation (0.50) than do cash flows of Investment T (0.20); therefore, even though the standard deviation is smaller, Investment S is the *more* risky of the two alternatives.

The Relationship Between Risk and Return

Understanding the trade-off between risk and required (or expected) rates of return is integral to effective decision making. For example, investors who purchase shares of common stock hope to receive returns that will exceed those that might be earned from alternative investments, such as a savings account, U.S. government bonds, or high-quality corporate bonds. Investors recognize that the expected return from common stock over the long run tends to be higher than the expected return from less risky investments. To receive higher returns, however, investors must be prepared to accept a higher level of risk.

Risk and Required Return

The relationship between risk and required return on an investment in either a physical asset or financial asset (security) can be defined as

$$\text{Required return} = \text{Risk-free return} + \text{Risk premium} \qquad [2.9]$$

The risk-free rate of return refers to the return available on an investment with no risk of default. For debt securities, no default risk means that promised interest and principal payments are guaranteed to be made. The best example of risk-free securities are short-term U.S. government securities, such as Treasury bills. There is no risk of default on these bonds because the U.S. government always can print more money. Of course, if the government recklessly prints money to pay its obligations, the purchasing power of the money will decline. So, risk-free returns equal the real rate of interest plus the expected rate of inflation. Nevertheless, the buyer of a

U.S. government bond is always assured of receiving the promised *principal* and *interest* payments.

A *risk premium* is a potential "reward" that an investor can expect to receive from making a risky investment. The risk may arise for any number of reasons. The borrower firm may default on its contractual repayment obligations (a default risk premium). The investor may have little seniority in presenting claims against a bankrupt borrower (a seniority risk premium). The investor may be unable to sell his security interest (a liquidity risk premium), or debt repayment may occur early (a maturity risk premium). Finally, the return the investor receives may be highly volatile, exceeding expectations during one period and plummeting below expectations during the next period. Investors generally are considered to be *risk averse;* that is, they expect, on average, to be compensated for any and all of these risks they assume when making an investment.

EXAMPLE

Risk-Return Trade-Offs in Stocks and Bonds

Investors require higher rates of return on securities subject to default risk. Bond rating agencies, such as Moody's, Standard and Poor's, Duff and Phelps, and Fitch, provide evaluations of the default risk of many corporate bonds in the form of bond ratings. Moody's, for example, rates bonds on a 9-point scale from Aaa through C, where Aaa-rated bonds have the lowest expected default risk. As can be seen in Table 2.9, the yields on bonds increase as the risk of default increases, reflecting the positive relationship between risk and required returns. Over time, the spread between the required returns on bonds having various levels of default risk varies, reflecting the economic prospects and the resulting probability of default.

Table 2.9 Relationship Between Default Risk and Required Returns

Security	Yield
U.S. Treasury bonds (25-year +)	5.06%
Aaa-rated corporate bonds	6.49
Aa-rated bonds	6.93
A-rated bonds	7.18
Baa-rated corporate bonds	7.80

Source: Board of Governors of the Federal Reserve System, *Federal Reserve Bulletin* (Washington, DC, July 2002), p. A26.

The risk versus return trade-off also can be illustrated by examining the returns *achieved* by investors in various securities over long periods of time. Table 2.10 shows the realized returns (and the standard deviation of those returns) from small company common stock (highest risk), the common stocks in the S&P 500 index (next highest risk), long-term corporate bonds (third highest risk), long-term U.S. government bonds (fourth highest risk), intermediate-term government bonds (fifth highest risk), and U.S. Treasury bills (lowest risk). The realized returns and the standard deviation (risk) of these returns over the period 1926–2005 are consistent with our expectation that the relationship between risk and return is positive.

Table 2.10 Relationship Between Realized Returns and Risk of Various Investments (1926–2002)

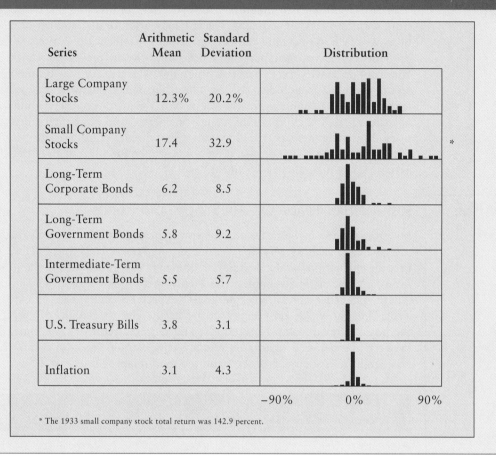

Series	Arithmetic Mean	Standard Deviation	Distribution
Large Company Stocks	12.3%	20.2%	
Small Company Stocks	17.4	32.9	*
Long-Term Corporate Bonds	6.2	8.5	
Long-Term Government Bonds	5.8	9.2	
Intermediate-Term Government Bonds	5.5	5.7	
U.S. Treasury Bills	3.8	3.1	
Inflation	3.1	4.3	

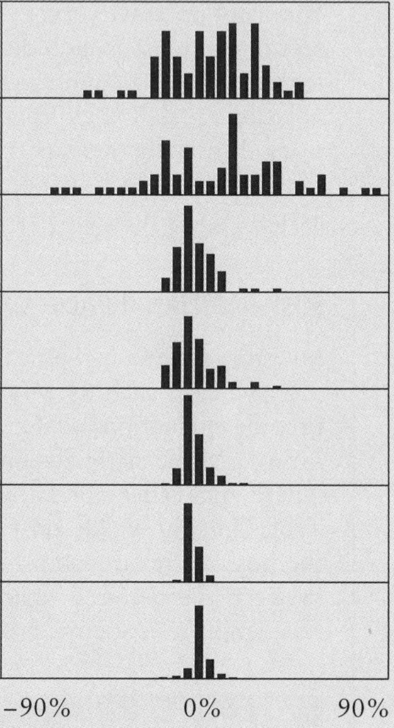

* The 1933 small company stock total return was 142.9 percent.

Source: *Stocks, Bonds, Bills and Inflation: 2006 Yearbook* (Chicago: Ibbotson Associates, Inc., 2006), Table 2–1, p. 31. Data reproduced with permission of Ibbotson Associates.

SUMMARY

- Demand and supply simultaneously determine equilibrium market price. The determinants of demand (supply) other than price shift the demand (supply) curve. A change in price alone leads to a change in quantity demanded (supplied) without any shift in demand (supply).
- The offer price demanders are willing to pay is determined by the marginal use value of the purchase being considered. The asking price suppliers are willing to accept is determined by the marginal cost of the product or service being supplied.
- The *marginal analysis* concept requires that a decision maker determine the additional (marginal) costs and additional (marginal) benefits associated with a proposed action. If the marginal benefits exceed the marginal costs (i.e., if the net marginal benefits are positive), the action should be taken.
- The *net present value* of an investment is equal to the present value of expected future returns (cash flows) minus the initial outlay.
- The net present value of an investment equals the contribution of that investment to the value of the firm

and, accordingly, to the wealth of shareholders. The net present value of an investment depends on the return required by investors (the firm), which, in turn, is a function of the perceived risk of the investment.

- *Risk* refers to the potential variability of outcomes from a decision alternative. It can be measured either by the *standard deviation* (an absolute measure of risk) or *coefficient of variation* (a relative measure of risk).
- A positive relationship exists between risk and required rates of return on securities and physical asset investments. Investments involving greater risks must offer higher expected returns.

Exercises

Answers to the exercises in blue can be found in Appendix C at the back of the book.

1. The Ajax Corporation has the following set of projects available to it:

Project*	Investment Required ($ millions)	Expected Rate of Return
A	500	23.0%
B	75	18.0
C	50	21.0
D	125	16.0
E	300	14.0
F	150	13.0
G	250	19.0

*Note: All projects have equal risk.

Ajax can raise funds with the following marginal costs:

First $250 million	14.0%
Next 250 million	15.5
Next 100 million	16.0
Next 250 million	16.5
Next 200 million	18.0
Next 200 million	21.0

Use the marginal cost and marginal revenue concepts developed in this chapter to derive an optimal capital budget for Ajax.

2. The demand for MICHTEC's products is related to the state of the economy. If the economy is expanding next year (an above-normal growth in GDP), the company expects sales to be $90 million. If a recession occurs next year (a decline in GDP), sales are expected to be $75 million. If next year is normal (a moderate growth in GDP), sales are expected to be $85 million. MICHTEC's economists estimate the chances that the economy will be either expanding, normal, or in a recession next year at 0.2, 0.5, and 0.3, respectively.
   a. Compute expected annual sales.
   b. Compute the standard deviation of annual sales.
   c. Compute the coefficient of variation of annual sales.
3. Two investments have the following expected returns (net present values) and standard deviation of returns:

Project	Expected Returns	Standard Deviation
A	$ 50,000	$ 40,000
B	$250,000	$125,000

Which one is riskier? Why?

4. An investment project has expected annual net cash flows of $100,000 with a standard deviation of $40,000. The distribution of annual net cash flows is approximately normal.
   a. Determine the probability that the annual net cash flows will be negative.
   b. Determine the probability that the annual net cash flows will be less than $20,000.
5. The manager of the aerospace division of General Aeronautics estimates the price it can charge for providing satellite launch services to commercial firms. Her most optimistic estimate (a price not expected to be exceeded more than 10 percent of the time) is $2 million. Her most pessimistic estimate (a lower price than this one is not expected more than 10 percent of the time) is $1 million. The price distribution is believed to be approximately normal.
   a. What is the expected price?
   b. What is the standard deviation of the launch price?
   c. What is the probability of receiving a price less than $1.2 million?
6. Amgen, Inc., uses state-of-the-art biotechnology to develop human pharmaceutical and diagnostic products. During 1983 and 1984 Amgen recorded losses of $4.9 million and $7.8 million, respectively. The firm barely broke even between 1985 and 1987 and had sizable losses ($8.2 million) in 1988. On the strength of royalty income from the sale of its Epogen product, a stimulator of red blood cell production, profits increased steadily from $19 million in 1989 to $355 million in 1993 to $670 million in 1996. Profits were expected to exceed $900 million per year by 1998–1999, according to forecasts prepared by the *Value Line Investment Survey. Value Line* rated the safety (a risk measure) of Amgen to be "average."
   a. Discuss the past, present, and projected performance of Amgen in the context of risk-return trade-offs.
   b. Amgen's 1993 return on equity (Net income ÷ Shareholders' equity) was about 30 percent. In 1993, its projected return on equity was 28.5 percent for 1995 and 22.5 percent during 1997–1999. The 1989 return on equity was 10.2 percent, and the 1985–1987 return on equity was about 0.9 percent. Do you believe Amgen is now earning "excessive profits" from its Epogen product? Why or why not?
7. Water is a necessity of life, and diamonds (at least cosmetic diamonds) are somewhat frivolous. Why then do diamonds almost always sell for a high market equilibrium price and water seldom does? Be complete in your answer.
8. Gasoline prices above $3 per gallon have affected what Enterprise rental car company can charge for various models of rental cars. SUVs are $37 with one-day return and subcompacts are $41 with one-day return. Why would the equilibrium price of SUVs such as Ford Explorers and Chevy Trailblazers be lower than the equilibrium price of subcompacts?

APPENDIX

2a

DIFFERENTIAL CALCULUS TECHNIQUES IN MANAGEMENT

Decision analysis involves determining the action that best achieves a desired goal or objective. It means finding the action that optimizes (that is, maximizes or minimizes) the value of an objective function. For example, we may be interested in determining the output level that maximizes profits. In a production problem, the goal may be to find the combination of inputs that minimizes the cost of producing a desired level of output. In a capital budgeting problem, the objective may be to select those projects that maximize the net present value of the investments chosen. Many techniques are available for solving optimization problems such as these. This appendix focuses on the use of differential calculus.

RELATIONSHIP BETWEEN MARGINAL ANALYSIS AND DIFFERENTIAL CALCULUS

In Chapter 2, marginal analysis was introduced as one of the fundamental concepts of microeconomic decision making. In the marginal analysis framework, resource allocation decisions are made by comparing the marginal benefits of a proposed change in the level of an activity with the marginal costs of that change. The proposed change should be made as long as the marginal benefits exceed the marginal costs. By following this basic rule, resources can be allocated efficiently and profits or shareholder wealth can be maximized.

Initially, let us assume that the objective we are seeking to optimize, Y, can be expressed algebraically as a function of *one* decision variable, X.

$$Y = f(X) \qquad [2A.1]$$

Recall that marginal profit is defined as the change in profit resulting from a one-unit change in output. In general, the marginal value of any variable Y, which is a function of another variable X, is defined as the change in the value of Y resulting from a one-unit change in X. The marginal value of Y, M_y, can be calculated from the change in Y, ΔY, that occurs as the result of a given change in X, ΔX:

$$M_y = \frac{\Delta Y}{\Delta X} \qquad [2A.2]$$

When calculated with this expression, different estimates for the amount ΔY may be obtained, depending on the size of the incremental change in X that we use in the computation. The true marginal value of a function is obtained from Equation 2A.2 when ΔX is made as small as possible. If ΔX can be thought of as a continuous

MANAGERIAL CHALLENGE

A Skeleton in the Stealth Bomber's Closet[1]

In 1990, the U.S. Air Force publicly unveiled its newest long-range strategic bomber, the B-2 or "Stealth" bomber. This plane is characterized by a unique flying wing design engineered to evade detection by enemy radar. The plane has been controversial because of its high cost. However, a lesser known controversy relates to its fundamental design.

The flying wing design originated from a secret study that concluded that a plane's maximum range could be achieved if virtually all the volume were contained in the wing. A complex mathematical appendix was attached to the study.

However, Professor of Engineering Joseph Foa discovered that a fundamental error had been made in the initial report. It turned out that the original researchers had taken the first derivative of a complex equation and found that it had two solutions. The original researchers mistakenly concluded that the all-wing design was the one that maximized range, when, in fact, it *minimized* range.

In this chapter we introduce some of the same optimization techniques applied to the Stealth bomber project. We develop tools designed to maximize profits or minimize costs. Fortunately, the mathematical functions we deal with in this chapter and throughout the book are much simpler than those that confronted the original "flying wing" engineers. We introduce techniques that can be used to check whether a function, such as profits or costs, is being minimized or maximized at a particular level of output.

[1] Based on W. Biddle, "Skeleton Alleged in the Stealth Bomber's Closet," *Science* (May 12, 1989), pp. 650–651.

Derivative
A measure of the marginal effect of a change in one variable on the value of a function. Graphically, it represents the slope of the function at a given point.

(rather than a discrete) variable that can take on fractional values,[2] then in calculating M_y by Equation 2A.2, we can let ΔX approach zero.

In concept, differential calculus takes this approach. The **derivative,** or, more precisely, *first derivative,*[3] dY/dX, of a function is defined as the *limit* of the ratio $\Delta Y/\Delta X$ as ΔX approaches zero; that is,

$$\frac{dY}{dX} = \underset{\Delta X \to 0}{\text{limit}} \frac{\Delta Y}{\Delta X} \qquad [2A.3]$$

Graphically, the first derivative of a function represents the *slope* of the curve at a given point on the curve. The definition of a derivative as the limit of the change in Y (that is, ΔY) as ΔX approaches zero is illustrated in Figure 2A.1(a).

Suppose we are interested in the derivative of the $Y = f(X)$ function at the point X_0. The derivative dY/dX measures the slope of the tangent line ECD. An estimate of this slope, albeit a poor estimate, can be obtained by calculating the marginal value of Y over the interval X_0 to X_2. Using Equation 2A.2, a value of

$$M_y' = \frac{\Delta Y}{\Delta X} = \frac{Y_2 - Y_0}{X_2 - X_0}$$

[2] For example, if X is a continuous variable measured in feet, pounds, and so on, then ΔX can in theory take on fractional values such as 0.5, 0.10, 0.05, 0.001, 0.0001 feet or pounds. When X is a continuous variable, ΔX can be made as small as desired.

[3] It is also possible to compute second, third, fourth, and so on, derivatives. Second derivatives are discussed later in this appendix.

Figure 2A.1 First Derivative of a Function

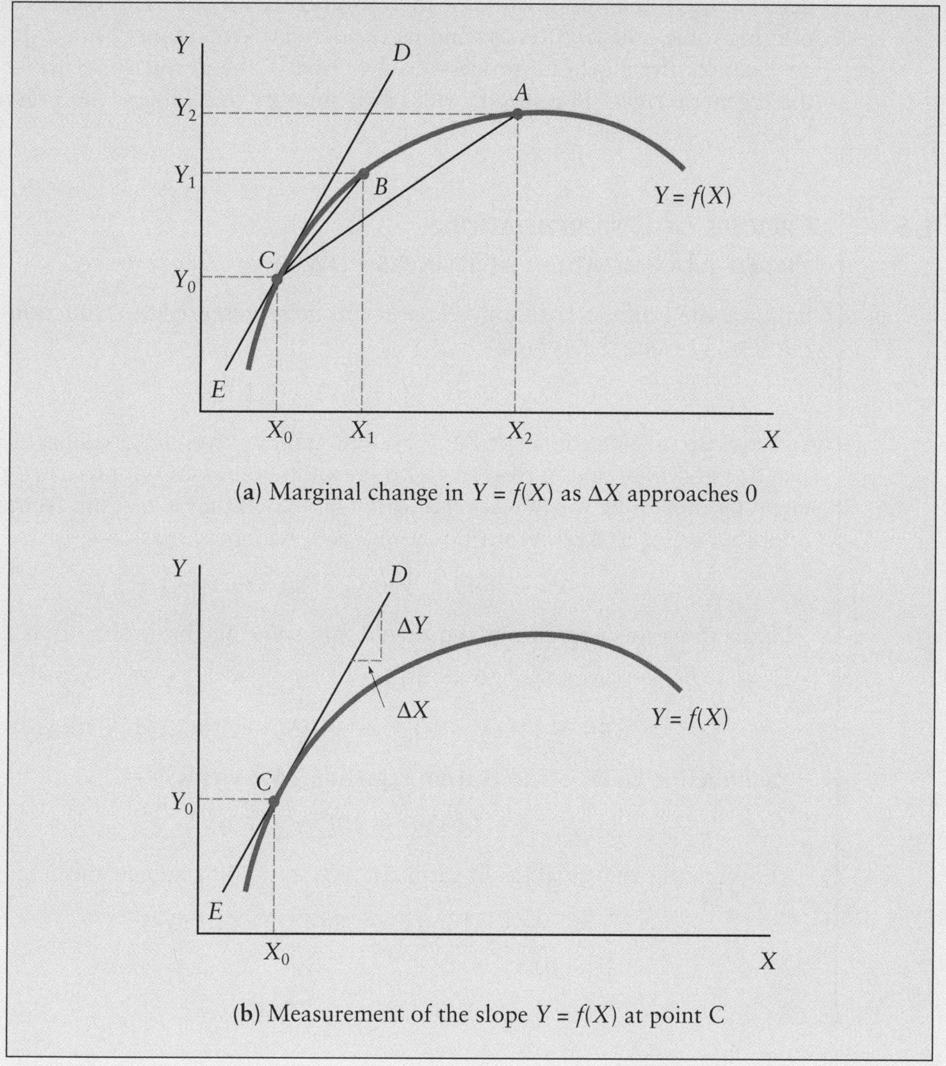

is obtained for the slope of the *CA* line. Now let us calculate the marginal value of *Y* using a smaller interval, for example, X_0 to X_1. The slope of the *CB* line, which is equal to

$$M_y'' = \frac{\Delta Y}{\Delta X} = \frac{Y_1 - Y_0}{X_1 - X_0}$$

gives a much better estimate of the true marginal value as represented by the slope of the *ECD* tangent line. Thus we see that the smaller the ΔX value, the better the estimate of the slope of the curve. Letting ΔX approach zero allows us to find the slope of the $Y = f(X)$ curve at point C. As shown in Figure 2A.1(b), the slope of the *ECD* tangent line (and the $Y = f(X)$ function at point C) is measured by the change in *Y*, or rise, ΔY, divided by the change in *X*, or run, ΔX.

Process of Differentiation

The process of differentiation—that is, finding the derivative of a function—involves determining the limiting value of the ratio $\Delta Y/\Delta X$ as ΔX approaches zero. Before offering some general rules for finding the derivative of a function, we illustrate with an example the algebraic process used to obtain the derivative without the aid of these general rules. The specific rules that simplify this process are presented in the following section.

EXAMPLE

Process of Differentiation: Profit Maximization at Illinois Power

Suppose the profit, π, of Illinois Power can be represented as a function of the output level Q using the expression

$$\pi = -40 + 140Q - 10Q^2 \quad [2A.4]$$

We wish to determine $d\pi/dQ$ by first finding the marginal profit expression $\Delta\pi/\Delta Q$ and then taking the limit of this expression as ΔQ approaches zero. Let us begin by expressing the new level of profit $(\pi + \Delta\pi)$ that will result from an increase in output to $(Q + \Delta Q)$. From Equation 2A.4, we know that

$$\pi + \Delta\pi = -40 + 140(Q + \Delta Q) - 10(Q + \Delta Q)^2 \quad [2A.5]$$

Expanding this expression and then doing some algebraic simplifying, we obtain

$$\begin{aligned} \pi + \Delta\pi &= -40 + 140Q + 140\Delta Q - 10[Q^2 + 2Q\Delta Q + (\Delta Q)^2] \\ &= -40 + 140Q - 10Q^2 + 140\Delta Q - 20Q\Delta Q - 10(\Delta Q)^2 \end{aligned} \quad [2A.6]$$

Subtracting Equation 2A.4 from Equation 2A.6 yields

$$\Delta\pi = 140\Delta Q - 20Q\Delta Q - 10(\Delta Q)^2 \quad [2A.7]$$

Forming the marginal profit ratio $\Delta\pi/\Delta Q$, and doing some canceling, we get

$$\begin{aligned} \frac{\Delta\pi}{\Delta Q} &= \frac{140\Delta Q - 20Q\Delta Q - 10(\Delta Q)^2}{\Delta Q} \\ &= 140 - 20Q - 10\Delta Q \end{aligned} \quad [2A.8]$$

Taking the limit of Equation 2A.8 as ΔQ approaches zero yields the expression for the derivative of Illinois Power's profit function (Equation 2A.4).

$$\begin{aligned} \frac{d\pi}{dQ} &= \lim_{\Delta Q \to 0} [140 - 20Q - 10\Delta Q] \\ &= 140 - 20Q \end{aligned} \quad [2A.9]$$

If we are interested in the derivative of the profit function at a particular value of Q, Equation 2A.9 can be evaluated for this value. For example, suppose we want to know the marginal profit, or slope of the profit function, at $Q = 3$ units. Substituting $Q = 3$ in Equation 2A.9 yields

$$\text{Marginal profit} = \frac{d\pi}{dQ} = 140 - 20(3) = \$80 \text{ per unit}$$

RULES OF DIFFERENTIATION

Fortunately, we do not need to go through this lengthy process every time we want the derivative of a function. A series of general rules, derived in a manner similar to the process just described, exists for differentiating various types of functions.

CONSTANT FUNCTIONS A constant function can be expressed as

$$Y = a \tag{2A.10}$$

where a is a constant (that is, Y is independent of X). The derivative of a constant function is equal to zero:

$$\frac{dY}{dX} = 0 \tag{2A.11}$$

For example, consider the constant function

$$Y = 4$$

which is graphed in Figure 2A.2(a). Recall that the first derivative of a function (dY/dX) measures the slope of the function. Because this constant function is a horizontal straight line with zero slope, its derivative (dY/dX) is therefore equal to zero.

POWER FUNCTIONS A power function takes the form of

$$Y = aX^b \tag{2A.12}$$

where a and b are constants. The derivative of a power function is equal to:

$$\frac{dY}{dX} = b \cdot a \cdot X^{b-1} \tag{2A.13}$$

Figure 2A.2 Constant, Linear, and Quadratic Functions

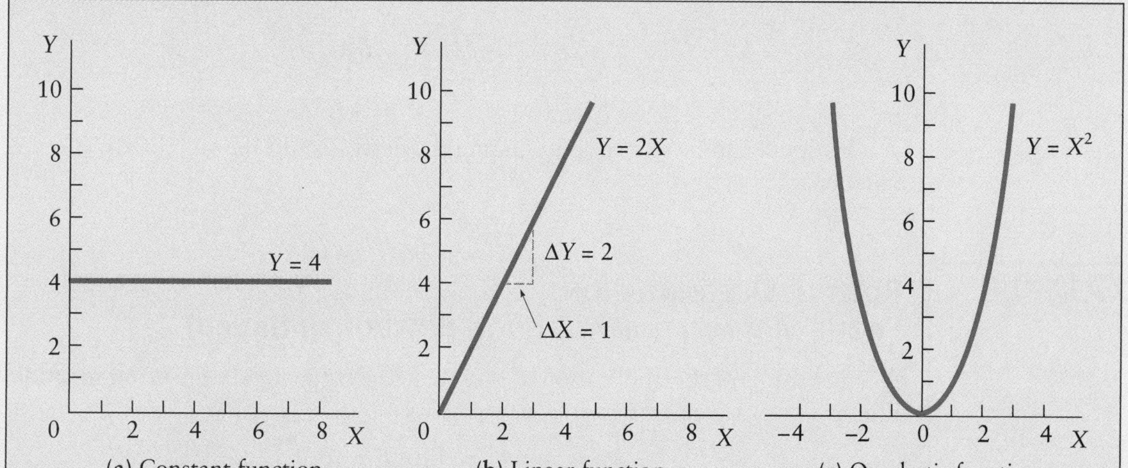

(a) Constant function (b) Linear function (c) Quadratic function

A couple of examples are used to illustrate the application of this rule. First, consider the function

$$Y = 2X$$

which is graphed in Figure 2A.2(b). Note that the slope of this function is equal to 2 and is constant over the entire range of X values. Applying the power function rule to this example, where $a = 2$ and $b = 1$, yields

$$\begin{aligned}\frac{dY}{dX} &= 1 \cdot 2 \cdot X^{1-1} \\ &= 2X^0 = 2\end{aligned}$$

Note that any variable raised to the zero power, e.g., X^0, is equal to 1.

Next, consider the function

$$Y = X^2$$

which is graphed in Figure 2A.2(c). Note that the slope of this function varies depending on the value of X. Application of the power function rule to this example yields ($a = 1$, $b = 2$):

$$\begin{aligned}\frac{dY}{dX} &= 2 \cdot 1 \cdot X^{2-1} \\ &= 2X\end{aligned}$$

As we can see, this derivative (or slope) function is negative when $X < 0$, zero when $X = 0$, and positive when $X > 0$.

Sums of Functions Suppose a function $Y = f(X)$ represents the sum of two (or more) separate functions, $f_1(X)$, $f_2(X)$, that is,

$$Y = f_1(X) + f_2(X) \qquad [2A.14]$$

The derivative of Y with respect to X is found by differentiating each of the separate functions and then adding the results:

$$\frac{dY}{dX} = \frac{df_1(X)}{dX} + \frac{df_2(X)}{dX} \qquad [2A.15]$$

This result can be extended to finding the derivative of the sum of any number of functions.

EXAMPLE

Rules of Differentiation: Profit Maximization at Illinois Power (continued)

As an example of the application of these rules, consider again the profit function for Illinois Power, given earlier in Equation 2A.4:

$$\pi = -40 + 140Q - 10Q^2$$

In this example Q represents the X variable and π represents the Y variable; that is, $\pi = f(Q)$. The function $f(Q)$ is the sum of *three* separate functions: a constant function, $f_1(Q) = -40$, and two power functions, $f_2(Q) = 140Q$ and $f_3(Q) - 10Q^2$. Therefore, applying the differentiation rules yields

$$\frac{d\pi}{dQ} = \frac{df_1(Q)}{dQ} + \frac{df_2(Q)}{dQ} + \frac{df_3(Q)}{dQ}$$

$$= 0 + 1 \cdot 140 \cdot Q^{1-1} + 2 \cdot (-10) \cdot Q^{2-1}$$

$$= 140 - 20Q$$

This result is the same as obtained in Equation 2A.9 by the differentiation process.

PRODUCT OF TWO FUNCTIONS Suppose the variable Y is equal to the product of two separate functions $f_1(X)$ and $f_2(X)$:

$$Y = f_1(X) \cdot f_2(X) \qquad [2A.16]$$

In this case the derivative of Y with respect to X is equal to the sum of the first function times the derivative of the second, plus the second function times the derivative of the first.

$$\frac{dY}{dX} = f_1(X) \cdot \frac{df_2(X)}{dX} + f_2(X) \cdot \frac{df_1(X)}{dX} \qquad [2A.17]$$

For example, suppose we are interested in the derivative of the expression

$$Y = X^2(2X - 3)$$

Let $f_1(X) = X^2$ and $f_2(X) = (2X - 3)$. By the preceding rule (and the earlier rules for differentiating constant and power functions), we obtain

$$\frac{dY}{dX} = X^2 \cdot \frac{dY}{dX}[(2X - 3)] + (2X - 3) \cdot \frac{dY}{dX}[X^2]$$

$$= X^2 \cdot (2 - 0) + (2X - 3) \cdot (2X)$$

$$= 2X^2 + 4X^2 - 6X$$

$$= 6X^2 - 6X$$

$$= 6X(X - 1)$$

QUOTIENT OF TWO FUNCTIONS Suppose the variable Y is equal to the quotient of two separate functions $f_1(X)$ and $f_2(X)$:

$$Y = \frac{f_1(X)}{f_2(X)} \qquad [2A.18]$$

For such a relationship the derivative of Y with respect to X is obtained as follows:

$$\frac{dY}{dX} = \frac{f_2(X) \cdot \dfrac{df_1(X)}{dX} - f_1(X) \cdot \dfrac{df_2(X)}{dX}}{[f_2(X)]^2} \qquad [2A.19]$$

As an example, consider the problem of finding the derivative of the expression

$$Y = \frac{10X^2}{5X - 1}$$

Letting $f_1(X) = 10X^2$ and $f_2(X) = 5X - 1$, we have

$$\begin{aligned}\frac{dY}{dX} &= \frac{(5X-1)\cdot 20X - 10X^2 \cdot 5}{(5X-1)^2} \\ &= \frac{100X^2 - 20X - 50X^2}{(5X-1)^2} \\ &= \frac{50X^2 - 20X}{(5X-1)^2} \\ &= \frac{10X(5X-2)}{(5X-1)^2}\end{aligned}$$

Functions of a Function (Chain Rule) Suppose Y is a function of the variable Z, $Y = f_1(Z)$; and Z is in turn a function of the variable X, $Z = f_2(X)$. The derivative of Y with respect to X can be determined by first finding dY/dZ and dZ/dX and then multiplying the two expressions together:

$$\begin{aligned}\frac{dY}{dX} &= \frac{dY}{dZ} \cdot \frac{dZ}{dX} \\ &= \frac{df_1(Z)}{dZ} \cdot \frac{df_2(X)}{dX}\end{aligned} \qquad [2A.20]$$

To illustrate the application of this rule, suppose we are interested in finding the derivative (with respect to X) of the function

$$Y = 10Z - 2Z^2 - 3$$

where Z is related to X in the following way:[4]

$$Z = 2X^2 - 1$$

First, we find (by the earlier differentiation rules)

$$\frac{dY}{dX} = 10 - 4Z$$

$$\frac{dY}{dX} = 4X$$

[4] Alternatively, one can substitute $Z = 2X^2 - 1$ into $Y = 10Z - 2Z^2 - 3$ and differentiate Y with respect to X.

Table 2A.1 Summary of Rules for Differentiating Functions

Function	Derivative
1. Constant Function	
$Y = a$	$\frac{dY}{dX} = 0$
2. Power Function	
$Y = aX^b$	$\frac{dY}{dX} = b \cdot a \cdot X^{b-1}$
3. Sums of Functions	
$Y = f_1(X) + f_2(X)$	$\frac{dY}{dX} = \frac{df_1(X)}{dX} + \frac{df_2(X)}{dX}$
4. Product of Two Functions	
$Y = f_1(X) \cdot f_2(X)$	$\frac{dY}{dX} = f_1(X) \cdot \frac{df_2(X)}{dX} + f_2(X) \cdot \frac{df_1(X)}{dX}$
5. Quotient of Two Functions	
$Y = \frac{f_1(X)}{f_2X}$	$\frac{dY}{dX} = \frac{f_2(X) \cdot \frac{df_1(X)}{dX} - f_1(X) \cdot \frac{df_2(X)}{dX}}{[f_2(X)]^2}$
6. Functions of a Function	
$Y = f_1(Z)$, where $Z = f_2(X)$	$\frac{dY}{dX} = \frac{dY}{dZ} \cdot \frac{dZ}{dX}$

and then

$$\frac{dY}{dX} = (10 - 4Z) \cdot 4X$$

Substituting the expression for Z in terms of X into this equation yields

$$\begin{aligned}\frac{dY}{dX} &= [10 - 4(2X^2 - 1)] \cdot 4X \\ &= (10 - 8X^2 + 4) \cdot 4X \\ &= 40X - 32X^3 + 16X \\ &= 56X - 32X^3 \\ &= 8X(7 - 4X^2)\end{aligned}$$

These rules for differentiating functions are summarized in Table 2A.1.

APPLICATIONS OF DIFFERENTIAL CALCULUS TO OPTIMIZATION PROBLEMS

The reason for studying the process of differentiation and the rules for differentiating functions is that these methods can be used to find optimal solutions to many kinds of maximization and minimization problems in managerial economics.

Maximization Problem

First-Order Condition
A test to locate one or more maximum or minimum points of an algebraic function.

As you recall from the discussion of marginal analysis, a necessary (but not sufficient) condition for finding the maximum point on a curve (e.g., maximum profits) is that the marginal value or slope of the curve at this point must be equal to zero. We can now express this condition within the framework of differential calculus. Because the derivative of a function measures the slope or marginal value at any given point, an equivalent necessary condition for finding the maximum value of a function $Y = f(X)$ is that the derivative dY/dX at this point must be equal to zero. This requirement is known as the **first-order condition** for locating one or more maximum or minimum points of an algebraic function.

EXAMPLE

First-Order Condition: Profit Maximization at Illinois Power (continued)

Using the profit function (Equation 2A.4)

$$\pi = -40 + 140Q - 10Q^2$$

discussed earlier, we can illustrate how to find the profit-maximizing output level Q by means of this condition. Setting the first derivative of this function (which was computed previously) to zero, we obtain

$$\frac{d\pi}{dQ} = 140 - 20Q$$

$$0 = 140 - 20Q$$

Solving this equation for Q yields $Q^* = 7$ units as the profit-maximizing output level. The profit and first derivative functions and optimal solution are shown in Figure 2A.3. As we can see, profits are maximized at the point where the function is neither increasing nor decreasing; in other words, where the slope (or first derivative) is equal to zero.

Second Derivatives and the Second-Order Condition

Second-Order Condition
A test to determine whether a point that has been determined from the first-order condition is either a maximum point or a minimum point of the algebraic function.

Setting the derivative of a function equal to zero and solving the resulting equation for the value of the decision variable does not guarantee that the point will be obtained at which the function takes on its maximum value. (Recall the Stealth bomber example at the start of the Appendix.) The slope of a U-shaped function will also be equal to zero at its low point and the function will take on its *minimum* value at the given point. In other words, setting the derivative to zero is only a *necessary* condition for finding the maximum value of a function; it is not a *sufficient* condition. Another condition, known as the **second-order condition,** is required to determine whether a point that has been determined from the first-order condition is either a maximum point or minimum point of the algebraic function.

This situation is illustrated in Figure 2A.4. At both points A and B the slope of the function (first derivative, dY/dX) is zero; however, only at point B does

Figure 2A.3 Profit and First Derivative Functions

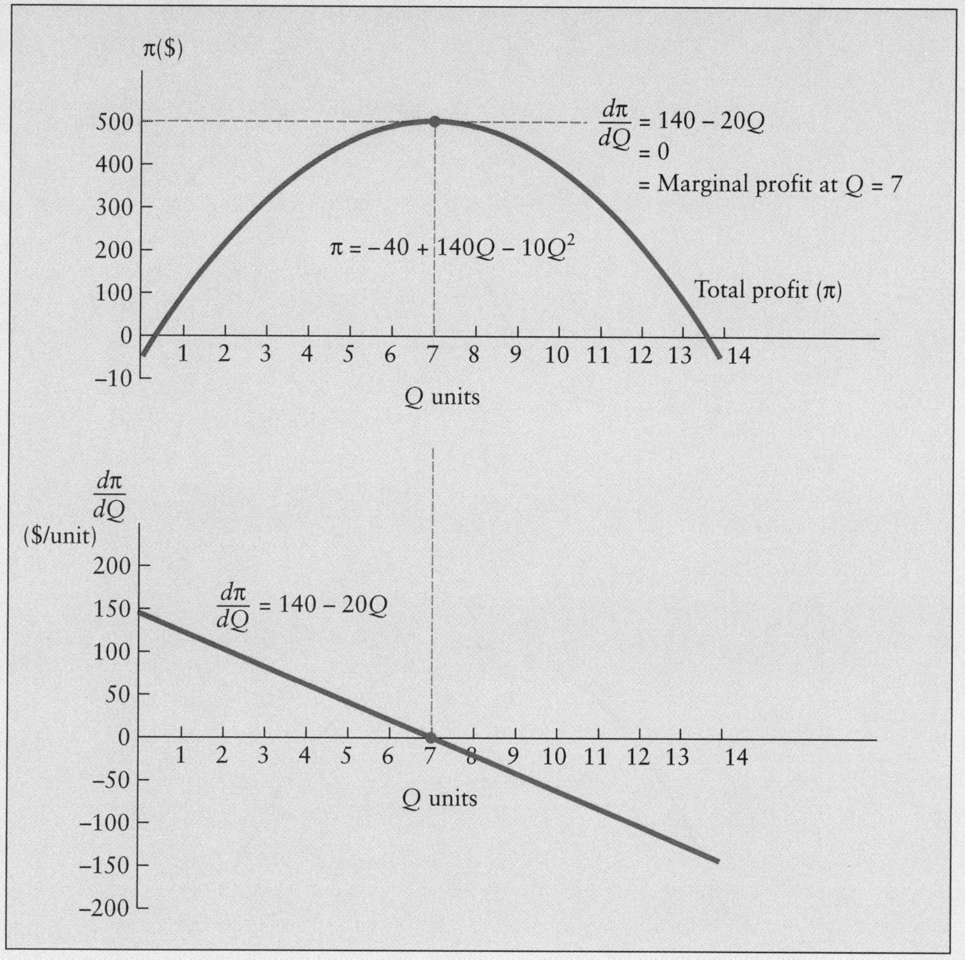

the function take on its maximum value. We note in Figure 2A.4 that the marginal value (slope) is continually *decreasing* in the neighborhood of the maximum value (point B) of the $Y = f(X)$ function. First the slope is positive up to the point where $dY/dX = 0$, and thereafter the slope becomes negative. Thus we must determine whether the slope's marginal value (slope of the slope) is declining. To test whether the marginal value is decreasing, take the derivative of the marginal value and determine whether it is negative at the given point on the function. In effect, we need to find the derivative of the derivative—that is, the *second derivative* of the function—and then test whether it is less than zero. Formally, the second derivative of the function $Y = f(X)$ is written as d^2Y/dX^2 and is found by applying the previously described differentiation rules to the first derivative. A *maximum point is obtained if the second derivative is negative; that is,* $d^2Y/dX^2 < 0$.

Figure 2A.4 Maximum and Minimum Values of a Function

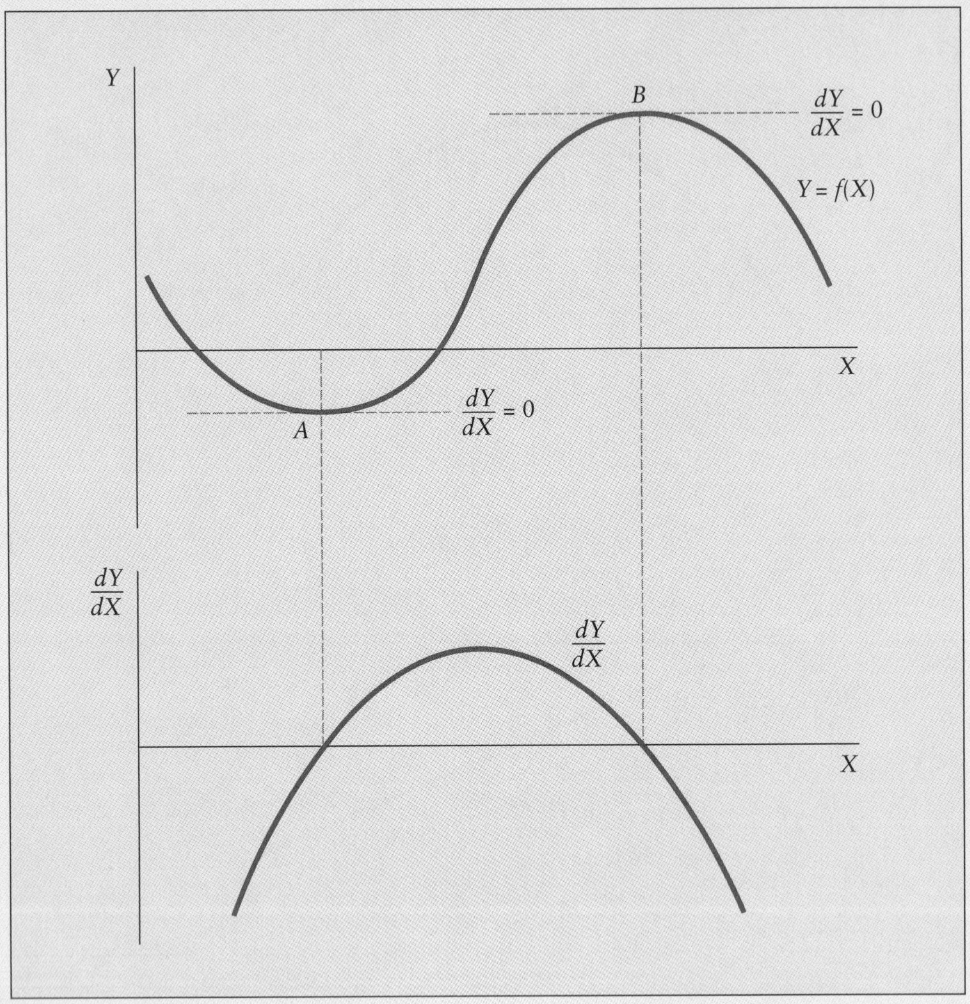

EXAMPLE

Second-Order Condition: Profit Maximization at Illinois Power (continued)

In the profit-maximization example, the second derivative is obtained from the first derivative as follows:

$$\frac{d\pi}{dQ} = 140 - 20Q$$

$$\frac{d^2\pi}{dQ^2} = 0 + 1 \cdot (-20) \cdot Q^{1-1}$$

$$= -20$$

Because $d^2\pi/dQ^2 < 0$, we know that a maximum-profit point has been obtained.

An opposite condition holds for obtaining the point at which the function takes on a minimum value. Note again in Figure 2A.4 that the marginal value (slope) is continually *increasing* in the neighborhood of the minimum value (point A) of the $Y = (X)$ function. First the slope is negative up to the point where $dY/dX = 0$, and thereafter the slope becomes positive. Therefore, we test to see whether $d^2Y/dX^2 > 0$ at the given point. *A minimum point is obtained if the second derivative is positive; that is,* $d^2Y/dX^2 > 0$.

MINIMIZATION PROBLEM

In some decision-making situations, cost minimization may be the objective. As in profit-maximization problems, differential calculus can be used to locate the optimal points.

EXAMPLE

COST MINIMIZATION: KEYSPAN ENERGY

Suppose we are interested in determining the output level that minimizes average total costs for KeySpan Energy, where the average total cost function might be approximated by the following relationship (Q represents output):

$$C = 15 - 0.040Q + 0.000080Q^2$$

Differentiating C with respect to Q gives

$$\frac{dC}{dQ} = -0.040 + 0.000160Q$$

Setting this derivative equal to zero and solving for Q yields

$$0 = 0.040 + 0.000160Q$$
$$Q^* = 250$$

Taking the second derivative, we obtain

$$\frac{d^2C}{dQ^2} = +0.000160$$

Because the second derivative is positive, the output level of $Q = 250$ is indeed the value that minimizes average total costs.

Summarizing, we see that *two* conditions are required for locating a maximum or minimum value of a function using differential calculus. The *first-order* condition determines the point(s) at which the first derivative dY/dX is equal to zero. After we obtain one or more points, a *second-order* condition is used to determine whether the function takes on a maximum or minimum value at the given point(s). The second derivative d^2Y/dX^2 indicates whether a given point is a maximum ($d^2Y/dX^2 < 0$) or a minimum ($d^2Y/dX^2 > 0$) value of the function.

Partial Differentiation and Multivariate Optimization

Thus far in the chapter, the analysis has been limited to a criterion variable Y that can be expressed as a function of *one* decision variable X. However, many commonly used economic relationships contain two or more decision variables. For example, a *demand function* relates sales of a product or service to such variables as price, advertising, promotion expenses, price of substitutes, and income.

Partial Derivatives

Consider a criterion variable Y that is a function of two decision variables X_1 and X_2.[5]

$$Y = f(X_1, X_2) \qquad [2A.21]$$

Partial Derivative
A measure of the marginal effect of a change in one variable on the value of a multivariate function, while holding constant all other variables.

Let us now examine the change in Y that results from a given change in either X_1 or X_2. To isolate the marginal effect on Y from a given change in X_1 (that is, $\Delta Y/\Delta X_1$), we must hold X_2 constant. Similarly, if we wish to isolate the marginal effect on Y from a given change in X_2 (that is, $\Delta Y/\Delta X_2$) the variable X_1 must be held constant. A measure of the marginal effect of a change in any one variable on the change in Y, holding all other variables in the relationship constant, is obtained from the **partial derivative** of the function. The partial derivative of Y with respect to X_1 is written as $\partial Y/\partial X_1$ and is found by applying the previously described differentiation rules to the $Y = f(X_1, X_2)$ function, where the variable X_2 is treated as a constant. Similarly, the partial derivative of Y with respect to X_2 is written as $\partial Y/\partial X_2$ and is found by applying the differentiation rules to the function, where the variable X_1 is treated as a constant.

EXAMPLE

Partial Derivatives: Indiana Petroleum Company

To illustrate the procedure for obtaining partial derivatives, let us consider the following relationship in which the profit variable, π, is a function of the output level of two products (heating oil and gasoline) Q_1 and Q_2:

$$\pi = -60 + 140Q_1 + 100Q_2 - 10Q_1^2 - 8Q_2^2 - 6Q_1Q_2 \qquad [2A.22]$$

Treating Q_2 as a constant, the partial derivative of π with respect to Q_1 is obtained:

$$\begin{aligned}\frac{\partial \pi}{\partial Q_1} &= 0 + 140 + 0 + 2\cdot(-10)\cdot Q_1 - 0 - 6Q_2 \\ &= 140 - 20Q_1 - 6Q_2 \qquad [2A.23]\end{aligned}$$

Similarly, with Q_1 treated as a constant, the partial derivative of π with respect to Q_2 is equal to

$$\begin{aligned}\frac{\partial \pi}{\partial Q_1} &= 0 + 0 + 100 - 0 + 2\cdot(-8)\cdot Q_2 - 6Q_1 \\ &= 100 - 16Q_2 - 6Q_1 \qquad [2A.24]\end{aligned}$$

[5] The following analysis is not limited to two decision variables. Relationships containing any number of variables can be analyzed within this framework.

EXAMPLE

PARTIAL DERIVATIVES: DEMAND FUNCTION FOR SHIELD TOOTHPASTE

Partial derivatives can be useful in demand analysis, especially in quantitative studies. Suppose the demand for Shield toothpaste is estimated as tubes per year,

$$Q = 14.6 + 2.2P + 7.4A \qquad [2A.25]$$

where Q = quantity sold, P = selling price, and A = advertising campaigns, the partial derivatives of Q with respect to P and A are

$$\frac{\partial Q}{\partial P} = -2.2 \text{ and } \frac{\partial Q}{\partial A} = 7.4$$

To take another example, for the multiplicative exponential demand function

$$Q = 3.0P^{-.50}A^{.25}$$

The partial derivative of Q with respect to P is

$$\begin{aligned}\frac{\partial Q}{\partial P} &= 3.0A^{.25}(-.50P^{-.50-1})\\ &= -1.5P^{-1.50}A^{.25}\end{aligned}$$

Similarly, the partial derivative of Q with respect to A is

$$\begin{aligned}\frac{\partial Q}{\partial P} &= 3.0P^{-.50}(.25A^{.25-1})\\ &= .75P^{-.50}A^{-.75}\end{aligned}$$

MAXIMIZATION PROBLEM

The partial derivatives can be used to obtain the optimal solution to a maximization or minimization problem containing two or more X variables. Analogous to the first-order conditions discussed earlier for the one-variable case, we set *each* of the partial derivatives equal to zero and solve the resulting set of simultaneous equations for the optimal X values.

EXAMPLE

PROFIT MAXIMIZATION: INDIANA PETROLEUM COMPANY (continued)

Suppose we are interested in determining the values of Q_1 and Q_2 that maximize the company's profits given in Equation 2A.22. In this case, each of the two partial derivative functions (Equations 2A.23 and 2A.24) would be set equal to zero:

$$0 = 140 - 20Q_1 - 6Q_2$$
$$0 = 100 - 16Q_2 - 6Q_1$$

This system of equations can be solved for the profit-maximizing values of Q_1 and Q_2.[6] The optimal values are $Q_1^* = 5.77$ units and $Q_2^* = 4.08$ units.[7] The optimal total profit is

$$\pi^* = -60 + 140(5.77) + 100(4.08) + 10(5.77)^2 - 8(4.08)^2 - 6(5.77)(4.08) = 548.45$$

[6] The second-order conditions for obtaining a maximum or minimum in the multiple-variable case are somewhat complex. A discussion of these conditions can be found in most basic calculus texts.

[7] Exercise 10 at the end of this appendix requires the determination of these optimal values.

SUMMARY

- *Marginal analysis* is useful in making decisions about the expansion or contraction of an economic activity.
- *Differential calculus,* which bears a close relationship to marginal analysis, can be applied whenever an algebraic relationship can be specified between the decision variables and the objective or criterion variable.
- The *first derivative* measures the slope or rate of change of a function at a given point and is equal to the limiting value of the marginal function as the marginal value is calculated over smaller and smaller intervals, that is, as the interval approaches zero.
- Various rules are available (see Table 2A.1) for finding the derivative of specific types of functions.
- A necessary, but not sufficient, condition for finding the maximum or minimum points of a function is that the first derivative be equal to zero, which is known as the *first-order condition.*
- A *second-order condition* is required to determine whether a given point is a maximum or minimum. The *second derivative* indicates that a given point is a maximum if the second derivative is less than zero or a minimum if the second derivative is greater than zero.
- The *partial derivative* of a multivariate function measures the marginal effect of a change in one variable on the value of the function, holding constant all other variables.

Exercises

Answers to the exercises in blue can be found in Appendix C at the back of the book.

1. **Define Q as the level of output produced and sold, and suppose that a firm's total revenue (TR) and total cost (TC) functions can be represented in tabular form as shown here.**

Output (Q)	Total Revenue (TR)	Total Cost (TC)	Output (Q)	Total Revenue (TR)	Total Cost (TC)
0	0	20	11	264	196
1	34	26	12	276	224
2	66	34	13	286	254
3	96	44	14	294	286
4	124	56	15	300	320
5	150	70	16	304	356
6	174	86	17	306	394
7	196	104	18	306	434
8	216	124	19	304	476
9	234	146	20	300	520
10	250	170			

   a. Compute the marginal revenue and average revenue functions.
   b. Compute the marginal cost and average cost functions.
   c. On a single graph, plot the total revenue, total cost, marginal revenue, and marginal cost functions.
   d. Determine the output level in the *graph* that maximizes profits (Profit = Total revenue − Total cost) by finding the point where marginal revenue equals marginal cost.
   e. Check your result in part (d) by finding the output level in the *tables* developed in parts (a) and (b) that likewise satisfies the condition that marginal revenue equals marginal cost.

2. Consider again the total revenue and total cost functions shown in tabular form in the previous problem.
   a. Compute the total, marginal, and average profit functions.
   b. On a single graph, plot the total profit and marginal profit functions.

c. Determine the output level in the graph and table where the total profit function takes on its maximum value.

d. How does the result in part (c) in this exercise compare with the result in part (d) of the previous exercise?

e. Determine total profits at the profit-maximizing output level.

3. Differentiate the following functions:

a. $TC = 50 + 100Q - 6Q^2 + .5Q^3$

b. $ATC = 50/Q + 100 - 6Q + .5Q^2$

c. $MC = 100 - 12Q + 1.5Q^2$

d. $Q = 50 - .75P$

e. $Q = .40X^{1.50}$

4. Differentiate the following functions:

a. $Y = 2X^3/(4X^2 - 1)$

b. $Y = 2X/(4X^2 - 1)$

c. $Y = 8Z^2 - 4Z + 1$, where $Z = 2X^2 - 1$ (differentiate Y with respect to X)

5. Define Q to be the level of output produced and sold, and assume that the firm's cost function is given by the relationship

$$TC = 20 + 5Q + Q^2$$

Furthermore, assume that the demand for the output of the firm is a function of price P given by the relationship

$$Q = 25 - P$$

a. Define total profit as the difference between total revenue and total cost, and express in terms of Q the total profit function for the firm. (*Note:* Total revenue equals price per unit times the number of units sold.)

b. Determine the output level where total profits are maximized.

c. Calculate total profits and selling price at the profit-maximizing output level.

d. If fixed costs increase from \$20 to \$25 in the total cost relationship, determine the effects of such an increase on the profit-maximizing output level and total profits.

6. Use the cost and demand functions in Exercise 5 to calculate the following:

a. Determine the marginal revenue and marginal cost functions.

b. Show that, at the profit-maximizing output level determined in part (b) of the previous exercise, marginal revenue equals marginal cost and illustrates the economic principle that profits are maximized at the output level where marginal revenue equals marginal cost.

7. Determine the partial derivatives with respect to all of the variables in the following functions:

a. $TC = 50 + 5Q_1 + 10Q_2 + .5Q_1Q_2$

b. $Q = 1.5L^{.60} K^{.50}$

c. $Q_A = 2.5P_A^{-1.30}Y^{.20}P_B^{.40}$

8. Bounds Inc. determined through regression analysis that its sales (S) are a function of the amount of advertising (measured in units) in two different media. This relationship is given by the following equation (X = newspapers, Y = magazines):

$$S(X,Y) = 200X + 100Y - 10X^2 - 20Y^2 + 20XY$$

a. Find the level of newspaper and magazine advertising that maximizes the firm's sales.

b. Calculate the firm's sales at the optimal values of newspaper and magazine advertising determined in part (a).

9. The Santa Fe Cookie Factory is considering an expansion of its retail piñon cookie business to other cities. The firm's owners lack the funds needed to undertake the expansion on their own. They are considering a franchise arrangement for the new outlets. The company incurs variable costs of \$6 for each pound of cookies sold. The fixed costs of operating a typical retail outlet are estimated to be \$300,000 per year. The demand function facing each retail outlet is estimated to be

$$P = \$50 - .001Q$$

where P is the price per pound of cookies and Q is the number of pounds of cookies sold. [*Note:* Total revenue equals price (P) times quantity (Q) sold.]

a. What price, output, total revenue, total cost, and total profit level will each profit-maximizing franchise experience?

b. Assume that the parent company charges each franchisee a fee equal to 5 percent of total revenues, and recompute the values in part (a).

c. The Santa Fe Cookie Factory is considering a combined fixed/variable franchise fee structure. Under this arrangement each franchisee would pay the parent company \$25,000 plus 1 percent of total revenues. Recompute the values in part (a).

d. What franchise fee arrangement do you recommend that the Santa Fe Cookie Factory adopt? What are the advantages and disadvantages of each plan?

10. Show that the optimal solution to the set of simultaneous equations in the Indiana Petroleum example are $Q_1^* = 5.77$ and $Q_2^* = 4.08$.

PART II

Demand and Forecasting

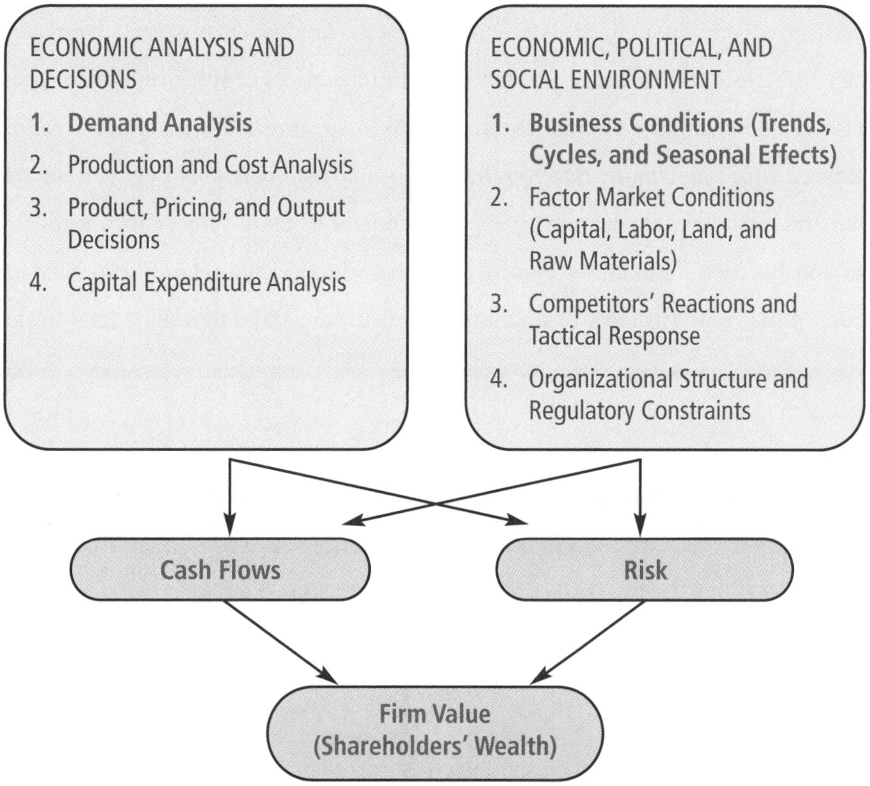

Part II (Demand and Forecasting) considers the elements determining the demand for a firm's output. Chapter 3 develops the theory of demand and introduces the elasticity properties of the demand function. Chapter 4 examines the procedures that may be used in making empirical estimates of demand and sales. Business and economic forecasting is the topic in Chapter 5. We consider forecasting at both the level of the firm and the overall economy. Chapter 6 examines the determinants of exchange rates, trade policy, and other factors crucial for effectively managing import-export trade. Understanding the determinants of both domestic and export demand is central to estimating the level and risk of the cash flows facing a firm.

CHAPTER

3

DEMAND ANALYSIS

CHAPTER PREVIEW Demand analysis serves two major managerial objectives. First, it provides the insights necessary to effectively manage demand. Second, it helps forecast sales and the revenue portion of a firm's cash flow stream. This chapter develops the theory of demand and introduces the elasticity properties of the demand function. The elasticity of demand is a measure of the responsiveness of quantity demanded to a change in one of the factors influencing demand, such as price, advertising, income levels, and the prices of substitute or complementary goods. Web Appendix A employs utility indifference curves to analyze consumer behavior in selecting housing and food items subject to a budget constraint. We then develop the relationship between cost-of-living price indices and new product introductions.

MANAGERIAL CHALLENGE

Health Care Reform and Cigarette Taxes[1]

When the Canadian government raised cigarette taxes enough to push the price per pack over $4, adult smoking declined by 38 percent and teenage smoking declined even more (by 61 percent). In 1997, a similar U.S. excise tax increase funded the "Tobacco settlement." Philip Morris, Reynolds Tobacco, Liggett, and other cigarette manufacturers agreed to pay $368 billion over 25 years to achieve immunity from civil liability in class action suits. The State Attorneys General had sued the cigarette manufacturers to recover the additional Medicare and Medicaid costs of smoking-related illnesses. Under the settlement, the average U.S. price of $1.43 per pack rose by 62 cents to $2.05 (by 35%).[2] Some critics of the proposal insisted at the time that the tobacco tax should be higher (perhaps as much as $1.50 higher) to deter young smokers from acquiring the habit. The stated objective for reducing teenage smoking was 30 percent in five years and 50 percent in seven years.

One important element of the debate regarding the "optimal" cigarette tax increase depends on how sensitive consumption is to changes in price. An excellent measure of this sensitivity is the price elasticity of demand, defined as the percentage change in quantity demanded that occurs as a result of some percentage change in price. Economists have estimated the price elasticity of adult cigarette demand to be −0.4, indicating that for a 10 percent increase in price, quantity demanded can be expected to decline by 4 percent. For teenagers, however, the price elasticity is thought to be much higher (−0.6), which indicates that for a 10 percent increase in price, quantity demanded can be expected to decline by 6 percent. So, a 35 percent increase in price would result in a 21 percent decline in teen smoking.

Unfortunately, however, this reduction is far below the stated goal of 30 percent reduction in teenage smoking. As a result, in 1999 the U.S. Congress decided to raise the federal excise

MANAGERIAL CHALLENGE

tax another 60 cents. State legislatures got involved as well, such that by 2002 the average price per pack reached $3.28 nationwide. Today, the price is even higher in most states. By 2006, New Jersey, Washington, Rhode Island, Michigan, and Arizona, for example, had imposed more than $2 a pack in state excise taxes, making the price of a pack $5 or more in those states.

In the ongoing debate over the amount of cigarette tax required for health care cost recovery, policy makers face a difficult set of trade-offs.

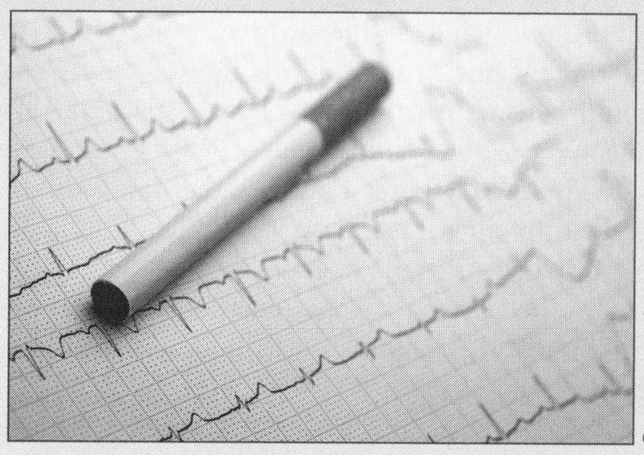

State Excise Tax Rates on Cigarettes (January 1, 2006)

State	Tax Rate (¢ Per Pack)	Rank	State	Tax Rate (¢ Per Pack)	Rank
Alabama	42.5	39	Nebraska	64	30
Alaska	160	7	Nevada	80	25
Arizona	118	16	New Hampshire	80	25
Arkansas	59	32	New Jersey	240	2
California	87	23	New Mexico	91	22
Colorado	84	24	New York	150	10
Connecticut	151	8	North Carolina	30	45
Delaware	55	35	North Dakota	44	38
Florida	33.9	44	Ohio	125	13
Georgia	37	41	Oklahoma	103	18
Hawaii	140	11	Oregon	118	16
Idaho	57	33	Pennsylvania	135	12
Illinois	98	21	Rhode Island	246	1
Indiana	55.5	34	South Carolina	7	51
Iowa	36	42	South Dakota	53	37
Kansas	79	27	Tennessee	20	48
Kentucky	30	45	Texas	41	40
Louisiana	36	42	Utah	69.5	29
Maine	200	4	Vermont	119	15
Maryland	100	19	Virginia	30	45
Massachusetts	151	8	Washington	202.5	3
Michigan	200	4	West Virginia	55	35
Minnesota	123	14	Wisconsin	77	28
Mississippi	18	49	Wyoming	60	31
Missouri	17	50	Dist. of Columbia	100	19
Montana	170	6	U.S. Median	80.0	

Source: Federation of Tax Administrators.

MANAGERIAL CHALLENGE

On the one hand, if the primary objective is to generate income to fund health care costs, the tax should be set such that it will maximize tax revenue. On the other hand, if the primary objective is to discourage smoking, a much higher tax could be justified. In either case, however, knowledge of the true price elasticity of demand is an essential element of this important policy decision. In this chapter, we investigate how to calculate and use such demand relationships.

[1] Based in part on "Add $2 to the Cost of a Pack of Cigarettes" and "And Even Teen Smokers May Kick the Habit," *Business-Week* (March 15, 1993), p. 18; "Critics Question Tobacco Pact's Effect on Teen Smoking," *Wall Street Journal* (August 19, 1997), p. A20; "Major Makers of Cigarettes Raise Prices," *Wall Street Journal* (August 31, 1999), p. A3; and "Politicians Are Hooked on Cigarette Taxes," *Wall Street Journal* (February 20, 2002), p. A2.

[2] The 35 percent price increase in the United States can be calculated by dividing the $0.62 tax increase by the average of the original $1.43 and the post-tax $2.05 price.

Demand Relationships

Demand relationships can be represented in the form of a schedule (table), graph, or algebraic function. Each of these forms of presentation provides insights into demand relationships. This section focuses on schedules and graphs; the next section discusses algebraic functions.

The Demand Schedule Defined

The demand schedule is the simplest form of the demand relationship. It is merely a list of prices and corresponding quantities of a product or service that would be demanded by some individual or group of individuals at uniform prices.[3] Table 3.1 shows the demand schedule for gasoline. This demand schedule indicates that *if* the price per gallon were $2.00, U.S. households would purchase 20 gallons per week. If the price were $3.00, household consumption would be 16 gallons

Table 3.1 U.S. Household Demand for Gasoline

Price ($/Gallon)	Quantity Purchased (Gallons Per Week)
$3.50	14
$3.00	16
$2.50	18
$2.00	20
$1.50	22
$1.00	24

[3] The terms *commodity, good,* and *product* are used interchangeably throughout the text to describe both physical goods and services.

per week. Note that the lower the price, the greater the quantity per week that would be demanded. This inverse or negative relationship between price and the rate of purchase is generally referred to as the "law of demand." At lower prices, people are able and willing to purchase more of a commodity than at a higher price.

CONSTRAINED UTILITY MAXIMIZATION AND DEMAND

The concept of demand is based on the theory of consumer choice. Each consumer faces a constrained optimization problem, where the objective is to choose among the combinations of goods and services that maximize satisfaction or utility, subject to a constraint on the amount of funds (i.e., the household budget) available. Think of a food and entertainment budget allowance from your employer while you are traveling on an extended business trip or, alternatively, a set of friends who share these expenses while rooming together. In this constrained utility-maximizing framework, economists have identified two basic reasons for the increase in quantity demanded as the result of a price reduction. These factors are known as *income* and *substitution effects.*

INCOME EFFECT When the price of a good—for example, apartment housing rent—declines, one effect of this decline is an increase in the real income or purchasing power of the consumer, known as the *income effect of the price change.* For example, if an individual normally purchases six hundred square feet at $1,000 per month, a price decline to $800 per month would enable the consumer to purchase the same amount of housing for $200 less per month. This savings of $200 represents an increase in real income of $200, which may be used to purchase greater quantities of housing (as well as other income-superior goods) each week.

Sometimes the income effect of a price reduction is miniscule because so little of the household's budget is expended on the good (like a salt canister purchased once every other year), but at other times the change in purchasing power is enormous. Consider a young family who spends 40 percent of their disposable income on apartment housing. In general, the sign and magnitude of the income effect of a price change has much to do with the positioning decision in the firm's marketing plan (i.e., at whom is the product or service targeted). French-American families, for example, spend almost twice as much of their disposable income on food (22%) as does the representative American family (12%). As a result, the quantity demanded of income-superior food items such as veal or wines we would expect to be much more price sensitive among French-American families.

SUBSTITUTION EFFECT When the price of a good such as movies declines, it becomes less expensive in relation to other substitute entertainment outings—for example, restaurant meals. As a result of the price decline, the rational consumer can increase his or her satisfaction or utility by purchasing more of the good whose price has declined and less of the substitutes. This situation is known as the *substitution effect of the price change.*

For example, suppose that the prices of movie admission and snacks versus a restaurant meal are $20 and $30, respectively. Furthermore, assume that an individual purchases one movie outing and two restaurant meals per week for a total entertainment expenditure of $80 per week. Suppose that the price of movies declines to $15.67. As a result of this price decrease, an individual who has a preference for movies may decide to increase his or her consumption to three movies per week and decrease his or her consumption of restaurant meal outings to one per week, which requires the same total expenditure of $50 per week. Thus, we see that a decrease in the relative price of movies to restaurant meals leads to an increase in the demand for movies, holding purchasing power constant.

In summary, because of the combined impact of the income and substitution effects, a decline in the price will always have a positive impact on the quantity demanded for income-superior goods and services (for which more is preferred to less as income rises). In this case, both the income and substitution effects dictate an increase in quantity demanded as prices fall. For income-*inferior* goods and services, such as efficiency apartments or riding the bus (for which less is preferred to more as income rises), the income and substitution effects have opposite and partially offsetting impacts on the quantity demanded. The net effect, even in the case of inferior goods, is usually that more goods and services will be demanded as the price declines.

Durable Good
A good that yields benefits to the owner over a number of future time periods.

Durable Goods Up to this point it has been implicitly assumed that we are considering the demand for consumer goods to be of a nondurable nature. These goods are purchased largely to meet current needs, and they generally provide service on a short-term basis. Food items, ball point pens, and virtually all services fall in this category, but autos and DVD players are clearly different. One reason is that by their very nature, **durable goods** *may be stored.* Another is that the replacement of a durable item may be delayed from period to period by performing additional repair and maintenance or by merely tolerating an old model. For example, an automobile may be repaired or its out-of-date styling merely endured; an electric furnace may be fixed again and again at considerably less cost than buying a new heating system.

Obsolescence in style, convenience, and prestige value play a larger role in affecting the replacement demand of durables. Also, consumer expectations regarding future levels of income, the availability of complements, and future product price play a major role in explaining the demand for durable goods. For example, a consumer may ask the following sorts of questions when embarking on a personal computer purchase:

- Will new products soon make my computer obsolete?
- Will my income be sufficient and steady enough to make the payments on the computer?
- Are prices likely to rise or fall over the next year?
- Will adequate software be available over the economic working life of my PC?

Because these expectational factors come into play in evaluating replacement demand, demand for durable goods is more volatile, and its analysis is more complex than a similar analysis for nondurables.

Producer's Good
A good that is not produced for direct consumption, but rather is the raw material or capital equipment that is used to produce a consumer good (or some other producer's good).

Derived Demand for Producer's Goods **Producer's goods** differ from consumer goods in that they are not produced for direct consumption but rather are the raw materials, capital equipment, and parts that are combined in manufacturing.

As such, the demand for producer's goods may be thought of as a *derived demand* because it is derived from some ultimate consumer desire. For example, the demand for aluminum, a raw material, is dependent on consumer desires and tastes for those products that are wholly or partially composed of aluminum, such as home siding and rain gutters, and for those services that are dependent on aluminum, such as plane travel. Therefore, when analyzing derived demand for producer's goods, an account must be taken of purchasing agent criteria and of the demand for the ultimate consumer goods for which the producer's goods are inputs.

THE PRICE ELASTICITY OF DEMAND

From a decision-making perspective, any firm needs to know the magnitude effects of changes in the determinants of demand. Some of these factors are under the control of management, such as price, advertising, product quality, and customer service. Other demand determinants, including disposable income and the prices of competitors' products, are outside the direct control of the firm. Nevertheless, effective demand management still requires that the firm be able to measure the impact of changes in these variables on the quantity demanded.

EXAMPLE

PIZZA HUT AND FORD DEALERS RESPOND TO DEFICIENT DEMAND

Pizza Hut anticipates a purchase frequency of 60 pizzas per night at a price of $9 and plans their operations accordingly. When fewer than the 60 customers arrive on a given evening, the Pizza Hut franchise does something different from what a Ford auto dealer might do in similar circumstances. The restaurant slashes orders; fewer pizza dough balls are flattened and spun out and baked. Instead of slashing prices in the face of deficient demand, restaurants tend delay their release-to-production orders. Why?

One insight hinges on the lack of customer traffic in a restaurant that might be attracted by a given discount to purchase more food on short notice. The demand by Pizza Hut customers is not as price sensitive as the final preparation stages of Pizza Hut supply are flexible. In other words, supply adjusts more easily than demand in this case. In contrast, in the auto business at the end of a model year, customer demand can be stimulated on short notice by sharp price discounts, while the supply schedule is rigid. Ford Motor Company assembles and ships a number of cars in response to firm orders by their retail dealers and then insists on a no-returns policy. Therefore, in the face of deficient demand (below the planned rate of sale), Ford dealerships slash their asking prices to clear the excess inventory.

Auto dealerships adopt price discounts as their primary adjustment mechanism, while restaurants slash orders. Fundamentally, what causes the difference in these two businesses? In the one case, demand is price sensitive and supply is not (retail autos at the end of the model year). In the other case, demand is price insensitive, and supply is quite flexible (restaurants). The difference is characterized by the price elasticity of demand and supply.

Price Elasticity Defined

ceteris paribus
Latin for "all other things held constant."

Price Elasticity of Demand
The ratio of the percentage change in quantity demanded to the percentage change in price, assuming that all other factors influencing demand remain unchanged. Also called *own* price elasticity.

The most commonly used measure of the responsiveness of quantity demanded to changes in any of the variables that influence the demand function is *elasticity*. In general, *elasticity* may be thought of as a ratio of the percentage change in one quantity (or variable) to the percentage change in another, ***ceteris paribus*** (all other things remaining unchanged). In other words, how responsive is some dependent variable to changes in a particular determinant of that variable? With this understanding of elasticity in mind, we define the **price elasticity of demand** (E_D) as the ratio of the percentage change in quantity demanded to a percentage change in price:

$$E_D = \frac{\%\Delta Q}{\%\Delta P}, \text{ ceteris paribus} \qquad [3.1]$$

where

$$\Delta Q = \text{change in quantity demanded}$$
$$\Delta P = \text{change in price}$$

Because of the normal inverse relationship between price and quantity demanded, the sign of the price elasticity coefficient will always be negative.

Arc Price Elasticity

The *arc* price elasticity of demand is a technique for calculating price elasticity between two prices.[4] It indicates the effect of a change in price, from P_1 to P_2, on the quantity demanded. The following formula is used to compute this elasticity measure:

$$E_D = \frac{\dfrac{Q_2 - Q_1}{\left(\dfrac{Q_2 + Q_1}{2}\right)}}{\dfrac{P_2 - P_1}{\left(\dfrac{P_2 + P_1}{2}\right)}} = \frac{Q_2 - Q_1}{P_2 - P_1} \cdot \frac{P_2 + P_1}{Q_2 + Q_1} = \frac{\Delta Q}{\Delta P}\frac{P_2 + P_1}{Q_2 + Q_1} \qquad [3.2]$$

where

$$Q_1 = \text{quantity sold before a price change}$$
$$Q_2 = \text{quantity sold after a price change}$$
$$P_1 = \text{original price}$$
$$P_2 = \text{price after a price change}$$

The fraction $(Q_2 + Q_1)/2$ represents average quantity demanded in the range over which the price elasticity is being calculated. $(P_2 + P_1)/2$ also represents the average price over this range.

[4] As we will see in the following section dealing with point price elasticities, the price elasticity of a straight-line demand curve is different at each point on the demand curve. Hence an arc price elasticity computed between two prices may be thought of as an average of the various point elasticities between the two prices.

Rearranging Equation 3.2 shows that the elasticity measurement depends on the inverse of the *slope* of the ordinary demand curve (i.e., the sensitivity of demand in the target market to price *changes*):

$$\frac{Q_2 - Q_1}{P_2 - P_1}$$

as well as to the *position* on the curve (i.e., the price point positioning) where elasticity is calculated:

$$\frac{P_2 + P_1}{Q_2 + Q_1}$$

Because the slope remains constant over the entire schedule of linear demand but the value of $(P_2 + P_1)/(Q_2 + Q_1)$ changes, depending on where on the demand curve elasticity is being calculated, *the value of the elasticity measured generally changes throughout the length of the demand curve.* Price elasticity at higher prices and smaller volume is therefore larger (in absolute value) than price elasticity for the same product and same demanders at lower price points and larger volume.

To illustrate, consider the demand schedule shown in Table 3.2 for men's Levi's jeans. Calculate the price elasticity between an original price of \$19 (14 units are demanded) and a new price of \$18. Substituting the relevant data from Table 3.2 into Equation 3.2 yields

$$E_D = \frac{\dfrac{16 - 14}{(16 + 14)/2}}{\dfrac{\$18 - \$19}{(\$18 + \$19)/2}}$$
$$= -2.46$$

A price elasticity of demand coefficient of −2.46 means that a 10 percent increase (decrease) in price can be expected to result in a 24.6 percent decrease (increase) in quantity demanded, *ceteris paribus.*

Table 3.2 Demand Schedule: Levi's Jeans

Price, *P* (\$/Unit)	Quantity Sold, Q_D (Units Per Period)
20	12
19	14
18	16
17	18
16	20
12	28
11	30

Now assume the original price was \$12, and a new price of \$11 is set. Determine the price elasticity of demand. Employing Equation 3.2 and the relevant data from Table 3.2 yields

$$E_D = \frac{\dfrac{30 - 28}{(30 + 28)/2}}{\dfrac{\$11 - \$12}{(\$11 + \$12)/2}} = -0.79$$

A price elasticity of demand of −0.79 means that a 10 percent increase (decrease) in price can be expected to result in a 7.9 percent decrease (increase) in quantity demanded, *ceteris paribus*.

We can also use Equation 3.2 to compute a price that would have to be charged to achieve a particular level of sales. Consider the NBA Corporation, which had monthly basketball shoe sales of 10,000 pairs (at \$100 per pair) before a price cut by its major competitor. After this competitor's price reduction, NBA's sales declined to 8,000 pairs a month. From the past experience, NBA estimated the price elasticity of demand to be about −2.0 in this price-quantity range. If the NBA wishes to restore its sales to 10,000 pairs a month, determine the price that must be charged.

Letting $Q_2 = 10{,}000$, $Q_1 = 8{,}000$, $P_1 = \$100$, and $E_D = -2.0$, the required price, P_2, may be computed using Equation 3.2:

$$-2.0 = \frac{\dfrac{10{,}000 - 8{,}000}{(10{,}000 + 8{,}000)/2}}{\dfrac{P_2 - \$100}{(P_2 + \$100)/2}}$$

$$P_2 = \$89.50$$

A price cut to \$89.50 would be required to restore sales to 10,000 pairs a month.

EXAMPLE

PRICE ELASTICITY OF DEMAND: THE *MACON TELEGRAPH*[5]

The *Macon Telegraph* newspaper is the principal sponsor of the Macon Labor Day Road Race, a 5K and 10K running event held annually in Macon, Georgia. The entry fee for the 1999 race was \$12 per runner. The fee was raised to \$20 per runner for the 2001 race, in hopes of increasing revenues from the race. Prior to the race, organizers heard complaints that the fee was too high for that kind of race and that it precluded many families from being able to afford entry fees.

The newspaper learned a lesson in price elasticity. In 1999 the race attracted 1,600 runners, and thus generated income of \$19,200. In 2001, under similar weather conditions, the race attracted only 900 runners, and thus generated income of only \$18,000. Because a (\$20 − \$12)/\$16 = 50 percent increase in price resulted in a massive (−700/1250) = 56 percent decrease in quantity demanded, the total revenue

[5] Based on Margaret Chivers, "They Voted with Their Feet," *Running Journal* (October 1991), pp. 1–2.

declined, and the price elasticity of demand over this range is "elastic" (greater than 1.0 in absolute value). Specifically, the price elasticity can be estimated as

$$\begin{aligned} E_D &= [(Q_2 - Q_1)/(Q_2 + Q_1)]/[(P_2 - P_1)/(P_2 + P_1)] \\ &= [(900 - 1{,}600)/(900 + 1{,}600)]/[(\$20 - \$12)/(\$20 + \$12)] \\ &= -1.12 \end{aligned}$$

That is, the $\%\Delta Q_D = -56$ percent is 1.12 times as large as the $\%\Delta P = 50$ percent; the demand percentage decrease exceeded the price percentage increase, and that amount is the difference by which total revenue declined.

In this case, the strategy of raising the price backfired because the newspaper misunderstood or incorrectly estimated the price elasticity of demand.

POINT PRICE ELASTICITY

The preceding formulas measure the *arc elasticity* of demand; that is, elasticity is computed over a discrete range of the demand curve or schedule. Because elasticity is normally different at each point on the curve, arc elasticity is a measure of the average elasticity over that range.

By employing some elementary calculus, the elasticity of demand at any *point* along the curve may be calculated with the following expression:

$$E_D = \frac{\partial Q_D}{\partial P} \cdot \frac{P}{Q_D} \qquad [3.3]$$

where

$\frac{\partial Q_D}{\partial P}$ = the partial derivative of quantity with respect to price (the inverse of the slope of the demand curve)

Q_D = the quantity demanded at price P

P = the price at some specific point on the demand curve

The partial derivative of quantity with respect to price, $\partial Q_D/\partial P$, is merely an indication of the rate of change in quantity demanded as the price changes. This incremental change ratio is analogous to

$$\frac{Q_2 - Q_1}{P_2 - P_1} = \frac{\Delta Q}{\Delta P}$$

the discrete change ratio in the arc elasticity measure.

The daily demand function for Christmas trees at sidewalk seasonal sales lots in mid-December can be used to illustrate the calculation of the point price elasticity. Suppose that demand can be written algebraically as quantity demanded per day:

$$Q_D = 45{,}000 - 2{,}500P + 2.5Y \qquad [3.4]$$

If one is interested in determining the point price elasticity when the price (P) is equal to \$40 and per capita disposable personal income (Y) is equal to \$30,000, taking the partial derivative of Equation 3.4 with respect to P yields

$$\frac{\partial Q_D}{\partial P} = -2{,}500 \text{ trees per dollar}$$

Substituting the relevant values of P and Y into Equation 3.4 gives

$$Q_D = 45{,}000 - 2{,}500(40) + 2.50(30{,}000) = 20{,}000$$

From Equation 3.4, one obtains

$$E_D = -2{,}500 \frac{\text{trees}}{\$}\left(\frac{\$8}{10{,}000 \text{ trees}}\right) = -2.0$$

EXAMPLE

Price Elasticity of Demand: The Case of Horse Race Pari-Mutuel Betting[6]

Faced with tight budgets and the need to raise additional revenues, many states have turned to various forms of state-operated legalized gambling. One of the earliest forms of betting, and still among the most prevalent, is the pari-mutuel wagering system of horse racing. The state revenue from horse race betting comes from a tax (called the "takeout rate") on the total of money wagered (called the "handle"). If the demand for horse race wagering is price inelastic, then states could increase their tax revenues by increasing the takeout rate. In contrast, if demand is price elastic, then increases in the takeout rate are likely to lead to declines in state revenues.

Two tracks in New York City lost revenue when they cut the takeout rate from 17 percent to 14 percent. With an inelastic demand, a reduction in "price" results in a decline in total revenue. At 22 other racetracks, in 21 instances, increases in the takeout rate resulted in increases in total revenues to both the state and the racing industry. These revenue effects suggest an inelastic demand for racetrack betting, insensitive to price increases.

Interpreting the Price Elasticity: The Relationship Between the Price Elasticity and Revenues

Once the price elasticity of demand has been calculated, it is necessary to interpret the meaning of the number obtained. The elasticity coefficient may take on *absolute values* over the range from 0 to ∞ (infinity). Values in the indicated ranges are described in Table 3.3.

When demand is *unit* elastic, a percentage change in price P is matched by an *equal* percentage change in quantity demanded Q_D. When demand is *elastic,* a

Table 3.3 Price Elasticity of Demand in Absolute Values

Range	Description
$E_D = 0$	Perfectly inelastic
$0 < \lvert E_D \rvert < 1$	Inelastic
$\lvert E_D \rvert = 1$	Unit elastic
$1 < \lvert E_D \rvert < \infty$	Elastic
$\lvert E_D \rvert = \infty$	Perfectly elastic

[6] Based on Donn R. Pescatrice, "The Inelastic Demand for Wagering," *Applied Economics* 12 (1980), pp. 1–10.

Figure 3.1 Perfectly Elastic and Inelastic Demand Curves

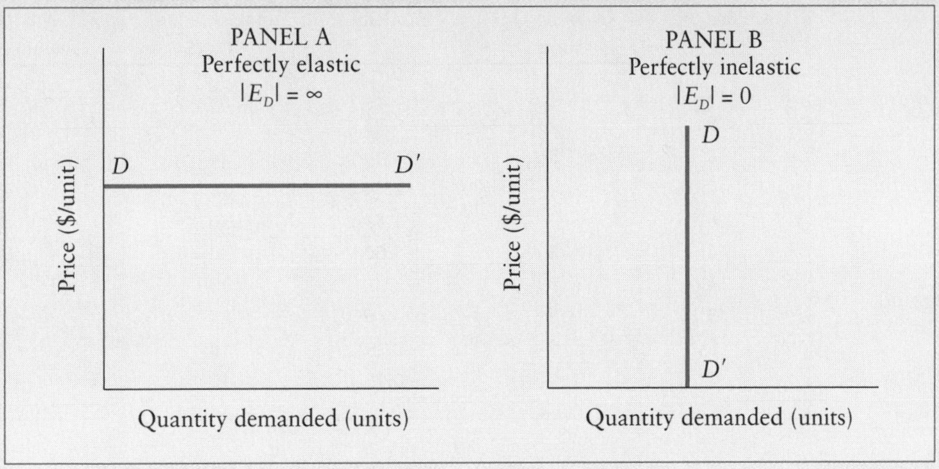

percentage change in P is exceeded by the percentage change in Q_D. For *inelastic* demand, a percentage change in P results in a smaller percentage change in Q_D. The theoretical extremes of perfect elasticity and perfect inelasticity are illustrated in Figure 3.1. AAA-grade January wheat sells on the Kansas City spot market with perfectly elastic demand facing any particular grain dealer; Panel A illustrates this case. Heroin addicts have almost perfectly inelastic demand; their quantity demanded is fixed no matter what the price, as indicated in Panel B. However, these extremes are rarely encountered. Rather, they illustrate the limits of price elasticity.

The price elasticity of demand indicates the effect a change in price will have on the total revenue that is generated. Because total revenue TR is equal to price (average revenue), P, times the number of units sold, Q_D, we may determine, from our knowledge of demand elasticity, the effect on total revenue when price changes.

When demand elasticity is less than 1 in absolute value (i.e., inelastic), an increase (decrease) in price will result in an increase (decrease) in total consumer expenditures ($P \cdot Q_D$). This occurs because inelastic demand implies that a given percentage increase (decrease) in price results in a smaller percentage decrease (increase) in quantity sold. Table 3.4 illustrates this point. When demand is *inelastic* ($|E_D| < 1$), an increase in price from \$2 to \$3, for example, results in an increase in total revenue from \$18 to \$24.[7]

In contrast, when demand is *elastic* ($|E_D| > 1$), a given percentage increase (decrease) in price is more than offset by a larger percentage decrease (increase) in quantity sold. An increase in price from \$9 to \$10 results in a reduction in total consumer expenditure from \$18 to \$10 (again, see Table 3.4).

When demand is *unit elastic,* a given percentage change in price is exactly offset by the same percentage change in quantity demanded, the net result being a constant total consumer expenditure. If the price is increased from \$5 to \$6, total revenue would remain constant at \$30, because the decrease in quantity demanded at the

[7] The expression $|E_D| < 1$ indicates that we are talking about the absolute value of the elasticity coefficient, rather than its actual negative value. This symbol (| |) is used whenever we refer to absolute values.

Table 3.4 The Relationship Between Elasticity and Marginal Revenue

Price, P (\$/Unit)	Quantity Q_D (Units)	Elasticity E_D	Total Revenue $P \cdot Q_D$ (\$)	Marginal Revenue (\$/Unit)
10	1		10	
9	2	−6.33	18	8
8	3	−3.40	24	6
7	4	−2.14	28	4
6	5	−1.44	30	2
5	6	−1.00	30	0
4	7	−0.69	28	−2
3	8	−0.46	24	−4
2	9	−0.29	18	−6
1	10	−0.15	10	−8

new price just offsets the price increase (see Table 3.4). When the price elasticity of demand $|E_D|$ is equal to 1 (or is unit elastic), the total revenue function is maximized. In the example, total revenue equals \$30 when price P equals either \$5 or \$6 and quantity demanded Q_D equals either 6 or 5.

The relationship among price, quantity, elasticity measures, marginal revenue, and total revenue is illustrated graphically in Figure 3.2. When total revenue is maximized, marginal revenue equals zero and demand is unit elastic. At any price higher than P_2, the demand function is elastic. Hence, successive equal percentage increases in price may be expected to generate higher and higher percentage decreases in quantity demanded because the demand function is becoming increasingly elastic. Alternatively, successive equal percentage reductions in price below P_2 may be expected to generate ever lower percentage increases in quantity demanded because the demand function is more inelastic at lower prices.

To summarize, a change in TR arises from two sources: a change in prices and a change in unit sales. Specifically,

$$\Delta TR = (\Delta P \cdot Q_0) + (\Delta Q \cdot P_1)$$

then, dividing by $P_1 \cdot Q_0$, yields the useful expression:

$$\begin{aligned} \%\Delta TR &= (\Delta P/P_1) + (\Delta Q/Q_0) \\ \%\Delta TR &= \%\Delta P + \%\Delta Q \end{aligned} \qquad [3.5]$$

That is, the percentage effect on sales revenue is the *signed* summation of the percentage change in price and in unit sales.

If Johnson & Johnson lowers the price on BAND-AIDs 10 percent and sales revenue goes up 24 percent, we can conclude that unit sales must have risen 34 percent, because applying Equation 3.5 gives us

$$24\% = -10\% + 34\%$$

Marginal Revenue
The change in total revenue that results from a one-unit change in quantity demanded.

The relationship between a product's price elasticity of demand and the marginal revenue at that price point is one of the most important in managerial economics. This relationship can be derived by analyzing the change in revenue resulting from a price change. To start, **marginal revenue** is defined as the change in total revenue resulting from lowering price to make an additional unit sale. Lowering price from

Figure 3.2 Price Elasticity over Demand Function

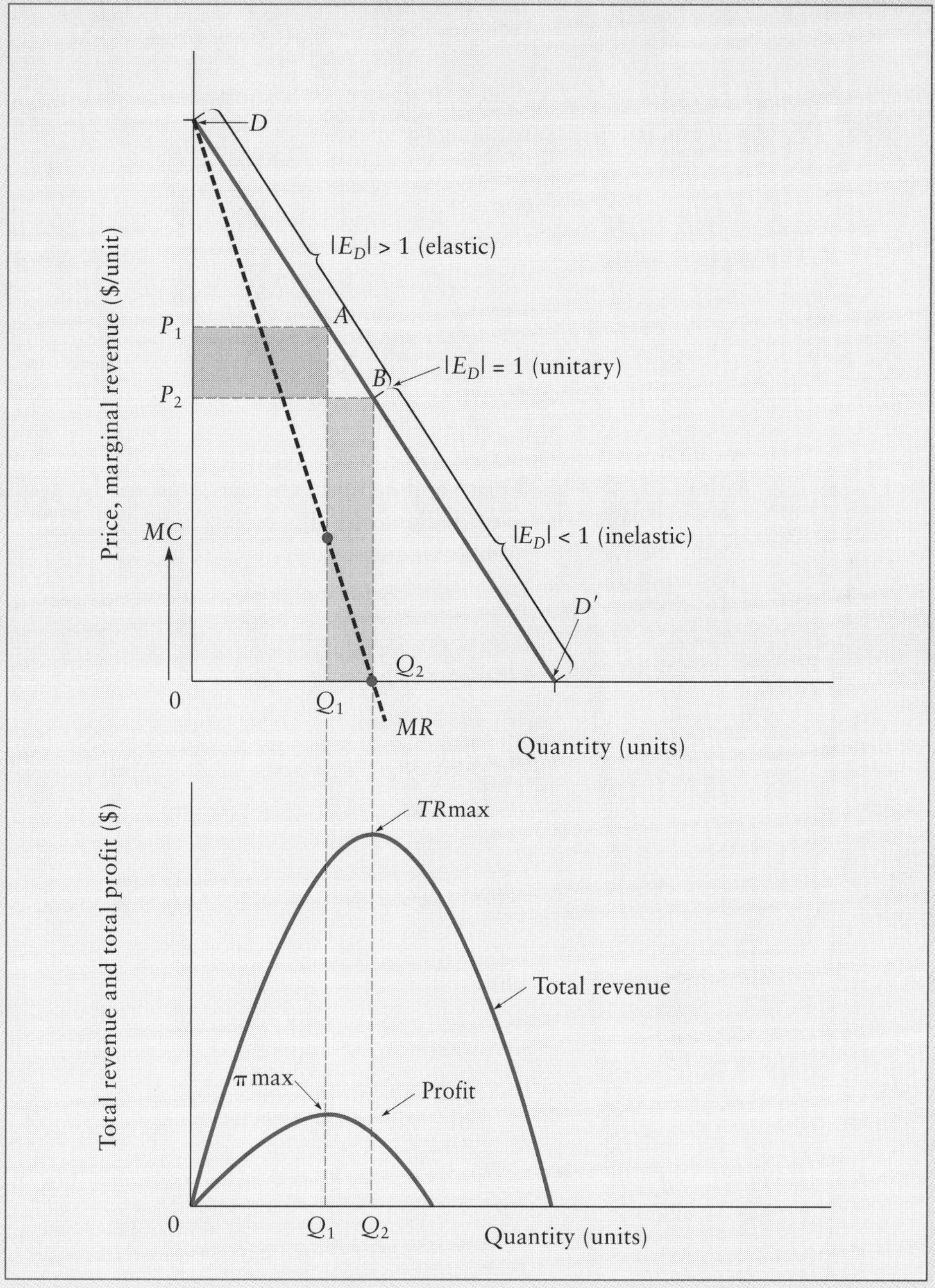

P_1 to P_2 in Figure 3.2 to increase quantity demanded from Q_1 to Q_2 results in a change in the initial revenue P_1AQ_10 to P_2BQ_20. The difference in these two areas is illustrated in Figure 3.2 as the two shaded rectangles. The horizontal shaded rectangle is the loss of revenue caused by the price reduction $(P_2 - P_1)$ over the previous units sold Q_1. The vertical shaded rectangle is the gain in revenue from selling $(Q_2 - Q_1)$

additional units at the new price P_2. That is, the change in total revenue from lowering the price to sell another unit can always be written as follows:

$$MR = \frac{\Delta TR}{\Delta Q} = \frac{P_2(Q_2 - Q_1) + (P_2 - P_1)Q_1}{(Q_2 - Q_1)} \qquad [3.6]$$

where $P_2(Q_2 - Q_1)$ is the vertical shaded rectangle and $(P_1 - P_2)Q_1$ is the horizontal shaded rectangle. Rearranging, we have

$$MR = P_2 + \frac{(P_2 - P_1)Q_1}{(Q_2 - Q_1)}$$

$$= P_2\left(1 + \frac{(P_2 - P_1)Q_1}{(Q_2 - Q_1)P_2}\right)$$

$$MR = P_2\left(1 + \frac{\Delta P Q_1}{\Delta Q P_2}\right)$$

The ratio term is the inverse of the price elasticity at the price point P_2 using the quantity Q_1. For small price and quantity changes, this number closely approximates the arc price elasticity in Equation 3.2 between P_1 and P_2. Therefore, the relationship between marginal revenue and price elasticity can be expressed algebraically as follows:[8]

$$MR = P\left(1 + \frac{1}{E_D}\right) \qquad [3.7]$$

[8] This equation also can be derived from the definitions of marginal revenue and price elasticity using calculus. Marginal revenue is equal to the first derivative of total revenue:

$$MR = \frac{d(TR)}{dQ_D} = \frac{d(P \cdot Q_D)}{dQ_D}$$

Using the rule for taking the derivative of a product (see Appendix 2A, Equation 2A.20) yields

$$MR = P \cdot \frac{dQ_D}{dQ_D} + Q_D\frac{dP}{dQ_D}$$

$$= P + Q_D\frac{dP}{dQ_D}$$

This equation may be rewritten as

$$MR = P\left(1 + \frac{Q_D}{P} \cdot \frac{dP}{dQ_D}\right)$$

Recall that the point price elasticity of demand is

$$E_D = \frac{dQ_D}{dP} \cdot \frac{P}{Q_D}$$

and the term $\frac{Q_D}{P} \cdot \frac{dP}{dQ_D}$ is the reciprocal of the point price elasticity measure.

Hence, substituting $\frac{1}{E_D}$ for $\frac{Q_D}{P} \cdot \frac{dP}{dQ_D}$ results in Equation 3.7:

$$MR = P\left(1 + \frac{1}{E_D}\right)$$

Using this equation, one can demonstrate that when demand is unit elastic, marginal revenue is equal to zero. Substituting $E_D = -1$ into Equation 3.7 yields

$$\begin{aligned} MR &= P\left(1 + \frac{1}{-1}\right) \\ &= P(0) \\ &= 0 \end{aligned}$$

EXAMPLE

CONTENT-PROVIDERS PRESS PUBLISHING COMPANIES TO LOWER PRICES

Entertainment and publishing companies pay composers, playwrights, and authors a fixed percentage of realized sales revenue as a royalty. The two groups often differ as to the preferred price and unit sales. In Figure 3.2, total revenue can be increased by lowering the price any time the quantity sold is less than Q_2. That is, at any price above P_2 (where marginal revenue remains positive), the total revenue will continue to climb only if prices are lowered and additional units sold. Composers, playwrights, patent holders, and authors often therefore press their licensing agents and publishers to lower prices whenever marginal revenue remains positive (i.e., to the point where demand is unit elastic). The publisher, on the other hand, will wish to charge higher prices and sell less quantity because operating profits arise from marginal revenue in excess of marginal cost. Unless marginal cost is zero, the publisher always wants a positive marginal revenue and therefore a price greater than P_2 (e.g., P_1).

A commission-based sales force and the management team have this same conflict; salespeople often develop ingenious hidden discounts to try to circumvent a company's list pricing policies. Lowering the price from P_1 to P_2 to set $|E_D| = 1$ will always maximize sales revenue, and therefore maximize total commissions.

The fact that total revenue is maximized (and marginal revenue is equal to zero) when $|E_D| = 1$ can be shown with the following example: Custom-Tees, Inc., operates a kiosk in Hanes Mall where it sells custom-printed T-shirts. The demand function for the shirts is

$$Q_D = 150 - 10P \qquad [3.8]$$

where P is the price in dollars per unit and Q_D is the quantity demanded in units per period.

The inverse demand curve can be rewritten in terms of P as a function of Q_D.

$$P = 15 - \frac{Q_D}{10} \qquad [3.9]$$

Total revenue (TR) is equal to price times quantity sold.

$$\begin{aligned} TR &= P \cdot Q_D \\ &= \left(15 - \frac{Q_D}{10}\right) Q_D \\ &= 15Q_D - \frac{Q_D^2}{10} \end{aligned}$$

Marginal revenue (MR) is equal to the first derivative of total revenue with respect to Q_D:

$$MR = \frac{d(TR)}{dQ_D}$$
$$= 15 - \frac{Q_D}{5}$$

To find the value of Q_D where total revenue is maximized, set marginal revenue equal to zero:[9]

$$MR = 0$$
$$15 - \frac{Q_D}{5} = 0$$
$$Q_D^* = 75 \text{ units}$$

Substituting this value into Equation 3.9 yields

$$P^* = 15 - \frac{75}{10} = \$7.50 \text{ per unit}$$

Thus, total revenue is maximized at $Q_D^* = 75$ and $P^* = \$7.50$. The following calculation provides a check of the results:

$$E_D = \frac{\partial Q_D}{\partial P} \cdot \frac{P}{Q_D} = (-10)\frac{(7.5)}{75} = -1$$
$$|E_D| = 1$$

In addition to showing that $|E_D| = 1$ when the total revenue function is at its maximum, this example also demonstrates that marginal revenue MR is equal to zero when total revenue is maximized. This finding is not surprising when we remember that the definition of marginal revenue is the increase in total revenue resulting from the sale of one additional unit. Beyond the output level where total revenue is maximized, marginal revenue becomes negative and total revenue declines; that is, $|E_D| < 1$.

The Importance of Elasticity-Revenue Relationships

Elasticity is often the key to marketing plans. A product-line manager will attempt to maximize sales revenue by allocating a marketing expense budget among price promotions, advertising, retail displays, trade allowances, direct mail, and in-store couponing. Knowing whether and at what magnitude demand is responsive to each of these marketing initiatives depends on careful estimates of the various demand elasticities of price, advertising, promotional displays, and so on.

[9] To be certain one has found values for P and Q_D, where total revenue is maximized rather than minimized, check the second derivative of TR to see that it is negative. In this case $d^2TR/dQ_D^2 = -1/5$, so the total revenue function is maximized.

EXAMPLE

VW's Invasion of North America

When Volkswagen entered the U.S. market with its no-frills automobile, the original Beetle, European excess inventory had stockpiled at ports and road terminals awaiting export to a new market. Consequently, VW focused for a time on any demand stimulus that would increase revenue. In the U.S. market, VW had no dealer network and initially provided sales and service only at the docks in New Jersey; Charleston, South Carolina; and Houston, Texas. General Motors and Ford were developing compact cars as well, so VW decided to enter the market at what appeared to be a ridiculously low promotional price of $800 (approximately $6,500 in 2007 U.S. dollars). Two years later, a 25 percent price increase was introduced. Although VW lost some potential customers at $1,000 who were willing to pay between $800 and $999, the extra $200 per car on all the cars they continued to sell easily offset the revenue loss at old $800 prices from a few lost sales. (Compare the two shaded areas in Figure 3.3.) The price elasticity of demand was in the inelastic range of demand. By 1960, VW had raised the price another 20 percent to $1,200, and again revenue rose. Finally, in 1964 at $1,350, the extra receipts from the $150 price increase across all remaining sales were just sufficient to offset the loss in revenue from the lost sales. At $1,350, price elasticity had reached the unit elastic price point (see Figure 3.3). Volkswagen then proceeded to build a U.S. dealer network. These changes increased the potential size of the market in the United States and shifted the demand for Volkswagen products to the right. At $1,350 with a dealer network and a larger quantity base, the measured price elasticity then declined (again into the inelastic range), and Volkswagen was again in a position to raise price.

In 1968, 562,000 Beetles were sold at a price of $1,500, and revenue again increased (to $843 million). Although the product remained inexpensive ($1,500 in 1968 is about $9,000 today), the Highway Safety Act of 1996, plus Ralph

Figure 3.3 Raising Price with Demand in the Inelastic Range

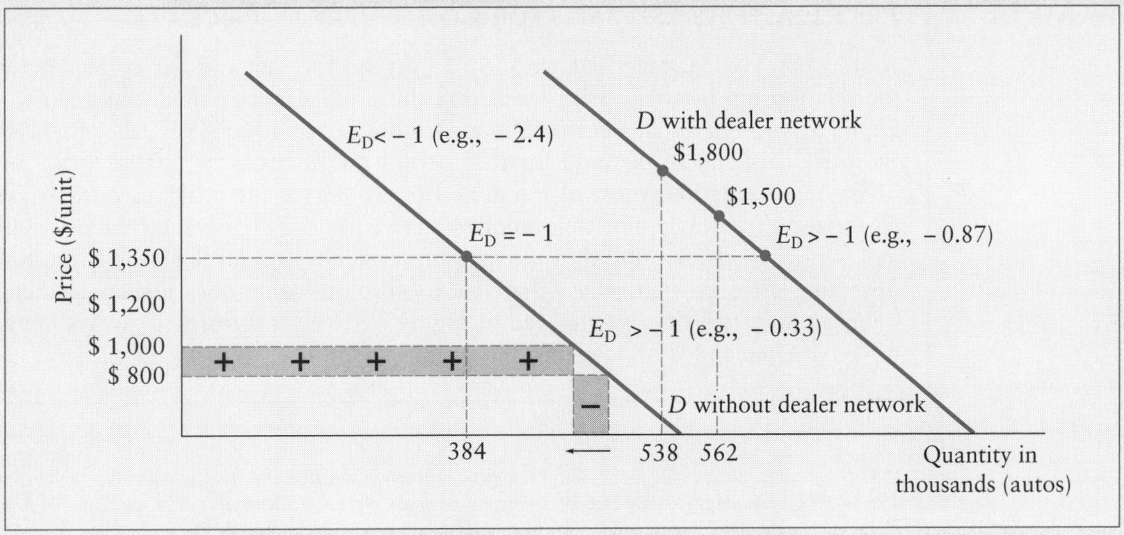

Nader's crusade against small rear-engine cars, plus low gasoline prices caused a loss of interest in Beetles among consumers who started buying large numbers of Mustangs, Camaros, and a new more powerful Super Beetle. In 1969, revenue and price of the Beetle increased one last time. At \$1,800, revenue was \$968 million (\$1,800 × 538,000 units sold). That is, demand remained in the inelastic range, and thus, a price increase from \$1,500 to \$1,800 resulted in higher total revenue.

One managerial insight illustrated by this example is that firms should always seek to raise prices for any products in the inelastic range of their demand. To lower prices in such a range would both *increase* costs (of producing and distributing additional output demanded at the lower prices) and also *decrease* revenue. It is far better to approach unit elasticity from below, raising prices thereby increasing revenue while at the same time saving the production and distribution costs. In fact, astute profit-maximizing firms will carry these price increases right on into the elastic range beyond the point of maximum revenue and unit elasticity (above and beyond point B at P_2 and Q_2 in Figure 3.2).

Starting from the other direction at zero output, a profit-maximizing firm will only lower price to increase revenue as long as the incremental change in total revenue (the MR in Figure 3.2) exceeds the positive change in total variable cost (labeled height MC). That is, the profit-maximizing output will always occur in the elastic region of the firm's demand—for example, at a price above the unit elastic price point.

As we saw earlier, unit elasticity is also of special significance for commission-based employees or anyone whose paycheck rises as sales revenue increases. In general, composers, playwrights, patent holders, authors, and e-business content providers want to maximize revenue. Because operating profits occur only when marginal revenue is in excess of marginal cost, managers want higher prices with somewhat reduced revenue, much reduced costs, and therefore higher profits. One solution to this incentives conflict is to involve the content providers in the company's profit-sharing plan.

EXAMPLE

Price Elasticity Estimates for Coffee Vary by Price[10]

A study by Huang, Siegfried, and Zardoshty on the demand for coffee confirms the relationship between price levels and the price elasticity of demand shown in Figure 3.2. After studying coffee demand for the period 1963–1977, they found that the price elasticity of demand for that period ranged from -0.10 for price levels prevailing throughout most of the period to -0.89 for the peak price level. Thus, coffee users are nearly nine times more sensitive to price changes at high prices than at low price levels. Because these are market-level, not firm-level, elasticity estimates, observing price elasticities less than 1.0 in absolute value does not contradict the managerial insight that is conveyed by Figure 3.3; that is, *firms* will always increase price until demand is no longer in the inelastic region.

[10] Cliff J. Huang, John J. Siegfried, and Farangis Zardoshty, "The Demand for Coffee in the United States, 1963–1977," *Quarterly Review of Economics and Business* 20, no. 2 (Summer 1980), pp. 36–50. Another more recent estimate of the demand elasticity for coffee can be found in Albert A. Okunade, "Functional Forms and Habits Effects in the U.S. Demand for Coffee," *Applied Economics* (November 1992).

FACTORS AFFECTING THE PRICE ELASTICITY OF DEMAND

The market demand for furniture, a durable good, is extremely price elastic (−3.04), whereas the market demand for caffeinated coffee (−0.16) is extremely price inelastic. As shown in Table 3.5, price elasticities vary greatly among different products

Table 3.5 Empirical Price Elasticities

Commodity (Good/Service)	Price Elasticity of Market Demand	Commodity (Good/Service)	Price Elasticity of Market Demand
Alcoholic beverages		Furniture	−3.04[m]
(consumed at home)		Glassware/China	−1.20[c]
Beer	−.84[e]	Household appliances	−.64[c]
Wine	−.55[e]	International air transportation	
Liquor	−.50[e]	United States/Europe	−1.25[h]
Apparel		Canada/Europe	−.82[h]
Market	−1.1[m]	Outdoor recreation	−.56[f]
Firms	−4.1[m]	School lunches	−.47[d]
Coffee		Shoes	−.73[c]
Regular	−.16[b]	Soybean meal	−1.65[j]
Instant	−.36[b]	Telephones	−0.10[a]
Credit charges on bank cards	−2.44[l]	Textiles	
Dental visits		Market	−1.5[m]
Adult males	−.65[g]	Firms	−4.7[m]
Adult females	−.78[g]	Tires	−0.60[c]
Children	−1.40[g]	Tobacco products	−.46[c]
Food		Tomatoes	−2.22[k]
Market	−1.0[n]	Wool	−1.32[i]
Firms	−3.8[n]		

[a] D. Cracknell and M. Knott, "The Measurement of Price Elasticities—The BT Experience," *International Journal of Forecasting* 11 (1995), pp. 321–329.

[b] Cliff J. Huang, John J. Siegfried, and Farangis Zardoshty, "The Demand for Coffee in the United States, 1963–1977," *Quarterly Review of Economics and Business* 20, no. 2 (Summer 1980), pp. 36–50.

[c] H. S. Houthakker and Lester D. Taylor, *Consumer Demand in the United States,* 2d ed. (Cambridge, MA: Harvard University Press, 1970).

[d] George A. Braley and P. E. Nelson, Jr., "Effect of a Controlled Price Increase on School Lunch Participation: Pittsburgh, 1973," *American Journal of Agricultural Economics* (February 1975), pp. 90–96.

[e] Dale Heien and Greg Pompelli, "The Demand for Alcoholic Beverages: Economic and Demographic Effects," *Southern Economic Journal* (January 1989), pp. 759–769.

[f] Russel L. Gum and W. E. Martin, "Problems and Solutions in Estimating the Demand for and Value of Rural Outdoor Recreation," *American Journal of Agricultural Economics* (November 1975), pp. 558–566.

[g] Willard G. Manning, Jr. and Charles E. Phelps, "The Demand for Dental Care," *The Bell Journal of Economics* 10, no. 2 (Autumn 1979), pp. 503–525.

[h] J. M. Cigliano, "Price and Income Elasticities for Airline Travel: The North Atlantic Market," *Business Economics* (September 1980), pp. 17–21.

[i] C. E. Ferguson and M. Polasek, "The Elasticity of Import Demand for Raw Apparel Wool in the United States," *Econometrica* 30 (1962), pp. 670–699.

[j] H. Knipscheer, L. Hill, and B. Dixon, "Demand Elasticities for Soybean Meal in the European Community," *American Journal of Agricultural Economics* (May 1982), pp. 249–253.

[k] Daniel B. Suits, "Agriculture," in *Structure of American Industry,* 7th ed., ed. W. Adams (New York: Macmillan, 1986).

[l] J. Starvins, "Can Demand Elasticity Explain Sticky Credit Card Rates?" *New England Economic Review* (July/August 1996), pp. 43–54.

[m] Richard D. Stone and D.A. Rowe, "The Durability of Consumers' Durable Goods," *Econometrica* 28 (1960), pp. 407–416.

[n] M. D. Shapiro, "Measuring Market Power in U.S. Industry," NBER Working Paper, No. 2212, 1987.

and services.[11] Some of the factors that account for the differing responsiveness of consumers to price changes are examined next.

Availability and Closeness of Substitutes The most important determinant of the price elasticity of demand is the availability and closeness of substitutes. The greater the number of substitute goods within the relevant market, the more price elastic is the demand for a product because a customer can easily shift from one good to a close substitute good if the price rises. The price elasticity of demand for Johnson & Johnson's BAND-AIDs is high because numerous companies offer a nearly identical product. The closeness of substitutes is a related but different concept. Intravenous feeding systems have distant substitutes for hospital patients in shock or otherwise unable to digest food, so the price elasticity of demand for that product is low. Sunbeam white bread, however, has close substitutes from Sarah Lee, from sourdough breads, from rolls and bagels. So, in that case, price elasticity of demand is high.

Durable Goods The demand for durable goods tends to be more price elastic than the demand for nondurables because of the ready availability of a relatively inexpensive substitute in many cases (e.g., the repair of a used television, car, or refrigerator, rather than buying a new one). In addition, consumers of durable goods are often in a position to wait for a more favorable price, a sale, or a special deal when buying these items.

Percentage of the Consumer's Budget The demand for relatively high-priced goods tends to be more price elastic than the demand for inexpensive items because expensive items account for a greater proportion of a person's budget. Consequently, we would expect the demand for housing to be more price elastic than the demand for children's toys. The greater the percentage of the budget spent on a good, the larger the purchasing power released by any given price reduction or absorbed by any given price increase. And the larger this "income effect," the greater the price elasticity for normal goods.

EXAMPLE

Determinants of the Price Elasticity of Demand for Housing in San Francisco, Kansas City, and Houston[12]

Residents of San Francisco spend 39.7 percent of their after-tax income on housing, while residents of Kansas City and Houston spend only 18.4 percent and 18.7 percent, respectively. This difference in the allocation of a typical household's budget implies that the increase in a San Franciscan's purchasing power for all goods and services, if housing costs in general fall by 10 percent, will be more than twice as large as the increase in purchasing power enjoyed by a Kansas Citian or Houstonian for the same 10 percent decline in housing costs. The demand for all "normal" or income-superior goods should rise more in San Francisco than in Kansas City or Houston. Because housing is an income-superior good, one might expect the percentage increase in demand for housing in San Francisco to be larger than in Kansas City or Houston for an equal percentage reduction in price in all three locations.

---

[11] Rothstein-Tauber, Inc. is one of a number of consulting firms that estimates price elasticities. You can access their Internet site at www.rti-dfd.com.

[12] Based on "The Home Front," *Wall Street Journal* (July 11, 1997), p. B6.

Recall that this reasoning assumes that all other factors influencing quantity demanded have remained unchanged (i.e., comparable neighborhoods, comparable size, comparable styles, etc.). If this assumption (*ceteris paribus*) is not met, the price elasticity of housing in the three cities may be quite different. This warning applies to all elasticity calculations and analysis.

TIME FRAME OF ANALYSIS Over time, the demand for many products tends to become more elastic because of the increase in the number of effective substitutes that become available. For example, in the short run, the demand for gasoline may be relatively price inelastic because the only available alternatives are not taking a trip or using some form of public transportation. Over time, as consumers replace their cars, they find another excellent substitute for gasoline—namely, more fuel-efficient vehicles. Also, other product alternatives may become available, such as electric cars or cars powered by natural gas.

Another reason the time frame of analysis affects the elasticity involves transaction costs. Almost all purchases necessitate a certain transportation and time expense on the part of both buyer and seller. In addition, to respond to a price decrease, potential customers must first learn about the discount and then incur the cost of adjusting their own schedules to complete a purchase during the sale period. Because both search and adjustment costs for consumers are higher if sale prices last only a few minutes, the demand response to price changes is diminished the shorter the time period of adjustment. Predictable end-of-model-year promotions in the auto industry lasting throughout the month of August stimulate much more elastic demand than unannounced "Midnight Madness" sales that last only a few hours.

INTERNATIONAL PERSPECTIVES

FREE TRADE AND THE PRICE ELASTICITY OF DEMAND: NESTLÉ YOGURT

The 1990s were characterized by an explosion of free-trade agreements among important trading partners. The Europe 1992 plan virtually eliminated trade barriers, and goods now flow freely and without tariffs from one European country to another. Increasing standardization of products in these markets will further reduce trading barriers. In 1994, the North American Free Trade Agreement (NAFTA) was ratified in the United States, Canada, and Mexico, and the General Agreement on Tariffs and Trade (GATT) was implemented, leading to a worldwide reduction in tariffs and other trade barriers. In 2001, the United States launched the Doha Round of free trade talks that continue to the present.

What are the implications of these reduced trade barriers for estimates of price elasticity of demand? Free trade results in an effective increase in the number of substitute goods that are available to consumers and businesses in any country. Consequently, as barriers to free trade come down, demand will become more price elastic for goods that historically have not been able to flow easily between countries. Nestlé's yogurt and custard products now travel from manufacturing sites in the British Midlands to Milan in 17 hours, whereas the customs processing and transportation bottlenecks once required 38 hours. Similarly, iron forging of crankshafts and engine blocks for U.S. autos now occurs primarily in Mexico, and transmissions for Detroit are often constructed as subassemblies in Japan. The winners in this globalization process should be consumers, who will have a wider variety of products to choose from at ever more competitive prices. The losers will be those firms that cannot compete in a global market on the basis of cost, quality, and service.

THE INCOME ELASTICITY OF DEMAND

Among the variables that affect demand, disposable income of the target market is often one of the most important. Business analysts compute an income elasticity of demand analogous to the price elasticity of demand.

INCOME ELASTICITY DEFINED

Income Elasticity

The ratio of the percentage change in quantity demanded to the percentage change in income, assuming that all other factors influencing demand remain unchanged.

Income elasticity of demand measures the responsiveness of a change in quantity demanded of some commodity to a change in income. It can be expressed as

$$E_y = \frac{\%\Delta Q_D}{\%\Delta Y}, \textit{ ceteris paribus} \qquad [3.10]$$

where

$$\Delta Q_D = \text{change in quantity demanded}$$
$$\Delta Y = \text{change in income}$$

Various measures of income can be used in the analysis. One commonly used measure is consumer disposable income, calculated on an aggregate, household, or per capita basis.

ARC INCOME ELASTICITY

The *arc* income elasticity is a technique for calculating income elasticity between two income levels. It is computed as

$$E_y = \frac{\dfrac{Q_2 - Q_1}{(Q_2 + Q_1)/2}}{\dfrac{Y_2 - Y_1}{(Y_2 + Y_1)/2}} = \frac{\Delta Q}{\Delta Y}\frac{(Y_1 + Y_2)}{(Q_1 + Q_2)} \qquad [3.11]$$

where Q_2 = quantity sold after an income change
Q_1 = quantity sold before an income change
Y_2 = new level of income
Y_1 = original level of income

For example, assume that an increase in disposable personal income in Rhode Island from \$1.00 billion to \$1.10 billion is associated with an increase in boat sales in the state from 5,000 to 6,000 units. Determine the income elasticity over this range. Substituting the relevant data into Equation 3.11 yields

$$E_y = \frac{\dfrac{6{,}000 - 5{,}000}{(6{,}000 + 5{,}000)/2}}{\dfrac{\$1.10 - \$1.00}{(\$1.10 + \$1.00)/2}} = \frac{1{,}000}{\$0.10}\frac{(\$2.10)}{(11{,}000)}$$
$$= 1.91$$

Thus, a 1 percent increase in income would be expected to result in a 1.91 percent increase in quantity demanded, *ceteris paribus*.

POINT INCOME ELASTICITY

The arc income elasticity measures the responsiveness of quantity demanded to changes in income levels over a range. In contrast, the *point* income elasticity provides a measure of this responsiveness at a specific point on the demand function. The point income elasticity is defined as

$$E_y = \frac{\partial Q_D}{\partial Y} \cdot \frac{Y}{Q_D} \qquad [3.12]$$

where Y = income

Q_D = quantity demanded of some commodity

$\frac{\partial Q_D}{\partial Y}$ = the partial derivative of quantity with respect to income

The algebraic demand function for Christmas trees (Equation 3.4) introduced earlier in the chapter can be used to illustrate the calculation of the point income elasticity. Suppose one is interested in determining the point income elasticity when the price is equal to \$40 and per capita personal disposable income is equal to \$30,000. Taking the partial derivative of Equation 3.4 with respect to Y yields

$$\frac{\partial Q_D}{\partial Y} = 2.50$$

Recall from the point price elasticity calculation described earlier in the chapter that substituting P = \$40 and Y = \$30,000 into Equation 3.4 gave Q_D equal to 20,000 units. Therefore, from Equation 3.12, one obtains

$$E_y = 2.50\left(\frac{\$30{,}000}{20{,}000}\right) = 3.75$$

Thus, from an income level of \$30,000, one could expect demand for Christmas trees to increase by 37.5 percent for each 10 percent increase in per capita disposable income, *ceteris paribus*.

INTERPRETING THE INCOME ELASTICITY For most products, income elasticity is expected to be positive; that is, $E_y > 0$. Such goods are referred to as *normal* or *income-superior goods*. Those goods having a calculated income elasticity that is negative are called *inferior goods*. Inferior goods are those that are purchased in smaller absolute quantities as the income of the consumer increases. Such food items as canned mackerel and dried beans, or subcompact autos are frequently cited as examples of inferior goods. They may compose a large part of a low-income diet or transportation budget, but may virtually disappear as income levels increase.

Income elasticity is typically defined as being *low* when it is between 0 and 1 and *high* if it is greater than 1. Goods that are normally considered luxury items generally have a high income elasticity, whereas goods that are necessities (or perceived as necessities) have low income elasticities.

Knowledge of the magnitude of the income elasticity of demand for a particular product is especially useful in relating forecasts of economic activity. In industries that produce goods having high income elasticities (such as new furniture), a major increase or decrease in economic activity will have a significant impact on demand. Knowledge of income elasticities is also useful in developing marketing strategies for products. For example, products having a high income elasticity can be promoted as being luxurious and stylish, whereas goods having a low income elasticity can be promoted as being economical.

EXAMPLE

Income Elasticities: Empirical Estimates

Estimates of the income elasticity of demand have been made for a wide variety of goods and services, as shown in Table 3.6. Note that the income elasticities for goods that are often perceived as necessities (e.g., many food items, housing) are less than 1.0, whereas the income elasticities for items that are usually viewed as luxuries (e.g., European travel) are greater than 1.0.

Table 3.6 Empirical Income Elasticities

Commodity (Good/Service)	Income Elasticity
International air transportation	1.91[a]
Apples	1.32[b]
Beef	1.05[b]
Chicken	.28[b]
Dental visits	
Adult males	.61[c]
Adult females	.55[c]
Children	.87[c]
Housing (low-income renters)	.22[d]
Milk	.50[a]
Oranges	.83[a]
Potatoes	.15[a]
Tomatoes	.24[a]

[a] J. M. Cigliano, "Price and Income Elasticities for Airline Travel: The North Atlantic Market," *Business Economics* (September 1980), pp. 17–21.

[b] Daniel B. Suits, "Agriculture," in *Structure of American Industry*, 7th ed., ed. W. Adams (New York: Macmillan, 1986).

[c] Willand G. Manning, Jr. and Charles E. Phelps, "The Demand for Dental Care," *The Bell Journal of Economics* 10, no. 2 (Autumn 1979), pp. 503–525.

[d] Elizabeth A. Roistacher, "Short-Run Housing Responses to Changes in Income," *American Economic Review* (February 1977), pp. 381–386.

Cross Price Elasticity of Demand

Cross Price Elasticity
The ratio of the percentage change in the quantity demanded of Good *A* to the percentage change in the price of Good *B*, assuming that all other factors influencing demand remain unchanged.

Another determinant of demand that substantially affects the demand for a product is the price of a related (substitute or complementary) product.

Cross Price Elasticity Defined

The **cross price elasticity** of demand, E_x, is a measure of the responsiveness of changes in the quantity demanded (Q_{DA}) of Product A to price changes for Product *B* (P_B).

$$E_x = \frac{\% \Delta Q_{DA}}{\% \Delta P_B}, \textit{ ceteris paribus} \qquad [3.13]$$

where ΔQ_{DA} = change in quantity demanded of Product A
ΔP_B = change in price of Product B

ARC CROSS PRICE ELASTICITY

The *arc* cross price elasticity is a technique for computing cross elasticity between two price levels. It is calculated as

$$E_x = \frac{\dfrac{Q_{A2} - Q_{A1}}{(Q_{A2} + Q_{A1})/2}}{\dfrac{P_{B2} - P_{B1}}{(P_{B2} + P_{B1})/2}} = \frac{\Delta Q_A}{\Delta P_B} \frac{(P_{B2} + P_{B1})}{(Q_{A2} + Q_{A1})} \qquad [3.14]$$

where Q_{A2} = quantity demanded of A after a price change in B
Q_{A1} = original quantity demanded of A
P_{B2} = new price for Product B
P_{B1} = original price for Product B

For example, suppose the price of butter, P_B, increases from \$1 to \$1.50 per pound. As a result, the quantity demanded of margarine, Q_A, increases from 500 pounds to 600 pounds a month at a local grocery store. Compute the arc cross price elasticity of demand. Substituting the relevant data into Equation 3.14 yields

$$E_x = \frac{\dfrac{600 - 500}{(600 + 500)/2}}{\dfrac{\$1.50 - \$1.00}{(\$1.50 + \$1.00)/2}} = \frac{100}{\$0.50} \frac{(\$2.50)}{(1{,}100)}$$
$$= 0.45$$

This result indicates that a 10 percent increase in the price of butter will lead to a 4.5 percent increase in the quantity demanded of margarine, which is, of course, a butter substitute.

POINT CROSS PRICE ELASTICITY

In similar fashion, the *point* cross price elasticity between Products A and B may be computed as

$$E_x = \frac{\partial Q_A}{\partial P_B} \cdot \frac{P_B}{Q_A} \qquad [3.15]$$

where P_B = price of Product B
Q_A = quantity demanded of Product A at price point P_B
$\dfrac{\partial Q_A}{\partial P_B}$ = the partial derivative of Q_A with respect to P_B

INTERPRETING THE CROSS PRICE ELASTICITY

If the cross price elasticity measured between Products *A* and *B* is *positive* (as might be expected in our butter/margarine example or between such products as plastic wrap and aluminum foil), the two products are referred to as *substitutes* for each other. The higher the cross price elasticity, the closer the substitute relationship. A *negative* cross price elasticity, on the other hand, indicates that two products are *complementary.* For example, a significant decrease in the price of DVD players would probably result in a substantial increase in the demand for DVDs.

ANTITRUST AND CROSS PRICE ELASTICITIES

The number of close substitutes may be an important determinant of the degree of competition in a market. The fewer and poorer the number of close substitutes that exist for a product, the greater the amount of the producing or selling firm's market power. An important issue in antitrust cases involves the appropriate definition of the relevant product market to be used in computing statistics of market control (e.g., market share). A case involving DuPont's production of cellophane was concerned with this issue. Does the relevant product market include just the product cellophane or does it include the much broader flexible packaging materials market?

The Supreme Court found the cross price elasticity of demand between cellophane and other flexible packaging materials to be sufficiently high so as to exonerate DuPont from a charge of monopolizing the market.[13] Had the relevant product been considered to be cellophane alone, DuPont would have clearly lost, because it produced 75 percent of all cellophane output and its only licensee, Sylvania, produced the rest. But when other flexible packaging materials were included in the product market definition, DuPont's share dropped to an acceptable 18 percent level. The importance of the definition of the relevant product market and the determination of the cross price elasticity of demand among close substitute products has often been emphasized by the Courts.[14]

EXAMPLE

WHY PAY MORE FOR FAX PAPER AND STAPLES AT STAPLES?[15]

Just what constitutes an available substitute has as much to do with the cross price elasticity of rival firm supply as it does with the cross price elasticity of demand. In a hotly contested recent merger proposal, the Federal Trade Commission (FTC) has argued that office superstores such as OfficeMax, Office Depot, and Staples are a separate relevant market from other smaller office supply retailers. Office Depot had 46 percent of the $13.22 billion in 1996 superstore sales of office supplies; Staples had 30 percent, and OfficeMax had the remaining 24 percent. Office Depot and Staples proposed to merge, thereby creating a combined firm with 76 percent of the market. Such mergers have been disallowed many times under the Sherman Antitrust Act's prohibition of monopolization.

[13] *U.S. v. DuPont*, 351 U.S. 377 (1956).

[14] See, for example, *U.S. v. Alcoa*, 148 F.2d., 416, 424; *Times Picayune Publishing Co. v. U.S.*, 345 U.S. 594; *Continental Can Co. v. U.S.*, 378 U.S., 441, 489. See John E. Kwoka and Lawrence J. White, *The Antitrust Revolution: Economics, Competition, and Policy* (New York: Oxford University Press, 1999) for a further discussion of some of the economic issues involved in antitrust laws.

[15] Based on "FTC Votes to Bar Staples' Bid for Rival," *Wall Street Journal* (March 11, 1997), p. A3.

The two companies insisted, however, that their competitors included not only OfficeMax but all office supply distribution channels, including small paper goods specialty stores, department stores, discount stores like Target, warehouse clubs like Sam's Club, office supply catalogs, and some computer retailers. This larger office supply industry is fragmented, easy to enter (or exit), and huge; 1996 sales topped $185 billion. By this latter standard, the proposed merger involved admittedly the largest players in the industry, but companies with only 3–5 percent market shares. Under this alternative interpretation of the relevant market, Office Depot and Staples should have been allowed to proceed with their merger.

Have superstores such as Home Depot and Lowes in do-it-yourself building supplies, PetSmart in pet supplies, and Office Depot, OfficeMax, and Staples created a new time-saving customer shopping experience and demand pattern in towns where they are clustered? Office supply products are search goods for which customers *can* detect quality prior to purchase and locate just the quality-price combination they desire. Brand name reputations should therefore have little effect on repeat purchase shopping patterns at Office Depot and Staples. Is this case devoid of a rationale for antitrust action? Have successful entrepreneurs simply created a new segment within the traditional relevant market for office products?

The FTC undertook two sets of experiments to advise the commissioners who voted to deny the proposed merger. Prices for everything from paper clips to fax paper were sampled in 40 cities and towns where Office Depot and Staples competed and in other similar locations where only one of the superstores was present. The prices were significantly higher in the single superstore markets. Apparently, despite an enormous rival supply of traditional office product retailers, target customers (e.g., secretaries responsible for securing resupply) are willing to pay more for staples at Staples.

As Wal-Mart demonstrated in other search good categories, shoppers will flock to a superstore despite numerous small retailers closer to the customer. So, despite the enormous preexisting supply of traditional rivals and the exceptional ease of entry (and exit) on a small scale, competition for superstore retailers comes only from other superstore retailers. As a result, the Sherman Act warrants denying the proposed merger in office supply superstores. Although stores such as Wal-Mart are entitled to become "category killers" on their own sales growth, the FTC has decided to bar superstore mergers as a route to obtaining near-monopoly status.

AN EMPIRICAL ILLUSTRATION OF PRICE, INCOME, AND CROSS ELASTICITIES

A study by Chapman, Tyrrell, and Mount examined the elasticity of energy use by residential, commercial, and industrial users during the period 1946–1972.[16] They hypothesized that the demand for electricity was determined by the price of electricity, income levels, and the price of a substitute good—natural gas.

Table 3.7 summarizes the electricity-use elasticities with respect to price, income, and the substitute product (here, natural gas) prices. As shown in the table, the price elasticity of demand for electricity was relatively elastic in all markets, with the highest price elasticity being in the industrial market. These findings are consistent with the

[16] D. Chapman, T. Tyrrell, and T. Mount, "Electricity Demand Growth and the Energy Crisis," *Science* (November 17, 1972), p. 705.

Table 3.7 Electricity-Use Elasticities

	Price Elasticity	Income Elasticity	Cross Elasticity (Gas)
Residential market	−1.3	0.3	0.15
Commercial market	−1.5	0.9	0.15
Industrial market	−1.7	1.1	0.15

observation that many assembly plants, foundries, and other heavy industrial users switch to self-generated power with natural gas-fired turbines when electricity prices spike. The positive cross elasticity shows that electricity and natural gas are, indeed, substitute goods.

Other Demand Elasticity Measures[17]

Advertising Elasticity

Advertising elasticity measures the responsiveness of sales to changes in advertising expenditures. It is measured by the ratio of the percentage change in sales to a percentage change in advertising expenditures. The higher the advertising elasticity coefficient, the more responsive sales are to changes in the advertising budget. An awareness of this elasticity measure may assist advertising or marketing managers in their determination of appropriate levels of advertising outlays relative to price promotions or display and packaging expenditures.

Elasticity of Price Expectations

In an inflationary environment or in projecting durable goods demand (housing demand, for example), the elasticity of price expectations may provide helpful insights. It is defined as the percentage change in *future* prices expected as a result of current percentage price changes. A coefficient that exceeds unity indicates that buyers expect future prices to rise (or fall) by a greater percentage amount than current prices. A positive coefficient that is less than unity indicates that buyers expect future prices to increase (or decrease) but by a lesser percentage amount than current price changes.

A positive coefficient of price expectations (especially one greater than unity) suggests consumers or intermediate producers may try to beat future price increases by stockpiling the commodity. The stockpiling by Folgers that occurs when crops freeze (e.g., coffee beans in South America) can be explained, at least in part, by the effects of a high elasticity of price expectations.

[17] In addition to demand elasticities, one can also define a price elasticity of supply. The price elasticity of supply measures the responsiveness of quantity supplied by producers to changes in prices. An inelastic supply function is one whose price elasticity coefficient is less than unity. It indicates that a 1 percent change in price will lead to a less than 1 percent change in quantity supplied. An elastic supply function has an elasticity coefficient greater than unity, indicating that a 1 percent change in price will result in a greater than 1 percent change in quantity supplied. Because producers are normally willing to supply more at higher prices, the sign of the price elasticity coefficient of supply will normally be positive.

THE COMBINED EFFECT OF DEMAND ELASTICITIES

When two or more of the factors that affect demand change simultaneously, one is often interested in determining their combined impact on quantity demanded. For example, suppose that a firm plans to increase the price of its product next period and anticipates that consumers' disposable incomes will also increase next period. Other factors affecting demand such as advertising expenditures and competitors' prices are expected to remain the same in the next period. From the formula for the price elasticity (Equation 3.1), the effect on quantity demanded of a price increase would be equal to

$$\%\Delta Q_D = E_D(\%\Delta P)$$

Similarly, from the formula for the income elasticity (Equation 3.11), the effect on quantity demanded of an increase in consumers' incomes would be equal to

$$\%\Delta Q_D = E_y(\%\Delta Y)$$

Each of these percentage changes (divided by 100 to put them in a decimal form) would be multiplied by current period demand (Q_1) to get the respective changes in quantity demanded caused by the price and income increases. Assuming that the price and income effects are *independent* and *additive,* the quantity demanded next period (Q_2) would be equal to current period demand (Q_1) plus the changes caused by the price and income increases:

$$Q_2 = Q_1 + Q_1\,[E_D(\%\Delta P)] + Q_1[E_y(\%\Delta Y)]$$

or

$$Q_2 = Q_1\,[1 + E_D(\%\Delta P) + E_y(\%\Delta Y)] \quad [3.16]$$

The combined use of income and price elasticities, illustrated here for forecasting demand, can be generalized to include any of the elasticity concepts that were developed in the preceding sections of this chapter.

EXAMPLE

PRICE AND INCOME EFFECTS: THE SEIKO COMPANY

Suppose Seiko is planning to increase the price of its watches by 10 percent in the coming year. Economic forecasters expect real disposable personal income to increase by 6 percent during the same period. From past experience, the price elasticity of demand has been estimated to be approximately -1.3 and the income elasticity has been estimated at 2.0. These elasticities are assumed to remain constant over the range of price and income changes anticipated. Seiko currently sells 2 million watches per year. Determine the forecasted demand for next year (assuming that the percentage price and income effects are independent and additive). Substituting the relevant data into Equation 3.16 yields

$$\begin{aligned} Q_2 &= 2{,}000{,}000\,[1 + (-1.3)(0.10) + (2.0)(0.06)] \\ &= 1{,}980{,}000 \text{ units} \end{aligned}$$

The forecasted demand for next year is 1.98 million watches assuming that other factors that influence demand, such as advertising and competitors' prices, remain unchanged. In this case, the positive impact of the projected increase in household income is more than offset by the decline in quantity demanded associated with a price increase.

SUMMARY

- Demand relationships can be represented in the form of a schedule (table), graph, or algebraic function.
- The demand curve is downward sloping, indicating that consumers are willing to purchase more units of a good or service at lower prices.
- Changes in price result in *movement* along the demand curve, whereas changes in any of the other variables in the demand function result in *shifts* of the entire demand curve. Thus "changes in quantity demanded along" a particular demand curve result from price changes. In contrast, when one speaks of "changes in demand," one is referring to shifts in the entire demand curve.
- Some of the factors that cause a shift in the entire demand curve are changes in the income level of consumers, the price of substitute and complementary goods, the level of advertising, competitors' advertising expenditures, population, consumer preferences, time period of adjustment, taxes or subsidies, and price expectations.
- Elasticity refers to the responsiveness of one economic variable to changes in another related variable. Thus *price elasticity* of demand refers to the percentage change in quantity demanded associated with a percentage change in price, holding constant the effects of other factors thought to influence demand. Demand is said to be relatively price *elastic* if a given percentage change in price results in a greater percentage change in quantity demanded. Demand is said to be relatively price *inelastic* if a given percentage change in price results in a lesser percentage change in quantity demanded.
- When demand is unit elastic, marginal revenue equals zero and total revenue is maximized. When demand is elastic, an increase (decrease) in price will result in a decrease (increase) in total revenue. When demand is inelastic, an increase (decrease) in price will result in an increase (decrease) in total revenue.
- Prices should always be increased in the inelastic region of the firm's demand because lower price points would result in reduced revenue, despite increased unit sales.
- *Income elasticity* of demand refers to the percentage change in quantity demanded associated with a percentage change in income, holding constant the effects of other factors thought to influence demand.
- *Cross elasticity* of demand refers to the percentage change in quantity demanded of Good *A* associated with a percentage change in the price of Good *B*.
- An understanding of the magnitude of various elasticity measures for a product can be extremely helpful when forecasting demand and formulating marketing or operations plans.

Exercises

Answers to the exercises in blue can be found in Appendix C at the back of the book.

1. The Potomac Range Corporation manufactures a line of microwave ovens costing $500 each. Its sales have averaged about 6,000 units per month during the past year. In August, Potomac's closest competitor, Spring City Stove Works, cut its price for a closely competitive model from $600 to $450. Potomac noticed that its sales volume declined to 4,500 units per month after Spring City announced its price cut.
   a. What is the arc cross price elasticity of demand between Potomac's oven and the competitive Spring City model?
   b. Would you say that these two firms are close competitors? What other factors could have influenced the observed relationship?
   c. If Potomac knows that the arc price elasticity of demand for its ovens is −3.0, what price would Potomac have to charge to sell the same number of units it did before the Spring City price cut?
2. The price elasticity of demand for personal computers is estimated to be −2.2. If the price of personal computers declines by 20 percent, what will be the expected percentage increase in the quantity of computers sold?
3. The Olde Yogurt Factory reduced the price of its popular Mmmm Sundae from $2.25 to $1.75. As a result, the firm's daily sales of these sundaes have increased from 1,500 per day to 1,800 per day. Compute the arc price elasticity of demand over this price and consumption quantity range.

4. The subway fare in your town just increased from 50 cents to $1.00 per ride. As a result, the transit authority notes a decline in ridership of 30 percent.
   a. Compute the price elasticity of demand for subway rides.
   b. If the transit authority reduces the fare back to 50 cents, what impact would you expect on the ridership? Why?
5. A number of empirical studies of automobile demand yielded the following estimates of income and price elasticities:

Study	Income Elasticity	Price Elasticity
Chow	+3.0	−1.2
Alkinson	+2.5	−1.4
Roos and Von Szeliski	+2.5	−1.5
Suits	+3.9	−1.2

Assume that income and price effects on automobile sales are *independent* and *additive*. Assume also that the auto companies intend to increase the average price of an automobile by about 6 percent in the next year and that next year's disposable personal income is expected to be 4 percent higher than this year's. If this year's automobile sales were 11 million units, how many would you expect to be sold under each pair of price and income demand elasticity estimates?

6. A typical consumer behaved in the following manner with respect to purchases of butter over the past eight years:

Year	Price of Butter ($/Pound)	Quantity of Butter Purchased (Pounds)	Real Income (Dollars)	Price of Margarine ($/Pound)
1	$.95	200	$11,000	$.65
2	1.10	180	11,000	.65
3	1.10	190	11,500	.65
4	1.10	200	11,500	.90
5	1.15	170	11,500	.90
6	.99	190	11,500	.90
7	.99	175	10,500	.90
8	.99	150	10,500	.65

Compute all meaningful price, income, and cross elasticity coefficients. (Remember that the effects of other factors need to be held constant when computing any one of these coefficients.)

7. If the marginal revenue from a product is $15 and the price elasticity of demand is −1.2, what is the price of the product?
8. The demand function for bicycles in Holland has been estimated to be

$$Q = 2{,}000 + 15Y - 5.5P$$

where Y is income in *thousands* of euros, Q is the quantity demanded in units, and P is the price per unit. When $P = 150$ euros and $Y = 15(000)$ euros, determine the following:
   a. Price elasticity of demand
   b. Income elasticity of demand
9. Two goods have a cross price elasticity of +1.2.
   a. Would you describe these goods as substitutes or complements?
   b. If the price of one of the goods increases by 5 percent, what will happen to the demand for the other product, holding constant the effects of all other factors?

10. In an attempt to increase revenues and profits, a firm is considering a 4 percent increase in price and an 11 percent increase in advertising. If the price elasticity of demand is −1.5 and the advertising elasticity of demand is +0.6, would you expect an increase or decrease in total revenues?
11. Between 2000 and 2005, the quantity of automobiles produced and sold declined by 20 percent. During this period the real price of cars increased by 5 percent, real income levels declined by 2 percent, and the real cost of gasoline increased by 20 percent. Knowing that the income elasticity of demand is +1.5 and the cross price elasticity of gasoline and cars is −0.3,
    a. Compute the impact of the decline in real income levels on the demand for cars.
    b. Compute the impact of the gasoline price increase on the demand for cars.
    c. Compute the price elasticity of the demand for cars during this period.
12. The demand function for school lunches in Pittsburgh has been estimated to be

$$Q = 16{,}415.21 - 131.372P$$

where Q = lunches served and P = price in cents.
    a. Compute the point elasticity of demand for school lunches at a price of
        (i) $1.00 per lunch
        (ii) 80 cents per lunch
    b. What is the arc price elasticity of demand between prices of 80 cents and $1.00?
13. Over the past six months Heads-Up Hair Care, Inc., has normally had sales of 500 bottles of A-6 Hair Conditioner per week. On the weeks when Heads-Up ran sales on its B-8 Hair Conditioner, cutting the price of B-8 from $10 to $8, sales of A-6 declined to 300 bottles.
    a. What is the arc cross elasticity of demand between A-6 and B-8?
    b. If the price of B-8 were increased to $12, what effect would you expect this to have on the quantity demanded of A-6?
    c. What does the evidence indicate about the relationship between B-8 and A-6?
14. A study of the long-term income elasticity of demand for housing by renters is in the range of 0.8 to 1.0, whereas the income elasticity for owner-occupants is between 0.7 and 1.15.
    a. If income levels are expected to increase at a compound annual rate of 4 percent per year for the next five years, forecast the impact of this increase in income levels on the quantity of housing demanded in the two markets (rental and owner-occupants) in five years (assume that the price of housing does not change over this period).
    b. What would be the impact of price increases during this period on the levels of demand forecasted in part (a)?
15. Given the following demand function:

Price P ($)	Quantity Q_D (Pounds of Steak)	Arc Elasticity E_D	Total Revenue ($)	Marginal Revenue ($/Unit)
$12	30	n.a.	______	n.a.
11	40	______	______	______
10	50	______	______	______
9	60	______	______	______
8	70	______	______	______
7	80	______	______	______
6	90	______	______	______
5	100	______	______	______
4	110	______	______	______

    a. Compute the associated arc elasticity, total revenue, and marginal revenue values.
    b. On separate graphs, plot the demand function, total revenue function, and marginal revenue function.

16. The Stopdecay Company sells an electric toothbrush for $25. Its sales have averaged 8,000 units per month over the last year. Recently, its closest competitor, Decayfighter, reduced the price of its electric toothbrush from $35 to $30. As a result, Stopdecay's sales declined by 1,500 units per month.
   a. What is the arc cross elasticity of demand between Stopdecay's toothbrush and Decayfighter's toothbrush? What does this elasticity indicate about the relationship between the two products?
   b. If Stopdecay knows that the arc price elasticity of demand for its toothbrush is −1.5, what price would Stopdecay have to charge to sell the same number of units as it did before the Decayfighter price cut? Assume that Decayfighter holds the price of its toothbrush constant at $30.
   c. What is Stopdecay's average monthly total revenue from the sale of electric toothbrushes before and after the price change determined in part (b)?
   d. Is the result in part (c) necessarily desirable? What other factors would have to be taken into consideration?
17. The demand for renting motorboats in a resort town has been estimated to be $Q_D = 5{,}000 - 50P$, where Q_D is the quantity of boats demanded (boat-hours) and P is the average price per hour to rent a motorboat. If this relationship holds true in the future:
   a. How many boat-hours will be demanded at rental prices of $10, $20, and $30 per hour?
   b. What is the *arc* price elasticity of demand between $10 and $20? Between $20 and $30?
   c. What is the *point* price elasticity of demand at $10, $20, and $30?
   d. If the number of boat rental hours was 4,250 last year, what would you expect the average rental rate per hour to have been?
18. If the price of DVD players declines by 20 percent and the total revenue from the sale of DVD players rises, what can you say about the price elasticity of demand for DVD players? Will this price reduction necessarily lead to an increase in profits for DVD player manufacturers?
19. The Sydney Transportation Company operates an urban bus system in New South Wales, Australia. Economic analysis performed by the firm indicates that two major factors influence the demand for its services: fare levels and downtown parking rates. Table 1 presents information available from 2005 operations. Forecasts of future fares and hourly parking rates are presented in Table 2.

Table 1

Average Daily Transit Riders (2005)	Average Downtown Round-Trip Fare	Parking Rate
5,000	$1.00	$1.50

Table 2

Year	Round-Trip Fare	Average Parking Rates
2006	$1.00	$2.50
2007	$1.25	$2.50

Sydney's economists supplied the following information so that the firm can estimate ridership in 2006 and 2007. Based on past experience, the coefficient of cross elasticity between bus ridership and downtown parking rates is estimated at 0.2, given a fare of $1.00 per round trip. This level of elasticity is not expected to change for a fare increase to $1.25. The price elasticity of demand is currently estimated at −1.1, given hourly parking rates of $1.50. It is estimated, however, that the price elasticity will change to −1.2 when parking rates increase to $2.50. Using these data, estimate the average daily ridership for 2006 and 2007.

20. Many states offer drivers an opportunity to express their individuality with their automobile license plates. For the privilege of having your license plate imprinted with your own custom message—such as SINGLE, PISCES, MY BENZ, B-PHIT—drivers normally pay a small premium to the state.

In 1985 when vanity license plates were introduced in Texas, they could be acquired for a mere $20 over the cost of a normal license plate. By 2005 the price had jumped to $50. At this price 154,000 Texans invested in "their own automotive identity." As Texas legislative leaders frantically scrambled for new sources of revenue, the Texas legislature tripled the price to $150. Sales tumbled to only 56,000 custom plates. Faced with this sudden decline in demand, the legislature cut the price to $80. The Texas legislators learned a quick lesson in the concept of price elasticity.

a. What assumptions do you believe led the legislature to increase the price threefold?

b. Compute the arc price elasticity of demand between $50 and $150, assuming no other factors affecting the demand for license plates changed. Given this calculation, why do you feel the legislature cut the price to $80?

c. What other factors should be considered in future pricing decisions by the legislature?

21. The Reliable Aircraft Company manufactures small, pleasure-use aircraft. Based on past experience, sales volume appears to be affected by changes in the price of the planes and by the state of the economy as measured by consumers' disposable personal income. The following data pertaining to Reliable's aircraft sales, selling prices, and consumers' personal income were collected:

Year	Aircraft Sales	Average Price	Disposable Personal Income (in Constant 2006 Dollars–Billions)
2006	525	$7,200	$610
2007	450	8,000	610
2008	400	8,000	590

a. Estimate the arc price elasticity of demand using the 2006 and 2007 data.

b. Estimate the arc income elasticity of demand using the 2007 and 2008 data.

c. Assume that these estimates are expected to remain stable during 2009. Forecast 2009 sales for Reliable assuming that its aircraft prices remain constant at 2008 levels and that disposable personal income will increase by $40 billion. Also assume that arc income elasticity computed in part (b) is the best available estimate of income elasticity.

d. Forecast 2009 sales for Reliable given that its aircraft prices will increase by $500 from 2008 levels and that disposable personal income will increase by $40 billion. Assume that the price and income effects are *independent* and *additive* and that the arc income and price elasticities computed in parts (a) and (b) are the best available estimates of these elasticities to be used in making the forecast.

22. Federal excise taxes on gasoline vary widely across the developed world. The United States has the lowest taxes at US$0.40 per gallon (or £0.07 per litre), Canada has taxes of US$0.60 per gallon, Japan and much of Europe are US$2.00 per gallon, while Britain has the highest tax at US$2.83 a gallon or £0.5 per litre. If gasoline taxes are intended to reduce the time losses from road congestion in urban environments and gasoline pretax costs about £0.40 per litre, why might the optimal tax in Canada be 50 percent higher than in the United States? What would be an explanation for why adjacent countries would have such different estimates of the price elasticity of demand for auto driving? [Based on "Fueling Discontent," *The Economist,* May 19, 2001, p. 69.]

CASE EXERCISE

POLO GOLF SHIRT PRICING

Complete the following demand and total revenue spreadsheet for daily sales of a golf shirt in each of Ralph Lauren's discount stores. What price maximizes sales revenue? What price maximizes operating profit? Why? Who would pursue the first objective? How could Ralph Lauren's managers provide an incentive for profit-maximizing behavior?

Quantity Sold	Uniform Price	Total Revenue	Marginal Revenue	Variable Cost
0	$50.00	$0	$0	$28
1	$48.00	$48	$48	$28
2	$46.00	$92	$44	$28
3	$45.00	$135	$43	$28
4	$44.00	$176	$41	$28
5	$42.00	$210	$34	$28
6	$40.00	$240	$30	$28
7	$38.31	$268	$28	$28
8	$36.50	$292	$24	$28
9	$34.50	$311	$19	$28
10			$16	$28
11			$13	$28
12			$10	$28
13			$7	$28
14			$4	$28
15			$0	$28
16			($1)	$28
17			($4)	$28
18			($7)	$28

CHAPTER

4

ESTIMATING DEMAND

CHAPTER PREVIEW The preceding chapter developed the theory of demand, including the concepts of price elasticity, income elasticity, and cross price elasticity of demand. A manager who is contemplating an increase in the price of one of the firm's products needs to know the impact of this increase on quantity demanded, total revenue, and profits. Is the demand elastic, inelastic, or unit elastic with respect to price over the range of the contemplated price increase? What growth of unit sales can be expected if consumer incomes increase or decrease as a result of an economic expansion or contraction? Managers in profit-seeking enterprises face these types of questions about the *magnitudes* of quantitative demand relationships every day.

Governments and not-for-profit institutions are also faced with similar questions. What will be the impact of an increase in bridge tolls? Will automobile commuting decrease by 5, 10, or 20 percent? Will a sales tax increase boost revenue enough to cover a projected budget shortfall? This chapter discusses some of the techniques and problems associated with making such magnitude estimates. The more knowledgeable a manager is regarding the quantitative demand relationships, the more likely that manager will be to take actions that can maximize the profits and cash flows accruing to the firm.

MANAGERIAL CHALLENGE

The Demand for Public Transportation[1]

Port Authority Transit (PAT) provides public transportation services to the residents of Allegheny County (Pittsburgh and suburbs). It operates a fleet of 997 buses and 55 light rail vehicles in providing 66 million transit trips (see graph on p. 113). In 2004 PAT adopted a $285 million operating budget that Pennsylvania state law requires not to exceed fare revenues plus federal, state, and county subsidies. PAT's cash (base) fare was increased from $1.25 to $1.60 in 2002, and a further increase to $1.75 is under consideration.

© KEITH BROFSKY/PHOTODISC GREEN/GETTY IMAGES

MANAGERIAL CHALLENGE

In analyzing the effects of this proposed fare increase, a number of issues need to be addressed. The most important are the following:

- How would the fare (price) increase affect demand and overall revenues?
- What other factors, besides fares, could affect demand?

Examination of the data in the graph on the following page gives some possible answers to these questions. Note that ridership declined whenever PAT raised fares (i.e., in 1971, 1976, 1980, 1982, 1992, and 2002). Note also that ridership increased during the mid to late 1970s when there were gasoline shortages and (relatively) higher gasoline prices, much like today. Finally, note that ridership

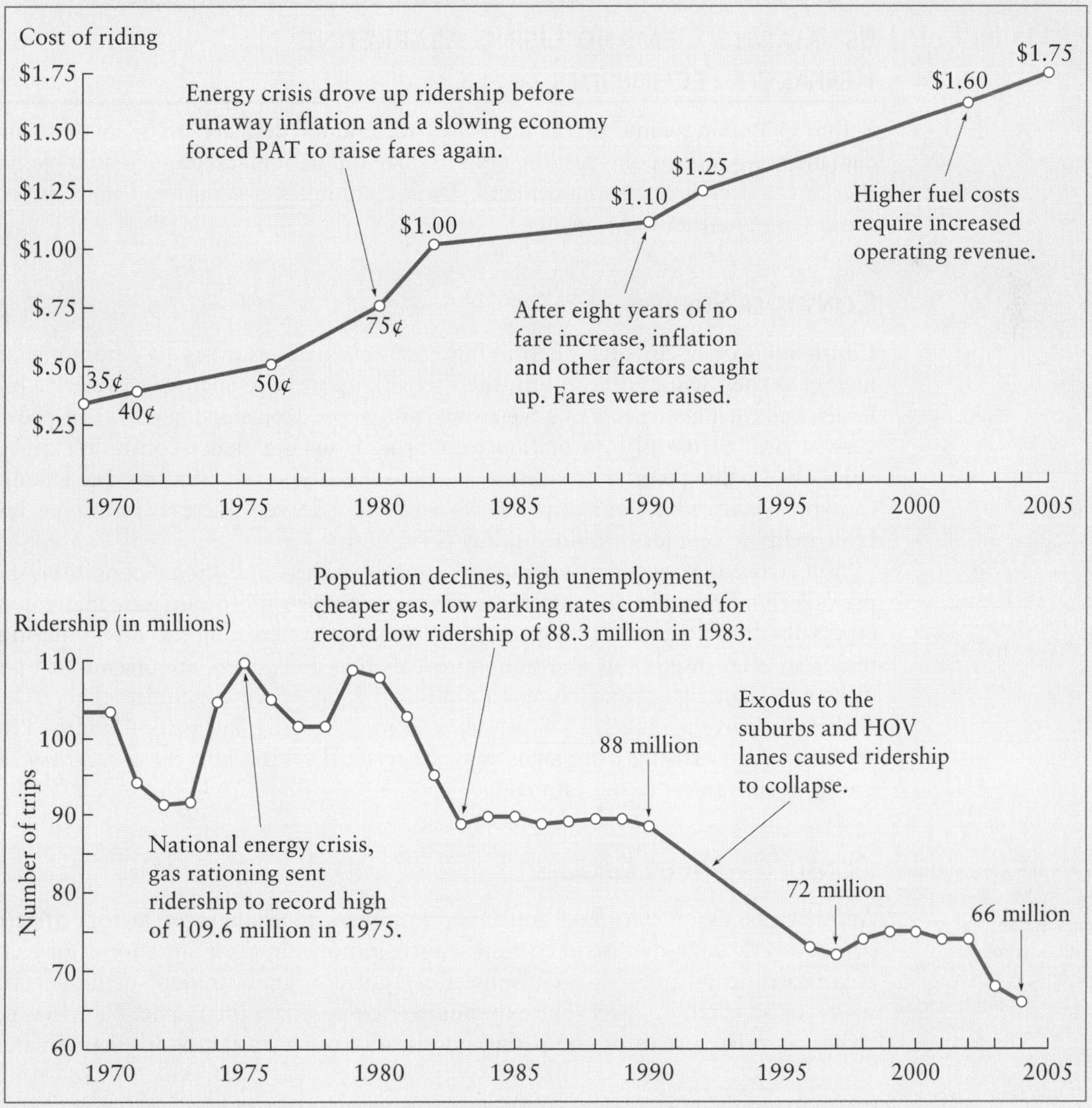

MANAGERIAL CHALLENGE

declined steeply once in the early 1980s—when there was higher unemployment, population declines in Pittsburgh itself, and (relatively) lower gasoline prices—and a second time in the early 1990s when high occupancy vehicle (HOV) lanes reserved for carpools opened on several of the major interstate highways leading from the distant suburbs into Pittsburgh.

Econometric models can be developed that incorporate price and other relevant variables in explaining transit demand in order to make forecasts of demand (and fare revenues). This chapter focuses on the techniques that are used in developing such models.

[1] Based on the National Transit Database, Allegheny County, PA (Area 3022).

Estimating Demand Using Marketing Research Techniques

Before examining some of the statistical techniques that are useful in estimating demand relationships, this section looks at three different marketing research methods that can be used in analyzing demand. These techniques are consumer surveys, focus groups, and market experiments.

Consumer Surveys

Consumer surveys involve questioning a sample of consumers to determine such factors as their willingness to buy, their sensitivity to price changes or relative price levels, and their awareness of advertising campaigns. Consumer surveys can provide a great deal of useful information to a firm. However, many consumers are not able or not willing to give accurate answers to these types of questions. For example, can you specify what your response would be to a 15-cent increase in the bus fare? How many fewer rides would you buy per month?

Still, consumer expectations about future business and credit conditions may provide significant insights into the consumers' propensity to purchase many items, especially durable goods. Using a little imagination and asking less direct questions may also offer insights. If questioning reveals that consumers are unaware of price differences among several competing goods, it might be concluded that at least within the current range of prices, demand may be price inelastic. Also, the effectiveness of advertising campaigns may be tested by sampling the awareness of a group of consumers to the campaign.

Consumer Focus Groups

Focus Group

A market research technique employing close observation of discussion among target consumers.

Another means of recording consumer responses to changes in factors affecting demand is through the use of consumer **focus groups**. In these situations, for example, experimental groups of consumers are given a small amount of money with which to buy certain items. The experimenter can observe the impact on actual purchases as price, prices of competing goods, and other variables are manipulated.[2]

[2] The use of laboratory experimentations to estimate demand elasticities is illustrated in J.F. Engle, *Consumer Behavior* (Hinsdale, IL: Dryden Press, 1993).

Then the group of consumers are closely observed discussing the choices they made and why.

Of course, the costs of setting up and running such a clinic are substantial, and consequently the number of consumers actually participating is likely to be quite small. Second, the participants are generally aware that their actions are being observed, and hence they may suspect that the experimenter is interested in sensitivity to prices and may be significantly more price conscious than otherwise would be the case.

MARKET EXPERIMENTS IN TEST STORES

Another approach that is sometimes used to garner information about the demand function is the *market experiment,* which examines the way consumers behave in controlled purchase environments. A test store may vary one or more of the determinants of demand, such as price or advertising or the presence of an NFL or NBA logo on a sweatshirt, and observe the impact on quantity demanded. This approach may be especially useful in developing measures of the promotion elasticity of demand for a product.

EXAMPLE

ESTIMATING CROSS ELASTICITY: SIMMONS MATTRESS COMPANY

The Simmons Mattress Company conducted an experiment involving the relative prices of its mattresses. Two identical types of mattresses, some with the Simmons label and others with an unknown brand name, were offered for sale at the same prices and varying price spreads to determine cross elasticity. It was found that with identical prices, Simmons outsold the unknown brand 15 to 1; with a $5 premium over the unknown brand, Simmons's sales were 8 times greater; and with a 25 percent premium, sales were about the same.

Sales effects are sometimes observed in poorly controlled experiments due to all sorts of disturbances, such as unusually bad weather, competitive advertising or competitive price reductions, and even local strikes or large layoffs that change consumer incomes significantly. The duration of market experiments is usually short, and the magnitude of price or advertising changes in many most experiments is usually small. In spite of these limitations, direct market experimentation may prove quite useful.

STATISTICAL ESTIMATION OF THE DEMAND FUNCTION

Effective decision making eventually requires the quantitative measurement of economic relationships. *Econometrics* is a collection of statistical techniques available for estimating such relationships. The principal econometric techniques used in measuring demand relationships are *regression* and *correlation analysis.* The simple (two-variable) linear regression model and the more complex cases of multiple linear regression models and nonlinear models (discussed in Appendix 4A) are presented here.

EXAMPLE

Variable Identification and Data Collection: Sherwin-Williams Company

Sherwin-Williams Company is attempting to develop a demand model for its line of exterior house paints. The company's chief economist feels that the most important variables affecting paint sales (Y) (measured in gallons) are

1. Promotional expenditures, A (measured in dollars), including expenditures on advertising (radio, TV, and newspapers), in-store displays and literature, and customer rebate programs.
2. Selling price, P (measured in dollars per gallon).
3. Disposable income per household, M (measured in dollars).

The chief economist decides to collect data on the variables in a sample of 10 company sales regions that are roughly equal in population.[3] Data on paint sales, promotional expenditures, and selling prices were obtained from the company's marketing department. Data on disposable income (per capita) were obtained from the Bureau of Labor Statistics. The data are shown in Table 4.1.

Table 4.1 Sherwin-Williams Company Data

Sales Region	Sales (Y) (×1,000 gallons)	Promotional Expenditures (A) (×$1,000)	Selling Price (P) ($/gallon)	Disposable Income (M) (×$1,000)
1	160	150	15.00	19.0
2	220	160	13.50	17.5
3	140	50	16.50	14.0
4	190	190	14.50	21.0
5	130	90	17.00	15.5
6	160	60	16.00	14.5
7	200	140	13.00	21.5
8	150	110	18.00	18.0
9	210	200	12.00	18.5
10	190	100	15.50	20.0

Specification of the Model

The next step is to specify the form of the equation, or regression relation, that indicates the relationship between the independent variables and the dependent variable(s). Normally the specific functional form of the regression relationship to be estimated is chosen to depict the true demand relationships as closely as possible. Many alternatives and variations may be tried. A clue to which functional form should initially be tried may be gained by graphing such relationships as the dependent variable over time (when working with time-series data) and each independent variable against the dependent variable. The results of this preliminary analysis often

[3] A sample size of 10 observations was chosen to keep the arithmetic simple. Much larger samples are used (when the data are available) in actual applications. The desired accuracy and the cost of sampling must be weighed in determining the optimal sample size to use in a given problem.

will tell, for example, whether a linear equation is most appropriate or whether logarithmic, exponential, or other transformations are more appropriate.[4]

LINEAR MODEL A linear demand model for Sherwin-Williams paint would be specified as follows:

$$Q = \alpha + \beta_1 A + \beta_2 P + \beta_3 M + \varepsilon \quad [4.1]$$

where α, β_1, β_2, and β_3 are the parameters of the model, and ε is the error term to reflect the fact that the observed demand value will seldom equal the exact value predicted by the model. The values of the parameters are estimated using the regression techniques described later in the chapter. Demand theory implies that price (P) would have a negative effect on gallons of paint sold (Q) (i.e., as the price rises, quantity demanded declines, holding constant all other variables) and that promotional expenditures (A) and income (M) would have a positive effect on paint sales.

The parameter estimates may be interpreted in the following manner. The constant or intercept term, α, has little economic significance in demand function of Equation 4.1 because it represents the quantity of paint demanded when all the independent variables (i.e., promotional expenditures, price, and income) are equal to zero. However, if we rearrange Equation 4.1 to solve for price (P), the intercept of the resulting *inverse demand function* identifies the maximum price that can be charged.

The value of each β coefficient provides an estimate of the change in quantity demanded associated with a *one-unit* change in the given independent variable, holding constant all other independent variables. The β coefficients are equivalent to the partial derivatives of the demand function:

$$\beta_1 = \frac{\partial Q}{\partial A}, \quad \beta_2 = \frac{\partial Q}{\partial P}, \quad \beta_3 = \frac{\partial Q}{\partial M} \quad [4.2]$$

Note that the elasticity of demand with respect to each independent variable is *not* constant, but instead varies with the point on the linear demand curve where it is measured. This relationship can be shown as follows for the price variable. Recall from Chapter 3 that the point price elasticity of demand was defined as

$$E_D = \frac{\partial Q}{\partial P} \cdot \frac{P}{Q} \quad [4.3]$$

Now substitute Equation 4.2 into this expression to yield

$$E_D = \beta_2 \cdot \frac{P}{Q} \quad [4.4]$$

Equations 4.3 and 4.4 show that price elasticity is a function of both the target market's price sensitivity ($\partial Q/\partial P$) and the price point positioning of the product (P/Q).

Linear demand equations have been used extensively in empirical work because of their ease of estimation and the realism with which they approximate many true demand relationships.

MULTIPLICATIVE EXPONENTIAL MODEL Another commonly used demand relationship is the multiplicative exponential model. In the Sherwin-Williams example, such a model would be specified as follows:

$$Q = \alpha A^{\beta_1} P^{\beta_2} M^{\beta_3} \quad [4.5]$$

[4] See Appendix 4A for a discussion of these transformations. See also any standard econometrics text, such as R. S. Pindyck and D. L. Rubinfeld, *Econometric Models and Economic Forecasts*, 4th ed. (New York: McGraw-Hill, 1999), for additional information concerning some of the alternative functional forms that may be tried.

This model is also popular because of its ease of estimation. For instance, Equation 4.5 may be transformed to a simple linear relationship in logarithms (adding an error term) as follows:

$$\log Q = \log \alpha + \beta_1 \log A + \beta_2 \log P + \beta_3 \log M + \varepsilon \qquad [4.6]$$

and the parameters log α, β_1, β_2, and β_3 can be easily estimated by any regression package. The intuitive appeal of this multiplicative exponential functional form is based on the fact that the marginal impact of a change in price on quantity demanded is dependent not only on the price change, but also on the level of promotional expenditures and income.

A feature of demand functions in the multiplicative exponential form is that the *elasticities are constant* over the range of data used in estimating the parameters and equal to the estimated values of the respective parameters. In the Sherwin-Williams data, for example, the price elasticity of demand is defined as

$$E_D = \frac{\partial Q}{\partial P} \cdot \frac{P}{Q} \qquad [4.7]$$

Differentiating Equation 4.5 with respect to price results in

$$\frac{\partial Q}{\partial P} = \beta_2 \alpha A^{\beta_1} P^{\beta_2 - 1} M^{\beta_3} \qquad [4.8]$$

$$E_D = \beta_2 \alpha A^{\beta_1} P^{\beta_2 - 1} M^{\beta_3} \left(\frac{P}{Q}\right) \qquad [4.9]$$

Substituting Equation 4.5 for Q in Equation 4.9 and canceling and then combining terms where possible yields

$$E_D = \beta_2$$

The property of constant elasticity at all points on the multiplicative exponential demand curve contrasts sharply with the elasticity of a linear demand function that changes continuously over the entire range of the demand curve. However, pricing analysts at Sherwin-Williams may be able to tell us that the percentage change in quantity demanded for either a 10 percent price increase or a 10 percent price cut is a constant 15 percent. And the same answer may apply at rather different price points when clearance sales or other promotional tie-ins occur. If so, a multiplicative exponential demand model is appropriate.

EXAMPLE

Linear, Not Exponential, Sales at Global Crossing Inc.[5]

In 2002 telecom network providers such as Global Crossing and WorldCom were wildly optimistic about the growth of telecom traffic, fueled by the projected growth of the Internet. Much like the adoption of color television, the penetration of the Internet into the American household has exhibited a classic S-shaped pattern of exponential growth fueled by the early adopters (1994–1996) followed now by a long period of much slower, approximately linear growth in demand. Purchasing and installing fiber optic cable networks as though the exponential demand growth

[5] Based on "Adoption Rate of Internet by Consumers Is Slowing," "Has Growth of the Net Flattened?" *Wall Street Journal,* July 16, 2001, pp. B1 and B8.

were continuing unabated led to a quick saturation of a market that would have been better specified with a linear time trend:

$$Q = \alpha + \beta_1 A + \beta_2 P + \beta_3 M + \beta_4 T + \varepsilon$$

where T is time (1996 = 0, 1997 = 1, etc.). The effect of these demand projections on Global Crossing is examined in the Managerial Challenge at the beginning of Chapter 5.

A Simple Linear Regression Model

The analysis in this section is limited to the simple case of one independent and one dependent variable, where the form of the relationship between the two variables is *linear*.

$$Y = \alpha + \beta X + \varepsilon \qquad [4.10]$$

The simple linear regression model that is used in this problem involves several basic underlying assumptions.

Assumptions Underlying the Simple Linear Regression Model

A standard convention in regression analysis, which will be followed here, is to use X to represent the independent variable and Y to represent the dependent variable.[6]

Assumption 1 The value of the dependent variable Y is postulated to be a random variable, which is dependent on fixed (i.e., nonrandom) values of the independent variable X.[7]

Assumption 2 A theoretical straight-line relationship (see Figure 4.1) exists between X and the expected value of Y for each of the possible values of X. This theoretical regression line

$$E(Y|X) = \alpha + \beta X \qquad [4.11]$$

has a slope of β and an intercept of α. The regression coefficients α and β constitute population parameters whose values are unknown, and we desire to estimate them.

Assumption 3 Associated with each value of X is a probability distribution, $p(y|x)$, of the possible values of the random variable Y. When X is set equal to some value x_i, the value of Y that is observed will be drawn from the $p(y|x_i)$ probability distribution and will not necessarily lie on the theoretical regression line. As illustrated in Figure 4.2, some values of $y|x_i$ are more likely than others, and the mean $E(y|x_i)$ lies on the theoretical regression line. If ε_i is defined as the *deviation* of the *observed* y_i value from the theoretical value y_i', then

$$\begin{aligned} y_i &= y_i' + \varepsilon_i \\ y_i &= \alpha + \beta x_i + \varepsilon_i \end{aligned} \qquad [4.12]$$

[6] Capitalized letters X and Y represent the *name* of the random variables. Lowercase x and y represent *specific values* of the random variables.

[7] Stochastic (i.e., random) values of the right-hand-side independent variable are addressed in Appendix 4A under simultaneous equations relationships.

Figure 4.1 Theoretical Regression Line

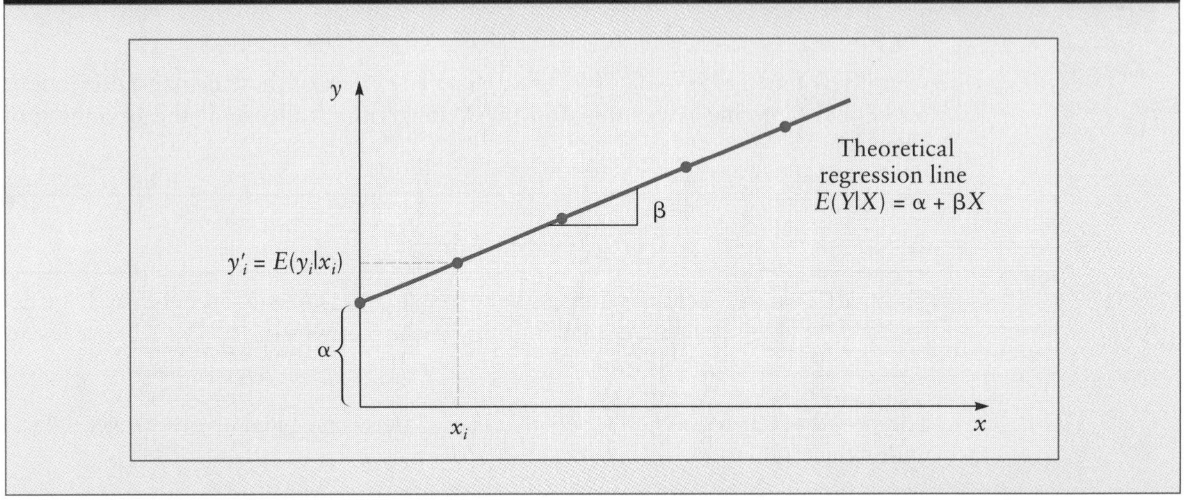

Figure 4.2 Conditional Probability Distribution of Dependent Variable

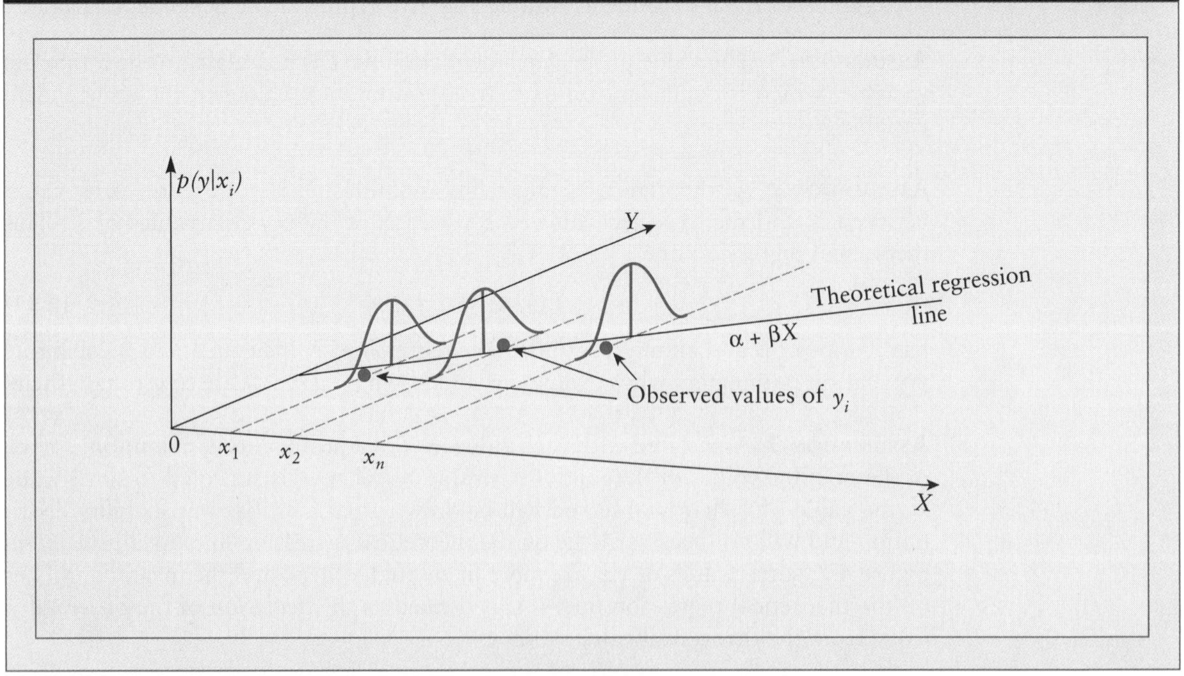

or, in general, the *linear regression relation* becomes (as illustrated in Figure 4.3)

$$Y = \alpha + \beta X + \varepsilon \quad [4.13]$$

where ε is a zero mean *stochastic disturbance* (or *error*) *term.*

Assumption 4 The disturbance term (ε_i) is assumed to be an independent random variable [that is, $E(\varepsilon_i \varepsilon_j) = 0$ for $i \neq j$] with an expected value equal to zero [that is,

Figure 4.3 Deviation of the Actual Observations About the Theoretical Regression Line

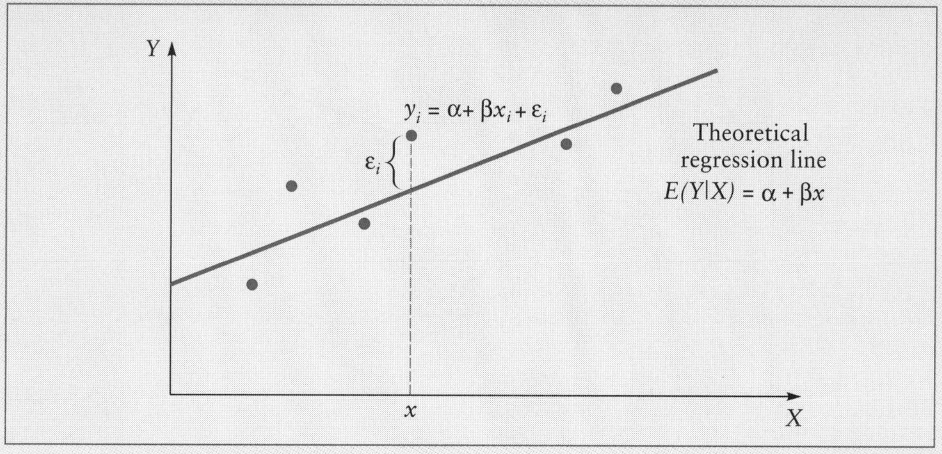

$E(\varepsilon_i) = 0$] and with a constant variance equal to σ_ε^2 [that is, $E(\varepsilon_i^2) = \sigma_\varepsilon^2$ for all i]. Furthermore, to perform the statistical tests of significance (i.e., t-tests and F-tests) later in the chapter, we also must assume that the disturbance term (ε_i) follows the normal probability distribution.

Together, Assumptions 1 and 4 imply that the disturbance term is expected to be uncorrelated with the independent variables in the regression model.

ESTIMATING THE POPULATION REGRESSION COEFFICIENTS

Once the regression model is specified, the unknown values of the population regression coefficients α and β are estimated by using the n pairs of sample observations $(x_1, y_1), (x_2, y_2), \ldots, (x_n, y_n)$. This process involves finding a *sample regression line* that best fits the sample of observations the analyst has gathered.

The sample estimates of α and β can be designated by a and b, respectively. The estimated or predicted value of Y, $\hat{y}_i$, for a given value of X (see Figure 4.4) is

$$\hat{y}_i = a + bx_i \qquad [4.14]$$

Letting e_i be the *deviation* of the *observed* y_i value from the *estimated value* $\hat{y}_i$, then

$$\begin{aligned} y_i &= \hat{y}_i + e_i \\ &= a + bx_i + e_i \end{aligned} \qquad [4.15]$$

or, in general, the *sample regression equation* becomes

$$Y = a + bX + e \qquad [4.16]$$

Although several methods can be used to determine the values of a and b (i.e., finding the regression equation that provides the best fit to the series of observations), the best known and most widely used is the method of *least squares*. The objective of least-squares analysis is to find values of a and b that *minimize* the sum of the squares of the e_i deviations. (By squaring the errors, positive and negative errors cumulate and

Figure 4.4 Deviation of the Observations about the Sample Regression Line

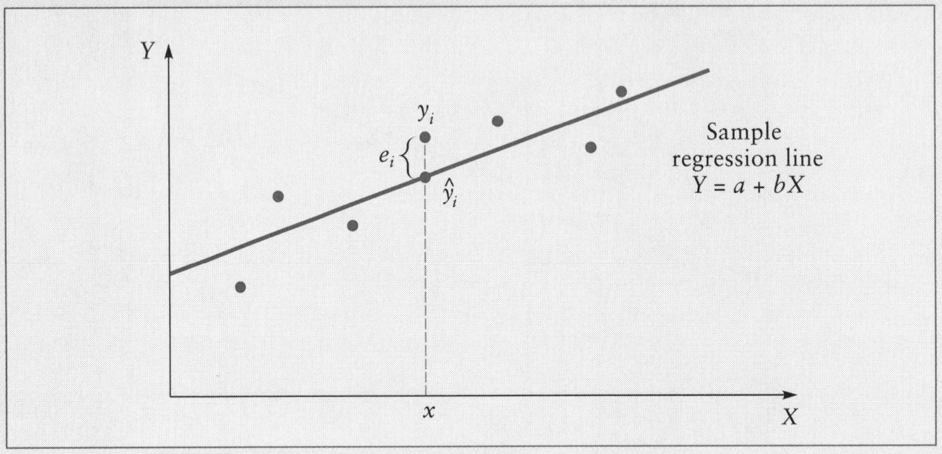

do not cancel each other.) From Equation 4.15, the value of e_i is given by

$$e_i = y_i - a - bx_i \tag{4.17}$$

Squaring this term and summing over all n pairs of sample observations, one obtains

$$\sum_{i=1}^{n} e_i^2 = \sum_{i=1}^{n} (y_i - a - bx_i)^2 \tag{4.18}$$

Using calculus, the values of a and b that minimize this sum of squared deviations expression are given by

$$b = \frac{n\Sigma x_i y_i - \Sigma x_i \Sigma y_i}{n\Sigma x_i^2 - (\Sigma x_i)^2} \tag{4.19}$$

$$a = \bar{y} - b\bar{x} \tag{4.20}$$

where $\bar{x}$ and $\bar{y}$ are the arithmetic means of X and Y, respectively (i.e., $\bar{x} = \Sigma x/n$ and $\bar{y} = \Sigma y/n$) and where the summations range over all the observations ($i = 1, 2, \ldots, n$).

EXAMPLE

Estimating Regression Parameters: Sherwin-Williams Company (continued)

Return to the Sherwin-Williams Company example and suppose that only promotional expenditures are used to predict paint sales. Using the notation of the simple linear regression model, Y will be used to represent paint sales and X to represent promotional expenditures. The regression model can be represented by Equation 4.13, discussed earlier. If promotional expenditures are used to predict paint sales in a given metropolitan area, then estimates of α and β must be calculated from the sample data presented earlier in Table 4.1. These data are reproduced here in columns 1–3 of Table 4.2 and shown graphically in Figure 4.5.

Table 4.2 Worksheet for Estimation of the Simple Regression Equation: Sherwin-Williams Company

Sales Region (1) i	Promotional Expenditures (× \$1,000) (2) x_i	Sales (× 1,000 gal) (3) y_i	(4) $x_i y_i$	(5) x_i^2	(6) y_i^2
1	150	160	24,000	22,500	25,600
2	160	220	35,200	25,600	48,400
3	50	140	7,000	2,500	19,600
4	190	190	36,100	36,100	36,100
5	90	130	11,700	8,100	16,900
6	60	160	9,600	3,600	25,600
7	140	200	28,000	19,600	40,000
8	110	150	16,500	12,100	22,500
9	200	210	42,000	40,000	44,100
10	100	190	19,000	10,000	36,100
Total	1,250	1,750	229,100	180,100	314,900
	Σx_i	Σy_i	$\Sigma x_i y_i$	Σx_i^2	Σy_i^2

$\bar{x} = \Sigma x_i/n = 1{,}250/10 = 125$

$\bar{y} = \Sigma y_i/n = 1{,}750/10 = 175$

The estimated slope of the regression line is calculated as follows using Equation 4.19:

$$b = \frac{10(229{,}100) - (1{,}250)(1{,}750)}{10(180{,}100) - (1{,}250)^2}$$
$$= 0.433962$$

Similarly, using Equation 4.20, the intercept is estimated as

$$a = 175 - 0.433962(125)$$
$$= 120.75475$$

Therefore, the equation for estimating paint sales (in thousands of gallons) based on promotional expenditures (in thousands of dollars) is

$$Y = 120.755 + 0.434X \qquad [4.21]$$

and is graphed in Figure 4.5. The coefficient of X (0.434) indicates that for a one-unit increase in X (\$1,000 in additional promotional expenditures), expected sales (Y) will increase by 0.434 (× 1,000) = 434 gallons in a given sales region.

USING THE REGRESSION EQUATION TO MAKE PREDICTIONS

A regression equation can be used to make predictions concerning the value of Y, given any particular value of X. This calculation is done by substituting the particular value of X, namely, x_p, into the sample regression equation (Equation 4.14):

$$\hat{y} = a + bx_p$$

Figure 4.5 Estimated Regression Line: Sherwin-Williams Company

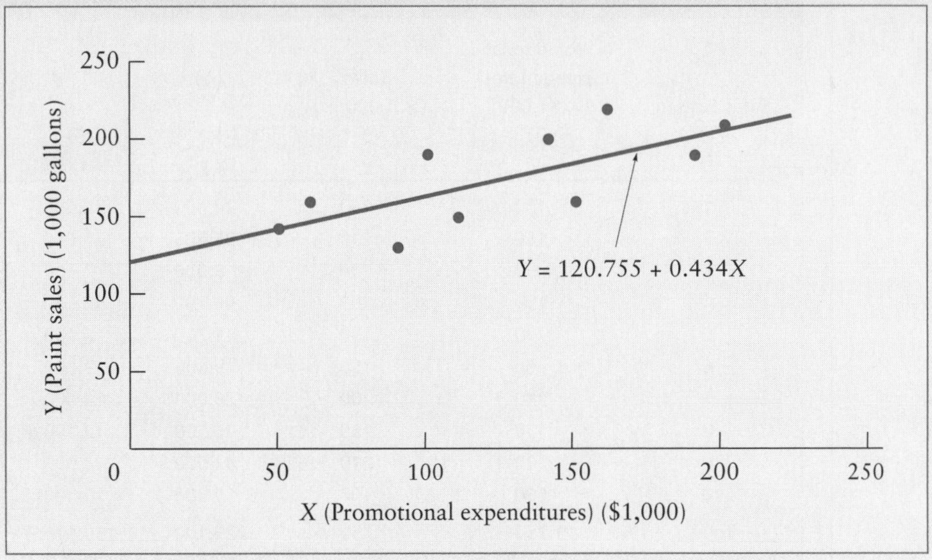

where, as you recall, $\hat{y}$ is the hypothesized expected value for the dependent variable from the probability distribution $p(Y|X)$.[8]

Suppose one is interested in estimating Sherwin-Williams' paint sales for a metropolitan area with promotional expenditures equal to $185,000 (i.e., $x_p = 185$). Substituting $x_p = 185$ into the estimated regression equation (Equation 4.21) yields

$$\begin{aligned}\hat{y} &= 120.755 + 0.434\,(185)\\ &= 201.045\end{aligned}$$

or 201,045 gallons.

Caution must be exercised in using regression models for prediction, particularly when the value of the independent variable lies *outside* the range of observations from which the model was estimated. In many cases the linear relationship is not valid for extremely large or small values of the independent variable. For example, suppose we want to estimate paint sales for a sales region with promotional expenditures equal to $300,000 (i.e., $x_p = 300$). Because this value of X falls well outside of the series of observations for which the regression line was calculated, we cannot be certain that the prediction of paint sales based on the linear regression model would be reasonable. Such factors as diminishing returns and the existence of saturation levels can cause relationships between economic variables to be nonlinear.

Standard Error of the Estimate

The standard deviation of the error term in a linear regression model.

A measure of the accuracy of estimation with the regression equation can be obtained by calculating the standard deviation of the errors of prediction (also known as the **standard error of the estimate**). The error term e_i was defined earlier in Equation 4.17 to be the difference between the observed and predicted values of the

[8] The expected value of the error term (e) is zero, as indicated earlier in Assumption 4.

dependent variable. The standard deviation of the e_i term is based on the summed squared error (SSE) Σe_i^2 normalized by the degrees of freedom:

$$s_e = \sqrt{\frac{\Sigma e_i^2}{n-2}} = \sqrt{\frac{\Sigma(y_i - a - bx_i)^2}{n-2}}$$

or, when this expression is simplified,[9]

$$s_e = \sqrt{\frac{\Sigma y_i^2 - a\Sigma y_i - b\Sigma x_i y_i}{n-2}} \quad [4.22]$$

If the observations are tightly clustered about the regression line, the value of s_e will be small and prediction errors will tend to be small. Conversely, if the deviations e_i between the observed and predicted values of Y are fairly large, both s_e and the prediction errors will be large.

In the Sherwin-Williams Company example, substituting the relevant data from Table 4.2 into Equation 4.22 yields

$$s_e = \sqrt{\frac{314{,}900 - 120.75475(1{,}750) - 0.433962(229{,}100)}{10-2}}$$
$$= 22.799$$

or a standard error of 22,799 gallons.

The standard error of the estimate (s_e) can be used to construct prediction *intervals* for y.[10] An *approximate* 95 percent prediction interval is equal to[11]

$$\hat{y} \pm 2s_e \quad [4.23]$$

Returning to the Sherwin-Williams Company example, suppose we want to construct an approximate 95 percent prediction interval for paint sales in a sales region with promotional expenditures equal to \$185,000 (i.e., $x_p = 185$). Substituting $\hat{y} = 201.045$ and $s_e = 22.799$ into Equation 4.23 yields

$$201.045 \pm 2(22.799)$$

or a prediction interval from 155.447 to 246.643 (i.e., from 155,447 gallons to 246,643 gallons).

INFERENCES ABOUT THE POPULATION REGRESSION COEFFICIENTS

For repeated samples of size n, the sample estimates of α and β (i.e., a and b) will tend to vary from sample to sample. In addition to prediction, often one of the purposes of

[9] This formula applies to the case of simple regression in Equation 4.16. As additional variables are added to the linear regression model, the degrees of freedom in the denominator of Equation 4.22 become smaller and smaller: $n - 3$, $n - 4$, $n - 5$, etc. See also footnote 15.

[10] An *exact* $(1 - k)$ percent prediction interval is a function of both the sample size (n) and how close x_p is to $\bar{x}$ and is given by the following expression:

$$\hat{y} \pm t_{k/2,n-s} s_e \sqrt{1 + \frac{1}{n} + \frac{(x_p - \bar{x})^2}{\Sigma(x_i - \bar{x})^2}}$$

where $t_{k/2,n-2}$ is the value from the t-distribution (with $n - 2$ degrees of freedom) in Table 2 of the Statistical Tables (Appendix B) in the back of the book.

[11] For large n ($n > 30$), the t-distribution approximates a normal distribution and the t-value for a 95 percent prediction interval approaches 1.96 or approximately 2. For most applications, the approximation methods give satisfactory results.

regression analysis is testing whether the slope parameter β is equal to some particular value β_0. One standard hypothesis is to test whether β is equal to zero.[12] In such a test the concern is with determining whether X has a significant effect on Y. If β is either zero or close to zero, then the independent variable X will be of no practical benefit in predicting or explaining the value of the dependent variable Y. When $\beta = 0$, a one-unit change in X causes Y to change by zero units, and hence X has no effect on Y.

To test hypotheses about the value of β, the sampling distribution of the statistic b must be known.[13] It can be shown that b has a t-distribution with $n - 2$ degrees of freedom.[14,15] The mean of this distribution is equal to the true underlying regression coefficient β, and an estimate of the standard deviation can be calculated as

$$s_b = \sqrt{\frac{s_e^2}{\Sigma x_i^2 - (\Sigma x_i)^2/n}} \qquad [4.24]$$

where s_e is the standard deviation of the error terms from Equation 4.22.

Suppose that we want to test the null hypothesis:

$$H_0\colon \beta = \beta_0$$

against the alternative hypothesis:

$$H_a\colon \beta \neq \beta_0$$

at the k percent level of significance.[16] We calculate the statistic

$$t = \frac{b - \beta_0}{s_b} \qquad [4.25]$$

and the decision is to reject the null hypothesis, if t is either less than $-t_{k/2,n-2}$ or greater than $+t_{k/2,n-2}$ where the $t_{k/2,n-2}$ value is obtained from the t-distribution

---

[12] The intercept parameter, α, is of less interest in most economic studies and will be excluded from further analysis.

[13] In addition to testing hypotheses about β, one can also calculate confidence intervals for β in a manner similar to Equation 4.23.

[14] A t-test is usually used to test for the significance of individual regression parameters when the sample size is relatively small (30 or less). For larger samples, tests of statistical significance may be made using the standard normal probability distribution, which the t-distribution approaches in the limit.

[15] *Degrees of freedom* are the number of observations beyond the minimum necessary to calculate a given regression coefficient or statistic. In a regression model, the number of degrees of freedom is equal to the number of observations less the number of parameters (α and βs) being estimated. For example, in a simple (two-variable) regression model, a minimum of two observations is needed to calculate the slope (β) and intercept (α) parameters—hence the number of degrees of freedom is equal to the number of observations minus two.

[16] The *level of significance* (k) used in testing hypotheses indicates the probability of making an incorrect decision with the decision rule by rejecting the null hypothesis when it is true. For example, with H_0: $\beta \geq 0$, setting k equal to 0.05 (i.e., 5 percent) indicates 1 chance in 20 that we will conclude an effect exists when no effect is present (i.e., a 5-percent chance of "false positive" outcomes).

Medical researchers trying to identify statistically significant therapies that could save lives, and research and development (R&D) researchers trying to identify potential blockbuster products worry more about reducing the risk of "false negatives" (i.e., of concluding they have discovered nothing when their research could save a life or a company). Medical and R&D researchers therefore often perform hypothesis tests with $k = 0.35$, meaning a 65 percent confidence that the null hypothesis $\beta = 0$ should be rejected. They are willing to increase from 5 to 35 percent the probability of false positives, or that they will conclude that β is positive for a treatment or therapy and can help the patient when in fact $\beta = 0$. This level of significance is preferred not because they wish to engender false hope but rather because a higher tolerance for false positives reduces the probability of "false negative" decisions that arise when they conclude that $\beta = 0$ when in fact β is positive. Ultimately, the question of what significance level to choose must be decided by the relative cost of false positives and false negatives in a given situation.

(with $n - 2$ degrees of freedom) in Table 2 (Appendix B).[17] Business applications of hypothesis testing are well advised to keep k small (i.e., no larger than 1 percent or 5 percent). One cannot justify building a marketing plan around advertising and retail displays incurring millions of dollars of promotional expense unless the demand estimation yields a high degree of confidence that promotional expenditures actually "drive" sales (i.e., $\beta \neq 0$).

In the Sherwin-Williams Company example, suppose that we want to test (at the $k = 0.05$ level of significance) whether promotional expenditures are a useful variable in predicting paint sales. In effect, we wish to perform a statistical test to determine whether the sample value—that is, $b = 0.433962$—is significantly different from zero. The null and alternative hypotheses are

$$H_0\text{: } \beta = 0 \text{ (no relationship between } X \text{ and } Y)$$
$$H_a\text{: } \beta \neq 0 \text{ (linear relationship between } X \text{ and } Y)$$

Because the sample used to compute the regression equation consisted of 10 observations, the sample statistic b will have a t-distribution with 8 (= $n - 2$) degrees of freedom. From the t-distribution (Table 2 of Appendix B), we obtain a value of 2.306 for $t_{.025,8}$. Therefore, if the calculated value of t is either less than -2.306 or greater than $+2.306$, the decision rule is to reject H_0 and conclude that $\beta \neq 0$, which means that a statistically significant relationship exists between promotional expenditures and paint sales.

Using Equation 4.24, s_b is calculated as

$$s_b = \sqrt{\frac{(22.799)^2}{180{,}100 - (1{,}250)^2/10}}$$
$$= 0.14763$$

The calculated value of t from Equation 4.25 becomes

$$t = \frac{0.433962 - 0}{0.14763}$$
$$= 2.939$$

Because this value is greater than $+2.306$, we reject H_0. Therefore, based on the sample evidence, we conclude that at the 5 percent level of significance a linear, positive relationship exists between promotional expenditures and paint sales.

CORRELATION COEFFICIENT

In correlation analysis we analyze the extent to which high (or low) values of one variable tend to be associated with high (or low) values of the other variable. The measure of the degree of association between two variables is called the *correlation coefficient*. Given n pairs of observations from the population, $(x_1, y_1), (x_2, y_2), \ldots, (x_n, y_n)$, the sample correlation coefficient is defined as

$$r = \frac{\Sigma(x_i - \bar{x})(y_i - \bar{y})}{\sqrt{\Sigma(x_i - \bar{x})^2 \Sigma(y_i - \bar{y})^2}}$$

[17] *One-tail* tests can also be performed. To test H_0: $\beta \leq \beta_0$ against H_a: $\beta > \beta_0$, one calculates t using Equation 4.25 and rejects H_0 at the k level of significance of $t > t_{k,n-2}$, where $t_{k,n-2}$ is obtained from the t-distribution (Table 2 of Appendix B) with $n - 2$ degrees of freedom. Similarly, to test H_0: $\beta \geq \beta_0$ against H_a: $\beta < \beta_0$, one calculates t using Equation 4.25 and rejects H_0 at the k level of significance if $t < -t_{k,n-2}$.

Figure 4.6 Correlation Coefficient

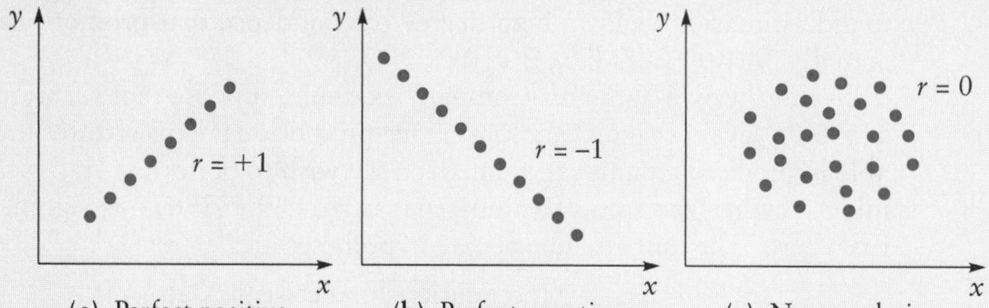

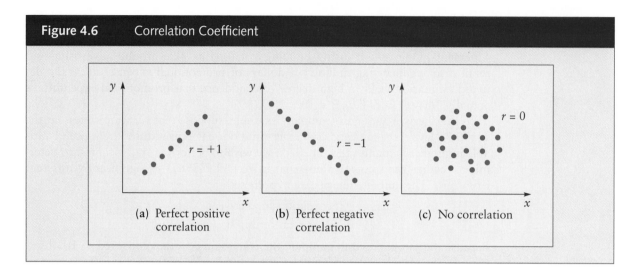

(a) Perfect positive correlation (b) Perfect negative correlation (c) No correlation

and, when this expression is simplified, it is calculated as

$$r = \frac{n\Sigma x_i y_i - \Sigma x_i \Sigma y_i}{\sqrt{[n\Sigma x_i^2 - (\Sigma x_i)^2][n\Sigma y_i^2 - (\Sigma y_i)^2]}} \quad [4.26]$$

The value of the correlation coefficient (r) ranges from +1 for two variables with perfect positive correlation to −1 for two variables with perfect negative correlation. In Figure 4.6, (a) and (b) illustrate two variables that exhibit perfect positive and negative correlation, respectively. Few, if any, relationships between economic variables exhibit perfect correlation. Figure 4.6 (c) illustrates zero correlation—no discernible relationship exists between the observed values of the two variables. A positive correlation coefficient indicates that high values of one variable tend to be associated with high values of the other variable, whereas a negative correlation coefficient indicates just the opposite—high values of one variable tend to be associated with low values of the other variable.

The Sherwin-Williams Company example discussed earlier can be used to illustrate the calculation of the sample correlation coefficient. Substituting the relevant quantities from Table 4.2 into Equation 4.26, we obtain a value of

$$r = \frac{10(229{,}100) - (1{,}250)(1{,}750)}{\sqrt{[10(180{,}100) - (1{,}250)^2][10(314{,}900) - (1{,}750)^2]}}$$
$$= 0.72059 \text{ or } 0.721$$

for the correlation between the sample observations of promotional expenditures and paint sales.[18]

Correlation analysis is useful in exploratory studies of the relationships among economic variables. The information obtained in the correlation analysis can then be used as a guide in building regression models.

[18] Statistical techniques exist for testing whether the degree of correlation within the population is significantly different from zero. See D. R. Anderson, D. J. Sweeney, and T. A. Williams, *Statistics for Business and Economics*, 9th ed. (St. Paul, MN: West, 2001), for a discussion of these techniques.

Figure 4.7 Partitioning the Total Deviation

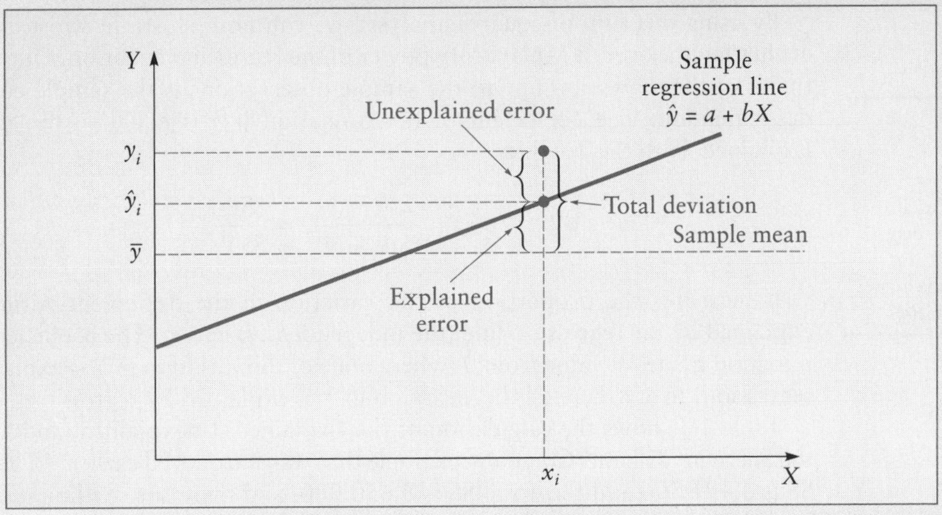

THE ANALYSIS OF VARIANCE

Earlier we illustrated a method for testing the statistical significance of individual regression coefficients. Now we will examine some techniques for evaluating the overall "fit" of the regression model to the sample of observations.

We begin by examining a typical observation (y_i) in Figure 4.7. Suppose we want to predict the value of Y for a value of X equal to x_i. While ignoring the regression line for the moment, what error is incurred if we use the average value of Y (that is, $\bar{y}$) as the best estimate of Y? The graph shows that the error involved, labeled the "Total deviation," is the difference between the observed value (y_i) and $\bar{y}$. Suppose we now use the sample regression line to estimate Y. The best estimate of Y, given $X = x_i$, is $\hat{y}_i$. As a result of using the regression line to estimate Y, the estimation error has been reduced to the difference between the observed value (y_i) and $\hat{y}_i$. In the graph, the total deviation $(y_i - \bar{y})$ has been partitioned into two parts: the unexplained portion of the total deviation $(y_i - \hat{y}_i)$ and that portion of the total deviation explained by the regression line $(\hat{y}_i - \bar{y})$; that is,

$$\text{Total deviation} = \text{Unexplained error} + \text{Explained error}$$
$$(y_i - \bar{y}) = (y_i - \hat{y}_i) + (\hat{y}_i - \bar{y})$$

If we decompose the total error of each observation in the sample using this procedure and then sum the squares of both sides of the equation, we obtain (after some algebraic simplification):[19]

$$\text{Total SS} = \text{Unexplained SS} + \text{Explained SS}$$
$$\text{SST} = \Sigma e_i^2 + \text{SSR} = \text{SSE} + \text{SSR}$$
$$\Sigma(y_i - \bar{y})^2 = \Sigma(y_i - \hat{y}_i)^2 + \Sigma(\hat{y}_i - \bar{y})^2 \qquad [4.27]$$

[19] A standard convention in statistics is to let the prefix "SS" represent the "Sum of Squares" as illustrated by SSE, the sum of squared errors.

This equation indicates that the total of the squared deviations from the mean, summed over all the observations in the sample, can be partitioned into two independent parts: the Unexplained SS and the Explained SS.

By using this sum-of-squares analysis, we can now illustrate two techniques for evaluating the overall explanatory power of the regression equation. One measure of the fit of the regression line to the sample observations is the sample **coefficient of determination.** The coefficient of determination (r^2) is equal to the ratio of the Explained SS to the Total SS:

Coefficient of Determination

A measure of the proportion of total variation in the dependent variable that is explained by the independent variable(s).

$$r^2 = \frac{\Sigma(\hat{y}_i - \bar{y})^2}{\Sigma(y_i - \bar{y})^2} = \frac{\text{SSR}}{\text{SST}} \qquad [4.28]$$

It measures the proportion of the variation in the dependent variable that is explained by the regression line (the independent variable). The coefficient of determination ranges in value from 0 (where none of the variation in Y is explained by the regression) to 1 (where all the variation in Y is explained by regression).

Table 4.3 shows the calculation of the Explained, Unexplained, and Total SS for the Sherwin-Williams Company example that was introduced earlier.[20] The Explained SS is 4,491.506 and the Total SS is 8,650.000, and therefore, by Equation 4.28 the coefficient of determination is

$$r^2 = \frac{4{,}491.506}{8{,}650.000}$$
$$= 0.519$$

Table 4.3 Calculation of the Explained, Unexplained, and Total SS for the Sherwin-Williams Company

i	x_i	y_i	$\hat{y}$ = 120.75475 + 0.433962 x_i	Explained SS $(\hat{y}_i - \bar{y})^2$	Unexplained SS $(y_i - \hat{y}_i)^2$	Total SS $(y_i - \bar{y})^2$
1	150	160	185.849	117.702	668.171	225.000
2	160	220	190.189	230.696	888.696	2,025.000
3	50	140	142.453	1,059.317	6.017	1,225.000
4	190	190	203.208	795.665	174.451	225.000
5	90	130	159.811	230.696	888.696	2,025.000
6	60	160	146.792	795.665	174.451	225.000
7	140	200	181.509	42.373	341.917	625.000
8	110	150	168.491	42.373	341.917	625.000
9	200	210	207.547	1,059.317	6.017	1,225.000
10	100	190	164.151	117.702	668.171	225.000
				4,491.506	4,158.504	8,650.000*
				$\Sigma(\hat{y}_i - \bar{y})^2$	$\Sigma(y_i - \hat{y}_i)^2$	$\Sigma(y_i - \bar{y})^2$

*"Total SS" differs slightly from the sum of "Explained SS" and "Unexplained SS" because of rounding.

[20] Only two of the three SS need to be calculated in the manner shown in Table 4.3, because the third SS can be obtained from Equation 4.27 once the other two SS are calculated.

Table 4.4 Analysis of Variance Table for Regression Model

Source of Variation	Sum of Squares	Degrees of Freedom
Regression (*explained variation*)	$SSR = \Sigma (\hat{y}_i - \bar{y})^2$ $= 4{,}491.5$	1
Error (*unexplained variation*)	$SSE = \Sigma (y_i - \hat{y}_i)^2$ $= 4{,}158.5$	$n - 2$
Total	$SST = \Sigma (y_i - \bar{y})^2$ $= 8{,}650$	$n - 1$

The regression model, with promotional expenditures as the sole independent variable, explains about 52 percent of the variation in paint sales in the sample. Note also that, in the simple linear regression model, the coefficient of determination is equal to the square of the correlation coefficient [i.e., $r^2 = 0.519 = (r)^2 = (0.72059)^2$].

A second technique for evaluating the explanatory power of the regression equation is an *F*-test of the sources of variation within the sample data.[21] Using the sum-of-squares framework discussed previously, an analysis of variance table is constructed, as shown in Table 4.4. The *F*-ratio

$$F = \frac{\text{SSR}}{\text{SSE}/d.f.} \qquad [4.29]$$

then can be used to test whether the estimated regression equation explains a significant proportion of the variation in the dependent variable. The decision is to reject the null hypothesis of no relationship between *X* and *Y* (that is, no explanatory power) at the *k* level of significance if the calculated *F*-ratio is greater than the $F_{k,1,n-2}$ value obtained from the *F*-distribution in Table 3 of the Statistical Tables (Appendix B).

An analysis of variance table for the Sherwin-Williams Company example appears in Table 4.4. Forming the *F*-ratio, we obtain

$$F = \frac{4{,}491.506}{4{,}158.5/8}$$
$$= 8.641$$

The comparable value of $F_{.05,1,8}$ from the *F*-distribution (Table 3 of Appendix B) is 5.32. Therefore, we reject, at the .05 level of significance, the null hypothesis that there is no relationship between promotion expenditures and paint sales. In other words, we conclude that the regression model *does* explain a significant proportion of the variation in paint sales in the sample.

ASSOCIATION AND CAUSATION

Based on the finding of a statistically significant regression relationship, one may be tempted to conclude that a causal economic relationship exists—the independent variable being the cause and the dependent variable being the effect. However, *the*

[21] For the multiple linear regression model, the *F*-test is used to test the hypothesis that *all* the regression coefficients are zero.

presence of association (correlation) does not necessarily imply causation. Statistical tests can establish only whether association exists between the variables. The existence of a cause-and-effect economic relationship can only be inferred from economic reasoning.

An association relationship may not imply a causal relationship for many reasons. First, even a 95-percent statistically significant association between two variables may result from 5-percent pure chance. Second, the association between two variables may be the result of the influence of a third common factor. For example, although per capita expenditures for food and clothing exhibit a close relationship over time, one cannot conclude that increases in food expenditures cause increases in clothing expenditures. The high degree of association between these two variables can be attributed to a third variable, namely, per capita income. As per capita income increases over time, people tend to spend more on both food and clothing. Finally, both variables may be the cause and the effect at the same time. In other words, a simultaneous or interdependent relationship may exist between the variables. One could, for example, hypothesize that a person's income is a function of his or her level of education—the more years of schooling the person has, the higher will be the income. However, one could instead argue that the opposite relationship is also true: Education level is a function of income. A higher income increases the likelihood that a person will be able to afford additional college or professional education.

Multiple Linear Regression Model

A linear relationship containing two or more independent variables is known as a *multiple linear regression model*. In the (completely) general multiple linear regression model, the dependent variable Y is hypothesized to be a function of m independent variables $X_1, X_2, \ldots, X_m$, and to be of the form

$$Y = \alpha + \beta_1 X_1 + \beta_2 X_2 + \ldots + \beta_m X_m + \varepsilon \qquad [4.30]$$

In the Sherwin-Williams Company example, paint sales (Y) were hypothesized to be a function of three variables: promotional expenditures (A), price (P), and household disposable income (M) (see Equation 4.1):

$$Q = \alpha + \beta_1 A + \beta_2 P + \beta_3 M + \varepsilon$$

Assumptions Underlying the Multiple Linear Regression Model

In addition to satisfying a set of four assumptions similar to those for the simple linear regression model, the application of the least-squares estimation procedure to the multiple linear regression model requires two further assumptions.

Assumption 5 The number of observations (n) must exceed the number of parameters to be estimated ($m + 1$).

Assumption 6 No exact linear relationships can exist between any of the independent variables. A definitional relationship or identity (e.g., cash in the register is equal to initial cash plus receipts) cannot be estimated unless some source of randomness is present in the data. For example, the clerk on duty may commit occasional errors in making change.

Figure 4.8 Computer Output: Sherwin-Williams Company

Dep var: SALES (Y) N: 10 Multiple R: 0.889 Multiple R squared: 0.790

Adjusted multiple R squared: 0.684 Standard error of estimate: 17.417

Variable	Coefficient	Std error	Std coef	Tolerance	T	P(2 tail)
CONSTANT	310.245	95.075	0.000	.	3.263	0.017
PROMEXP (X_1)	0.008	0.204	0.013	0.3054426	0.038	0.971
SELLPR (X_2)	−12.202	4.582	−0.741	0.4529372	−2.663	0.037
DISPINC (X_3)	2.677	3.160	0.225	0.4961686	0.847	0.429

Analysis of Variance

Source	Sum-of-squares	DF	Mean-square	F-ratio	P
Regression	6829.866	3	2276.622	7.505	0.019
Residual	1820.134	6	303.356		

USE OF COMPUTER PROGRAMS

Using matrix algebra, procedures similar to those explained for the simple linear regression model can be employed for calculating the estimated regression coefficients (α and βs) of Equation 4.30, and for testing the statistical significance of the individual independent variables and overall explanatory power of the regression equation. In most practical applications of multiple regression analysis, generalized computer programs are used to perform these procedures.

Although many different programs are available for doing multiple regression analysis, the output of these programs is fairly standardized. The output normally includes the estimated regression coefficients, *t*-statistics of the individual coefficients, R^2, analysis of variance, and *F*-test of overall significance. The particular program that is illustrated here is MYSTAT.[22]

Putting the data in Table 4.1 for the Sherwin-Williams Company along with the appropriate control statements into the MYSTAT program yields the output shown in Figure 4.8.

ESTIMATING THE POPULATION REGRESSION COEFFICIENTS

From the computer output (coefficient column) the following regression equation is obtained:

$$Y = 310.245 + 0.008A - 12.202P + 2.677M \qquad [4.31]$$

The coefficient of the P variable (−12.202) indicates that, *all other things being equal,* a \$1.00 price increase will reduce expected sales by $-12.202 \times 1{,}000 = 12{,}202$ gallons in a given sales region.

[22] MYSTAT is a product of Systat, Inc., Evanston, Illinois.

Using the Regression Model to Make Forecasts

As in the simple linear regression model, the multiple linear regression model can be used to make point or interval forecasts. Point forecasts can be made by substituting the particular values of the independent variables into the estimated regression equation.

In the Sherwin-Williams example, suppose we are interested in estimating sales in a sales region where promotional expenditures are \$185,000 (i.e., $A = 185$), selling price is \$15.00 (P), and disposable income per household is \$19,500 (i.e., $M = 19.5$). Substituting these values into Equation 4.31 yields

$$\hat{y} = 310.245 + 0.008(185) - 12.202(15.00) + 2.677(19.5) = 180.897 \text{ gallons}$$

Whether to include one, two, or all three independent variables in predicting $\hat{y}$ depends on the mean prediction error (e.g., here 185,000 − 180,897 = 4,103) in this and subsequent out-of-sample forecasts.

The standard error of the estimate (s_e) from the output in Figure 4.8 can be used to construct prediction intervals for Y. An *approximate* 95 percent prediction interval is equal to

$$\hat{y} \pm 2s_e$$

For a sales region with the characteristics cited in the previous paragraph (i.e., $A = 185$, $P = \$15.00$, and $M = 19.5$), an *approximate* 95 percent prediction interval for paint sales is equal to

$$180.897 \pm 2(17.417)$$

or 146,063 to 215,731 gallons.

Inferences about the Population Regression Coefficients

Most regression programs test whether *each* of the independent variables (Xs) is statistically significant in explaining the dependent variable (Y). This tests the null hypothesis:

$$H_0: \beta_i = 0$$

against the alternative hypothesis:

$$H_a: \beta_i \neq 0$$

The decision rule is to reject the null hypothesis at the k level of significance if the t-value (labeled T) from the computer output ($t = b/s_b$) is either less than $-t_{k/2,n-m-1}$ or greater than $+t_{k/2,n-m-1}$ where the $t_{k/2,n-m-1}$ value is obtained from the t-distribution (with $n - m - 1$ degrees of freedom) in Table 2 (Appendix B).[23]

To test the null hypothesis of no relationship between paint sales (Y) and each of the independent variables at the .05 significance level, we would reject the null hypothesis if the respective t-value for each variable is less than $-t_{.025,6} = -2.447$ or greater than $t_{.025,6} = +2.447$. As shown in Figure 4.8, only the calculated t-value for the P variable is less than −2.447. Hence, we can conclude that only selling price (P) is statistically significant (at the .05 level) in explaining paint sales. This inference might determine that marketing plans for this type of paint should focus on price

[23] Rather than having to look up the $t_{k/2,n-m-1}$ in the table, MYSTAT calculates the significance level at which one can reject the null hypothesis ($\beta_i = 0$). For example, if we are testing the null hypothesis at the $k = .05$ significance level, we would reject the null hypothesis (no relationship between Y and X_i) if the P (two-tail) value from the computer output is less than .05.

and not on the effects of promotional expenditures or the disposable income of the target households.

THE ANALYSIS OF VARIANCE

Techniques similar to those described for the simple linear regression model are used to evaluate the *overall* explanatory power of the multiple linear regression model.

The multiple coefficient of determination (r^2) is a measure of the overall "fit" of the regression model. The squared multiple R value of 0.790 in Figure 4.8 indicates that the three-variable regression equation explains 79 percent of the total variation in the dependent variable (paint sales).

The F-value (labeled F-ratio in the computer output of Figure 4.8) is used to test the hypothesis that all the independent variables ($X_1, X_2, \ldots, X_m$) together explain a significant proportion of the variation in the dependent variable (Y). One is using the F-value to test the null hypothesis:

$$H_0\text{: All } \beta_i = 0$$

against the alternative hypothesis:

$$H_a\text{: At least one } \beta_i \neq 0$$

In other words, we are testing whether at least one of the explanatory variables contributes information for the prediction of Y. The decision is to reject the null hypothesis at the k level of significance if the F-value from the computer output is *greater* than the $F_{k,m,n-m-1}$ value from the F-distribution (with m and $n - m - 1$ degrees of freedom). Table 3 (Appendix B) provides F-values.

In the Sherwin-Williams example, suppose we want to test whether the three independent variables explain a significant (at the .05 level) proportion of the variation in income. The decision rule is to reject the null hypothesis (no relationship) if the calculated F-value (7.505 in Figure 4.8) is greater than $F_{.05,3,6} = 4.76$. Rather than having to look up the $F_{.05,3,6}$ critical value in tables of the F-distribution, MYSTAT calculates the significance level at which we can reject the null hypothesis (H_0: All $\beta_i = 0$) and prints the result in the column labeled P. Because $F = 7.505$ has a P-value of 0.019, we reject the null hypotheses and conclude that the independent variables *are* useful in explaining paint sales with $(1 - 0.019) = 98.1$ percent confidence.

EXAMPLE

THE ESTIMATED DEMAND FOR NEW AUTOMOBILES[24]

New car registrations of recently purchased autos vary over time in predictable ways. This economic theory reasoning can identify the explanatory variables to include in an empirical model of new car demand. First, any consumer durable demand increases with rising population of the target customer group. Therefore, one must either control for population size as an explanatory variable or, alternatively, divide registrations by population, thereby creating a dependent variable of new car demand per capita, as in Table 4.5. Second, many new car purchases are financed, so minimum cash deposit requirements and auto financing rates are as important as the sale price in triggering a decision to purchase during one month rather than another. Third, one would expect changes in disposable income to affect a household's decision to replace its prior car. Higher household income would be

[24] Based on "An Econometric Model of New Car Demand in the UK," *Managerial and Decision Economics* (1986), 7, pp. 19–23.

associated with increased demand for superior models. Geopolitical events such as the Iraq War with its attendant gas price spikes should also affect demand for autos because gasoline is the primary complement in consumption of automobiles. Finally, as with other fad items, the introduction of popular new models enhances subsequent purchase decisions, so higher auto sales last period should have a positive effect on additional auto sales this period. These positive lagged effects of past sales should dampen as one gets further away from the product introductions that triggered the initial surge in sales.

Table 4.5 reports the empirical results. These multiplicative exponential models are similar to Equations 4.5 and 4.6. Thus, the dependent variable and each of the explanatory variables are in logarithms,[25] and therefore the parameter estimates themselves can be interpreted as elasticities (price elasticity of demand, income elasticity of demand, interest rate elasticity of demand, minimum deposit elasticity of demand, etc.).

The British researchers who performed this study found, first of all, that market demand for new car registrations per capita was price inelastic (−0.341), suggesting some substantial pricing power for many models. Next, a minimum deposit elasticity of −0.105 means that a 20 percent increase in cash deposit leads to a 2.1 percent decrease in demand (i.e., 0.2 × −0.105 = 0.021). As expected, a 50 percent increase in auto financing rates from, say, 6 percent to 10 percent, leads to a 22 percent decline in auto demand (i.e., 0.5 × −0.436 = −0.22). Autos appear to be income elastic (1.947)

Table 4.5 OLS Estimates of the Determinants of the U.K. Per Capita Demand for New Autos

Explanatory Variables	Coefficient
Constant	−15.217
	(−5.66)[a]
log Price	−0.341
	(−2.25)[b]
log Minimum Deposit	−0.105
	(−1.78)[c]
log Interest Rate	−0.436
	(−5.31)[a]
log Income	1.947
	(10.94)[a]
Oil Crisis Dummy	−0.146
	(−4.45)[a]
log New Car_{t-1}	0.404
	(3.24)[a]
Adjusted R^2	0.965
Durbin-Watson	2.11
F	91.62
N	20

Notes: *t*-statistics in parentheses. Hypotheses tests are one-tailed.

[a,b,c] Statistical significance at the 1%, 5%, and 10% levels, respectively.

[25] The one exception is that the 0/1 Oil Crisis dummy variable is added to the regression model directly, without taking logs, because the logarithm of zero is equal to negative infinity and is therefore an undefined value in the regression programs. As a consequence, the elasticity of demand with respect to the 0/1 event is $e^{\beta}-1$ (or in this case, $e^{-0.146}-1 = 0.864 - 1 = -13.6\%$). Hence, we conclude −14%.

such that a 10 percent increase in disposable income results in a 19.5 percent rise in auto demand. Gas shortages and time waiting in queues to buy the complement gasoline led to a 14 percent reduction in auto demand during the OPEC oil embargo. Finally, one period lagged demand, New Auto_{t-1}, had a significant positive effect on current purchases with the coefficient being between 0 and 1, as expected.[26] Overall, this model explained 96 percent of the time-series variation in new car sales per capita.

[26] In contrast, a coefficient greater than 1 (or less than −1) on the lagged dependent variable would imply inherently unstable dynamics of exponentially accelerating demand growth (or decay).

SUMMARY

- Empirical estimates of the demand for relationships are essential if the firm is to achieve its goal of shareholder wealth maximization. Without good estimates of the demand function facing a firm, it is impossible for that firm to make profit-maximizing price and output decisions.
- Consumer surveys involve questioning a sample of consumers to determine such factors as their willingness to buy, their sensitivity to price changes or levels, and their awareness of promotional campaigns.
- Focus groups make use of carefully directed discussion among groups of consumers. The results may be influenced by significant experimental bias.
- Market experiments observe consumer behavior in real-market situations. By varying product characteristics, price, advertising, or other factors in some markets but not in others, the effects of these variables on demand can be determined. Market experiments are expensive.
- Statistical techniques are often found to be of great value and relatively inexpensive as a means to make empirical demand function estimates. Regression analysis is often used to estimate statistically the demand function for a good or service.
- The linear model and the multiplicative exponential model are the two most commonly used functional relationships in demand studies.
- In a *linear* demand model, the coefficient of each independent variable provides an estimate of the change in quantity demanded associated with a one-unit change in the given independent variable, holding constant all other variables. This marginal impact is constant at all points on the demand curve. The elasticity of a linear demand model with respect to each independent variable (e.g., price elasticity and income elasticity) is not constant, but instead varies over the entire range of the demand curve.
- In a multiplicative exponential demand model, the marginal impact of each independent variable on quantity demanded is not constant, but instead varies over the entire range of the demand curve. However, the elasticity of a multiplicative exponential demand model with respect to each independent variable is constant and is equal to the estimated value of the respective parameter.
- The objective of *regression analysis* is to develop a functional relationship between the dependent and independent (explanatory) variable(s). Once a functional relationship (that is, regression equation) is developed, the equation can be used to make forecasts or predictions concerning the value of the dependent variable.
- The *least-squares* technique is used to estimate the regression coefficients. Least squares minimizes the sum of the squares of the differences between the observed and estimated values of the dependent variable over the sample of observations.
- The t-test is used to test the hypothesis that a specific independent variable is useful in explaining variation in the dependent variable.
- The F-test is used to test the hypothesis that *all* the independent variables ($X_1, X_2, \ldots, X_m$) in the regression equation explain a significant proportion of the variation in the dependent variable.
- The *coefficient of determination* (r^2) measures the proportion of the variation in the dependent variable that is explained by the regression equation (that is, the entire set of independent variables).
- The presence of association does not necessarily imply causation. Statistical tests can only establish whether or not an association exists between variables. The existence of a cause-and-effect economic relationship should be inferred from economic reasoning.

Exercises

Answers to the exercises in blue can be found in Appendix C at the back of the book.

1. Consider the Sherwin-Williams Company example discussed in this chapter (see Table 4.1). Suppose one is interested in developing a simple regression model with paint sales (Y) as the dependent variable and selling price (P) as the independent variable.
   a. Determine the estimated regression line.
   b. Give an economic interpretation of the estimated intercept (a) and slope (b) coefficients.
   c. Test the hypothesis (at the .05 level of significance) that there is no relationship ($\beta = 0$) between the variables.
   d. Calculate the coefficient of determination.
   e. Perform an analysis of variance on the regression, including an F-test of the overall significance of the results (at the .05 level).
   f. Based on the regression model, determine the best estimate of paint sales in a sales region where the selling price is \$14.50. Construct an *approximate* 95 percent prediction interval.
   g. Determine the price elasticity of demand at a selling price of \$14.50.
2. In a study of the demand for life insurance, Executive Insurers, Inc., is examining the factors that affect the amount of life insurance held by executives. The following data on the amount of insurance and annual incomes of a random sample of 12 executives were collected.

Observation	Amount of Life Insurance (× \$1,000)	Annual Income (× \$1,000)
1	90	50
2	180	84
3	225	74
4	210	115
5	150	104
6	150	96
7	60	56
8	135	102
9	150	104
10	150	108
11	60	65
12	90	58

   a. Given the nature of the problem, which would be the dependent variable and which would be the independent variable?
   b. Plot the data.
   c. Determine the estimated regression line. Give an economic interpretation of the slope (b) coefficient.
   d. Test the hypothesis that there is no relationship ($\beta = 0$) between the variables.
   e. Calculate the coefficient of determination.
   f. Perform an analysis of variance on the regression, including an F-test of the overall significance of the results.
   g. Determine the best estimate, based on the regression model, of the amount of life insurance held by an executive whose annual income is \$80,000. Construct an *approximate* 95 percent prediction interval.
3. The Pilot Pen Company has decided to use 15 test markets to examine the sensitivity of demand for its new product to various prices, as shown in the following table.

Advertising effort was identical in each market. Each market had approximately the same level of business activity and population.

a. Using a linear regression model, estimate the demand function for Pilot's new pen.

b. Evaluate this model by computing the coefficient of determination and by performing a *t*-test of the significance of the price variable.

c. What is the price elasticity of demand at a price of 50 cents?

Test Market	Price Charged	Quantity Sold (thousands of pens)
1	50¢	20.0
2	50¢	21.0
3	55¢	19.0
4	55¢	19.5
5	60¢	20.5
6	60¢	19.0
7	65¢	16.0
8	65¢	15.0
9	70¢	14.5
10	70¢	15.5
11	80¢	13.0
12	80¢	14.0
13	90¢	11.5
14	90¢	11.0
15	40¢	17.0

4. In a study of housing demand, the county assessor is interested in developing a regression model to estimate the market value (i.e., selling price) of residential property within her jurisdiction. The assessor feels that the most important variable affecting selling price (measured in thousands of dollars) is the size of house (measured in hundreds of square feet). She randomly selected 15 houses and measured both the selling price and size, as shown in the following table.

Observation i	Selling Price (× \$1,000) Y	Size (× 100 ft^2) X_2
1	265.2	12.0
2	279.6	20.2
3	311.2	27.0
4	328.0	30.0
5	352.0	30.0
6	281.2	21.4
7	288.4	21.6
8	292.8	25.2
9	356.0	37.2
10	263.2	14.4
11	272.4	15.0
12	291.2	22.4
13	299.6	23.9
14	307.6	26.6
15	320.4	30.7

a. Plot the data.

b. Determine the estimated regression line. Give an economic interpretation of the estimated slope (b) coefficient.

c. Determine whether size is a statistically significant variable in estimating selling price.

d. Calculate the coefficient of determination.

e. Perform an F-test of the overall significance of the results.

f. Construct an *approximate* 95 percent prediction interval for the selling price of a house having an area (size) of 15 (hundred) square feet.

5. a. Fill in the missing information (blanks) in the following multiple regression computer output.

DEPENDENT VARIABLE: SALES

VARIABLE	DF	PARAMETER ESTIMATE	STANDARD ERROR	T-RATIO
INTERCEPT	1	________	1.105	2.205
PRICE	1	−.3750	________	−1.570
INCOME	1	________	0.140	2.780
ADVERTISING	1	−6.2500	1.950	________

SOURCE OF VARIATION	DF	SUM OF SQUARES	MEAN SQUARES
REGRESSION	________	1187.343	________
RESIDUAL	________	________	18.625
TOTAL	25	________	
R-SQUARE:	________		
F-RATIO:	________		

b. Determine which of the variables (if any) are statistically significant (at the .05 level).

c. Determine whether the independent variables explain a significant (.05 level) proportion of the variation in the dependent variable.

6. Cascade Pharmaceuticals Company developed the following regression model, using time-series data from the past 33 quarters, for one of its nonprescription cold remedies:

$$Y = -1.04 + 0.24X_1 - 0.27X_2$$

where Y = quarterly sales (in thousands of cases) of the cold remedy

X_1 = Cascade's quarterly advertising (×\$1,000) for the cold remedy

X_2 = competitors' advertising for similar products (×\$10,000)

Here is additional information concerning the regression model:

$$s_{b_1} = 0.032 \qquad s_{b_2} = 0.070$$

$$R^2 = 0.64 \qquad s_e = 1.63 \qquad F\text{-statistic} = 31.402$$

$$\text{Durbin-Watson } (d) \text{ statistic} = .4995$$

a. Which of the independent variables (if any) appear to be statistically significant (at the .05 level) in explaining sales of the cold remedy?

b. What proportion of the total variation in sales is explained by the regression equation?

c. Perform an F-test (at the .05 level) of the overall explanatory power of the model.

d. How do the results in part (d) affect your answers to parts (a), (b), and (c)?

e. What additional statistical information (if any) would you find useful in the evaluation of this model?

7. The following equation was estimated as the demand function for gasoline (number of observations equals 1,682, and standard errors are in parentheses):

$$\begin{aligned} \ln Q = {} & \underset{(1.51)}{3.95} - \underset{(0.105)}{0.525} \ln P - \underset{(0.920)}{0.263} \ln \text{Age} + \underset{(0.65)}{0.129} \ln Y - \underset{(0.156)}{0.211} \ln P_c \\ & + \underset{(0.063)}{0.796} \text{ Ln D} - \underset{(0.031)}{0.103} \text{ U} + \underset{(0.036)}{0.182} \text{ R} \quad \text{with R-squared} = 0.39, \end{aligned}$$

where Q = gallons of gas demanded per week by a household, P = price per gallon of gasoline, Age = age of the head of household, Y = income level, and P_c = an index of the price for automobiles, D = Number of drivers, U = urban (inner city) location, R = rural (not suburban) location.

a. Interpret the coefficients of the various variables in the preceding demand equation.

b. How much confidence do you have in each of these coefficient estimates?

8. Moyer Winery is the maker of a high-quality white grape juice. A linear regression model used to estimate the demand function for Moyer's white grape juice yielded the following results:

$$Q_D = \underset{(4{,}215)}{10{,}425} - \underset{(1{,}010)}{2{,}910P_x} + \underset{(0.004)}{0.028A} + \underset{(3{,}542)}{11{,}100P_{op}}$$

where Q_D = quantity demanded
P_x = price of Moyer white grape juice
A = Moyer Winery advertising in dollars
P_{op} = percentage of the U.S. population over 21

a. Determine the point price elasticity for prices of \$5 and \$10, when A = \$1,000,000 and P_{op} = .05.

b. Determine the point advertising elasticity at an advertising level of \$2,000,000, if price remains at \$5 and P_{op} = .05.

c. The standard error for each coefficient is given in parentheses. If you know that the demand function was estimated using 25 observations, can you reject at the 95 percent confidence level the hypothesis that there is no relationship between each of the independent variables and Q_D?

9. General Cereals is using a regression model to estimate the demand for Tweetie Sweeties, a whistle-shaped, sugar-coated breakfast cereal for children. The following (multiplicative exponential) demand function is being used:

$$Q_D = 6{,}280P^{-2.15}A^{1.05}N^{3.70}$$

where Q_D = quantity demanded, in 10 oz. boxes
P = price per box, in dollars
A = advertising expenditures on daytime television, in dollars
N = proportion of the population under 12 years old

a. Determine the point price elasticity of demand for Tweetie Sweeties.

b. Determine the advertising elasticity of demand.

c. What interpretation would you give to the exponent of N?

10. The demand for jewelry sold by the Topaz Mining Company has been estimated as

$$Q_B = .22P_B^{-.95}I^{1.4}A_B^{.3}P_C^{.2}P_{op}^{.6}$$

where Q_B = carats of topaz sold each week
P_B = price per carat charged by Topaz Mining
I = level of per capita disposable personal income in the target market area
A_B = dollar amount of advertising expenditures
P_C = price per carat charged by competitors
P_{op} = population in target market area

a. What interpretation can you give to the exponents of P_B, I, A_B, P_C, and P_{op}?

b. Are these values consistent with your expectations?

c. If Topaz Mining ceased advertising, what would be the impact on demand according to this demand equation? What problem does this factor illustrate in an interpretation of demand functions?

11. The demand for haddock has been estimated as

$$\log Q = a + b \log P + c \log I + d \log P_m$$

where Q = quantity of haddock sold in New England
P = price per pound of haddock
I = a measure of personal income in the New England region
P_m = an index of the price of meat and poultry

If $b = -2.174$, $c = 0.461$, and $d = 1.909$,

a. Determine the price elasticity of demand.
b. Determine the income elasticity of demand.
c. Determine the cross price elasticity of demand.
d. How would you characterize the demand for haddock?
e. Suppose disposable income is expected to increase by 5 percent next year. Assuming all other factors remain constant, forecast the percentage change in the quantity of haddock demanded next year.

12. An estimate of the demand function for household furniture produced the following results:

$$F = 0.0036Y^{1.08}R^{0.16}P^{-0.48} \qquad r^2 = 0.996$$

where F = furniture expenditures per household
Y = disposable personal income per household
R = value of private residential construction per household
P = ratio of the furniture price index to the consumer price index

a. Determine the point price and income elasticities for household furniture.
b. What interpretation would you give to the exponent for R? Why do you suppose R was included in the equation as a variable?
c. If you were a supplier to the furniture manufacturer, would you have preferred to see the analysis performed in physical sales units rather than dollars of revenue? How would this change alter the interpretation of the price coefficient, presently estimated as -0.48?

13. Consider again the Sherwin-Williams Company example discussed in this chapter (see Table 4.1). Suppose one is interested in developing a multiple regression model with paint sales (Y) as the dependent variable and promotional expenditures (A) and selling price (P) as the independent variables.

a. Determine the estimated regression line.
b. Give an economic interpretation of the estimated slope (b) coefficients.
c. Test the hypothesis (at the .05 level of significance) that there is no relationship between the dependent variable and each of the independent variables.
d. Determine the coefficient of determination.
e. Perform an analysis of variance on the regression, including an F-test of the overall significance of the results (at the .05 level).
f. Based on the regression model, determine the best estimate of paint sales in a sales region where promotional expenditures are \$80(000) and the selling price is \$12.50.
g. Determine the point promotional and price elasticities at the values of promotional expenditures and selling price given in part (f).

14. The county assessor (see Exercise 4) feels that the use of more independent variables in the regression equation might improve the overall explanatory power of the model.

In addition to size, the assessor feels that the total number of rooms, age, and whether the house has an attached garage might be important variables affecting selling price. These data for the 15 randomly selected dwellings are shown in the following table.

a. Using a computer regression program, determine the estimated regression equation with the four explanatory variables shown in the table.

b. Give an economic interpretation of each of the estimated regression coefficients.

c. Which of the independent variables (if any) are statistically significant (at the .05 level) in explaining selling price?

d. What proportion of the total variation in selling price is explained by the regression model?

e. Perform an *F*-test (at the .05 significance level) of the overall explanatory power of the model.

f. Construct an *approximate* 95 percent prediction interval for the selling price of a 15-year-old house having 1,800 square feet, 7 rooms, and an attached garage.

Observation I	Selling Price ($\times$ \$1,000) Y	Size ($\times$ 100 ft^2) X_1	Total No. of Rooms X_2	Age X_3	Attached Garage (No = 0, Yes = 1) X_4
1	265.2	12.0	6	17	0
2	279.6	20.2	7	18	0
3	311.2	27.0	7	17	1
4	328.0	30.0	8	18	1
5	352.0	30.0	8	15	1
6	281.2	21.4	8	20	1
7	288.4	21.6	7	8	0
8	292.8	25.2	7	15	1
9	356.0	37.2	9	31	1
10	263.2	14.4	7	8	0
11	272.4	15.0	7	17	0
12	291.2	22.4	6	9	0
13	299.6	23.9	7	20	1
14	307.6	26.6	6	23	1
15	320.4	30.7	7	23	1

CASE EXERCISES

SOFT DRINK DEMAND ESTIMATION

Demand can be estimated with experimental data, time-series data, or cross-section data. Sara Lee Corporation generates experimental data in test stores where the effect of an NFL-licensed Carolina Panthers logo on Champion sweatshirt sales can be carefully monitored. Demand forecasts usually rely on time-series data. In contrast, cross-section data appear in Table 1. Soft drink consumption in cans per capita per year is related to six-pack price, income per capita, and mean temperature across the 48 contiguous states in the United States.

QUESTIONS

1. Estimate the demand for soft drinks using a multiple regression program available on your computer.
2. Interpret the coefficients and calculate the price elasticity of soft drink demand.
3. Omit price from the regression equation and observe the bias introduced into the parameter estimate for income.

4. Now omit both price and temperature from the regression equation. Should a marketing plan for soft drinks be designed that relocates most canned drink machines into low-income neighborhoods? Why or why not?

Table 1

Soft Drink Demand Data

	Annual Cans Per Capita	Price Per Six-Pack	Income Per Capita	Mean Temp.
Alabama	200	2.19	13	66
Arizona	150	1.99	17	62
Arkansas	237	1.93	11	63
California	135	2.59	25	56
Colorado	121	2.29	19	52
Connecticut	118	2.49	27	50
Delaware	217	1.99	28	52
Florida	242	2.29	18	72
Georgia	295	1.89	14	64
Idaho	85	2.39	16	46
Illinois	114	2.35	24	52
Indiana	184	2.19	20	52
Iowa	104	2.21	16	50
Kansas	143	2.17	17	56
Kentucky	230	2.05	13	56
Louisiana	269	1.97	15	69
Maine	111	2.19	16	41
Maryland	217	2.11	21	54
Massachusetts	114	2.29	22	47
Michigan	108	2.25	21	47
Minnesota	108	2.31	18	41
Mississippi	248	1.98	10	65
Missouri	203	1.94	19	57
Montana	77	2.31	19	44
Nebraska	97	2.28	16	49
Nevada	166	2.19	24	48
New Hampshire	177	2.27	18	35
New Jersey	143	2.31	24	54
New Mexico	157	2.17	15	56
New York	111	2.43	25	48
North Carolina	330	1.89	13	59
North Dakota	63	2.33	14	39
Ohio	165	2.21	22	51
Oklahoma	184	2.19	16	82
Oregon	68	2.25	19	51
Pennsylvania	121	2.31	20	50
Rhode Island	138	2.23	20	50
South Carolina	237	1.93	12	65
South Dakota	95	2.34	13	45
Tennessee	236	2.19	13	60
Texas	222	2.08	17	69
Utah	100	2.37	16	50
Vermont	64	2.36	16	44
Virginia	270	2.04	16	58
Washington	77	2.19	20	49
West Virginia	144	2.11	15	55
Wisconsin	97	2.38	19	46
Wyoming	102	2.31	19	46

APPENDIX

4a

Problems in Applying the Linear Regression Model

Introduction

When the simple linear and multiple linear regression models were discussed in Chapter 4, several assumptions were made about the nature of the relationships among the variables. Questions naturally arise on the applicability or validity of these assumptions in the actual analysis of economic relationships and data. How can we determine whether the assumptions are being violated in a given situation? How does the violation of the assumptions affect the parameter estimates and prediction accuracy of the model? What methods (if any) exist for overcoming the difficulties caused by the inapplicability of the assumptions in a given situation?

Econometrics provides answers to some, but not all, of these questions. A thorough treatment of them is beyond the scope of this text. The (more limited) objective of this appendix is to make the reader aware of some of the potential problems that can arise in actual applications of the regression models and to suggest possible techniques for overcoming some of these problems. Some of the problems that may invalidate the regression results include the following:

1. Autocorrelation
2. Heteroscedasticity
3. Specification and measurement errors
4. Multicollinearity
5. Simultaneous equation relationships and the identification problem
6. Nonlinearities

All these problems are discussed in this appendix.

Autocorrelation

In many economic modeling and prediction problems, empirical data are in the form of a *time series*—a series of observations taken on the variables at different points in time. For example, we may be interested in predicting total (domestic U.S.) television sales by using disposable income as the independent variable. The data used to calculate estimates of the regression parameters (a and b) might consist of a series of yearly (or quarterly) measurements of the number of television sets sold and disposable income for a period of 10 to 15 years. In working with time-series data, a problem known as autocorrelation can arise.

Recall that one of the assumptions underlying the regression model (specifically, Assumption 4) is that the disturbance term e_t must be an independent random variable.

Figure 4A.1 Types of Autocorrelation (Numbers 1, 2, 3, . . . , 10 refer to successive time periods.)

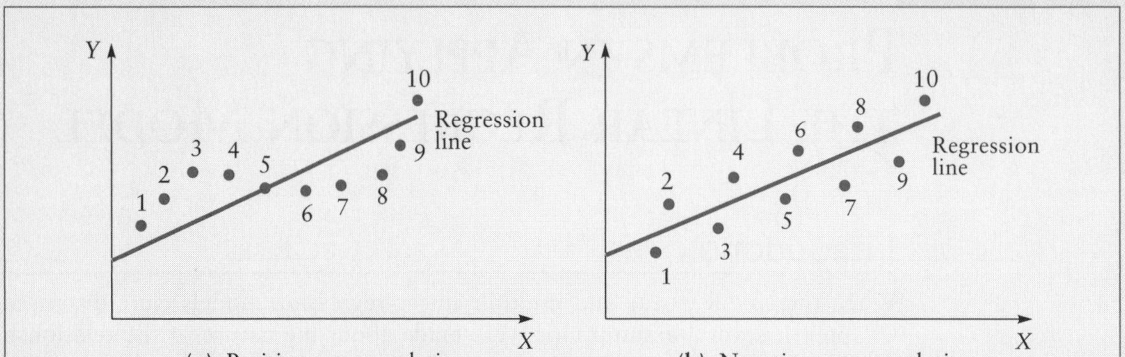

(a) Positive autocorrelation (b) Negative autocorrelation

Autocorrelation

An econometric problem characterized by the existence of a significant pattern in the successive values of the error terms in a linear regression model.

In other words, we assume that each successive error, e_t, is independent of earlier and later errors so that the regression equation produces no predictable pattern in the successive values of the disturbance term. The existence of a significant pattern in the successive values of the error term constitutes **autocorrelation**. Successive values of the disturbance term can exhibit either positive or negative autocorrelation. Positive autocorrelation, as shown in Figure 4A.1 (a), is inferred whenever successive positive (or negative) disturbances tend to be followed by disturbances of the *same* sign. Negative autocorrelation, as shown in Figure 4A.1 (b), is inferred whenever successive positive (or negative) disturbances tend to be followed by disturbances of the *opposite* sign.

Negative autocorrelation reflects an undershooting and overshooting process such as purchases of storable consumer goods. If a household buys too much breakfast cereal one week, that household will probably buy less than average the next week, and again more than average the following week. Financial market returns can also exhibit such patterns. Returns temporarily above capital market equilibrium values will set in motion arbitrage activity that corrects (perhaps overcorrects) the return back toward the trend.

Positive autocorrelation can result from several factors. One is the existence of cyclical and seasonal variation in economic variables. The overall growth of the economy coupled with business cycles causes most economic time series to have an overall upward trend with periodic upturns and downturns around this trend. Likewise, seasonal patterns can cause weekly, monthly, or quarterly data to rise and fall in a predictable manner each year. Another cause of positive autocorrelation is self-reinforcing trends in consumer purchase patterns, for example, in fashion retailing. If Hermes scarves are in fashion, each successive week of sales data will be further above trend than the previous week until the fad slows and the Hermes look goes out of fashion. Either positive or negative autocorrelation may also result if significant explanatory variables are omitted from the regression equation or if nonlinear relationships exist.

As a safeguard when working with time-series data, the disturbances (e_t values) should be examined for randomness. Statistical tests are also available to check for autocorrelation. One commonly used technique is the Durbin-Watson statistic. It is calculated as follows:[1]

$$d = \frac{\sum_{t=2}^{n}(e_t - e_{t-1})^2}{\sum_{t=1}^{n} e_t^2} \qquad [4.A1]$$

where e_t is the estimated error term in period t and e_{t-1} is the error term in period $t - 1$. The Durbin-Watson statistic tests for first-order autocorrelation, that is, whether the error in period t, is dependent on the error in the preceding period $t - 1$. The value of d ranges from 0 to 4. If there is *no* first-order autocorrelation, the expected value of d is 2. Values of d less than 2 indicate the possible presence of *positive* autocorrelation, whereas values of d greater than 2 indicate the possible presence of *negative* autocorrelation.

Formal hypothesis tests for first-order autocorrelation can be performed using the d statistic and the Durbin-Watson table (Table 6 in Appendix B). The critical value of d from the table (at the .025 significance level for a one-tail test, that is, a test for positive autocorrelation or a test for negative autocorrelation, or at the .05 significance level for a two-tail test) is a function of both the number of observations (n) and the number of independent variables (m). The decision rules are summarized in Figure 4A.2.

For example, suppose we wish to test for the presence of positive autocorrelation (at the .025 level of significance) in a regression equation with four independent variables (not counting the constant term) estimated from 25 observations. For $m = 4$ and $n = 25$, the values of d_L and d_U are 0.94 and 1.65, respectively (see Table 6, Appendix B). If the calculated d value is less than $d_L = 0.94$, one would *reject* H_0 and conclude that there is statistically significant evidence of the presence of positive autocorrelation. If the calculated d value is between 0.94 and 1.65, no conclusion could be drawn concerning the possible presence of positive autocorrelation. Finally, if the calculated d value is greater than 1.65, one would *not reject* H_0 and conclude that there is *no* statistically significant evidence of the presence of positive autocorrelation.

The presence of autocorrelation leads to several undesirable consequences in the regression results. First, although the estimates of α and β will be unbiased, the least-squares procedure will misestimate the sampling variances of these estimates. [An estimator is unbiased if its expected value is identical to the population parameter being estimated. The computed a and b values are unbiased estimators of α and β, respectively, because $E(a) = \alpha$ and $E(b) = \beta$.] In particular, the standard error (s_e in Equation 4.22) will either be inflated or deflated depending on whether we have positive or negative autocorrelation. As a result, the use of the t-statistic to test hypotheses about these parameters may yield incorrect conclusions about the importance of the individual predictor (i.e., independent) variables. Second, overall measures of the fit and explanatory power of the regression model, such as the coefficient of determination (r^2) and F-test, will no longer provide reliable information

[1] Most computer regression programs will compute the Durbin-Watson statistic when specified by the user in the control statements.

Figure 4A.2 Testing for the Presence of First-Order Autocorrelation

	One-Tail Tests		Two-Tail Tests*
Type of Autocorrelation	Positive Autocorrelation	Negative Autocorrelation	Positive and Negative
Hypothesis			
Null	H_0: No Positive autocorrelation	H_0: No negative autocorrelation	H_0: No positive or negative autocorrelation
Alternative	H_a: Positive autocorrelation	H_a: Negative autocorrelation	H_a: Positive or negative autocorrelation
Decision Rule			
Reject H_0	$d < d_L$	$d > (4 - d_L)$	$d < d_L$ or $d > (4 - d_L)$
Do not reject H_0	$d > d_U$	$d < (4 - d_U)$	$d_U < d < (4 - d_U)$
Test is inconclusive (No conclusion can be made concerning the possible presence of autocorrelation)	$d_L \leq d \leq d_U$	$(4 - d_U) \leq d \leq (4 - d_L)$	$d_L \leq d \leq d_U$ or $(4 - d_U) \leq d \leq (4 - d_L)$

*Note that for a two-tail test, the significance level is double that shown in Table 6 in Appendix B.

about the significance of the economic relationships obtained. Finally, the use of the regression equation for prediction purposes will yield predictions with unnecessarily large sampling variances.

Several procedures are available for dealing with autocorrelation.[2] If one can determine the functional form of the dependence relationship in the successive values of the residuals, then the original variables can be transformed by a lag structure to remove this pattern. Another technique that may help to reduce autocorrelation is to include a new linear trend or time variable in the regression equation.[3] A third procedure is to calculate the first differences in the time series of each of the variables (i.e., $Y_{t+1} - Y_t$, $X_{1,t+1} - X_{1,t}$, $X_{2,t+1} - X_{2,t}$, and so on) and then calculate the regression equation using these transformed variables. A fourth method is to include additional variables of the form X_1^2 or X_1X_2 in the regression equation. Usually one of these procedures will yield satisfactory results consistent with the independent errors assumption.

[2] See R. Pindyck and D. Rubinfeld, *Econometric Models and Econometric Forecasting* (Boston, MA: Irwin/McGraw-Hill, 1997) for a much more detailed discussion of procedures for dealing with autocorrelation.

[3] A linear trend variable is one in which each observation in the time series is given a successively larger integer value, such as 1, 2, 3, . . . , *n*, when *n* is the number of observations.

HETEROSCEDASTICITY

In developing the ordinary least-squares regression model, another of the assumptions (Assumption 4) is that the error terms have a constant variance. In other words, we assume that the observations have uniform variability about the theoretical regression line. This property is referred to as *homoscedasticity.* Departure from this assumption is known as **heteroscedasticity**, which is indicated whenever a systematic relationship is evident between the absolute magnitude of the error term and the magnitude of one (or more) of the independent variables. Graphic or tabular comparisons between the absolute values of disturbance terms and the values of each of the independent variables will help to detect the existence of significant heteroscedasticity.

Heteroscedasticity

An econometric problem characterized by the lack of a uniform variance of the error terms about the regression line.

The presence of heteroscedasticity causes the estimate of the variance of the error terms (s_e) to be dependent on the particular set of values of the independent variables that were chosen. Another set of observations may yield a much different estimate of this variance. As a result, tests of the statistical significance of the individual regression coefficients (the t-test) and overall explanatory power of the regression equation (the F-test, r^2) may prove to be misleading.

One form of heteroscedasticity occurs when the variance of the error term increases with the size of the independent variable, such as in the case illustrated in Figure 4A.3. For example, consider a regression model in which savings by households is postulated to be a function of household income. In this case it is likely that more variability will be found in the savings of high-income households compared with low-income households simply because high-income households have more money available for potential savings. Another example arising frequently with cross-sectional sales data is that the error variance with large retail stores, divisions,

Figure 4A.3 Illustration of Heteroscedasticity

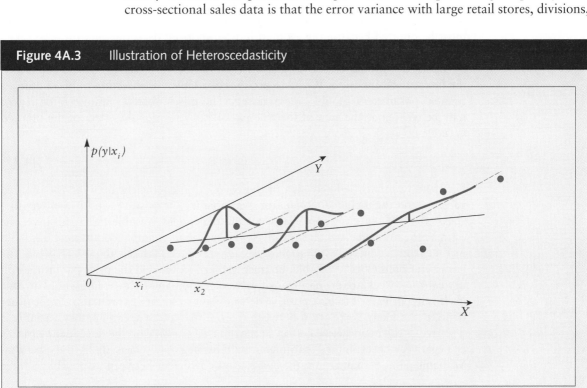

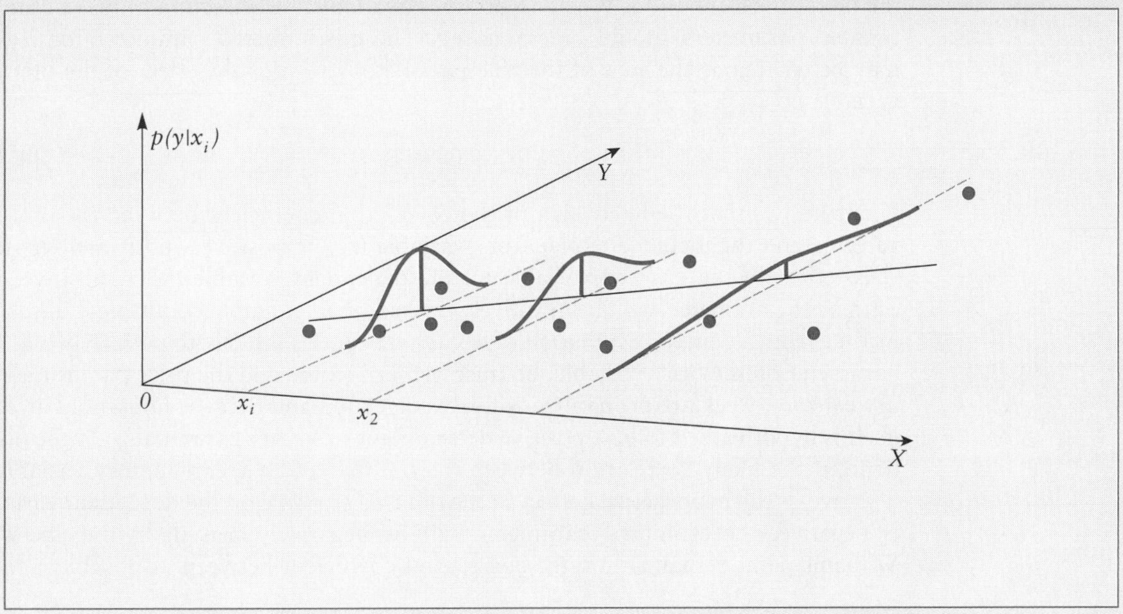

or firms exceeds the error variance for smaller entities. In many cases this form of heteroscedasticity can be reduced or eliminated by dividing all the variables in the regression equation by the independent variable that is thought to be causing the heteroscedasticity and then applying the least-squares analysis to the resulting set of transformed variables. This transformation, however, *does* alter the form of the hypothesized relationship among the variables and thus may be inappropriate in some situations. Another method for dealing with heteroscedasticity is to take logarithms of the data. Again, this transformation alters the form of the hypothesized relationship among the variables. More advanced, generalized least-squares techniques can account for the nonuniform error variance and preserve the original, hypothesized relationship.

SPECIFICATION AND MEASUREMENT ERRORS

Specification errors can result whenever one or more significant explanatory variables are not included in the regression equation. If the omitted variable is moderately or highly correlated with one of the explanatory variables included in the regression equation, then the effect of the missing variable will be represented in the coefficient (b value) of the included variable. It may lead to overestimating or underestimating the economic effect of the explanatory variable included in the regression equation, that is, a bias in the least-squares estimates of the theoretical regression coefficients (α, β). The omission of a significant explanatory variable from a time-series regression equation (e.g., a time trend) may also produce autocorrelation problems.[4]

The formulation of a correctly specified model must therefore occupy a prominent role in the estimation of any economic relation. Sometimes relevant variables must be omitted because the estimation is supporting decisions that must be taken prior to complete data availability. In such cases, a close proxy variable is often available and should be substituted for the omitted variable. The closer the proxy, the better the estimation. When no proxy is available, the direction of bias in the estimated parameters should be diagnosed. The misestimated parameter for $X_1(b_1)$ may be written as the sum of the true parameter (β_1) plus the effect of the omitted variable j:

$$b_1 = \beta_1 + \beta_j r_{1,j} \quad [4.A2]$$

If one knows that the likely sign of the correlation coefficient between the omitted variable and the included explanatory variable ($r_{1,j}$) is positive, and if the hypothesized effect of the omitted variable on the dependent variable (β_j) is positive, the estimated parameter will be positively biased. For example, omitting household income from a demand estimation of luxury car rentals is likely to positively bias the parameter on the price variable, because higher income and the price paid for a luxury car for a week are probably positively correlated and because household income itself is hypothesized to be a positive determinant of luxury car rentals. On the other hand, if the likely correlation between the omitted and the explanatory variable is negative or the hypothesized effect of the omitted variable on the dependent variable is negative, the estimated parameter will be negatively biased. In the Sherwin-Williams paint demand data, the correlation coefficient between disposable income

[4] Inclusion of irrelevant explanatory variables has a similar effect on the standard error of the residuals (s_e).

Figure 4A.4 Correlation Coefficients: Sherwin-Williams Company

	SALES Y	PROMEXP X_1	SELLPR X_2	DISPINC X_3
SALES Y	1.000			
PROMEXP X_1	0.721	1.000		
SELLPR X_2	−0.866	−0.739	1.000	
DISPINC X_3	0.615	0.710	−0.514	1.000

and price is −0.514 (see Figure 4A.4). Omitting DISPINC from that demand estimation in Figure 4.8 would lead to a negative bias in the estimated effect of price on sales. Although these diagnoses of the omitted variable bias can never replace a fully and correctly specified model, they do allow much more informed decision making based on incomplete data.

The estimation of the parameters of the regression equation requires that a series of measurements be made on both the dependent and independent variables that are to be included in the relationship. Despite the many precautions taken, errors in the measurement of economic variables can arise. For example, the values of many economic variables (such as unemployment, GDP, and prices) are obtained from samples, and sampling error is inherent in the data. Also, data based on a complete census of the population can contain errors caused by missing observations, interviewer biases, recording errors, and so forth. Finally, proxy variables always introduce some measurement error. Measurement errors in the dependent variable do not affect the validity of the assumptions underlying the regression model or the parameter estimates obtained by the least-squares procedure because these errors become part of the overall residual or unexplained error. However, measurement error in the explanatory variables introduces a stochastic component in the Xs and may cause the values of the error term e_i to be correlated with the observed values of these explanatory variables. Consequently, the assumption that the disturbance terms are independent random variables (Assumption 4) is violated, and the resulting least-squares estimates of the regression coefficients (α, β) are biased.

Simultaneous equation estimation techniques discussed in a later section are one method of dealing with stochastic explanatory variables. Measurement error can also be modeled, if the form of the error in the X variables can be specified.

MULTICOLLINEARITY

Whenever a high degree of correlation exists among some or all of the explanatory variables in the regression equation, it becomes difficult to determine the separate influences of each of the explanatory variables on the dependent variable because the standard deviations (s_b) of their respective regression coefficients become large. Whenever two or more explanatory variables are highly correlated (or collinear), the t-test is no longer a reliable indicator of the statistical significance of the individual explanatory variables. Under such a condition, the least-squares procedure tends

Multicollinearity

An econometric problem characterized by a high degree of intercorrelation among some or all of the explanatory variables in a regression equation.

to yield highly unstable estimates of the regression coefficients from one sample to the next. The presence of **multicollinearity**, however, does not necessarily invalidate the use of the regression equation for prediction purposes. Provided that the correlation pattern among the explanatory variables persists into the future, the equation can produce reliable forecasts of the value of the dependent variable.

A number of techniques exist for dealing with multicollinearity. One technique is to alter the model by removing all but one of the set of highly correlated variables. For example, consider the variables that were used to explain paint sales in the Sherwin-Williams example discussed earlier. The correlation coefficients between each of the variables are shown in Figure 4A.4. The correlation coefficients between each of the possible pairs of explanatory (independent) variables are shown in the enclosed area of the table. Note the high degree of intercorrelation (in absolute value terms) between promotional expenditures and selling price and between promotional expenditures and disposable income, indicating that the standard deviations of the estimates of these three regression coefficients may be inflated. Therefore, the analyst may want to consider dropping one of these variables from the regression.[5]

When working with time-series data, another technique is to use cross-sectional data to obtain independent estimates of some of the regression parameters. Finally, the elimination of trends, through deflation procedures, such as using a trend variable or first differences, will often reduce the multicollinearity problem.

Simultaneous Equation Relationships and the Identification Problem

Many economic relationships are characterized by simultaneous interactions. For example, recognition of simultaneous relationships is at the heart of marketing plans. The optimal advertising expenditure for a product line such as Hanes Her Way hosiery depends on sales (i.e., on the quantity Hanes expects to sell). However, sales obviously also depend on advertising; a particularly effective ad campaign that just happens to match a random swing in customer fashion will drive sales substantially upward. And this sales boost will increase spending on advertising. Sales (i.e., demand) and advertising are simultaneously determined.

Identification Problem

A difficulty encountered in empirically estimating a demand function by regression analysis. This problem arises from the simultaneous relationship between two functions, such as supply and demand.

In attempting to estimate the parameters of simultaneous equation relationships with single equation models, one encounters the **identification problem**. For example, in developing demand functions from empirical data, one is faced with the simultaneous relationship between the demand function and the supply function. Suppose demand can be written as a function of price (P), income (M), and a random error ε_1,

$$Q_d = \beta_1 + \beta_2 P + \beta_3 M + \varepsilon_1 \qquad [4A.3]$$

and supply can be written as a function of price, input costs (I), and a random error ε_2,

$$Q_s = \alpha_1 + \alpha_2 P + \alpha_3 I + \varepsilon_2 \qquad [4A.4]$$

or, rearranging,

$$P = \frac{-\alpha_1}{\alpha_2} + \frac{1}{\alpha_2}(Q_s - \varepsilon_2) - \frac{\alpha_3}{\alpha_2} I \qquad [4A.5]$$

[5] The analyst must carefully observe the effect of this procedure on the other parameters, however, because removing a partially collinear but relevant explanatory variable introduces omitted variable bias into the estimation.

Because quantity demanded will equal quantity supplied in market-clearing equilibrium (i.e., $Q_d = Q_s$), we can substitute Equation 4A.3 for Q_s in 4A.5 to obtain

$$P = \frac{-\alpha_1}{\alpha_2} + \frac{1}{\alpha_2}(\beta_1 + \beta_2 P + \beta_3 M + \varepsilon_1 - \varepsilon_2) - \frac{\alpha_3}{\alpha_2} I \qquad [4A.6]$$

$$P = \frac{1}{\alpha_2 - \beta_2}(-\alpha_1 + \beta_1 + \beta_3 M + \varepsilon_1 - \varepsilon_2 - \alpha_3 I). \qquad [4A.7]$$

The price variable in this rearranged supply function, Equation 4A.7, is quite obviously a stochastic explanatory variable; observed values of P will be correlated with the disturbance term in the demand function ε_1. An ordinary least-squares regression of Equation 4A.3 therefore violates Assumption 4 that disturbance terms must be independent of the Xs, or $E(P_i\varepsilon_i) = 0$. As a result, the price coefficient in Equation 4A.3 (β_2) will be biased.

To see the problem this situation poses when estimating the shape of an empirical demand function, note that one may observe only one actual price-output combination at any point in time. If one sought to estimate the demand curve for computer memory chips, one might observe historical data on quantity bought (sold) and the price at a specific time. A next step would be to plot these data on a graph, as shown in Figure 4A.5. Is the line DD', drawn by connecting the four observed price-output

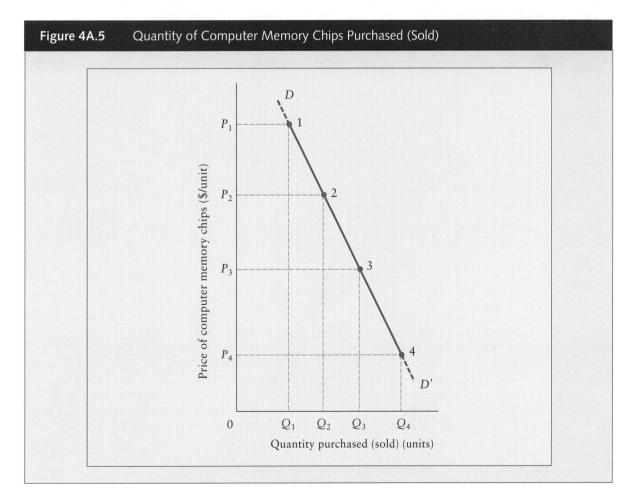

Figure 4A.5 Quantity of Computer Memory Chips Purchased (Sold)

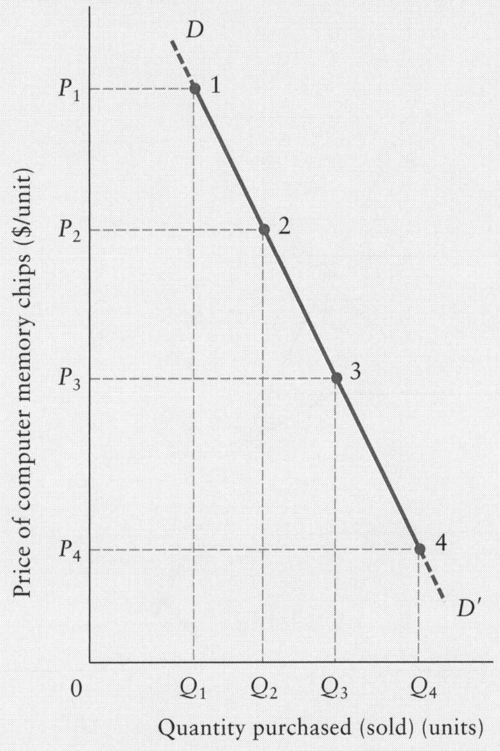

combinations, equivalent to the demand curve for memory chips? Usually not. Although it does have the traditional negative slope of a demand curve, one cannot conclude that it represents the true demand-price relationship.

To see why, recall that the price-output combinations actually observed result from an interaction of the supply and demand curves at a point in time, as illustrated in Figure 4A.6. If D_1, D_2, D_3, and D_4 represent the true demand curves at four different points in time and S_1, S_2, S_3, and S_4 the corresponding supply curves, one would have been seriously misled to conclude that the true demand relationship was depicted by DD' and was generally inelastic, when in fact demand was quite elastic and shifting (as was the supply curve). During the four successive time periods in which price-output combinations were observed, both the demand and supply curves had shifted. Recall from Chapter 3 that to obtain a true estimate of the actual demand curve, one must hold constant the effects of all other variables in the demand functions, allowing only price and quantity demanded to vary.

Under what circumstances may valid empirical estimates of the demand curve be made? If both curves retain their original shape and position from one time period to the next, nothing can be learned of the true demand curve because all observed price-output combinations will coincide, or at least be closely clustered. If,

Figure 4A.6 Quantity of Computer Memory Chips Purchased (Sold) with Shifting Supply and Demand

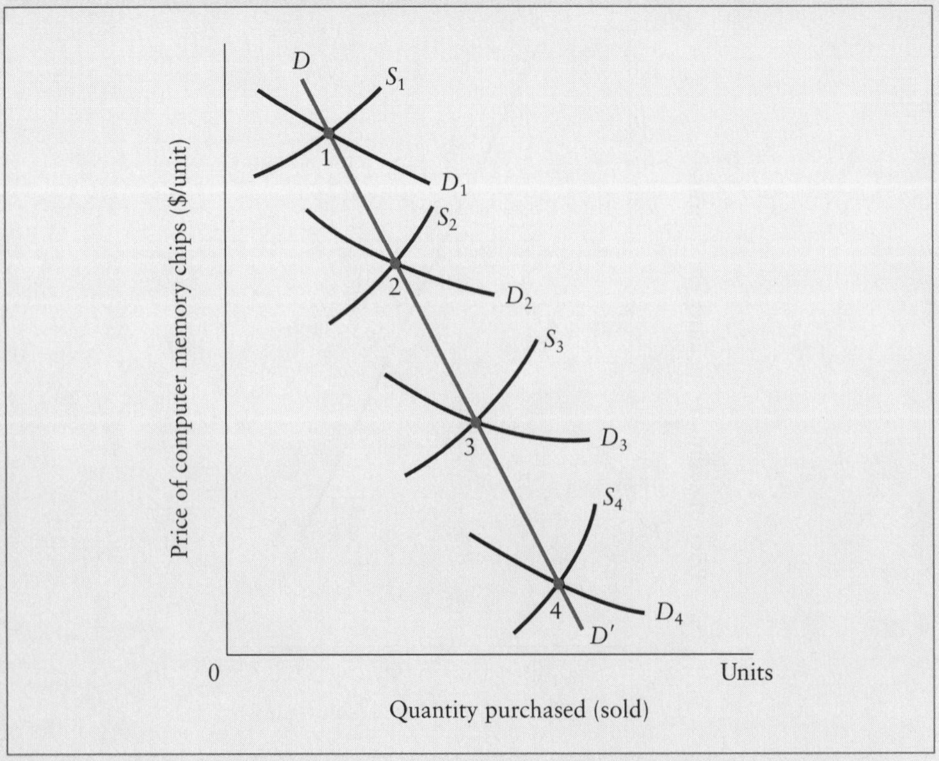

Figure 4A.7 Quantity of Computer Memory Chips Purchased (Sold) with Stable Demand and Shifting Supply

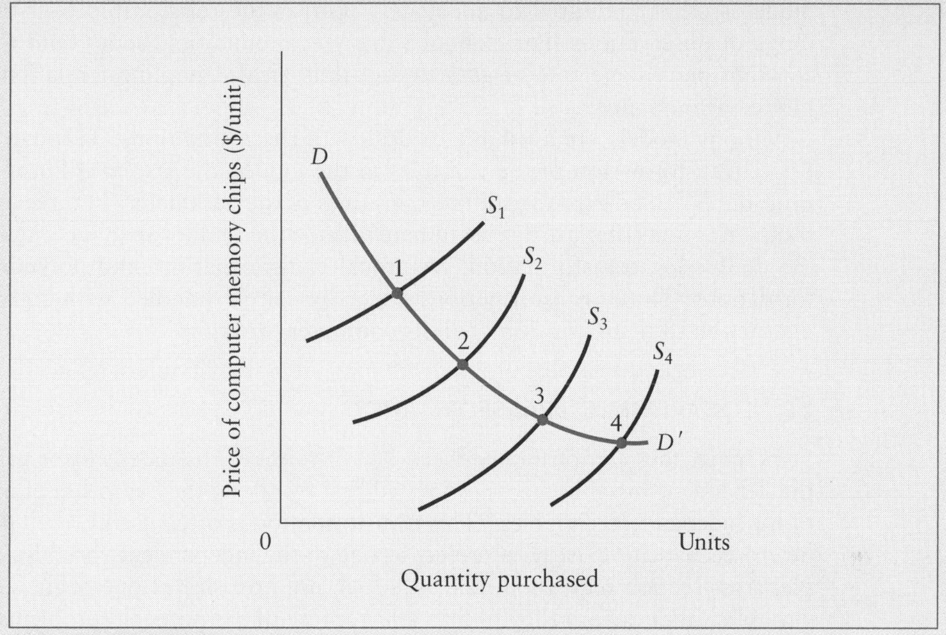

however, the supply curve shifts but the demand curve remains constant, observed price-output combinations will trace out the true demand curve as illustrated in Figure 4A.7. If, for example, technological advances were being introduced in the production of computer memory chips during Periods 1, 2, 3, and 4, then the supply curve would shift downward and to the right, from S_1 to S_4, tracing out the actual demand curve.

A final possibility is that both curves have shifted during the time period under consideration, but one has enough information to *identify* how each curve has shifted. When these types of simultaneous relationships occur, the ordinary least-squares (OLS) curve-fitting techniques discussed earlier in Chapter 4 may *break down and yield results that bear little or no relationship to the actual equation being sought.* Separating the effects of simultaneous relationships in demand analysis requires that more than just price-output data be available. In other words, other variables, such as income and advertising, that may cause a shift in the demand function must also be included in the model. Alternative statistical estimation techniques, such as two-stage least-squares (2SLS), must often be used to separate supply curve shifts from shifts in the demand curve.[6]

[6] A discussion of these alternative estimation procedures is beyond the scope of this book. The reader is referred to R. Pindyck and D. Rubinfeld, *Econometric Methods and Forecasting,* 3rd ed. (Boston, MA: Irwin/McGraw-Hill, 1997) Chapter 12, for a further discussion of the identification problem and alternative estimation techniques. See also Ernst R. Berndt, *The Practice of Econometrics: Classic and Contemporary* (Reading, MA: Addison-Wesley Publishing Company, 1991), especially Chapter 8.

Nonlinear Regression Models

Although the relationships among many economic variables can be satisfactorily represented using a linear regression model, situations do occur in which a nonlinear model is clearly required to adequately portray the relationship over the relevant range of observations. For example, many economic time series tend to exhibit a constant percentage rate of growth and thus yield a nonlinear relationship when plotted against time.

Various models are available to deal with these situations. Through an appropriate transformation of the variables in the model, the standard linear regression procedures can be used to estimate the values of the parameters of these models. The transformations that are discussed here include the semilogarithmic transformation, the double-log transformation, reciprocal transformation, and polynomial transformations. These transformations normally can be handled with an appropriate instruction to the regression analysis computer program.

Semilogarithmic Transformation

Sometimes, the relationship between one or more of the independent variables and the dependent variable can be estimated best by taking the logarithm of one or more of the independent variables.[7] This transformation is often useful when problems of heteroscedasticity exist with respect to one of the independent variables. For example, cross-section regression models, which use firm size as one of the independent variables, often take the log of firm size because of the potential problems caused by including in the same equation firms of $10 million in assets with firms of $10 billion in assets.

A semilog transformation is of the form

$$Y = a + b \log S + cX + dZ \qquad [4A.8]$$

where Y is the dependent variable, X and Z are independent variables expressed in a normal form, and $\log S$ is an independent variable expressed in a logarithmic form. Standard least-squares techniques can be used to estimate Equation 4A.8.

Double-Log Transformation

In Chapter 4, we saw that a multiplicative exponential model (see Equation 4.5 and Table 4.5) is often used in demand studies. Likewise, as will be seen in Chapter 7, such models are useful for relating the quantities of various inputs used in a production process to the quantity of output obtained. A three-variable exponential regression function can be represented as

$$Z = AV^{\beta_1}W^{\beta_2} \qquad [4A.9]$$

where V and W are the explanatory variables; A, β_1, and β_2 are the parameters to be estimated. Multiplicative exponential functions such as these can be transformed to linear relationships. In Equation 4A.9, taking logarithms of both sides of the equation yields

$$\log Z = \log A + \beta_1 \log V + \beta_2 \log W$$

---

[7] It is possible to transform many, but not all, nonlinear forms into a linear expression.

By defining the following transformations: $Y = \log Z$, $\alpha = \log A$, $X_1 = \log V$, $X_2 = \log W$, and adding an error term ε, the following multiple linear regression model is obtained:

$$Y = \alpha + \beta_1 X_1 + \beta_2 X_2 + \varepsilon$$

Again, least-squares procedures can be used to estimate these regression coefficients.

EXAMPLE

CONSTANT ELASTICITY DEMAND: PEPSI

If the data on soft drinks in Case Exercise 2 at the end of Chapter 4 (see Table 2) represent firm-level unit sales, marketing analysts in the company (PepsiCo, Inc.) may confirm that price elasticity coefficients have been similar at several price points in recent years. If the same results of nearly constant elasticity estimates have arisen from detailed studies of income elasticity in upper- and lower-income neighborhoods, then a demand specification such as Equation 4A.9 and a double-log estimation of the data in Table 2 would be indicated. Results of such an estimation are listed here:

$$\underset{(1.72)}{\text{Log } Q = 1.050} \; - \underset{(-4.92)}{3.196 \text{ LogPrice}} + \underset{(1.19)}{0.221 \text{ LogIncome}} + \underset{(4.23)}{1.119 \text{ LogTemp}}$$

$$SSE = 0.111 \qquad R^2 = 0.671$$

Numbers in parentheses are *t*-score statistics.

RECIPROCAL TRANSFORMATION

Another transformation, which is useful in relationships that exhibit an asymptotic behavior, is the reciprocal transformation. The two possible cases are shown in Figure 4A.8. In Figure 4A.8 (a) the relationship is of the form

$$Y = \alpha + \frac{\beta}{Z} \qquad [4A.10]$$

Figure 4A.8 Reciprocal Transformations

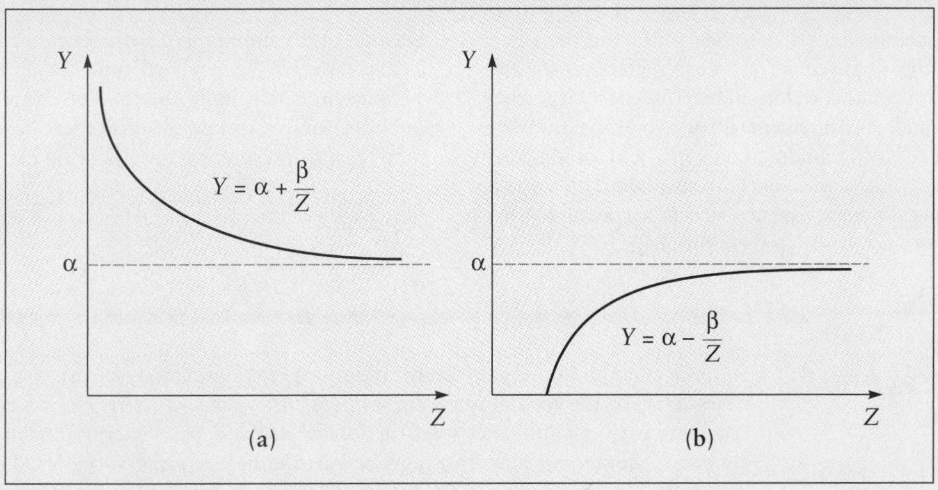

and in Figure 4A.8 (b) it is of the form

$$Y = \alpha - \frac{\beta}{Z} \qquad [4A.11]$$

Defining the transformation $X = 1/Z$, Equations 4A.10 and 4A.11 yield the following respective simple linear regression models:

$$Y = \alpha + \beta X + \varepsilon$$

and

$$Y = \alpha - \beta X + \varepsilon$$

whose parameters can be estimated by the usual least-squares procedures.

Polynomial Transformation

As will be seen in Chapter 8, the cost-output function for a firm is often postulated to follow a quadratic or cubic pattern. This type of relationship can be represented by means of a *polynomial function*. For example, a third-degree (that is, cubic) polynomial function can be represented as

$$Y = \alpha + \beta_1 Z + \beta_2 Z^2 + \beta_3 Z^3 \qquad [4A.12]$$

Letting $X_1 = Z$, $X_2 = Z^2$, $X_3 = Z^3$, Equation 4A.12 can be transformed into the following multiple linear regression model:

$$Y = \alpha + \beta_1 X_1 + \beta_2 X_2 + \beta_3 X_3$$

Standard least-squares procedures can be used in estimating the parameters of this model.

The transformations discussed illustrate the possibilities that are available to the model builder. These various transformations may, of course, be combined and used in the same equation. Further discussions of these and other more complex transformations are found in most econometrics books.

Summary

- Various methodological problems can occur when applying the single-equation linear regression model. These include autocorrelation, heteroscedasticity, specification and measurement errors, multicollinearity, simultaneous equation relationships, and nonlinearities. Many of these problems can invalidate the regression results. In some cases, methods are available for detecting and overcoming these problems.
- Because of the simultaneous equation relationship that exists between the demand function and the supply function in determining the market-clearing price and quantity, analysts must exercise great care when estimating and interpreting empirical demand functions.

Exercises

Answers to the exercises in blue can be found in Appendix C at the back of the book.

1. Suppose an appliance manufacturer is doing a regression analysis, using quarterly time-series data, of the factors affecting its sales of appliances. A regression equation was estimated between appliance sales (in dollars) as the dependent variable and disposable personal income and new housing starts as the independent variables. The statistical tests of the model showed large *t*-values for both independent variables, along with a

high r^2 value. However, analysis of the residuals indicated that substantial autocorrelation was present.

a. What are some of the possible causes of this autocorrelation?

b. How does this autocorrelation affect the conclusions concerning the significance of the individual explanatory variables and the overall explanatory power of the regression model?

c. Given that a person uses the model for forecasting future appliance sales, how does this autocorrelation affect the accuracy of these forecasts?

d. What techniques might be used to remove this autocorrelation from the model?

2. In the case exercise at the end of Chapter 4 on soft drink demand, what problem might arise if the given data are for Pepsi and the researcher decides to add the price of Coca-Cola in each state to the model?

3. A product manager has been reviewing selling expenses (advertising, sales commissions, etc.) associated with marketing a line of household cleaning products. The manager suspects some sort of diminishing marginal returns relationship exists between selling expenses and the resulting sales generated by these expenditures. After examining the selling expense and sales data for various regions (all regions are similar in sales potential) shown in the following table and graph, however, the manager is uncertain about the nature of the relationship.

Region	Selling Expense ($000)	Sales (100,000 Units)	Log (Selling Expense)	Log (Sales)
A	5	1	3.6990	5.0000
B	30	4.25	4.4771	5.6284
C	25	4	4.3979	5.6021
D	10	2	4.0000	5.3010
E	55	5.5	4.7404	5.7404
F	40	5	4.6021	5.6990
G	10	1.75	4.0000	5.2430
H	45	5	4.6532	5.6990
I	20	3	4.3010	5.4771
J	60	5.75	4.7782	5.7597

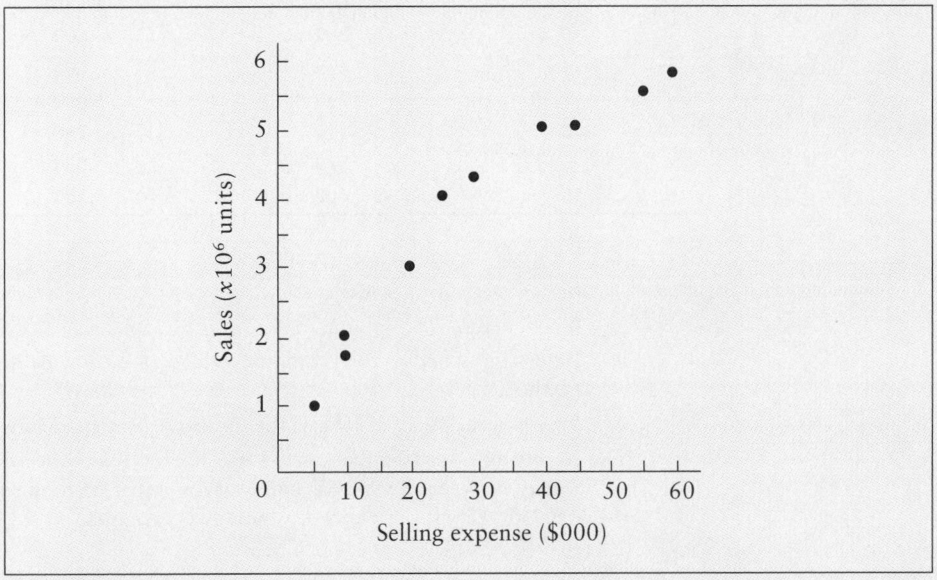

a. Using the linear regression model

$$Y = \alpha + \beta X$$

where Y is sales and X is selling expenses, estimate α, β, and the r^2 statistic by the least-squares technique.

b. Using the exponential function model

$$Y = \alpha X^{\beta}$$

apply the double-logarithmic transformation to obtain a linear relationship that can be estimated by the least-squares technique.

c. Applying the least-squares technique, estimate α, β, and the r^2 statistic for the transformed (linear) model in part (b). (Note that the logarithms of the X and Y variables needed in the calculations are given in the table.)

d. Based on the r^2 statistics calculated in parts (a) and (c), which model appears to give a better fit of the data?

e. What implications does the result in part (d) have for the possible existence of a diminishing marginal returns relationship between sales and selling expenses as suggested by the manager?

f. What other transformations of the variables might we try to give a better fit to the data?

Note: The following problems require the use of a multiple regression computer program, such as JMP, Minitab, SAS, SPSS, MYSTAT, or Excel.

4. a. Using the data in Table 4.1 for the Sherwin-Williams Company, estimate a multiplicative exponential demand model (see Equation 4.5) for paint sales.

b. Compare the results in part (a) (i.e., parameter estimates, standard errors, statistical significance) with the linear model developed in Chapter 4.

5. The following table presents data on sales (S), advertising (A), and price (P):

Observation	Sales (S)	Advertising (A)	Price (P)
1	495	900	150
2	555	1,200	180
3	465	750	135
4	675	1,350	135
5	360	600	120
6	405	600	120
7	735	1,500	150
8	435	750	150
9	570	1,050	165
10	600	1,200	150

a. Estimate the following demand models:

(i) $S = \alpha + \beta_1 A + \beta_2 P$

(ii) $S = \alpha A^{\beta_1} P^{\beta_2}$

b. Determine whether the estimated values of β_1 and β_2 are statistically significant (at the .05 level).

c. Based on the value of R^2 and the F-ratio, which model gives the best fit?

6. The county assessor (see Exercise 14 in Chapter 4) is concerned about possible multicollinearity between the size (X_1) and total number of rooms (X_2) variables. Calculate the correlation coefficient between these two variables.

CHAPTER

5

BUSINESS AND ECONOMIC FORECASTING

CHAPTER PREVIEW "With over 50 models of cars already on sale here in the U.S., the Japanese auto industry isn't likely to carve out a big slice of the U.S. market for itself."

—*BusinessWeek,* 1958

"Internet traffic doubles every hundred days."

—U.S. Department of Commerce, 1998

One of the central concerns of managers in all enterprises is forecasting the future demand and input costs for their products. As the quotations indicate, forecasting is often quite difficult. Forecasts at the firm level depend on the performance of the overall economy, including the growth rate in gross national product, the level of interest rates, the rate of unemployment, the value of the dollar in foreign exchange markets, and the rate of inflation. These macroeconomic forecasts are provided by economists employed by the government, large firms, and economic forecasting organizations. The forecasting models for the future macroeconomic environment are complex and require considerable judgment in their use.

In this chapter we discuss several classes of forecasting techniques suitable for use at the firm level and consider the strengths and weaknesses of each, including time-series analysis, smoothing techniques, barometric indicators, survey and opinion polling, and econometric methods. Because the value of a firm depends on expected levels of future cash flows, accurately forecasting the components of these future cash flows is essential if managers wish to make shareholder wealth-maximizing decisions.

MANAGERIAL CHALLENGE

Excess Fiber Optic Capacity at Global Crossing Inc.[1]

The capacity of U.S. fiber optic networks to transmit high-speed data and voice signals recently outstripped telecom demand so much that 97 percent of the installed capacity in the United States was idle "silent fiber." Indeed if all telecom network traffic in the United States were routed through Chicago, only one-quarter of that city's fiber optic capacity would be in use. With all this excess capacity in the market, fiber optic network providers such as Global Crossing Inc. saw their pricing power collapse. A one-megabyte data connection between New York and Los Angeles that in 1995 had sold for as much as $12,000 per year declined by 2001 to $3,000 and by 2002 to $1,200. As their sales revenue plummeted, more than fifty telecom network companies sought bankruptcy protection from their creditors.

How did this extreme excess capacity situation develop? First, an innovation in signal compression

MANAGERIAL CHALLENGE

technology caused capacity to outpace the growth of the market. Between 1995 and 2003, dense wave divisional multiplexing (DWDM) expanded the transmission capacity of a single strand of fiber optic cable from 25,000 one-page e-mails per second to 25 million per second, a thousand-fold increase. In addition, however, telecom network providers such as Global Crossing and WorldCom were wildly optimistic about the growth of telecom traffic, fueled by the projected growth of the Internet, so they continued to lay additional cable. UUNet, a subsidiary of WorldCom, forecasted that Internet use would continue to double every 100 days. This exponential tenfold growth per year (1,000 percent) was an extrapolation of the sales growth UUNet actually experienced in 1995–1996.

When the U.S. Department of Commerce and the Federal Communications Commission repeated this forecast, network providers continued to buy and bury redundant fiber optic cable. Between 2001 and 2002, U.S. fiber optic total capacity grew from 8,000 gigabytes per second to 80,000, but by 2003, the growth rate of demand had slowed (from 1,000 percent) to only 40 percent per year. Global Crossing's failure to forecast this demand slowdown proved disastrous.

As we saw in Chapter 4, the penetration of the Internet into the American household has followed a classic S-shaped pattern. Initially, the Internet experienced exponential growth by the early adopters, then linear growth, and eventually fractional growth. This S-shaped penetration curve is drawn in Figure 5.1. It took both color television and the Internet only 8 years (1947 to 1955 for color TVs and 1993 to 2001 for direct Internet access) to reach approximately 60 percent of U.S. households. However, color television adoptions then hit a wall, requiring another 30 years (1955 to

Figure 5.1 Market Penetration Curves of the Color Television and the Internet

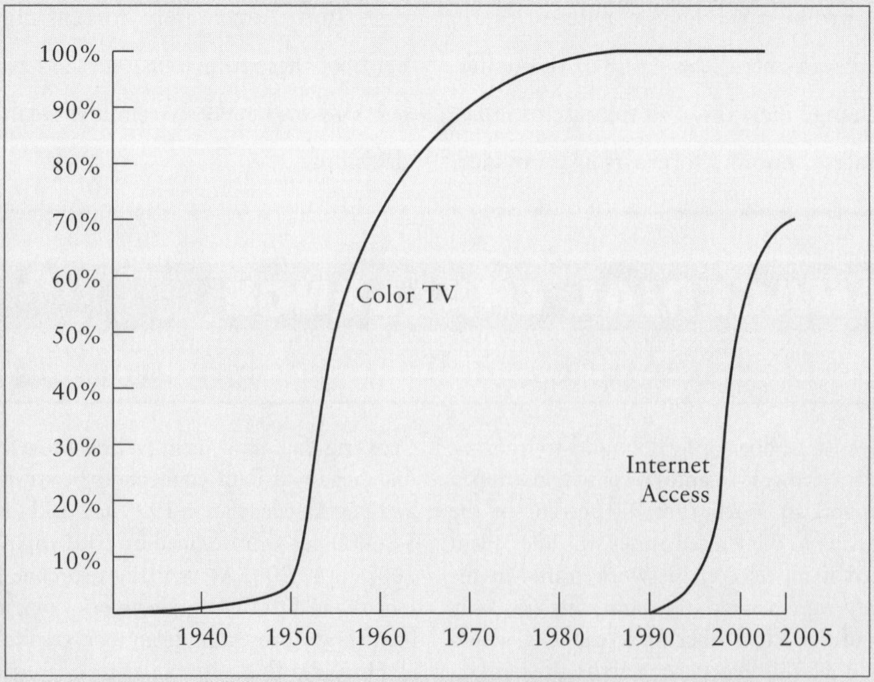

MANAGERIAL CHALLENGE

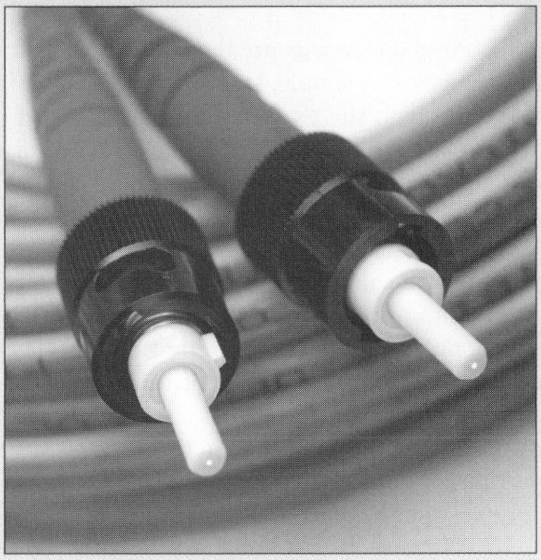

© DON FARRALL/PHOTODISC RED/GETTY IMAGES

1985) to achieve 98 percent penetration. Similarly with the Internet, customers who did not adopt high-speed home computer connections early are resistant to adopt now for several reasons: (1) the Internet is often available at work and can be used for some personal use; and (2) availability of movies and other entertainment through high-speed Internet lines is limited. Consequently, demand-related growth will likely continue to slow in the United States.

[1] Based on "Adoption Rate of Internet by Consumers Is Slowing," *Wall Street Journal,* July 16, 2001, pp. B1; "Has Growth of the Net Flattened," *Wall Street Journal,* July 16, 2001, pp. B8; "Behind the Fiber Glut," and *Wall Street Journal,* July 26, 2001, p. B1; and "Innovation Outpaced the Marketplace," September 26, 2002, p. B1.

THE SIGNIFICANCE OF FORECASTING

Accurately forecasting future business prospects is one of the most important functions of management. Sales forecasts are necessary for operations managers to plan the proper future levels of production. The financial manager requires estimates of not only future sales revenue but also disbursements and capital expenditures. Forecasts of credit conditions must also be made so that the cash needs of the firm may be met at the lowest possible cost.

Public administrators and managers of not-for-profit institutions must also forecast. City government officials, for example, forecast the level of services that will be required of their various departments during a budget period. How many police officers will be needed to handle the public safety concerns of the community? How many streets will require repair next year, and how much will the repairs cost? What will next year's school enrollment be at each grade level? The hospital administrator must forecast the health care needs of the community and the amount and cost of charity patient care.

SELECTING A FORECASTING TECHNIQUE

The forecasting technique used in any particular situation depends on a number of factors.

HIERARCHY OF FORECASTS

The highest level of economic aggregation that is normally forecast is that of the national economy. The usual measure of overall economic activity is gross domestic product (GDP); however, a firm may be more interested in forecasting some of the specific components of GDP. For example, a machine tool firm may be concerned about expected plant and equipment expenditures. Retail establishments are concerned about future levels and changes in disposable personal income rather than the overall GDP estimate.

The next levels in the hierarchy of economic forecasts are the industry sales forecast, followed by individual firm sales forecasts. A simple, single firm forecast might take the industry sales estimate and relate it to the expected market share of the individual firm. Future market share might be estimated on the basis of historical market shares as well as on changes that are anticipated because of new marketing strategies, new products and model changes, and relative prices.

Within the firm, a hierarchy of forecasts also exists. Managers often estimate company-wide or regional dollar sales and unit sales by product line. These forecasts are used by operations managers in planning orders for raw materials, employee-hiring needs, shipment schedules, and production runs. In addition, marketing managers use sales forecasts to determine optimal sales force allocations, to set sales goals, and to plan promotions. The sales forecast also constitutes a crucial part of the financial manager's forecast of the cash needs of the firm. Long-term forecasts for the economy, the industry, and the firm are used in planning long-term capital expenditures for plant and equipment and for charting the general direction of the firm.

Criteria Used to Select a Forecasting Technique

Some forecasting techniques are quite simple, rather inexpensive to develop and use, and best suited for short-term projections, whereas others are extremely complex, require significant amounts of time to develop, and may be quite expensive. The technique used in any specific instance depends on a number of factors, including the following:

1. The cost associated with developing the forecasting model compared with potential gains resulting from its use
2. The complexity of the relationships that are being forecast
3. The time period of the forecast (long term or short term)
4. The lead time necessary for making decisions based on the forecast
5. The accuracy required of the forecasting model

Evaluating the Accuracy of Forecasting Models

In determining the accuracy, or reliability, of a forecasting model, one is concerned with the magnitude of the differences between the observed (actual) (Y) and the forecasted values ($\hat{Y}$). Various measures of model accuracy are available. For example, in the discussion of regression analysis in the previous chapter, the coefficient of determination, or R^2, was used as a measure of the "goodness of fit" of the predicted values from the model to the patterns in the actual data. In addition, the average forecast error, or root mean square error,

$$\text{RMSE} = \sqrt{\frac{1}{n}\Sigma(Y_t - \hat{Y}_t)^2} \qquad [5.1]$$

is often used to evaluate the accuracy of a forecasting model (where n is the number of observations). The smaller the value of the RMSE, the greater the accuracy.

ALTERNATIVE FORECASTING TECHNIQUES

The managerial economist may choose from a wide range of forecasting techniques that can be classified in the following general categories:

- Deterministic time-series analysis
- Smoothing techniques
- Barometric indicators
- Survey and opinion polling techniques
- Econometric models
- Stochastic time-series analysis
- Forecasting with input-output tables

DETERMINISTIC TIME-SERIES ANALYSIS

Time-Series Data
A series of observations taken on an economic variable at various past points in time.

Cross-Sectional Data
Series of observations taken on different observation units (e.g., households, states, or countries) at the same point in time.

Data collected for use in forecasting the value of a particular variable may be classified into two major categories: time-series or cross-sectional data. **Time-series data** are defined as a sequence of the values of an economic variable at different points in time. **Cross-sectional data** are an array of the values of an economic variable observed at the same time, such as the data collected in a census across many individuals in the population. No matter what type of forecasting model is being used, one must decide whether time-series or cross-sectional data are most appropriate.

COMPONENTS OF A TIME SERIES

In the analysis of time-series data, time in years, months, or weeks is represented on the horizontal axis, and the values of the dependent variable are on the vertical axis. The variations that are evident in the time series in Figure 5.2 can be decomposed into four components:

Secular Trends
Long-run changes (growth or decline) in an economic time-series variable.

Cyclical Variations
Major expansions and contractions in an economic series usually lasting longer than a year in duration.

Seasonal Effects
Variations in a time series during a year that tend to appear regularly from year to year.

1. ***Secular trends.*** These long-run trends cause changes in an economic data series [*solid line* in Panel (a) of Figure 5.2]. For example, in empirical demand analyses, such factors as increasing population size or evolving consumer tastes may result in trend increases or decreases of a demand series over time.
2. ***Cyclical variations.*** These major expansions and contractions in an economic series are usually greater than a year in duration [*broken line* in Panel (a) of Figure 5.2]. For example, the housing industry appears to experience regular expansions following contractions in demand. When cyclical variations are present, regression estimates using the raw data will be distorted due to the presence of positive autocorrelation. Care must then be taken to specify an appropriate lag structure to remove the autocorrelation.
3. ***Seasonal effects.*** Seasonal variations during a year tend to be more or less consistent from year to year. The data in Panel (b) of Figure 5.2 (*broken line*) show significant seasonal variation. For example, two-thirds of Hickory Farms' (a retailer of holiday food gifts) annual sales occur between November and January.
4. ***Random fluctuations.*** Finally, an economic series may be influenced by random factors that are unpredictable [*solid line* in Panel (b) of Figure 5.2], such as hurricanes, floods, and tornados as well as extraordinary government actions like a wage-price freeze or a declaration of war.

Figure 5.2 Secular, Cyclical, Seasonal, and Random Fluctuations in Time Series Data

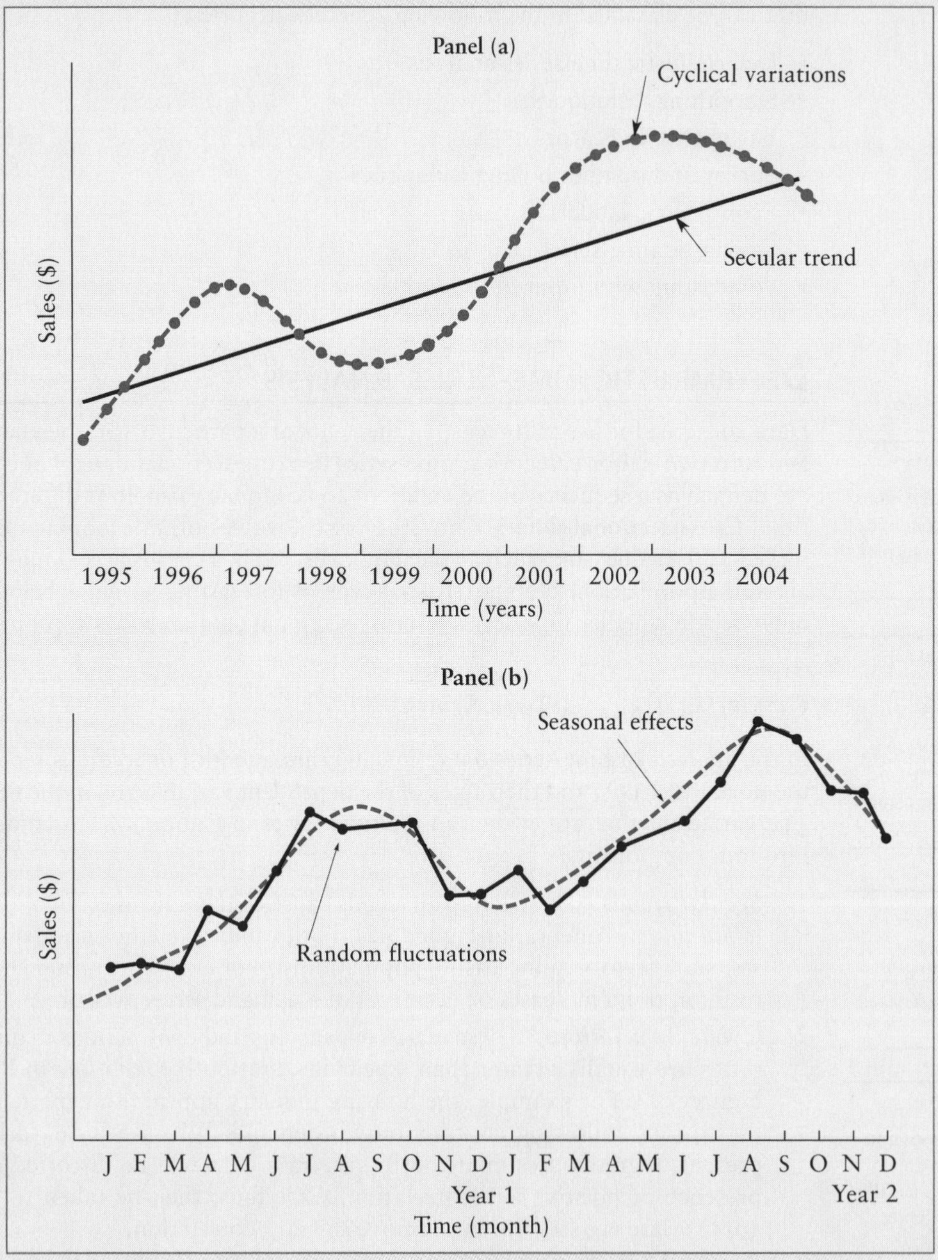

Some Elementary Time-Series Models

The simplest time-series model states that the forecast value of the variable for the next period will be the same as the value of that variable for the present period:

$$\hat{Y}_{t+1} = Y_t \qquad [5.2]$$

Table 5.1 Buckeye Brewing Company's Monthly Beer Sales (thousands of barrels)

	Year		
Month	2005	2006	2007
January	2,370	2,446	2,585
February	2,100	2,520	2,693
March	2,412	2,598	2,738
April	2,376	2,533	
May	3,074	3,250	
June	3,695	3,446	
July	3,550	3,986	
August	4,172	4,222	
September	3,880	3,798	
October	2,931	2,941	
November	2,377	2,488	
December	2,983	2,878	

For example, consider the sales data shown in Table 5.1 for the Buckeye Brewing Company. To forecast monthly sales, the model uses *actual* beer sales for March 2007 of 2,738 (000) barrels as the forecast value for April.

Where changes occur slowly and the forecast is being made for a relatively short period in the future, such a model may be quite useful. However, because Equation 5.2 requires a knowledge of this month's sales, the forecaster may be faced with the task of speeding up the collection of actual data. Another problem with this model is that it makes no provision for incorporating special promotions by the firm (or its competitors) that could cause large sales deviations.

Further examination of the Buckeye beer sales data in Table 5.1 indicates a slight upward trend in sales—beer sales in most months are higher than in the same month of the previous year. Second, we note that sales are somewhat seasonal—beer sales are high during the summer months and low during the winter. The tendency for recent increases to trigger further increases in beer sales may be incorporated by adjusting Equation 5.2 slightly to yield this equation:

$$\hat{Y}_{t+1} = Y_t + (Y_t - Y_{t-1}) \quad [5.3]$$

For example, Buckeye's sales forecast for April 2007 using this model would be

$$\begin{aligned}\hat{Y}_{t+1} &= 2{,}738 + (2{,}738 - 2{,}693)\\ &= 2{,}783(000) \text{ barrels}\end{aligned}$$

Other forecasting models that incorporate trends and seasonal effects such as these are discussed next.

SECULAR TRENDS

Long-run changes in an economic time series can follow a number of different types of trends. Three possible cases are shown in Figure 5.3. A *linear* trend is shown in Panel (a). Panels (b) and (c) depict *nonlinear* trends. In Panel (b), the economic time

Figure 5.3 Time-Series Growth Patterns

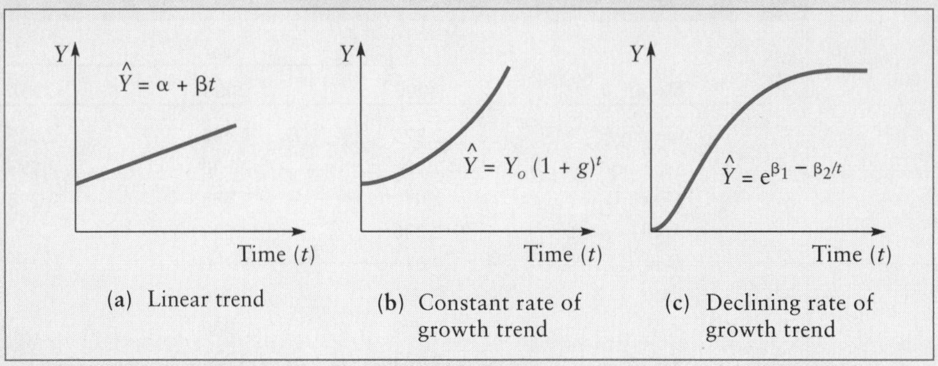

series follows a *constant rate of growth* pattern. The earnings of many corporations follow this type of trend. Panel (c) shows an economic time series that exhibits a declining rate of growth. Sales of a new product may follow this pattern. As market saturation occurs, the rate of growth will decline over time.

LINEAR TRENDS A linear time trend may be estimated by using least-squares regression analysis to provide an equation of a straight line of "best fit." (See Chapter 4 for a further discussion of the least-squares technique.) The equation of a linear time trend is given in the general form

$$\hat{Y}_t = \alpha + \beta t \qquad [5.4]$$

where $\hat{Y}_t$ is the forecast or predicted value for period t, α is the y intercept or constant term, t is a unit of time, and β is an estimate of this trend factor.

EXAMPLE

LINEAR TREND FORECASTING: PRIZER CREAMERY[2]

Suppose one is interested in forecasting monthly ice cream sales of the Prizer Creamery for 2007. A least-squares trend line could be estimated from the ice cream sales data for the past four years (48 monthly observations), as shown in Figure 5.4. Assume that the equation of this line is calculated to be

$$\hat{Y}_t = 30{,}464 + 121.3\,t$$

where $\hat{Y}_t$ = predicted monthly ice cream sales in gallons in month t
30,464 = number of gallons sold when $t = 0$
t = time period (months) (where December 2002 = 0, January 2003 = 1, February 2003 = 2, March 2003 = 3, etc..)

[2] The Marketsearch Company offers a fee-based Internet guide to approximately 25 market research and forecasting studies for ice cream and frozen desserts.

The coefficient (121.3) of t indicates that sales may be expected to increase by 121.3 gallons on the average each month. Based on this trend line and ignoring any seasonal effects, forecasted ice cream sales for August 2007 (t = 56) would be

$$\begin{aligned} Y_{56} &= 30{,}464 + 121.3(56) \\ &= 37{,}257 \text{ gallons} \end{aligned}$$

This *seasonally unadjusted* forecast is given by the August 2007 point (⊙) on the trend line in Figure 5.4. As can be seen in the graph, ice cream sales are subject to seasonal variations. Later in this section we will show how this seasonal effect can be incorporated into the forecast.

Figure 5.4 Prizer Creamery: Monthly Ice Cream Sales

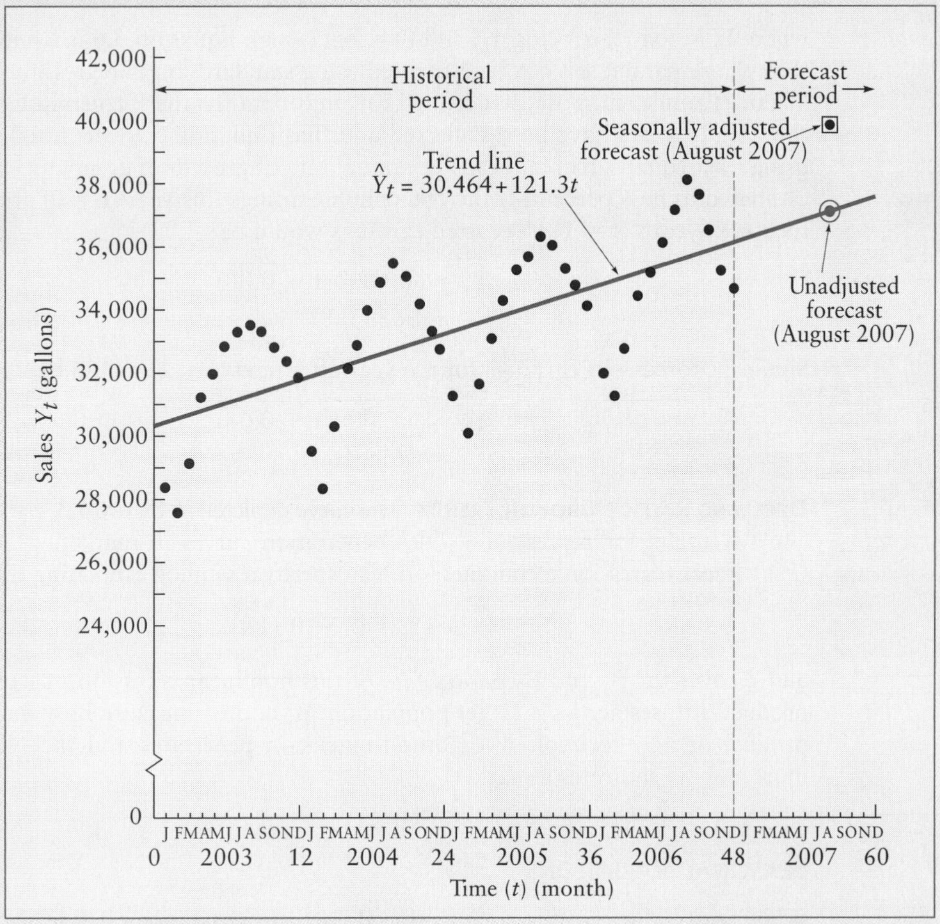

Linear time trend forecasting is easy and inexpensive to do, but it is generally too simple and inflexible to be used in many forecasting circumstances. Constant rate of growth time trends is one alternative.

Constant Rate of Growth Trends The formula for the constant rate of growth forecasting model is

$$\hat{Y}_t = Y_0(1 + g)^t \qquad [5.5]$$

where $\hat{Y}_t$ is the forecasted value for period t, Y_0 is the initial ($t = 0$) value of the time series, g is the constant growth rate per period, and t is a unit of time. The predicted value of the time series in period t ($\hat{Y}_t$) is equal to the initial value of the series (Y_0) compounded at the growth rate (g) for t periods. Because Equation 5.5 is a nonlinear relationship, the parameters cannot be estimated directly with the ordinary least-squares method. However, taking logarithms of both sides of the equation gives

$$\log \hat{Y}_t = \log Y_0 + \log(1 + g) \cdot t$$

or

$$\hat{Y}'_t = \alpha + \beta t \qquad [5.6]$$

where $\hat{Y}'_t = \log \hat{Y}_t$, $\alpha = \log Y_0$, and $\beta = \log(1 + g)$. Equation 5.6 is a linear relationship whose parameters can be estimated using standard linear regression techniques.

For example, suppose that annual earnings data for the Fitzgerald Company for the past 10 years have been collected and that Equation 5.6 was fitted to the data using least-squares techniques. The annual rate of growth of company earnings was estimated to be 6 percent. If the company's earnings this year ($t = 0$) are \$600,000, then next year's ($t = 1$) forecasted earnings would be

$$\hat{Y}_1 = 600{,}000(1 + 0.06)^1$$
$$= \$636{,}000$$

Similarly, forecasted earnings for the year after next ($t = 2$) would be

$$\hat{Y}_2 = 600{,}000(1 + 0.06)^2$$
$$= \$674{,}160$$

Declining Rate of Growth Trends The curve depicted in Figure 5.3, panel (c) is particularly useful for representing sales penetration curves in marketing applications. Using linear regression techniques, one can specify a semilog estimating equation,

$$\log \hat{Y}_t = \beta_1 - \beta_2(1/t)$$

and recover the β_1 and β_2 parameters of this nonlinear diffusion process as a new product diffuses across a target population. β_1 and β_2 measure how quickly a new product or new technology or brand extension penetrates and then slowly (ever more slowly) saturates a market.

Seasonal Variations

When seasonal variations are introduced into a forecasting model, its short-run predictive power may be improved significantly. Seasonal variations may be estimated in a number of ways.

Ratio to Trend Method One approach is the *ratio to trend method*. This method assumes that the trend value is multiplied by the seasonal effect.

EXAMPLE

SEASONALLY ADJUSTED FORECASTS: PRIZER CREAMERY (continued)

Recall in the Prizer Creamery example discussed earlier that a linear trend analysis (Equation 5.4) yielded a sales forecast for August 2007 of 37,257 gallons. This estimate can be adjusted for seasonal effects in the following manner. Assume that over a four-year period (2003–2006) the trend model predicted the August sales patterns shown in Table 5.2 and that actual sales are as indicated. These data indicate that, on the average, August sales have been 7.0 percent higher than the trend value. Hence, the August 2007 sales forecast should be seasonally adjusted *upward* by 7.0 percent to 39,865. The seasonally adjusted forecast is shown by the point (⊡) above the trend line in Figure 5.4. If however, the model predicted February 2007 ($t = 50$) sales to be 36,529, but similar data indicated February sales to be 10.8 percent below trend on the average, the forecast would be adjusted *downward* to 36,529(1 − 0.108) = 32,584 gallons.

Table 5.2 Prizer Creamery's August Ice Cream Sales

(August)	Forecast	Actual	Actual/Forecast
2003	31,434	33,600	1.0689
2004	32,890	35,600	1.0824
2005	34,346	36,400	1.0598
2006	35,801	38,200	1.0670
2007	37,257	—	—
			Sum = 4.2781

Adjustment factor = 4.2781/4 = 1.0695 (i.e., 1.07)

DUMMY VARIABLES Another approach for incorporating seasonal effects into the linear trend analysis model is the use of *dummy variables*. A dummy variable is a variable that normally takes on one of two values—either 0 or 1. Dummy variables, in general, are used to capture the impact of certain qualitative factors in an econometric relationship, such as sex: male-0 and female-1. This method assumes that the seasonal effects are added to the trend value. If a time series consists of quarterly data, then the following model could be used to adjust for seasonal effects:

$$\hat{Y}_t = \alpha + \beta_1 T + \beta_2 D_{1t} + \beta_3 D_{2t} + \beta_4 D_{3t} \quad [5.7]$$

where $D_{1t} = 1$ for first-quarter observations and 0 otherwise, $D_{2t} = 1$ for second-quarter observations and 0 otherwise, $D_{3t} = 1$ for third-quarter observations and 0 otherwise, and α and β are parameters to be estimated using least-squares techniques. In this model the values of the dummy variables (D_{1t}, D_{2t}, D_{3t}) for observations in the fourth quarter of each year (base period) would be equal to zero. In the estimated model the value β_2, D_{1t} represents the impact of a first-quarter observation (D_1) on values of the forecast, Y_t, relative to the forecast from the omitted class (4th quarter), when D_{2t} and D_{3t} take values of 0.

EXAMPLE

Dummy Variables and Seasonal Adjustments: Value-Mart Company

The Value-Mart Company (a small chain of discount department stores) is interested in forecasting quarterly sales for next year (2008) based on Equation 5.7. Using quarterly sales data for the past eight years (2000–2007), the following model was estimated:

$$\hat{Y}_t = 22.50 + 0.250t - 4.50\,D_{1t} - 3.20\,D_{2t} - 2.10\,D_{3t} \qquad [5.8]$$

where $\hat{Y}_t$ = predicted sales ($ million) in quarter t

22.50 = quarterly sales ($ million) when $t = 0$

t = time period (quarter) (where the fourth quarter of 1999 = 0, first quarter of 2000 = 1, second quarter of 2000 = 2, . . .)

The coefficient of t (0.250) indicates that sales may be expected to increase by $0.250 million on the average each quarter. The coefficients of the three dummy variables (−4.50, −3.20, and −2.10) indicate the change (i.e., reduction because the coefficients are negative) in sales in Quarters 1, 2, and 3, respectively, because of seasonal effects. Based on Equation 5.8, Value-Mart's quarterly sales forecasts for 2008 are shown in Table 5.3.

Table 5.3 Value-Mart's Quarterly Sales Forecast (2008)

Quarter	Time Period t	Dummy Variable D_{1t}	D_{2t}	D_{3t}	Sales Forecast ($ Millions) $\hat{Y} = 22.50 + 0.250t - 4.50\,D_{1t} - 3.20\,D_{2t} - 2.10\,D_{3t}$
1	33	1	0	0	26.25
2	34	0	1	0	27.80
3	35	0	0	1	29.15
4	36	0	0	0	31.50

The introduction of these trend and seasonality factors into a forecasting model should significantly improve the model's ability to predict short-run turning points in the data series, provided the historical causal factors have not changed significantly.[3]

The models of time-series forecasting discussed in this section may have substantial value in many areas of business. However, the business forecaster must not rely too heavily on time-series models alone. These models do not seek to relate changes in a data series to the causes underlying observed values in the series, so they are highly susceptible to making poor predictions when the underlying causal factors change. For example, the nation's money supply series has at times proved useful for forecasting inflationary pressure in the economy. But narrow definitions of the nation's money supply gradually broadened to include bank-card lines of credit, which may have become a more important measure of household purchasing power.

[3] See more extensive discussion of these issues in F. Diebold, *Elements of Forecasting*, 2nd ed. (Cincinnati: South-Western College Publishing, 2001).

Figure 5.5 Actual and Expected Inflation

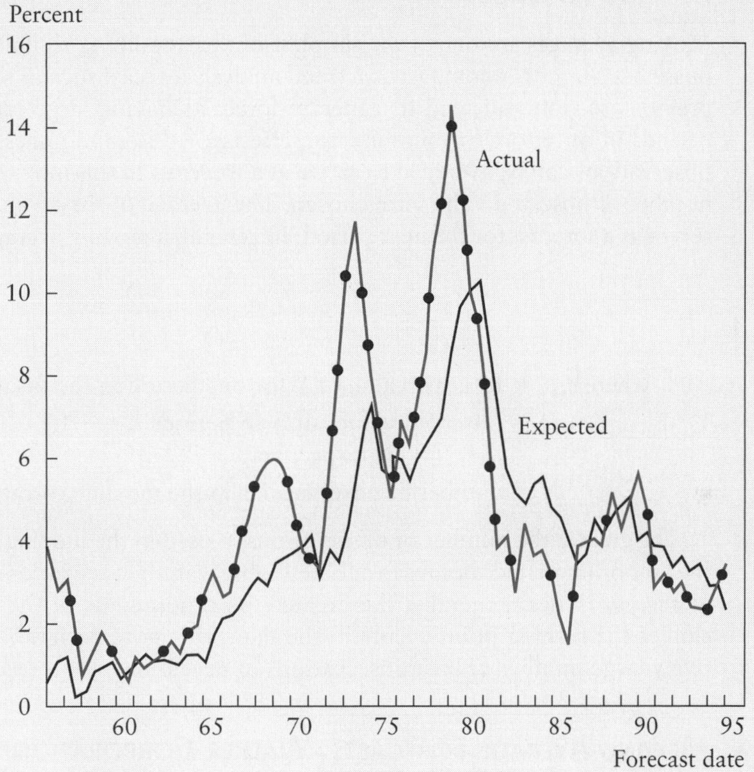

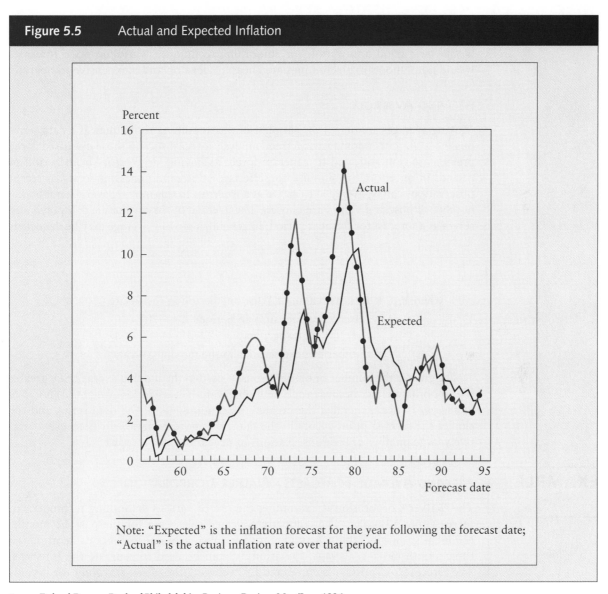

Note: "Expected" is the inflation forecast for the year following the forecast date; "Actual" is the actual inflation rate over that period.

Source: **Federal Reserve Bank of Philadelphia, *Business Review,* May/June 1996.**

Inflation forecasts based on narrow money supply measures today would yield large errors between the actual and predicted inflation (see Figure 5.5).

SMOOTHING TECHNIQUES

Smoothing techniques are another type of time-series forecasting model that assumes a repetitive underlying pattern can be found in the historical values of the variable being forecast. It is assumed that these historical observations represent not only the underlying pattern but also random variations. By taking some form of an average of past observations, smoothing techniques attempt to eliminate the distortions arising from random variation in the series and to base the forecast on a smoothed average of several past observations.

In general, smoothing techniques work best when a data series tends to change slowly from one period to the next with few turning points. Housing price forecasts would be a good application for smoothing techniques. Gasoline price forecasts would not. Smoothing techniques are cheap to develop and inexpensive to operate.

Moving Averages

Moving averages are one of the simplest of the smoothing techniques. If a data series possesses a large random factor, a trend analysis forecast such as those discussed in the previous section will tend to generate forecasts having large errors from period to period. In an effort to minimize the effects of this randomness, a series of recent observations can be averaged to arrive at a forecast. In this moving average method, a number of observed values are chosen. The average of these values is computed and serves as a forecast for the next period. In general, a moving average may be defined as

$$\hat{Y}_{t+1} = \frac{Y_t + Y_{t-1} + \cdots + Y_{t-N+1}}{N} \quad [5.9]$$

where $\hat{Y}_{t+1}$ = forecast value of Y for one period in the future

Y_t, Y_{t-1}, Y_{t-N+1} = observed values of Y in periods $t, t-1, \ldots, t-N+1$, respectively

N = number of observations in the moving average

The greater the number of observations N used in the moving average, the greater the smoothing effect because each new observation receives less weight ($1/N$) as N increases. Hence, generally, the greater the randomness in the data series and the slower the turning point events in the data, the more preferable it is to use a relatively large number of past observations in developing the forecast.

EXAMPLE

Moving Average Forecasts: Walker Corporation

The Walker Corporation is examining the use of various smoothing techniques to forecast monthly sales. The company collected sales data for the past 12 months (2006) as shown in Table 5.4 and Figure 5.6. One technique under consideration is a three-month moving average. Equation 5.9 can be used to generate the forecasts. The forecast for Period 4 is computed by averaging the observed values for Periods 1, 2, and 3.

$$\hat{Y}_4 = \frac{Y_3 + Y_2 + Y_1}{N} \quad [5.10]$$

$$= \frac{1{,}925 + 1{,}400 + 1{,}950}{3}$$

$$= 1{,}758$$

Similarly, the forecast for Period 5 is computed as

$$\hat{Y}_5 = \frac{Y_4 + Y_3 + Y_2}{N} \quad [5.11]$$

$$= \frac{1{,}960 + 1{,}925 + 1{,}400}{3}$$

$$= 1{,}762$$

Table 5.4 Walker Corporation's Three-Month Moving Average Sales Forecast Table

t	Month	Sales ($1,000) Actual Y_t	Forecast $\hat{Y}_t$	Error $(Y_t - \hat{Y}_t)$	$(Y_t - \hat{Y}_t)^2$
1	January 2006	1,950	—	—	—
2	February	1,400	—	—	—
3	March	1,925	—	—	—
4	April	1,960	1,758	202	40,804
5	May	2,800	1,762	1,038	1,077,444
6	June	1,800	2,228	−428	183,184
7	July	1,600	2,187	−587	344,569
8	August	1,450	2,067	−617	380,689
9	September	2,000	1,617	383	146,689
10	October	2,250	1,683	567	321,489
11	November	1,950	1,900	50	2,500
12	December	2,650	2,067	583	339,889
13	January 2007	*	2,283	—	—
					Sum = 2,837,257

$$\text{RMSE} = \sqrt{2{,}837{,}257/9} = \$561(000)$$

Note that if one subtracts $\hat{Y}_4$ from $\hat{Y}_5$, the result is the change in the forecast from $\hat{Y}_4$, or

$$\begin{aligned}\Delta\hat{Y}_4 &= \hat{Y}_5 - \hat{Y}_4\\ &= \frac{Y_4 + Y_3 + Y_2}{N} - \frac{Y_3 + Y_2 + Y_1}{N}\\ &= \frac{Y_4}{N} - \frac{Y_1}{N}\end{aligned} \qquad [5.12]$$

Adding this change to $\hat{Y}_4$, the following alternative expression for $\hat{Y}_5$ can be derived:

$$\hat{Y}_5 = \hat{Y}_4 + \frac{Y_4}{N} - \frac{Y_1}{N} \qquad [5.13]$$

or, in general,

$$\hat{Y}_{t+1} = \hat{Y}_t + \frac{Y_t}{N} - \frac{Y_{t-N}}{N} \qquad [5.14]$$

which indicates that each moving average forecast is equal to the past forecast, $\hat{Y}_t$, plus the weighted effect of the most recent observation, Y_t/N, minus the weighted effect of the oldest observation that has been dropped, Y_{t-N}/N. As N becomes larger, the smoothing effect increases because the new observation, $\hat{Y}_t$, has a small impact on the moving average.

As shown in Table 5.4, Walker's forecast for January 2007 (t = 13) is $2,283(000). Note also that the root mean square error (RMSE) of the three-month (N) moving average period is $561(000).

Figure 5.6 Walker Corporation's Three-Month Moving Average Sales Forecast Chart

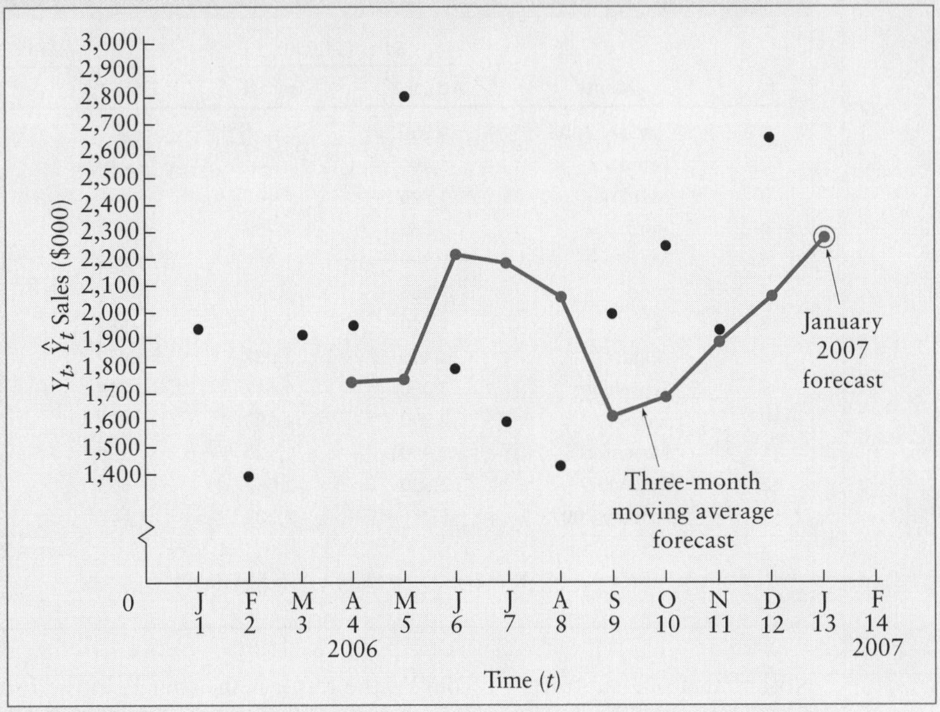

The choice of an appropriate moving average period, that is, the choice of N, should be based on a comparison of the results of the model in forecasting past observations. For example, the forecaster might try a three-period average, a five-period average, and a seven-period average, and compare the accuracy of the alternatives. The best moving average is chosen on the basis of the value of N that minimizes the root mean square error (Equation 5.1).

First-Order Exponential Smoothing

One criticism of moving averages as smoothing techniques is that they normally give equal weight (a weight of $1/N$) to all observations used in preparing the forecast, even though intuition often indicates that the most recent observation probably contains more immediately useful information than more distant observations. Exponential smoothing is designed to overcome this objection.[4]

Consider the following alternative forecasting model:

$$\hat{Y}_{t+1} = wY_t + (1 - w)\hat{Y}_t \qquad [5.15]$$

[4] More complex double exponential smoothing models generally give more satisfactory results than first-order exponential smoothing models when the data possess a linear trend over time. See Newbold and Bos, *Introductory Business Forecasting* (Cincinnati: South-Western College Publishing, 1994).

This model weights the most recent observation by w (some value between 0 and 1 inclusive), and the past forecast by $(1 - w)$. A large w indicates that a heavy weight is being placed on the most recent observation.[5]

Using Equation 5.15, a forecast for $\hat{Y}_t$ may also be written as

$$\hat{Y}_t = wY_{t-1} + (1 - w)(\hat{Y}_{t-1}) \qquad [5.16]$$

By substituting Equation 5.16 into 5.15, we get

$$\hat{Y}_{t+1} = wY_t + w(1 - w)Y_{t-1} + (1 - w)^2\hat{Y}_{t-1} \qquad [5.17]$$

By continuing this process of substitution for past forecasts, we obtain the general equation

$$\hat{Y}_{t+1} = wY_t + w(1 - w)Y_{t-1} + w(1 - w)^2Y_{t-2} + w(1 - w)^3Y_{t-3} + \cdots \qquad [5.18]$$

Equation 5.18 shows that the general formula (Equation 5.15) for an exponentially weighted moving average is a weighted average of all past observations, with the weights defined by the geometric progression:

$$w,\ (1 - w)w,\ (1 - w)^2w,\ (1 - w)^3w,\ (1 - w)^4w,\ (1 - w)^5w, \ldots \qquad [5.19]$$

For example, a w of 2/3 would produce the following series of weights:

$$\begin{aligned} w &= 0.667 \\ (1 - w)w &= 0.222 \\ (1 - w)^2w &= 0.074 \\ (1 - w)^3w &= 0.024 \\ (1 - w)^4w &= 0.0082 \\ (1 - w)^5w &= 0.0027 \end{aligned}$$

With a high initial value of w, heavy weight is placed on the most recent observation, and rapidly declining weights are placed on older values.

Another way of writing Equation 5.15 is

$$\hat{Y}_{t+1} = \hat{Y}_t + w(Y_t - \hat{Y}_t) \qquad [5.20]$$

This formula indicates that the new forecast is equal to the old forecast plus w times the error in the most recent forecast. A w that is close to 1 indicates a quick adjustment process for any error in the preceding forecast. Similarly, a w closer to 0 suggests a slow error correction process.

It should be apparent from Equations 5.15 and 5.20 that exponential forecasting techniques can be easy to use. They only require last period's forecast, last period's observation, plus a value for the weighting factor, w. The optimal weighting factor is normally determined by making successive forecasts using past data with various values of w and choosing the w that minimizes the root mean square error (RMSE) given in Equation 5.1.

---

[5] The greater the amount of serial correlation (correlation of values from period to period), the larger will be the optimal value of *w*.

EXAMPLE

Exponential Smoothing: Walker Corporation (continued)

Consider again the Walker Corporation example discussed earlier. Suppose that the company is interested in generating sales forecasts using the first-order exponential smoothing technique. The results are shown in Table 5.5. To illustrate the approach, an exponential weight w of 0.5 will be used. To get the process started, one needs to make an initial forecast of the variable. This forecast might be a weighted average or some simple forecast, such as Equation 5.2:

$$\hat{Y}_{t+1} = Y_t$$

The latter approach will be used. Hence the forecast for Month 2 made in Month 1 would be \$1,950(000) ($\hat{Y}_{t+1} = 1{,}950$). The Month 3 forecast value is (using Equation 5.20)

$$\begin{aligned}\hat{Y}_3 &= 1{,}950 + 0.5(1{,}400 - 1{,}950) \\ &= 1{,}950 - 275 = \$1{,}675(000)\end{aligned}$$

Similarly, the Month 4 forecast equals

$$\begin{aligned}\hat{Y}_4 &= 1{,}675 + 0.5(1{,}925 - 1{,}675) \\ &= \$1{,}800(000)\end{aligned}$$

The remaining forecasts are calculated in a similar manner.

As can be seen in Table 5.5, Walker's sales forecast for January 2007 using the first-order exponential smoothing technique is \$2,322(000). Also, the root mean square error of this forecasting method (with $w = 0.50$) is \$491(000).

Table 5.5 Walker Corporation: First-Order Exponential Smoothing Sales Forecast

		Sales (\$1,000)		Error	
t	Month	Actual Y_t	Forecast $\hat{Y}_t$	$(Y_t - \hat{Y}_t)$	$(Y_t - \hat{Y}_t)^2$
1	January 2006	1,950	—	—	—
2	February	1,400	1,950	−550	302,500
3	March	1,925	1,675	250	62,500
4	April	1,960	1,800	160	25,600
5	May	2,800	1,880	920	846,400
6	June	1,800	2,340	−540	291,600
7	July	1,600	2,070	−470	220,900
8	August	1,450	1,835	−385	148,225
9	September	2,000	1,642	358	128,164
10	October	2,250	1,821	429	184,041
11	November	1,950	2,036	−86	7,396
12	December	2,650	1,993	657	431,649
13	January 2007	—	2,322	—	—
					Sum = 2,648,975

$$\text{RMSE} = \sqrt{2{,}648{,}975/11} = \$491(000)$$

BAROMETRIC TECHNIQUES

The time-series forecasting models already discussed assume that future patterns in an economic time series may be predicted by projecting a repeat of past patterns, but few economic time series exhibit consistent enough cyclical variations to make simple projection forecasting reliable. For example, Table 5.6 conveys why the prediction of a business cycle's turning point proves to be so difficult. Although the duration of postwar U.S. business cycles averages 67 months (from peak to peak), three cycles have lasted 100 months or more, while others have been as short as 32 and even 18 months. Economists, however, have long recognized that if it were possible to isolate sets of time series that exhibited a close correlation, and if one or more of these time series normally *led* (in a consistent manner) the time series in which the forecaster had interest, then this leading series could be used as a predictor or barometer.

Although the concept of leading or barometric forecasting is not new,[6] current barometric forecasting is based largely on the work done at the National Bureau of Economic Research (www.nber.org). The barometric forecasting model developed there is used primarily to identify potential future changes in general business conditions, rather than conditions for a specific industry or firm.

LEADING, LAGGING, AND COINCIDENT INDICATORS

Economic indicators may be classified as leading, coincident, or lagging indicators, depending on their timing relative to business cycle peaks and troughs (see Figure 5.7).

Table 5.6 Duration of U.S. Business Cycles (in months)

				Business Cycle	
		Contraction*	Expansion†	Trough to Trough	Peak to Peak
Oct 1945	Nov 1948	8	37	88	45
Oct 1949	July 1953	11	45	48	56
May 1954	Aug 1957	10	39	55	49
Apr 1958	Apr 1960	8	24	47	32
Feb 1961	Dec 1969	10	106	34	116
Nov 1970	Nov 1973	11	36	117	47
Mar 1975	Jan 1980	16	58	52	74
July 1980	July 1981	6	12	64	18
Nov 1982	July 1990	16	92	28	108
Mar 1991	Mar 2001	8	120	100	116
Nov 2001		8		128	128
Average post-war cycle		10	57	67	67

* Months from previous peak to trough.
† Months from trough to next peak.

Source: "U.S. Business Cycle Expansions and Contractions," National Bureau of Economic Research at www.nber.org

[6] Andrew Carnegie used to count the number of smoke-belching chimneys in Pittsburgh to forecast the level of business activity and consequently the demand for steel.

Figure 5.7 Barometric Indicators

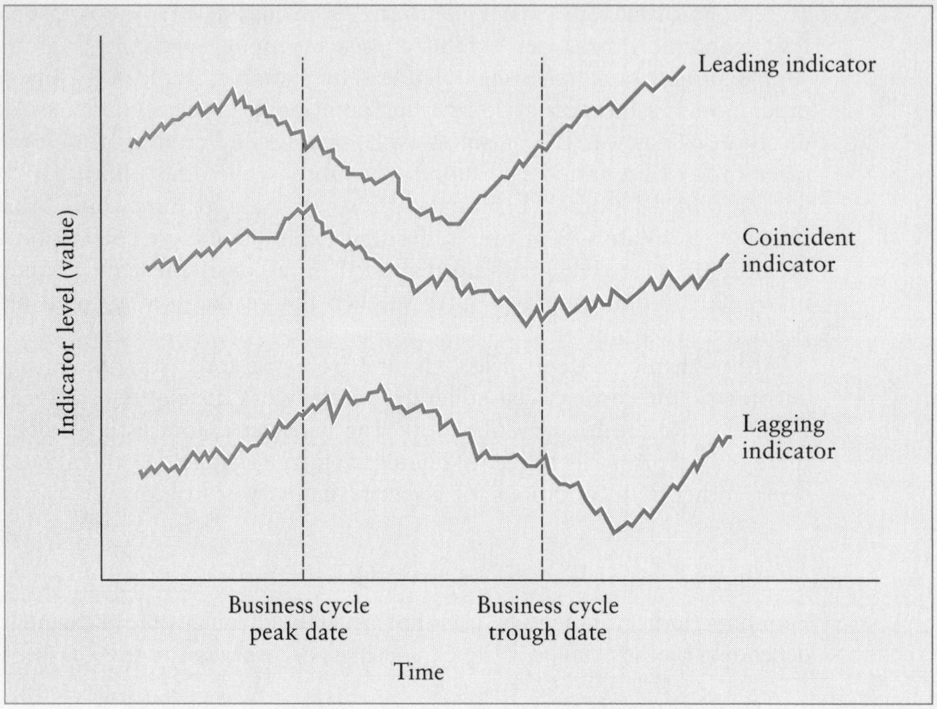

The *Conference Board,* a private not-for-profit research institute in New York, identified 11 series that tend to lead the peaks and troughs of business cycles, 4 series of roughly coincident indicators of economic activity, and 7 series that tend to lag the peaks and troughs of economic activity. Table 5.7 lists the title of each series and the mean lead or lag of the series in relation to peaks and troughs of economic activity.

The rationale for the use of many of the series listed in this table is obvious. Many of these series represent commitments to future levels of economic activity. Building permits precede housing starts, and orders for durable goods precede their actual production. For some of the other indicators, the nature of the causal relationships involved is not quite so clear. The value of any particular time series as a predictor of future changes in another series depends on a number of factors. First, the user must be concerned with the success of the series in predicting the turning points in economic activity. Even the best series exhibit only 80–90 percent accuracy. In addition, a series is more valuable not only if it consistently leads (lags) business cycles but also if it lacks a large variability in the *length* of the lead (lag). Finally, a series that is free of large random or seasonal fluctuations should be rated high because it will not give as many false signals.

The main value of leading and lagging indicators is in predicting the *direction* of future change in economic activity. These indicators reveal little or nothing about the *magnitude* of the changes.

EXAMPLE

LEADING INDICATORS CHANGE[7]

The Index of Leading Economic Indicators, which can be accessed at http://www.conference-board.org, is constantly under scrutiny by both private and public forecasting agencies. When any series appears outdated or begins to generate misleading signals, a replacement can often emerge from a consensus of best practices in business forecasting. Three of the series in Table 5.7 have been ranked "Poor" at predicting recessions and recoveries in the last decade by the Conference Board, a prominent trade association of major corporations that collects, analyzes, and distributes business cycle data. Two of the three (i.e., manufacturers' unfilled orders for durables and the change in sensitive materials prices) were removed from the Index and replaced by the interest rate spread between 10-year Treasury bond yields and 3-month Treasury bill yields.

The interest rate spread is an attempt to capture the effects of monetary policy on the business cycle. A long-bond yield at least 1.21 percent higher than the T-bill yield implies less than a 0.05 probability of recession four quarters ahead. If the Federal Reserve tightens credit, however, such that short-term interest rates rise 0.82 percent above long-term rates, the probability of recession increases to 50 percent and more. At an interest rate spread of 2.40 percent, the probability of recession four quarters ahead rises to 90 percent. This new indicator of credit conditions should effectively supplement the generally poor third predictor, the M2 measure of the nation's money supply. However, because oil price hikes have returned to a position of prominence in business planning, the sensitive materials price series may soon be restored to the Index. For descriptions of recent revisions in this index, see http://www.tcb-indicators.org.

DIFFUSION AND COMPOSITE INDEXES

To overcome some of the weaknesses associated with forecasting based on leading series, economists have developed the *diffusion index*. The primary advantage of this index is that it reduces the chances of making a false prediction based on a short-term fluctuation in one series alone. When all indicators in the index are rising, the diffusion index equals 100; when all are falling, it equals 0; and when one-fourth are rising, it equals 25. During business cycle expansions, the National Bureau of Economic Research has found that this index is normally above 50 percent, and during contractions it is normally below 50 percent. Diffusion indexes may be constructed using any combination of indicator series that the forecaster feels is appropriate.

Composite indexes, which are weighted averages of several indicators, are also designed to overcome the problem of making false predictions based on short-term fluctuations in a single series. The performances of the composite indexes for the 11 leading, 4 coincident, and 7 lagging indicators are summarized in Table 5.7. For example, consider the composite index of 4 coincident indicators (listed at line 920 in Table 5.7). This index missed the July 1990 peak by one month (−1 meaning one month late) but exactly coincided with the March 1991 business cycle trough.

[7] Based on "Makeup of Leading Indicators May Shift," *Wall Street Journal,* August 11, 1996, p. A2.

Table 5.7 Cyclical Leads (−) and Lags (+) for Leading, Coincident, and Lagging Indicators (length in months)

		At Reference Peaks[1]									
Series No.	Series Title	July 1990	July 1981	Jan. 1980	Nov. 1973	Dec. 1969	Apr. 1960	Aug. 1957	July 1953	Nov. 1948	Mean
	LEADING INDICATORS										
1	Average weekly hours, manufacturing	−15	−7	−10	−7	−14	−11	−21	−3	−11	−11.0
5	Average weekly initial claims for unemployment insurance (inverted)[2]	−22	0	−16	−9	−11	−12	−23	−10	−13	−12.9
8	Manufacturers' new orders in 1987 dollars, consumer goods and materials	−2	−2	−13	−8	−13	−13	−25	−3	−5	−9.3
32	Vendor performance, slower deliveries diffusion index	+1	−3	−9	0	−4	−14	−28	−12	−7	−8.4
20	Contracts and orders for plant and equipment in 1987 dollars	−7	−3	−10	−1	−11	−13	−9	−5	−7	−7.3
29	Building permits, new private housing units	−21	−10	−19	−11	−10	−17	−30	−8	−13	−15.4
92	Change in manufacturers' unfilled orders in 1987 dollars, durable goods (smoothed)[3]	−3	−6	−13	−6	−7	−12	−19	−26	−3	−10.6
99	Change in sensitive materials prices (smoothed)[3]	+2	−7	−7	+3	−10	−17	−17	−9	n.a.	−7.8
19	Index of stock prices, 500 common stocks	−1	−8	NST	−10	−12	−9	−13	−6	−30	−11.1
106	Money supply M2 in 1987 dollars	−7	NST	−24	−10	−11	NST	−16	NST	−17	−14.2
83	Index of consumer expectations	−18	−2	−38	−15	−10	−2	−9	−5	n.a.	−12.4
910	Composite index of 11 leading indicators	−18	−8	−15	−9	−11	−11	−20	−5	−7	−11.6
940	Ratio, coincident index to lagging index	−4	−4	−15	−11	−9	−12	−27	−9	−10	−11.2
	COINCIDENT INDICATORS										
41	Employees on nonagricultural payrolls	−1	0	+2	+11	+3	0	−5	−1	−2	+0.8
51	Personal income less transfer payments in 1987 dollars	−3	+1	0	0	NST	+1	0	−1	−1	−0.4
47	Index of industrial production	+2	0	+2	0	−2	−3	−5	0	−4	−1.1
57	Manufacturing and trade sales in 1987 dollars	−4	−6	−10	0	−2	−3	−6	−3	+1	−3.7
920	Composite index of 4 coincident indicators	−1	+1	0	0	−2	−3	−5	0	−1	−1.2
	LAGGING INDICATORS										
91	Average duration of unemployment (inverted)[1]	−13	+5	−6	−2	−2	+2	+1	+2	0	−1.4
77	Ratio, manufacturing, and trade inventories to sales in 1987 dollars	+6	+15	+5	+16	+11	+9	+8	+5	+8	+9.2
62	Change in index of labor cost per unit of output, manufacturing (smoothed)[3]	+8	+6	+5	+16	+1	+10	+6	+6	0	+6.4
109	Average prime rate charged by banks	−14	+1	+3	+10	+2	+3	+4	+7	NST	+2.0
101	Commercial and industrial loans outstanding in 1987 dollars	0	+14	+2	+10	+8	NST	+1	−1	+3	+4.6
95	Ratio, consumer installment credit to personal income	−10	NST	−7	+5	NST	+8	+5	+5	NST	+1.0
120	Change in Consumer Price Index for services (smoothed)[3]	+2	+2	+5	+11	+4	−6	−5	n.a.	n.a.	+1.9
930	Composite index of 7 lagging indicators	−8	+3	+3	+13	+3	+3	+4	+5	NST	+3.1

[1] *Note:* Reference peaks and troughs are the cyclical turning points in overall business activity; specific peaks and troughs are the cyclical turning points in individual series. This table lists, for the composite indexes and their components, the leads (−) and lags (+) of the specific peaks and troughs in relation to the corresponding reference peaks and troughs. See National Bureau of Economic Research information on the selection of cyclical peaks and troughs available at http://www.nber.org. Data for the March 2001 turning point are not comparable and therefore are unreported.

n.a. Not available. Data needed to determine a specific turning point are not available.

NST No specific turn. No specific turning point is discernible in the data.

Table 5.7 Cyclical Leads (−) and Lags (+) for Leading, Coincident, and Lagging Indicators (length in months) (*continued*)

Series No.	Series Title	At Reference Troughs[1] July 1990	July 1981	Jan. 1980	Nov. 1973	Dec. 1969	Apr. 1960	Aug. 1957	July 1953	Nov. 1948	Mean
	LEADING INDICATORS										
1	Average weekly hours, manufacturing	+1	−1	0	0	−2	−2	0	−1	−6	−1.2
5	Average weekly initial claims for unemployment insurance (inverted)[1]	0	−2	−2	0	−1	0	0	+4	0	−0.1
8	Manufacturers' new orders in 1987 dollars, consumer goods and materials	0	−1	−2	0	0	0	−2	−7	−4	−1.8
32	Vendor performance, slower deliveries diffusion index	0	−8	−2	−1	+1	−11	−4	−6	−7	−4.2
20	Contracts and orders for plant and equipment in 1987 dollars	+3	+4	−2	+9	−1	+1	−1	−2	−6	+0.6
29	Building permits, new private housing units	−2	−13	−3	0	−10	−2	−2	−8	−9	−5.4
92	Change in manufacturers' unfilled orders in 1987 dollars, durable goods (smoothed)[2]	+20	−2	−1	+1	−3	−9	−2	−5	−4	−0.6
99	Change in sensitive materials prices (smoothed)[2]	0	−5	0	−2	−2	−1	−4	−4	−4	−2.4
19	Index of stock prices, 500 common stocks	−5	−4	NST	−3	−5	−4	−4	−8	−4	−4.6
106	Money supply M2 in 1987 dollars	−2	NST	−2	−2	−7	NST	−3	NST	−15	−5.2
83	Index of consumer expectations	−5	−8	−4	−1	−6	−3	+1	−6	n.a.	−4.0
910	Composite index of 11 leading indicators	−2	−10	−2	−1	−1	−2	−2	−4	−4	−3.1
940	Ratio, coincident index to lagging index	−2	−10	−2	0	−8	−1	0	−5	0	−2.9
	COINCIDENT INDICATORS										
41	Employees on nonagricultural payrolls	+11	0	0	+1	0	0	+1	+3	0	+1.8
51	Personal income less transfer payments in 1987 dollars	+8	0	0	−1	NST	−2	0	−1	−3	+0.1
47	Index of industrial production	0	+1	0	0	0	0	0	−1	0	0
57	Manufacturing and trade sales in 1987 dollars	−2	+1	−1	0	0	−1	0	−5	−3	−1.2
920	Composite index of 4 coincident indicators	0	+1	0	0	0	0	0	+2	0	+0.3
	LAGGING INDICATORS										
91	Average duration of unemployment (inverted)[1]	+19	+8	+6	+10	+19	+5	+6	+12	+8	+10.3
77	Ratio, manufacturing, and trade inventories to sales in 1987 dollars	+36	+14	+6	+44	+27	+14	+13	+12	+9	+17.4
62	Change in index of labor cost per unit of output, manufacturing (smoothed)[2]	+6	+10	+7	+8	+12	+7	+6	+11	+1	+9.7
109	Average prime rate charged by banks	+35	+8	+1	+25	+16	+57	+4	+14	NST	+17.9
101	Commercial and industrial loans outstanding in 1987 dollars	+24	+11	+8	+18	+15	NST	+4	+3	−1	+10.2
95	Ratio, consumer installment credit to personal income	+21	0	NST	+11	NST	+9	+7	+6	NST	+9.0
120	Change in Consumer Price Index for services (smoothed)[2]	+18	+2	+3	+5	+27	+5	+8	n.a.	n.a.	+9.7
930	Composite index of 7 lagging indicators	+36	+7	+3	+21	+15	+6	+4	+9	NST	+9.3

Source: *Survey of Current Business,* U.S. Department of Commerce, through December 1995, no. C52. Thereafter, these data are available from The Conference Board, Business Cycle Indicators Project at http://www.conference-board.org.

[2] This series is inverted (i.e., low values are peaks and high values are troughs).

[3] This series is smoothed by an autoregressive-moving-average filter developed) by Statistics Canada.

Survey and Opinion-Polling Techniques

Survey and opinion polling are other forecasting tools that may be helpful in making short-period forecasts. These techniques may be used for forecasting the overall level of economic activity, or they may be used within the firm for forecasting future sales. The rationale for the use of survey and opinion polling is that certain attitudes having an impact on economic decisions may be identified in advance of the actual implementation of the decision. If individuals who are responsible for making these decisions are polled, they may provide insights into their intended actions. Business firms normally plan additions to plant and equipment well in advance of the actual expenditures; consumers plan expenditures for autos, vacations, and education in advance of the actual purchase; and governments at all levels prepare budgets indicating priorities and amounts of intended expenditures.

The greatest value of survey and opinion polling techniques is that they may help to uncover changes in past relationships that the quantitative techniques assume will remain stable. If consumer tastes are changing or if business executives begin to lose confidence in the economy, survey techniques may be able to uncover these trends before their impact is felt.

Forecasting Macroeconomic Activity

Some of the best-known surveys available from private and governmental sources include the following:

1. *Plant and equipment expenditure plans.* Surveys of business intentions regarding plant and equipment expenditures are conducted by McGraw-Hill, the National Industrial Conference Board, the U.S. Department of Commerce, *Fortune* magazine, the Securities and Exchange Commission, and a number of individual trade associations. The McGraw-Hill survey, for example, is conducted twice yearly and covers all large corporations and many medium-sized firms. The survey reports plans for expenditures on fixed assets, as well as for expenditures on research and development. More than 50 percent of all new investment is accounted for by the McGraw-Hill survey.

   The Department of Commerce–Bureau of Economic Analysis plant and equipment expenditures survey is conducted quarterly and published regularly in the *Survey of Current Business.* The sample is larger and more comprehensive than that used by McGraw-Hill.

   The National Industrial Conference Board surveys capital appropriations commitments made by the board of directors of 1,000 manufacturing firms. The survey picks up capital expenditure plans that are to be made sometime in the future and for which funds have been appropriated. It is especially useful to firms that sell heavily to manufacturers and may aid in picking turning points in plant and equipment expenditures. This survey is published in the *Survey of Current Business.* You can access the *Survey of Current Business* on the Internet at http://www.bea.gov.

2. *Plans for inventory changes and sales expectations.* Business executives' expectations about future sales and their intentions about changes in inventory levels are reported in surveys conducted by the U.S. Department of Commerce, McGraw-Hill, Dun and Bradstreet, the Institute for Supply Management, and

the National Association of Purchasing Agents. The National Association of Purchasing Agents survey, for example, is conducted monthly, using a large sample of purchasing executives from a broad range of geographical locations and industrial activities in manufacturing firms.

3. *Consumer expenditure plans.* Consumer intentions to purchase specific products such as household appliances, automobiles, and homes are reported by the Survey Research Center at the University of Michigan (http://www.isr.umich.edu/src/) and by the Census Bureau. The Census Bureau survey, for example, is aimed at uncovering varying aspects of consumer expenditure plans, including income, holdings of liquid and nonliquid assets, the likelihood of making future durable goods purchases, and consumer indebtedness.

SALES FORECASTING

Opinion polling and survey techniques are also used on a micro level within the firm for forecasting sales. Some of the variations of opinion polling that are used include the following:

1. *Sales force polling.* Some firms survey their own salespeople in the field about their expectations for future sales by specific geographical area and product line. The idea is that the employees who are closest to the ultimate customers may have significant insights into the state of the future market.
2. *Surveys of consumer intentions.* Some firms (especially in durable goods industries) conduct their own surveys of specific consumer purchases. Consider an auto dealer who pursues a "customer for life" relationship with his or her target market. Such a dealer, or a furniture company, may conduct a mail survey to estimate target households' intentions of purchasing replacement autos or furniture.

ECONOMETRIC MODELS

Another forecasting tool that is available to the managerial economist is econometric modeling. Econometrics is a combination of theory, statistical analysis, and mathematical model building to explain economic relationships. Econometric models may vary in their level of sophistication from the simple to the extremely complex. Econometric techniques for demand estimation were discussed in Chapter 4.

ADVANTAGES OF ECONOMETRIC FORECASTING TECHNIQUES

Forecasting models based on econometric methodology possess a number of significant advantages over time-series analysis (e.g., trend projection) models, barometric models, and survey or opinion poll-based techniques. The most significant advantage is that they identify independent variables (such as price or advertising expenditures in a demand model) that the manager may be able to manipulate.

Another advantage of econometric models is that they predict not only the direction of change in an economic series, but also the magnitude of that change. This capability represents a substantial improvement over the trend projection models, which failed to identify turning points, and the barometric models, which do not forecast the magnitudes of expected changes.

A third advantage of econometric models is their adaptability. On the basis of a comparison between forecast values and actual values, the model can be modified (i.e., existing parameters may be reestimated and new variables or relationships developed) to improve future forecasts.

SINGLE-EQUATION MODELS

The simplest form of an econometric model is the single-equation model, as was developed for explaining the demand for Sherwin-Williams house paint in Chapter 4. Once the parameters of the demand equation are estimated, the model can be used to make forecasts of demand for house paint in a given region.

EXAMPLE

SINGLE-EQUATION FORECASTS: THE DEMAND FOR GAME-DAY ATTENDANCE IN THE NFL[8]

Welki and Zlatoper report a model that explains the major determinants of the demand for game-day attendance at National Football League games. This type of forecasting model might be used by a team to plan the most opportune times for special promotions and to predict demand for items sold at the stadium concession outlets. These variables were used to estimate the model that follows:

ATTENDANCE	game attendance
PRICE	average ticket price
INCOME	real per capita income
COMPCOST	price of parking at one game
HMTMRECORD	season's winning proportion of the home team prior to game day
VSTMRECORD	season's winning proportion of the visiting team prior to game day
GAME	number of regular season games played by the home team
TEMP	high temperature on game day
RAIN	dummy variable 1 = rain, 0 = no rain
DOME	dummy variable 1 = indoors, 0 = outdoors
DIVRIVAL	dummy variable 1 = teams are in same division, 0 = teams are not in same division
CONRIVAL	dummy variable 1 = conference game, 0 = nonconference game
NONSUNDAY	dummy variable 1 = game day is not Sunday, 0 = game day is Sunday
SUNNIGHT	dummy variable 1 = game moved to Sunday night for coverage on ESPN, 0 otherwise
BLACKOUT	dummy variable = 1 if game is blacked out for local TV, 0 otherwise

[8] Andrew M. Welki and Thomas J. Zlatoper, "U.S. Professional Football: The Demand for Game-Day Attendance in 1991," *Managerial and Decision Economics* (September–October 1994), pp. 489–495.

Independent Variable	Expected Sign	Estimated Coefficient	*T*-Statistic
INTERCEPT		98053.00	11.49
PRICE	−	−642.02	−3.08
INCOME	?	−1.14	−3.12
COMPCOST	−	574.94	1.34
HMTMRECORD	+	16535.00	6.38
VSTMRECORD	?	2588.70	1.05
GAME	?	−718.65	−3.64
TEMP	?	−66.17	−1.27
RAIN	−	−2184.40	−1.23
DOME	?	−3171.70	−1.66
DIVRIVAL	+	−1198.00	−0.70
CONRIVAL	?	−1160.00	−0.58
NONSUNDAY	+	4114.80	1.74
SUNNIGHT	+	804.60	0.28
BLACKOUT	−	−5261.00	−3.15

These results indicate that weather conditions have little impact on the attendance at games. Fans appear to favor games played outdoors rather than in domed stadiums. Conference and divisional rivalries do not appear to impact demand greatly. Higher prices negatively impact attendance, but demand appears to be inelastic at current price levels. The quality of the team, as measured by its winning percentage, has a significant positive impact on attendance. A similar model could be used as the basis for forecasting demand for any type of athletic event.

MULTI-EQUATION MODELS

Although in many cases single-equation models may accurately specify the relationship that is being examined, frequently the interrelationships may be so complex that a system of several equations becomes necessary. To illustrate, we examine a simple model of the national economy:

$$C = \alpha_1 + \beta_1 Y + \varepsilon_1 \qquad [5.21]$$

$$I = \alpha_2 + \beta_2 P_{t-1} + \varepsilon_2 \qquad [5.22]$$

$$T = \beta_3 GDP + \varepsilon_3 \qquad [5.23]$$

$$GDP = C + I + G \qquad [5.24]$$

$$Y = GDP - T \qquad [5.25]$$

where C = consumption expenditures
I = investment
P_{t-1} = profits, lagged one period
GDP = gross domestic product
T = taxes
Y = national income
G = government expenditures

Table 5.8 Characteristics of Three Econometric Models of the U.S. Economy

	Model		
Characteristic	Wharton Econometric Forecasting Associates	Chase Econometric Associates	Townsend-Greenspan
Approximate number of variables forecasted	10,000	700	800
Forecast horizon (quarters)	2	10–12	6–10
Frequency of model updates (times per year)	12	12	4
Date model forecast first regularly issued	1963	1970	1965
Forecasting techniques			
(a) Econometric model	60%	70%	45%
(b) Judgment	30%	20%	45%
(c) Time-series methods	—	5%	—
(d) Current data analysis	10%	5%	10%

Source: Stephen K. McNees, "The Record of Thirteen Forecasters," *New England Economic Review,* September–October 1981, pp. 5–21; and Andrew Bauer et al., "Transparency, Expectations, and Forecasts," *Federal Reserve Bank St. Louis Review,* September–October, 2003, pp. 1–25.

Equations 5.21, 5.22, and 5.23 are behavioral or structural equations, whereas Equations 5.24 and 5.25 are identities or definitional equations. Once parameters of a system of equations have been estimated,[9] forecasts may be generated by substituting known or estimated values for the independent variables into the system and solving for a forecast.

Complex Models of the U.S. Economy A number of complex multiple-equation econometric models of the U.S. economy have been developed and are used to forecast business activity. Information on three of these models and the forecasting techniques they employ is summarized in Table 5.8. As can be seen, some of the large econometric models still rely heavily on the judgment of their staffs of economists.

Consensus Forecasts: Blue Chip Forecaster Surveys

The Federal Reserve Bank of Philadelphia (Livingston surveys) and Blue Chip Economic Indicators in Aspen, CO conduct semiannual surveys of leading U.S. economists regarding their forecasts of unemployment, inflation, stock prices, and economic growth. The 50 to 60 economists who are regularly surveyed represent a cross-section from large corporations and banks, labor unions, government, investment banking firms, and universities. The Livingston and Blue Chip Forecaster surveys have been used by federal and state budget offices and many corporations to gauge the expectation of businesses regarding future economic growth and inflation.

[9] See, for example, Ernest R. Berndt, *The Practice of Econometrics* (Reading, MA: Addison-Wesley Publishing Co., 1991), Chapter 8.

Figure 5.8 Livingston and Blue Chip Forecasts of GDP Growth

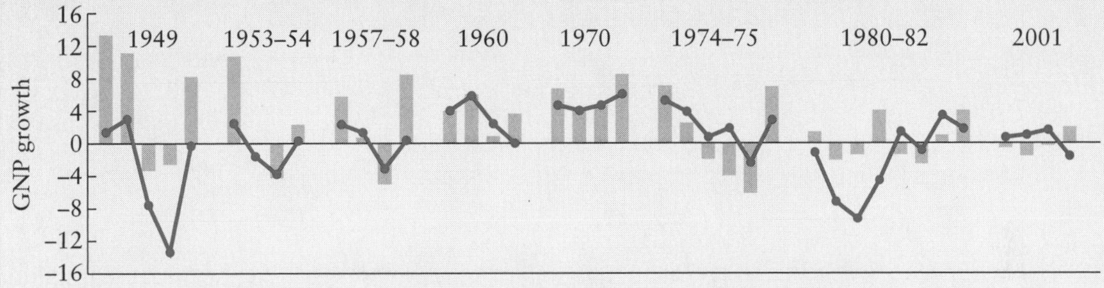

Note: Bars indicate actual values. Lines connecting dots reflect forecasts.

As a broad-based consensus forecast, the Livingston and Blue Chip survey data tend to be more stable over time than any individual forecast. Refer again to Figure 5.5 and notice the evidence that economists have tended to underestimate both increases and decreases in the inflation rate.[10] Figure 5.8 indicates the record of the Livingston and Blue Chip forecasts in predicting major expansions and recessions. As can be seen, economists have tended to predict well the relatively moderate recessions and expansions but have not predicted sharp short recessions such as the ones that occurred in 1974–75 and in 2001.[11]

STOCHASTIC TIME-SERIES ANALYSIS

Finally, consider two forecasting approaches that capitalize on the interdependencies in business data: stochastic time-series analysis and input-output analysis. Deterministic time-series analysis, discussed earlier, was concerned with extrapolating deterministic past trends in the data (e.g., seasonal effects and population growth time trends). In contrast, stochastic time-series analysis attempts to remove deterministic time trends and instead model, estimate, and hopefully replicate the stochastic process generating any remaining patterns in the data across successive time periods (i.e., any remaining autocorrelation patterns). Autocorrelation was discussed in Appendix 4A.

Consider a simple autoregressive first-order process with positive drift α,

$$y_t = \alpha + \beta y_{t-1} + \varepsilon_t \qquad \varepsilon \overset{iid}{\sim} N(0, \sigma_\varepsilon^2) \qquad [5.26]$$

where $\beta = 1$ by hypothesis and where ε_t is a pure white noise disturbance drawn independently each period from a zero-mean, constant-variance normal probability distribution (an iid, independent and identically distributed, disturbance). As illustrated

[10] Based on Herb Taylor, "The Livingston Surveys: A History of Hopes and Fears," *Business Review*, Federal Reserve Bank of Philadelphia, May–June 1996, pp. 15–25.

[11] Based on Kevin Kliesen, "The 2001 Recession," *Federal Reserve Bank St Louis Review*, September–October 2003, pp. 23–38.

Figure 5.9 Random Walks Illustrated

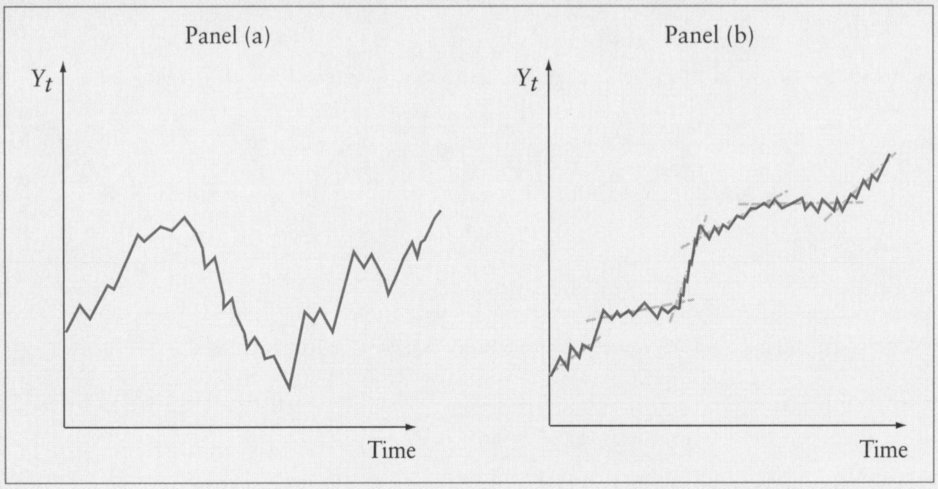

in Figure 5.9 Panel (a), when α equals zero, such a series has no tendency to revert to any particular value (no "mean reversion"). In contrast, such series wander, and are inherently unforecastable, and therefore the last realization of y_t is the best prediction of the next realization of the series. Similarly, when α is nonzero, the level of y_t has no tendency to mean revert to any particular trend line; each innovation can result in a new trend line as illustrated in Figure 5.9 Panel (b). This famous "random walk" model is applicable to the level of stock prices. Under the efficient markets hypothesis, a stock price such as y_t in Equation 5.26 is "fully informative" in the sense that it incorporates all publicly available information that could possibly be useful in forecasting next period's stock price. For business forecasters, the difficulty is that commodity prices, exchange rates, interest rates, and possibly other macroeconomic variables such as real GDP and the overall price index may also exhibit these random walk properties.

Random walk variables pose several problems if one tries to make a forecast based on OLS regression analysis. For one thing, two random walk variables with positive (negative) drift will almost certainly exhibit spurious correlation. Because each series is trending upward (downward) and not reverting to its mean, an OLS estimation on two variables generated by the process in Equation 5.26 will indicate a significant positive relationship between the variables when no causal link between the two exists. For example, even though real GDP and the overall price index of the economy (the GDP price deflator) have random shocks that may be totally unrelated, and even though real growth and inflation may have unrelated structural determinants (e.g., population growth versus monetary expansions), the *t* score in a simple OLS regression of real GDP on the price index can easily be as high as 12.0 (i.e., 99-percent confidence in a positive relationship). This result can be misleading to the forecaster seeking leading indicators for use in a business plan; imagine selling your firm's senior officers on the idea that because inflation is up, the firm can expect substantial real growth in demand next period. You might well be sent on an extended unpaid leave or even fired.

Of course, not all business time series exhibit these random walk properties. For example, a firm's profitability and earnings *do* mean revert in response to competitive entry and exit whenever they move substantially above or below the risk-adjusted mean for the industry, and therefore profits and earnings are not a random walk.[12] Hence, it is crucial to know whether the data one is working with are, or are not, generated by a random walk process.

The second problem posed by random walks is that the level of y_T after a number of periods T is

$$y_T = y_0 + \sum_{i=0}^{T} (\alpha + \varepsilon_{T-i}) \qquad [5.27]$$

$$= y_0 + T\alpha + \Sigma\,\varepsilon_t \qquad [5.28]$$

the cumulative sum of the drift parameter plus all the white noise errors up to period T. Another way of describing this phenomenon is to say that all innovations to random walk variables result in *permanent* effects; the shocks just continue to cumulate and don't wash out as the time series lengthens. Therefore, "trends" in business data have two meanings. Some trends are deterministic like the upward and downward sales trends for bathing suits in the spring and summer versus the fall and winter buying seasons. Other trends, however, are stochastic; stochastic trends are the permanent effects of innovations in a random walk process like Equation 5.26. Since the $\Sigma\varepsilon_t$ do not cancel out, it is appropriate to think of them as trends too. The problem is that the variance of y_T as the time series lengthens is equal to $T\sigma_\varepsilon^2$—that is, the variance of the stock price or interest rate has no limit! This issue makes it quite difficult to reduce root mean square error (RMSE) with the forecasting techniques we have seen so far. For example, even long lag structures in OLS regression models of stock price changes often have R^2 as low as 0.02 to 0.05 and very large RMSEs. Again, such series have enormous variance as T increases.

Although many advanced techniques beyond the scope of this text are motivated by the random walk stochastic process,[13] two simple methods we have already introduced at least partially address both of the complications just mentioned. First, all random walk-like processes have long, slowly decaying autocorrelation functions. The first-order autoregressive AR(1) random walk process with drift α in Equation 5.26 is said to be *integrated of order one*—*written* $I(1)$—because the coefficient on the first autoregressive lag is by hypothesis $\beta = 1$. Indeed, this particular first-order autocorrelation function never decays. Consequently, the Durbin-Watson statistic introduced in Equation 4A.1 and Figure 4A.2 can be used to detect the presence of severe autocorrelation in such variables. The DW statistic will definitely fall well below 2.0 for data generated by Equation 5.26—i.e., below d_L for positively autocorrelated series and above $(4\text{-}d_L)$ for negatively autocorrelated series generated by a process like Equation 5.26 with $\beta = -1$. So, one can use the DW statistic as a diagnostic instrument to detect the possibility of a non-mean-reverting, random walk process.

---

[12] See E. Fama and K. French, "Forecasting Profitability and Earnings," *Journal of Business*, April 2000, pp. 164–175.

[13] Several useful introductions to additional techniques in stochastic time-series analysis are F. Diebold, *Elements of Forecasting*, 2nd ed. (Cincinnati, OH: South-Western, 2001); W. Enders, *Applied Econometric Time-Series* (New York: John Wiley and Sons, 2004).

Moreover, the I(1) property of an AR(1) random walk implies that taking the first difference of the price or interest rate series in Equation 5.26,

$$\Delta y_t = \alpha + (\beta - 1)\, y_{t-1} + \varepsilon_t \qquad [5.29]$$

would leave us with a process that did mean revert (i.e., a process that reverted to the drift parameter α) if in fact $\beta = 1$. It is straightforward to estimate the first difference of the time series in Equation 5.29 or, more generally, to estimate a vector autoregression in first differences,

$$\Delta y_t = \alpha + (\beta - 1)\, y_{t-1} + \sum_{t=1}^{\infty} \Delta y_{t-1} + \varepsilon_t \qquad [5.30]$$

and conclude whether the null hypothesis $\beta = 1$ is true or false.[14] If true, any series with these properties should be differenced and incorporated into the forecasting regressions as first differences, not as levels.[15] If the situation as described in Equations 5.27, 5.28, and 5.29 pertains to both the dependent and an explanatory variable, the entire forecasting model should be specified in first differences. In that case, these two series are said to be **cointegrated time series** and will exhibit a nonspurious co-movement with one another, the presence of which could prove quite important to achieving the standard forecasting objective of low RMSE.

Cointegrated Time Series

Stochastic series with a common order of integration and exhibiting an equilibrium relationship such that they do not permanently wander away from one another.

Forecasting with Input-Output Tables

Another forecasting approach that capitalizes on the cross-sectional interdependence between various intermediate product and final product industries is *input-output analysis*. Input-output analysis enables the forecaster to trace the effects of an increase in demand for one product to other industries. An increase in the demand for automobiles will first lead to an increase in the output of the auto industry, which will increase the demand for steel, glass, plastics, tires, and upholstery fabric. In addition, secondary impacts will occur as the increase in the demand for upholstery fabric, for example, requires an increase in the production of fibers used to make the fabric. The demand for machinery may also increase as a result of the fabric demand, and so the pattern continues. Input-output analysis permits the forecaster to trace through all the interindustry effects that occur as a result of the initial increase in the demand for automobiles. The Bureau of Economic Analysis of the U.S. Department of Commerce produces a complicated set of tables specifying the interdependence among the various industries in the economy.[16]

[14] These tests can be performed with the t-statistic on the $(\beta - 1)$ parameter on y_{t-1} but require using a modified set of Dickey-Fuller critical values. See Appendix B, Table 7.

[15] If $\beta = 1$ is rejected, each series in question should be differenced again, and the second differences tested in exactly the same fashion. If in that case $\beta = 1$, second differences would be incorporated rather than first differences. If neither first nor second differences indicate a I(1) or I(2) series, the forecaster proceeds using the levels of the original data.

[16] The most recent input-output tables may be found for 16 industry groups and 432 detailed industries in "Input-Output Tables" on the U.S. Bureau of Economic Analysis website at http://www.bea.gov.

INTERNATIONAL PERSPECTIVES

LONG-TERM SALES FORECASTING BY GENERAL MOTORS IN OVERSEAS MARKETS

General Motors has an extensive forecasting system for both its North American and its overseas operations that is implemented by the Corporate Product Planning and Economics staff. The process generates short- and long-term forecasts of the U.S. vehicle market and long-term forecasts for overseas markets. A discussion of the overseas forecasting process follows.

General Motors produces forecasts for motor vehicle sales in nearly 60 countries. These countries vary in the number of cars per 1,000 people (car density), from less than 10 to over 500. The primary factor used to explain the growth in car density is the level of and changes in income in each country. In the first step of the forecasting process, the macroeconomic relationship between key economic variables, including income levels and motor vehicle sales, is estimated. Specifically, estimates are made of the income elasticity of demand in each country. The second step attempts to monitor changes over time in the relationships established in Step 1.

The third step consists of consultations between the Product Planning and Economics Staff and the Marketing Staffs of each GM overseas operation. The objective of this phase is to identify any special factors in each country that might require a significant modification in the forecasts generated from the econometric models. For example, in the early and mid-1980s, many believed that certain voluntary restraint policies adopted by the Japanese government would hold down demand by up to 50 percent, relative to the forecasts from the econometric model. When these policy barriers were removed, Japanese car sales skyrocketed up to levels predicted by the econometric model. More recently, the entry of China into the World Trade Organization has caused a shift upward in the future projected net exports (exports minus imports) of cars to China.

The final step provides models of alternative future scenarios that reflect the impact of major changes in the economic environment for which full information is unavailable. For example, GM developed a scenario plan for the opening of the Chinese market; it predicted more sales by 2010 in the fast-growing markets of China and India than in all other foreign locations combined. To derive cash flow forecasts from foreign sales, GM must model (and manage) its exchange rate risk exposure, which is discussed in the next chapter on managing exports.

SUMMARY

- A forecast is a prediction concerning the future.
- The choice of a forecasting technique depends on the cost of developing the forecasting model relative to the potential benefits to be derived, the complexity of the relationship being forecast, the time period for the forecast, the accuracy required of the model, and the lead time required to obtain inputs for the forecasting model.
- Data used in forecasting may be in the form of a time series (i.e., a series of observations of a variable over a number of past time periods), or they may be cross-sectional (observations taken at a single point in time for a sample of individuals, firms, geographic regions, communities, or some other set of observable units).
- Deterministic time-series forecasting models are based on an extrapolation of past values into the future. Time-series forecasting models may be adjusted for seasonal, secular, and cyclical trends in the data. Stochastic time-series forecasting models investigate the randomness-generating process in the underlying data.
- When a data series possesses a great deal of randomness, *smoothing techniques,* such as moving averages and exponential smoothing, may improve the forecast accuracy.
- Neither trend analysis models nor smoothing techniques are capable of identifying major future changes in the direction of an economic data series.

- *Barometric techniques,* which employ leading, lagging, and coincident indicators, are designed to forecast changes in the direction of a data series but are poorly suited for forecasting the magnitude of the change.
- *Survey and opinion polling techniques* are often useful in forecasting such variables as business capital spending and major consumer expenditure plans and for generating product-specific or regional sales forecasts for a firm.
- *Econometric methods* seek to explain the reasons for a change in an economic data series and to use this quantitative, explanatory model to make future forecasts. Econometric models are among the most useful business forecasting tools, but they tend to be expensive to develop and maintain. Their net benefit hinges on their success in reducing root mean forecast error in out-of-sample forecasting environments.
- Trends in business data are either deterministic or stochastic. Stochastic trends introduced by random walk variables such as stock prices require careful diagnosis and special methods.

Exercises

Answers to the exercises in blue can be found in Appendix C at the back of the book.

1. The forecasting staff for the Prizer Corporation has developed a model to predict sales of its air-cushioned-ride snowmobiles. The model specifies that sales S vary jointly with disposable personal income Y and the population between ages 15 and 40, Z, and *inversely* with the price of the snowmobiles P. Based on past data, the best estimate of this relationship is

$$S = k\frac{YZ}{P}$$

where k has been estimated (with past data) to equal 100.

   a. If $Y = \$11{,}000$, $Z = \$1{,}200$, and $P = \$20{,}000$, what value would you predict for S?
   b. What happens if P is reduced to \$17,500?
   c. How would you go about developing a value for k?
   d. What are the potential weaknesses of this model?

2. a. Fred's Hardware and Hobby House expects its sales to increase at a constant rate of 8 percent per year over the next three years. Current sales are \$100,000. Forecast sales for each of the next three years.
   b. If sales in 2004 were \$60,000 and they grew to \$100,000 by 2008 (a four-year period), what was the actual annual compound growth rate?

3. Metropolitan Hospital estimated its average monthly bed needs as

$$N = 1{,}000 + 9X$$

where X = time period (months); January 2003 = 0
N = monthly bed needs

Assume that no new hospital additions are expected in the area in the foreseeable future. The following monthly seasonal adjustment factors have been estimated, using data from the past five years:

Month	Adjustment Factor
January	+5%
April	−15%
July	+4%
November	−5%
December	−25%

   a. Forecast Metropolitan's bed demand for January, April, July, November, and December of 2006.

b. If the following actual and forecast values for June bed demands have been recorded, what seasonal adjustment factor would you recommend be used in making future June forecasts?

Year	Forecast	Actual
2006	1,045	1,096
2005	937	993
2004	829	897
2003	721	751
2002	613	628
2001	505	560

4. Stowe Automotive is considering an offer from Indula to build a plant making automotive parts for use in that country. In preparation for a final decision, Stowe's economists have been hard at work constructing a basic econometric model for Indula to aid the company in predicting future levels of economic activity. Because of the cyclical nature of the automotive parts industry, forecasts of future economic activity are quite important in Stowe's decision process.

Corporate profits (P_{t-1}) for all firms in Indula were about \$100 billion. *GDP* for the nation is composed of consumption *C*, investment *I*, and government spending *G*. It is anticipated that Indula's federal, state, and local governments will spend in the range of \$200 billion next year. On the basis of an analysis of recent economic activity in Indula, consumption expenditures are assumed to be \$100 billion plus 80 percent of national income. National income is equal to *GDP* minus taxes *T*. Taxes are estimated to be at a rate of about 30 percent of *GDP*. Finally, corporate investments have historically equaled \$30 billion plus 90 percent of last year's corporate profits (P_{t-1}).

a. Construct a five-equation econometric model of the state of Indula. Include a consumption equation, an investment equation, a tax receipt equation, an equation representing the *GDP* identity, and a national income equation.

b. Assuming that all random disturbances average to zero, solve the system of equations to arrive at next year's forecast values for *C*, *I*, *T*, *GDP*, and *Y*. (*Hint:* It is easiest to start by solving the investment equation and then working through the appropriate substitutions in the other equations.)

5. A firm experienced the demand shown in the following table.

Year	Actual Demand	5-Year Moving Average	3-Year Moving Average	Exponential Smoothing (w = 0.9)	Exponential Smoothing (w = 0.3)
1995	800	xxxxx	xxxxx	xxxxx	xxxxx
1996	925	xxxxx	xxxxx	—	—
1997	900	xxxxx	xxxxx	—	—
1998	1025	xxxxx	—	—	—
1999	1150	xxxxx	—	—	—
2000	1160	—	—	—	—
2001	1200	—	—	—	—
2002	1150	—	—	—	—
2003	1270	—	—	—	—
2004	1290	—	—	—	—
2005	*	—	—	—	—

*Unknown future value to be forecast.

a. Fill in the table by preparing forecasts based on a five-year moving average, a three-year moving average, and exponential smoothing (with a $w = 0.9$ and a $w = 0.3$). *Note:* The exponential smoothing forecasts may be begun by assuming $\hat{Y}_{t+1} = Y_t$.

b. Using the forecasts from 2000 through 2004, compare the accuracy of each of the forecasting methods based on the RMSE criterion.

c. Which forecast would you have used for 2005? Why?

6. The economic analysis division of Mapco Enterprises estimated the demand function for its line of weed trimmers as

$$Q_D = 18{,}000 + 0.4N - 350P_M + 90P_S$$

where N = number of new homes completed in the primary market area
P_M = price of the Mapco trimmer
P_S = price of its competitor's Surefire trimmer

In 2006, 15,000 new homes are expected to be completed in the primary market area. Mapco plans to charge $50 for its trimmer. The Surefire trimmer is expected to sell for $55.

a. What sales are forecast for 2006 under these conditions?

b. If its competitor cuts the price of the Surefire trimmer to $50, what effect will it have on Mapco's sales?

c. What effect would a 30-percent reduction in the number of new homes completed have on Mapco's sales (ignore the impact of the price cut of the Surefire trimmer)?

7. The sales of Cycle City, a large motorcycle and moped distributor, grew significantly during the 1990s. This past history of sales growth is indicated in the following table:

Year	Sales
1990	$100,000
1991	130,000
1992	166,400
1993	209,664
1994	259,983
1995	317,180
1996	380,615
1997	449,126
1998	520,986
1999	593,924
2000	665,195

a. What was the compound annual rate of growth in sales for Cycle City over this 10-year period?

b. Based on your answer in Part (a), what sales would you have forecasted for the next year (2001)?

c. Graph the growth in sales over the 10 years. What happened to the rate of growth over this period?

d. Based on your answer to Part (c), what sales would you have forecasted for 2001?

8. The Questor Corporation experienced the following sales pattern over a 10-year period:

Year	Sales ($000)
1997	121
1998	130
1999	145
2000	160
2001	155
2002	179
2003	215
2004	208
2005	235
2006	262
2007	*

*Unknown future value to be forecast.

a. Compute the equation of a trend line (similar to Equation 5.4) for these sales data to forecast sales for the next year. (Let 1997 = 0, 1998 = 1, etc., for the time variable.) What does this equation forecast for sales in the year 2007?

b. Use a first-order exponential smoothing model with $w = 0.9$ to forecast sales for the year 2007.

9. Bell Greenhouses estimated its monthly demand for potting soil to be the following:

$$N = 400 + 4X$$

where N = monthly demand for bags of potting soil
X = time periods in months (March 2004 = 0)

Assume this trend factor is expected to remain stable in the foreseeable future. The following table contains the monthly seasonal adjustment factors, which have been estimated using actual sales data from the past five years:

Month	Adjustment Factor
March	+2%
June	+15%
August	+10%
December	−12%

a. Forecast Bell Greenhouses' demand for potting soil in March, June, August, and December 2005.

b. If the following table shows the forecasted and actual potting soil sales by Bell Greenhouses for April in five different years, determine the seasonal adjustment factor to be used in making an April 2006 forecast.

Year	Forecast	Actual
2005	500	515
2004	452	438
2003	404	420
2002	356	380
2001	308	320

10. Savings-Mart (a chain of discount department stores) sells patio and lawn furniture. Sales are seasonal, with higher sales during the spring and summer quarters and lower sales during the fall and winter quarters. The company developed the following quarterly sales forecasting model:

$$\hat{Y}_t = 8.25 + 0.125t - 2.75D_{1t} + 0.25D_{2t} + 3.50D_{3t}$$

where $\hat{Y}_t$ = predicted sales ($ million) in quarter t

8.25 = quarterly sales ($ million) when $t = 0$

t = time period (quarter) where the fourth quarter of 2000 = 0, first quarter of 2001 = 1, second quarter of 2001 = 2, . . .

$$D_{1t} = \begin{cases} 1 \text{ for first-quarter observations} \\ 0 \text{ otherwise} \end{cases}$$

$$D_{2t} = \begin{cases} 1 \text{ for second-quarter observations} \\ 0 \text{ otherwise} \end{cases}$$

$$D_{3t} = \begin{cases} 1 \text{ for third-quarter observations} \\ 0 \text{ otherwise} \end{cases}$$

Forecast Savings-Mart's sales of patio and lawn furniture for each quarter of 2006.

11. The demand for tea has been estimated as

$$Q = 7{,}000 - 550P + 210I + 425P_c$$

where Q = thousands of pounds of tea sold

P = price per pound of tea

I = per capita disposable personal income in thousands of dollars

P_c = price per pound of coffee

a. If next year's tea price is forecast to be $3, per capita disposable personal income is estimated to be $15,000 (i.e., 15), and the price per pound of coffee is estimated to be $4, compute the expected quantity demanded for the coming year.

b. Economic forecasters believe the probability of a major recession next year is high and would reduce per capita income to $13,000 (13). In addition, a frost in Brazil is likely to increase the price of coffee to $7 per pound. What impact would these changes in the economic outlook have on the demand for tea?

12. Use the monthly series on the Consumer Price Index (all items) from the previous two years to produce a forecast of the CPI for each of the next three years. Is the precision of your forecast greater or less at 36 months ahead than at 12 months ahead? Why? Compare your answer to that of Moody's online U.S. Macro Model at http://www.economy.com/.

CASE EXERCISES

SOUTH POLE ICE CREAM COMPANY

Monthly sales (× \$100,000) of the South Pole Ice Cream Company are shown in the following table.

Month	2005	2006	2007
January	2.30	2.65	3.30
February	2.60	2.80	3.60
March	2.70	3.00	3.60
April	2.85	3.20	4.20
May	3.25	3.85	4.20
June	3.30	3.90	5.00
July	3.25	3.80	—
August	3.35	3.90	—
September	3.20	3.60	—
October	3.10	3.55	—
November	2.75	3.30	—
December	2.65	3.20	—

QUESTIONS

1. Plot the data on a graph with time on the horizontal axis and sales (in hundred thousands) on the vertical axis.
2. Fit a linear trend equation to the data using the least-squares method. (*Note:* This calculation can be made using either a calculator or a computer.)
3. Based on your answer to Question 2, forecast (seasonally unadjusted) sales for each of the last six months of 2007.
4. Calculate seasonally adjusted monthly sales by the ratio-to-trend method for the last six months of 2007.

CRUISE SHIP ARRIVALS IN ALASKA

The summer months bring warm weather, megafauna (bears), and tourists to the coastal towns of Alaska. At the top of the Inland Passage, Skagway was the entrance to the Yukon in the nineteenth century. Today this town attracts multiple cruise ships per day; literally thousands of passengers disembark into a town of 800 for a taste of the Alaskan frontier experience between 10 A.M. and 5 P.M. Some ride steam trains into the mountains, others wander the town spending money in galleries, restaurants, and souvenir shops. The Skagway Chamber of Commerce is trying to decide which transportation mode in the following table should receive the highest priority in the tourist promotions for next season.

QUESTIONS

1. Plot the raw data on arrivals for each transportation mode against time, all on the same graph. Which mode is growing the fastest? Which the slowest?
2. Plot the logarithm of arrivals for each transportation mode against time, all on the same graph. Which now appears to be growing the fastest?

Logarithms are especially useful for comparing series with two divergent scales because 10 percent growth always looks the same, regardless of the starting level. When absolute levels matter, the raw data is more appropriate, but when growth rates are what's important, log scales are better.

3. Now create an index number to represent the growth of arrivals in each transportation mode by dividing the first (smallest) number in each column into the remaining numbers in the column. Plot these index numbers for each transportation mode against time, all in the same graph. Which is growing the fastest?

4. In attempting to formulate a model of the passenger arrival data on cruise ships over time would a nonlinear (perhaps a multiplicative exponential) model be preferable to a linear model of cruise ship arrivals against time? What about in the case of the passenger arrivals by ferry against time?

5. Estimate the double-log (log linear) time trend model for log cruise ship arrivals against log time. Estimate a linear time trend model of cruise ship arrivals against time. Calculate the root mean square error between the predicted and actual value of cruise ship arrivals. Is the root mean square error greater for the double log time trend model or for the linear time trend model?

Skagway Visitor Arrival Statistics

Year	Cruise	Ferry	Highway	Air
1983	48,066	25,288	72,384	3,500
1984	54,907	25,196	79,215	3,750
1985	77,623	31,522	89,542	4,000
1986	100,695	30,981	91,908	4,250
1987	119,279	30,905	70,993	4,953
1988	115,505	31,481	74,614	5,957
1989	112,692	29,997	63,789	7,233
1990	136,512	33,234	63,237	4,799
1991	141,284	33,630	64,610	4,853
1992	145,973	37,216	79,946	7,947
1993	192,549	33,650	80,709	10,092
1994	204,387	34,270	81,172	10,000
1995	256,788	33,961	87,977	17,000
1996	299,651	35,760	86,536	20,721
1997	438,305	27,659	91,849	11,466
1998	494,961	31,324	100,784	20,679
1999	525,507	31,467	92,291	15,963

Source: *The Skagway News*, November 16, 1999.

LUMBER PRICE FORECAST

QUESTIONS

1. One of the most important variables that must be forecasted accurately to project the cost of single-family home construction is the price of Southern pine framing lumber. Use the following data to forecast two- and four-year-ahead lumber prices.

2. Compare the forecast accuracy of at least two alternative forecasting methods.

Lumber Price Index

2005	173.2	1984	101.3
2004	160.0	1983	101.2
2003	137.1	1982	93.8
2002	134.5	1981	96.4
2001	140.2	1980	95.2
2000	146.4	1979	99.0
1999	176.3	1978	90.9
1998	168.4	1977	77.9
1997	182.7	1976	67.7
1996	168.7	1975	58.3
1995	162.7	1974	60.5
1994	168.9	1973	58.3
1993	163.2	1972	47.6
1992	137.5	1971	41.9
1991	123.9	1970	37.4
1990	121.7	1969	41.3
1989	118.9	1968	37.3
1988	111.5	1967	32.9
1987	105.8	1966	33.0
1986	100.7	1965	31.6
1985	100.0	1964	31.4

Source: Forest Product Market Prices and Statistics, Annual Yearbooks, Random Length Publications, Inc., Eugene, OR, various issues.

CHAPTER

6

Managing Exports

CHAPTER PREVIEW Business plans today involve supply chains, manufacturing operations, and targeted marketing on several continents. Many U.S., German, Japanese, Brazilian, and Korean companies engage in foreign direct investment and manufacture through subsidiaries abroad. Other companies outsource manufacturing to low-wage partners in places such as China, Mexico, Portugal, Indonesia, and the Caribbean. Still others buy parts and supplies or preassembled components from foreign firms. And almost all firms face competition from imports or produce a product to sell abroad. Indeed, export markets are increasingly the primary source of sales growth for many U.S. manufacturers, and consequently, the United States is both the world's largest exporter and importer. Careful analysis and accurate forecasting of these international purchases and international sales provide pivotal information for capacity planning, for production scheduling, and for pricing, promotion, and distribution plans in many companies.

In this chapter, we investigate the relationship between exchange rates and import/export sales. International trade in merchandise and services plus international capital flows determine long-term trends in exchange rates, which we analyze with standard demand and supply tools in the market for U.S. dollars as foreign exchange (FX). Purchasing power parity provides a way to assess these FX trends and incorporate cash flow from export sales in business scenario planning. We then explore the reasons for and patterns of trade in the world's economy with special attention to regional trading blocs and emergent economies, such as the European Union, NAFTA, and China. The chapter closes with perspectives on the U.S. trade deficit. Our attention throughout is focused on a management approach to international trade and policy.

MANAGERIAL CHALLENGE

Export Market Pricing at Toyota[1]

In February 2002, the U.S. dollar exchanged for as much as ¥135. A popular performance sports car, the Toyota Celica GT-S Coupe, made in Japan and shipped to U.S. dealers sold for $21,165, meaning that each sale realized almost ¥3 million (i.e., ¥2,857,275) in revenue. Just 18 months earlier in June of 2000, the dollar had exchanged for only ¥104. The 25 percent lower value of the dollar in 2000 made Japanese exports to the United States potentially much less profitable. To recover costs and earn the same profit margin back home in Japan, Toyota would have had to price the 2000

MANAGERIAL CHALLENGE

GT-S Coupe at $27,474 in order to again realize ¥2,857,275 (because ¥2,857,275 ÷ (¥104/US$) = $27,474). Rather than pricing their sporty performance street machine well ahead of the competition and trying to limit the erosion of market share by emphasizing horsepower, style, or manufacturing quality, Toyota instead slashed profit margins. Specifically, Toyota only charged $21,555 for the 2000 GT-S, earning just ¥2,241,720 in revenue, and successfully protected their foreign market share.

As we shall see in this chapter, different companies react in different ways to the challenges presented by such severe currency fluctuations. GM and Ford tend to maintain margins and sacrifice market share. In contrast, Toyota tends to slash margins to maintain or even grow market share. Because of these pricing and related decisions between 1987 and 2007, Toyota's share of the North American car market rose from 6 percent to 18 percent, while General Motors share fell from 35 percent to 24 percent. Is one approach right for Toyota and the opposite approach right for GM? Why or why not?

[1] Based on G. Gardner, "The Fading Big Three Car Market," *Ward's Automotive World* (September 1997), pp. 41–46; and Jack Gillis, *The Car Book* (1997).

INTRODUCTION

Around the globe, the reduction of trade barriers and the opening of markets to foreign imports increased competitive pressure on manufacturers who once dominated their domestic industries. Tennis shoes and dress footwear once produced in large factories in Britain and the United States now come from Korea, China, and Italy. Automobile manufacturing once dominated by Ford, General Motors, and Chrysler now occurs in large numbers in Japan. In addition, Toyota owns 11 assembly and parts plants in North America, 4 in South America, 6 in Europe, 4 in India and Pakistan, and 22 across Asia. In retailing, McDonald's operates in more than 100 foreign countries, Wal-Mart sells $200 billion overseas, and Coca-Cola, Kellogg, Gillette, and Pampers international sales will exceed those in the United States. Boeing and Microsoft are the two largest U.S. exporters, but exports have become the key to growth for many leading manufacturing firms, service companies, and franchise retailers.

Similarly, outsourcing components and customer service to foreign companies has become a standard supply chain management practice for U.S. manufacturers. For a minivan, DaimlerChrysler may decide to cast engine blocks in Mexico, acquire electronics from Taiwan, perform machine tooling of ball bearings in Germany, and locate final assembly in Canada. Wood furniture "made in the U.S.A." now includes foreign components equal to 38 percent of the total value added. So, when 32 percent of Canadian output and 25 percent of Mexican, or Malaysian output flows into the United States as imports, much of that flow is preassembled components owned by U.S. companies. These data explain in large measure why 26 percent of

U.S. corporate profits in 2003 came from overseas operations.[2] The world of business has truly become a matter of managing in the global economy.

Import-Export Sales and Exchange Rates

As illustrated in the Managerial Challenge, import/export sales and/or profit margins are sensitive to changes in exchange rates. Over the 1970s, 1980s, 1990s, and 2000–2005, foreign exchange (FX) rates were four times more volatile than interest rates and ten times more volatile than inflation rates. Figure 6.1 shows that £/$ and DM/$ exchange rates in the mid-1980s and the €/$ exchange rate between 2000 and 2005 were particularly volatile. Analyzing and forecasting the cash flow effects of such massive FX rate changes provides crucial information for the marketing,

Figure 6.1 The Value of the Dollar: Recent Exchange Rates (U.S. Dollar Against Several Major Currencies)

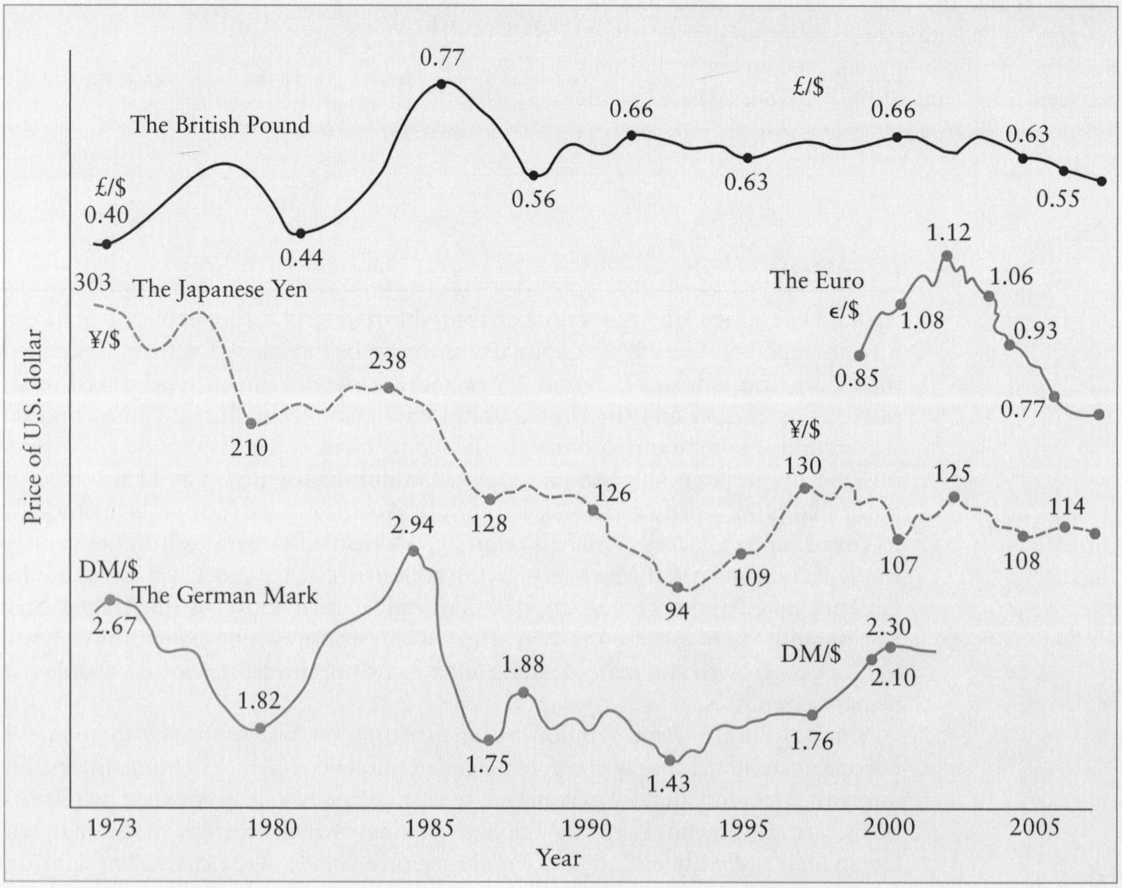

[2] "Dollar's Dive Helps U.S. Companies," *Wall Street Journal* (April 21, 2003), p. A2.

operations, and merger plans of companies such as Boeing, Microsoft, and DaimlerChrysler.

THREE TYPES OF FX RISK

Foreign Exchange Translation Risk Exposure

An accounting adjustment in the home currency value of foreign assets or liabilities.

Such FX risk exposure is of three types. **Foreign exchange translation risk exposure** occurs when a company's foreign assets (or liabilities) are affected by exchange rate movements. Accordingly, the accounting books in the home country must translate these balance sheet adjustments back into home country currency. A $200 million assembly plant owned by Daimler-Benz and located in the United States may need to be written down on the company's German balance sheet when the U.S. dollar falls from 1.12 €/$ in 2001 to 0.8 €/$ in 2006 (again, see Figure 6.1). This €64 million translation risk exposure, $(€1.12 - €0.8)/\$ \times \$200$ million, is easily offset with balance sheet hedges. A balance sheet hedge would be achieved by a merger or acquisition that matched the magnitude of Daimler-Benz company liabilities in U.S. dollars to those of the dollar assets held by Daimler's foreign subsidiary, the Chrysler Corporation. Then an offsetting €64 million reduction in liabilities (say, in the euro cost of $200 million in pension plan contractual commitments to Chrysler workers) would leave the net asset position of the foreign subsidiary unchanged.

In general, balance sheet fluctuations due to exchange rate risk are often ignored. FX translation risk exposure receives more attention, however, during financial crises when companies worry about violating their bond covenants because of excessive balance sheet debt/asset ratios (e.g., during the Asian currency crisis in 1998–2000 and in financially distressed companies such as airlines).

Foreign Exchange Transaction Risk Exposure

A change in cash flows resulting from contractual commitments to pay in or receive foreign currency.

Foreign exchange transaction risk exposure is a much more generally significant problem in managing exports. Transaction risk exposure occurs when a purchase agreement or sales contract (a specific "transaction") commits the company to make future payables or accept future receivables in a foreign currency. Over the time period between executing the contract and actually making or receiving the payments, the company has FX transaction risk exposure. Many financial derivatives such as FX forward contracts, FX swap contracts, and FX options contracts have emerged to assist corporate treasurers in reducing transaction risk exposure. A later section discusses the use of these derivative instruments to construct covered hedges that eliminate the transaction risk exposure for a modest risk premium known and fixed in advance.

Foreign Exchange Operating Risk Exposure

A change in cash flows from foreign or domestic sales resulting from currency fluctuations.

Finally, exchange rate fluctuations that result in substantial changes in the operating cash flow of foreign subsidiaries, such as those befalling Toyota in the Managerial Challenge, are examples of **foreign exchange operating risk exposure.** Operating risk exposures are more difficult to forecast than transaction risk exposures and more difficult to lay off than translation risk exposures. As a result, operating risk exposures necessitate still more managerial attention and careful analysis.

For one thing, the deterioration of export revenues from sales in foreign subsidiaries is just one side of the problem that a rising domestic currency poses. In addition, depending on the viability of global competition, operating risk exposures may entail a substantial deterioration of domestic sales as well, because competing import products become cheaper in the home market. These relationships are well illustrated by the export and domestic business of the Cummins Engine Co. of Columbus, Indiana.

The effect of these massive 1980–1985 and 2001 dollar appreciations on Cummins's export sales was catastrophic. For a German trucking company to buy a

INTERNATIONAL PERSPECTIVES

The Collapse of Export and Domestic Sales at Cummins Engine[3]

U.S. manufacturer Cummins Engine Co. is the world's leading producer of replacement diesel engines for trucks. Like all durable equipment manufacturers, Cummins's revenues are highly cyclical, declining steeply in economic downturns. If households buy fewer appliances, clothing, and furniture, less shipping by truck is required to deliver inventories from warehouses to restock store shelves. Less shipping means less truck mileage, and less truck mileage means a slower replacement demand for diesel engines. For example, in the mild U.S. recession of 2001, Cummins's sales fell off 15 percent, operating margins collapsed from 7.4 percent to 5.3 percent, and cash flow plummeted by 68 percent. As the U.S. economy improved sharply during 2002, Cummins's sales and margins remained flat. Why? What went wrong? By 2004, Cummins's sales, margins, and cash flow were all at record levels. Why? What went so right?

Cummins Engine (with a 70% domestic market share) competes against rivals Caterpillar (20%) and Detroit Diesel (10%). But Cummins sells 47 percent of its replacement diesel engines in the *export* market, competing primarily against Mercedes-Benz diesels. The euro or British pound price that a Cummins engine can sell for in Munich or London (and still recover its cost plus a profit) is as important to Cummins's cash flow as metal costs or wage bargains with the United Machinists union. A $40,000 Cummins Series N diesel sold for approximately DM 72,000 in 1978, 1988, and again in 1998. In each of those years, the exchange rate between the deutsche mark and the U.S. dollar stood at approximately 1.8 (i.e., 1.8 deutsche marks per dollar). In one intervening time period, however, the U.S. dollar appreciated substantially against the mark. Between 1980–1985, the value of the dollar soared almost 47 percent from DM 1.82 to DM 2.94 (see Figure 6.1).[4] Similarly, in both 1999 and 2003 a Cummins $40,000 Series N diesel sold for €34,000 (0.85€/$ × $40,000) in Munich whereas in the interim (i.e., in 2001) the dollar soared 27 percent to €1.12/$.

[3] Based on *Value Line Investment Survey, Part III: Ratings and Reports*, various issues.

[4] Similar exchange rate movements occurred against the British pound, against which the U.S. currency appreciated 54 percent between 1980 and 1985 (from £0.44/$ to £0.77/$). Exchange rate percentage changes are calculated as the difference from one period to the next divided by the average exchange rate over the period. For example, a change from £0.44 per U.S. dollar to £0.77 equals a 0.33/0.5(0.44 + 0.77) = 0.33/0.605 = 54% change. Similarly, DM 1.82 to DM 2.94 equals a 1.12/2.38 or 47 percent change.

The reason for this midpoint procedure is that when the DM/$ exchange rate returns by 1988 to very nearly its original level (i.e., see DM 1.88 for 1988 in Figure 6.1), the midpoint calculation yields a downward adjustment of −44 percent, nearly equal and opposite to the +47 percent rise.

$40,000 Cummins diesel engine at the dollar's peak in 1985 required (DM2.94/$) × $40,000 = DM 117,600 and in 2001 (€1.12/$) × $40,000 = €44,800 or, in the former currency, DM 103,000! No feature of the equipment had changed. No service offering had changed. No warranty had changed. The export diesels from the United States to Germany had simply become much more expensive solely because the domestic currency of those European buyers had become much less valuable. Such enormous price increases of the Cummins export product made substitute products, such as a domestically produced €40,000 Mercedes-Benz diesel, substantially more attractive to German buyers than before the change in the exchange rate.

Moreover, in 2001, Mercedes-Benz perceived a huge opportunity to sell its own replacement diesels into Cummins's home territory in the United States. An import diesel made by Mercedes-Benz (which had sold in Boston, Cleveland, and Chicago for €34,000/0.85 = $40,000 in 1999 and would do so again in 2003) could cover cost and a small profit while selling for just €34,000/1.12 = $30,357 at the peak of the dollar in 2001. Consequently, Mercedes-Benz diesels sold well that year throughout the United States. Not only did Cummins's export sales collapse, but so did Cummins's domestic sales (and margins). The steep appreciation of the dollar in 1980–1985 and again in 2001 put U.S. manufacturers of traded goods, such as autos, VCRs, airplanes, and diesel engines, at a big disadvantage. U.S. exports sharply declined, U.S. imports steeply increased, and the U.S. trade deficit skyrocketed.

Subsequently, as the U.S. dollar weakened against the euro (throughout 2003–2005, again see Figure 6.1), American exporters experienced a turnaround and profited from booming European sales. Seven percent of IBM's reported 11 percent sales growth in 2003 Q1 was attributed to currency fluctuations. Similarly, Colgate-Palmolive and Microsoft, respectively, reported two-thirds of a 20 percent sales increase in Europe and nine-tenths of a 12 percent sales increase in Europe, the Middle East, and Africa were attributable to the lower in-country prices emergent from a weaker U.S. dollar.[5]

OUTSOURCING

One lasting effect of all the international competitive pressure on U.S. manufacturers in the strong dollar years of 2000–2002 has been a laser-like dedication to cost-cutting. With just-in-time delivery of component subassemblies, production to order, and other lean manufacturing techniques, U.S. companies have sliced inventory costs, reduced scrapwork, and cut manufacturing cycle times enough to boost productivity 25 percent since the recession of 2001.[6] That is, the ratio of merchandise produced to input cost has risen sharply at firms such as Cummins, Caterpillar, General Electric, and Boeing. One reason is better operations management techniques, but another is the outsourcing of IT, less complex assembly, and raw materials handling tasks to places such as Mexico, Korea, Malaysia, and now India and China.

An HP personal computer is 95 percent outsourced, with components from 8 countries, assembled in Shanghai by Quanta, a Taiwanese-owned firm, air-freighted to Memphis, and delivered then by FedEx (see Figure 6.2). Outsourcing is not new. U.S. companies such as Merck and DuPont and IBM have outsourced for decades to Germany, France, Ireland, and now India in order to access skilled people for analytical jobs in R&D. In addition, basic manufacturing of low-skill, low-wage jobs has always moved offshore, first from Europe to America, then to Canada, Brazil, Mexico, Portugal, Malaysia, Thailand, India, and now China.

One reason is that shipping costs from Shanghai to New York for a 40-foot container filled with 6,000 garments runs just $3,900 (66 cents per garment) for the 30-day ocean voyage through the Panama Canal, and $5,000 (85 cents per garment)

---

[5] "Dollar's Dive Helps U.S. Companies," *Wall Street Journal* (April 21, 2003), p. A2.

[6] Based on "Lean and Unseen," *The Economist* (July 1, 2006), pp. 55–56; and Murray Weidenbaum, "Outsourcing: Pros and Cons," *Business Horizons* (2005), pp. 311–315.

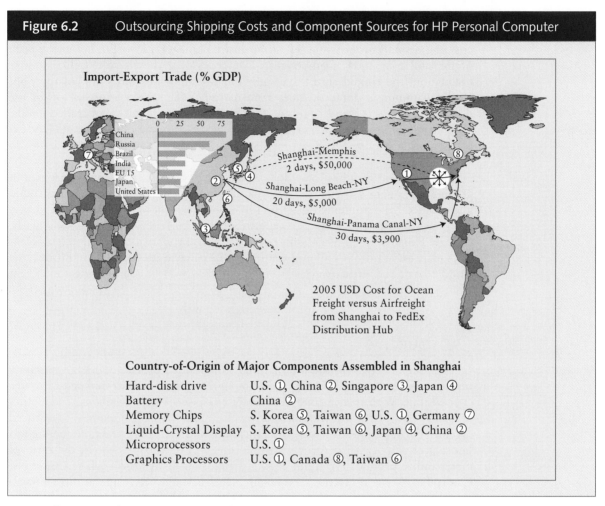

Figure 6.2 Outsourcing Shipping Costs and Component Sources for HP Personal Computer

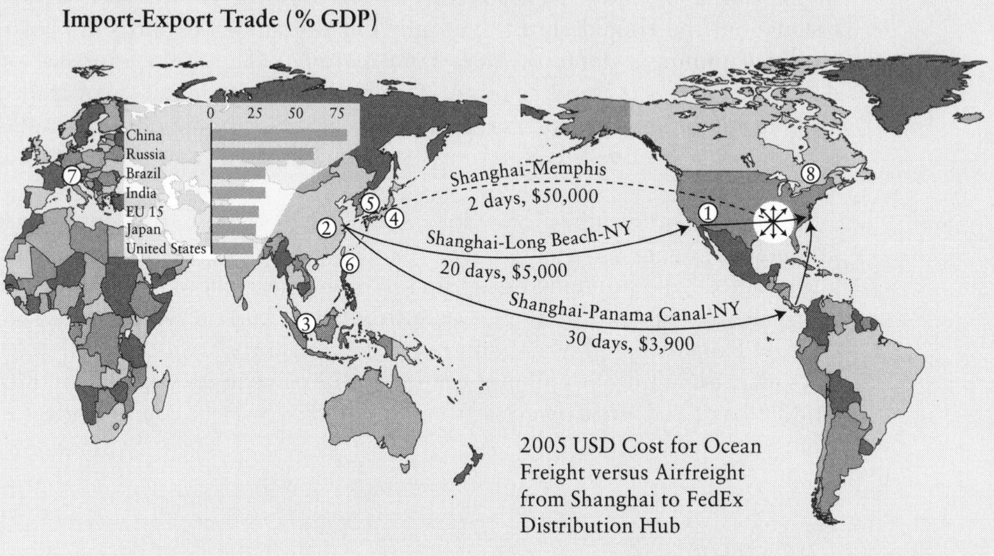

Country-of-Origin of Major Components Assembled in Shanghai

Hard-disk drive	U.S. ①, China ②, Singapore ③, Japan ④
Battery	China ②
Memory Chips	S. Korea ⑤, Taiwan ⑥, U.S. ①, Germany ⑦
Liquid-Crystal Display	S. Korea ⑤, Taiwan ⑥, Japan ④, China ②
Microprocessors	U.S. ①
Graphics Processors	U.S. ①, Canada ⑧, Taiwan ⑥

Source: *Wall Street Journal,* June 9, 2005, p. B1., World Trade Organization, Thomson Datastream.

for the 20-day intermodal service through the Long Beach, California, harbor and then onto trucks (see Figure 6.2). Across all types of cargo, ocean shipping adds only about 1 percent to the delivered price of a product. Hewlett-Packard PCs, on the other hand, warrant the $50,000 cost for an air freighter from Shanghai to the FedEx hub in Memphis, Tennessee. However, full costs offshore include not just these obvious additional shipping costs for overseas production but substantial additional costs for careful vendor selection, intellectual property protection insurance, and compensation for expatriate managers. For example, Hewitt Associate LLC estimates that to transfer a director-level U.S. employee to Beijing or Shanghai requires $190,000 additional compensation and a $60,000 housing allowance. By one estimate, $5-an-hour call-center jobs in India or $1-an-hour factory jobs in China require another $12 to cover these additional costs of outsourcing. Many U.S. employees not interested in minimum wage work are of course available at $13 to $17 per hour.

Outsourcing is as much about importing competitiveness as it is about exporting jobs. Time to market and the capacity to innovate have become more important in auto manufacturing, for example, than the cost of the next shipment of three-speed transmissions. If Toyota and Nokia and AMD introduce major product innovations on two-year, six-month, and three-week timetables, respectively, and if those cycles have become the key to customer acceptance, then GM, Motorola, and Intel have no choice but to access the people and processes that can match that capability. If those people are Indian software engineers, Mexican electronics assemblers, and Chinese garment workers, then the best hope for American workers is to sell those developing economies tractors, cell phones, appliances, aircraft, network servers, management consulting, and banking and legal services.

CHINA TRADE BLOSSOMS

An amazing story is unfolding in the People's Republic of China (PRC) along the Yellow, Yangtse, and Pearl River systems and in the port megacities of Shanghai, Guangzhou, Dalian, and Zhuhai. A decade ago China accounted for a relatively insignificant 2.8 percent of world trade despite a highly educated workforce and an immense population of 1.3 billion. But in the last three years, China's import-export trade increased by a startling 40 percent as a percentage of world trade (from 3.8 percent in 2002 to 6.4 percent in 2005, see Figure 6.2). That 6.4 percent of $22 trillion in world trade in 2005 is $1.5 trillion, 75 percent of China's GDP. This $2 trillion economy (fourth largest behind the United States, Germany, and Japan) experienced from 8 percent to 10 percent real GDP growth per annum, 1995–2005. The trade share of China with the United States rose from 10.73 percent of all U.S. imports in 2003 to 14.51 percent in 2005. Such growth is unprecedented both in its decade longevity and double-digit magnitude.

China's largest trading partners are Japan, Taiwan, the United States, South Korea, and Hong Kong. The principal categories of exports are clothing to Hong Kong, machinery, toys, furniture, shoes, and clothing to the United States, textiles to Japan, and telecommunications equipment to Germany. In many cases Chinese factories are assembling components in facilities that emerged as joint venture investments of the PRC's China International Trust and Investment Corporation with Taiwanese, Japanese, European, and U.S. multinationals. For example, HP personal computers are assembled in Shanghai in factories owned by the Quanta Corporation of Taiwan as a partner in HP's supply chain. With wage rates of $1 per hour for assembly-line work, China has quickly become the world's largest producer of televisions, personal computers, toys, bicycles, steel, and wood furniture.

Chinese import flows reflect the goods and services needed to sustain such astounding growth (i.e., electrical machinery and aircraft from the United States, steel from South Korea, autos and chemicals from Japan, and rubber, ships, and cement from Hong Kong). Two events in 2000 and 2001 set this story in motion. In 2001, China joined the World Trade Organization and agreed to drop some restrictions on foreign investment and to abide by the WTO standards for protecting patents and copyright. The year before, the U.S. Congress normalized trade relations by extending to China permanent most-favored-nation status, which removed innumerable U.S. tariffs. From successful joint ventures in auto parts supply chains to the failed joint venture with McDonnell Douglas to design and build aircraft, international business in China is a balancing act. One must balance caution in staging the co-investment and protecting intellectual property against the unbridled enthusiasm associated with a growth opportunity of a lifetime.

The Market for U.S. Dollars as Foreign Exchange

Because American manufacturers, such as Cummins Engine, still incur many of their expenses at domestic manufacturing sites in the United States, American manufacturers tend to require that export purchase orders be made payable in U.S. dollars. This receivables policy requires that Munich buyers of Cummins diesels transact simultaneously in the foreign exchange and diesel markets. To buy a Cummins diesel, Munich customers (or their financial intermediaries) will supply euros and demand dollars to secure the currency required for the dollar-denominated purchase order and payment draft awaited by the Cummins shipping department. This additional demand for the dollar and the concurrent additional supply of euros drive the price of the dollar higher than it otherwise would have been. Thus, the equilibrium price of the dollar as foreign exchange (in euros per dollar on the vertical axis in Figure 6.3) rises. In general, any such unanticipated increase in export sales results in this appreciation of the domestic currency.

Similarly, any unanticipated decrease in export sales results in a depreciation of the domestic currency. For example, in 2001–2005 Boeing experienced an unanticipated collapse of export sales in competition with Europe's Airbus, and this shift

Figure 6.3 The Market for U.S. Dollars as Foreign Exchange (Depreciation of the Dollar, 2001–2005)

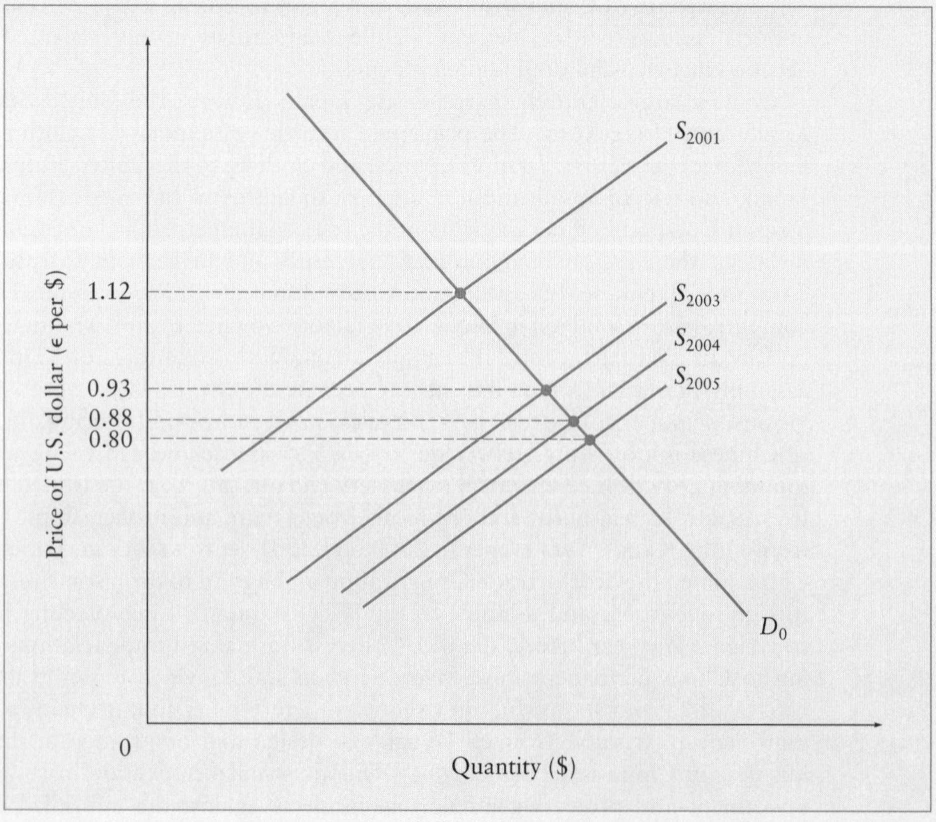

contributed to the dollar's collapse against the euro over that period (see Figure 6.3). These downward FX trends of the dollar assisted Cummins in stabilizing its sales and cash flows both at home and abroad. With the dollar worth fewer euros, the dollar cost of American imports from Mercedes-Benz and Airbus became more expensive, while American exports priced in euros by Cummins and Boeing sales reps in Germany became cheaper. This automatic self-correcting adjustment of flexible exchange rates in response to trade flow imbalances is one of the primary arguments for adopting a freely fluctuating exchange rate policy.

IMPORT/EXPORT FLOWS AND TRANSACTION DEMAND FOR A CURRENCY

To examine these effects more closely, let's turn the argument around and trace the currency flows when Americans increase their demand for imported goods. The Mazda and BMW dealers would have some inventory stock on hand, but suppose an unexpectedly large number of baby boomers wish to recapture their youth by purchasing sporty Miata or BMW convertibles. Just as Cummins Engine prefers to be paid in U.S. dollars, so too BMW wishes to be paid in euros. Therefore, BMW purchase orders must be accompanied by euro cash payments. The local BMW dealer in Charlotte therefore requests a wire transfer from her banker at Bank of America. BOA debits the dollar account of the dealer, then authorizes payment from the euro cash balances of BOA and presents a wire transfer for an equivalent sum (minus fees) to the Munich branch of Deutsche Bank for deposit in the BMW account. Both import buyer and foreign seller have done business in their home currencies and exchanged a handsome new car. And the merchandise trade account of the U.S. balance of payments would show one additional import transaction valued at the BMW convertible's purchase price.

If Bank of America anticipated fewer such import transactions and euro requests than actually occurred, the bank's foreign currency portfolio would now be out of balance. Euro balances must be restored to support future anticipated export transactions. Bank of America therefore goes (electronically) into the interbank foreign currency markets and demands euros. Although the American bank might pay with any currency in excess supply in its foreign currency portfolio, it would normally pay in U.S. dollars. In particular, if no other unanticipated import or export flows (and no unanticipated capital flows) have occurred, BOA would pay in U.S. dollars. Therefore, unanticipated demand by Americans for German imports both raises the demand for euros and (as the flip side of that same transaction) *increases* the supply of U.S. dollars.

THE EQUILIBRIUM PRICE OF THE U.S. DOLLAR

In the market for U.S. dollars as foreign exchange (see Figure 6.3), the supply curve shifts to the right. This shift of market supply represents Bank of America and many other correspondent banks supporting import transactions by selling dollars to acquire other foreign currencies. The equilibrium price on the y-axis of Figure 6.3 is the price of the dollar expressed in amounts of any foreign currency (e.g., British pounds per U.S. dollar, yen per U.S. dollar, or euros per U.S. dollar). As the supply of U.S. dollars increases, S_{2001} to S_{2005}, the equilibrium price of the dollar declines.

For example, as imports of Airbus airplanes increased 2002–2005, the supply of U.S. dollars in the foreign currency market had to increase. Again, American consumers and companies needed to acquire euros to purchase German imports. U.S. financial intermediaries supplied dollars to acquire the foreign currency their local customers requested. Thus, the spectacular dollar appreciation of the previous three years 1999–2001 slowed and the dollar began to depreciate (see Figure 6.1). The dollar's price decline is expressed quite naturally as a falling exchange rate in Figure 6.3 from €1.12 per U.S. dollar in 2001 to €0.93 in 2003 and eventually to €0.80 in 2005.

Speculative Demand, Government Transfers, and Coordinated Intervention

The U.S. dollar depreciation of 2001–2005 reflects several factors besides transaction demand. In addition, currency value also depends upon speculative demand, government transfers, and central bank interventions. Speculative demand is highly volatile. Transfers can involve either debt repayment (reducing the supply of a currency as a debtor nation takes money out of circulation and returns it to the lender nation's treasury) or foreign aid (increasing the supply of a currency). Interventions can be coordinated across several central banks or uncoordinated and can be sterilized or unsterilized. **Sterilized interventions** involve offsetting transactions in the relevant government bond market. For example, the Federal Reserve might sell dollars in the foreign currency markets, but then turn around and acquire dollars by selling an equal dollar volume of T-bonds, leaving the supply of dollars in international exchange essentially unchanged.

Sterilized Interventions

Central bank transactions in the foreign exchange market accompanied by equal offsetting transactions in the government bond market, in an attempt to alter short-term interest rates without affecting the exchange rate.

What is the proportionate weight of each of these factors in determining the equilibrium value of a currency? An important first perspective is that only one out of five foreign exchange transactions supports an import or export trade flow; the other four support international capital flows. In 2005, for example, the average *daily* volume of foreign currency transactions in the 43 largest foreign currency markets had a dollar value of almost $2 trillion. The average *daily* volume of world exports was $30 billion. So, the dollar volume of currency outstrips the dollar volume of trade flows by 65 to 1. Short-term foreign currency transactions therefore reflect international capital flows, much of which is speculative and transitory.

Intervention in the foreign currency markets by any one central bank therefore has almost no chance of affecting the equilibrium value of a currency. Take the Bank of Japan, for instance. In September 2002, the central bank of Japan had official reserves of foreign currencies equal (at existing exchange rates) to $440 billion and further reserves of gold equal to $7 billion.[7] By comparison, the European Central Bank in this same month had $230 billion in foreign currency reserves and $115 billion in gold reserves. China had $240 billion in reserves, while the U.S. Federal Reserve had $70 billion in currency and $75 billion in gold.

Suppose the Bank of Japan decided to try to initiate a depreciation of the yen to improve the competitiveness of their export sector. Investing half of their entire reserves ($220 billion), the Bank of Japan's intervention could be easily overwhelmed in one day by the sheer enormity of the 10 times greater $2 trillion mobile capital awash daily in the international capital markets. Indeed, the official reserves of all

[7] "Official Reserves," *The Economist*, September 21, 2005, p. 97.

the developed countries *total* only $1.8 trillion, approximately equal to *one day's worth* of foreign currency transactions.

It takes coordinated intervention by several large central banks with deep reserves to have any real chance of permanently affecting a currency's value. One such coordinated intervention took place as a result of the Plaza Accords in 1985 when the G7 nations (the United States, Britain, Japan, Germany, France, Italy, and Canada) agreed to a sustained sale of dollars from their reserves over 1986 and 1987. It was this coordinated intervention that contributed to the steep decline of the dollar from DM 2.94/$ to DM 1.75/$ over 1986 and 1987, illustrated in Figure 6.1. In September 2000, the Bank of England, the European Central Bank, the Bank of Japan, and the U.S. Federal Reserve Bank again coordinated selling of dollar reserves.

EXAMPLE

A Coordinated Intervention to Support the Euro

Beginning Friday, September 22, 2000, several central banks joined the European Central Bank in selling U.S. dollars and buying euros to support the European Union's new currency. Right from its inception in January 1999, the euro fell in value against the dollar almost 20 percent (again see Figure 6.1). With fully 30 percent of Intel, Sun Microsystems, Hewlett-Packard, IBM, and Oracle worldwide sales in Europe, the U.S. Federal Reserve was motivated by concern about projected declines in the U.S. export sector if dollar appreciation continued. One of Intel's chief competitors, Siemens of Germany, reported record chip sales the same day that Intel warned that earnings would slump because of weaker demand in Europe. That Friday, Intel stock declined in value 23 percent (or $97 billion). The central banks of Japan and England had similar reasons to avoid export sector collapses by intervening to support the euro. Coordinated intervention for several days resulted in a 7 percent appreciation of the euro. Soon thereafter the U.S. dollar continued its climb, peaking a year later in mid-2001.

Short-Term Exchange Rate Fluctuations

The transaction demand determinants of long-term annual trends in exchange rates are fundamentally different from the determinants of day-to-day exchange rate fluctuations. Short-term exchange rate movements from week to week, day to day, or even hour to hour are determined by arbitrage activity in the international capital markets and by speculative demand, rather than by the transaction demand determinants of trade flows and long-term international capital investments. Speculative demand is motivated by arbitrage and driven by volatile investor expectations of what other investors are likely to do. Arbitrage activity is triggered by temporary violations of arbitrage equilibrium conditions, such as equal real rates of return on 90-day government bonds (adjusted for any differences in default risk). When such conditions do not hold, opportunities for arbitrage profits exist, and arbitrage activity will appear quickly, proceed at huge volume, and continue until the relevant arbitrage equilibrium conditions are reestablished.[8]

Arbitrage
Buying cheap and selling elsewhere for an immediate profit.

Speculation
Buying cheap and selling later for a delayed profit (or loss).

[8] **Arbitrage** is the act of buying real assets, commodities, stocks, bonds, loans, or even televisions and radios cheaply and selling them at higher prices later. If the buying and selling prices and terms of delivery can be arranged simultaneously, then the transaction is one of pure arbitrage. If the second transaction is delayed, we often call the activity **speculation.**

Again, the sheer magnitude of the international capital flows committed to this financial arbitrage between nations is astounding. Remember, the dollar value of the flow *per day* in the world's capital markets is $2 trillion. These enormous floodtides of arbitrage capital quickly (within hours or even minutes) close the window of arbitrage profit opportunity in government bills and FX trading.

Foreign Exchange Risk Management

Internal Hedge

A balance sheet offset or foreign payables offset to fluctuations in foreign receipts attributable to exchange rate risk.

To reduce the potentially wide swings in cash flows and net assets resulting from currency fluctuations, companies use financial hedges and internal hedges. **Internal hedges** may be either operating hedges or balance sheet hedges. Operating hedges reduce operating cash flow risk exposure by matching anticipated foreign sales receipts against projected foreign operating expenses in that same currency. A few companies such as Nestlé and Unilever have so many foreign operations and so many global brands (Nestlé Crunch, Carnation, Perrier, Kit Kat, Lipton Tea, Dove Soap, Wishbone, Bird's Eye, Obsession) that their operating hedges circumvent the need for further risk management. And 72 percent of all U.S., Asian, and U.K. companies consider operating hedges an important focus of FX risk management.

EXAMPLE

South Carolina Plant Helps BMW Internally Hedge Its Operations Risk

The North American subsidiary of BMW can now accept purchase orders with payment in U.S. dollars and then use those same dollar receipts to cover BMW marketing expenses in the United States. In addition, in 1995, BMW built a Spartanburg, South Carolina, plant to assemble its popular 325 model convertibles and more recently Z3, Z4, and X5s. This massive facility along the major East Coast Interstate I-85 incurs tens of millions of dollars of annual labor and local materiel expenses. Such offsetting positions payable in U.S. dollars are a way of hedging the operating risk exposure of BMW receivables in U.S. dollars. With an internal hedge provided by a German ball-bearing plant, Cummins Engine could accomplish the same thing.

In contrast, balance sheet hedges address primarily translation risk exposure by matching assets and liabilities in various countries and their respective currencies. Fewer than 25 percent of all U.S., Asian, and U.K. companies consider translation risk important.

Value at Risk

The notional value of a transaction exposed to appreciation or depreciation because of exchange rate risk.

Financial hedges in a manufacturing or service company reduce transaction risk exposure by setting up positions in financial derivative contracts to offset cash flow losses from currency fluctuations. More than 93 percent of U.S., Asian, and U.K. companies employ forward contracts to manage transaction risk exposure.[9] Goldman Sachs estimates that a financial hedge for $100 million of risk exposure costs about $5.2 million, approximately 5 percent of the **value at risk.** As the dollar appreciated steeply against the euro in 2000, Goodyear decided that these hedging costs were prohibitive and ended up earning $68 million profit on their European

[9] Andrew P. Marshall, "Foreign Exchange Risk Management in Multinational Companies," *Journal of Multinational Financial Management,* 10 (2000), pp. 185–211.

INTERNATIONAL PERSPECTIVES

TOYOTA AND HONDA BUY U.S. ASSEMBLY CAPACITY[10]

From 1980–1995, the Japanese share of the North American auto market rose from 20 to 30 percent, and the U.S. demand for the Toyota Camry and Honda Accord began to outdistance the capacities of Japanese factories. Total quality management and cost-cutting initiatives made it possible to hold price increases on Camrys and Accords to a minimum. As a result, the Toyota Camry became the highest-volume model of any car sold in the United States.

The U.S. Congress responded with "voluntary import restraints" on Japanese cars and imposed a 25 percent tariff on Japanese light trucks. In part to ease the trade policy pressure, to exempt their cars and trucks from U.S. tariffs, and to improve the delivery time and reliability for their most popular models, Toyota and Honda each purchased four assembly plants in North America. By 1996, Honda assembled in North America 80 percent (and Toyota assembled 60 percent) of their vehicles sold in North America.

When a manufacturer's home currency is strong, foreign direct investment in overseas plant and equipment is especially attractive. From 1985 to 1993, the yen rocketed from ¥238 per U.S. dollar to ¥94 per U.S. dollar (see Figure 6.1), as Honda and Toyota employed the strengthening yen to acquire their U.S. manufacturing capacity. A $1 billion U.S. assembly plant that drew down balance sheet cash by ¥94 billion in 1993 would have drawn down ¥238 billion cash or would have introduced a ¥238 billion debt liability on the balance sheet 10 years earlier. These reduced liabilities in acquiring new fixed assets provided a balance sheet hedge offsetting the ever-lower yen receipts 1980–1995 from the U.S. sale of another Camry or Accord. Nevertheless, the U.S. assembly plants were clearly a response to U.S. protectionist trade policy, and not motivated by the balance sheet hedges.

[10] Based on "Japanese Carmakers Plan Major Expansion of American Capacity," *Wall Street Journal* (September 24, 1997), p. A1; and "Detroit Is Getting Sideswiped by the Yen," *BusinessWeek* (November 11, 1996), p. 54.

operations rather than the $92 million ($97 gross profit – $5 million hedging cost) they would have earned with a fully hedged position.[11] In contrast, Coca-Cola established a covered hedge for their euro net cash flow risk exposure that year.

COVERED HEDGES: FORWARDS, OPTIONS, AND SWAPS

By establishing a short position in the foreign currency forward or options markets, a company can hedge the domestic cash flow from their export sales receipts. For example, suppose Cummins Engine had sales contracts with its German dealers for future delivery in 2001 of €5 million of diesel engines. Cummins has risk exposure to a decline in the value of these export sales receipts. So, to lay off this exchange rate risk, in 2000 Cummins sells a euro forward contract in the foreign exchange derivative markets to establish a hedge. Cummins's transaction is described as a covered hedge because Cummins anticipates euro receivables (from their German dealers) equal to the amount of their short forward position. That is, their contract sales receipts "cover" their obligation to deliver as a seller of euro forward contracts.

[11] "Business Won't Hedge the Euro Away," *BusinessWeek* (December 4, 2000), p. 157.

EXAMPLE

Cummins Engine Goes Short

Selling forward contracts in 2000 at some prespecified forward price (say, \$1.00/€) that agreed to deliver €5 million at a future settlement date in 2001 made money for Cummins Engine because the dollar appreciated and the euro receipts from foreign sales declined in dollar value. In particular, at €1.12 per dollar in 2001 (i.e., \$0.89/€), Cummins was entitled to receive \$1.00/€ for European currency that it could purchase in the spot market in 2001 for \$0.89/€. Therefore, Cummins "cancelled" its forward position and collected from the futures market settlements process a gain of \$0.11/€ × 5 million euros = \$550,000. This cash flow was just sufficient to cover their \$1.00 to \$0.89 per euro loss in value on the €5 million in 2001 sales receipts from their German dealers. As intended, these two cash flows from a covered hedge just offset one another.

Besides setting up internal hedges or short forward positions, Cummins Engine and BMW could also have entered into a currency-swap contract to exchange their anticipated future streams of dollar and euro cash flows from export sales. BMW would swap a prespecified amount of their anticipated dollar receipts from auto sales in North America for a prespecified amount of Cummins's anticipated euro sales receipts in Germany.[12] However, these swap contract alternatives to demanding payment in their domestic (home) currency impose some costs on BMW and Cummins Engine. Therefore, BMW generally will offer its best fixed price on an export transaction to an American or other foreign buyer on a purchase order payable in euros. And for the same reason, the best fixed price from Cummins Engine generally will be available on a purchase order payable only in U.S. dollars.

The Determinants of Long-Run Trends in Exchange Rates

Short-term movements in FX rates are caused by speculative demand. Sometimes current events set speculators off in support of demanding and holding a currency (a long position), sometimes the reverse (a short position). Behaviorally, each speculator tries to guess what the others will do, and much herd-like stampeding behavior ensues.

Long-run trends in FX rate are quite different. Understanding the magnitude, the timing, and the forces that set in motion the exchange-rate-induced swings in sales and profits is crucial for effectively managing export business. Quarter-to-quarter or year-to-year trends depend on three factors: real growth rates, real interest rates, and anticipated cost inflation rates. We now discuss each of these determinants in turn.

The Role of Real Growth Rates

As we have seen, a primary determinant of the year-to-year exchange rate fluctuations in Figure 6.1 is the net direction of trade flows. Unanticipated increases in

[12] At each future settlement date in a swap contract, the difference between the spot market exchange rate and the forward rates prespecified at the start of the swap contract actually determine who pays whom. For complete explanations of the use of forwards, options, and swap contracts in managing foreign exchange risk, see C. Eun and B. Resnick, *International Finance,* 3rd ed. (Burr Ridge, IL: McGraw-Hill, 2003).

imports lower a local currency's value, whereas unanticipated increases in exports raise a local currency's value. The stimulus underlying such trade flow imbalances may be either business cycle–based, productivity-based, or may arise from the introduction of protectionist trade barriers. In a business cycle– or productivity-based domestic expansion, consumption (including import consumption) increases, causing exports from a country's trading partners to increase; in a domestic contraction, import consumption decreases, causing exports from the trading partners to decline.

EXAMPLE

A European Slowdown Decreases DuPont's Exports[13]

"Beggar thy neighbor" became the rallying cry for trade policy in the mercantilist centuries (1500–1750), during which punitive tariffs and other forms of protectionism isolated city, state, and national economies. Today, however, rather than attempting self-sufficiency, most nations are better off recognizing mutual interdependence, encouraging both import and export activities, and specializing in accordance with comparative advantage. In that freer trade environment, growing neighbors are the best neighbors.

In the late 1990s, an economic slowdown in Europe undercut the export sales of American manufacturers and U.S. multinationals. Not only Cummins Engine (28%), Sun Microsystems (36%), and DuPont (39%), but even Wrigley Chewing Gum (41%) and McDonald's (37%) realized a large proportion of their 1997 revenue in Europe. Across all S&P 500 U.S. companies, 21 percent of 1997 sales revenue came from European sales. After several years of steady increases, import demand by households and companies flattened in Germany and France, and it actually declined in Italy and the United Kingdom during 1998. The U.S. industrial sector was particularly hard hit; chemicals shipments from the United States to Europe, for example, declined 20 percent on a year-to-year basis.

During the years 2002–2005, U.S. gross domestic product (GDP) grew at 1.6 percent, 2.7 percent, 4.2 percent, and 3.5 percent, respectively, in real terms (i.e., adjusted for inflation) (see Table 6.1). The United States had an accelerating economy. In those same years, Euro area real GDP, on the other hand, exhibited anemic growth at 0.9 percent, 0.5 percent, 1.8 percent, and 1.4 percent. Although Canadian growth rates were comparable to the United States, both Mexico and Japan had slower growth than the United States (again, see Table 6.1). Among the five largest U.S. export trading partners, only China was growing faster than the United States (at 8.3%, 9.5%, 9.5%, and 9.0%). These growth-rate trends led to decreased exports from the United States of goods such as computer software, PCs, grains, aircraft, professional services, and diesel engines, while causing increased imports into the United States of goods such as autos, textiles, furniture, and consumer electronics.

As U.S. net exports (exports minus imports) fell 2002–2005, foreign buyers had to acquire fewer dollars to complete transactions with U.S. companies such as Microsoft, IBM, ADM, Boeing, McKinsey, and Cummins Engine. In the market for

[13] "Weak Growth in Europe Threatens U.S. Exports," *Wall Street Journal* (March 11, 1999), p. A1.

Table 6.1 Transaction Determinants of Long-Term Exchange Rate Trends

	United States			Germany/Euro Area			Japan			China		
	Real GDP	Real r	PPI	Real GDP	Real r	PPI	Real GDP	Real r	PPI	Real GDP	Real r	PPI
1995	2.7	3.1	1.9	2.0	3.2	2.0	1.9	1.3	−0.6	10.5	−6.7	14.1
1996	3.7	2.5	2.7	1.0	1.4	1.0	2.6	0.5	−1.4	9.6	0.7	6.8
1997	4.5	3.3	0.4	1.9	1.4	1.8	1.4	−1.1	0.2	8.8	5.8	2.0
1998	4.2	4.0	−0.8	1.8	2.5	0.5	−1.9	0.0	0.3	7.8	5.5	−0.9
1999	4.4	3.1	1.8	2.9	1.9	3.9	−0.1	0.5	−0.9	7.1	4.6	−0.8
2000	3.7	3.1	3.8	4.0	2.3	7.1	2.9	0.9	−0.2	8.0	2.9	2.4
2001	0.8	0.9	1.9	2.0	1.9	2.0	0.4	0.8	−0.7	7.5	2.7	2.8
2002	1.6	0.1	−1.3	1.0	1.0	−0.1	0.1	1.0	−0.9	8.3	3.5	1.3
2003	2.7	−1.1	3.2	0.8	0.3	1.4	1.8	0.34	−0.5	9.5	1.5	3.1
2004	4.2	−1.1	3.6	1.8	0.0	2.3	2.3	0.03	1.4	9.5	−0.7	7.5
2005	3.5	0.1	4.9	1.4	0.0	4.1	2.6	0.33	2.0	9.0	1.5	4.6

Sources: Federal Reserve Bank of St. Louis, *International Economic Trends* (July 2006); European Central Bank, *Statistics Pocketbook* (2006).
Notes: Real GDP refers to the growth rate of gross domestic product adjusted for price changes by the GDP deflator. Real r refers to the short-term interest rate on government debt minus the annual percentage change in consumer prices. PPI is the annual percentage change in producer prices.

dollars as foreign exchange depicted in Figure 6.4, this decline of net exports decreased the demand for dollars; D_{2001} shifts to the left to D_{2002} and on to D_{2004}. At the same time, increased purchases of foreign imports by Americans will increase the supply of dollars. That is, in the market for dollars as foreign exchange, S_{2001} shifts right to S_{2005}. Both factors cause a depreciation of the U.S. dollar, such as occurred in 2001–2004. In sum, the decrease in exports and increase in imports led to a fall in the price of the dollar against the euro from €1.12 per dollar in 2001 to €0.80 per dollar in 2004 and against the yen from ¥125 per dollar in 2002 to ¥108 per dollar in 2004. The market demand and supply shifts 2001–2004 shown in Figure 6.4 mirror the collapse of the €/$ and ¥/$ exchange rates depicted over this period at the right of Figure 6.1.

The uptick of both exchange rates in 2005, to ¥114/$ and €0.82/$, reflects a coordinated intervention by the Singapore and Chinese central banks in the first quarter of 2005. Unstopped decay in the dollar's value not only threatened to derail the competitiveness of Chinese exports, but also threatened the value of a massive Chinese asset. In particular, in 2005 the Chinese alone held $800 billion in official dollar reserves. Thus, these two and a few other developing country central banks in Asia purchased $269 billion of U.S. Treasury securities in an attempt to end the decay in the dollar's value,[14] thereby bolstering the value of their remaining U.S. dollar reserves.

[14] By accepting a U.S. T-bill promissory note in exchange for official dollar reserves, the Chinese and Singaporan central banks effectively reduced the supply of U.S. dollars in circulation. As before, reduced supply in Figures 6.3 or 6.4 implies a higher equilibrium price. See "The Dollar U-Turn," Federal Reserve Bank at St Louis, *International Economic Trends* (February 2006,) p. 1.

Figure 6.4 The Market for U.S. Dollars as Foreign Exchange (Depreciation Against the Yen and the Euro 2001–2004; Appreciation in 2005)

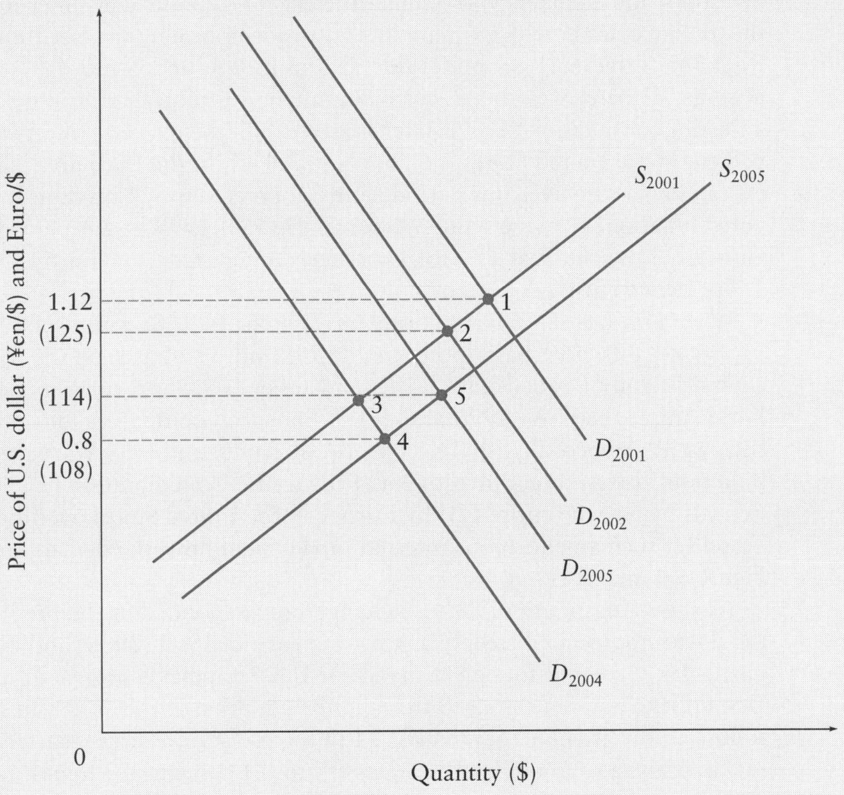

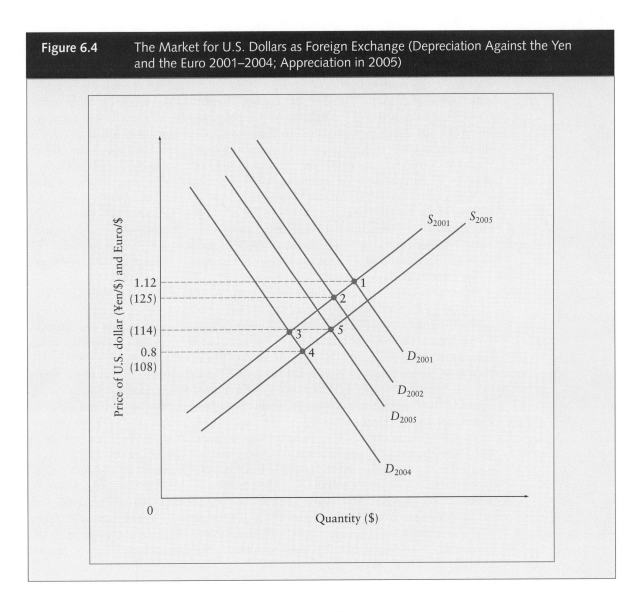

THE ROLE OF REAL INTEREST RATES

The second factor determining long-run trends in exchange rates is comparable interest rates adjusted for inflation. The higher the real rate of interest in an economy, the greater the demand for the financial assets offered by that economy. If a Japanese, German, or Swiss investor can earn higher returns (for equivalent risk) from U.S. Treasury bills than from Euromoney or Japanese government bills, foreign owners of capital will move quickly to rebalance their portfolios to incorporate more U.S. assets. Since the New York Federal Reserve Bank auctioning off new T-bills; Salomon Brothers underwriting a new issue of DuPont bonds; Merrill-Lynch selling T-bills, T-bonds, and DuPont bonds in the secondary (resale) market; and the New York Stock Exchange settlements department all require payment in U.S. dollars, the foreign investor who desires U.S. financial assets must first acquire U.S. dollars to complete his or her transactions. So, a higher real interest rate in the United States (relative to European, Japanese, and British rates) implies international capital inflow into the United States and an increased demand for and appreciation of U.S. dollars.

What really matters in triggering these international capital flows is an investor's expectation of domestic value of the foreign interest earned when capital invested overseas is redeemed and the interest paid is converted back from the foreign to the investor's home currency. Nominal interest rates minus consumer inflation rates in the foreign country approximate this post-redemption return (see the column labeled Real r in Table 6.1). In mid-1999, U.S. 3-month and 6-month T-bills yielded on average 5.3 percent with a 2.2 percent inflation forecast, returning 3.1 percent after adjusting for inflation. A year later in mid-2000, the real rate of return remained 3.1 percent in the United States (i.e., 6.5% − 3.4%). In the Euro area, short-term interest rates also rose over this period from 3.0 percent to 4.4 percent, but so did anticipated inflation, growing from 1.1 percent in mid-1999 to 2.1 percent in mid-2000. Consequently, the real rate of short-term interest across Europe increased from 1.9 percent to just 2.3 percent.

With 120 basis points favoring investment in U.S. assets in 1999 [(0.031 − 0.019) × 100], 150 basis points in 1998, and 190 basis points in 1997, foreign capital literally flooded into T-bills and other U.S. short-term money instruments. For example, between 1996 and 2000, European companies and investment funds such as BP Amoco, British Telecom, BASF, Bayer, and UBS-Warburg invested $650 billion in foreign direct investment (FDI) in the United States. This four-year figure exceeds by half the entire FDI by Europe in the United States over the past 50 years. To reflect such an enormous international capital flow, the demand for the dollar in Figure 6.4 increases.

As shown in Figure 6.1, the exchange rate responded in the predicted fashion as the dollar appreciated steeply against the euro in 1999, 2000, and on into 2001. In particular, increased foreign demand for U.S. financial assets raised the demand for U.S. dollars, and hence raised the equilibrium price of the dollar. In 2002, however, following the attack of September 11 in the midst of a three-quarter U.S. recession, real interest rates in the United States fell to 0.1 percent, the lowest rate in 40 years, and then continued lower to −1.07 percent in 2003 and −1.11 percent in 2004. Predictably, based on this real interest rate factor, the dollar then collapsed against the euro (see Figure 6.1).

The Role of Expected Inflation

Inflationary expectations provide an important third determinant of long-term trends in exchange rates. Suppose you were entering into a long-term contract to replace the diesel engines installed in a fleet of trucks over the next three to five years. Would you be inclined to approach and enter into negotiation with Cummins Engine, where recent material costs have been low, cost-saving productivity increases have been substantial, and union bargaining pressure may be declining? Or would you approach a substitute supplier such as Mercedes-Benz, where all those factors are reversed, suggesting the strong possibility of a surging inflationary trend in input costs that underlay the price you could negotiate for a German diesel engine over the next several quarters?

Cost inflation is usually compared across economies by examining an index of producer prices. From 2003 to 2005, the percentage change in producer prices in the United States was 3.2 percent, 3.6 percent, and 4.9 percent, respectively, whereas in the Euro area, producer prices increased by less (i.e., 1.4%, 2.3%, and 4.1%). Clearly, the lower price in a long-term fixed price contract for replacement diesels would not be available from Cummins, the company in a country experiencing higher cost-push inflation. Consequently, export sales on U.S. traded goods such as Cummins diesels would decrease.[15]

In Figure 6.4, the D_{2003} (not shown), D_{2004}, and D_{2005} demands for the U.S. dollar all shift to the left, and the dollar depreciates still further. Indeed, the relative purchasing power parity (PPP) hypothesis says that goods arbitrage of this sort will continue until the €/$ exchange rate adjusts upward sufficiently to reflect entirely the inflation differential. That is, between the United States and Europe, a 1.8 percent (3.2% − 1.4%) differential in the producer price index favoring Europe should, according to PPP, depreciate the value of the dollar by approximately 1.8 percent. We discuss purchasing power parity in the next section.

PURCHASING POWER PARITY

When no significant transportation, legal, or cultural costs or other barriers are associated with moving goods or services between markets, then the price of each product should be the same from one international market to another. This conclusion is known as the *law of one price*. When the different markets represent different countries, the law of one price says that prices will be the same in each country after making the appropriate conversion from one currency to another. Alternatively, one can say that exchange rates between two currencies will equal the ratio of the price indexes between the countries. In international finance and trade, this relationship is known as the absolute version of purchasing power parity.

Absolute purchasing power parity implies that core inflation that results in a doubling of U.K. prices for a Dickens novel (and other traded goods) will result in a depreciation of the British currency by 50 percent. For example, if after a sustained period of British inflation, one needs £20 to buy a Dickens novel that before the inflation cost £10, and if Japanese publishers will continue to print and sell that same novel (in English) for ¥1000, the novel will be exported to Britain, driving down the pound. Such imports by the British will persist, and the supply of pounds to support these import transactions will continue to grow until the exchange rate reflecting the price of the British pound declines from ¥1000/£10 = ¥100/£ all the way to ¥50/£. At that point the two prices for acquiring a Dickens novel will again be the same in the two economies, £20 from Britain and ¥1000 from Japan. Goods arbitragers in global book supply chains prevent the delivered prices in Britain and Asia from remaining different for long. Does this example imply global supply chains will displace all country manager processes?

Relative Purchasing Power Parity (PPP)
A relationship between differential inflation rates and long-term trends in exchange rates.

A less restrictive form of the law of one price is known as **relative purchasing power parity (PPP)**. The relative PPP principle states that in comparison to a period when exchange rates between two countries are in equilibrium, changes in the differential rates of inflation between two countries will be offset by equal, but opposite, changes in the future spot exchange rate. For example, if prices in the

[15] Eventually, if producer cost inflation differentials between the United States and Germany persist, import-export companies that specialize in capital equipment transactions between the United States and Germany will join the surging demand for American products and buy replacement diesels cheaply in the United States for resale at a profit in Germany. This goods arbitrage activity, discussed in the next section, limits the extent to which such cost differentials can persist for long periods of time.

WHAT WENT RIGHT • WHAT WENT WRONG

FORD MOTOR CO. AND EXIDE BATTERIES: ARE COUNTRY MANAGERS HERE TO STAY?[16]

As export growth outstripped domestic growth for many U.S. firms in the 1990s, multinationals such as Ford Motor, Procter & Gamble, and Exide Batteries wrestled with the question of whether to organize worldwide operations by product line or by country. That is, should operations and marketing decisions be controlled by global business units for Tide detergent, Pampers diapers, and Crest toothpaste, or should country managers in Spain, Germany, and China call the shots on input contracts, manufacturing standards, assembly location, pricing, and promotion?

By developing global product lines, Ford Motor claimed $5 billion in savings from 1995–1998 when it eliminated overlapping plants, standardized suppliers, realized volume discounts on components, and brought new products to market faster. A consolidated worldwide design team and centralized manufacturing authority saved money. However, Ford Europe's market share slipped from 13 percent in 1995 to 8.8 percent in 1999; untargeted marketing and inflexible pricing divorced from local market conditions were to blame.

Exide pursued the same path from 1998–2002 by organizing its global business units around its automotive, industrial, and network telecom batteries. Major plants were spread out as far apart as China, Brazil, and Germany, because subassembly components from these far-flung sources often cut labor costs tenfold and shortened lead times from three months to five weeks. Yet, Exide found that some regional sales teams continued to excel in ways global sales teams could not, and so the North American industrial battery operation has again become a separate division. As a result, relationship marketing between Exide–North America and Ford headquarters in Detroit secured a major new account in automotive batteries for Exide.

[16] "Place vs. Product: It's Tough to Choose a Management Model," *Wall Street Journal* (June 21, 2001), p. A1; and "The World as a Single Machine," *The Economist* (June 20, 1998), pp. 3–18.

United States rise by 4 percent per year and prices in Europe rise by 6 percent per year, then relative PPP asserts that the euro will weaken relative to the U.S. dollar by approximately 2 percent.

The exact relative purchasing power parity relationship is

$$\text{Relative PPP: } \left(\frac{S_1}{S_0}\right) = \left(\frac{1 + \pi_h}{1 + \pi_f}\right) \qquad [6.1]$$

where S_1 is the expected future spot rate at time period 1, S_0 is the current spot rate, π_h is the expected home country (U.S.) inflation rate, and π_f is the expected foreign country inflation rate. Using the previous example, if U.S. prices are expected to rise by 4 percent over the coming year, prices in Europe are expected to rise by 6 percent during the same time, and the current spot exchange rate (S_0) is \$0.60/€, then the expected spot rate in one year (S_1) will be

$$S_1/\$0.60 = (1 + 0.04)/(1 + 0.06)$$
$$S_1 = \$0.5887$$
$$= \$0.60\ (1 - 0.0189)$$

Figure 6.5 Purchasing Power Parity (DM/$, 1973–2001)

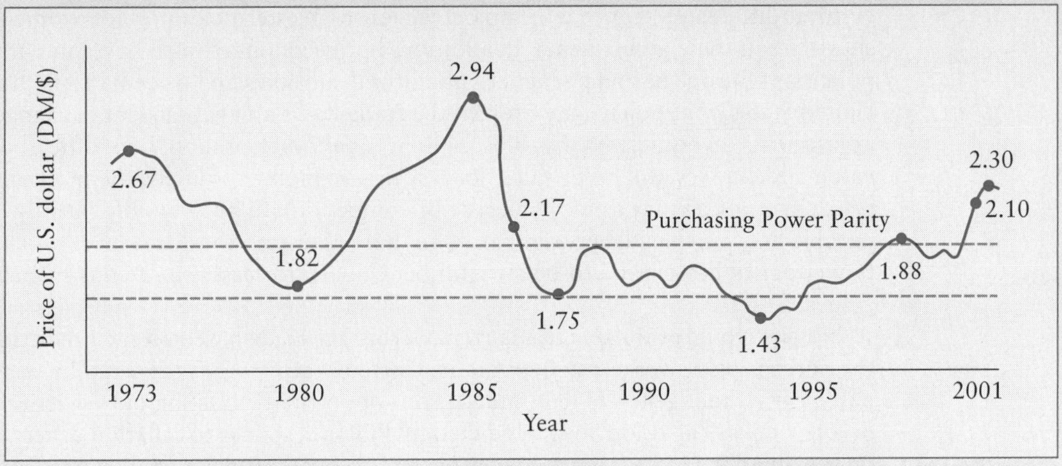

The higher European inflation rate can be expected to result in a decline in the future spot value of the euro relative to the dollar by 1.89 percent.[17]

The dashed lines in Figure 6.5 indicate purchasing power parity between the deutsche mark and the U.S. dollar, accounting for cumulative inflation in the United States and Germany from 1973–2000. Over this period, the consumer price index in Germany rose from 67.1 to 137.2 (a 104% increase), and the consumer price index in the United States rose from 49.3 to 166.7 (a 238% increase). Starting from a March 1973 exchange rate of DM 2.81/$, the predicted equilibrium exchange rate in 2000 implied by the hypothesis of relative purchasing power parity would be (DM 2.81/$1.00) × (204/338) = 1.70, close to the actual 1997 exchange rate of DM 1.76/$ but far below the 2000 exchange rate of 2.30. Therefore, as shown in Figure 6.5, the dollar was substantially above its purchasing power parity level in 1984–1986, and again in 1999–2001. In each case, a subsequent sharp decline in value against European currencies ensued. Between 2001 and 2005, for example, the dollar lost 34 percent of its value against the euro (see Figure 6.1).

QUALIFICATIONS OF PPP

Purchasing power parity calculations can be sensitive to the starting point for the analysis. In 1972, the DM/$ exchange rate averaged DM 3.19/$, whereas in 1973 the average value of the dollar fell to DM 2.67/$. The 1972 starting point implies a 2000 exchange rate predicted by PPP of DM 1.93/$, while the 1973 starting point implies a predicted 2000 exchange rate of only DM 1.70/$. Clearly, the difference is nontrivial, and many such applications of the PPP hypothesis will hinge on which year the analyst chooses to start. Figure 6.5 indicates this qualification by displaying a band of exchange rates within which PPP holds.

17 Several other parity conditions in international finance are discussed in R. C. Moyer, W. Kretlow, and J. McGuigan, *Contemporary Financial Management,* 10th ed. (Cincinnati, OH: Thomson/South-Western, 2003), Chapter 22.

Purchasing power parity has several other qualifications as well. For the full PPP adjustments to take place in exchange rates as domestic prices inflate, the traded goods must be nearly identical in quality and use in the two economies. Cross-cultural differences (e.g., the Islamic aversion to Western clothing for women) can short-circuit these adjustments. In addition, both economies must have similar trade policies. If Europe has much higher agricultural subsidies and trade barriers than the United States, that policy may prevent the trade flows and subsequent exchange rate adjustments hypothesized by PPP. Similar qualifications apply to differences in value-added taxes and other sales taxes across economies. Finally, the markups and profit margins arising from the degree of competition in an economy must be comparable for purchasing power parity to hold. Despite these caveats, purchasing power parity has proved to be a useful benchmark for assessing trends in currency values.

No one would ever execute a currency arbitrage trade based on the predictions of the purchasing power parity hypothesis. Currency arbitrage is triggered by unanticipated events that generate temporary profit opportunities lasting only several hours or a few days. The trade flows predicted by PPP in response to inflation differentials, on the other hand, are a much longer-term process requiring several quarters or even years. Companies with a substantial proportion of their sales abroad must identify these longer-term trends in exchange rates, and purchasing power parity proves useful for just that purpose. For example, a realization that the dollar was well above purchasing power parity levels in 1984–1985 and again in 1999–2001 should have influenced production and pricing policies at the start of the twenty-first century.

Being attuned to the international business environment of exchange rate trends does not allow fine tuning, but it does allow better medium-term planning of production volume, proactive pricing, targeted marketing, and segmented distribution channels, all of which may offer profit advantages. Some companies make these considerations a focus of their business plans and prosper in international markets; others are less successful.

EXAMPLE

What Went Wrong? GM, Nissan, and the Value of the Dollar 1980–1988[18]

In 1980, with exchange rates at ¥226/$ and DM 1.82/$, the Buick Century sold for approximately $10,000. Nissan priced its competing four-door standard sedan, the Maxima, at ¥2,250,000, or $9,956. As the dollar appreciated spectacularly in 1980–1984 against the German mark (i.e., 1.82 to 2.94) and appreciated somewhat against the yen (i.e., 226 to 238), GM took four price increases averaging 10.2 percent per year across all its models, which added 48 percent ($1.102^4 = 1.48$) to the domestic (dollar) price of cars such as the Century. Nissan took four price increases averaging 13.8 percent, which added 68 percent to the dollar price of a Maxima sold in the United States The dollar had risen 5 percent, so Nissan's effective price increase in their home currency was 63 percent in yen (68% − 5%). For GM, the export price to Japan was 53 percent (48% + 5%) higher.

[18] Based on "General Motors and the Dollar," Harvard Business School, Publishing Division, Harvard University (1989); and "Foreign-Owned Plants Produce Growing Share of U.S. Autos," *Investors Business Daily* (March 30, 1998), p. A4.

Consider, however, the net price increases for GM products in deutsche marks. Because the dollar had risen 47 percent against the mark in 1980–1984, the net price increase for overseas sales in Germany in 1985 was a whopping 95 percent (48% + 47%) higher in deutsche marks. The Opel Division of General Motors found it difficult to explain to potential German customers why asking prices should essentially double in so short a period. Accordingly, Opel received permission to roll back many of these price increases.

In the subsequent period, 1985–1988, the dollar depreciated almost as spectacularly as it had risen in 1980–1984 (i.e., −44% against the mark and −60% against the yen). It is instructive to examine how Nissan and GM reacted when their roles in managing the exchange rate trends reversed. Now, Nissan had to deal with a strengthening currency and the deterioration of export sales that might follow, the same problem GM had faced in 1980–1984. Nissan's response was to slash their profit margins by taking only 5.7 percent per-year dollar price increases (i.e., $1.057^4 = 1.25$ = 25% price increase) at a time when their currency was steeply appreciating by 60 percent. Over this four-year period, therefore, the net receipts in yen from selling a Maxima in the United States export market declined by 35 percent (25% − 60%). That is, the 25 percent additional dollars charged were worth so much less yen that the net receipts in the home currency actually fell by 35 percent. General Motors, in this 1985–1988 time period, took 7.2 percent price increases, raising dollar receipts 32 percent ($1.072^4 = 1.32$).

Altogether, between 1980 and 1988, the cumulative dollar price increases on the competing cars were similar. A $10,000 GM car rose in price to $19,479, and a competing $9,956 Nissan car rose in price to $20,837. However, the exchange rate trend from ¥226/$ in 1980 to ¥128/$ in 1988 reveals that the Japanese accepted a much smaller price increase in their home currency. Multiplying $20,837 by ¥128 to the dollar identifies the Nissan gross receipts on an export Maxima in 1988 as ¥2,667,136. This figure represents only a *cumulative* 20 percent yen price increase over the eight years, while GM's cumulative dollar price increase was 95 percent. Not surprisingly, the Japanese share of the U.S. new car market grew rapidly over this period, from 19.8 percent to 23.7 percent. General Motors' market share plummeted from 45.9 percent in 1980 to 36.1 percent in 1988.

Why did GM and Nissan have such different pricing and markup policies? One might suspect that costs were higher in the United States during 1980–1988. In fact, the unit labor costs in auto manufacturing were lower in the United States than in Japan over this period. Perhaps Nissan sought greater sales volume to realize scale economies or take advantage of learning curve-related reductions in unit cost as cumulative volume increased. Total quality initiatives in Japanese manufacturing in this period did realize much-heralded cost savings on the assembly plant floor as more vehicles passed quality inspections without requiring rework. And cost savings from manufacturing quality initiatives are related to volume. Nissan's plant in Smyrna, Tennessee, is heralded as the most efficient assembly line in America, with worker productivity almost 35 percent higher than the average GM plant. Finally, Toyota, Honda, and Nissan certainly are export-driven companies. Between 1985 and 1988, Nissan generated 50 percent of its sales abroad (fully 45% in the United States alone).

General Motors, in contrast, had 72 percent domestic sales, 12 percent export sales, and 16 percent sales from overseas production divisions. Consequently, GM does not focus marketing and operations planning on export sales. Every company should, however, always analyze their import market competition. Fundamentally,

GM simply maintained higher net profit margins (i.e., 3.2% return on sales) over 1980–1988, while Nissan cut net margins (i.e., from 2.4% to 1.2%) to achieve market penetration and realize cost savings on greater production volume. Nissan's response to ¥/$ exchange rate fluctuations is typical of Japanese manufacturers, who tend to absorb approximately half of any unfavorable exchange rate moves (appreciations of the yen) by reducing margins.

The Appropriate Use of PPP: An Overview

What, then, is the appropriate role of purchasing power parity in managing international business? First, one should be aware that PPP is a long-run proposition. Arbitrage activities are motivated whenever the price of auto tires or canned green beans in one economy departs markedly from the price of similar goods in another economy, not far distant. In such circumstances, entrepreneurs emerge to buy cheap in one location and sell dear in the other, but goods arbitrage takes time. Goods arbitrage requires logistical infrastructure such as freight terminals, distribution networks or reliable relationships, and effective transnational marketing campaigns. Until all these matters can be resolved, international markets remain somewhat segmented, thereby preventing the complete convergence of prices of identical products between the United States and Japan, between EU countries, between the United States and the United Kingdom, and even between the United States and Canada. Unlike arbitrage in financial markets, the goods arbitrage underlying PPP may take months, years, or even decades. As a result, the variance of prices for like goods across countries is larger (often 10 times larger) than the variance of prices through time within an economy.[19]

In the short run, therefore, when the prices of traded goods in the United States diverge from those in the United Kingdom, nominal exchange rates may not respond to fully offset the price differentials, as predicted by PPP. Instead, price stickiness in traded goods combined with the lemming-like behavior of herds of FX (foreign exchange) speculators leads to more volatile nominal exchange rates than would characterize a fully adjusting price regime. In particular, nominal exchange rates may overshoot or undershoot their equilibrium levels in adjusting to demand or monetary shocks. To avoid the problem of comparing prices across countries at contemporaneous exchange rates that may bias the assessment, many analysts perform cross-border comparisons of price levels or trade statistics using purchasing power parity estimates for the prior 15-year period.

For example, if one observes in June 2004 that 10 feet of 0.019-gauge gutter pipe sells in do-it-yourself stores in the United States for $3.36 and that in mid-2004 the value of the British pound is $1.80/£ (i.e., £0.55/$), it might be misleading to calculate that identically priced gutter pipe should sell for £1.84 in the United Kingdom (i.e., $3.36 × £0.55/$). Even if the British are paying £2.10, the apparent arbitrage profit of (£2.10 − £1.84) × $1.80/£ = $0.47 per 10 feet may not be available. Consequently, rushing out to organize the distribution and export of U.S. gutter pipe for sale in Great Britain every time the exchange rate overshoots or undershoots does

[19] C. Engel and J. H. Rogers, "How Wide Is the Border?" *American Economic Review,* 86 (1996), pp. 1112–1125; and "Goods Prices and Exchange Rates," *Journal of Economic Literature,* 35 (1997), pp. 1243–1272.

not make sense. Instead, one should multiply the $3.36 U.S. price by a £0.63/$ purchasing power parity value of the pound over 1990–2004 (see Figure 6.1). It would imply that gutter pipe in British stores selling for as much as £2.12 would not be overpriced relative to the United States. And, in light of the confidence bounds around PPP conditions, one might consider a British price of £2.12 ± 10 percent (£1.91 to £2.33) consistent with the absence of arbitrage opportunities in gutter pipe.

EXAMPLE

ARE DIRTY DISHES MOBILE? DIXAN AND GENERIC *PATTI SCALA* FROM SCALA S.P.A.

Sometimes purchasing power parity (PPP) fails to characterize the price of identical items for sale in different currencies because some complementary factors in consumption or production are immobile. Especially unique land is one immobile factor; dirty dishes are another. In July 2001, after a 35 percent, two-year appreciation of the U.S. dollar to 2,284 lira and 1.18 euros, Tuscan villagers found themselves serving mountains of *primi patti* (first dishes) of various pastas to throngs of U.S. tourists. As a result, dirty dishes piled up in many Italian sinks.

As elsewhere, dirty dishes in Italy eventually require *patti scala* (dish soap), and Scala S.p.A. from Castrocielo, France, supplies lemon-scented generic Patti Scala throughout the grocery stores of Tuscany. Generic Patti Scala at 1,900 lira competes directly against Dixan, a popular branded dish soap at 2,600 lira, both in regular size 750-milliliter plastic containers. What is extraordinary at first glance about these Italian prices is that in July 2001, the 1,900 lira and 2,600 lira equated to $0.84 and $1.14, respectively, much less than the price of equivalent dish soaps in U.S. stores (e.g., Harris Teeter sells 750 milliliters of generic dish soap for $1.80; Joy, Palmolive, and Dawn sell for $1.99, $2.49, and $2.79 in roughly comparable sizes—see Table 6.2). Do these differences imply that Joy, Palmolive, and Dawn should anticipate massive erosion of their U.S. market share because of an invasion of lower priced Dixan imports from Italy?

The answer is definitely no, for three reasons. First, of course, customers of Joy, Palmolive, and Dawn in the United States do not recognize the Dixan brand. A massive advertising and promotional campaign by Dixan would be necessary to overcome the brand name barriers to entry in the U.S. market. International

Table 6.2 Competing Dish Soap Products in the United States and Italy

Branded Products	June 2001 Price	Unit Volume (ml.)
Joy	$1.99	740
Palmolive	$2.49	739
Dawn	$2.79	740
Dixan (June 2001)	$1.14 (2,600 lira) + 30% shipping = $1.45	750
Dixan (June 1999)	$1.56 (2,600 lira) + 30% shipping = $2.03	750
Generic Products		
Harris Teeter Dish Soap	$1.80	828
Patti Scala (June 2001)	$0.84 (1,900 lira) + 30% shipping = $1.09	750
Patti Scala (June 1999)	$1.15 (1,900 lira) + 30% shipping = $1.48	750

arbitrage in goods and full attainment of PPP is partially prevented by the customer-switching costs imposed by these brand names. Most branded products compete in at least partially segmented domestic markets.

Second, even in the absence of branded products, PPP may fail to hold in the generic dish soap market because dirty dishes are immobile. Although the chemical ingredients, lemon scents, and hand softeners in Scala S.p.A.'s Patti Scala are virtually identical to those in Harris Teeter Dish Soap, and despite the availability of surplus Patti Scala at 1,900 lira in Italy, the immobile dirty dish complements in consumption are located in the United States. One must therefore incorporate a transportation cost into these price comparisons. A delivered price of Patti Scala in the United States would be 1,900/2,284 lira = $0.84, plus perhaps 30 percent shipping cost (i.e., $1.09). Transportation costs explain a substantial portion of the observed price differential between identical products priced in different currencies.

Still, one should ask, why do the prices of generic dish soap products shipped into another currency's domestic market in the summer of 2001 differ by as much as $1.09 to $1.80? The answer lies in recognizing that purchasing power parity is a hypothesis about long-term price dynamics. Exchange rates often overshoot/undershoot their equilibrium levels, and consequently the ratio of retail prices in one economy to the exchange-rate-adjusted retail prices in another economy should be computed over several years. For example, two years earlier the Italian lira was much stronger than in the summer 2001; specifically, in June 1999 the U.S. dollar exchanged for just 1,665 lira, versus 2,248 lira in June 2001. With the suggested retail prices of Patti Scala and Dixan the same in 1999 as in 2001, Patti Scala at (1,900/1,665 lira =) $1.14 + 30% transportation cost = $1.47 for 750 milliliters (i.e., $0.0020 per milliliter). This unit price in Italy is closely aligned with Harris Teeter's unit price of $0.0022 per milliliter for 828 milliliters of generic dish soap at $1.80. Furthermore, Dixan at (2,600/1,665 lira =) $1.56 + 30% transportation cost = $2.03 for 750 milliliters is nearly identical to Joy's $1.99 price for 740 milliliters of branded dish soap.

In conclusion, successful brand name campaigns, the immobility of complements, and temporary exchange rate overshooting/undershooting may create significant gaps between the final product prices of like products sold in different currencies. Nevertheless, a judicious use of PPP calculations can be very revealing.

EXAMPLE

The Big Mac Index of Purchasing Power Parity[20]

Big Mac hamburgers sold in 120 countries around the world are as close to identical as the McDonald's parent corporation can make them, yet individual country managers have complete discretion in setting the price. In 1974, the Big Mac sold for approximately $1.00 in the United States and DM 2.50 in Germany. In that same year, 2.50 German marks exchanged for one U.S. dollar in the foreign currency markets. The Big Mac index of PPP for a hamburger (i.e., DM 2.50/$1.00) just equaled the actual exchange rate.

By 1996, the cost of a Big Mac in downtown Munich had risen to $4.90, slightly higher than implied by the 93 percent cumulative German inflation between 1974–1996 (i.e., 1.93 × DM 2.50 = DM 4.82). In 1996 in Atlanta, on the other

[20] Based on "McCurrencies: Where's the Beef?" *The Economist* (April 27, 1996), p. 110; "Big MacCurrencies," *The Economist* (April 9, 1994), p. 88; and "Big MacCurrencies," *The Economist* (April 6, 2005).

hand, the Big Mac sold for \$2.36, considerably lower than implied by the 219 percent cumulative U.S. inflation 1974–1996 (i.e., 3.19 × \$1.00 = \$3.19). Consequently, the Big Mac index of purchasing power parity (i.e., DM 4.90/\$2.36 = 2.08) at the end of 1996 implied that the U.S. dollar should exchange for DM 2.08. With the actual exchange rate in 1996 at DM 1.76/\$1 (see Figure 6.1), PPP implied that the dollar was substantially undervalued. Sustained dollar appreciation against the mark in 1997–2000 from DM 1.76/\$ to DM 2.30/\$ suggests that "burger economics" has merit.

The Big Mac relationships are not a perfect application of the relative PPP hypothesis for several reasons: (1) because the 17 percent European Union VAT tax exceeds the U.S. sales tax, (2) because downtown land rents and utilities in Munich substantially exceed those in Atlanta, and (3) because the degree of fast-food industry competition facing a Munich McDonald's is lower than that facing an Atlanta McDonald's. Also, of course, a prepared Big Mac cannot be purchased in Munich for effective resale in Atlanta; goods arbitrage with perishable commodities is infeasible. Nevertheless, such PPP measures can help evaluate trends in currency value.

When the dollar reached DM 2.10/\$ in 1999, the Big Mac index of PPP predicted that any additional increases in dollar value would constitute overshooting. Sure enough, as conveyed in Figure 6.1, no sooner had the U.S. dollar risen to DM 2.30/\$ and €1.12/\$ in 2001, then it collapsed 34 percent during 2002–2004 against European currencies (i.e., to €0.80/\$). Even the trade-weighted index value of the dollar declined steeply (see Figure 6.6), despite the fact that Canada, Mexico, Japan, and China are now more prominent than Germany, France, and the other European countries in U.S. trade.

Figure 6.6 Trade-Weighted Effective Exchange Rate Index, U.S. Dollar (1981–2006)

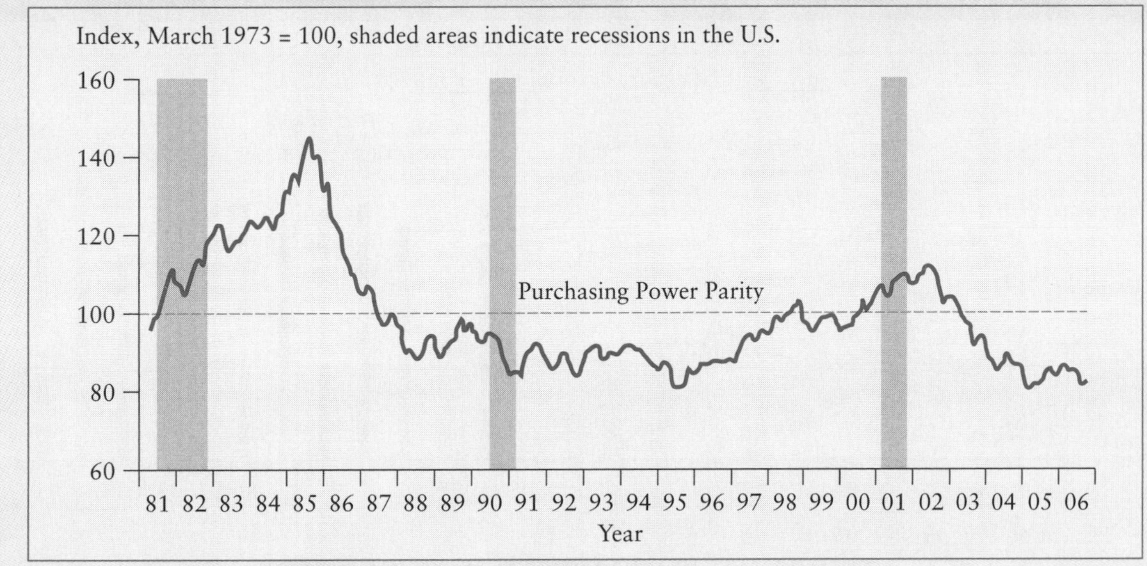

Source: *National Economic Trends,* Federal Reserve Bank of St. Louis, quarterly.

The Trade-Weighted Exchange Rate Index

Figure 6.6 shows the value of the U.S. dollar against the currencies of the United States' largest trading partners from 1981–2006. This trade-weighted exchange rate, sometimes called the effective exchange rate (EER), calculates the weighted average value of the dollar against 19 currencies, where the weights are determined by the volume of import plus export trade between the United States and each of its trading partners. The EER for the United States is therefore defined as

$$\mathrm{EER}_t^{\$} = \sum_i \mathrm{eI}_{\mathrm{it}}^{\$}\mathrm{w}_{\mathrm{it}} \qquad [6.2]$$

where w_{it} is the relative proportion of total import and export trade from and to country i in time period t (e.g., 0.049 for the United Kingdom in 2003 but only 0.034 in 2005) and where $\mathrm{eI}_{\mathrm{it}}^{\$}$ is the exchange rate index for the dollar in period t against the currency of country i. For Britain, $\mathrm{eI}_{£05}^{\$}$ is calculated as the £/$ exchange rate in 2005 divided by the £/$ exchange in the base year, multiplied by 100 [i.e., (£0.63/$ ÷ £0.40/$) × 100 = 1.58 × 100 = 158].

From 1995–2001, the trade-weighted U.S. dollar appreciated substantially. All three factors determining long-run trends in exchange rates were involved. Real growth rates in the United States declined over this period relative to several of the United States' largest trading partners. Real interest rates on U.S. T-bills were high and rising relative to those same trading partners. And finally, cost inflation in the U.S. producer price index was at a post-World War II low relative to the United States' largest trading partners. So, U.S. export trade rose dramatically and capital flowed into the United States.

As it had been for their Japanese and European competitors in the 1980s, export trade provided the engine of growth for many U.S. companies in the 1990s. Panel (a) of Figure 6.7 shows that from the 1960s to the late 1990s, the share of exports

Figure 6.7 The Growth of the Export Sector in U.S. Economy

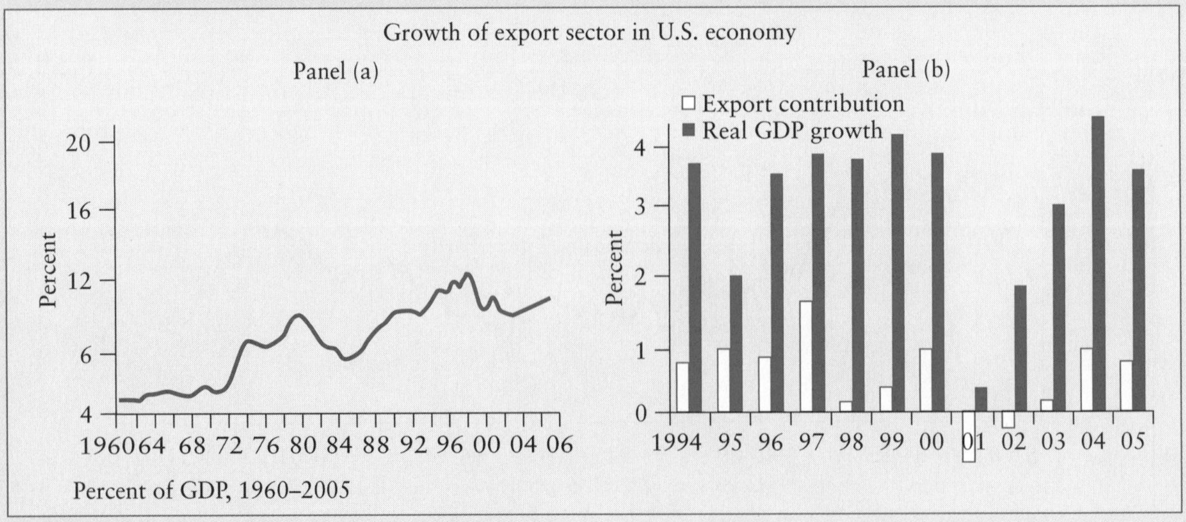

Source: U.S. Department of Commerce, Bureau of Economic Analysis.

relative to U.S. GDP grew from 4 percent to 12 percent. By 1994, one fifth of real U.S. GDP growth was attributable to exports. Between 1994 and 1997, that contribution of exports to GDP growth doubled (see Figure 6.7, Panel (b)). Between 1998 and 2002, the U.S. export sector decayed, primarily because the value of the dollar had appreciated above purchasing power parity (see Figure 6.6). However, at its highest recent peak values of ¥134 in mid-1998, DM 2.30 in mid-2000, and €1.12 in 2001, the U.S. dollar was still well below its spectacular 1985 peak of ¥238 and DM 2.94. This historical perspective can prove useful, because it took only a 34 percent depreciation of the dollar 2001–2004 to restart the U.S. export sector. Figure 6.7 shows that in recent years 2004 and 2005 exports have again begun to exceed 10 percent of GDP and are again contributing approximately one-fifth to U.S. GDP growth.

INTERNATIONAL TRADE: A MANAGERIAL PERSPECTIVE

SHARES OF WORLD TRADE AND REGIONAL TRADING BLOCS

As we explained earlier, the United States is both the largest exporter and the largest importer in the world's economy. Thus, the United States generates the largest share of the $22 trillion in bilateral world trade (13%), comprising 10 percent of all exports and 15.7 percent of all imports. The next eight countries with the largest shares of world trade in 2005 were Germany (9%), China (6%), Japan (5%), Britain (5%), France (5%), the Netherlands (5%), Italy (4%), and Canada (3%). Although these largest trading nations are predominantly Western-developed economies, the next six largest trading nations are predominantly rapidly developing Asian economies: Hong Kong (3%), South Korea (2%), Spain (3%), Singapore (2%), Mexico (2%), and Taiwan (2%). Altogether, the World Trade Organization (WTO) includes 149 nations who have agreed to share trade statistics, coordinate the liberalization of trade policy (i.e., the opening of markets), and cooperatively resolve their trade disputes in accordance with WTO rules and procedures.

Figure 6.8 shows that over the last two decades the import and export trade flows to and from the United States have grown to represent fully 27 percent of GDP (only 10.5% being exports). Some nations are much more export-driven. South Korean exports average 34 percent of GDP; Taiwanese and Indonesian exports are 50 percent of GDP; Chinese exports are 60 percent of GDP, and Malaysian exports are 93 percent of GDP! In Europe, German exports run 35 percent of GDP. And within North America, Mexican and Canadian exports are 34 percent and 43 percent of GDP, respectively.

Most nations continue to protect with tariffs and other trade barriers some infant or politically sensitive industries. France, for example, remains a largely agricultural polity and therefore lowers its agricultural subsidies only after great hand-wringing and extended periods of tough negotiations with its European neighbors. The WTO's Doha round of tariff-reduction negotiations was suspended in mid-2006 primarily because the European Union refused to give up its €47 billion common agricultural policy (CAP). France receives €10.6 billion of these CAP subsidies, 80 percent of which go not to rustic French family farms but rather to large French landholders for intensive industrial farming.

The United States is hardly blameless as agricultural subsidies in sugar and crop price support programs for small family farmers are embedded in American populist politics. Although the agriculture sector contributes only 1 percent to U.S. GDP, during the 1993–2003, the U.S. increased agricultural subsidies from 19 percent to 22 percent of total agricultural value, while the European Union reduced agricultural subsidies from

Figure 6.8 U.S. Imports and Exports as a Percentage of GDP

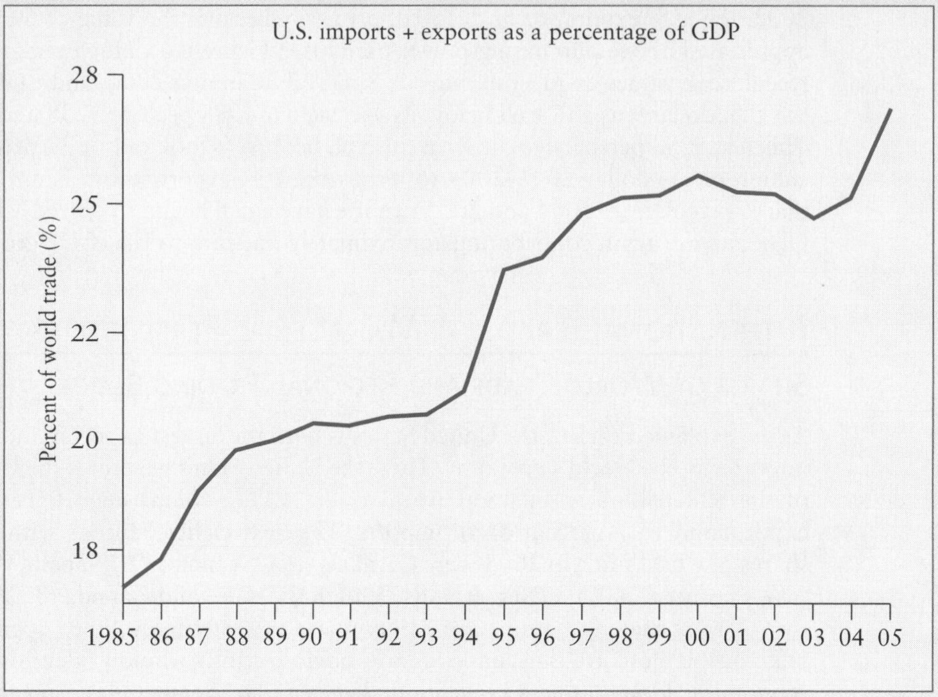

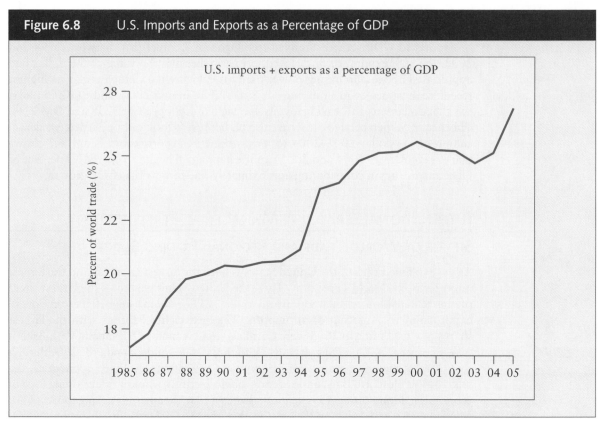

Source: **U.S. Department of Commerce, Bureau of Economic Analysis.**

47 percent to 35 percent. And until recently, the U.S. imposed import restraints on Japanese automobiles and maintained 30 percent tariffs on textiles, apparel, and carbon steel imports. Fortunately, regional trading blocs such as the European Union (EU) and the North American Free Trade Agreement (NAFTA) were highly successful in the 1990s at removing trade barriers, negotiating multilateral reductions in tariffs, and promoting free trade as a mechanism of peaceful competition between nations.

EXAMPLE

MERCOSUR Averts a Trade War

MERCOSUR was formed as a free trade area to secure the free flow of goods and services in the cone at the base of South America. The dominant trading partners Brazil and Argentina joined with Uruguay and Paraguay and pledged under the Treaty of Asunción in 1991 to avoid punitive tariffs and import quotas (later extended to the associate members Chile and Bolivia). These commitments were sorely tested during a recession in 1998–1999. GDP growth plummeted from 7.1 percent to −3 percent in Brazil, while Argentina slowed from 8.6 percent to 1.8 percent but continued to grow.

To jump-start its economy, Brazil devalued the *real* (which immediately raised the cost of imports by 40%) and adopted an industrial policy of offering tax breaks, free land, and other subsidies to any Argentine automobile parts suppliers, shoe manufacturers, and corporate farms that would move to Brazil. Argentina retaliated by threatening to place tariffs on Brazilian textile exports, claiming that said exports were so heavily subsidized that their prices fell below replacement cost. The WTO allows any member to impose antidumping duties on export products sold below cost. However, under MERCOSUR's procedures, Brazil and Argentina agreed instead to negotiate a reduction in the subsidies and a removal of the threat of punitive tariffs while attempting to harmonize their fiscal policies and inflation targets, much like the European Union experience with the Maastricht Treaty. A nasty trade war was narrowly averted.

Across the world economy, six such regional trading blocs have emerged (see Figure 6.9). In South America, Argentina, Brazil, Paraguay, Uruguay, Bolivia, and Chile formed one trading block (MERCOSUR) that is now approaching \$250 billion of merchandise trade. The Andean group (Venezuela, Peru, Colombia, Bolivia, and Ecuador) formed another; both are attempts to mirror NAFTA, the free trade agreements of Canada, the United States, and Mexico. Seven Southeast Asian (ASEAN) and 16 trans-Pacific economies including Japan and Mexico (APEC) also formed trading blocs. From 1980–1999, trade *within* these trading blocs swelled to dominate the member states' total trade, especially in NAFTA and the European Union

Figure 6.9 Regional Trading Zones (Percentage of World Trade)

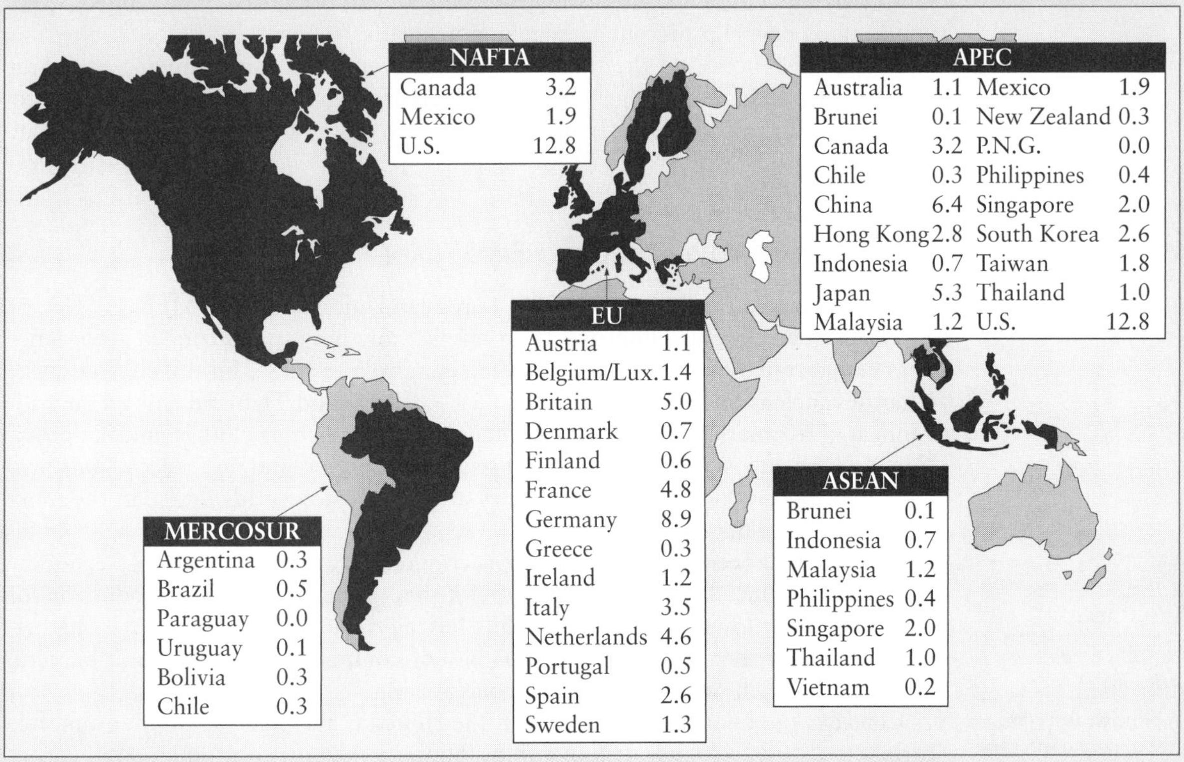

NAFTA
Canada 3.2
Mexico 1.9
U.S. 12.8
APEC
Australia 1.1
Brunei 0.1
Canada 3.2
Chile 0.3
China 6.4
Hong Kong 2.8
Indonesia 0.7
Japan 5.3
Malaysia 1.2
Mexico 1.9
New Zealand 0.3
P.N.G. 0.0
Philippines 0.4
Singapore 2.0
South Korea 2.6
Taiwan 1.8
Thailand 1.0
U.S. 12.8
EU
Austria 1.1
Belgium/Lux. 1.4
Britain 5.0
Denmark 0.7
Finland 0.6
France 4.8
Germany 8.9
Greece 0.3
Ireland 1.2
Italy 3.5
Netherlands 4.6
Portugal 0.5
Spain 2.6
Sweden 1.3
ASEAN
Brunei 0.1
Indonesia 0.7
Malaysia 1.2
Philippines 0.4
Singapore 2.0
Thailand 1.0
Vietnam 0.2
MERCOSUR
Argentina 0.3
Brazil 0.5
Paraguay 0.0
Uruguay 0.1
Bolivia 0.3
Chile 0.3

Source: World Trade Organization.

Table 6.3 Intraregional Trade as a Percentage of a Region's World Trade

	1980	1990	1999
European Union	57	66	61
NAFTA	33	37	47
MERCOSUR	13	14	22
Andean Community	4	5	10
ASEAN	14	14	18

Source: International Monetary Fund, *Direction of Trade Statistics*.

but not in MERCOSUR and the Andean Community (see Table 6.3). For example, Canada-United States-Mexico trade grew from 33 percent to 47 percent of U.S. trade between 1993 and 2000, while Japan-U.S. trade shrank from 15 percent to 10 percent of U.S. trade. Because fully 88 percent of Mexican trade now involves its two NAFTA partners, 34 nations in Central and South America have pursued forming a Free Trade Area of the Americas (FTAA) to include Canada, Mexico, and the United States, encompassing 840 million people and combined output equal to $14 trillion.

The Brazilian ($604 billion) and Mexican ($596 billion) economies are comparable in size, about one-half as large as Canada and one-twentieth the size of the U.S. economy. Brazil, Mexico, and Argentina have large industrial bases protected by 14–16 percent import tariffs, whereas Paraguay, Bolivia, and Guatemala are commodity-based economies employing 6–8 percent import tariffs. The United States and Canada have 4.5 percent average import tariffs.

These differences and the trade dispute between Brazil and United States over steel, sugar, and frozen orange juice hinder further progress on the FTAA. Therefore, MERCOSUR (see Figure 6.10) and NAFTA are likely to move forward as separate free trade areas.

Comparative Advantage and Free Trade

Within a regional trading bloc such as European Union, NAFTA, MERCOSUR, or APEC, each member can improve its economic growth by specializing in accordance with comparative advantage and then engaging in free trade. Intuitively, low-wage countries such as Spain, Mexico, Puerto Rico, China, and Thailand enjoy a cost advantage in the manufacture of labor-intensive goods such as clothes and the provision of labor-intensive services, such as sewing or coupon and insurance claims processing. Suppose one of these economies also enjoys a cost advantage in the more capital-intensive manufacturing of auto assembly. One of the powerful insights of international microeconomics is that in such circumstances, the low-cost economy should not produce both goods, but rather it should specialize in that production for which it has the lower relative cost, while buying the other product from its higher-cost trading partner. Let's see how this **law of comparative advantage** in bilateral trade reaches such an apparently odd conclusion.

Law of Comparative Advantage

A principle defending free trade and specialization in accordance with lower relative cost.

Consider the bilateral trade between the United States and Japan in automobile carburetors and computer memory chips. Suppose the cost of production of carburetors in Japan is ¥10,000 compared to $120 in the United States. At an exchange rate of ¥100/$, the Japanese cost-covering price of $100 is lower than the U.S.

Figure 6.10 Gross Domestic Product, Merchandise Exports as a Percentage of GDP, and Average Import Tariffs for MERCOSUR Countries

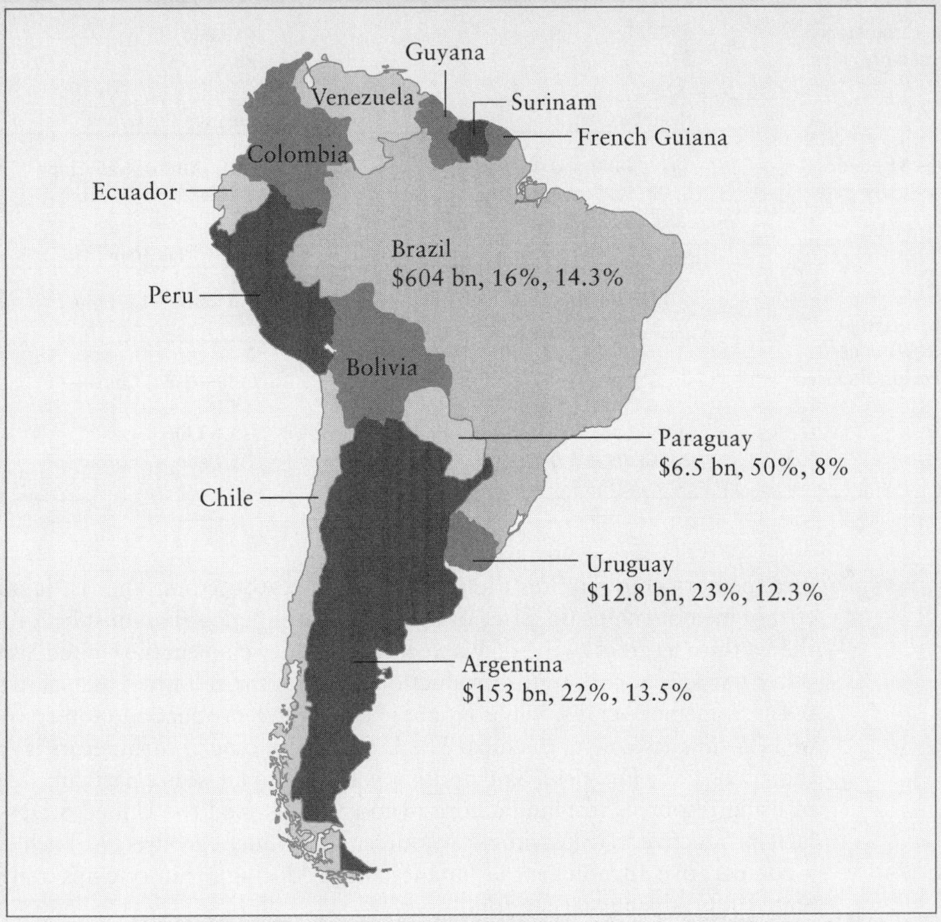

Absolute Cost Advantage

A comparison of nominal costs in two locations, companies, or economies.

Real Terms of Trade

Comparison of relative costs of production across economies.

cost-covering price of $120. Suppose, in addition, that memory chips cost ¥8,000 in Japan compared to $300 in the United States. Again, the price of the Japanese product (i.e., $80) is lower than the price of the U.S. product. Japan is said to enjoy an **absolute cost advantage** in the manufacture of both products. However, Japan is 83 percent (i.e., $100/$120) as expensive in producing carburetors as the United States while being only 27 percent (i.e., $80/$300) as expensive in producing memory chips. Japan is said to have a comparative advantage in memory chips and should specialize in the manufacture of that product.

The gains from specialization in accordance with comparative advantage and subsequent trade are best demonstrated using the real terms of trade. **Real terms of trade** identify what amounts of labor effort, material, and other resources are required to produce a product in one economy relative to another. In Japan, the manufacture of memory chips requires the sacrifice of resources capable of manufacturing 0.8 carburetors (see Table 6.4), whereas in the United States the manufacture

Table 6.4 Real Terms of Trade and Comparative Advantage

	Absolute Cost, U.S.	Absolute Cost, Japan
Automobile carburetors	\$120	¥10,000
Computer memory chips	\$300	¥8,000
	Relative Cost, U.S.	**Relative Cost, Japan**
Automobile carburetors	\$120/\$300 = 0.4 Chips	¥10K/¥8K = 1.25 Chips
Computer memory chips	\$300/\$120 = 2.5 Carbs	¥8K/¥10K = 0.8 Carbs
	Gains from Trade, U.S.	**Gains from Trade, Japan**
Initial Goods	1.0 Carb + 1.0 Chip	1.0 Carb + 1.0 Chip
After specialization:		
Carburetors produced	(1.0 + 2.5) Carbs	0
Memory chips produced	0	(1.0 + 1.25) Chips
Trade	+1.0 Chip	+1.5 Carb
	−1.5 Carb	−1.0 Chip
Net goods	2.0 Carbs + 1.0 Chip	1.5 Carbs + 1.25 Chips

of a memory chip requires the sacrifice of 2.5 carburetors. That is, Japan's relative cost of memory chips (in terms of carburetor production that must be forgone) is less than a third as great as the relative cost of memory chips in the United States. On the other hand, U.S. carburetor production requires the resources associated with only 0.4 U.S. memory chips, while Japanese carburetor production requires the sacrifice of 1.25 Japanese memory chips. The U.S. relative cost of carburetors is much lower than that of the Japanese. Said another way, the Japanese are particularly productive in using resources to manufacture memory chips, and the United States is particularly productive in using similar resources to produce carburetors. Each country has a comparative advantage: the Japanese in producing memory chips and the United States in producing carburetors.

Assess what happens to the total goods produced if each economy specializes in production in accordance with comparative advantage and then trades to diversify its consumption. Assume that the United States and Japan produced one unit of each product initially, that labor is immobile, that no scale economies are present, and that the quality of both carburetors and both memory chips is identical. If the Japanese cease production of carburetors and specialize in the production of memory chips, they increase memory chip production to 2.25 chips (see Table 6.4). Similarly, if the United States ceases production of memory chips and specializes in the production of carburetors, it increases carburetor production to 3.5 carburetors. In these circumstances, the United States could offer Japan 1.5 carburetors for a memory chip, and both parties would end up unambiguously better off. The United States would enjoy a residual domestic production after trade of 2.0 carburetors plus the import of one memory chip. And the Japanese would enjoy a residual domestic production after trade of 1.25 memory chips plus the import of 1.5 carburetors. As demonstrated in Table 6.4, each economy would have replaced all the products they initially produced, plus each would enjoy additional amounts of both goods (i.e., unambiguous gains from trade).

IMPORT CONTROLS AND PROTECTIVE TARIFFS

In the Mercantilist period from 1500 to 1750, many nations rejected free-trade policies and instead attempted to restrain the purchase of foreign imports in order to expand the production of their domestic industries (as Brazil attempted in 1999). To bar imports, some nations adopted protective tariffs that raised the domestic prices of foreign goods. Others tried direct import controls, such as a maximum allowable quota of a specific type of foreign import. England, for example, banned the export of Cotswold wool to French cloth manufacturers in Flanders in hopes of retaining the cloth weaving, finishing, and dyeing industries in Britain. When excess inventories of expensive British cloth accumulated, Flanders cloth imports were restricted. Between 1500 and 1603, the unintended consequence of these import-export quotas was a 500 percent inflation in cloth prices in Britain.

A few of these ill-advised import control ideas even survive to the present day (e.g., the U.S. voluntary import restraint, or VIR, agreement with Japanese automobile manufacturers in the mid-1980s and threats by the U.S. Congress to impose similar controls on textiles from China today). Again, the net results of import controls are often unintended by their proponents. In the face of the VIRs, Toyota and Honda simply built assembly plants all over the United States, and still more GM, Ford, and Chrysler workers were laid off. In general, national income and employment in the country barring imports eventually falls below the potential income available under freer trade policies.

One reason why is because imports increase when trading partners experience export growth. Following almost a decade of subpar growth, as the Japanese economy accelerated 2003–2005 at real GDP growth rates of 1.8, 2.3, and 2.6 percent, Japanese households increased import consumption of merchandise from the Gap to Prada by 40 percent. A second reason for higher national income when import barriers are avoided hinges on an understanding of exchange rates and trade balances. Import controls lead inevitably to a reduction in the supply of a nation's currency in the foreign exchange market. For example, when some American households are prohibited from completing import purchases of Toyotas and Hondas they would otherwise have bought, those households fail to request the yen they would have needed to accomplish the import purchases. Accordingly, they also fail to supply the U.S. dollars that would have been exchanged for the requisite foreign currency.

A reduction in the supply of dollars, all other things being the same, implies that the dollar must appreciate; therefore, reduced imports implies a rise in value of the domestic currency. However, this exchange rate adjustment raises the price of American exports because the number of yen, euros, or yuan a foreign buyer must pay to acquire dollar-denominated goods and services inevitably rises, and U.S. exports then decline. These consequences normally unfold even if the domestic producers attempt to offset their currency's appreciation with reduced profit margins. Ultimately, therefore, the attempt to improve domestic output and raise national income by imposing import controls often results in a collapse of the export sector sufficient to worsen the trade balance (exports minus imports) and actually decreases national income.

Free trade and open markets offer the prospect of higher national income. Developing countries with open economies grew by 4.5 percent per year in the 1970s and 1980s, whereas those with import controls and protective tariffs grew by only 0.7 percent per year. Rich country comparisons also favored free trade: 2.3 percent to, again, 0.7 percent. In the 1990s, this gap widened still further. Those developing countries whose import plus export trade as a percentage of GDP ranked in the top 50 percentile of developing countries had GDP growth per person of 5 percent. Those in the bottom 50 percentile saw GDP growth per person actually shrink by 1 percent.[21] Clearly, globalization and trade enhance prosperity, even in the lesser-developed countries.

EXAMPLE

President Bush's 2002 Steel Tariffs: Justified Sanctions or Hypocritical Protectionism?[22]

Despite its heavy weight and high transportation cost, steel is sourced from factories around the globe. At \$350/ton, sheet steel from Brazil and South Korea can be shipped to the United States for \$70/ton and still sell \$55 below the \$475/ton cost of the big integrated hot-rolled steel producers in the United States, such as Bethlehem and Republic Steel (see Table 6.5). As a result, 15 of 17 such integrated U.S. producers who convert iron ore in blast furnaces using 160,000 United Steel Workers (USW) are operating under bankruptcy protection from their creditors. Their market share fell from 80 percent in 1976 to 40 percent in 2002. The United States is ranked fourth in world steel production after the European Union, China, and Japan (see Figure 6.11).

Only AK Steel, U.S. Steel, Nucor, and other mini-mill producers are profitable. Nucor employs one-third as many workers as the integrated mills, using less expensive

Table 6.5 Sheet Steel, \$ Cost per Ton

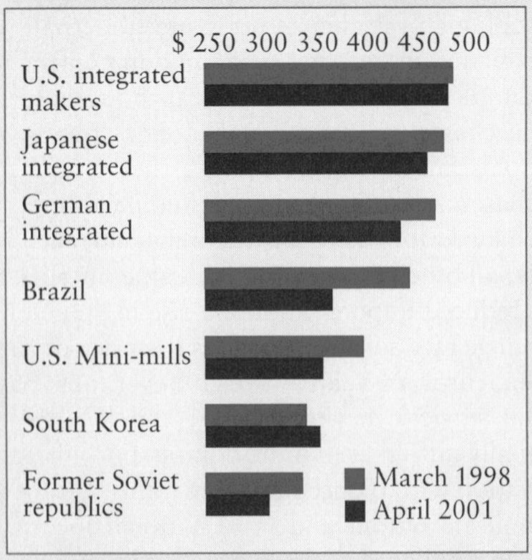

Source: *World Steel Dynamics*, 2002.

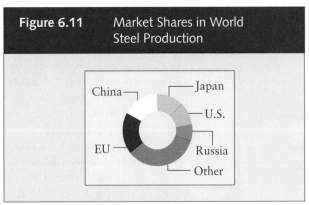

Figure 6.11 Market Shares in World Steel Production

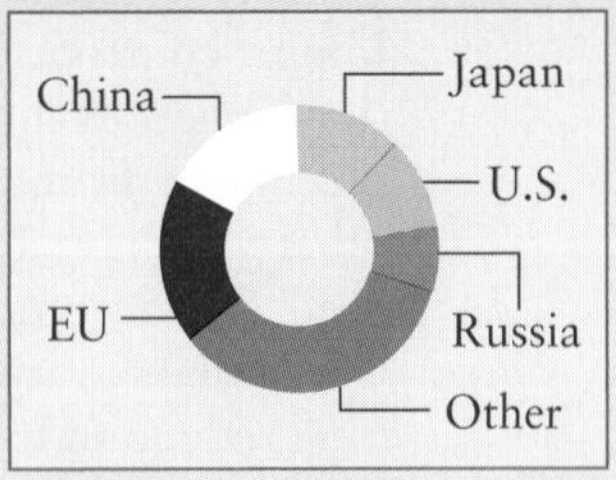

Source: *The Economist*, February 16, 2002.

[21] "Globalization, Growth and Poverty," World Bank report, December 2001.

[22] Based on "Rust Never Sleeps," *The Economist* (March 9, 2002), p. 61; "U.S. Companies Cry Foul," *Wall Street Journal* (March 19, 2002), p. A2; "U.S. Protectionism Imperils Free Trade Talks with Latins," *Wall Street Journal* (March 20, 2002), p. A15; and "WTO Trade Negotiations Hit a Snag," *Wall Street Journal* (March 18, 2003), p. A2.

electric arc furnaces. In addition, because Nucor starts with scrap metal, not iron ore, their principal input cost is highly correlated with final steel sheet and steel slab prices, a highly effective internal hedge. For example, when slab steel prices sank from $300 to $200 recently, the price of Nucor's scrap steel input plummeted to all-time lows as well. Finally, a nonunion workforce allows Nucor to avoid the so-called "legacy costs" of the USW contracts with the integrated steel producers (i.e., detailed work rules that stifle innovation and extraordinary health care benefits). In short, U.S. integrated mill steel-making is a highly competitive business that makes use of a high-priced artificially scarce factor, namely, unionized steel workers. In such circumstances, international trade theory predicts internal consumption of domestic production with little export trade and massive foreign imports.

Yet, the USW is a powerful political lobby, and U.S. International Trade Commission hearings plus World Trade Organization (WTO) antidumping rules and dispute resolution procedures provided the vehicle for President Ford and the Second President Bush to consider imposing tariff sanctions to protect the domestic steel industry. In March 2002, Bush decided to impose quotas on Brazilian steel and 30 percent tariffs on steel slab and steel sheet from several other nations for three years. Predictably, such trade restrictions will increase the cost of steel supplies in the United States. For example, Precision Technologies of Houston estimated it would raise their costs $3 million on $57 million in sales of high-stress steel tubing for the drilling industry.

There *are* several valid arguments for trade restrictions (import quotas or tariffs): (1) to protect *infant industries* until they reach minimum efficient scale, (2) to offset government subsidies provided to foreign competitors with one's own *countervailing duties,* and (3) to impose antidumping sanctions for foreign goods sold below their domestic cost. Chilean salmon, Argentine honey, and Brazilian frozen orange juice concentrate and slab steel have all been subject to U.S. antidumping duties in recent years. The Brazilians, in particular, claim that their export prices simply reflect a countervailing reduction relative to their domestic cost in order to offset the enormous $30 billion in farm subsidies that the United States makes available to its agricultural sector. The United States does spend $20,000 per full-time farmer to subsidize agricultural products (third behind Switzerland's $27,000 and Japan's $23,000).

The WTO is sorting out these claims and counterclaims on agricultural subsidies and steel duties. Whether the United States will ultimately be sustained in imposing antidumping sanctions on $8 billion of steel or whether Brazil will be sustained in their countervailing duties to offset the massive U.S. agricultural subsidies remains to be seen.

THE CASE FOR STRATEGIC TRADE POLICY

Although the logic of free trade has dominated academic debate since 1750, and the twentieth century saw the repeal of many import controls and tariffs, a few exceptions are worth noting. The WTO has effectively spearheaded the negotiation of *mutual* trade liberalization policies. However, *unilateral* reduction of tariffs when trading partners stubbornly refuse to relax import controls or open their domestic markets seldom makes sense. The United States has found it necessary to threaten tariffs on Japanese consumer electronics, for example, in order to negotiate successfully the opening of Japanese markets to U.S. cellular phones and computer chips.

This threat bargaining and negotiated mutual reduction of trade barriers illustrates the concept of "strategic trade policy."

In the spring of 1999, continued EU import controls on U.S.-based Dole and Chiquita bananas from Central America led the United States to impose WTO-sanctioned duties on $180 million of European products from Louis Vuitton plastic handbags and British cashmere sweaters to French Roquefort cheese and foie gras. The British and French former colonies in the Caribbean such as St. Lucia enjoy approximately $150 million in banana farm profits as a result of the European Union's quota limiting the importing of U.S. bananas into Europe. But the cost to EU consumers has been estimated at $2 billion in higher priced fruit. Strategic trade policy by the United States induced the European Union to relax its banana import controls.

EXAMPLE

Intel's Chip Market Access Improves in Japan[23]

In the mid-1980s, Japanese semiconductor producers grabbed much of the world market in the dynamic random access memory chips (DRAMs) used in personal computers. Through a combination of aggressive pricing and an almost closed domestic market, Japanese semiconductors achieved massive economies of scale and much reduced unit cost. When the retail price of PCs declined steeply in 1986, the American and European manufacturers such as Intel ceased production of basic memory chips.

That same year, an international dumping complaint at the WTO proved that many Japanese chips had been sold in the United States and Europe below cost. The U.S. Department of Commerce then imposed punitive tariffs on Japanese chips, laptop computers, and televisions. To avoid these higher tariffs, the Japanese then agreed to open access to their domestic market and set a 20 percent target for foreign memory chip sales in Japan. Intel, Siemens, and other producers expanded, and the Japanese producers Sharp and Toshiba cut production. Although the Japanese did not renew the chip access accords when the second round expired in 1995, the U.S., German, and Japanese semiconductor manufacturers have formed joint ventures to codesign and jointly manufacture subsequent generations of flash memory chips. In this instance, strategic trade policy opened markets and expanded the national income of all the participating nations.

Increasing Returns

Another motivation for strategic trade policy arises in markets where domestic producers encounter increasing returns. Suppose the Boeing Corp. and Airbus find that learning curve effects in airframe manufacturing offer a 1 percent reduction in *variable* cost for every market share point above 30 percent. A firm with a 40 percent market share of the world output of new wide-body aircraft (such as the Boeing 777) will experience variable costs only 90 percent as great as smaller competitors. A firm with 50 percent market share will experience variable costs only 80 percent

[23] Based on "America Chips Away at Japan," *The Economist* (March 27, 1993); and "Foreign Chip Sales Up in Japan," *Financial Times* (December 16, 1994).

as great as smaller competitors, and so forth. These circumstances are rare indeed in the industrial sector of the economy; they imply that diminishing returns in production are more than offset by economies of scope or learning curve advantages at higher output. However, where such circumstances exist, some nations use these so-called industrial policies to jump-start the preemptive development of new aircraft models with public subsidies to research and development. Others impose import controls or protective tariffs to assure the attainment of the 30 percent market share baseline volume required to trigger the emergence of learning curve advantages. This approach also entails strategic trade policy.

EXAMPLE

NETWORK EXTERNALITIES AT MICROSOFT AND APPLE: A ROLE FOR PROTECTIVE TARIFFS?

The information economy has a higher incidence than the industrial economy of these increasing returns phenomena. Frequently, in the information economy context, cost reductions at larger market share are associated with externalities in the installation of a network or the adoption of a technical standard. As the installed base of Windows software expands, Microsoft finds it increasingly less difficult to convince new customers to adopt their product. Computer users find it much easier to exchange documents and explain new applications, for example, if their PCs employ the same operating system. As a result, the marketing cost to secure the next adoption from a marginal buyer actually declines, the larger the market share that Windows attains. The same thing holds for Apple's operating system. The greater the installed base, the more software the independent programmers will write for use on a Mac. The more software available for use on a Mac, the lower the variable cost to Apple of successfully marketing the next PC.

Should strategic trade policy in the United States protect a company with the possibility of achieving increasing returns? Microsoft and Apple pose a good case in point. *Without* import controls and protective tariffs, Microsoft successfully achieved a larger dollar volume of export trade than any other American company. Had the sole U.S. competitor been Apple rather than Microsoft, a serious question would have arisen. Could Apple have secured a 30 percent-plus market share in the absence of import controls and protective tariffs against a foreign Microsoft?

Is it an appropriate role of the government to pursue such cost advantages for one domestic company or an alliance of domestic companies? Or should government pursue the consumer interest of lowest prices wherever that product is produced? These questions are hotly debated in strategic trade policy today. The case exercise on reciprocal protectionism at the end of Chapter 12 looks at these strategic trade policy questions in the context of Boeing and Airbus.

FREE TRADE AREAS: THE EUROPEAN UNION AND NAFTA

Free trade and specialization in accordance with comparative advantage leaves economies vulnerable to trade interruptions and punitive tariffs on essential inputs. Nevertheless, the formation of the European Union provides an example of what can be accomplished. Starting with the Treaty of Rome in 1957, 12 original European

Free Trade Area

A group of nations that have agreed to reduce tariffs and other trade barriers.

Community members established the groundwork for a **free trade area,** which they subsequently consolidated in the Single Europe Act of 1986. Between 1986 and 1992, 12 dissimilar European economies realized 5 percent additional cumulative growth of GDP attributable to the increased intra-European trade.

Increased specialization in accordance with comparative advantage has the relatively low-wage Spaniards and Portuguese assembling high value-added German components for BMWs and Blaupunkt radios. Reduced trade barriers at borders have cut transportation time. The English Channel ferry now unloads in 15 minutes rather than the previous 90 minutes, and yogurt from Nestlé's subsidiary in Birmingham, England, now speeds across Europe to target customers in Milan in 11 hours rather than the previous 38. Reduced intra-European tariffs on foodstuffs, beer, wine, and autos markedly reduced the cost of living. Although corporate tax rates still differ from 45 percent in Italy and Germany to 30 percent in Ireland, wide differences in value-added taxes have been reconciled at uniform 17 percent rates in most cases. Just the mere act of exchanging money, which employed 1 in every 200 full-time employees in Europe, became much more efficient with a single European currency.

Optimal Currency Areas

How far and wide a single currency should be adopted as the official monetary unit depends on a complex mix of economic, social, and political factors. The benefits of a single currency are the avoidance of exchange rate risk on intraregional trade and the reduction of conversion costs. Because hedging does cost 5 percent of the value at risk, and recall that the total value of world trade (equal to $22 trillion per year) pales in comparison to the total value of worldwide currency trading (equal to $2 trillion *per day*), companies such as the German pharmaceutical firm Hoeschst AG estimated that it would save more than DM 10 million in covered forward hedge contract costs previously incurred to lay off risk exposure on European currencies. Competitiveness was also enhanced when European auto companies secured volume purchase discounts from their cheapest suppliers rather than spreading their parts purchases across Europe as an internal hedge, matching expenditures in local currencies to their anticipated car revenues.

The boundary of an optimal currency area hinges on three factors: the magnitude of intraregional trade, the mobility of labor, and the correlation of macroeconomic shocks between countries within the proposed currency area.

EXAMPLE

If Europe, What About One Currency for NAFTA?[24]

Should the Mexican peso, the Canadian dollar, and the U.S. dollar be replaced by a single currency for NAFTA, just as eleven European currencies were replaced in 1999 by the euro? Even as early as 1992, every nation of the European Union traded more with other EU members than with the rest of the world (see Table 6.6). In some cases

[24] See O. Blanchard and J. Wolfers, "The Role of Shocks and Institutions in the Rise of European Unemployment," *Economic Journal* (March 2000); R. Mundell, "Threat to Prosperity" *Wall Street Journal* (March 30, 2000), p. A30; and M. Chriszt, "Perspectives on a North American Currency Union," *Fed Atlanta Economic Review,* 4 (2000), pp. 29–36.

(Belgium, Luxembourg, and Ireland), exports make up a majority of their GDP, and the countertrade patterns that underlay the hopes and dreams of the Treaty of Rome have clearly emerged. Similarly, in NAFTA countries, exports plus imports account for 70 percent of GDP in Canada and 58 percent in Mexico, with 79 percent of Canadian trade and 88 percent of Mexican trade involving the United States.

However, two critical social and political factors limit the effectiveness of the European currency union, and three of the European Union's 15 members (Britain, Sweden, and Denmark) decided to opt out. With monetary policy constrained to reflect European-wide perceptions about the need for credibility in fighting inflation, and with fiscal policy constrained by rigid guidelines for membership in the currency union, labor mobility must adjust rapidly to stabilize swings in unemployment caused by localized market conditions. For example, if Italy is in a slump, Germany and France are growing slowly, and Ireland and Portugal are booming, a common monetary policy and little fiscal autonomy require that labor move quickly from Continental Europe to the fringes of the European Union. Although such mobility occurs easily in the United States where a family can find similar schools, houses, and language in moving from one state to another, the same cannot be said in Europe. Relocation costs in the United States of $25,000 are one third as great as in Europe.

In addition, of course, most cultural differences are enormous from one corner of the European Union to another. While European professionals have trained in foreign capitals and accepted diversity in mannerisms and cultural practices for centuries, working-class Europeans tend to be more culturally prejudicial. Thus, even those who would take the initiative to cross national and cultural borders in pursuit of transitory jobs typically will experience less than full acceptance as "guest workers." Knowing this likelihood, fewer unemployed or underemployed Western European workers desire to relocate than would be the case in the United States. Thus, the average level of European unemployment has increased from less than 2 percent in the 1960s to 12 percent in 2002. The expansion of the EU free trade area into Eastern Europe will exacerbate the problem of inadequate labor mobility among Western Europeans.

European countries differ in the strength of their unions, payroll taxes, minimum wages, layoff restrictions, and unemployment insurance. Europe's many separate labor markets cause common macroeconomic shocks to result in a growing dispersion of natural rates of unemployment from 4 percent in Ireland to 20 percent in Spain. A one-size-fits-all monetary policy and little fiscal autonomy may be inappropriate for both Europe and North America. Although Canadian macroeconomic shocks and responses are highly correlated with the United States, Mexico is a petroleum exporter with business cycles more similar to Venezuela than to the United States. For the same reason that Britain opted out of a common currency, so should Mexico.

The European Union's original free trade and single currency agreements occurred in a region where the output per capita differs by 100 percent between wealthy Milan, Munich, and the Rhineland versus poor Greece, Southern Italy, Spain, and Portugal. Manufacturing-unit-labor cost runs close to $34 per hour in Denmark, $32 in Germany, $20 in Spain, and only $14 in Greece. Marketing plans are just as divergent. The peak penetration of TV into Spanish households (20% viewership) occurs at 2 to 4 in the afternoon. Only 5 percent of Spanish households are tuned in from 6 to 8 in the evening when the 22 percent peak British audience

Table 6.6 Price Differentials in Europe

Largest Mean Difference by Country			
1992	Coca-Cola (1.5L)	Ecu 0.69 (Belgium)	Ecu 1.45 (Denmark)
	Heinz Ketchup	Ecu 0.86 (UK)	Ecu 1.92 (Spain)
	Clothes Washer	Ecu 407 (UK)	Ecu 565 (Italy)
	Portable TV	DM 434 (Germany)	DM 560 (Italy)
	VCR	DM 1383 (Germany)	DM 1873 (Spain)
1998	Big Mac	Ecu 1.75 (Spain)	Ecu 2.10 (Belgium)
	Ford Mondeo	DM 32,000 (Spain)	DM 48,000 (Germany)
2004	Compact Disk	€13.50 (France)	€21.80 (Ireland)
	Pampers	€6.75 (Hungary)	€21.00 (Denmark)
	Big Mac Meal	€2.80 (Estonia)	€8.80 (Norway)
	Coca-Cola	€0.65 (Lithuania)	€2.50 (France)
	Movie Ticket	€4.00 (Lithuania)	€15.00 (Britain)
	Milk (1G)	€2.20 (Czech Rep.)	€4.86 (Norway)
% Standard Deviation Across Europe, Euro-11 price index, pretax			
1998	Household Insurance		51%
	Coca-Cola by the glass		29
	Local Phone Service		25
	Yogurt		20
	Gasoline		14
	Levi's 501 Jeans		10
	VW Golf		5

Source: *Financial Times, The Economist,* various issues.

is "watching the telly." The Spanish consider packaged pet food a luxury and purchase yogurt through the pharmacy. Milanese brag about overpaying for a Sony television, while Munich shoppers search for days to find 5 percent discounts on Sony products. In short, few pan-European marketing plans succeed; segmented markets characterize the European Union.

These issues are easily demonstrated by examining the price variation for standard goods across the European Union. In Table 6.6, at the origin of the Common Market in 1992, Coca-Cola and Heinz Ketchup were approximately twice as expensive in Denmark and Spain as in Belgium and the United Kingdom. Twelve years later in 2004, food products such as Coca-Cola and milk remained twice as expensive in Norway as in Hungary or the Czech Republic. Appliances and consumer electronics can be easily bought in one location and sold in another. Hence in 1992, clothes washers and portable TVs only differed in price from one country to another by about 20 percent.

As one would expect, VW Golf cars and other easily arbitraged goods such as Levi's 501 jeans exhibit the smallest price variation, and immobile services (e.g., insurance) and perishable food (e.g., soft drinks by the glass and yogurt) exhibit the highest price variation across the Union. Still, with 2004 compact disks sold in France for €13.50 and in Ireland for €21.80, intra-European trade dominates the landscape. Italy, Germany, and France do 55 to 60 percent of their total trade with other European countries, and Spain does 70 percent. Ireland, Portugal, and the Benelux countries do close to 80 percent. Even Britain trades more with its regional trading bloc partners than with the rest of the world combined.

THE LARGEST U.S. TRADING PARTNERS: THE ROLE OF NAFTA

Canada, not Japan, is by far the largest trading partner of the United States with almost twice the share (23.6%) of American goods exported there than anywhere else in the world's economy (see Figure 6.12). U.S. exports to Canada include everything from merchandise, such as Microsoft's software and DaimlerChrysler's automobile components for assembly at an automated minivan plant in Ontario, to professional services such as strategic management consulting by McKinsey & Co. Canada is also the largest source of U.S. imports (17%), with natural resources and finished goods manufacturing leading the list. China provides 14.5 percent of U.S. imports, especially clothing, textiles, shoes, and telecom equipment, and purchases 4.7 percent of U.S. exports, especially machinery, autos, and aircraft.

Mexico consumes and assembles a 13.5 percent share of U.S. exports (up 50% since 1996) and provides 10 percent of U.S. imports. Mexico supplies large quantities of auto parts, steel, and oil to the United States. From 1993–2003, following the passage of NAFTA, Mexican tariffs declined from 40 percent to 16 percent, and exports to the United States increased from 67 percent to 88 percent of total Mexican exports. NAFTA also reduced the trade barriers for American companies such as General Motors and Wal-Mart to sell in Mexico. Wal-Mart now operates 520 retail

Figure 6.12 Largest U.S. Trading Partners

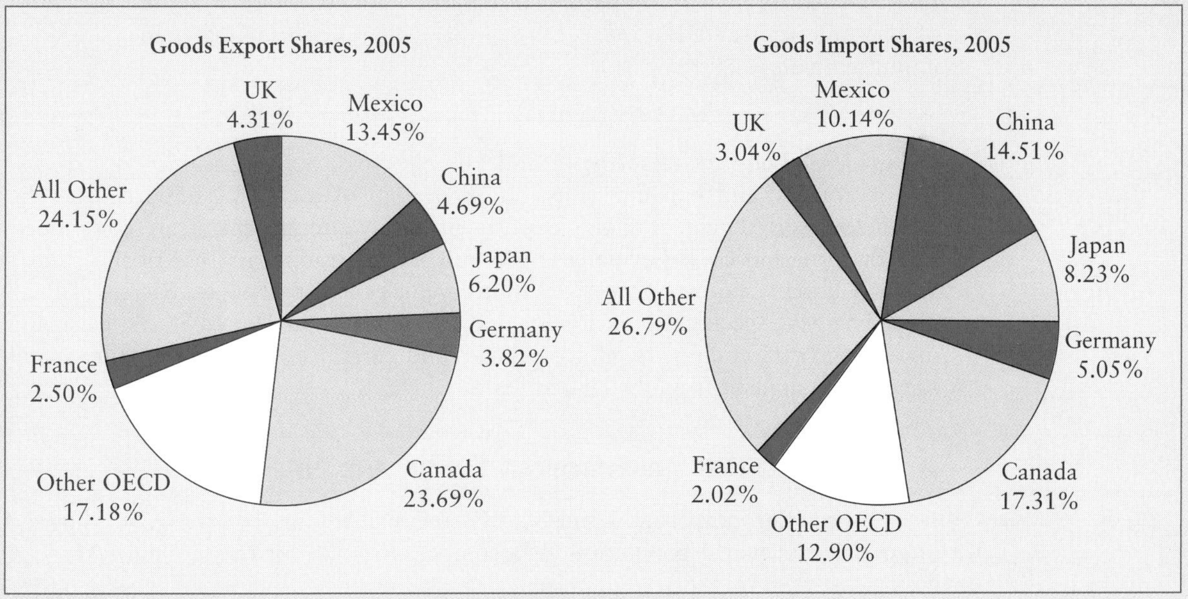

Source: National Economic Trends, *Federal Reserve Bank of St. Louis.*

stores across Mexico. U.S.-owned manufacturing and processing plants have long employed semiskilled labor at $2/hour in Mexico. This trade activity mirrors the labor-intensive assembly that German manufacturing companies perform in Spain and Portugal. For example, with untariffed import of subassemblies NAFTA lowered Mexican production costs for heavy equipment assembler Freightliner by $2,500 per truck between 1992 and 1998, enough to warrant opening a second **maquiladora** assembly plant in Mexico. NAFTA's million and a half new Mexican jobs have caused wage rates to begin to rise. Consequently, some of the assembly line, call center, and data processing jobs have now moved to still lower wage areas in Argentina, India, and China, respectively.

Maquiladora

A foreign-owned assembly plant in Mexico that imports and assembles duty-free components for export and allows owners to pay duty only on the "value added."

EXAMPLE

A Household Iron Manufacturer in Mexico Becomes a Major Engine-Block Supplier to Detroit[25]

Since its passage in 1994, NAFTA has made Mexico into a leading outsourcing location for the worldwide auto parts industry. Duty-free access to the United States for auto subassemblies such as transmissions and wiring harnesses, plus a growing sector of skilled nonunionized workers, induced GM, Ford, DaimlerChrysler, and Volkswagen as well as Mexican firms such as San Luis Corporation and Grupo Industrial Saltillo SA to invest billions in auto plants and equipment.

Cifunsa SA is a Grupo subsidiary that specialized immediately after WWII in the manufacture of metal castings for household appliances, especially hand irons. Today, Cifunsa has converted its aluminum and steel casting expertise to the production of engine blocks. Indeed, Cifunsa has the dominant position as a supplier of engine monoblocks to the North American car companies. Other Mexican metal casters play a major role in supplying heavy axles and coil springs for trucks and SUVs. Many windshields installed on U.S.-assembled cars and trucks also come from Mexico. Although some of this import-export trade is motivated by lower wage rates at Mexican than at comparable U.S. parts suppliers, another factor is the desire of the American and European car companies to decrease their dependence on unionized plants.

Japanese goods such as Toyota and Honda autos, Sony consumer electronics, Canon copiers, and Fuji film constitute 8 percent of total U.S. imports, and the Japanese absorb 6 percent of U.S. exports, primarily aircraft, chemicals, computers, timber, corn, and coal. Germany is the fifth largest trading partner of the United States. Germany exports principally motor vehicles and parts (e.g., Mercedes-Benz diesel engines), specialized machinery, and chemicals to the United States; Germany imports aircraft, computers, motor vehicles and parts (e.g., Cummins engines), and scientific equipment from the United States.

A Comparison of the European Union and NAFTA

Between the European Union and NAFTA regional trading blocs, NAFTA has the larger share of world population (6% compared to 5% for the original European

[25] Based on "Mexico Is Becoming Auto-Making Hot Spot," *Wall Street Journal* (June 23, 1998); and "Mexico Becomes a Leader in Car Parts," *Wall Street Journal* (March 30, 1999), p. A21.

Table 6.7 Destination of U.S. Goods Exports

1970–1975		1998–2003	
Country	Share (%)	Country	Share (%)
Canada	21.4	Canada	24.0
Japan	10.2	Mexico	13.5
Germany	5.4	Japan	9.4
United Kingdom	4.9	United Kingdom	5.2
Mexico	4.4	Germany	3.9
Netherlands	3.9	Korea	3.8
France	3.1	Taiwan	3.2
Italy	2.9	Netherlands	2.9
Brazil	2.7	France	2.8
Belgium-Luxembourg	2.3	China	2.4

Source: Federal Reserve Bank of St. Louis, *Review* (March/April 1999).

Union) and the same share of $61 trillion of world output in 2005 (21%), but the European Union has the larger share of world trade (32% compared to 24% for the NAFTA in 2005). Recall, however, that much of the EU trade (even prior to 1992) was always with other Western European countries *inside* the regional trading bloc. Table 6.7 shows this same type of relationship was also true of United States–Canada trade, but not true for trade with Mexico. Twenty years pre-NAFTA, Mexico purchased only 4.4 percent of U.S. exports. After the reduction in trade barriers associated with NAFTA, Mexican growth boomed, and only then in 1998–2003 did Mexico become the second-largest purchaser of U.S. exports (with a 13.5% share).

Another important contrast between the European Union and NAFTA is the "structural funds" the European Union allocates to upgrade roads, bridges, and port infrastructure in less-developed regions of Europe. Between 2000 and 2006, €42 billion went to Spain, €28 billion to southern Italy, €27 billion to former East Germany, and €20 billion to Greece and Portugal. However, these redistributive efforts, restrictive labor laws, and social programs in Europe impose a heavy burden on manufacturing competitiveness. Six weeks' paid vacation in Germany is now standard, and the Germans spend 8.4 percent of GDP on pension payments. Compare two weeks' paid vacation in the United States and the 5 percent of GDP Americans spend on pension payments. Opting out of the European Union's social program has allowed the British economy to stay almost head-to-head with U.S. total labor costs. As a consequence, although wages for time worked in the U.S., British, and German manufacturing sectors are similar (approximately $15 per hour), labor costs for holiday and leave pay add $5.70 an hour in Germany and only $1.03 an hour in the United States. When pensions and health care coverage are included, the total labor cost in Germany rises to $27.70 an hour versus $20.75 an hour in the United States. These massive cost differentials suggest that the world competitiveness of many European manufacturers remains in doubt.

In addition, workers on the senior management councils of German corporations often vote against plant closings. Plant closing legislation in Japan and the United

States, on the other hand, has sensibly left the ultimate decision-making and contracting authority with boards of directors. Also, French labor law makes it nearly impossible to lay off and furlough workers. Consequently, few entrepreneurial businesses in France proceed beyond small sole proprietorships. One interesting development in France has been the emergence of foreign subsidiaries operating under less restrictive EU labor regulations, such as Mercedes-Benz building its Swatch minicar in France.[26]

These factors all demonstrate that the institutional arrangements in the country surrounding a company are as important to its ultimate competitive success as the business plan, the quality of management decisions, and the commitment of dedicated employees. The enhanced competitive pressure arising from free trade and the opening of markets has served to accentuate the disadvantages of inefficient institutional arrangements. Rather than struggle against regulations that raise costs, global supply chain managers just take their business elsewhere.

Grey Markets, Knockoffs, and Parallel Importing

The prices charged for identical goods varied widely across Europe both before and after the formation of the Common Market (again see Table 6.6). For example, six years after the official lowering of trade barriers, a Ford Mondeo still cost 50 percent more in Germany than in Spain. To lower overall consumer prices and to improve competitiveness throughout the Union, the European Commission (EC) often adopts policies to encourage price competition. Goods arbitragers who want to buy Black and Decker power tools in Spain and sell them in Germany or buy Kawaski motorcycles in Holland and sell them in Britain are encouraged to do so. Volkswagen was fined €15 million for refusing to supply Northern Italian VW dealers who sold cars to large numbers of Munich weekenders traveling across the Alps for the Verona opera (and the inexpensive German car prices available in Italy). The EC also eliminated any contractual link between product sales and after-market service; any government-certified repair shop can purchase parts to perform VW, Nikon, or Sony maintenance and service. The problem, of course, is that such grey markets may lead to counterfeit sales and substandard service passed off as branded sales and authorized service.

EXAMPLE

EU Ban on Some Parallel Imports Pleases European but not U.S. and Japanese Manufacturers[27]

Manufacturers often seek to maintain different prices in different franchise territories for identical branded goods such as Levi's jeans, Nike shoes, Microsoft Windows, or Apple iPods. A recent ruling of the European Court of Justice (the

[26] Two useful surveys on these issues are "Business in Europe Survey," *The Economist* (November 23, 1996); and "Survey of the World Economy," *The Economist* (September 20, 1997).

[27] Based on "Setback for Parallel Imports," *BBC World Service* (July 16, 1998); "Parallel Imports," *Financial Times* (May 20, 1996); "Music Market Indicators," *The Economist* (May 15, 1999); D. Wilkinson, "Breaking the Chain: Parallel Imports and the Missing Link," *European Intellectual Property Review* (1997); and "Prozac's Maker Confronts China Over Knockoffs," *Wall Street Journal* (March 25, 1998), p. B9.

ECJ) held that copyright and trademark protection for Silhouette sunglasses, an Austrian export product, was infringed by an Austrian retailer who purchased the sunglasses at deep discount in Bulgaria and then reimported the product for sale in Austria at prices below those suggested by the manufacturer. Sourcing a product cheaply wherever it can be purchased around the world and then backshipping at discounted prices into the high-valued markets is a commonplace occurrence for many trading companies. The policy question is whether the discounted product can be effectively distinguished by customers from knockoff counterfeit products and whether the brand-name reputation of the manufacturer is thereby diminished.

Parallel Imports
The purchase of a foreign export product in one country to resell as an unauthorized import in another country.

Prior EU rulings had allowed such **parallel imports,** which occur any time a foreign export product is purchased in one EU country for resale in another EU country. For example, Tesco, a British retailer, purchased Levi's jeans and Nike shoes overseas and offered them for sale at a discount in Britain where the Levi- and Nike-authorized distribution channels had much higher price points. Similarly, Merck pharmaceuticals produced in Germany and sold at substantial discount in Spain had been backshipped into Germany by discount German retailers without prohibition (*Merck v. Primecrown* and *Beecham v. Europharm*). What was new about the Silhouette case was that Silhouette was itself an EU manufacturer, and the sourcing was obtained outside the European Union. The ECJ decided to extend to *European* brand-name products (such as Silhouette sunglasses) intellectual property protection not extended to *foreign* brand-name products. The purchase in Bulgaria for resale in Germany of a German-manufactured product at new product prices below the authorized retail price was prohibited.

In addition to this new European rule strengthening EU property rights to brand names and trademarks, Japan's high court prohibited computer software sales in violation of manufacturer-authorized distribution agreements. Under bilateral trade pressure from the United States, Japan supported Microsoft's international intellectual property rights. However, at the same time, Japan allowed the parallel importing of grey-market Steinway pianos and some music CDs and DVDs. As the world's largest exporter in the $38.7 billion music industry and the $90 billion computer software industry, the United States has threatened retaliation unless major trading partners aggressively punish violators of international copyright and trademark protection. Clearly, the status of parallel import policy is in flux, and businesses must plan accordingly.

The price impact of a policy prohibiting parallel imports can be enormous. Australians carefully protect intellectual property by aggressively prosecuting gray-market sellers of music. Cheap imitations and counterfeit substitutes are rare in Sydney or Melbourne, but the result is that popular music DVDs sold for $6.33 more in Australia than in other Far Eastern economies. The United Kingdom and China, therefore, choose the opposite policy for selected products. China permits the copying of patented medicines. Eli Lilly's Prozac, an antidepressant, sells for $1.73 per capsule, but a chemically identical "knockoff" from Shanghai Zhong Qi Pharmaceutical and Jiangsu Changzhov Pharmaceutical sells for $1.02 per capsule under the brand name You Ke. Similarly, the English obtain almost 10 percent of their pharmaceuticals and more than 30 percent of their wine, liquor, and beer through parallel importing.

Perspectives on the U.S. Trade Deficit

International trade is just one component of a country's balance of payments with the rest of the world. Capital flows (such as the sale of massive quantities of U.S. Treasury bonds and bills to foreign borrowers, Vodaphone's $66 billion purchase of Air Touch Communications, and BP's $55 billion purchase of Amoco) as well as transfer payments (such as U.S. financial support to the United Nations and other foreign aid) are other important components. Figure 6.13 shows that only once in the last 25 years has the United States generated a trade surplus. Instead, typically the services trade surplus (e.g., from McKinsey & Co. exporting management consulting and Haliburton exporting oil field development) is overwhelmed by a massive merchandise trade deficit. In 2005, a merchandise trade deficit of $792 billion when added to a $75 billion trade surplus in services led to a $717 billion trade *deficit* (5.8% of U.S. GDP).

Several factors contributed to this doubling of the U.S. trade deficit relative to the 2.7 percent 25-year average. First, U.S. manufacturers of Bali bras and Ford autos increasingly outsource the production of components and subassemblies to lower-wage Caribbean, Mexican, and Chinese partners and subsidiaries. These goods show up in the trade statistics as imports when they return for final assembly to the United States, even if they are produced by foreign subsidiaries owned by U.S. firms. Second, between 1998 and 2000, literally 60 percent of total fixed investment in the United States was for information technology (i.e., computers, servers, telecommunications equipment). The importance of the investment in new technology bought from abroad versus increased import consumption of cars, wine, and DVD players can be determined by examining Figure 6.14. In 1990, the proportion of capital goods imports was 22 percent of total U.S. merchandise imports. At the end of the 20th century, U.S. capital goods imports had skyrocketed to 50 percent of total imports.

Finally, recall that Figure 6.6 shows that the U.S. dollar exhibited a sustained appreciation against the currencies of almost all U.S. trading partners for almost a

Figure 6.13 The U.S. Trade Balance (Exports-Imports) as a Percentage of GDP

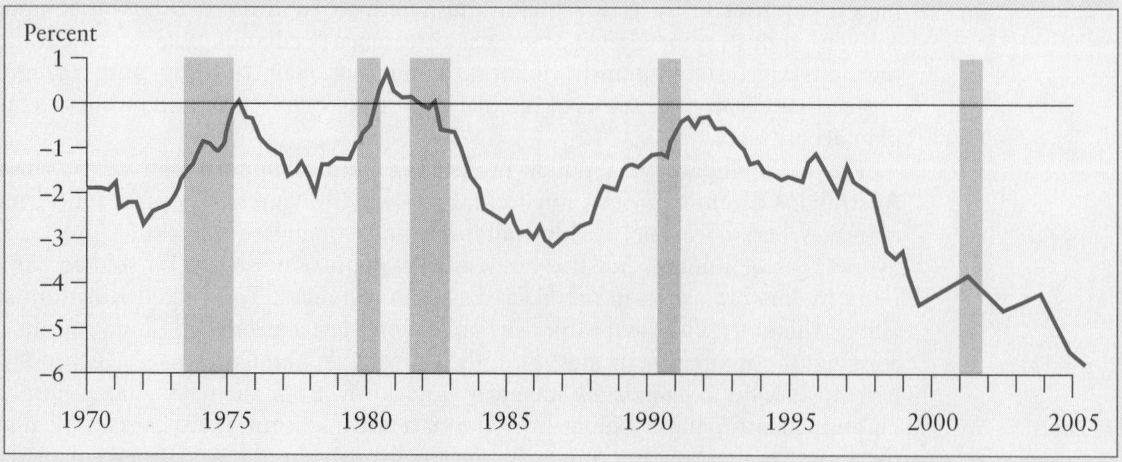

Source: *Review,* Federal Reserve Bank of St. Louis.

Figure 6.14 Capital Goods Imports/Total Merchandise Imports, United States

Source: *Review,* Federal Reserve Bank of St. Louis.

decade during 1995–2002. Ultimately, as we have seen in this chapter, such trends in exchange rates have a significant detrimental effect on net export trade flows. With the dollar depreciating below purchasing power parity in 2003–2005, U.S. exports surged, and the U.S. trade deficit will perhaps begin a long-awaited decline.

SUMMARY

- Export sales are sensitive to changes in exchange rates. Exports become more expensive (cheaper) in the foreign currencies of the importing countries when the domestic (i.e., home) currency of the manufacturer strengthens (weakens).
- Outsourcing to lower-wage manufacturing plants is a centuries-old phenomenon. Outsourcing often imports innovation and access to highly skilled analytical capabilities in testing and design as well as exporting lower-skilled jobs. Containerized ocean shipping is cheap and yet, outsourcing costs must include increased costs of vendor selection, quality control, intellectual property insurance, and expatriate management compensation.
- Major currencies are traded in the foreign exchange markets that include markets for U.S. dollars, British pounds, Japanese yen, and so on. Demand and supply in these markets reflects the speculative and transactions demands of investors, import-export dealers, corporations, financial institutions, the International Monetary Fund, central bankers, and governments throughout the global economy.
- Companies often demand payment and offer their best fixed-price quotes in their domestic currency because of transaction risk exposure and operating risk exposure to exchange rate fluctuations. Alternatively, such companies can manage the risk of exchange rate fluctuations themselves by setting up internal or financial

hedges involving forward, option, or currency swap contracts.

- Internal hedges may be either balance sheet hedges addressing translation risk or operating hedges matching anticipated foreign sales receipts with anticipated expenses in that same foreign currency. Financial hedges often address transaction risk exposure by setting up positions in financial derivative contracts to offset cash flow losses from currency fluctuations. Such hedging costs about 5 percent of the value at risk.
- Foreign buyers (or their financial intermediaries) usually must acquire euros to execute a purchase from Mercedes-Benz, U.S. dollars to purchase from General Motors, or yen to purchase from Toyota. Each buyer in these international sales transactions usually supplies their own domestic currency. Additional imports by Americans of Japanese automobiles would normally therefore result in an increased demand for the yen and an increased supply of dollars in the foreign currency markets (i.e., a dollar depreciation).
- Long-term trends in exchange rates are determined by transaction demand, government transfer payments, and central bank or IMF interventions.
- Three transaction demand factors are real (inflation-adjusted) growth rates, real (inflation-adjusted) interest rates, and expected cost inflation. The lower the expected cost of inflation, the lower the real growth rate, and the higher the real rate of interest in one economy relative to another, the higher the exports, the lower the import demand, and the higher the demand for financial instruments from that economy. All three determinants imply an increased demand or decreased supply of the domestic currency (i.e., a currency appreciation).
- Consumer price inflation serves as a good predictor of the combined effect of all three transaction demand factors on post-redemption returns to foreign asset holders. Projected changes in consumer inflation therefore directly affect international capital flows, which can easily overwhelm the effect of trade flows on exchange rates.
- The relative strength of a currency is often measured as an effective exchange rate index, a weighted average of the exchange rates against major trading partners, with the weights determined by the volume of import plus export trade.
- Free trade increases the economic growth of both industrialized and developing nations. Tariffs, duties, and import quotas sometimes play a role in strategic trade policy to force multilateral reduction of tariffs, open markets, or secure increasing returns.
- Trade restrictions (quotas or tariffs) may be warranted under special circumstances to protect infant industries, to offset government subsidies with countervailing duties, or to impose antidumping sanctions on foreign imports sold at a price below their domestic cost.
- Speculative demand especially influences short-term changes in exchange rates. Because the total dollar volume of foreign-currency trading worldwide is $2 trillion *per day,* these short-term fluctuations can be quite volatile.
- International capital flows and the flow of tradable goods across nations respond to arbitrage opportunities. Arbitrage trading ceases when parity conditions are met. One such condition is relative purchasing power parity.
- Relative purchasing power parity (PPP) hypothesizes that a doubling of consumer prices in one economy will lead to trade flows that cut in half the value of the currency. Over long periods of time and on an approximate basis, exchange rates do appear related to differential rates of inflation across economies. PPP serves a useful benchmark role in assessing long-term trends in exchange rates.
- The European Union (EU) and the North American Free Trade Agreement (NAFTA) are two of several large trading blocs that have organized to open markets to free trade. The European Union is the largest producer of world output with dissimilar economies that have reduced trade barriers and specialized in accordance with comparative advantage. Marketing across the European Union must address clusters of distinctly different consumers.
- Whether a nation should join a (single) currency union depends on (1) the magnitude of intraregional trade, (2) the mobility of labor, and (3) the correlation of macroeconomic shocks.
- The United States is both the largest single-nation exporter and the largest importer in the world economy. The largest trading partner of the United States is Canada, followed by China, Mexico, Japan, United Kingdom, and Germany. China is by far the fastest growing nation in world trade. The U.S. share of world trade (14%) has grown in recent years, while that of Germany and other EU nations has declined. Extensive social programs, supplemental labor costs, and institutions that discourage business formation in Europe seem responsible for these trends.
- The trade flows of the United States are often in deficit (i.e., imports exceed exports); the last time the United States experienced a trade surplus was during the recession of 1981–1982. The balance of trade deficit of the United States is normally offset by international capital flows into the United States plus the occasional transfer of official reserves. The balance of payments accounts reflect this accounting identity.

- The U.S. 2005 trade deficit of $717 billion was generated by $792 billion more merchandise imported into the United States than exported. Services generated a $75 billion trade surplus. In recent years, these trade deficits have been approximately 5–6 percent of a $12 trillion gross domestic product in the United States.

Exercises

Answers to the exercises in blue can be found in Appendix C at the back of the book.

1. If the U.S dollar depreciates 20 percent, what are the effects on the export and domestic sales of a U.S. manufacturer? Explain.
2. If the U.S. dollar were to appreciate substantially, what steps could a domestic manufacturer such as Cummins Engine Co. of Columbus, Indiana, take in advance to reduce the effect of the exchange rate fluctuation on company profitability?
3. After an unanticipated dollar appreciation occurs, what would you recommend a company such as Cummins Engine do with its strong domestic currency?
4. What is the difference between transaction demand, speculative demand, and autonomous transactions by central banks, the World Bank, and the IMF in the foreign exchange markets? Which of these factors determines the long-term quarterly trends in exchange rates?
5. Would increased cost inflation in the United States relative to its major trading partners likely increase or decrease the value of the U.S. dollar? Why?
6. If the domestic prices for traded goods rose 50 percent over 10 years in Japan and 100 percent over that same 10 years in the United States, what would happen to the yen/dollar exchange rate? Why?
7. If Boeing's aircraft prices in dollars increase 20 percent and the yen/dollar exchange rate declines 15 percent, what effective price increase is facing Japan Air Lines for the purchase of a Boeing 747? Would Boeing's margin likely rise or fall if the yen then depreciated and competitor prices were unchanged? Why?
8. Unit labor costs in Germany exceed $32 per hour, whereas in Britain unit labor costs are only about $17 per hour. Why would such a large difference persist between two members of the EU free trade area?
9. If U.S. citizens and corporations earn more investment income on their foreign investments than is paid to foreigners on their U.S. investments, and if foreigners purchase more U.S. securities, loans, and real assets than U.S citizens and corporations purchase abroad, will the United States be a net importer or net exporter? Explain.
10. From 2000 (Q4) to 2002 (Q4) the net foreign direct investment in U.S. equities declined steadily from $87 billion to $9 billion per quarter. How does a reduced flow of international capital into the U.S. stock markets affect the dollar's exchange rate, and why? Would expectations of continuing withdrawals from U.S. markets have any additional effect on exchange rates? Why?
11. Unit labor costs in Spain and Portugal rose 3.5 percent from a low base in 1999–2001, while producer price indices also rose 2.6 percent and 6.0 percent, respectively. In contrast, unit labor costs in Germany declined 1.5 percent and producer prices were unchanged. What effect should these factors, by themselves, have on export trade, and why?
12. What three factors determine whether two economies with separate fiscal and monetary authorities should form a currency union? Give an illustration of each factor using NAFTA economies.
13. Would yogurt or Prada handbags have wider price variation in a free trade area such as the European Union? Why?
14. If core price inflation has grown at a compound growth rate of 2.13 percent per annum in the United States and 0.04 percent in Japan for the past eight years, what exchange rate represents purchasing power parity today if the two currencies eight years ago in 1998 were in parity and exchanged at the rate of ¥130/$?

CASE EXERCISES

PREDICTING THE LONG-TERM TRENDS IN VALUE OF THE U.S. DOLLAR DM AND EURO

1. Analyze the following data on inflation rates, interest rates, and growth rate forecasts to determine what the likely long-term trend movement of the U.S. dollar would have been during 1998–1999 against the German deutsche mark. Would you have expected the DM/$ exchange rate to increase or decrease? Why?

	1996, %	1997, %	Forecasted 1998, %
U.S. nominal interest rate (90-day bills)	5.23	5.43	
German nominal interest rate (90-day bills)	3.18	3.40	
Quarterly U.S. consumer inflation	2.2	1.5	
Quarterly German consumer inflation	2.1	2.3	
U.S. real growth rate of GDP	3.7	4.5	2.5
German real growth rate of GDP	0.8	2.4	2.9
U.S. producer price index	2.8	−1.2	
German producer price index	1.0	1.8	

2. Analyze the following data on inflation rates, interest rates, and growth rate forecasts to determine what the likely long-term trend movement of the euro would have been during 2000 against the U.S. dollar. Would you have expected the euro/$ exchange rate to increase or decrease? Why?

	1998, %	1999, %	Forecasted 2000, %
U.S. nominal interest rate (90-day bills)	5.5	5.3	
Euro-11 nominal interest rate (90-day bills)	3.8	3.0	
U.S. consumer inflation	1.6	2.2	
Euro-11 consumer inflation	1.1	1.1	
U.S. real growth of GDP	4.3	4.2	3.9
Euro-11 real growth of GDP	2.3	2.5	3.3
U.S. producer price index	0.0	3.0	
Euro-11 producer price index	1.0	1.0	

3. After the recession of 2001–2002, the U.S. economy grew at 2.7 percent in 2003, and the European economy grew at 0.8 percent. Usually the American economy does *lead* out of world business cycle downturns. To further assure this development, the U.S. Federal Reserve lowered the rate at which federal banks borrow short term from the Fed. As a result of the new Fed policy and a weakness in the demand for new investment by business, 3-month T-bill real rates declined to near zero in 2003–2004. With Euro area 3-month bonds yielding 1.05 percent as a real rate, Producer costs (as measured by the producer price index) rising in both the United States and Europe at 3.2 percent and 1.4 percent, respectively, analyze how each of the above-mentioned factors will affect the €/$ exchange rate, which presently stands at near-parity 1.01 €/$.

U.S. ENERGY POLICY, OIL IMPORTS, AND THE PRICE OF GASOLINE[28]

From 1973–2003, U.S. dependence on foreign oil grew as oil imports rose from 40 percent to 60 percent of U.S. oil consumption (19.5 million barrels per day). Over this 30-year period, inflation-adjusted retail gasoline prices in the United States were highly volatile, but they started and finished at approximately the same $1.50 per gallon (see the following figure). At times in the interim, retail gasoline cost as much as $2.20 per gallon (in 1980–1981) and at other times as little as $1.10 per gallon (in 1998). A 100 percent input price variation of this sort can easily cause profitable business plans in transportation industries (e.g., trucking and airlines) to run huge deficits. You work at an oil company, and your chief operating officer (COO) has asked that you prepare a study detailing the likely sources of future price variation.

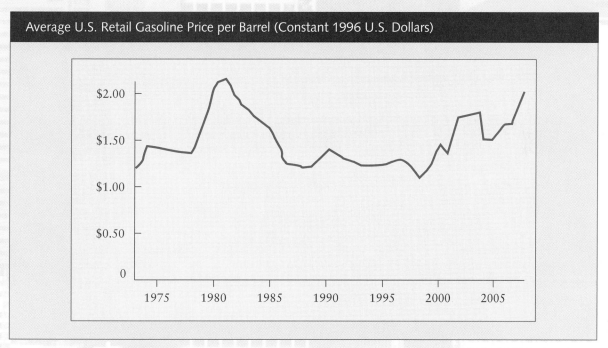

Average U.S. Retail Gasoline Price per Barrel (Constant 1996 U.S. Dollars)

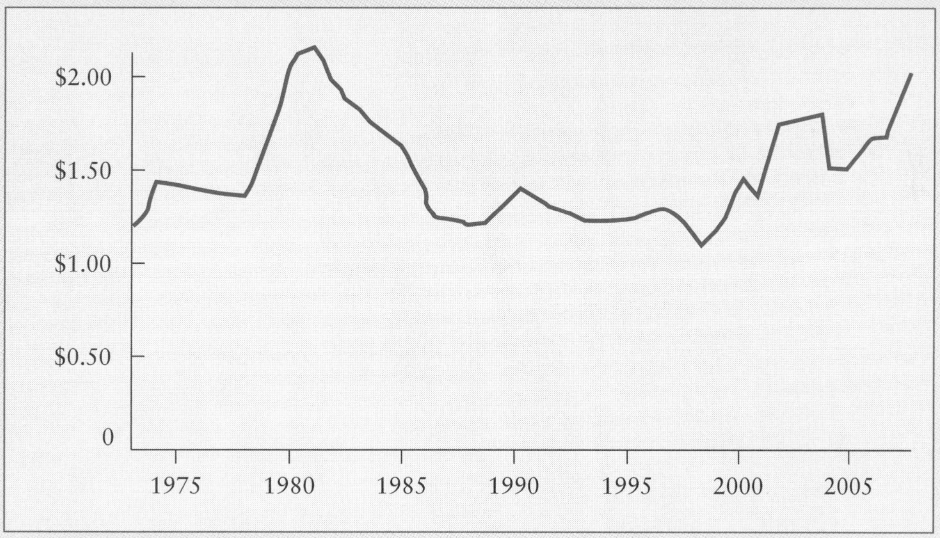

Source: U.S. Department of Energy.

U.S. energy policy contributed to some of the peaks and troughs of retail gasoline prices. President Carter championed a synthetic fuel oil program using coal and shale in 1979–1980, but that initiative was quickly dismissed as uneconomic when President Reagan took office. More stringent fuel efficiency standards for autos were imposed by the U.S. Congress in 1983 and again in 1997. More recently, in 2002, President Bush backed a $1.7-billion publicly funded research effort to develop hydrogen-powered fuel cells as a substitute for gasoline engines in automobiles.

The successes and failures of the Organization of Petroleum Exporting Countries (OPEC) cartel have also been involved in explaining peaks and troughs of U.S.

---

28 Based on "Why the U.S. Is Still Hooked on Oil Imports," *Wall Street Journal* (March 18, 2003), p. A1; and "Iraq's Crude Awakening," *Time* (May 18, 2003), p. 49.

gasoline prices. Although only 20 percent of U.S. crude oil imports come from the Persian Gulf, members of OPEC effectively set the price by controlling two thirds of proven reserves, possessing 90 percent of excess capacity to pump and pipe and ship additional crude oil, and by developing by far the lowest-priced operations. Incremental barrels of crude oil that cost $1.00 to extract in Iraq and $2.50 in Saudi Arabia cost fully $5 in the North Sea oil fields and $10 in the United States.

Because 50 percent of the inputs for the production of gasoline for cars and trucks in North America come from crude oil imports, you hypothesize that the price of U.S. retail gasoline will also fluctuate in accordance with the value of the U.S. dollar in foreign exchange markets. As the dollar appreciates, import prices decline, and thus gasoline retail prices decline. As the dollar depreciates, import prices rise, and thus gasoline retail prices rise. Using Figure 6.6, analyze the changes in the value of the U.S. dollar in various years leading up to peaks and troughs of gas prices from 1973–2003. Analyze the relationship between U.S. energy policy initiatives and the average U.S. gasoline price. Advise your boss about the likelihood of $3.00 per gallon oil prices by 2006. What could cause the gasoline price to fall to $1.50?

PART III
Production and Cost

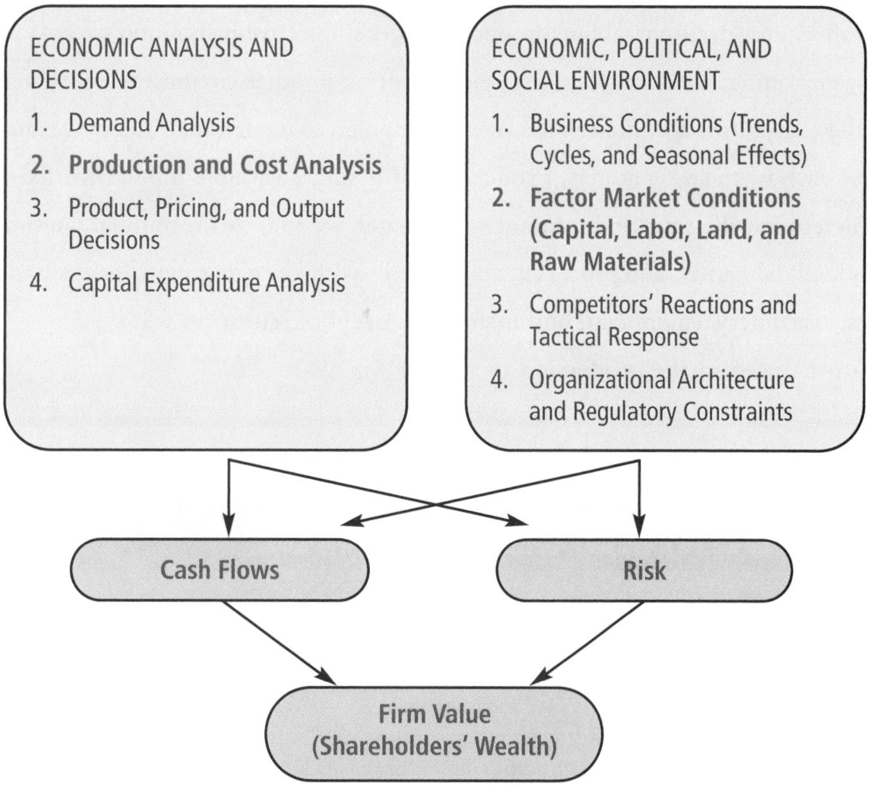

Part III deals with the production and cost analysis decisions facing managers. In Chapter 7 the theory of production decisions is developed using primarily graphical tools of analysis. Production decisions include the determination of the type and amount of resources (land, labor, materials, capital equipment, and managerial skills) that are used in the production of a desired amount of output. The objective is to combine these inputs in the most efficient manner to produce a given type of output. Appendix 7A examines constrained optimization techniques, using calculus, to assist production decision making. Web Appendix C looks at real-world process choice decisions in a linear programming framework. In Chapter 8 the theory of cost analysis is developed. Cost measures are combined with revenue estimates to determine optimal levels and mixes of output. Chapter 9 discusses the applications of cost theory, including the measurement of short- and long-run cost relationships, the use of break-even and contribution analysis, and operating leverage concepts. The learning curve concept, as applied to manufacturing, is developed in Appendix 9A.

CHAPTER

7

PRODUCTION ECONOMICS

CHAPTER PREVIEW Managers are required to make resource allocation decisions about production operations, marketing, financing, and personnel. Although these decisions are interrelated, it is useful to discuss each of them separately. Production decisions determine the type and amount of inputs—such as land, labor, raw and processed materials, factories, machinery, equipment, and managerial talent—to be used in the production of a desired quantity of output. The production manager's objective is to minimize cost for a given output or, in other circumstances, to maximize output for a given input budget. First, we analyze the choice of a single variable input with fixed input prices. Later, we analyze the optimal multi-input combination with changing input prices and introduce the concept of returns to scale.

MANAGERIAL CHALLENGE

What Went Wrong in California's Deregulation of Electricity?[1]

Large-scale electric power plants entail huge capital investments, with pollution abatement technology in coal-fired plants and redundant safety devices in nuclear plants running into the hundreds of millions of dollars. Pacific Gas and Electric's (PG&E) Diablo Canyon nuclear power plant near Santa Barbara cost $5.8 billion. Nuclear-powered and coal-fired plants have much lower variable costs than smaller-scale natural gas-powered and fuel oil-powered electricity generating plants. For coal and nuclear, the operating cost is only $20 per megawatt hour (mwh) versus $35/mwh for natural gas-fired and fuel oil-fired plants. The trade-off between investing in low-fixed-cost plants with higher and much more volatile variable costs versus high-fixed-cost plants with lower and stable variable costs has come into focus during the electricity deregulation crisis in California.

In 1998, California implemented legislation to decouple electricity generation and distribution, allowing large retail and industrial customers to purchase electricity from long-distance suppliers. As a result, two California utilities, Pacific Gas and Electric and Southern Cal Edison, scaled back their generating plant expansion plans and began to meet peak demand by purchasing 25 percent of their power in wholesale spot markets. It has been estimated that as much as 55 percent of the variation in peak-hour daily wholesale prices is attributable to extraordinary transmission line fees from bottlenecked long-distance suppliers and to the small-scale fuel oil and natural gas independent generating plants that fire up to meet the last 5 percent of peak demand (see the following graph). As a result, 11 times between June 2000 and June 2001 the peak-hour daily price in Southern California rose above $400/mwh.

Between 1998 and 2001, the monthly average wholesale price of electricity in California shot up from $25–$50 to $198–$231/mwh. California

MANAGERIAL CHALLENGE

Edison and PG&E were restrained by a $54/mwh price cap set by the public utility commission from passing through to their retail customers almost $11 billion in higher wholesale costs. Not surprisingly, therefore, almost no Californians elected to switch away from their assigned utility providers, whereas 12 percent of Pennsylvanians, 5 percent of Ohioans, 3 percent of New Yorkers, and 30 percent of British citizens did so within two years after electricity deregulation.

With the onslaught of rolling blackouts in 2001, the California Public Utility Commission approved a 46 percent increase in retail electricity rates. Still PG&E declared bankruptcy, and the State of California has been forced to arrange an expensive long-term bailout. In light of this California "energy

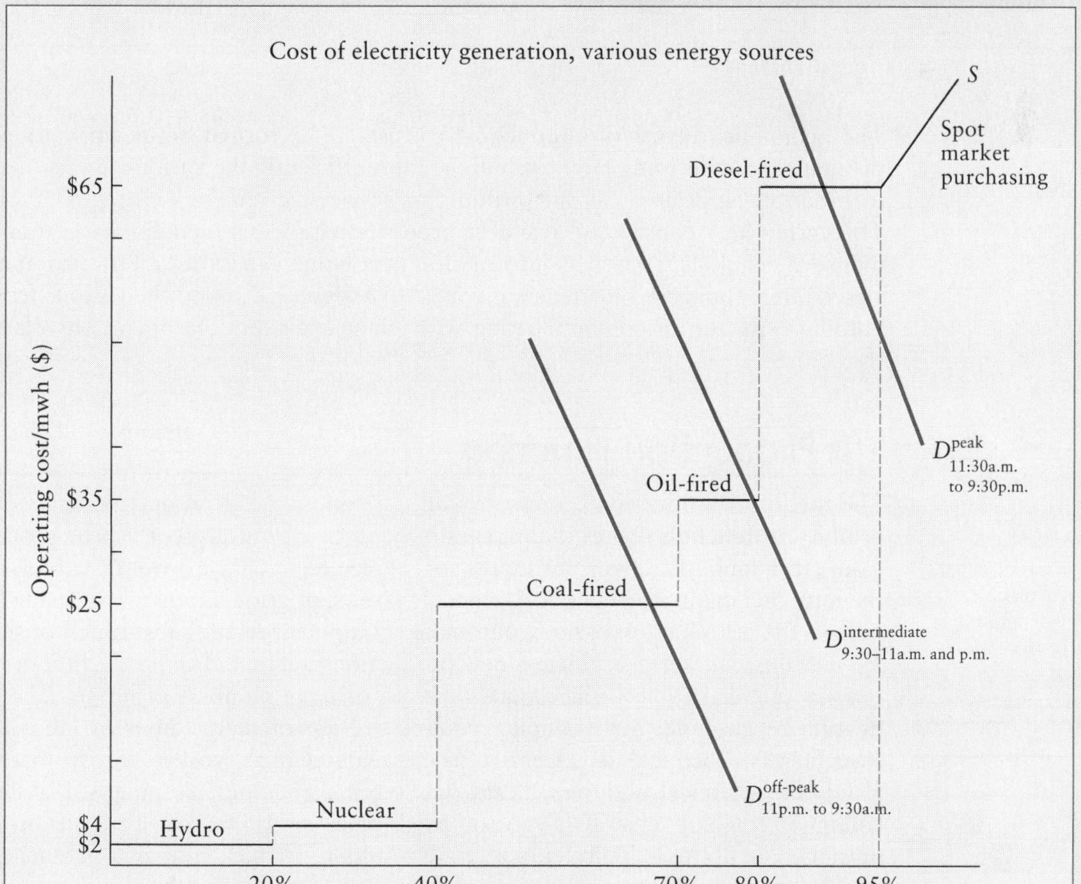

MANAGERIAL CHALLENGE

nightmare," three Western states (Montana, Nevada, and Oregon) and six others across the country revised or delayed their electricity deregulation initiatives. Fourteen states, including Florida, Georgia, and North and South Carolina, rejected electricity deregulation altogether, and are pursuing other alternatives.

One alternative approach is to charge electricity customers a variable rate per mwh to reflect differential cost at different hours of the day, days of the week, and seasons of the year. We discuss such real-time differential pricing in Chapter 14. A second new approach is *distributed generation* by extremely small-scale diesel generators or natural gas-fired microturbine generators in factories and commercial establishments. Operating costs of the microturbines are \$70–\$120/mwh, much higher than utility-supplied electricity. Yet, the capital cost that must be recovered is less than one 1/1000th of traditional power plants. La Quinta Motels, for example, saved \$20,000 in one year with a microturbine at one of its Dallas properties. Puget Sound Energy, the largest investor-owned utility in the state of Washington, began installing microturbines in substations near growing neighborhoods that are forecasted to be sources of peak demand on capacity. In this chapter, we will study the dilemma of whether to substitute higher cost variable inputs for fixed inputs entailing substantial capital investment.

[1] Based on "The Lessons Learned" and "Think Small," *Wall Street Journal* (September 17, 2001), pp. R4, R13, R15, and R17; "Are Californians Starved for Energy?" *Wall Street Journal* (September 16, 2002), p. A1; and "How to Do Deregulation Right," *BusinessWeek* (March 26, 2001), p. 112.

The economic theory of production consists of a formal framework to assist the manager in deciding how to combine most efficiently the various inputs[2] needed to produce the desired output (product or service), given the existing technology. This technology consists of available production processes, equipment, labor and management skills, as well as information-processing capabilities. Production analysis is often applied by managers involved in assigning costs to the various feasible output levels and in communicating with plant engineers the operations plans of the company.

The Production Function

Production Function

A mathematical model, schedule (table), or graph that relates the maximum feasible quantity of output that can be produced from given amounts of various inputs.

Input

A resource or factor of production, such as a raw material, labor skill, or piece of equipment, that is employed in a production process.

The theory of production centers around the concept of a production function. A **production function** relates the maximum quantity of output that can be produced from given amounts of various inputs for a given technology. It can be expressed in the form of a mathematical model, schedule (table), or graph. A change in technology, such as the introduction of more automated equipment or the substitution of skilled for unskilled workers, results in a new production function. The production of most outputs (goods and services) requires the use of large numbers of **inputs.** The production of gasoline, for example, requires the use of many different labor skills (roughnecks, chemical engineers, refinery maintenance workers), raw materials (crude oil, chemical additives, heat), and types of equipment (boilers, distillation columns, cracking chambers). Also, production processes often result in joint outputs. For example, petroleum refining results in jet fuel, propane, butane, gasoline, kerosene, lubricant oil, tar, and asphalt.

[2] The terms *input, factor,* and *resource* are used interchangeably throughout the chapter.

Cobb-Douglas Production Function

A particular type of mathematical model, known as a multiplicative exponential function, used to represent the relationship between the inputs and the output.

Letting L and K represent the quantities of two inputs (labor L and capital K) used in producing a quantity Q of output, a production function can be represented in the form of a mathematical model, such as

$$Q = \alpha L^{\beta_1} K^{\beta_2} \qquad [7.1]$$

where α, β_1, and β_2 are constants. This particular multiplicative exponential model is known as the **Cobb-Douglas production function** and is examined in more detail later in the chapter. Production functions also can be expressed in the form of a *schedule* (or table), as illustrated in the following ore-mining example.

EXAMPLE

An Illustrative Production Function: Deep Creek Mining Company

The Deep Creek Mining Company uses capital (mining equipment) and labor (workers) to mine uranium ore. Various sizes of ore-mining equipment, as measured by its brake horsepower (bhp) rating, are available to the company. The amount of ore mined during a given period (Q) is a function only of the number of workers assigned to the crew (L) operating a given type of equipment (K). The data in Table 7.1 show the amount of ore produced (measured in tons) when various sizes of crews are used to operate the equipment.

A two-input, one-output production function at Deep Creek Mining can also be represented *graphically* as a three-dimensional production surface, where the height of the square column associated with each input combination in Figure 7.1 indicates the amount of iron ore output produced.

Fixed and Variable Inputs

In deciding how to combine the various inputs (L and K) to produce the desired output, inputs are usually classified as being either fixed or variable. A *fixed* input is defined as one required in the production process but whose quantity employed

Table 7.1 Total Output Table—Deep Creek Mining Company

		Capital Input *K* (bhp, Brake Horsepower)							
		250	500	750	1,000	1,250	1,500	1,750	2,000
Labor Input *L* (Number of Workers)	1	1	3	6	10	16	16	16	13
	2	2	6	16	24	29	29	44	44
	3	4	16	29	44	55	55	55	50
	4	6	29	44	55	58	60	60	55
	5	16	43	55	60	61	62	62	60
	6	29	55	60	62	63	63	63	62
	7	44	58	62	63	64	64	64	64
	8	50	60	62	63	64	65	65	65
	9	55	59	61	63	64	65	66	66
	10	52	56	59	62	64	65	66	67

Figure 7.1 The Production Function—Deep Creek Mining Company

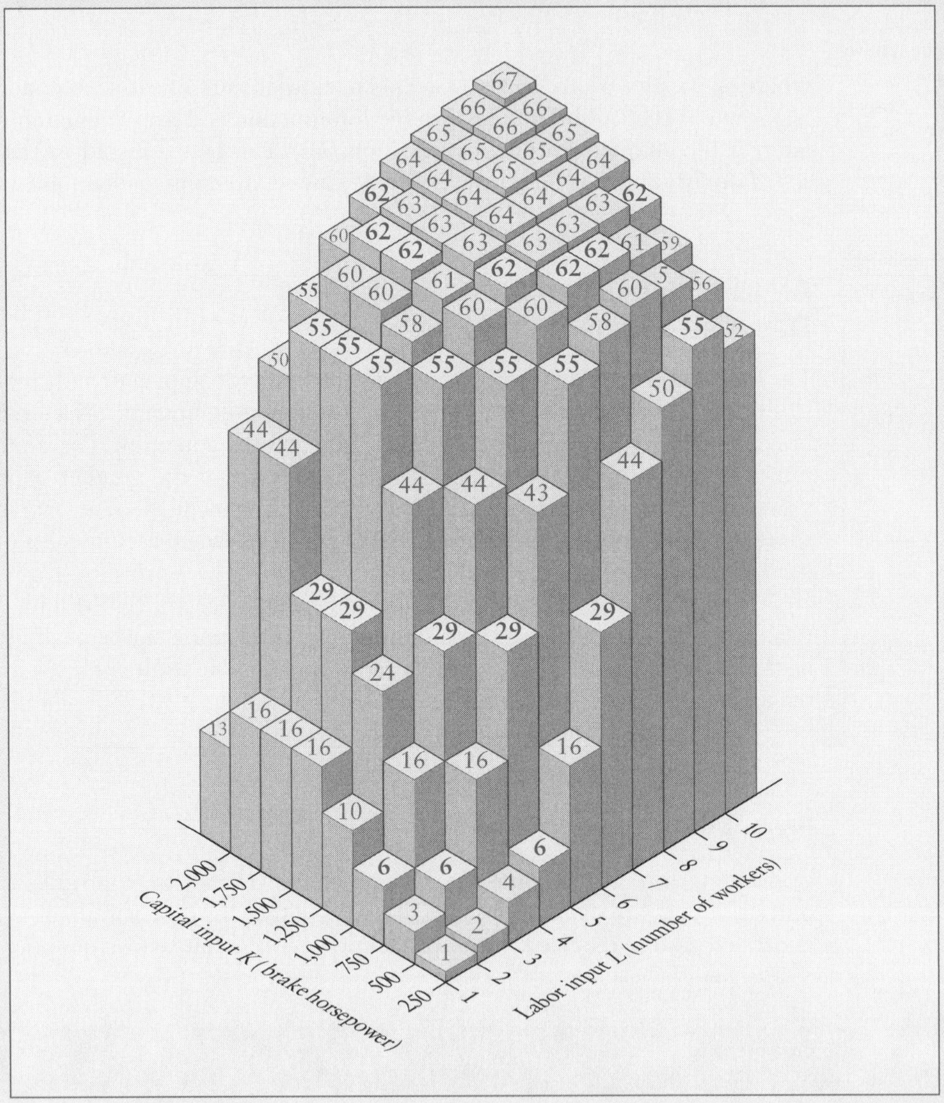

in the process is constant over a given period of time regardless of the quantity of output produced. The costs of a fixed input must be incurred regardless of whether the production process is operated at a high or a low rate of output. A *variable* input is defined as one whose quantity employed in the process changes, depending on the desired quantity of output to be produced.

Short Run

The period of time in which one (or more) of the resources employed in a production process is fixed or incapable of being varied.

The **short run** corresponds to the period of time in which one (or more) of the inputs is fixed. To increase output, then, the firm must employ more of the variable input(s) with the given quantity of fixed input(s). Thus, for example, with an auto assembly plant of fixed size and capacity, the firm can increase output only by employing more labor, such as by scheduling additional shifts.

As the time period under consideration (the planning horizon) is lengthened, however, more of the fixed inputs become variable. Over a planning horizon of about six months, most firms can acquire or build additional plant capacity and order more manufacturing equipment. In lengthening the planning horizon, a point is eventually reached where all inputs are variable. This period of time is called the **long run.**

Long Run
The period of time in which *all* the resources employed in a production process can be varied.

In the short run, because some of the inputs are fixed, only a subset of the total possible input combinations is available to the firm. By contrast, in the long run, all possible input combinations are available.

PRODUCTION FUNCTIONS WITH ONE VARIABLE INPUT

Suppose, in the Deep Creek Mining Company example of the previous section, that the amount of capital input K (the size of mining equipment) employed in the production process is a fixed factor. Specifically, suppose that the firm owns or leases a piece of mining equipment having a 750-bhp rating. Depending on the amount of labor input L used to operate the 750-bhp equipment, varying quantities of output will be obtained, as shown in the *750* column of Table 7.1 and again in the Q column of Table 7.2.

Marginal Product
The incremental change in total output that can be obtained from the use of one more unit of an input in the production process (while holding constant all other inputs).

MARGINAL AND AVERAGE PRODUCT FUNCTIONS

Once the total product function is given (in tabular, graphic, or algebraic form), the marginal and average product functions can be derived. The **marginal product** is defined as the incremental change in total output ΔQ that can be produced by the

Table 7.2 Total Product, Marginal Product, Average Product, and Elasticity—Deep Creek Mining Company (Capital input, bhp = 750)

Labor Input (Number of Workers)	Total Product TP_L (= Q) (Tons of Ore)	Marginal Product of Labor, MP_L ($\Delta Q \div \Delta L$)	Average Product of Labor, AP_L ($Q \div L$)	Production Elasticity, E_L ($MP_L \div AP_L$)
0	0	—	—	—
1	6	+ 6	6	1.0
2	16	+10	8	1.25
3	29	+13	9.67	1.34
4	44	+15	11	1.36
5	55	+11	11	1.0
6	60	+ 5	10	0.50
7	62	+ 2	8.86	0.23
8	62	0	7.75	0.0
9	61	− 1	6.78	−0.15
10	59	− 2	5.90	−0.34

Figure 7.2 Total Product, Marginal Product of Labor, and Average Product of Labor Deep Creek Mining Co.

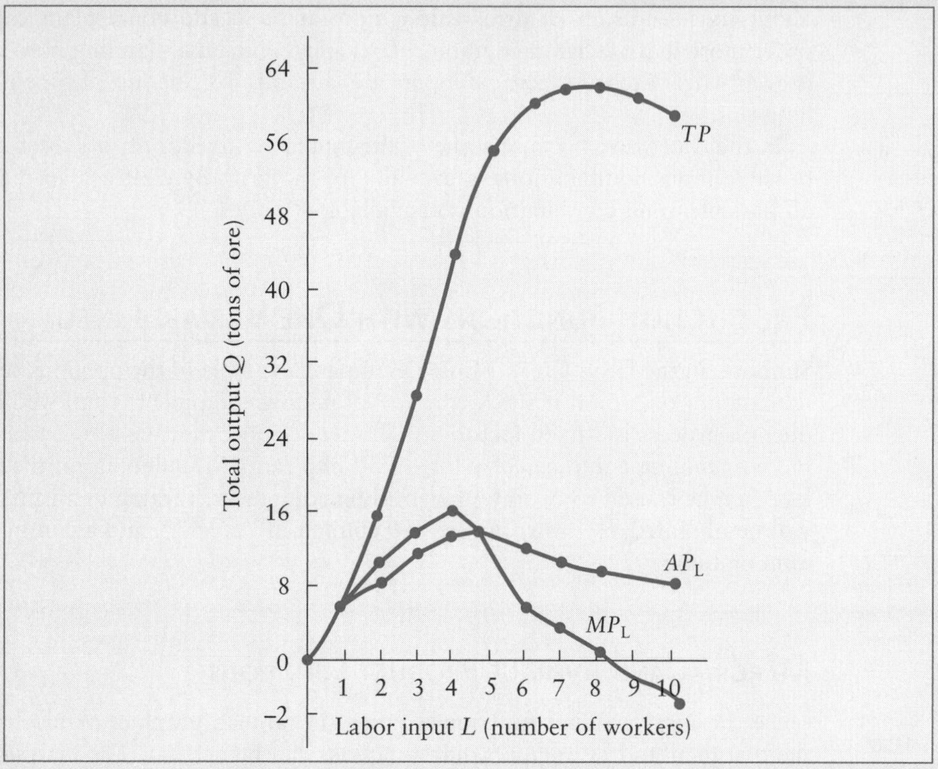

use of one more unit of the variable input ΔL, while K remains fixed. The marginal product is defined as[3]

$$MP_L = \frac{\Delta Q}{\Delta L} \text{ or } \frac{\partial Q}{\partial L} \quad [7.2]$$

for discrete and continuous changes, respectively.

The marginal product of labor in the ore-mining example is shown in the third column of Table 7.2 and as MP_L in Figure 7.2.

Average Product

The ratio of total output to the amount of the variable input used in producing the output.

The **average product** is defined as the ratio of total output to the amount of the variable input used in producing the output. The average product of labor is

$$AP_L = \frac{Q}{L} \quad [7.3]$$

The average product of labor for the Deep Creek ore-mining example is shown in the fourth column of Table 7.2.

[3] Strictly speaking, the ratio $\Delta Q/\Delta L$ represents the *incremental* product rather than the *marginal* product. For simplicity, we continue to use the term *marginal* throughout the text, even though this and similar ratios are calculated on an incremental basis.

WHAT WENT RIGHT • WHAT WENT WRONG

FACTORY BOTTLENECKS AT A BOEING ASSEMBLY PLANT[4]

The Boeing Company assembles wide-body aircraft (747s, 767s, and 777s) at its 4.3-million-square-foot Everett, Washington, assembly plant, the largest building in the world. Fifteen railcars a day deliver parts that are directed to five assembly lines by overhead cranes cruising on 31 miles of networked track. The variable inputs in this production process are millions of parts and thousands of skilled assemblers.

As Boeing ramped up production from 244 aircraft deliveries in 1995 to 560 in 1999, the Everett plant went to three shifts of 6,000, 4,000, and 1,500 workers, and twice as many parts poured in. But crowding effects descended on the Everett plant. Although final assembly of an aircraft body continued to take its normal 21 workdays, overtime was required to maintain this roll-out schedule, in large part because of lost, defective, and reworked parts. At times, piles of redundant parts would appear on the shop floor, while at other times, shortages of seats and electronic gear caused delays. As a result, work-in-progress inventory skyrocketed and work orders got out of sequence. By late 1997, overtime was running almost a billion dollars over budget, and the production operations at Everett were "hopelessly snarled."

To resolve the problem, in 1999 Boeing scrapped its antiquated parts-tracking system and adopted lean production techniques. It cut parts order sizes and outsourced subassembly work away from bottlenecked points on the final assembly line. By 2001, a continuous stream of fewer parts arrived at autonomous worker cells just in time, as required to complete a smoothly flowing assembly process for 527 aircraft deliveries.

[4] "Boeing's Secret," *BusinessWeek* (May 20, 2002), pp. 113–15; "Gaining Altitude," *Barron's* (April 29, 2002), pp. 21–25; and Everett plant tours.

THE LAW OF DIMINISHING MARGINAL RETURNS

The tabular production function just discussed illustrates the production law of diminishing marginal returns. Initially, the assignment of more workers to the crew operating the mining equipment allows greater labor specialization in the use of the equipment. As a result, the marginal output of each worker added to the crew at first increases, and total output increases at an increasing rate. Thus, as listed in Table 7.2 and graphed in Figure 7.2, the addition of a second worker to the crew results in 10 additional tons of output; the addition of a third worker results in 13 additional tons of output; and the addition of a fourth worker yields 15 additional tons.

A point is eventually reached, however, where the marginal increase in output for each worker added to the crew begins to decline. This decrease in output occurs because only a limited number of ways exist to achieve greater labor specialization and because each additional worker introduces crowding effects. Thus, the addition of a fifth worker to the crew yields a marginal increase in output of 11 additional tons, compared with the marginal increase of 15 additional tons for the fourth worker. Similarly, the additions of the sixth and seventh workers to the crew yield successively smaller increases of 5 and 2 tons, respectively. With enough additional workers, the marginal product of labor may become zero or even negative. Some work is just more difficult to accomplish when superfluous personnel are present.

Increasing Returns with Network Effects

Network Effects

An exception to the law of diminishing marginal returns that occurs when the installed base of a network product makes the efforts to acquire new customers increasingly more productive.

The law of diminishing marginal returns is *not* a mathematical theorem, but an empirical assertion that has been observed in almost every economic production process as the amount of the variable input increases. An interesting exception occurs, however, with **network effects.** The greater the installed base of a network product, such as Microsoft Office and Outlook, the larger the number of compatible network connections and therefore the more possible value for a new customer. Consequently, as the software's installed base increases, Microsoft's promotions and other selling efforts to acquire new customers become increasingly more productive.

A manufacturer's product line costs usually now include marketing and distribution activities as well as the labor and material direct costs of standard production and assembly. The reason is that, like service firms, many manufacturers today compete on customer inquiry systems, change order responsiveness, delivery reliability, and technological updates, not just on delivery times and warranty repairs. Qualifying for and actually winning a customer order often requires quality characteristics and support services beyond the physical unit of production. For example, Ford Motor wants all its manufacturing suppliers to meet the ISO 9000 manufacturing quality standards for continuous improvement processes. Wal-Mart requires that its fashion clothing suppliers deliver shipments just in time (JIT) for planned departure from Wal-Mart distribution centers. Disney World gift shops choose manufacturers who can alter their production schedules on short notice in order to provide much greater change-order responsiveness than traditional make-to-order manufacturing of Mickey Mouse coffee mugs.

EXAMPLE

Increasing Returns at Sony HDTV

At times, additional marketing and distribution activities can lead to increasing returns and declining marginal costs. For example, securing the adoption of an industry standard favorable to one's own product (e.g., Sony's digital high-definition television—HDTV standard) involves promotional and other selling efforts, which grow *more productive* the more widely the product is adopted by consumers. The more Sony digital TV receivers there are, the more programs are independently produced to be transmitted with this technology. And the more digital programs that are available, the easier and cheaper it is for Sony to sell HDTV sets to even more customers.

A similar reason for increasing returns at Microsoft is that the more adoptions Microsoft Windows secures, the more Windows-compatible applications will be introduced by independent software programmers. And the more applications introduced, the greater the chance will be for further adoptions. Normal sales penetration or saturation curves (like the MP_L curve in Figure 7.2) exhibit initially increasing marginal returns to promotional expenses followed by eventually diminishing marginal returns. However, with the adoption of new industry standards or a network technology, increasing returns can persist. Once Sony HDTV achieves a 30 percent adoption, increasing returns in marketing its product offering introduce a disruptive technology that displaces other competitors. Netscape's once dominant Internet search engine experienced exactly this sort of displacement by Microsoft's Windows, which bundled for free Internet Explorer (IE). IE then grew to a 92 percent market share in Internet browsers.

Selling efforts are generally subject to diminishing returns, but when the number of other users of a network-based device reaches a 30 to 40 percent share, the next 40–50 share points are cheaper and cheaper to promote. These relationships are depicted in Figure 7.3. From 0 percent to 30 percent market share, the selling efforts required to achieve each additional share point have a diminishing effect on the probability of adoption by the next potential user (note the reduced slope of the sales penetration curve). Consequently, additional share points become more and more expensive over this range.

Beyond the 30 percent *inflection point,* however, each additional share point of users leads to an increasing probability of adoption by another user; hence a decrease in the marketing expense required to secure another unit sale (note the increased slope of the sales penetration curve in this middle range). These network-based effects of compatibility with other users reflect increased value to the potential adopter. When Sony HDTV achieves more than 30 percent acceptance in the marketplace, it effectively becomes an industry standard. Eventually, beyond a market

Figure 7.3 Increasing Returns with Network Effects

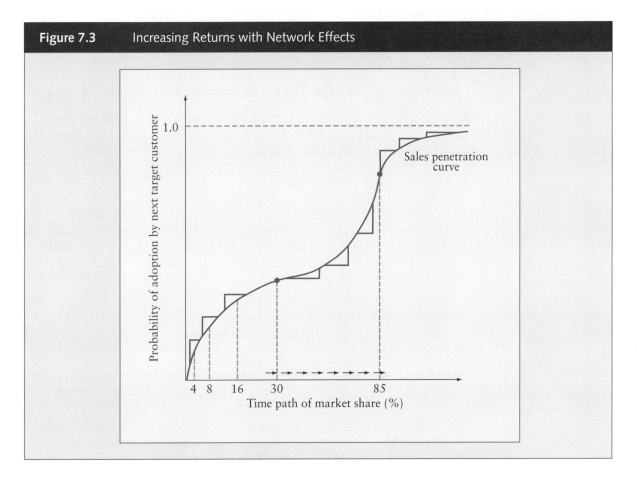

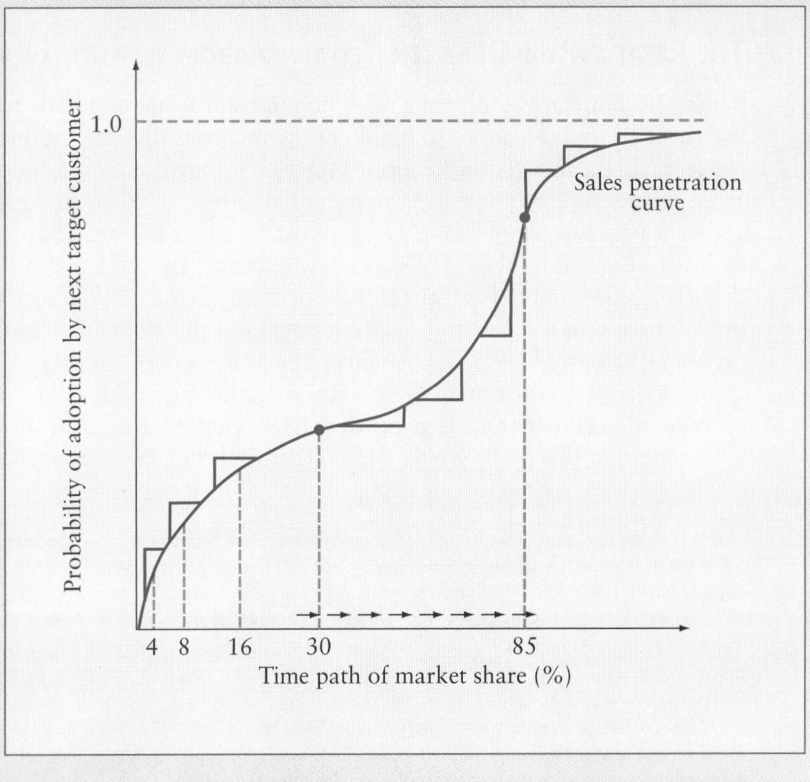

share of 80–90 percent, securing the final adopters becomes increasingly expensive because selling efforts have again become subject to diminishing returns.

Producing Information Services in the "New Economy"

It is insightful to compare the production economics of old-economy companies that produce *things* to new-economy companies that produce *information*. Things, when sold, the seller ceases to own. Information, when sold, the seller can sell again (at least until information spillovers overwhelm the target market). Things must be replicated through expensive manufacturing processes. Information is replicable at almost zero incremental cost. Things exist in one location. Information can exist simultaneously in many locations. The production and marketing of things are subject to eventually diminishing returns. The marketing (and maybe the production) of information is subject to increasing returns. That is, the more people who use my information, the more likely it is that another person will want to acquire it (for any given marketing cost) or, said another way, the cheaper it is to secure another sale. Things often involve economies of scale in production. Information is produced by small companies at comparably low costs. Things focus a business on supply-side thinking and the high costs of distribution. Information products focus a business on demand-side thinking and have almost no costs of distribution. By getting the next customer to adopt, one can set in motion a "virtuous circle" of higher customer value, lower overhead costs, and lower prices and costs for the next customer. Hence, Microsoft evolved to dominate an information-oriented business like computer network software. Chapter 11 discusses increasing returns as a source of dominant firm market power.

The Relationship Between Total, Marginal, and Average Product

Figure 7.4 illustrates a production function total value added or total product (TP) with a single variable input to highlight the relationships among the TP, AP, and MP concepts. In the first region labeled "Increasing returns," the TP function is increasing at an *increasing rate*. Because the marginal value added or marginal product (MP) curve measures the slope of the TP curve ($MP = \partial Q/\partial L$), the MP curve is increasing up to L_1. In the region labeled "Decreasing returns," the TP function is increasing at a *decreasing rate*, and the MP curve is decreasing up to L_3. In the region labeled "Negative returns," the TP function is *decreasing*, and the MP curve continues decreasing, becoming negative beyond L_3. An inflection point occurs at L_1. Next, if a line is drawn from the origin 0 to any point on the TP curve, the slope of this line, Q/L, measures the average value added or average product (AP). Hence we see that the AP curve reaches a maximum at this point where the average and the marginal products are equated.[5]

[5] Note also that the marginal product MP equals the average product AP at L_2, because the marginal product MP is equal to the slope of the TP curve ($MP = \partial Q/\partial L$), and at L_2 the average product AP is also equal to the slope of the TP curve.

Consider, for example, the following analogy: A baseball player's batting *average* for the season is 0.250. If that player has an excellent night at bat (his *marginal* performance) and goes 4 for 4 (1.000), then his season average will be pulled up. On the other hand, if he goes hitless, this poor *marginal* performance will pull down his season average. If he goes 1 for 4, this marginal performance will have no impact on his season average (marginal performance equals average performance). Hence the MP curve will always intersect with the AP curve when it is at a maximum. As we will see in the next chapter, a firm's marginal cost curve always intersects the average cost curve at its minimum point, for the same reason.

Figure 7.4 The Relationships between Total, Average, and Marginal Product Curves

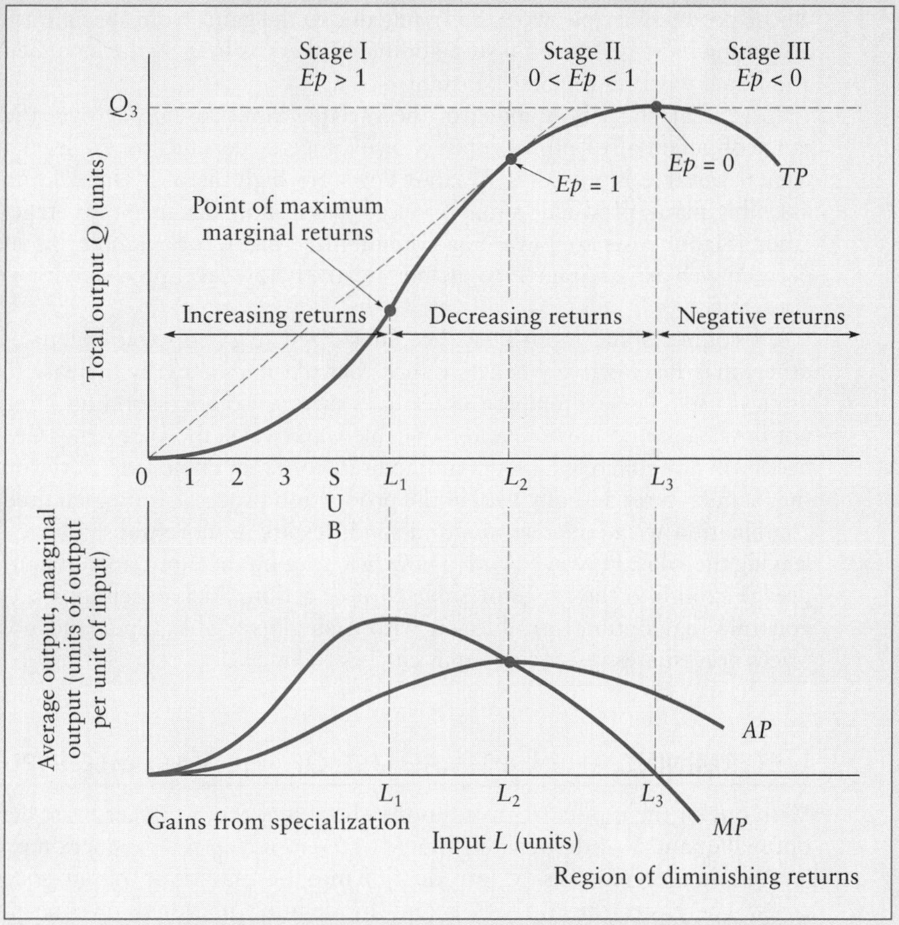

THREE STAGES OF PRODUCTION

In analyzing the production function, economists have identified three different stages of production based on the relationships among the *TP*, *AP*, and *MP* functions. Stage I is defined as the range of *L* over which the average product (AP) is increasing; it occurs from the origin (0) up to L_2 (perhaps from 0 up to 3 assembly line workers plus a substitute apprentice) and represents the region of net gains from specialization. Stage II corresponds to the range of *L* from the point at which the average product is at a maximum (L_2) to the point where the marginal product (*MP*) declines to zero (L_3). Note the endpoint of Stage II thus corresponds to the point of maximum output on the *TP* curve. Stage III encompasses the range of *L* over which the total product is declining or, equivalently, the marginal product is negative. Stage III thus corresponds to all values of *L* greater than (i.e., to the right of) L_3, where crowding effects overwhelm any output attributable to additional workers.

To determine of the optimal quantity of labor input *L* to employ, first note that the rational producer would not operate the production process over the excessive range of values of input L contained in Stage III, because the marginal product of input L is negative beyond L_3. Even if the variable input were free, the rational producer would not wish to proceed into Stage III. By the same token, no manager whose productivity per worker is rising due to the gains from specialization (i.e., AP increasing in Stage I) should stop adding workers as long as the incremental cost for additional workers remains constant.

In general, then, how much of the variable input to employ over the remaining range of potentially optimal input choice (Stage II) depends on the level of the incremental variable input costs. If labor costs are high, as in a United Auto Workers' assembly plant, production may proceed just a short distance into Stage II in hiring labor. If labor costs are lower in a nonunionized plant, for example, labor hiring may proceed well across Stage II to include relatively low-level productivity workers, like apprentices.

Of course, some input costs are subsidized (e.g., job training programs), and others may be effectively negative such that *revenues* actually increase the more the input is used. For example, in order to ensure that dredge spoil once removed does not flow back into harbors and navigable waterways, the U.S. Army Corps of Engineers will pay concrete block manufacturers for every cubic yard of the muddy slurry the manufacturer actually uses in the production process. Too much dredge spoil, in combination with concrete mix and sand, results in more unusable cracked blocks leaving the kilns. However, with a *negative* price on the input, manufacturers employ dredge spoil into the range of Stage III production. Such exceptions prove the general rule that optimal production with a single variable input and positive input prices necessitates restricting input choices to Stage II.

Determining the Optimal Use of the Variable Input

With one of the inputs (K) fixed in the short run, the producer must determine the optimal quantity of the variable input (L) to employ in the production process. Such a determination requires the introduction into the analysis of output prices and labor costs. Therefore, the analysis begins by defining marginal revenue product and marginal factor cost.

Marginal Revenue Product

Marginal Revenue Product (MRP_L)

The amount that an additional unit of the variable production input adds to total revenue. Also known as *marginal value added.*

Marginal revenue product (MRP_L) is defined as the amount that an additional unit of the variable input adds to total revenue, or

$$MRP_L = \frac{\Delta TR}{\Delta L} \quad [7.4]$$

where ΔTR is the change in total revenue associated with the given change (ΔL) in the variable input, and MRP_L is equal to the marginal product of L (MP_L) times the marginal revenue (MR_Q) resulting from the increase in output obtained:

$$MRP_L = MP_L \cdot MR_Q \quad [7.5]$$

Consider again the Deep Creek Mining Company example (Table 7.2) of the previous section where K (capital) is fixed at 750 bhp. Suppose that the firm can sell all the ore it can produce at a price of \$10 per ton; for example in a perfectly

Table 7.3 Marginal Revenue Product and Marginal Factor Cost—Deep Creek Mining Company

Labor Input L (Number of Workers)	Total Product $Q = (TP_L)$ (Tons of Ore)	Marginal Product of Labor MP_L (Tons Per Worker)	Total Revenue $TR = P \cdot Q$ (\$)	Marginal Revenue $MR_Q = \frac{\Delta TR}{\Delta Q}$ (\$/Ton)	Marginal Revenue Product $MRP_L = MP_L \cdot MR_Q$ (\$/Worker)	Marginal Factor Cost MFC_L (\$/Worker)
0	0	—	0	—	—	—
1	6	6	60	10	60	50
2	16	10	160	10	100	50
3	29	13	290	10	130	50
4	44	15	440	10	150	50
5	55	11	550	10	110	50
6*	60	5	600	10	50	50
7	62	2	620	10	20	50
8	62	0	620	10	0	50

*Indicates the optimal input level.

competitive market, the firm would realize a constant marginal revenue equal to the going market equilibrium price. The marginal revenue product of labor (MRP_L) is computed using Equation 7.5 and is shown in Table 7.3.[6]

Sometimes in practice this concept is referred to as the marginal value added—that is, the amount by which potential sales revenue is increased as a result of employing an additional unit of variable input to increase output. In Europe, for example, rather than taxing the final retail sales value of goods, instead each level of production from raw material to finished goods distribution is taxed on its marginal value added at each stage of production.

MARGINAL FACTOR COST

Marginal Factor Cost (MFC_L)
The amount that an additional unit of the variable input adds to total cost.

Marginal factor cost (MFC_L) is defined as the amount that an additional unit of the variable input adds to total cost, or

$$MFC_L = \frac{\Delta TC}{\Delta L} \quad [7.6]$$

where ΔTC is the change in cost associated with the given change (ΔL) in the variable input.

In the ore-mining example, suppose that the firm can employ as much labor (L) as it needs by paying the workers \$50 per shift (C_L). In other words, the labor market is assumed to be *perfectly competitive.* Under these conditions, the marginal factor cost (MFC_L) is equal to C_L, or \$50 per worker. It is constant regardless of the level of operation of the mine (see the last column of Table 7.3).

[6] Input levels in Stage III ($MP_L < 0$) have been eliminated from consideration.

Optimal Input Level

Given the marginal revenue product and marginal factor cost, we can compute the optimal amount of the variable input to use in the production process. Recall from the discussion of marginal analysis in Chapter 2 that an economic activity should be expanded as long as the marginal benefits exceed the marginal costs. For the short-run production decision, the optimal level of the variable input occurs where

$$MRP_L = MFC_L \qquad [7.7]$$

As can be seen in Table 7.3, the optimal input is $L = 6$ workers because $MRP_L = MFC_L = \$50$ at this point. At fewer than six workers, $MRP_L > MFC_L$ and the addition of more labor (workers) to the production process will increase revenues more than it will increase costs. Beyond six workers the opposite is true—costs will increase more than revenues.

Production Functions with Multiple Variable Inputs

Using the Deep Creek Mining Company example, suppose now that both capital (measured by the maximum brake horsepower rating of the equipment) and labor (measured by the number of workers) are variable inputs to the ore-mining process. The firm can choose to operate the production process using any of the capital-labor combinations shown previously in Table 7.1.

Production Isoquants

Production Isoquant

An algebraic function or a geometric curve representing all the various combinations of two inputs that can be used in producing a given level of output.

A production function with two variable inputs can be represented graphically by a set of two-dimensional production isoquants. A **production isoquant** is either a geometric curve or an algebraic function representing all the various combinations of the two inputs that can be used in producing a given level of output. In the Deep Creek example, a production isoquant shows all the alternative ways in which the number of workers and various sizes of mining equipment can be combined to produce any desired level of output (tons of ore). Several of the production isoquants for the ore-mining example are shown in Figure 7.5. For example, an output of 6 tons can be produced using any of three different labor-capital combinations: 1 worker and 750 bhp equipment, 2 workers and 500 bhp equipment, or 4 workers and 250 bhp equipment. Similarly, as seen in the graph, an output of 62 tons can be produced using any one of five different labor-capital combinations.

Although each isoquant indicates how quantities of the two inputs may be *substituted* for one another, these choices are normally limited for two reasons: first, some input combinations in Figure 7.5 employ an excessive quantity of one input. Just as more than eight workers result in negative marginal returns in choosing a single variable input for Deep Creek Mining (see Figure 7.2), so too here with 750-bhp machinery, crowding effects introduced by the presence of a ninth worker would actually reduce output. Similarly, more than 1,750-bhp machinery would result in negative marginal returns to capital equipment with only five workers. Because all such inefficient mixes of capital and labor increase the input requirements (and therefore costs) without increasing output, they should be eliminated from consideration in making input substitution choices.

Second, input substitution choices are also limited by the technology of production, which often involves machinery that is not divisible. Although one can find

Figure 7.5 Production Isoquants—Deep Creek Mining Company

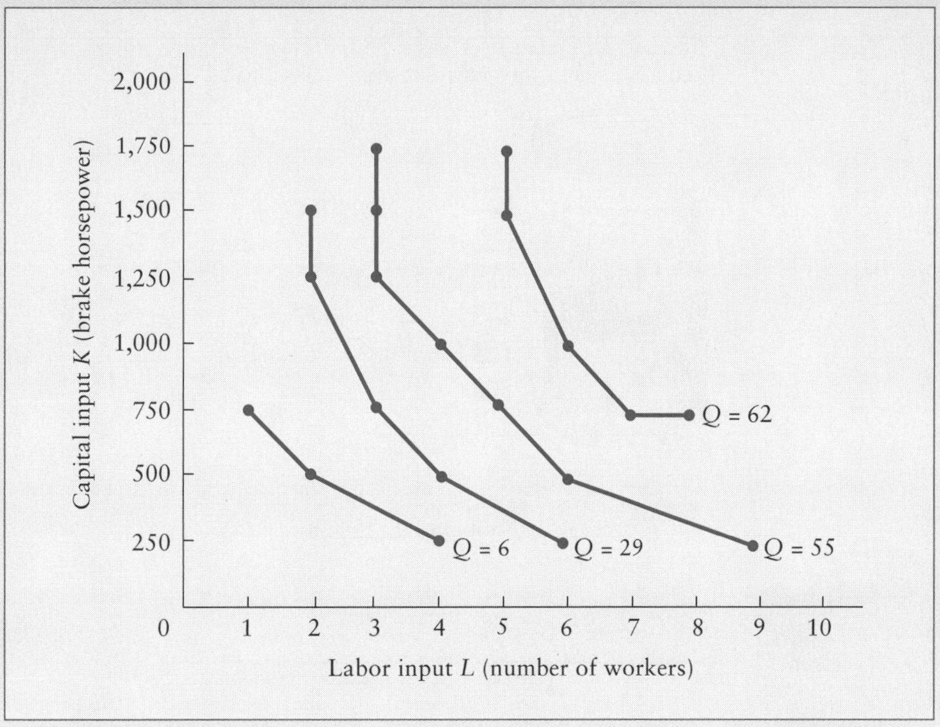

smaller and larger mining equipment, not every brake horsepower machine listed on the K axis of Figure 7.5 will be available. The industrial engineering of mining operations often requires that we select from three or four possible fixed proportions production processes involving a particular size drilling machine and a requisite size labor force to run it.

EXAMPLE

JUST WHAT EXACTLY IS A REFINERY, AND WHY WON'T ANYONE BUILD ONE?[7]

New petroleum refineries are underway in Kuwait and in Saudi Arabia that will be capable of processing 600,000 barrels of crude per day (bpd) and 450 bpd, respectively. However, no petroleum refinery has been built in the United States in more than 30 years. Why not? To answer this question requires knowing a little about what a refinery is and what it does.

In essence, refineries are enormous chemical plants that begin by superheating various grades of crude oil in large vessels and then pass the vapors that boil off through fractional distillation columns where they phase change back into various liquids as the distillates cool (see Figure 7.6). Crude oil contains literally hundreds of

[7] Based on "Working Knowledge: Oil Refineries," *Scientific American* (June 2006), pp. 88–89.

Figure 7.6 Crude Oil Is Made Into Different Fuels from Distillation/Cracking/Reformer Processes

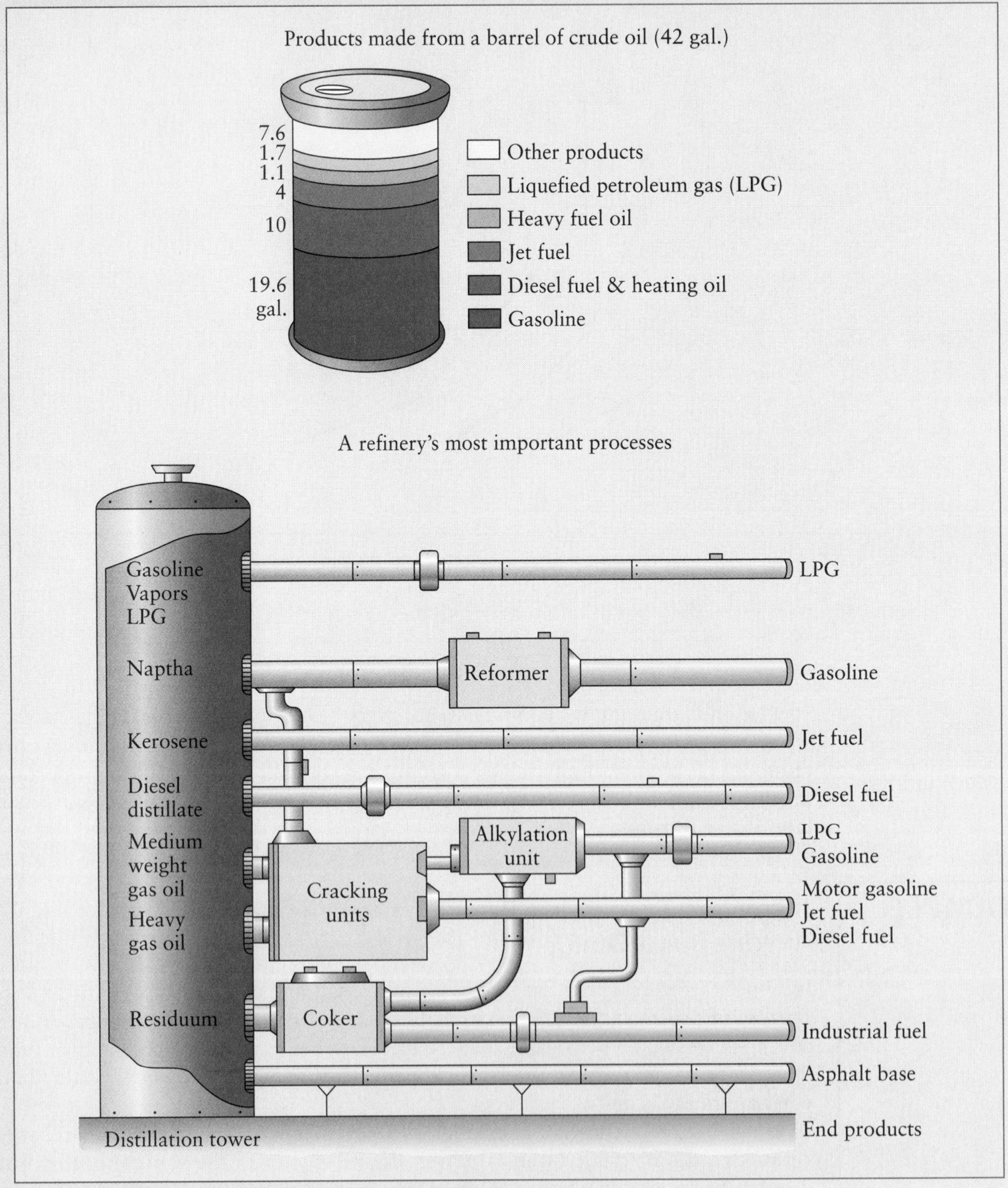

Source: **Energy Information Administration, U.S. Department of Energy.**

hydrocarbons, and the distillates run the gamut from lubricants and grease which "cool" to a liquid at a whopping 450 °C near the bottom of the column to propane at the top. Jet fuel, diesel, and some gasoline liquefy at 250 °C with the help of a catalytic cracking process in a separate converter, and farther up the column naptha distillate yields gasoline after passing through a reformer. Kerosene, butane, and polyethylene (the basic building block for plastic) also distill out.

Refining is a classic variable proportions production process. The chemical cracking process of breaking long chains of hydrocarbons can use more or less pressure, more or less heat, more or less high quality but expensive light sweet crude or sulfurous heavy crude. From one 42-gallon barrel of crude, the input mix can be optimized to achieve about 20 gallons of gasoline and 7 gallons of diesel. Much of the equipment involved is 10 stories high and expensive. The fixed cost investment today for a major refinery totals $2 billion. Cost recovery must emanate from just 22 percent of the final product price of gasoline, whereas crude itself commands 54 percent of the final product price. Profit margins in refining come to just a few cents per gallon, much like the thin margins in gasoline retailing.

Percent of Final Product Price of Gasoline by Stage of Production (2006)

Exploration and development and extraction of crude oil	54%
Federal and state excise taxes	16
Refining	22
Distribution and retail	8

THE MARGINAL RATE OF TECHNICAL SUBSTITUTION

In addition to indicating the quantity of output that can be produced with any of the various input combinations that lie on the isoquant curve, the isoquant also indicates the *rate* at which one input may be substituted for another input in producing the given quantity of output. Suppose one considers the meaning of a shift from point A to point B on the isoquant labeled "$Q = 29$" in Figure 7.7. At point A, 3 workers and a 750-bhp machine are being used to produce 29 tons of output, whereas at point B, 4 workers and a 500-bhp machine are being used to produce the same amount of output. In moving from point A to point B, one has substituted 1 additional unit of labor for 250 units of capital. The rate at which capital has been replaced with labor in producing the given output is equal to 250/1 or 250 units of capital per unit of labor. The rate at which one input may be substituted for another input in the production process, while total output remains constant, is known as the **marginal rate of technical substitution,** or *MRTS*.

Marginal Rate of Technical Substitution (MRTS)

The rate at which one input may be substituted for another input in producing a given quantity of output.

MRTS is given by the slope of the curve relating K to L—that is, the slope of the isoquant. The slope of the AB segment of the isoquant in Figure 7.7 is equal to the ratio of AC to CB. Algebraically, $AC = K_1 - K_2$ and $CB = L_1 - L_2$; therefore, the slope is equal to $(K_1 - K_2) \div (L_1 - L_2)$. Because the slope is negative and one wishes to express the substitution rate as a positive quantity, a negative sign is attached to the slope:

$$MRTS = -\frac{K_1 - K_2}{L_1 - L_2} = -\frac{\Delta K}{\Delta L} \qquad [7.8]$$

Figure 7.7 The Production Isoquant Curve—Deep Creek Mining Company

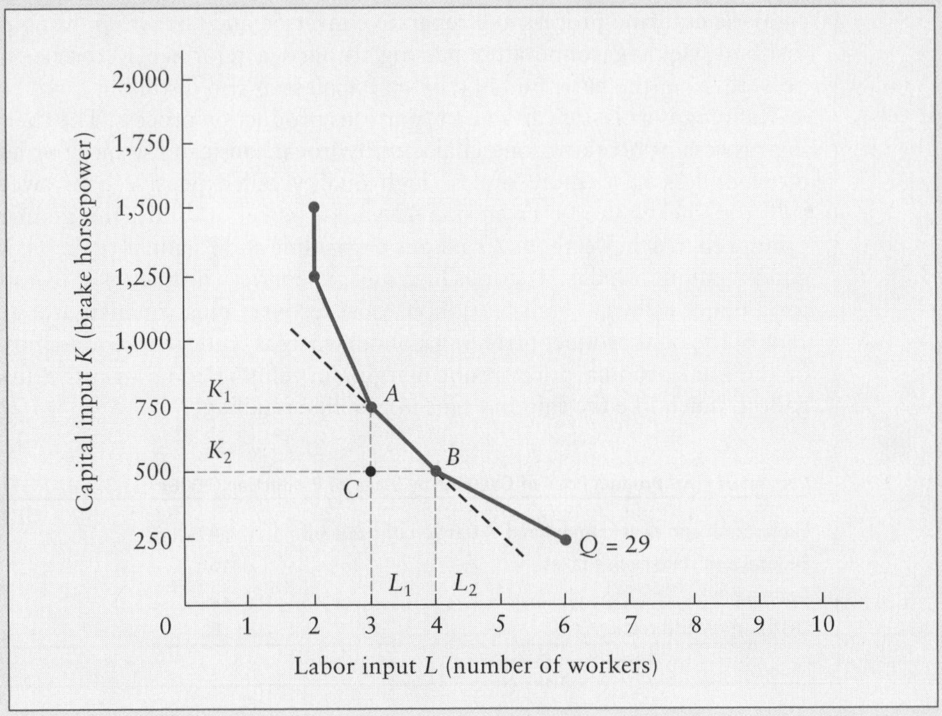

In the Deep Creek Mining Company example, $\Delta L = 3 - 4 = -1$, $\Delta K = 750 - 500 = 250$. Substituting these values into Equation 7.8 yields

$$MRTS = -\frac{250}{-1} = 250$$

Therefore, along $Q = 29$ between input combinations A and B, 250 bhp substituted for one worker.

It can be shown that the $MRTS$ is equal to the ratio of the marginal products of L and K by using the definition of the marginal product (Equation 7.2). This definition yields $\Delta L = \Delta Q/MP_L$ and $\Delta K = \Delta Q/MP_K$. Substituting these expressions into Equation 7.8 (and dropping the minus sign) yields

$$MRTS = \frac{\Delta Q/MP_K}{\Delta Q/MP_L}$$

$$MRTS = \frac{MP_L}{MP_K} \quad [7.9]$$

Perfect Substitute and Complementary Inputs

Production inputs vary in the degree to which they can be substituted for one another in a given process. The extreme cases are *perfect substitutes* and *perfect complements*. Isoquants for these two cases are shown in Figure 7.8. The isoquants for inputs that

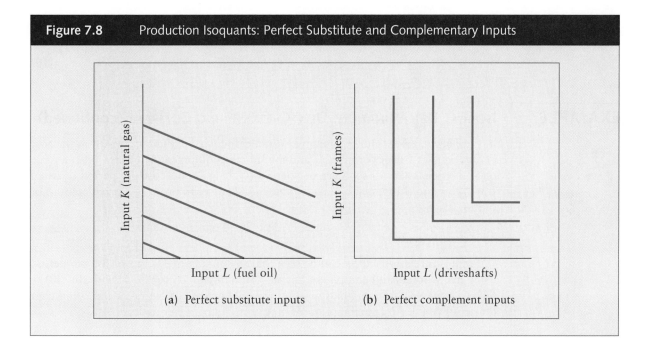

Figure 7.8 Production Isoquants: Perfect Substitute and Complementary Inputs

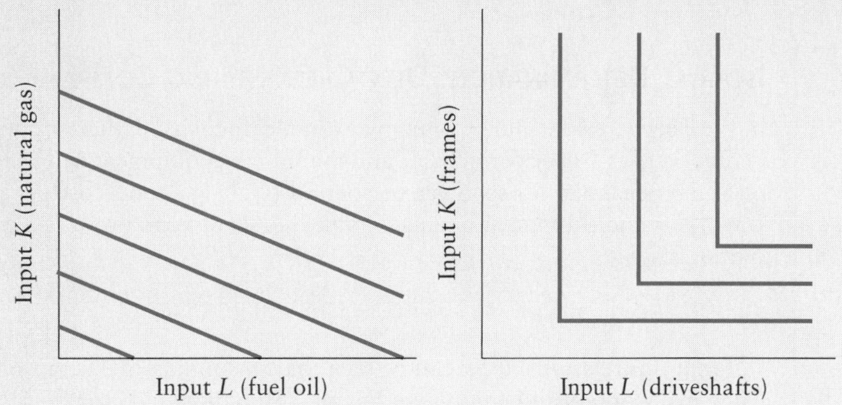

(a) Perfect substitute inputs (b) Perfect complement inputs

are *perfect substitutes* for one another consist of a series of parallel lines, as shown in Panel (a). Examples of perfect substitutes are the use of alternative fuels (inputs), such as fuel oil or natural gas in the production of electricity, or the use of soybeans or oats in the production of nutrients in animal feeds. The isoquants for inputs that are *perfect complements* for one another consist of a series of right angles, as shown in Panel (b). Such inputs are said to have zero substitutability. Examples of perfect complements include component parts that must be combined in fixed proportions, such as drive shafts and frames for automobiles or foundations and roofs for houses.

Production inputs usually fall somewhere between the extreme cases of perfect complements and perfect substitutes. For most production functions, isoquants are convex to the origin, as shown earlier in Figure 7.7. This shape implies that the production inputs are imperfectly substitutable and that the rate of substitution declines as one input is substituted for another.

DETERMINING THE OPTIMAL COMBINATION OF INPUTS

As shown in the previous section, a given level of output can be produced using any of a large number of possible combinations of two inputs. The firm needs to determine which combination will minimize the total costs for producing the desired output.

ISOCOST LINES

The total cost of each possible input combination is a function of the market prices of these inputs. Assuming that the inputs are supplied in perfectly elastic fashion in competitive markets, the per-unit price of each input will be constant, regardless of the amount of the input that is purchased. Letting C_L and C_K be the per-unit prices of inputs L and K, respectively, the total cost (C) of any given input combination is

$$C = C_L L + C_K K \qquad [7.10]$$

EXAMPLE

Isocost Determination: Deep Creek Mining Company (continued)

In the Deep Creek Mining Company example discussed earlier, suppose that the cost per worker is \$50 per period (C_L) and that mining equipment can be leased at a price of \$0.20 per brake horsepower per period (C_K). The total cost per period of using L workers and equipment having K brake horsepower to produce a given amount of output is

$$C = 50L + 0.20K \qquad [7.11]$$

From this relationship, it can be seen that the mining of 55 tons of ore per period using five workers and equipment having 750 bhp would cost $50(5) + 0.20(750) =$ \$400. However, this combination is not the only mixture of workers and equipment that costs \$400. Any combination of inputs satisfying the equation

$$\$400 = 50L + 0.20K$$

would cost \$400. Solving this equation for K yields

$$K = \frac{\$400}{0.20} - \frac{50}{0.20}L$$
$$= \$2{,}000 - 250L$$

Thus, the combinations $L = 1$ and $K = 1{,}750$; $L = 2$ and $K = 1{,}500$; $L = 3$ and $K = 1{,}250$ (plus many other combinations) all cost \$400.

The combinations of inputs costing \$400 can be represented as the *isocost line* in Figure 7.9 labeled "$C = \$400$." An isocost line exists for every possible total cost C. Solving Equation 7.11 for K gives the equation of each isocost line in Figure 7.9. Note that only the y-intercept $C/0.20$ changes as one moves from one isocost line to another.

$$K = \frac{C}{0.20} - 250L \qquad [7.12]$$

That is, all the isocost lines are parallel, each one having a slope of -250.

Once the isoquants and isocosts are specified, it is possible to solve for the optimum combination of inputs. The production decision problem can be formulated in two different ways, depending on the manner in which the production objective or goal is stated. One can solve for the combination of inputs that either

1. Minimizes total cost subject to a given constraint on output
2. Maximizes output subject to a given total cost constraint

Figure 7.9 Isocost Lines—Deep Creek Mining Company

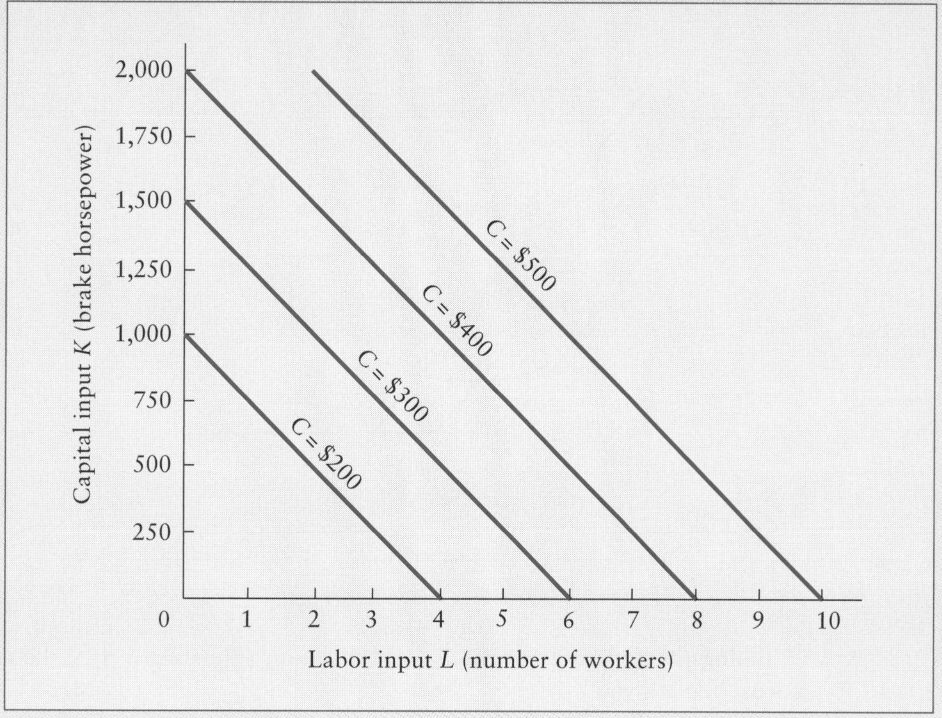

Constrained cost minimization in Option 1 is the dual problem to the constrained output maximization problem in Option 2.

MINIMIZING COST SUBJECT TO AN OUTPUT CONSTRAINT

Consider first the problem in which the director of operations desires to release to production a number of orders for at least $Q^{(2)}$ units of output. As shown in Figure 7.10, this constraint requires that the solution be in the feasible region containing the input combinations that lie either on the $Q^{(2)}$ isoquant or on isoquants that fall above and to the right having larger output values (the shaded area). The total cost of producing the required output is minimized by finding the input combinations within this region that lie on the lowest cost isocost line. Combination D on the $C^{(2)}$ isocost line satisfies this condition. Combinations E and F, which also lie on the $Q^{(2)}$ isoquant, yield higher total costs because they fall on the $C^{(3)}$ isocost line. Thus, the use of L_1 units of input L and K_1 units of input K will yield a (constrained) minimum cost solution of $C^{(2)}$ dollars.

At the optimal input combination, the slope of the given isoquant must equal the slope of the $C^{(2)}$ lowest isocost line. As in the previous section, the slope of an isoquant is equal to dK/dL and

$$-\frac{dK}{dL} = MRTS = \frac{MP_L}{MP_K} \quad [7.13]$$

Figure 7.10 Cost Minimization Subject to an Output Constraint

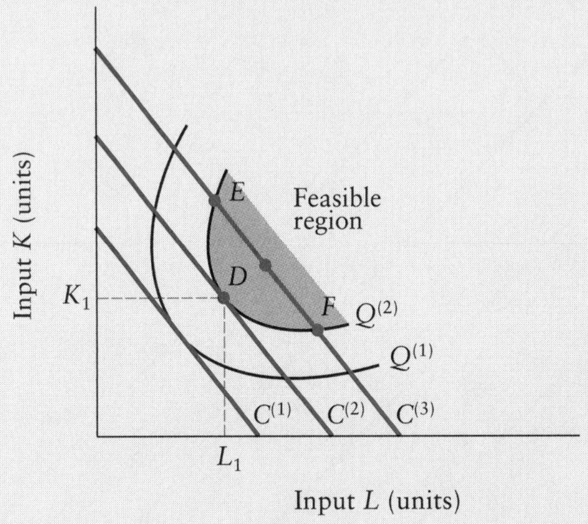

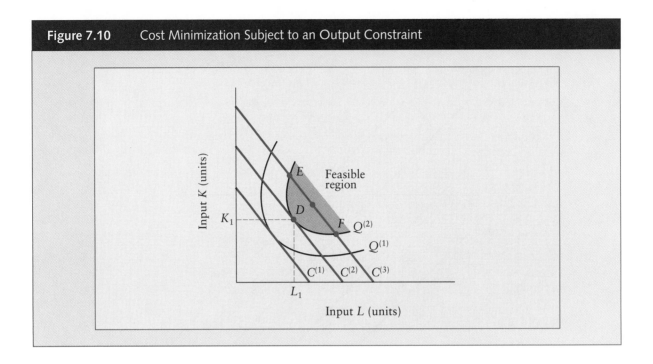

Taking the derivative of the isocost equation (Equation 7.12), the slope of the isocost line is given by

$$\frac{dK}{dL} = -\frac{C_L}{C_K} \qquad [7.14]$$

Multiplying Equation 7.14 by (-1) and setting the result equal to Equation 7.13 yields

$$-\frac{dK}{dL} = -\left(-\frac{C_L}{C_K}\right)$$

$$= \frac{MP_L}{MP_K}$$

Thus, the following equilibrium condition, the "equimarginal criterion"

$$\frac{MP_L}{MP_K} = \frac{C_L}{C_K}$$

or, equivalently,

$$\frac{MP_L}{C_L} = \frac{MP_K}{C_K} \qquad [7.15]$$

must be satisfied in order for an input combination to be an optimal solution to the problem of minimizing cost subject to an output constraint. Equation 7.15 indicates that the marginal product per dollar input cost of one factor must be equal to the marginal product per dollar input cost of the other factor.

Figure 7.11 Output Maximization Subject to a Cost Constraint

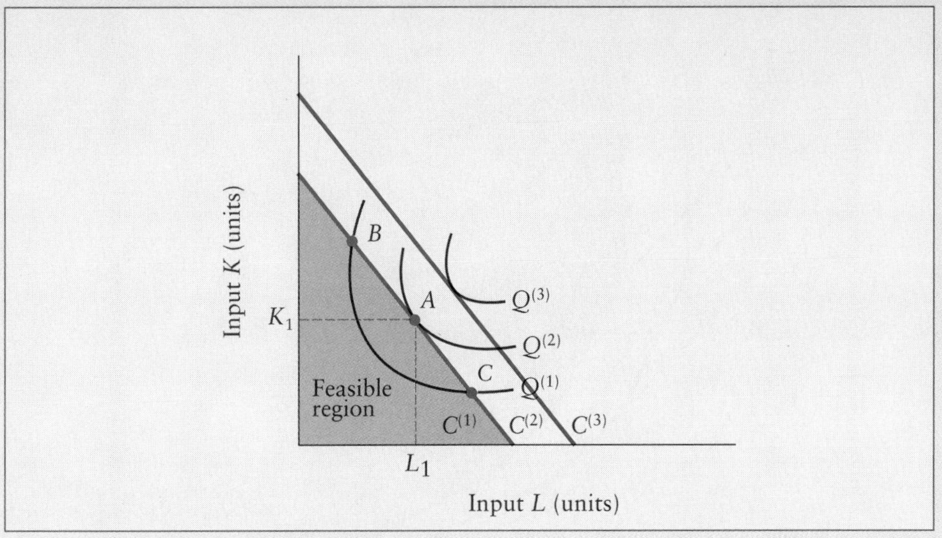

Note in Figure 7.11 that maximizing output subject to a feasible region demarcated by the $Q^{(2)}$ cost constraint yields exactly the same (L_1, K_1) optimal input combination that satisfies the equimarginal criterion.

A Fixed Proportions Optimal Production Process

The previous section analyzed the least-cost combination of divisible inputs in variable proportions production, where one input substituted continuously for another. However, Deep Creek Mining's production choices involve indivisible capital equipment, such as one small or one large mining drill and a predetermined number of workers to run the chosen equipment. Similarly, an auto fender stamping machine in an assembly plant must be used in fixed proportion to labor and sheet metal supplies. And 3 hours of setup, maintenance, and cleaning may be required to support a 5-hour printing press run. Three additional hours of work by maintenance personnel would be required for a second press run, and a third shift of maintenance workers would be required for 24-hour printing operations. Although a higher output rate can be achieved by scaling up all the inputs, each of these production processes is one of fixed, not variable, proportions.

Linear programming techniques are available to determine the least-cost process for fixed proportions production. The Deep Creek Mining Company example can be used to illustrate the graphic approach to finding such a solution.

EXAMPLE

Cost Minimization: Deep Creek Mining Company (continued)

Suppose one is interested in finding the combination of labor input and capital equipment that minimizes the cost of producing at least 29 tons of ore. Assume that the isocost lines are the ones defined by Equation 7.11 and graphed in Figure 7.9

Figure 7.12 A Fixed Proportions Production Decision—Deep Creek Mining Company

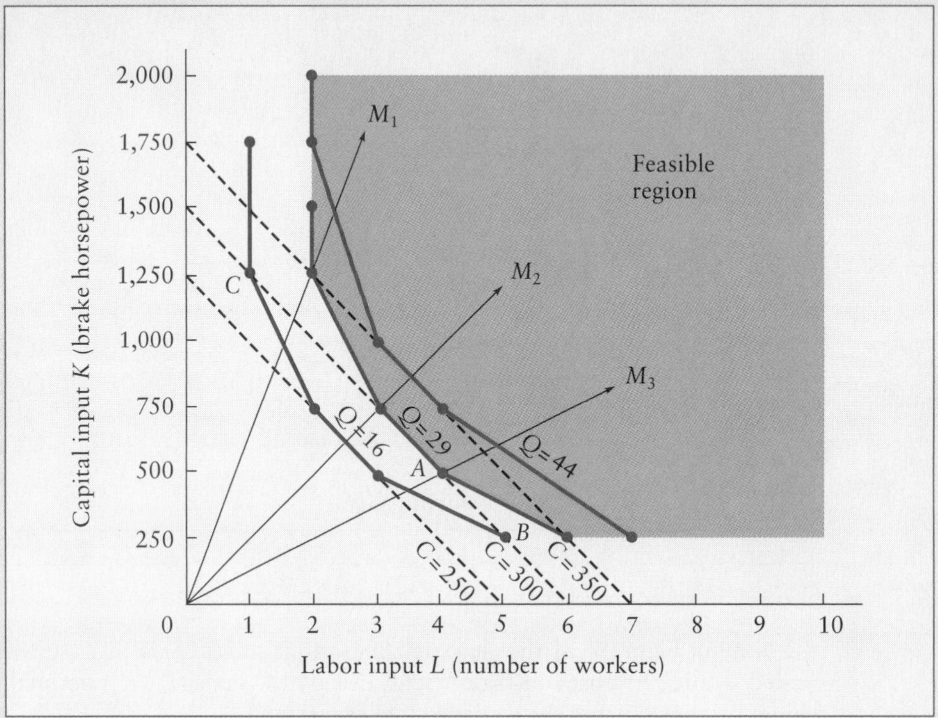

earlier in this section. Figure 7.12 combines several isoquants and isocost lines for the ore-mining problem. The shaded area in the graph represents the set of feasible input combinations, that is, those labor and capital production processes that yield at least $Q = 29$ tons of output. Processes M_2 and M_3 minimize the cost of producing 29 tons at \$300. M_1 imposes higher costs of \$350.

Production Processes and Process Rays

Production Process
A fixed-proportions production relationship.

A **production process** can be defined as one in which the inputs are combined in fixed proportion to obtain the output. By this definition, a production process can be represented graphically as a ray through the origin having a slope equal to the ratio of the number of units of the respective resources required to produce one unit of output. Three production process rays for Deep Creek Mining are shown in Figure 7.12. Along Process Ray M_1, the inputs are combined in the ratio of two workers to a 1,250 bhp drilling machine. Hence, Ray M_1 has a slope of 625 bhp per mine worker.

Operating multiple production processes like M_1, M_2, and M_3 can offer a firm flexibility in dealing with unusual orders, interruptions in the availability of resources, or binding resource constraints. However, not all fixed proportions production processes are equally efficient. The firm will prefer to use one or two production processes exclusively if they offer the advantage of substantial cost savings. Mine 1 employs process M_1 to produce 29 tons with 2 workers and a 1,250 bhp drilling machine at a total cost of 50 (2) + 0.20 (1,250) = \$350 or \$350/29 = \$12.07 per ton. Mine 2 uses a more labor-intensive process (M_2) with 3 workers and a smaller 750 bhp machine and incurs a lower total cost of \$300. Mine 2 is the benchmark operation for Deep Creek in that this M_2 process produces 29 tons at minimum cost—specifically, \$300/29 = \$10.34 per ton.

MEASURING THE EFFICIENCY OF A PRODUCTION PROCESS

Allocative Efficiency

A measure of how closely production achieves the least-cost input mix or process, given the desired level of output.

Mine 1 with production process M_1 is said to be allocatively inefficient because it has chosen the wrong input mix; the mine has allocated its input budget incorrectly. Its 1,250-bhp machine is too large for the number of workers hired and the output desired. By producing 29 tons of output for \$350 relative to the lowest cost benchmark at \$300, process M_1 exhibits only \$300/\$350 = 85.7 percent **allocative efficiency.**

In addition to allocative inefficiency involving the incorrect input mix, a production operation can also exhibit technical inefficiency. For example, the industrial engineering indicated by the production isoquants in Figure 7.12 suggests that the process M_3 also should be capable of producing 29 tons. The "C = \$300" isocost line is tangent to the boundary of the feasible region (i.e., the "Q = 29" isoquant) at not only 3 workers and a 750-bhp machine (M_2), but also at 4 workers and 500-bhp machine (M_3). In principle, both production processes yield the desired 29 tons of ore at a minimum total cost of \$300 and will thereby satisfy the condition in Equation 7.15.

Technical Efficiency

A measure of how closely production achieves maximum potential output given the input mix or process.

However, suppose Mine 2 has been unable to achieve more than 27 tons of output. Although it has adopted a least-cost process, Mine 2 would then be characterized as *technically inefficient.* In particular, Mine 2 exhibits only 27 tons/29 tons = 93 percent **technical efficiency** by comparison to the benchmark plant. Despite adopting the least-cost process, Mine 2's 93 percent technical efficiency may be inadequate. Benchmark plants often do substantially better, with many processes meeting 98 percent and 99 percent of their production goals.

EXAMPLE

GM'S A-FRAME SUPPLIER ACHIEVES 99.998 PERCENT TECHNICAL EFFICIENCY

As technically inefficient plants approach the current standard of excellence, continuous quality improvement initiatives frequently raise the standards. Just-in-time delivery systems accentuate the need for high reliability to produce on time as promised with near zero defects. One A-frame supplier to General Motors assembly plants reduced defective parts to 5 per million (i.e., 0.002 of 1%) and agreed to pay a \$4,000 *per minute* "charge back" for any late deliveries that cause GM assembly line delays. Such a company must constantly monitor and proactively solve production problems before they arise in order to ensure near 100 percent technical efficiency.

Overall Production Efficiency
A measure of technical and allocative efficiency.

Overall production efficiency is defined as the product of technical, scale, and allocative efficiency. If a 100 percent scale-efficient plant has 93 percent technical efficiency and 85.7 percent allocative efficiency, then its overall production efficiency is $0.93 \times 0.857 = 0.797$, or 79.7 percent. Your job as an operations manager might be to decide which least-cost process Mine 1 in Figure 7.12 should now adopt. Because M_2 and M_3 are both allocatively efficient for 29 tons of output, but process M_2 experienced technical inefficiency problems resulting in an inability to realize its maximum potential output, Process M_3 would be preferred.

EXAMPLE

TECHNICAL AND ALLOCATIVE EFFICIENCY IN COMMERCIAL BANKS[8]

Wave after wave of bank merger activity may be motivated by the potential for substantial improvements in operating efficiency. Combining loan officers, facilities, and deposits of various kinds, the representative commercial bank in the United States "produces" only 63 percent of the loan value not in default (so-called "current status loans") that the most efficient benchmark banks produce. In contrast, natural gas-fired power plants average 93 percent operating efficient. The problem (and opportunity for improvement) in commercial banks is twofold. First, some banks adopt inefficient processes such as allowing the borrower to pick one, single senior loan officer who will review the loan application. Linear programming studies show that allocative efficiency in U.S. commercial banking averages only 81 percent, meaning that the least-cost process is 19 percent cheaper. Then one bank may need to jettison its own and imitate another bank's borrower screening or loan monitoring process.

When several banks do manage to adopt identical least-cost processes, yet one produces more current-status loans or larger loans than the others, the maximum feasible potential output in that type of institution can be identified. Technical efficiency then measures the observed bank output divided by the maximum potential output of the benchmark bank with identical processes. The smaller a bank's loan value not in default, the lower the technical efficiency. The representative commercial bank in the United States is only 78 percent technically efficient.

Bank takeovers, buyouts, and mergers often result in a concerted effort to improve allocative and technical efficiency. Afterward, the ratio of noninterest operating expenses to total bank income often declines enough, and capitalized value often rises enough to allow recovery of a merger premium of up to 20–30 percent paid by the new owners in excess of the bank's premerger value.

THE EFFECT OF A CHANGE IN INPUT PRICES

As already shown, the optimal combination of inputs in both the cost-minimization and output-maximization problems is a function of the relative prices of the inputs, that is, C_L and C_K. As the price of input L rises, one would expect the firm to use less of this input and more of the other input K in the production process, all other things being equal. This shift is demonstrated in Figure 7.13. The firm is interested in

[8] Based on D. Wheelock and P. Wilson, "Evaluating the Efficiency of Commercial Banks," *St. Louis Federal Reserve Review* (July/August 1995), pp. 39–52; and A. Kleit and D. Terrell, "Measuring Potential Efficiency Gains from Deregulation of Electricity Generation," *Review of Economics and Statistics* (August 2001), pp. 523–550.

Figure 7.13 The Effect of a Change in Input Prices

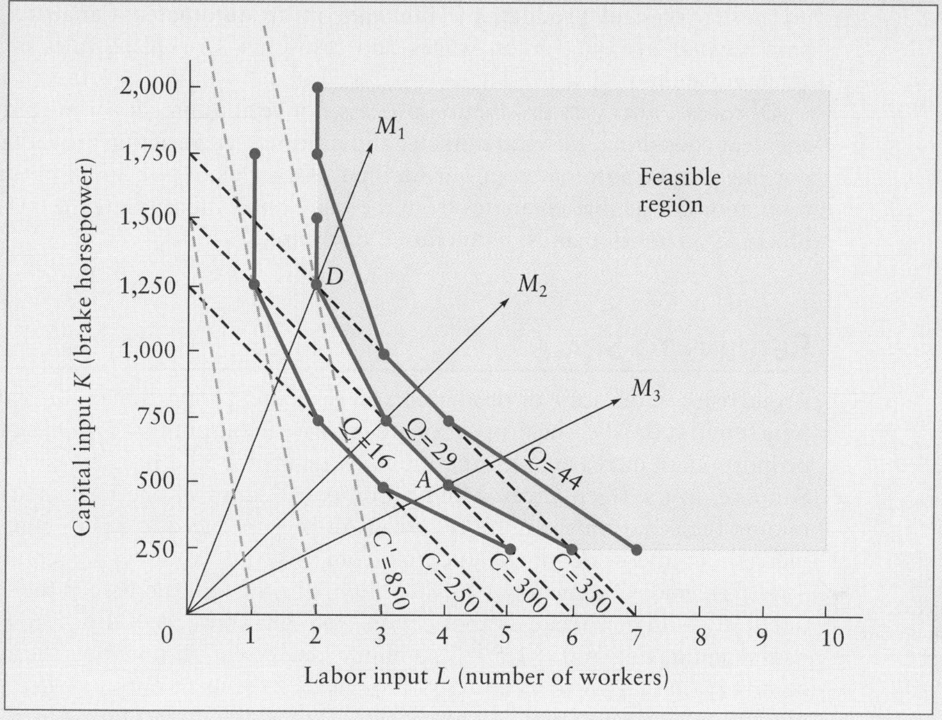

minimizing the cost of producing a given quantity of output $Q = 29$. Initially, the prices of inputs are $C_L = \$50$ and $C_K = \$0.20$ resulting in the isocost line $C = 300$. Given these conditions, the firm would operate at tangency A, using 4 units of labor input and 500 units of the capital input. Now suppose that the price of labor is increased to \$300 itself. This change has the effect of increasing the slope of the isocost lines, as shown in the graph. A \$300 input budget, before the labor price increase, purchased 1,500-bhp machinery or six workers; now \$300 purchases the same 1,500-bhp machine or just one worker. To produce $Q = 29$ units of output at minimum cost, the firm would operate at tangency D using a 1,250-bhp machine and two workers.

Cost for 29 tons of ore has risen from \$300 to \$850 [(1,250 × \$0.2) + (2 × \$300) = \$850], but the cost is far less than if the original process at A had been continued. In that case, cost for 29 tons would have risen from \$300 to \$1,300 [i.e., (500 × \$0.2) + (4 × \$300) = \$1,300]. Oftentimes, these *input substitution effects* are reinforced by a negative *output effect*—that is, higher input costs are passed through (as higher prices) to consumers who respond by cutting back their consumption. As less output than $Q = 29$ is ordered, the amount of more-expensive labor hired may fall substantially below two workers.

From this analysis, one can see that as the price of one input increases, the firm will substitute away from this input and use more of the relatively less expensive input. Since at least the Industrial Revolution, a similar phenomenon has been observed in the shift toward more automated capital-intensive production processes (i.e., greater use of labor-saving equipment), because the price of labor has increased relative to the price of capital. DaimlerChrysler Corporation decided to assemble its most successful product, the minivan, in an automated Canadian factory, in part because of rising union wages and restrictive workplace rules in its Detroit assembly plants.

Of course, not every production process can be automated. Airline piloting, management consulting, hospital nursing, and motion picture acting are services that are not likely to be automated in our lifetimes. Other examples entail products whose reputation for quality emanates from the high labor intensity involved in their manufacture: Steinway pianos, handcrafted furniture, sculptural art.

Returns to Scale

Returns to Scale
The proportionate increase in output that results from a given proportionate increase in *all* the inputs employed in the production process.

An increase in the scale of production consists of a proportionate increase in all inputs simultaneously. The proportionate increase in output that results from the given proportionate increase in all the inputs is defined as the physical **returns to scale.** Suppose, in the Deep Creek Mining Company example, one is interested in determining the effect on the number of tons of ore produced (output) of a 1.50 factor increase in the scale of production from a given labor-capital combination of 4 workers and equipment having 500 bhp. A 1.50 factor increase in the scale of production would constitute a labor-capital combination of $4 \times 1.5 = 6$ workers and equipment having $500 \times 1.5 = 750$ bhp. From Table 7.1, note that the labor-capital combination of 4 workers and 500 bhp yields 29 tons of output, whereas the combination of 6 workers and 750 bhp yields 60 tons of output. Output increased by the ratio of $60/29 = 2.07$. Thus, a 1.50 factor increase in input use has resulted in more than a 1.50 factor output increase (specifically, 2.07).

Measuring Returns to Scale

An increase in the scale of production can be represented graphically in a two-dimensional isoquant map, as is shown in Figure 7.14. Increasing the scale of production by a factor of $\lambda = 2$ from the combination of 10_1 units of input L and 100_1 units of input K to 20 units of input L and 200 units of K results in an increase in the quantity of output from $Q^{(1)}$ to $Q^{(2)}$. Three possible relationships that can exist between the increase in inputs and the increase in outputs are as follows:

1. *Increasing* returns to scale: Output increases by *more than* λ; that is, $Q^{(2)} > \lambda Q^{(1)}$.
2. *Decreasing* returns to scale: Output increases by *less than* λ; that is, $Q^{(2)} < \lambda Q^{(1)}$.
3. *Constant* returns to scale: Output increases by *exactly* λ; that is, $Q^{(2)} = \lambda Q^{(1)}$.

Figure 7.14 illustrates three different production functions that exhibit these three types of returns to scale. In Panel (a), showing increasing returns to scale, doubling input L from 10 to 20 units and input K from 100 to 200 units yields more than double the amount of output (i.e., an increase from 100 to 250). In Panel (b), showing decreasing returns to scale, a similar doubling of two inputs, L and K, yields less than double the amount of output (i.e., an increase from 10,000 to 15,000). Finally, in Panel (c), showing constant returns to scale, a similar doubling

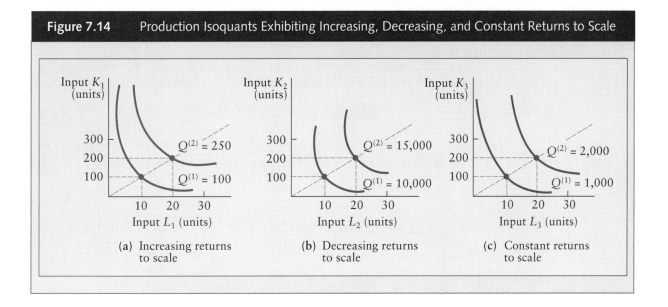

Figure 7.14 Production Isoquants Exhibiting Increasing, Decreasing, and Constant Returns to Scale

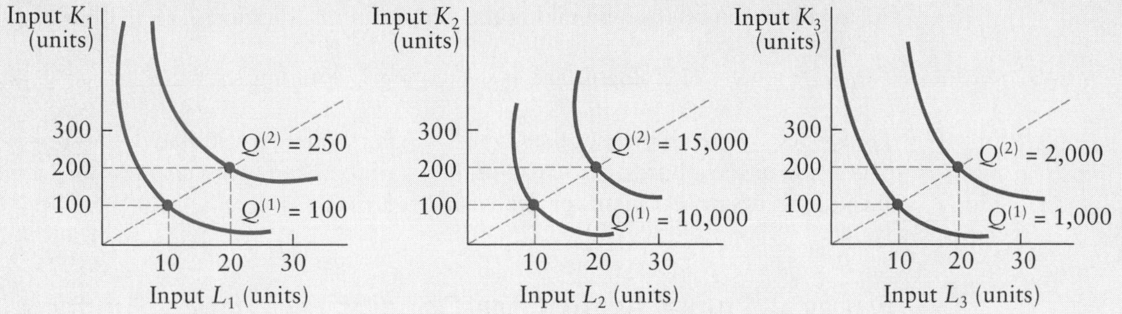

(a) Increasing returns to scale (b) Decreasing returns to scale (c) Constant returns to scale

of inputs L and K yields exactly double the amount of output (i.e., an increase from 1,000 to 2,000).

INCREASING AND DECREASING RETURNS TO SCALE

In addition to satisfying the law of diminishing marginal returns discussed earlier, a firm's production function is often characterized by first increasing and then decreasing returns to scale. A number of industrial engineering arguments have been presented to justify this characteristic of the production function. The major argument given for initial increasing returns, as the scale of production is first increased, is the opportunity for *specialization in the use of capital and labor.* As the scale of production is increased, equipment that is more efficient in performing a limited set of tasks can be substituted for less efficient all-purpose equipment. Similarly, the efficiency of workers in performing a small number of related tasks is greater than that of less highly skilled, but more versatile, workers.

A principal argument given for the existence of decreasing returns to scale thereafter is the increasingly complex *problems of coordination and control* faced by management as the scale of production is increased. For example, mangers may be limited in their ability to transmit and receive status reports over a wider and wider span of control. This may diminish the effectiveness of management in exercising control and coordination. As a result, proportionate increases in all of the inputs of the production process, including the input labeled "management," may eventually yield less than proportionate increases in total output.

THE COBB-DOUGLAS PRODUCTION FUNCTION

The Cobb-Douglas production function has returns to scale determined by the sum of the parameters $(\beta_1 + \beta_2)$:

$$Q = \alpha L^{\beta_1} K^{\beta_2} \qquad [7.16]$$

Depending on whether $n = \beta_1 + \beta_2$ is less than, equal to, or greater than 1, the Cobb-Douglas production function will exhibit decreasing, constant, or increasing returns, respectively.

The multiplicative exponential Cobb-Douglas function can be estimated as a linear regression relation by taking the logarithm of Equation 7.16 to obtain

$$\log Q = \log \alpha + \beta_1 \log L + \beta_2 \log K. \qquad [7.17]$$

Thus, once the parameters of the Cobb-Douglas model are estimated, the sum of the exponents of the labor (β_1) and capital (β_2) variables can be used to test for the presence of increasing, constant, or decreasing returns to scale.

Empirical Studies of the Cobb-Douglas Production Function

This section examines three Cobb-Douglas production function studies that illustrate the basic methodology used and the type of results obtained: first, a study employing aggregate time-series data on the economy; second, a study using cross-sectional data on individual industries; and third, a study that develops a production function for major league baseball.

EXAMPLE

A Time-Series Analysis of the U.S. Manufacturing Sector

In their original study, Cobb-Douglas fitted a production function of the form in Equation 7.16 to indices of production Q, labor L, and capital K in the U.S. manufacturing sector. Q was an index of physical volume of manufacturing; L was an index of the average number of employed wage earners only (i.e., salaried employees, officials, and working proprietors were excluded); and K was an index of the value of plants, buildings, tools, and machinery reduced to dollars of constant purchasing power. With the sum of the exponents restricted to one (constant returns to scale), the following function was obtained:

$$Q = 1.01\, L^{.75} K^{.25} \qquad [7.18]$$

In later studies Cobb-Douglas made several modifications that altered their results somewhat. These modifications included revisions in the output and labor indices, removing the secular trend from each index by expressing each yearly index value as a percentage of its overall trend value, and dropping the assumption of constant returns to scale. With these modifications the estimated production function for the manufacturing sector was

$$Q = 0.84\, L^{.63} K^{.30} \qquad [7.19]$$

A 10 percent increase in labor input results in about a 6 percent increase in output, and a 10 percent increase in capital input results in approximately a 3 percent increase in output. Also, the resulting sum of the exponents of the labor and capital variables is slightly less than 1, which indicates the presence of decreasing returns to scale in the broadly defined manufacturing sector.

EXAMPLE

A CROSS-SECTIONAL ANALYSIS OF U.S. MANUFACTURING INDUSTRIES

Moroney used cross-sectional data to estimate Cobb-Douglas production functions for 18 U.S. manufacturing industries.[9] Using aggregate data on plants located within each state, the following three-variable model was fitted:

$$Q = \alpha\, L_p^{\beta_1} L_n^{\beta_2} K^{\beta_3} \qquad [7.20]$$

where Q is the value added by the production plants, L_p is production worker work-hours, L_n is nonproduction work-years, and K is gross book values of depreciable and depletable assets.[10] The results for several of the industries are shown in Table 7.4. The sum of the exponents ($\beta_1 + \beta_2 + \beta_3$) ranged from a low of 0.947 for petroleum to a high of 1.109 for furniture. In 13 of the 18 industries studied, the statistical tests showed that the sum of the exponents was not significantly different from 1.0. This evidence supports the hypothesis that most manufacturing industries exhibit constant returns to scale.

Table 7.4 Production Elasticities for Several Industries

Industry	Capital Elasticity* β_1	Production Worker Elasticity β_2	Nonproduction Worker Elasticity β_3	Sum of Elasticities $\beta_1 + \beta_2 + \beta_3$
Food and beverages	.555 (.121)	.439 (.128)	.076 (.037)	1.070* (.021)
Textiles	.121 (.173)	.549 (.216)	.335 (.086)	1.004 (.024)
Furniture	.205 (.153)	.802 (.186)	.103 (.079)	1.109* (.051)
Petroleum	.308 (.112)	.546 (.222)	.093 (.168)	.947 (.045)
Stone, clay, etc.	.632 (.105)	.032 (.224)	.366 (.201)	1.029 (.045)
Primary metals	.371 (.103)	.077 (.188)	.509 (.164)	.958 (.035)

Number in parentheses below each elasticity coefficient is the standard error.
*Significantly greater than 1.0 at the 0.05 level (one-tailed test).
Source: John R. Moroney, "Cobb-Douglas Production Functions and Returns to Scale in U.S. Manufacturing Industry," *Western Economic Journal* 6, no. 1 (December 1967), Table 1, p. 46.

[9] John R. Moroney, "Cobb-Douglas Production Functions and Returns to Scale in U.S. Manufacturing Industry," *Western Economic Journal* 6, no. 1 (December 1967), pp. 34–51.

[10] "Book values" of assets are the *historic* values of these assets as they appear on the balance sheet of the firm. Book values may differ significantly from current replacement values and hence may overstate or understate the actual amount of capital employed in the firm. Nonproduction workers are management and other staff personnel.

EXAMPLE

AN EMPIRICAL ESTIMATION OF THE PRODUCTION FUNCTION FOR MAJOR LEAGUE BASEBALL[11]

Team sports such as Major League Baseball are similar to other enterprises in that they attempt to provide a product (team victories) by employing various skills of team members. In acquiring team members through trades, the free agent market, and minor leagues/colleges, the owner is faced with various input trade-offs. For example, a baseball team owner may have to decide whether to trade a starting pitcher to obtain a power hitter or whether to sign a free agent relief pitcher in exchange for a frequent base stealer. These decisions are all made in the context of an intuitive baseball production function, possibly subject to various constraints (e.g., budgetary limits, league rules).

In an attempt to quantify the factors that contribute to the team's success, a Cobb-Douglas production function was developed using data from 26 major league baseball teams. Output (Q) was measured by team victories. Inputs (X_1, X_2, X_3, etc.) from five different categories were included in the model:

- *Hitting*. This factor involves two different subskills: hitting frequency, as measured by the team *batting average*, and hitting with power, as measured by the team's *home runs*.
- *Running*. One measure of speed is a team's *stolen base total*.
- *Defense*. This factor also involves two subskills: catching those chances that the player is able to reach, as measured by *fielding percentage*, and catching difficult chances that many players would not be able to reach, as measured by *total chances accepted*. Because these two variables are highly correlated with one another (i.e., multicollinear), separate regressions were run with each variable.
- *Pitching*. The most obvious measure of the pitching factor is the team's earned run average (ERA). However, ERA depends not only on pitching skill, but also on the team's defensive skills. A better measure of pure pitching skills is the *strikeouts-to-walks* ratio for the pitching staff.
- *Coaching*. Teams often change managers when they are performing unsatisfactorily, so this factor is thought to be important. However, the ability of a manager (coach) is difficult to measure. Two different measures are used in this study—the manager's *lifetime won-lost percentage* and *number of years spent managing in the major leagues*. Separate regressions are run with each variable.

Finally, a dummy variable ($NL = 0$, $AL = 1$) was used to control for any differences between leagues, such as the designated hitter rule.

The results of four regressions are shown in Table 7.5. Several conclusions can be drawn from these results:

1. Hitting average contributes almost six times as much as pitching to a team's success. This finding tends to contradict conventional wisdom, which says that pitching and defense wins championships.
2. Home runs contribute about twice as much as stolen bases to a team's success.
3. Coaching skills are not significant in any of the regression equations.

[11] Charles E. Zech, "An Empirical Estimation of a Production Function: The Case of Major League Baseball," *The American Economist*, 25, no. 2 (Fall 1981), pp. 19–23.

Table 7.5 Empirical Estimates of Baseball Production Functions

Variable	Equation 1	Equation 2	Equation 3	Equation 4
Constant	.017	.018	.010	.008
League dummy	−.002	−.003	.004	.003
Batting average	2.017*	1.986*	1.969*	1.927*
Home runs	.229*	.299*	.208*	.215*
Stolen bases	.119*	.120*	.110*	.112*
Strikeouts/walks	.343*	.355*	.324*	.334*
Total fielding chances	1.235	1.200		
Fielding percentage			5.62	5.96
Manager *W/L* percentage		−.003		−.004
Manager years	−.004		−.002	
$\bar{R}^2$ (coef. of determination)	.789	.790	.773	.774

*Statistically significant at the 0.05 level.
Source: Charles Zech, op. cit.

4. Defensive skills are not significant in any of the regression equations.
5. Finally, the sums of the statistically significant variables in each of the four equations range from 2.588 to 2.709. Because these are all much greater than 1.0, the baseball production functions examined all exhibit *increasing returns to scale.* Better ballplayers and better managers yield more than proportional increases in games won.

SUMMARY

- A *production function* is a schedule, graph, or mathematical model relating the maximum quantity of output that can be produced from various quantities of inputs.
- For a production function with one variable input, the *marginal product* is defined as the incremental change in total output that can be produced by the use of one more unit of the variable input in the production process.
- For a production function with one variable input, the *average product* is defined as the ratio of total output to the amount of the variable input used in producing the output.
- The *law of diminishing marginal returns* states that, with all other productive factors held constant, the use of increasing amounts of the variable factor in the production process beyond some point will result in diminishing marginal increases in total output. *Increasing returns* can arise with *network effects.*
- In the short run, with one of the productive factors fixed, the optimal output level (and optimal level of the variable input) occurs where marginal revenue product equals marginal factor cost. *Marginal revenue product* is defined as the amount that an additional unit of the variable input adds to total revenue. *Marginal factor cost* is defined as the amount that an additional unit of the variable input adds to total cost.
- A *production isoquant* is either a geometric curve or algebraic function representing all the various combinations of inputs that can be used in producing a given level of output.
- The *marginal rate of technical substitution* is the rate at which one input may be substituted for another input in the production process, while total output remains constant. It is equal to the ratio of the marginal products of the two inputs.
- In the long run, with both inputs being variable, minimizing cost subject to an output constraint (or

maximizing output subject to a cost constraint) requires that the production process be operated at the point where the marginal product per dollar input cost of each factor is equal.

- The degree of *technical efficiency* of a production process is the ratio of observed output to the maximum potentially feasible output for that process, given the same inputs.
- The degree of *allocative efficiency* of a production process is the ratio of total cost for producing a given output level with the least-cost process to the observed total cost of producing that output.
- Physical *returns to scale* is defined as the proportionate increase in the output of a production process that results from a given proportionate increase in all the inputs.
- The Cobb-Douglas production function, which is used extensively in empirical studies, is a multiplicative exponential function in which output is a (nonlinear) monotonically increasing function of each of the inputs.
- The Cobb-Douglas production function has various properties that allow one to draw conclusions, based on parameter estimates, about returns to scale.

Exercises

Answers to the exercises in blue can be found in Appendix C at the back of the book.

1. In the Deep Creek Mining Company example described in this chapter (Table 7.1), suppose again that labor is the variable input and capital is the fixed input. Specifically, assume that the firm owns a piece of equipment having a 500-bhp rating.

   a. Complete the following table:

Labor Input L (No. of Workers)	Total Product TP_L (= Q)	Marginal Product MP_L	Average Product AP_L
1	____	____	____
2	____	____	____
3	____	____	____
4	____	____	____
5	____	____	____
6	____	____	____
7	____	____	____
8	____	____	____
9	____	____	____
10	____	____	____

   b. Plot the (i) total product, (ii) marginal product, and (iii) average product functions.

   c. Determine the boundaries of the three stages of production.

2. From your knowledge of the relationships among the various production functions, complete the following table:

Variable Input L	Total Product TP_L (= Q)	Average Product AP_L	Marginal Product MP_L
0	0	–	–
1	____	____	8
2	28	____	____
3	____	18	____
4	____	____	26
5	____	20	____
6	108	____	____
7	____	____	−10

3. The amount of fish caught per week on a trawler is a function of the crew size assigned to operate the boat. Based on past data, the following production schedule was developed:

Crew Size (Number of Workers)	Amount of Fish Caught Per Week (Hundreds of lbs.)
2	3
3	6
4	11
5	19
6	24
7	28
8	31
9	33
10	34
11	34
12	33

a. Over what ranges of workers are there (i) increasing, (ii) constant, (iii) decreasing, and (iv) negative returns?

b. How large a crew should be used if the trawler owner is interested in maximizing the total amount of fish caught?

c. How large a crew should be used if the trawler owner is interested in maximizing the average amount of fish caught per person?

4. Consider Exercise 3 again. Suppose the owner of the trawler can sell all the fish caught for \$75 per 100 pounds and can hire as many crew members as desired by paying them \$150 per week. Assuming that the owner of the trawler is interested in maximizing profits, determine the optimal crew size.

5. Consider the following short-run production function (where L = variable input, Q = output):

$$Q = 6L^2 - 0.4L^3$$

a. Determine the marginal product function (MP_L).

b. Determine the average product function (AP_L).

c. Find the value of L that maximizes Q.

d. Find the value of L at which the marginal product function takes on its maximum value.

e. Find the value of L at which the average product function takes on its maximum value.

6. Consider the following short-run production function (where L = variable input, Q = output):

$$Q = 10L - 0.5L^2$$

Suppose that output can be sold for \$10 per unit. Also assume that the firm can obtain as much of the variable input (L) as it needs at \$20 per unit.

a. Determine the marginal revenue product function.

b. Determine the marginal factor cost function.

c. Determine the optimal value of L, given that the objective is to maximize profits.

7. Suppose that as the result of recent labor negotiations, wage rates are *reduced* by 10 percent in a production process employing only capital and labor. Assuming that other conditions (e.g., productivity) remain constant, determine what effect this

decrease will have on the desired proportions of capital and labor used in producing the given level of output at minimum total cost. Illustrate your answer with an isoquant-isocost diagram.

8. A firm uses two variable inputs, labor (L) and raw materials (M), in producing its output. At its current level of output:

$$C_L = \$10/\text{unit} \qquad MP_L = 25$$
$$C_M = \$2/\text{unit} \qquad MP_M = 4$$

a. Determine whether the firm is operating efficiently, given that its objective is to minimize the cost of producing the given level of output.
b. Determine what changes (if any) in the relative proportions of labor and raw materials need to be made to operate efficiently.

9. Suppose that a firm's production function is given by the following relationship:

$$Q = 2.5\sqrt{LK} \qquad (\text{i.e., } Q = 2.5L^{.5}K^{.5})$$

where Q = output
L = labor input
K = capital input

a. Determine the percentage increase in output if labor input is increased by 10 percent (assuming that capital input is held constant).
b. Determine the percentage increase in output if capital input is increased by 25 percent (assuming that labor input is held constant).
c. Determine the percentage increase in output if *both* labor and capital are increased by 20 percent.

10. Based on the production function parameter estimates reported in Table 7.4:
a. Which industry (or industries) appears to exhibit decreasing returns to scale? (Ignore the issue of statistical significance.)
b. Which industry comes closest to exhibiting constant returns to scale?
c. In which industry will a given percentage increase in capital result in the largest percentage increase in output?
d. In what industry will a given percentage increase in production workers result in the largest percentage increase in output?

11. Consider the following Cobb-Douglas production function for the bus transportation system in a particular city:

$$Q = \alpha L^{\beta_1} F^{\beta_2} K^{\beta_3}$$

where L = labor input in worker hours
F = fuel input in gallons
K = capital input in number of buses
Q = output measured in millions of bus miles

Suppose that the parameters (α, β_1, β_2, and β_3) of this model were estimated using annual data for the past 25 years. The following results were obtained:

$$\alpha = 0.0012 \quad \beta_1 = 0.45 \quad \beta_2 = 0.20 \quad \beta_3 = 0.30$$

a. Determine the (i) labor, (ii) fuel, and (iii) capital input production elasticities.
b. Suppose that labor input (worker hours) is increased by 2 percent next year (with the other inputs held constant). Determine the approximate percentage change in output.

c. Suppose that capital input (number of buses) is decreased by 3 percent next year (when certain older buses are taken out of service). Assuming that the other inputs are held constant, determine the approximate percentage change in output.

d. What type of returns to scale appears to characterize this bus transportation system? (Ignore the issue of statistical significance.)

e. Discuss some of the methodological and measurement problems one might encounter in using time-series data to estimate the parameters of this model.

12. *Extension of the Cobb-Douglas Production Function*—The Cobb-Douglas production function (Equation 7.16) can be shown to be a special case of a larger class of production functions having the following mathematical form:[12]

$$Q = \gamma[\partial K^{-\rho} + (1 - \partial)L^{-\rho}]^{-\nu/\rho}$$

where γ is an efficiency parameter that shows the output resulting from given quantities of inputs; ∂ is a distribution parameter ($0 \leq \partial \leq 1$) that indicates the division of factor income between capital and labor; ρ is a substitution parameter that is a measure of substitutability of capital for labor (or vice versa) in the production process; and ν is a scale parameter ($\nu > 0$) that indicates the type of returns to scale (increasing, constant, or decreasing). Show that when $\nu = 1$, this function exhibits constant returns to scale. [*Hint:* Increase capital K and labor L each by a factor of λ, or $K^* = (\lambda)K$ and $L^* = (\lambda)L$, and show that output Q also increases by a factor of λ, or $Q^* = (\lambda)(Q)$.]

13. Lobo Lighting Corporation currently employs 100 unskilled laborers, 80 factory technicians, 30 skilled machinists, and 40 skilled electricians. Lobo feels that the marginal product of the last unskilled laborer is 400 lights per week, the marginal product of the last factory technician is 450 lights per week, the marginal product of the last skilled machinist is 550 lights per week, and the marginal product of the last skilled electrician is 600 lights per week. Unskilled laborers earn $400 per week, factory technicians earn $500 per week, machinists earn $700 per week, and electricians earn $750 per week.

Is Lobo using the lowest cost combination of workers to produce its targeted output? If not, what recommendations can you make to assist the company?

CASE EXERCISE

THE PRODUCTION FUNCTION FOR WILSON COMPANY

Economists at the Wilson Company are interested in developing a production function for fertilizer plants. They collected data on 15 different plants that produce fertilizer (see the following page).

QUESTIONS

1. Estimate the Cobb-Douglas production function $Q = \alpha L^{\beta_1} K^{\beta_2}$, where Q = output; L = labor input; K = capital input; and α, β_1, and β_2 are the parameters to be estimated.

2. Test whether the coefficients of capital and labor are statistically significant.

3. Determine the percentage of the variation in output that is "explained" by the regression equation.

[12] See R. G. Chambers, *Applied Production Analysis* (Cambridge: Cambridge University Press, 1988).

4. Determine the labor and capital estimated parameters and give an economic interpretation of each value.

5. Determine whether this production function exhibits increasing, decreasing, or constant returns to scale. (Ignore the issue of statistical significance.)

Plant	Output (000 Tons)	Capital ($000)	Labor (000 Worker Hours)
1	605.3	18,891	700.2
2	566.1	19,201	651.8
3	647.1	20,655	822.9
4	523.7	15,082	650.3
5	712.3	20,300	859.0
6	487.5	16,079	613.0
7	761.6	24,194	851.3
8	442.5	11,504	655.4
9	821.1	25,970	900.6
10	397.8	10,127	550.4
11	896.7	25,622	842.2
12	359.3	12,477	540.5
13	979.1	24,002	949.4
14	331.7	8,042	575.7
15	1064.9	23,972	925.8

APPENDIX

7a

Maximization of Production Output Subject to a Cost Constraint

Using graphical analysis, we illustrated in the chapter that the following condition (Equation 7.15)

$$\frac{MP_L}{C_L} = \frac{MP_K}{C_K}$$

must be satisfied in determining the combination of inputs (L and K) that minimizes total cost subject to an output constraint. It turns out that the same result arises in maximizing output subject to a cost constraint, the mathematical dual of the earlier constrained minimization problem.

Given the production function to identify potential output possibilities,

$$Q = f(L, K) \qquad [7A.1]$$

and the cost constraint

$$C = C_L L + C_K K \qquad [7A.2]$$

we define an artificial variable λ (lambda) and form the Lagrangian function

$$L_Q = Q - \lambda(C_L L + C_K K - C) \qquad [7A.3]$$

Differentiating L_Q with respect to L, K, and λ and setting the (partial) derivatives equal to zero (condition for a maximum) yields

$$\frac{\partial L_Q}{\partial L} = \frac{\partial f(L, K)}{\partial L} - \lambda C_L = 0 \qquad [7A.4]$$

$$\frac{\partial L_Q}{\partial K} = \frac{\partial f(L, K)}{\partial K} - \lambda C_K - 0 \qquad [7A.5]$$

$$\frac{\partial L_Q}{\partial \lambda} = C_L L + C_K K - C = 0 \qquad [7A.6]$$

Recognizing that $\frac{\partial f(L, K)}{\partial L} = MP_L$ and $\frac{\partial f(L, K)}{\partial K} = MP_K$, and solving Equations 7A.4 and 7A.5 for λ yields

$$\lambda = \frac{MP_L}{C_L} \qquad [7A.7]$$

$$\lambda = \frac{MP_K}{C_K} \qquad [7A.8]$$

Setting Equations 7A.7 and 7A.8 equal to each other gives the optimality condition

$$\frac{MP_L}{C_L} = \frac{MP_K}{C_K} \qquad [7A.9]$$

Exercise

Answers to the exercises in blue can be found in Appendix C at the back of the book.

1. The output (Q) of a production process is a function of two inputs (L and K) and is given by the following relationship:

$$Q = 0.50LK - 0.10L^2 - 0.05K^2$$

The per-unit prices of inputs L and K are \$20 and \$25, respectively. The firm is interested in maximizing output subject to a cost constraint of \$500.

a. Formulate the Lagrangian function:

$$L_Q = Q - \lambda(C_L L + C_K K - C)$$

b. Take the partial derivatives of L_Q with respect to L, K, and λ, and set them equal to zero.

c. Solve the set of simultaneous equations in Part (b) for the optimal values of L, K, and λ.

d. Based on your answers to Part (c), how many units of L and K should be used by the firm? What is the total output of this combination?

e. Give an economic interpretation of the λ value determined in Part (c).

f. Check to see whether the optimality condition (Equation 7A.9) is satisfied for the solution you obtained.

CHAPTER

8

COST ANALYSIS

CHAPTER PREVIEW Economic cost refers to the cost of attracting a resource from its next best alternative use (the opportunity cost concept). Managers seeking to make the most efficient use of resources to maximize value must be concerned with both short-run and long-run opportunity costs. Short-run cost-output relationships help managers to plan for the most profitable level of output, given the capital resources that are immediately available. Long-run cost-output relationships involve attracting additional capital to expand or contract the plant size and change the scale of operations. Achieving scale economies is often the key to the firm's operations strategy.

MANAGERIAL CHALLENGE

US Airways Cost Structure[1]

US Airways Corporation (USAir) was formed through the merger of several diverse regional airlines, including Allegheny, Mohawk, Lake Central, Pacific Southwest, Piedmont Airlines, and America West. Although these mergers led to a "national" competitor in the airline industry, USAir's market strength remained in the Northeast and far West. USAir has a major or dominant presence in Pittsburgh, Charlotte, Philadelphia, the Baltimore/Washington area, New York, Phoenix, and Boston.

Unlike the much more successful Southwest Airlines, which flies only one type of plane, the Boeing 737, US Airways possesses a diverse fleet of aircraft. This diversity results in higher costs of maintenance and crew training and a much more complex crew scheduling problem. In addition, USAir is burdened with restrictive work rules that increase labor costs, which account for 40 percent of total airline operating costs. The net result is that USAir's cost per available seat mile is close to the highest in the industry at 10.89 cents per available seat mile. This cost compares to 11.62 cents for Delta, 10.86 cents for Northwest, 9.80 cents for American Airlines, 10.56 cents for Continental, 7.7 cents for Southwest, and 6.74 cents for JetBlue.

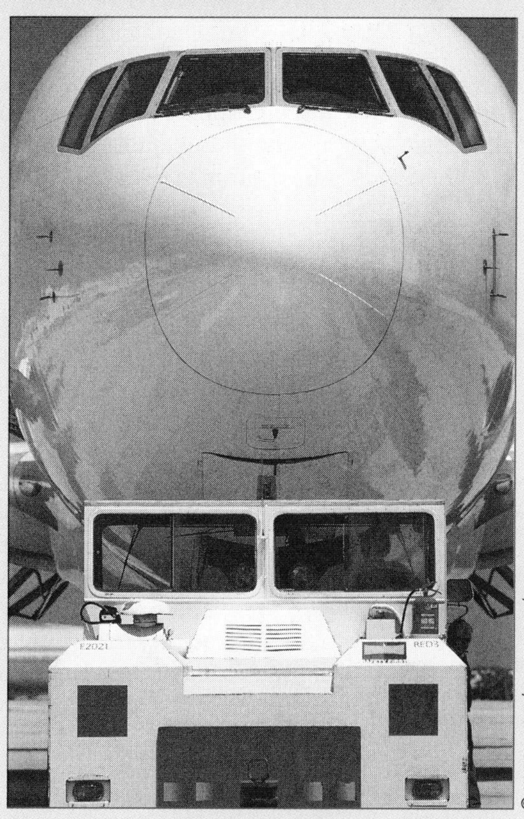

MANAGERIAL CHALLENGE

Because of the traditionally weak competition in its Northeast market stronghold, USAir has the highest average passenger fare received for each revenue passenger mile flown: 18.8 cents, compared with 14.21 cents for United, 15.18 cents for American, 12.76 cents for Continental, and 12.37 cents for Southwest. In 2005, USAir merged with America West, a low-cost discounter with Phoenix and Las Vegas hubs and a 7.68 cent operating cost per available seat mile.

The combination of high fares and high costs per available seat mile invited competition. After emerging from bankruptcy with a new, lower cost structure, Continental announced a major restructuring of its route system to compete head on with USAir in much of its core business area. In addition, Southwest Air began to enter some of USAir's traditional markets (particularly Baltimore/Washington).

As a result of massive losses due to the downturn in travel after September 11, 2001, and its high cost structure, USAir declared bankruptcy in 2002. After taking various steps to reduce costs, including negotiating lower wage contracts with its employee unions, the carrier emerged from bankruptcy in 2003. Cost control is a difficult problem in any corporation. It is, however, especially difficult in a heavily unionized capital-intensive industry such as airlines.

In this chapter we consider many of the important cost relationships that are essential to a firm's long-term competitive success.

[1] Based on "UAL Latest Cost Cuts," *Wall Street Journal* (May 12, 2005), p. A10.

THE MEANING AND MEASUREMENT OF COST

In its most elementary form, cost simply refers to the sacrifice incurred whenever an exchange or transformation of resources takes place. This association between forgone opportunities and economic cost applies in all circumstances. However, the appropriate manner to measure costs is a function of the purpose for which the information is to be used.

ACCOUNTING VERSUS ECONOMIC COSTS

Accountants have been primarily concerned with measuring costs for *financial reporting purposes*. As a result, they define and measure cost by the *historical outlay of funds* that takes place in the exchange or transformation of a resource. Thus, whenever *A* sells a product or commodity to *B*, the *price* paid by *B*, expressed in dollars, measures the accounting cost of the product to *B*. When *A* exchanges labor services for money or other items of value, the *wages* that *A* receives represent the accounting cost of *A*'s services to the employer. Similarly, the *interest* paid to the bondholder or lending institution is used to measure the accounting cost of funds to the borrower.

Opportunity Costs

The value of a resource in its next best alternative use. Opportunity cost represents the return or compensation that must be forgone as the result of the decision to employ the resource in a given economic activity.

Economists have been mainly concerned with measuring costs for *decision-making purposes*. The objective is to determine the present and future costs of resources associated with various alternative courses of action. Such an objective requires a consideration of the opportunities forgone (or sacrificed) whenever a resource is used in a given course of action. So, although both the accounting cost and the economic cost of a product will include such *explicit* costs as labor, raw materials, supplies, rent, interest, and utilities, economists will also include the implicit **opportunity costs** of time and capital that the owner-manager has invested in the enterprise. The opportunity cost of the owner's time is measured by the most attractive salary or other form of compensation that the owner could have received by applying his or her talents, skills, and experience in the management of a similar (but second-best) business owned by someone else. Similarly, the opportunity cost of the capital is measured by the profit or return that could have been received if the owner had chosen to employ capital in the second-best (alternative) investment of comparable risk.

Economic profit is defined as the difference between total revenues and total economic costs. Algebraically, economic profit is given by

$$\text{Economic profit} = \text{Total revenues} - \text{Explicit costs} - \text{Implicit costs} \quad [8.1]$$

EXAMPLE

OPPORTUNITY COSTS AT BENTLEY CLOTHING STORE

Robert Bentley owns and operates the Bentley Clothing Store. A traditional income statement for the business is shown in Panel (a) of Table 8.1. The mortgage on the store has been paid, and therefore no interest expenses are shown on the income statement.

Table 8.1 Profitability of Bentley Clothing Store

(a) Accounting Income Statement		
Net sales		$650,000
Less: Cost of goods sold		250,000
Gross profit		400,000
Less: Expenses		
Employee compensation*	150,000	
Advertising	30,000	
Utilities and maintenance	20,000	
Miscellaneous	10,000	
Total		210,000
Net profit before taxes		$190,000
(b) Economic Profit Statement		
Total revenues		$650,000
Less: Explicit costs		
Cost of goods sold	250,000	
Employee compensation*	150,000	
Advertising	30,000	
Utilities and maintenance	20,000	
Miscellaneous	10,000	
Total		460,000
Accounting profit before taxes		190,000
Less: Implicit costs		
Salary (manager)	130,000	
Rent on building	88,000	
Total		218,000
Economic profit (or loss) before taxes		($ 28,000)

*Employee compensation does not include any salary to Robert Bentley.

Also, the building has been fully depreciated and thus no depreciation charges are shown. From an *accounting* standpoint and from the perspective of the Internal Revenue Service, Bentley is earning a *positive accounting profit* of $190,000 (before taxes).

However, consider the store's profitability from an *economic* standpoint. As indicated earlier in the chapter, implicit costs include the opportunity costs of time and capital that the entrepreneur has invested in the firm. Suppose that Bentley could go to work as a clothing department manager for a large department or specialty store chain and receive a salary of $130,000 per year. Also assume that Bentley could rent his building to another merchant for $88,000 (net) per year. Under these conditions, as shown in Panel (b) of Table 8.1, Bentley is earning a *negative economic profit* (−$28,000 before taxes). By renting his store to another merchant and going to work as manager of a different store, he could make $28,000 more than he is currently earning from his clothing store business. Thus, accounting profits, which do not include opportunity costs, are not always a valid indication of the economic profitability (or loss) of an enterprise.

When one recognizes that such first-best and second-best uses change over time, it becomes clear that the historical outlay of funds to obtain a resource at an earlier date (the accounting cost basis) may not be the appropriate measure of opportunity cost in a decision problem today. For example, consider the following three cases of a substantive distinction between economic cost and accounting cost.

Capital Asset
A durable input that depreciates with use, time, and obsolescence.

DEPRECIATION COST MEASUREMENT The production of a good or service typically requires the use of licenses and plant and equipment. As these **capital assets** are used, their service life is expended; the assets wear out or become obsolete. Depreciation is the cost of using these assets in producing the given output. If the Phillips Tool Company owns a machine that has a current market value of $8,000 and is expected to have a value of $6,800 after one more year of use, then the opportunity cost of using the machine for one year (the economist's measure of depreciation cost) is $8,000 − $6,800 = $1,200. Assuming that 2,000 units of output were produced during the year, the depreciation cost would be $1,200 ÷ 2,000 units = $.60 per unit.

Unfortunately, it is often difficult, if not impossible, to determine the service life of a capital asset and the future changes in its market value.[2] Some assets are unique (patents); others are not traded in liquid resale markets (plants); and still others are rendered obsolete with little predictability (computers). To overcome these measurement problems with economic depreciation cost, accountants have adopted certain procedures for allocating a portion of the acquisition cost of an asset to each accounting time period, and in turn to each unit of output that is produced within that time period. This allocation is typically done by estimating the service life of the asset and then arbitrarily assigning a portion of the historical cost of the asset against income during each year of the service life. If the machine is purchased by Phillips for

[2] This concept of the future cost of the partially consumed asset is termed the *replacement cost* of the asset rather than the *historical acquisition cost* of the asset.

$10,000 and is expected to have a 10-year life and no salvage value, the straight-line method of depreciation ($10,000 ÷ 10 = $1,000) would calculate the depreciation cost of this asset each year. Assuming that 2,000 units of output are produced in a given year, then $1,000 ÷ 2,000 = $.50 would be allocated to the cost of each unit produced by Phillips. Note from this example that the straight-line method described for allocating depreciation costs is arbitrary, and the calculated accounting depreciation cost does not equal the economic depreciation cost actually incurred, if in fact the market value of the machine drops to $6,800 after one year.

INVENTORY VALUATION Whenever materials are stored in inventory for a period of time before being used in the production process, the accounting and economic costs may differ if the market price of these materials has changed from the original purchase price. The accounting cost is equal to the actual *acquisition* cost, whereas the economic cost is equal to the current *replacement* cost. As the following example illustrates, the use of the acquisition cost can lead to incorrect production decisions.

EXAMPLE

INVENTORY VALUATION AT WESTSIDE PLUMBING AND HEATING

Westside Plumbing and Heating Company is offered a contract for $100,000 to provide the plumbing for a new building. The labor and equipment costs are calculated to be $60,000 for fulfilling the contract. Westside has the materials in inventory to complete the job. The materials originally cost the firm $50,000; however, prices have since declined and the materials could now be purchased for $37,500. Material prices are not expected to increase in the near future and hence no gains can be anticipated from holding the materials in inventory. The question is: Should Westside accept the contract? An analysis of the contract under both methods for measuring the cost of the materials is shown in Table 8.2. Assuming that the materials are valued at the acquisition cost, the firm should not accept the contract because an apparent loss of $10,000 would result. By using the replacement cost as the value of the materials, however, the contract should be accepted, because a profit of $2,500 would result.

To see which method is correct, examine the income statement of Westside at the end of the accounting period. If the contract *is not* accepted, then at the end of the accounting period the firm will have to reduce the cost of its inventory by $12,500 ($50,000 − $37,500) to reflect the lower market value of this unused

Table 8.2 Effect of Inventory Valuation Methods on Measured Profit—Westside Plumbing and Heating Company

	Acquisition Cost	Replacement Cost
Value of contract	$100,000	$100,000
Costs		
Labor, equipment	60,000	60,000
Materials	50,000	37,500
	110,000	97,500
Profit (or loss)	($10,000)	$ 2,500

inventory. The firm will thus incur a loss of $12,500. If the contract *is* accepted, then the company will make a profit of $2,500 on the contract, but will also incur a loss of $12,500 on the materials used in completing the contract. The firm will thus incur a *net* loss of only $10,000. Hence, acceptance of the contract results in a smaller overall loss to Westside than does rejection of the contract. For decision-making purposes, replacement cost is the appropriate measure of the cost of materials in inventory, and Westside should accept the contract.

Sunk Cost of Underutilized Facilities The Dunbar Manufacturing Company recently discontinued a product line and was left with 50,000 square feet of unneeded warehouse space. The company rents the entire warehouse (200,000 square feet) from the owner for $1 million per year (i.e., $5 per square foot) under a long-term (10-year) lease agreement. A nearby company that is expanding its operations offered to rent the 50,000 square feet of unneeded space for one year for $125,000 (i.e., $2.50 per square foot). Should Dunbar accept the offer to rent the unused space, assuming that no other higher offers for the warehouse space are expected?

One could argue that Dunbar should reject the offer because the additional rent (revenue) of $2.50 per square foot is less than the lease payment (cost) of $5 per square foot. Such reasoning, however, will lead to an incorrect decision. The lease payment ($5 per square foot) represents a **sunk cost** that must be paid regardless of whether the other company rents the unneeded warehouse space. As shown in Table 8.3, renting the unneeded warehouse space *reduces* the net cost of the warehouse from $1 million to $875,000, a savings of $125,000 per year to Dunbar. The relevant comparison is between the incremental revenue ($125,000) and the incremental costs ($0 in this case). Thus, sunk costs (such as the lease payment of $5 per square foot in this example) should not be considered relevant costs because such costs are unavoidable, independent of the course of action chosen.

Sunk Cost

A cost incurred regardless of the alternative action chosen in a decision-making problem.

Conclusions Several conclusions can be drawn from this discussion of the concept of cost:

1. Costs can be measured in different ways, depending on the purpose for which the cost figures are to be used.
2. The costs appropriate for financial reporting purposes are not always appropriate for decision-making purposes. Typically, changes and modifications have to

Table 8.3 Warehouse Rental Decision—Dunbar Manufacturing Company

	Decision	
	Do Not Rent	Rent
Total lease payment	$1,000,000	$1,000,000
Less: Rent received on unused space	—	125,000
Net cost of warehouse to Dunbar Manufacturing Company	$1,000,000	$ 875,000

be made to reflect the opportunity costs of the various alternative actions that can be chosen in a given decision problem. The *relevant cost* in economic decision making is the opportunity cost of the resources rather than the historical outlay of funds required to obtain the resources.

3. Sunk costs, which are incurred regardless of the alternative action chosen, should seldom be considered in making operating decisions.
4. The opportunity costs of a given action in a decision problem are sometimes highly subjective, but often the more objective accounting cost estimates may be arbitrary.

SHORT-RUN COST FUNCTIONS

Cost Function

A mathematical model, schedule, or graph that shows the cost (such as total, average, or marginal cost) of producing various quantities of output.

In addition to measuring the costs of producing a given quantity of output, economists are also concerned with determining the behavior of costs as output is varied over a range of possible values. The relationship between cost and output is expressed in terms of a **cost function**: a schedule, graph, or mathematical relationship showing the minimum achievable cost of producing various quantities of output.

The discussion in Chapter 7 concerning the inputs used in the production process distinguished between fixed and variable inputs. A fixed input was defined as an input that is required in the production process, but whose quantity used in the process is constant over a given period of time regardless of the level of output produced. Short-run questions relate to a situation in which one or more of the inputs to the production process are fixed. Long-run questions relate to a situation in which *all* inputs are variable; that is, no restrictions are imposed on the amount of a resource that can be employed in the production process.

Capital-Intensive Cost Function

A characteristic of costs associated with a high proportion of fixed to variable inputs, usually due to extensive investment in plant and equipment.

The actual period of time corresponding to the long run for a given production process will depend on the nature of the inputs employed in the production process. Generally, the more capital equipment used relative to labor and other inputs (i.e., the more **capital intensive** the process), the longer will be the period of time required to increase significantly all the factors of production and the scale of operations. A period of five or more years may be required for a new or expanded electric utility–generating facility, steel mill, or oil refinery to be constructed and put into operation. Before the expansion is completed (i.e., in the short run), increases in production output can only be achieved by operating existing production facilities at higher rates of use through the utilization of greater amounts of labor and other variable inputs. In comparison, a service-oriented production process (such as a trucking company or consulting firm) that uses a relatively small amount of capital equipment may have a long-run planning horizon of only a few months, especially if the company rents or short-term leases much of its equipment. Such a company can abruptly change the scale of operations as business conditions dictate. Associated with the short-run and long-run planning periods are short-run and long-run cost functions.

TOTAL COST FUNCTION

Fixed Costs

The costs of inputs to the production process that are constant over the short run.

The total cost of producing a given quantity of output is equal to the sum of the costs of each of the inputs used in the production process. In discussing short-run cost functions, it is useful to classify costs as either *fixed* or *variable costs*. **Fixed costs** represent the costs of all the inputs to the production process that are fixed or constant over the short run. These costs will be incurred regardless of whether a small or large quantity of output is produced during the period. **Variable costs** consist of the costs of all the variable inputs to the production process. Whereas variable costs may not change in direct proportion to the quantity of output produced, they will increase (or decrease) in some manner as output is increased (or decreased).

Variable Costs

The costs of the variable inputs to the production process.

EXAMPLE

Short-Run Cost Functions: Deep Creek Mining Company

To illustrate the nature of short-run costs and show how the short-run cost function can be derived from the production function for the firm, consider again the Deep Creek Mining Company example that was discussed in Chapter 7. It was assumed that two inputs, capital and labor, are required to produce or mine ore. Various-sized pieces of capital equipment, as measured by their brake horsepower rating K, are available to mine the ore. Each of these pieces of equipment can be operated with various-sized labor crews L. The amount of output (tons of ore) that can be produced in a given period with each capital-labor input combination is shown again in Table 8.4. It was also assumed that the rental cost of using the mining equipment per period is \$0.20 per brake horsepower and that the cost of each worker (labor) employed per period is \$50. This yielded the following total cost equation for any given combination of labor L and capital K (Equation 7.21):

$$C = 50L + 0.20K$$

Suppose that Deep Creek has signed a lease agreeing to rent, for the next year, a 750-brake-horsepower piece of mining equipment (capital). During the ensuing year (the short run), the amount of capital that the company can employ in the ore-mining process is fixed at 750 brake horsepower. Therefore, for each period a fixed cost of $\$0.20 \times 750 = \$150$ will be incurred, regardless of the quantity of

Table 8.4 Production Function—Deep Creek Mining Company

		Capital Input K (Brake Horsepower)							
		250	500	750	1,000	1,250	1,500	1,750	2,000
Labor Input L (Number of Workers)	1	1	3	6	10	16	16	16	13
	2	2	6	16	24	29	29	44	44
	3	4	16	29	44	55	55	55	50
	4	6	29	44	55	58	60	60	55
	5	16	43	55	60	61	62	62	60
	6	29	55	60	62	63	63	63	62
	7	44	58	62	63	64	64	64	64
	8	50	60	62	63	64	65	65	65
	9	55	59	61	63	64	65	66	66
	10	52	56	59	62	64	65	66	67

Table 8.5 Short-Run Cost Functions—Deep Creek Mining Company

Output	Variable Cost		Fixed Cost		Total Cost	Average Fixed Cost	Average Variable Cost	Average Total Cost	Marginal Cost
Q	Labor Input L	$VC = \$50 \cdot L$	Capital Input K	$FC = \$150$	$TC = FC + VC$	$AFC = \frac{FC}{Q}$	$AVC = \frac{VC}{Q}$	$ATC = \frac{TC}{Q}$	$MC = \frac{\Delta TC}{\Delta Q}$
0	0	$ 0	750	$150	$150	—	—	—	—
6	1	50	750	150	200	$25.00	$8.33	$33.33	$\frac{50}{6}$ = $8.33
16	2	100	750	150	250	9.38	6.25	15.63	$\frac{50}{10}$ = 5.00
29	3	150	750	150	300	5.17	5.17	10.34	$\frac{50}{13}$ = 3.85
44	4	200	750	150	350	3.41	4.55	7.95	$\frac{50}{15}$ = 3.33
55	5	250	750	150	400	2.73	4.55	7.27	$\frac{50}{11}$ = 4.55
60	6	300	750	150	450	2.50	5.00	7.50	$\frac{50}{5}$ = 10.00
62	7	350	750	150	500	2.42	5.65	8.06	$\frac{50}{2}$ = 25.00

ore that is produced. The firm must operate the production process at one of the capital-labor combinations shown in the third column of Table 8.4. Output can be increased (decreased) by employing more (less) labor in combination with the given 750-brake-horsepower capital equipment. Labor is thus a variable input to the production process.

The short-run cost functions for Deep Creek are shown in Table 8.5.[3] The various possible output levels Q and the associated capital-labor input combinations L and K are obtained from Table 8.4. The short-run variable cost VC is equal to $50 times the number of workers (L) employed in the mining process. The short-run fixed cost FC is equal to the rental cost of the 750-brake-horsepower equipment ($150). The total cost in the short run is the sum of the fixed and variable costs:

$$TC = FC + VC \quad [8.2]$$

In Figure 8.1 the three curves from the data given in Table 8.5 are plotted. Note that the TC curve has an identical shape to that of VC, being shifted upward by the FC of $150.

[3] The rational producer would not employ more than seven workers in the short run because the use of additional workers will not result in any increase in the quantity of ore that is produced. That is, labor has a negative marginal value added beyond seven workers.

Figure 8.1 Short-Run Variable, Fixed, and Total Cost Functions—Deep Creek Mining Company

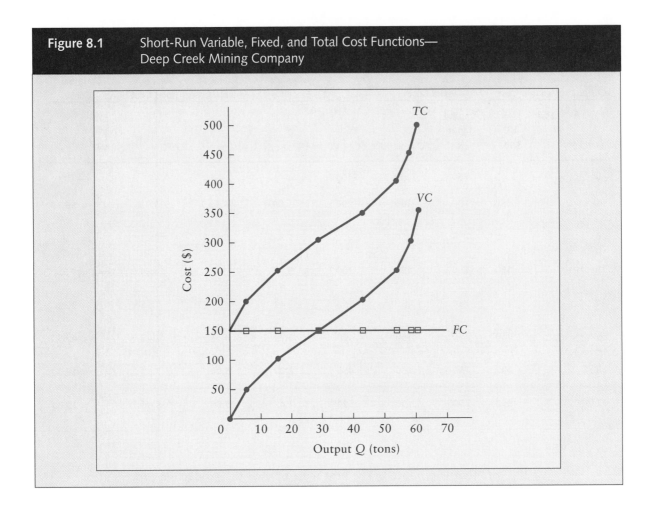

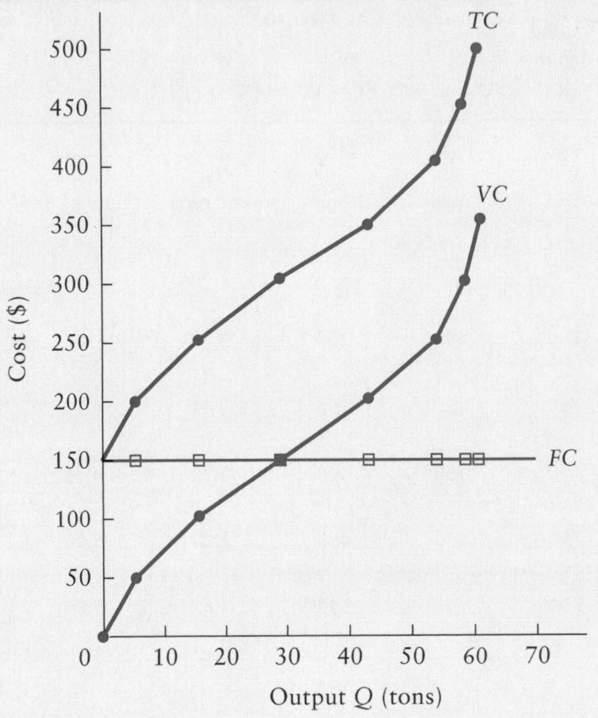

Average and Marginal Cost Functions

Once the total cost function is determined, one can then derive the average and marginal cost functions. The average fixed cost AFC, average variable cost AVC, and average total cost ATC are equal to the respective fixed, variable, and total costs divided by the quantity of output produced:

$$AFC = \frac{FC}{Q} \tag{8.3}$$

$$AVC = \frac{VC}{Q} \tag{8.4}$$

$$ATC = \frac{TC}{Q} \tag{8.5}$$

Also,

$$ATC = AFC + AVC \tag{8.6}$$

Marginal Cost

The incremental increase in total cost that results from a one-unit increase in output.

Marginal cost is defined as the incremental increase in total cost that results from a one-unit increase in output, and is calculated as[4]

$$MC = \frac{\Delta TC}{\Delta Q} \tag{8.7}$$

$$= \frac{\Delta VC}{\Delta Q}$$

or, in the case of a continuous TC function, as

$$MC = \frac{d(TC)}{dQ} \tag{8.8}$$

$$= \frac{d(VC)}{dQ} \tag{8.9}$$

The average and marginal costs for Deep Creek that were calculated in Table 8.5 are plotted in the graph shown in Figure 8.2. Except for the AFC curve, which is

Figure 8.2 Short-Run Average and Marginal Cost Functions—Deep Creek Mining Company

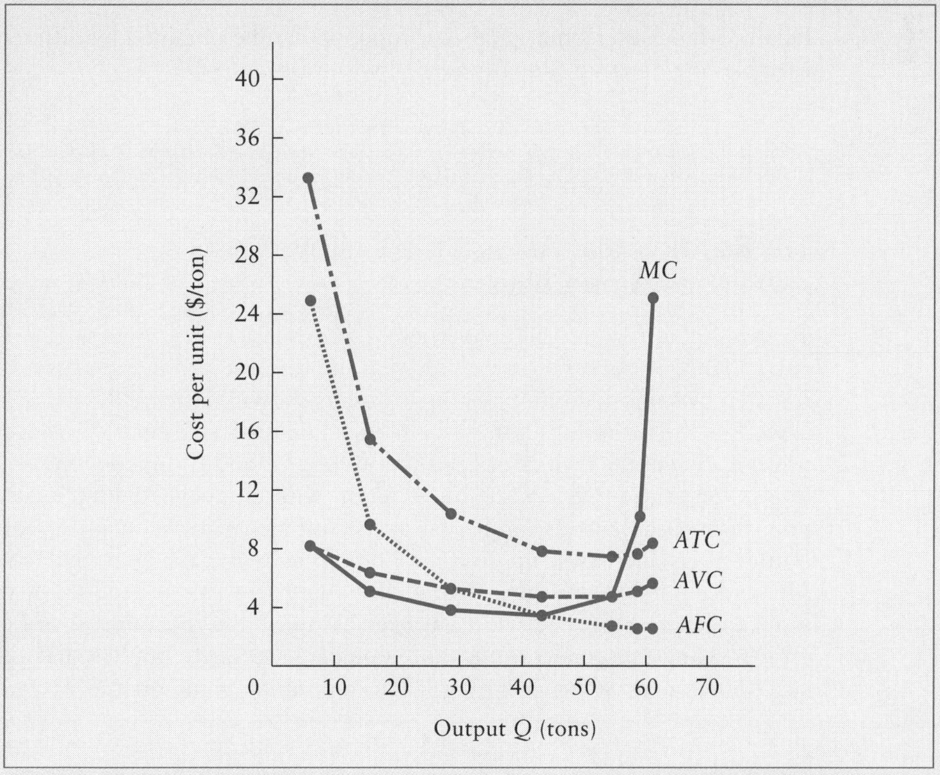

[4] Technically, the ratio $\Delta TC/\Delta Q$ represents the *incremental* cost associated with a discrete change in output by more than one unit rather than the *marginal* cost associated with *one* additional unit of output.

continually declining, note that all other average and marginal cost curves are U-shaped.

The Deep Creek example illustrated the derivation of the various cost functions when the cost data are given in the form of a schedule (tabular data). Consider another example where the cost information is represented in the form of an algebraic function. Suppose fixed costs for the Manchester Company are equal to \$100, and the company's variable costs are given by the following relationship (where Q = output):

$$VC = 60Q - 3Q^2 + 0.10Q^3 \qquad [8.10]$$

Given this information, one can derive the total cost function using Equation 8.2:

$$TC = 100 + 60Q - 3Q^2 + 0.10Q^3$$

Next, AFC, AVC, and ATC can be found using Equations 8.3, 8.4, and 8.5, respectively, as follows:

$$AFC = \frac{100}{Q}$$

$$AVC = 60 - 3Q + 0.10Q^2$$

$$ATC = \frac{100}{Q} + 60 - 3Q + 0.10Q^2$$

Finally, Manchester's marginal cost function can be obtained by differentiating the variable cost function (Equation 8.10) with respect to Q:

$$MC = \frac{d(VC)}{dQ} = 60 - 6Q + 0.30Q^2$$

The Relationships Among the Various Cost and Production Curves

To investigate further the properties of and relationships among the various cost and production curves, assume now that the cost and production curves can be represented by smooth continuous functions, as shown in Figure 8.3. Also assume that input L is the variable factor, with an associated variable cost VC; that the per-unit price of each of the factors of production (i.e., C_L and C_K) is *constant* over all usage levels; and that input K is the fixed factor, with an associated fixed cost FC. First, note that variable costs (and total costs) initially increase at a decreasing rate as output Q is increased up to Q_1. Correspondingly, the marginal cost function MC is declining. Over this range of output, the marginal product of the variable input L is increasing. Because it has been assumed that the unit cost of L is constant, an increasing marginal product for input L necessarily implies that the marginal cost function must be declining.[5] The minimum point on the MC curve at Q_1

[5] The relationship can be shown algebraically in the following way: MC is defined as $\Delta TC/\Delta Q$, which is also equal to $\Delta VC/\Delta Q$. ΔVC is equal to $C_L \Delta L$, where C_L is the unit cost of the variable input L. Thus, $MC = C_L(\Delta L/\Delta Q)$. However, the marginal product of input L, MP, was defined in Equation 7.2 as $\Delta Q/\Delta L$, or, in reciprocal form, $1/MP = \Delta L/\Delta Q$. Substituting $1/MP$ in the relationship for MC, we obtain $MC = C_L(1/MP)$. Because the marginal productivity of L is increasing, the marginal cost must be decreasing.

Figure 8.3 Short-Run Cost and Production Functions

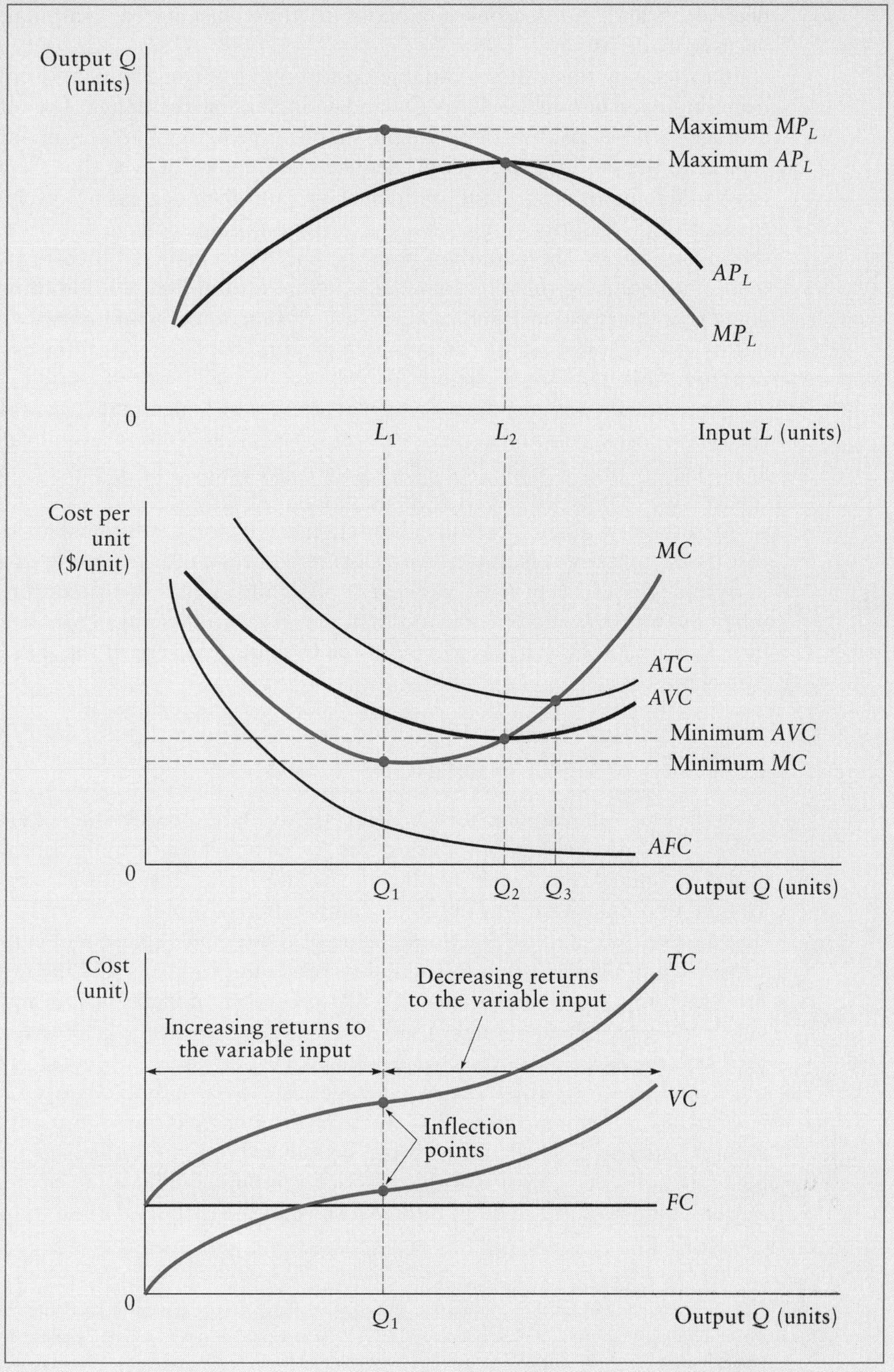

corresponds to the maximum point on the MP_L curve at L_1. Beyond Q_1, variable (and total) costs increase at an increasing rate and, correspondingly, the marginal cost curve is increasing. Over this range of output, the marginal product of L is decreasing and, for reasons analogous to those just noted, marginal cost must necessarily be rising.

In examining the average variable cost curve, AVC, in Figure 8.3, note that it is declining over output levels to Q_2 and is increasing thereafter. The shape of the average variable cost function, like the shape of the marginal cost function, is closely related to the production function defined in Chapter 7. Given that the unit cost of the variable input is constant, an increasing (and then decreasing) average product for input L necessarily implies that the average variable cost will be decreasing (and then increasing).[6] The minimum point on the AVC curve at Q_2 corresponds to the maximum point on the AP_L curve at L_2. Note also in Figure 8.3 that the marginal cost curve intersects the average variable cost function at its minimum value, which necessarily follows because the marginal product curve intersects the average product curve at its maximum value.

The average total cost curve, which is equal to the sum of the vertical heights of the average fixed cost and average variable cost curves, likewise initially declines and subsequently begins rising beyond some level of output. At a level of output of Q_3 the average total cost curve is at its minimum value.

As discussed in the previous chapter, specialization in the use of the variable resources initially results in increasing returns and declining average and marginal costs. Eventually, however, the gains from specialization are overwhelmed by crowding effects, and then marginal and average costs begin increasing. This reasoning is used to explain the U-shaped pattern of the ATC, AVC, and MC curves.

Long-Run Cost Functions

Over the long-run planning horizon, using the available production methods and technology, the firm can choose the plant size, types and sizes of equipment, labor skills, and raw materials that, when combined, yield the lowest cost of producing the desired amount of output. Once the optimum combination of inputs is chosen to produce the desired level of output at least cost, some of these inputs (plant and equipment) become fixed in the short run. If demand increases unexpectedly and the firm wishes to produce not Q_1, as planned, but rather Q_2 as shown in Figure 8.4, it may have little choice but to lay on additional variable inputs such as overtime labor and expedite the rush-order delivery of supplies to meet its production goals. Of course, such arrangements are expensive, and short-run average cost will temporarily rise to C_2'.

Should this demand persist, a larger fixed input investment in plant and equipment is warranted. Then, unit cost can be reduced to C_2. Another short-run average cost function, SAC_2, exists for this new set of inputs. In theory, an optimum combination of inputs and a minimum total cost exists for each level of output. Associated

[6] This relationship can be shown using the previously defined expressions for the average product AP and average variable cost AVC. AVC is equal to VC/Q. VC is equal to $C_L \cdot L$ where C_L is the unit cost of the variable input. Thus, $AVC = (C_L \cdot L)/Q$. The average product is defined as Q/L or, in reciprocal form, $1/AP = L/Q$. Substituting this form in the expression for AVC, we obtain $AVC = C_L(1/AP)$. Thus, if the average product is increasing, the average variable cost must be decreasing, and vice versa.

Figure 8.4 Long-Run and Short-Run Average Cost Functions

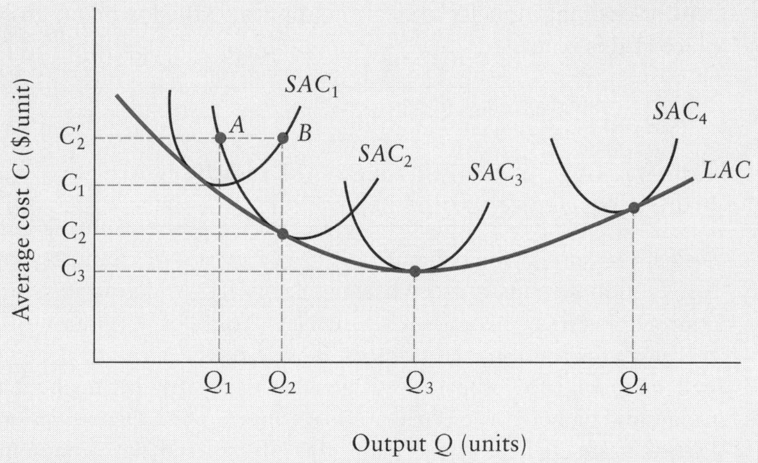

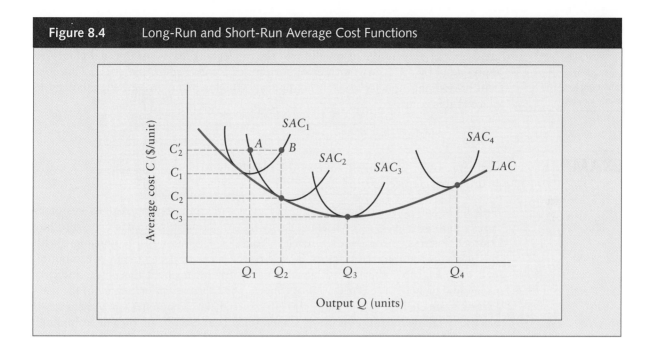

with the fixed inputs in each of these optimum combinations is a short-run average cost function. Several of these other short-run average cost functions (SAC_3, SAC_4) are shown in Figure 8.4. The long-run average cost function consists of the *lower boundary* or *envelope* of all these short-run curves. No other combination of inputs exists for producing each level of output Q at an average cost below the cost that is indicated by the LAC curve.[7]

Optimal Capacity Utilization: Three Concepts

Optimal Output for a Given Plant Size

Output rate that results in lowest average total cost for a given plant size.

Optimal Plant Size for a Given Output Rate

Plant size that results in lowest average total cost for a given output.

To assess capacity utilization, assume the firm has been producing Q_1 units of output using a plant of size "1," having a short-run average cost curve of SAC_1. The average cost of producing Q_1 units is therefore C_1, and Q_1 is the optimal output for the plant size represented by SAC_1. **Optimal output for a given plant size** is a short-run concept of capacity utilization.

Suppose that the firm now wishes to expand output to Q_2. What will the average cost be of producing this higher volume of output? In the short run, as we saw earlier, the average cost would be C_2'. However, in the long run, it would be possible for the firm to build a plant of size "2," having a short-run average cost curve of SAC_2. With this larger plant, the average cost of producing Q_2 units of output would be only C_2. Thus, because the firm has more options available to it in the long run, average total cost of any given output generally can be reduced. SAC_2 represents the **optimal plant size for a given output rate Q_2**.

[7] From the graph one can see that the long-run average cost of producing any given level of output, in general, does *not* occur at the point where short-run average costs are minimized. Only at the output level Q_3, corresponding to the minimum cost point on the *LAC* curve, does the long-run average cost equal the minimum short-run average cost.

However, if the firm can execute a marketing plan to sell still more output, a still more efficient allocation of resources is available. Only when optimal output increases to Q_3, where the firm will build the universally least-cost **optimal plant size** represented by SAC_3, will further opportunities for cost reduction cease. This concept of optimal capacity utilization applies to the long run, given the technology in place at this plant.

Optimal Plant Size
Plant size that achieves minimum long-run average total cost.

EXAMPLE

The Average Cost per Kilowatt Hour in Underutilized Power Plants[8]

Under pressure from regulators, the electric power industry opened its customer distribution systems to freewheeling electricity. A factory in Ohio can choose to buy contract electricity from Michigan, New York, or Virginia power companies. With the new competition, the price of electricity is certain to decline, and consumption will increase. However, excess capacity is present in much of the power industry today, and higher-cost electric utilities will soon find themselves priced out of the market. As more efficient power plants are constructed, some estimates show the price of electricity falling by 1.8 cents using conventional coal-fired steam turbine technology and by as much as 3.0 cents using nuclear and other technologies. These savings imply an \$18.00 to \$30.00 reduction per month in the residential electricity bill for a customer who switches to the lower-cost firms.

The flip side, however, is that firms left behind will find themselves with "stranded costs" too high to retain customers, yet too low to shutter the facility and close the power plant. Instead, such underutilized plants will likely come on line during peak demand and at other times be relegated to stand-by status. Unfortunately, this underutilization will raise the already-high average cost per kilowatt hour (say, C_2 at Q_2 on SAC_2), still further to C_2' at the lower output Q_1 on SAC_1 in Figure 8.4.

Short-run average total cost with underutilization of capacity at Point A or overutilization of capacity at Point B in Figure 8.4 is always higher than the minimum average total cost in the long run (LAC) when the production manager can vary plant and equipment, matching capacity to his or her output requirements. The LAC can be obtained using the **expansion path** of input combinations that satisfy the condition:

Expansion Path
The input combinations that minimize cost for a given level of output.

$$\frac{MP_L}{C_L} = \frac{MP_K}{C_K} \qquad [8.11]$$

As shown in Figure 8.5, the expansion path can be represented by a line that connects these various tangency points between the isoquants and isocost lines, and the

[8] Based on M. Maloney, R. McCormick, and R. Sauer, *Customer Choice, Consumer Value: An Analysis of Retail Competition in America's Electric Industry* (Washington, DC: Citizens for a Sound Economy, 1996).

Figure 8.5 Expansion Path

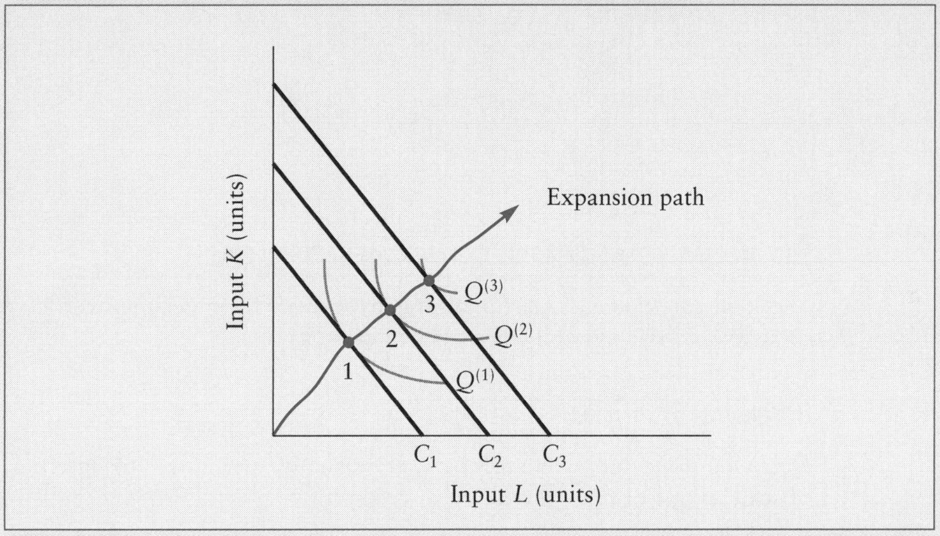

Figure 8.6 Long-Run Total Cost Function

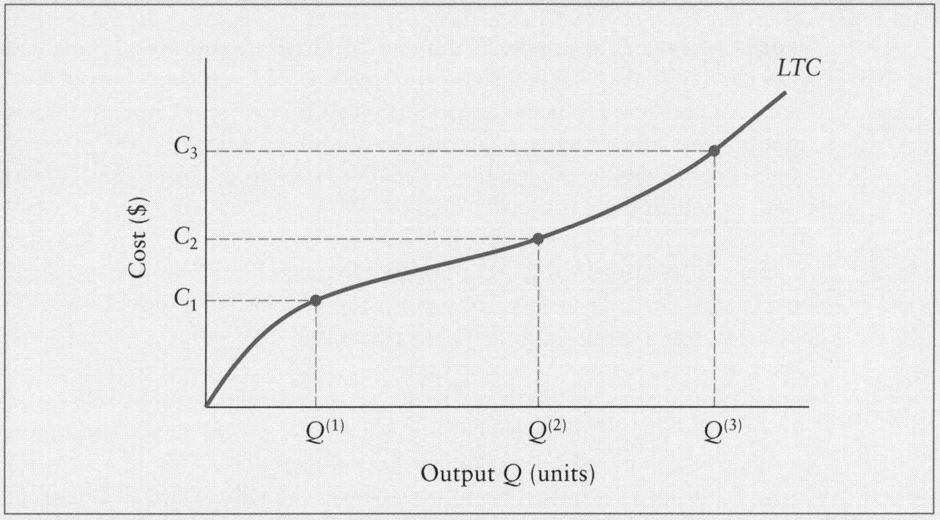

long-run total cost function can be obtained from the corresponding cost and output values. Thus, for example, from Point 1 in Figure 8.5 one obtains the cost-output combination (C_1, $Q^{(1)}$), which is then plotted in Figure 8.6.

The cost-output combinations (C_2, $Q^{(2)}$) and (C_3, $Q^{(3)}$) are obtained in a similar manner. Connecting these points yields the long-run total cost (*LTC*) curve shown in

Figure 8.6. The long-run average cost (LAC) and long-run marginal cost (LMC) curves are defined and calculated in a manner similar to their short-run counterparts:[9]

$$LAC = \frac{LTC}{Q} \quad [8.12]$$

$$LMC = \frac{\Delta LTC}{\Delta Q} \quad [8.13]$$

ECONOMIES AND DISECONOMIES OF SCALE

The long-run *average* cost function is hypothesized to decline over lower ranges of capacity and rise over higher ranges of capacity.

INTERNAL ECONOMIES OF SCALE

Internal Economies of Scale
Declining long-run average costs as the rate of output for a product, plant, or firm is increased.

Declining long-run average costs are usually attributed to **internal economies of scale** at one of three levels:

- *Product-level economies*: Internal economies of scale related to the output of one product.
- *Plant-level economies*: Internal economies of scale related to the total output (of multiple products) of one plant.
- *Firm-level economies*: Internal economies of scale related to the total output of a firm's operations.

PRODUCT-LEVEL ECONOMIES A number of different sources of scale economies are associated with producing larger volumes of a single product. Special-purpose equipment, which is more efficient in performing a limited set of operations, can be substituted for less efficient general-purpose equipment. Likewise, the production process can be broken down into a series of smaller tasks, and workers can be assigned to the tasks for which they are most qualified. Workers are then able to acquire additional proficiency through higher repetition of the tasks to which they are assigned.

Learning Curve Effect
Declining unit cost attributable to greater cumulative volume.

External Economy of Scale
Volume discounts in purchasing inputs.

In manufacturing, a related phenomenon called the **learning curve effect** is often observed; that is, the amount of labor input required to produce each unit of output decreases for successive increases in the cumulative volume of output (e.g., during long production runs of 767 airframes at Boeing). In general, internal economies of scale can be distinguished from learning curve effects or volume discounts (so-called **external economies of scale**) because the latter always result from increases in the cumulative volume of output no matter how small the output rate per time period. As such, they may well not be associated with any change in scale. Instead, purchasing manages may be simply buying inputs less frequently in bigger order sizes. The learning curve concept is discussed further in Appendix 9A.

PLANT-LEVEL ECONOMIES Sources of scale economies at the plant level include capital investment, overhead, and required reserves of maintenance parts and personnel.

[9] Alternatively, the long-run cost function can be derived algebraically from the production function. Such a derivation for the Cobb-Douglas production function is examined in Appendix 8A.

With respect to *capital investment,* capital costs tend to increase less than proportionately with the productive capacity of a plant, particularly in process-type industries. For example, consider oil pipeline operations. A pipeline with twice the radius of another pipeline can be constructed for perhaps as little as twice the cost, yet have four times the capacity (i.e., $\pi(2r)^2 = 4\pi r^2$ versus πr^2) of the smaller one.

EXAMPLE

IBM AND INTEL FABRICATE MONSTER SILICON WAFERS[10]

The semiconductor industry produces thin wafers of silicon and then etches them with electrical circuit lines 1/1000th the width of a human hair in superclean "wafer fab" factories. Such intermediate products are then sliced and diced into the tiny memory chips in our PCs and PDAs. One 12-inch wafer yields enough memory chips to store 5,000 sets of the *Encyclopaedia Britannica*. Until recently, the standard wafer measured about 8 inches across and cost $5,500 to produce in a $1.4 billion wafer fab. New monster wafers are almost 12 inches across, cost $8,000 to produce in $2 billion wafer fabs but their 125 percent greater surface area yields 575 chips per wafer as opposed to only 240 chips from the standard 8-inch wafer. That is, for a 45 percent increase in cost, the monster wafers yield 140 percent more chips than the standard wafer. As a result, the unit cost of a chip falls to $14 from $23.

Internal scale economies can also be realized in equipment maintenance. *Reserves of replacement parts and maintenance personnel* needed to deal with randomly occurring equipment breakdowns normally increase less than proportionately with increases in the size of the plant. Finally, another source of scale economies is overhead costs, which include such items as administrative costs (e.g., management salaries) and other indirect expenditures (e.g., paperwork documentation associated with regulatory compliance costs). Overhead costs can be spread over a higher volume of output in a larger plant or facility, thus reducing average costs per unit.

EXAMPLE

REFUSE COLLECTION AND DISPOSAL IN ORANGE COUNTY

Private for-profit trash collectors in California have demonstrated the scale economies of landfills. The environmental safety issues at a landfill require enormous investment in environmental impact studies, lining the site, monitoring for seepage and leeching of toxins, and scientific follow-up studies. Spreading these overhead costs across a larger rate of output has led an Orange County company to seek refuse as far away as the northern suburbs of San Diego, almost an hour down the California coast. The trucks from Orange County pass right by several municipal landfills en route. However, the fees charged for dumping at these intermediate sites are much higher. Apparently, the variable transportation costs of hauling a ton of trash prove to be less than the higher start-up costs and environmental monitoring costs per ton at smaller-scale landfills. By state law, all of these municipalities must charge a dumping fee that covers their fully allocated cost, so reduced long-run average total cost provides a substantial price advantage for the large-scale Orange County site.

[10] Based on "Chips on Monster Wafers," *BusinessWeek* (November 4, 2002), pp. 112–126.

Firm-Level Economies In addition to product-level and plant-level economies of scale, other scale economies are associated with the overall size of the firm. Often these latter scale economies can only be realized by the large multiproduct, multiplant firm. One possible source of firm-level scale economies is in *distribution*. For example, multiplant operations may permit a larger firm to maintain geographically dispersed plants. Delivery costs are often lower for a geographically dispersed multiplant operation compared with one (larger) plant.

Another possible source of scale economies to the firm is in *raising capital funds*. Because flotation costs increase less than proportionately with the size of the security (stock or bond) issue, average flotation costs per dollar of funds raised is smaller for larger firms. Similar scale economies also exist in *marketing and sales promotion*. These scale economies can take such forms as (1) quantity discounts in securing advertising media space and time, or (2) the ability of the large firm to spread the fixed costs of advertising preparation over greater output. In addition, the large firm may be able to achieve a relatively greater degree of brand recognition and brand loyalty for any given level of sales promotion expenditures.

A final source of firm-level scale economies is in *technological innovation*. Unlike smaller firms, large firms can afford sizable research and development (R&D) laboratories and costly specialized equipment and research personnel. Also, the large firm is better able to undertake a diversified portfolio of R&D projects and can thus reduce the risk associated with the failure of any one (or small number) of the projects. The smaller firm, in contrast, may be unwilling to undertake a large R&D project, because failure of the project could result in bankruptcy.

EXAMPLE

Economies of Scale: Superscale Money-Center Versus Community Banks

The number of large money-center banks—banks that are 1,000 times larger than the typical community bank in smaller towns and cities—is growing in the United States. Shaffer and David examined the economies of scale in these superscale banks, which range in size from \$2.5 billion to \$120.6 billion in assets.[11] Their results indicate that long-run average costs decline until superscale banks range between \$15 billion and \$37 billion in assets. The superscale banks have come to dominate credit card issuance, corporate lending, and custodial asset management (see Figure 8.7), perhaps because of the massive information technology investments required in these businesses. In contrast, community banks thrift institutions, and credit unions dominate retail banking, where diseconomies of scale (rising long-run average costs) set in beyond \$50 million in assets.[12]

Diseconomies of Scale

Diseconomies of Scale
Rising long-run average costs as the level of output is increased.

Rising long-run average costs at higher rates of output are attributed to **diseconomies of scale.** A primary source of diseconomies of scale associated with an

[11] S. Shaffer and E. David, "Economies of Superscale in Commercial Banking," *Applied Economics* 23 (1991), pp. 283–293.

[12] T. Gilligan, M. Smirlock, and W. Marshall, "Scale and Scope Economies in the Multi-Product Banking Firm," *Journal of Monetary Economics* 13 (1984), pp. 393–405.

Figure 8.7 Bank Market Shares in Four Businesses, 2000

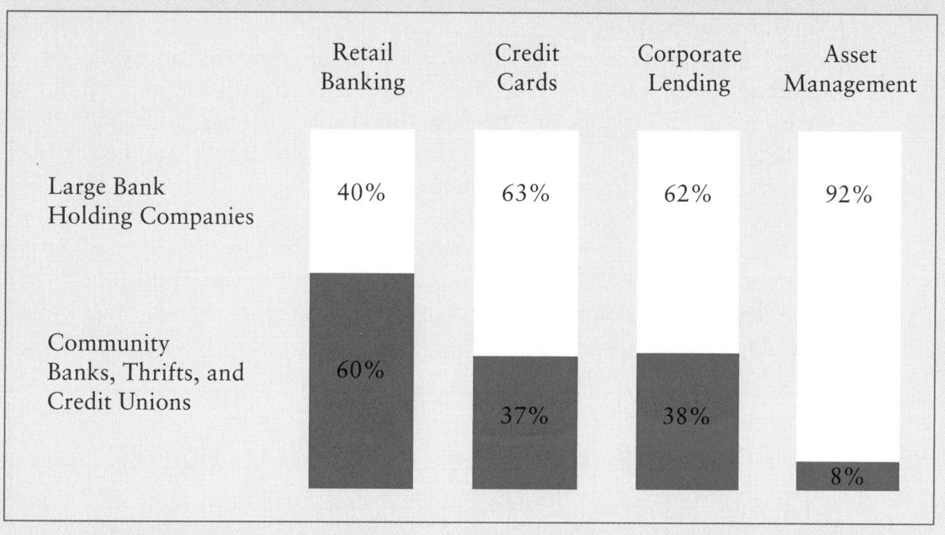

Source: *Wall Street Journal* (April 23, 2001), p. B12.

individual production plant is *transportation costs.* Another possible source of plant diseconomies is labor requirements; higher wage rates or costly worker recruiting and relocation programs may be required to attract the necessary personnel, particularly if the plant is located in a sparsely populated area. Finally, large-scale plants are often inflexible operations designed for long production runs of one product, based often on forecasts of what the target market wanted in the past.

Diseconomies of scale at the firm level result from problems of coordination and control encountered by management as the scale of operations is increased. First, the size of management staffs and their associated salary costs may rise more than proportionately as the scale of the firm is increased. Also, less direct and observable costs may occur, such as the losses arising from delayed or faulty decisions and weakened or distorted managerial incentives. Contemporary examples of these problems include General Motors and AT&T.

EXAMPLE

Flexibility and Operating Efficiency: Ford Motor Company's Flat Rock Plant[13]

Ford Motor Company spent an estimated $200 million in the early 1970s to construct a massive plant in Flat Rock, Michigan, to build cast iron engine blocks. The plant produced V8 blocks exclusively on five ultra-high-speed assembly lines at the rate of 8,000 engine blocks per day. In the 1980s, however, Ford executives decided to close the Flat Rock plant and move production to an older Cleveland engine block plant. Ford's Cleveland plant had ten smaller and slower production

[13] Based on articles in *The Economist* (January 11, 2001), p. 58; *AI* (February 1998); and *Wall Street Journal* (September 16, 1981).

lines; the Cleveland plant was clearly the less efficient of the two factories. However, Ford executives realized it would cost less to convert Cleveland's smaller production lines to the new high-performance six- and four-cylinder engines that had become popular.

When Flat Rock was designed, Ford could count on long V8 production runs of perhaps 1 million units of its most popular Ford Mustang model. But in the 1980s, variety in the product line became the key business strategy. By 1998, Ford's top-selling Explorer (383,852 units), Taurus (357,162 units), and Escort (283,898 units) reflected the fragmented auto marketplace. Only the F-series pickup (746,111 units) warranted Flat Rock's massive scale. As George Booth, iron-operations manager for the casting division at Ford, explained, "Flat Rock was built to make a few parts at very high volumes. But the plant turned out to be very inflexible for conversion to making new types and different sizes of engine blocks. Sometimes you really can be too big."

The Overall Effects of Scale Economies and Diseconomies

For some industries, such as textile and furniture manufacturing, long-run average costs for the firm remain constant over a wide range of output once scale economies are exhausted. In such cases, many plant sizes are consistent with least-cost production, as shown in Figure 8.8. In other industries (e.g., steel ingot production and engine block casting), long-run average costs rise at a large scale. The possible presence of both economies and diseconomies of scale leads to the hypothesized long-run average cost function for a typical manufacturing firm being U-shaped with a flat middle area. Up to some **minimum efficient scale (MES)**, that is, the smallest scale at which minimum long-run average total costs are attained, economies of scale are present. In most industries, it is possible to increase the size of the firm beyond this MES without incurring diseconomies of scale. Over this range, average costs per unit

Minimum Efficient Scale (MES)
The smallest scale at which minimum costs per unit are attained.

INTERNATIONAL PERSPECTIVES

How Japanese Companies Deal with the Problems of Size[14]

Many large, successful U.S. corporations, such as General Electric, Hewlett-Packard, Sara Lee, and Johnson & Johnson, are attempting to deal with the problems of excessive size by decentralizing their operations. These companies did so by setting up independent business units, each with its own profit-and-loss responsibility, thereby giving managers more flexibility and freedom in decision making.

Like their counterparts in the United States, Japanese corporations are often collections of hundreds of individual companies. For example, Matsushita Electrical Industrial Company consists of 161 consolidated units. Another example is Hitachi, Ltd., which is composed of 660 companies, with the stock of 27 of these companies being publicly traded. James Abegglen, an expert on Japanese management, has observed that "As something new comes along . . . it gets moved out to a subsidiary so the elephant does not roll over and smother it. If all goes well, it becomes a successful company on its own. If not, it gets pulled back in."

[14] Based on an article entitled "Is Your Company Too Big?" *BusinessWeek* (March 17, 1989), pp. 84–94.

Figure 8.8 Long-Run Average Cost Function and Scale Economies

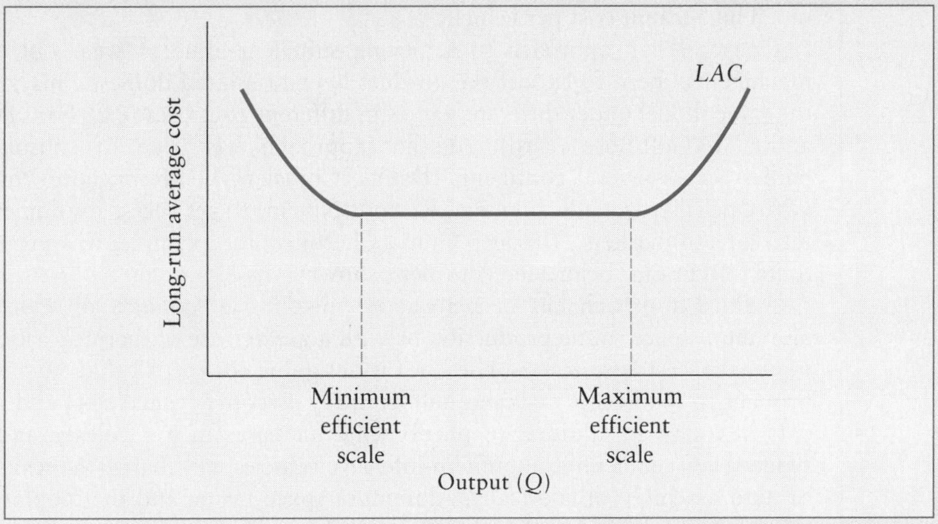

are relatively constant. However, expansion beyond the maximum efficient scale eventually will result in problems of inflexibility, lack of managerial coordination, and rising long-run average costs.

EXAMPLE

Aluminum-Intensive Vehicle Lowers the Minimum Efficient Scale at Ford[15]

For decades, the largest fixed asset on the auto assembly line has been a $30 million body-stamping machine. This massive piece of capital equipment bends sheet metal into hoods, trunks, and fenders and hydraulically presses steel plate into floor pan and door pillar shapes. Because a body-stamping machine has a physical working life of 600,000 vehicles, it has been the source of substantial scale economies in the production of most auto models. Only the top-selling Ford Focus (902,008), F-series pickup (869,001), VW Golf (795,835), Opel Astra (770,003), Chevy pickup (644,084) had sufficient sales volume in 1999 to fully depreciate a body-stamping machine within the model year. Most moderately successful auto models sell fewer than 100,000 units per year. Therefore, a six-year period is required to physically "wear out" a body-stamping machine as it makes repetitive presses for a typical model.

Should Ford change body shapes and structural components every two to three years to keep their model "current"? Or should they forgo the body style changes

[15] Based on "Aluminum Cars," *The Economist* (April 15, 2000), p. 89; *Consumer Report* (April 1997), p. 26; "The Global Gambles of GM," *The Economist* (June 24, 2000), p. 67; and "Daimler-Chrysler Merger," *Wall Street Journal* (May 8, 1998), p. A10.

and fully depreciate their body-stamping machines over a six-year period or longer? The former decision necessitates scrapping a machine with substantial physical working life remaining and recovering the capital equipment investment with a much higher unit cost per vehicle.

One common approach to achieving sufficient scale to wear out a stamping machine has been to export the product beyond limited domestic markets and sell the same model under different names in different countries (e.g., Ford Focus/Fiesta and VW Golf/Bora/Vento). Another approach has been to consolidate companies across several continents (DaimlerChrysler-Mitsubishi, Ford-Volvo-Mazda, GM-Opel-Fiat-Isuzu-Suzuki, and Renault-Nissan) to get access for domestic models into foreign markets. The Jeep Grand Cherokee, for example, was projected to do quite well in European Mercedes-Benz showrooms.

A third approach has been to avoid this classic economy of scale issue with aluminum space frame production or with a greater use of thermoplastics. The aluminum space-frame automobile Ford is designing (or the A2 that Audi has already brought to market) is not even half as heavy as conventional steel and sheet metal cars of today. In addition to phenomenal increases in gas mileage and markedly reduced CO_2 emissions, aluminum-intensive vehicles will change the scale economies of auto assembly dramatically. Aluminum space frame and thermoplastic components are cast, forged, and extruded into different thicknesses depending upon where strength is needed. Neither require a body stamping machine.

Although an aluminum space frame vehicle is 10 percent more costly on average than the typical steel and sheet metal vehicle, the minimum efficient scale of an aluminum-intensive auto assembly process is only 50,000 cars. As illustrated in Figure 8.9, a marketing plan for smaller volume niche products such as the Ford Mustang, Pontiac Firebird, and Jeep Wrangler can achieve minimum efficient scale at Point *A* with these new aluminum production techniques. Previously with sheet metal and steel automobiles, production runs at this reduced scale would have

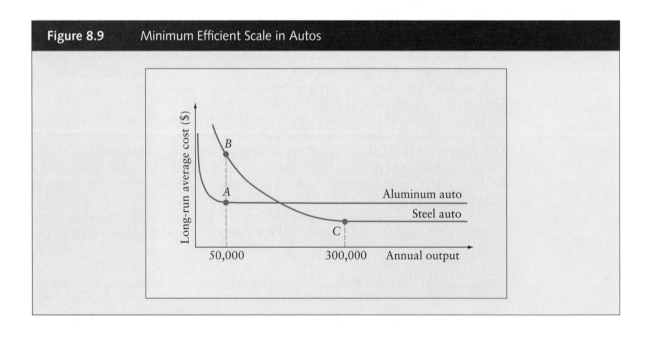

Figure 8.9 Minimum Efficient Scale in Autos

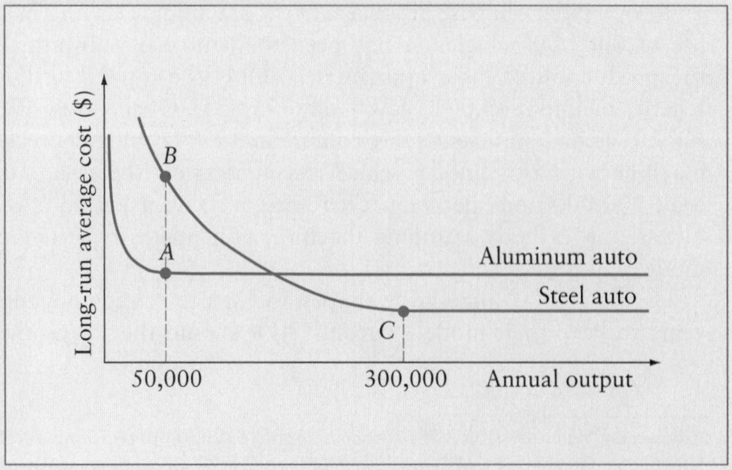

resulted in unit costs at Point *B*, more than twice as high as those of a 300,000-unit vehicle such as the VW Passat (322,493); compare Point *C* in Figure 8.9. Cost discrepancies this great can seldom be overcome no matter how popular the design. By moving to thermoplastic and aluminum components, niche vehicles can remain cost competitive.

SUMMARY

- *Cost* is defined as the sacrifice incurred whenever an exchange or transformation of resources takes place.
- Different approaches are used in measuring costs, depending on the purposes for which the information is to be used. For financial reporting purposes, the historical outlay of funds is usually the appropriate measure of cost, whereas for decision-making purposes, it is often appropriate to measure cost in terms of the opportunities forgone or sacrificed.
- A *cost function* is a schedule, graph, or mathematical relationship showing the minimum achievable cost (such as total, average, or marginal cost) of producing various quantities of output.
- Short-run *total costs* are equal to the sum of *fixed* and *variable costs.*
- *Marginal cost* is defined as the incremental increase in total cost that results from a one-unit increase in output.
- The short-run average variable and marginal cost functions of economic theory are hypothesized to be U-shaped, first falling and then rising as output is increased. Falling short-run unit costs are attributed to the gains available from specialization in the use of capital and labor. Rising short-run unit costs are attributed to diminishing returns in production.
- The theoretical long-run average cost function is often found to be L-shaped due to the frequent presence of scale economies and frequent absence of scale diseconomies. *Economies of scale* are attributed primarily to the nature of the production process or the factor markets, whereas *diseconomies of scale* are attributed primarily to problems of coordination and inflexibility in large-scale organizations.
- Volume discounts in purchasing inputs and learning curve effects, both of which result from a larger cumulative volume of output, can be distinguished from scale effects, which depend on the firm's rate of output per time period. Learning curve advantages often, therefore, arise in small-scale plants able to make long production runs.
- *Minimum efficient scale* is achieved by a rate of output sufficient to reduce long-run average total cost to the minimum possible level. Smaller rates of output imply smaller plant sizes to reduce unit cost, albeit to higher levels than would be possible if a firm's business plan could support minimum efficient scale production.

Exercises

Answers to the exercises in blue can be found in Appendix C at the back of the book.

1. Kay Evans just completed her B.S. degree and is considering pursuing doctoral (Ph.D.) studies in economics. If Kay takes a job immediately after graduation, she can earn $35,000 during the first year, with an anticipated raise of $4,000 per year over the next five years. If Kay pursues the doctorate, five more years of school are required. Kay has been offered an assistantship paying $9,500 per year plus tuition. Books and computer purchases needed for her study will cost an average of $1,500 per year. These costs will not be incurred if Kay takes a job immediately. Upon graduation, Kay expects an annual income level of $55,000 during her first year of teaching. The growth rate in Kay's teaching salary is expected to equal the growth rate of the income she would make if she did not pursue the Ph.D. How should Kay evaluate her decision to pursue a Ph.D.? What other information do you need? What factors other than salary should be considered?
2. US Airways owns a piece of land near the Pittsburgh International Airport. The land originally cost US Airways $375,000. The airline is considering building a new training center on this land. US Airways determined that the proposal to build the new facility

is acceptable if the original cost of the land is used in the analysis, but the proposal does not meet the airline's project acceptance criteria if the land cost is above \$850,000. A developer recently offered US Airways \$2.5 million for the land. Should US Airways build the training facility at this location?

3. Howard Bowen is a large-scale cotton farmer. The land and machinery he owns has a current market value of \$4 million. Bowen owes his local bank \$3 million. Last year Bowen sold \$5 million worth of cotton. His variable operating costs were \$4.5 million; accounting depreciation was \$40,000, although the actual decline in value of Bowen's machinery was \$60,000 last year. Bowen paid himself a salary of \$50,000, which is not considered part of his variable operating costs. Interest on his bank loan was \$400,000. If Bowen worked for another farmer or a local manufacturer, his annual income would be about \$30,000. Bowen can invest any funds that would be derived, if the farm were sold, to earn 10 percent annually. (Ignore taxes.)
   a. Compute Bowen's accounting profits.
   b. Compute Bowen's economic profits.
4. Mary Graham worked as a real estate agent for Piedmont Properties for 15 years. Her annual income is approximately \$100,000 per year. Mary is considering establishing her own real estate agency. She expects to generate revenues during the first year of \$2 million. Salaries paid to her employees are expected to total \$1.5 million. Operating expenses (i.e., rent, supplies, utility services) are expected to total \$250,000. To begin the business, Mary must borrow \$500,000 from her bank at an interest rate of 15 percent. Equipment will cost Mary \$50,000. At the end of one year, the value of this equipment will be \$30,000, even though the depreciation expense for tax purposes is only \$5,000 during the first year.
   a. Determine the (pretax) accounting profit for this venture.
   b. Determine the (pretax) economic profit for this venture.
   c. Which of the costs for this firm are explicit and which are implicit?
5. From your knowledge of the relationships among the various cost functions, complete the following table.

Q	*TC*	*FC*	*VC*	*ATC*	*AFC*	*AVC*	*MC*
0	125						
10							5
20				10.50			
30			110				
40	255						
50						3	
60							3
70				5			
80			295				

6. Economists at General Industries have been examining operating costs at one of its parts manufacturing plants in an effort to determine whether the plant is being operated efficiently. From weekly cost records, the economists developed the following cost-output information concerning the operation of the plant:
   a. *AVC* (average variable cost) at an output of 2,000 units per week is \$7.50.
   b. At an output level of 5,000 units per week, *AFC* (average fixed cost) is \$3.
   c. *TC* (total cost) increases by \$5,000 when output is increased from 2,000 to 3,000 units per week.
   d. *TVC* (total variable cost) at an output level of 4,000 units per week is \$23,000.

e. *AVC* (average variable cost) decreases by \$0.75 per unit when output is increased from 4,000 to 5,000 units per week.

f. *AFC* plus *AVC* for 8,000 units per week is \$7.50 per unit.

g. *ATC* (average total cost) decreases by \$0.50 per unit when output is decreased from 8,000 to 7,000 units per week.

h. *TVC* increases by \$3,000 when output is increased from 5,000 to 6,000 units per week.

i. *TC* decreases by \$7,000 when output is decreased from 2,000 to 1,000 units per week.

j. *MC* (marginal cost) is \$16 per unit when output is increased from 8,000 to 9,000 units per week.

Given the preceding information, complete the following cost schedule for the plant. (*Hint:* Proceed sequentially through the list, filling in all the related entries before proceeding to the next item of information in the list.)

Output (Units Per Week)	*TFC*	*TVC*	*TC*	*AFC*	*AVC*	*ATC*	*MC*
0				x	x	x	x
1,000							
2,000							
3,000							
4,000							
5,000							
6,000							
7,000							
8,000							
9,000							

7. A manufacturing plant has a potential production capacity of 1,000 units per month (capacity can be increased by 10% if subcontractors are employed). The plant is normally operated at about 80 percent of capacity. Operating the plant above this level significantly increases variable costs per unit because of the need to pay the skilled workers higher overtime wage rates. For output levels up to 80 percent of capacity, variable cost per unit is \$100. Above 80 and up to 90 percent, variable costs on this additional output increase by 10 percent. When output is above 90 and up to 100 percent of capacity, the additional units cost an additional 25 percent over the unit variable costs for outputs up to 80 percent of capacity. For production above 100 percent and up to 110 percent of capacity, extensive subcontracting work is used and the unit variable costs of these additional units are 50 percent above those at output levels up to 80 percent of capacity. At 80 percent of capacity, the plant's fixed costs per unit are \$50. Total fixed costs are not expected to change within the production range under consideration. Based on the preceding information, complete the following table.

Q	*TC*	*FC*	*VC*	*ATC*	*AFC*	*AVC*	*MC*
500							
600							
700							
800							
900							
1,000							
1,100							

8. The Blair Company's three assembly plants are located in California, Georgia, and New Jersey. Previously, the company purchased a major subassembly, which becomes part of the final product, from an outside firm. Blair has decided to manufacture the subassemblies within the company and must now consider whether to rent one centrally located facility (e.g., in Missouri, where all the subassemblies would be manufactured) or to rent three separate facilities, each located near one of the assembly plants, where each facility would manufacture only the subassemblies needed for the nearby assembly plant. A single, centrally located facility, with a production capacity of 18,000 units per year, would have fixed costs of $900,000 per year and a variable cost of $250 per unit. Three separate decentralized facilities, with production capacities of 8,000, 6,000, and 4,000 units per year, would have fixed costs of $475,000, $425,000, and $400,000, respectively, and variable costs per unit of only $225 per unit, owing primarily to the reduction in shipping costs. The current production rates at the three assembly plants are 6,000, 4,500, and 3,000 units, respectively.

   a. Assuming that the current production rates are maintained at the three assembly plants, which alternative should management select?
   b. If demand for the final product were to increase to production capacity, which alternative would be more attractive?
   c. What additional information would be useful before making a decision?

9. Kitchen Helper Company decides to produce and sell food blenders and is considering three different types of production facilities ("plants"). Plant A is a labor-intensive facility, employing relatively little specialized capital equipment. Plant B is a semiautomated facility that would employ less labor than A but would also have higher capital equipment costs. Plant C is a completely automated facility using much more high-cost, high-technology capital equipment and even less labor than B. Information about the operating costs and production capacities of these three different types of plants is shown in the following table.

	Plant Type		
	A	B	C
Unit variable costs			
Materials	$3.50	$3.25	$3.00
Labor	4.50	3.25	2.00
Overhead	1.00	1.50	2.00
Total	$9.00	$8.00	$7.00
Annual fixed costs			
Depreciation	$ 60,000	$100,000	$200,000
Capital	30,000	50,000	100,000
Overhead	60,000	100,000	150,000
Total	$150,000	$250,000	$450,000
Annual capacity	75,000	150,000	350,000

   a. Determine the average total cost schedules for each plant type for annual outputs of 25,000, 50,000, 75,000, . . . , 350,000. For output levels beyond the capacity of a given plant, assume that multiple plants of the same type are built. For example, to produce 200,000 units with Plant A, three of these plants would be built.
   b. Based on the cost schedules calculated in part (a), construct the long-run average total cost schedule for the production of blenders.

10. The ARA Railroad owns a piece of land along one of its right-of-ways. The land originally cost ARA $100,000. ARA is considering building a new maintenance facility on this land. ARA determined that the proposal to build the new facility is acceptable if the original cost of the land is used in the analysis, but the proposal does not meet the railroad's project acceptance criteria if the land cost is above $500,000. An investor has recently offered ARA $1 million for the land. Should ARA build the maintenance facility at this location?

CASE EXERCISE

COST ANALYSIS

The Leisure Products (LP) Company manufactures lawn and patio furniture. Most of its output is sold to do-it-yourself warehouse stores (e.g., Lowe's Home Improvement) and to retail hardware and department store chains (e.g., True Value and JCPenney), who then distribute the products under their respective brand names. LP is not involved in direct retail sales. Last year the firm had sales of $35 million.

One of LP's divisions manufactures folding (aluminum and vinyl) chairs. Sales of the chairs are highly seasonal, with 80 percent of the sales volume concentrated in the January–June period. Production is normally concentrated in the September–May period. Approximately 75 percent of the hourly workforce (unskilled and semiskilled workers) is laid off (or takes paid vacation time) during the June–August period of reduced output. The remainder of the workforce, consisting of salaried plant management (line managers and supervisors), maintenance, and clerical staff, are retained during this slow period. Maintenance personnel, for example, perform major overhauls of the machinery during the slow summer period.

LP planned to produce and sell 500,000 of these chairs during the coming year at a projected selling price of $7.15 per chair. The cost per unit was estimated as follows:

Direct labor	$2.25
Materials	2.30
Plant overhead*	1.15
Administrative and selling expense*	0.80
TOTAL	$6.50

*These costs are allocated to each unit of output based on the projected annual production of 500,000 chairs.

A 10 percent markup ($0.65) was added to the cost per unit in arriving at the firm's selling price of $7.15 (plus shipping).

In May, LP received an inquiry from Southeast Department Stores concerning the possible purchase of folding chairs for delivery in August. Southeast indicated that they would place an order for 30,000 chairs if the price did not exceed $5.50 each (plus shipping). The chairs could be produced during the slow period using the firm's existing equipment and workforce. No overtime wages would have to be paid to the workforce in fulfilling the order. Adequate materials were on hand (or could be purchased at prevailing market prices) to complete the order.

LP management was considering whether to accept the order. The firm's chief accountant felt that the firm should *not* accept the order because the price per chair was less than the total cost and contributed nothing to the firm's profits. The firm's chief economist argued that the firm should accept the order *if* the incremental revenue would exceed the incremental cost.

The following cost accounting definitions may be helpful in making this decision:

- Direct labor: Labor costs incurred in converting the raw material into the finished product.
- Material: Raw materials that enter into and become part of the final product.
- Plant overhead: All costs other than direct labor and materials that are associated with the product, including wages and salaries paid to employees who do not work directly on the product but whose services are related to the production process (line managers, maintenance, and janitorial personnel); heat; light; power; supplies; depreciation; taxes; and insurance on the assets employed in the production process.
- Selling and distribution costs: Costs incurred in making sales (e.g., billing and salespeople's compensation), storing the product, and shipping the product to the customer. (In this case the customer pays all shipping costs.)
- Administrative costs: Items not listed in the preceding categories, including general and executive office costs, research, development, engineering costs, and miscellaneous items.

QUESTIONS

1. Calculate the incremental, or marginal, cost per chair to LP of accepting the order from Southeast.
2. What assumptions did you make in calculating the incremental cost in Question 1? What additional information would be helpful in making these calculations?
3. Based on your answers to Questions 1 and 2, should LP accept the Southeast order?
4. What additional considerations might lead LP to reject the order?

APPENDIX

8a

Long-Run Costs with a Cobb-Douglas Production Function

In Chapter 8, the shape of the firm's long-run unit cost structure (the *LAC*) was shown to depend on whether economies or diseconomies of scale were present. *A priori* hypotheses about the shape of the firm's *LAC* can be derived, before examining cost data, by postulating a production function for the firm. Consider the Cobb-Douglas production function

$$Q = \alpha L^{\beta_1} K^{\beta_2} \quad [8A.1]$$

where L is the amount of labor, K is the amount of capital used in producing Q units of output, and α, β_1, and β_2 are constants. The total cost of employing L units of labor and K units of capital in a production process is equal to

$$C = C_L L + C_K K \quad [8A.2]$$

where C_L and C_K are the per-unit prices of labor and capital, respectively. Using Lagrangian multiplier techniques, one can determine the total cost (C) of producing any level of output.

The objective is to minimize the total cost (C) of producing a given level of output $Q = Q_0$. We begin by forming the Lagrangian function

$$L_C = C + \lambda(Q - Q_0) \quad [8A.3]$$

$$= C_L L + C_K K + \lambda(\alpha L^{\beta_1} K^{\beta_2} - Q_0) \quad [8A.4]$$

Differentiating L_C with respect to L, K, and λ and setting these derivatives equal to zero yields:

$$\frac{\partial L_C}{\partial L} = C_L + \lambda(\beta_1 \alpha L^{\beta_1 - 1} K^{\beta_2}) = 0 \quad [8A.5]$$

$$\frac{\partial L_C}{\partial K} = C_K + \lambda(\beta_2 \alpha L^{\beta_1} K^{\beta_2 - 1}) = 0 \quad [8A.6]$$

$$\frac{\partial L_C}{\partial \lambda} = \alpha L^{\beta_1} K^{\beta_2} - Q_0 = 0 \quad [8A.7]$$

Solving these equations yields the following cost-minimizing values of L and K:

$$L^* = \left(\frac{Q_0}{\alpha}\right)^{1/(\beta_1+\beta_2)}\left(\frac{\beta_1 C_K}{\beta_2 C_L}\right)^{\beta_2/(\beta_1+\beta_2)} \qquad [8A.8]$$

$$K^* = \left(\frac{Q_0}{\alpha}\right)^{1/(\beta_1+\beta_2)}\left(\frac{\beta_1 C_L}{\beta_2 C_K}\right)^{\beta_1/(\beta_1+\beta_2)} \qquad [8A.9]$$

Substituting Equation 8A.8 for L and Equation 8A.9 for K in Equation 8A.2 and doing some algebraic operations gives the total cost (C) of producing any level of output (Q):

$$C = C_L^{\beta_1/(\beta_1+\beta_2)} C_K^{\beta_2/(\beta_1+\beta_2)}\left[\left(\frac{\beta_2}{\beta_1}\right)^{\beta_1/(\beta_1+\beta_2)} + \left(\frac{\beta_2}{\beta_1}\right)^{-\beta_2/(\beta_1+\beta_2)}\right]\left(\frac{Q}{\alpha}\right)^{1/(\beta_1+\beta_2)}$$

This cost equation indicates that total costs are a function of the output level (Q), the per-unit costs of labor (C_L) and capital (C_K), and the parameters (α, β_1, and β_2) of the Cobb-Douglas production function.

Several examples can be used to illustrate the implied shapes of the firm's long-run average cost (LAC) and long-run total cost (LTC). In the following examples, assume that $\alpha = 4.0$ and that the per-unit costs of labor (C_L) and capital (C_K) are \$2 and \$8, respectively.

Constant Returns

$\beta_1 = 0.50$, $\beta_2 = 0.50$ (Because $\beta_1 + \beta_2 = 1.0$, this equation is an example of *constant* returns to scale.)

$$LTC = (2)^{.50}(8)^{.50}[1 + 1]\left(\frac{Q}{4.0}\right)^1$$
$$= 2.0Q$$
$$LAC = \frac{LTC}{Q} = \frac{2.0Q}{Q}$$
$$= 2.0$$

These LAC and LTC functions are graphed in Panel (a) of Figure 8A.1. Note that when the Cobb-Douglas production function exhibits constant returns to scale, total costs increase linearly with output, and average total costs are constant, or independent of output.

Decreasing Returns

$\beta_1 = 0.25$, $\beta_2 = 0.25$ (Because $\beta_1 + \beta_2 < 1.0$, this equation is an example of *decreasing* returns to scale.)

$$LTC = (2)^{.50}(8)^{.50}[1 + 1]\left(\frac{Q}{4.0}\right)^2$$
$$= 0.50Q^2$$
$$LAC = 0.50Q$$

Figure 8A.1 Long-Run Average Cost and Long-Run Total Cost Functions for a Cobb-Douglas Production Function

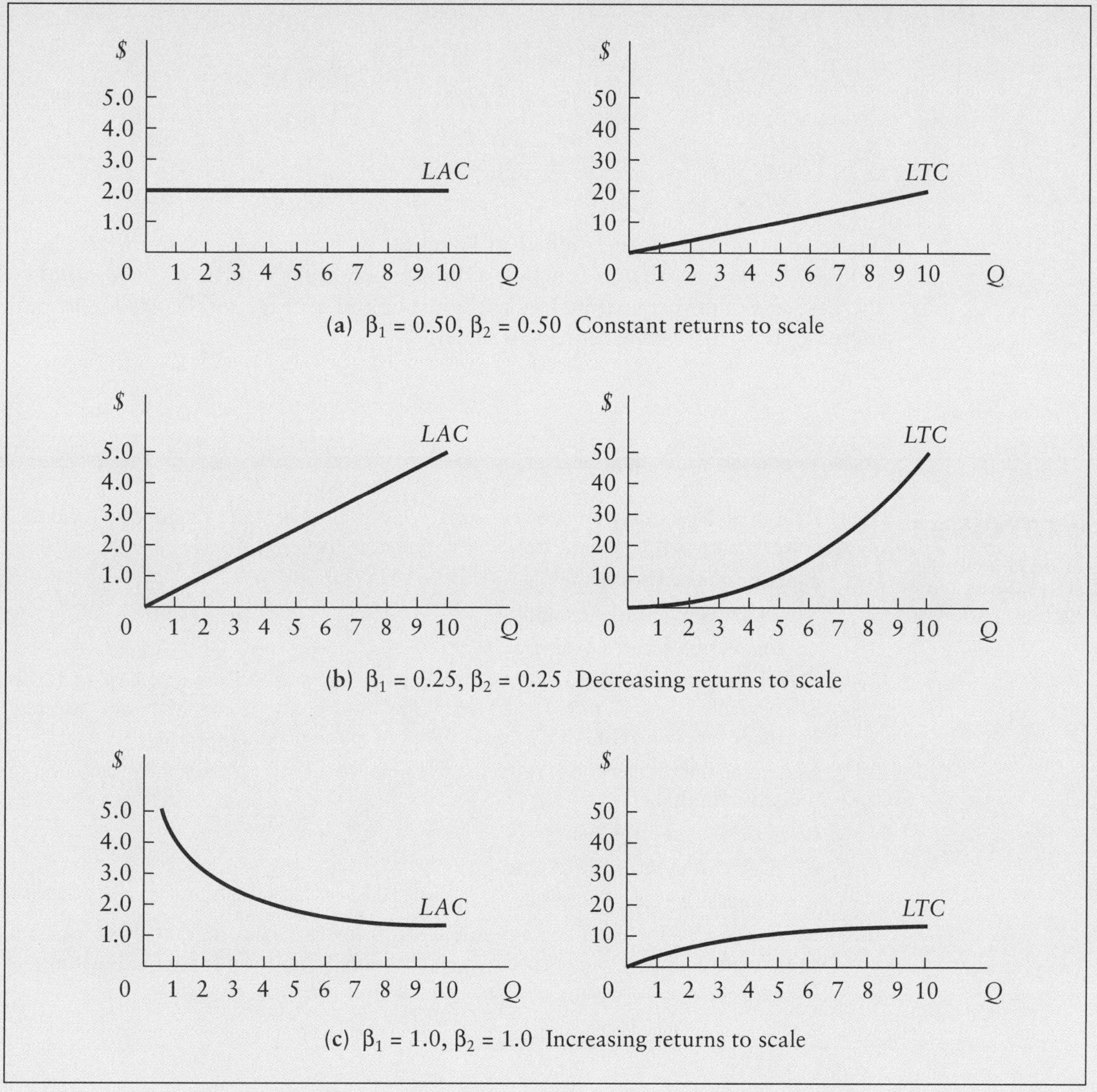

These cost functions are graphed in Panel (b) of Figure 8A.1. Note that when the Cobb-Douglas production function exhibits decreasing returns to scale, total costs increase more than proportionately with output, and average total costs rise as output increases (i.e., decreasing returns to scale).

Increasing Returns

$\beta_1 = 1.0$, $\beta_2 = 1.0$ (Because $\beta_1 + \beta_2 > 1.0$, this equation is an example of *increasing* returns to scale.)

$$LTC = (2)^{.50}(8)^{.50}[1 + 1]\left(\frac{Q}{4.0}\right)^{.50}$$
$$= 4.0\,Q^{.50}$$
$$LAC = \frac{4.0}{Q^{.50}}$$

These cost functions are graphed in Panel (c) of Figure 8A.1. Note that when the Cobb-Douglas production function exhibits increasing returns to scale, total costs increase less than proportionately with output and average total costs fall as output increases (i.e., increasing returns to scale).

Exercises

Answers to the exercises in blue can be found in Appendix C at the back of the book.

1. Determine how many units of labor (L^*) and capital (K^*) are required to produce five units of output (Q_0) for the production function given in the
   a. Constant returns example.
   b. Decreasing returns example.
   c. Increasing returns example.
2. Recompute your answers to Exercise 1, assuming that the per-unit cost of labor increases from $C_L = \$2$ to $C_L' = \$4$. How has the increase in the labor rate affected the optimal proportions of labor and capital used in the production process?
3. Determine the total cost of producing five units of output (Q_0) for the production function given in the
   a. Constant returns example.
   b. Decreasing returns example.
   c. Increasing returns example.
4. Use the data in Table 8.4 and a multiple regression analysis program on your computer to estimate a Cobb-Douglas production function of the form shown in Equation 8A.1. Do you observe increasing, decreasing, or constant returns to scale?

CHAPTER

9

Applications of Cost Theory

CHAPTER PREVIEW This chapter examines some of the techniques that have been developed for estimating the cost functions of production processes in actual firms. In the short run, a knowledge of the firm's cost function is essential when deciding whether to accept an additional order, perhaps at less than "full cost"; whether to schedule overtime for workers; or whether to temporarily suspend operations but not close the plant. In the long run, a knowledge of cost-function relationships will determine the capital investments to make, the production technology to adopt, the markets to enter, and the new products to introduce. The first part of the chapter examines various techniques for empirically estimating short-run and long-run cost functions. The second part of the chapter deals with break-even and contribution analysis—an application of cost theory that is useful in examining the profitability of a firm's operations. Appendix 9A discusses mass customization and learning curves.

MANAGERIAL CHALLENGE

How Exactly Have Computerization and Information Technology Lowered Costs at Chevron, Timken, and Merck?[1]

Computerization has made output per worker higher and therefore lowered unit labor cost when it comes to processing insurance claims or typesetting newspapers and magazines. Personal computers have decreased many-fold the time and talent required to perform routine work done previously with paper forms and time-consuming repetitive human tasks. However, not every business uses large numbers of PCs. How have computerization and information technology raised productivity and lowered cost so widely across other industries?

One key seems to be enhanced analytical and R&D capability provided by computers and information technology (IT) systems. Chevron Corporation once spent anywhere from $2 million to $4 million each to drill 10 to 12 exploratory wells before finding oil. Today, Chevron finds oil once in every five wells. The reason for the cost savings is a new technology that allows Chevron to display three-dimensional graphs of the likely oil and gas deposits in potential oil fields. New fast parallel processors allow more calculation-intensive 3-D simulation modeling. Using only seismic data as inputs, Chevron can now model how the oil and gas deposits will shift and flow as a known field is pumped out. This model allows a much more accurate location of secondary wells. As a result, overall production costs declined 16 percent industry-wide since 1991.

MANAGERIAL CHALLENGE

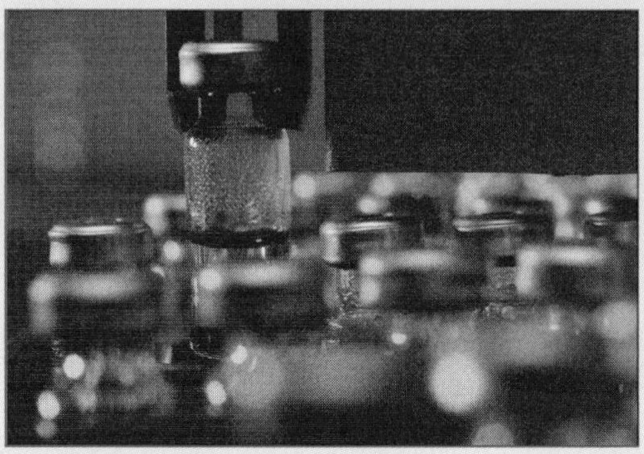
© PHOTOLINK/PHOTODISC GREEN/GETTY IMAGES

Timken, a $4 billion ball-bearing manufacturer has also used digital 3-D modeling to reconfigure production processes and implement small production runs of high profit margin products. Timken's newest facility in North Carolina is a so-called flexible manufacturing system where order taking, limited customization of design, production scheduling, and the actual factory itself are all IT enabled and networked. Networked machine tools make it possible to build-to-order against precise specifications deliverable within four hours rather than stockpile enormous inventories of subassemblies or request that customers wait six to eight weeks, as was the practice before IT. Nissan recently estimated that $3,600 in the final price of an auto is tied up in inventory expense. The build-to-order system could save the auto industry as much as $50 billion per year out of its $80 billion inventory cost.

Pharmaceutical research and development has experienced a similar benefit from computerization. Drug industry basic research always starts with biochemical or biogenetic modeling of the disease mechanism. In the past, once a mechanism for Hodgkins disease or pancreatic cancer became well understood, researchers at Merck or Pfizer experimented on known active compounds one by one in time-consuming chemical trials. Successful therapies emerged only after human trials on the promising compounds that showed efficacy with few side effects. Total time to introduction of a new pharmaceutical was often longer than a decade and entailed $1.5 billion investments.

Today, the first stage of the basic research process remains much the same, but the second stage of dribbling chemicals into a petri dish has ended. Instead, machines controlled and automated by microchips perform thousands of reactions at once and tally the results. Human researchers then take the most likely reagents and perform much more promising experiments that culminate in human trials. The total time to discovery has been cut by more than two thirds, and all attendant costs have declined sharply.

[1] Based on "The Innovators: The Rocket Under the High-Tech Boom," *Wall Street Journal* (March 30, 1999); "Mass Customization," *The Economist* (July 14, 2001), pp. 64–67; and "The Flexible Factory," *BusinessWeek* (May 5, 2003), pp. 90–101.

TYPES OF COST FUNCTIONS

A *cost function* is a schedule, graph, or mathematical relationship showing the total, average, or marginal cost of producing various quantities of output. Two different cost functions can be defined and derived: the *short-run* and the *long-run* cost functions. The short-run cost function is relevant to decisions in which one or more of the inputs to the production process are fixed or incapable of being altered. To make optimal pricing and production decisions, the firm must have knowledge of the shape and characteristics of its short-run cost function. For example, to decide whether to accept or refuse an order offered at some particular price, the firm must identify exactly what variable cost and direct fixed costs the order entails. In contrast, the long-run cost function is associated with the longer-term planning period in which all the inputs to the production process are variable and no restrictions are placed on the amount of an input that can be employed in the production process. Consequently, all costs, including indirect fixed costs such as headquarters facility costs, are avoidable. To make optimal investment decisions on everything from new production facilities to new product introductions, the firm must have knowledge of the behavior of its long-run cost function.

ESTIMATING SHORT-RUN COST FUNCTIONS[2]

To measure statistically a firm's cost function, one usually observes the dynamic actual cost of various output levels at different points in time. Comparing such estimates across firms is problematic and must be approached with care and judgment for several reasons.

DIFFERENCES IN COST DEFINITION AND MEASUREMENT Recall from Chapter 8 that differences exist between the economic and accounting concepts of cost. Economic cost is represented by the value of opportunities forgone, whereas accounting cost is measured by the outlays that are incurred. Some companies such as Deep Creek Mining record the cost of their own output (the crude oil, coal, or gas) shipped downstream to their refining and processing operations as expenses at the world market price on the day of shipment (i.e., at their opportunity cost). Other companies account for these same resources as their out-of-pocket expenses. If extraction costs of the company being studied are low (e.g., with Kentucky coal or West Texas intermediate crude or Persian Gulf oil), these two cost methods will diverge because the equilibrium market price is always determined by the considerably higher cost of the marginal producer (e.g., an oil platform in the North Sea).

Similar problems arise in measuring variable costs (i.e., costs that vary with output). Some companies employ only direct accounting costs, including materials, supplies, direct labor costs, and any direct fixed costs avoidable by refusing the batch order in question. Direct costs exclude all overhead and any other fixed cost that must be allocated (so-called indirect fixed costs). For batch decisions about whether to accept or refuse an order for a proposed charter air flight, a special production run, or a customer's proposed change order, these estimates of variable plus direct fixed costs are needed. For other questions, such as offering a customized design, however, some indirect accounting cost for the IT system that allows customized design would be an appropriate inclusion in the cost data.

Several other cost measurement issues arise with depreciation. Conceptually, depreciation can be divided into two components: *Time depreciation* represents the decline in value of an asset associated with the passage of *time,* and *use depreciation* represents the decline in value associated with *use.* For example, annual body style changes in the automobile industry or technical progress in speed and memory of personal computers renders products and production processes obsolete. Note that such time depreciation is completely independent of the rate of output at which the asset is actually operated. Because only use depreciation varies with the rate of output, only use depreciation is relevant in determining the shape of the cost-output relationship. However, accounting data on depreciation seldom break out use depreciation costs separately. Instead, the depreciation of

[2] Much of this discussion is based on the work of Joel Dean, who pioneered the development of statistical cost functions. See Joel Dean, *Statistical Cost Estimation* (Bloomington, IN: Indiana University Press, 1976), pp. 3–35, for an expanded treatment of the problems associated with the measurement of cost functions.

the value of an asset over its life cycle is usually determined by arbitrary tax regulations. Finally, capital asset values (and their associated depreciation costs) are often stated in terms of historical costs rather than in terms of replacement costs. In periods of rapidly increasing price levels, this approach will tend to understate true economic depreciation costs. These limitations need to be kept in mind when interpreting the cost-output relationship for a firm with numerous capital assets, such as an airline.

Controlling for Other Variables In addition to being a function of the output level of the firm, cost is a function of other factors, such as output mix, the length of production runs, employee absenteeism and turnover, production methods, input costs, and managerial efficiency.

To isolate the cost-output relationship itself, one must control for these other influences by:

- *Deflating or detrending the cost data.* Whenever wage rates or raw material prices change significantly over the period of analysis, one can deflate the cost data to reflect these changes in factor prices. Provided suitable price indices are available or can be constructed, costs incurred at different points in time can be restated as dollars of equivalent purchasing power.[3]
- *Using multiple regression analysis.* Suppose a firm believes that costs should decline gradually over time as a result of innovative worker suggestions. One way to incorporate this effect into the cost equation would be to include a time trend t as an additional explanatory variable:

$$C = f(Q, t) \quad [9.1]$$

Other possible control variables include the number of product lines, the number of customer segments, and the number of distribution channels.

The Form of the Empirical Cost-Output Relationship Polynomial Function The total cost function in the short run (STC), as hypothesized in economic theory, is an S-shaped curve that can be represented by a cubic relationship:

$$STC = a + bQ + cQ^2 + dQ^3 \quad [9.2]$$

The familiar U-shaped marginal and average cost functions then can be derived from this relationship. The associated marginal cost function is

$$MC = \frac{d(STC)}{dQ} = b + 2cQ + 3dQ^2 \quad [9.3]$$

The average total cost function is

$$ATC = \frac{STC}{Q} = \frac{a}{Q} + b + cQ + dQ^2 \quad [9.4]$$

[3] Two assumptions are implicit in this approach: No substitution takes place between the inputs as prices change, and changes in the output level have no influence on the prices of the inputs. For more automated plants that incorporate only maintenance personnel, plant engineers, and material supplies, these assumptions fit the reality of the production process quite well.

Figure 9.1 Polynomial Cost-Output Relationships

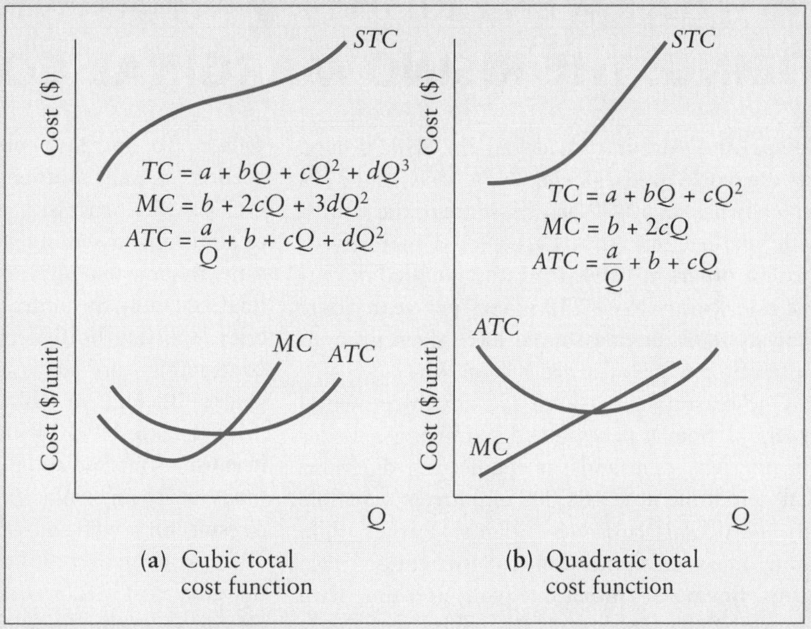

The cubic total cost function and its associated marginal and average total cost functions are shown in Figure 9.1(a). If the results of a regression analysis indicate that the cubic term (Q^3) is not statistically significant, then short-run total cost can be represented by a quadratic relationship:

$$STC = a + bQ + cQ^2 \quad [9.5]$$

as illustrated in Figure 9.1(b). In this quadratic case, total costs increase at an increasing rate throughout the typical operating range of output levels. The associated marginal and average cost functions are

$$MC = \frac{d(STC)}{dQ} = b + 2cQ \quad [9.6]$$

$$ATC = \frac{STC}{Q} = \frac{a}{Q} + b + cQ \quad [9.7]$$

As can be seen from Equation 9.6, this quadratic total cost relationship implies that marginal costs increase linearly as the output level is increased.

But rising, not constant, marginal cost (such as Boeing experienced in assembling wide-body jets) is characteristic of essentially all manufacturing environments. Information services companies such as IBM Global Services or network-based software companies such as Microsoft may at times experience declining marginal costs.

WHAT WENT RIGHT • WHAT WENT WRONG

BOEING: THE RISING MARGINAL COST OF 747s[4]

Boeing and Airbus provide all the wide-bodied jets the world needs. Boeing 747s, 767s, and 777s typically have a 60–70 percent share of the worldwide market, but Airbus accepted a majority of the new orders in 1994–1995 and doubled its output rate from 126 to 232 planes per year. Some analysts think Boeing should have given up even more of the wide-body order flow. Why?

One reason is that until recently, incremental orders at Boeing necessitated redrawing and duplicating the thousands of engineering diagrams that determine how 200,000 employees assemble any particular customer's plane. Rather than doing mass customization from common platforms, Boeing assembles one plane at a time with new drawings for each $150 million wide-body ordered. Eventually, incremental variable costs must rise as designers and shop floors get congested with new instructions and new diagrams.

With backorders running to almost 1,000 planes companywide in the mid-1990s, Boeing boosted production from 180 to 560 commercial jets per year. At the final assembly plant for Boeing wide-bodies in Everett, Washington, just north of Seattle, throughput was increased from 15 planes per month to 21 planes per month (i.e., by 40%). To increase production rates, Boeing needed to split bottlenecked assembly stations into parallel processes, which entailed the hiring of additional assembly workers and massive overtime. Boeing also increased the production rate of final assembly by contracting out more subassemblies. Splitting bottlenecked assembly stations or contracting out subassemblies substantially increases Boeing's variable costs.

In the late 1990s, wide-body prices did not rise because of intense competitive pressure from Airbus, but Boeing's marginal costs certainly did. As a result, for a while in the late 1990s, every Boeing 747 plane delivered had a price less than its marginal cost (i.e., a negative gross profit margin). Of course, eventually such orders must be refused. In 2000, Boeing did slow the production throughput rate at Everett back to 15 wide-bodies per month in order to return to profitability. Today, the well-equipped 747-400 aircraft earns as much as $45 million in operating profits above its variable cost.

[4] Based on "Boeing's Trouble," *Wall Street Journal* (December 16, 1998), p. A23; and Everett, Washington, site visit.

LOGARITHMIC FUNCTION A logarithmic function also can be used to represent empirical cost-output relationships. A simple cost relationship could take the form

$$lnSTC = a + b\ lnQ \qquad [9.8]$$

where $lnSTC$ and lnQ are the natural logarithms of short-run total cost and output, respectively, and a and b are the parameters to be estimated by regression analysis.[5] Such a relationship is shown in Figure 9.2. In actual applications, for a multiproduct, multi-input firm or production process, the equation can become much more complex with the addition of linear, quadratic, and cross-product terms for all the different products and input prices.

[5] A *natural* logarithm, lnX, is a logarithm to the base e, where $e = 2.71828. \ldots$ A logarithm to the base 10 is represented as log X.

Figure 9.2 Logarithmic Cost-Output Relationship

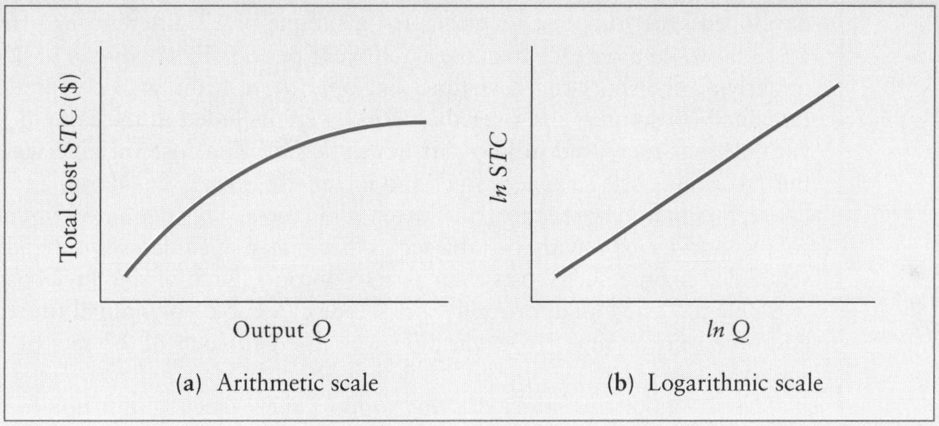

EXAMPLES OF STATISTICALLY ESTIMATED SHORT-RUN COST FUNCTIONS

Short-run cost functions have been estimated for firms in a large number of different industries—for example, food processing, furniture, railways, gas, coal, electricity, hosiery, steel, and cement.[6]

EXAMPLE

SHORT-RUN COST FUNCTIONS: MULTIPLE-PRODUCT FOOD PROCESSING

In a study of a British food processing firm, Johnston constructed individual cost functions for 14 different products and an overall cost function for the firm.[7] Weekly data for nine months were obtained on the physical production of each type of product and total direct costs of each product (subdivided into the four categories of materials, labor, packing, and freight). Indirect costs (such as salaries, indirect labor, factory charges, and laboratory expenses) remained fairly constant over the time period studied and were excluded from the analysis. A price index for each category of direct costs for each product was obtained from government sources and used to deflate all four sets of input costs, yielding a weekly deflated direct cost for each product. For the individual products, output was measured by physical production (quantity). For the firm as a whole, an index of aggregate output was constructed by weighting the quantities of each product by its selling price and summing over all products produced each period.

For the 14 different products and for the overall firm, the linear cost function gave an excellent fit between direct cost and output. Therefore, Johnston concluded that total direct costs were a linear function of output and marginal costs were constant over the observed ranges of output.

[6] See A. A. Walters, "Production and Cost Functions: An Econometric Survey," *Econometrica 31*, no. 1–2 (January/April 1963), pp. 1–66, for a summary of these studies.

[7] See Jack Johnston, *Statistical Cost Analysis* (New York: McGraw-Hill, 1960), pp. 87–97.

EXAMPLE

Short-Run Cost Functions: Electricity Generation[8]

Another study by Johnston of the costs of electric power generation in Great Britain developed short-run cost functions for a sample of 17 different firms from annual cost-output data on each firm over a 20-year period. To satisfy the basic conditions underlying the short-run cost function, only those firms whose capital equipment remained constant in size over the period were included in the sample. The output variable was measured in kilowatt-hours (kWh). The cost variable was defined as the "working costs of generation" and included (1) fuel; (2) salaries and wages; and (3) repairs and maintenance, oil, water, and stores. This definition of cost does not correspond exactly with variable costs because it includes some fixed costs (i.e., scheduled maintenance costs even at zero output). Each of the three cost categories was deflated using an appropriate price index. A cubic polynomial function with an additional linear time trend variable was fitted to each of 17 sets of cost-output observations.

The results of this study did *not* support the existence of a nonlinear cubic or quadratic cost function. The cubic term, Q^3, was not statistically significant in any of the regressions, and the quadratic term, Q^2, was statistically significant in only 5 of the 17 cost equations. A typical linear total cost function is given by

$$C = 18.3 + 0.889Q - 0.639T$$

where C = variable costs of generation, Q = annual output (millions of kilowatt-hours), and T = time (years). The equation "explained" 97.4 percent of the variation in the cost variable.

The results of the two preceding studies are similar to those found in many other cost studies—namely, that short-run total costs tend to increase *linearly* over the ranges of output for which cost-output data are available. In other words, short-run average costs tend to decline and marginal costs tend to be constant over the "typical" or "normal" operating range of the firm. At higher rates of output, we would expect to see exponentially increasing total cost and rising marginal cost. But, of course, this circumstance is exactly what firms try to avoid. Recall Boeing's experience in producing too many 747s per month.

Long-Run Cost-Output Relationships

The long-run cost function consists of the least-cost combination of inputs for producing any level of output when *all* of the inputs to the production process are variable. As is indicated in Figure 9.3, the theoretical long-run average cost function (LAC) consists of the lower boundary, or envelope, of the various short-run average cost functions (SAC).

Statistical Estimation of Long-Run Cost Functions

Long-run costs can be estimated over a substantial period of time in a single plant (time-series data) or with multiple plants operating at different rates of output

[8] Ibid., pp. 44–63.

Figure 9.3 Long-Run Average Cost Function

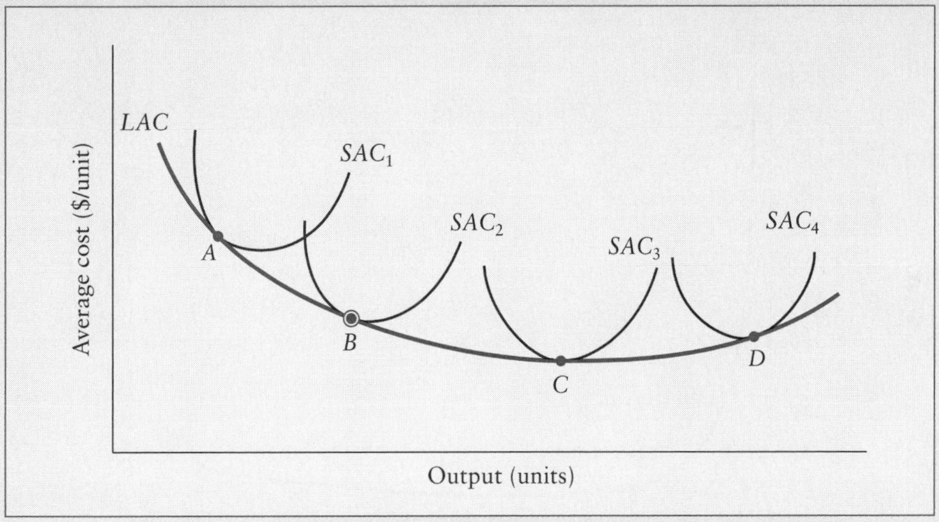

(cross-sectional data). The use of cross-sectional data assumes that each firm is operating as efficiently as possible given its fixed plant and equipment inputs—that is, that the four firms having the four short-run average cost functions labeled SAC_1, SAC_2, SAC_3, and SAC_4 in Figure 9.3 are operating at points *A*, *B*, *C*, and *D*, respectively. The use of time-series data assumes that input prices, the production technology, and the products offered for sale remain unchanged. Both methods, therefore, require heroic assumptions, but cross-sectional data are more prevalent in estimating long-run cost functions.

EXAMPLE

LONG-RUN COST FUNCTIONS: ELECTRICITY GENERATION

In his study of electrical power generation by British firms, Johnston developed long-run cost functions using both time-series and cross-sectional data.[9] In the time-series analysis, a cubic cost function with a linear trend variable was fitted to each of 23 firms whose capital equipment had *not* remained constant over the 1928–1947 period. The cubic term was not statistically significant in any of the regression equations, and the quadratic term was statistically significant in only six of the regression equations. Regardless of whether a linear time trend was included in the regression model, a linear model between cost and output tended to give the best fit.

In a cross-sectional study of U.S. electric utility companies, Christensen and Greene used a logarithmic model to test for the presence of economies and diseconomies of scale.[10] The long-run average cost curve (*LAC*) using data on 114 firms is shown in Figure 9.4. The bar below the graph indicates the number of firms in

[9] Ibid., pp. 64–86.

[10] L. R. Christensen and W. H. Greene, "Economies of Scale in U.S. Electric Power Generation," *Journal of Political Economy* 84, no. 4 (August 1976).

Figure 9.4 Average Cost Function for U.S. Electric Utility Firms

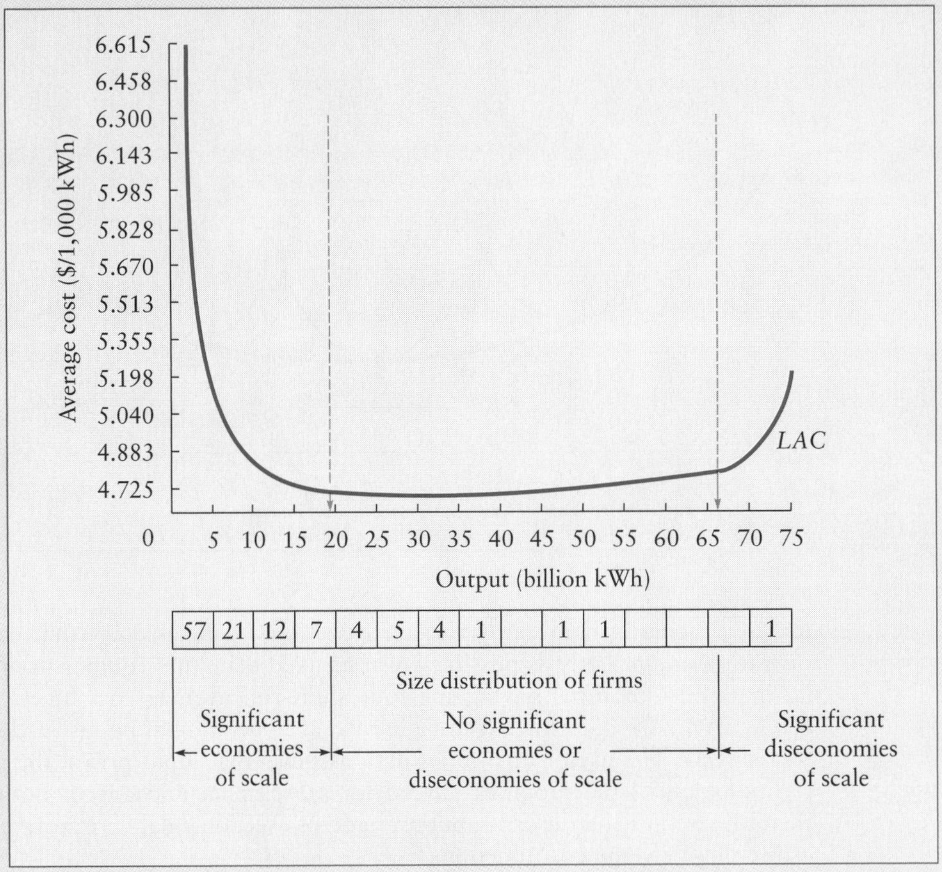

each interval. Below 19.8 billion kWh (left arrow in graph), significant economies of scale were found to exist. The 97 firms in this range accounted for 48.7 percent of the total output. Between 19.8 and 67.1 billion kWh (right arrow in the graph), no significant economies of scale were present. The 16 firms in this range accounted for 44.6 percent of the total output. Above 67.1 billion kWh, diseconomies of scale (one firm and 6.7 percent of total output) were found.

Determining the Optimal Scale of an Operation

The size at which a company should attempt to establish its operations depends on the extent of the scale economies and the extent of the market. Some firms can operate at minimum unit cost using a small scale. Consider a licensed street vendor of leather coats. Each additional sale entails variable costs for the coat, a few minutes of direct labor effort to answer potential customers' questions, and some small allocated cost associated with the step-van or other vehicle where the inventory is stored and hauled from one street sale location to another. Ninety-nine percent of the operating cost is the variable cost of an additional leather coat per additional sale. Long-run average cost will be essentially flat, constant at approximately the wholesale cost of a leather coat. As a result, in street vending, a small-scale operation will be just as efficient as a large-scale operation.

In contrast, the hydroelectric power plants, depicted in Figure 9.4, have few variable costs of any kind. Instead, essentially all the costs are fixed costs associated with buying the land that will be flooded, constructing the dam, and purchasing the huge electrical generator equipment. Thereafter, the only variable inputs required are a few lubricants and maintenance workers. Consequently, a hydroelectric power plant has long-run average total costs that decline continuously as the company spreads its enormous fixed cost over additional sales by supplying power to more and more households. Similarly, electric distribution lines (the high-tension power grids and neighborhood electrical conduits) are a high-fixed-cost and low-variable-cost operation. In the electrical utility industry, large-scale operations therefore incur lower unit cost than small-scale operations, as demonstrated in Figure 9.4.

EXAMPLE

SCALE ECONOMIES IN THE TRADITIONAL CABLE INDUSTRY: TIME-WARNER[11]

Telephone landlines and traditional cable TV businesses have cost characteristics similar to electric utilities. Once the wires have been put in place, the incremental cost of extending TV or telephone service to another household is small. The extent of the scale economies in such industries may warrant licensing only one cable company or one local telephone service provider. In fact, municipalities have historically issued an exclusive service contract to such public utilities. The rationale was that one firm could service the whole market at much lower cost than several firms dividing the market and failing therefore to realize all of the available scale economies.

However, remember that the optimal scale of operation of any facility, even a declining cost facility, is limited by the extent of the market. The expansion of the cable TV market has always been limited by the availability of videocassette recorders, DVD players, and services such as NetFlix because they are inexpensive, convenient entertainment substitutes. As a result, the potential scale economies suggested by industrial engineering studies of cable TV operations have never been fully realized.

In addition, both telephone and cable TV companies are now facing new wireless alternative technologies. Satellite-based digital television and cell phones have cut deeply into the market once reserved exclusively for monopoly-licensed communications companies. As a result, the average unit cost in these cable-based businesses increased from B to A as volume declined (see Figure 9.5). Consequently, the price required to break even has necessarily risen. Of course, the higher the cost-covering price, the more customers the cable TV and telephone companies lose to wireless alternatives.

[11] See W. Emmons and R. Prager, "The Effects of Market Structure in the U.S. Cable Television Industry," *Rand Journal of Economics* 28, no. 4 (Winter 1997), pp. 732–750.

Figure 9.5 Fixed Costs Stranded by Freewheeling Electricity and Satellite-Based TV Signals

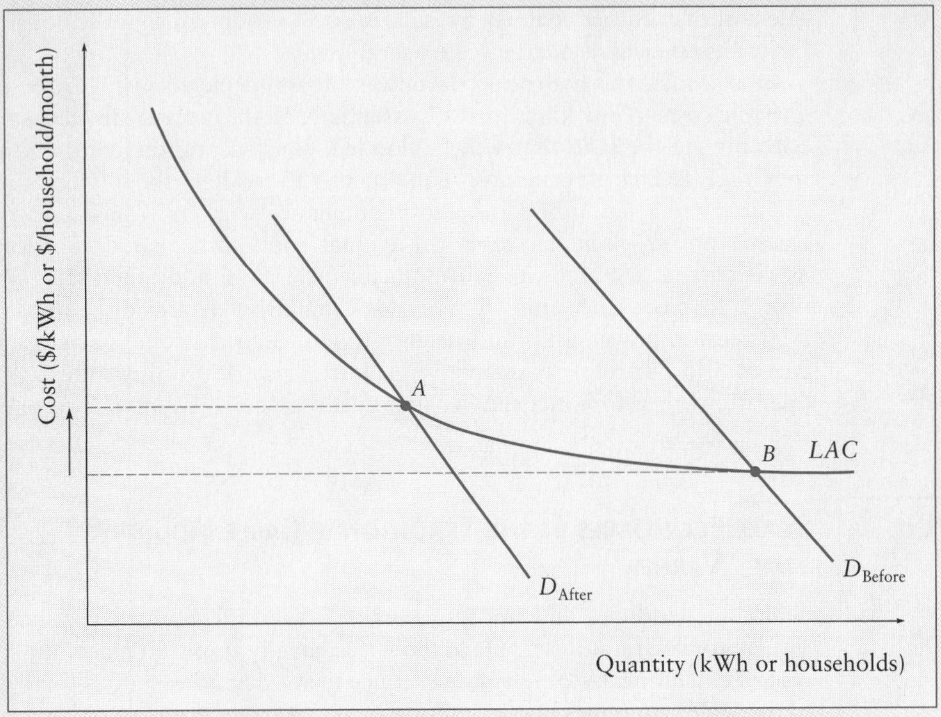

"Freewheeling" in the electrical utility industry has similar effects. When industrial and commercial electricity buyers (e.g., a large assembly plant or hospital) were allowed in January 2003 to contract freely with low-cost power suppliers elsewhere in the state or even several states away, the local public utility experienced "stranded costs." That is, the high initial fixed costs of constructing dams, power plants, and distribution lines were left behind as sales volume declined and local customers opted out. If the costs involved had been mostly variable, the local power utilities could simply cut costs and operate profitably at smaller scale. Unfortunately, however, the costs are mostly fixed and unavoidable, so unit costs will unavoidably rise as the number of customers served declines. Consequently, the advantages of additional competition for lowering prices to consumers are projected to be almost completely offset by the rise in unit costs caused by reduced scale.[12]

Economies of Scope
Economies that exist whenever the cost of producing two (or more) products jointly by one plant or firm is less than the cost of producing these products separately by different plants or firms.

Economies of Scale Versus Economies of Scope

Economies of scope occur whenever inputs can be shared in the production of different products. For example, in the airline industry, the cost of transporting both passengers and freight on a single airplane is less than the cost of using two airplanes

[12] M. Maloney and R. McCormick, *Customer Choice, Consumer Value,* (Washington, DC: Citizens for a Sound Economy Foundation, 1996).

to transport passengers and freight separately. Similarly, commercial banks who manage both credit card-based unsecured consumer loans and deeded property-secured mortgage loans can provide each activity at lower cost than they could be offered separately. These cost savings occur independent of the scale of operations; hence they are distinguished from economies of scale.

EXAMPLE

ECONOMIES OF SCOPE IN THE BANKING INDUSTRY

A number of empirical studies have attempted to estimate economies of scale and scope in the banking industry, which includes commercial banks, savings and loan associations, and credit unions. A survey article by Jeffrey Clark compiled the results of 13 of these studies.[13] Possible sources of production economies in financial institutions include the following:

- *Specialized labor.* A larger depository institution may be able to employ more specialized labor (e.g., computer programmers, cash managers, investment specialists, and loan officers) in producing its services. If the expertise of these workers results in the processing of a higher volume of deposit and loan accounts per unit of labor, then larger institutions will experience lower per-unit labor costs compared with smaller institutions.
- *Computer and telecommunications technology.* Once the large setup, or fixed, costs are incurred, computer and electronic funds transfer systems can be used to process additional transactions at small additional costs per transaction. Spreading the fixed costs over a higher volume of transactions may permit the larger firm to achieve lower average total costs.
- *Information.* Credit information about loan applicants must be gathered and analyzed before lending decisions are made. However, once gathered, this credit information can be reused, usually at little additional cost, in making decisions about lending to the institution's customers. For example, credit information gathered in making mortgage loans can also be used in making automobile and other personal loans. Thus, larger financial institutions, which offer a wide array of different types of credit, may realize economies of scope in information gathering. That is, the cost of mortgage and auto installment lending done jointly is lower than the total cost of both when each is done separately.

All the studies reviewed by Clark employed a logarithmic cost function. The following conclusions were derived:

- Some evidence indicates economies of scope between consumer and mortgage lending.
- Significant overall (i.e., firm-specific) economies of scale occur only at relatively low levels of output (less than \$100 million in deposits). Beyond that point, most studies found an L-shaped long-run average cost curve where average total cost falls steeply at low levels of output and then flattens out and becomes horizontal. In this respect, banking *LAC* closely mirrors the shape of the *LAC* in representative manufacturing.

[13] Jeffrey A. Clark, "Economies of Scale and Scope at Depository Financial Institutions: A Review of the Literature," Federal Reserve Bank of Kansas City, *Economic Review* (September/October 1988), pp. 16–33.

ENGINEERING COST TECHNIQUES

Engineering Cost Technique
A method of estimating cost functions by deriving the least-cost combination of labor, capital equipment, and raw materials required to produce various levels of output, using only industrial engineering information.

Engineering cost techniques provide an alternative to estimating long-run cost functions without using accounting cost data. Using production data, the engineering approach attempts to determine the least-cost combination of labor, capital equipment, and raw materials required to produce various levels of output. Engineering methods offer a number of advantages over statistical methods in examining economies of scale. First, it is generally much easier with the engineering approach to hold constant such factors as input prices, product mix, and product efficiency, allowing one to isolate the effects on costs of changes in output. Second, use of the engineering method avoids some of the cost-allocation and depreciation problems encountered when using accounting data.

In a study designed to isolate the various sources of scale economies within a plant, Haldi and Whitcomb collected data on the cost of individual units of equipment, the initial investment in plant and equipment, and on operating costs. They noted that "in many basic industries such as petroleum refining, primary metals, and electric power, economies of scale are found in very large plant sizes (often the largest built or contemplated)."[14] Few (if any) firms were observed operating beyond these minimum efficient scale plant sizes.

THE SURVIVOR TECHNIQUE

Survivor Technique
A method of estimating cost functions from the shares of industry output coming from each size class over time. Size classes whose shares of industry output are increasing (decreasing) over time are presumed to be relatively efficient (inefficient) and have lower (higher) average costs.

It is also possible to detect the presence of scale economies or diseconomies without having access to any cost data. The **survivor technique** involves classifying the firms in an industry by size and calculating the share of industry output coming from each size class over time.[15] If the share decreases over time, then this size class is presumed to be relatively inefficient and to have higher average costs. Conversely, an increasing share indicates that the size class is relatively efficient and has lower average costs. The rationale for this approach is that competition will tend to eliminate those firms whose size is relatively inefficient, allowing only those size firms with lower average costs to survive.

Despite its appeal, the survivor technique does have one serious limitation. Because the technique does not use actual cost data in the analysis, it cannot assess the *magnitude* of the cost differentials between firms of varying size and efficiency.

EXAMPLE

THE SURVIVOR TECHNIQUE: STEEL PRODUCTION

The survivor technique has been used to examine the long-run cost functions in steel ingot production by open-hearth or Bessemer processes. Based on the data in Table 9.1, Stigler developed the sleigh-shaped long-run average cost function for steel ingot production shown in Figure 9.6. Because of the declining percentages at the lowest levels of output and at extremely high levels of output, Stigler concluded that both were relatively inefficient size classes. The intermediate size classes (from

[14] J. Haldi and D. Whitcomb, "Economies of Scale in Industrial Plants," *Journal of Political Economy* 75, no. 1 (August 1967), pp. 373–385.

[15] G. J. Stigler, *The Organization of Industry* (Homewood, IL: Richard D. Irwin, 1968), Chapter 7. For other examples of the use of the survivor technique, see H. E. Ted Frech and Paul B. Ginsburg, "Optimal Scale in Medical Practice: A Survivor Analysis," *Journal of Business* (January 1974), pp. 23–26.

Table 9.1 Distribution of Steel Ingot Capacity by Relative Size of Company

Company Size (Percentage of Total Industry Capacity)	Percentage of Industry Capacity			Number of Companies		
	1930	1938	1951	1930	1938	1951
Under ½	7.16	6.11	4.65	39	29	22
½ to 1	5.94	5.08	5.37	9	7	7
1 to 2½	13.17	8.30	9.07	9	6	6
2½ to 5	10.64	16.59	22.21	3	4	5
5 to 10	11.18	14.03	8.12	2	2	1
10 to 25	13.24	13.99	16.10	1	1	1
25 and over	38.67	35.91	34.50	1	1	1

Source: George J. Stigler, "The Economies of Scale," *Journal of Law and Economics* (October 1958). Reprinted by permission.

Figure 9.6 Long-Run Average Costs of Steel Ingot Production

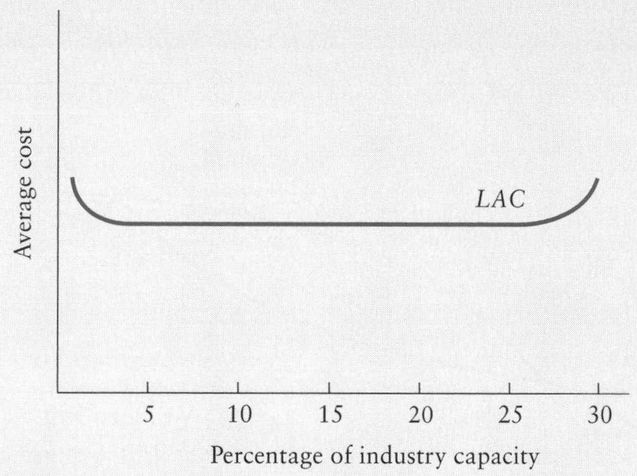

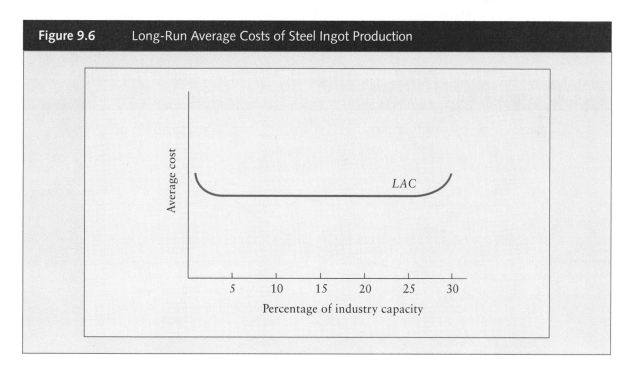

2.5 to 27.5 percent of industry capacity) represented the range of optimum size because these size classes grew or held their shares of capacity. Stigler also applied the survivor technique to the automobile industry and found an L-shaped average cost curve, indicating no evidence of diseconomies of scale at large levels of output.

One final note of caution: The concept of average total costs per unit of output (i.e., so-called "unit costs"), so prominent in our recent discussion of scale economies, is seldom useful for managerial decision making. Get in the habit of avoiding the use of unit costs in your decision problem reasoning. Reserve unit costs for describing, debating, and planning issues related to scale economies and diseconomies alone.

Break-Even Analysis Versus Contribution Analysis

Break-Even Analysis
A technique used to examine the relationship among a firm's sales, costs, and operating profits at various levels of output.

Many of the planning activities that take place within a firm are based on anticipated levels of output. The study of the interrelationships among a firm's sales, costs, and operating profit at various anticipated output levels is known as **break-even analysis.**

Break-even analysis is based on the revenue-output and cost-output functions of microeconomic theory. These functions are shown together in Figure 9.7. Total revenue is equal to the number of units of output sold multiplied by the price per unit. Assuming that the firm can sell additional units of output only by lowering the price, the total revenue curve *TR* will be concave (inverted U shaped), as indicated in Figure 9.7. The total cost curve *TC* shown in the figure is a static short-run cost function analogous to that shown earlier in Chapter 8 (Figure 8.3). It indicates the relationship between costs and output for a given production process in which one or more of the factors of production (e.g., plant and production technology) are fixed.[16] Short-run total costs consist of a fixed-cost component and a variable-cost component.

The difference between total revenue and total cost at any level of output represents the total profit that will be obtained. In Figure 9.7, total profit *TP* at any output level is given by the vertical distance between the total revenue *TR* and total cost *TC*

Figure 9.7 Generalized Break-Even Analysis

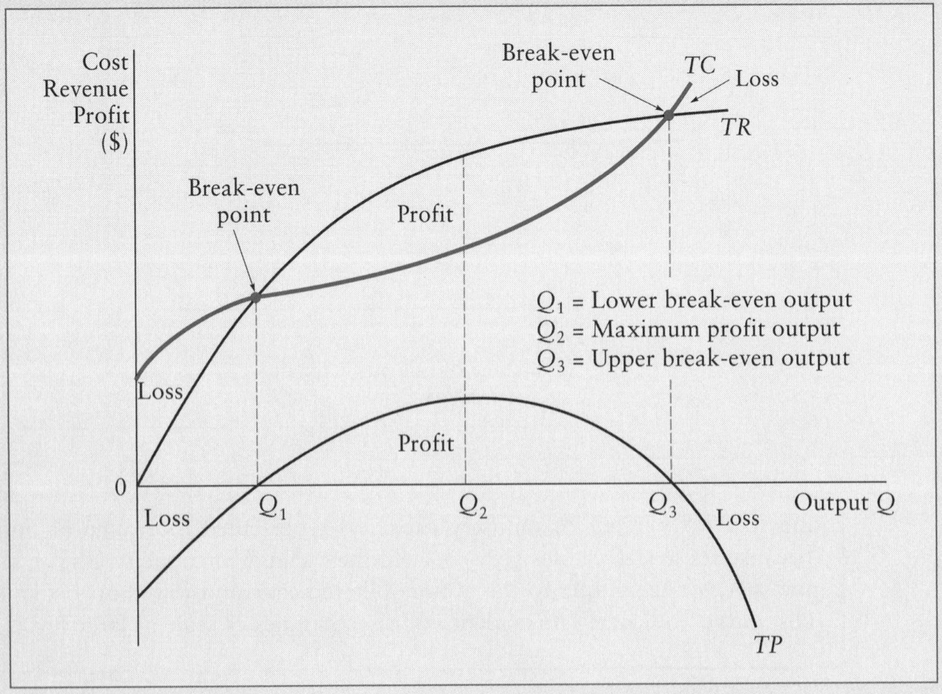

[16] An additional assumption of break-even analysis is that all the units produced during the period are sold during the period or that all production is in response to firm orders; that is, no inventory-planning decisions are required.

curves. A break-even situation (zero profit) occurs whenever total revenue equals total cost. In Figure 9.7, note that a break-even condition occurs at two different output levels: Q_1 and Q_3. Below an output level of Q_1, losses will be incurred because $TR < TC$. Between Q_1 and Q_3, profits will be obtained because $TR > TC$. At output levels above Q_3, losses will occur again because $TR < TC$. Total profits are maximized within the range of Q_1 to Q_3; the vertical distance between the TR and TC curves is greatest at an output level of Q_2.

LINEAR BREAK-EVEN ANALYSIS

Break-even analysis is one of the most frequently used techniques of business planning. We discuss both the graphical and algebraic methods of solving break-even problems.

GRAPHICAL METHOD

Over the output range Q_1 to Q_2 in Figure 9.7, the linearity of total cost and total revenue can be assumed as a simplifying approximation. Constant selling price per unit and a constant variable cost per unit yield the linear TR and TC functions illustrated in Figure 9.8, which shows a basic linear break-even chart. Total cost is computed as the sum of the firm's fixed costs F, which are independent of the output level, and the variable costs, which increase at a constant rate of VC per unit of output. Earnings before interest and taxes, or *EBIT*, is equal to the difference between total revenues (TR) and total (*operating*) costs (TC).

The break-even point occurs at point Q_b in Figure 9.8, where the total revenue and the total cost functions intersect. If a firm's output level is below this break-even

Figure 9.8 Linear Break-Even Analysis Chart

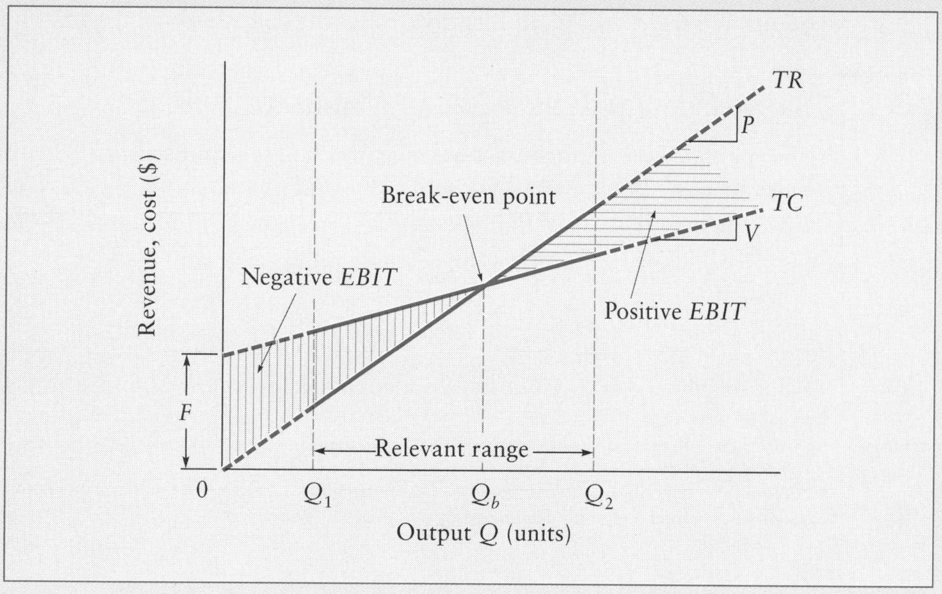

point (i.e., if $TR < TC$), it incurs *operating losses,* defined as a *negative EBIT.* If the firm's output level is above this break-even point (if $TR > TC$), it realizes *operating profits,* defined as a *positive EBIT.*

Algebraic Method

To determine a firm's break-even point algebraically, one must set the total revenue and total (operating) cost functions equal to each other and solve the resulting equation for the break-even volume. Total revenue is equal to the selling price per unit times the output quantity:

$$TR = P \times Q \qquad [9.9]$$

Total (operating) cost is equal to fixed plus variable costs, where the variable cost is the product of the variable cost per unit times the output quantity:

$$TC = F + (V \times Q) \qquad [9.10]$$

Setting the total revenue and total cost expressions equal to each other and substituting the break-even output Q_b for Q results in

$$TR = TC$$

or

$$PQ_b = F + VQ_b \qquad [9.11]$$

Finally, solving Equation 9.11 for the break-even output Q_b yields[17]

$$PQ_b - VQ_b = F$$

$$(P - V)Q_b = F$$

$$Q_b = \frac{F}{P - V} \qquad [9.12]$$

Contribution Margin
The difference between price and variable cost per unit.

The *difference* between the selling price per unit and the variable cost per unit, $P - V$, is referred to as the **contribution margin.** It measures how much each unit of output contributes to meeting fixed costs and operating profits. Thus, the break-even output is equal to the fixed cost divided by the contribution margin.

EXAMPLE

Break-Even Analysis: Allegan Manufacturing Company

Assume that Allegan manufactures one product, which it sells for \$250 per unit (P). Variable costs (V) are \$150 per unit. The firm's fixed costs (F) are \$1 million. Substituting these figures into Equation 9.12 yields the following break-even output:

$$Q_b = \frac{\$1,000,000}{\$250 - \$150}$$

$$= 10,000 \text{ units}$$

Allegan's break-even output can also be determined graphically, as shown in Figure 9.9.

[17] Break-even analysis also can be performed in terms of dollar *sales* rather than *units* of output. The break-even dollar sales volume S_b can be determined by the following expression:

$$S_b = \frac{F}{1 - V/P}$$

where V/P is the variable cost ratio (calculated as variable cost per dollar of sales).

Figure 9.9 Linear Break-Even Analysis Chart for the Allegan Manufacturing Company

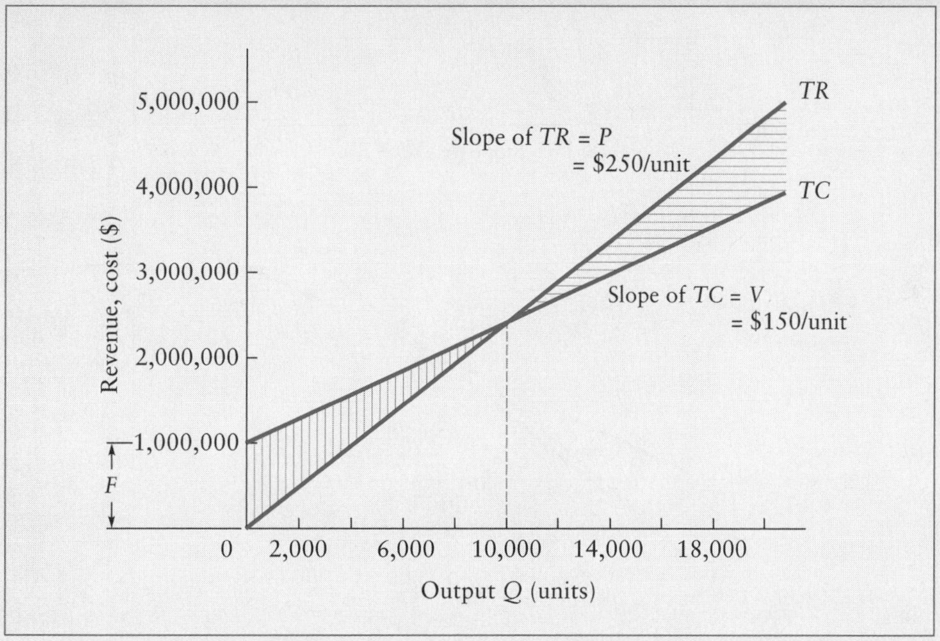

Another illustration would be to use break-even analysis to approve or reject a batch sale promotion. Suppose that in the previous example, the \$1 million is a trade rebate to elicit better shelf location for Allegan's product. If the estimated effect of this promotion is additional sales of 9,000 units, which is less than the break-even output, the change in total contributions will fall below the \$1 million promotion cost [i.e., $(\$250 - \$150) \times 9{,}000 < \$1{,}000{,}000$]. Therefore, the promotion plan should be rejected.

Because a firm's break-even output is dependent on a number of variables—in particular, the price per unit, variable (operating) costs per unit, and fixed costs—the firm may wish to analyze the effects of changes in any one (or more) of the variables on the break-even output. For example, it may wish to consider either of the following:

1. Change the selling price.
2. Substitute fixed costs for variable costs.

EXAMPLE

BREAK-EVEN ANALYSIS: ALLEGAN MANUFACTURING COMPANY (continued)

Assume that Allegan increased the selling price per unit P' by \$25 to \$275. Substituting this figure into Equation 9.12 gives a new break-even output.

$$Q_b' = \frac{\$1{,}000{,}000}{\$275 - \$150}$$
$$= 8{,}000 \text{ units}$$

Figure 9.10 Linear Break-Even Analysis Chart for the Allegan Manufacturing Company Showing the Effects of a Price Increase

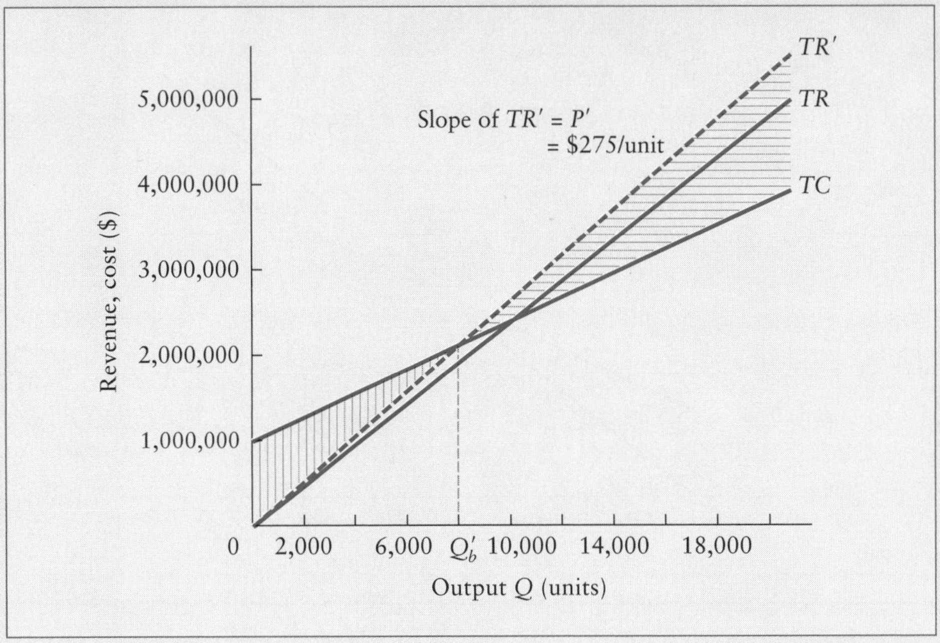

This outcome can also be seen in Figure 9.10, in which an increase in the price per unit increases the slope of the total revenue function TR' and reduces the break-even output.

Rather than increasing the selling price per unit, Allegan's management may decide to substitute fixed costs for variable costs in some aspect of the company's operations. For example, as labor wage rates increase over time, many firms seek to reduce operating costs through automation, which in effect represents the substitution of fixed-cost capital equipment for variable-cost labor. Suppose Allegan determines that it can reduce labor costs by $25 per unit by leasing $100,000 of additional equipment. Under these conditions, the firm's new level of fixed costs F' would be $1,000,000 + $100,000 = $1,100,000. Variable costs per unit V' would be $150 − $25 = $125. Substituting P = $250 per unit, V' = $125 per unit, and F' = $1,100,000 into Equation 9.12 yields a new break-even output:

$$Q_b' = \frac{\$1{,}100{,}000}{\$250 - \$125}$$
$$= 8{,}800 \text{ units}$$

As we can see in Figure 9.11, the effect of this change in cost fixity of the operations is to raise the intercept on the vertical axis, decrease the slope of the total (operating) cost function TC', and reduce the break-even output.

Figure 9.11 Linear Break-Even Analysis Chart for the Allegan Manufacturing Company Showing the Effects of Substituting Fixed Costs for Variable Costs

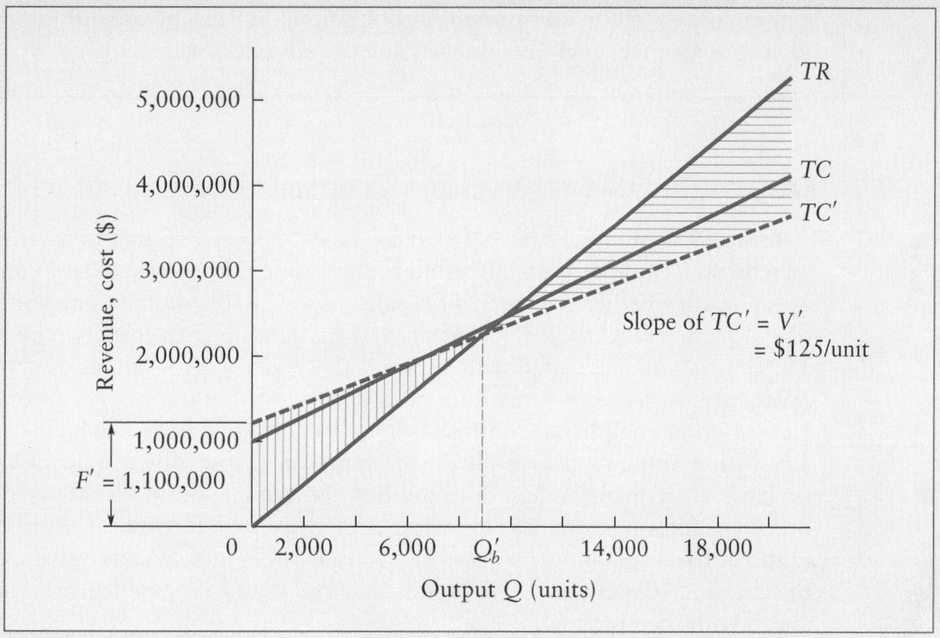

EXAMPLE

FIXED COSTS AND PRODUCTION CAPACITY AT GENERAL MOTORS[18]

In an industry with 17 million unit sales annually, GM admitted in March 2002 that it needed to reduce automobile production capacity by 1 million cars per year to match its current sales of 5 million cars. It represented the second time in its 100-year history (1988 being the earlier event) that the company had significantly shrunk its capacity. As part of its decision to reduce its size, GM planned to close 10 of its U.S. automobile assembly lines.

In the past, GM alternated between (1) building all the cars it could produce and then using costly clearance sales to attract buyers, and (2) reducing output by running plants below capacity through a slowdown in the pace of the assembly line or elimination of an entire shift. The new strategy called for the company to use 100 percent of its American automobile production capacity five days a week with two shifts per day. When automobile demand increased above this capacity level,

[18] Jacob M. Schlesinger, "GM to Reduce Capacity to Match Its Sales," *Wall Street Journal* (April 25, 1988), p. 2; Lawrence Ingrassia and Joseph B. White, "GM Plans to Close 21 More Factories, Cut 74,000 Jobs, Slash Capital Spending," *Wall Street Journal* (December 19, 1991), p. A3; and "A Duo of Dunces," *The Economist* (March 9, 2002), p. 63.

third-shift operations would be used to boost production. Ford had been following this strategy for some time.

In effect, GM and Ford were trading off lower fixed costs over the entire business cycle against (the possibility of) having to incur higher variable costs (e.g., use of higher cost overtime and third-shift operations) during periods of strong demand. As a consequence, GM's break-even output point declined sharply.

Doing a Break-Even Versus a Contribution Analysis

A break-even analysis assumes that all types of cost except the narrowly defined incremental variable cost (V) of additional unit sales are avoidable and asks the question of whether sufficient unit sales are available at the contribution margin ($P - V$) to cover all these relevant costs. If so, they allow the firm to earn a net profit. These questions normally arise at entry and exit decision points where a firm can avoid essentially all its costs if the firm decides to stay out or get out of a business. Contribution analysis, in contrast, applies to questions such as whether to adopt an advertising campaign, introduce a new product, shut down a plant temporarily, or close a division. What distinguishes these contribution analysis questions is that some fixed costs remain unavoidable and are therefore irrelevant to the decision (indirect fixed costs), while other fixed costs will be newly committed as a result of the decision (direct fixed costs) and therefore could be avoided by refusing to go ahead with the proposal.

More generally, contribution analysis always asks whether enough additional revenue arises from the ad campaign, the new product, or the projected sales of the plant or division to cover the additional fixed plus variable costs. That is, **contribution analysis** calculates whether sufficient gross operating profits result from the incremental sales (ΔQ) attributable to the ad, the new product, or the promotion to offset the proposed increase in fixed cost. In other words, are the total contributions to cover fixed cost increased by an amount greater than the increase in direct fixed cost avoidable by the decision?

Contribution Analysis
A comparison of the additional operating profits to the direct fixed costs attributable to a decision.

$$\begin{aligned}(P - V)\,\Delta Q &> \Delta \text{ Total Fixed Cost} \\ &> \Delta \text{ Indirect Fixed Cost} + \Delta \text{ Direct Fixed Cost} \qquad [9.13] \\ &> 0 + \Delta \text{ Direct Fixed Cost}\end{aligned}$$

Such decisions are not break-even decisions because they ignore (abstract from) the indirect fixed costs that, by definition, cannot be avoided by rejecting the ad campaign or new product introduction proposal or by closing the plant temporarily. For example, headquarters facility cost and other corporate overhead are indirect fixed costs that cannot be avoided by any of these decisions. So, corporate overhead is not a relevant cost in making these decisions and is therefore ignored in the contribution analysis done to support making such decisions.

In contrast, corporate overhead is prominent in the preceding examples of break-even analysis done to decide how or whether to enter a new business in the first place. Business certification, licensing, or franchise fees would be a good example of this concept of corporate overhead. The case exercise on charter airline operating decisions at the end of this chapter illustrates the use of contribution analysis as distinguished from break-even analysis.

EXAMPLE

TACO BELL CHIHUAHUA DRIVES SALES

Consider the Taco Bell ad campaign with the cute little dog that was designed to pulse twenty-five 15-second spot commercials over several weeks. The ad agency quoted a cost of $750,000 per spot to secure prime-time network television reaching 176 million households. To decide whether to buy this ad campaign, we need to know just two things: (1) the incremental sales that demand analysis suggests will be stimulated by this campaign, and (2) the contribution margin in dollars. Suppose the incremental sales are estimated at 2,100 Taco Bell meals per day for 90 days across 48 states, totaling 9,072,000 meals. If $7.99 is the average price per realized unit sale and variable costs are $5.00, should Taco Bell go ahead with the ad? The answer is yes, because when we apply Equation 9.13

$$(\$7.99 - \$5.00)\ 907{,}200 > 0 + (25 \times \$750{,}000)$$
$$\$27{,}125{,}280 > \$18{,}750{,}000$$

we see that Taco Bell would increase its operating profit by $8.4 million and make further contributions toward covering fixed cost and profit if it authorized the proposed ad campaign.

SOME LIMITATIONS OF BREAK-EVEN AND CONTRIBUTION ANALYSIS

Break-even analysis has a number of limitations that arise from the *assumptions* made in constructing the model and developing the relevant data.

COMPOSITION OF OPERATING COSTS In doing break-even analysis, one assumes that costs can be classified as either fixed or variable. In fact, some costs are partly fixed and partly variable (e.g., utility bills). Furthermore, some fixed costs increase in a stepwise manner as output is increased; they are *semivariable*. For example, machinery maintenance is scheduled after 10 hours or 10 days or 10 weeks of use. These direct fixed costs must be considered variable if a batch production decision entails this much use.

MULTIPLE PRODUCTS The break-even model also assumes that a firm is producing and selling either a *single* product or a *constant mix* of different products. In many cases the product mix changes over time, and problems can arise in allocating fixed costs among the various products.

UNCERTAINTY Still another assumption of break-even analysis is that the selling price and variable cost per unit, as well as fixed costs, are known at each level of output. In practice, these parameters are subject to uncertainty. Thus, the usefulness of the results of break-even analysis depends on the accuracy of the estimates of the future selling price and variable cost.

INCONSISTENCY OF PLANNING HORIZON Finally, break-even analysis is normally performed for a planning period of one year or less; however, the benefits received from some costs may not be realized until subsequent periods. For example, research and development costs incurred during a specific period may not result in new products for several years. For break-even analysis to be a dependable decision-making tool, a firm's operating costs must be matched with resulting revenues for the planning period under consideration.

Operating Leverage[19]

Operating Leverage

The use of assets having fixed costs (e.g., depreciation) in an effort to increase expected returns.

Degree of Operating Leverage (DOL)

The percentage change in a firm's earnings before interest and taxes (EBIT) resulting from a given percentage change in sales or output.

Operating leverage involves the use of assets that have fixed costs. A firm uses operating leverage in the hope of earning returns in excess of the fixed costs of the assets, thereby increasing the returns to the owners of the firm. A firm's **degree of operating leverage** (DOL) is defined as the multiplier effect resulting from the firm's use of fixed operating costs. More specifically, DOL can be computed as the *percentage change* in earnings before interest and taxes (EBIT) resulting from a given *percentage change* in sales (output):

$$\text{DOL at } Q = \frac{\text{Percentage change in EBIT}}{\text{Percentage change in Sales}}$$

This relationship can be rewritten as follows:

$$\text{DOL at } Q = \frac{\dfrac{\Delta\text{EBIT}}{\text{EBIT}}}{\dfrac{\Delta\text{Sales}}{\text{Sales}}} \qquad [9.14]$$

where ΔEBIT and ΔSales are the changes in the firm's EBIT and Sales, respectively.

Because a firm's DOL differs at each sales level, it is necessary to indicate the sales point, Q, at which operating leverage is measured. The degree of operating leverage is analogous to the elasticity of demand concept (e.g., price and income elasticities) because it relates percentage changes in one variable (EBIT) to percentage changes in another variable (sales). Equation 9.14 requires the use of two different values of sales and EBIT. Another equation (derived from Equation 9.14) that can be used to compute a firm's DOL more easily is

$$\text{DOL at } Q = \frac{\text{Sales} - \text{Variable costs}}{\text{EBIT}} \qquad [9.15]$$

The variables defined in the previous section on break-even analysis can also be used to develop a formula for determining a firm's DOL at any given output level. Because sales are equivalent to TR (or $P \times Q$), variable cost is equal to $V \times Q$, and EBIT is equal to total revenue (TR) less total (operating) cost, or $(P \times Q) - F - (V \times Q)$, these values can be substituted into Equation 9.15 to obtain the following:

$$\text{DOL at } Q = \frac{(P \cdot Q) - (V \cdot Q)}{(P \cdot Q) - F - (V \cdot Q)}$$

or

$$\text{DOL at } Q = \frac{(P - V)Q}{(P - V)Q - F} \qquad [9.16]$$

[19] This section can be omitted without loss of continuity.

EXAMPLE

OPERATING LEVERAGE: ALLEGAN MANUFACTURING COMPANY (continued)

In the earlier discussion of break-even analysis for the Allegan Manufacturing Company, the parameters of the break-even model were determined as $P = \$250/\text{unit}$, $V = \$150/\text{unit}$, and $F = \$1{,}000{,}000$. Substituting these values into Equation 9.16 along with the respective output (Q) values yields the DOL values shown in Table 9.2. For example, a DOL of 6.00 at an output level of 12,000 units indicates that, from a base output level of 12,000 units, EBIT will increase by 6.00 percent for each 1 percent increase in output.

Note that Allegan's DOL is largest (in absolute value terms) when the firm is operating near the break-even point (where $Q = Q_b = 10{,}000$ units). Note also that the firm's DOL is negative below the break-even output level. A negative DOL indicates the percentage *reduction* in operating *losses* that occurs as the result of a 1 percent *increase* in output. For example, the DOL of −1.50 at an output level of 6,000 units indicates that, from a base output level of 6,000 units, the firm's operating *losses* will be *reduced* by 1.5 percent for each 1 percent *increase* in output.

Table 9.2 DOL at Various Output Levels for Allegan Manufacturing Company

Output *Q*	Degree of Operating Leverage DOL
0	0
2,000	−0.25
4,000	−0.67
6,000	−1.50
8,000	−4.00
10,000	(undefined) Break-even level
12,000	+6.00
14,000	+3.50
16,000	+2.67
18,000	+2.25
20,000	+2.00

A firm's DOL is a function of the nature of the production process. If the firm employs large amounts of equipment in its operations, it tends to have relatively high fixed operating costs and relatively low variable operating costs. Such a cost structure yields a high DOL, which results in large operating profits (positive EBIT) if sales are high and large operating losses (negative EBIT) if sales are depressed.

BUSINESS RISK

Business Risk

The inherent variability or uncertainty of a firm's operating earnings (earnings before interest and taxes).

Business risk refers to the inherent variability or uncertainty of a firm's EBIT. It is a function of several factors, one of which is the firm's DOL. The DOL is a measure of how sensitive a firm's EBIT is to changes in sales. The greater a firm's DOL, the larger the change in EBIT will be for a given change in sales. Thus, *all other things being equal*, the higher a firm's DOL, the greater the degree of business risk.

Other factors can also affect a firm's business risk, including the variability or uncertainty of sales. A firm with high fixed costs and stable sales will have a high DOL, but it will also have stable EBIT and, therefore, low business risk. Public utilities and pipeline transportation companies are examples of firms having these operating characteristics.

Another factor that may affect a firm's business risk is uncertainty concerning selling prices and variable costs. A firm having a low DOL can still have high business risk if selling prices and variable costs are subject to considerable variability over time. A cattle feedlot illustrates these characteristics of low DOL but high business risk; both grain costs and the selling price of beef at times fluctuate wildly.

In summary, a firm's DOL is only one of several factors that determine the firm's business risk.

Break-Even Analysis and Risk Assessment

The break-even unit sales figure can also be used to assess the business risk to which a firm is exposed. If one forecasts the mean unit sales for some future period of time, the standard deviation of the distribution of unit sales, and makes an assumption about how actual sales are distributed, one can compute the probability that the firm will have operating losses, meaning it will sell fewer units than the break-even level.

The probability of having operating losses (selling fewer than Q_b units) can be computed using the following equation and the standard normal probability distribution as

$$z = \frac{Q_b - \overline{Q}}{\sigma_Q} \qquad [9.17]$$

where the probability values are from Table 1 in Appendix B, $\overline{Q}$ is the expected unit sales, σ_Q is the standard deviation of unit sales, and Q_b is (as defined earlier) the break-even unit sales. The probability of operating profits (selling more than Q_b units) is equal to 1 minus the probability of operating losses.

EXAMPLE

Business Risk Assessment: Allegan Manufacturing Company (continued)

For the Allegan Manufacturing Company discussed earlier, suppose that expected sales are 15,000 units with a standard deviation of 4,000 units. Recall that the break-even volume was 10,000 units. Substituting $Q_b = 10{,}000$, $\overline{Q} = 15{,}000$, and $\sigma_Q = 4{,}000$ into Equation 9.17 yields

$$z = \frac{10{,}000 - 15{,}000}{4{,}000} = -1.25$$

In other words, the break-even sales level of 10,000 units is 1.25 standard deviations *below* the mean. From Table 1 in Appendix B, the probability associated with −1.25 standard deviations is 0.1056 or 10.56 percent. Thus, Allegan faces a 10.56 percent chance that it will incur operating losses and an 89.44 percent chance (100% − 10.56% chance of losses) that it will record operating profits from selling more than the break-even number of units of output.

SUMMARY

- In estimating the behavior of short-run and long-run cost functions for firms, the primary methodological problems are (1) differences in the manner in which economists and accountants define and measure costs, and (2) accounting for other variables (in addition to the output level) that influence costs.
- Many statistical studies of *short-run* cost-output relationships suggest that total costs increase linearly (or quadratically) with output, implying constant (or rising) marginal costs over the observed ranges of output.
- Many statistical studies of *long-run* cost-output relationships indicate that long-run cost functions are L-shaped. Economies of scale (declining average costs) occur at low levels of output. Thereafter, long-run average costs remain relatively constant over large ranges of output. Diseconomies of scale are observed in only a few cases, probably because few firms can survive with costs attributable to excessive scale.
- *Engineering cost techniques* are an alternative approach to statistical methods in estimating long-run cost functions. With this approach, knowledge of production facilities and technology is used to determine the least-cost combination of labor, capital equipment, and raw materials required to produce various levels of output.
- The *survivor technique* is a method of determining the optimum size of firms within an industry by classifying them by size and then calculating the share of industry output coming from each size class over time. Size classes whose share of industry output is increasing over time are considered to be more efficient and to have lower average costs.
- *Break-even analysis* is used to examine the relationship among a firm's revenues, costs, and operating profits (EBIT) at various output levels. Frequently the analyst constructs a break-even chart based on linear cost-output and revenue-output relationships to determine the operating characteristics of a firm over a limited output range.
- The *break-even point* is defined as the output level at which total revenues equal total costs of operations. In the linear break-even model, the break-even point is found by dividing fixed costs by the difference between price and variable cost per unit, the *contribution margin*.
- *Contribution analysis* is used to examine operating profitability when some fixed costs (indirect fixed costs) cannot be avoided and other direct fixed costs can be avoided by a decision. Decisions on advertising, new product introduction, shutdown, and downsizing are often made by doing a contribution analysis.
- *Operating leverage* occurs when a firm uses assets having fixed operating costs. The *degree of operating leverage* (DOL) measures the percentage change in a firm's EBIT resulting from a 1-percent change in sales (or units of output). As a firm's fixed operating costs rise, its DOL increases.
- *Business risk* refers to the variability of a firm's EBIT. It is a function of several factors, including the firm's DOL and the variability of sales. All other things being equal, the higher a firm's DOL, the greater is its business risk.

Exercises

Answers to the exercises in blue can be found in Appendix C at the back of the book.

1. A study of 86 savings and loan associations in six northwestern states yielded the following cost function:[20]

$$C = \underset{(2.84)}{2.38} - \underset{(2.37)}{.006153Q} + \underset{(2.63)}{.000005359Q^2} + \underset{(2.69)}{19.2X_1}$$

where C = average operating expense ratio, expressed as a percentage and defined as total operating expense ($ million) divided by total assets ($ million) times 100 percent

Q = output, measured by total assets ($ million)

X_1 = ratio of the number of branches to total assets ($ million)

[20] Holton Wilson, "A Note on Scale Economies in the Savings and Loan Industry," *Business Economics* (January 1981), pp. 45–49.

Note: The number in parentheses below each coefficient is its respective *t*-statistic.

a. Which variable(s) is(are) statistically significant in explaining variations in the average operating expense ratio?

b. What type of cost-output relationship (e.g., linear, quadratic, or cubic) is suggested by these statistical results?

c. Based on these results, what can we conclude about the existence of economies or diseconomies of scale in savings and loan associations in the Northwest?

2. Referring to Exercise 1 again:

a. Holding constant the effects of branching (X_1), determine the level of total assets that minimizes the average operating expense ratio.

b. Determine the average operating expense ratio for a savings and loan association with the level of total assets determined in Part (a) and

(i) 1 branch

(ii) 10 branches

3. A study of the costs of electricity generation for a sample of 56 British firms in 1946–1947 yielded the following long-run cost function:[21]

$$AVC = 1.24 + .0033Q + .0000029Q^2 - .000046QZ - .026Z + .00018Z^2$$

where AVC = average variable cost (i.e., working costs of generation), measured in pence per kilowatt-hour (kWh). (A pence was a British monetary unit equal, at that time, to 2 cents U.S.)

Q = output, measured in millions of kWh per year

Z = plant size, measured in thousands of kilowatts

a. Determine the long-run variable cost function for electricity generation.

b. Determine the long-run marginal cost function for electricity generation.

c. Holding plant size constant at 150,000 kilowatts, determine the short-run average variable cost and marginal cost functions for electricity generation.

d. For a plant size equal to 150,000 kilowatts, determine the output level that minimizes short-run average variable costs.

e. Determine the short-run average variable cost and marginal cost at the output level obtained in Part (d).

4. Assuming that all other factors remain unchanged, determine how a firm's break-even point is affected by each of the following:

a. The firm finds it necessary to reduce the price per unit because of increased foreign competition.

b. The firm's direct labor costs are increased as the result of a new labor contract.

c. The Occupational Safety and Health Administration (OSHA) requires the firm to install new ventilating equipment in its plant. (Assume that this action has no effect on worker productivity.)

5. Cool-Aire Corporation manufactures a line of room air conditioners. Its break-even sales level is 33,000 units. Sales are approximately normally distributed. Expected sales next year are 40,000 units with a standard deviation of 4,000 units.

a. Determine the probability that Cool-Aire will incur an operating loss.

b. Determine the probability that Cool-Aire will operate above its break-even point.

---

[21] Johnston, *Statistical Cost Analysis*, Chapter 4.

6. McKee Corporation has annual fixed costs of $12 million. Its variable cost ratio is .60.
   a. Determine the company's break-even dollar sales volume.
   b. Determine the dollar sales volume required to earn a target profit of $3 million.
7. Smithton Company's sales in 2006 were $5 million. Its fixed costs were $1.5 million and its variable cost ratio was .60.
   a. Determine the company's DOL.
   b. Based on your answer to Part (a), forecast the percentage change in Smithton's EBIT for 2007, assuming that fixed costs and the variable cost ratio remain the same and that sales increase by 3 percent.

CASE EXERCISES

COST FUNCTIONS

The following cost-output data were obtained as part of a study of the economies of scale in operating a charter high school in Wisconsin:[22]

Students in Average Daily Attendance (A)	Midpoint of Values in Column A (B)	Operating Expenditure per Student (C)	Number of Schools in Sample (D)
143–200	171	$531.9	6
201–300	250	480.8	12
301–400	350	446.3	19
401–500	450	426.9	17
501–600	550	442.6	14
601–700	650	413.1	13
701–900	800	374.3	9
901–1,100	1,000	433.2	6
1,101–1,600	1,350	407.3	6
1,601–2,400	2,000	405.6	7

QUESTIONS

1. Plot the data in columns B and C in an output- (enrollment) cost graph and sketch a smooth curve that would appear to give a good fit to the data.
2. Based on the scatter diagram in Question 1, what kind of mathematical relationship would appear to exist between enrollment and operating expenditures per student? In other words, do operating expenditures per student appear to (i) be constant (and independent of enrollment), (ii) follow a linear relationship as enrollment increases, or (iii) follow some sort of nonlinear U-shape (possibly quadratic) relationship as enrollment increases?

[22] John Riew, "Economies of Scale in High School Operation," *Review of Economics and Statistics* 48, no. 3 (August 1966), pp. 280–287.

As part of this study, the following cost function was developed:

$$C = f(Q, X_1, X_2, X_3, X_4, X_5)$$

where C = operating expenditures per student in average daily attendance (measured in dollars)
Q = enrollment (number of students in average daily attendance)
X_1 = average teacher salary
X_2 = number of credit units ("courses") offered
X_3 = average number of courses taught per teacher
X_4 = change in enrollment between 1957 and 1960
X_5 = percentage of classrooms built after 1950

Variables X_1, X_2, and X_3 were considered measures of teacher qualifications, breadth of curriculum, and the degree of specialization in instruction, respectively. Variable X_4 measured changes in demand for school services that could cause some lagging adjustments in cost. Variable X_5 was used to reflect any differentials in the costs of maintenance and operation due to the varying ages of school properties. Statistical data on 109 selected high schools yielded the following regression equation:

$$\begin{aligned} C = 10.31 - &\underset{(.063)^*}{.402Q} + \underset{(.000023)^*}{.00012Q^2} + \underset{(.013)^*}{.107X_1} + \underset{(.640)}{.985X_2} - \underset{(11.95)}{15.62X_3} \\ &+ \underset{(.189)^*}{.613X_4} - \underset{(.109)}{.102X_5} \\ r^2 &= .557^* \end{aligned}$$

Notes: The numbers in parentheses are the standard deviations of each of the respective (b) coefficients. An asterisk (*) indicates that the result is statistically significant at the .01 level.

3. What type of cost-output relationship (linear, quadratic, cubic) is suggested by these statistical results?
4. What variables (other than enrollment) would appear to be most important in explaining variations in operating expenditures per student?
5. Holding constant the effects of the other variables (X_1 through X_5), determine the enrollment level (Q) at which average operating expenditures per student are minimized. (*Hint:* Find the value of Q that minimizes the ($\partial C/\partial Q$ function.)
6. Again, holding constant the effects of the other variables, use the $\partial C/\partial Q$ function to determine, for a school with 500 students, the reduction in per-student operating expenditures that will occur as the result of adding one more student.
7. Again, holding the other variables constant, what would be the saving in per-student operating expenditures of an increase in enrollment from 500 to 1,000?
8. Based on the results of this study, what can we conclude about the existence of economies or diseconomies in operating a public high school?

CHARTER AIRLINE OPERATING DECISIONS

Firm-specific demand in the *scheduled airline industry* is segmented by customer class and is highly uncertain so that an order may not lead to realized revenue and a unit sale. Airlines respond to this dynamic, highly competitive environment by tracking reservations at preannounced fares and reassigning capacity to the various market segments ("buckets") as business travelers, vacationers, and convention groups book the flights above or below expected levels several days and even weeks before scheduled departure. This systems management process combining marketing, operations, and finance is referred to as revenue management or yield management and is discussed in Chapter 14.

The *charter airline business*, on the other hand, is much less complicated because capacity requirements are known far in advance and all confirmed orders lead to realized revenue. We consider the following three decisions for a charter airline: (1) the entry/exit break-even decision, (2) the operate/shut down decision to fly/not fly a charter that has been proposed, and (3) the output decision as to how many incremental seats to sell if the airline decides to operate the charter flight.

Suppose the following costs for a 10-hour round-trip flight apply to the time frame and expenses of an unscheduled 5-hour charter flight from New York to Oakland (and return) on a 3-year-old Boeing 757 with 180 occupied seats.[23] Some costs have been aggregated up to the flight level from a seat-level decision. Others have been allocated down to the flight level from an entry/exit company-level decision. Still other costs vary with the go/no go flight-level decision itself. Your job is to analyze each cost item and figure out the "behavior of cost," or how the decision varies with cost.

Fuel and landing fees	**$5,200**
Quarterly airframe maintenance re: FAA certificate	**1,000**
Unscheduled engine maintenance per 10 flight hours	**1,200**
Pro rata time depreciation for 3rd year of airframe	**7,200**
Flight pay for pilots per round-trip flight	**4,200**
Long-term hangar facility lease	**6,600**
Annual aircraft engine operating lease	**7,100**
Base salaries of headquarters personnel	**2,000**
Food service with seat-by-seat JIT delivery at each departure	**900**
Airport ground crew baggage handling for each flight arrival	**450**

QUESTIONS

1. What are the variable costs for the decision to send one more person aboard a charter flight that is already 80 percent booked?

2. In making an entry/exit decision, if competitive pressure is projected to force the price down to $300, what is the break-even unit sales volume this company should have projected as part of its business plan before entering this market and should reconsider each time it considers leaving (exiting) this business altogether?

[23] The aerodynamics of the plane and its fuel efficiency do change as the number of seats occupied falls below 180, but you may ignore this effect.

3. Identify the indirect fixed, direct fixed, and variable costs for the go/no go decision to operate rather than not fly the charter service for a particular one of many such charters this month.

4. If one were trying to decide whether to operate (fly) or not fly an unscheduled round trip charter flight, what would be the total indirect fixed costs?

5. In the same choice situation, what would be the total direct fixed costs plus variable costs of the flight?

6. Charter contracts are negotiable, and charter carriers receive many contract offers that do not promise $300 prices or 80-percent-full planes. Should the airline accept a charter flight proposal from a group that offers to guarantee the sale of 90 seats at $250? Why or why not?

7. What are the total contributions of the charter flight with 90 seats at $250 per seat?

8. What are the net income losses this period if the airline refuses the charter, stays in business, but temporarily shuts down? What are the net income losses if it decides to operate and fly the charter that has been proposed?

9. What is the segment-level contribution of a separate group that is willing to join the 90-seat-at-$250-per-seat charter on the same plane and same departure, but only wishes to pay $50 per seat for 10 seats?

10. Should you accept their offer? What problems do you anticipate if both charter groups are placed on the 757?

APPENDIX

9a

MASS CUSTOMIZATION AND THE LEARNING CURVE[1]

Learning Curve Effect
The amount of inputs, such as labor, and associated costs required to produce each unit of output is observed to decrease with greater cumulative volume.

Mass customization is a new trend in operations management designed to standardize at least some of the production processes associated with fulfilling custom orders. Lee Jeans' customers can choose their own back pocket stitching and number of prior stone washings at a mall kiosk, but then Lee actually assembles the custom order from stockpiles of subassemblies produced with long production runs. The customer is pleased with the special attention, yet Lee Jeans maintains high-volume production. Especially in manufacturing, the quantity of resources (inputs) required to complete each successive unit of output is often observed to decrease as the *cumulative* volume of output increases. This **learning curve effect** of cumulative volume in reducing unit cost is distinguished from scale economies and increasing returns to scale that are associated with the flow rate of throughput (i.e., the output per unit time period).[2] Such learning effects are most commonly observed in the behavior of labor costs. The number of work-hours necessary to obtain one unit of output may decline for a variety of reasons as more units of the product are produced. These factors include increased familiarization with the tasks by workers and supervisors, improvements in work methods and the flow of work, and the need for fewer skilled workers as the tasks become more repetitive. Raw material costs per unit may also be subject to the learning curve effect if less scrap and waste occur as workers become more familiar with the production process. Most other variable costs are not subject to the learning process, however. For example, transportation costs per unit normally do not decline with greater cumulative volume.

The learning curve principle was first applied in airframe manufacturing, shipbuilding, and appliance manufacturing. Forecasts of declining personnel and raw material costs based on the learning curve have been used in scheduling production, in setting prices, and in evaluating the price quotations of input suppliers.

LEARNING CURVE RELATIONSHIP

The learning curve relationship is usually expressed as a constant percentage. This percentage represents the proportion by which the amount of an input (or cost) per unit of output is reduced each time production is doubled. For example, consider a

[1] An excellent survey on mass customization is found in M. Agrawal, T. V. Kumaresh, and G. A. Mercer, "The False Promise of Mass Customization," *McKinsey Quarterly* (November 3, 2001). See also "A Long March," *The Economist* (July 14, 2001), pp. 63–65.

[2] Other names given to the learning curve relationship include *learning-by-doing, progress curve, experience curve,* and *improvement curve.*

Figure 9A.1 Learning Curve: Arithmetic Scale

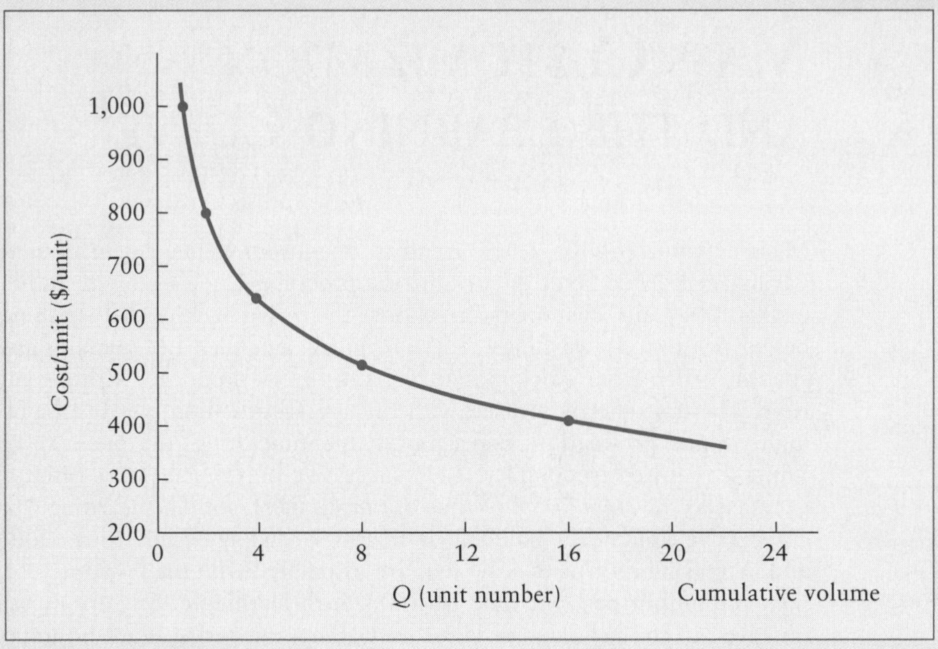

production process in which labor input and costs follow an 80 percent learning curve. Assume that the *first* unit requires labor costs of $1,000 to produce. Based on the learning curve relationship, the *second* unit costs $1,000 × 0.80 = $800, the *fourth* unit costs $800 × 0.80 = $640, the *eighth* unit costs $640 × 0.80 = $512, the *sixteenth* unit costs $512 × 0.80 = $409.60, and so on.

This learning curve relationship is shown in Figures 9A.1 and 9A.2. When plotted on an *arithmetic scale,* as shown in Figure 9A.1, the cost-output relationship is a curvilinear function. When plotted on a *logarithmic scale,* as shown in Figure 9A.2, the cost-output relationship is a linear function.

The learning curve relationship can be expressed algebraically as follows:

$$C = aQ^b \quad [9A.1]$$

where C is the input cost of the Qth unit of output, Q is consecutive units of output produced, *a* is the theoretical (or actual) input cost of the first unit of output, and *b* is the rate of reduction in input cost per unit of output. Because the learning curve is downward sloping, the value of *b* is normally negative. It should be noted that *b* is *not* the same as the learning curve percentage. Taking logarithms of both sides of Equation 9A.1 yields

$$\log C = \log a + b \log Q \quad [9A.2]$$

When the learning curve is expressed in logarithmic form, *b* represents the slope of the function.

Figure 9A.2 Learning Curve: Logarithmic Scale

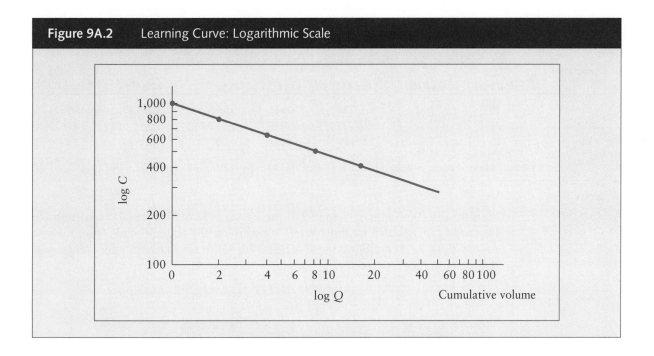

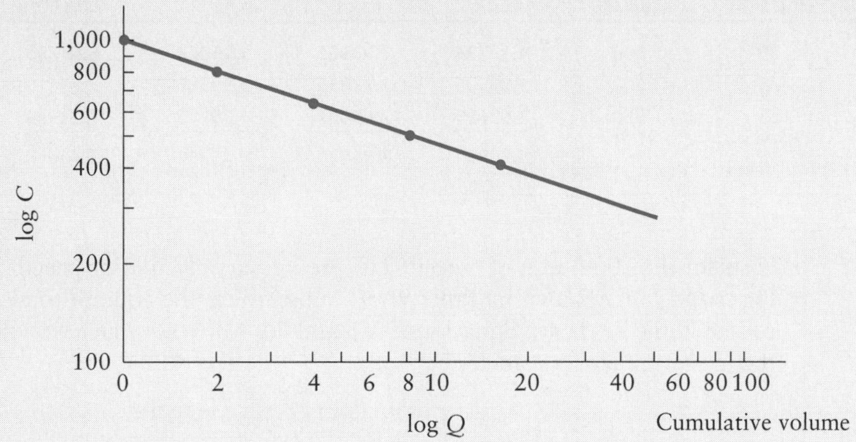

ESTIMATING THE LEARNING CURVE PARAMETERS

Application of the learning curve in forecasting costs requires that one first determine the values of the log a and b parameters in Equation 9A.2. In the absence of any historical cost-output data for the production process, one would have to make subjective estimates of these parameters based on prior experience with similar types of production operations. For a production process that has been operating for a period of time and for which historical cost-output data are available, however, regression analysis can be used to estimate the parameters. In the learning curve equation (Equation 9A.2), log C is the dependent variable and log Q is the independent variable. Applying the least-squares procedure to the series of cost-output observations yields the following equations for estimating the learning curve parameters:

$$b = \frac{n\sum(\log Q_i \log C_i) - (\sum \log Q_i)(\sum \log C_i)}{n\sum(\log Q_i)^2 - (\sum \log Q_i)^2} \quad [9A.3]$$

$$\log a = \frac{\sum \log C_i - b\sum \log Q_i}{n} \quad [9A.4]$$

where n is the number of observations.

EXAMPLE

LEARNING CURVES: EMERSON CORPORATION

The Emerson Corporation, a manufacturer of airplane landing gear equipment, is trying to develop a learning curve model to help forecast labor costs for successive units of one of its products. From past data, the firm knows that labor costs of the 25th, 75th, and 125th units were \$800, \$600, and \$500, respectively. Develop the learning curve equation from these data and use the resulting model to predict labor

Table 9A.1 Learning Curve: Preliminary Calculations

Observation i	Q_i (Unit No.)	C_i (Dollars)	Log Q_i	Log C_i	$(\text{Log } Q_i)^2$	$(\text{Log } C_i)^2$	$(\text{Log } Q_i) \times (\text{Log } C_i)$
1	25	800	1.39794	2.90309	1.95423	8.42793	4.05834
2	75	600	1.87506	2.77815	3.51585	7.71811	5.20920
3 $(=n)$	125	500	2.09691	2.69897	4.39703	7.28444	5.65950
Sum			5.36991	8.38021	9.86711	23.43048	14.92704

costs for the 200th unit of output. The preliminary calculations needed to determine log a and b are shown in Table 9A.1. Substituting the column totals from the last row of Table 9A.1 into Equations 9A.3 and 9A.4 provides the following estimates of the learning curve parameters:

$$b = \frac{3(14.92704) - (5.36991)(8.38021)}{3(9.86711) - (5.36991)^2}$$

$$= -0.28724$$

$$\log a = \frac{8.38021 - (-0.28724)(5.36991)}{3}$$

$$= 3.30755$$

The learning curve equation for labor costs is

$$\log C = 3.30755 - 0.28724 \log Q \qquad [9A.5]$$

Using this model, the estimated cost of the 200th unit of output is obtained as follows:

$$\log C = 3.30755 - 0.28724 \log 200$$

$$= 3.30755 - 0.28724\,(2.30103)$$

$$= 2.64660$$

$$C = \$443.20$$

The Percentage of Learning

The percentage of learning, which is defined as the proportion by which an input (or its associated cost) is reduced when output is doubled, can be estimated as follows:

$$L = \frac{C_2}{C_1} \times 100\% \qquad [9A.6]$$

where C_1 is the input (or cost) for the Q_1 unit of output and C_2 is the cost for the $Q_2 = 2Q_1$ unit of output.

EXAMPLE

PERCENTAGE OF LEARNING: EMERSON CORPORATION (continued)

To illustrate the calculation of the percentage of learning, consider the Emerson Corporation example again. Using the learning curve model developed earlier (Equation 9A.5), labor costs for the $Q_1 = 50$th unit of output are $C_1 = \$659.98$ and labor costs for the $2Q_1 = 100$th unit of output are $C_2 = \$540.84$. Substituting these values into Equation 9A.6 yields

$$L = \frac{\$540.84}{\$659.98} \times 100\%$$

$$= 81.9\%$$

The percentage of learning for labor costs in the production of these landing gear units is thus approximately 82 percent—indicating that labor costs decline by about 18 percent each time output is doubled.

Exercise

Answers to the exercises in blue can be found in Appendix C at the back of the book.

1. Ajax Controls Company uses a learning curve to estimate labor costs for its products. The firm recently introduced a new line of process control devices and collected the following cost data:

Unit No.	Labor Cost
100	$1,250
300	1,000
600	850

   a. Determine the learning curve for the labor costs required to produce this product.
   b. What is the percentage of learning for labor costs?
   c. Estimate the labor costs of the 800th unit based on the learning curve developed in Part (a).

PART

IV

Pricing and Output Decisions: Strategy and Tactics

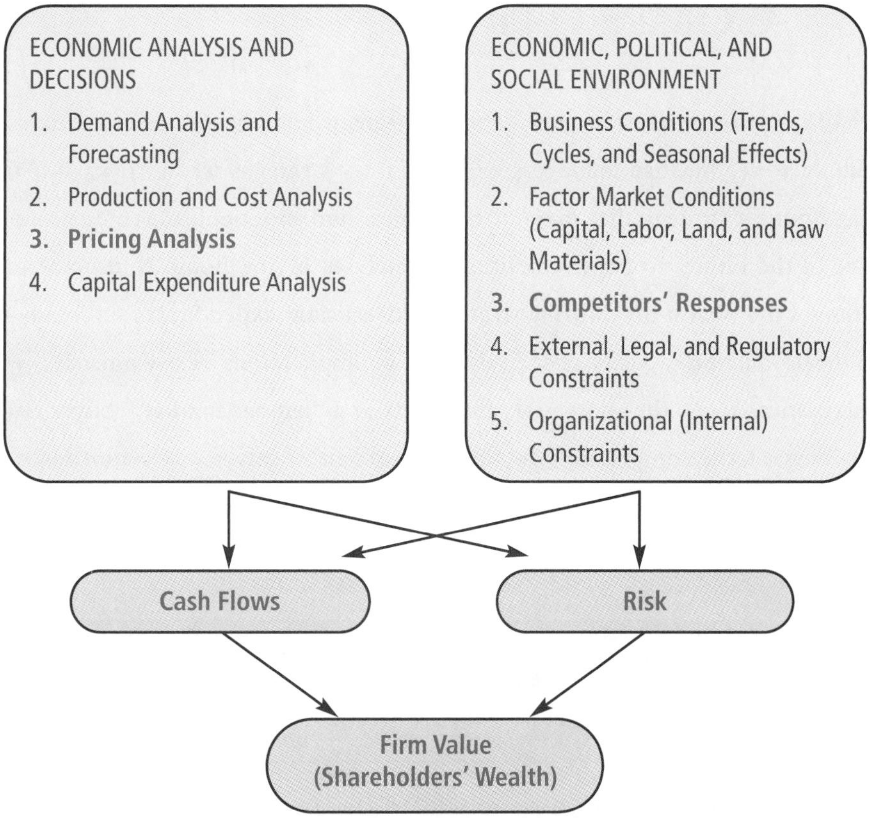

In the previous chapters we developed the theories and modeling techniques useful in analyzing demand, production, and cost relationships in a firm. In this part we consider the profit-maximizing price-output decisions, especially as they relate to the firm's strategic choices in competitive markets (Chapter 10). Asymmetric information conditions as well as ideal full information exchanges are discussed. Chapters 11 and 12 consider price and output determination in dominant-firm monopoly and oligopoly markets. Chapter 13 presents a game-theory framework for analyzing rival response tactics.

Chapter 14 examines value-based differential pricing in theory and practice and presents the concept of revenue management. Web Appendix E addresses specialized pricing problems, including pricing for the multiproduct firm, pricing of joint products, and transfer pricing.

CHAPTER

10

PRICES, OUTPUT, AND STRATEGY: PURE AND MONOPOLISTIC COMPETITION

CHAPTER PREVIEW If the goal of business is to maximize stockholder wealth, then managers will seek a pricing and output strategy that maximizes the present value of the future profits to the firm. The determination of the wealth-maximizing strategy depends on the production capacity, cost levels, demand characteristics, and the potential for immediate- and longer-term competition. In this chapter we provide an introduction to competitive strategic analysis and discuss Michael Porter's Five Forces strategic framework. We also distinguish pure and monopolistic competition with detailed analyses of the home contractor industry and of advertising expenditures in ready-to-eat cereals. The implications of asymmetrically informed sellers in a "lemons market," buyer reticence, and the problem of adverse selection in competitive markets are also discussed.

MANAGERIAL CHALLENGE

Resurrecting Apple[1]

In the 1980s, Apple Macs revolutionized personal computing by introducing a graphical user interface (GUI). The GUI was reverse engineered and quickly imitated by Microsoft whose PC operating system Windows captured a 92 percent market share by 1997. IBM and then Compaq, Dell, and Hewlett-Packard came to dominate the PC assembly business. Apple retained PC market leadership only in the education, graphics design, and publishing sectors. Because 55 percent of all PC and operating systems sales are in industry, 33 percent are in the home, 7 percent in government, and only 5 percent are in education, Apple's market share of total PC sales slipped from 9.4 percent in 1993 to 5.2 percent in 1996, 2.6 percent in 1997, and 2.3 percent in 2004.

Today, the assembly of personal computers is outsourced to a wide variety of suppliers in China and Taiwan, operating at minimum-efficient-scale. Dell, for example, assembles whatever components the buyer wants and delivers by direct mail order. With little inventory and just-in-time manufacturing on a masterfully managed supply chain, Dell's direct-to-the-consumer business model drove down costs. The company achieved a 20 percent market share and became the most profitable company in the personal computer industry.

With few outsourced components, in-house manufacturing, large overhead, and extensive R&D costs, Apple's least expensive product offering was \$1,700, whereas "comparable" IBM machines were \$1,100 and Dell's PCs were as low as \$600. Recently, the highly regarded MacPro line of laptops retailed for \$1,900, roughly twice what competing HP laptops cost. Apple initially sold primarily through retail outlets such as Computree, but to target the consumer sector rather than chief

MANAGERIAL CHALLENGE

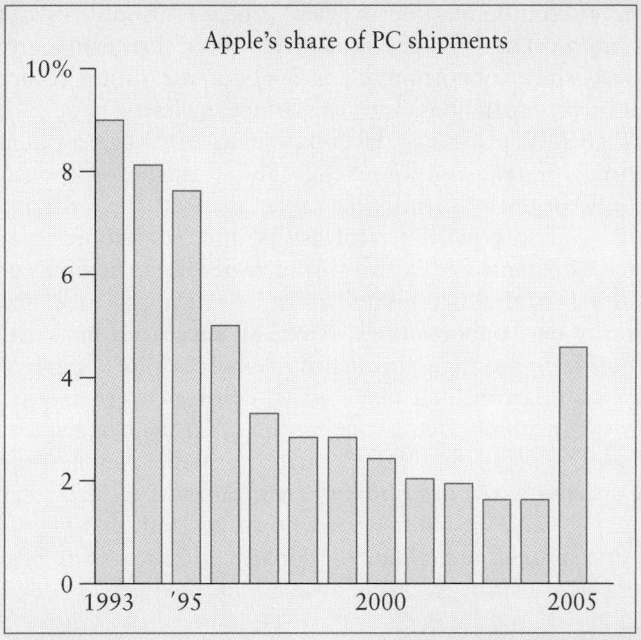

information officers in corporations, Apple recently launched dozens of company-owned stores.

In addition, Apple chose a closed (proprietary, unlicensable) operating system architecture. This approach sacrifices the numerous complementary relationships that would be available with the installed base of Microsoft customers running applications on Intel chips. A huge installed base of customers attracts independent software vendors to write applications programs. Without compatibility to this Wintel installed base, Apple's software stagnated until 2005 when Apple and Intel agreed to codevelop chips for Apple products.

In 1999, Steve Jobs regained the leadership of the company intent on restoring the brand image of the once highly innovative Apple machines. The introduction of the spiffy iMac PC made a good start and allowed Apple's market share in the $75 billion home computer market to climb back from 2 percent in 2004 to 5.4 percent in 2006. Jobs also oversaw Apple's effort to reinvent itself and revolutionized another industry by introducing the iPod. What prices to charge for iPods, distribution channels to use, and alliances to form had to be decided.

This time Apple was ready with layer upon layer of enhanced capabilities for each new generation of

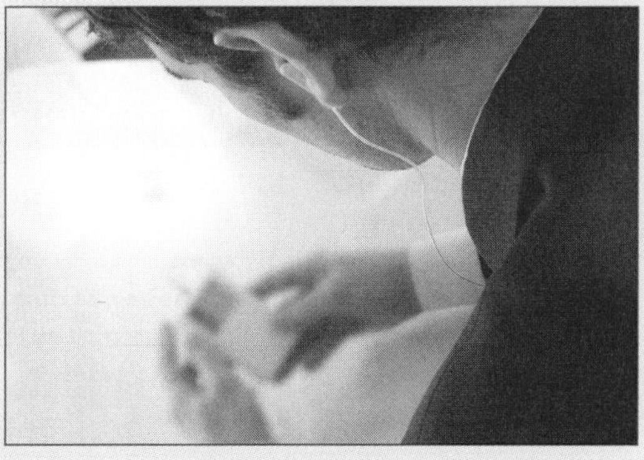

© JUNOPHOTO/fSTOP/GETTY IMAGES

its digital music products. No competitors have yet matched their compelling appeal. iPod's competitive advantages are process-based (rather than product-based) and rely on its iTunes Music Store and its partnership with Disney Inc. and record labels. Apple maintains a 70 percent share of the $9 billion digital music industry and was named the top corporate performer of 2005 by *BusinessWeek* magazine.

[1] Based on *Apple Computer 1992, 1995 (A), 1996, and 1997,* Harvard Business School Publishing; "The Road Ahead," *Wall Street Journal* (June 28, 2000), p. A3; "Is Apple Losing Its Sheen?" *Wall Street Journal* (June 28, 2004), p. B1; "Just What Apple Needs: Intel," *BusinessWeek* (January 9, 2006), p. 1; and "The Best Performers," *BusinessWeek* (March 23, 2006), p. 1.

Introduction

To remain competitive, many companies today commit themselves to strategic planning and continuous improvement processes. Competitive strategic analysis provides a framework for thinking proactively about threats to a firm's business model, about new business opportunities, and about the future reconfigurations of the firm's resources, capabilities, and core competencies.

Figure 10.1 displays the components of a business model within the context of a firm's prerequisite knowledge and strategic decisions. All successful business models begin by identifying *target markets* (i.e., what businesses one wants to enter and stay in). Physical assets, human resources, and intellectual property (such as patents and licenses) sometimes limit the firm's capabilities, but potential business models are limited only by the ability of entrepreneurial managers to identify new opportunities. Next, all successful business models lay out a ***value proposition*** grounded in customer expectations of perceived value, and then identify what part of the *value chain* the firm plans to create. Business models always must clarify *how and when revenue will be realized* and analyze the sensitivity of *gross and net margins* to various possible changes in the firm's cost structure. By specifying *required investments,* business models also assess the potential for creating *value in network relationships* with complementary businesses and in joint ventures and alliances. Finally, all successful business models develop a competitive strategy.

Value Proposition
Basis for customer willingness to pay more than cost-covering prices.

Figure 10.1 The Strategy Process

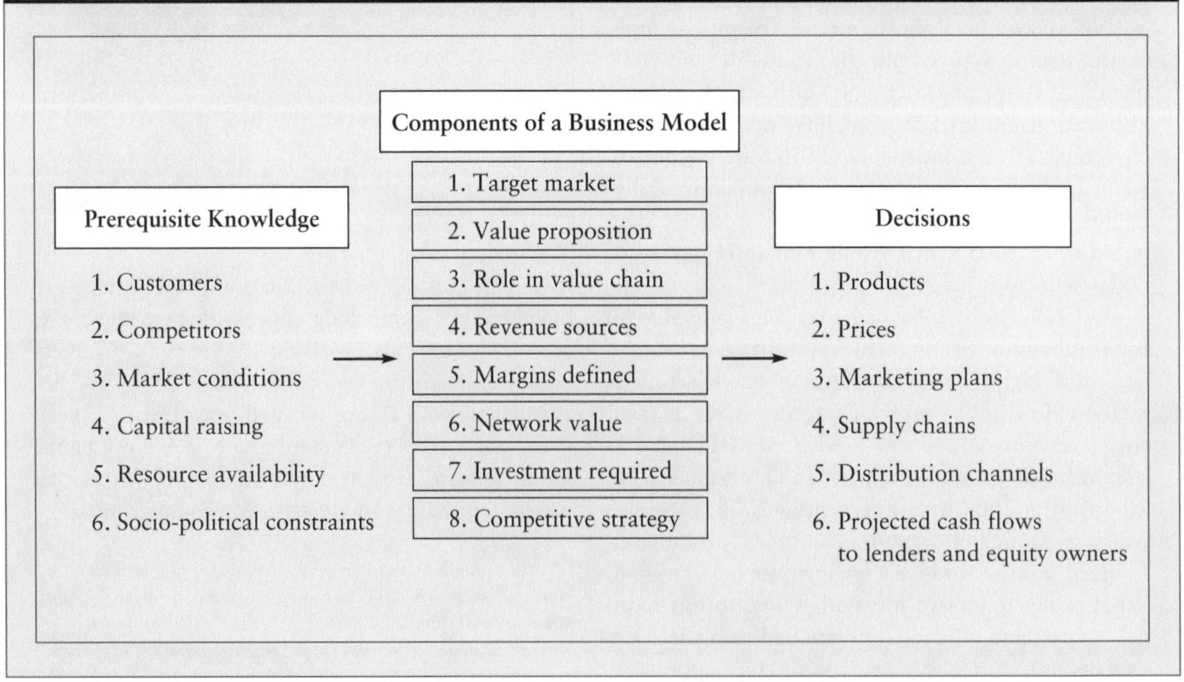

Source: Adapted from H. Chesbrough, *Open Innovation* (Cambridge, MA: Harvard University Press, 2003).

COMPETITIVE STRATEGY

The essence of competitive strategy is threefold: resource-based capabilities, business processes, and adaptive innovation.[2] First, competitive strategy analyzes how the firm can secure differential access to key resources such as patents or distribution channels. From humble beginnings as an Internet bookseller that contracted out its warehousing and book delivery service, Amazon managed to become the preferred fulfillment agent for Internet sales in general. That is, Amazon acquired enough regular customers searching for CDs, office products, tools, and toys that companies such as Toys "R" Us adopted Amazon as their Internet sales channel. Second, competitive strategy attempts to design business processes that are difficult to imitate and capable of creating unique value for the target customers. For example, the high-frequency point-to-point streamlined operations processes of Southwest Airlines prove difficult for hub-and-spoke airlines to imitate, and as a result in 2005 Southwest had a market capitalization equal to that of all the major U.S. carriers combined.

Similarly, both Dell and Compaq had $12 billion in net sales and approximately $1 billion in net income in 1998. But Compaq's business model required $6 billion in net operating assets (i.e., inventories plus net plant and equipment plus working capital) to earn $1 billion while Dell's required only $2 billion. How could Dell produce the same net income with one third as much plant and equipment, inventories, and working capital? The answer is that Dell created a direct-to-the-customer sales process; it builds to order with subassembly components bought just in time from outside contractors, and it realizes cash from a sale within 48 hours. These value-creating business processes generated 50 percent ($1 billion/$2 billion) return on investment at Dell, whereas the comparable ROI at Compaq was just 16 percent ($1 billion/$6 billion).[3]

Finally, competitive strategy provides a road map for sustaining a firm's profitability through innovation. As industries emerge, evolve, and morph into other product spaces (e.g., think of cameras, calculators, and mobile phones), firms must anticipate these changes and plan how they will sustain their positioning in the industry, and ultimately migrate their business to new industries. IBM, the dominant mainframe leasing company in the 1970s, reinvented itself twice—first in the 1980s as a PC manufacturer, and a second time in the 1990s as a systems solution provider. In contrast, some firms such as Xerox or Kodak become entrenched in outdated competitive strategic positions.

Industry Analysis
Assessment of the strengths and weaknesses of a set of competitors or line of business.

Core Competencies
Technology-based expertise or knowledge on which a company can focus its strategy.

GENERIC TYPES OF STRATEGY[4]

Strategic thinking initially focuses on **industry analysis** (i.e., identifying industries in which it would be attractive to do business). Michael Porter's Five Forces model (discussed in a later section) illustrates this approach. Soon thereafter, however, strategists want to conduct *competitor analysis* to learn more about how firms can sustain their relative profitability in a group of related firms. Efforts to answer these questions are often described as competitive *strategic positioning*. Finally, strategists try to isolate what **core competencies** any particular firm possesses as a result of its

[2] This section is based on H. Chesbrough, *Open Innovation* (Boston, MA: Harvard Business Press, 2003), pp. 73–83.

[3] Return on invested capital is defined as net income divided by net operating assets (i.e., net plant and equipment plus inventories plus net accounts receivable.)

[4] This section is based in part on C. deKluyver and J. Pearce, *Strategy: A View from the Top* (Upper Saddle River, NJ: Prentice Hall, 2003).

▲WHAT WENT RIGHT ▼WHAT WENT WRONG

XEROX[5]

Xerox invented the chemical paper copier and thereafter realized phenomenal 15 percent compound growth rates throughout the 1960s and early 1970s. When their initial patents expired, Xerox was ready with a plain paper copier (PPC) that established a first-mover technology advantage, but ultimately the company failed to receive any broad patent extension.[6] Xerox's target market was large corporations and government installations who valued high-quality, high-volume leased machines with an enormous variety of capabilities and full-service maintenance contracts, even though supplies and usage fees were expensive.

Unable to compete on product capabilities, Japanese competitors Canon and Ricoh realized that tremendous market potential lay in small businesses where affordability per copy was a major value proposition issue. Installation and service were outsourced to highly competitive independent dealer networks, and the smaller volume copy machine itself was sold at low initial cost with self-service replacement cartridges being the principal source of profitability.

As with later events at Apple, Xerox insisted on closed architecture software and built all of its copier components in house rather than pursuing partnerships that could reduce cost and trigger a larger installed base of machines. Competitors pursued just the opposite open architecture and partnership strategy to achieve network effects and drive down costs.

Between 1975 and 1985, Xerox copier sales more than doubled from $4 billion to $9 billion while those of Canon grew 25-fold from $87 million to $2.2 billion. During this "lost decade," Xerox's market share fell to 40 percent worldwide, and Canon and Ricoh both became $2 billion firms in a copier business that Xerox had totally dominated only 15 years earlier. Failure to adapt its once-dominant business model doomed Xerox to nearly second-rank status.

[5] Based on Chesbrough, op. cit.; and C. Bartlett and S. Ghoshal, *Transnational Management* (Boston, MA: Irwin-McGraw-Hill, 1995), Case 4-1.

[6] In fact, because of Xerox's 93 percent monopoly of the copier industry in 1971, the U.S. Federal Trade Commission forced Xerox in 1975 to license its PPC technology at low royalty rates.

Sustainable Competitive Advantages
Difficult-to-imitate features of a company's processes or products.

resource-based capabilities in order to identify **sustainable competitive advantages** over their competitors in a relevant market.

PRODUCT DIFFERENTIATION STRATEGY

Product Differentiation Strategy
A business-level strategy that relies upon differences in products or processes affecting perceived customer value.

Profitability clearly depends on the ability to create sustainable competitive advantages. Any one of three generic types of strategies may suffice. A firm may establish a product differentiation strategy, a lowest-delivered-cost strategy, or an information technology (IT) strategy. **Product differentiation strategy** usually involves competing on capabilities, brand naming, or product endorsements. Xerox in copiers and Kodak in paper and chemicals for film development compete on product capabilities. Coca-Cola is by far the world's most widely recognized brand, with almost 80 percent of its sales outside the United States. Marlboro, Gillette, P&G's Pampers, Nestlé, Nescafe, and Kellogg each have more than 50 percent of their sales outside their home markets. All of these branded products command a price premium worldwide simply because of the product image and lifestyle associated with their successful branding.

EXAMPLE

Rawlings Sporting Goods Waves Off the Swoosh Sign[7]

A third type of product differentiation strategy is based on endorsements. Even though $200 million Rawlings competes against heavily branded Nike with annual sales of $14 billion, Rawlings gloves are extremely profitable. The key is that they are used by more than 50 percent of major leaguers, such as St. Louis Cardinal Albert Pujols. These superstars receive only $10,000 to $20,000 for licensing their autographs to Rawlings for engraving on Little League gloves. But player after player can talk about a feature of Rawlings equipment that keeps them coming back year after year. Rawlings is attentive to this feedback and will lengthen the webbing or stiffen the fingers on a new model in just a few weeks to please their celebrity endorsers. Quick adaptation to the vagaries of the consumer marketplace is a requisite part of any product differentiation strategy.

Competitive Scope
The number and type of product lines and market segments, the number of geographic locations, and the network of horizontally and vertically integrated businesses in which the company decides to invest.

Which of the three generic types of strategy (differentiation, cost, or IT) will be most effective for a particular company depends in part on a firm's choice of **competitive scope**: the number and type of product lines and market segments, the number of geographic locations, and the network of horizontally and vertically integrated businesses in which the company decides to invest. For example, the most profitable clothing retailer in the United States (The Gap) undertook to expand its competitive scope by opening a new chain of Old Navy stores. Old Navy's bargain-priced khakis, jeans, and sweaters immediately began cannibalizing sales at its mid-priced parent. Even fashion-conscious teens could see little reason to pay $16.50 for a Gap-emblazoned t-shirt when Old Navy's branding offered style and a nearly identical product for $12.50. The configuration of a firm's resource capabilities, its business opportunities relative to its rivals, and a detailed knowledge of its customers intertwine to determine the preferred competitive scope.

Cost-Based Strategy
A business-level strategy that relies upon low-cost operations, marketing, or distribution.

Cost-Based Strategy

Competitive scope decisions are especially pivotal for **cost-based strategy**. A firm such as Southwest Airlines with a *focused cost strategy* must limit its business plan to focus narrowly on point-to-point, medium distance, nonstop routes.

EXAMPLE

Think Small to Grow Big: Southwest Airlines[8]

Southwest adopts operations processes for ticket sales, boarding, plane turnaround, crew scheduling, flight frequency, maintenance, and jet fuel hedging that deliver exceptionally reduced operating costs to target customers in their price-sensitive market niche. Anything that works against this focus must be jettisoned from the business plan. Southwest has clearly accomplished its goal. As air travel plummeted in the months following the September 11, 2001 attacks on the World Trade Center, only Southwest had a break-even that was low enough to continue to make money. Southwest can cover all of its costs at 64 percent load factors (unit sales/seat capacity). After September 11, American Airlines, United, Delta, US Airways, and America West operated well below their break-even points of 84 percent to 94 percent.

[7] Based on "I've Got It," *Wall Street Journal* (April 1, 2002), p. A1.

[8] "United's Bid to Cut Labor Costs," *Wall Street Journal* (February 25, 2003), p. A1; and Booz Allen Hamilton, *Airlines: A New Operating Model* (2003).

Much has been made of the difference in labor cost (i.e., that Southwest has labor costs covered by 36% of sales dollars while United, American, and US Airways have labor costs covered by 48% of sales dollars), but the 7 cent gap between United's $0.12 cost per revenue passenger mile (rpm) and Jet Blue's $0.05 and Southwest's $0.06 cost per rpm results primarily from different processes. Booz Allen Hamilton found that only 15 percent of the operating cost difference between full-service and low-cost carriers was labor cost. Rather, the large source of cost difference was process differences in ticket taking and reservations and crew scheduling and maintenance, as well as a different pace of operations (i.e., the famed 15-minute turnaround at Southwest).

On the other hand, Dell's *cost leadership strategy* allows it to address a wide scope of PC product lines at prices that make its competitors wish to exit the market, as IBM did in 1999. Gateway was unable to keep pace with Dell's cost-cutting and by 2006 found itself at 5.3 percent market share versus a 10.6 percent peak in 1999.

EXAMPLE

Dell's Cost Leadership in PC Assembly[9]

Dell sells over the phone and over the Internet direct to the consumer, then assembles and delivers mass-customized PCs usually within 48 hours. In contrast, Compaq's large dealer network requires 35 days to convert a sale into realized cash. Even rival mail-order company Gateway takes 16 days. Having no dealer network and realizing cash quickly might be processes to imitate, but Michael Dell pushed the just-in-time approach down his supply chain. Every company that builds critical components for Dell must warehouse within fifteen minutes travel time of a Dell factory. Consequently, Dell does not even order components until the customer commits to a purchase. Even after developing Internet distribution channels, Compaq's slower production process requires that subassembly components sit on the shelves for months. Lower inventory levels at Dell means tying up less working capital, and less working capital means lower cost.

Between 1990 and 1998, Dell drove PC prices down, and as a result, even Dell's gross margin (the difference between net sales revenue and the direct costs of goods sold as a percentage of net sales revenue) also fell, from 33 percent to 23 percent. However, Dell's net profit margin actually increased from 8 percent to 11 percent over this period. How could this happen? Dell's selling, general, and administrative expense (SG&A) declined from 21 percent of sales to 9 percent of sales. Again, less overhead means lower cost, and lower cost can mean higher profitability, even in an era of steeply falling prices.

The overall effect of this cost leadership strategy on market share, profits, and capitalized value has been stunning. Between 1996 and 2001, Dell's market share in PC shipments grew from 7 percent to 24 percent. Dell's net income increased tenfold from $260 million in 1996 to $2.3 billion in 2001. And Dell's market capitalization grew from $6 billion to $70 billion, which was the fastest growing valuation among NYSE-listed companies in several of those years.

[9] Based on "The New Economy Is Stronger Than You Think," *Harvard Business Review* (November/December 1999), pp. 104–105; Chesbrough, op. cit., p. 55; and "How Dell Fine Tunes Its Pricing," *Wall Street Journal* (June 8, 2001), p. A1.

INFORMATION TECHNOLOGY STRATEGY

Information Technology Strategy

A business-level strategy that relies on IT capabilities.

Finally, firms can seek their sustainable competitive advantage among relevant market rivals by pursuing an **information technology strategy.** In addition to assisting in the recovery of stolen vehicles, satellite-based GPS has allowed Allstate Insurance to confirm that certain cars on a family policy are not being driven to work, while other less expensive cars are exposed to the driving hazards of commuting. This information allows Allstate to cut some insurance rates and win more business from their competitors. Southland Corporation's 7-Eleven convenience stores in 6,000 locations across Japan provide another good example.

EXAMPLE

THE E-COMMERCE OF LUNCH AT 7-ELEVENS IN JAPAN[10]

Japanese office workers put in long hours, often arriving at 8 A.M. and staying well into the evening. In the midst of this long day, most take a break to go out on the street and pick up lunch. Boxed lunches, rice balls, and sandwiches are the routine offerings, but the fashion-conscious Japanese want to be seen eating what's "in." This situation makes an excellent opportunity for Southland Corporation's 7-Eleven, which is the biggest retailer in Japan and twice as profitable as the country's second largest retailer, the clothing outlet Fast Retailing. Half of sales revenue at 7-Eleven comes from these lunch items. The key to 7-Eleven Japan's success has been electronic commerce and its information technology strategy.

7-Eleven Japan collects sales information by proprietary satellite communication networks from 8,500 locations three times a day. Like other retailers, 7-Eleven Japan uses the data for merchandising studies to improve its product packaging and shelf placements with laboratory-like experiments in matched-pair stores throughout the country. But it does more—much more. 7-Eleven Japan built systems to analyze the entire data inflow in just 20 minutes. Specifically, 7-Eleven is interested in what sells this morning and what sold yesterday evening (and the local weather) as a forecast of what sandwiches to prepare for the lunch crowd rush hour today. As customers become more fickle, product fashion cycles in sandwiches are shortening from 7 weeks to, in some cases, as little time as 10 days. 7-Eleven Japan forecasts the demand daily on an item-by-item, store-by-store basis.

Of course, such short-term demand forecasting would be useless if food preparation were a production-to-stock process with many weeks of lead time required. Instead, supply chain management practices are closely monitored and adapted continuously with electronic commerce tools. Delivery trucks carry bar code readers that upload instantaneously to headquarters databases. Orders for a particular sandwich at a particular store are placed before 10 A.M., processed through the supply chain to all component input companies in less than 7 minutes, and delivered by 4 P.M. for the next day's sales. Most customers praise the extraordinary freshness, quality ingredients, and minimal incidence of out-of-stock items. All this competitive advantage over rival grocers and noodle shops has led to consistent price premiums for 7-Eleven's in-house brand.

In conclusion, a company's strategy can result in higher profits if the company configures its resource-based capabilities, business processes, and adaptive innovations in

[10] Based on "Over the Counter Commerce," *The Economist* (May 26, 2001), pp. 77–78.

such as way as to obtain a sustainable competitive advantage. Whether cost-based strategy, product differentiation strategy, or information technology strategy provides the most effective route to competitive advantage depends in large part on the firm's strategic focus. IT-based strategy is especially conducive to broad target market initiatives. In addition to using IT for merchandizing lunch items, 7-Eleven Japan "drives" customer traffic to its convenience stores by allowing Internet buyers to pick up their Web purchases and pay at the 7-Eleven counter. Is 7-Eleven Japan a convenience store, an Internet fulfillment agent like Amazon, or a warehouse and distribution company? In some sense, 7-Eleven Japan fills all of these roles. Unlike Southwest Airlines' focused cost strategy, 7-Eleven Japan has a much broader IT-based strategy that conveys a competitive advantage across several relevant markets.

The Relevant Market Concept

Relevant Market
A group of firms belonging to the same strategic group of competitors.

A **relevant market** is a group of firms that interact with each other in a buyer-seller relationship. Relevant markets often have both spatial and product characteristics. For example, the market for Microsoft's Windows operating system is worldwide, whereas the market for Minneapolis-origin air travel is confined to suppliers in the upper Midwest. Similarly, the market for large, prime-rate commercial loans includes large banks and corporations from all areas of the United States, whereas the market for bagged cement is confined to a 250-mile radius around the plant.

Concentrated Market
A relevant market with a majority of total sales occurring in the largest four firms.

Fragmented Market
A relevant market whose market shares are uniformly small.

Consolidated Market
A relevant market whose number of firms has declined through acquisition, merger, buyout, or other event.

The *market structure* within these relevant markets varies tremendously. The four largest producers of breakfast cereals control 86 percent of the total U.S. output—a **concentrated market.** In contrast, the market for concrete block and brick is **fragmented,** with the largest four firms accounting for only 8 percent of the total U.S. output. Recently, the share of the total U.S. output produced by the largest four firms in the women's hosiery industry has **consolidated,** growing from 32 percent to 58 percent. These differences in market structures and changes in market structure over time have important implications for the determination of price levels, price stability, and the likelihood of sustained profitability in these relevant markets.

Porter's Five Forces Strategic Framework

Michael Porter[11] developed a conceptual framework for identifying the threats from competition in a relevant market. Incumbent firms attempt to secure competitive advantages through their choice of management strategy. Porter's Five Forces framework conceptualizes management strategy in terms of the likelihood of sustained profitability for a particular industry or line of business. Figure 10.2 displays Porter's Five Forces: the threat of substitutes, the threat of entry, the power of buyers, the power of suppliers, and the intensity of rivalry.

The Threat of Substitutes

First, an incumbent's profitability is determined by the threat of substitutes. Is the product generic, like AAA-grade January wheat, two-bedroom apartments, and

[11] Michael Porter, *Competitive Strategy* (Cambridge, MA: The Free Press, 1998). See also Cynthia Porter and Michael Porter, eds., *Strategy: Seeking and Securing Competitive Advantage* (Cambridge, MA: Harvard Business School Publishing, 1992).

Figure 10.2 Porter's Five Forces Strategic Model

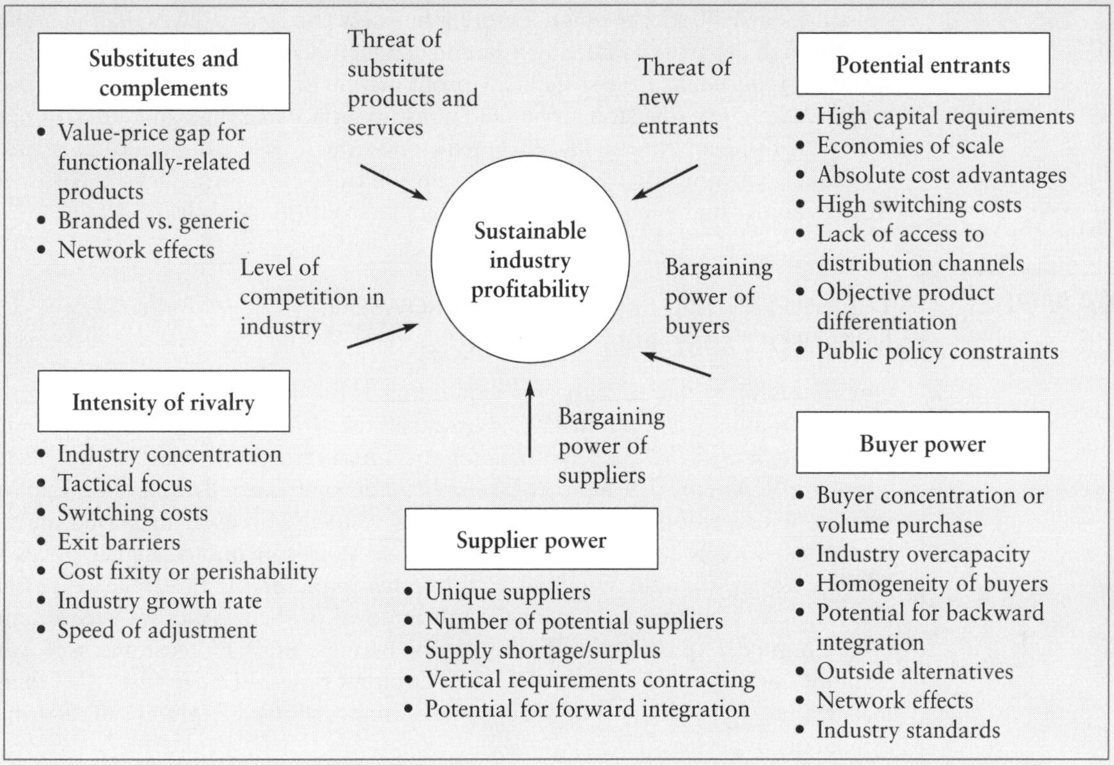

Source: Adapted from M. Porter, *Competitive Strategy* (Cambridge, MA: *The Free Press*, 1998).

office supplies, or is it branded, like Gillette razors, Coca-Cola, and Campbell's soup? The more brand loyalty, the less the threat of substitutes and the higher the incumbent's sustainable profitability will be. Also, the more distant the substitutes outside the relevant market, the less price responsive will be demand, and the larger will be the optimal markups and profit margins. For example, as video conferencing equipment improves, the margins in business air travel will decline. A video conferencing projector and sound system now leases for just $279 per month. Similarly, flavored and unflavored bottled water and other noncarbonated beverages such as juice, tea, and sports drinks are growing as much as eight times faster than U.S. soda sales. This trend will tend to erode the loyalty of Pepsi and Coke drinkers. If so, profitability will decline.

Network effects are available to enhance profitability if companies can find complements (i.e., independent firms who enhance the customer value associated with using the primary firms product, thereby raising profitability). For example, Microsoft Windows has obtained such a lock-in on PC customers for which independent software providers (ISPs) write highly valued Windows applications for which Microsoft pays nothing. Similarly, Apple's iPod attracts ISPs who enhance the customer value, price point, and positioning of iPod.

The closeness or distance of substitutes often hinges not only on consumer perceptions created by advertising, but also on segmentation of the customers into separate distribution channels. Pantyhose distributed through convenience stores have few substitutes at 9:00 P.M. the night before a business trip, many fewer than pantyhose sold through department store distribution channels. Consequently, the threat of substitutes is reduced, and the sustainable profit margin on convenience store pantyhose is higher. Similarly, one-stop service and nonstop service in airlines are different products with different functionality. United's one-stop service from Chicago provides a distant substitute for Minneapolis-origin air travelers. Consequently, Northwest Airlines enjoys high margins on nonstop service from Minneapolis.

EXAMPLE

The Relevant Market for Web Browsers: Microsoft's Internet Explorer[12]

One of the recurring antitrust policy questions is the definition of the relevant market for computer software. In 1996, Netscape's user-friendly and pioneering product Navigator had an 82 percent share of the Internet browser market. But during 1996–1999, Microsoft's Internet Explorer made swift inroads. Bundling Explorer with its widely adopted Windows operating system, Microsoft marketed an integrated software package pre-installed on PCs. Microsoft quoted higher prices for Windows alone than for Windows with Internet Explorer and threatened PC assemblers such as Compaq and Gateway with removal of their Windows license unless they mounted Explorer as a desktop icon. Because most PC customers do want Windows pre-installed on their machines, Explorer penetrated deep into the browser market quickly. By the start of 2000, some estimates showed Explorer's market share as high as 59 percent.

If the relevant market for these products is an integrated PC operating system (OS), then Microsoft simply incorporated new Web browser and media player technology into an already dominant Windows OS product. An analogy might be the interlock between an automobile's ignition and steering system to deter auto theft. If, on the other hand, Internet browsers (or more recently, media players) are a separate relevant market, like stereo equipment for automobiles, then Microsoft should not be entitled to employ anticompetitive practices, such as refusals to deal, to extend their dominance of PC operating systems into this new software market.

Microsoft's spectacular growth in sales of Windows 98 was not the issue. Winning a near monopoly of 85 percent market share in the previously fragmented OS software industry indicated a superior product, a great business plan, and good management. But allowing Microsoft to extend that market power into a new line of business using tactics that would be ineffective and self-defeating in the absence of the dominant market share in the original business is just what the antitrust laws were intended to prevent. Twenty states attorney general in the United States and the European antitrust authorities pursued this line of reasoning. The EU insisted on multiple versions of Windows with (and without) Media Player stripped out and fined Microsoft $624 million in March 2004.

[12] Based on "U.S. Sues Microsoft over PC Browser," *Wall Street Journal* (October 21, 1997); "Personal Technology," *Wall Street Journal* (October 30, 1997); "Microsoft's Browser: A Bundle of Trouble," *The Economist* (October 25, 1997); and *U.S. News and World Report,* Business and Technology (December 15, 1997).

THE THREAT OF ENTRY

A second force determining the likely profitability of an industry or product line is the threat of potential entrants. The higher the barriers to entry, the more profitable an incumbent will be. Barriers to entry can arise from several factors. First, consider high capital costs. The bottling and distribution business in the soft drink industry necessitates a \$50 million investment. Although a good business plan with secure collateral will always attract loanable funds, unsecured loans become difficult to finance at this size. Fewer potential entrants with the necessary capital imply a lesser threat of entry and higher incumbent profitability.

Second, economies of scale and absolute cost advantages can provide another barrier to entry. In the traditional cable TV industry, the huge infrastructure cost of laying wire throughout the community deterred multiple entrants. The first-mover had a tremendous scale economy in spreading fixed cost across a large customer base. An absolute cost advantage arises with proprietary IT technology that lowers a company's cost (e.g., at 7-Eleven Japan). Of course, wireless technology for satellite-based TV may soon lower this barrier, and then numerous suppliers of TV content will exhibit similar unit cost. These new threats of entry imply lower industry profitability in cable TV.

Third, if customers are brand loyal, the costs of inducing a customer to switch to a new entrant's product may pose a substantial barrier to entry. Year after year, hundreds of millions of dollars of cumulative advertising in the cereal industry maintains the pulling power of the Tony the Tiger Frosted Flakes brand. Unadvertised cereals go unnoticed. To take another example, hotel corporations raise the switching costs for their regular customers when they issue frequent guest giveaways. Committing room capacity to promotional giveaways raises barriers to entry. A new entrant therefore has a higher cost associated with becoming an effective entry threat in these markets.

EXAMPLE

POTENTIAL ENTRY AT OFFICE DEPOT/STAPLES[13]

In 1997 Office Depot (a \$6 billion company) and Staples (a \$4 billion company) proposed to merge. Their combined sales in the \$13 billion office supply superstore industry totaled 76 percent. From another perspective, their potential competitors included not only OfficeMax but all small paper goods specialty stores, department stores, discount stores such as Kmart, warehouse clubs like Sam's Club, office supply catalogs, and some computer retailers. This much larger office supply industry is fragmented, easy to enter, and huge (\$185 billion). Using this latter standard, the combined market share of Staples and Office Depot was only 6 percent.

The profit margins of Office Depot, OfficeMax, and Staples are significantly higher when only one office supply superstore locates in a town, which suggests that the small-scale office suppliers offer little threat of entry into the superstore market. The exceptional ease of entry (and exit) at a small scale moderates the markups and profit margins of incumbent specialty retailers such as stationery stores, but not

[13] Based on "FTC Rejects Staples' Settlement Offer," *Wall Street Journal* (April 7, 1997), p. A3; and J. Baker, "Econometric Analysis in *FTC* v. *Staples*," *Journal of Public Policy and Marketing* 18, no. 1 (Spring 1999), pp. 11–21.

office supply superstores. High capital requirement and scale economies in warehousing and distribution appear responsible for the barriers to entry in the office supply superstore market.

Access to distribution channels is another potential barrier that has implications for the profitability of incumbents. The shelf space in grocery stores is limited; all the slots are filled. A new entrant would therefore have to offer huge trade promotions (i.e., free display racks or slot-in allowances) to induce grocery store chains to displace one of their current suppliers. A related barrier to entry has emerged in the satellite television industry where DirecTV and EchoStar control essentially all the channel slots on satellites capable of reaching the entire U.S. audience. Government regulatory agencies also can approve or deny access to distribution channels. For example, the FDA approves prescription drugs for certain therapeutic uses but not for others. The FDA also approves or denies exceptions to the Orphan Drug Act that gives firms patent-like exclusive selling rights when public policy pressure warrants doing so. Biogen's highest sales product, Avonex (a weekly injection for multiple sclerosis patients), received an exception to the Orphan Drug Act. Other similarly situated firms have been denied approval; such a barrier to entry may prove insurmountable.

Preexisting competitors in related product lines provide a substantial threat of entry as well. Netflix's one-day mailing service for DVD movie rentals acquired 3 million U.S. customers in its first three years in operation. Charging $17.99 a month for an unlimited number of movie rental (three at one time) and prepaying the minor mailing fees, Netflix revolutionized the movie rental business. However, by 2005 the video rental giant Blockbuster decided to enter the online DVD rental business and drove prices down to $14.99. Netflix responded with a cut-rate service of one movie at a time for $9.99 per month, which drove the net profit right out of the business.

EXAMPLE

Eli Lilly Poses a Threat of Potential Entry for AstraZeneca[14]

Eli Lilly markets a pharmaceutical product, Evista, long approved by the FDA for the treatment of osteoporosis. Preliminary tests suggested a therapeutic potential for Evista in the prevention of breast cancer. Lilly promptly released an Evista study in which the incidence of developing cancer over a three-year period was reduced 55 percent in 10,575 women with high-risk factors for developing breast cancer. Zeneca Group PLC then sued to stop Lilly trade representatives from making any such product claims. In 2000, AstraZeneca's cancer treatment Nolvadex became the first drug ever approved for reducing the risk of breast cancer in presently healthy women. AstraZeneca's lawsuit undoubtedly slowed Lilly's marketing efforts, but the real barrier to entry would come if the FDA denies the use of Evista for breast cancer treatment. Without such a denial, Nolvadex faces a formidable direct competitor from a preexisting supplier in the adjacent relevant market.

[14] "Zeneca Sues Eli Lilly Over Evista Promotion," *Wall Street Journal* (February 26, 1999), p. B6.

Finally, a barrier to entry may be posed by product differentiation. If the differences between products are objective (e.g., dot matrix quality in a copier or shutter speed technology in a camera), the entrant can reverse engineer the copier or camera. Perceived product differentiation is actually harder to imitate and poses therefore a more effective barrier.

EXAMPLE

OBJECTIVE VERSUS PERCEIVED PRODUCT DIFFERENTIATION: XEROX

Shielded from competition by patents on its landmark dry paper copier, Xerox enjoyed essentially a monopoly and 15 percent compound earnings growth through the 1960s and early 1970s. During this period, its research lab in Palo Alto, California, spun off one breakthrough device after another. One year it was the graphical user interface that Apple later brought to market as a user-friendly PC. In 1979, Xerox scientists and engineers developed the Ethernet, a first local area network for connecting computers and printers. Yet, Xerox was able to commercialize almost none of these R&D successes. As a result, Japanese copier companies such as Canon and IKON reverse engineered the Xerox product, imitated its processes, and ultimately developed better and cheaper copiers.

Especially with the increasing globalization of commerce, objective product differentiation is always subject to reverse engineering, violations of intellectual property, and offshore imitation even of patented products. In contrast, product differentiation based on customer perceptions of lifestyle images and product positioning (e.g., Coca-Cola) can erect barriers to entry that allow incumbent firms to better survive competitive attack. In sum, the higher any of these barriers to entry, the lower the threat of potential entrants and the higher the potential industry profitability will be.

THE POWER OF BUYERS AND SUPPLIERS

The profitability of incumbents is determined in part by the bargaining power of buyers and suppliers. Buyers may be highly concentrated, such as Boeing, Lockheed, and Airbus in the purchase of large aircraft engines, or extremely fragmented, such as restaurants that are customers of wholesale grocery companies. If industry capacity approximately equals or exceeds demand, concentrated buyers can force price concessions that reduce an incumbent's profitability. On the other hand, fragmented buyers have little bargaining power unless excess capacity and inventory overhang persist.

Unique suppliers may also reduce industry profitability. The Coca-Cola Co. establishes exclusive franchise arrangements with independent bottlers. No other supplier can provide the secret ingredients in the concentrate syrup. Bottler profitability is therefore rather low. In contrast, Coke's own suppliers are numerous; many potential sugar and flavoring manufacturers would like to win the Coca-Cola account, and the syrup inputs are nonunique commodities. These factors raise the likely profitability of the concentrate manufacturers because of the lack of power among their suppliers.

Supply shortages, stockouts, and a backorder production environment can alter the relative power of buyers and suppliers in the value chain. One of the few levers a supplier has against huge category-killer retailers like Toys "R" Us to prevent their expropriating all the net value is to refuse to guarantee on-time delivery for triple orders of popular products. A deeply discounted wholesale price should never receive 100 percent delivery reliability.

Finally, buyers and suppliers will have more bargaining power and reduce firm profitability when they possess more outside alternatives and can credibly threaten to vertically integrate into the industry. HMOs can negotiate low fees from primary care physicians precisely because the HMO has so many outside alternatives. Buyers who control the setting of industry standards can also negotiate substantial reductions in pricing and profitability from manufacturers who may then be in a position to capture network effects. Companies favored by having their product specs adopted as an industry standard often experience increasing returns to their marketing expenditures.

The Intensity of Rivalrous Tactics

In the global economy, few companies can establish and maintain dominance in anything beyond niche markets. Reverse engineering of products, imitation of advertising images, and offshore production at low cost imply that General Motors (GM) cannot hope to rid itself of Ford and DaimlerChrysler, and Coca-Cola cannot hope truly to defeat Pepsi. Instead, to sustain profitability in such a setting, companies must avoid intense rivalries and elicit passive, more cooperative responses from close competitors. The intensity of the rivalry in an industry depends on several factors: industry concentration, the tactical focus of competition, switching costs, the presence of exit barriers, the industry growth rate, and the ratio of fixed to total cost (termed the **cost fixity**) in the typical cost structure.

Cost Fixity

A measure of fixed-to-total cost that is correlated with gross profit margins.

What firms and what products offer close substitutes for potential customers in the relevant market determine the degree of industry concentration. One measure of industry concentration is the sum of the market shares of the four largest or eight largest firms in an industry. The larger the market shares and the smaller the number of competitors, the more interdependence each firm will perceive, and the less intense the rivalry. The ready-to-eat cereal industry has more intense rivalry than the soft drink industry, in part because Kellogg's (37 percent), General Mills (25 percent), Post (15 percent), and Quaker Oats (8 percent) together enjoy 85 percent of the market. When two firms enjoy 60–90 percent of industry shipments (e.g., Pepsi and Coke), their transparent interdependence can lead to reduced intensity of rivalry if the firms tacitly collude. Similarly, because Titleist and Spalding dominate the golf ball market, the rivalrous intensity is less than in the fragmented golf club business.

Sustainable profitability is increased by tactics that focus on nonprice rather than price competition. Airlines are more profitable when they can avoid price wars and focus their competition for passengers on service quality (e.g., delivery reliability, change-order responsiveness, and schedule convenience). But trunk route airlines between major U.S. cities provide generic transportation with nearly identical service quality and departure frequency. Consequently, fare wars are frequent, and the resulting profitability of trunk airline routes is low. In contrast, long-standing rivals Coca-Cola and Pepsi have never discounted their cola concentrates. This absence of "gain-share discounting" and a diminished focus on price competition tactics in general increases the profitability of the concentrate business. Airlines tried to control gain-share discounting by introducing "frequent flyer" programs to increase the customers' *switching cost* from one competitor to another. This idea to reduce the intensity of rivalry worked well for a time, until business travelers joined essentially all the rival frequent flyer programs.

EXAMPLE

PRICE COMPETITION AT THE SODA FOUNTAIN: PEPSICO INC.[15]

Soft drinks are marketed through several distribution channels at different prices. The channels of distribution include independent beverage resellers, vending machine companies, and company-owned bottlers that supply supermarkets, convenience stores, and vending machines, which account for 31 percent, 12 percent, and 11 percent, respectively, of all soft drink sales. Shelf slots in the store channels are full, and bottlers compete on stocking services and retailer rebates for prime shelf space and vending machine locations in an attempt to grow their brands. With roughly the same percent market shares in the stores, the Coca-Cola- and PepsiCo-owned bottlers attempt to avoid head-to-head price competition, which would simply lower profits for both firms, and instead seek predictable patterns of company-sponsored once-every-other-week discounts. Where independent beverage resellers have established a practice of persistent gain-share discounting, the Coca-Cola Company and PepsiCo have often attempted to purchase the franchises and replace them with company-owned bottlers. Vending operations are high margin businesses, and PepsiCo and Coca-Cola increasingly service vending machines directly from their company-owned bottlers. To date, little price competition has emerged in the vending channel, in part because independents must purchase from exclusive franchise bottlers in their areas.

Price competition is heating up, however, in the fountain drink side of the business. As more and more families eat more and more meals outside the household, the fountain drink channel accounted for 37 percent of total sales. Coca-Cola has long dominated the fountain drink business. At restaurants and soda shops in 2000, Coke enjoyed a 59 percent share to Pepsi's 23 percent. Recently, PepsiCo declared an intent to vigorously pursue fountain drink sales through discount pricing tactics if necessary. This development threatens continuing profitability in this important channel of the soft drink industry.

Sometimes price versus nonprice competition simply reflects the lack of product differentiation available in commodity-like markets (e.g., in selling cement). However, the incidence of price competition is also determined in part by the cost structure prevalent in the industry. Where fixed costs as a percentage of total costs are high, margins will tend to be larger. If so, firms are tempted to fight tooth and nail for incremental customers because every additional unit sale represents a substantial contribution to covering the fixed costs. All other things being the same, gain-share discounting will therefore tend to increase the greater the fixed cost is. For example, gross margins in the airline industry reflect the enormous fixed costs for aircraft leases and terminal facilities, often reaching 80 percent. Consider the following **break-even sales change analysis** for an airline that seeks to increase its total contributions by lowering its prices 10 percent:

Break-Even Sales Change Analysis

A calculation of the percentage increase in unit sales required to justify a price discount, given the gross margin.

$$\begin{aligned}(P_0 - MC)\, Q_0 &< (0.9\, P_0 - MC)\, Q_1 \\ &< (0.9\, P_0 - MC)\, (Q_0 + \Delta Q)\end{aligned} \quad [10.1]$$

[15] Based on "Cola Wars Continue," Harvard Business School Case Publishing (1994); "Pepsi Hopes to Tap Coke's Fountain Sales," *USA Today* (November 6, 1997), p. 3B; and "Antitrust Suit Focuses on Bottlers' Pricing and Sales Practices," *Wall Street Journal* (January 20, 1999), p. B7.

where revenue minus variable cost ($MC \times Q$) is the *total contribution*. If discounting is to succeed in raising total contributions, the change in sales ΔQ must be great enough to more than offset the 10 percent decline in revenue per unit sale. Rearranging Equation 10.1 and dividing by P_0 yields

$$\frac{(P_0 - MC)\, Q_0}{P_0} < \left[\frac{P_0 - MC}{P_0} - 0.1\,\frac{P_0}{P_0}\right](Q_0 + \Delta Q)$$

$$(PCM)\, Q_0 < (PCM - 0.1)(Q_0 + \Delta Q)$$

where PCM is the price-cost margin, often referred to as the contribution margin. That is,

$$\frac{PCM}{(PCM - 0.1)} < \frac{(Q_0 + \Delta Q)}{Q_0}$$

$$\frac{PCM}{(PCM - 0.1)} < 1 + \frac{\Delta Q}{Q_0} \qquad [10.2]$$

Using Equation 10.2, an 80 percent price-cost margin implies that a sales increase of only 15 percent is all that one requires to warrant cutting prices by 10 percent. Here's how one reaches that conclusion:

$$\frac{0.8}{[0.8 - 0.1]} < 1 + \frac{\Delta Q}{Q_0}$$

$$1.14 < 1 + \frac{\Delta Q}{Q_0}$$

$$1.14 < 1 + 0.15$$

In contrast, in paperback book publishing, a price-cost margin of 12 percent implies sales must increase by better than 500 percent in order to warrant a 10-percent price cut (i.e., $0.12/0.02 < 1 + 5.0^{+}$). Because a marketing plan that creates a 15 percent sales increase from a 10 percent price cut is much more likely than one that creates a 500 percent sales increase from a 10 percent price cut, the airline industry is more likely to focus on pricing competition than the paperback book publishing industry.

EXAMPLE

Contribution Margins at Hanes Discourage Discounting

First-quality white cotton T-shirts and briefs have long been the mainstay of the Hanes Corporation. Selling these "blanks" to other companies that perform value-added finishing, dyeing, embroidering, or custom stitching, Hanes captures only the initial stages in the value chain. At a wholesale price of \$1.25 and with \$0.85 direct cost of goods sold, the gross margin for Hanes briefs of \$0.40 must recover all fixed costs plus all distribution and selling expenses to earn a profit. With a \$0.15 commission per unit sale as a selling expense, the contribution margin in dollars (*CM*) is \$0.25, and the contribution margin percentage (*PCM*) is \$0.25/\$1.25 = 20%.

Because of the price-elastic demand, price discounted by as little as 15 percent can double unit sales. However, with contribution margins (*PCM*) as low as 20 percent, the additional sales triggered by the discount are much less attractive than one might think. Break-even sales change analysis using Equation 10.2 confirms that a

Table 10.1 Hanes Sales Volume Required to Maintain Operating Profit with a 15 Percent Price Cut

	Given Data	With 15% Price Cut	Double Sales Volume	Triple Sales Volume	Quadruple Sales Volume
Price	1.25	1.0625	2.125	3.1875	4.25
DCGS (VC only)	−0.85	−0.85	−1.70	−2.55	−3.40
Commission	−0.15	−0.15	−0.30	−0.45	−0.60
CM	0.25	0.0625	0.125	0.1875	0.25

doubling of sales volume is less than the incremental sales change required to restore total contributions to the levels earned before the price cut:

$$PCM/(PCM - \Delta P) = 0.20/(0.20 - 0.15) = 4.0$$

The interpretation here is that unit sales must increase by 300 percent $(1 + 300\%\Delta Q)$ in order to restore total contributions to their preexisting level. That is, the price reduction must more than *quadruple* unit sales in order to raise total contributions (operating profit). The data displayed in Table 10.1 demonstrate this conclusion in a spreadsheet format.

Barriers to Exit

Economic losses resulting from nonredeployable assets or contractual constraints upon business termination.

Barriers to exit increase the intensity of rivalry in a tight oligopoly. If remote plants specific to a particular line of products (e.g., aluminum smelting plants) are nonredeployable, the tactics will be more aggressive because no competitor can fully recover its sunk cost should margins collapse. In addition to capital equipment, nonredeployable assets can include product-specific display racks (L'eggs); product-specific showrooms (Ethan Allen); and intangible assets that prove difficult to carve up and package for resale (unpatented trade secrets and basic research). Trucking companies, on the other hand, own highly redeployable assets (i.e., trucks and warehouses). If a trucking company attacks its rivals, encounters aggressive retaliation, and then fails and must liquidate its assets, the owners can hope to receive nearly the full value of the economic working life remaining in their trucks and warehouses. As a result, competitive tactics in the trucking industry are not as effective in threatening rivals, so competitive rivalrous intensity is lower and profitability is higher.

Finally, industry demand growth can influence the intensity of rivalry. When sales to established customers are increasing and new customers are appearing in the market, rival firms are often content to maintain market share and realize high profitability. When demand growth declines, competitive tactics sharpen in many industries, especially if capacity planning has failed to anticipate the decline. Furniture companies discount steeply when housing demand slows. Airline prices and profits declined sharply when demand for air travel leveled off unexpectedly after the Gulf War. Between 1965 and 1975, soft drink consumption in the United States grew by 49 percent. Again, between 1975 and 1985, demand growth was 53 percent. However, from 1985 to 1995, U.S. demand grew by only 24 percent. Sales in the United States flattened out by 1992; annual consumption had reached a plateau of approximately 50 gallons per person (i.e., a gallon per week). Porter's model predicts that flat soft drink demand would lead to more intense rivalry and lower profitability at PepsiCo Inc. and Coca-Cola Co. Recently, Coca-Cola deflected many initiatives to its fast-growing international division in an attempt to reduce the likelihood of intense rivalry with PepsiCo here in the United States.

EXAMPLE

Intensity of Rivalry at Northwest Airlines[16]

The Minneapolis hub of Northwest Airlines is a concentrated terminal facility; Northwest has more than 80 percent of the flights. Thus, Northwest's market share is comparable to Microsoft's dominance of the operating system business with Windows XP. However, high indirect fixed costs for aircraft leases and facilities imply high margins that make it tempting for airlines to attract incremental customers through price discounting. In contrast, Windows is seldom, if ever, discounted. Also, exit barriers are low in airlines but rather high in computer software, where massive sunk-cost expenses for research and development create largely unpatentable trade secrets that are not easily resold. Finally, industry demand growth is low in airlines but extremely high in computer software. Consequently, in one-stop flights from Minneapolis, Northwest is subject to intense rivalry but Microsoft Windows is not.

Frequent price competition, low exit barriers, and flat growth all imply tremendous rivalrous intensity in the airline industry and downward competitive pressure on Northwest Airline's profit margins. The opposite is true in Microsoft's OS software business. Windows XP is seldom discounted and remains extremely profitable. In short, airlines have industry characteristics that incline the performance results of even a dominant firm to be more nearly competitive, whereas a dominant firm in computer operating systems faces less intense rivalry.

Finally, the speed of adjustment of rivalrous actions and reactions matters. Recall that if incumbents are slow to respond to tactical initiatives of hit-and-run entrants, then profitability may be driven down to the break-even levels in so-called contestable markets. In contrast, if incumbents are easily provoked and exhibit fast adjustment speeds, then profitability is often more sustainable.

The Myth of Market Share

In summary, the key to profitability in many businesses is to design a strategy that reduces the threat of substitutes, the power of buyers and suppliers, and the threat of entry. Then, firms must adopt tactics and elicit tactical responses from their rivals so that the profit potential in their effective business strategy is not eroded away. This strategy often means forsaking gain-share discounting and other aggressive tactics that would spiral the industry into price wars. Price premiums reflecting true customer value are difficult to win back once buyers have grown accustomed to a pattern of deep discount rivalry between the competitors or predictably timed clearance sales. Airlines and department store retailers are painfully aware of these tactical mistakes.

[16] Based on "Mergers, Monopolies, and the Soaring Cost of Flying," *The Margin* (March/April 1990), p. 19; and "Flying to Charlotte Is Easy," *Wall Street Journal* (June 14, 1995), p. S1.

More generally, discounting and excessive promotions designed to grab market share are seldom a source of long-term profitability and often result in lower capitalized value. The soft-drink bottler 7-Up doubled and tripled its market share in the late 1970s largely through discounting. But profits declined, and the company was eventually acquired by Cadbury Schweppes. Hon Industries makes twice the return on investment of Steelcase in the office equipment market even though Hon is one third of Steelcase's size. Boeing was much more profitable allowing a slight majority of wide-bodied orders to go to government-subsidized Airbus rather than tie up their own assembly-line operations with hundreds of additional orders triggered by the low prices.

After the initial penetration of a new product or new technology into a relevant market, market share should never become an end in itself. Increasing market share is the means to achieve scale economies and learning curve-based cost advantages. But additional share points at any cost almost always mean a reduction in profits, not the reverse.

A Continuum of Market Structures

The relationship between individual firms and the relevant market as a whole is referred to as the industry's *market structure* and depends upon the following factors:

1. The number and relative size of firms in the industry
2. The degree of product differentiation among the products sold by the firms of the industry
3. The extent to which decision making by individual firms is independent, not interdependent or collusive
4. The conditions of entry and exit

Four specific market structures are often distinguished: pure competition, monopoly, monopolistic competition, and oligopoly. If we were to graph the structures on a continuum with the extremes at either end, it would look like the following:

Pure Competition — **Monopolistic Competition** — **Oligopoly** — **Monopoly**

Pure Competition

Pure Competition

A market structure characterized by a large number of buyers and sellers of a homogeneous (nondifferentiated) product, where entry and exit from the industry is costless or nearly so; information is freely available to all market participants; and no collusion occurs among firms in the industry.

The **pure competition** industry model has the following characteristics:

1. A large number of buyers and sellers, each of which buys or sells such a small proportion of the total industry output that a single buyer's or seller's actions cannot have a perceptible impact on the market price
2. A homogeneous product produced by each firm; that is, no product differentiation, as with licensed taxi cab services or AAA-grade January wheat
3. Complete knowledge of all relevant market information by all firms, each of which acts totally independently, such as the 117 home builders of standardized two-bedroom subdivision homes in a large city
4. Free entry and exit from the market; that is, minimal barriers to entry and exit

The single firm in a purely competitive industry is, in essence, a price taker. Because the products of each producer are almost perfect substitutes for the products

Figure 10.3 Pure Competition in the Tract Home Building Industry

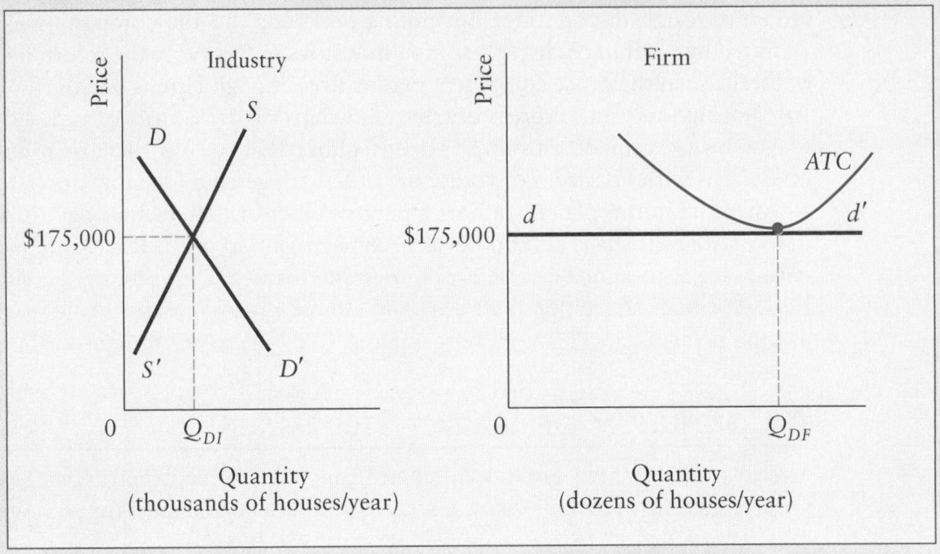

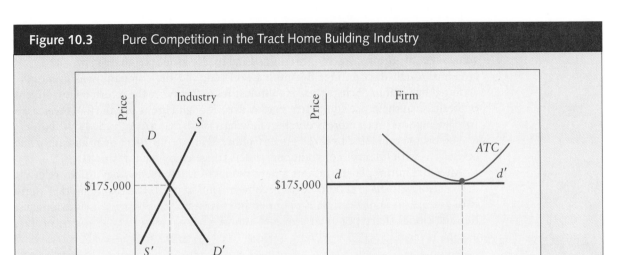

of every other producer, the single firm in pure competition can do nothing but offer its entire output at the going market price. As a result, the individual firm's demand curve approaches perfect elasticity at the market price. It can sell nothing at a higher price because all buyers will rationally shift to other sellers. If the firm sells at a price slightly below the long-run market price, it will lose money.

For example, Figure 10.3 indicates the nature of the industry and firm demand curves under pure competition in tract home building. Line *DD'* represents the total industry or market demand curve for tract houses and *S'S* is the market supply curve. At price $175,000, the market price, a total of Q_{DI} houses will be demanded by the sum of all firms in the industry. Line *dd'* represents the demand curve facing each individual firm. The individual firm sells its entire output, Q_{DF}, at the market price $175,000. By definition the quantity Q_{DF} represents only a small fraction of the total industry demand of Q_{DI}.

Why get involved in industries where revenues per sale ($175,000 in Figure 10.3) are just sufficient to cover fully allocated unit costs of $175,000? The reason is that these sales at a "hairline margin" are the ticket to the occasional windfalls when demand increases and price rises enough to generate excess profits (for a few months in the tract home business, a few days in the wildcatter oil business, a few hours in the AAA Kansas City wheat business, or a few minutes in the T-bond resale market). Note that the timing and magnitude of these windfalls are not predictable. Otherwise the respective real estate development land, oil leases, and grain silos would rise in value, and the expected excess profit would again reduce to a hairline break-even. Also, remember that at competitive equilibrium the business owner-manager is getting a salary or other return as great as could be received in his or her next best activity. In short, it is not the business environment where venture capital and entrepreneurial returns of 40 percent on invested capital occur regularly, but it does provide perhaps a 12 percent return with good managerial skills and cost controls interrupted occasionally when windfall profits erupt for a short time.

CONTESTABLE MARKETS A contestable market is an extreme case of purely competitive markets. In this market structure, break-even performance often occurs with just a handful of firms, perhaps only one. The reasons are free entry and costless exit. Consequently, the mere threat of "hit and run" entry is sufficient to drive prices down to the zero-profit, full cost-covering level. Incumbents in such markets are often slower to react than the hit-and-run firms that impose all this competitive pressure. An example is the bond markets where financial arbitrage by hedge funds triggers enormous bets (perhaps tens of billions of dollars) that any government bond or bill prices currently out of line will converge back to their equilibrium levels. Similarly, airlines might seem to be a contestable market; aircraft would seem to be the ultimate mobile asset, but landing slots are not, and incumbents react quickly and aggressively to hit-and-run entrants in these markets.

MONOPOLY

Monopoly

A market structure characterized by one firm producing a highly differentiated product in a market with significant barriers to entry.

The **monopoly** model at the other extreme of the market structure spectrum from pure competition is characterized as follows:

1. Only one firm producing some specific product line (in a specified market area), such as an exclusive cable TV franchise
2. Low cross price elasticity of demand between the monopolist's product and any other product, or no close substitute products
3. No interdependence with other competitors because the firm is a monopolist in its relevant market
4. Substantial barriers to entry to prevent competition from entering the industry, including any of the following:
   a. Absolute cost advantages of the established firm, resulting from economies in securing inputs or from patented production techniques
   b. Product differentiation advantages, resulting from consumer loyalty to established products
   c. Scale economies that increase the difficulty for potential entrant firms of financing an efficient-sized plant or building up a sufficient sales volume to achieve lowest unit costs in such a plant
   d. Large capital requirements, exceeding the financial resources of potential entrants
   e. Legal exclusion of potential competitors, as is the case for public utilities, and for those companies with patents and exclusive licensing arrangements
   f. Trade secrets not available to potential competitors

By definition, the demand curve of the individual monopoly firm is identical with the industry demand curve, because the firm is the entire relevant market. As we will see in Chapter 11, the identity between the firm and industry demand curves allows decision making for the monopolist to be a relatively simple matter, compared to the complexity of rivalrous tactics with few close competitors in tight oligopoly groups, discussed in Chapter 12.

Monopolistic Competition

A market structure much like pure competition, with the major distinction being the existence of a differentiated product.

MONOPOLISTIC COMPETITION

E. H. Chamberlin and Joan Robinson coined the term **monopolistic competition** to describe industries with characteristics both of competitive markets (i.e., many firms) and of monopoly (i.e., product differentiation). The market structure of monopolistic competition is characterized as follows:

1. A few dominant firms and a large number of competitive fringe firms
2. Dominant firms selling products that are differentiated in some manner: real, perceived, or just imagined
3. Independent decision making by individual firms
4. Ease of entry and exit from the market as a whole but substantial barriers to effective entry among the leading brands

By far the most important distinguishing characteristic of monopolistic competition is that the outputs of each firm are differentiated in some way from those of every other firm. In other words, the cross price elasticity of demand between the products of individual firms is much lower than in purely competitive markets (i.e., among tract home builders, oil wildcatters, AAA January wheat suppliers, or T-bill resellers). Product differentiation may be based on exclusive features (Disney World), trademarks (Nike's swoosh), trade names (Blackberry), packaging (L'Eggs hosiery), quality (Coach handbags), design (Apple iPod), color and style (Swatch watches), or the conditions of sale (Dooney & Bourke). These conditions may include such factors as credit terms, location of the seller, congeniality of sales personnel, after-sale service, warranties, and so on.

Because each firm produces a differentiated product, it is difficult to define an industry demand curve in monopolistic competition. Thus, rather than well-defined industries, one tends to get something of a continuum of products. Generally, it is rather easy to identify groups of differentiated products that fall in the same industry, such as light beers, after-shave colognes, or perfumes.

OLIGOPOLY

Oligopoly

A market structure in which the number of firms is so small that the actions of any one firm are likely to have noticeable impacts on the performance of other firms in the industry.

The **oligopoly** market structure describes a market having a few closely related firms. The number of firms is so small that actions by an individual firm in the industry with respect to price, output, product style or quality, terms of sale, and so on, have a perceptible impact on the sales of other firms in the industry. In other words, oligopoly is distinguished by a noticeable degree of *interdependence* among firms in the industry. The products or services that are produced by oligopolists may be homogeneous (air travel, 40-foot steel I-beams, aluminum, and cement) or they may be differentiated (automobiles, cigarettes, and cruise ships).

Although the degree of product differentiation is an important factor in shaping an oligopolist's demand curve, the degree of interdependence of firms in the industry is of even greater significance. Primarily because of this interdependence, defining a single firm's demand curve is complicated. The relationship between price and output for a single firm is determined not only by consumer preferences, product substitutability, and level of advertising, *but also by the responses that other competitors may make to a price change by the firm.* A full discussion of rival response expectations will be deferred until Chapter 12.

PRICE-OUTPUT DETERMINATION UNDER PURE COMPETITION

As discussed previously, the individual firm in a purely competitive industry is effectively a price taker because the products of every producer are perfect substitutes for the products of every other producer. This situation leads to the familiar horizontal or perfectly elastic demand curve of the purely competitive firm. Although we rarely find instances where all the conditions for pure competition are met, securities exchanges and the commodity markets approach these conditions. For instance, the individual wheat farmer or T-bill reseller has little choice but to accept the going market price.

SHORT RUN

A firm in a purely competitive industry may either make transitory profits (in excess of normal returns to capital and entrepreneurial labor) or operate at a loss in the short run.

In pure competition, the firm must sell at the market price (p_1 or p_2), and its demand curve is represented by a horizontal line (D_1 or D_2) at the market price, as shown in Figure 10.4. In the purely competitive case, marginal revenue MR is equal to price P, because the sale of each additional unit increases total revenue by the price of that unit (which remains constant at all levels of output). For instance, if

$$P = \$8/\text{unit}$$

then

$$\begin{aligned}\text{Total revenue: } TR &= P \cdot Q \\ &= 8Q\end{aligned}$$

Figure 10.4 The Firm in Pure Competition: The Short Run

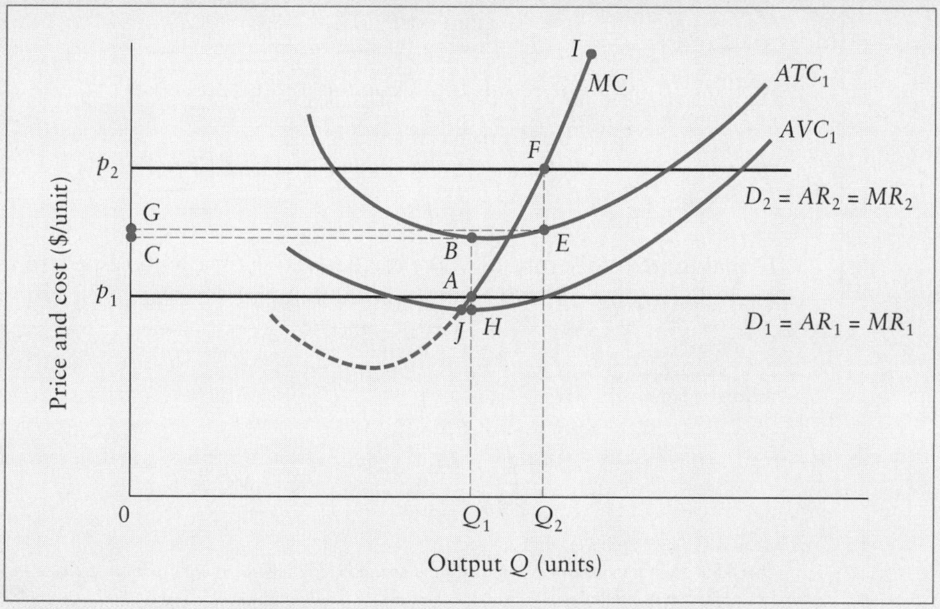

Marginal revenue is defined as the change in total revenue resulting from the sale of one additional unit, or the derivative of total revenue with respect to Q:

$$MR = \frac{dTR}{dQ} = \$8/\text{unit}$$

and marginal revenue equals price.

The profit-maximizing firm will produce at that level of output where marginal revenue equals marginal cost. Beyond that point, the production and sale of one additional unit would add more to total cost than to total revenue ($MC > MR$), and hence total profit ($TR - TC$) would decline. Up to the point where $MC = MR$, the production and sale of one more unit would increase total revenue more than total cost ($MR > MC$), and total profit would increase as an additional unit is produced and sold. *Producing at the point where marginal revenue MR equals marginal cost MC is equivalent to maximizing the total profit function.*[17]

EXAMPLE

Profit Maximization Under Pure Competition in the Short Run: Adobe Corporation

This example illustrates the profit-maximization conditions for a firm operating in a purely competitive market environment in the short run. Assume Adobe Corporation faces the following total revenue and total cost functions:

$$\text{Total revenue: } TR = 8Q$$
$$\text{Total cost: } TC = Q^2 + 4Q + 2$$

Marginal revenue and marginal cost are defined as the first derivative of total revenue and total cost, or

$$\text{Marginal revenue: } MR = \frac{dTR}{dQ} = \$8/\text{unit}$$

$$\text{Marginal cost: } MC = \frac{dTC}{dQ} = 2Q + 4$$

Similarly, total profit equals total revenue minus total cost:

$$\begin{aligned}\text{Total profit: } (\pi) &= TR - TC \\ &= 8Q - (Q^2 + 4Q + 2) \\ &= -Q^2 + 4Q - 2\end{aligned}$$

To maximize total profit, we take the derivative of π with respect to quantity, set it equal to zero, and solve for the profit-maximizing level of Q. (It is also necessary

---

[17] This can be proven as follows:

$$\pi = TR - TC$$

$$\frac{d\pi}{dQ} = \frac{dTR}{dQ} - \frac{dTC}{dQ} = MR - MC = 0$$

or, $MR = MC$ when profits are maximized.

Check for profit maximization by taking the second derivative of π with respect to Q, or $\frac{d^2\pi}{dQ^2}$. If it is less than zero, then π is maximized.

to check the second derivative to be certain we have found a maximum, not a minimum.)[18]

$$\frac{d\pi}{dQ} = -2Q + 4 = 0$$

$$Q^* = 2 \text{ units}$$

But because $MR = \$8/\text{unit}$ and $MC = 2Q + 4 = 2(2) + 4 = \$8/\text{unit}$, when total profit is maximized, we are merely setting $MC = MR$.

The individual firm's supply function in Figure 10.4 is equal to that portion of the MC curve from point J to point I. At any price level below point J the firm would shut down because it would not even be covering its variable costs (i.e., $P < AVC$). Temporary shutdown would result in limiting the losses to fixed costs alone.

In Figure 10.4, if price $P = p_1$, the firm would produce the level of output Q_1, where $MC = MR$ (profits are maximized or losses minimized). In this case the firm would incur a loss per unit equal to the difference between average total cost ATC and average revenue or price. This amount is represented by the height BA in Figure 10.4. The total loss incurred by the firm at Q_1 level of output and price p_1 equals the rectangle p_1CBA. Total loss may be conceptually thought of as the loss per unit (BA) times the number of units produced and sold (Q_1). At price p_1 losses are minimized, because average variable costs AVC have been covered and a contribution remains to cover part of the fixed costs (AH per unit times Q_1 units). If the firm did not produce, it would incur losses equal to the entire amount of fixed costs (BH per unit times Q_1 units). Hence we may conclude that in the short run a firm will produce and sell at that level of output where $MR = MC$, as long as the variable costs of production are being covered ($P > AVC$).

If price were p_2, the firm would produce Q_2 units and make a profit per unit of EF, or a total profit represented by the rectangle $FEGp_2$. The supply curve of the competitive firm is therefore often identified as the marginal cost schedule above minimum AVC (i.e., the MC schedule from J to I). Industry supply is the horizontal summation of these firm supply curves.

EXAMPLE

GASOLINE PRICE RISES TO RECORD LEVELS REFLECTING A SPIKE IN CRUDE OIL INPUT COSTS[19]

Throughout 2004, 2005, and early 2006, the price of gasoline in the United States galloped upward to reach \$3 per gallon. Why? Competitive pressure at the retail level prevents gas stations from gouging retail customers. Excise taxes average only \$0.40 across the United States and have been largely unchanged for two decades. Refinery and pipeline bottlenecks were partially to blame after Gulf Coast hurricanes

[18] The check for profit maximization goes as follows:

$$\frac{d^2\pi}{dQ^2} = -2$$

Because the second derivative is negative, we know we have found a maximum value for the profit function.

[19] Based on "Special Report: The Oil Industry," *The Economist* (April 22, 2006), pp. 55–73.

Katrina and Rita. But the principal source of the run up in gasoline prices was a spectacular increase in crude oil input prices.

Figure 10.5 (a) shows that six times in the last 30 years, crude oil prices have risen steeply. In each prior case, supply disruptions due to armed conflicts in the Middle East or cartel restrictions of output were responsible. In 1973 and 1999–2000, the OPEC I and OPEC III oil cartels successfully enforced reduced output quotas on members, thereby restraining supply and driving the market price of crude oil higher. In 1978, 1981, and 1990, three military conflicts massively restricted the supply of crude oil leaving the Persian Gulf. In 2004–2006, however, not supply but demand factors are involved. Demand growth in India, China, and the United States during 2004–2006 drove scarce input prices right up the rising marginal cost schedule exhibited in Figure 10.5 (b).

Oil in the Persian Gulf region is cheapest to find, develop, and extract at a unit cost of \$3 per barrel. In contrast, Venezuelan and Russian oil breaks even at \$9 per barrel, West Texas oil at \$13 per barrel, and the North Sea fields necessitate offshore rigs and expensive extraction technology that generate \$20-per-barrel average total cost. The full delivered costs of Alaskan North Slope oil runs \$30 per barrel. These oil field production firms and their associated output trace out a traditional upward-sloping long-run supply curve (here a step function) for the crude oil industry. See Figure 10.5 (b).

By mid-year 2006, at crude oil prices between \$70 and \$80, Missouri and Iowa farmers were putting up \$34,000 to join coops created to build and operate \$65 million corn-fed ethanol plants. The Brazilians have been hugely successful with sugar cane-fed ethanol plants, and in 2007 will declare energy independence from foreign oil. Now it appears the bread basket of the U.S. Plains states will become the next major source of energy for internal combustion vehicles.

Long Run

In the long run, all inputs are free to vary. Hence, no conceptual distinction exists between fixed and variable costs. Under long-run conditions in purely competitive markets, average cost will tend to be just equal to price, and all excessive profits will be eliminated (see Point *A* where $p_1 = AC_1$ in Figure 10.6). If, on the other hand, a price above p_1 exceeds average total costs, then more firms will enter, the industry supply will increase (as illustrated by the parallel shift outward to the right of the $\Sigma_{SR}S_{FIRM}$ along market demand D^2_{MKT} in Figure 10.6), and market price will again be driven down toward the equilibrium, zero-profit level p_1.

In addition, as more firms bid for the available factors of production (say, skilled labor or natural resources like crude oil), the cost of these factors will tend to rise. In that event, the entire cost structure of MC_1 and AC_1 will rise to reflect the higher input costs along an upward-sloping input supply schedule such as the one for crude oil in Figure 10.5 (b). This higher input cost results in a shift up of the firm's cost structure to AC_2 (see Figure 10.6) and imposes a two-way squeeze on excess profit. Such a scenario is referred to as an **external diseconomy of scale.** External scale diseconomies are distinguished from internal scale economies and diseconomies in that the latter reflect unit cost changes as the rate of output increases, *assuming no change in input prices,* whereas the former reflect exactly the bidding up of input prices as the industry expands in response to an increase in market demand.

External Diseconomy of Scale

An increase in unit costs reflecting higher input prices.

Figure 10.5 Crude Oil Prices and Costs

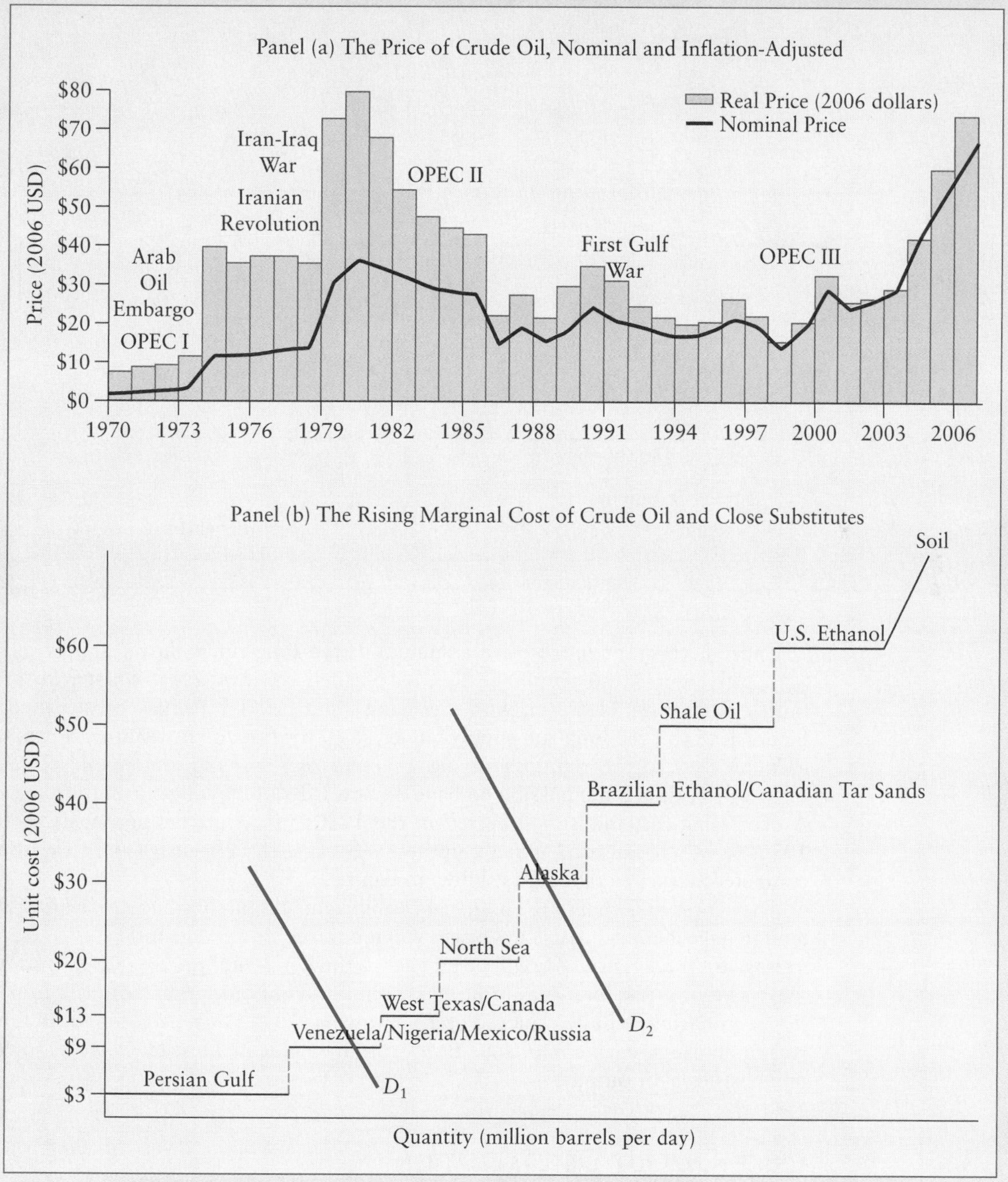

Figure 10.6 Long-Run Equilibrium Under Pure Competition (in an Increasing Cost Industry)

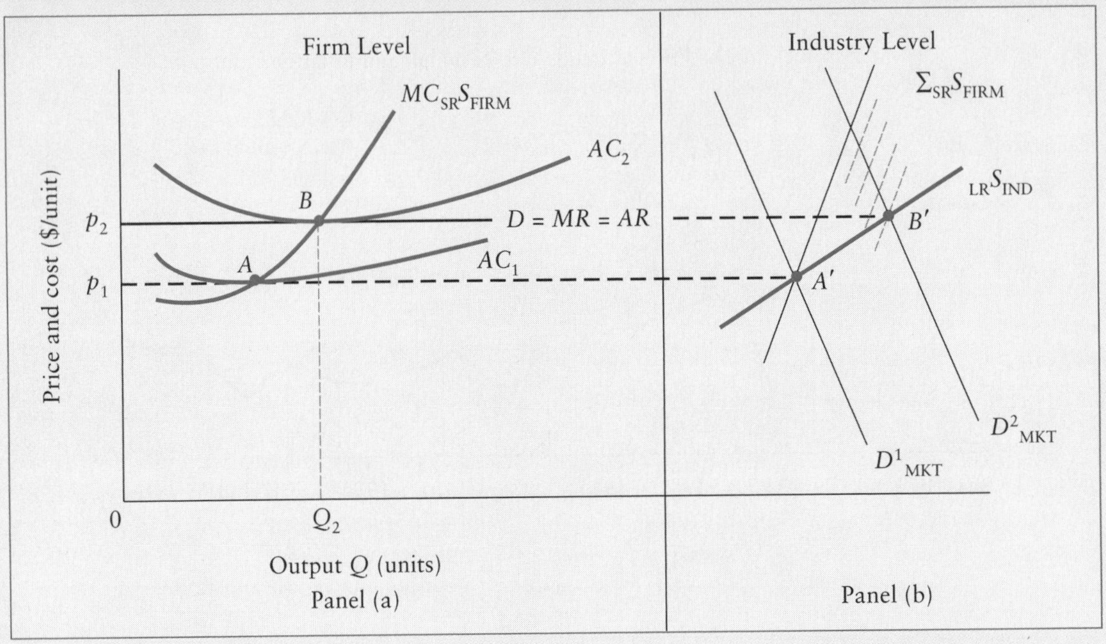

Under a constant input price assumption, the long-run industry supply curve $_{LR}S_{IND}$ in Figure 10.6 would be flat, a so-called *constant-cost industry* such as timber harvesting. However, with the rising input prices for crude oil depicted in Figure 10.5 (b), the long-run supply curve $_{LR}S_{IND}$ for the downstream final product gasoline rises to the right, signifying an *increasing-cost industry,* as depicted in Figure 10.6. (It is quite possible to have downward-sloping long-run supply curves. A decreasing-cost industry occurred in the 1980s in calculators and again in the 1990s in PCs because computer chip inputs became less expensive as the personal computer market expanded, as shown in Figure 10.7.)

The net result is that in the long-run equilibrium, all purely competitive firms will tend to have identical costs, and prices will tend to equal average total costs (i.e., the average total cost curve AC will be tangent to the horizontal price line p_2). Thus, we may say that at the long-run profit-maximizing level of output under pure competition, equilibrium will be achieved at a point where $P = MR = MC = AC$. In long-run equilibrium, each competitive firm is producing at its most efficient (its lowest unit cost) level of output.

Price-Output Determination Under Monopolistic Competition

Monopolistic competition is a market structure with a relatively large number of firms, each selling a product that is differentiated in some manner from the products of its fringe competitors, and with substantial barriers to entry into the group of leading firms.

Figure 10.7 The Computer Price Index and U.S. Final Sales of Personal Computers

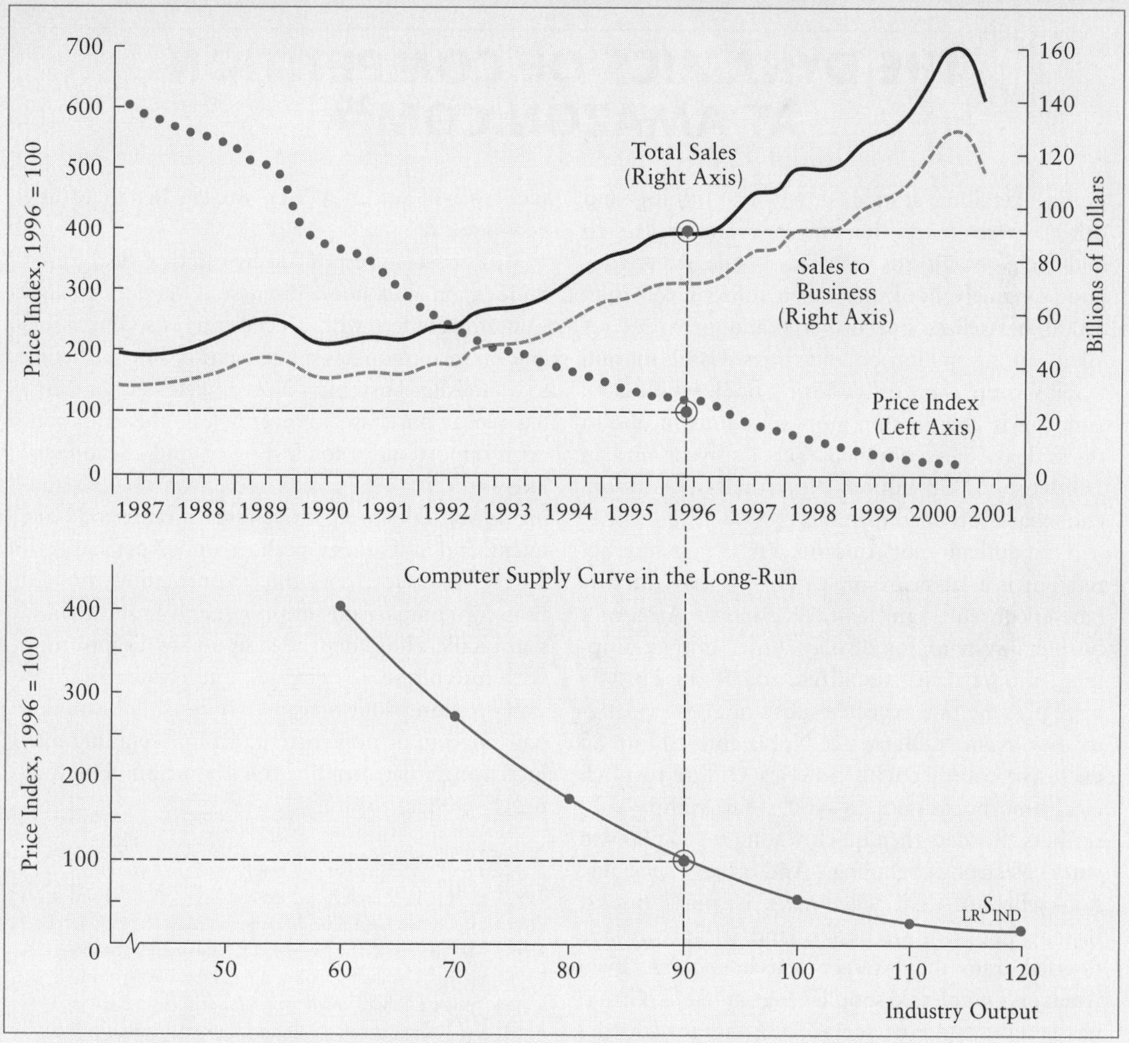

Source: **St. Louis Federal Reserve Bank, *National Economic Trends,* May 2001.**

Product differentiation may be based on special product characteristics, trademarks, packaging, quality perceptions, distinctive product design, or conditions surrounding the sale, such as location of the seller, warranties, and credit terms. The demand curve for any one firm is expected to have a negative slope and be extremely elastic because of the large number of close substitutes. The firm in monopolistic competition has some limited discretion over price, as distinguished from the firm in pure competition, which has none because of customer loyalties arising from real or perceived product differences. Profit maximization (or loss minimization) again occurs when the firm produces at that level of output and charges that price at which marginal revenue equals marginal cost.

WHAT WENT RIGHT • WHAT WENT WRONG

THE DYNAMICS OF COMPETITION AT AMAZON.COM[20]

Online retailing started slowly in clothing and other search goods that buyers want to "touch and feel," but it has excelled in one experience good—namely, books. Amazon stocks fewer than 1,000 bestsellers but displays and provides reviews on 2.5 million popular titles. Using Ingram Book Group, the world's largest book wholesaler, Amazon is able to ship most selections in one to three days. Sales doubled each half-year and in 2004 topped $2 billion. Nevertheless, Amazon.com shares declined in value.

One difficulty for Amazon.com is that Internet retailing is a classic example of a business with low barriers to entry and exit. As soon as Amazon's business systems for display, order taking, shipping, and payments stabilized, and because profits were present, one expected substantial entry activity. For example, Barnes & Noble entered into an exclusive contract with America Online to pitch electronic book sales to AOL's 8.5 million subscribers. Borders then quickly announced plans to enter electronic retailing. And many specialist booksellers of Civil War books, jet plane books, history books, auto books, and so forth, have flooded onto the Internet search engines. Even Amazon's wholesale supplier Ingram Book Group has entered the fray; for $2,500, Ingram support services will set up a Web site on behalf of any new book retailer.

Amazon.com responded by offering customized notification and book discussion services to add value for readers with special interests. The information revolution has made relationship marketing to established customers a pivotal element in securing repeat purchases. Nevertheless, the numerous open opportunities for fast, easy, and cheap entry likely will erode the profits in electronic book retailing down to the competitive rates of return on time, talent, and investment, perhaps only 7 percent.

The imperfect consumer information, limited time for comparison shopping, and brand loyalty that retailers have depended upon are disappearing with Internet search engines, and retailing's traditionally slim profit margins are quickly becoming hairline thin or nonexistent. Online retailing may increasingly perform like tract home building (i.e., purely competitively).

[20] Based on "Web Browsing," *The Economist* (March 29, 1997), p. 71; "In Search of the Perfect Market: A Survey of Electronic Commerce," *The Economist* (May 10, 1997); "The Net: A Market Too Perfect for Profits," *BusinessWeek* (May 11, 1998), p. 20; "Comparison Shopping Is the Web's Virtue—Unless You're a Seller," *Wall Street Journal* (July 23, 1998), p. A1; and *Value Line, Ratings and Reports,* various issues.

SHORT RUN

Just as in the case of pure competition, a monopolistically competitive firm may or may not generate a profit in the short run. For example, consider a demand curve such as $D'D'$ in Figure 10.8, with marginal revenue equal to MR'. Such a firm will set its prices where $MR' = MC$, resulting in price P_3 and output Q_3. The firm will earn a profit of EC dollars per unit of output. However, the low barriers to entry in a monopolistically competitive industry will not permit these short-run profits to be earned for long. As new firms enter the industry, industry supply will increase, causing the equilibrium price to fall, as reflected in the downward movement in the demand curve facing any individual firm.

Figure 10.8 Long-Run Equilibrium in Monopolistic Competition

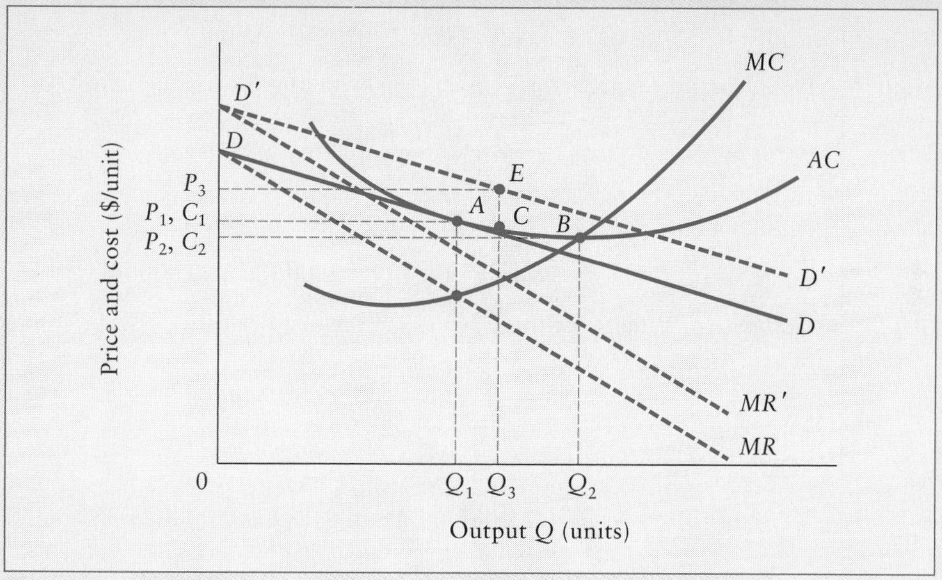

LONG RUN

With relatively free entry and exit into the competitive fringe, average costs and a firm's demand function will be driven *toward* tangency at a point such as A in Figure 10.8. At this price, P_1, and output, Q_1, marginal cost is equal to marginal revenue. Hence a firm such as an airline is producing at its optimal level of output. Any price lower or higher than P_1 will result in a loss to the firm because average costs will exceed price.

Because the monopolistic competitor produces at a level of output where average costs are still declining (between Points A and B in Figure 10.8), monopolistically competitive firms produce with "excess" capacity. Of course, this argument overlooks the extent to which idle capacity may be a source of product differentiation. Idle capacity means a firm, such as an airline, can operate with high delivery reliability and change order responsiveness, which can be especially important to business travelers on congested planes, and that warrants a price premium relative to competitive fringe airlines.

EXAMPLE

LONG-RUN PRICE AND OUTPUT DETERMINATION: VIDEO MAGIC, INC.

The market for video rentals in Charlotte, North Carolina, can best be described as monopolistically competitive. The demand for video rentals is estimated to be

$$P = 10 - 0.004Q$$

where Q is the number of weekly video rentals. The long-run average cost function for Video Magic is estimated to be

$$LRAC = 8 - 0.006Q + 0.000002Q^2$$

Video Magic's managers want to know the profit-maximizing price and output levels, and the level of expected total profits at these price and output levels.

First, compute total revenue:

$$TR = P \cdot Q = 10Q - 0.004Q^2$$

Next, compute marginal revenue (MR) by taking the first derivative of TR:

$$MR = \frac{dTR}{dQ} = 10 - 0.008Q$$

Compute total cost (TC) by multiplying $LRAC$ by Q:

$$TC = LRAC \cdot Q = 8Q - 0.006Q^2 + 0.000002Q^3$$

Compute marginal cost (MC) by taking the first derivative of TC:

$$MC = \frac{dTC}{dQ} = 8 - 0.012Q + 0.000006Q^2$$

Next, set $MR = MC$:

$$10 - 0.008Q = 8 - 0.012Q + 0.000006Q^2$$
$$0.000006Q^2 - 0.004Q - 2 = 0$$

Use the quadratic formula to solve for Q. Q^* is equal to 1,000.[21] At this quantity, price is equal to

$$\begin{aligned} P^* &= 10 - 0.004\,(1{,}000) \\ &= 10 - 4 \\ &= \$6 \end{aligned}$$

Total profit is equal to the difference between TR and TC, or

$$\begin{aligned} \pi &= TR - TC \\ &= 10Q - 0.004Q^2 - [8Q - 0.006Q^2 + 0.000002Q^3] \\ &= 10(1{,}000) - 0.004(1{,}000)^2 - [8(1{,}000) - 0.006(1{,}000)^2 \\ &\quad + 0.000002(1{,}000)^3] \\ &= \$2{,}000 \end{aligned}$$

The MR and MC at these price and output levels are \$2.

The fact that Video Magic expects to earn a profit of \$2,000 suggests that the firm can anticipate additional competition, resulting in price cutting, which will ultimately eliminate this profit amount.[22]

[21] The solution of the quadratic formula, $aQ^2 + bQ + c = 0$, is

$$Q = \frac{-b \pm \sqrt{b^2 - 4ac}}{2a} = \frac{-(-.004) \pm \sqrt{(-.004)^2 - 4(0.000006)(-2)}}{2(0.000006)}$$
$$= 1{,}000;\ -333.33$$

Only the positive solution is feasible.

[22] Recall that the TC function includes a "normal" level of profit. Hence this \$2,000 represents an economic *rent* above a normal profit level.

SELLING AND PROMOTIONAL EXPENSES

In addition to varying price and quality characteristics of their products, firms may also vary the amount of their advertising and other promotional expenses in their search for profits. This kind of promotional activity generates two distinct types of benefits. First, demand for the general product group may be shifted upward to the right as a result of the individual firm and industry advertising activities. The greater the number of firms in an industry, the more diffused will be the effects of a general demand-increasing advertising campaign by any one firm. In contrast, a monopolist such as an electric utility, or a highly concentrated oligopoly such as computer operating systems, will be more inclined to undertake an advertising campaign.

The second, more widespread incentive for advertising is the desire to shift the demand function of a particular firm at the expense of other firms offering similar products. This strategy will be pursued both by oligopolists such as the Philip Morris division of Altria and General Mills and by firms in more monopolistically competitive industries such as AT&T, MCI, and Sprint.

DETERMINING THE OPTIMAL LEVEL OF SELLING AND PROMOTIONAL OUTLAYS

Selling and promotional activities, often collectively referred to as advertising, are one of the most important tools of nonprice competition.

To illustrate the effects of advertising expenditures and to determine the optimal selling expenses of a firm, consider the case where price and product characteristics already have been determined, and all retailers are selling at the manufacturer's suggested retail price.

The determination of the optimal advertising outlay is a straightforward application of the marginal decision-making rules followed by profit-maximizing firms. Define MR to be the change in total revenue received from a one-unit increase in output (and the sale of that output). For fixed-price settings, MR just equals the price, P. Define MC to be the change in total costs of producing and distributing (but not of advertising) an additional unit of output. The marginal profit or contribution margin from an additional unit of output is:

$$PCM = P - MC \tag{10.3}$$

The marginal cost of advertising (MCA) associated with the sale of an additional unit of output is defined as the change in advertising expenditures (ΔAk) where k is the unit cost of an advertising message, A, or

$$MCA = \frac{\Delta Ak}{\Delta Q} \tag{10.4}$$

The optimal level of advertising outlays is the level of advertising where the marginal profit contribution (PCM) is equal to the marginal cost of advertising, or

$$PCM = MCA \tag{10.5}$$

As long as a firm receives a greater contribution margin than the MCA it incurs to sell an additional unit of output, the advertising outlay should be made. If PCM is less than MCA, the advertising outlay should not be made and the level of advertising should be reduced until $PCM = MCA$. This marginal analysis also applies to other types of nonprice competition such as after-sale service and product replacement guarantees.

EXAMPLE

Optimal Advertising at Parkway Ford

The marginal profit contribution from selling Ford automobiles at Parkway Ford averages \$1,000 across the various models it sells. Parkway estimates that it will have to incur \$550 of additional promotional expenses per vehicle to increase its sales per day. Should the outlay for promotion be made?

Because $PCM > MCA$ (i.e., \$1,000 > \$550), Parkway's operating profit will be increased by \$450 if it incurs an additional \$550 of promotional expenses. Parkway should continue to make additional promotional outlays (which are likely to be less and less effective at triggering additional sales per day) up to the point where the marginal cost of advertising equals the expected (marginal profit) contribution margin.

If Parkway were then to find that MCA was greater than PCM, they should cut back on promotional outlays until the contribution margin rose enough to again equate $PCM = MCA$.

Optimal Advertising Intensity

Optimal expenditure on demand-increasing costs such as promotions, coupons, direct mail, and media advertising can be compared across firms. For example, the total contributions from incremental sales relative to the advertising cost of beer ads can be compared to the total contributions relative to the advertising cost of cereal ads. Advertising is often placed in five media (network TV, local TV, radio, newspapers, and magazines). The "reach" of a TV ad is measured as audience thousands per minute of advertising message; reach is directly related to the advertising message's cost (k). A manager should fully fund in the marketing budget any ad campaign for which

$$(P - MC)\,(\Delta Q/\Delta A) > k \qquad [10.6]$$

where $(P - MC)$ is the contribution margin and $(\Delta Q/\Delta A)$ is the increase in demand (i.e., a shift outward in demand) attributable to the advertising.[23]

EXAMPLE

Ford and P&G Tie Ad Agency Pay to Sales

Historically, ad agencies earned more income each time their clients bought another expensive 30-second slot on network TV (or other media), whatever the performance of the ad in generating incremental sales. More recently, Ford and Procter & Gamble, two of the world's biggest advertisers, announced that all agency billings would need to be performance based. These incentive payment plans include a fixed

[23] Sometimes, the price points at which the product can be sold change after a successful ad campaign. If so, the appropriate valuation of the incremental sales in Equation 10.6 is the new contribution margin.

fee for designing ad campaigns plus incentive pay based on the incremental sales traceable to the ad. The idea is to encourage agencies to search for database marketing, Internet, and event sponsorships that far exceed the marginal media buy in advertising productivity, $\Delta Q/\Delta A$.

Expanding Equation 10.6 identifies the two determinants of the optimal advertising expenditure per dollar sales or "advertising intensity." Ak/PQ is determined by the gross margin $(P - MC)/P$ and by the advertising elasticity of demand E_a:

$$\frac{Ak}{PQ} = \frac{(P - MC)}{P}\frac{A}{Q}(\Delta Q/\Delta A) \quad [10.7]$$

$$\frac{Ak}{PQ} = \frac{(P - MC)}{P}E_a \quad [10.8]$$

Both factors are important. With high margins (near 70%) and effective ads, Kellogg spends 30 percent of every dollar of sales revenue on cereal advertising. In contrast, the jewelry industry has 92 percent margins, the highest of all four-digit industries, but Zales's advertising inserts in the weekend paper simply do not trigger many jewelry sales. The advertising elasticity of jewelry is low; consequently, a company such as Zales spends less than 10 percent of its sales revenue on advertising. Campbell Soup has relatively high advertising elasticity of demand given its strong brand name, but the margins on canned goods are low (less than 5%); consequently, Campbell Soup spends just one tenth of what Kellogg spends on advertising as a percentage of sales revenue—just 3 percent of sales revenue.

EXAMPLE

Optimal Advertising Intensity at Kellogg and General Mills[24]

The ready-to-eat (RTE) cereal industry spends 55 percent of its sales revenue on marketing and promotion—30 percent on advertising alone. In part, this resource allocation decision reflects the fact that cereal demand is sensitive to successful ad campaigns such as Kellogg's Tony the Tiger or General Mills' Wheaties, The Breakfast of Champions. In addition, however, RTE cereal margins are among the highest of any four-digit industry. Kellogg's Raisin Bran sells for \$4.49 and has a direct fixed plus variable manufacturing cost of \$1.63. That calculates as a $(4.49 - 1.63)/4.49 =$ 70 percent gross margin. Frosted Flakes' margin is 72 percent, and Fruit Loops' margin is 68 percent. These margins reflect brand loyalties built up over many years of advertising investments as well as Kellogg's 37 percent market share. In the highly concentrated RTE cereal industry, Quaker Oats (8%), Post (15%), General Mills (25%), and Kellogg control 85 percent of the market.

Until recently, advertising and retail displays were the predominant form of competition in cereals. Like Coca-Cola and PepsiCo, the dominant RTE cereal companies concluded that price discounting would be mutually ruinous and ultimately ineffective. Therefore, each company decided independently to refrain from discounting prices to attempt to gain market share. However, in June 1996, 20 percent

[24] Based on "Cereals," *Winston-Salem Journal* (March 8, 1995), p. A1; and "Denial in Battle Creek," *Forbes* (October 7, 1996), pp. 44–46.

price cuts swept through the industry, in part in response to the growth of private-label cereals (e.g., Kroger Raisin Bran), which had collectively grabbed close to 10 percent of the market. Margins on some leading brand-name products fell to 50 percent with ingredients (15%), packaging (10%), wages (10%), and distribution (15%) accounting for the rest of the selling price.

The Net Value of Advertising

Traditional economic analysis has tended to conclude that the primary impacts of advertising are to raise prices to consumers and to lead to the creation and maintenance of monopoly power.[25]

George Stigler and Phil Nelson[26] used the theory of the economics of information to argue that by giving consumers price information, advertising is expected to reduce the price paid. The discovery of price information may be costly and time consuming in the absence of price advertising. If, for example, it costs a consumer $10 in time costs to discover the store that will offer a saving of $8 on the price of an item, the search for price information is not worthwhile. But if price advertising makes all consumers aware of the lowest price supplier of an item at an additional cost of only $1, then the great majority of consumers will be better off as a result of this advertising. For example, Benham[27] found the price of eyeglasses to be substantially lower in states that permitted price advertising than in those that prohibited such advertising. Similar results have been found for dental, medical, and legal services.

In addition, Nelson found that advertisers of all products have substantial incentives to provide useful and truthful information to customers. High-quality information can reduce the search cost for consumers as they seek to make a choice between alternative goods. Because consumers can assess the truthfulness of the information contained in an advertisement and because advertising creates brand awareness (both for good and inferior brands), advertisers who misrepresent their product will not be successful in generating future (and repeat) business.

Competitive Markets Under Asymmetric Information [Optional Advanced Section]

In competitive markets for newsprint, crude oil, auto rentals, and delivered pizza, both buyers and sellers have full knowledge of the capabilities and after-sale performance of the standard products. Equilibrium price just covers the supplier's cost of production for a product of known reliable quality. If suppliers were to charge more, rival offers and entry would quickly erode their sales. If suppliers were to charge less, they could not afford to stay in business. This message has been the one given so far in Chapter 10: In competitive markets under ideal information conditions, you get what you pay for. Such markets differ enormously from competitive markets under

[25] Evidence in support of this view is presented in William Comaner and Thomas Wilson, *Advertising and Market Power* (Cambridge, MA: Harvard University Press, 1974).

[26] George J. Stigler, "The Economics of Information," *Journal of Political Economy* (June 1961), pp. 213–225; and Philip Nelson, "The Economic Consequences of Advertising," *Journal of Business* (April 1975), pp. 213–241.

[27] Lee Benham, "The Effect of Advertising on the Price of Eyeglasses," *Journal of Law and Economics* (October 1972), pp. 337–352.

asymmetric information, which are sometimes called *lemons markets*. One prominent example of asymmetric information in a lemons market is used automobiles, in which the true quality of mechanical repairs or other features often is known only to the seller. Other goods sold under asymmetric information include house paint, mail-order computer components, and common cold remedies.

In a lemons market, the buyers discount all unverifiable claims by the sellers, who market only lower quality products as the reduced prices buyers are willing to offer. This disappearance of higher-quality products from the marketplace illustrates the concept of adverse selection (i.e., the lower-quality products are selected in and the higher-quality products are adversely selected out). To resolve the marketing problems posed by adverse selection requires credible commitment mechanisms such as warranties, brand-name reputations, collateral, or price premiums for reliable repeat-purchase transactions.

Incomplete Versus Asymmetric Information

Incomplete Information
Uncertain knowledge of payoffs, choices, and other factors.

One distinction that can sharpen our understanding of these complicating factors in competitive exchange is that between asymmetric information and **incomplete information.** Incomplete information is associated with uncertainty, and uncertainty is pervasive. Practically all exchanges, whether for products, financial claims, or labor services, are conducted under conditions of uncertainty. On the one hand, decision makers often face uncertainty as to the effect of random disturbances on the outcome of their actions. This uncertainty typically leads to insurance markets. On the other hand, decision makers are sometimes uncertain as to the payoffs or even types of choices they face. This condition typically leads to intentionally incomplete contracting.

Asymmetric Information
Unequal, dissimilar knowledge.

Asymmetric information exchange, in contrast, refers to situations in which either the buyer or the seller possesses information that the other party cannot verify or to which the other party does not have access. For example, mail-order suppliers of computer components or personal sellers of used cars often have an informationally advantaged position relative to the buyers. The sellers know the machine's capabilities, deficiencies, and most probable failure rate, but these matters are difficult for the buyer to assess from reading magazine ads or kicking the tires. And the typical 90-day warranty does nothing to alter this information asymmetry. Both buyer and seller face uncertainty against which they may choose to insure, but one has more information or better information than the other.

Search Goods Versus Experience Goods

In services, retailing, and many manufacturing industries, buyers generally search the market to identify low-price suppliers. Sometimes this search is accomplished by asking for recommendations from recent purchasers, by scouring the catalogs and ads, or by visiting showrooms and sales floors. In selecting a supplier, many customers are also intensely interested in multiple dimensions of product and service quality, including product design, durability, image, conformance to specifications, order delay, delivery reliability, change order responsiveness, and after-sale service. Customers often spend as much time and effort searching the market for the desired quality mix as they do searching for lowest price. Retailers and service providers understand this and often offer many quality combinations at various prices to trigger

Search Goods

Products and services whose quality can be detected through market search.

Experience Goods

Products and services whose quality is undetectable when purchased.

a purchase of these **search goods.** Consider, for example, the many price-quality alternatives available in clothing, sporting goods, furniture stores, and hotel chains.

On the other hand, some products and services have important quality dimensions that *cannot* be observed at the point of purchase. Consider, again, used cars and other resale machinery, nonprescription remedies for the common cold, house paint, and mail-order computer components. The quality of these items can be detected only through experience in using the products. Hence, products and services of this type are termed **experience goods** and are distinguished from search goods.

Ultimately the problem with experience goods in competitive market exchange is the unverifiability of asymmetric information. The seller knows how to detect the difference between high- and low-quality products (e.g., between lemons and cream puffs in the used-car market), but cannot credibly relay this information to buyers, at least not in chance encounters between strangers. Fraudulent sellers will claim high quality when it is absent, and realizing this tendency, buyers rationally discount all such information. Because of the private nature of the product quality information, the seller's claims and omissions can never be verified without experiencing for oneself the reliability of the auto, the efficacy of the common cold remedy, the durability of the house paint, or the capability of the computer component.

All of these factors do not mean that the buyers of experience goods are without recourse or that the sellers are without ingenuity as to how to market their products. Warranties and investments in reputations provide mechanisms whereby the sellers of house paint and computer components can credibly commit to delivering a high-quality product. The essential point is that in the absence of these bonding or hostage mechanisms, the experience-good buyer will rationally disbelieve the seller's claims. Consequently, the honest seller of truly high-quality experience goods will find little market for his or her higher-cost, higher-priced product. The "bad apples drive out the good" in many experience-good markets.

Adverse Selection and the Notorious Firm

Suppose customers recognize that unverifiable private information about experience-good quality is present, yet knowledge of any fraudulent high-price sale of low-quality products spreads almost instantaneously throughout the marketplace. Is this extreme reputational effect sufficient to restore the exchange of high-quality/high-price experience goods? Or, can the notorious firm continue to defraud customers here and elsewhere? The answer depends on the conditions of entry and exit discussed earlier in this chapter, but not in the way you might expect.

Consider the cost structure and profits of such a notorious firm, depicted in Figure 10.9. If offered the low price P_l, the firm operates in competitive equilibrium at Q_1 where the price just covers the marginal cost and average total cost ($SAC_{\text{low quality}}$) for Q_1 units of the low-quality product. Alternatively, if offered the high price P_h, the firm can either competitively supply Q_1 of the high-quality experience good and again just break even against the higher costs of $SAC_{\text{high quality}}$,[28] or the firm can deliver a low-quality experience good at Q_2 and continue to incur the lower costs $SAC_{\text{low quality}}$. The third alternative entails an expansion of output along $MC_{\text{low quality}}$

[28] The minimum cost output for the plant configuration and cost structure associated with high quality could shift right or left, but to simplify, assume that the *SAC* just increases vertically from Point *C* to Point *A*.

Figure 10.9 Low-Quality Experience Goods Emerge from Competitive Markets

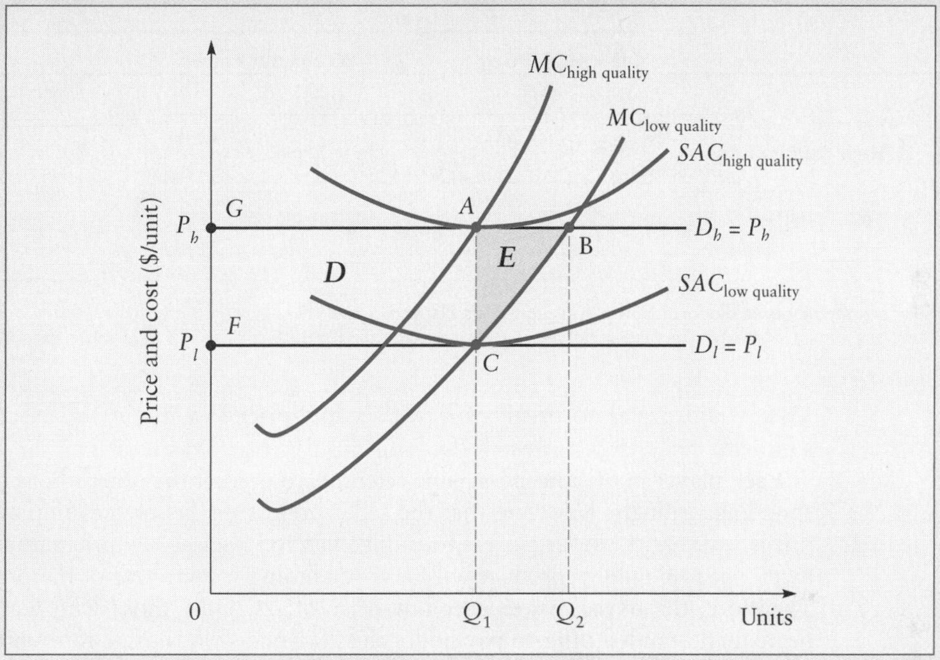

in response to the price rise and generates profits. That is, the incremental output ($Q_2 - Q_1$) earns incremental profit equal to the difference between P_h and $MC_{\text{low quality}}$—namely, the shaded area *ABC* (labeled bold **E**)—and in addition, the original output Q_1 earns a fraudulent rent of area *GACF* (labeled bold **D**). Although the supplier observes its own cost directly and therefore detects the availability of **D** + **E**, the problem for the experience-good buyer is that in terms of point-of-sale information, high-price transactions at Point *B* on $MC_{\text{low quality}}$ and at Point *A* on $MC_{\text{high quality}}$ are indistinguishable. Both types of products have an asking price of P_h, and only the seller observes the output rate Q_1 versus Q_2.

Of course, the supplier is not indifferent between the two alternatives. The high-quality transaction offers a cash flow from operations just sufficient to cover capital costs and break even at Point *A*, whereas the fraudulent transaction (a low-quality product at a high price at Point *B*) offers a net profit for at least one period. Table 10.2 depicts this interaction between experience-good buyers and a potentially fraudulent firm as a payoff matrix. The seller can produce either low or high quality, and the buyer can offer either low or high prices. The row player (the seller) gets the below-diagonal payoffs in each cell, and the column player (the buyer) gets the above-diagonal payoffs in each cell. The buyer prefers to cover the high cost of high-quality products (in the northwest cell) rather than pay less and only cover the lower cost of low-quality products (in the southeast cell). However, the buyer is worst off when the seller fails to deliver a high-quality product for which the buyer has paid a high price (in the southwest cell). The buyer also recognizes that getting more than what was paid for (in the northeast cell) would impose losses on the seller,

Table 10.2 Experience-Good Payoff Matrix

		Buyer: Offer High Price	Buyer: Offer Low Price
Seller	High Quality	Better / Break even	Best / Loss $(-D)$
	Low Quality	Worst / Profit $(D + E)$	Worse / Break even

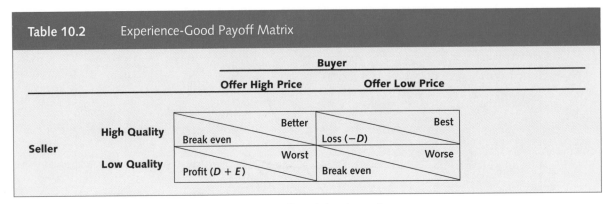

Note: Column-player payoffs are above diagonal. Row-player payoffs are below diagonal.

who would prefer to break even with a low-price/low-quality transaction in the southeast cell.

Each player in this business game attempts to predict the other's behavior and respond accordingly. Knowing that the seller prefers profits to breaking even at high prices and that the seller prefers breaking even to losses at low prices, the buyer predicts that low-quality product will be forthcoming irrespective of the price offered. Therefore, the buyer makes only low-price offers. Only those who wish to be repeatedly defrauded offer to pay high prices for one-shot transactions with strangers offering experience goods.

Adverse Selection

A limited choice of lower-quality alternatives attributable to asymmetric information.

Lemons Market

Asymmetric information exchange leading to low-quality products and services driving out higher-quality products and services.

This reasoning motivates **adverse selection** by the rational seller in an experience-good market. Because sellers can anticipate only low-price offers from buyers, the sellers never produce high-quality products. That is, the market for experience goods will be incomplete in that not all product qualities will be available for sale. Anticipating that buyers will radically discount their unverifiable high-quality "cream puffs," individual sellers of used cars choose to place only low-quality **"lemons"** on the **market.** The "cream puffs" often are given away to relatives. Similarly, jewelers in vacation locations, anticipating that out-of-town buyers will radically discount high-grade, uncertified gemstones, choose to sell only lower quality gemstones. And unbranded mail-order computer components are inevitably of lower quality. Adverse selection always causes competitive markets with asymmetric information to be incomplete. Again, the bad apples drive out the good.

Insuring and Lending Under Asymmetric Information: Another Lemons Market

This same adverse selection reasoning applies beyond experience-good product markets whenever asymmetric information is prominent. Consider the transaction between a bank loan officer and a new commercial borrower, or between an insurance company and a new auto insurance policyholder. Through an application and interview process and with access to various databases and credit references, the lender or insurer attempts to uncover the private, impacted information about the applicant's credit or driving history. Nevertheless, just as in the case of claims made by the itinerant seller of an experience good, verification remains a problem. The applicant has an incentive to omit facts that would tend to result in loan or insurance denial (e.g., prior business failures or unreported accidents), and knowing this, the lender may offer only higher rate loans and the insurer higher rate policies.

The problem is that higher rate loans and expensive insurance policies tend to affect the composition of the applicant pool resulting in adverse selection. Some honest, well-intentioned borrowers and good-risk insurance applicants will now drop out of the applicant pool because of concern about their inability to pay principal and interest and insurance premiums on time as promised. But other applicants who never intended to repay (or drive carefully), or more problematically, those who will try less hard to avoid default or accidents, are undeterred by the higher rates. The asymmetric information and higher rates have adversely selected out precisely those borrowers and drivers the lender and auto insurance company wanted to attract to their loan portfolio and insurance risk pool. Recognizing this problem, the creditors and insurers offer a restricted and incomplete set of loan and insurance contracts. Credit rationing that excludes large segments of the population of potential borrowers and state-mandated protection against uninsured motorists are reflections of the adverse selection problem resulting from asymmetric information in these commercial lending and auto insurance markets.

SOLUTIONS TO THE ADVERSE SELECTION PROBLEM

In both theory and practice, two approaches elicit the exchange of high-quality experience goods, commercial loans to new borrowers, or auto insurance policies to new residents. The first involves regulatory agencies such as the Federal Trade Commission, the Food and Drug Administration, and the Consumer Product Safety Commission. These agencies can attempt to set quotas (e.g., on minimum product durability, on minimum lending in "red-lined" underprivileged communities, or on minimum auto liability insurance coverage). They may also impose restrictions (e.g., on the sale of untested pharmaceuticals), enforce product safety standards (e.g., on the flammability of children's sleepwear), and monitor truth in advertising laws. We discuss public regulation at greater length in Chapter 16.

MUTUAL RELIANCE: HOSTAGE MECHANISMS SUPPORT ASYMMETRIC INFORMATION EXCHANGE

A second, quite different approach involves self-enforcing private solution mechanisms where each party relies on the other. Such **reliance relationships** often involve the exchange of some sort of hostage, such as a reputational asset, an escrow account, or a surety bond. In general, **hostage or bonding mechanisms** are necessary to induce unregulated asymmetric information exchange. For this second approach to the adverse selection problem to succeed, buyers must be convinced that fraud is more costly to the seller than the cost of delivering the promised product quality. Then and only then will the customers pay for the seller's additional expected costs attributable to the higher-quality products.

Reliance Relationship
Long-term, mutually beneficial agreements, often informal.

Hostage or Bonding Mechanism
A procedure for establishing trust by assigning valuable property contingent on your nonperformance of an agreement.

One simple illustration of the use of a hostage mechanism to support asymmetric information exchange is a product warranty, perhaps for an auto tire. Tires are an experience good in that blowout protection and tread wear life are product qualities not detectable at the point of purchase. Only by driving many thousands of miles and randomly encountering many road hazards can the buyer ascertain these tire qualities directly. However, if a tread wear replacement warranty and a tire blowout warranty make the sellers conspicuously worse off should they fail to deliver high-quality tires, then buyers can rely on that manufacturer's product claims. As a consequence, buyers will be willing to offer higher prices for the unverifiably higher-quality product.

Hostage mechanisms can be either self-enforcing or enforced by third parties. Like warranties, a seller's representations about after-sale service and product replacement guarantees are ultimately contractual agreements that will be enforced by the courts. However, other hostage mechanisms require no third-party enforcement. Suppose DuPont's industrial chemicals division reveals to potential new customers the names and addresses of several satisfied current customers. This practice of providing references is not only to assist potential buyers in gauging the quality of the product or service for sale but also to deliver an irretrievable hostage. Once new customers have the easy ability to contact regular customers and blow the whistle on product malfunctions or misrepresentations, the seller has an enhanced incentive to deliver high quality to both sets of buyers. Connecting all suppliers and customers in a real-time information system is a natural extension of this familiar practice of providing references. The total quality movement's (TQMs) ISO 9000 standards recommend that companies insist on just such information links to their suppliers.

EXAMPLE

Credible Product Replacement Claims: Dooney & Bourke

The women's handbag market has a wide selection of brand names, prices, and qualities. Leather products have several search good characteristics in that one can touch and feel the material in order to assess the fineness or coarseness of the grain, the evenness of the tanning process, the suppleness of the leather, and other qualities. In these respects, one can search for just that quality for which one is willing to pay. However, the susceptibility to discoloring with age or exposure to the elements and the quality of the stitching is much harder to detect at the point of purchase. As a result, some aspects of handbag purchase are an experience good exchange. Therefore, one wonders how the wide variety of prices and qualities can be sustained. Dooney & Bourke resolved this question by offering an almost preposterous replacement guarantee. Like Revo sunglasses, Dooney & Bourke offered to replace any handbag for the life of the customer. Because each state attorney general will assist any customer in enforcing this promise, the commitment was credible, and the replacement guarantee provides a hostage that supports high-price, high-quality exchanges. In particular, customers can easily discern that Dooney & Bourke is better off producing an exceptionally high-quality handbag to deliver at the first transaction rather than an unlimited series of replacements.

Brand-Name Reputations as Hostages

A marketing mechanism that supports asymmetric information exchange is a brand-name reputation such as Sony Trinitron Wega digital televisions, Apple Macintosh computers, Pepperidge Farm snacks, and Toyota Lexus automobiles. Branding requires a substantial investment over extended periods of time. Moreover, brand names are capital assets that provide future net cash flows from repeat-purchase customers as long as the brand reputation holds up. To defraud customers by delivering less quality than the brand reputation promised would destroy the capitalized market value of the brand name. Buyers anticipate that value-maximizing managers will not intentionally destroy brand-name capital. Brand names therefore deliver a hostage, providing assurances to buyers that the seller will not misrepresent the quality of an experience good.

Ultimately, brand-name capital provides such a hostage because the disreputation effects on the brand name that result from delivering fraudulent product quality cannot be separated from the salable brand asset. Successful brands can be extended to sell other products; Nestlé's original hot chocolate brand can be extended to sell cereal-based candy bars, and Oreo cookies can be extended to sell ice cream. But the product failure of Texas Instruments (TI) personal computers means that now the TI brand name cannot be easily extended to other consumer electronic products. All the potential buyers have to figure out is whether the seller would be worse off sacrificing the value of the brand name but economizing on production expenses rather than simply incurring the extra expense to produce a high-quality product while retaining the brand value. A brand-name asset such as Pepperidge Farm may suggest one answer, whereas Joe's Garage suggests another.

EXAMPLE

CUSTOMERS FOR LIFE AT SEWELL CADILLAC[29]

The most profitable luxury automobile dealership in the United States is operated in Dallas, Texas, by Carl Sewell. Several decades ago, Sewell realized that the critical success factor in his business was establishing repeat-purchase transactions with regular customers. Many potential buyers shop for lowest price in the new automobile market, sometimes with no more inconvenience than browsing the Internet. And because the alternatives are many, and the information on posted prices is great, many dealerships spend several hundred dollars per car on personal selling costs with little prospect of repeat business. Carl Sewell decided instead to expend similarly large amounts attracting "customers for life." He began by making the apparently preposterous claim that he would dispatch Sewell Cadillac emergency roadside service to any Sewell Cadillac customer experiencing car trouble anywhere in the state of Texas. To economize on the need for such trips, Sewell developed an extensive dealer-based maintenance schedule and instituted one of the first total quality management (TQM) programs in his service department.

Because these policies introduced new process-based competitive advantages, they were difficult for other dealers to imitate. These process innovations cost plenty, but the word-of-mouth reputation effects every time the dealership delivered on its promise spread the name and quality image of Sewell Cadillac across North Texas. Soon customers were driving in from surrounding cities for the privilege of doing high-margin business with Carl Sewell. And even more importantly, these same customers came back time and time again with little additional cost to the dealership.

If brand-name assets could be sold separately from their reputations (or disreputations), then this hostage mechanism would cease to support experience-good exchange. Assets that can be easily redeployed are not hostages. Easy entry and exit,

[29] See Carl Sewell and Paul B. Brown, *Customers for Life* (New York: Simon & Schuster, 1992).

which worked to ensure break-even prices just sufficient to cover costs in the normal competitive markets, may have undesirable consequences here in asymmetric information experience-good markets.

Price Premiums with Nonredeployable Assets[30]

Recall that if buyers offer prices that just cover high-quality cost, sellers of experience goods prefer the profit from defrauding customers by delivering low-quality products. But suppose buyers offered reliable sellers a continuing price premium above the cost of high-quality products. At P_{hh} in Figure 10.10, the non-notorious firm produces Q_1' high-quality product and earns a continuous stream of profits ($IJAG + JKA$), labeled $T + U$. These anticipated future profits may now exceed (in present value) the notorious firm's one-time-only fraudulent rent from production at Q_2'—namely, $D + T$, plus incremental profit $E + U + V$. That is,

$$(T + U)/d > [(D + T) + (E + U + V)]/(1 + d) \qquad [10.9]$$

where d is an appropriate discount rate (e.g., the firm's weighted average cost of capital, perhaps 12%). By Equation 10.9, lower discount rates or faster rising marginal cost (i.e., a smaller incremental profit from the expansion of output, shaded area V in Figure 10.10) decreases the likelihood of fraudulent behavior. If reliable delivery

Figure 10.10 High-Quality Experience Goods Earn a Price Premium

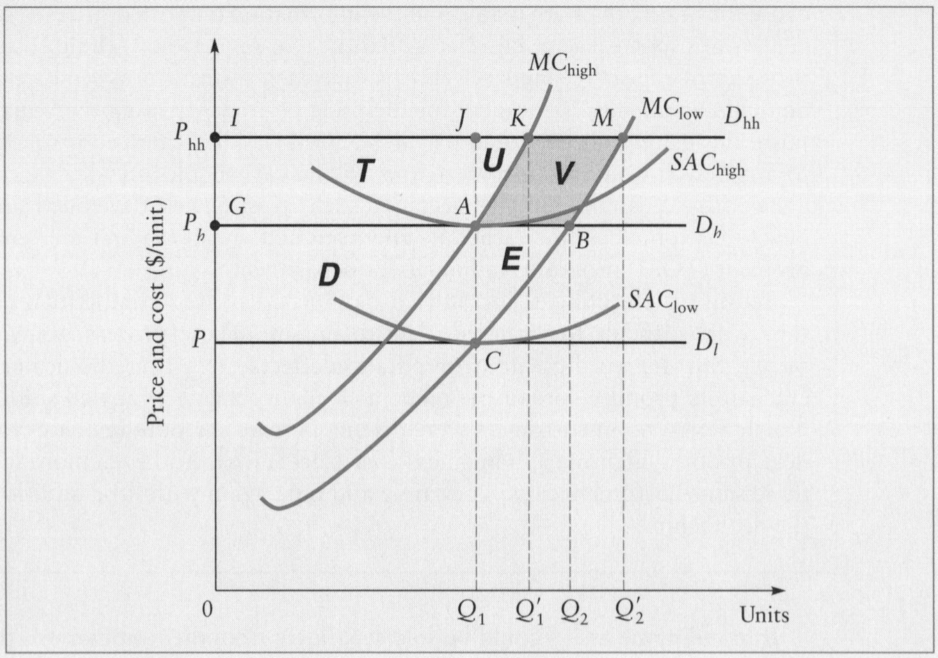

[30] See B. Klein and K. Leffler, "The Role of Market Forces in Assuring Contractual Performance," *Journal of Political Economy* 89, no. 4 (1981), pp. 615–641.

of a high-quality product does in fact earn long-term net profit in excess of the one-time-only profit from fraud, sellers will offer both low- and high-quality products at P_l and P_{hh}, respectively, and some buyers will purchase in each market.

However, transitory profits alone do not eliminate adverse selection. When profits attract entry in competitive markets, the price premiums will erode, and notorious firm behavior will then return. What is missing is a mechanism to drive out the rent from the price premiums. If the sellers invest the high-quality price premiums in firm-specific assets, such as L'eggs retail displays for convenience stores or Ethan Allen's interiors for their showrooms, then new entrants will encounter higher entry barriers. Potential entrants perceive these barriers as reducing potential net profit and therefore a deterrent to entry. L'eggs' or Ethan Allen's operating profits in excess of the production cost can then persist, and high-quality, high-price experience goods can survive in the marketplace.

To avoid the hit-and-run entry that would recur each time high-quality prices rose above cost, rent-dissipating investments must not be in generic retail sites easily redeployable to the next tenant or capital equipment easily redeployable to the next manufacturer (e.g., corporate jet aircraft). New entrants would use that redeployability to move in on the business for a short time and then sell off their assets in thick resale markets when profits eroded. Then, competitive equilibrium would again induce adverse selection in experience-good markets. Instead, the investment that dissipates the operating profit from high-quality products must be sunk cost investment in nonredeployable assets.

Nonredeployable Assets
Assets whose value in second-best use is near zero.

Asset Specificity
The difference in value between first-best and second-best use.

Nonredeployable assets are assets whose liquidation value in second-best use is low. This situation usually occurs when the assets depend on a firm-specific input such as a L'eggs or Ethan Allen brand name. Without the brand name, no firm has a use for the egg-shaped retail racks designed for L'eggs original packaging or the lavish Ethan Allen showrooms. Many such nonredeployable assets have high value in their first-best use. The difference between value in first-best use and liquidation value is a measure of **asset specificity**. Highly specific assets make the best hostages to convince customers that asymmetric information transactions will be nonfraudulent.

In summary, asymmetric information causes competitive markets for experience goods to differ significantly from the competitive markets for search goods. Long-run equilibrium for high-quality experience goods requires revenues in excess of total unit cost. These profits are invested by reliable sellers of experience goods in highly specific assets. Potentially notorious firms with redeployable assets attract only customers seeking low-price/low-quality experience goods. In experience-good markets, you get what you pay for when reputations matter or other hostage mechanisms establish the seller's credibility.

EXAMPLE

Efficient Uncut Diamond Sorting at DeBeers[31]

Another illustration of experience-good exchange is block booking by the DeBeers diamond cartel, which controls more than 80 percent of the uncut wholesale diamond business. DeBeers offers groupings of diamonds of various grades to approved wholesale buyers. Because buyers are not allowed to cull the less valuable stones, the quality of the diamonds in any given grouping is unverifiable at the point of

[31] Based on R. Kenney and B. Klein, "The Economics of Block Booking," *Journal of Law and Economics* 26 (1983), pp. 497–540.

purchase—hence, the term *sights*. If these arrangements were one time only, no buyer would purchase high-price sights or agree to the culling restrictions. But because block booking reduces the need for inspection of rejected stones that would otherwise result, DeBeers can consistently offer its sights at net costs below the value at which the diamonds grade out. Buyers therefore have a reason for purchasing high-quality experience goods from DeBeers. If a competitor offered no culling restrictions and lower prices, the diamond merchants would carefully weigh the additional cost of sorting the diamonds themselves against the price premiums at DeBeers and might well decide to continue doing business with DeBeers. Because of its reputation, few potential competitors ever challenge DeBeers despite high markups and margins in the uncut diamond wholesale business. DeBeers' reputation for passing on its cost savings in diamond sorting to buyers is the hostage that brings buyers back time and time again.

Summary

- Competitive strategy entails an analysis of the firm's resource-based capabilities, the design of business processes that can secure sustainable competitive advantage, and the development of a road map for innovation.
- Types of strategic thinking include industry analysis, competitor analysis, strategic positioning, and identification of core competencies derived from resource-based capabilities.
- Sustainable competitive advantage may arise from product differentiation strategy (product capabilities, branding, and endorsements), from focused cost or cost leadership strategy, or from information technology strategy.
- The choice of competitive strategy should be congruent with the breadth or narrowness of the firm's strategic focus.
- A successful competitive strategy includes an ongoing process of reinvention and reconfiguration of capabilities and business models.
- A relevant market is a group of economic agents that interact with each other in a buyer-seller relationship. Relevant markets often have both spatial and product characteristics.
- The Five Forces model of business strategy identifies threat of substitutes, threat of entry, power of buyers, power of suppliers, and the intensity of rivalry as the determinants of sustainable incumbent profitability in a particular industry.
- The threat of substitutes depends on the number and closeness of substitutes as determined by the product development, advertising, brand-naming, and segmentation strategies of preexisting competitors. Complements in consumption can be an enormous source of network effects, raising sustainable profitability.
- The threat of entry depends on the height of barriers to potential entrants including capital requirements, economies of scale, absolute cost advantages, switching costs, access to distribution channels, and trade secrets and other difficult-to-imitate forms of product differentiation.
- The bargaining power of buyers and suppliers depends on their number, their size distribution, the relationship between industry capacity and industry demand, the uniqueness of the inputs, the potential for forward and backward integration, the ability of the buyers to influence the setting of an industry standard, and the extent to which each party to the bargain has outside alternatives.
- The intensity of rivalry depends on the number and size distribution of sellers in the relevant market, the relative frequency of price versus nonprice competition, switching costs, the proportion of fixed to total cost, the barriers to exit, the growth rate of industry demand, and the incumbents' speed of adjustment.
- The *demand* for a good or service is defined as the various quantities of that good or service that consumers are willing and able to purchase during a particular period of time at all possible prices. The *supply* of a good or service is defined as the quantities that sellers are willing to make available to purchasers at all possible prices during a particular period of time.

- In general, a profit-maximizing firm will desire to operate at that level of output where marginal cost equals marginal revenue.
- In a purely competitive market structure, the firm will operate in the short run as long as price is greater than average variable cost.
- In a purely competitive market structure, the tendency is toward a long-run equilibrium condition in which firms earn just normal profits, price is equal to marginal cost and average total cost, and average total cost is minimized.
- In a monopolistically competitive industry, a large number of firms sell a differentiated product. In practice, few market structures can be best analyzed in the context of the monopolistic competition model. Most actual market structures have greater similarities to the purely competitive market model or the oligopolistic market model.
- Advertising expenditures are optimal from a profit-maximization perspective if they are carried to the point where the marginal profit contribution from an additional unit of output is equal to the marginal cost of advertising. The optimal level of advertising intensity (the advertising expenditure per sales dollar) varies across products and industries; it is determined by the marginal profit contribution from incremental sales and by the advertising elasticity of demand.
- Exchange under incomplete information and exchange under asymmetric information differ. *Incomplete information* refers to the uncertainty that is pervasive in practically all transactions and motivates insurance markets. *Asymmetric information,* on the other hand, refers to private information one party possesses that the other party cannot independently verify.
- Asymmetric information in *experience-good* markets leads to *adverse selection* whereby high-price/high-quality products are driven from the market by low-quality products whose low quality is indistinguishable at the point of sale. Buyers in such *lemons markets* refuse to offer prices high enough to cover the cost of high quality because under competitive conditions suppliers will predictably commit fraud, and then perhaps move on to conduct business with unsuspecting customers under other product or company names.
- To escape adverse selection and elicit high-quality experience goods necessitates either intrusive and expensive regulation or some sort of bonding mechanism to induce *self-enforcing reliance relationships* between buyers and sellers. Warranties, independent appraisals, leases with a high residual, collateral, irrevocable money-back guarantees, contingent payments, and brand names all provide assurance to buyers that the seller will not misrepresent the product quality. Hostage mechanisms support asymmetric information exchange.
- Another way to escape adverse selection is for buyers to offer price premiums and repeat-purchase transactions to firms that resist fraudulently selling low-quality experience goods for high prices. These profits are invested by reliable sellers in *nonredeployable, highly specific assets.* Potentially *notorious firms* with redeployable assets continue to attract only customers seeking low-price/low-quality products. Under asymmetric information, at best you get what you pay for, never more than that.

Exercises

Answers to the exercises in blue can be found in Appendix C at the back of the book.

1. The profitability of the leading cola syrup manufacturers PepsiCo and Coca-Cola and of the bottlers in the cola business is different. PepsiCo and Coca-Cola enjoy an 81 percent operating profit as a percentage of sales; bottlers experience only a 15 percent operating profit as a percentage of sales. Perform a Porter's Five Forces analysis that explains why one type of business is potentially so profitable relative to the other.
2. Television channel operating profits vary from as high as 45–55 percent at MTV and Nickelodeon down to 12–18 percent at NBC and ABC. Provide a Porter Five Forces analysis of each type of network. Why is MTV so profitable relative to the major networks?
3. The costs of producing steel declined substantially from building a conventional hot-rolled steel mill down to the new minimill technology that requires only scrap metal, an electric furnace, and 300 workers rather than iron ore raw materials, enormous blast furnaces, rolling mills, reheating furnaces, and thousands of workers. What effect on the potential industry profitability would Porter's Five Forces framework suggest this new technology has? Why?

4. Ethanol is again viewed as one part of a solution to the problem of shortages of petroleum products. Ethanol is made from a blend of gasoline and alcohol derived from corn. What would you expect the impact of this program to be on the price of corn, soybeans, and wheat?
5. The demand function for propane is

$$Q_D = 212 - 20P$$

The supply function for propane is

$$Q_S = 20 + 4P$$

   a. What is the equilibrium price and quantity?
   b. If the government establishes a price ceiling of \$6, what quantity will be demanded and supplied?
   c. If the government establishes a price floor (minimum price) of \$9, what quantity will be demanded and supplied?
   d. If supply increases to

   $$Q'_S = 20 + 6P$$

   what is the new equilibrium price and quantity?
   e. If demand increases to

   $$Q'_D = 250 - 19P$$

   and the supply is as given in Part (d), what is the new equilibrium price and quantity?
6. Assume that a firm in a perfectly competitive industry has the following total cost schedule:

Output (Units)	Total Cost (\$)
10	\$110
15	150
20	180
25	225
30	300
35	385
40	480

   a. Calculate a marginal cost and an average cost schedule for the firm.
   b. If the prevailing market price is \$17 per unit, how many units will be produced and sold? What are profits per unit? What are total profits?
   c. Is the industry in long-run equilibrium at this price?
7. Royersford Knitting Mills, Ltd., sells a line of women's knit underwear. The firm now sells about 20,000 pairs a year at an average price of \$10 each. Fixed costs amount to \$60,000, and total variable costs equal \$120,000. The production department estimates that a 10 percent increase in output would not affect fixed costs but would reduce average variable cost by 40 cents.

   The marketing department advocates a price reduction of 5 percent to increase sales, total revenues, and profits. The arc elasticity of demand with respect to prices is estimated at −2.

   a. Evaluate the impact of the proposal to cut prices on (i) total revenue, (ii) total cost, and (iii) total profits.
   b. If average variable costs are assumed to remain constant over a 10 percent increase in output, evaluate the effects of the proposed price cut on total profits.

8. The Poster Bed Company believes that its industry can best be classified as monopolistically competitive. An analysis of the demand for its canopy bed resulted in the following estimated demand function for the bed:

$$P = 1760 - 12Q$$

The cost analysis department estimates the total cost function for the poster bed as

$$TC = \frac{1}{3}Q^3 - 15Q^2 + 5Q + 24{,}000$$

a. Calculate the level of output that should be produced to maximize short-run profits.
b. What price should be charged?
c. Compute total profits at this price-output level.
d. Compute the point price elasticity of demand at the profit-maximizing level of output.
e. What level of fixed costs is the firm experiencing on its bed production?
f. What is the impact of a \$5,000 increase in the level of fixed costs on the price charged, output produced, and profit generated?

9. A firm operating in a purely competitive environment is faced with a market price of \$250. The firm's total cost function (short run) is

$$TC = 6{,}000 + 400Q - 20Q^2 + Q^3$$

a. Should the firm produce at this price in the short run?
b. If the market price is \$300, what will total profits (losses) be if the firm produces 10 units of output? Should the firm produce at this price?
c. If the market price is greater than \$300, should the firm produce in the short run?

10. Jordan Enterprises estimated the contribution margin $(P - MC)/P$ for its Air Express model of basketball shoes to be 40 percent. Based on market research and past experience, Jordan estimates the following relationship between the sales for Air Express and advertising/promotional outlays:

Advertising/Promotional Outlays	Sales Revenue
\$500,000	\$4,000,000
600,000	4,500,000
700,000	4,900,000
800,000	5,200,000
900,000	5,450,000
1,000,000	5,600,000

a. What is the marginal revenue from an additional dollar spent on advertising if the firm is currently spending \$1 million on advertising?
b. What level of advertising would you recommend to Jordan's management?

11. Which of the following products and services are likely to encounter adverse selection problems: golf shirts at traveling pro tournaments, certified gemstones from Tiffany's, graduation gift travel packages, or mail-order auto parts? Why or why not?

12. Without employing a tread wear warranty contract, how could the sellers of tires credibly commit to the delivery of high-quality products with long tread wear life?

13. If notorious firm behavior (i.e., defrauding a buyer of high-priced experience goods by delivering low-quality) becomes known throughout the marketplace only with a lag of three periods, profits on high-quality transactions remain the same, and interest rates rise slightly, are customers more likely or less likely to offer high prices for an experience good? Explain.

14. The average retail price of DVD players fell by two-thirds in four years from $360 in 1998 to $120 in 2002. In the same period, HDTV sets fell in price by only one-third from $3,000 to $2,000. You observe that many ISPs are writing applications for the DVDs that movie production companies inevitably release in DVD format today. How could this factor help explain why digital television sets have not caught on as yet and continue to remain few in number and high in price?

CASE EXERCISES

HP AND DELL PERSONAL COMPUTERS

Consider the following questions about competitive strategy in personal computers.

QUESTIONS

1. Does easy access to distribution channels at Best Buy, Office Depot, and direct-to-the consumer on the Internet, and small minimum efficient scale in assembly operations indicate high or low entry threat in the PC business? Why?
2. Do suppliers appropriate little or most of the value in the PC value chain? Why?
3. What factors determine the intensity of rivalry in an industry? Is the intensity of rivalry in the PC industry high or low? Why?

SAVING SONY MUSIC

Explore the crisis that Internet file-sharing of copyrighted music recordings has caused for Vivendi Universal, Sony Music, EMI, and AOL Time Warner Music, who together formerly supplied 70 percent of the global music industry.

QUESTIONS

1. How would the Internet firms Napster, Kazaa, and Apple's iTunes Music Store be reflected in a Porter Five Forces industry analysis?
2. Why was the Internet a disruptive technology for Sony?
3. What should be Sony's competitive strategy in response to this crisis? Include a discussion of resource-based capabilities, business opportunities, and a road map of future innovation.
4. Is your competitive strategy for Sony Music a product differentiation strategy, a low-cost strategy, or an information technology strategy? What is your strategic focus?

CHAPTER 11

PRICE AND OUTPUT DETERMINATION: MONOPOLY AND DOMINANT FIRMS

CHAPTER PREVIEW In this chapter we analyze how firms that operate in monopoly or near-monopoly markets make output and optimal pricing decisions. In such markets the dominant firm does not have to accept the market price as a given. These firms base their price-cost markups on other factors. In this chapter, we identify the reasons for single-firm dominance and analyze the components of the contribution margin and the gross margin for such firms. In addition to considering the price and output determination for "unregulated" monopolies and near-monopolies, we also look at these decisions for regulated industries: electric power, natural gas distribution and transmission, and broadcast communications. Deregulation continues to be a topic of debate, and it is important that any policy changes be consistent with microeconomic principles to avoid some of the problems that we face as part of the current system of utility regulation.

MANAGERIAL CHALLENGE

Dominant Microprocessor Company Intel Adapts to Next Trend[1]

With continuous innovation, ever-faster, more powerful chip designs, and a business plan riveted on supplying the $200 billion PC industry, Intel Corporation dominates the high-end market in microprocessors. After being forced out of the dynamic random access memory (DRAM) chip business by Japanese rivals in 1986, Intel reinvented itself as the lead supplier of microprocessors for PCs. Intel has an 85 percent market share in the microprocessor chips for laptops and 75 percent market share for desktops. In addition, Intel sells 90 percent of the chip sets that control the flow of data from the microprocessor to the display screens, modems, and graphical user interface. Its market dominance provides it with enormous economies of scale in production and increasing returns on its marketing expenditures, which allow it to beat out its smaller rivals. The result is high markups and margins (for mass-produced electronics products); for example, the Pentium series of microprocessors earned 25 percent net profit margins.

Because intellectual property is the company's most important asset, Intel protects its proprietary trade secrets about chip design and manufacture by using tight nondisclosure agreements with its customers. Some Intel chip purchasers found, however, that Intel would withhold vital information about technical specifications required to fully integrate

MANAGERIAL CHALLENGE

the chips into new products unless it was given access to its customers' new technologies. Intergraph, a maker of high-end workstations for media applications, alleged recently that Intel withheld information about subtle bugs in some Intel chips until Intergraph agreed to license its graphical user interface technology to the chip supplier.

With $300 desktop computers and $600 laptops causing a surge of demand that was unexpected, the worldwide PC market continues to grow at 15 percent per year. The market for digital telephones, handheld computers, video-game players, and set-top control boxes for digital televisions may be even bigger than the PC market. Such devices require inexpensive flash memory chips that quickly process data, not high-end Intel chips designed to run Microsoft's complex software. Samsung and Advanced Micro Devices (AMD) are the leaders in this new chip segment.

Former Intel president Andy Grove says Intel must prepare to sell lower-end chip products for under $40, despite the fact that Intel's chips previously

©TAYLOR S. KENNEDY/NATIONAL GEOGRAPHIC/GETTY IMAGES

sold for $87 to $200. Fortunately for Intel, Apple and Disney recently entered into a joint venture with Intel to develop new chips for multimedia entertainment applications.

[1] Based on "Hand-Held Combat," *Wall Street Journal* (February 12, 1998), p. A1; "Showdown Looms Over Chip Giant's Power," *Wall Street Journal* (June 8, 1998), p. B1; "Intel's Surge," *Wall Street Journal* (July 20, 2005), p. B1; and "Intel Outside," *The Economist* (May 27, 2006), pp. 59–63.

Monopoly Defined

Monopoly is defined as a market structure with significant barriers to entry in which one firm produces a highly differentiated product. Without any close substitutes for the product, the demand curve for a monopolist is often an entire relevant market demand. Just as purely competitive market structures (e.g., for AAA January wheat in Kansas City) are rare, so too pure monopoly markets are also rare.

EXAMPLE

The Mickey Mouse Monopoly: Disney

When it began, Disneyland in Anaheim, California, was unique. Other theme parks that were later developed, such as Six Flags, reduced Disney's monopoly power. In an attempt to restore its near-monopoly position, Disney created Disney World in Orlando, Florida, but Universal Studios, SeaWorld, and other attractions throughout the Orlando area quickly offered additional theme park experiences. Were they a complement or a substitute for Disney World? Negative cross price elasticity of demand evidence suggests that they are complementary relationships. Seventy percent of Disney World's business is repeat business; more variety inside or outside the park means more frequent returns for longer vacations. Because it anticipated these developments, Disney long ago became a major property owner throughout the Orlando area.

THE SOURCES OF MARKET POWER FOR A MONOPOLIST

Monopolists or near-monopoly dominant firms enjoy several sources of market power. First, a firm may possess a *patent* or *copyright* that prevents other firms from producing the same product. For example, Pharmacia & Upjohn, Inc., has a patent on the product Rogaine, the hair growth stimulator for balding men.

Second, a firm may *control critical resources*. De Beers Consolidated Mines Limited owns or controls most of the diamond production in South Africa and until recently, had marketing agreements with other major diamond-producing countries, including the former Soviet Union. This control of raw materials enabled De Beers to maintain high world prices for cut diamonds for nearly three-quarters of a century.

EXAMPLE

IMPERMANENT CONTROL OF A DENVER AIRPORT HUB: UNITED AIRLINES[2]

The market power that comes from the control of critical resources is often temporary. After the deregulation of airlines, some major carriers developed "fortress" hubs. US Airways, United, Delta, and Northwest control most of the gates at their hubs in Charlotte, Denver, Atlanta, and Minneapolis, respectively. These dominant carriers created barriers to entry by signing long-term leases with airport authorities. Local customer loyalty then supported 20 to 27 percent price premiums based on the delivery reliability, change order responsiveness, and nonstop scheduling convenience at these hubs.

By the mid-1990s, however, small start-up airlines threatened to break into the hubs of these market leaders. Delta encountered strong challenges from Kiwi and AirTran, whose presence in Atlanta caused margins on competing routes to dwindle. Frontier Airlines attracted discount and drive-in traffic at Denver. Consequently, United fares to and from Denver declined. US Airways may still control the majority of the departures from Charlotte, but its high fares caused the city council to approach Southwest Airlines and AirTran about possible entry.

A third source of monopoly power may be a *government-authorized franchise*. In most U.S. cities, one firm is chosen to provide cable TV services to the community. The same type of monopoly power occurs when a government agency such as the FCC adopts an industry standard that favors one company over another.

Monopoly power also happens in natural monopolies because of significant *economies of scale* over a wide range of output. The first entrant firm will enjoy declining long-run average costs. Under these circumstances, one supplier of the good or service is the only one able to produce the output more cheaply than can a group of smaller competitors. These so-called natural monopolies are usually closely regulated by government agencies to restrict the profits of the monopolist.

THE INCREASING RETURNS FROM NETWORK EFFECTS

Finally, *increasing returns in network-based businesses* can be a source of monopoly market power. When Microsoft managed to achieve a critical level of adoption for

[2] "Air Fares Decline in Denver," *Wall Street Journal* (February 6, 1996), p. B1.

its Windows graphical user interface (GUI), the amount of marketing and promotional expenditure required to secure the next adoption actually began to fall.

Marketing and promotions are generally subject to diminishing returns, as depicted in Figure 11.1. From 0 to 30 percent market share, the marketing required to achieve each additional share point has a diminishing effect on the probability of adoption by the next potential user (note the reduced slope of the sales penetration curve). Consequently, additional share points become more and more expensive over this range. When the number of other users of a network-based device reaches a 30 percent share, the next 50 or so share points are cheaper to promote. That is, beyond the 30 percent inflection point, each additional share point of users connected to Windows increases the probability that another user will adopt. Therefore, the marketing expense required to secure another unit sale decreases. (Note the increased slope of the sales penetration curve in the middle portion of Figure 11.1.) Then beyond 85 percent diminishing returns again set in.

These network-based effects of compatibility with other users increase the value to the potential adopter. The same thing occurs as more independent software vendors (ISVs) write applications for an operating system like Windows that has effectively become an industry standard by achieving more than 30 percent acceptance in the marketplace. The inflection points in the sales penetration curve make it likely that Microsoft will achieve an 85 percent monopoly control of the operating system

Figure 11.1 How the Adoption of a Technology Leads to Increasing Returns

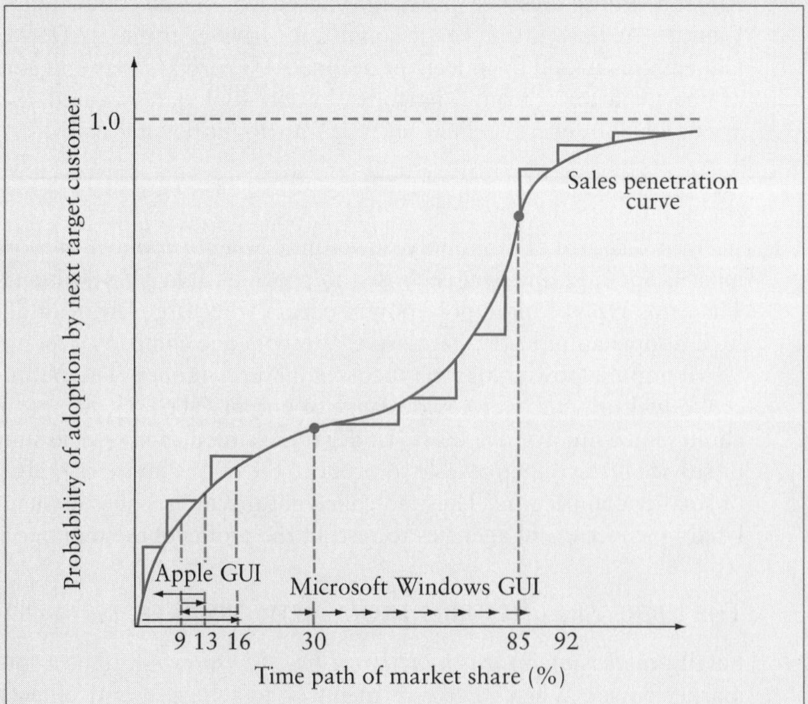

Network Effect

A source of unit cost reduction based on network value rather than scale of operations or volume purchase discounts.

market. Whatever customer relationships preexisted, once Microsoft achieved a 30 percent share, its increasing returns in marketing caused a disruptive technology **network effect** that displaced other competitors. Microsoft's share then grew to 92 percent. Netscape's Internet search engine experienced similar displacement by Microsoft's Internet Explorer when Microsoft achieved a 30 percent-plus penetration by bundling Internet Explorer with Windows. In effect, it gave away the search engine for free to reach the middle sales penetration range of increasing returns.

EXAMPLE

WHAT WENT RIGHT AT MICROSOFT BUT WRONG AT APPLE COMPUTER[3]

Throughout much of its history, Apple Computer, discussed in the *Managerial Challenge* at the beginning of Chapter 10, hovered at 7–10 percent market share in the U.S. personal computer market. Twice in its early history, Apple reached double-digit share points (16 percent in 1986 and 13 percent in 1993). Apple never did come close to achieving the inflection point (depicted at 30 percent in Figure 11.1). Apple therefore pursued increasing returns by attempting to become an industry standard in several personal computer submarkets such as the desktop publishing, journalism, media-based advertising, and entertainment industries. In addition, despite fiercely defending its graphical user interface (GUI) code for almost two decades with patent applications and trade secret infringement suits, in 1998–1999 Apple reversed its course and began discussing broad licensing and alliance agreements with both Microsoft and IBM. Compatibility with other operating systems had been easy to achieve, but widespread adoption of Mac programming code by independent software vendors (ISVs) had not. Consequently, to obtain a critical mass of adoptions that would trigger ISVs to begin writing software applications for the Mac, Apple reversed its company policy on the closed architecture of its GUI. The GUI code at Apple was clearly technically superior to the early-generation Windows products. However, the technically superior product lost out to the product that first reached increasing returns—namely, Microsoft Windows GUI running on IBM-clone PCs.

Netscape, too, once controlled 80 percent of the Internet browser market, but lost shares rapidly once Microsoft's Internet Explorer reached increasing returns. When Internet Explorer achieved 55 percent of the market share, Netscape made its browser services compatible and instead began positioning itself as a portal for Wintel machines to use in accessing the Net. Netscape wanted to avoid Apple's mistake of refusing to recognize an evolving industry standard and then finding itself buried by Microsoft's increasing returns.

Even with increasing returns set off by network effects, monopoly is always the outcome for three reasons. First, innovative new products can easily offset the cost savings from increasing returns. Second, network effects tend to occur in technology-based industries that are also experiencing external economies of scale (i.e., falling input prices). Figure 11.2 shows that between 1997 and 2002, the cost per megahertz for silicon computer chips fell from $2.00 to $0.10, and between 1998

[3] Based on "Netscape to Woo Microsoft's Customers," *Reuters* (October 1, 1998); W. Brian Arthur, "Increasing Returns and the New World of Business," *Harvard Business Review* (July–August 1996); and "Sorting Out the Deal," *U.S. News and World Report* (August 18, 1997), p. 20.

Figure 11.2 How Declining Component Costs Lead to External Economies of Scale in the Computer and Telecom Industries

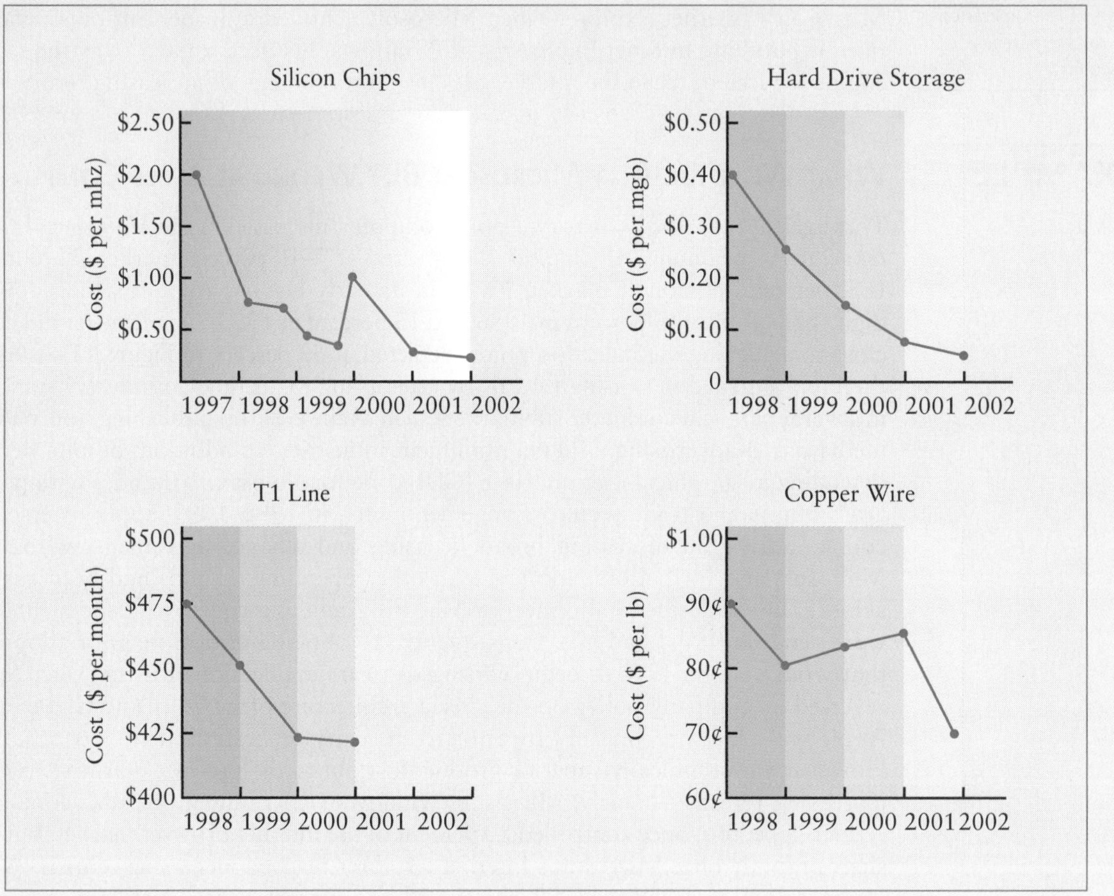

Source: **"A Spoonful of Poison,"** ***Wired*****, March 2002, p. 57.**

and 2002, hard drive storage device cost per megabyte fell from \$0.40 to \$0.05, cost per month for a T1 high-speed data transmission line fell from \$475 to \$420, and even copper wire fell from \$0.90 to \$0.70 per pound. During the same period, Corning fiber-optic cable became essentially free to anyone who would carry it off. In short, as these input suppliers grew to serve the expanding product markets in computer equipment and telecom devices, they encountered new productivity from learning curves and innovative design breakthroughs that drove down their costs. Because flash memory chips and telecom equipment markets tend to be highly competitive, the cost savings of input suppliers such as AMD and Corning get passed along to the final product producers, including Hewlett-Packard, PC-assembler Dell, cell phone manufacturer Nokia, and router manufacturer Cisco. Consequently, generally lower costs for all inputs offset in large part the advantage from increasing returns in promotion and selling expenses for companies such as Microsoft, Dell, and Palm.

WHAT WENT RIGHT • WHAT WENT WRONG

PILOT ERROR AT PALM[4]

PalmPilot, the once-dominant product in handheld computers, demonstrates how fragile is the position of even an industry leader with increasing returns to promotional spending in a technology business. Despite having 80 percent of the handheld operating system market and despite producing 60 percent of the handheld hardware at its peak in 2000, Palm, Inc., lost market share to rivals. Palm grew so fast (165% year-over-year sales increases) that it gave little attention to operational issues such as managing the supply of inputs and forecasting demand. In 2001, it mistimed the announcement of its m500 product upgrades, which were delayed by supply chain bottlenecks, and customers stopped buying older models. Handspring, Sony, Hewlett-Packard, Microsoft's Pocket PC, and the popular Blackberry drove prices lower and offered newer product features. Almost overnight, excess Palm IV and V inventories piled up on shelves, and inquiries about Microsoft's Pocket PC shot way up. Customers were awaiting the new model, and Palm was forced to take a $300 million write-down on their inventory losses. The stock price fell from $25 to $2 a share.

[4] Based on "How Palm Tumbled," *Wall Street Journal* (September 7, 2001), p. A1.

Third, technology products whose primary value lies in their intellectual property (e.g., computer software, pharmaceuticals, and telecom networks) have revenue sources that are dependent on renewals of governmental licensures and product standards. Unlike autos or steel, once R&D costs have been recouped, the marginal cost of additional copies of the software, additional doses of the medicine, or additional users on the wireless system are close to zero; every single unit sold thereafter is close to pure profit. Competitor firms who have incurred the up-front fixed costs but not succeeded in reaching the inflection point of increasing returns will rationally spend enormous sums seeking to recoup these rents through the political process and in the courts. For example, Genentech's first commercial success was a multiple sclerosis drug that avoided direct challenge to a broad Schering-Plough Corporation patent by employing a special FDA rule. Xerox was forced to license its wet paper copier technology at low royalty fees. Netscape and Sun succeeded during Microsoft's long antitrust trial of 1997–2002 in restricting their competitor (e.g., court-ordered restrictions on Microsoft's installation agreements for Windows and prohibition of Microsoft's refusal to deal with Windows licensees who install Netscape's competing Web browser software).

How can firms get around the inflection point of Figure 11.1 and achieve increasing returns? Free trials for a limited period of use is one approach. Another is giving the technology away if it can be bundled with other revenue-generating product offerings. Microsoft gave away Internet Explorer (IE) for free without being charged with predatory pricing because IE's variable cost was $0.004; that is, it rounded to zero. Another approach is to undertake consolidation mergers and acquisitions; this strategy drove IBM's acquisition of a host of smaller software companies, including Lotus, Glucode Software, and FileNet, and Oracle's hostile takeover of PeopleSoft. Some companies such as Sun Microsystems also provide JAVA and Linux programming subsidies to independent software vendors whose applications will provide network effects as complements to Sun's JAVA-based OS. Finally, having a product adopted as an industry standard leads to increasing returns. Motorola continues to work toward this end with its HDTV standard for the U.S. market.

Price and Output Determination for a Monopolist

Recall that the demand curve of a pure monopolist is the same as the industry demand curve because one firm constitutes the entire industry. Figure 11.3 shows the price-output decision for a profit-maximizing monopolist.

Just as in pure competition, profit is maximized at the price and output combination, where $MC = MR$. This point corresponds to a price of P_1, output of Q_1, and total profits equal to BC profit per unit times Q_1 units. For a negatively sloping demand curve, the MR function is not the same as the demand function. In fact, for any linear, negatively sloping demand function, the marginal revenue function will have the same intercept on the P axis as the demand function and a slope that is twice as great as that of the demand function. If, for example, the demand function were of the form

$$P = a - bQ$$

then

$$\begin{aligned}\text{Total revenue} &= TR = P \cdot Q \\ &= aQ - bQ^2\end{aligned}$$

Figure 11.3 The Price and Output Determination of a Pure Monopoly

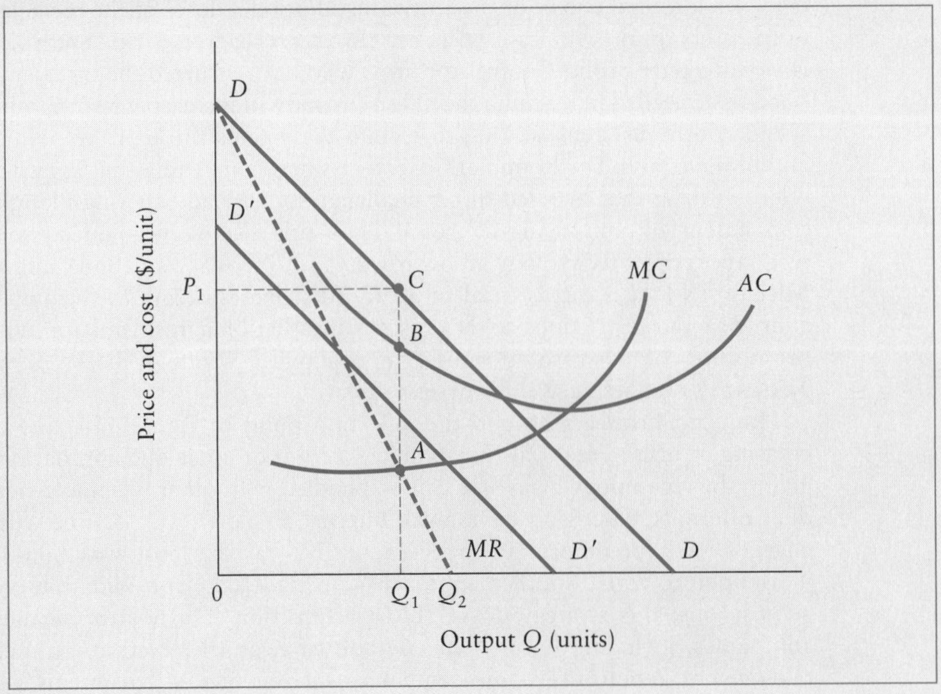

and

$$MR = \frac{dTR}{dQ} = a - 2bQ$$

The slope of the demand function is $-b$, and the slope of the MR function is $-2b$.

EXAMPLE

PROFIT MAXIMIZATION FOR A MONOPOLIST

Assume a monopolist is faced with the following demand function:

$$Q = 400 - 20P$$

and short-run total variable cost function:

$$TC = 5Q + \frac{Q^2}{50}$$

To maximize profits, it would produce and sell that output where $MC = MR$, and charge the corresponding price:

$$MC = \frac{dTC}{dQ} = 5 + \frac{Q}{25}$$

MR may be found by rewriting the demand function in terms of Q:

$$P = \frac{-Q}{20} + 20$$

and then multiplying by Q to find TR:

$$\begin{aligned} TR &= P \cdot Q \\ &= -\frac{Q^2}{20} + 20Q \end{aligned}$$

$$MR = \frac{dTR}{dQ} = -\frac{Q}{10} + 20$$

Setting $MR = MC$ yields

$$-\frac{Q^*}{10} + 20 = 5 + \frac{Q^*}{25}$$

$$Q^* = 107 \text{ units}$$

Substituting Q^* back into the demand equation, we may solve for P^*:

$$\begin{aligned} P^* &= \frac{-107}{20} + 20 \\ &= \$14.65/\text{unit} \end{aligned}$$

Hence the profit-maximizing monopolist would produce 107 units and charge a price of \$14.65 each, which would yield a profit of

$$\begin{aligned}\pi^* &= TR - TC \\ &= (P^* \cdot Q^*) - \left(5Q^* + \frac{Q^{*2}}{50}\right) \\ &= 14.65(107) - \left(5(107) + \frac{(107)^2}{50}\right) \\ &= \$803.57\end{aligned}$$

The Importance of the Price Elasticity of Demand

Recall from Chapter 3 that marginal revenue (MR), the incremental change in total revenue arising from one more unit sale, can be expressed in terms of price (P) and the price elasticity (E_D), or

$$MR = P\left(1 + \frac{1}{E_D}\right) \quad [11.1]$$

Equating MR with MC (as shown in Figure 11.3) yields the profit-maximizing relationship in terms of price and price elasticity, or

$$MC = P\left(1 + \frac{1}{E_D}\right) \quad [11.2]$$

For the monopoly case, price will be greater than marginal cost. For example, if price elasticity $E_D = -2.0$, price will equal

$$\begin{aligned}MC &= P\left(1 + \frac{1}{-2}\right) \\ MC &= 0.5P \\ P &= 2MC\end{aligned}$$

Note from Equation 11.2 that a monopolist will never operate in the area of the demand curve where demand is price inelastic (i.e., $|E_D| < 1$). If the absolute value of price elasticity is less than 1 ($|E_D| < 1$), then the reciprocal of price elasticity ($1/E_D$) will be less than -1, and marginal revenue $\left[P\left(1 + \frac{1}{E_D}\right)\right]$ will be negative. In Figure 11.3, the inelastic range of output is output beyond level Q_2. A negative marginal revenue means that total revenue can be increased by reducing output (through an increase in price). But we know that reducing output must also reduce total costs, resulting in an increase in profit. A firm will continue to raise prices (and reduce output) as long as the price elasticity of demand is in the inelastic range. Therefore, for a monopolist, the price-output combination that maximizes profits must occur where $|E_D| \geq 1$.

Equation 11.2 also demonstrates that the more elastic the demand (suggesting the existence of better substitutes), the lower the price (relative to marginal cost) any given firm can charge. This relationship can be illustrated with the following example.

EXAMPLE

PRICE ELASTICITY AND PRICE LEVELS FOR MONOPOLISTS

Consider a monopolist with the following total cost function:

$$TC = 10 + 5Q$$

The marginal cost (MC) function is

$$MC = dTC/dQ = 5$$

The price elasticity of demand has been estimated to be −2.0. Setting $MC = MR$ (where MR is expressed as in Equation 11.1) results in the following price rule for a profit-maximizing monopolist:

$$MC = \$5 = P(1 + 1/-2.0) = MR$$
$$P = 5/(0.5) = \$10/\text{unit}$$

If, however, demand is more price elastic, such as $E_D = -4.0$, the profit-maximizing monopolist would set the price at

$$P = \$5/(0.75) = \$6.67/\text{unit}$$

THE OPTIMAL MARKUP, CONTRIBUTION MARGIN, AND CONTRIBUTION MARGIN PERCENTAGE

Sometimes it is useful and convenient to express these relationships among optimal price, price elasticity, and marginal cost as a markup percentage or contribution margin percentage. Rearranging Equation 11.2 to solve for optimal price yields

$$P = \frac{E_D}{(E_D + 1)} MC \qquad [11.3]$$

where the multiplier term ahead of MC is 1.0 plus the percentage markup.[5] For example, the case of $E_D = -3$ is a product with a $-3/(-3 + 1) = 1.5$ multiplier, a 50 percent markup. The optimal profit-maximizing price recovers the marginal cost and then marks up MC another 50 percent. If $MC = \$6$, this item would sell for $1.5 \times \$6 = \$9$ and the profit-maximizing markup is \$3, or 50 percent more than the marginal cost.

Contribution Margin
The difference between the profit-maximizing price and marginal cost, often expressed as a percentage of the price. When more than one unit sale is involved, contribution margin is the difference between revenue and incremental variable cost.

The difference between price and marginal cost (i.e., the absolute dollar size of the markup) is often referred to as the **contribution margin**. With the incremental variable cost already covered, these additional dollars are available to contribute to covering fixed cost and earning a profit. They are often expressed as a percentage of the total price. In the previous example, the \$3 markup above and beyond the \$6 marginal cost represents a 33 percent contribution to fixed cost and profit, that is, a 33 percent contribution margin on the \$9 item. To summarize, an elasticity of −3.0 implies that the profit-maximizing markup is 50 percent, and that 50 percent markup implies a 33 percent contribution margin. Using Equation 11.3 and $E_D = -3$,

$$\frac{(P - MC)}{P} = \frac{1.5\ MC - 1.0\ MC}{1.5\ MC}$$
$$\text{Contribution Margin } \% = 0.5/1.5 = 33\%$$

[5] The symbol MC may be understood to refer to the accountant's narrow definition of *variable costs,* operating costs that vary with the least aggregated unit sale in the business plan.

Price elasticity information therefore carries implications for the marketing plan. Combining the contribution margin percentage (33%) with incremental variable cost information indicates what dollar markups and product prices to announce.

EXAMPLE

Markups and Contribution Margins on Chanel No. 5, Ole Musk, and Whitman's Sampler

Consider three products available at the typical drugstore counter: Chanel No. 5, Whitman's Sampler, and the store brand fragrance Ole Musk. Chanel has a loyal following of regular buyers and a price elasticity of −1.1. Whitman's has some rather close substitutes but substantial name recognition and packaging familiarity; its price elasticity measures −1.86. Finally, customers perceive many close substitutes for the generic fragrance Ole Musk, whose price elasticity is therefore −12.0.

Table 11.1 shows the optimal prices, markups, and contribution margins for these three products. Using Equation 11.3, the multiplier on *MC* for Chanel No. 5 is $-1.1/(-1.1 + 1) = 11.0$, and the optimal markup is therefore 1,000 percent (i.e., 10 times the incremental variable cost of the essences and the bottle). Because optimal price is 11.0 *MC*, the contribution margin percentage on Chanel No. 5 calculates as 10.0 *MC*/11.0 *MC* = 91%. Whitman's Sampler has a multiplier of $-1.86/(-1.86 + 1) = 2.16$: an optimal markup of 116 percent and a contribution margin of 1.16 *MC*/2.16 *MC* = 54%. In contrast, Ole Musk with the greatest price elasticity has a multiplier of $-12/(-12 + 1) = 1.09$: a markup of 9 percent, and a contribution margin percentage of 0.09 *MC*/1.09 *MC* = 8%.

Table 11.1 Optimal Prices, Markups, and Margins

	E_D	Price	Contribution Margin	Markup %	Contribution Margin %
Chanel No. 5 ($85/½oz.)	−1.1	11.00 *MC*	10.00 *MC*	1000%	91%
Whitman's Sampler ($8/lb.)	−1.86	2.16 *MC*	1.16 *MC*	116%	54%
Ole Musk ($6/4 oz.)	−12.0	1.09 *MC*	0.09 *MC*	9%	8%

Thus, the more elastic the demand function for a monopolist's output, the lower the price that will be charged, *ceteris paribus*. At the limit, consider the case of a firm in pure competition with a perfectly elastic (horizontal) demand curve. In this case the price elasticity of demand approaches $-\infty$; hence, 1 divided by the price elasticity approaches 0 and marginal revenue in Equation 11.1 becomes equal to price. Thus, the profit-maximizing rule in Equation 11.2 becomes "Set price equal to marginal cost," and the profit-maximizing markup in Equation 11.3 is zero (i.e., the marginal cost multiplier is 1.0). Of course, this conclusion is the same price-cost solution developed in Chapter 10 in the discussion of price determination under pure competition.

COMPONENTS OF THE GROSS PROFIT MARGIN

Gross Profit Margin

Revenue minus the sum of variable cost plus direct fixed cost, also known as direct costs of goods sold in manufacturing.

Gross profit margin (or just "gross margin") is a term often used in manufacturing to refer to the contribution margin after *direct* fixed costs are subtracted. For example, in a carpet plant the gross margin on each product line would be the plant's wholesale revenue minus the sum of variable costs plus machinery setup costs for the production runs involving that type of carpet. A manufacturer's income statement identifies variable costs plus direct fixed manufacturing cost as the "direct cost of goods sold" (DCGS). Thus, the gross margin is revenue minus direct cost of goods sold.[6]

Gross profit margins differ across industries and across firms within the same industry for a variety of reasons. First, some industries are more capital intensive than others. Airlines have 70–80 percent gross profit margins, not because they are particularly profitable relative to other industries, but because airlines have high fixed costs; the capital asset cost of the aircraft are a large proportion of the total cost structure. A distinction must be made between operating profits (net income on an income statement) and net cash flow available to owners after interest and other fixed costs for capital assets have been paid. The first component of the gross profit margin percentage, then, is capital costs per sales dollar.

Second, differences in gross margins reflect differences in advertising, promotion, and selling costs. Leading brands in the ready-to-eat cereal industry have 70 percent gross margins, but half of that price-cost differential (35% of every sales dollar) is spent on advertising and promotion. The automobile industry also spends hundreds of millions of dollars on advertising but only 9 percent per sales dollar. The second component of the gross profit margin percentage is advertising and selling expenses per sales dollar.

Third, differences in gross margins arise because of differential overhead in some businesses. The pharmaceutical industry has high gross margins, in large part because of the enormous expenditures on research and development to find new drugs. To conduct business in that product line, other pharmaceutical firms then incur patent fees and licensing costs, which raise their overhead costs and set the industry-level prices. Overhead costs also may differ if headquarters salaries and other general administrative expenses are high in certain firms but not others.

Finally, after accounting for any differences in capital costs, selling expenses, or overhead, the remaining differences in gross margins do reflect differential profitability.

EXAMPLE

COMPONENTS OF THE GROSS MARGIN AT KELLOGG CO.[7]

As we noted in Chapter 10, Kellogg's profit margin of 70 percent on Raisin Bran [($4.49 − $1.63)/$4.49] reflects brand loyalties built up over many years by massive and continuous advertising investments. On the leading brands, Kellogg spends

[6] The gross margin definition can be applied to retail firms but not to service firms whose direct cost of goods sold is undefined by accountants. In services, the contribution margin definition of unit profit is prevalent, and activity-based costing (ABC) determines what costs are variable to a product line or an account.

[7] Based on "Cereals," *Winston-Salem Journal* (March 8, 1995), p. A1; and "Denial in Battle Creek," *Forbes* (October 7, 1996), pp. 44–46.

30 percent of each sales dollar on advertising, and adds another 5 percent on couponing, slot-in shelf space allowances, rebates, and other promotional expenses. Capital costs entail approximately 22 percent per sales dollar. Expenditures on headquarters, general administrative, R&D, and all other overheads total 8 percent. That leaves a net profit margin of about 5 percent.

Successful restaurants have almost twice the gross margin of convenience stores on food items sold (60% versus 32%), and much of that differential (perhaps 25%) reflects net profit. Not so in Kellogg's business where, as we have seen, most of its 70 percent gross margin goes to recover advertising, capital equipment, and other fixed costs. The much higher net profit margin in a successful restaurant is a reward for bearing high risk of failure. Long term, the incidence of success in restaurants is really quite low; three out of five lose money.

Monopolists and Capacity Investments

Because monopolists do not face the discipline of strong competition, they tend to install excess capacity or, alternatively, fail to install enough capacity. A monopolist that wants to restrain entry of new competitors into the industry may install excess capacity in order to threaten to flood the market with supply and lower prices, which makes entry less attractive. Even in regulated monopolies such as electric utility companies, considerable evidence shows that regulation often provides incentives for a firm to overinvest or underinvest in generating capacity. Because utilities are regulated so that they have an opportunity to earn a "fair" rate of return on their assets, if the allowed return is greater (less) than the firm's true cost of capital, the company will be motivated to overinvest (underinvest) in new plant and equipment.

Limit Pricing

Maximizing *short-run* profits by setting marginal revenue equal to marginal cost in order to yield an optimal output of Q_1 and an optimal price of P_1 may not necessarily maximize the *long-run* profits (or shareholder wealth) of the firm. By keeping prices high and earning monopoly profits, the dominant firm encourages potential competitors to commit R&D or advertising resources in an effort to obtain a share of these profits. Instead of charging the short-run profit-maximizing price, the monopolist firm may decide to engage in *limit pricing,* where it charges a lower price, such as P_L in Figure 11.4, in order to discourage entry into the industry by potential rivals. With a limit-pricing strategy, the firm forgoes some of its short-run monopoly profits in order to maintain its monopoly position in the long run. The limit price, such as P_L in Figure 11.4, was set below the minimum point on a potential competitor's average total cost curve, (AC_{pc}). The appropriate limit price is a function of many different factors.[8]

[8] The limit-pricing model illustrates the importance of *potential* competition as a control device on existing firms. See D. Carlton and J. Perloff, *Modern Industrial Organization,* 3d ed. (New York: Harper-Collins, 1999), Chapter 10, for an expanded discussion of the limit-pricing concept.

Figure 11.4 Limit-Pricing Strategy

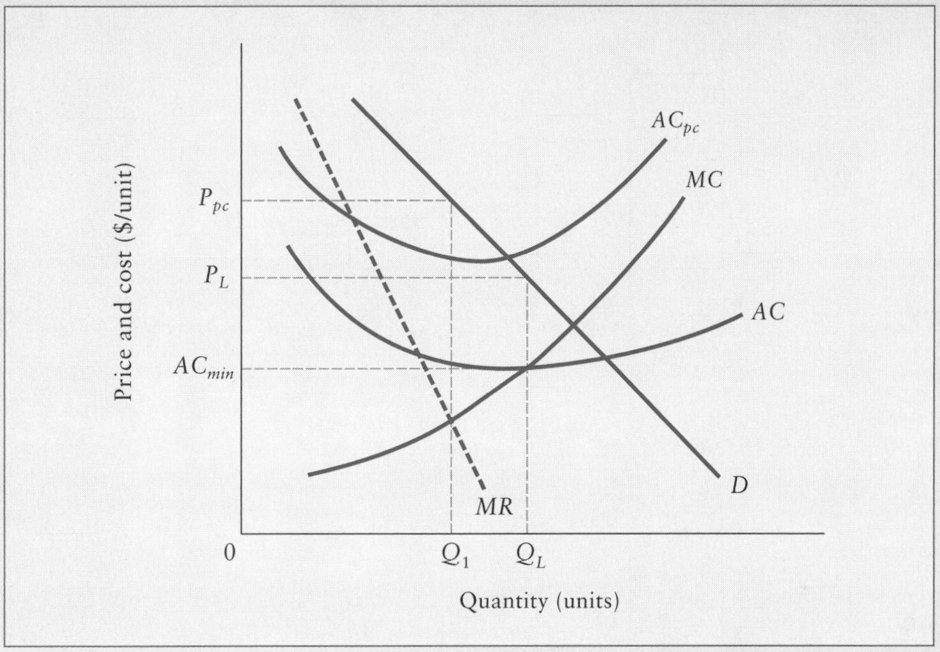

The effect of the two different pricing strategies on the dominant firm's profit stream is illustrated in Figure 11.5. By charging the (higher) short-run profit-maximizing price, the firm's profits are likely to decline over time at a faster rate, as in Panel (a), than by charging a limit price as shown in Panel (b). The firm should engage in limit pricing if the present value of the profit stream from the limit-pricing strategy exceeds the present value of the profit stream associated with the short-run profit-maximization rule of $MR = MC$. Such a decision is more likely the higher the discount rate is. Choosing a high discount rate will place relatively higher weight on near-term profits in the calculation of present discounted value and relatively lower weight on profits that occur further into the future. A high discount rate is justified when the firm's long-term pricing policy, and hence profits, are subject to a high degree of risk or uncertainty. The higher the risk, the higher is the appropriate discount rate.

EXAMPLE

USING LIMIT PRICING TO HAMPER THE SALES OF GENERIC DRUGS[9]

Patent protection is the key to financial success in the pharmaceutical industry. The typical patented drug emerges from tests on 250 chemical compounds, requires 15 years of research and FDA approval processes, and accumulates total costs of entry averaging $350 million.

[9] Based on "Too Clever by Half," *The Economist* (September 20, 1997), p. 68; "Time's Up," *Wall Street Journal* (August 12, 1997), p. A1; "Industry Merger Wave Heads to Europe," *Wall Street Journal* (November 12, 1999), p. A15; "Wearing Off: Schering-Plough Faces a Future Without Claritin," *Wall Street Journal* (March 22, 2002), p. A1.

Figure 11.5 The Effect of Pricing Strategies on Profit Streams as a Patent Expires

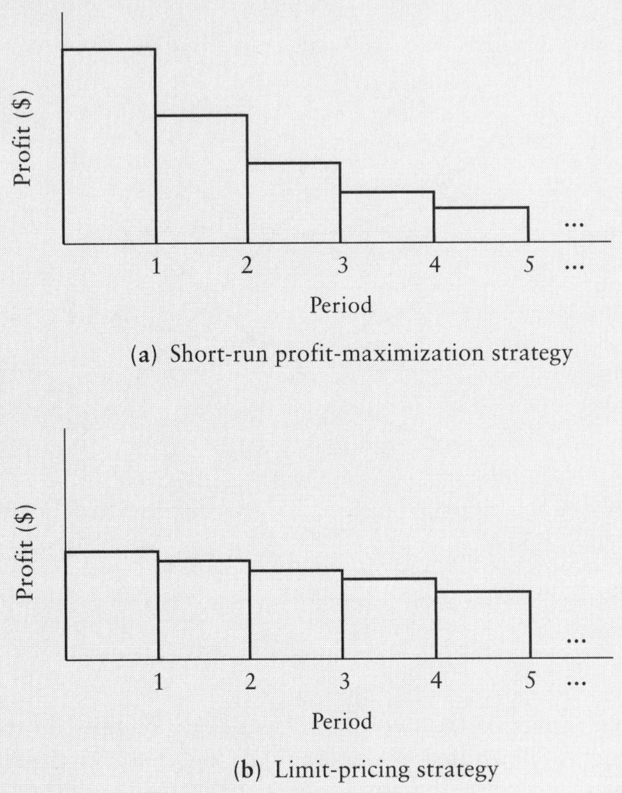

Capoten is Bristol-Myers Squibb's (BMS) hypertension drug for use in reducing heart-attack risk. Rather than limit pricing, BMS maintained Capoten's 57-cents-per-pill price right to the end of its 20-year patent protection in February 1996. Competition from generics selling for 3 cents per pill was swift and disastrously effective. In early 1996, BMS introduced its own generic product that cannibalized sales of the branded product still further. By the fourth quarter of 1996, Capoten sales had collapsed to $25 million from $146 million the year before. In order to restore profitability, BMS and other leading pharmaceutical companies are merging in order to take advantage of economies of scale in R&D through follow-on drugs with improved efficacy or reduced side effects.

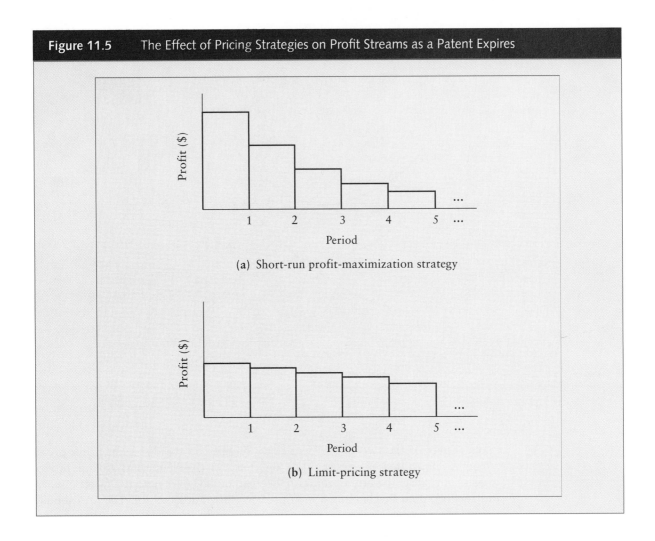

In contrast, Eli Lilly and Schering-Plough chose limit pricing and advertising for their leading medications, the antidepressant Prozac and the allergy treatment Claritin. Prozac lost patent protection in 2001, as did Claritin in 2003. One reason Schering-Plough chose a different (limit) pricing strategy is that Claritin has no improved follow-on drug available, the FDA demoted the prescription-only product to over-the-counter status at an identical dosage, and as a consequence $100-per-month-per-patient revenue was projected to decline to $9 if short-run profit maximization continued. At a gross profit margin of 79 percent, Schering-Plough was facing a monumental loss of $2.1 billion in operating profits on $2.7 billion in Claritin sales.

In general, new biotechnologies have allowed imitation pharmaceuticals to appear much faster in during the past 15 years. Indeed, the first hypertension drug, Inderal, enjoyed almost a decade from 1968–1977 of pure monopoly sales after Capoten lost its patent protection. Prozac, on the other hand, met competition from imitators within four years of its 1988 introduction. And Recombinate, a breakthrough drug for hemophiliacs newly patented in 1992, encountered copycat products by 1994. Tactics such as limit pricing become all the more important in the presence of such quick and relatively easy imitation by fast-second competitors.

REGULATED MONOPOLIES

Public Utilities

A group of firms, mostly in the electric power, natural gas, and communications industries, that are closely regulated by one or more government agencies. The agencies control entry into the business, set prices, establish product quality standards, and influence the total profits that may be earned by the firms.

Several important industries in the United States operate as regulated monopolies. In broad terms, the regulated monopoly sector of the U.S. economy includes **public utilities** such as electric power companies, natural gas companies, and communications companies. In the past, much of the transportation industry (airlines, trucking, railroads) also were regulated closely, but these industries have been substantially deregulated over the past 10 to 25 years.

ELECTRIC POWER COMPANIES

Investor-owned electric power companies make up one large industry subject to economic regulation. Electric power is made available to the consumer through a production process characterized by three distinct stages. First, the power is generated in generating plants. Next, in the transmission stage, the power is transmitted at high voltage from the generating site to the locality where it is used. Finally, in the distribution stage, the power is distributed to the individual users. The complete process may take place as part of the operations of a single firm, or the producing firm may sell power at wholesale rates to a second enterprise that carries out the distribution function. In the latter case, the distribution firm often is a department within the local municipal government or a consumers' cooperative.

Firms that produce electric power are subject to regulation at several levels. Integrated firms that carry out all three stages of production are usually regulated by state public utility commissions. These commissions set the rates to be charged to the final consumers. The firms normally receive exclusive rights to serve individual localities through franchises granted by local governing bodies. As a consequence of their franchises, electric power companies have well-defined markets within which they are the sole provider of output. Finally, the Federal Energy Regulatory Commission (FERC) has the authority to set rates on power that crosses state lines and on wholesale power sales. Some states are continuing to partially or totally deregulate the power production and transmission elements of this industry. The California crisis with deregulated electricity raises questions about the desirability of fully deregulated competition at the retail (distribution) level.[10]

[10] See M. Maloney, R. McCormick, and R. Sauer, *Consumer Choice, Consumer Value: An Analysis of Retail Competition in America's Electric Utility Industry* (Washington, DC: Citizens for a Sound Economy, 1996); "Electric Utility Deregulation Sparks Controversy," *Harvard Business Review* (May/June 1996); and A. Faruqui and K. Eakin, eds., *Pricing in Competitive Electricity Markets* (Boston: Kluwer, 2000).

WHAT WENT RIGHT • WHAT WENT WRONG

THE PUBLIC SERVICE COMPANY OF NEW MEXICO

The Public Service Company of New Mexico (PNM) provides electric power service (generation and distribution) and natural gas distribution services to most of New Mexico's population. This monopoly position is regulated by the Public Service Commission of the State of New Mexico and, to a lesser extent, by the Federal Energy Regulatory Commission. These commissions determine the rates charged to various classes of customers for the services provided. The rates are based on the cost of providing service, including a "fair return" on the capital invested.

PNM earned a 4.9 percent return on common equity during 1992, 8.0 percent on common equity during 1995, and 7.5 percent on common equity between 1997 and 1999. The industry average return on equity was 11–12 percent, according to *Value Line*. PNM earned extraordinarily low returns even though PNM is authorized by its regulatory commission to charge rates consistent with its earning a return of 12.5 percent on common equity. Why has this monopoly supplier of utility services (and many other utility companies) been unable to earn its authorized return?

During the 1970s, PNM experienced high growth in the demand for its services as the Sunbelt prospered and industry grew in the region. One large user of power was the growing uranium mining industry in New Mexico that was serving the needs of nuclear power plants being built by other electric utilities. Faced with rapid growth in demand and increasing costs for its traditional fuel, natural gas, PNM embarked on a major program to expand and modernize its power-generating capacity. As the managers of the utility planned for the future, they made projections of future demand. PNM's managers examined a number of alternatives to meet the growing demand, including purchasing power from nearby utilities, building large coal-fired plants close to New Mexico's abundant coal resources, and building nuclear power plants. The objective of PNM's management was to meet the projected demand at the lowest cost. Having seen what happened to the price of natural gas in the early 1970s, these managers also were aware of the desirability of having a diverse mix of fuel sources. PNM ultimately decided to participate with other regional utilities in the construction of several large coal-fired plants in the Four Corners region of northwest New Mexico, to build additional coal-fired plants of its own, and to participate with other utilities in the construction of a five-unit nuclear power plant called Palo Verde.

As time passed, load growth did not materialize as expected. In the aftermath of the disaster at Three Mile Island, demand for uranium ore declined and lower-cost alternative sources were developed. The New Mexico uranium mining industry virtually shut down. The state of New Mexico required that expensive pollution control devices, called scrubbers, be installed at the coal plants being constructed, thereby dramatically increasing their cost and the cost of power produced from these plants. The Palo Verde project was plagued by cost overruns, delays, and extensive and costly safety modifications. Ultimately, two of the five units of Palo Verde were canceled. When the construction program was completed, PNM found itself with capacity nearly 80 percent in excess of peak demand (a 20-percent reserve margin is more normal).

The regulatory process facing utilities does not ensure that a company will earn its authorized returns. Consequently, the New Mexico state regulatory commission refused to permit PNM to recover the costs of this excess capacity in rates charged to its present customers. Even in the absence of regulation, PNM would probably be unable to fully recover the costs of this excess capacity.

Natural Gas Companies

The highly regulated natural gas industry furnishes natural gas to users in a three-stage process. The first stage is the production of the gas in the field. Transportation to the consuming locality through pipelines is the second stage. Distribution to the final user makes up the third stage. The FERC historically set the field price of natural gas that is moved out of the production stage. The regulation of natural gas prices at the wellhead has been effectively phased out. In addition, the FERC oversees the interstate transportation of gas by approving pipeline routes and by controlling the wholesale rates charged by pipeline companies to distribution firms. The distribution function may be carried out by a private firm or by a municipal government agency. In either event, the rates charged to final users also are controlled because the distribution firm often has a monopoly in its service area.

Communications Companies

In the communications industry, the most important activities are radio, cable, television, and telephone service that are regulated by the Federal Communications Commission (FCC). Local service in the intrastate markets, which may be provided either by one of the former Bell System companies or by one of the so-called local telephone independents, is regulated by state commissions. Radio station ownership continues to become more concentrated; perhaps 70 percent of the stations in the top 100 markets are now controlled by two companies.

The Economic Rationale for Regulation

As described in the preceding section, regulated industries furnish services that are critical to the functioning of the economy. Apart from this factor, do the regulated industries share any other common characteristics that account for the regulation imposed on them? What are the justifications for imposing economic regulation on certain industries?

Natural Monopoly Argument

Natural Monopoly
An industry in which maximum economic efficiency is obtained when the firm produces, distributes, and transmits all of the commodity or service produced in that industry. The production of natural monopolists is typically characterized by increasing returns to scale throughout the relevant range of output.

Firms operating in the regulated sector are often **natural monopolies** in which a single supplier tends to emerge because of a production process characterized by increasing returns to scale. In other words, as all inputs are increased by a given percentage, the average total cost of a unit of output decreases. Consequently, the long-run unit cost of output declines throughout the relevant range of output. This situation is illustrated in Figure 11.6 for a firm in long-run stable equilibrium.

Suppose that the market demand curve for output is represented by the curve DD in Figure 11.6. The socially optimal level of output would then be Q^*; at that level of output, price would be well below the average total cost per unit AC^* but equal to short-run and long-run marginal cost. A single producer is able to realize economies of scale that are unavailable to firms in the presence of competition. From a social perspective, competition would result in inefficiency in the form of higher costs such as unit cost (AC_C) for the competitive firm than the unit cost (AC_M) for the monopoly firm that is six times as large. The argument follows that production

Figure 11.6 The Price-Output Determination of a Natural Monopoly

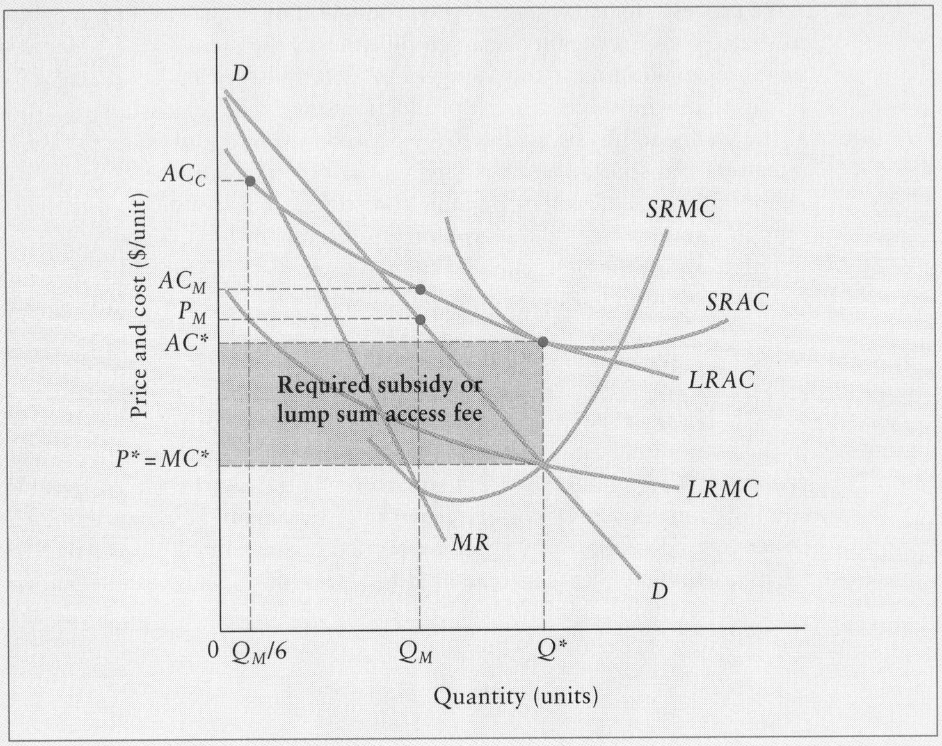

relations like those in Figure 11.6 will lead to the emergence of a single supplier. Competing firms will realize that their costs decrease as output expands. As a consequence, they will have an incentive to cut prices as long as *MR* exceeds *LRMC* to increase sales volume and spread the fixed cost. During this period, prices will be below average cost, resulting in losses for the producing firms. Unable to sustain such losses, the weaker firms gradually leave the industry, until only a single producer remains. Thus, competitive forces contribute to the emergence of the natural monopoly.

If a monopolistic position were to exist in the absence of regulation, the monopolist would maximize profit by equating marginal revenue and marginal cost at an output Q_M, leading to a higher price P_M and lower output. Thus, intervention through regulation is required to achieve the benefits of the most efficient organization of production. In its simplest form, this is the explanation of regulation based on the existence of natural monopolies.

EXAMPLE

Are Large-Scale Electricity Generating Plants Becoming Extinct?

The electric utility industry in the United States has always faced intense regulation of its prices, service standards, and the choice of production technologies it employs. Regulation is provided by state utility commissions and the Nuclear Regulatory Commission.

Many of the power plants constructed during the 1980s and 1990s were large base-load generating plants using coal or nuclear energy as their fuel. During that time, industry experts believed that these larger plants would provide the lowest-cost sources of power due to their economies of large scale. However, in some cases the final cost of these plants greatly exceeded initial estimates.

The situation, as the electric utility industry enters an era of deregulation and faces market competition, calls into question these old assumptions of economies of scale. Independent power producers, who produce electricity for sale to utility companies or directly to end users, have built many smaller, less capital-intensive plants. These plants substitute a cheap variable input, natural gas, for the expensive fixed capital equipment required in nuclear and coal-fired power plants, which means substantial cost savings.

Deregulation will likely accelerate this trend toward distributed generation of electricity in smaller plants with considerably less economies of scale.

Figure 11.6 illustrates one problem stemming from a genuine natural monopoly. Suppose that a regulatory agency succeeds in establishing the socially optimal price for output, P^*. As the cost curves indicate, this price would lead to losses for the producing firm, because price would be below the average total cost AC^*. This is obviously an unsustainable result. In this situation the regulating agency normally sets prices at average cost to make sure revenues are sufficient to cover all costs. The most efficient way to realize revenue, however, is to charge a per-unit price equal to $LRMC$ (P^*) and collect the shaded deficit area in Figure 11.6 as a *lump sum* access fee, perhaps divided equally among customers. Alternatively, with time-of-day metering, the lump sum access fees can depend on when the customer uses power—higher lump sum access fees charged at peak periods such as 4 P.M. to 8 P.M.

PEAK-LOAD UTILITY RATES

When output cannot be stored in inventory, and the power utility ordinarily stands ready to satisfy user demand, the cost of producing a unit of output varies according to a time dimension. For simplicity, suppose that demand happens at only two levels: an afternoon peak period when the demand is high and the rest of the day (an off-peak period) when the demand is below the level of afternoon demand. Because of the way in which electricity is produced, the generating capacity required to produce power for the afternoon period stands idle for the remainder of the firm's operating cycle; that is, excess generating capacity is available except during peak demand. The firm can produce additional output during the morning, for instance, at a relatively low marginal cost (the cost of the additional fuel used). In contrast, to produce an additional unit of output during the afternoon period, the firm would have to install an additional unit of generating capacity, which means the marginal cost of that unit of output would be quite high. Because expanding output in the peak period requires the expansion of productive capacity, the basic principle of $MR = MC$ suggests that peak and off-peak output be priced differently to reflect the differences in marginal cost.

To determine an appropriate pricing policy during peak loads, consider the situation shown in Figure 11.7 where two independent demand periods are assumed.

Figure 11.7 Peak-Load Pricing

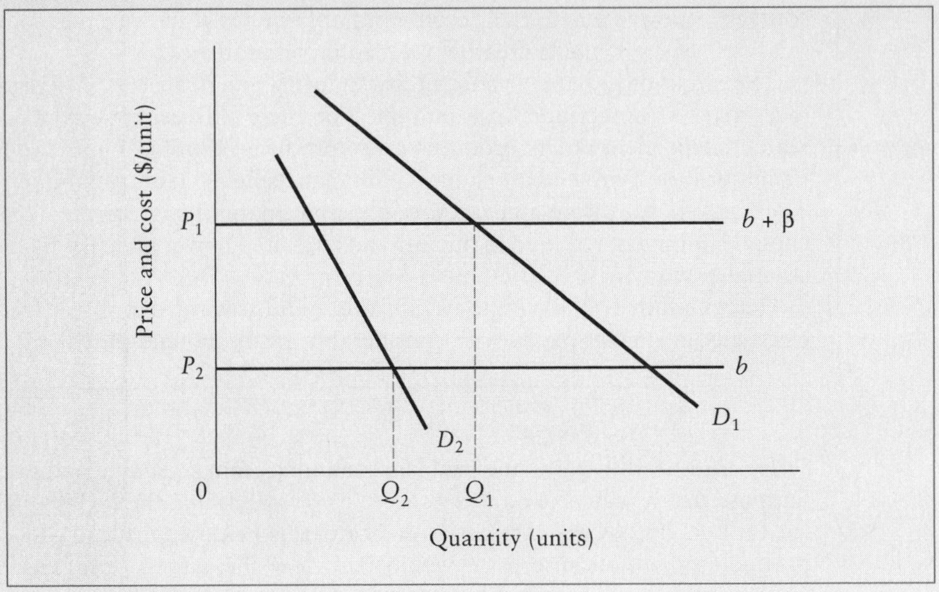

In the peak period (late afternoon), demand is represented by curve D_1; in the off-peak period, demand is shown by D_2. All units of output require the use of fuel at a constant rate, assumed to be b per unit. In addition, capital or generating capacity, which costs β per unit, is also required to produce all output; however, the capacity is not fully used except in the peak period.

The supply curve relevant for determining price and output during the late afternoon is the curve $b + \beta$, which reflects the marginal (and average) cost of supplying an additional unit of output during the peak period. At price $P_1 = b + \beta$, day users are just willing to pay the cost of producing a unit of output, making it the appropriate price for peak service. At this price, Q_1 units of output are produced, the level of capacity installed.

At what price should off-peak output be sold? With total capacity at Q_1, the appropriate price of off-peak output is P_2, which is equal to the marginal cost of fuel alone. Providing off-peak service imposes no other costs. As a result, the price should be no higher than b per unit at which Q_2 units of output are sold.[11]

Peak-Load Pricing

The process of charging a higher price during those periods of time when demand is heaviest and lower prices when demand is light.

This simplified example illustrates the basic principles of **peak-load pricing.** This policy encourages the most efficient use of existing capacity. Notice that in the usual case, users would be expected to purchase both peak and off-peak output, because air conditioner use between 4 P.M. and 8 P.M. has price inelastic demand.

[11] If base-load generation has high capital costs (i.e., if $\beta > b$), peak-load pricing can motivate many consumers to shift their clothes drying and some cooking to off-peak times, for example, through the use of interruptible service, or highly efficient water heaters that allow customers to heat water at night, rather than on demand. In this situation, the peak period may shift to the current off-peak period. Then, the original peak-load prices will be incorrect. The solution is to charge a fraction of the capital cost during each period.

SUMMARY

- Monopoly is a market structure with significant barriers to entry in which one firm produces a differentiated product.
- In a pure monopoly market structure, firms will generally produce a lower level of output and charge a higher price than would exist in a more competitive market structure. This conclusion assumes no significant economies of scale that might make a monopolist more efficient than a large group of smaller firms.
- The primary sources of monopoly power include patents and copyrights, control of critical resources, government "franchise" grants, economies of scale, and increasing returns in networks of users of compatible complementary products.
- Increasing returns from network effects are limited by input cost reductions among competitors, by innovative new product introductions, and by lobbying efforts.
- Monopolists will produce at that level of output where $MR = MC$ if their goal is to maximize short-run profits.
- The price charged by a profit-maximizing monopolist will be in that portion of the demand function where demand is elastic (or unit elastic). The greater the elasticity of demand facing a monopolist, the lower will be its price relative to marginal cost, *ceteris paribus*.
- Contribution margins are defined as revenue minus incremental variable cost, or revenue minus marginal cost when only one unit is sold.
- *Contribution margins* and *markups* are inversely related to the price elasticity of demand.
- *Gross margins* are defined as revenue minus direct costs of goods sold (incremental variable cost plus direct fixed cost), and serve to recover capital costs, selling costs, and overhead as well as earn profits.
- Limit pricing—pricing a product below the short-run profit-maximizing level—is a strategy used by some monopolists to discourage rivals from entering an industry.
- Public utilities are firms, mostly in the electric power, natural gas distribution, natural gas pipeline, and communications industries, that are closely regulated with respect to entry into the business, prices, service quality, and total profits.
- The rationales for public utility regulation are many. The *natural monopoly* argument is applied in cases where a product is characterized by increasing returns to scale. The one large firm can theoretically furnish the good or service at a lower cost than a group of smaller competitive firms. Regulators then set utility rates to prevent monopoly price gouging, ideally allowing the regulated firm to earn a return on investment just equal to its cost of capital.
- Price discrimination by utilities is often economically desirable on the basis of cost justifications and demand justifications.
- *Peak-load pricing* is designed to charge customers a greater amount for the services they use during periods of greater demand. Long-distance phone services typically have been priced on a peak-load basis.

Exercises

Answers to the exercises in blue can be found in Appendix C at the back of the book.

1. Information Resources, Inc. (IRI), collects data on consumer packaged goods at 32,000 scanner checkout counters and in panel surveys of 70,000 households. IRI records indicate that department store-brand pantyhose sell for a gross margin of 43 percent and a contribution margin of 29 percent, and the store inventory turns over 14 times per year.
   a. What expenses explain the difference between 43 percent and 29 percent?
   b. What percentage change in unit sales is required to increase total contributions if price is cut by 10 percent?
   c. Compare store-brand pantyhose with the products in Table 11.1. Why should Whitman's Sampler sell for a contribution margin of 54 percent when store-brand pantyhose sell for 29 percent?
2. You have been retained as an analyst to evaluate a proposal by your city's privately owned water company to increase its rates by 100 percent. The company has argued that at the present rate level, the firm is earning only a 2 percent rate of return on invested equity capital. The company believes a 16 percent rate of return is required in today's capital markets.

Assume that you agree with the 16 percent rate of return proposed by the company.

a. What factors need to be considered when setting rates designed to achieve this objective?
b. Would your analysis differ if you knew that the law prohibited individuals from drilling their own wells? What impact would this condition have on the price elasticity of demand?
c. Water companies have a large proportion of fixed costs compared to variable costs. How does this fact influence your analysis?

3. Ajax Cleaning Products is a medium-sized firm operating in an industry dominated by one large firm—Tile King. Ajax produces a multiheaded tunnel wall scrubber that is similar to a model produced by Tile King. Ajax decides to charge the same price as Tile King to avoid the possibility of a price war. The price charged by Tile King is \$20,000.

Ajax has the following short-run cost curve:

$$TC = 800{,}000 - 5{,}000Q + 100Q^2$$

a. Compute the marginal cost curve for Ajax.
b. Given Ajax's pricing strategy, what is the marginal revenue function for Ajax?
c. Compute the profit-maximizing level of output for Ajax.
d. Compute Ajax's total dollar profits.

4. One and Only, Inc., is a monopolist. The demand function for its product is estimated to be

$$Q = 60 - 0.4P + 6Y + 2A$$

where Q = quantity of units sold
P = price per unit
Y = per capita disposable personal income (thousands of dollars)
A = hundreds of dollars of advertising expenditures

The firm's average variable cost function is

$$AVC = Q^2 - 10Q + 60$$

Y is equal to 3 (thousand) and A is equal to 3 (hundred) for the period being analyzed.

a. If fixed costs are equal to \$1,000, derive the firm's total cost function and marginal cost function.
b. Derive a total revenue function and marginal revenue function for the firm.
c. Calculate the profit-maximizing level of price and output for One and Only.
d. What profit or loss will One and Only earn?
e. If fixed costs were \$1,200, how would your answers change for Parts (a) through (d)?

5. The Lumins Lamp Company, a producer of old-style oil lamps, estimated the following demand function for its product:

$$Q = 120{,}000 - 10{,}000P$$

where Q is the quantity demanded per year and P is the price per lamp. The firm's fixed costs are \$12,000 and variable costs are \$1.50 per lamp.

a. Write an equation for the total revenue (TR) function in terms of Q.
b. Specify the marginal revenue function.
c. Write an equation for the total cost (TC) function in terms of Q.
d. Specify the marginal cost function.

e. Write an equation for total profits (π) in terms of Q. At what level of output (Q) are total profits maximized? What price will be charged? What are total profits at this output level?

f. Check your answers in Part (e) by equating the marginal revenue and marginal cost functions, determined in Parts (b) and (d), and solving for Q.

g. What model of market pricing behavior has been assumed in this problem?

6. Unique Creations holds a monopoly position in the production and sale of magnometers. The cost function facing Unique is estimated to be

$$TC = \$100{,}000 + 20Q$$

a. What is the marginal cost for Unique?

b. If the price elasticity of demand for Unique is currently -1.5, what price should Unique charge?

c. What is the marginal revenue at the price computed in Part (b)?

d. If a competitor develops a substitute for the magnometer and the price elasticity increases to -3.0, what price should Unique charge?

7. The Jenkins Tool Company estimated the following demand equation for its product:

$$Q_D = 12{,}000 - 4{,}000P$$

where

$$P = \text{price/unit}$$
$$Q_D = \text{quantity demanded/year}$$

The firm's total costs are \$4,000 when nothing is being produced. These costs increase by 50 cents for each unit produced.

a. Write an equation for the total cost function.

b. Specify the marginal cost function.

c. Write an equation for total revenue in terms of Q.

d. Specify the marginal revenue function.

e. Write an equation for total profits, π, in terms of Q. At what level of output are total profits maximized (i.e., find the maximum of the total profit function)? What price will be charged? What will total profit be?

f. Check your answers in Part (e) by equating marginal cost and marginal revenue and solving for Q.

g. What model of market pricing behavior has been assumed in this problem?

8. Exotic Metals, Inc., a leading manufacturer of beryllium, which is used in many electronic products, estimates the following demand schedule for its product:

Price (\$/Pound)	Quantity (Pounds/Period)
\$25	0
18	1,000
16	2,000
14	3,000
12	4,000
10	5,000
8	6,000
6	7,000
4	8,000
2	9,000

Fixed costs of manufacturing beryllium are $14,000 per period. The firm's variable cost schedule is as follows:

Output (Pounds/Period)	Variable Cost (Per Pound)
0	$0
1,000	10.00
2,000	8.50
3,000	7.33
4,000	6.25
5,000	5.40
6,000	5.00
7,000	5.14
8,000	5.88
9,000	7.00

a. Find the total revenue and marginal revenue schedules for the firm.

b. Determine the average total cost and marginal cost schedules for the firm.

c. What are Exotic Metals' profit-maximizing price and output levels for the production and sale of beryllium?

d. What is Exotic's profit (or loss) at the solution determined in Part (c)?

e. Suppose that the federal government announces it will sell beryllium, from its extensive wartime stockpile, to anyone who wants it at $6 per pound. How does this affect the solution determined in Part (c)? What is Exotic Metals' profit (or loss) under these conditions?

9. Wyandotte Chemical Company sells various chemicals to the automobile industry. Wyandotte currently sells 30,000 gallons of polyol per year at an average price of $15 per gallon. Fixed costs of manufacturing polyol are $90,000 per year and total variable costs equal $180,000. The operations research department has estimated that a 15 percent increase in output would not affect fixed costs but would reduce average variable costs by 60 cents per gallon. The marketing department has estimated the arc elasticity of demand for polyol to be −2.0.

a. How much would Wyandotte have to reduce the price of polyol to achieve a 15 percent increase in the quantity sold?

b. Evaluate the impact of such a price cut on (i) total revenue, (ii) total costs, and (iii) total profits.

10. Tennis Products, Inc., produces three models of high-quality tennis rackets. The following table contains recent information on the sales, costs, and profitability of the three models:

Model	Average Quantity Sold (Units/ Month)	Current Price	Total Revenue	Variable Cost Per Unit	Contribution Margin Per Unit	Contribution Margin*
A	15,000	$30	$ 450,000	$15.00	$15	$225,000
B	5,000	35	175,000	18.00	17	85,000
C	10,000	45	450,000	20.00	25	250,000
Total			$1,075,000			$560,000

*Contribution to fixed costs and profits.

The company is considering lowering the price of Model *A* to \$27 in an effort to increase the number of units sold. Based on the results of price changes that have been instituted in the past, Tennis Products' chief economist estimates the arc price elasticity of demand to be −2.5. Furthermore, she estimates the arc cross elasticity of demand between Model *A* and Model *B* to be approximately 0.5 and between Model *A* and Model *C* to be approximately 0.2. Variable costs per unit are not expected to change over the anticipated changes in volume.

a. Evaluate the impact of the price cut on the (i) total revenue, and (ii) contribution margin of Model *A*. Based on this analysis, should the firm lower the price of Model *A*?

b. Evaluate the impact of the price cut on the (i) total revenue, and (ii) contribution margin for the entire line of tennis rackets. Based on this analysis, should the firm lower the price of Model *A*?

11. The Public Service Company of the Southwest is regulated by an elected state utility commission. The firm has total assets of \$500,000. The demand function for its services has been estimated as

$$P = \$250 - \$0.15Q$$

The firm faces the following total cost function:

$$TC = \$25{,}000 + \$10Q$$

(The total cost function does not include the firm's cost of capital.)

a. In an unregulated environment, what price would this firm charge, what output would be produced, what would total profits be, and what rate of return would the firm earn on its asset base?

b. The firm has proposed charging a price of \$100 for each unit of output. If this price is charged, what will be the total profits and the rate of return earned on the firm's asset base?

c. The commission has ordered the firm to charge a price that will provide the firm with no more than a 10 percent return on its assets. What price should the firm charge, what output will be produced, and what dollar level of profits will be earned?

12. The Odessa Independent Phone Company (OIPC) is currently engaged in a rate case that will set rates for its Midland-Odessa area customer base. OIPC has total assets of \$20 million. The Texas Public Utility Commission has determined that an 11 percent return on assets is fair. OIPC has estimated its annual demand function as follows:

$$P = 3{,}514 - 0.08Q$$

Its total cost function (not including the cost of capital) is

$$TC = 2{,}300{,}000 + 130Q$$

a. OIPC has proposed a rate of \$250 per year for each customer. If this rate is approved, what return on assets will OIPC earn?

b. What rate can OIPC charge if the commission wants to limit the return on assets to 11 percent?

c. What problem of utility regulation does this exercise illustrate?

CASE EXERCISE

DIFFERENTIAL PRICING OF PHARMACEUTICALS: THE HIV/AIDS CRISIS[12]

The HIV/AIDS crisis has been called the worst pandemic since the fourteenth-century Black Plague. The first incident of HIV/AIDS was discovered by the U.S. Centers for Disease Control in 1981. Over the next two decades, 60 million people became infected, and 22 million died. Most HIV/AIDS cases are reported in the developing world, where 95 percent of those with HIV live today. Beyond social welfare and humanitarian concerns, as a result of globalization and the fastest-growing international business opportunities in China and India, AIDs is now everybody's business. Because the pharmaceutical industry especially relies upon governmental authority to approve formularies for reimbursement, to protect its monopoly patent rights, and to prevent importation of unauthorized, unlicensed imitation medicines, the question of how to price AIDS drugs is a public issue.

Although no one has yet developed a cure for HIV, a number of companies have patented drugs that inhibit either the virus's ability to replicate or its ability to enter host cells. Without further drug discovery, however, the best that can be done at present once a person contracts HIV is to partially and temporarily suppress the virus, thus delaying progression of the infection. The drugs that suppress HIV are called antiretrovirals, and the first, known as Retrovir (also known by its generic name zidovudine or AZT), was introduced in 1987 by Burroughs Wellcome (now GlaxoSmithKline) and was the only approved therapy available to treat HIV until 1991. Since then, several new antiretrovirals have been developed by large pharmaceutical companies such as Abbott Labs, Bristol-Myers Squibb, Merck, Roche, and smaller biotech companies such as Agouron, Gilead Sciences, Triangle Pharmaceuticals, and Trimeris. Largely as a result of these drugs, the rate of increase of AIDS-related diseases (e.g., opportunistic infections) dramatically slowed in the United States from 1992–1995 and actually decreased in 1996 for the first time.

Yet, even in the early days of antiretroviral drug development, HIV/AIDS drug pricing was a serious and contentious issue. Burroughs Wellcome faced an enormous wave of protest in the late 1980s in the United States and Europe over its pricing of AZT and subsequently reduced the drug's price by 20 percent in 1987 and another 20 percent in 1989. The core problem is the fact that most HIV/AIDS cases are outside what the UN classifies as "rich countries" such as the United States. North America registered about 980,000 cases of individuals living with HIV/AIDS and fewer than 10,000 deaths due to AIDS in 2002, but the comparative numbers for sub-Saharan Africa were nearly 30 million cases and more than two million deaths in 2002. Similarly, the U.S. adult infection rate was estimated at slightly more than one half of a percent in 2002 versus almost nine percent in sub-Saharan Africa, with a high of 38.8 percent in Botswana (UN AIDS). If the affordability of HIV/AIDS drugs in the United States (with a GDP per capita in excess of $30,000) is a serious issue, the problem is even more acute in the hardest hit countries, whose GDPs per capita often are less than one-tenth of the U.S. GDP, in many cases even below $1,000. Compounding the problem is the fact that many new AIDS drugs, especially

[12] E. Berndt, "Pharmaceuticals in U.S. Health Care: Determinants of Quality and Price," and M. Kremer, "Pharmaceuticals and the Developing World," *Journal of Economic Perspectives* (Fall 2002), pp. 45–90.

those designed to attack the growth in drug-resistant HIV, grow ever more expensive. Trimeris and Roche introduced Fuzeon in early 2003, for example, at a wholesale price of €20,245 per annum, at least three times the price of any existing HIV/AIDS drug. The pricing decision sparked immediate protests in the United States and abroad. Even many providers of Medicaid, the state-based health assistance program for the indigent in the United States (and now the buyer of more than 50 percent of HIV/AIDS drugs in the United States), immediately suggested that they could not contemplate how they would possibly pay for such an expensive therapy.

GlaxoSmithKline and Roche, the leading HIV/AIDS drug manufacturers, and their cohorts now find they must balance the fiscal realities of their expensive, R&D-intensive business model against enlarged, global, corporate social responsibilities. A nation-state specific pricing policy across global markets has resulted in a tenfold differential between the highest priced market, the United States, and the price charged in the poorest countries. Glaxo and Roche management teams face many serious business ethics issues in this highly charged environment. Is such a tenfold price differential sustainable? How does one manage the resulting problem of parallel importing and secure trade protection from unauthorized reimportation of export drugs? What should they do if even 90 percent price reductions still leave the therapies too expensive for the majority of patients in less-developed countries? Will abrogation of intellectual property in the developing world threaten intellectual property protection at home? Will a public affairs backlash in high-priced markets force drug price discounts? If so, how can the massive R&D investment required for ongoing drug discovery and development be recovered? Are these companies facing such a public relations disaster that their corporate brand equity could be radically affected? What are big pharmaceutical companies' corporate responsibilities in a public health crisis? Should Glaxo (or Roche) go it alone, or instead pursue collaborative strategies with other big pharmaceutical rivals?

QUESTIONS

1. Is the monopoly on patented pharmaceuticals secure? What barrier to entry prevents the reimportation into the United States of pharmaceuticals sold at lower prices abroad (say, in Canada)?

2. Analyze the contribution margin percentage on pharmaceuticals relative to ready-to-eat cereals. Identify three reasons why pharmaceutical margins are higher.

3. Suggest an approach to the big pharmaceutical company problem of differential pricing in the United States, Western Europe, and Japan versus the less-developed world.

CHAPTER

12

PRICE AND OUTPUT DETERMINATION: OLIGOPOLY

CHAPTER PREVIEW The previous two chapters analyzed price and output decisions of firms that competed in markets with either a large number of sellers (i.e., pure competition and monopolistic competition) or essentially no other sellers (i.e., monopoly). In pure competition, the firm made its price and output decisions independently of the decisions of other firms. The monopoly firm did not need to consider the pricing actions of rival firms, because it did not have any competitors. This chapter examines price and output decisions by firms in oligopoly market structures with a small number of competitors, where each firm's decisions are likely to evoke a response from one (or more) of these rivals. To maximize shareholder wealth, each oligopoly firm must take into account these rival responses in its own decision making. In the next chapter, game theory analysis is introduced to help you predict how your rivals will respond.

MANAGERIAL CHALLENGE

Are Nokia's Margins on Cell Phones Collapsing?[1]

From a stodgy Finnish industrial conglomerate selling everything from rubber boots and wire cable to toilet paper and televisions, Nokia transformed itself into a relentlessly focused technology company. When Sweden's telecommunications-equipment giant Ericsson developed a cellular network across Scandinavia in the 1980s, Nokia provided the wireless but bulky radio telephones. Nokia recognized this situation as a strategic opportunity, so it spun off other business in the 1990s and focused its attention on the enormous market potential of a digital (not analog) cell phone. Nokia grew from 22 percent market share in 1985 (half of Motorola's 45 percent) to overtake the market leader in 1998. By 2004, 35 percent of the $70 billion sales in cell phones belonged to Nokia, relative to Motorola's 14 percent. Other major suppliers include Samsung (10%), Siemens (9%), and Sony-Ericsson (5%). The 1.4 billion cell phones in service exceed the number of land lines. With huge scale economies and a snazzy branded product, Nokia's cell phone margins, at 23 percent, outstrip Motorola's paltry 3 percent, but are Nokia's margins sustainable?

First, Third Generation (3G) high-speed worldwide mobile phone networks threaten to rewrite the telecommunications landscape. Nokia's European partners went deeply into debt to pay $125 billion for 3G licenses and spent another $100 billion for 3G network equipment. Nokia, NEC, and Panasonic first offered innovative cell phones with a built-in digital camera. But 3G technology allows the introduction of much enhanced wireless Web products into the handset marketplace: handheld computers by Dell, pocket audiovisual terminals by Palm and Blackberry, and game consoles from Sony-Ericsson.

MANAGERIAL CHALLENGE

Second, these enhanced mobile handsets create value principally through their software applications provided by third-party independent software vendors (ISVs). And the ISVs will want their share of the gross margins that have made Nokia so profitable. The power of these ISV suppliers was virtually nonexistent in the voice-only mobile phone business, but it's not just about voice messaging anymore.

Third, the developed world is nearly saturated with wireless handsets, which have achieved 60 percent penetration in North America and 78 percent in Europe. Consequently, demand is projected to grow at only 7 percent over the next few years, rather than the 12–20 percent of the past. Europe's dominant cell phone operator Vodaphone recently secured $73 color screen cell phones for British customers where the lowest color handset price had been $180.

Fourth, the threat of entry is real. Two Japanese consumer electronics manufacturers, NEC and Panasonic, have adapted the 3G technology into the first wireless Internet devices. High-end camera phones from Sharp and Samsung are the hottest sellers across Asia where new design features, color screens, and slide bars change as often as the whims of a fad-driven marketplace. Cycle times for new products are down to six months versus two years at the start of the millennium. Moreover, Chinese demand is soaring but local vendors now control distribution, and price wars are commonplace.

Should Nokia invest heavily in product design or focus on the projected growth in the low end of the camera phone market, especially in China and Latin America? If neither, what else should Nokia do to grow its future cash flows?

[1] Based on "Nokia: A Finnish Tale," *The Economist* (October 14, 2000), pp. 83–85; "Cellphone Squeeze Play," *Wall Street Journal* (November 17, 2005), p. B1; "Special Report: Mobile Telephones," *The Economist*, (May 1, 2004), pp. 71–76.

OLIGOPOLISTIC MARKET STRUCTURES

An oligopoly is characterized by a relatively small number of firms offering a similar product or service. The product or service may be branded, as in soft drinks, cereals, and athletic shoes, or unbranded as in crude oil, aluminum, and cement. The main distinction of oligopoly is that the number of firms is small enough that actions by any individual firm in the industry on price, output, product style or quality, introduction of new models, and terms of sale have a perceptible impact on the sales of other firms in the industry. In this easily recognizable interdependence among the firms in the industry, each firm knows that any new move, such as introducing a price cut or launching a large promotional campaign, is likely to evoke a countermove from its rivals.

In all oligopoly markets, rival response expectations are therefore the key to firm-level analysis. If rival firms are expected to match price increases and price cuts as in airlines, a share-of-the-market demand curve may adequately illustrate the sales response to the pricing initiatives of one firm (such as Southwest Airlines); see Figure 12.1, Panel (a). On the other hand, if rival firms are slow to match price

Figure 12.1 Rival Response Expectations Determine Firm Demand

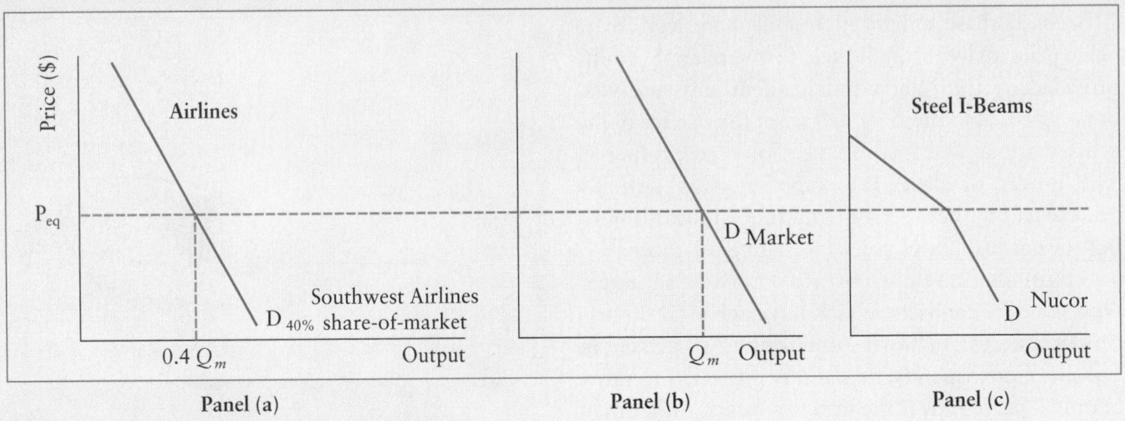

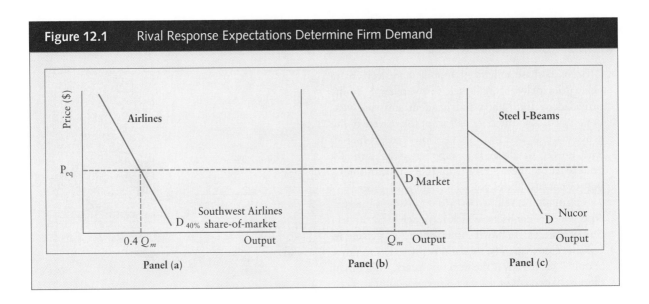

increases and cuts, oligopolists can discount to gain share and will lose share in response to price hikes. In markets such as I-beam steel, rivals match price cuts but ignore price increases. Consequently, Nucor faces a much more price elastic demand above the going equilibrium price than the share-of-the-market demand below that price. These asymmetric rival response expectations lead to kinked oligopoly firm demand schedules discussed later in the chapter and illustrated in Figure 12.1, Panel (c).

Oligopoly in the United States: Relative Market Shares

Much of U.S. industry is best classified as oligopolistic in structure with a wide range of industry configurations. At one extreme are the markets for shaving razors, cigarettes, digital printers, tea, athletic shoes, and cell phones where Gillette (80%), Phillip Morris (67%), Hewlett-Packard (49%), Lipton (37%), Nokia (35%), and Nike (47%) are all several times larger than their next largest competitors (see Table 12.1).

EXAMPLE

Hewlett-Packard's Dominance in Printers[2]

At 49 percent market share, sales of HP printers are five times larger than their closest rivals Xerox and Lexmark, which have 10 percent and 8 percent of the market, respectively. The HP business plan for printers calls for a razor-and-blades approach of relatively inexpensive machines followed by a long period of selling lucrative ink and toner replacement cartridges. In 2001, HP printers and supplies made $410 million in operating profits on $5 billion in sales revenue. This represents two-thirds of HP's $647 million overall profit on only one-tenth of the $49 billion in sales. Despite vicious price wars for market share in the sub-$100 and sub-$200 segments, the printer business has clearly been a cash cow for HP. On the horizon for high-end products, HP plans to launch a digital printing press to replace the plates and film required today for commercial offset printing. In the mass market targeted by Lexmark, Canon,

[2] Based on "HP Sees Room for Growth in Printer Market," *Wall Street Journal* (June 28, 2001), p. B10.

Table 12.1 Largest U.S. Market Shares in Oligopolistic Industries

Shaving Razors and Blades (2004)	
Gillette	80%
Schick	17
Bic	3
Tobacco (2004)	
Altria	67%
R.J. Reynolds	13
Lorillard	11
Brown and Williamson	9
Digital Printers (2001)	
Hewlett-Packard	49%
Xerox	10
Lexmark	8
IBM	4
Canon	3
Tea (2001)	
Lipton	37%
Celestial Seasonings	10
Bigelow	10
Tetley	10
Luzianne	6
Athletic Shoes (2005)	
Nike	33%
Adidas	15
Reebok	10
Cell phones (2005)	
Nokia	35%
Motorola	15
Samsung	10
Siemens	9
Sony-Ericsson	5
Crackers (1998)	
Nabisco	45%
Keebler	22
Pepperidge Farm	7
Confectionary (2002)	
Hershey	30%
Mars	17
Wrigley	7
Nestlé	7
Appliances (2004)	
Sears	36%
Lowe's	14
Home Depot	9
Best Buy	7
U.S. Beer (2001)	
Anheuser-Busch	49%
Miller	20
Coors	11
Soft Drinks (2003)	
Coca-Cola	44%
PepsiCo	32
Cadbury Schweppes	16
Search Engines (2004)	
Google	36%
Yahoo!	31
MSN	14
Tires (2003)	
Goodyear/Sumitomo	28%
Michelin	23
Bridgestone/Firestone	21
Batteries (2005)	
Duracell	43%
Energizer	33
Rayovac	11
Credit Cards (1999)	
Visa	51%
MasterCard	25
American Express	18
Textbooks (2002)	
Pearson	27%
Thomson	22
McGraw-Hill	13
Long-Distance Telephone (2005)	
SBC/AT&T	43%
Verizon/MCI	21
Sprint	9
Qwest	5
U.S. Autos (2005)	
General Motors	26%
Ford	20
Toyota	18
DaimlerChrysler	14
Honda	11
Trucks (2001)	
Freightliner	30%
International	17
Mack	13
Peterbuilt	12
Kenworth	11
Volvo Truck	10
Music Recording (2001)	
Universal/Polygram	23%
Sony	15
EMI	13
Warner	12
BMG	8
Personal Computers (2000)	
Dell	20%
Compaq	17
HP	11
Gateway	9
IBM	6
Computer Storage (2002)	
EMC	34%
HP	30
IBM	16
Sun	11
Wireless (2005)	
Cingular Wireless	28%
Verizon Wireless	24
AT&T Wireless	20
Sprint/Nextel	21
T-Mobile	18

Sources: "Industry Surveys," *Net Advantage Database,* Standard & Poor's; and *Market Share Reports,* Gale Research, annual issues.

and Epson, penetration of PCs into American households and businesses has reached a plateau, but printing volume (and therefore demand for HP supplies) may continue to grow because of the printing of digital photographs and Web pages.

In crackers, beer, soft drinks, aircraft, candy, and databases, not one but two firms dominate (see Table 12.1). In snack foods, Nabisco's 45 percent market share and Keebler's 22 percent overshadow Pepperidge Farms' 7 percent. Similarly, Coke and Pepsi dominate the soft drink market, Anheuser-Busch and Miller Brewing dominate the beer market, and Boeing and Airbus dominate the wide-bodied aircraft market. These duopoly pairs of dominant firms often study complex tactical scenarios of moves and probable countermoves against one another. In still other cases, three firms circle warily, planning their tactical initiatives and retreats: tires (Goodyear 28%, Bridgestone/Firestone 21%, Michelin 23%); batteries (Duracell 44%, Energizer 33%, Rayovac 11%); cereals (Kellogg 30%, General Mills 30%, Post 13%); long-distance telephone service (AT&T 32%, Verizon 12%, SBC 10%, MCI 9%, Sprint 12%); and credit cards (Visa 51%, MasterCard 25%, and American Express 18%). Although no airline has a dominant market share nationally, a number of airlines have dominant positions at various airports around the country. For example, American has a 65 percent share at Dallas/Fort Worth, Northwest has an 84 percent share at Minneapolis/St. Paul and an 80 percent share at Detroit, and US Airways has a 93 percent share at Charlotte.

EXAMPLE

Airlines Deconcentrate While Telephone and Retail Gasoline Firms Consolidate: Southwest Airlines, AT&T, and Exxon/Mobil

The market share distributions in Table 12.1 are seldom static. Instead, the dynamics of the share distribution often tell important insights. For example, over the 14-year period 1992–2005, the rank order of the leading airlines was largely unchanged, but every one of the major hub-and-spoke carriers lost two to three share points to the point-to-point discounters Southwest and America West (see the data in Table 12.2). In cereals, General Mills' new product introductions continued to take share points from Kellogg during 1993–1999. But it was Post/Nabisco that was the big loser to private-label discount cereals (Kroger Raisin Bran) and their contract supplier

Table 12.2 Market Share Distributions over Time in Airlines, Cereals, and Wide-Bodied Aircraft

Airlines				Cereals				Wide-Bodied Aircraft			
1992		2002		1993		1999		1998		2005	
American	21%	American	19%	Kellogg	35%	Kellogg	30%	Boeing	70%	Boeing	51%
United	20	United	17	General Mills	25	General Mills	30	Airbus	30	Airbus	49
Delta	15	Delta	15	Post/Nabisco	18	Post/Nabisco	13				
Northwest	14	Northwest	11	Quaker	8	Private Label	11				
Continental	11	Continental	9	Private Label	6	Ralston	7				
US Airways	9	Southwest	7	Ralston	5	Quaker	6				

Sources: *Wall Street Journal* (December 21, 2001), p. A8; (December 27, 1996), p. A3; (October 16, 1998), p. B4; and (July 14, 2006), p. B1.

Ralston/Purina. In wide-bodied aircraft, Boeing ceded market share to Airbus, lowered its final assembly rate of production, removing bottlenecks and making itself much more profitable.

In telephone land lines and retail gasoline, consolidation occurred. The four survivors of the seven regional phone companies created by the breakup of AT&T [SBC Communications (formerly Southwestern Bell, Pacific Telesis, and Ameritech), Verizon (formerly Bell Atlantic and NYNEX), Bell South, and Quest (formerly USWest)] have become larger in market value than the long-distance carriers AT&T, MCI, and Sprint who engage in nearly continuous price wars. In 2005, SBC reacquired AT&T's long-distance unit. The top three long-distance carriers had 56 percent of the relevant market in 1999, whereas by 2005 the top three firms had 73 percent. See Figure 12.2. Massive consolidation also occurred in the retail gasoline industry, where company after company sought a large partner with whom to merge. Scale economies in exploration and development as well as the closing of redundant gas stations drove the trend.

Finally, Table 12.1 shows several industries in which the share distributions are more equal but where the strong interdependencies between leading firms, so

Figure 12.2 The Relative Sizes of Competitors in the Cable and Gasoline Industries

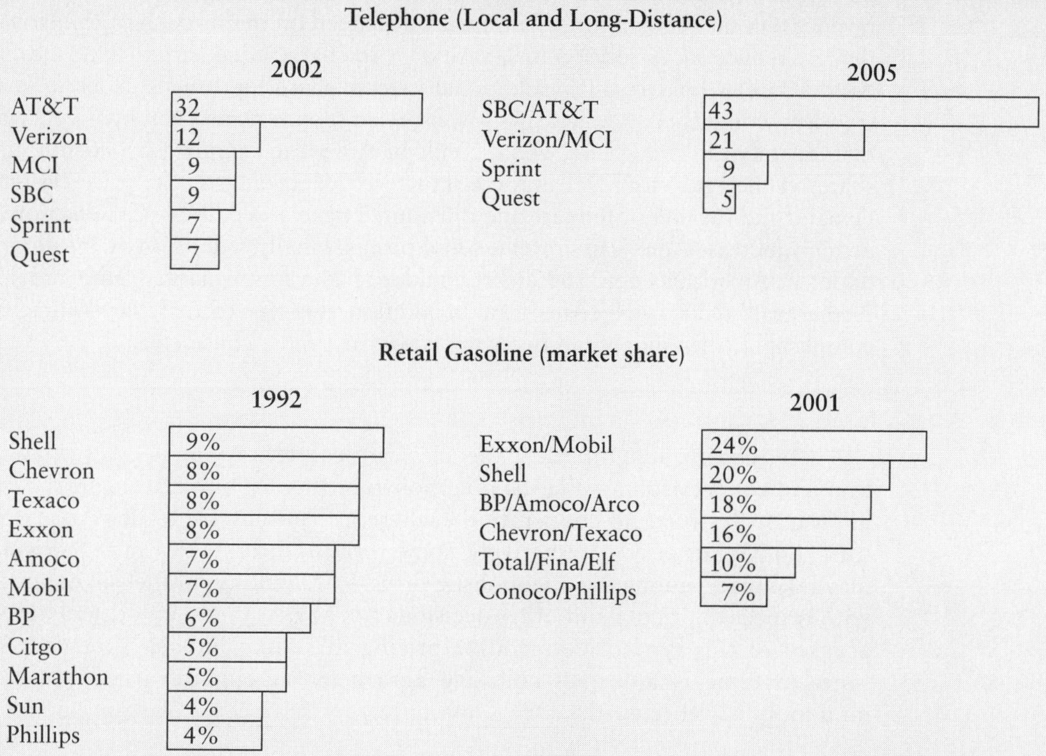

Source: *Wall Street Journal* (December 21, 2001), p. A8; (January 21, 1992), p. B6; (Nov 1, 2005), p. A2.

characteristic of oligopoly, remain prominent in each firm's business planning. Sales in the U.S. auto and truck markets are dispersed across five or six companies. And in four industries heavily influenced by the disruptive technology of Internet computing (namely, music recording, PCs, computer file storage devices, and wireless system operators), the forces of competition have dispersed the shares across a half dozen firms.

Interdependencies in Oligopolistic Industries

The nature of interdependencies in oligopolistic industries can be illustrated using an airline pricing example.

EXAMPLE

Airline Pricing: The Pittsburgh Market

Consider the case of the airline route between Pittsburgh and Dallas. One can fly this route on a number of different airlines, but only American and US Airways offer nonstop service between these cities. (Flights on other airlines require a stopover and change of planes, which many travelers prefer to avoid.) Prior to the introduction of American's new fare, both airlines were charging $1,054 for a round-trip coach-class ticket. American's new fare was $640, a reduction of $414. US Airways was then faced with the decision of whether to maintain its current $1,054 fare (or some other fare above American's new fare), match American's new $640 fare, or undercut American's $640 fare. American's demand function (and revenues) in the Pittsburgh-Dallas market depended on the reaction of US Airways to the fare reduction. A decision by US Airways to charge a higher fare (e.g., the current $1,054 fare) would result in additional market share for American, because many travelers would choose American's lower-priced service. A decision by US Airways to match American's new fare would result in American retaining its existing market share on the Pittsburgh-Dallas route. However, depending on the price elasticity of demand and the mix of full fare and discounted tickets sold, the price reduction could actually increase American's revenues and profits. Finally, a decision by US Airways to undercut American's new $640 fare would lead to a lower market share and a likely further price reduction by American. In addition, this type of analysis gets much more complicated when more than two competitors are under consideration.

These recognizable interdependencies can lead to varying degrees of competition and cooperation among the oligopolistic firms. At one extreme is the case of intense rivalry (i.e., no cooperation), where a firm may try to drive its competitor(s) out of business. Alternatively, some form of informal, or tacit, cooperation may take place among the oligopolistic firms—"conscious parallelism of action"—with respect to pricing and other decisions.[3] NASDAQ security dealers have been accused of this type of cooperative pricing in setting bid-ask spreads.[4] At the other extreme is a formal collusive agreement among the firms to act as a monopoly cartel (e.g., the OPEC oil cartel) by setting prices to maximize total

[3] See F. M. Scherer and David Ross, *Industrial Market Structure and Economic Performance,* 3d ed. (Chicago, IL: Rand McNally, 1990), pp. 339–346, for a discussion of the conscious parallelism doctrine.

[4] "U.S. Examines Alleged Price-Fixing on NASDAQ," *Wall Street Journal* (October 20, 1994), p. C1.

industry profits. Because of the wide scope of industry configurations in Table 12.1 that fall under the oligopoly classification, several normative models can be used to describe oligopolists' competitive behavior regarding price, output, and other market conditions.

IGNORING INTERDEPENDENCIES

The simplistic approach to the interdependency problem among oligopolists is merely to ignore it; that is, for a firm to act as if it does not exist at all and assume that competitors will do likewise.

THE COURNOT MODEL

One oligopoly model, proposed by the French economist Augustin Cournot, asserts that each firm, in determining its profit-maximizing output level, *assumes that the other firm's output will not change.*

For example, suppose that two duopolists (Firms A and B) produce identical products. If Firm A observes Firm B producing Q_B units of output in the current period, then Firm A will seek to maximize its own profits assuming that Firm B will continue producing the same Q_B units in the next period. Firm B acts in a similar manner. It attempts to maximize its own profits under the assumption that Firm A will continue producing the same amount of output in the next period as Firm A did in the current period. In the Cournot model this pattern continues until reaching the long-run equilibrium point where output and price are stable and neither firm can increase its profits by raising or lowering output. The following example illustrates the determination of the long-run Cournot equilibrium.

EXAMPLE

THE COURNOT OLIGOPOLY SOLUTION: SIEMENS AND THOMSON-CSF

Suppose that two European electronics companies, Siemens (Firm S) and Thomson-CSF (Firm T), jointly hold a patent on a component used in airport radar systems. Demand for the component is given by the following function:

$$P = 1{,}000 - Q_S - Q_T \qquad [12.1]$$

where Q_S and Q_T are the quantities sold by the respective firms and P is the (market) selling price. The total cost functions of manufacturing and selling the component for the respective firms are

$$TC_S = 70{,}000 + 5Q_S + 0.25Q_S^2 \qquad [12.2]$$

$$TC_T = 110{,}000 + 5Q_T + 0.15Q_T^2 \qquad [12.3]$$

Suppose that the two firms act independently, with each firm seeking to maximize its own total profit from the sale of the component.

Siemens's total profit is equal to

$$\begin{aligned}\pi_S &= PQ_S - TC_S \\ &= (1{,}000 - Q_S - Q_T)\,Q_S - \left(70{,}000 + 5Q_S + 0.25Q_S^2\right) \\ &= -70{,}000 + 995\,Q_S - Q_TQ_S - 1.25Q_S^2 \qquad [12.4]\end{aligned}$$

Note that Siemens's total profit depends on the amount of output produced and sold by Thomson (Q_T). Taking the partial derivative of Equation 12.4 with respect to Q_S yields

$$\frac{\partial \pi_S}{\partial Q_S} = 995 - Q_T - 2.50Q_S \quad [12.5]$$

Similarly, Thomson's total profit is equal to

$$\begin{aligned}\pi_T &= PQ_T - TC_T \\ &= (1{,}000 - Q_S - Q_T)\,Q_T - \left(110{,}000 + 5Q_T + 0.15Q_T^2\right) \\ &= -110{,}000 + 995Q_T - Q_SQ_T - 1.15Q_T^2\end{aligned} \quad [12.6]$$

Note also that Thomson's total profit is a function of Siemens's output level (Q_S). Taking the partial derivative of Equation 12.6 with respect to Q_T yields

$$\frac{\partial \pi_T}{\partial Q_T} = 995 - Q_S - 2.30Q_T \quad [12.7]$$

Setting Equations 12.5 and 12.7 equal to zero yields

$$2.50Q_S + Q_T = 995 \quad [12.8]$$

$$Q_S + 2.30Q_T = 995 \quad [12.9]$$

Solving Equations 12.8 and 12.9 simultaneously gives the optimal levels of output for the two firms: $Q_S^* = 272.32$ units and $Q_T^* = 314.21$ units. By substituting these values into Equation 12.1, we calculate an optimal (equilibrium) selling price of $P^* = \$413.47$ per unit. The respective profits for the two firms are obtained by substituting Q_S^* and Q_T^* into Equations 12.4 and 12.6 to obtain $\pi_S^* = \$22{,}695.00$ and $\pi_T^* = \$3{,}536.17$.

Cartels and Other Forms of Collusion

Cartel

A formal or informal agreement among firms in an oligopolistic industry that influences such issues as prices, total industry output, market shares, and the division of profits.

Oligopolists sometimes reduce the inherent risk of being so interdependent by either formally or informally agreeing to cooperate or collude in decision making. Collusive agreements between oligopolists are called **cartels.** In general, collusive agreements of are illegal in the United States under the Sherman Antitrust Act of 1890; however, some important exceptions exist. For example, prices and quotas of various agricultural products (e.g., milk, oranges) are set by growers in many parts of the country with the approval of the federal government. The International Air Transport Association (IATA), composed of airlines flying transatlantic routes, sets uniform prices for these flights. And ocean shipping rates are set by hundreds of collusive "conferences" on each major transoceanic route.

Illegal collusive arrangements, however, also arise from time to time. For example, cement and paving companies as well as cardboard box manufacturers often are indicted for price fixing. In a celebrated 1994 case, General Electric was accused of conspiring with De Beers Centenary AG to fix industrial diamond prices on machine tooling and drilling products; in 2004 De Beers paid a $10 million fine.[5] The grain-processing giant Archer-Daniels-Midland (ADM) pled guilty in 1996 to organizing an explicit quota and pricing system among five firms in the lysine market (see Figure 12.3); lysine is an amino acid food supplement that speeds the growth of livestock. ADM paid $100 million in antitrust penalties, and ADM executives went to jail.[6]

[5] "De Beers to Pay," *Wall Street Journal* (July 14, 2004), p. A3.

[6] "In ADM Saga, Executives Now on Trial," *Wall Street Journal* (July 9, 1998), p. B10.

Figure 12.3 • Lysine Manufacturers Who Pled Guilty to Price Fixing

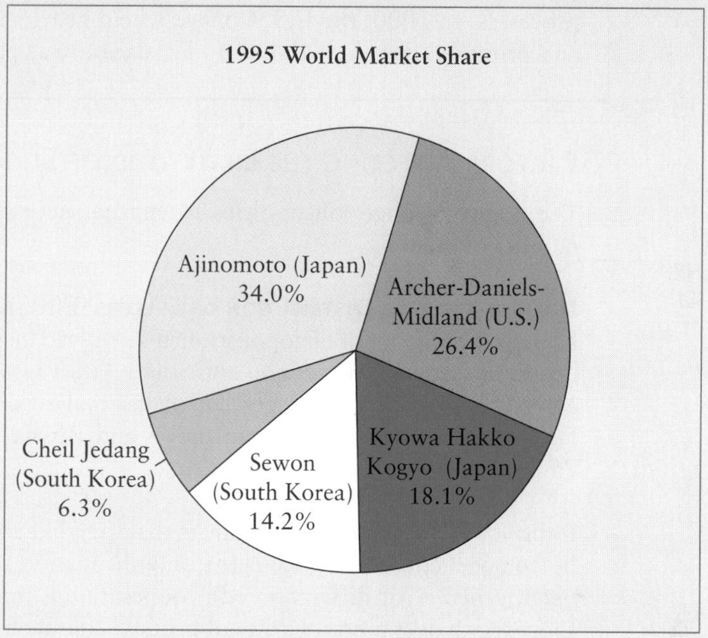

Source: *Wall Street Journal* (July 9, 1998).

Roche and BASF, large Swiss and German industrial conglomerates in pharmaceuticals, chemicals, fragrances, and vitamins, agreed to pay $500 million and $225 million fines, respectively, to the U.S. Justice Department for their leadership of a price-fixing conspiracy in vitamin supplements. This 1999 antitrust settlement reduced Roche's profitability by 30 percent.[7] Worldwide the fines arising from the vitamin price-fixing conspiracy totaled $1.6 billion. These severe penalties indicate how serious the inefficiencies arising from cartelization of an industry can be. Businesses are wise not to ignore the prohibition against price fixing.

EXAMPLE

How Ocean Shipping Conferences Have Affected Shipping Rates[8]

Since the Shipping Act of 1916, ocean freight companies have been exempted from the antitrust laws of the United States. Shipping rates on a transoceanic route are set jointly by 10 to 50 competitors acting as a "shipping conference." Two studies in 1993 and 1995 by the U.S. Agriculture Department and the FTC found that rates were 18 or 19 percent lower when ocean-shipping companies broke out of these conference arrangements and negotiated as independents. Nevertheless, the conferences maintain their market power by signing exclusive-dealing contracts with large volume customers. The enormous capacity of the shipping conferences

[7] "Scandal Costs Roche," *Wall Street Journal* (May 25, 1999), p. A20.

[8] Based on "Making Waves," *Wall Street Journal* (October 7, 1997), p. A1; J. Yong, "Excluding Capacity-Constrained Entrants through Exclusive Dealing: Theory and Applications to Ocean Shipping," *Journal of Industrial Economics* 46, no. 2 (June 1996); and "Shipmates," *Wall Street Journal* (February 20, 2003), p. A1.

allows more schedule frequency and greater reliability than the independents can offer. In exchange for exclusive contracts, shipping conferences have offered attractive settlement of disputed cargo claims, using speedy liquidated damages processes. In 2000, the U.S. Congress held hearings about this antitrust immunity and proposed its removal, but no legislation was passed.

Factors Affecting the Likelihood of Successful Collusion

The ability of oligopolistic firms to engage successfully in collusion depends on a number of factors:

Number and Size Distribution of Sellers Effective collusion generally is more difficult as the number of oligopolistic firms involved increases. In the 1990s, the De Beers diamond cartel in Switzerland and South Africa was effective in part because Russia agreed in 1995 to sell 95 percent of its total wholesale supply through De Beers. De Beers's central selling organization and Russia alone accounted for more than 75 percent of world supply at that time.

Product Heterogeneity Products that are alike in their characteristics are said to be homogeneous, and price is the only distinction that matters. When products are *heterogeneous* (or differentiated), cooperation is more difficult because competition is occurring over a broad array of product characteristics, such as durability, fashion timing, warranty, and after-sale policies.

EXAMPLE

DRAM Chipmakers Pay Enormous Fines for Forming a Global Cartel[9]

The world's top four manufacturers of inexpensive random access memory chips that are the key component of all consumer electronic devices agreed to fines and jail terms for several executives because of 1999–2002 price-fixing. The criminal conspiracy raised prices 400 percent in a six-month period from $1 to $4 per 100 megabits and then orchestrated maintaining the price at $3. DRAM chips are generic and easily substitutable between suppliers. As a result, a cartel agreement to limit production and maintain $3 prices emerged. Samsung and Hynix, two Korean firms that produce the majority of the chips, paid $300 million and $185 million fines, respectively. Infineon Technologies of Germany paid a $160 million fine, and four executives went to jail for several months and paid individual fines of $250,000. Micron Technology of Boise, Idaho, received immunity for cooperating with the prosecutors and complainants Dell and HP in making the case.

Cost Structures The more cost functions differ among competing firms, the more difficult it will be for firms to collude on pricing and output decisions. Also, successful collusion is more difficult in industries where fixed costs are a large part of total costs. A higher percentage of fixed costs implies higher contribution margins to

[9] Based on "Samsung to Pay," *Wall Street Journal* (October 14, 2005), p. A3; and "Hynix Pleads Guilty," *Wall Street Journal* (April 22, 2004), P. B6.

recover those fixed costs. And, as we saw in Equation 10.2 in Chapter 10, higher margins mean a lower break-even sales change which makes discounting more attractive. Therefore, breakdowns in collusively high prices often occur in industries that require highly capital-intensive production processes, such as petroleum refining, steel making, and airlines.

SIZE AND FREQUENCY OF ORDERS Successful oligopolistic cooperation also depends on the size distribution of customer orders over time. Effective collusion is more likely when orders are small, frequent, and received regularly. When large orders are received infrequently at irregular intervals as in the purchase of aircraft engines, it is more difficult for firms to collude on pricing and output decisions. Hence, Pratt & Whitney, Rolls-Royce, and General Electric have never colluded on jet engines, despite the fact that GE did collude with other manufacturers in hydroelectric power plant equipment.

THREAT OF RETALIATION An oligopolistic firm will be less tempted to grant secret price concessions to selected customers if it feels that other cartel members would detect these price reductions and then retaliate. The toilet tissue manufacturers' collusive agreement allegedly operated through public bids for institutional customers such as schools and hospitals. Sealed bids might have prevented the collusion, surprisingly.

PERCENTAGE OF EXTERNAL OUTPUT Most cartels contain the seeds of their own destruction. Rising prices and profits attract the entry of new competitors. Any increase in supply from outside the cartel means larger restrictions on output for cartel members in order to sustain any given market price. At one point in 1999, De Beers had to purchase for its own inventory $3.96 billion in diamonds (in only an $8-billion market) in order to stabilize prices because so many Canadian, Australian, and Russian diamonds (external to the De Beers cartel) had flooded the market.[10]

Finally, in 2000, with 37 percent of total diamond supply outside the cartel, De Beers declared the end of its 65-year cartel. Similar events ended the OPEC I cartel when Mexican, Venezuelan, and Norwegian oil flooded onto the market. Ocean shipping prices are breaking down today because the rate-setting "conferences" now control less than 70 percent of the $85 billion North Atlantic market and less than 50 percent of the $262 billion trans-Pacific market. External suppliers reduce the likelihood of successful ccoordination among cartel members to maintain prices above their competitive level.

CARTEL PROFIT MAXIMIZATION AND THE ALLOCATION OF RESTRICTED OUTPUT

Under both legal cartels and secret collusive agreements, firms attempt to increase prices and profits above the level that would prevail in the absence of collusion. The profit-maximization solution for a two-firm cartel, E and F, is shown graphically in Figure 12.4. The *industry* demand D, marginal revenue MR, and marginal cost ΣMC curves are shown in the third panel. The industry marginal cost curve is

[10] Based on "De Beers to Abandon Monopoly," *Wall Street Journal* (July 13, 2000), p. A20; and "Atlantic Ocean Shipping Cartel Makes Concessions," *Wall Street Journal* (February 7, 1997), p. A2.

Figure 12.4 Price-Output Determination for a Two-Firm Cartel

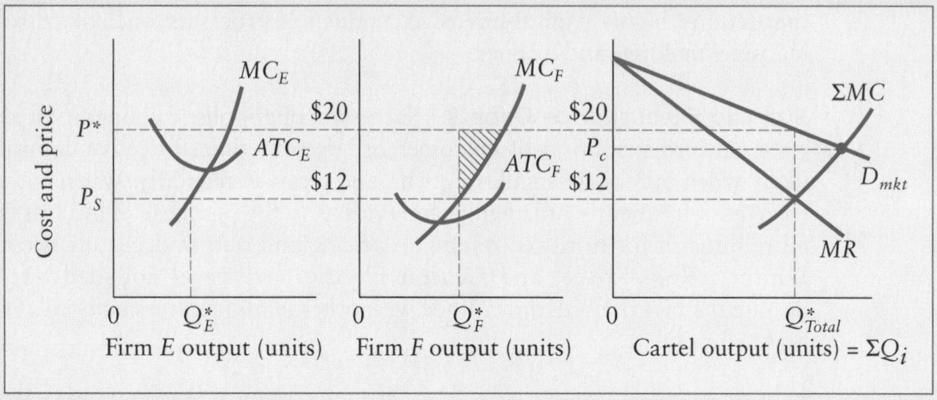

obtained by summing horizontally across outputs the marginal cost curves of the individual firms in the first two panels: that is, $\Sigma MC = MC_E + MC_F$. Total industry profits are maximized by setting total industry output (and consequently price) at the point where industry marginal revenue equals industry marginal cost (i.e., Q^*_{Total} units of output at a price of P^* per unit).

If the cartel maximizes its total profits, the market share (or quota) for each firm should be set at a level where marginal cost of all firms is identical and industry (summed) $MC = MR$. The optimal output is for Firm *E* to produce a quota of Q_E^* units and for Firm *F* to produce a quota of Q_F^* units. If Firm *E* were producing at a level where its marginal costs exceeded Firm *F*'s, cartel profits could be increased by shifting output from *E* to *F* until marginal costs were equal.[11]

Cartel pricing agreements are hard to reach, but the central problem for a cartel lies in monitoring these output shares or quotas. Detecting quota violations and effectively enforcing punishment schemes are nearly impossible. Consequently, most cartels are unstable, like the price-fixing agreements among cardboard box manufacturers: These collusive agreements form approximately once a quarter and break up within a few weeks. The longevity of the Organization of Petroleum Exporting Countries (OPEC) and the De Beers diamond cartel is exceptional. Let's return to Figure 12.4 and see why.

Suppose you are Firm *F* facing a cartel-determined price for crude oil P^* of \$20 per barrel. Your marginal costs are presently running \$12 per barrel at your assigned quota of Q_F/Q_{Total}. The Aramco pipelines, which once consolidated all your throughput from the production wells to shipping terminals, have now been superseded by numerous independent shipping terminals, many within your own nation. In addition, your crude is relatively undifferentiated from that of many other OPEC members. Should you abide by your quota commitment? Is it in your best interest to do so? The answer depends on whether your additional sales beyond quota are detectable and whether your additional output will increase total supply enough to

[11] Note that the average total costs of the two firms are not necessarily equal at the optimal (profit-maximizing) output level. Note also that Firm *E* is given a sizable share of the total output even though its average total costs are higher than Firm *F*'s.

place downward pressure on the cartel price. If the answer to both questions is no, then because a 40 percent profit margin ($8) awaits your selling another barrel, a profit maximizer will be tempted to increase output and capture the hatched area of incremental profit in the middle panel of Figure 12.4.

Of course, the problem is that other cartel members may think exactly the same way. If everyone takes the cartel price as given and independently profit maximizes, then cartel supply increases to ΣMC, and black market price must fall to the competitive level P_c of perhaps $17 just to clear the market. Enforcement of the ideal quotas Q_F and Q_E is the weak point of every cartel. In OPEC, Saudi Arabia plays a pivotal role in absorbing quota violations by other OPEC members and thereby stabilizing the cartel.

EXAMPLE

COFFEE PRICING AGREEMENT DISSOLVES AMIDST DILEMMA[12]

The top Colombian and Brazilian coffee producers along with several African and Central American smaller producers often agree in principle to withhold millions of tons of coffee beans from the market in an effort to raise collapsing wholesale prices. Brazilian producers may propose to hold back 2 million bags of a projected 18-million-bag crop. Colombian producers may agree to hold back 1.3 million bags. However, both countries opposed a formal quota system that assigns production ceilings, imposes monitoring mechanisms, and penalizes violators. In 1989 and again in 1993, International Coffee Agreements collapsed over the refusal to accept assigned quotas.

In both cases when the harvest was larger than expected, coffee bean prices plummeted. If all major coffee bean producers could rely upon one another to withhold extraordinarily large production in exceptionally good weather years, all would have higher profitability. Instead, some cartel members maximize self-interest by releasing excess supplies to the world market at just below the official agreed-upon price. Because other cartel members think that same way, equilibrium market price then plummets. Only dupes then continue to restrain output when world market prices erode, signaling that other coffee producers are violating the agreement.

EXAMPLE

WHY U.S. GASOLINE PRICES ROSE SO RAPIDLY TO $3 PER GALLON[13]

In recent years, the OPEC III cartel has been overshadowed by the Iraq War and by unanticipated growth of gasoline consumption in China and India. Despite OPEC total output that exceeded the sum of agreed-upon member quotas by 40 percent in 2005, crude oil reached $80 per barrel in 2006, and gasoline prices flirted with $3 per gallon. Why?

One explanation might be that state and federal excise taxes or state and local sales taxes have risen, but they have remained approximately $0.60 per gallon for

[12] "Brazil, Colombia Form Cartel for Coffee Exports," *Wall Street Journal* (September 8, 1991), p. B12.

[13] Based on "Oil Nations Move Closer to a New Round of Cuts," *Wall Street Journal* (March 12, 1999), p. A3; "Crude Cuts: Will Oil Nations Stick or Stray?" *Wall Street Journal* (March 26, 1999), p. A19; "The Next Oil Shock," *The Economist* (March 6, 1999); "Standstill Britain," *The Economist* (September 16, 2000), p. 64; and "At OPEC Some Say There's Enough Oil," *Wall Street Journal* (September 12, 2000), p. A2.

Figure 12.5 Components of the Price of Gasoline Per Gallon (1990–2005)

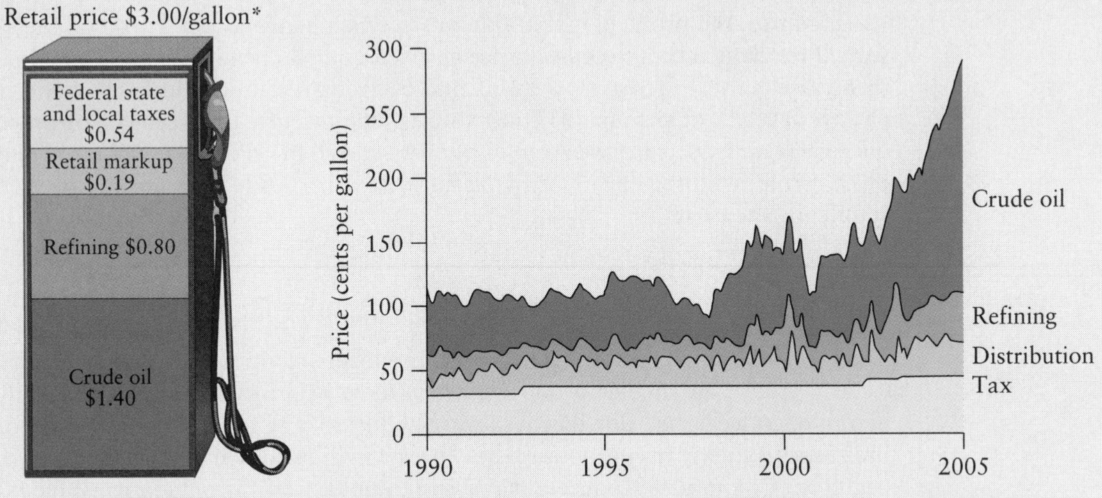

Sources: "The Truth about Oil", *Fortune*, October 3, 2005; *Changing Gasoline Prices*, Federal Trade Commission, June, 2005
*Note: Includes $0.07 Marketing and Distribution Cost

a decade (see Figure 12.5 for the detailed breakdown of a $3.00 price per gallon). Another explanation might be that retail station owners are gouging customers, but perfect competition characterizes the retail gas market, and consequently, retail margins are low and have also remained unchanged at $0.15 to $0.20 for many years. Distribution bottlenecks occasionally are responsible for price spikes in a local region when pipelines break, but in general, only $0.07 of the price of gas is attributable to distribution costs. Scarcity of refining capacity is another explanation, and $0.89 of the $3.38 is attributable to refining costs that have risen somewhat in recent years.

Nevertheless, by far the largest component cost reflected in gas prices is crude oil (again, see Figure 12.5). Fully half of the cost of $3 per gallon gasoline ($1.54) is attributable to the cost of crude oil itself. And it is this component that has increased enormously from $35 per barrel in 2004 to $70–$80 per barrel in 2005–2006.

Saudi Arabia has an enormous 264 billion barrels of known but untapped crude oil reserves, expected to last well into the twenty-second century. By comparison, at current rate of output, the United States has only 21 billion barrels and three years of reserves left, although Canada has many decades of oil sands. The last time crude oil and gasoline prices spiked in the early 1980s, the United States responded with conservation and the development of alternative fuels, reducing energy dependency by almost half.

Therefore, the Saudis prefer to discourage the emergence of alternative fuels such as sugar cane-based ethanol in Brazil, corn-based ethanol in the United States, and

INTERNATIONAL PERSPECTIVES

THE ORGANIZATION OF PETROLEUM EXPORTING COUNTRIES (OPEC) CARTEL

The Organization of Petroleum Exporting Countries (OPEC) was founded in 1960 by five Persian Gulf nations that hosted ARAMCO, a joint venture set up in 1947 by the international oil companies for exploration and development of the Mideast oil fields. ARAMCO set the price of crude oil and paid oil concession royalties to the host nations who were gradually purchasing ARAMCO's assets. With 80 percent of world petroleum output in 1973–1974, OPEC I was able to sustain a 400 percent increase in the price of crude oil from $3 to $12 per barrel. Saudi Arabia is the most influential member of this price-fixing cartel because of the tremendous size of its production capacity—almost one half of OPEC's total output at the inception of OPEC and still 32 percent of OPEC output today. By the early 1980s, the price of oil ranged from $32 to $41 ($80 in 2006 dollars); covert price cutting was rampant. Nigeria, for example, engaged in secret price cutting by reducing income taxes for the oil companies working there. Other OPEC members bartered and extended payment terms for oil purchases, thereby reducing interest expenses on the funds required to finance the purchase.

During this period (often referred to as OPEC II), Saudi Arabia regularly stabilized declining oil prices by acting as a "swing producer," cutting its production to as low as 2 million barrels per day (bpd) in 1980 when its authorized quota was 4.35 million and its capacity was 10 million bpd. OPEC II ended effectively in October 1985, when Saudi Arabia reversed its policy and began increasing its output to as much as 6 million bpd. When the Saudis utilized their full capacity, the equilibrium market price of crude fell as low as $12.[14]

OPEC now controls less than 40 percent of world oil output, half of what they once did. For most of the 1990s, crude oil traded at approximately $20–$25 per barrel. That price stimulated enormous increases in production in nontraditional oil-producing regions. Major production emerged in Prudhoe Bay, Alaska; in Russia; and in the North Sea despite extraction costs three to five times higher than the $3-per-barrel exploration, development, and extraction cost in the Middle East (see Figure 12.5). Venezuela has publicly challenged the role of Saudi Arabia as swing producer and price leader, especially in the Western hemisphere.[15] With 9.27 million bpd, Russia has posed the same challenge in other parts of the world.

With production breaking out all over, in 1998 and early 1999 crude oil prices again collapsed to $9.96 (see Figure 12.6). To stabilize the marekt, OPEC members agreed in March 1999 (and again in September 2000) to a production quota system. As in the cartel's heyday of the late 1970s, the largest cartel members agreed to larger cutbacks. Saudi Arabia accepted a 585,000-barrel-per-day cutback, which equaled 7 percent of its February 1999 average daily production of 8.8 million barrels. Iran, with a 12 percent share, agreed to a 264,000-barrel cutback, which also equaled a 7 percent reduction of its 3.6-million-barrel output. Venezuela accepted a 125,000-barrel-per-day cutback, which equaled a 4 percent reduction of its 3.4-million-barrel output. Overall, these cuts plus other reductions by non-OPEC members Mexico and Norway reduced the supply on world markets by 2 million bpd of the 76-million-barrel-per-day world consumption. Crude oil prices responded almost immediately, rising more than threefold from a $10 trough to $33 per barrel in 15 months (again see Figure 12.6). The OPEC III cartel was in place, effectively restricting output to raise prices.

[14] "Why the Saudis Won't Back Down Soon," *Wall Street Journal* (April 8, 1986); and J. Griffin and W. Xiong, "The Incentive to Cheat: An Empirical Analysis of OPEC," *Journal of Law and Economics* 60, no. 2 (1997).

[15] *The Economist* (March 16, 1996), p. 68; and "Jump Start," *Wall Street Journal* (August 14, 1997).

Figure 12.6 How OPEC III Production Quotas and Record Demands Have Affected Crude Oil Prices

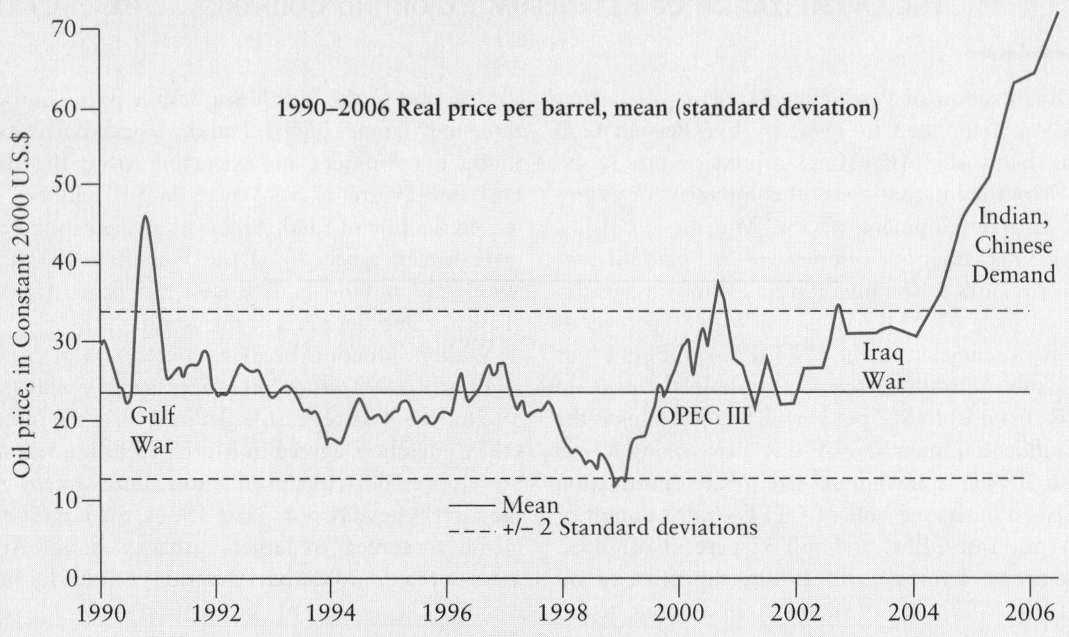

Source: Federal Reserve Bank, St. Louis, *National Economic Trends* (September 2000); FedDallas, Regional Economic Data, 2006.

the extraction facilities for the extensive tar sands in Canada. On the other hand, OPEC countries with lesser petroleum reserves (Libya, Iran, Algeria) often price their oil at the high end of the range in an attempt to maximize their returns before their oil runs out. In this sense, U.S. oil interests in Texas are often at odds with Saudi Arabia and aligned instead with the smaller OPEC producers.

EXAMPLE

Cartel Pricing and Output Decisions: Siemens and Thomson-CSF

The profit-maximizing price and output levels for a two-firm cartel can also be determined algebraically when the demand and cost functions are given. Consider again the Siemens (Firm *S*) and Thomson-CSF (Firm *T*) example discussed in the previous section. The demand function was given by Equation 12.1 and the cost functions for the two firms were given by Equations 12.2 and 12.3. Suppose that Siemens and Thomson decide to form a cartel and act as a monopolist to maximize total profits from the production and sale of the components.

Total industry profits (π_{Total}) are equal to the sum of Siemens's and Thomson's profits and are given by the following expression:

$$\begin{aligned}\pi_{\text{Total}} &= \pi_S + \pi_T \\ &= PQ_S - TC_S + PQ_T - TC_T\end{aligned} \qquad [12.10]$$

Substituting Equations 12.1, 12.2, and 12.3 into this expression yields

$$\begin{aligned}\pi_{\text{Total}} &= (1{,}000 - Q_S - Q_T)\,Q_S - \left(70{,}000 + 5Q_S + 0.25Q_S^2\right) \\ &\quad + (1{,}000 - Q_S - Q_T)\,Q_T - \left(110{,}000 + 5Q_T + 0.15Q_T^2\right) \\ &= 1{,}000Q_S - Q_S^2 - Q_SQ_T - 70{,}000 - 5Q_S - 0.25Q_S^2 \\ &\quad + 1{,}000Q_T - Q_SQ_T - Q_T^2 - 110{,}000 - 5Q_T - 0.15Q_T^2 \\ &= -180{,}000 + 995Q_S - 1.25Q_S^2 + 995Q_T \\ &\quad -1.15Q_T^2 - 2Q_SQ_T \end{aligned} \qquad [12.11]$$

To maximize π_{Total}, take the *partial* derivatives of Equation 12.11 with respect to Q_S and Q_T:

$$\frac{\partial \pi_{\text{Total}}}{\partial Q_S} = 995 - 2.50Q_S - 2Q_T$$

$$\frac{\partial \pi_{\text{Total}}}{\partial Q_T} = 995 - 2.30Q_T - 2Q_S$$

Setting these expressions equal to zero yields

$$2.5Q_S + 2Q_T - 995 = 0 \qquad [12.12]$$

$$2Q_S + 2.3Q_T - 995 = 0 \qquad [12.13]$$

Solving Equations 12.12 and 12.13 simultaneously gives these optimal output levels: $Q_S^* = 170.57$ units and $Q_T^* = 284.39$ units.

Substituting these values into Equations 12.10 and 12.11 gives an optimal selling price and total profit for the cartel of $P^* = \$545.14$ per unit and $\pi_{\text{Total}}^* = \$46{,}291.43$, respectively. The marginal costs of the two firms at the optimal output level are equal to

$$\begin{aligned} MC_S^* = \frac{d(TC_S)}{dQ_S} &= 5 + 0.50Q_S \\ &= 5 + 0.50(170.57) = \$90.29 \\ MC_T^* = \frac{d(TC_T)}{dQ_T} &= 5 + 0.30Q_T \\ &= 5 + 0.30(284.29) = \$90.29 \end{aligned}$$

As in the graphical solution illustrated earlier in Figure 12.2, the optimal output (or market share) for each firm in the cartel occurs where the marginal costs of the two firms are equal.

How a Cournot Equilibrium Affects a Cartel's Pricing: Siemens-Thomson Example

Table 12.3 summarizes the results of the Siemens and Thomson example: (a) where the two companies acted independently to maximize their own company profits (Cournot equilibrium), and (b) where they formed a cartel to maximize total industry profits. Several conclusions can be drawn from this comparison. First, total industry output (Q_{Total}^*) is lower and selling price (P^*) is higher when the firms collude. Also, total industry profits (π_{Total}^*) are higher when the firms set

Table 12.3 Comparison of Pricing, Output, and Profits for Siemens and Thomson

Optimal Value	(a) No Collusion: Siemens and Thomson Act Independently to Maximize Their Own Company's Profits	(b) Collusion: Siemens and Thomson Form a Cartel to Maximize Total Industry Profits
Q_S^* (Siemens's output)	272.32 units	170.57 units
Q_T^* (Thomson's output)	314.21 units	284.29 units
$Q_{Total}^* = Q_S^* + Q_T^*$ (Total industry output)	586.53 units	454.86 units
P^* (Selling price)	\$413.47/unit	\$545.14/unit
π_S^* (Siemens's profit)	\$22,695.00	\$14,858.15
π_T^* (Thomson's profit)	\$3,536.17	\$31,433.28
$\pi_{Total}^* = \pi_S^* + \pi_T^*$ (Total industry profit)	\$26,231.17	\$46,291.43

prices and output jointly than when they act independently. Finally, although it may not be true in all collusive agreements, one firm's profits (i.e., Siemens's) are actually lower under the cartel solution than when it acts independently. Therefore, to get Siemens to participate in the cartel, Thomson probably would have to agree to share a significant part of the cartel's additional profits with Siemens.

EXAMPLE

A Sports Cartel: Major League Baseball[16]

Major League Baseball (MLB), a cartel of professional team owners, has been exempted from the antitrust laws since a U.S. Supreme Court decision in 1922. MLB restricts entry, approves transfers of ownership, and regulates the selection and employment of apprentice players for their first six years in professional baseball. In 1975, Curt Flood of the St. Louis Cardinals successfully challenged baseball's restrictive labor practices (the "reserve clause") for major leaguers beyond their sixth year, and a collective bargaining agreement then granted such players free agency status. Experienced players could then offer their services to the highest bidder whenever their contracts were due for renewal.

As a result, salaries skyrocketed, and star players concentrated in the biggest markets (New York and Los Angeles) where owners with larger ticket revenue, higher concession sales, and bigger television contract licensing fees offered to pay more. Even the average player profited from the end of baseball's reserve clause. Average salary for major leaguers rose in inflation-adjusted dollars from \$160,000 in 1972 to \$1,015,000 in 1992. Because owners spend 58 percent of team revenue on salaries and another 13 percent on the scouting system and the minor league apprentice teams, the MLB cartel intervened to preserve competition among the teams. When perceived competitive imbalance continued to plague the sport, MLB began a

[16] Based on "Let the Market Rule," *Wall Street Journal* (November 10, 1998), p. A22; "Just Not Cricket," *The Economist* (May 31, 2003), p. 34; and Gerald Scully, *The Market Structure of Sports* (Chicago: Chicago University Press, 1995).

revenue-sharing system characteristic of cartels. Currently, the wealthiest teams are taxed 34 percent of total revenue to subsidize salaries for teams with a smaller fan base, either because of smaller markets (Minneapolis) or less success on the field (Montreal). One question is whether these subsidies, totaling more than $260 million in 2003, might actually provide incentives to cut payroll, rather than hire better players and attempt to attract more fans.

PRICE LEADERSHIP

Price Leadership

A pricing strategy followed in many oligopolistic industries. One firm normally announces all new price changes. Either by an explicit or an implicit agreement, other firms in the industry regularly follow the pricing moves of the industry leader.

Another model of price-output determination in some oligopolistic industries is **price leadership.** Many industries exhibit a pattern where one or a few firms normally set a price and others tend to follow, frequently with a time lag of a few days. In the case of basic steel products, for example, the price that prevails within a week is generally uniform from one producer to another.

Effective price leadership can only happen if price movements initiated by the leader have a high probability of sticking and no maverick or nonconforming firms exist. The fewer the number of firms in the industry (i.e., the greater the interdependencies of decision outcomes among firms), the more effective price leadership is likely to be. Two major price leadership patterns have been observed in various industries from time to time: *barometric* and *dominant price leadership*.

BAROMETRIC PRICE LEADERSHIP

In barometric price leadership, one firm announces a change in price that it hopes will be accepted by others. The leader need not be the largest firm in the industry. In fact, this leader may actually change from time to time. The leader must, however, be reasonably correct in its interpretation of changing demand and cost conditions so that suggested price changes will be accepted and stick. In essence, the barometric price leader merely initiates a reaction to changing market conditions that other firms find in their best interest to follow. These conditions might include such things as cost increases (or decreases) and sluggish (or brisk) sales accompanied by inventory buildups (or shortages) in the industry.

EXAMPLE

BAROMETRIC PRICE LEADERSHIP: AMERICAN AIRLINES AND CONTINENTAL AIRLINES[17]

In the second week of March 2002, American Airlines announced a de facto increase in business airfares. Three-day advance purchase fares were no longer available on many nonstop routes from American hubs. Instead, American returned to the old 7-day-advance-purchase requirement to obtain a 20 percent off full coach class fares ($1,629 from Dallas to New York or $1,684 from Dallas to Miami, for example). Other much cheaper Saturday overnight fares bought 7 days or even 14 days in advance were not affected because those prices primarily target leisure travelers.

American Airlines was hoping that its major competitors, Continental, Delta, United, US Airways, and Northwest, would take this opportunity to follow its lead and increase margins. Only Continental did so. Indeed, Northwest took advantage of the

[17] Based on "Airfare Skirmish Shows Why Deals Come and Go," *Wall Street Journal* (March 19, 2002), p. B1.

situation and promoted a steeply discounted \$198 round-trip fare on American's principal nonstop routes. Within a few days, American rescinded its pricing changes on routes where it competed with Northwest but retained them where it had a dominant hub, as at Dallas-Ft. Worth. In addition, American simultaneously announced a week of \$198 fares on 10 nonstop routes from United's Chicago hub, 10 nonstop routes from Delta's Atlanta hub, 10 nonstop routes from US Airways' Pittsburgh hub, and 10 nonstop routes from Northwest's Minneapolis hub. Only Continental was spared.

Dominant Firm Price Leadership

In dominant firm price leadership, one firm establishes itself as the leader because of its larger size, customer loyalty, or lower cost structure in relation to other competing firms. The leader may then act as a monopolist in its segment of the market. What is the incentive for followers to accept the established price? In some cases it may be a fear of cutthroat retaliation from a low-cost dominant firm that keeps smaller firms from undercutting the prevailing price. In other cases, following a price leader may be viewed as simply a convenience.

The price-output solution for the dominant-firm model is shown in Figure 12.7. D_T shows total market demand for the product, MC_L represents the marginal cost curve for the dominant (leader) firm, and ΣMC_F constitutes the horizontal *summation* of the marginal cost curves for the follower firms, each of which may well have costs higher than MC_L. In the following analysis, assume that the dominant firm sets the price knowing that follower firms will sell as much output as they wish at this price. The dominant firm then supplies the remainder of the market demand.

Figure 12.7 Price-Output Determination for the Dominant Firm

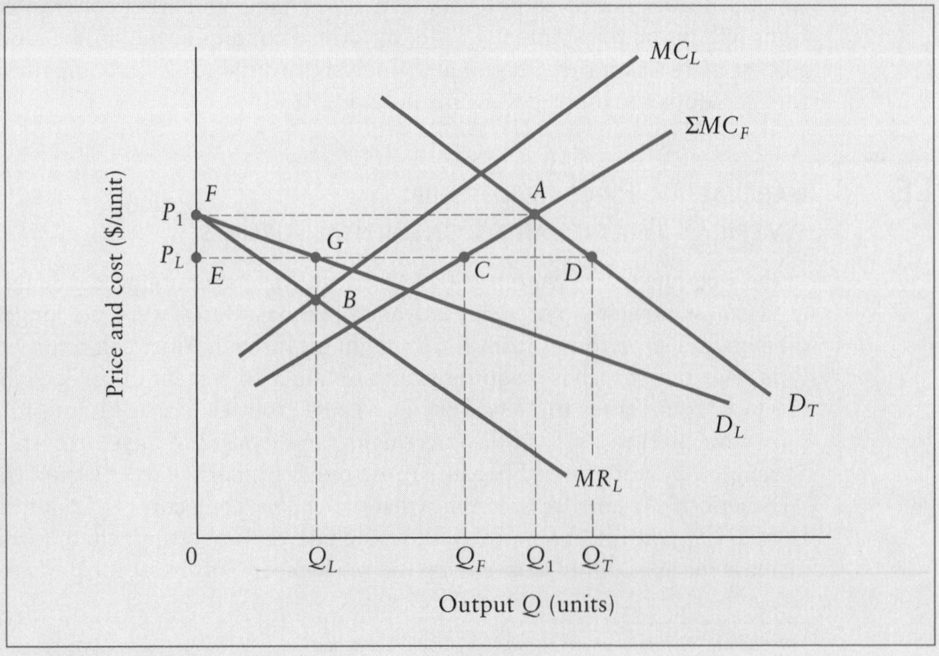

Given that the follower firms can sell as much output as they wish at the price P_L established by the dominant firm, they are faced with a horizontal demand curve and a perfectly competitive market situation. The follower firms view the dominant firm's price P_L as their marginal revenue and maximize profits, producing that level of output where their marginal cost equals the established price. The ΣMC_F curve therefore shows the total output that will be *supplied* at various prices by the follower firms. The dominant firm's residual demand curve D_L is obtained by subtracting the amount supplied by the follower firms ΣMC_F from the total market demand D_T at each price. For example, at a price of P_L, Point G on the D_L curve is obtained by subtracting EC from ED. Other points on the D_L curve are obtained in a similar manner. At a price of P_1 the quantity supplied by the follower firms Q_1 is equal to total market demand (Point A), and the dominant firm's residual demand is therefore zero (Point F). The dominant firm's marginal revenue curve MR_L is then obtained from its residual demand curve D_L.

The dominant firm maximizes its profits by setting price and output where marginal cost equals marginal revenue. As shown in Figure 12.7, $MR_L = MC_L$ at Point B. Therefore, the dominant firm should sell Q_L units of output at a price of P_L per unit. At a price of P_L, total demand is Q_T units, and the follower firms supply $Q_T - Q_L = Q_F$ units of output.

The following example illustrates the application of these concepts.

EXAMPLE

PRICE LEADERSHIP: AEROTEK

Aerotek and six other smaller companies produce an electronic component used in small planes. Aerotek (L) is the price leader. The other [follower (F)] firms sell the component at the same price as Aerotek. Aerotek permits the other firms to sell as many units of the component as they wish at the established price. The company supplies the remainder of the demand itself. Total demand for the component is given by the following function:

$$P = 10{,}000 - 10Q_T \qquad [12.14]$$

where

$$Q_T = Q_L + Q_F \qquad [12.15]$$

that is, total output (Q_T) is the sum of the leader's (Q_L) and followers' (Q_F) output. Aerotek's marginal cost function is

$$MC_L = 100 + 3Q_L \qquad [12.16]$$

The aggregate marginal cost function for the other six producers of the component is

$$\Sigma MC_F = 50 + 2Q_F \qquad [12.17]$$

We are interested in determining the output for Aerotek and the follower firms and the selling price for the component given that the firms are interested in maximizing profits.

Aerotek's profit-maximizing output is found at the point where

$$MR_L = MC_L \qquad [12.18]$$

Its marginal revenue function (MR_L) is obtained by differentiating the firm's total revenue function (TR_L) with respect to Q_L. Total revenue (TR_L) is given by the following expression:

$$TR_L = P \cdot Q_L \qquad [12.19]$$

Q_L is obtained from Equation 12.15:

$$Q_L = Q_T - Q_F \qquad [12.20]$$

Using Equation 12.14, one can solve for Q_T:

$$Q_T = 1{,}000 - 0.10P \qquad [12.21]$$

To find Q_F, we note that Aerotek lets the follower firms sell as much output (i.e., components) as they wish at the given price (P). Therefore, the follower firms are faced with a horizontal demand function. Hence

$$MR_F = P \qquad [12.22]$$

To maximize profits, the follower firms will operate where

$$MR_F = \Sigma MC_F \qquad [12.23]$$

Substituting Equations 12.22 and 12.17 into Equation 12.23 gives

$$P = 50 + 2Q_F \qquad [12.24]$$

Solving this equation for Q_F yields

$$Q_F = 0.50P - 25 \qquad [12.25]$$

Substituting Equation 12.21 for Q_T and Equation 12.25 for Q_F in Equation 12.20 gives

$$\begin{aligned} Q_L &= (1{,}000 - 0.10P) - (0.50P - 25) \\ &= 1{,}025 - 0.60P \end{aligned} \qquad [12.26]$$

Solving Equation 12.26 for P, one obtains

$$P = 1{,}708.3333 - 1.6667Q_L \qquad [12.27]$$

Substituting this expression for P in defining total revenue yields

$$\begin{aligned} TR_L &= (1{,}708.3333 - 1.6667Q_L)\, Q_L \\ &= 1{,}708.3333Q_L - 1.6667Q_L^2 \end{aligned} \qquad [12.28]$$

Differentiating this expression with respect to Q_L, one obtains Aerotek's marginal revenue function:

$$\begin{aligned} MR_L &= \frac{d(TR_L)}{dQ_L} \\ &= 1{,}708.3333 - 3.3334Q_L \end{aligned} \qquad [12.29]$$

Substituting Equation 12.29 for MR_L and Equation 12.16 for MC_L and equating the two gives the following optimality condition:

$$1{,}708.3333 - 3.3334Q_L^* = 100 + 3Q_L^* \qquad [12.30]$$

Solving this equation for Q_L^* yields

$$Q_L^* = 253.945 \text{ units}$$

or an optimal output for Aerotek of 253.9 units of the component. Substituting this value of Q_L into Equation 12.27 gives

$$\begin{aligned} P^* &= 1{,}708.3333 - 1.6667\,(253.945) \\ &= \$1{,}285.083 \end{aligned}$$

or an optimal selling price of \$1,285.08. The optimal output for the follower firms is found by substituting this value of P into Equation 12.25,

$$Q_F^* = 0.50\ (1{,}285.083) - 25$$
$$= 617.542 \text{ units}$$

or an optimal output of 617.5 units.

THE KINKED DEMAND CURVE MODEL

Sometimes when an oligopolist cuts its prices, competitors quickly feel the decline in their sales and are forced to match the price reduction. Alternatively, if one firm raises its prices, competitors rapidly gain customers by maintaining their original prices and hence have little or no motivation to match a price increase. In this situation, the demand curve facing an individual oligopolist would be far more elastic for price increases than for price decreases. If an oligopolist *raises* its price and others do not follow, the increase in price will lead to a declining share of the market as illustrated in Figure 12.8. Demand segment KD' is the *share-of-the-market demand curve* where all rivals match price and this firm's market share remains unchanged, perhaps at 21 percent. For price increases above P, however, if rival firms do not match price, the demand segment facing this firm is more elastic. For price increases, its market share declines, perhaps to 15 percent.

The oligopolist's demand curve is therefore DKD' with the prevailing price as P and output as Q. The marginal revenue curve is discontinuous because of the kink

Figure 12.8 The Kinked Demand Curve Model

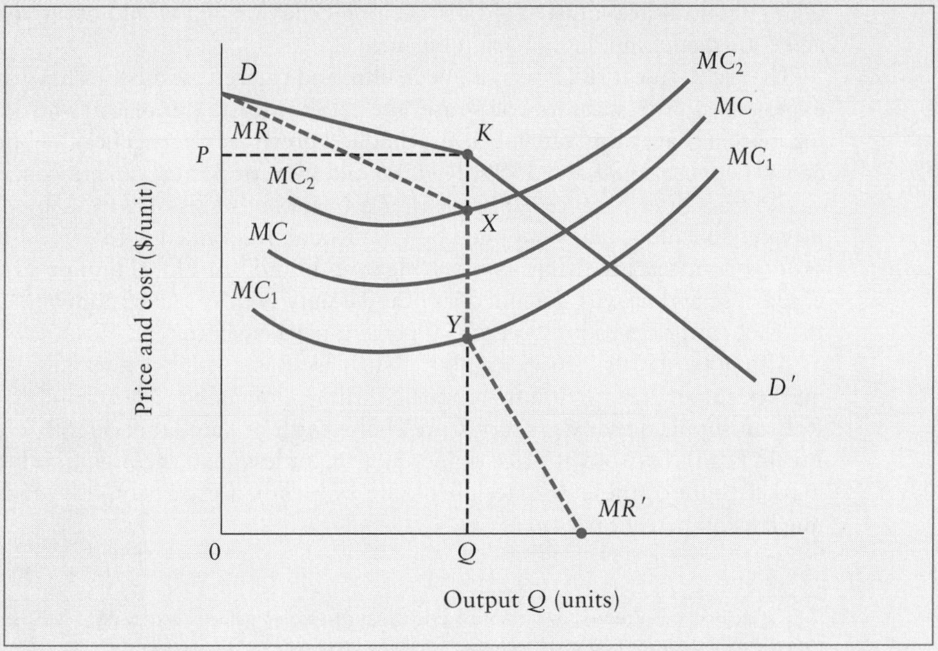

in the demand curve at *K*. Hence, marginal revenue is represented by the two line segments *MRX* and *YMR'*. If the marginal cost curve *MC* passes through the gap *XY* in the marginal revenue curve, the most profitable alternative is to maintain the current price-output policy.[18] The profit-maximizing level of price and output remains constant for the firm, which perceives itself to be faced with a fixed unit price, even though costs may change over a rather wide range (e.g., MC_2 and MC_1). Similarly, shifts in the demand curve either to the right (an increase in demand) or to the left (a decrease in demand) may not change the price decisions of the firm. Because the kink is determined at the *prevailing price,* a shift in demand shifts the gap *XY* in the marginal revenue curve to the right or left. If *MC* still passes through the gap, the prevailing price is maintained, although output will either increase or decrease.

A number of criticisms have been made of the kinked demand curve model as a general model of oligopoly behavior. Although the model does explain why stable prices have been observed to exist in some oligopolistic industries, it takes the prevailing price as given and offers no reason why that price level rather than some other is the prevailing price. Therefore, the kinked demand model of oligopolistic pricing must be viewed as incomplete.

Avoiding Price Wars

Knowing how to avoid a price war has become a critical success factor for many high-margin businesses in tight oligopolistic groups. Recall from our discussion of break-even sales change analysis in Chapter 10 that the higher the margin, the more tempted companies are to use price discounting to increase incremental sales. Because each additional sale incurs few additional costs, high margins encourage price discounting to gain market share. So building a business plan or adopting a strategy that reduces the power of substitutes, entrants, buyers, and suppliers and thereby generates high profit margins is no guarantee of success. To sustain profitability, oligopoly firms also must avoid discounting behavior that would otherwise be characteristic tactics in a high-margin business.

The ready-to-eat (RTE) cereal, beer, film, and cigarette industries have all recently experienced price wars. In each case, the catalyst for the price war was the fast rising market share of private labels in what had previously been a heavily branded category. Between 1989 and 1999, Kodak Gold film for 35mm cameras declined from a $3.49 list price to a $2 list price after a blistering series of attacks by discounted private-label films, many supplied by Fuji. Kodak responded with a good-better-best product strategy involving its own "fighting brand" of film, Funtime Film, for everyday use and heavily defended its brand equity with "Kodak moment" ads but, in the end, cut prices to preserve its 70 percent market share.

Also in the 1990s, generic cigarettes such as "Basic" took a substantial amount of market share from premium brands Marlboro, Winston, Merit, and Salem. And Ralston supplied many grocery store chains with private label cereals (e.g., Kroger Raisin Bran) that sold at price points 30 percent less than the premium brands. The market share of these private label store brands had grown rapidly, sometimes as much as 30 percent per year.

[18] Profit may not be increased by increasing price (and decreasing output) because $MR > MC$, and this difference would increase with a price increase. Similarly, profit may not be increased by decreasing price (and increasing output) because $MR < MC$, and this difference would also increase with a price decrease.

EXAMPLE

PRICE WARS AT GENERAL MILLS AND POST[19]

In both cereals and cigarettes, the price cut that triggered a price war was 20 percent discount per unit. This amount represented a $1.00 price discount on the $4.80 average price for a full-size box of RTE cereal, and a $0.40 discount off the $1.92 average price per pack of premium brand cigarettes. The price war in cereals was started by Post Cereals, the distant third player in the industry with a 13 percent market share. At the same time, Quaker Oats with a 7 percent market share began selling branded cereals such as Cap'n Crunch and Life in large "value-priced" bags for $3.50 in the Target and Wal-Mart distribution channels. Post had carefully analyzed the tactical situation and decided it could better maintain regular customers and compete for price-sensitive new customers if Kellogg and General Mills reduced advertising. Post believed they would do so only in response to a massive industry-wide price cut.

General Mills was experiencing a slowly eroding 25 percent market share, while Kellogg faced a rapidly declining 35 percent market share. Every share point in the U.S. ready-to-eat cereal industry is worth $80 million in sales. In part because of a panic-stricken determination to arrest the erosion of their market shares, both Kellogg and General Mills quickly decided to match the Post price cut. Full-size boxes of branded products such as General Mills' Wheaties and Kellogg's Frosted Flakes were cut in price from $4.80 to $3.88. Just as Post had predicted, each of the leading firms then scaled back their advertising campaigns. Cereals such as Post Raisin Bran and Post Grape Nuts then gained share rapidly, at least for a short time until Kellogg matched the Post price cut on two-thirds of its premium brands. Two years later, cereal prices in the all-important grocery store distribution channel began to return to their pre-price-war levels.

Kellogg has the strongest brands in the cereals industry with 12 of the 15 top-selling cereals. Rather than match Post's price cuts, Kellogg might have poured not two but three scoops of raisins into every box of Kellogg's Raisin Bran. In the first two months after the price cuts by Post and General Mills, Kellogg lost three share points (from 35 percent to 32 percent) and Post gained four (from 16 percent to 20 percent). At $80 million per share point and 55 percent gross margins (on average across the affected brands), Kellogg's contributions on the lost sales totaled $132 million ($-3 \times$ $80 million $\times$ 0.55). To retrieve that $132-million-per-year operating profit, Kellogg slashed prices 19 percent on two-thirds of its brands, sacrificing more than $305 million ($-0.19 \times$ $2.4 billion sales $\times$ 0.66). Market share continued to decline to 29 percent in 1999, and the capitalized value of Kellogg fell by $7 billion. Many observers wondered whether expending $305 million (or half that much) on product innovation or on advertising would have accomplished more.

One key to avoiding price wars in tight oligopolies is to recognize the ongoing nature of the pricing rivalry and attempt to mitigate the intensity of the price competition by growing the market. United Airlines cannot hope to get rid of American Airlines. Kodak foresees a perpetual rivalry with Fuji Film. And Pepsi is stuck with Coke. Consequently, each rival must anticipate retaliation for aggressive discounting

[19] Based on "Denial in Battle Creek," *Forbes* (October 7, 1996); "Cereal Thriller," *The Economist* (June 15, 1996); and P. Cummins, "Cereal Firms in Cost-Price Squeeze," Reuters News Service (May 15, 1996).

WHAT WENT RIGHT • WHAT WENT WRONG

GOOD-BETTER-BEST PRODUCT STRATEGY AT KODAK[20]

Marriott Corporation and Kodak have responded to fierce price competition in their respective industries by introducing upscale, high-quality midrange, and down-market product lines to their respective target customers. Ritz-Carlton, Courtyards by Marriott, and Fairfield Inns all operate as subsidiary hotel chains under the parent Marriott Corporation but as distinct offerings.

Similarly, in the early 1990s, in response to declining perceived quality differentials, collapsing market share, and price pressure from private label film, Kodak introduced a new lineup that included Royal Gold, Kodak Gold Plus, and Funtime Film. Successful segmentation is the key to such a product strategy for avoiding ruinous price discounting. Funtime Film and the Kodak disposable cameras that followed are positioned for everyday use to capture the hundreds of events, posed people, and scenery that highly accessible cheap film sold through convenience store distribution channels make possible. These photo shots customers will later find "lost" in great stacks in file cabinets, desk drawers, and old shoeboxes. Although not generally used to memorialize anything of significance, the snapshot accentuates the experiential event, as it happens.

"Kodak moments," however, pursue a different set of value drivers. Kodak Royal Gold provided exceptional picture resolution in many different light conditions. Although slower, Gold Plus is also able to memorialize subtleties of expressions of surprise, exaltation, pride in fulfilling challenging tasks, and so on. Kodak's marketing research found that many of its customers would pay a price premium to memorialize a personal emotion (such as when a woman demonstrably triumphs amidst the worst whitewater rapids in a raft filled with her brothers). Heavy advertising and event marketing further established this product image.

[20] Based on "Film-War Spoils: A Buck a Roll?" *Wall Street Journal* (November 11, 1998), p. B1; "Eastman Kodak Company: Funtime Film," Harvard Business School Publishing (1998); and "Kodak Is Rolling Out Digital Photo Processing," *Wall Street Journal* (February 9, 1999), p. A4.

designed to attract away the other company's regular customers. It is better to maintain high prices and expect your rivals to do the same. Then, each company can focus on opening new markets and selling more volume to established customers. Coke Classic now sells an average of six servings per day to heavy Coke drinkers. In the last five years, Coke introduced dozens of new soft drinks to countries throughout the world. As a result, the Coca-Cola concentrate syrup has never been discounted in 80 years.

Customer segmentation with differential pricing is another way to avoid price wars. If low-cost new entrants attack a major airline, one effective response that avoids initiating a price war with other major carriers involves matching prices to a targeted customer segment and then carefully controlling how much capacity is released for sale to that segment. "Fencing" restrictions such as 10-day advance-purchase requirements and Saturday night stayovers prove crucial in segmenting the price-sensitive discretionary traveler from the regular business expense-account customer. The incumbent carriers can "meet the competition" in these restricted fare classes while reserving sufficient capacity for those who desire to pay for the reliability, convenience, and change order responsiveness of business class and full-coach seats. Most importantly, established competitors can maintain high prices on unaffected departures, segments, and routes. In Chapter 13, we discuss how revenue management techniques can help accomplish these goals.

In addition to segmenting the target customers into more and less price-sensitive submarkets, product line extensions can reduce gainshare price discounting by providing reference prices and framing effects that help sell the mid-range product at full (undiscounted) price. Consumers of unbranded products typically remember the last price they encountered on the shelf in deciding whether to purchase at the quoted price today. Branded products, however, trigger long reference pricing. Discounting with a major branded item such as Tide detergent tends to etch in the customer's mind a new lowball price that can be expected thereafter for many months. Therefore, what one really might like to do in the face of private-label discount competition is to introduce a super premium product offered at price points well above your traditional product. Loyal customers of the regular brand will remember these high references prices. Because the opportunity losses in going from mid-range to bargain-basement products (while saving $2, for example) tend to weigh more heavily upon consumers than the perceived satisfaction of moving upscale to super premiums (at an equal $2 cost), the mid-range products are expected to sell even better in the presence of the framing provided by super premium products. In the late 1990s, Kodak introduced super premium digital photography with a product line called Picture CD. Max and Advantrix film were also introduced by Kodak at price points 15 percent above the Gold Films, now sold in discounted multipacks through Sam's Club, Wal-Mart, and Kmart. Max and Advantrix soon provided 38 percent of Kodak's sales with relatively little discounting.

Another way to avoid or at least reduce the effects of price wars is to differentiate through innovation. Rather than matching price cuts, a higher-priced brand can highlight conspicuous product innovations the discounters have missed. Sony's Mavica is an easy-to-use point-and-shoot digital camera that records images onto a 3-inch CD-R/RW disk. The disk pops out of the camera and into any PC for easy and immediate printing. While digital camera competitors Kodak and Casio were improving picture resolution to justify complicated expensive peripherals, Sony simplified the process and increased customer value. As a result, the Mavica earned a premium price relative to its competitors.

EXAMPLE

WHAT WENT RIGHT AT INTERLINK SURGICAL STEEL AND GILLETTE?[21]

In the 1980s and early 1990s, Interlink sold replacement hypodermic syringes by the thousands to hospitals for 10 cents per syringe. Each time a catheter was changed, a new hypodermic syringe would be inserted into the patient's vein. A Japanese surgical steel company entered the market with an identical product for 3 cents each. Interlink promptly introduced a replacement device that only needs insertion one time; that is, any new saline or pharmaceutical drip lines can be hooked directly to an Interlink syringe device that need not be removed and replaced. This new process reduces the risk of patient infection and the inherent hazard to the nursing staff of exposure to patient blood. Interlink again dominates the market, and prices have stabilized at higher levels than before.

[21] Based on "How to Fight a Price War," *Harvard Business Review* (March/April 2000), pp. 107–116; "How to Escape a Price War," *Fortune* (June 13, 1994), pp. 82–90; and "Gillette to Launch," *Wall Street Journal* (January 16, 2004), p. A8.

Similarly, Gillette Co. responded to a four-bladed new product introduction of Quattro by Schick-Wilkinson Sword. Quattro had stolen 3 percent of Gillette's 83 percent market share in the men's razor market. Instead of an ongoing parade of discounts, coupons, and promotions, Gillette rolled out its own innovation: a battery-powered vibrating razor called Mach3Power. M3Power improves the closeness and longevity of the shave by exciting chin hairs to push up out of their follicles. The new product costs two-thirds more than the Gillette Mach3Turbo it replaced, and replacement cartridges are 20 percent higher-priced.

Figure 12.9 analyzes an oligopolistic market with extreme brand loyalty based on innovation, customer risk avoidance, or effective brand name advertising. Kellogg's Raisin Bran faces an inverse demand segment, ($\$11 - Q^d$) = Price, that includes the highest willingness-to-pay customers. Setting *MR* in this segment, $\$11 - 2Q^d$, equal to a marginal cost of \$1, Kellogg's Raisin Bran maximizes operating profit at $Q^* =$ 5(000) and a price per box of (\$11 − 5) = \$6. Without as established a brand image, Post Raisin Bran must sell under \$6 and accordingly faces a different segment whose inverse demand may be written as ($\$6 - Q^d$) = Price (i.e., the line segment from \$6 downward to the right along *D* in Figure 12.9). Setting *MR* at Post, $\$6 - 2Q^d$, equal to a higher \$2 marginal cost per box yields a profit-maximizing output for Post of 2(000) at a profit-maximizing price of (\$6 − \$2) = \$4 per box. These (5/11 = 45%) and (2/11 = 19%) market shares for Kellogg and Post, respectively, approximate their actual market shares in the ready-to-eat cereal market for raisin bran products.

Figure 12.9 Segmented Oligopoly with Extreme Brand Loyalty

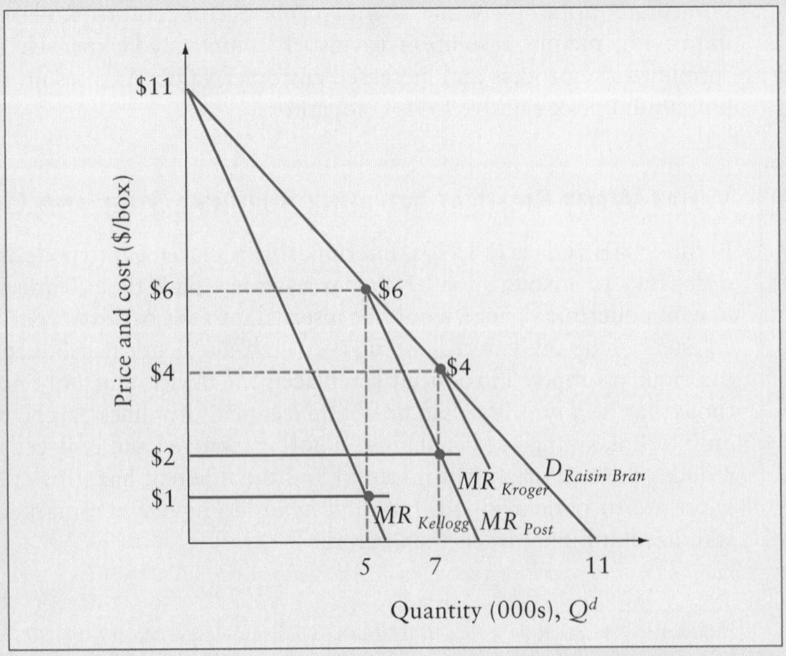

Additional firms with still less brand loyalty, such as Kroger Raisin Bran, would supply the remaining segments illustrated still farther downward to the right.

Perhaps the best way to avoid a price war in a small oligopolistic rivalry group is to not start one in the first place. If someone else does start a price war, often the best response is simply to match the competition and then accentuate nonprice elements of the marketing mix by increasing services or advertising. When Phillip Morris cut 20 percent from the price of premium cigarettes such as Marlboro, rather than furthering the downward price spiral, Reynolds matched the price cut only in its premium brands, Winston and Salem, and expanded advertising. At the \$2.00 per pack all-time high price before the price war, the heavy smoker had a \$35 per week incentive to quit. For Marlboro, with an 82 percent contribution margin, the 20 percent price cut necessitated a 32 percent [$0.82/(0.82 - 0.20) = 1.32$] increase in incremental sales to achieve increased short-term profit. Instead, Marlboro market share rose only about 17 percent.

EXAMPLE

NONPRICE TACTICS IN A PRICE WAR: COORS[22]

Coors implemented exactly the same nonprice response in the midst of a costly price war between Anheuser-Busch and Miller Brewing. As Miller and Bud products reduced the category to more and more of a commodity with ever deeper discounts, Coors and Stroh's decided to realign their product positioning with Corona and Heineken. Amidst heavy advertising, Coors gained two share points despite prices \$2-per-case higher than Miller and Bud.

A final key in avoiding price wars comes through the tactical insights often available from game theory analysis. Being able identify a rival's payoffs using competitor surveillance helps predict the competitor's response to one's own price cuts. In other circumstances, cooperative high-price outcomes may arise out of mutual interest. Simply recognizing the detailed structure of the pricing "game" can be a first step in altering the competitive environment in ways that increase profitability. In the following chapter, we present game theory techniques that provide managerial insights for effective tactical decision making.

[22] Based on "Big Brewers Find Price War," *Wall Street Journal* (July 2, 1998), p. B6, and (January 4, 1999), p. R6.

SUMMARY

- An *oligopoly* is an industry structure characterized by a relatively small number of firms in which recognizable *interdependencies* exist among the actions of the firms. Each firm is aware that its actions are likely to evoke countermoves from its rivals.
- In the *Cournot* model of oligopoly behavior, each of the firms, in determining its profit-maximizing output level, assumes that the other firm's output will remain constant.
- A *cartel* is a formal or informal agreement among oligopolists to cooperate or collude in determining outputs, prices, and profits. If the cartel members can enforce agreements and prevent cheating, they can act as a monopolist and maximize industry profits.

- A number of factors affect the ability of oligopolistic firms to engage successfully in some form of formal (or informal) cooperation, including the number and size distribution of sellers, product heterogeneity, cost structures, size and frequency of orders, secrecy and retaliation, and the percentage of industry output from outside the cartel.
- *Price leadership* is a pricing strategy in an oligopolistic industry in which one firm sets the price and, either by explicit or implicit agreement, the other firms tend to follow the decision.
- In the *kinked demand curve* model, it is assumed that if an oligopoly firm reduces its prices, its competitors will quickly feel the decline in their sales and will be forced to match the reduction. Alternatively, if the oligopolist raises its prices, competitors will rapidly gain customers by maintaining their original prices and will have little or no motivation to match a price increase. Hence, the demand curve for individual oligopolists is much more elastic for price increases than for price decreases and may lead oligopolists to maintain stable prices.
- To avoid price wars, oligopoly firms can grow the market, engage in product line extensions, expand into new geographic areas, segment customers and employ differential pricing, or innovate to retain profitable customers.

Exercises

Answers to the exercises in blue can be found in Appendix C at the back of the book.

1. Assume that two companies (C and D) are duopolists that produce identical products. Demand for the products is given by the following linear demand function:

$$P = 600 - Q_C - Q_D$$

where Q_C and Q_D are the quantities sold by the respective firms and P is the selling price. Total cost functions for the two companies are

$$TC_C = 25{,}000 + 100\,Q_C$$
$$TC_D = 20{,}000 + 125\,Q_D$$

Assume that the firms act *independently* as in the Cournot model (i.e., each firm assumes that the other firm's output will not change).

a. Determine the long-run equilibrium output and selling price for each firm.

b. Determine the total profits for each firm at the equilibrium output found in Part (a).

2. Assume that two companies (A and B) are duopolists who produce identical products. Demand for the products is given by the following linear demand function:

$$P = 200 - Q_A - Q_B$$

where Q_A and Q_B are the quantities sold by the respective firms and P is the selling price. Total cost functions for the two companies are

$$TC_A = 1{,}500 + 55Q_A + Q_A^2$$
$$TC_B = 1{,}200 + 20Q_B + 2Q_B^2$$

Assume that the firms act *independently* as in the Cournot model (i.e., each firm assumes that the other firm's output will not change).

a. Determine the long-run equilibrium output and selling price for each firm.

b. Determine Firm A, Firm B, and total industry profits at the equilibrium solution found in Part (a).

3. Consider Exercise 2 again. Assume that the firms form a *cartel* to act as a monopolist and maximize total industry profits (sum of Firm A and Firm B profits).

a. Determine the optimum output and selling price for each firm.

b. Determine Firm A, Firm B, and total industry profits at the optimal solution found in Part (a).

c. Show that the marginal costs of the two firms are equal at the optimal solution found in Part (a).

4. Compare the optimal solutions obtained in Exercises 2 and 3. Specifically:
   a. How much higher (lower) is the optimal selling price when the two firms form a cartel to maximize industry profits, compared to when they act independently?
   b. How much higher (lower) is total industry output?
   c. How much higher (lower) are total industry profits?
5. Alchem (L) is the price leader in the polyglue market. All 10 other manufacturers [follower (F) firms] sell polyglue at the same price as Alchem. Alchem allows the other firms to sell as much as they wish at the established price and supplies the remainder of the demand itself. Total demand for polyglue is given by the following function ($Q_T = Q_L + Q_F$):

$$P = 20{,}000 - 4Q_T$$

Alchem's marginal cost function for manufacturing and selling polyglue is

$$MC_L = 5{,}000 + 5Q_L$$

The aggregate marginal cost function for the other manufacturers of polyglue is

$$\Sigma MC_F = 2{,}000 + 4Q_F$$

   a. To maximize profits, how much polyglue should Alchem produce and what price should it charge?
   b. What is the total market demand for polyglue at the price established by Alchem in Part (a)? How much of total demand do the follower firms supply?
6. Chillman Motors, Inc., believes it faces the following segmented demand function:

$$P = \begin{cases} 150 - 0.5Q & \text{when } 0 \le Q \le 50 \\ 200 - 1.5Q & \text{for } Q > 50 \end{cases}$$

   a. Indicate both verbally and graphically why such a segmented demand function is likely to exist. What type of industry structure is indicated by this relationship?
   b. Calculate the marginal revenue functions facing Chillman. Add these to your graph from Part (a).
   c. Chillman's total cost function is

$$TC_1 = 500 + 15Q + 0.5Q^2$$

   Calculate the marginal cost function. What is Chillman's profit-maximizing price and output combination?
   d. What is Chillman's profit-maximizing price-output combination if total costs increase to

$$TC_2 = 500 + 45Q + 0.5Q^2$$

   e. If Chillman's total cost function changes to either

$$TC_3 = 500 + 15Q + 1.0Q^2$$

   or

$$TC_4 = 500 + 5Q + 0.25Q^2$$

   what price-output solution do you expect to prevail? Would your answer change if you knew that all firms in the industry witnessed similar changes in their cost functions?

7. *Library Research Project*. Examine the literature on the price-fixing agreements that occurred in the electrical equipment industry during the 1950s. For example, see Richard Austin Smith, "The Incredible Electrical Conspiracy," *Fortune* (April/May 1961).
   a. What firms and products were involved in the conspiracy?
   b. What measures did the executives use to keep their meetings secret?
   c. How did the companies determine who should get contracts and orders?
   d. What market-sharing formulas (quotas) were used in allocating demand?
   e. What were some of the problems encountered in maintaining the price-fixing agreements?
8. It was observed in the chapter that collusion among oligopolists can be facilitated in part by information sharing. As a consequence, the sharing of price information among rival oligopolists can violate U.S. antitrust laws. You can see how the U.S. Supreme Court has interpreted antitrust law as it pertains to sharing price information by reading a summary of the case of *U.S. v. U.S. Gypsum Co. et al.* (438 U.S. 422), which is available at: www.stolaf.edu/people/becker/antitrust/summaries/438us422.htm.

   In what manner was price information shared, and why did the court find these actions to be an antitrust violation?

CASE EXERCISE

CELL PHONES DISPLACE MOBILE PHONE SATELLITE NETWORKS

Motorola's Iridium, a go-anywhere mobile phone system that beamed signals down from 66 satellites, was called "the eighth wonder of the world" by Motorola CEO Chris Galvin. However, at $1,500 for a handset the size of a brick, consumers balked, and few business customers needed the security and reliability offered in remote corners of the globe like Katmandu. As a result, Motorola's 25 percent market share in cell phones declined steadily to 13 percent in 2001, and Motorola stock fell 16 percent from 1997–2001, during a period when the S&P 500 was up 76 percent.

QUESTIONS

1. Characterize the product space for mobile phones when Iridium began.
2. What trends did Nokia pursue as it designed mobile phone products in the late 1990s? (Refer to the Managerial Challenge at the beginning of this chapter.)
3. What might a more proactive Motorola have done differently had it correctly perceived the steps its rival Nokia would take?

CHAPTER

13

Best-Practice Tactics: Game Theory

CHAPTER PREVIEW Businesses and potential entrants into product markets who compete against a few rivals need effective tactics for effective decision making. Effective tactics in turn require anticipating rival response and counterresponse. Noncooperative simultaneous and sequential games were designed for just this purpose, including entry deterrence and accommodation games, bidding games, manufacturer-distributor games, product development or research and development games, and pricing and promotion games.

All such noncooperative games prohibit side payments and binding contracts between rivals. Instead, they depend on self-enforcing relationships to maintain strategic equilibrium. For example, each airline in a posted pricing game must decide whether it is in its own best interest to resist discounting to gain market share, based on the best reply responses it anticipates from rivals. In some circumstances, mutual discounting proves to be a dominant strategy that provides protection from renegade discounters, while in other situations, mutual forbearance leads to higher margins.

The order of play can matter in such games if credible threats and commitments influence the endgame outcomes. In this chapter we explore the role that first-mover and last-mover advantages, nonredeployable assets, credible punishment schemes, hostage mechanisms, matching price guarantees, and imperfect information can play in business strategy.

MANAGERIAL CHALLENGE

Large-Scale Entry Deterrence of Low-Cost Discounters: Southwest, People Express, Value Jet, Kiwi, and JetBlue[1]

Since the deregulation of the U.S. airlines industry, legacy carriers such as United, American, US Airways, and Delta have faced a progression of low-cost competitors. Beginning with Southwest Airlines, continuing though People Express, Value Jet (now Air Tran), Kiwi, Independence Air, and now JetBlue, these firms established point-to-point operations in unserved or underserved cities and thereby created profitable business models at much lower prices. For example, from San Antonio to Los Angeles, Southwest is profitable at $300 for last-minute walk-up one-way service whereas

MANAGERIAL CHALLENGE

American Airlines charges \$520. From San Antonio to Philadelphia, Southwest's cost-covering fare is \$280, whereas American's is \$495.

Not surprisingly, one focus of the low-cost discounters has been the relentless pursuit of cost savings. Point-to-point service simplifies a carrier's operations, and Southwest with 15-minute turnarounds gets 10.3 flight hours per plane per day, 46 percent more than the industry average. By increasing capacity utilization 46 percent, Southwest lowers its indirect fixed cost per seat for interest, overhead, and time depreciation on the airframes by 31 percent ($1 - 1/1.46 = 1 - 0.69$). By stripping out the first-class seats and the galley, Southwest increases its seating capacity by 33 percent from 90 to 119 seats on Boeing 737s, thereby lowering direct fixed costs per seat for flight crews, fuel, and maintenance by 25 percent ($1 - 1/1.33 = 1 - 0.75$). In addition, the low-cost start-ups have remained largely nonunionized with labor costs well below industry averages; as a result, legacy carriers have gone back time and time again to their machinist and flight crew unions seeking wage and salary concessions. In 2005, the total cost per available seat mile (ASM) varied from a high of 11.62 cents at Delta and 10.89 at US Airways to 7.70 cents at Southwest and 6.74 at Jet Blue. American and United were in the middle at 9.80 cents and 10.12, respectively.

Two prominent game theory questions in such settings involve the discounter's optimal capacity choice and the legacy airline's optimal pricing to deter or accommodate the entry. Southwest's entry strategy in any new city is to offer a uniform low-price, no-frills seat with high-frequency scheduling. By unbundling all services, adopting quick turnaround times, working longer crew shifts, and converting all first-class and galley space into additional coach-class seats, Southwest typically achieves 20 percent to 25 percent lower operating cost than American. Southwest's prototypical target customer is a manufacturer's trade representative who often needs to travel on short notice, but is seldom fully reimbursed through a company expense account.

In essence, a Southwest entry creates a new segment of the market not previously served by much more expensive and infrequently scheduled legacy carriers (e.g., passengers who often drove rather than took the plane). These new low willingness-to-pay customers often quickly reserve most if not all of Southwest's capacity, leaving almost none available to other air travelers. As a result, a Southwest entry may not erode the market for higher-priced incumbent airlines but rather creates a so-called "Southwest effect" of increased volume and load factors throughout the market, but at much lower prices. Eventually, this lower price environment drags down the profitability of all carriers. The established airlines have to decide whether to match Southwest's deeply discounted fares right away or accommodate Southwest by maintaining high fares. Southwest has to decide whether to enter with a large or small capacity. In this chapter, we will see how businesses use game theory reasoning in making such decisions.

[1] Based on "UAL Hopes Latest Cost Cuts Will Yield," *Wall Street Journal* (May 12, 2005), p. A10; "Southwest's Dallas Duel," *Wall Street Journal* (May 10, 2005), p. B1; and F. Harris, "Large Scale Entry Deterrence of Low-Cost Discounters: An Early Success of Revenue Management," *International Journal of Revenue Management* 1, no. 1, (2007).

OLIGOPOLISTIC RIVALRY AND GAME THEORY

Most oligopolistic competition takes place today in product submarkets between a few rival incumbent firms, each with some market power over price. Consider Bayer Aspirin, Bufferin, Excedrin, and St. Joseph's in pain relievers; Pepsi and Coke in colas; Six Flags and Disney in theme parks; and Delta, US Airways, and American in air travel to Florida. Smaller competitors selling more generic products are often present in peripheral markets, but these oligopolists are notable because of some brand name or other barrier to effective entry and their extraordinary *interdependence*.

Recall that in a purely competitive industry, such as real estate development of tract home subdivisions, each competitor can act quite independently. Each takes price as "given," that is, determined externally in the open market, because any decision to expand or embargo his or her own supply has no appreciable effect on the enormously larger industry supply. Even if one real estate developer were to purchase many subdivisions in a community, the barriers to entry are so low that any price above cost would surely attract enough new competitors to restore the competitive price-taking equilibrium.

In contrast, each firm in an oligopolistic market must pay close attention to the moves and countermoves of its rivals. Correctly anticipating entry and exit, product development, pricing, and promotions several steps ahead of actual events and at least one step ahead of the competition is often the key to a successful business. Despite one's best efforts, sometimes a competitor takes the lead, and then quickly adaptive behavior is preferable to reactive behavior. The best option of all is proactive behavior, and proactive behavior requires accurate and reliable predictions of rival initiatives and rival response.

The managerial purpose of game theory is to provide these predictions of rival behavior. To execute defensive strategy as well as plan strategic initiatives, each oligopolist must try to predict well in advance the actions, responses, and counterresponses of their rivals and then choose optimal strategies accordingly. Modern **game theory** was invented for precisely this purpose.

Game Theory

A theory of interdependent decision making by the participants in a conflict-of-interest or opportunity-for-collaboration situation.

A CONCEPTUAL FRAMEWORK FOR GAME THEORY ANALYSIS

A general definition of a **strategy game** is any consciously interdependent choice behavior engaged in by purposeful individuals or hierarchical groups who share a common goal (e.g., tribes, sports teams, or value-maximizing companies). As such, strategy games have always been a part of human interactions. Some of the earliest formal analyses of strategy games involved strategic voting in the Roman Senate, bargaining among Phoenician traders, and the ancient Chinese military tactics of Sun Tzu.

Strategy Game

A decision-making situation with consciously interdependent behavior between two or more of the participants.

Consider, for example, how the private property rights to a person's belongings might evolve in a setting like the TV show *Survivor*. Table 13.1 displays the normal form of the strategy game in which communities of hunter-gatherers had to decide between agricultural pursuits combined with guarding consolidated property versus continuously hunting and marauding against targets of opportunity. History records that the private property consolidators (the Aggies) won out; let's see why.

Two competing players (Randle and Kahn) struggle for resources by selecting between two actions: *Maraud,* which occasionally yields unguarded windfall treasures but leaves one's own possessions vulnerable to counterattack; or *Guard,* which frees time between defensive struggles for consolidating and multiplying the fruits of one's labors with agriculture. Kahn has a tactical advantage in marauding against anything

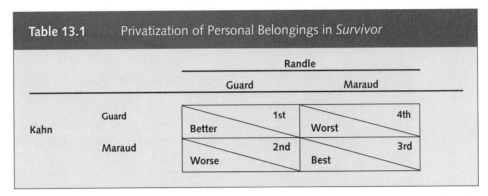

Table 13.1 Privatization of Personal Belongings in *Survivor*

		Randle	
		Guard	Maraud
Kahn	Guard	Better / 1st	Worst / 4th
	Maraud	Worse / 2nd	Best / 3rd

Note: Column-player payoffs are above the diagonal. Row-player payoffs are below the diagonal. Randle ranks outcomes from 1st to 4th. Kahn ranks outcomes from best to worst.

but strongly guarded positions. However, no matter what action Kahn decides to take, an examination of the payoff matrix in Table 13.1 reveals that the Aggie named Randle is always better off selecting Guard. In particular, the outcome in the NW cell (above the diagonal) is ranked first by Randle whereas the outcome in the NE cell (again above the diagonal) is ranked fourth. Similarly, the outcome in the SW cell (above the diagonal) is ranked second by Randle versus the outcome in the SE cell which is ranked third. Therefore, no matter what action Kahn decides to take, Randle is always better off guarding his own consolidated property rather than marauding himself.

Dominant Strategy

An action rule that maximizes the decision maker's welfare independent of the actions of other players.

Guard is Randle's **dominant strategy** because his outcomes from Guard exceed the outcomes from any alternative strategy, regardless of the opponent's behavior. Knowing this fact or discovering it through trial and error, Kahn predicts his rival Randle will continue to guard. On that presumption, Kahn then iterates back to his own choice decision and finds he prefers guard himself. {Guard, Guard} therefore emerges as a strategic equilibrium, and the game provides a sense of how and why private property arrangements evolved.

Components of a Game

The essential elements of all strategy games are present in the preceding example and include the following: players, actions, information sets, payoffs, an order of play, focal outcomes of interest, strategies, and equilibrium strategies. Let's illustrate each component in a game of service quality competition. Suppose two copier repair *players*, Lanier Now and Sharp ER, must choose whether to offer fast-response copier repair service six and seven territories removed from their respective regional headquarters located in two different cities 100 miles apart (see Figure 13.1). Six versus seven territories of fast-response service repair are the *actions*. The *payoffs* from the decisions, which must be announced simultaneously at next week's industrial trade show, are shown in Table 13.2. This payoff matrix is the **normal form of the game,** which is an appropriate way of representing any simultaneous-play (versus sequential-play) game.

Normal Form of the Game

A representation of payoffs in a simultaneous-play game.

Sharp finds that fast-response service repair in the more distant seventh territory is expensive. Cutting back to six territories reduces cost by $15 per week per customer and raises Sharp's profit from $55 to $70 per week when Lanier also cuts back, and from $45 to $60 per week when Lanier does not. The improved effectiveness of Sharp's service in the remaining six territories lowers the prices that rival Lanier can charge and reduces its profit from an initial $45 down to only $30 should Lanier

Figure 13.1 Fast-Response Copier Service and Repair

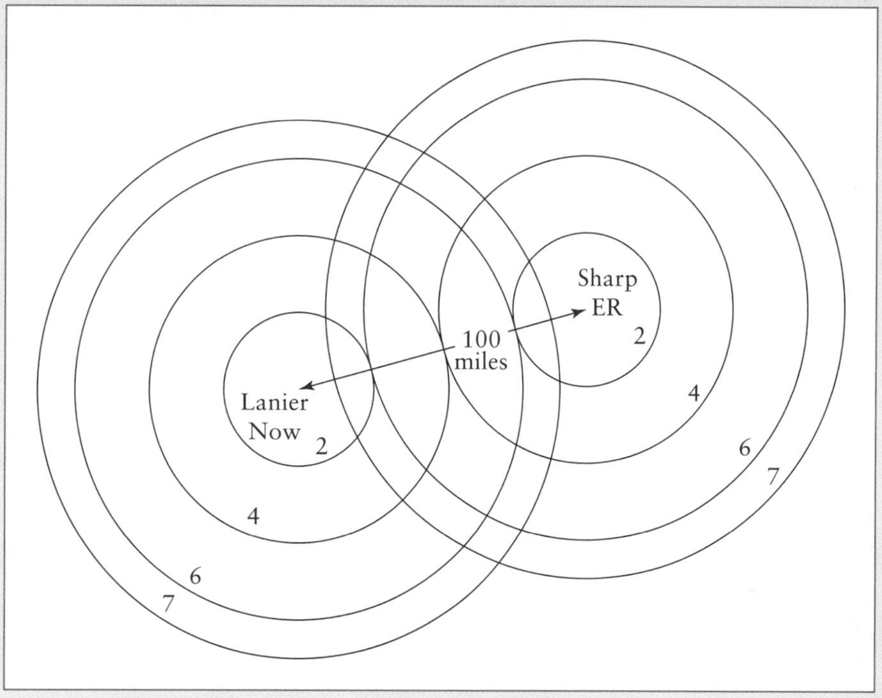

Table 13.2 Six or Seven Territories?

		Sharp: Six Territories	Sharp: Seven Territories
Lanier	Six Territories	$40 / $70	$35 / $55
	Seven Territories	$30 / $60	$45 / $45

Notes: Payoffs are profits. Sharp payoffs are above the diagonal, and Lanier payoffs are below the diagonal.

continue servicing all seven territories. By cutting back to six territories itself, Lanier can restrict its losses to just $5 ($45 now to $40). The common *information set* known to both players includes knowledge of all these payoffs.

What strategy should Lanier adopt? First, using the concept of *dominant strategy,* it is clear that Sharp ER will discontinue service in the seventh territory. Sharp is better off cutting back to six territories independent of what Lanier does. For Sharp, seven territories is *dominated* (unambiguously less preferred than six territories). Lanier wishes it were not so, because its most successful operation entails head-to-head, seven-territory competition against Sharp. Nevertheless, predictable reality lies elsewhere, and Lanier must predict six-territory behavior on the part of its rival and proceed to reexamine its remaining options. Having eliminated Sharp's dominated strategy in the second column, Lanier now has an unambiguously preferred *strategy* of providing fast-response repairs in only six territories itself. {Six, Six} is therefore the *equilibrium strategy* pair. That is, by applying the concept of a dominant strategy equilibrium to the prediction of its rival's behavior, Lanier can iterate back to analyze its own best action. {Six, Six} is therefore referred to as an **iterated dominant strategy** equilibrium.

Iterated Dominant Strategy
An action rule that maximizes self-interest in light of the predictable dominant-strategy behavior of other players.

This concept of eliminating dominated strategies in simultaneous games and then iterating back to one's remaining choices first appeared in *The Theory of Games and Economic Behavior* (1944) by John von Neumann and Oskar Morgenstern.[2] Von Neumann and Morgenstern confined their analysis primarily to cooperative games, in which players can form coalitions, arrange side payments, and enter into binding agreements. John Nash, Reinhard Selten, and John Harsanyi won the 1994 Nobel Prize in economics for their extension of strategic equilibrium concepts to noncooperative games, sequential games, and games of imperfect information. John Nash's life was celebrated in the book by Sylvia Nasar, *A Beautiful Mind,* and the subsequent movie starring Russell Crowe.

EXAMPLE

The Nobel Prize Goes to Three Game Theorists

Nash, Selten, and Harsanyi won the 1994 Nobel Prize for their work on equilibrium strategies in sequential games ranging from chess and poker to central bank interventions, limit pricing to deter entry, research and development competitions, and the auctioning of the radio magnetic spectrum. Not infrequently, multiple equilibria arise in such games. Another implication is that the order of play can affect strategic decisions; moving first in a preemptive product development can often bar a competitor's threatened entry. In other circumstances, making the last response in the endgame, as dynamic technology takes a new direction, can secure a strategic advantage. Distinguishing between these and other complex paths to the most profitable strategy is the role of equilibrium strategies in game theory.

Cooperative and Noncooperative Games

Cooperative Games
Game structures that allow coalition formation, side payments, and binding third-party enforceable agreements.

The fact that in a **cooperative game** players can form coalitions, make side payments, and communicate to one another their private information about their own prices, profit margins, or variable costs has limited the usefulness of cooperative game theory in business settings. An illustration of a side payment in cooperative games is the mandatory compensation scheme a manufacturer might impose when one sales representative violates another's exclusive territory. Or, suppose in the previous Lanier Now and Sharp ER example that the two firms got together to arrange a side payment to ensure a strategic equilibrium of {Six, Six}. As you may already suspect, most such cooperative game agreements between arm's-length competitors to exchange price information or arrange side payments are per se violations of the

[2] Two other useful volumes on modern game theory are A. Dixit and S. Skeath, *Games of Strategy* (New York, Norton, 1999), and Eric Rasmussen, *Games and Information,* 2d ed. (Cambridge, MA: Basil Blackwell, 1993).

antitrust laws in the United States and Western Europe.[3] For these reasons, business strategists paid relatively little attention to game theory until *noncooperative* strategic equilibrium concepts were developed.

Noncooperative Games

Game structures that prohibit collusion, side payments, and binding agreements enforced by third parties.

Noncooperative games prohibit collusive communication, side payments, and third-party enforceable binding agreements. Instead, such games focus on self-enforcing reliance relationships to characterize strategic equilibrium and predict rival response. One example we already encountered in Chapter 10 is the mutual reliance between buyers of high-priced experience goods such as used cars and sellers with nonredeployable assets (e.g., CARMAX advertising). Other examples include computer companies who build operating systems to a common standard that can communicate across PC platforms, or competing airlines who announce high fares day after day despite the quick but short-lived attraction of breaking out as a renegade discounter. Clearly, these noncooperative games differ from cooperative games in important ways that make them more applicable to business strategy.

OTHER TYPES OF GAMES

Strategy games are also classified according to the number of players involved, the compatibility of their interests, and the number of replays of the game. We analyzed both these games as *single-period ("one-shot") games.* The ongoing rivalry between the players in "Guarder-Marauder" and in "Six or Seven Territories" is highly pertinent to the strategic situation; we will turn our attention next to the distinct and somewhat paradoxical implications of so-called *repeated games.* In a *two-person game,* each player attempts to obtain as much as possible from the other player through whatever methods of cooperation, bargaining, or threatening are available. *N-person games* are more difficult to analyze because subsets of players can form coalitions to impose solutions on the rest of the players. Coalitions can be of any size and can break up and re-form as the game proceeds. Parliamentary government is the classic example of *n*-person games. Although the possibility of coalitions adds greatly to the richness of the types of situations that can be considered by game theory, coalitions add substantial complexity to the theory required to analyze such games.

Two-Person Zero-Sum Games

Game in which net gains for one player necessarily imply equal net losses for the other player.

In a **two-person zero-sum game,** the players have exactly opposite interests; one player's gain is the other player's loss, and vice versa. "Guarder-Marauder" serves as an intuitive example. Although a number of parlor games and some military applications can be analyzed with zero-sum games, most real-life conflict-of-interest situations do not fit within this category. In contrast, in a *two-person non-zero-sum game,* both players may gain or lose depending on the actions each chooses to take. "Six or Seven Territories" is a non-zero-sum game; limiting competition to six territories raises the total profit from the interaction to $110 rather than $90. In all such games at least one outcome is jointly preferred, and consequently, the players may be able to increase their payoffs through some form of coordination. Perhaps the most famous generic structure for non-zero-sum games is the *Prisoner's Dilemma.* Many real-world situations, such as duopoly pricing between Pepsi and Coke, experience good transactions for a used car, and bargaining with channel partners in manufacturer-distributor games, can be represented as a Prisoner's Dilemma.

[3] For example, the antitrust opinions in *U.S. v. National Gypsum,* 428 U.S. 422 (1978) and *U.S. v. Airline Tariff Publishing Co., et al.,* 92-52854 (1992) expressly prohibited the exchange of preannouncement price lists between competitors.

Analyzying Simultaneous Games

The Prisoner's Dilemma

In the Prisoner's Dilemma, two suspects are accused of jointly committing a crime. To convict the suspects, however, a confession is needed from one or both of them. They are separated and no information can pass between them, making it a noncooperative game. If neither suspect confesses, the prosecutor will be unable to convict them of the crime and each suspect will receive only a short-term (1-year) prison sentence. If one suspect confesses (i.e., turns state's evidence) and the other does not, then the one confessing will receive a suspended sentence, and the other will receive a long 15-year prison sentence. If both suspects confess, then each will receive an intermediate 6-year prison sentence. Each suspect must decide, under these conditions, whether to confess. This conflict-of-interest situation can be represented in a game matrix such as the one shown in Table 13.3.

Maximin Strategy

A criterion for selecting actions that minimize absolute losses.

This game can be examined by using the concept of a minimum security level that arises when players "worst case" the situation. A **maximin strategy** then selects the maximum payoff when worst-case scenarios arise. For Suspect 2 (the column player), the minimum payoff from his choosing "Not Confess" is a 15-year prison sentence arising when Suspect 1 confesses (in the bottom row) and the minimum payoff from his choosing "Confess" is a 6-year prison sentence arising again when Suspect 1 confesses. So, maximizing the security level would therefore motivate Suspect 2 to choose the second alternative of confessing in order to avoid the possibility of a still worse outcome from not confessing. Similar reasoning holds true for Suspect 1, and she also would be motivated to choose the alternative of confessing her guilt. Thus, the second alternative for each player "Confess" dominates the other strategy "Not Confess" and {Confess, Confess} constitutes a dominant strategy equilibrium strategy pair and isolates the predictable solution of the players.[4]

In this game both suspects would clearly receive a larger payoff (i.e., a shorter sentence) if they both decided to choose their first alternatives ("Not Confess").

Table 13.3 Prisoner's Dilemma Payoff Matrix

		Suspect 2: Not Confess	Suspect 2: Confess
Suspect 1	Not Confess	1-year prison term for each suspect	15-year prison term for Suspect 1 Suspended sentence for Suspect 2
	Confess	Suspended sentence for Suspect 1 15-year prison term for Suspect 2	6-year prison term for each suspect

[4] Maximin strategy will often yield actions that are not aligned with dominant strategy equilibrium if the decision maker is focused on maximizing gains or expected value of net gains rather than just minimizing absolute losses. A related strategy focuses on the minimization of opportunity losses, sometimes called minimax regret.

However, in seeking to maximize their predictable payoffs (or, more accurately, to maximize their security levels), the first alternative is not a rational choice for either suspect. The players could of course agree in advance to maintain their innocence. But without strong sanctions to force one another to adhere to the agreement, each would be tempted to double-cross the other by confessing his or her guilt. Whichever suspect breaks the agreement first has the possibility of reducing his or her sentence from a six-year prison term to a suspended sentence.

The analogy to pricing and output decisions among firms in oligopolistic industries is striking. Consider two cruise lines—Carnival and Royal Caribbean—that operate the only three-day Caribbean cruises from Miami. If each firm acts independently to maximize its own profits, the long-run (Cournot equilibrium) profit-maximizing price is \$300 per person. If two firms act jointly to maximize total industry profits, the profit-maximizing price is \$450. Assume that these two prices are the only prices under consideration.

Simultaneous Game

A strategy game in which players must choose their actions simultaneously.

Sequential Game

A game with an explicit order of play.

Both firms must decide their action without knowing their rival's decision, which is the essence of a **simultaneous game.** Although **sequential game** reasoning is critical to the successful conduct of some business strategy, many decisions must be made simultaneously with one's rivals. Consider offers in a silent auction, release dates for fashion clothing collections, promotional ads to meet a newspaper deadline, and posted price announcements at an electronic clearinghouse sponsored by the airline or cruise ship industry.

The payoffs to each cruise ship firm are shown in Table 13.4. The below-diagonal number in each cell is the payoff to Royal Caribbean, and the above-diagonal number is the payoff to Carnival. Each firm is reluctant to choose the (jointly) more profitable \$450 price. If either firm reneges and discounts to \$300, then the firm that charges \$450 will earn significantly lower profits than the rival. This game has a typical Prisoner's Dilemma ordering of outcomes. As we have seen, unilaterally cooperating by announcing high prices under such circumstances is foolish. For example, the payoff for Carnival from unilateral defection (\$375,000) exceeds the payoff from mutual cooperation at high prices (\$275,000), which itself exceeds the payoff from mutual defection at low prices (\$185,000), which finally exceeds the payoff from unilateral cooperation (\$60,000), which makes Carnival's dominant strategy to defect.

Royal Caribbean (RC) has no such dominant strategy. However, because RC can predict Carnival's behavior, by eliminating the prospect of Carnival's dominated

Table 13.4 Cruise Ship Pricing with Dominant Strategy

		Carnival \$450	Carnival \$300
Royal Caribbean	\$450	\$275 (above diagonal) / \$350 (below diagonal)	\$375 (above diagonal) / \$50 (below diagonal)
	\$350	\$60 (above diagonal) / \$320 (below diagonal)	\$185 (above diagonal) / \$175 (below diagonal)

Notes: Column-player payoffs (in thousands) are above the diagonal. Row-player payoffs are below the diagonal.

$450 strategy, RC can iterate to a preferable strategy itself. Therefore, Royal Caribbean's behavior is also quite predictable, and the iterated dominant strategy equilibrium proves to be {$300, $300} or {Defect, Defect} just as in Prisoner's Dilemma itself. The Prisoner's Dilemma facing Royal Caribbean and Carnival is a noncooperative positive-sum game of coordination. In the next section we will study how to escape the dilemma by changing the structure of such games.

Dominant Strategy and Nash Equilibrium Strategy Defined

Note that a dominated strategy is not necessary for both cruise ship companies to reach an iterated dominant strategy equilibrium. The reason is that a dominant strategy requires no particular optimal or suboptimal response behavior on the part of anyone else. It is defined as an action for player i that is an optimal action $\{a_i^*\}$ in the strong sense that no matter what other players do, the payoff for player i, $\Pi_i\,\{a_i^*, a_{-i}\}$ exceeds the payoff for player i from any other action, $\Pi_i\,\{a_i, a_{-i}\}$[5]

$$\Pi_i\,\{a_i^*, a_{-i}\} > \Pi_i\,\{a_i, a_{-i}\} \qquad [13.1]$$

Consequently, one dominant strategy is quite enough to predict rival behavior and therefore strategic equilibrium in any two-person one-shot simultaneous game. Once Carnival's dominant strategy (i.e., to defect and cut prices to $300) has been identified, Royal Caribbean's behavior (i.e., to also defect) is easily predictable. We have seen this outcome in "Six or Seven Territories?" and in "Marauder-Guarder."

What about simultaneous games without any dominant strategy? To examine this question we now turn to a one-shot simultaneous price announcement game between PepsiCo and Coca-Cola. Each week both firms must choose whether to maintain or discount in their grocery store distribution channels. The payoffs per week per store are shown in Table 13.5. As shown in the northeast cell, if Coca-Cola unilaterally defects to discounting, then Coca-Cola's payoff increases from $13,000 to $16,000, while PepsiCo's payoff declines by 25 percent from $12,000 to $9,000. Similarly, PepsiCo can turn the tables on Coca-Cola by unilaterally discounting to increase operating profits by 16% from $12,000 to $14,000 while Coca-Cola profits would decline from 13,000 to $10,500. Table 13.5 shows no dominant strategy. PepsiCo wants to discount when Coca-Cola maintains higher prices ($14,000 > $12,000), but just as clearly PepsiCo wants to maintain higher prices when Coca-Cola discounts ($9,000 > $6,300). And the same ambiguity is present for Coca-Cola. What criteria allow the prediction of rival behavior in this game of "Renegade Discounting"?

Best-Reply Response
An action that maximizes self-interest from among feasible choices.

Nash Equilibrium Strategy
An equilibrium concept for nondominant strategy games.

The answer lies in a reflexive application of the concept of **best-reply response.** If an action were the best reply to a rival's action, which in turn was the best reply to the original action, the parties would have identified an equilibrium strategy. More formally, a **Nash equilibrium strategy** is defined as an action for player i that is conditionally optimal $\{a_i^*\}$ in that the payoff for player i, given best-reply responses by rivals $\Pi_i\,\{a_i^*, a_{-i}^*\}$, exceeds the payoff for player i from any other action $\Pi_i\,\{a_i, a_{-i}^*\}$ given best-reply responses of rivals:

$$\Pi_i\,\{a_i^*, a_{-i}^*\} > \Pi_i\,\{a_i, a_{-i}^*\} \qquad [13.2]$$

In Renegade Discounting, the two pure Nash equilibria are {Maintain_p^*, Discount_c^*} and {Discount_p^*, Maintain_c^*} where the subscripts refer to PepsiCo and Coca-Cola.

[5] A starred action refers to a maximizing choice; here, it is an action that results from maximizing profit.

Table 13.5 Renegade Discounting in Soft Drinks with No Dominant Strategy

		Coca-Cola: Maintain High Prices	Coca-Cola: Discount Low Prices
PepsiCo	Maintain High Prices	$12,000 \ $13,000	$9,000 \ $16,000
	Discount Low Prices	$14,000 \ $10,500	$6,300 \ $8,000

Note: Column-player payoffs (in thousands) are above the diagonal. Row-player payoffs are below the diagonal.

Recall that the order of play is not important in this game; we could have just as easily reversed these strategy pairs and listed Coca-Cola rather than PepsiCo first. The actual rivals appear to have perceived precisely this point because, for 42 weeks in 1992, they took turns discounting on the endcaps in grocery stores.

What is notable about these Nash equilibrium strategies is that they are nonunique. The multiple equilibria occur because the Nash equilibrium concept is less demanding (i.e., easier to satisfy) than dominant strategy equilibrium. The latter requires that an action be optimal for every possible rival response, whereas Nash equilibrium requires only that an action be optimal for a best-reply rival response. However, this knowledge does not help solve PepsiCo's problem as to what price to announce next. Remember that each bottler is announcing its price without knowing until afterwards what its rival announced.

If PepsiCo believed Coca-Cola would discount half the time and maintain half the time, the expected value of PepsiCo's maintaining is $10,500 (namely, 0.5 × $12,000 + 0.5 × $9,000), whereas the expected value of PepsiCo's discounting is smaller (i.e., only $10,150). These results would seem to suggest a preference for maintaining high prices, but again, if PepsiCo kept its prices predictably high, Coca-Cola could unilaterally defect and earn $16,000, whereas PepsiCo would then realize only $9,000. So how can PepsiCo avoid tipping its hand and ending up with the $9,000 outcome rather than its own $14,000 defection outcome too often?

The answer lies in PepsiCo's randomizing the pricing process. PepsiCo must figure out what automated pricing response would make Coca-Cola indifferent between maintaining and discounting and thereby willing to randomize its own price announcement. That is, what probability of discounting by PepsiCo would make Coca-Cola indifferent by equating Coca-Cola's expected payoff from maintaining to its expected payoff from discounting? Interestingly, because the payoffs are asymmetrical, the desired probability is not 0.5. Let's see what the solution is. Using p to represent the probability that PepsiCo maintains and $(1 - p)$ if it discounts, we calculate

$$(p)\$13{,}000 + (1 - p)\$10{,}500 = (p)\$16{,}000 + (1 - p)\$8{,}000 \qquad [13.3]$$

where the Coca-Cola payoffs are arranged to correspond to the columns of Table 13.5. The solution probabilities $p = 0.454$ and $(1 - p) = 0.546$ make Coca-Cola indifferent and therefore PepsiCo less vulnerable to unilateral defection.

Note the mirror-image reflexivity associated with this Nash equilibrium solution: Coca-Cola faces a comparable payoff structure and strategy dilemma to that of PepsiCo, and would presumably want to know the probabilities of maintaining and discounting that would make PepsiCo indifferent between the two choices. Calculating as before

$$(p')\$12{,}000 + (1 - p')\$9{,}000 = (p')\$14{,}000 + (1 - p')\$6{,}300 \qquad [13.4]$$

where the PepsiCo payoffs are arranged to correspond to the rows of Table 13.5, we obtain $p' = 0.574$ and $(1 - p') = 0.426$. If randomized choice by PepsiCo is a best-reply response to Coca-Cola, and if Coca-Cola can then do no better, this renegade discounting game must have a third Nash equilibrium strategy—namely, {Maintain by PepsiCo with $p = 0.454$, Maintain by Coca-Cola with $p' = 0.574$}. This strategy pair is called a **mixed Nash equilibrium strategy.** A 0.454 probability weight on maintaining and a 0.546 probability weight on discounting by PepsiCo yields \$11,634 expected value for each of Coca-Cola's price announcement strategies. Similarly, a 0.574 probability weight on maintaining and a 0.426 probability weight on discounting by Coca-Cola yields \$10,720 expected value for each of PepsiCo's price announcement strategies. The strategic equilibrium solution for this game therefore contains two pure and one mixed Nash strategy: {Maintain_p^*, Discount_c^*}, {Discount_p^*, Maintain_c^*}, and {$\text{Maintain}_p^* = 0.454$, $\text{Maintain}_c^* = 0.574$}.

Mixed Nash Equilibrium Strategy
A strategic equilibrium concept involving randomized behavior.

Using a computer program that randomizes an unfair coin toss is one way to implement this mixed Nash strategy. In principle, however, none of these three Nash equilibrium strategies is preferable to any other. In a one-shot play of Renegade Discounting, all four cells in Table 13.5 still arise. The {\$6,300, \$8,000} outcome in the southeast cell and the {\$12,000, \$13,000} outcome in the northwest cell as well as the two asymmetric outcomes that correspond to our two pure Nash strategies will all sometimes arise. In a noncooperative simultaneous one-shot game that allows no communication in advance, no side payments, and no binding agreements, players simply cannot avoid this multiplicity of possible strategic equilibria. In practice, therefore, a one-shot play of any of the three Nash strategies in the Renegade Discounting game can work out well or badly.

Of course, the {\$12,000, \$13,000} outcome is best of all. In the next section we will see how to secure this win-win outcome by introducing repeated plays, imperfect information, and credibility mechanisms to convert this simultaneous game into a sequential game. Barry Nalebuff, Yale professor and author of the widely read *Thinking Strategically,* calls it "changing the nature of competition" and distinguishes it from "collusion," which would violate the antitrust laws.[6]

THE ESCAPE FROM PRISONER'S DILEMMA

MULTIPERIOD PUNISHMENT AND REWARD SCHEMES IN REPEATED PLAY GAMES

In this section, we relax the assumptions of single-play, complete, and perfect information games. Let's again look at the PepsiCo and Coca-Cola example with the Prisoner's Dilemma payoff structure as shown in Table 13.6. Both PepsiCo and Coca-Cola are worse off if either unilaterally defects from maintaining high prices.

[6] See A. Dixit and B. Nalebuff, *Thinking Strategically* (New York: Norton, 1993); and "Businessman's Dilemma," *Forbes* (October 11, 1993), p. 107.

Table 13.6 Repeated Prisoner's Dilemma in Soft Drinks

		Coca-Cola	
		Maintain High Prices	Discount
PepsiCo	Maintain High Prices	$12,000 \ $12,000	$6,000 \ $17,000
	Discount	$17,000 \ $6,000	$8,000 \ $8,000

Each soft drink bottler would like to pursue the $12,000 payoff, but the only way to avoid the vulnerability of a unilateral defection is by defecting oneself! Dominant strategy drives both players to discount their 12-packs in the one-shot game. However, surely PepsiCo and Coca-Cola recognize they are engaged in an ongoing competitive process, not a one-shot (i.e., single-play) game. Week after week, they will encounter one another in many future replays of this pricing game at grocery and convenience stores nationwide. Consequently, tacit cooperation rather than dogmatic price cutting has a chance to evolve.

Grim Trigger Strategy
A strategy involving infinitely long punishment schemes.

Suppose Coca-Cola begins the process by announcing a high price in Period 1. Coke's intention is to play that price continuously until PepsiCo defects and thereafter to never announce High again, which is a so-called **grim trigger strategy.** Any move by PepsiCo away from cooperative High pricing, and Coca-Cola's punishment is immediate and never-ending. Multiperiod punishment schemes are a key to inducing cooperation in Prisoner's Dilemma games, whether it is cruise ship, airline, or soft drink companies. In this case, PepsiCo compares the perpetuity opportunity loss of ($12,000 − $8,000) discounted at the interest rate r per period to the one-time gain from defection of ($17,000 − $12,000):

$$\$4{,}000/r > \$5{,}000 \quad \text{if} \quad r < 0.8 \qquad [13.5]$$

Folk Theorem
A conclusion about cooperation in repeated Prisoner's Dilemma.

The interpretation is straightforward. At any discount rate less than 80 percent, PepsiCo's future gains from cooperatively maintaining high prices outweigh the one-time gains from defection. Thus, the dominant strategy to defect in one-shot games is no longer attractive. This calculation and conclusion reflect a generalizable **Folk theorem,** which states that for any payoff structure, a discount rate always exists that is low enough to induce cooperation in an infinitely repeated Prisoner's Dilemma. So, a grim trigger strategy can induce cooperation in an infinitely repeated Prisoner's Dilemma.[7]

However, because companies do not last forever, the Folk theorem raises an obvious question, "What about for shorter periods, say 20 weeks?" The 20-period calculation is easily done; r now must be less than 79 percent. But if 20 weeks, what about 10, and if 10, what about for 2 weeks? Suppose it is now the beginning of

Trembling Hand Trigger Strategy
A punishment mechanism that forgives random mistakes and miscommunications.

[7] Of course, one transparent disadvantage of grim trigger strategies is that cooperative outcomes cannot survive a single small mistake in reasoning or miscommunication by either player. Selten's concept of a **trembling hand trigger strategy** allows one grace period of misplay by the other party before imposing the grim punishment for defection. Of course, a wily rival who understands this strategy will take advantage of its opponent by claiming just as many one-period "mistakes" of defection as it can get away with.

Week 2. We know we are out of this "cooperative" structure next week (i.e., Week 3), so our remaining incentive to maintain high prices is only $4,000/(1 + *r*), and our incentive to defect is $5,000. Now all of a sudden, for any discount rate, each player is better off defecting. This result is also generalizable. The last play of a finitely repeated Prisoner's Dilemma has the same incentives as a one-shot Prisoner's Dilemma; everybody defects. Therefore, one period away from the endgame of a finitely repeated play Prisoner's Dilemma, neither party has an incentive to maintain its reputation for cooperating.

Unraveling and the Chain Store Paradox

Unraveling Problem
A failure of cooperation in games of finite length.

Infinitely Repeated Games
A game that lasts forever.

Endgame Reasoning
An analysis of the final decision in a sequential game.

The prospects for cooperation in any *finitely* repeated Prisoner's Dilemma are poor, because what is true for a 2-period game must be true by backwards induction for a 3-period game. If you know in the 2-period game that it pays to defect, then in the 3-period game you must know that a certain defection is only one period away, therefore, you should defect now. And if that is so for a 3-period game, then so too for a 4-period game, and so on, even for a 20-period game. Reinhard Selten investigated this **unraveling problem** for finitely repeated Prisoner's Dilemmas in the context of chain store incumbents facing repeated entry threats from rivals.[8] In a Prisoner's Dilemma setting like those we've been examining, the established firm has a dominant strategy to accommodate the new entrant. But one's intuition says that in the face of enough repetitions of the chain store competition, the established firm's reputation for fighting entry can pay off. And in the extreme, this intuition is absolutely correct. In **infinitely repeated games,** the Folk theorem does apply. However, with any fewer repetitions, in even the enormous number of chain store competitions that might face a McDonald's or a Wal-Mart, the cooperative equilibrium unravels.

Reinhard Selten invented the concept of **endgame reasoning** to show this paradoxical result and to emphasize the sequential nature of reputation effects. Endgame reasoning always entails looking ahead to the last play in an ordered sequence of plays, identifying the player whose decisions will control the outcome of the endgame, and then predicting that player's best-reply response. In Figure 13.2 we have a chain store Incumbent (I) who accommodates or fights in response to a Potential Entrant (PE) who stays out or enters. Accommodation forgoes $20,000 of the incumbent chain store's profit ($100,000 − $80,000) and induces future entry, but fighting the present entry to acquire a reputation for toughness in future possible entry situations entails actual losses now (−$10,000). Conceive of the displayed game tree as the last three encounters of a 20-chain store competition perceived by both players from the start. Looking ahead to the endgame, it is clear that the incumbent will accommodate in the last submarket. At decision C, the $100,000 to accommodate exceeds the $60,000 to fight, and the $80,000 to accommodate at decision B exceeds the −$10,000 to fight. More importantly, a tough reputation gains no future payoff thereafter because it is truly the endgame. Because the Potential Entrant also knows it is the endgame, entry will surely take place in that last submarket.

[8] See J. Harsanyi and R. Selten, *A General Theory of Equilibrium Selection in Games* (Cambridge: MIT Press, 1988); or for a less technical treatment, E. Rasmussen, *Games and Information,* 2d ed. (Cambridge: Blackwell, 1994), Chapter 5.

Figure 13.2 The Chain Store Paradox

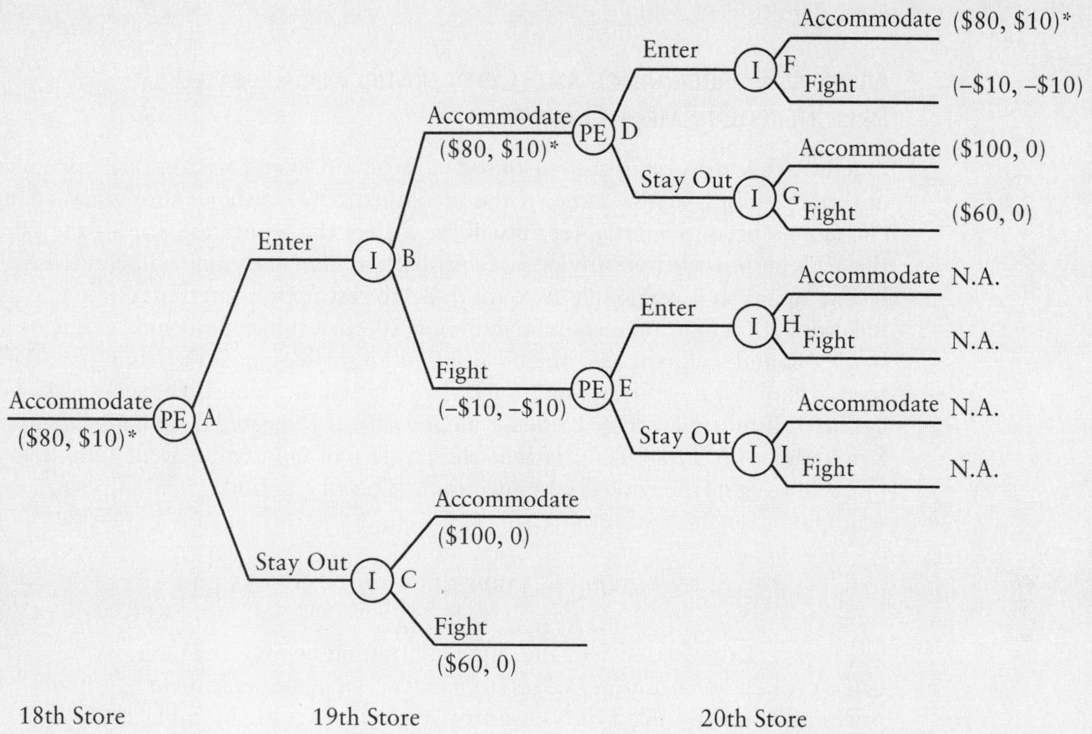

Note: Payoffs are listed (Incumbent, Potential Entrant) in thousands. N.A. (not applicable).

Now, in looking back to the previous submarket (i.e., the 19th store), the incumbent realizes that its rival's subsequent entry in the 20th submarket is certain and therefore that, again, any attempt to aquire an enhanced reputation for fighting is useless in that 19th submarket. Accommodate is therefore the best-reply response in the proper subgame from Node B onward to the endgame. Because the entrant can predict this decision as well, entry occurs in the 19th submarket at Node A. But what is true of the 19th must therefore be true of the 18th, and the 17th, and so forth, right back to the start of the game.

Chain Store Paradox

A prediction of always-accommodative behavior by incumbents facing entry threats.

This *backwards induction reasoning* leads to the **chain store paradox.** We can calculate in Submarket 1 that at reasonable rates of discount the incumbent may well have a sufficient net present value of profits from deterring future entry to justify fighting now rather than accommodating. Yet, the predictability of its future accommodation jeopardizes the credibility of the incumbent's present fighting. This predictability of selecting accommodation as a best-reply response all the way out to the endgame means the reputation effects of any present fighting unravel. Accommodation therefore occurs in every submarket or every period in the 20-submarket/20-period game just as we argued earlier it would in the 2-submarket/2-period game.

Our intuition tells us otherwise, especially when a long line of potential entrants is waiting in the wings. Hence, the term chain store *paradox*. And, as we shall now see, changing some other features of the chain store decision problem can overturn this counterintuitive result.

Mutual Forbearance and Cooperation in Repeated Prisoner's Dilemma Games

One way to short-circuit the reasoning of the chain store paradox is to introduce an uncertain ending of the game. If the incumbent can never be sure whether future encounters beyond Submarket 20 will arise, then the reputation effect of fighting in the 19th period returns. Any positive probability that the game will continue is sufficient (again, at low enough discount rates) to restore the deterrent effect of fighting in Period 20. If fighting is rational in Period 20, then the incumbent is willing to fight in 19, 18, and so forth, back to Period 1. And if the incumbent is willing in Period 1, then it may not have to because the other firm will not enter. The analogous implication in a finitely repeated pricing game such as Repeated Prisoner's Dilemma in Soft Drinks (in Table 13.6) is that the rivals will cooperate by maintaining high prices as long as the endgame is uncertain. With one period remaining, we can then write Equation 13.5 as

$$\$4{,}000 + \$4{,}000 \times \frac{1}{(1 + r)} \times p > \$5{,}000 \qquad [13.6]$$

where p is the probability of the game continuing beyond the next period. For $r = 0.1$, a probability as low as 0.28 is sufficient to elicit cooperation in maintaining high prices and a {\$12,000, \$12,000} northwest cell outcome in Table 13.6. Therefore, infinite repetition is not required to induce cooperation in Prisoner's Dilemmas; an uncertain ending will suffice.

EXAMPLE

A Violation of the Chain Store Paradox: Semiconductor Pricing at Intel, NEC, and AMD[9]

These insights seem especially important in industries with fast-changing technology, such as computer chips and consumer electronics, where cost disadvantages that might end an incumbent's business are seldom permanent because the technology changes so often. One illustration is the semiconductor industry, where Intel, AMD, and Motorola have recently returned to dominance after almost being displaced by Japanese firms such as Hitachi, NEC, and Toshiba in the 1990s.

With each successive generation of chips (see Table 13.7), the market leaders practice life cycle pricing techniques. After a period of high target pricing and value-based pricing, Intel, with more than 70 percent of the worldwide market, limits price rather than accommodate AMD with 21 percent, Motorola with 5 percent and numerous smaller competitors. That is, chip prices are slashed in an attempt to deter entry by the imitators. Then, with uncertain timing, the whole process repeats itself. New chips are introduced at high prices, imitators reverse-engineer the design, and limit pricing begins again. The uncertain endpoint of the successive

[9] Based on *Investor's Business Daily* (January 13, 1998), p. A8.

Table 13.7 Major Intel Microprocessors and Clock Speed

Year	Microprocessor	MHz	Year	Microprocessor	MHz
1979	8088	5	1997	Pentium II	233
1982	286	6	1999	Pentium III	333
1985	386	16	2002	Pentium IV	550
1989	486	25	2004	Celeron M	1200
1993	Pentium	60	2005	Pentium M	1600
1995	Pentium Pro	150	2006	Core2 Duo	2130

chip generation games leads to a violation of the chain store paradox and increased likelihood of higher prices, just as in soft drink pricing between Coca-Cola and PepsiCo.

Bayesian Reputation Effects

A second ingenious escape from Prisoner's Dilemma incorporates Bayesian reputation effects about opponent type, based on the work of Nobel laureate John Harsanyi. It involves estimating the likelihood of various opponent moves based on past events. If some irrational "crazies" who do not always maximize their payoffs are known to exist in the market, a perfectly sane incumbent might end up taking actions that seem crazy. The intent of the incumbent is to secure an asymmetric information pooling equilibrium in which the incumbent is indistinguishable from the crazies.[10] An example would be an automobile manufacturing incumbent that "predates"—that is, prices its product below its variable cost, even though the operating losses from such a strategy may not be recoverable in excess profits later. Japanese automobile manufacturers are often accused of such "dumping" in the offshore auto markets, especially in Europe.

EXAMPLE

Brown and Williamson's Reputation for Predating

The U.S. Supreme Court has addressed these issues and thereby set a standard for judging predatory pricing behavior by U.S. firms. In *Brooke Group Ltd. v. Brown and Williamson Tobacco Company,* 113 U.S. 2578 (1993), the Court held that pricing generic cigarettes below cost was not evidence of an undesirable predatory intent to monopolize a market because Brown and Williamson had no opportunity thereafter to earn excess profits and recoup its losses from the alleged predatory period. Similarly, when Kodak priced its Instamatic film camera at $11.95 despite a $28 direct manufacturing cost, it faced little prospect of later recovering the $16.05 operating loss per camera. Instead, this pricing tactic was reasonable as an attempt to clear inventory quickly before exiting the Instamatic submarket.

Whether the Court in these cases looked deeply enough into the long-term effect of deterring effective entry through pricing reputation effects is a hotly debated antitrust

[10] See R. Gibbons, "An Introduction to Applicable Game Theory," *Journal of Economic Perspectives* 11, no. 1 (Winter 1997), pp. 140–147; and Rasmussen, op. cit., pp. 352–356.

issue. Under incomplete information about opponent types, behaving like a "crazy," who predatorily prices below cost when it's unlikely to recover the losses, may deter an opponent's entry. This reputation effect of becoming known as a firm who might well price below cost is more valuable when the cost of new entrants is high, brand loyalty to incumbents is weak, and the number of potential entrants is large.

American Airlines discouraged the discounters Vanguard, Sunjet, and Western Pacific from remaining in the Dallas–Ft. Worth airline market using such tactics. In May 2001, American's indictment for predation was dismissed on the grounds that at no point did American lower price below its average variable cost. Hard-nosed competitive tactics that remain within the boundaries of recovering average variable cost are legal, because antitrust law exists to protect competition (encouraging lower prices for consumers), not to protect individual competitors.

Winning Strategies in Evolutionary Computer Tournaments: Tit for Tat

Robert Axelrod was intrigued by the reasons why people who are ardently pursuing their own goals often end up cooperating with competitors in long-term interactions.[11] He investigated the question of optimal strategy in repeated Prisoner's Dilemma by conducting a computer simulation in which 151 strategies competed against one another 1,000 times. He discovered that those strategies that finished highest in the computer tournament had several characteristics in common. First, winning strategies are clear and simple in order to avoid triggering mistakes by one's rival cooperators. Second, winning strategies make unilateral attempts to cooperate; they never initiate defection. Third, as we would expect, all winning strategies are provokable—they have credible commitments to some punishment rule. Interestingly, limited-duration punishment schemes that displayed forgiveness won out over maximal-punishment grim trigger strategies that do not. The reason seemed to be that winning strategies recover from misperceptions, miscommunications, and strategic mistakes; reprisals need not be self-perpetuating.

What types of actual strategies would you guess best fit these winning criteria? Surprisingly, "Tit for Tat" won the tournament! Repeating what your opponent did on the last round is simple and clearly provokable, but consistent with unilaterally initiating cooperation yourself. And perhaps most importantly, "Tit for Tat" is forgiving. After a single-period punishment, it reverts to cooperating as soon as the opponent/cooperator does so.

For example, one possible approach to managing competition for cruise ship companies Carnival and Royal Caribbean (RC) in Table 13.8 is to follow a Tit-for-Tat (TFT) decision rule. Royal Caribbean, who has a dominant $300 strategy, could signal a **conspicuous focal point** by promoting "staterooms" (rather than smaller, less well-appointed "cabins") as an industry standard and then choosing the $450 pricing strategy in the first period. Thereafter, Royal Caribbean would select the same pricing strategy in the next period as Carnival chose in the previous period. For example, if Carnival charges $450 in the current period, then Royal Caribbean

Conspicuous Focal Point

An outcome that attracts mutual cooperation.

[11] Robert Axelrod, *The Evolution of Cooperation* (New York: Basic Books, 1984). See also "Evolutionary Economics," *Forbes* (October 11, 1993), p. 110; and Jill Neimark, "Tit for Tat: A Game of Survival," *Success* (May 1987), p. 62.

Table 13.8 Cruise Ship Pricing with Price Matching

		Carnival Pricing Policy		
		$450	$300	"Match"
Royal Caribbean Pricing Policy	$450	$350 \ $275	$150 \ $375	$350 \ $275
	$300	$320 \ $160	$175 \ $185	$175 \ $185
	"Match"	$350 \ $275	$175 \ $185	$350 \ $275

Note: Column-player payoffs above the diagonal in $ thousands.

would do likewise in the next period. On the other hand, if Carnival defects and charges $300 in the current period, then Royal Caribbean would retaliate by charging the same $300 price next period. Through repeated plays, the participants may learn the Tit-for-Tat decision rule being applied by their competitor.

PRICE-MATCHING GUARANTEES

How should Carnival respond to a Tit-for-Tat decision rule by Royal Caribbean? Let's look at the analogies between this limited duration punishment scheme and a matching price guarantee. In Table 13.8, a matching price guarantee by Royal Caribbean substantially reduces Carnival's incentive to discount down to $300 when RC has announced $450 prices. Under the heading "$300" in the second column, one sees that Carnival's $300 discounted price can no longer generate the $375,000 payoff of the first row but instead simply realizes the $185,000 payoff from a matching price policy by RC. This $185,000 payoff that arises is the same when both firms discount to $300. Because RC's customers will monitor and enforce RC's matching price guarantee by requesting rebates of ($450 − $300 =) $150 from RC whenever Carnival discounts to $300, Carnival cannot hope to gain a significant share of RC's customers by discounting.

To place Royal Caribbean in the same position, Carnival will likely announce a matching price guarantee as protection in those times when RC might try a sneak discount attack on Carnival's market share. Assuming, as we did earlier, that Royal Caribbean initiates play with a $450 price announcement, both cruise companies will maintain $450 prices, effectively playing "Match, Match" and escaping the Prisoner's Dilemma by realizing the {$350,000, $275,000} payoff in the far northwest and far southeast cells. Like double-the-difference price guarantees, matching price guarantees increase the expected price level and hence the profitability in a tight oligopoly market.

Now, how does this outcome compare to Tit for Tat? Assume that no "Match" alternative is available in the game. Nevertheless, Carnival should see Royal Caribbean's TFT decision rule as a delayed matching price guarantee. That is, with a one-period lag, Royal Caribbean is going to match any discount that Carnival tries and subsequently match (again with a one-period lag) any return to high prices as soon as Carnival returns. These payoff paths are certain; no amount of apologizing by Carnival about mistakes and miscommunications can prevent RC's one-period punishment. Therefore, Carnival simply compares the profits from discounting unilaterally this period (\$375,000 − \$275,000) to a discounted opportunity loss from punishment next period (\$275,000 − \$160,000):

$$\$100{,}000 < \$115{,}000/(1 + r) \quad \text{if} \quad r < 0.15 \qquad [13.7]$$

As long as the discount rate is less than 15 percent and the continuation of this particular cruise route is certain for both firms, Carnival should not discount and thereby defect on the industry leader's pricing policy of \$450.

Of course, if the probability of continuance (p) falls below 1.0, a limited duration punishment scheme such as Tit for Tat becomes much less effective immediately. For example, multiplying the future opportunity loss from punishment next period by just 10 percent less than certainty of continuance,

$$\begin{aligned} \$100{,}000 &< \$115{,}000\,(1 - 0.1)/(1 + r) = \$103{,}500/(1 + r) \\ \$100{,}000 &< \$103{,}500/(1 + r) \quad \text{if} \quad r > 0.035 \end{aligned} \qquad [13.8]$$

implies that Carnival will defect and discount to attempt to gain market share any time the interest rate is greater than 3.5 percent.[12] Tit for Tat therefore is a more effective coordination device for oligopolists that expect to encounter one another again and again, such as PepsiCo and Coca-Cola, Nike and Reebok, United and American Airlines, Kodak and Fuji, Anheuser-Busch and Miller, and Carnival and Royal Caribbean.

Because the {\$450, \$450} actions yield \$90,000 more for Royal Caribbean than the iterated dominant strategy equilibrium {\$300, \$300}, Royal Caribbean may well initiate cooperation and thereafter play Tit for Tat. With rational, unconfused, and well-informed competitors, communication of conspicuous focal points and multiperiod punishment schemes can induce conditional cooperation in repeated Prisoner's Dilemma. Perhaps for this reason, the Third Federal Circuit Court prohibited airlines from signaling such coordination information to one another through their centralized reservation systems (see the following example). Business rivals often use self-enforcing reliance mechanisms to establish credible commitments precisely because they are limited by the antitrust statutes.

EXAMPLE

Signaling a Punishment Scheme: Northwest[13]

In the summer of 1989, America West announced a \$50 fare reduction for 21-day advance purchase tickets on the busy Minneapolis–Los Angeles route. Rather than cutting its own \$308 fare from its Minneapolis hub to match the America West \$258

[12] Equation 13.8 can also be written to highlight the interplay between p and r as

$$\$100{,}000 < \$115{,}000\,(0.9)/(1 + r) = \$115{,}000/(1 + R)$$

where R is the effective rate of interest $1/(1 + R) = (p/(1 + r) = 0.9/(1 + r)$. In the Tit for Tat example, because the probability of continuance is near 1.0, the effective rate of interest and the actual rate of interest are quite similar. For $r =$ 10 percent and $p = 0.9$, $p/(1 + r) = 0.9/1.1 = 0.82$, and therefore the effective rate of interest is 22 percent: $1/(1 + 0.22) = 0.82$. As p gets smaller, the effective and actual rates of interest diverge exponentially. For example, for an actual interest rate of 10 percent and $p = 0.55$, $p/(1 + r) = 0.55/1.1 = 0.5$, and therefore the effective rate of interest is 100 percent: $1/(1 + 1.0) = 0.5$.

[13] Based on "Fare Game," *Wall Street Journal* (June 28, 1990), p. A1; "Fare Warning," *Wall Street Journal* (October 9, 1990), p. B1; and "Why Northwest Gives Competition a Bad Name," *BusinessWeek* (March 16, 1998), p. 34.

fare, Northwest announced a $40 reduction (from $208 to $168) for 21-day advance purchase tickets on the busy Phoenix–New York route. America West's hub is in Phoenix. This retaliatory fare was labeled on the Airline Tariff Publishing computer system as available for only the next two days, with possible renewal thereafter. Five days later, America West canceled its $50 promotion on West Coast travel.

Price Signaling

A communication of price change plans, prohibited by antitrust law.

Antitrust law makes it illegal for companies to conspire to fix prices. **Signaling** the particulars of a multiperiod punishment scheme in order to elicit cooperation in maintaining high prices is seen as a violation of this provision of the Robinson-Patman Act. Northwest defended its actions as "competitive initiatives and responses consistent with independent self-interest" and therefore thoroughly legal. However, the Third Circuit Appeals Court was quite clear; signaling a limited-duration punishment schemes involving prices is not legal. *U.S. v. Airline Tariff Publishing Co. et al.*, 92-52854 (1992), expressly prohibited such preannouncements of price changes that might facilitate price coordination.

One reason is indicated by the pricing outcome in another of Northwest's routes (Detroit–Philadelphia) after a similar round of anticompetitive tactics. When Spirit Airline, a tiny discount carrier, entered that market in June 1996, one-way fares declined from $170 to $49 on all Northwest flights. Northwest increased flight frequency and drove Spirit from the market. Subsequently, Northwest cut flights and returned in 1997 to $230 one-way fares.

INDUSTRY STANDARDS AND REGULATORY CONSTRAINTS

Unlike in chess or poker, in any business strategy game the players are free to change the rules (i.e., the structure of the game itself). Mandatory industry standards or regulatory constraints are often a way of changing the structure of a simultaneous-play business rivalry into a sequential-play game. Java programming language for the Internet, the digital signal specifications for cell phones (CDMA, TDMA, GSM, and iDEN) or the specifications for high-definition television (the Motorola versus Sony standard) are examples of industry standards used in this way. By restricting the flexibility of one another's responses, rivals can often secure an escape from the dominant strategy payoffs of a Prisoner's Dilemma and achieve more profitable outcomes.

Consider the business-to-business sale of electrical equipment illustrated in Figure 13.3. General Electric would like to manufacture and distribute a high specifications ("Gold-plated") halogen recessed lighting fixture supported with full installation and after-sale service. Unfortunately, however, the GE distributor has higher payoffs from not providing full installation. Under those circumstances, GE is better off manufacturing a fixture that meets only minimal specifications. Because of the distributor's dominant strategy, the two companies earn payoffs {Worse, Better} and find themselves in a Prisoner's Dilemma. They would prefer the northwest cell {Better, Best}, but each would then be vulnerable to a defection by the other company, resulting in their Worst outcome.

By enlisting third parties (TP) such as Underwriters' Laboratory in specifying an installation standard or encouraging the adoption of local building codes that require full installation, General Electric and its distributors can escape the Prisoner's Dilemma. A General Electric distributor would then be engaged in an illegal ("below code") sale if it provided anything less than full installation, so General Electric can

Figure 13.3 Electrical Industry Standard Allows GE Distributor to Escape Prisoner's Dilemma

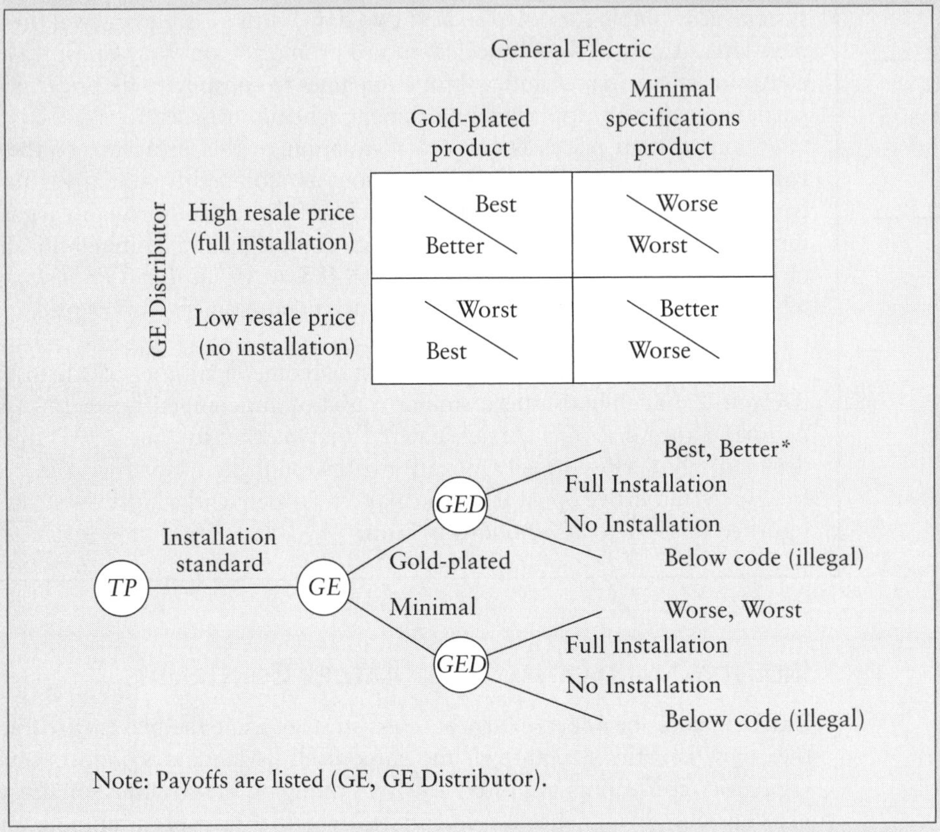

anticipate full installation and will therefore proceed to manufacture the high specifications product. The payoffs will then improve to {Better, Best}.

The same argument is often made by manufacturers who wish to limit their distributors' flexibility to initiate price discounts. Resale price maintenance (RPM) agreements prohibit retailers from cutting the price at which they resell the product below a manufacturer's suggested retail price. Most such restrictions on the vertical pricing relationship between manufacturers and distributors or distributors and retailers are illegal, especially when they appear motivated by the desire of competing retail dealers to reduce price competition. For example, Chevrolet dealers in Los Angeles once approached GM about using an RPM agreement to sanction the steep discounting of a "renegade" dealer who had markedly cut everyone's possible profit margins. In *United States v. GM* (1966), the Supreme Court declared this anticompetitive practice illegal per se.

Occasionally, however, a manufacturer or distributor can demonstrate a "legitimate manufacturer's interest" in regulatory or industry standards that place a floor under the resale prices of its products (e.g., a rare book distributor or Apple Computers).[14]

[14] See L. Telser, "Why Should Manufacturers Want Fair Trade II?" *Journal of Law and Economics* 33 (October 1990), pp. 409–417.

When one of these special exceptions is made and an RPM agreement is allowed, the parties have succeeded in using a regulatory mechanism to escape a Prisoner's Dilemma.

EXAMPLE

RESALE PRICE MAINTENANCE AGREEMENT: STRIDERITE[15]

In the late 1990s, Nintendo, New Balance Athletic, and StrideRite all paid multimillion dollar fines to settle charges that the manufacturers cut shipments to retail outlets that refused to charge the full MSRP (manufacturer's suggested retail price). In StrideRite's case, leading retailers were cut off if they refused to sell six styles of women's Keds at MSRP prices from \$20 to \$45. Although StrideRite insisted that it could suspend contracts with retailers who violated other company marketing policies and procedures, the government found that StrideRite had refused to deal with only those particular dealers who discounted Keds. The courts ruled StrideRite guilty of an anticompetitive business practice because the suspended dealers had been pressured by StrideRite to raise prices. Vertical requirements contracting between dealers and manufacturers about matters *other than resale price* is widespread and perfectly legal. Such mechanisms are a standard business contracting solution to the Prisoner's Dilemma problem in Figure 13.3.

ANALYZYING SEQUENTIAL GAMES

To illustrate the importance of the sequential order of play in many tactical situations, consider another manufacturer-distributor coordination game that arises between heavy truck manufacturers and independent retail distributors. The payoffs for the promotion and sale of a heavy truck like those sold by Volvo-GM Truck are displayed in normal form in Table 13.9. Let's first examine the actions and payoffs in the left-hand column. The manufacturer wants the retail distributors to continue providing personal selling efforts and all after-sales service, rather than discontinue these activities, and thereby increase their retail margins. In return, the manufacturer

Table 13.9 Simultaneous Manufacturer/Distributor 1

		Truck Manufacturer	
		Price increase Advertise	No price increase Do not advertise
Retail Distributor	Increase margins (Discontinue services)	\$280,000 \$120,000	\$150,000 \$130,000
	Continue services	\$300,000 \$180,000	\$380,000 \$60,000

[15] Based on "StrideRite Agrees to Settle," *Wall Street Journal* (September 28, 1993), p. A5.

agrees to advertise the product. If services continue and advertising occurs, the customers will tolerate higher prices. The manufacturer will also assist in the realization of this higher revenue by announcing an increase in the manufacturer's suggested retail price (MSRP). In that case, the retail distributor and the manufacturer can earn additional profits of $180,000 and $300,000, respectively. However, if retail selling efforts and some after-sales services are discontinued and if MSRP increases (as in the northwest cell of Table 13.9), unit sales volume declines so sharply that the retail distributor receives only $120,000 while the manufacturer clears $280,000 per day.

Independent retail distributors may feel tempted to deliver less service than they promise, especially if they suspect a lack of manufacturer-based advertising of this product will make their time and effort spent on other products more valuable. Sales volume will eventually decline, but how does the manufacturer know whether the decline is due to a retailer's lack of effort or just bad luck? In fact, a few weeks of apparently bad luck at a substantially higher margin may be in the retail distributor's best interests. This outcome is represented in the northeast cell of Table 13.9; with retail selling effort discontinued and no manufacturer-based advertising, both parties would incur fewer expenses and realize substantial incremental profit (i.e., $130,000 for the retailer but only $150,000 for the manufacturer). If the MSRP remains unchanged and the manufacturer does not advertise, but retailer services continue (i.e., the southeast cell), manufacturer profit skyrockets to $380,000 but the retailer only clears $60,000 because of much higher expenses.

What would you do as the dealer/distributor in this situation? Would you try for the increased margin by economizing on selling expenses and after-sale services? Remember that your best payoff occurs when the manufacturer anticipates your continuation of full selling effort and after-sales services, and chooses therefore to advertise and raise the customers' expectations by announcing a higher price point. And the manufacturer's best payoff occurs when you provide extensive dealer services, and manufacturer economizes on advertising expenses and does not raise prices. Perhaps you could take turns? One period the manufacturer would maintain lower prices; the next period the manufacturer could raise prices, while you would maintain extensive dealer services continuously. After each such initiative, however, one player or the other has an incentive to destabilize the relationship. Note that Table 13.9 contains no pure Nash equilibrium strategies! So, how would you coordinate this on again–off again pricing relationship, assuming that merging the two entities into one vertically integrated firm is infeasible? What if such volatile pricing policies caused you to miss repeat business opportunities? What if it didn't?

As these questions multiply, one quickly realizes that the coordination of business activities in a simultaneous game can be a real challenge. In Chapter 14, we will see how these coordination problems can be resolved by, and indeed motivate, private voluntary contracting over vertical requirements between manufacturers and distributors. For now, simply note how much additional predictability of rival behavior emerges in this coordination game if we introduce a small but pivotal change in the structure of the game: a sequential order of play.

A Sequential Coordination Game

Suppose that the manufacturer (M) must commit first to the release of a product update that warrants higher pricing or no update, and that this decision is easily observable and irreversible. Then the retail distributor (R) must decide whether to continue personal selling effort and after-sale services or discontinue, and finally the manufacturer will thereafter decide on whether to contribute to cooperative advertising with the retailer (MA). It turns out that introducing this sequential order to the decision making will make it possible to predict the optimal strategic behavior by both parties and resolve the ambiguity of the simultaneous game.

Game Tree

A schematic diagram of a sequential game.

The new structure of the sequential game can be represented as Figure 13.4, which is referred to as a **game tree** or *decision tree.* The order of the decisions is read from left to right, and each circle represents a decision node. *Update* or *Not update* identifies possible *actions* that the Player *M* can take at the first decision node M. *Continue* or *Discontinue* identifies possible actions of player *R* at the second decision nodes R1 to R2, and *Advertise* or *Not Advertise* identifies possible actions of the manufacturer at nodes M1 to M4. The *payoffs* for the retailer and then for the manufacturer, associated with each sequence of possible actions, are listed in the last two columns.

The manufacturer can look ahead and foresee that an *Update* of the product will make it advantageous for the retail distributor to *Discontinue* full retail selling effort. Out of self-interest, the manufacturer commits to an update, increases MSRP prices, and follows through with advertising. That is, the manufacturer can look ahead and analyze what subsequent choices are in the retail distributor's best interest (i.e., best-reply responses) and then reason back to detect what actions are in its own (the manufacturer's) self-interest. Each party in Figure 13.4 is able to look ahead and reason back using the concept of best-reply response to predict the rival's

Figure 13.4 A Sequential Coordination Game: Manufacturer/Distributor II

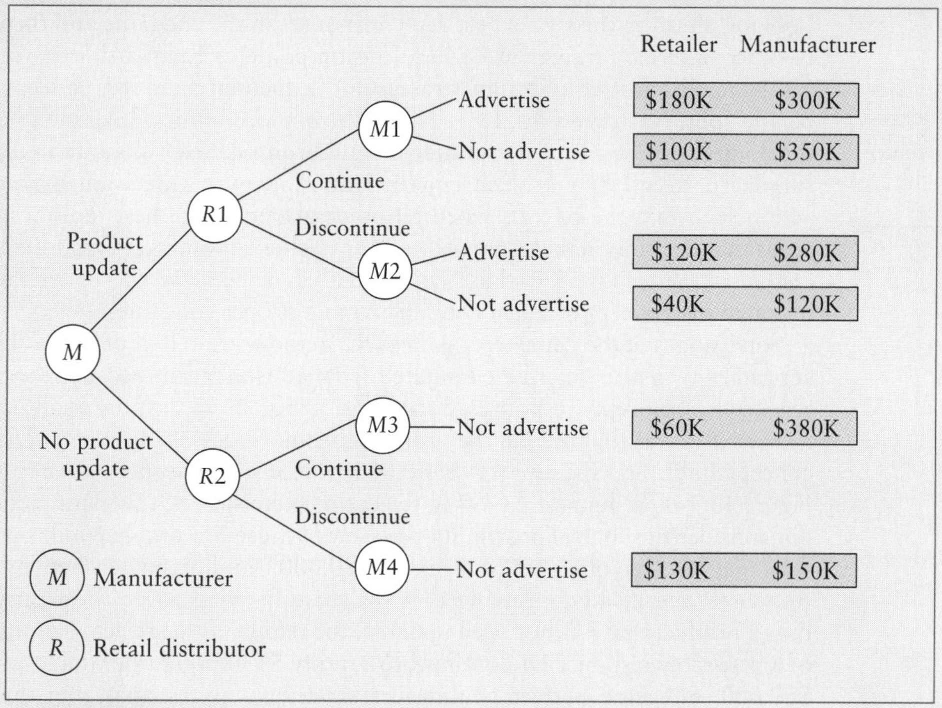

behavior. None of this sequential reasoning was available in the simultaneous-play version of the game.

Endgame reasoning always entails looking ahead to the last play in an ordered sequence of plays, identifying the player whose decisions will control the outcome of the endgame, and then predicting that player's best reply response. In this instance, knowing that the manufacturer controls the outcome from node M1 and that the manufacturer is better off with $350,000 from *Not Advertise* allows the retail distributor to ignore the possibility of the $180,000 outcome in the first row. That outcome is not consistent with best-reply response by the manufacturer who does control the endgame. Therefore, that branch should be removed ("pruned") from the game tree; the retail distributor should assume that if the product is updated and the retailer continues extensive selling effort, the manufacturer will not engage in cooperative advertising. Therefore {$100,000, $350,000} is the predictable outcome of deciding to Continue at Node M1. However, your analysis is far from finished.

Backwards Induction

Reasoning in reverse time sequence from later consequences back to earlier decisions.

These outcomes of endgame reasoning allow you to employ **backwards induction** and rethink whether you wish to *Continue* or *Discontinue* at node R1. If the manufacturer's best-reply response from M2 is to *Advertise* (which yields $280,000 rather than $120,000 for M and $120,000 for you), it appears that self-interest at the prior node R1 is to *Discontinue*. The strategy pair that provides a Nash equilibrium for the subgame beyond R1 is then {*Discontinue, Advertise*} implying distributor and manufacturer payoffs of {$120,000, $280,000}, respectively. By analogous reasoning, the strategy triplet that provides a Nash equilibrium for the sequential coordination game Manufacturer-Distributor II is then {*Update, Discontinue, Advertise*}.

Subgame Perfect Equilibrium in Sequential Games

Subgame Perfect Equilibrium Strategy

An equilibrium concept for noncooperative sequential games.

Looking ahead to the rival's best-reply responses in the endgame and then reasoning back to preferred strategy at earlier decision points is Reinhard Selten's concept of a **subgame perfect equilibrium strategy** for sequential games, a concept for which he and John Nash won the 1994 Nobel Prize in economics. Like many other path-breaking ideas, this intuitive strategic equilibrium concept is quite deceptive in its simplicity. Recall that a Nash equilibrium strategy is a decision maker's optimal action such that the payoff, when all other players make best-reply responses, exceeds that decision maker's payoff from any other action, again assuming best-reply responses. Selten applied this Nash equilibrium concept to sequential play and invented the concept of Nash equilibrium in a proper subgame.

Some nodes of the game tree, such as R2 in the bottom half of Figure 13.4 and the subgames thereafter, can be eliminated from consideration because they cannot be reached by best-reply responses. Such decision points are "off the equilibrium path." Selten's idea was that only in the proper subgame nodes would the Nash equilibrium concept hold. Specifically, the $380,000 outcome in the next to bottom row of Figure 13.4 is the highest payoff in the entire exercise. Yet, the manufacturer should not consider this logical possibility precisely because M3 and beyond is not a proper subgame; the payoffs {$60,000 and $380,000} cannot be reached by best-reply responses. Specifically, knowing that the manufacturer never cooperatively advertises a product that has not been updated, the retailer at R2 rejects Continue in favor of a best-reply response Discontinue, to capture $130,000 rather than the alternative $60,000. Subgame perfect equilibrium strategy requires analyzing the outcomes associated with actions and best-reply responses at R1 and M2, the only proper subgame nodes of Figure 13.4.[16] Again, {*Update, Discontinue, Advertise*} proves then to be the subgame perfect equilibrium strategy for Manufacturer-Distributor II.

Sometimes this identification of proper and improper subgames can get quite complicated when many endgames are possible. To illustrate, consider the three-way comparative advertising duel in Exercise 6 at the end of this chapter. With varying degrees of success, three firms attack one another with comparative advertising in pairwise, sequential competitions until just one firm remains. It can take two complete rounds of advertising attacks and almost 20 endgames to analyze the subgame perfect equilibrium strategy for that problem.

EXAMPLE

BUSINESS GAMING AT VERIZON[17]

Former Verizon chair Ray Smith employed the techniques, exercises, and lessons of game theory throughout his organization. In "war games," teams of Verizon managers assumed the role of major competitors and explored tactics that could defeat Verizon's business plans. Other teams detailed future contingencies in a large game tree that allowed Verizon to map its future moves and countermoves as well as uncover the competitive effects of new technological developments (e.g., digital voice and video transmission) before they happened. Traditional planning models lock managers into assumptions the importance of which they can only gauge through sensitivity analysis. But sequential game analysis constantly reminds managers to shape the game, not just play it. It can mean reversing the order of play by recommending preemptive strikes in some circumstances (e.g., merging with Nynex) but highlighting the value of "fast-second" best-reply responses in other circumstances (e.g., in following rather than leading basic research and product development at Lucent Technologies).

In addition, Verizon has learned to recognize endgames that are unfavorable to the company and reshape the structure of the competitive rivalry in those businesses. Verizon recently redefined the scope of the telephone industry's local network strategy game by winning approval in the courts for telephone companies to own the content transmitted over their phone lines. Verizon managers are now hard at work analyzing the new larger game that includes business directories, digitized movies, and video production.

BUSINESS RIVALRY AS A SELF-ENFORCING SEQUENTIAL GAME

It is important to emphasize that the subgame perfect equilibrium concept is self-enforcing. It predicts stable rival response, not because of effective monitoring and third-party enforcement, but because each party would be worse off departing from the equilibrium strategy pair than it would be implementing it. Ultimately, it is this

[16] The reader may wonder about the relevance of M1 if a miscommunication or strategic mistake is made by the retail distributor at Node R1. This concern is valid because mistakes and miscommunication do happen in the reality of business rivalry. Indeed, a refinement of subgame perfect equilibrium strategy allows for just such mistakes and describes equilibrium strategy for the manufacturer in this game less uniquely as {Update and Advertise if Retailer Discontinues} but {Update and Do Not Advertise if Retailer Makes a Strategic Mistake and Continues}.

[17] Based on "Business as a War Game: Report from the Battlefront," *Fortune* (September 30, 1996), pp. 190–193.

best-reply response idea that identifies whether a commitment is credible. And credibility can work both ways; credible commitments can also become credible threats. Let's see how.

Consider a well-established pharmaceutical manufacturer of ulcer relief medicine, who presently markets the only effective ulcer therapy, possessing no known side effects, and earns $100,000. This incumbent (let's call the firm "Pastense") faces a small potential entrant ("Potent" for short). Potent has discovered a new therapeutic process that also has the potential to cure stomach ulcers. Potent must decide whether to enter the monopoly market or stay out and license its trade secrets to any one of several interested buyers. Pastense must decide whether to maintain its present high prices, moderate its prices, or radically discount its prices. The payoffs are displayed in Figure 13.5. If the potential entrant Potent enters, and the incumbent Pastense does not moderate or discount to lower price points, suppose all the ulcer relief business goes to the new entrant and the incumbent realizes nothing. In contrast, with entry and discount prices, suppose the incumbent's product enjoys a slight cost advantage and earns a $10,000 greater payoff (i.e., $50,000 and $40,000 in the third row of Figure 13.5). Moderate incumbent prices result in a $35,000 payoff for Pastense and a $50,000 payoff for Potent.

To prevent the reduction of its profit from $100,000 as a monopolist to $50,000 post-entry, Pastense itself might be a prime candidate for the purchase of Potent's trade secret. Realistically, however, it is liable to run up against antitrust constraints that restrict mergers between dominant incumbents and new entrants. Note also from node I2 in Figure 13.5 that what another established pharmaceutical manufacturer will pay to license the trade secret, with all the attendant technology transfer problems and more extensive distribution and marketing experience, bears little correlation to what Potent itself could hope to earn upon entry. Potent receives its second highest payoff ($60,000) when it licenses its trade secret in a moderate price environment. Potent earns the least (namely, $20,000) when it stays out and licenses, and Pastense discounts anyway.

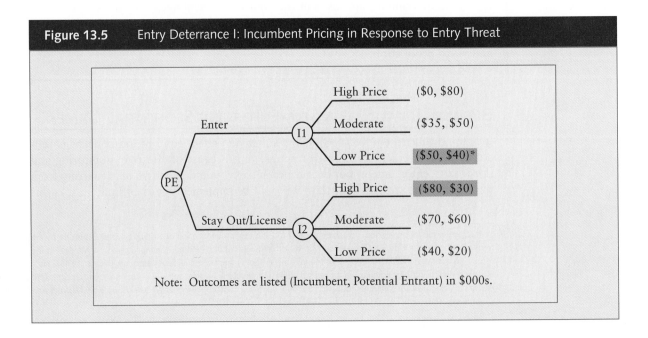

Figure 13.5 Entry Deterrance I: Incumbent Pricing in Response to Entry Threat

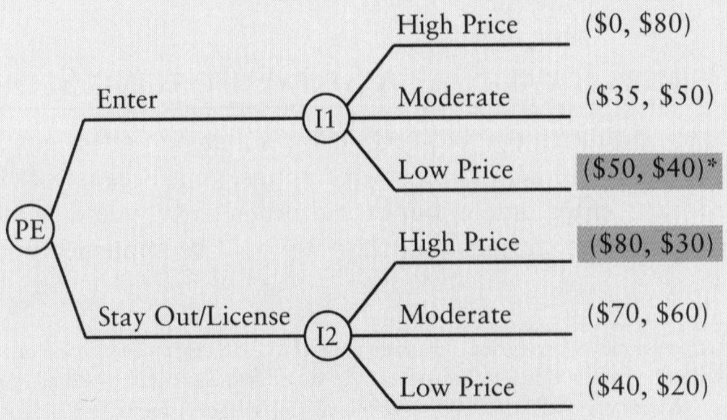

Note: Outcomes are listed (Incumbent, Potential Entrant) in $000s.

FIRST-MOVER AND FAST-SECOND ADVANTAGES

As is now obvious, "Who can do what, when?" is the essence of any sequential strategy game. The order of play determines who initiates and who replies, which determines the best-reply response in the endgame, and thus the strategic equilibrium. If Potent enters, Pastense strongly prefers a Low pricing response, because $50,000 far exceeds the zero or $35,000 outcomes from either the High or Moderate alternatives. This analysis of the incumbent's best-reply response allows Potent to predict that its own $80,000 and $50,000 outcomes are infeasible. Even though each is theoretically associated with its entry, neither can be obtained if Pastense makes a best-reply response in this proper subgame.

Similarly in the bottom endgame node I2, if Potent stays out, its royalty payoffs of $60,000 cannot be obtained, because Pastense will price High to secure $80,000 for itself rather than accept its lower $70,000 and $40,000 alternatives. Only two **focal outcomes of interest** remain for Potent in making its entry decision: the shaded payoffs of $40,000 from entering and $30,000 from staying out. Being a value-maximizing firm, Potent decides to enter, predictably, and the events of the subgame perfect strategic equilibrium {Enter, Discount} then unfold. Notice that both players could be better off with the {$70,000, $60,000} outcome in the lower node, but Potent cannot expect Pastense to respond with Moderate rather than High prices should Potent stay out and license.

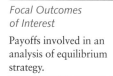

Focal Outcomes of Interest
Payoffs involved in an analysis of equilibrium strategy.

However, to illustrate the pivotal importance of the order of play, let's mix things up a bit. From the incumbent's point of view too, the outcomes {$50,000, $40,000} are not entirely satisfactory. Given its second-mover timing, Pastense did as well as could be expected. But the incumbent may wonder whether seizing the first-mover initiative would have worked to its advantage. However, no general rule on this point exists; sometimes it will, and sometimes it will not. Each sequential game situation is in this way unique.

To analyze the question, in Figure 13.6 we reverse the order of play in Entry Deterrence II. Now, the potential entrant controls the endgame, and the incumbent

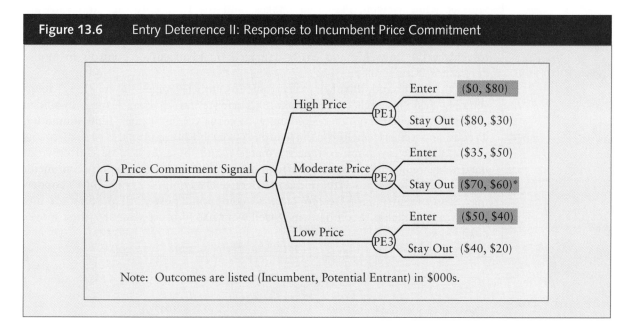

Figure 13.6 Entry Deterrence II: Response to Incumbent Price Commitment

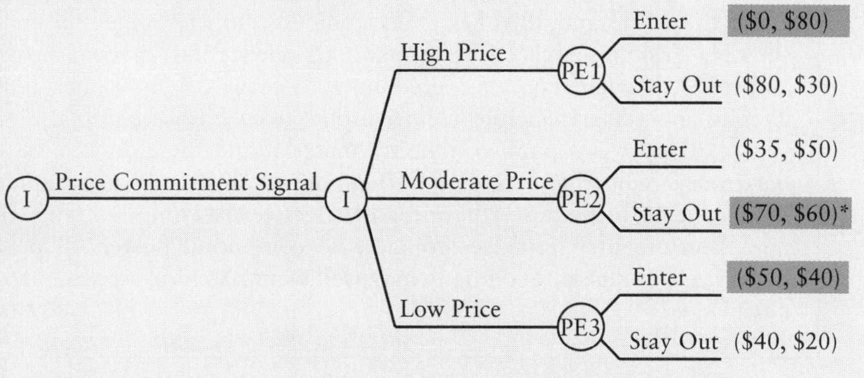

Note: Outcomes are listed (Incumbent, Potential Entrant) in $000s.

must announce irreversible pricing policies in advance. Saying they are irreversible does not make it so, but more on that in the next section. Analyzing the three endgame nodes, Pastense realizes that Potent will choose to enter when high prices are precommitted, stay out when moderate prices are precommitted, or enter when discount prices are precommitted. Knowing these outcomes, Pastense announces a moderate pricing policy, and the starred {Moderate, Stay Out} strategic equilibrium is the result. Not only has the potential entrant's behavior changed, but in addition, the payoff to Pastense has risen from $50,000 to $70,000. In this instance, a first-mover advantage proved to be just what the name implies.

EXAMPLE

Technology Leader or Fast-Second: IBM[18]

Whether to secure first-mover advantages in the development of new computing technologies or instead engage in a pattern of quick imitation (i.e., a fast-second strategy) poses a more difficult choice than one might think. In the absence of sunk-cost investments as a barrier to entry, hit-and-run entry often proves effective. Apple Computer commercialized the graphical user interface (GUI) that Xerox invented, and Apple's breathtaking but unsuccessful Newton led the way for Palm. Microsoft quickly challenged Netscape's early dominance of Internet browsers. And Sun Microsystems developed the reduced instruction-set computing (RISC) that IBM pioneered. Even in consumer perishables, Dunkin Donuts' Coolatta is fast imitating one of Starbuck's most profitable offerings, Frappuccino.

By restraining up-front investments in basic research and focusing instead on the development of products, IBM has recently switched from a technology leader to a "first of a kind" systems problem solver for high-margin customers. One example has been a blending of computer imaging and voice-recognition devices that allows hospital radiologists and surgeons to superimpose X-ray images and text on any PC throughout the local area network in a medical center. Doctors speak to one another while viewing PC-based images, and the IBM hardware and software creates a digital transcript of their diagnostic findings and expert opinions. Other examples would be IBM's wireless modem for the cellular industry and eraser-heads to replace the unwieldy and easily damaged trackball cursor controls in mouse devices for PCs.

On the other hand, IBM Microelectronics recently leveraged the company's long-standing basic research effort in materials science into a breakthrough in silicon chips. IBM's engineers discovered how to form copper rather than aluminum circuits and yet prevent the copper atoms from bleeding into the surface of the silicon. Copper is a more conductive material and therefore can be laid down in narrower circuits than aluminum. The more circuits etched on a square centimeter of silicon, the more powerful and cost effective the computer chip. IBM's copper-on-silicon circuitry promises to increase computing power 40 percent for any given size chip. Here, a company may well want patent protection of its first-mover advantage.

[18] Based on "Einstein and Eraser-Heads," *Wall Street Journal* (October 6, 1997), p. 1.

CREDIBLE THREATS AND COMMITMENTS

In multiperiod games, the credibility of all threats and commitments ultimately derive from whether the threat maker or commitment maker successfully identifies and adopts subgame perfect strategies. In Entry Deterrence I (see Figure 13.5), Pastense's threat to discount the ulcer relief medicine if Potent entered was credible precisely because discounting was, in fact, a best-reply response. Any other response would have made Pastense worse off (i.e., lowered its payoff). A **credible threat** is therefore defined as a conditional strategy that the threat maker is worse off ignoring than implementing. By the same token, a commitment by Pastense to maintain high prices (i.e., not to discount and thereby spoil the royalty value of Potent's trade secret) if Potent would stay out of the market is a credible commitment. Again, the reason is that this action is the incumbent's best-reply response to Potent's staying out and just earning royalties from the ongoing value of its trade secret. Therefore, without any monitoring or third-party enforcement whatsoever, one can fully rely upon Pastense to honor its commitment, because it would not be in its own best interest to do otherwise.

Credible Threat

A conditional strategy the threat maker is worse off ignoring than implementing.

In Figure 13.5, if Potent wanted to secure a commitment from Pastense to price at the *moderate* level in exchange for some portion of the much larger $60,000 royalties, Potent would need to employ a binding, third-party-enforceable contractual agreement. It is simply not in Pastense's best-reply-response interest to fulfill such a commitment otherwise.

You can now begin to see why purposeful individual behavior and a shared objective in groups is so critical to game theory reasoning. To predict choices of highly interdependent players, one must know what makes them tick, what true goals they seek, and what the consequence of various actions is on those goals, which is sometimes harder than it sounds. For example, performance-based incentives and takeover threats often align management objectives quite closely with stockholder value, but what motivates a closely held, family-run business is sometimes difficult to fathom. Moreover, consistently transmitted signals of business strategy are often jammed or misinterpreted by the receiver. Therefore, to ensure the effective communication of credible threats and credible commitments requires some guidelines. This situation can be illustrated by returning to the Entry Deterrence game.

As we have seen, Pastense found the switch to first-mover status highly advantageous. By committing to maintain moderate prices rather than discount, its profits increased from $50,000 to $70,000 when Potent sold out rather than entered. The question we must now reexamine, however, is "Why did Potent believe Pastense would maintain Moderate prices?" After all, it is clear from the original game tree in Figure 13.5 that once Potent licensed its trade secret to another less capable potential entrant (let's call the new firm "Impotent"), Pastense was really better off raising its price back to the high level it had once enjoyed. Note that thereby Pastense would then receive the $80,000 payoff from high prices rather than a $70,000 payoff from moderate prices. Thus, Pastense's commitment to maintain a moderate price was not a **credible commitment** because Pastense was worse off making good on the commitment than ignoring it.

Credible Commitment

A promise that the promise-giver is worse off violating than fulfilling.

One might be inclined to respond that likewise Potent can renege on its commitment to stay out of the ulcer relief business. Licensing a trade secret for royalty revenue today need not preclude Potent's potential entry tomorrow. Indeed, such royalty agreements seldom include a no-competition clause. However, the difference here is that Potent's payoff is maximized by staying out! Its commitment to staying out if the incumbent maintains moderate prices *is* in Potent's own best interest. Staying out is a best-reply response; therefore it is a credible commitment.

Mechanisms for Establishing Credibility[19]

As second mover, Potent controls the endgame and therefore finds itself in a position to insist on the necessary assurances from Pastense. Among the alternative mechanisms for establishing credibility, Pastense might establish a bond or contractual side payment, which would be forfeited if Pastense raised prices. Some such contracts, referred to as maximum resale price maintenance agreements, do exist between retailers and their suppliers. Another possible credibility mechanism would be for Pastense to invest heavily in its moderate price strategy to establish a reputation for moderate prices. Loss of this **nonredeployable reputational asset** would discourage reneging on its commitment to maintain moderate prices. Third, Pastense could short-circuit or interrupt the repricing process by preselling its ulcer relief medicine with forward contracts. Forward sale contracts establish credible commitments because the courts generally refuse to excuse forwards or futures contract breaches for any reason. Fourth, Pastense could enter into teamwork or an alliance relationship with Potent that would sufficiently dilute the rewards from reneging on its commitment, perhaps by taking an equity stake in Potent. Fifth, Pastense could change the structure of the game to require that both it and Potent only "take small steps." In the next section, we analyze leasing as a way to pursue this credibility mechanism.

Nonredeployable Reputational Asset

A reputation whose value is lost if sold or licensed.

And finally, the most practical response to this situation would be for Pastense to arrange an irreversible and irrevocable **hostage mechanism,** whereby likely future customers were granted a moderate price guarantee. Sometimes referred to as "most favored nation" clauses, these price guarantees promise double refunds if the customer discovers any lower-price Pastense transaction during the next or the previous year. As long as Potent observed at least one moderate price transaction before licensing its trade secret, it could rest assured that Pastense had now offered a credible commitment not to raise prices. The resulting double refunds, should Pastense raise prices, and the sacrifice of future transactions with its own repeat-purchase customers, should it renege on the refunds, ensure that Pastense will finally be better off honoring its commitment to moderate prices than ignoring it. And again, notice that these agreements are entirely self-enforcing.

Hostage Mechanism

A mechanism for establishing the credibility of a threat or commitment.

EXAMPLE

Double-the-Difference Price Guarantees: Circuit City

At times, Circuit City offers to rebate twice the differential purchase price of a DVD player to preferred customers should those customers find the same DVD player selling for less anywhere in the local area over the next three months. This rebate guarantee will be enforced by the courts. As in the simultaneous-play pricing game

[19] This section relies heavily on A. Dixit and B. Nalebuff, *Thinking Strategically: The Competitive Edge in Business, Politics, and Everyday Life* (New York: Norton, 1993), especially Chapters 5 and 6.

between PepsiCo and Coca-Cola, Circuit City normally would be better off discounting (maybe even steeply discounting) when competitors such as Best Buy and Sound Warehouse maintain high prices. But in the face of this double-the-difference low-price guarantee, Circuit City would lose more money on rebates than it could possibly gain from any amount of incremental business it could reasonably expect to take away from the competitors. In effect, Circuit City has given its competitors a hostage that supports a commitment to maintain high prices.

In Figure 13.7, Circuit City provides a bond of its intentions to maintain high prices by preannouncing the double-the-difference price guarantee. Sound Warehouse must then decide whether to discount or maintain high prices in light of the Circuit City rebate program. Like all good hostage mechanisms, the hostage is worth more to the hostage giver than its value in use to the recipient. That is, Sound Warehouse *could* trigger double-rebate payments at Circuit City by discounting its own price. And harming a competitor is a reasonable secondary goal, but it's only secondary. Securing your own highest payoff perhaps through legal cooperation with a competitor is the primary goal. Because Circuit City would respond to a Sound Warehouse discount by matching the lower price point, Sound Warehouse would gain nothing by using the hostage in this way. Indeed, for the hostage recipient such a decision would lead to the payoff labeled "Worse" in the top right-hand corner of Figure 13.7.

Figure 13.7 Double-the-Difference Price Guarantees

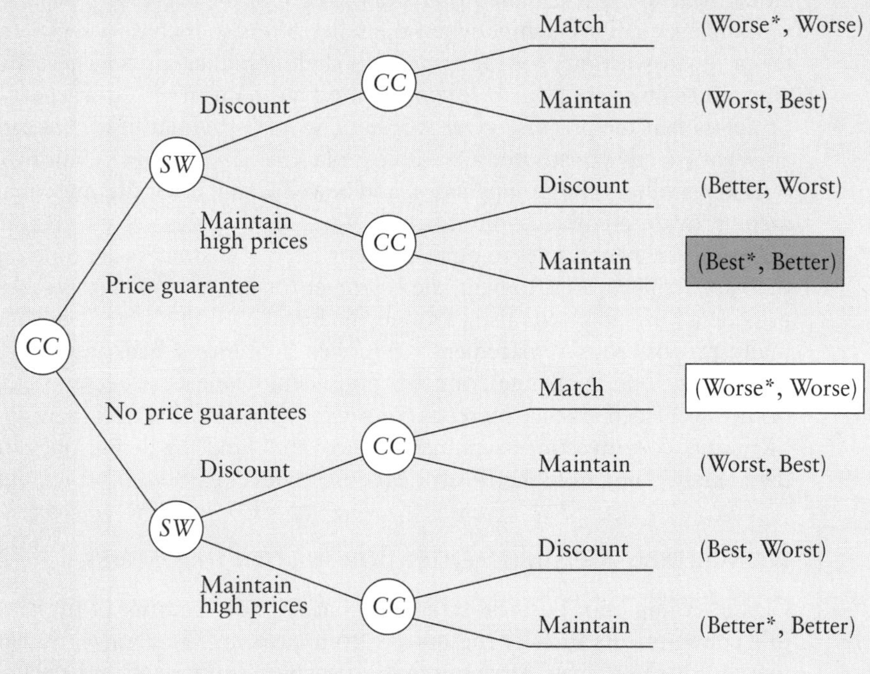

Note: Payoffs are listed (Circuit City CC, Sound Warehouse SW).

Knowing that Circuit City controls the endgame and that it would be in Circuit City's best interest after announcing the rebate program to match a discount price, Sound Warehouse finds itself preferring to maintain high prices. Because Circuit City is also best off by maintaining high prices, the payoff {Best*, Better} results. Thus, by introducing a price guarantee that limited its own ability to take advantage of its opponent's vulnerability at high prices, Circuit City secured first-best outcomes when the alternative was Worse (i.e., compare the shaded and unshaded boxed payoffs in Figure 13.7). A hostage mechanism that establishes one's credible commitment to maintain high prices if the rival maintains high prices will often elicit high prices from that rival. Thus, from the point of view of both companies, double-the-difference low-price guarantees are unambiguously preferred. Of course, consumer advocates will not rejoice, but complaining about double-the-difference price guarantees attracts few sympathizers to the consumer cause.

Replacement Guarantees

As we discussed in Chapter 10, all buyers rationally discount experience goods such as used cars and computer components if they cannot verify independently at the point of purchase the seller's quality claims. A replacement guarantee or a product performance repair warranty are other good examples of hostage mechanisms—in this case, hostage mechanisms that establish the credibility of a seller's commitment to deliver high-quality components in the goods it offers for sale. Should the seller violate his or her commitment, a third party (usually the courts) will impose on the seller monetary judgments that are larger than the incremental cost of upgrading from lower to higher quality inputs in the first place. Therefore, the buyer is assured of a higher quality machine when the seller offers to include a replacement guarantee or repair warranty for the same (or a slightly higher) price. These guarantees and warranties illustrate a *credible commitment* mechanism (i.e., third-party-enforceable promises that the promise-giver would be worse off violating than keeping).

What exactly constitutes a credible replacement guarantee? Claims by Dooney & Bourke handbags, Revo sunglasses, and Sewell Cadillac for lifetime repair or replacement provide credible commitments. Why? The key is repeat customer business. Because incremental sales to established or referral customers are much less expensive than attracting new customers, the customer-for-life relationships at these companies provide a hostage mechanism. Dooney & Bourke's, Revo's, or Sewell Cadillac's normally preposterous replacement or service guarantees backed by a brand name, unique distribution channel, or other nonredeployable asset become credible because of the seller's dependence on repeat or referral business. In effect, Sewell Cadillac says "My sunk cost investments cannot be recovered (and, by definition, cannot be liquidated at anything near their historical cost) unless I earn your repeat business."

EXAMPLE

Noncredible Commitments: Burlington Industries

Classic examples of business strategies that flounder because of the absence of credible commitments include the quota "commitments" in a cartel and the "commitment" not to compete after purchasing surplus equipment in a declining industry. Burlington Industries has experienced many problems with its overseas sales of old textile looms, often acquired in mergers and then liquidated at scrap value. The foreign buyers restore the old equipment and then backship their production into the

United States despite no-competition clauses in the equipment purchase contracts. Burlington has now begun to destroy old equipment, not just dismantle it, especially in declining product lines where it wishes to pursue a niche strategy as "the last iceman."[20] The idea is to preserve high margins by becoming the last company to sell a particular textile product, or block ice, or manual typewriters (Smith Corona, Brother, or Olivetti). To this purpose, IBM bought up Amdahl Millennium and Hitachi Skyline mainframe computers and physically crushed them in a scrap yard.

HOSTAGES SUPPORT THE CREDIBILITY OF COMMITMENTS

In Chapter 10 we encountered a noncooperative sequential games mechanism for securing cooperation in a repeated Prisoner's Dilemma game through the use of credible commitments. Potentially notorious firms selling low-quality experience goods (e.g., PC components) for high prices were identifiable in Table 10.2 as firms with entirely redeployable assets. That is, firms selling out of temporary locations, with unbranded products and no company reputation, could be reasonably expected to follow the dominant strategy of producing low quality. Consider eNow Components illustrated in Figure 13.8. This company is not likely to plan on more than one

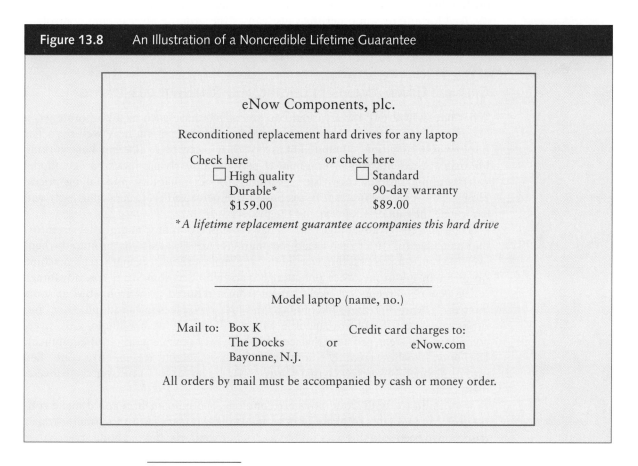

Figure 13.8 An Illustration of a Noncredible Lifetime Guarantee

eNow Components, plc.

Reconditioned replacement hard drives for any laptop

Check here	or check here
☐ High quality	☐ Standard
Durable*	90-day warranty
$159.00	$89.00

**A lifetime replacement guarantee accompanies this hard drive*

____
Model laptop (name, no.)

Mail to: Box K
The Docks
Bayonne, N.J.

or

Credit card charges to:
eNow.com

All orders by mail must be accompanied by cash or money order.

[20] Kathryn Harrigan has written about this superficially curious strategy in "Endgame Strategy," *Forbes* (July 1987), pp. 181–196.

transaction with any customer. It may not even plan on doing business through its present post office box or e-business site for long. Consequently, these are firms to whom no customer would offer a high price.

On the other hand, we argued that firms who asked high prices but also exhibited verifiable sunk cost investments that dissipate the rent from such prices, were much better bets. Reputational advertising of nontransferable company logos (say, Apple Computers or CARMAX) or investment in nonredeployable assets, such as product-specific showrooms (Ethan Allen) and unique retail displays (L'eggs), present a hostage to buyers. Because sellers offering hostages are worse off if they fail to deliver on the promise of high quality, a buyer can rely on these credible commitments even if unable to verify quality at the point of purchase. Although the credible commitments are noncontractual in nature, they establish reliance relationships that are as predictable as enforceable contracts.

Finally, credibility arises from cooperative game mechanisms that involve binding (third-party-enforceable) contracts such as franchise agreements, escrow bonds, and refund guarantees. These contractual mechanisms also provide hostages that support win-win exchange despite a dominant strategy that would otherwise lead players to defect. The key to the credibility of such mechanisms is the same as in noncooperative games. First, in the light of its warranty obligations, is the promise-giver better off fulfilling its promise than ignoring it? And second, can the warranty or bond *be revoked* for any reason other than just causes the promise-giver cannot control? If the answer to both questions is yes, then these contract commitments are credible and consistent with best-reply response.

Credible Commitments in Leasing and Renewable Licensing

What buyers will pay for a capital equipment purchase such as a corporate jet, a mainframe computer, or a business license depends in part on how well the seller resolves some credible commitment issues. If a piece of equipment has working life that will extend over several market periods, an early adopter of a new model worries about obsolescence risk, uncertain product reliability, and falling prices. How well a manufacturer addresses these three perceived risks of buying early will determine the rate of adoption and the prices paid.

The competitive advantages IBM's newest supercomputer might offer an information technology user such as a direct marketer are seriously compromised whenever IBM introduces a still newer model and makes the direct marketer's machine obsolete. In addition, other potential buyers who see somewhat less advantage in the new equipment will likely benefit from a reduced price from IBM at some later date. Knowing these likelihoods, the first buyer hesitates, adopts later, and offers to pay less than he or she otherwise would for the new technology. To overcome this persistent problem that comes with every new generation of equipment, IBM must somehow credibly commit to maintaining high prices and to a controlled rate of planned obsolescence that allows early buyers time to recover their investment costs.

In an industry with slow-moving technology, a dominant firm could make contractual commitments to phase in new updated equipment. At times, tractor-trailer trucks have been sold this way, and to a certain extent, the limited body style change from year to year in some automobile models (Impalas, Camrys, and Accords) reflects the same idea. However, in the mainframe computer industry, even IBM cannot afford such restrictions; technology simply moves too fast. So what alternatives remain? Buyers of updated capital equipment can't be expected to risk a lot of capital soon after the rollout of a new model; yet, companies such as IBM cannot lock themselves into delays of future upgrades.

Versioning

A new product rollout strategy to encourage early adoption at higher prices.

One approach is to continuously upgrade the product at higher and higher prices, what Carl Shapiro and Hal Varian call **versioning.**[21] Microsoft adopted this model upgrade strategy with their Windows operating system. The buyer is told, in effect, don't hesitate and wait for the price to fall; the next model will be even more expensive. But of course operating systems are not consumed on the spot, and they don't wear out. Like any durable goods monopolist, Microsoft's biggest competitor for Windows XP is Windows NT, just as the best substitute for Windows NT was Windows 2000. Another approach, therefore, is to ask buyers to take small steps by leasing the equipment one market period at a time. Although this approach fails to slow (and may actually quicken) the pace of new product introductions, buyers risk less up-front capital and therefore can be induced more easily to take on the new model and update their capital equipment more frequently *at higher prices*. IBM employed exactly this approach for many years by offering only to lease their mainframe computers.

Similarly, Dell Computer advertises "How many companies will let you return your computer when it becomes obsolete?" and leases its PCs for $99 per month with the opportunity to renew for a new updated computer two years later. And BMW auto leases provide bumper-to-bumper scheduled maintenance and unexpected repairs for the lifetime of the lease. So leasing mitigates obsolescence and maintenance risk. But what about the early adopters' risk of subsequent price reductions? How does leasing address that risk?

EXAMPLE

LEASING DIGITAL MOVIEHOUSE PROJECTORS: HUGHES-JVC[22]

George Lucas's *Star Wars* movies are now filmed entirely on digital movie cameras. Cinema companies such as General Cinema and Carmike much prefer digital film over the sixty-pound celluloid film prints that often reach diameters of five feet. Downloading compressed-signal digital films right off a satellite using high-speed secure data networks will allow the movie houses much more flexibility in their scheduling. In addition, the sound and projection quality will no longer deteriorate after a few dozen showings. The movie production companies also like the new technology because a full national rollout of a celluloid movie requires 5,000 prints that cost approximately $2,000 each to produce, and it necessitates a large fleet of trucks to move the film canisters about the country.

The biggest hurdle to the fast adoption of this new technology is the $150,000 replacement cost for each of the projectors in a small (five-screen) cinema. With the U.S. movie theatre industry badly overbuilt (some estimates suggest by as many as 10,000 more cinemas than needed), General Cinema, Carmike, and others are understandably hesitant to commit a half-million dollars of additional capital per movie house. Each would like to wait for the discounted digital projector prices that they believe will come later. Hughes-JVC, who manufactures one of the projectors,

[21] See C. Shapiro and H. Varian, "Versioning: The Smart Way to Sell Information," *Harvard Business Review* (November–December 1998), pp. 106–118.

[22] Based on "Curtains for Celluloid," *The Economist* (March 27, 1999), p. 81.

and CineComm Digital Cinema plan to lease the projectors to cinemas. Distribution will be handled by satellite to cut operating costs enough that leasing fees for the projectors can be tied to actual showings. This allows lower-revenue cinemas in overbuilt markets to participate in earlier adoption of the new technology.

Closed-End Leases with Residual Values: The Tactical Advantage

Understanding the tactical advantage of leasing requires careful analysis of the manufacturer's asymmetric information in making planned obsolescence and price discount decisions. Because the manufacturer knows the marketing plans and can estimate the pace of technology and the risk of obsolescence much better than the end user, one would think that lease terms can be more favorable when the seller undertakes to absorb the risk of price promotions and planned obsolescence. That is, in a competitive marketplace for capital equipment leases (i.e., the corporate jet lease market), one would expect sellers to offer closed-end leases with residual values that reflect their accurate estimates of what a two-year-old corporate jet will be worth. This residual value is what really establishes the credibility of the manufacturer's commitment over the lease period to refrain from discounting or introducing a new model that would render the current model obsolete. If the leasewriter (the lessor) violated this promise, the assets returned at the end of the lease would be worth less than the residual value at which the manufacturer-lessor has agreed to take them back. In effect, the manufacturer has given a hostage to the leaseholder (the lessee). By agreeing to take back the capital equipment for a preset amount and dispose of it in the resale market, the manufacturer-lessor credibly commits to a limited set of price promotions and to a limited rate of planned obsolescence.

EXAMPLE

NetJets Fractional Ownership Plans for Learjet and Gulfstream Aircraft[23]

FlexJets offers guaranteed access on four hours' notice to a fleet of Learjet and Challenger business aircraft for as little as $175,000 per year cost. NetJets, a division of Warren Buffett's Berkshire Hathaway Company, offers fractional shares in "the world's largest and finest fleet of 450 Gulfstream aircraft with guaranteed availability, guaranteed costs, and guaranteed liquidity of your asset." NetJets expects to schedule more than 400,000 flights in 2006. A one-sixteenth share of a Citation seven-passenger jet leases for $620,000 upfront plus a $7,909 monthly fee, plus $1,675 per flight hour to cover operating cost. These contractual arrangements are essentially operating leases.

One indication that these fractional ownership-leasing arrangements are designed to establish the credible commitment of the lessor to resale price stability is that NetJets continues to offer a $44-million Gulfstream VI, the top-of-the-line business jet, for $10.1 million up front plus $56,516 per month plus operating costs of $3,118 per hour in flight, despite a $7 to $10 million collapse of the resale value of the plane NetJets takes back at the end of the lease. A used Gulfstream comparable to the two-year-old lease-end aircraft in late 2002 sold for $18 million, when more

[23] "Prices on Private Planes Dive," *Wall Street Journal* (September 5, 2002); and "The Bargain Jaguar," *Wall Street Journal* (March 20, 2003), p. D1.

normal resale prices would be \$25–\$28 million. Again, someone (either lessor or lessee) must bear these repricing risks, but leasing offers a credible commitment from manufacturers to early adopters that such asset price collapses will not result from seller price promotions subsequent to an early adopter's purchase decision.

In contrast, deal making on luxury new car sales in 2003 drove the resale value of two-year-old Lexus LS 430s and Saab 9-5s down by 23.4 percent from \$53,500 to \$41,000 in just one year, compared to a 14.7 percent reduction for two-year-old models one year earlier.

Of course, the risk of technological developments and competitor discounts that the manufacturer cannot control still remain. The lessor and lessee have credibly committed some things and left others to chance. All such remaining risks will be priced into the terms of the residual value lease. As a result, over the lifetime of the equipment it will not be cheaper to lease rather than to buy. In other words, the buyer who insists on a product warranty means that the seller-lessor has to absorb the risk of product failure; this risk is then fully priced into a higher lease payment.

Closed-End Lease with Residual Value

A credible commitment mechanism for limiting the rate of planned obsolescence and establishing delays in price promotion.

Nevertheless, manufacturers need some way of credibly committing themselves to maintaining high asking prices and a limited rate of planned obsolescence over the buyer's holding period. Only then will early adopters pay the higher prices manufacturers wish to charge in the early mature phase of an upgraded product's life cycle. **Closed-end leases with fixed residual values** agreed in advance offer such a credible commitment because they demonstrate and certify just what the manufacturer's best estimates of forward value truly are. Such leases therefore shore up purchase prices paid by early adopters of durable equipment.

EXAMPLE

The Licensing of Taxi Medallions and Cell Phones[24]

Similarly, by selling a taxi medallion or a cellular phone authorization as a renewable license, a municipality can credibly limit the supply of the city's transportation and communication infrastructure. If the city were to insist on an outright purchase, taxi and cellular entrepreneurs would be concerned that soon thereafter the city would flood the market with additional taxis and cell phone companies. Consequently, the amounts bid for the right to do business would decline substantially. For example, in Washington, D.C., the city council authorized essentially open entry, attracted 12 cabs for every 1,000 residents, and found that the equilibrium entry fee was \$25. In contrast, New York City has restricted entry to 11,797 taxi medallions, 2 taxis per 1,000 residents, and as a result the New York taxi medallion asset transfers for \$140,000.

The point is not that potential license holders wish to avoid being duped, although of course all of us *are* motivated to avoid embarrassments. Instead, it's that licenses authorizing a business are a property right that the license holders may need to resell. Random events happen to every company, and license holders cannot assume that they will be able to operate forever. Licenses are durable capital assets,

[24] "New York Taxi Policy," *Wall Street Journal* (March 17, 1992), p. A14; and "Put the Brakes on Taxicab Monopolies," *Wall Street Journal* (November 6, 1984), p. A20.

and their resale value is as much a concern as would be the value of a mainframe computer or corporate jet. Municipalities can raise more money, therefore, with renewable leases for all business licenses.[25]

Even though renewable licensing and leasing offers tactical advantages in establishing credible commitments not obtainable with outright sales, leasing will not necessarily be cheaper than buying. Any costs imposed on the seller by the credibility mechanisms (e.g., a higher residual value) will be priced into the lease. The point is simply that some credible commitments impose additional costs on the asymmetrically informed manufacturer as a lessor that are lower than the reduction in price that would be required to accomplish a comparable sale. Consequently, manufacturer profitability increases with renewable licensing and leasing, relative to the alternative profitability available from the outright sale of durable equipment, business licenses, or patents.

[25] What occurs in business licensing by municipal and state governments also occurs in the licensing of trade secrets and patents. Again, credible commitments by seller-lessors to actions that will maintain forward asset values are the key to eliciting higher buyer-lessee willingness to pay among early adopters.

Summary

- Proactive oligopolists require accurate predictions of rival initiatives and rival response. The managerial purpose of game theory is to predict just such rival behavior. In a *game theory* analysis, each analyzes its competitors' optimal decision-making strategy, and then chooses its own best counterstrategy.
- Business strategy games may be classified as simultaneous-play or sequential-play, one-shot or repeated, zero-sum or non-zero-sum, two-player or *n*-player, and cooperative or noncooperative.
- *Cooperative games* allow coalition formation, side payment agreements, and third-party enforceable contracts whereas noncooperative games prohibit these characteristics.
- Simultaneous-play games occasionally arise in pricing and promotion rivalry, but the essence of business strategy is sequential reasoning.
- Dominant strategy equilibrium entails actions that maximize at least one decision maker's payoff, no matter what any other player chooses to do.
- Nash equilibrium strategy involves actions that maximize each decision maker's payoff, given best-reply responses of the other players.
- Nash equilibrium for simultaneous games identifies pure and mixed strategies. In both cases, players' choices reflect best-reply reactions of rivals and therefore provide stability.
- Most Nash equilibrium strategies are non-unique; multiple pure Nash strategies exist.
- Mixed strategy provides an optimal rule for randomizing one's actions among multiple Nash equilibrium strategies.
- Mutual cooperation in a repeated Prisoner's Dilemma game can be secured with the uncertain endgame timing, adoption of an industry standard, multiperiod punishment schemes such as Tit for Tat or grim trigger strategy, and strategic hostage or bonding mechanisms for establishing credible commitments and threats.
- Cooperation in noncooperative games is more likely if strategies are clear, provokable, take cooperative initiatives unilaterally, and are forgiving so as not to perpetuate mistakes. The Tit-for-Tat strategy has these characteristics.
- Playing against Tit-for-Tat strategies necessitates comparing the additional profit from unilateral defection against the discounted opportunity loss from limited-duration certain punishment next period. As the probability of continued replay declines, Tit for Tat becomes a less-effective coordination device for escaping the Prisoner's Dilemma than a matching price policy.
- The order of play matters in sequential games of coordination between manufacturers and distributors, entry deterrence and accommodation, service competition, R&D races, product development, and so on, because rivals must predict best-reply responses and counterresponses all the way out to an endgame.
- Endgame reasoning looks ahead to the last play in an ordered sequence of plays, identifies the player whose

decisions control the available outcomes in the endgame, and then predicts that player's preferred action.

- Subgame perfect equilibrium strategy looks ahead to analyze endgame outcomes and then reasons back to prior best-reply responses.
- Credible threats and credible commitments are the key to endgame reasoning, and therefore credibility mechanisms are the key to subgame perfect equilibrium strategy.
- Advantages may accrue to either first-movers or fast-seconds in a business rivalry. The former can credibly threaten or credibly precommit and therefore preempt some outcomes, whereas the latter replies and can determine the best-reply response in the endgame. Which is more advantageous depends on the particulars of the tactical and strategic situation.
- A credible threat is a conditional strategy the threat maker is worse off ignoring than implementing. A credible commitment is an obligation the commitment maker is worse off ignoring than fulfilling.
- Mechanisms for establishing credibility include establishing a bond or contractual side payment, investing in a nonredeployable reputation asset, short-circuiting or interrupting the response process, entering into a profit-sharing alliance, taking small steps, or arranging an irreversible and irrevocable hostage mechanism.
- Closed-end leases with preset residual values are a mechanism for establishing a durable goods manufacturer's credible commitment to early adopters of new models not to discount deeply after the sale.

Exercises

Answers to the exercises in blue can be found in Appendix C at the back of the book.

1. Suppose that two Japanese companies, Hitachi and Toshiba, are the sole producers (i.e., duopolists) of a microprocessor chip used in a number of different brands of personal computers. Assume that total demand for the chips is fixed and that each firm charges the same price for the chips. Each firm's market share and profits are a function of the magnitude of the promotional campaign used to promote its version of the chip. Also assume that only two strategies are available to each firm: a limited promotional campaign (budget) and an extensive promotional campaign (budget). If the two firms engage in a limited promotional campaign, each firm will earn a quarterly profit of $7.5 million. If the two firms undertake an extensive promotional campaign, each firm will earn a quarterly profit of $5.0 million. With this strategy combination, market share and total sales will be the same as for a limited promotional campaign, but promotional costs will be higher and hence profits will be lower. If either firm engages in a limited promotional campaign and the other firm undertakes an extensive promotional campaign, then the firm that adopts the extensive campaign will increase its market share and earn a profit of $9.0 million, whereas the firm that chooses the limited campaign will earn a profit of only $4.0 million.
   a. Develop a payoff matrix for this decision-making problem.
   b. In the absence of a binding and enforceable agreement, determine the dominant advertising strategy and minimum payoff for Hitachi.
   c. Determine the dominant advertising strategy and minimum payoff for Toshiba.
   d. Explain why the firms may choose not to play their dominant strategies whenever this game is repeated over multiple decision-making periods.
2. Consider the following payoff matrix:

		Player B Strategy	
		1	2
Player A Strategy	1	$1,000 $2,000	−$2,000 −$1,000
	2	−$1,000 −$2,000	$2,000 $1,000

a. Does Player A have a dominant strategy? Explain why or why not.

b. Does Player B have a dominant strategy? Explain why or why not.

3. Suppose that two mining companies, Australian Minerals Company (AMC) and South African Mines, Inc. (SAMI), control the only sources of a rare mineral used in making certain electronic components. The companies have agreed to form a cartel to set the (profit-maximizing) price of the mineral. Each company must decide whether to *abide* by the agreement (i.e., not offer secret price cuts to customers) or *not abide* (i.e., offer secret price cuts to customers). If both companies abide by the agreement, AMC will earn an annual profit of $30 million and SAMI will earn an annual profit of $20 million from sales of the mineral. If AMC does not abide and SAMI abides by the agreement, then AMC earns $40 million and SAMI earns $5 million. If SAMI does not abide and AMC abides by the agreement, then AMC earns $10 million and SAMI earns $30 million. If both companies do not abide by the agreement, then AMC earns $15 million and SAMI earns $10 million.

a. Develop a payoff matrix for this decision-making problem.

b. In the absence of a binding and enforceable agreement, determine the dominant strategy for AMC.

c. Determine the dominant strategy for SAMI.

d. If the two firms can enter into a binding and enforceable agreement, determine the strategy that each firm should choose.

4. Two insurance companies that manage employee benefit programs are bidding for additional business in their area of expertise at a market rate of $200 per hour. The potential customers refuse to leave their current suppliers and award benefit management contracts to the new firms unless billing rates are cut by $50. Abbott, Abbott & Daughters (AA&D) decides to do just that. Your firm, Zekiel, Zekiel & Sons (ZZ&S), must decide whether to match the price cut and then allow customers to choose randomly between the two firms, or whether to lower rates still further to $100 per hour. Past experience suggests, however, that the price cutting may well not stop there. The clients will surely take their best current offer back and forth between the two firms, forcing a downward price spiral. The question therefore is "How low will you go?" Crucially, this game has a stopping rule: at a price below your $40 cost, the additional business becomes unprofitable and must be refused. AA&D has higher costs at $66 per hour.

Again, your decision depends on an analysis of the sequence of predictable future events represented with a game tree or decision tree. Provide one. To simplify, assume that all rate cuts must be in $50 increments, that customers choose quickly between equal rate quotes using fair coin tosses (represented by capital letter *N* for *Nature*), that once a rate quote has been matched it cannot be lowered, and that many potential customers are present in the market. It is now your turn at node Z1 with rates at the $150-per-hour level. What should you do? Match rates or cut rates further?

5. How does the analysis and the strategic equilibrium outcome differ in Exercise 4 if the other firm enjoys a cost advantage (e.g., $35 at AA&D)? Then does the order of play (i.e., who goes first in making price cuts) matter in this bidding game with asymmetric costs?

6. Consider an ongoing sequence of pairwise marketing competitions between three companies with promotional campaigns of varying degrees of success. Each campaign involves comparative advertising belittling the target company. The company with the most loyal customers (call this firm "Most") enjoys 100 percent success when it attacks either of the others. The company with the least loyal customers ("Least") has a 30 percent success rate when it belittles either Most or "More." More experiences an 80 percent success rate. The firms each launch their advertising attacks one at a time in an arbitrary sequence. Least goes first and can attack either Most or More. More attacks second, and Most attacks third. If more than one of the opponents survives

the first round of competition, the order of play repeats itself: Least, then More, then Most. Any player can skip his or her turn; that is, the three actions available to Least to initiate the game are as follows: attack More, attack Most, or do nothing and pass the turn.

Diagram the game tree and employ subgame perfect equilibrium analysis to identify the strategic equilibrium. What should the most vulnerable firm with the least loyal customers do to initiate play? What would be More's best-reply response if attacked and More survives? What if Least did nothing? What would Most do when and if its turn arose?

7. Why should the early adopters of an information technology system provided by IBM Systems Solutions be willing to pay more for a closed-end lease of the servers and other hardware required than for an outright purchase?

8. People who are regularly late often don't bother to carry watches. In response, other people tend to adjust to their tardiness by starting meetings 10 minutes after they're scheduled, coming to lunch appointments 10 minutes late, and so on. Analyze the following coordination game and explain why.

		Harry: Be Punctual	Harry: Always Late
Tom	Be Punctual	100, 100	50, 70
	Always Late	70, 50	95, 95

9. Nike and Adidas face the following coordination problem in trying to decide whether to conduct heavy or light combative advertising against the other firm. What should each firm do?

		Nike: Light Ads	Nike: Heavy Ads
Adidas	Light Ads	$10 M, $12 M	$4 M, $6 M
	Heavy Ads	$5 M, $4 M	$8 M, $9 M

10. The outcomes in the bottom half of the game tree describing the last (the 20th) submarket of the chain store paradox in Figure 13.2 are labeled N.A. (not applicable). Why? What specific equilibrium concept in sequential games rules out the applicability of these outcomes? *Hint:* How would you describe the game tree from Node E onward as opposed to the game tree from Node D onward?

11. What problems arise in PepsiCo's couponing customers every other week to try to attract additional business? Would mail-order segmentation of PepsiCo versus Coca-Cola customers help this process? How?

12. Suppose you have announced you will "meet the competition" in response to entry threats by a potential rival who has done marketing research in your target market and

is offering a lower price point. What difference does it make, if any, if technology is moving very fast in the market so that this game proves to be one-time-only simultaneous play?

13. Analyze the following sequential game and advise Kodak about whether they should introduce the new product Picture CD.

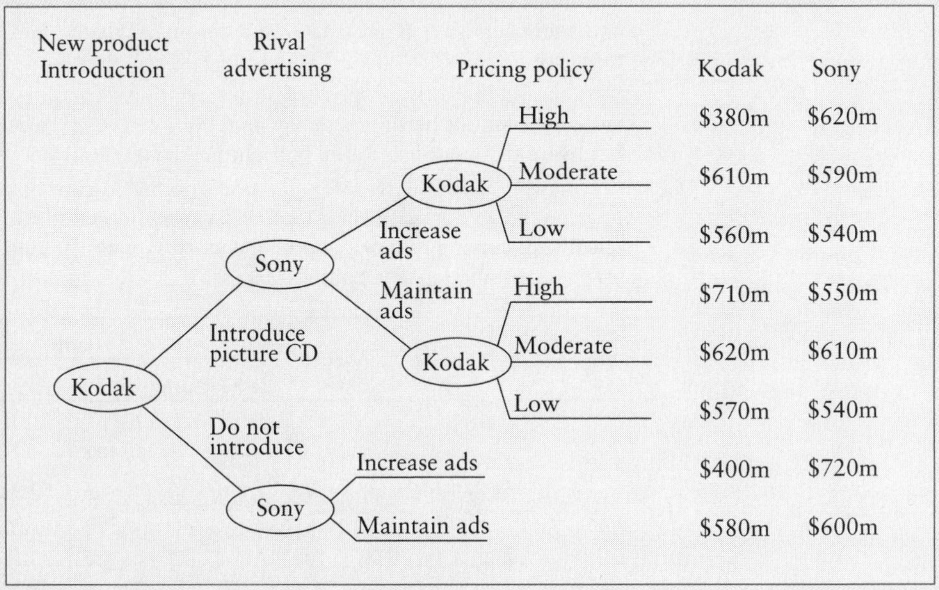

14. Calculate the 8-hour-shift costs of operating a taxi with a medallion license that cost $125,000 borrowed at 10 percent interest assuming two shifts for 365 days per year, plus a $25,000 car that depreciates 50 percent in one year, plus $22 for gas and maintenance per shift per day. Would you pay $60/shift for a taxi operator's license? Why or why not?

15. A math graduate student explains to her friends how to approach a group of smart attractive guys who have brought along famous actor Russell Crowe. What should her friend do? Ignore Russell Crowe or fixate on Russell Crowe? Explain the equilibrium reasoning underlying your answer.

		Student 1	
		Ignore R.C.	**Fixate on R.C.**
Student 2	**Ignore R.C.**	No date tonight (Worse) / No date tonight (Worse)	Date with R.C. (Best) / Date with other guys (Better)
	Fixate on R.C.	Date with other guys (Better) / Date with R.C. (Best)	No date ever (Worst) / No date ever (Worst)

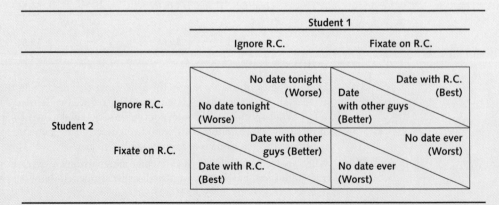

Note: Best payoff—date with R.C., Better—date with other guys, Worse—no date tonight, Worst—no date ever with any of these guys.

CASE EXERCISE

INTERNATIONAL PERSPECTIVES

THE SUPERJUMBO DILEMMA[26]

Boeing and Airbus build wide-bodied commercial aircraft in several sizes at the rate of about one per day. Customers first pay a deposit of one third of \$84–\$127 million for a 767, one third of \$134–\$185 million for a 777, and one third of \$165–\$200 million for a 747, depending on how the planes are equipped. The second third is due after final assembly when the aircraft is painted, and the final third is due at delivery. Final assembly requires 15–25 days, the entire production schedule is 11 months long, and of course, design modifications add months to the front end of each project. The largest of the Boeing planes (the 747-400) carries 432 passengers or 300 plus freight; by comparison, the largest Airbus planes (the A320 and A380) carry 330 and 550 passengers, respectively.

As early as 1993, Boeing and Airbus entered into discussions to jointly develop a very large commercial transport (VLCT) with perhaps 1,000 seats. If each firm proceeded independently, the market for VLCTs is so small relative to the massive R&D costs that sizeable losses were assured. Either firm had superior profit available if it proceeded alone. Analyze this noncooperative product development game and predict what Boeing and Airbus would do and why.

In contrast, the two competitors decided to enter into a strategic alliance with the option to develop a superjumbo or withdraw and maintain a wide-bodied aircraft focus. Analyze Boeing's decision in light of its \$45 million contribution margin on each 747 produced and sold. Net operating profit is about \$15 million.

Boeing\Airbus	Enter Strategic Alliance and Jointly Develop VLCT	Enter Strategic Alliance but Don't Agree to Develop VLCT
Enter Strategic Alliance and Jointly Develop VLCT	Reduced development risk Cannibalize wide-bodied business	Loss from alliance costs Max default risk, possibly net profit
Enter Strategic Alliance but Don't Agree to Develop VLCT	Max default risk, possibly a net profit Loss from alliance costs but preserve wide-bodied business	Loss from alliance costs Ongoing net profit of \$15mm per wide-bodied plane

[26] Based on M. Kretschmer, "Game Theory: The Developer's Dilemma, Boeing v. Airbus," Booz, Allen, and Hamilton, *Strategy & Business* (Second Quarter 1998); "Towards the Wild Blue Yonder," *The Economist* (April 27, 2002), p. 67; "Giving 'em Away," *BusinessWeek* (March 5, 2001), pp. 52–55; "Global Dogfight," *Wall Street Journal* (June 1, 2005), p. A1.

QUESTIONS

1. Why did Airbus go ahead with the A380 Superjumbo with its 550 seats, $10.7 billion development cost, and 250 planes required to break even by 2010?

2. In 2004, Boeing produced fewer planes than Airbus (see Figure 13.9). If Boeing finds itself less profitable at 60 percent market share than at 45 percent, what is the likely impact on the Airbus-Boeing tactical competition?

Figure 13.9 Wide-Bodied Aircraft Deliveries by Year

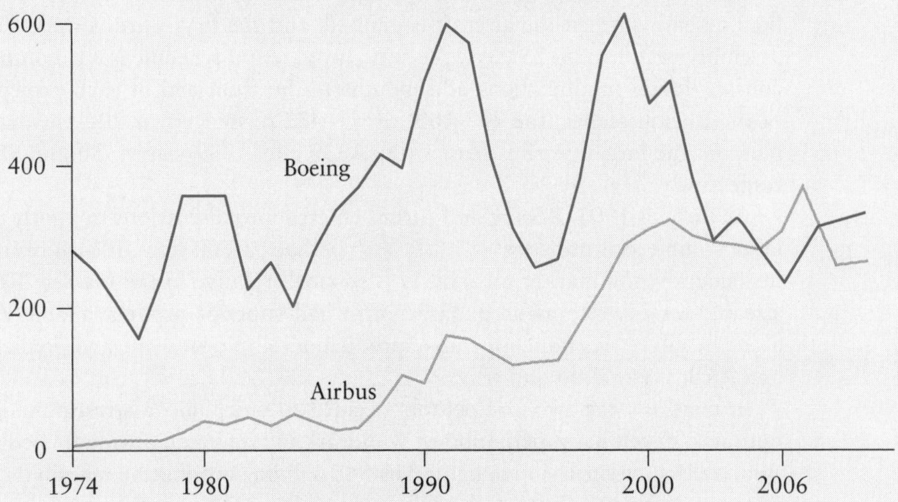

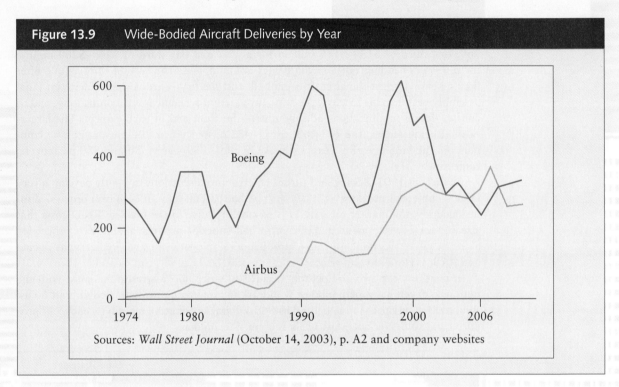

Sources: *Wall Street Journal* (October 14, 2003), p. A2 and company websites

3. The EU claims that Boeing was given $3.2 billion in tax exemptions by the State of Washington to support the Boeing Dreamliner 787 project. The United States claims that Airbus received $6 billion in loans that do not need to be repaid to support the research, development, and launch aid for the Airbus 380 Superjumbo. These charges and countercharges at the World Trade Organization address whether either firm is "dumping" when it brings the first 787s and 380s to market. Name some categories of cost that should be covered by the early penetration prices in order to avoid such charges of predatory pricing.

APPENDIX

13a

Entry Deterrence and Accommodation Games

In this appendix, we examine the tactical issues that arise when an incumbent firm faces an imminent threat of entry. We analyze whether to accommodate or attempt to deter the potential entrant and what capacity planning or limit pricing or sunk cost investment tactics to employ in that effort. At the end, we characterize contestable markets as dependent on both entry and exit barriers.

Excess Capacity As a Credible Threat

One type of credible threat or commitment that can markedly influence the subsequent competition is an investment in nonredeployable excess capacity. Irreversible investment in excess capacity credibly commits a high-priced incumbent to serve the price-sensitive new customers who might be attracted into the market by a potential entrant's discounting. If these and other regular customers can be expected to favor doing business with the incumbent, then excess capacity investment can substantially enhance the deterrent effect of an incumbent's threat to cut prices in response to entry.

Why exactly does excess capacity enhance an incumbent's threat to reduce prices should low-price entrants appear in the market? Is it that the incumbent can thereby prevent the new entrant from acquiring a large market share? Is it that the incumbent can deny the new entrant a unique reputation for low prices? Is it that the incumbent can become more profitable than before the entry threat? The answer to all these questions is no. The sole reason any action or communication is credible is if it makes the threat-maker worse off ignoring the threat than carrying out the threat. In Figure 13A.1, the competitive firm that invests in excess capacity by expanding from Plant 1 to Plant 2 is worse off with unchanged output Q_1 and unit costs of \$180 at A than selling the larger output Q_2 with unit costs of \$120 at B. A noncompetitive firm that must lower price to carry out a threat thereby increases sales and also moves from Q_1 to Q_2. Ignoring the threat would leave the incumbent worse off with higher unit costs at A now that Plant 1 has been replaced by Plant 2.

EXAMPLE

Excess Capacity Declines in the World Car Market: Samsung and Hyundai[1]

Sales in the three biggest and most profitable car markets in the United States, Europe, and Japan are stagnant. Worldwide, auto and light truck sales only grew from

[1] Based on Ward's Automotive *Yearbook*, "Car Making in Asia: Politics of Scale," *The Economist* (June 24, 2000), pp. 68–69, and "In Asia, GM Pins Hopes on a Delicate Web," *Wall Street Journal* (October 23, 2001), p. A23.

Figure 13A.1 Excess Capacity Enhances Credibility in Entry Deterrence

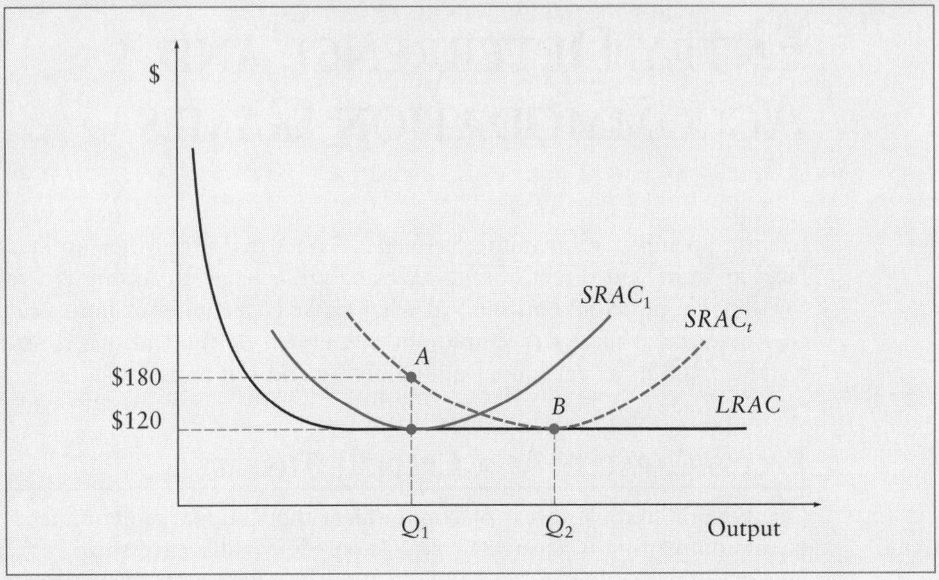

57 to 58 million vehicles between 2003–2006. Vehicle manufacturers reduced surplus capacity from 40% in 2003 with 79 million being produced to 16% in 2006 with 67 million vehicles projected. Nissan and Mitsubishi in Japan and DaimlerChrysler, Ford and General Motors all lost from 7 to 12% of sales volume in the first eight months of 2006. Among large manufacturers, Hyundai and Honda increased sales volume at 5% over 2005, and Toyoda experienced 11% unit sales growth, sufficient to move ahead of Ford as the second-largest auto manufacturer (see Table 13A.1). Why add excess capacity in such a business environment?

Economies of scale do not seem to be involved. Toyoda and Hyundai have already reached minimum efficient scale. Moreover, the GM Opel-Fiat-Saab-Daewoo and Ford-Jaguar-Volvo-Land Rover-Mazda global alliances focus on designing common platforms for vehicle families so that multimillion-dollar body-stamping machines and assembly plants can produce Opel Astra sedans one week and Fiat Zafira seven-seat minivans the next. Increasingly, up to a dozen different vehicles share the same

Table 13A.1 2005 Worldwide Auto and Light Truck Sales (Top 10)

General Motors	14.5%	Peugot Group	5.4%
Toyoda	11.4%	Honda	5.4%
Ford	10.3%	Nissan	5.4%
VW Group	8.3%	Hyundai Group	4.6%
DaimlerChrysler	6.9%	Renault Group	4.2%

Source: International Organization of Motor Vehicle Manufacturers

platform and assembly line. Even with less popular vehicles, minimum efficient scale has therefore become much less difficult to achieve.

A second explanation for capacity expansions highlights the location of the new capacity, much of which is appearing in Asia, especially South Korea and Thailand. Two thirds of the growth in new car sales between 2000–2010 is projected to come in the developing countries of China and India. Korean conglomerate Samsung recently opened a new robot-equipped 500,000-vehicle plant at an investment of $5 billion even though Korean production (at 6 million vehicles) is already substantially ahead of domestic consumption (1.5 million vehicles) plus export sales (3.5 million vehicles). Predictably, local retail auto prices in Korea collapsed as the looming overcapacity forced profit margins down to levels that no longer attract new auto industry investment.

But that may have been exactly the idea. Incumbent manufacturers like Hyundai and Kia want to deter further entry into an economy that can easily ship to the Asian growth market. Precommitting to enough capacity that no potential entrant will doubt their threat to aggressively cut prices is a way to defend market share. If this tactical initiative works and potential entrants stay out, the incumbent firms will never have to make good on their threat.

PRECOMMITMENTS USING NON-REDEPLOYABLE ASSETS

To address the tactical ramifications of installing excess capacity, consider the capacity decision of a well-established hospital that faces an entry threat from an outpatient clinic specializing in obstetrics and elective plastic surgery. The hospital is constructing a new surgical wing. The hospital's business manager can build a new facility to meet the future demand projected at their currently high prices, or she can include some considerable excess capacity in her expansion plans. Suppose that the birthing rooms and type of operating theater used in obstetrics and plastic surgery are not redeployable to general surgical or other specialized uses. Instead, the excess capacity, if built, will serve as a non-redeployable excess capacity precommitment by the hospital to compete for all the new price-sensitive business that a lower-priced outpatient surgical clinic might attract into the market.

The structure of this game is presented in the decision tree in Figure 13A.2. The hospital chooses excess capacity or not; the outpatient surgical clinic chooses thereafter to enter or stay out, and the hospital then controls the pricing endgame. If the hospital builds excess capacity, it is more likely to cut prices in the face of entry, and the clinic is then better off staying out. If the hospital does not build excess capacity, it is more likely to accommodate the entrant by maintaining high prices, and the clinic is then better off entering. Therefore, looking ahead to predict the hospital and the clinic's best-reply responses in the various proper subgames and endgames, the hospital's likely choices narrow to two strategies shaded in Figure 13A.2: {Excess Capacity, Stay Out, Limit Pricing} and {No Excess Capacity, Enter, Accommodate with Moderate Price}.

Clearly, business as usual is no longer an option. In particular, the very profitable prior business with high prices, no excess capacity, and no competition in the top row of the game tree is no longer a focal outcome of interest. The entry threat may require that the incumbent hospital now maximize its remaining profit by precommiting itself to constructing some excess capacity. In that scenario, then, the clinic

Figure 13A.2 Excess Capacity Precommitment Game

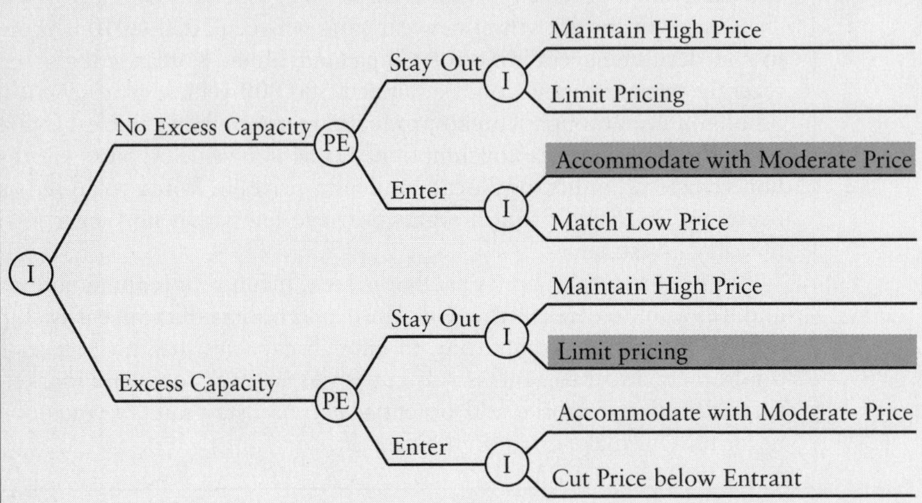

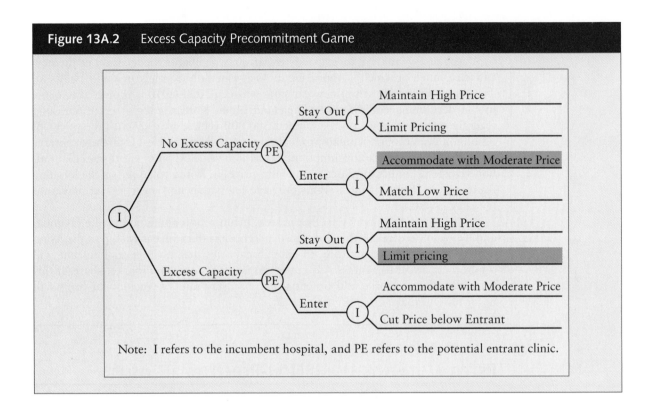

Note: I refers to the incumbent hospital, and PE refers to the potential entrant clinic.

will consider hit-and-run entry, but probably decide instead to stay out and enter the same market in another community with less capacity present or projected.

In general, whether incumbents will choose to deter potential entrants (e.g., in the bottom half of the game tree in Figure 13A.2) by the use of excess capacity precommitments or will actually prefer to accommodate (in the top half of the game tree) by retaining their smaller capacities and lowering prices is a complex question that depends on several factors. As we saw earlier, the answer depends in part on whether the incumbent can secure a first-mover advantage. Without it, in Entry Deterrence I, the incumbent Pastense discounted, but with it in Entry Deterrence II Pastense moderated prices.

This deterrence/accommodation decision also depends on whether the post-entry competition will be in prices among differentiated product sellers, each with some market power over price, or in quantities among homogeneous product sellers with no market power over price. Finally, the decision to deter or accommodate depends on how old and new customers in various segments of the market sort between an incumbent with excess capacity and a capacity-constrained lower-priced new entrant.

Customer Sorting Rules

If the entrant attracts only new price-sensitive customers, that's one thing. If, on the other hand, the new entrant takes away high-willingness-to-pay regular customers of the incumbent, that's something else. Not surprisingly, the former situation more typically leads to accommodation; the latter often leads to deterrence.

Brand Loyalty

A customer sorting rule favorable to incumbents.

Efficient Rationing

A customer sorting rule in which high-willingness-to-pay customers absorb the capacity of low-price entrants.

Inverse Intensity Rationing

A customer sorting rule that assures that low-willingness-to-pay customers absorb the capacity of low-price entrants.

Random Rationing

A customer sorting rule reflecting randomized buyer behavior.

Probably the simplest customer sorting pattern of all is extreme **brand loyalty** to incumbents. In this case, even in the face of differentially higher prices, customers reject the new entrant's offered capacity and instead backorder and reschedule when denied service at the incumbent. Competitive pressure from imitators normally erodes this degree of market power, but Microsoft Windows and popular local restaurants provide examples of products and services whose brand loyalty has sustained such a customer sorting pattern. At the other extreme, **efficient rationing** allocates the fixed-priced capacity of new entrant discounters in a manner that achieves maximum consumer surplus. This customer sorting rule implies that those with the highest willingness to pay will exert the effort, time, and inconvenience to seek out, queue up, and order early to secure low-priced capacity. Of course, one obvious qualification is that these customers may also have the highest opportunity cost of their time.

A third alternative, then, is **inverse intensity rationing,** a much less threatening customer sorting pattern posed by new low-priced capacity in a segmented market. In this instance, the low-willingness-to-pay customers quickly absorb all the capacity of the low-priced entrant. Starting with a customer just willing to pay the entrant's low price, one proceeds conceptually up the demand curve only as far as required to stock out the new entrant. In this instance, the demand of the incumbent may be largely unaffected if the discounter's capacity remains relatively small. Finally, there is **random rationing** of the low-priced capacity. Under random rationing, all customers willing to pay the low prices—i.e., both regular customers of the incumbent and the new customers attracted into the market by the entrant's discounting—have an equal chance of securing the low-priced capacity. For example, if 70 customers were present in the market at the incumbent's original high price, and 30 additional customers appear in response to the discounts, the probability of any 1 of the 100 potential customers securing service from 40 units of low-priced capacity is $40/100 = 0.4$. Conversely, the probability of not being served is $(1 - 0.4) = 0.6$, such that any customer may need to seek out higher-priced capacity with this probability. Under random rationing, therefore, the incumbent's expected demand falls as a result of the entry from 70 to $(70 \times 0.6) = 42$.

Because of the pivotal nature of the decision timing and of these customer sorting rules in predicting deterrence versus accommodation behavior, game-theoretic analysis must often be intertwined with an industry study in order to discriminate among the many possible implications. Otherwise, the rational business decisions of incumbents in these models may vary over a wide range of alternatives from the relatively passive acquisition of excess capacity all the way to the aggressive incumbent who occasionally predates by pricing below cost with no prospect of later recovering the loss. For the purpose of predicting rival behavior, this state of game-theoretic knowledge presents something of an embarrassment of riches. Hence, we reiterate the importance of doing sufficient field research to discover the particulars of the industry or firm-specific situation.

In Web Appendix D, we explore the entry deterrence and accommodation game between US Airways and People Express and between United and Jet Blue. Detailed cost, price, and realized revenue data allow us to distinguish among several pricing and capacity choice implications of sequential game theory. The analysis lends support to the importance of customer sorting "rules" in explaining why People Express met with little resistance and indeed was accommodated by incumbents in mid-Atlantic city-pair markets, but encountered effective deterrence from US Airways in the Southeastern city-pair markets. Eventually, People Express was forced to withdraw and exit from all of its Southeastern routes.

A Role for Sunk Costs in Decision Making

In both theory and practice, sequential games of entry deterrence and accommodation have uncovered a very rich variety of strategic incumbent behavior in response to entry or potential entry. These include the excess capacity precommitments just discussed as well as credible price discount threats. However, they also include price discrimination and capacity allocation schemes. Such yield management or revenue management systems can provide incumbents with an effective way to deter new entrant discounters. We discuss revenue management in Chapter 14.

Finally, entry deterrence and accommodation strategy may also be expressed through advertising campaigns or other promotional investments in non-redeployable assets. As we mentioned in Chapter 13, some examples would be reputational investments in company logos (such as CARMAX), unique stand-alone retail stores like McDonald's, or L'eggs retail displays unusable for selling anything other than egg-shaped products. All three investments precommit the incumbent to aggressively defend market share and cash flow in order to recover the cost of these non-redeployable investments.

Non-redeployable investments in specific assets are a reality in many businesses; these fixed asset expenses are said to be "sunk." Industrial machinery is often specialized to the purpose at hand and sometimes even to a particular supplier. For decades, Sara Lee Hosiery bought twisted nylon fiber for their highest quality hosiery from a sole source supplier, MacField Industries; the upstream nylon production equipment and the downstream hosiery spinning equipment were only usable as complements to this one supplier's twisted fiber input. Similarly, much of the trade secret knowledge discovered by Microsoft programmers is not easily packaged and separated out for redeployment and sale to another firm. Even airplanes cannot be redeployed to routes and trip distances for which they are not designed. Markets in which non-redeployable assets are common will be markets whose sunk cost conditions deter entry.

Perfectly Contestable Markets

Contestable Market

An industry with exceptionally open entry and easy exit where incumbents are slow to react.

Contestable markets are strategic industry groups in which new firms can enter and exit on short notice without anticipating losses due to sunk costs. Even if only a few firms dominate such a market, prices seldom rise above break-even levels because of the constant "hit and run" tactics of the frequent entrants. Rival firms jump in and scallop off the profits whenever prices rise and then escape quickly once the profits are dissipated. This hit and run entry/exit pattern ensures little divergence from cost-covering competitive equilibrium.

In the perfectly contestable markets scenario, incumbents react more slowly to entry threats than their regular customers, who chase after the most inexpensive supplier of the moment. In contrast, as we have seen in Figure 13A.2, proactive incumbents invest in excess capacity and non-redeployable assets in order to deter entry. That may sound like sunk-cost reasoning, and indeed it is. Recognizing the sequential nature of business strategy and the role of credible threats and credible commitments therein has led to a rehabilitation of the role of sunk costs in managerial decision making.

In fact, it is precisely because firms can do nothing about their sunk-cost investments, precisely because they are irreversible, irrevokable, and otherwise unrecoverable, that a particular threatened plan of action involving the use of these non-redeployable assets is credible. The player with sunk-cost investments has burned bridges. No better alternatives exist than to deliver on credible threats and to make credible commitments to remain in the business of serving repeat customers until the equipment becomes obsolete or wears out. Again, best-reply reasoning is the key to credibility, and credibility is the key to subgame perfect equilibrium strategy.

EXAMPLE

CONTESTABLE MARKET IN BICYCLE HELMETS: BELL SPORTS[2]

Bell Sports began as a motorcycle helmet manufacturer with a small side-bet business in bicycle helmets and accessories. Today Bell has $100 million sales of bicycle helmets, 85 percent of which occur in the United States. Twenty-seven states have initiated regulations making bicycle helmets mandatory for young riders. The potential growth in Europe, where bicycle helmets have become a fashion statement, is even greater. Prices range from $30 for colorful hard-shell designs to $140 for ultra-lightweight models.

The trouble with running a fast-growing niche business is that without sunk-cost investments, Bell inevitably attracted many new entrant competitors. Bicycle helmets are easy to fabricate and quickly sell themselves. All one needs is plastic molding machines and a foam extrusion process. These technologies are easily converted from many other industries, and more importantly, can be redeployed back to those other uses upon exit. The product sells well in bike shops and such discount stores as Kmart and Wal-Mart without any significant sales force, point-of-sale actions, or after-sale service required of the retail distributors. Consequently, the bicycle helmet market is a classic case of *contestable markets*. Bell Sports is constantly subject to hit-and-run entry from other niche manufacturers—i.e., Giro, Aurora, and Troxel Cycling.

The theory of contestable markets suggests that with no barriers to entry or exit and low customer costs of switching manufacturers, Bell Sports can never make more than a competitive profit in this business. As soon as prices rise above cost, temporary competitors enter the business, customers switch their allegiance, and Bell must lower prices. As a consequence, gross margins are low (averaging 8 percent) and fluctuate by as much as 50 percent from year to year. Bell's only alternatives are to outdo the hit-and-run entrants on new designs or to commit enough marketing investment dollars to establish a non-redeployable brand asset "Bell Helmets," like they have established in the motorcycle business. Until then, entry deterrence will prove infeasible, and entry accommodation must continue.

BRINKMANSHIP AND WARS OF ATTRITION

Sometimes the question of tactical interest is not one of deterring or accommodating the entry of other firms but rather how long should your own firm stay in an obviously declining business. In competing to win an exclusive license (e.g., to host the Olympics), to define an industry standard (e.g., for digital HDTV), to earn FDA

[2] Based on "Bell Sports," *Forbes* (February 13, 1995), pp. 67–68.

Figure 13A.3 A War of Attrition for HDTV Industry Standard

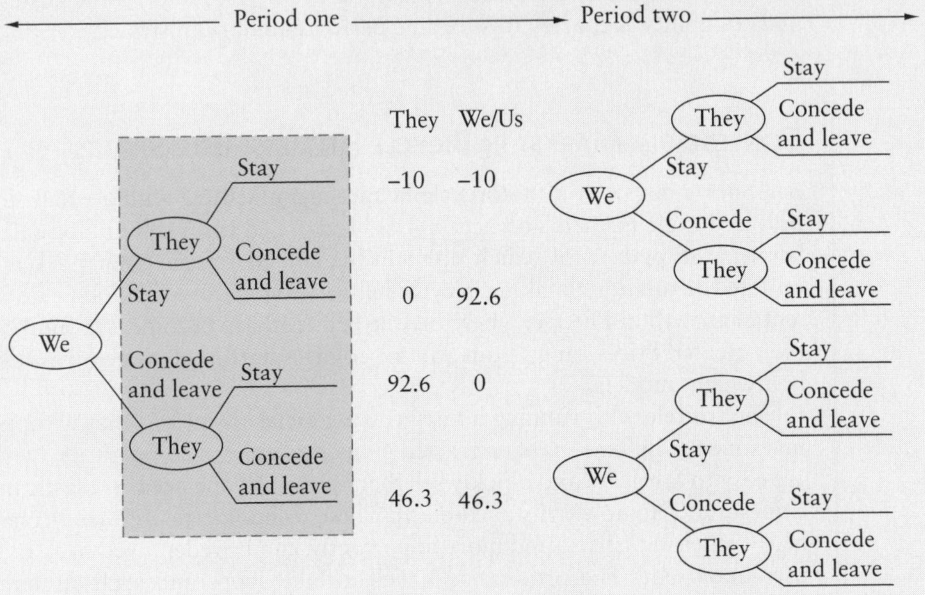

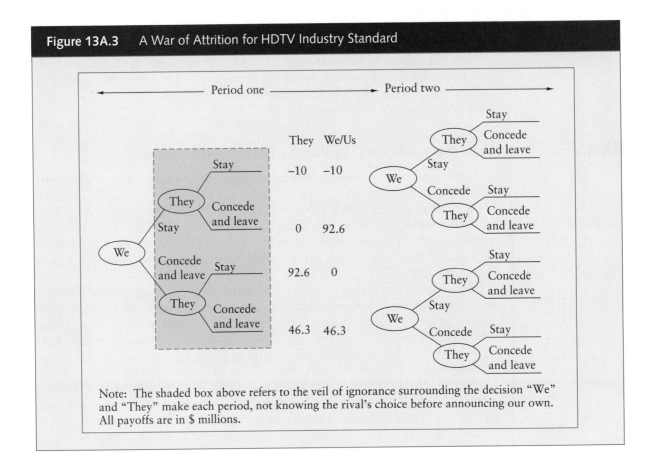

Note: The shaded box above refers to the veil of ignorance surrounding the decision "We" and "They" make each period, not knowing the rival's choice before announcing our own. All payoffs are in $ millions.

approval for a new class of drugs, or to capture the product loyalty of fickle customers with advertising, successive rounds of bloodletting by multiple competitors may prevent profitability until someone concedes and drops out. Hence, these tactical encounters are seen as an entry/exit game sometimes called "wars of attrition."

The first period of a multi-period sequential game representing a "war of attrition" is displayed on the left-hand side of Figure 13A.3. Each period requires a \$10 million "ante" at the start of the period just to remain in the game. No competitor knows her rivals' decision about staying when deciding whether to "hold 'em or fold 'em." It's as though auction bids were sealed and then opened simultaneously. If either firm concedes and leaves, it pays nothing, and the other firm's \$10 million ante is immediately recoverable by the firm who stays.

The market payoffs come at the end of the year and are equal to \$100 million if one firm concedes and \$50 million if both concede. These market prizes occur every year until the end of the game. If at the start of any period the rivals ("They") leave and concede the \$100 million market to "Us," a payoff of [$\$100/(1 + r)$] awaits—e.g., at 8 percent interest rates, ($\$100/1.08) - \$10 + \$10 = \$92.6$ million. If "We" concede when "They" stay, \$92.6 million awaits as their payoff. If both firms concede, they immediately merge, and the market is split 50–50 with no further cost. If "They" hang tough and stay in competition, and "We" do the same, both firms lose \$10 million—i.e., no one wins the prize that period. Then "We" proceed to the decision as to whether to spend another \$10 million ante to compete in the next period. The question is "How long should you stay?"

Consider the three-period game. If "We" leave now, the payoff is zero when "They" stay, and \$50 million when "They" concede. Let p be the probability that our opponent is a type who will concede immediately. Then the expected payoff from conceding immediately ourselves is just[3]

$$\$50p + 0(1 - p) \geq 0 \qquad [13A.1]$$

If we leave at the start of the second period, our expected payoff would be equal to

$$\$100p + \$50q - \$10 \geq 0 \qquad [13A.2]$$

where q is the probability that our rival will concede at the start of the second period, and $(1 - p - q)$ is the probability "They" will stay until the third period, never conceding. If we stay to the end, our expected payoff is as follows:

$$\$200p + \$100q - \$20 \geq 0 \qquad [13A.3]$$

Setting Equation 13A.1 equal to 13A.2 and 13A.2 equal to 13A.3, then solving simultaneously, yields the values of p and q that would leave "Us" just indifferent between conceding and hanging tough. Collecting terms and simplifying, we have

$$50p + 50q = 10 \qquad [13A.4]$$

$$-100p - 50q = -10 \qquad [13A.5]$$

which together imply $p = 0$, $q = 0.2$, and $(1 - p - q) = 0.8$.

In other words, "We" are indifferent as to conceding or hanging tough and paying \$10 million each of the first two periods to stay until the endgame if and only if there is no less than a 20-percent chance "They" will leave in the second period and no more than an 80-percent chance "They" will stay until the endgame. "We" decide whether to stay or leave by assessing the actual situation and actual rival and then comparing these 20 percent and 80 percent derived probability break points against our subjective probability estimates of the actual situation.

TACTICAL INSIGHTS ABOUT SLIPPERY SLOPES

Slippery Slope
A tendency for wars of attrition to generate mutual losses that worsen over time.

Note that $p = 0$ implies that neither party concedes immediately. Instead, $q = 0.2$ indicates a middle ground strategy of opponent types who test the competitive waters before conceding at the start of Period 2. This positive probability of "middle grounders" is a reflection of a **slippery slope.** Once you enter into a war of attrition and make your own first "ante" of -10 (because the Bayesian probability of Hang Toughers was less than 0.8), the probability of middle grounders who will step on that slippery slope with you is NOT zero. Instead, we have seen in the simultaneous solution to equations 13A.4 and 13A.5 that the equilibrium probability of middle grounders in this game is 0.2. That is, with the parameters assumed in this war of attrition, there is a 0.8 probability of a sequence of mutual losses, a death spiral until the less deep pocket is empty. Hence, these so-called "brinkmanship" games have serious and largely uncontrollable consequences even for the player with an

[3] In the discussion that follows, we ignore discounting to simplify the analysis. The payoff of \$92.6 million therefore becomes \$100 million.

apparently advantaged position. If you misestimate the depth of an opponent's pocket, 80% of the time you will be up against Hang Toughers and stepping onto a slippery slope to financial ruin; your own financial ruin.

What is a best-reply response in the n period game? Continuing to ignore the discounting of future cash flows for the moment to simplify the analysis, if we hang tough until the rivals leave and if the rivals leave in period t, we realize the \$100 million market prize for $n - t$ periods and pay \$10 million for t periods. Since if we leave now, zero (i.e., $\$50p = 0$) is the payoff, and the expected value of all other alternatives can be no worse than this; otherwise we'll just leave now. Combining these facts

$$(n - t)\ \$100 - t\ \$10 > 0 \qquad [13A.6]$$

$$0.91n > t \qquad [13A.7]$$

where 0.91 is the ratio of the \$100-million prize to the sum of (the periodic cost \$10 million plus the \$100 million prize).

How should we interpret equation 13A.7? If "We" believe the rivals will stay 91 percent of the total time or less, we should stay ourselves. If we believe "They" will stay more than 91 percent (or, with discounting, 90.25 percent) of the total time, we should concede immediately and save our \$10 million ante to invest in another competition elsewhere. For the three-period case, if "We" believe the rivals will stay less than $0.9025 \times 3 = 2.71$ years, we should hang tough and stay to the end ourselves.

Obviously, these calculations apply equally to the symmetrically-positioned "They" as well, so wars of attrition quickly become a matter of bluffing and signaling. The most useful insight the above analysis offers in such entry/exit games is that each player should assess the probability of her rivals' leaving in light of all the available evidence and should hinge her own decision on the ratio of the prize to the sum of the prize plus periodic cost. Very much like playing straight draw poker, you hold rather than fold the bigger the prize and the smaller the periodic cost of hanging tough and calling your rivals' bluff.

SUMMARY

- Incumbents may seek to deter potential entrants through the use of excess capacity precommitments or credible threats of advertising campaigns and price discounts.
- Whether incumbents deter or accommodate potential entrants depends in general on the presence or absence of first-mover advantages, on the structure of competition in prices versus quantities, and on how customers sort across alternative firms when the low-priced capacity stocks out.
- Customer sorting patterns include the following: random rationing in which all customers are equally likely to obtain the low-priced capacity; efficient rationing in which the highest (then next highest) willingness-to-pay customers obtain the low-priced capacity until it is exhausted; extreme brand loyalty in which none of the regular customers seek the low-priced capacity; and inverse intensity rationing in which the lowest (then next lowest) willingness-to-pay customers obtain the low-priced capacity until it is exhausted. With inverse intensity rationing, the customer sorting implies a segmented market and is most likely to lead to accommodation of entry.
- In wars of attrition, whether to hang tough and stay in competition for a market price or concede defeat and leave depends on the ratio of the prize to the sum of the prize plus the periodic cost of competing.

Exercises

1. Dunkin Donuts and McDonald's MacCafe have entered the specialty coffee business pioneered at Starbuck's 5,439 locations. Prices are 20% lower (99 cent espresso shots versus $1.45 at Starbuck's), orders are simpler (Large Mocha Swirl Latte at $2.69 versus Venti Caffe Mocha at $3.35), and the wait time is under a minute versus three to five.[4] Have Starbucks Frappacino's become an affordable luxury? Or is espresso coffee and flavored coffee going mainstream where Dunkin and McDonald's have 17% and 15% of the fast-food outlet brewed coffee business, respectively, to Starbuck's 6%? Which is happening in your city? Moreover, as MacCafe approaches Starbuck's market, what customer sorting rule will likely apply? Is there any reason to believe Starbuck's will have a different strategy in responding to Dunkin Donuts 4,100 stores versus the several hundred MacCafe's under development? Why?
2. Consumer electronics has often been a brutally competitive business with retailers offering one price promotion after another (10% below the best price elsewhere, 20% below, 30% below) to try to attract business away from rivals. Circuit City with $4.4 billion in sales in 2004 got 35% of its revenue from consumer electronics, 24% from audio products and entertainment software, and 41% from videos, video games, and video game equipment. Best Buy with $11.6 billion in sales in 2004 got 37% from consumer electronics, 19% from entertainment software, 6% from appliances, and 38% from home office equipment. If Best Buy and Circuit City were to enter a war of attrition today, which one would be forced to exit first? Why?

[4] Based on "Latte versus Latte," *Wall Street Journal* (February 10, 2004), p. B1.

CHAPTER

14

Pricing Techniques and Analysis

CHAPTER PREVIEW This chapter builds on the price and output determination models developed in Chapters 10 through 13 as it considers more complex pricing issues. The first two sections examine a value-based pricing conceptual framework. Then we characterize differential pricing in segmented markets where different target customers are charged nonuniform prices for identical products at different times or places. Differential pricing is often accomplished with bundled pricing, couponing, and two-part tariffs (an access or entry fee combined with a user fee). Finally, we discuss the concept of pricing throughout the product life cycle including target pricing, penetration pricing, price skimming, pricing for organic growth, limit pricing, and niche pricing. We conclude with a section on pricing of goods and services sold over the Internet. Finally, applications of revenue management in airlines, fashion clothing, and baseball are explained. Together, the pricing practices presented in this chapter provide an extensive overview of the way managers actually apply pricing techniques to maximize shareholder wealth.

Two additional pricing topics closely related to accounting (pricing of joint products and transfer pricing) are presented in Web Appendix E.

MANAGERIAL CHALLENGE

Pricing of Apple Computers: Market Share Versus Current Profitability[1]

Apple Computer manufactures and sells MacBook and iMac personal computers, Mac mini home entertainment systems as well as the famous iPod. All these products are innovative in design and stylistically striking. Some people compare the lifestyle choice of a Mac to driving a sports car rather than a sedan. The recent alliance between Apple, Disney, and Intel promises to deliver a home entertainment product line of breakthrough quality.

Historically, Apple priced its products higher than similar models of other computer makers. For example, despite price cuts throughout the 2000s by both Apple and Dell, MacBooks are still priced $300 to $500 higher than somewhat comparable Dell machines. Consequently, except for an upswing attributable to the opening of several high-profile retail stores in 2005–2006, Apple's market share fell from 2001 to 2004. Nevertheless, Apple's margins increased (from 24 percent to 29 percent).

By emphasizing current profit over market share, Apple emphasized the high value-in-use of its distinctive products but discouraged independent software providers (ISPs) from writing software

MANAGERIAL CHALLENGE

© RUBBERBALL/RUBBERBALL PRODUCTIONS/GETTY IMAGES

applications for the Mac. Some observers believe that the company would have to increase its market share to as much as 20 percent to accomplish the ISP objective. Ian Diery, Apple's sales vice president, defended the company's high prices, saying that Apple had to improve its balance sheet so that it could continue research and marketing efforts and idea creation. Is Apple's decision to charge premium prices for its products the right approach?

Steve Jones, longtime chief marketing officer of Coca-Cola, agrees that a company with leading-edge products must remain positioned at a high-end price point. "This world was not created by an accountant? No, the universe was created by the combustion of a creative explosion. Fire and explosion started everything; then order came on top."[2] His advice for generating organic growth in settings such as Apple's is to "provide an ignition source, create sparks, engage in reverse process thinking, clarify the innovation, define the destination for the brand, inspire and then get out of the way." Company staff and trend-setter customers will then co-create the new sources of customer value.

[1] Jim Carlton, "Apple's Choice: Preserve Profits or Cut Prices," *Wall Street Journal* (February 22, 1995), p. B1; and "Apple Gets Vote of Confidence," *Wall Street Journal* (September 14, 2006), p. B1.

[2] Remarks at the Wake Forest MBA Marketing Summit, "Using Advertising and Creativity to Drive Your Brand," Winston-Salem, North Carolina (February 13, 2006).

A CONCEPTUAL FRAMEWORK FOR PROACTIVE, SYSTEMATIC-ANALYTICAL, VALUE-BASED PRICING

In the past, pricing decisions were often treated as an afterthought. Companies either routinely marked up prices or reacted in an ad hoc fashion to a competitor's discounting. Today, systematically analyzing which orders to accept and which to refuse at many different value-based price points has become a critical success factor for many businesses.

Proactive pricing is tactically astute and internally consistent with a company's operations strategy. A high-cost, full-service, hub-and-spoke airline cannot slash prices dramatically even if it means 10 or 20 percent increases in market share in a high-margin segment. It must instead anticipate a matching price reaction by its lower-cost rivals, perhaps followed by still further price cuts below its own cost. Knowing these possibilities in advance makes discounting to gain market share much less attractive despite additional incremental sales in a high-margin business.

Pricing decisions must also be systematic and analytical, based on hard facts instead of ad hoc hunches. In the men's aftershave business, an incumbent recently encountered a new entrant with a penetration price 40 percent below the leading brands Skin Bracer, Old Spice, and Aqua Velva. The incumbent increased advertising but maintained its original price point and was astounded to observe a 50 percent decline in market share through its grocery store distribution channel. Only after-the-fact was a systematic analysis undertaken. Careful demand estimations showed that customers in the grocery store channel were price elastic and advertising inelastic.

Most importantly, pricing should be value-based. Prestone and Zerex sell leading anticorrosive radiator fluids whose product characteristics warrant a price premium. Under apparent price pressure, Zerex often simply matches any competitor's discount as long as competing prices on generic radiator fluid cover cost. A thorough value analysis reveals, however, that this reactive cost-based pricing failed to realize about one-third of Zerex's sustainable profit margin. Cost-based pricing has been called one of the "five deadly business sins" by Peter Drucker; what firms should do instead is "price-based costing." That is, firms should segment customers, perform an extensive value analysis, and then develop products whose costs allow substantial profitability in each product line the firm chooses to enter. Each firm's marketing and operations capabilities are the key to then sustaining that profitability.

Costs are not irrelevant. Indeed, a key to effective pricing management is to know precisely what activity-based costs are associated with each type of order from each customer segment. Knowing these costs allows firms to adopt differential pricing and allows value-based pricing managers to discern *which orders to refuse*. This insight—that every company has orders that it should refuse—is the key to a new set of pricing techniques known as "yield management" or more generally "revenue management (RM)." In an RM approach, costs become the consequence of a value-based pricing and product development strategy.

Value–in-Use
The difference between the value customers place on functions, cost savings, and relationships attributable to a product or service and the life cycle costs of acquiring, maintaining, and disposing of the product or service.

The appropriate conceptual framework for setting prices is to "know thy customer" through an analysis of the target customer's **value-in-use**. Value-in-use is the cost savings that arise from pursuing any given customer goal through the use of your product or service. A faster commute on a toll road or a nonstop jet to a distant second-tier city saves the $220-an-hour attorney or accountant exactly that much time value per hour. A Google ad with a documented click-through rate saves the advertising expenditure on additional magazine ads or cable TV commercials. An integrated and easy to use Kodak digital photography system saves time, money, and inconvenience in image capture, photo editing, developing, distribution, and storage.

EXAMPLE

Coated Coronary Stents Reduce the Cost of Later Surgeries[3]

Several angioplasty heart surgeries are performed every day in every major hospital worldwide. Through a non-invasive, relatively simple surgical procedure, a ballon is threaded into the femoral artery along the thigh and then directed upwards into a clogged coronary artery, where is is inflated to clear the blockage. Eighty percent of the time an $800 medical device (a stent) made of coiled wire resembling the spring

[3] Based on "Stents: Hospitals Wrangle Over More Expensive Stents," *Triad Business Journal* (May 30, 2002); "Guidant Stops Trials," *Wall Street Journal* (March 8, 2002), p. B8; "Preliminary Results of Large Scale U.S. Study with CYPHERT," www.jnj.com (May 22, 2002); "Medical Device Maker Sees Vast Market for Cardiac Stent," *Miami-Herald* (March 16, 2003); and "How Doctors Are Rethinking Drug-Coated Stents," Wall Street Journal (December 9, 2006), p. A1.

in a ball point pen is then inserted into the coronary artery to hold it open. The coronary stent market grew from introduction in the mid 1990s to $6 billion worldwide in 2006 with over a millions stents sold annually in the U.S. and an almost equal number sold abroad. In 15 to 30 percent of these cases, however, scar tissue grows around the wire stent reclosing the artery. That complication then necessitates $42,500 for follow-up open heart surgical procedures and additional treatments.

Recent advances by Cordis, a subsidiary of Johnson & Johnson, and by Boston Scientific, Guidant, and Medtronic have coated the coronary stent with an antibiotic or a cell-killing cancer drug to stop the scar tissue from forming. In its most advanced form, hollow stents can be made to eleut just the right amount of time-release pharmaceutical over a 45-day post-op period to prevent the vessel wall scarring. J&J's Sirolimus eleuting stent called CYPHER has practically eliminated the problem in routine angioplasties, reducing the incidence of reblockage to 3 percent in various human trials. Achieving a 12 to 27 percent reduction in the likelihood of $42,500 open heart surgery saves the patient $5,100 × (0.12 × $42,475) to $11,475 (0.27 × $42,500) in expected future medical expenses as well as avoiding the risks of the additional surgeries.

Hospitals and their attending surgeons charge on average $9,700 for the overnight stay plus the angioplasty with stent insertion. The original uncoated stent is billed to patients at an additional $1,165, for a total average bill of $10,865. The drug-eleuting stent device will be billed to patients at about $4,150 for a total average bill of $13,850. The almost $2,985 increase in price for a coated stent is well below the patient's $5,100 to $11,475 value-in-use from avoiding the need for subsequent open-heart surgery.

Table 14.1 lists various tangible and psychological sources of value-in-use, including product specifications and ease of use, delivery reliability, frequency, change order responsiveness, loyalty programs, and empathy in order processing. Many of these sources of cost savings are functional points of differentiation, but others are relationship-based. In addition, marketing communications seeks to position and brand the product through advertising, personal selling, and event marketing. Viral marketing identifies trend setters among the target customer group and seeks to place the product with those individuals, hoping that others will follow their lead. Because consumers strive to avoid psychological dissonance, products that affirm a particular lifestyle or group identity can often generate perceived value well beyond tangible cost savings. Coca-Cola and Starbucks each offer a lifestyle association and identity that would otherwise necessitate much larger clothing, travel, auto, and entertainment expenditures to achieve a similar result.

Importantly, lowest price is seldom what triggers a purchase. Instead, a target customer's purchase is triggered by a firm's generating customer value through functions, cost-savings, and relationships that exceed the product asking price or a ratio of value to asking price greater than a competitor's ratio. In Table 14.1, $0.50 is not the lowest price for a digital photography print, but Kodak's offering will trigger a purchase nevertheless if the excess customer value with the Kodak digital photography system ($2 − $0.50) exceeds the excess value from cheaper $0.29 products—perhaps ($1 − $0.29).

Consequently, firms often begin their pricing decisions by identifying the value-drivers in each and every customer segment. Business air travelers, for example, value conformance to the schedule, delivery reliability, and the ability to change

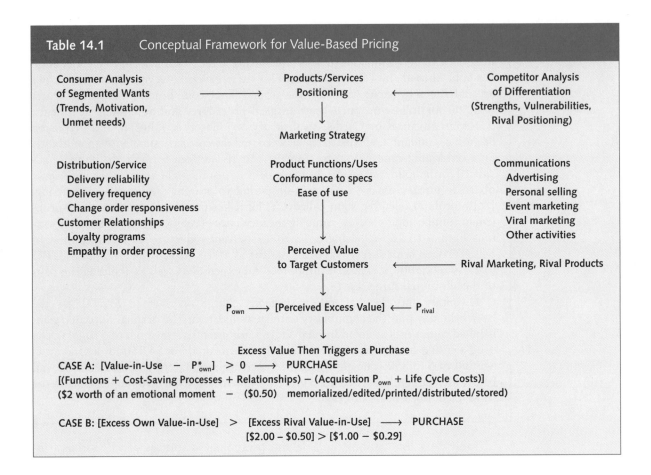

Table 14.1 Conceptual Framework for Value-Based Pricing

Consumer Analysis of Segmented Wants (Trends, Motivation, Unmet needs) ⟶ **Products/Services Positioning** ⟵ **Competitor Analysis of Differentiation (Strengths, Vulnerabilities, Rival Positioning)**

↓

Marketing Strategy

Distribution/Service
- **Delivery reliability**
- **Delivery frequency**
- **Change order responsiveness**

Customer Relationships
- **Loyalty programs**
- **Empathy in order processing**

Product Functions/Uses
- **Conformance to specs**
- **Ease of use**

Communications
- **Advertising**
- **Personal selling**
- **Event marketing**
- **Viral marketing**
- **Other activities**

↓

Perceived Value to Target Customers ⟵ **Rival Marketing, Rival Products**

↓

P_{own} ⟶ [Perceived Excess Value] ⟵ P_{rival}

↓

Excess Value Then Triggers a Purchase

CASE A: [Value-in-Use − P^*_{own}] > 0 ⟶ PURCHASE
[(Functions + Cost-Saving Processes + Relationships) − (Acquisition P_{own} + Life Cycle Costs)]
($2 worth of an emotional moment − ($0.50) memorialized/edited/printed/distributed/stored)

CASE B: [Excess Own Value-in-Use] > [Excess Rival Value-in-Use] ⟶ PURCHASE
[$2.00 − $0.50] > [$1.00 − $0.29]

itineraries on short notice more than frequent flights, good meals, and wide seats. Because that first set of process-based value drivers is harder to imitate, sustainable price premiums are often associated with those operations processes rather than the product or service characteristics of flights, meals, and seats. Because business travelers account for only 27 percent of the traffic but 80 percent of the profitability, a critical success factor for legacy airlines is to have hub processes and route planning that sustain these hard-to-imitate processes on nonstop flights.

In sum, pricing decisions should be proactive and systematically analytical, not reactive and ad hoc. Most importantly, pricing should be value-based, not cost-based. The value-in-use conceptual framework leads naturally to a differential pricing environment in which mass-produced products or services are customized to the requirements of target customer classes.

Optimal Differential Price Levels

The first step in setting optimal differential prices is then to estimate demand by market segment—say, for each of two customer classes (business and nonbusiness air travelers) on the Thursday 11:00 A.M. flight from DFW to LAX. The expense account business traveler tends to make less flexible travel plans and reserve space later and thus faces fewer close substitute alternatives than the nonbusiness traveler. Average

Figure 14.1 Optimal Differential Pricing and Capacity Allocation (45 Days in Advance) for Thursday 11:00 A.M. Flight from Dallas to Los Angeles

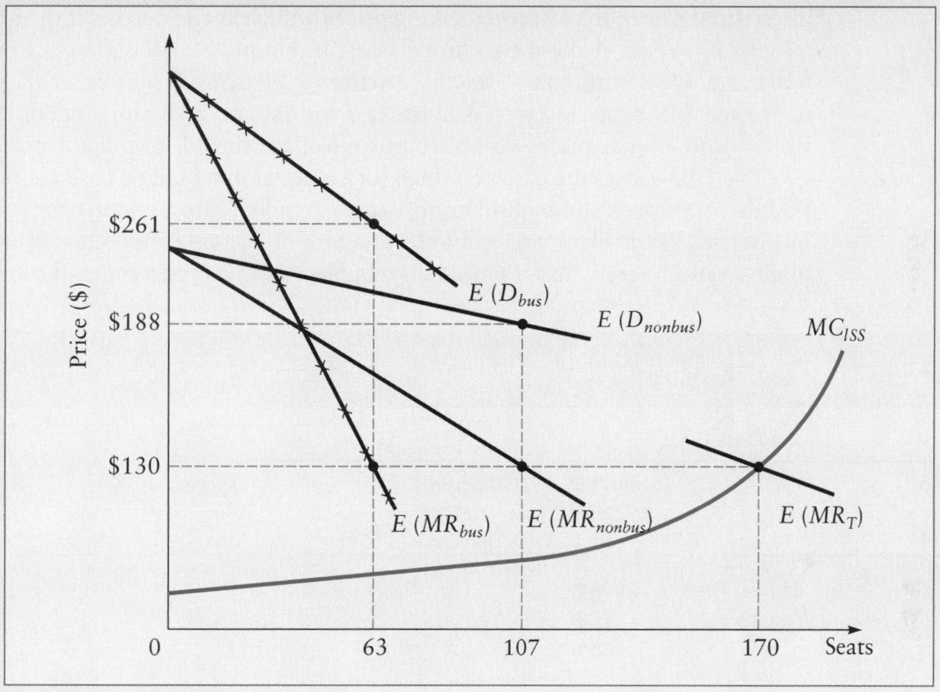

revenue and marginal revenue schedules for business travelers therefore prove to be less price elastic than for nonbusiness travelers, as indicated in Figure 14.1.

Previously, the airline's capacity planning department will have summed all the expected marginal revenues $E(MR)$ from the various segments and determined an optimal total capacity by setting summed marginal revenue $[\Sigma E(MR)]$ equal to the marginal cost of the last seat sold (MC_{lss}).[4] The result in Figure 14.1 is that a plane with 170 seats should be scheduled for the Thursday 11:00 A.M. flight departure.

One may think of the optimal differential pricing decision as determining how this total capacity of 170 seats should be allocated across the customer segments. Because at the margin a firm forgoes revenue unless the last customer in each segment contributes a marginal revenue equal to the marginal cost of the last seat sold (MC_{lss}), the optimal allocation of seating capacity results from equating the segment-level MRs to one another:

$$MR_{\text{bus}} = (MC_{\text{lss}}) = MR_{\text{nonbus}} \quad [14.1]$$

which in Figure 14.1 is at $MR = \$130$. Consider a case in which this condition does not hold. Suppose the 62nd seat sold in the business class contributed \$150 of marginal revenue and the 108th seat sold in the nonbusiness class contributed \$120. Clearly,

[4] To find aggregate demand, remember that individual demands (and *MRs*) are horizontally summed for rival goods that cannot be shared (such as airplane seats and bite-sized candy bars), whereas demands for nonrival goods (e.g., outdoor statues, tennis courts, and national defense) are vertically summed.

one could raise \$30 additional revenue for unchanged costs by selling one less seat in nonbusiness and one more in business, leaving both classes with, say, an $MR = \$130$.[5]

What prices can achieve the capacity allocation of 63 seats to the business class and 107 seats to the nonbusiness class? The answer is deceptively simple. Optimal differential prices are whatever asking prices will clear the market if the firm supplies 63 and 107 seats in these two fare classes. In Figure 14.1 the answer appears to be \$261 and \$188 with some effective barrier or "fencing," that prevents resale from the lower to the higher fares. The trick, of course, is predicting demand sufficiently well to know what prices will have this effect for the 11 A.M. flight next Thursday.

Table 14.2 shows the data on which such a decision would be based in practice. The first three columns show number of seats demanded, fares, and marginal revenue for business-class travelers. For example, at a fare of \$1,084, only one seat on the entire plane would be sold, and it would go to a business-class passenger. If the fare falls to

Table 14.2 Allocating Airline Capacity with Differential Fares for Leisure and Business

Business Class			Leisure Class				
Expected Seat Demand	Fare	Expected Marginal Revenue	Expected Seat Demand	Fare	Expected Marginal Revenue	Total Seats	Marginal Cost
1	\$1,084	\$1,084				1	\$87
2	1,032	980				2	87
3	974	858				3	87
4	907	705				4	87
5	835	550				5	87
10	613	390				10	87
			1	\$342	\$342		87
			2	331	320		95
			3	319	294		95
			4	311	288		95
20	456	280	5	305	280	25	95
			10	280	256		95
			20	260	240		95
30	381	230	30	250	230	60	100
			40	240	210		100
			50	231	194		100
40	331	180	60	222	180	100	112
			70	214	162		112
50	295	150	80	206	150	130	112
			90	198	140		120
60	268	133	100	192	133	160	125
63	261	130	107	188	130	170	130
			110	186	128		140
70	252	122	120	181	122	190	155
			130	176	115		170
80	235	110	140	173	110	220	190

[5] Note that the *MR* of each segment is not set equal to *MC*. Rather, the summed *MR* of all segments has been set equal to *MC*. The individual *MR*s are set equal to the *MC* of the last unit sold (i.e., \$130), and therefore equal to one another.

$1,032, two seats are taken by business-class passengers. At a fare of $974, three seats are taken, and so on. Expected marginal revenue is the increase in total revenue realized from selling one more seat in the business class. For example, when a single seat is sold at $1,084, total revenue is also $1,084. When two seats are sold at a fare of $1,032, however, total revenue jumps to $2,064, and marginal revenue, which is the difference in total revenue realized from selling one more seat, is $2,064 minus $1,084, or $980. Similarly, the marginal revenue associated with the third seat sold is $2,922 minus $2,064, or $858.

Table 14.2 also shows corresponding information for leisure class passengers. Note that the first leisure class seat is sold at $342, the second at $331, and so on. The last two columns depict total seats sold and marginal cost, which is the variable cost associated with serving one additional passenger in either class.

Using this simple two-booking-class example, marginal revenue equals rising marginal cost at $130 per seat. (Marginal cost increases by steps with the addition of flight attendants needed to serve additional passengers and the additional fuel consumed because of worsening aerodynamics at high load factors.) At MC = $130, optimal fares are obtained by equating individual marginal revenues of both segments and the marginal cost of the last seat expected to be sold (the 170th seat in this example). Business and leisure traveler marginal revenues equal $130 at 63 and 107 seats, respectively, and fares of $261 and $188 are optimal at these seat allocation levels.

MULTIPLE-PRODUCT PRICING

Figure 14.2 illustrates a situation of a firm with five products, D_1 represents the demand for Product 1, D_2 for Product 2, and so on. Again, profits are maximized when

Figure 14.2 Multiple-Product Pricing

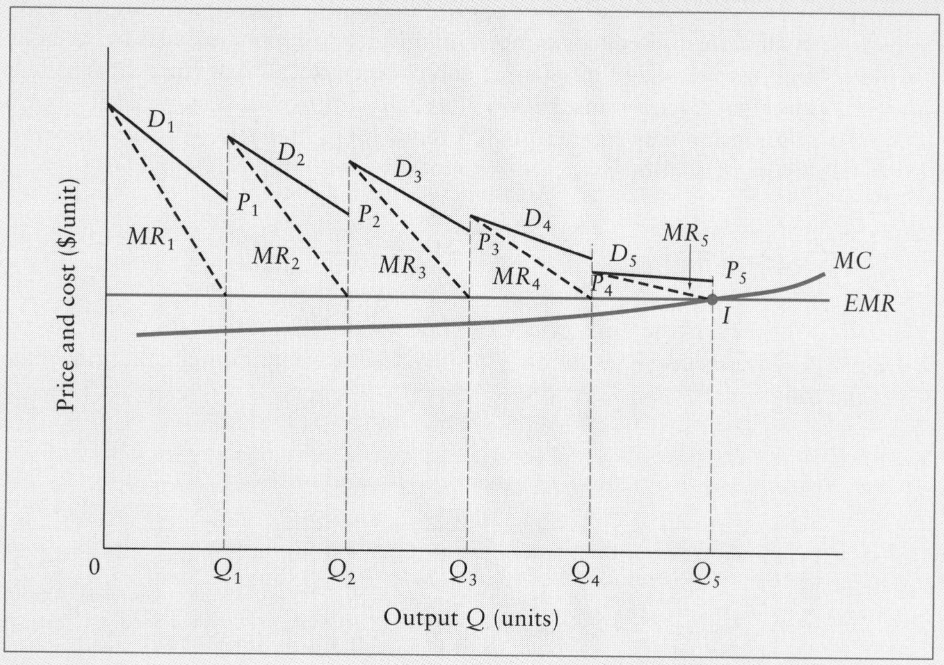

the firm produces and sells quantities of the five products such that marginal revenue is equal in all markets and equal to marginal cost. The line *EMR* represents *equal marginal revenue,* the firm's marginal revenue opportunity in other product lines. Because it is assumed that new product markets were entered in order of their profitability, the prices charged for the five products are arranged in declining order, from P_1 to P_5, and the elasticity of demand increases from D_1 to D_5. The height of the *EMR* line is determined by the intersection of the firm's marginal cost curve *MC* and the marginal revenue curve for the last product market that may be profitably served, MR_5 *at* Q_5.

The equilibrium condition in the marginal market D_5 where *P*, *MR*, and *MC* are virtually equivalent, illustrates the well-known fact that nearly all firms produce some products that generate little or no incremental operating profit and are on the verge of being dropped or replaced because the contribution margin approaches zero.

EXAMPLE

Multiple-Product Pricing: Supermarket Pricing

Supermarkets provide an illustration of this multiple-product pricing model. One of the primary productive resources of a supermarket is shelf space, which can be allocated among a wide variety of product categories (meat, dairy products, canned goods, frozen foods, and produce). Canned goods have only a 1–2 percent profit margin. Generally the markups and profit margins on staple items, such as bread, milk, and soap, are lower than on nonstaple items, such as imported foods and deli items. In an effort to increase their overall profitability, many supermarkets have added higher profit-margin categories, such as delicatessens, in-store bakeries, fresh fish, and floral departments by reallocating existing shelf space.[6]

Differential Pricing and the Price Elasticity of Demand

In all of the preceding examples, an inverse relationship exists between optimal price and price elasticity in separate submarkets. Recall that for profits to be maximized, marginal revenue must be equal in each of the separate submarkets. In Chapter 3 the relationship between marginal revenue (*MR*) and price (*P*) was shown to be the following (Equation 3.7):

$$MR = P\left(1 + \frac{1}{E_D}\right) \qquad [14.2]$$

where E_D is the price elasticity of demand. If P_1, P_2, E_1, and E_2 represent the prices and price elasticities in the two submarkets, we may equate marginal revenue by setting equal

$$MR_1 = P_1\left(1 + \frac{1}{E_1}\right) \quad \text{and} \quad MR_2 = P_2\left(1 + \frac{1}{E_2}\right) \qquad [14.3]$$

[6] Allocation of shelf space within each product category also involves a consideration of profit margins when making decisions about stocking private label versus national brand canned goods, prepackaged versus fresh-cut meat, and so on.

Hence,

$$P_1\left(1 + \frac{1}{E_1}\right) = P_2\left(1 + \frac{1}{E_2}\right)$$

$$\frac{P_1}{P_2} = \frac{\left(1 + \frac{1}{E_2}\right)}{\left(1 + \frac{1}{E_1}\right)} \qquad [14.4]$$

Perhaps JetBlue Airways has determined that the price elasticity of demand for two customer segments (New York to Los Angeles unrestricted coach and Super Saver Saturday night stayovers) is −1.25 and −2.50, respectively. To determine the relative prices (P_1/P_2) that JetBlue should charge if it is interested in maximizing profits on this route, substitute $E_1 = -1.25$ and $E_2 = -2.50$ into Equation 14.4 to yield

$$\frac{P_1}{P_2} = \frac{\left(1 + \frac{1}{-2.50}\right)}{\left(1 + \frac{1}{-1.25}\right)}$$

$$= 3.0$$

or

$$P_1 = 3.0\,P_2$$

Thus the price of an unrestricted coach seat (P_1) should be 3.0 times the price of a Super Saver coach seat (P_2).

Price elasticity is the key; the larger the number of close substitutes, the higher the price elasticity, and therefore the lower the optimal markup and price-cost margin. In electricity pricing, industrial customers such as factories and hospitals can now buy their power from competing public utilities. The industrial customer has so many more close substitute alternatives that the price per kilowatt hour is less than half the price of residential or small commercial users. Again, the higher the price elasticity, the lower the optimal price, ceteris paribus.

The increase in profitability from engaging in differential pricing as opposed to uniform pricing across all customer segments can be illustrated with the following example.

EXAMPLE

DIFFERENTIAL PRICING AT TAIWAN INSTRUMENT CO.

Taiwan Instrument Company (TIC) makes computer memory chips in Formosa, which it ships to computer manufacturers in Japan (Market 1) and the United States (Market 2). Demand for the chips in the two markets is given by the following functions:

$$\text{Japan: } P_1 = 12 - Q_1 \qquad [14.5]$$

$$\text{United States: } P_2 = 8 - Q_2 \qquad [14.6]$$

where Q_1 and Q_2 are the respective quantities sold (in millions of units), and P_1 and P_2 are the respective prices (in dollars per unit) in the two markets. TIC's total cost function (in millions of dollars) for these memory chips is

$$C = 5 + 2(Q_1 + Q_2) \qquad [14.7]$$

Case I: Differential Prices TIC's total combined profit in the two markets equals

$$\pi = P_1Q_1 + P_2Q_2 - C \qquad [14.8]$$

$$= (12 - Q_1)Q_1 + (8 - Q_2)Q_2 - [5 + 2(Q_1 + Q_2)]$$
$$= 12Q_1 - Q_1^2 + 8Q_2 - Q_2^2 - 5 - 2Q_1 - 2Q_2$$
$$= 10Q_1 - Q_1^2 + 6Q_2 - Q_2^2 - 5 \qquad [14.9]$$

To maximize profit with respect to Q_1 and Q_2, find the partial derivatives of Equation 14.9 with respect to Q_1 and Q_2, set them equal to zero, and solve for Q_1^* and Q_2^*:

$$\frac{\partial \pi}{\partial Q_1} = 10 - 2Q_1 = 0$$
$$Q_1^* = 5 \text{ (million) units}$$
$$\frac{\partial \pi}{\partial Q_2} = 6 - 2Q_2 = 0$$
$$Q_2^* = 3 \text{ (million) units}$$

Substituting Q_1^* and Q_2^* into the appropriate demand and profit equations yields

$$P_1^* = \$7 \text{ per unit}$$
$$P_2^* = \$5 \text{ per unit}$$
$$\pi^* = \$29 \text{ (million)}$$

The optimal solution is illustrated graphically in Figure 14.3 Panel (a).

Maximizing π with respect to Q_1 and Q_2 is equivalent to setting $MR_1 = MR_2$. The equivalence of MR_1 and MR_2 may be proved by taking the partial derivatives of the *TR* function with respect to Q_1 and Q_2:

$$TR = P_1 \cdot Q_1 + P_2 \cdot Q_2$$
$$= (12 - Q_1)\, Q_1 + (8 - Q_2)\, Q_2$$
$$= 12Q_1 - Q_1^2 + 8Q_2 - Q_2^2 \qquad [14.10]$$

and substituting the solution values, $Q_1^* = 5$ and $Q_2^* = 3$:

$$MR_1 = \frac{\partial TR}{\partial Q_1} = 12 - 2Q_1$$
$$MR_1^* = 12 - 2(5) = \$2 \text{ per unit}$$
$$MR_2 = \frac{\partial TR}{\partial Q_2} = 8 - 2Q_2$$
$$MR_2^* = 8 - 2(3) = \$2 \text{ per unit}$$

which equals the total marginal cost, that is, the derivative of Equation 14.7 with respect to $(Q_1 + Q_2)$.

The respective elasticities in the Japanese and U.S. markets at the optimal solution are

$$E_1 = \frac{dQ_1}{dP_1} \cdot \frac{P_1}{Q_1}$$
$$= -1\left(\frac{7}{5}\right) = -1.40$$

Figure 14.3 Demand and Cost Functions for Memory Chips: Taiwan Instrument Company

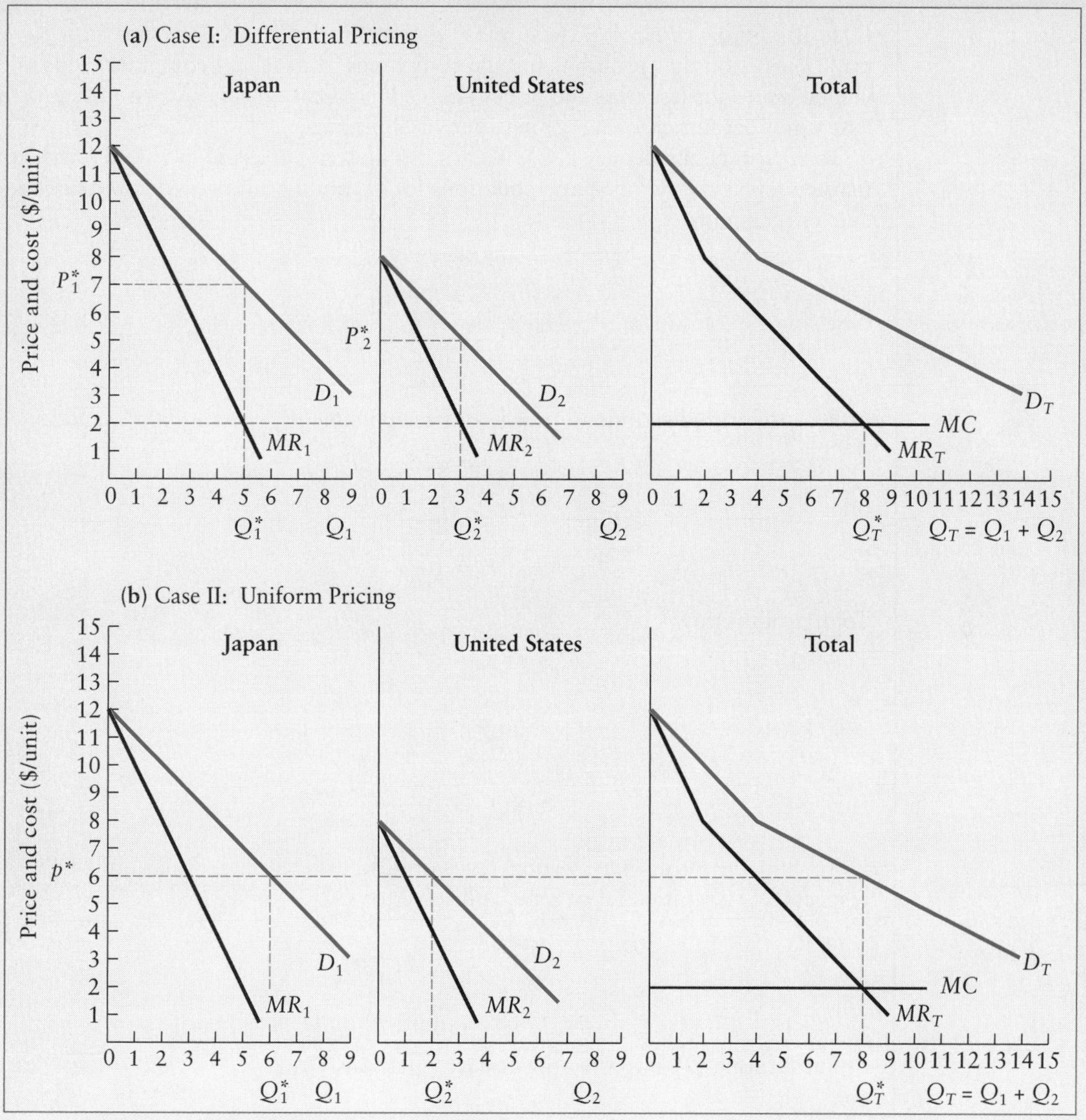

and

$$E_2 = \frac{dQ_2}{dP_2} \cdot \frac{P_2}{Q_2}$$

$$= -1\left(\frac{5}{3}\right) = -1.67$$

Hence we see that, as in the JetBlue Airways example, when the elasticity of demand is less (in absolute value) in Japan (Market 1) than in the United States (Market 2), the price in Japan is greater than in the United States.

Case II: Uniform Prices Now suppose that the U.S. Congress passes protectionist trade legislation that prohibits foreign companies from selling computer chips in the United States for less than the prices charged in Japan. In other words, assume that TIC is not permitted to engage in differential pricing.

To determine the profits TIC will earn if it does not discriminate between the two markets, solve the two demand equations for Q_1 and Q_2 and add them to get a total demand function:

$$\begin{aligned} Q_1 &= 12 - P_1 \\ Q_2 &= 8 - P_2 \\ Q_T &= Q_1 + Q_2 \\ &= 12 - P_1 + 8 - P_2 \end{aligned}$$

Because price discrimination is no longer possible, P_1 must equal P_2, and

$$Q_T = 20 - 2P$$

or

$$P = 10 - \frac{Q_T}{2}$$

Total profit is now

$$\begin{aligned} \pi &= PQ_T - C \\ &= 10Q_T - \frac{Q_T^2}{2} - 5 - 2Q_T \\ &= 8Q_T - \frac{Q_T^2}{2} - 5 \end{aligned} \tag{14.11}$$

To find the profit-maximizing level of Q_T, differentiate Equation 14.11 with respect to Q_T, set it equal to zero, and solve for Q_T^*:

$$\begin{aligned} \frac{d\pi}{dQ_T} &= 8 - Q_T = 0 \\ Q_T^* &= 8 \text{ (million) units} \end{aligned}$$

Substituting Q_T^* into the appropriate equations yields

$$\begin{aligned} P^* &= 10 - \frac{Q_T}{2} = \$6 \text{ per unit} \\ \pi^* &= 8Q_T - \frac{Q_T^2}{2} - 5 = \$27 \text{ (million)} \\ Q_1^* &= 12 - 6 = 6 \text{ (million) units} \\ Q_2^* &= 8 - 6 = 2 \text{ (million) units} \\ MR_1^* &= 12 - 2(6) = \$0 \text{ per unit} \\ MR_2^* &= 8 - 2(2) = \$4 \text{ per unit} \end{aligned}$$

The optimal solution is illustrated graphically in Figure 14.3 Panel(b).

The two cases are summarized in Table 14.3. Note that TIC's profits are higher when it engages in differential pricing ($29 million) than when it does not ($27 million).

Table 14.3 Taiwan Instrument Company: Effects of Price Discrimination

	Case I Differential Pricing		Case II Uniform Pricing	
Market	1 (Japan)	2 (U.S.)	1 (Japan)	2 (U.S.)
Price P^* ($/unit)	7	5	6	6
Quantity Q^* (million units)	5	3	6	2
Marginal Revenue MR^* ($/unit)	2	2	0	4
Profit π^* ($ million)	29		27	

The preceding example shows that by charging different prices to different groups of customers, companies may always increase their profits above the level they can achieve if no market segmentation is attempted, as long as resale can be prevented.

DIFFERENTIAL PRICING IN TARGET MARKET SEGMENTS

After identifying the different value drivers for various segments of the target market and setting an optimal differential price, firms must prevent resale between the segments using a variety of "fences." Two of the most frequent methods of direct segmentation that prevent resale involve intertemporal pricing of services or perishable products by time-of-day or day-of-week and differential pricing by delivery location.

Congestion-based pricing at peak-demand periods on roadways, bridges, and subway systems is an example of intertemporal pricing, illustrated in Figure 14.4. Peak-period drivers place demands on the Dulles toll road between 6:00 A.M. and 9:00 A.M. far in excess of its carrying capacity (Q_C). Charging commuters a toll equal to just the wear and tear imposed by their vehicle passing over the toll road pavement (i.e., an off-peak marginal cost, MC_{OP}) induces many more cars to enter the highway (Q_{PEAK}) than can be accommodated (i.e., $Q_P > Q_C$). The result is slowdowns, stoppages, and a markedly increased travel time for each commuter. Beyond Q_C, the traffic volume at which this congestion begins, MC_P rises steeply representing the incremental fuel and time costs imposed (by one additional car) on all the other drivers along a 10-mile stretch of congested toll road.

The advantage of a congestion toll such as $(P_P - MC_{OP}) = \$2$ is that it induces discretionary peak-period travelers to switch to other travel times and alternative modes of transportation. If a toll road authority set peak-period prices of $3 just sufficient to cover this congestion cost plus the off-peak MC, traffic volume would decline from Q_{PEAK} (P_{OP}) to Q_P, and the equilibrium differential prices P_P and P_{OP} would emerge. Such **congestion pricing** places the true resource cost on the scarce transportation system capacity at peak travel times.

Congestion Pricing

A fee that reflects the true marginal cost imposed by demand in excess of capacity.

Figure 14.4 Congestion Tolls with Peak and Off-Peak Demand: Dulles Toll Road

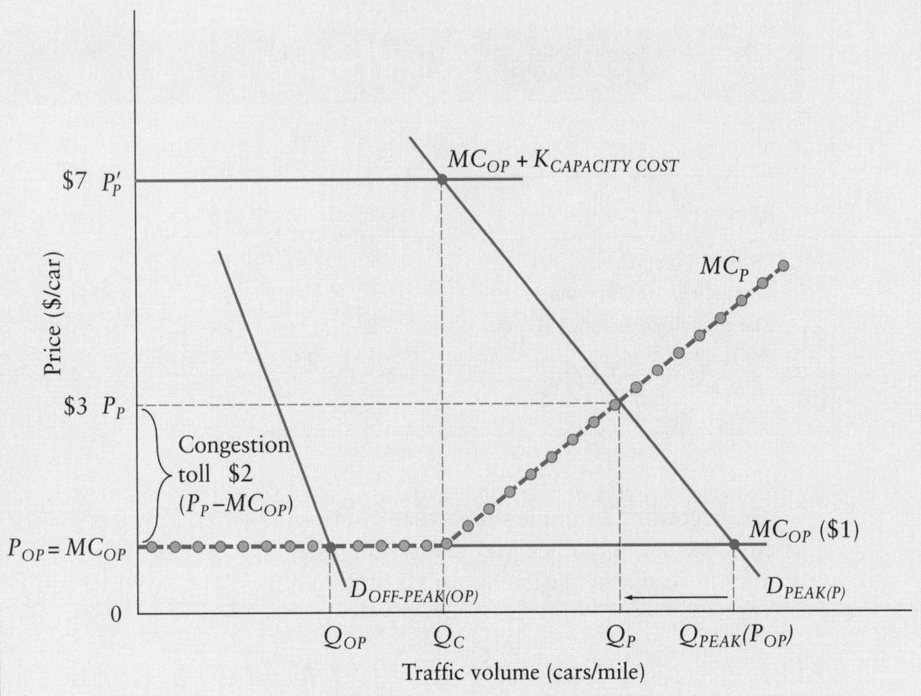

Notes : *P* refers to peak period; *OP* refers to off-peak period.

EXAMPLE

Congestion Tolls on Los Angeles, Houston, and Dulles Toll Roads[7]

The typical American spent 40 hours per year in traffic jams in 1995 due to peak-period road congestion. Urban traffic then grew by 20 percent during 1995–2005 but urban roadways increased by only 2 percent. The federal excise tax on gasoline of 18.4 cents per gallon (which is earmarked to repair and build federal highways) has not increased since the early 1990s. But is the answer simply more highways? Communities in Southern California, New Jersey, Houston, and Washington, D.C., think not.

Congestion tolls that charge commuters for the incremental time loss and fuel increase their cars impose on other drivers present during peak periods have been adopted on several public and private toll roads around the United States. Every day,

[7] Based on "How to Make Traffic Jams a Thing of the Past," *Fortune* (March 31, 1997), p. 34; "A Survey of Commuting," *The Economist* (September 5, 1998), p. 62; *The Economist Technology Quarterly* (June 12, 2004), pp. 30–32; and "Steep Increases Set for Toll Roads," *Wall Street Journal* (April 12, 2005), p. D1.

24,000 drivers pay a peak-period congestion toll of $3.30 per trip for a 10-mile stretch of true expressway in Orange County, California. Toll booths, which themselves cause delays, have been replaced by credit-card-size transponders mounted in dashboards from which overhead wireless receivers assess tolls as the cars speed by. Such on-board-units (OBUs) will be commonplace on all cars and trucks by 2010, and they may become the communications hub of the vehicle, offering information on road conditions ahead, directions to inexpensive gas stations, and emergency dispatch services based on the built-in global positioning satellite (GPS) device.

In Figure 14.4 the cost of additional vehicles on increased peak-period road congestion raises the peak period toll to $3 from an off-peak toll of $1. Electronic debits for driving on inner-city streets in London costs £5/day in and around Westminster. The congestion toll expenses of a typical commuter mount up quickly. But the effect of the tolls has been noticeable; traffic in London's designated congestion zone is down 30 percent in the first year. And time is money, so faced with the slow 25–40 m.p.h. commute on adjacent "freeways," many peak-period travelers in Los Angeles, Houston, and Washington, D.C., are opting for the differential pricing of a 65 m.p.h. toll road.

Like peak–off-peak roadway pricing, many other examples of differential pricing entail charging differential prices for the same capacity *at different times*. Hence, such customers are not in rivalry for the same capacity. Parking meters can now raise price between 10 A.M. and 2 P.M. Coca-Cola has new cold drink machines that vary the price by time of day, as well as by the predicted high temperature for the day. Matinee ($5) and evening movie theaters ($9) segment demanders not in rivalry for the same theater seats. First-run movies and subsequent movie videos, hardback and later paperback editions of books, seasonal discounts in the resort and cruise ship businesses, and weekend discounts in hotels all represent effective segmentation of different target customer classes by time of purchase.

DIRECT SEGMENTATION WITH "FENCES"

Direct segmentation of target customer classes not in rivalry with one another for the same capacity can also be accomplished by selling various versions of a product customized for target segments, or by varying the price by delivery location. Customers who arrive at the suburban neighborhood rental counters of Hertz and Avis have flexibly timed, convenience-based uses for rental cars. Consequently, demand is much more price sensitive than the demand at the airport by business travelers. A recent study found that weekday rates for a midsize sedan were $43 in neighborhood rental locations versus $69 on average in airport rental locations.[8] Because round-trip taxi fares from airports to the neighborhood locations would typically far exceed the $26 price difference, Avis and Hertz customers are effectively segmented by rental location.

Another example of location-based segmentation would be fashion clothing from France's Arche or Ralph Lauren sold less expensively in discount outlets along

[8] "Playing the Car-Rental Game," *Wall Street Journal* (July 31, 2002), p. D3; and "Highway Nirvana at a Price," *Wall Street Journal* (July 6, 2004), p. A15.

interstate highways than in suburban storefronts or vacation resorts. Outlet mall shoppers almost never overlap with the customers these companies find in their trendy boutiques. Hence, geographic segmentation works. Outlet shoppers will also buy a less costly, less durable version of the product (e.g., a lighter weight chemise cloth in Polo golf shirts), so in differential pricing, Ralph Lauren accomplishes more than just inventory clearance without any danger of cannibalizing full-price sales.

Hal Varian and Carl Shapiro argued that such "versioning" is an especially good way to sell information economy items such as software.[9] A voice recognition package sells for $79 as general-purpose Voice ProPad, for $795 as Office Talk, and for $7,995 as Voice Ortho, a special-purpose medical transcriptor for surgical theatres. All three versions derive from the same source code, but the more comprehensive version generates 100 times as much value to particular target customers. In contrast, when Amazon sells the *same* book or DVD at different prices to customers with different clickstreams, that degree of differential pricing for identical versions of the product often leads to adverse customer reactions. Coca-Cola is finding the same resistance to its differential time-of-day pricing in soft drink machine. As a result, many sellers adopt the techniques of *indirect segmentation* using two-part tariffs, couponing, and bundling. With indirect segmentation, the customer herself selects what differential price to pay from a variety of available alternatives.

Two-Part Tariffs

Two-part tariffs entail charging both a lump-sum entry fee for access to the facility or service and a per-unit user fee for each unit sale consumed. Amusement parks, nightclubs, golf and tennis clubs, copier leasing companies, cellular phone providers, Internet access providers, and rental car companies often employ such pricing. Their revenue per unit sale is a nonlinear function of two parts: a lump-sum monthly or daily fee that provides access to the facility, phone, computer, or rental car independent of use, and a per-hour or per-minute or per-mile fee that varies with usage. The magnitude per unit of user fees should at least cover marginal costs, so that heavy demanders "pay the freight" through higher total user fees. Tying the price for a leased copier to a metering counter that effectively measures intensity of use results in a differential monthly leasing fee across customer segments plus a cheap incremental cost per copy.

Companies differ on whether to set high or low entry fees and whether to charge high or low user fees. AT&T Wireless and Gillette practically give away their cell phones and razors but then charge steep prices for the calls and blades. iPods, in contrast, are pricey at the front end but iTunes thereafter are quite cheap. Similarly, most golf and tennis clubs charge substantial membership fees and annual dues, but thereafter adopt trivial user fees (e.g., $5 per court hour or $25 for greens fees).[10] As we will see, just how much above marginal cost to set the optimal user fee depends on how dissimilar are the segments of customer demand.

---

[9] C. Shapiro and H. Varian, "Versioning," *Harvard Business Review* (November/December 1998), pp. 106–114.

[10] When the Pebble Beach golf course and the Wimbledon tennis club have $350 greens fees for a round of golf or two sets of tennis, those user fees reflect congestion-based pricing rather than optimal two-part tariffs.

EXAMPLE

CALIFORNIA CONSUMERS PREFER TWO-PART TARIFFS FOR ELECTRICITY[11]

In principle, as experience has shown in Britain, Australia, and New Zealand, deregulation of electricity can work well if peak-load customers are asked to pay a price that reflects marginal cost. As much as 55 percent of the variation in intraday cost is attributable to extraordinary transmission line fees and old inefficient plants fired up to meet the last 5 percent of peak demand. For example, running a clothes dryer at 6 P.M. in August imposes wholesale costs on Pacific Gas and Electric of $220 per megawatt hour, relative to approximately $100 at 10 p.m. in August, and $20/mwh in April.

Industrial customers expect that such two-part pricing will lower their overall power costs by as much as 30 percent. The real success or failure of the deregulatory initiative in electricity will hinge on whether residential customers will conserve energy when the marginal cost is high or, alternatively (as happened in the California electricity crisis in 2000–2001), whether they pressure their politicians to cap the price of electricity and then overburden the scarce capacity of underfunded electric companies. One alternative is to charge uniform prices per kilowatt hour for interruptible (brownout) service but add on access fees that industrial customers such as hospitals and computer system operators would pay for noninterruptible service.

Let's investigate how to analyze an optimal two-part tariff. Consider the situation depicted in Figure 14.5 for separate customer segments with relatively elastic (D_1) and relatively inelastic demand (D_2) for rental autos. These might be young couples who are renting cars for vacationing (D_1) and manufacturers' trade representatives renting cars for making sales calls (D_2). The challenge is to find a uniform daily rate (the lump sum access fee) and a mileage charge that maximize profit and keep both segments in the market. One alternative would be to price the mileage at its marginal cost $(MC) = OA$ and elicit Q_1 and Q_2 usage while realizing from both customer segments the maximum daily rate (a lump sum access fee) that the price-sensitive D_1 demanders will pay (namely, hatched area AEF).

Perhaps, however, a better alternative is available. Suppose the car rental agency raises the price to P^* and reduces the daily access fee to the hatched and shaded area P^*DF in Figure 14.5. Mileage will decline in both segments, and area P^*DEA will be net revenue lost by virtue of the reduced daily access fee in both segments. However, the additional net revenue from mileage charges (P^*DGA in one segment and P^*HIA in the other segment) will more than offset the lost access fees.

Consequently, in addition to charging a positive lump-sum access fees, a price-discriminating monopolist will adopt two-part tariffs that price usage above its marginal cost. The more similar the price elasticity of demands of the target customer segments, the closer the optimal user fee should be to marginal cost. The more dissimilar the segment demands are, the higher the optimal unit price above MC should be.

[11] Based on "How to Do Deregulation Right," *BusinessWeek* (March 26, 2001), p. 112; "PG&E Gropes for a Way Out," *Wall Street Journal* (January 4, 2001), p. A1; and A. Faruqui and K. Eakin, eds., *Pricing in Competitive Electricity Markets* (New York: Kluwer, 2000).

Figure 14.5 Optimal Two-Part Tariffs for Auto Rentals

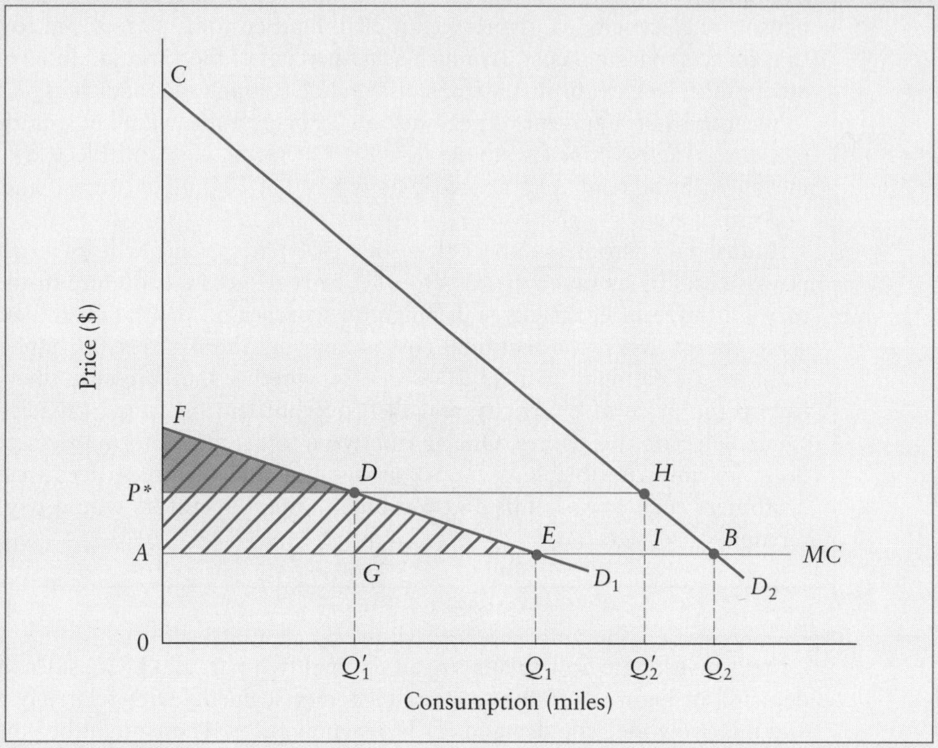

COUPONING

Another pricing mechanism for indirectly segmenting the market and allowing the customer to select what level of consumption and total price to pay is couponing. The $49 billion spent on direct-mail marketing with accompanying rebate and coupon offers passed the amount spent on newspaper ($45 billion) and television ($43 billion) advertising for the first time in the United States in 2003. A growing trend focuses marketing and promotions to a particular mailing address. This approach is made possible by successful forecasting initiatives based on consumer spending patterns. Companies have access to cash register and credit card data as well as property tax and public utility usage records. These sources allow Lowe's Home Improvement, for example, to project with more than 80 percent accuracy the month in which a particular household will buy a gas grill.

Such laser-like precision in targeting encourages differential pricing. If coupons worth 25 cents off the price of a box of cereal, 40 percent off the price of fashion clothing, or $50 rebates off the price of a home computer are redeemed religiously by some segments but ignored by others, Kellogg, Neiman Marcus, and Dell will segment the market with these direct mail promotions. The price-sensitive customers who constantly redeem coupons and file for rebates receive a lower net price, consistent with Equation 14.4.

▲WHAT WENT RIGHT ▼WHAT WENT WRONG

$19.95 FOR "UNLIMITED ACCESS" AT AOL TIME WARNER[12]

In triggering repeat purchases, customer service and availability are often as important as low price. Internet online provider America Online (AOL) offers computer help by phone and downloadable help files as well as Internet access. Internet access is a limited-capacity service either as dial-up, DSL, or cable-based broadband for which assured availability may be expensive. AOL, which has combined with Time Warner Cable, has infrastructure costs for high-speed modems, routers, servers, and other equipment that run $8.00 per month for the average one-hour-per-day customer. The larger the established customer base, the lower are these direct fixed costs of online access per customer. AOL has a direct fixed cost of only $0.27 per customer per hour for basic access. In contrast, help lines and other online customer support impose a variable cost of $8 per customer per hour—30 times larger. Neophyte users who make frequent requests of the help desk are therefore big money losers, whereas cyberspace veterans at $24 per month for basic access generate high profit margins of 67 percent.

To attract more high-margin customers who require almost no online support, AT&T Comcast was the first to offer a flat-rate access fee ($19.95 per month) with no user charge per hour. The rest of the industry quickly followed suit, and a battle for market share erupted. For $19.95 a month, AOL users became entitled to an unlimited amount of attempted access to the Net. As customers quickly discovered, however, "unlimited access" did not mean unlimited use. The need to make 20 sign-on attempts before achieving an Internet connection led to frustrated customers and a "D" service rating from *PC World* in 1998. With this radical degradation of service quality, AOL quickly lost market share and its profit margins suffered.

The solution proved to be two-part pricing packages that tied the total customer expense to the desired degree of availability and intensity of use. AOL offered a Light Usage Plan for $4.95 a month for the first three hours of Internet use plus $2.50 for each additional hour. MCI Internet offered $3 for 3 hours per month plus $1.80 for each additional hour. CompuServe offered 5 hours for $9.95 plus $2.95 for each additional hour and found they were able to deliver Internet connection on the customers' first try 97 percent of the time.

When capacity was insufficient to absorb peak demand, two-part pricing proved to be an efficient way to discourage trivial uses of the scarce capacity and recover capacity cost sufficient to fund additional capital equipment investment. When Road Runner, AOL Time Warner, and Vonage offered unlimited access for a flat fee of $24 to $40 per month, connection speed and reliability again declined.

[12] Based on "Why Internet $19.95 Deals May Not Last," *Wall Street Journal* (December 24, 1996), p. B1; "Net Firms Tinker with Service Pricing," *Investor's Business Daily* (April 4, 1998), p. A1; "Satellite's Hot Pursuit of Cable," *BusinessWeek* (May 24, 2004), p. 46; and "Cable Deal Brings Expansion to AOL," *Wall Street Journal* (August 21, 2004), p. B1.

Pillsbury measured the price elasticity of demand for its cake mix customers who redeem coupons and found it to be −0.43, whereas that of the nonredeemers is −0.21. Similarly, Purina measured the price elasticity of coupon redeemers among its cat food customers as −1.13 and among nonredeemers −0.49. Coupons for frozen potato dishes at Ore-Ida are redeemed by households with price elasticity of −1.33, and nonredeeming households have price elasticity of −1.97. Clearly, in all these cases, couponing is a way to segment the market and offer a discount to the more price sensitive segment.

BUNDLING

Bundling is another highly effective pricing mechanism that sellers use to capture profit from differential pricing across target customer segments. Have you ever wondered why Time Warner Cable offers Showtime, the channel for popular first-run movies, only in a bundled package that includes the History Channel? One insight is that this paired bundle of product offerings occurs because some other Time Warner customer is a history buff who is wondering why the History Channel comes with access to largely unwatched movies. That is, the operating profit to a seller from bundling negatively correlated demands is always larger than the operating profit from selling equally costly products separately. Let's see why.

Reservation Price

The maximum price a customer will pay to reserve a product or service unto their own use.

Suppose that two sets of customers have the following **reservation prices** for two cable channels, each of which incurs variable licensing fees of \$1 for a single showing to a single household. Movie buffs would pay \$9 for access to first-run movies and \$2 for access to historical documentaries. History buffs would pay \$8 for access to the History Channel and \$3 for access to Showtime. If the channels are priced uniformly to both customer segments as separate products, Time Warner can realize at most \$8 (or \$9 − \$1) on Showtime and \$7 (or \$8 − \$1) on the History Channel for a total of \$15 operating profit.[13] However, note that both types of customers would pay up to \$11 for the combined pair of channels rather than do without. If Time Warner made them available only as a bundled package, sales revenue would be \$22 minus \$4 licensing fees for a total of \$18 operating profit, which is greater than the \$15 calculated.

As long as one customer is willing to pay more for product A that another customer wants less than product B, the seller who is restricted to charging the two customers the same uniform price will always be better off bundling the two items, assuming all reservation prices exceed variable cost. Such inversely correlated demands occur in many settings. All-inclusive Caribbean resorts such as \$495 per day Bitter End on Virgin Gorda or Hotel Isle de France in St Bart's have guests who value \$75 gourmet lunches and \$350 per night fabulous cabanas but would not pay much for all the water sports activities and equipment while other guests value \$70 per day water sports activities but would not pay such high prices for better food or cabanas. Similarly, Elizabeth Arden's \$225 all-inclusive half-day spas have clients who would not pay high margin \$50 prices for at least one of the following: facials, mud wraps, massage, manicures, pedicures, and hair styling. Bundling all these services together always raises profitability when target customer demand is inversely correlated across the offerings as long as variable costs of the separate components are below the customers' willingness to pay for each.

Now suppose the variable costs are higher at, say, \$3. The History Channel valued at \$2 by the movie buff is no longer a profitable sale. Pure bundling includes this

[13] In this example, selling both products separately to both customer segments does not pay because of the much lower prices required. Specifically, Showtime priced separately into both segments would have to sell for as little as \$3, thereby earning operating profits of \$6 − \$2 = \$4, and the History Channel would have to sell for as little as \$2, earning \$4 − \$2 = \$2. Thus, the total profit of \$6 from selling all products to all customers at a uniform price would substantially diminish the potential profit of \$15 from selling each product to its target market alone. If the asymmetric demands in the two segments were not so different, this result could reverse, as long as all reservation prices were greater than variable cost.

Figure 14.6 Reservation Prices for Three Customer Segments

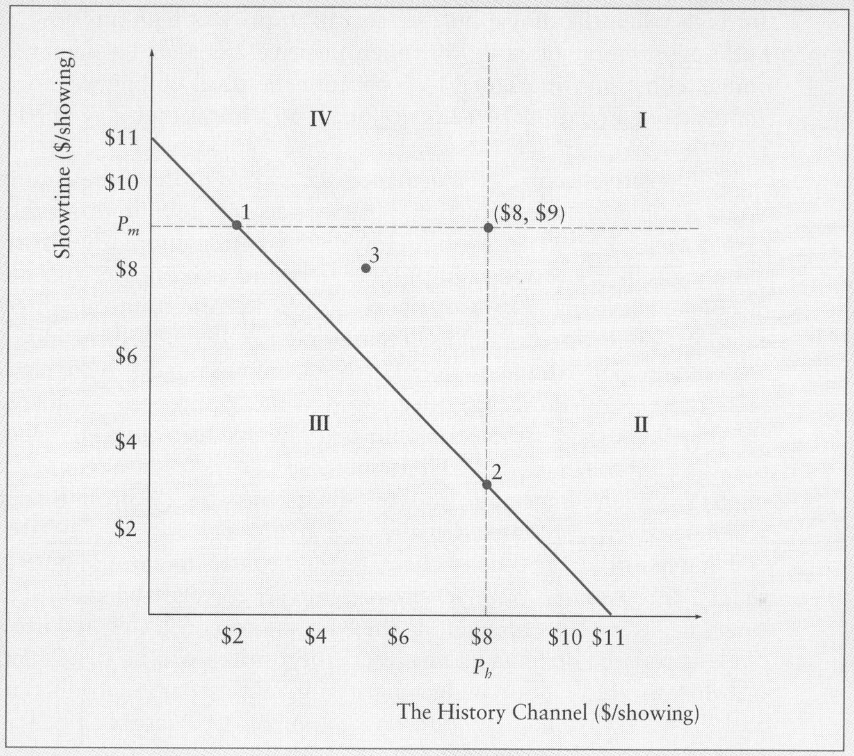

unprofitable sale and generates the same $22 revenue but now incurs $12 of total variable cost, yielding a profit of only $10. Forgoing the sale of the History Channel to the movie buff by selling each product separately at a $9 price for Showtime and an $8 price for the History Channel generates $6 (or $9 − $3) on Showtime and $5 (or $8 − $3) on the History Channel, yielding a total of $11 operating profit. Quite intuitively, pure bundling will be less attractive than pricing separately when some of the bundled sales are unprofitable.

It is also easy to see why positively correlated demand across customers works against bundling. Figure 14.6 displays reservation prices along a "budget" line that our customers in the earlier example are willing to spend on the two products.[14] The y-intercept is the total willingness-to-pay constraint for the two products—namely, $P_h + P_m = \$11$. With movie channel reservation prices on the vertical axis and History Channel reservation prices on the horizontal axis, each customer's mix of reservation prices lies along the line,

$$P_m = \$11 - 1P_h \qquad [14.12]$$

The −1 in Equation 14.12 signifies the perfect negative correlation between the reservation prices (demand) of our movie buff and those of our history buff. But

[14] This budget line is analogous to the budget line of a household making consumption decisions, except in this case it is the firm that is constrained by the maximum expenditure the customer is willing to make on the two goods.

suppose Time Warner has a third type of customer whose reservation prices are positively correlated with those of the movie buffs—that is, a third type of customer who values Showtime at $8 and the History Channel at $5. These reservation prices are high when the movie buff's reservation price is high and low when the movie buff's reservation price is low. Such positively correlated demand lies above the budget constraint in Figure 14.6 because the total willingness to pay on the left-hand side of Equation 14.12 is no longer $11 but rather is now $13, as shown for Point 3.

Mixed Bundling
Selling multiple products both separately and together for less than the sum of the separate prices.

With positively correlated demands across two of the three customer types, Time Warner could sell the Showtime-History Channel bundle to all three for $11 and earn $15 [3 × ($11 − $6)].[15] However, a better alternative is available. **Mixed bundling** sells the products both separately and as a bundle with the bundled price discounted below the sum of the two separate prices. In our three-customer-type example, Time Warner could sell Showtime for $9 and sell the History Channel for $8, while making the Showtime-History Channel bundle available for the package price of $13. The third type of customer would opt for the bundle, whereas each of the other types of customers would buy one product only. Revenue for this mixed bundling approach totals $30, but only four license fees are required, therefore earning $18 in profit. In general, pure bundling generates less profit than mixed bundling when positively correlated demands are involved.

Figure 14.6 can be used to characterize the attractiveness of pure bundling for the seller. If all customers have perfectly negatively correlated demands, their reservation prices lie, as we have seen, along the $11 budget constraint. If customers have positively correlated demands, their reservation prices will lie consistently either above or below this reservation budget constraint. With separate product prices of $P_m = \$9$ and $P_h = \$8$, customers with reservation prices in Quadrant I will always buy both products rather than one of the separate products alone (Quadrants II and IV) while those in Quadrant III will never buy either product sold separately. In addition, however, we know that customers with reservation prices above the reservation budget constraint will buy the bundled package and those below will not. Optimally, Customer 3 will therefore purchase the bundle, Customer 1 will purchase Showtime alone, and Customer 2 will purchase the History Channel alone. Only mixed bundling can achieve this result.

EXAMPLE

McDonald's Introduces Mixed Bundles as "Extra Value Meals"

In the United States, fast food consumption skyrocketed in the last two decades as 70 percent of households became two-worker households, and families began eating out several times a week. Beer and pizza or a soft drink, burger, and fries became the standard supper for many high time-cost households. With greater health consciousness, however, not everyone who wanted a burger wanted the fries. In other cases, some consumers wanted the fries but not the burger, and preferred lower fat chicken sandwiches instead. McDonald's Corporation has done its best to respond to these customer dissimilarities by introducing "Extra Value Meals" that bundled chicken sandwiches, with fries and a medium soft drink.

[15] Here we are again assuming that variable costs are at the higher level of $3 per showing.

The 2006 prices for some of McDonald's most popular menu items are listed here:

Menu Item	Separate Price Total If Purchased	Bundled Price	Separately
Large French Fries	$1.39		
Medium Soft Drink	$1.09		
McGrill Chicken Sandwich	$2.69	$4.29	$5.17
Chicken McNuggets	$2.79	$4.29	$5.27
McChicken Sandwich	$1.00	$3.39	$3.48
Big and Tasty Burger	$1.59	$3.49	$4.07
Double Cheeseburger	$1.00	$3.39	$3.48
Big Mac	$2.19	$3.79	$4.67
Quarter Pounder	$2.19	$3.79	$4.67

Examining only the last two columns, we see that some single-item specialty customers are getting almost as much of a per-item discount as the bundled "Extra Value Meal" customers.

To summarize, two-part tariffs, couponing, and bundling are pricing mechanisms that motivate customers to segment themselves indirectly. Two-part tariffs are particularly effective in capturing higher profits than uniform prices when customer segments are more nearly identical in their price elasticity of demand. Couponing works best when target segments are extraordinarily different in their price elasticity of demand. Bundling captures additional profit when segmented target customer demand is inversely correlated across multiple products.

PRICE DISCRIMINATION

Price Discrimination

The act of selling the same good or service, distributed in a single channel, at different prices to different buyers during the same period of time.

Price discrimination is defined as selling the same product or service out of the same distribution channel at different prices to different buyers during the same period of time. Examples of price discrimination include the following:

- Doctors, dentists, hospitals, lawyers, and tax preparers who charge clients who reside in wealthy zip codes more for the same service than those who reside in poorer zip codes
- Dell Inc.'s ultralight laptop, which it sells for $2,307 to small business customers, for $2,228 to health care companies, and for $2,072 to state and local governments
- Firms that sell the exact same product under two different labels at widely varying prices (Hotpoint and Kenmore appliances, Michelin and Sears Roadhandler radial tires)
- Athletic teams that sponsor family nights and ladies' nights at discount prices, while other customers pay the full price
- Hotels, restaurants, and other businesses that offer discounts to senior citizens
- Nationwide and GMAC auto insurance that lower rates based on the theft and collision risk exposure of the places you drive, as detected by the GPS device in your car
- Differentially priced seats in coach class on a particular flight based on how far ahead you booked the reservation or Saturday night stayovers

- Korean TV manufacturers who sell products direct to the customer at a lower price in the United States than in Japan

Most differential pricing to a firm's retail customers is perfectly legal.[16] It raises profits because it transfers some of the excess customer value (the satisfaction gained from the purchase of the product) from buyer to seller relative to the excess value generated for customers who pay a lower uniform price.

If a coffee aficionado were willing to pay $4.00 for a large cup of fresh brewed java for which Dunkin' Donuts charges $1.95, and $5.00 for the same cup of fresh brewed java bundled (on request) with a shot of espresso for which Starbucks charges $3.50, the consumer's excess value would decline from $2.05 at Dunkin' Donuts to $1.50 at Starbucks. Nevertheless, in the case where this customer declines the shot of espresso, Starbucks must have offered something else of value because the customer's willingness to pay rose from $4.00 to $5.00. If this customer kept returning to Starbucks, we should assume that the lifestyle and group identity available at Starbucks attracted his or her business.

EXAMPLE

eBusiness Clickstreams Allow Price Discrimination: Personify and Virtual Vineyards[17]

Personify, an Internet service company, created software that allows Web businesses to categorize buyers based on their clickstream patterns. Using this software, Virtual Vineyards, CDNow, and Amazon.com have experimented with charging different prices for the same wine, CD, or book based on the clickstream path. Let's see how this capability might work for Virtual Vineyards.

Incremental variable plus direct fixed costs in making table wines run at least $8 for the following inputs: $0.50 for the bottle itself, $0.30 for the cork, $0.20 for the label, $2 per bottle for the quickly decaying barrel used for aging, plus anywhere from $5 to $50 for the grapes. If it costs $220 to produce and stock a case of 20 bottles, and if five customers will pay $24 a bottle while another fifteen customers will pay $10 a bottle, uniform pricing across all 20 customers will result in a $20 loss [($10 × 20 = $200) − $220 = −$20]. At a $10 uniform price, all 20 customers will buy but the Virtual Vineyards will stop producing this wine. Similarly, at a $24 price, only five customers will buy, and the Virtual Vineyards again discontinues this wine because of now even more substantial loses [($24 × 5 = $120) − $200 = −$100].

But suppose five customers are asked to pay $20 per bottle, while fifteen more are asked to pay $9. Each group pays less than their willingness to pay and less than their proposed uniform prices of $24 and $10, yet the winery now stands to make a profit: (5 × $20) + (15 × $9) = $235 − $220 = $15. Virtual Vineyards could perhaps segment this market and prevent resale by charging $20 in the retail distribution channel and $9 for limited quantities at the winery. Alternatively, they could price discriminate by the clickstream of the customers visiting their Web site. New customers who first clicked through to the history of the awards won by the winery

[16] The Robinson-Patman Act prohibits price discrimination in wholesale business-to-business transactions where the product is going to be resold but allows whatever the market will bear in retail transactions not accompanied by duress, misrepresentation, or outright fraud.

[17] Based on "I Got It Cheaper Than You," *Forbes* (November 2, 1998), pp. 83–84; and "The Art and Science of Pricing Wine," *CNet* (July 3, 2003).

would be asked to pay $20 for the new release whereas returning customers who renew their membership online in the frequent buyer program and whose last purchase order was a case would be asked to pay $9 for the new release.

In the limiting case of *perfect price discrimination* (PPD), sometimes called *first degree* price discrimination, the seller discovers the maximum price each individual is willing to pay for each unit purchased. A PPD monopolist then charges each purchaser this maximum reservation price in order to capture the consumer's entire perceived excess value above the cost-covering price. However, because the information required for such pricing is so extensive, perfect price discrimination almost never occurs. Instead, as we have seen in studying two-part tariffs, couponing, and bundling, firms often price discriminate by allowing customers within indirectly segmented groups to determine their own price through intensity of use, redemption behavior, or selection of packages of products (so-called *second degree* price discrimination). Finally, firms may attempt to price discriminate through directly segmenting classes of customers by time or location of purchase and then charging one uniform price within each customer class (so-called *third degree* price discrimination).

PRICING IN PRACTICE

To this point, the chapter discussed firms that seek to maximize short-run profits. However, pricing is an area where a longer-run life cycle view of the firm's decision making is helpful.

PRODUCT LIFE CYCLE FRAMEWORK[18]

Life Cycle Pricing
Pricing that varies throughout the product life cycle.

In the early stages of **life cycle pricing**, the marketing, operations, and financial managers decide what the customer will value, how the firm can manage the supply chain to consistently deliver those characteristics, and how much it will cost, including the financing costs. If the value-based prices can cover this long-run full cost, the product becomes a prototype. Each proposed product or service then proceeds to marketing research, where the demand at various price points in several distribution channels usually is explored. Marketing research will identify a target price that the cross-functional product manager or the general managers will know is required on average over the product life cycle in order for the new product to provide sufficient revenue to cover fully allocated cost.

Once a product or service rollout takes place (usually at target price levels), the marketing plan often authorizes promotional discounts. In this stage of the life cycle, the firm is interested in penetrating the market. To do so requires coupons, free samples, name recognition advertising, and slot-in allowances on retail shelves. *Penetration pricing* therefore characterizes this early stage of the product life cycle at which net prices to the manufacturer fall below the firm's target price, as shown in Figure 14.7.

When a new product is introduced by a firm, pricing for that product is a difficult and critical decision, especially if the product is a durable good—one that has a relatively long useful life. The difficulty of pricing the new product comes from not knowing the level of demand with confidence. If the price is initially set too low,

[18] For a discussion of the conceptual framework of value-based pricing over a product's life cycle, see T. Nagle, *The Strategy and Tactics of Pricing,* 3rd ed. (Englewood Cliffs, NJ: Prentice Hall, 2001), Chapter 7.

Figure 14.7 The Price Life Cycle

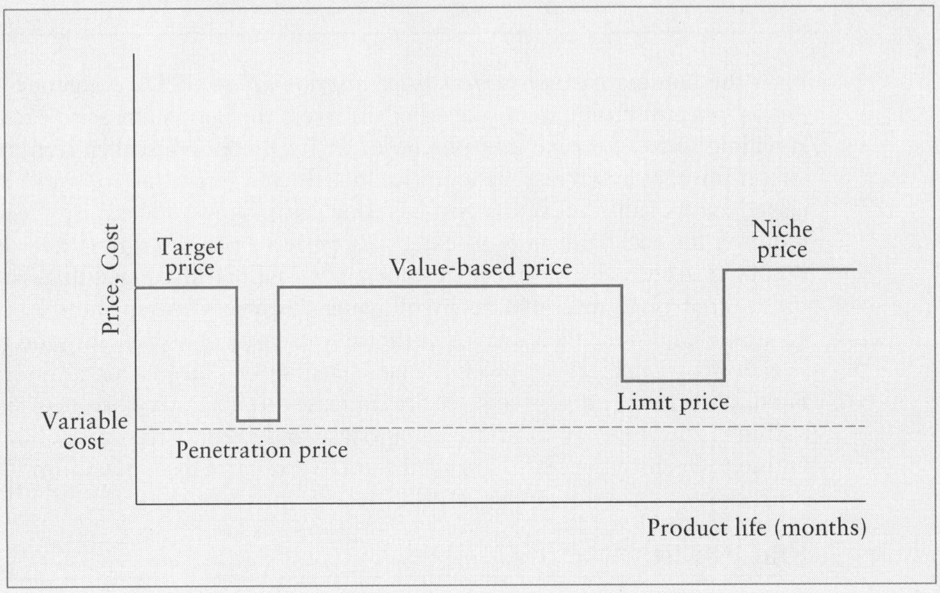

some potential customers will be able to buy the product at a price below what they are willing to pay. These lost profits will be gone forever. This problem is accentuated when the firm initially has limited production capacity for the new product.

Price Skimming

A new-product pricing strategy that results in a high initial product price being reduced over time as demand at the higher price is satisfied.

Under these circumstances, many firms adopt a strategy of **price skimming,** or pricing down along the demand curve. The initial price is set at a high level, even though the firm fully intends to make later price reductions. When the product is first introduced, a group of fashion-conscious or technology-conscious early adopters will pay the high price established by the firm. Once this source of demand is exhausted, the price is reduced to attract a new group of customers. Flat screen TVs and handheld computers such as the Blackberry and Palm's Treo are excellent examples of this phenomenon. As we discussed in Chapter 13, manufacturers who engage in price skimming on industrial equipment (e.g., mainframe computers and corporate jets) need credibility mechanisms to assure early full-price customers that later discounting will be limited.

In the mature stage of the product or service life cycle, organic growth comes from focusing on product differentiation and commitment to building the brand. Marketing team initiatives will add value in both product refinements and order management processes through brand-name advertising, product updates, or increased flexibility in accepting change orders from regular customers. Each decision at this mature stage is motivated by a desire to realize the highest *value-based pricing* allowed by the competitive conditions and potential entry threats. Although at times this approach to pricing can be overwhelmed by the necessity of short-term tactics to defend market share, the product life cycle remains a planning framework to which the pricing manager often returns.

At a late mature stage of the product or service life cycle, product managers may decide to limit price, reducing it well below the value-based pricing level in order to deter entry. *Limit pricing* appears to be inconsistent with profit maximization but in fact is motivated by a long-term profitability objective.

EXAMPLE

LOSS OF PATENT PROTECTION LIMITS THE PRICE OF PROZAC: ELI LILLY

When brand-name pharmaceuticals reach the end of their 20-year patent protection, sales may plummet unless prices are radically reduced. Some formerly patented drugs lost as much as 80 percent of their sales in the *first year* after generic substitutes were introduced. The ulcer relief medicine Zantac, which was at the time Glaxo's biggest seller, plummeted 51 percent in the first half year after loss of patent protection. By year-end, 10 rival products were on the shelves. Zovinax, an antiherpes medication, lost 39 percent in the first six months after generics costing only 20 percent of Zovinax's price appeared in the marketplace. And sales of Bristol-Myers Squibb's Capoten, at 57 cents per pill, declined 83 percent the year that a 3-cents-per-pill substitute generic was introduced.

In light of these disastrous experiences throughout the pharmaceutical industry, Eli Lilly limited the price of the depression treatment Prozac to variable plus direct fixed costs in order to arrest or at least slow the onslaught of imitators into its antidepressants market. We saw in Chapter 11 that such limit pricing strategies can raise the discounted present value of long-term cash flow to stockholders relative to maximizing short-run profitability.

Because competitors are constantly devising lower-cost ways of imitating leading products, limit pricing sometimes has only temporary success. If the entry threat materializes into a real live new entrant, many incumbent firms then decide to accommodate by raising prices in a particular high-price, high-margin market niche. This pricing practice is often referred to as *niche pricing*. Concluding that declining market share from entry into the mass market is inevitable, the incumbent moves upmarket and sells its experience and expertise at high prices in the top-end segments of the market, much as it did at the start of the product life cycle.

EXAMPLE

NICHE PRICING AT PFIZER[19]

After Pfizer's LDL cholesterol-reducing drug Lipitor, which has almost $10 billion in sales and another five years of patent life, Novasc is Pfizer's second flagship product, with $4.34 billion in sales. Unfortunately for Pfizer, the patent on this leading hypertension drug expires in 2007. Pfizer estimates that 3 million of the 30 million Americans who suffer from both hypertension and high cholesterol are being treated for both diseases. These patients are candidates for a combined pill Caduet (Novasc + Lipitor) that should preserve the pricing power on Novasc as it experiences an onslaught of generic competition. The profit potential from such combo pharmaceuticals is substantial relative to the 85 percent discounts that would otherwise be necessary to limit entry into Novasc's stand-alone market. Niche pricing is always of limited applicability, and Pfizer must expect that competitors will work hard to chip away at the appeal of one high-priced pill relative to a generic pill plus high-priced Lipitor.

[19] "Drug Makers' Combo," *Wall Street Journal* (January 29, 2004), p. B1.

Full-Cost Pricing Versus Incremental Contribution Analysis

Full-Cost Pricing

A method of determining prices that cover overhead and other indirect fixed costs, as well as the variable and direct fixed costs.

Some inadvisable pricing practices are widely adopted: two examples are full-cost pricing and target return-on-investment pricing. **Full-cost pricing** requires that not only direct fixed costs of a particular product line such as licensing and maintenance and advertising be considered in pricing, but even indirect fixed costs of overhead and capital financing be added to variable costs to arrive at a final price. Indirect costs may be allocated among a firm's several products in a number of ways. One typical method is to estimate total indirect fixed costs assuming the firm operates at a standard level of output, such as 70–80 percent of capacity.

EXAMPLE

Full-Cost Pricing Results in the Loss of a Big Contract at JPMorgan: British Telephone

Telecommunications is a fiercely competitive business. British Telephone once found that its $13 million bid to provide secure long-distance microwave business communications for the investment bank JPMorgan ended up $4 million higher per year than Sprint's rival bid of $9 million. When BT executives did a follow-up study to see why they had been so undercut by Sprint, they discovered that the vice president of the BT subsidiary in the United States had attempted to recover the entire annual overhead for the subsidiary headquarters from this one account. Needless to say, BT lost JPMorgan's business with a full-cost bid of $13 million when Sprint had offered to do essentially the same thing for $9 million. Full-cost pricing always runs the risk of such undercutting by rivals.

Target Return-on-Investment Pricing

A method of pricing in which a target profit, defined as the (desired profit rate on investment × total gross operating assets) is allocated to each unit of output to arrive at a selling price.

Target return-on-investment pricing begins by selecting an acceptable profit rate on investment, usually defined as earnings before interest and depreciation divided by total gross operating assets. This return is then prorated over the number of units expected to be produced over the planning horizon. Advocates of full-cost and target pricing argue that it is important to allocate all fixed costs among the various products produced by the firm and that each product should be forced to bear its fair share of the fixed-cost burden.

Incremental Contribution Analysis

An incremental managerial decision that analyzes the change in operating profits (revenue − variable costs − direct fixed costs) available to cover indirect fixed costs.

However, each product should instead be viewed in the light of its incremental contributions to covering the business plan's fixed costs. **Incremental contribution analysis** provides a better basis for considering whether the manufacture and sale of a product should be expanded, maintained, or discontinued in favor of some higher-profit alternative. Every firm should have an effective control system in which a general manager continually monitors the overall contribution of the firm's complete product line. This person can then ensure that value-based prices contribute to both the variable cost of each product and the total fixed costs of the firm. Such target pricing is especially relevant at the launch of a product line and later at the decision to exit (see Figure 14.7).

EXAMPLE

Incremental Analysis at Continental Airlines

At one point Continental was filling only about 50 percent of its available seats, or about 15 percent less than the industry average. Eliminating 5 percent of its flights would have resulted in a substantial increase in this load factor but would have reduced profits as well. The airline industry is characterized by extremely high indirect fixed costs, which are incurred whether a plane flies or not: time depreciation costs on the aircraft, interest charges, and the cost of continuous pilot training, the expense of ground crews, as well as headquarters staff overhead. Consequently, Continental has found it profitable to operate a flight as long as it covers variable plus direct fixed costs of the flight.

The analysis of whether to operate a flight proceeds as follows: First, management examines the majority of scheduled flights to be certain that depreciation, overhead, and insurance expenses are met for this basic schedule. Then the possibility of scheduling additional flights is considered, based on their impact on corporate net profit. If revenues on a flight exceed *actual variable costs* plus direct fixed costs, the flight should be added. These relevant costs are determined by soliciting inputs from every operating department that specify exactly what extra expenses are incurred as a result of the additional flight's operation. For instance, if a ground crew that can service the additional flight is already on duty, none of the costs of this service are included in actual operating costs. If, on the other hand, overtime must be paid to service this flight, then that direct fixed cost varies with the decision to operate this flight and should be included among its costs.

Another example of such incremental analysis is the case of a late-night Continental flight from Colorado Springs to Denver and an early morning return flight. Even though the flights often go without a passenger and little or no freight, the cost of operating them is less than an overnight hanger rental in Colorado Springs. Hence the flights are maintained.

In performing this type of incremental analysis, two important points must be stressed. First, someone in management must have coordinating authority to ensure that overall objectives are met before facing decisions based solely on incremental analysis. In the case of Continental, the vice president of flight planning assumed this task. Second, every reasonable attempt must be made to identify *actual* incremental costs and revenues associated with a particular decision. Once this information is determined, incremental analysis becomes a useful and powerful tool in considering a wide range of decision problems facing the firm.

PRICING ON THE INTERNET[20]

E-business encounters several problems unique to Web-based transactions. First is the anonymity of buyers and sellers who often are identified by only a Web address. Offers to buy (and sell) may be reneged, receivables may never be collected, and items delivered may not be what buyers thought they bought. The incidence of all these events is much greater in the virtual sales environment. As a result, offers are higher, and bids are lower. From another perspective, the bid-ask spread in an Internet transaction rises to cover the cost of fraud insurance.

A second problem that the Internet accentuates is the inability to confirm variable product quality with hands-on examination. Internet pricing of commodity products such as crude oil, sheet metal, and newsprint paper, shown in Table 14.4, often

[20] An excellent survey of pricing strategy for Internet products is provided in John Figueriredo, "Finding Sustainable Profitability in Electronic Commerce," *Sloan Management Review* (Summer 2000), pp. 41–52. See also "The Click Here Economy," *BusinessWeek* (June 22, 1998), pp. 122–126.

Table 14.4 Pricing Strategy for Various Internet Products

Commodity Products	Quasi-Commodity Products	Look-and-Feel Search Goods	Experience Goods Variable Quality
Crude oil Newsprint Sheet metal Paper clips	Books CDs Videos	Suits Homes New autos Toys	PCs Produce Tires Lumber
Low-cost, low-price strategy	Differentiate with reliable delivery and extra services	Employ differential pricing based on brands and time of adoption in fashion cycle	Customize and build to order with low- and high-price tiers

pursues a low-cost strategy. The availability of quick resale at predictable commodity prices reassures buyers and sellers, and here Internet pricing at tight bid-ask spreads proves quite efficient. However, as one moves to the right in Table 14.4, product quality becomes harder and harder to detect at the point of sale. Firms such as Amazon and CDNow seek to substitute brand equity for the inability of customers to examine the product. America Online, Amazon, and Priceline spent tens of millions of dollars establishing their brand equity.

When it comes to toys, suits, homes, and new autos, consumers search for that look-and-feel for which they're willing to pay. Brands again play an important role in certifying quality, but in this case it is product branding (e.g., Game Boy, Hart Schaffner Marx, Harris Tweed) that matters, not Web site brands. Customers rely on the hostage associated with the sunk cost investment in the product brand names to establish credibility. Finally, with highly variable quality in tires, PCs, produce, and lumber, only strong warranties, escrow accounts, and replacement guarantees or deep discounts can replace the reputation effects that help sell these experience goods in nonvirtual settings.

Internet sellers can add value and reduce some transaction costs in these markets by customizing and selling direct to the customer like Dell, who provides order fulfillment and manufactures almost nothing. For this reason, services have grown quickly on the Net; the travel industry itself accounted for 35 percent of all online sales in 2002. Table 14.5 shows that the growth rate of services far surpassed growth in consumer products online.

In business-to-business (B2B) transactions, pricing is more complex than in business-to-consumer transactions. In B2B, multiple attributes come into play in the price negotiation. B2B customers haggle over date of shipment, delivery costs, warranty service times and locations, delivery reliability, and replacement guarantees. These additional considerations typically mean pricing is a part of a two- or three-step process. First, customers match their nonnegotiable requirements to the suppliers with those attributes, and those firms become the order-qualified suppliers. Then, the remaining attributes may be negotiated away against demands for a lower price point. In the heyday of the Internet bubble, B2B Internet sales grew twenty-fold from $8 billion in 1997 to $183 billion in 2002; see Table 14.5.

Dynamic Pricing

A price that varies over time based on the balance of demand and supply, often associated with Internet auctions.

Internet pricing in these B2B settings requires a matching process to qualify for an order and then a **dynamic pricing** algorithm to trade off the remaining attributes. Information technology complexity in these B2B transactions arises because customers

Table 14.5 Growth in Online Sales

	Internet Bubble Years 1997	2001	Compound Annual Growth Rate
Consumer Services			
Travel	$654 million	$ 7.4 billion	83%
Event Tickets	79 million	2 billion	124%
Financial Services	1.2 billion	5 billion	43%
Consumer Products			
Apparel	$ 92 million	$514 million	53%
Books/CDs	156 million	1.1 billion	63%
PCs	863 million	3.8 billion	45%
B2B	$ 8 billion	$ 183 billion	119%

Sources: *BusinessWeek,* Forrester Research.

are heterogeneous, and the attributes that qualify a firm to supply one group of customers may not match the requirements of other customers. In addition, as we shall see in the next section, delivery reliability (i.e., the probability of stockout and backorder) is a continuous variable that should be optimized with a revenue management solution, not a simple on-again/off-again attribute to promise or refuse a potential customer in exchange for a somewhat larger or smaller markup.

THE PRACTICE OF REVENUE MANAGEMENT, ADVANCED MATERIAL[21]

Differential pricing is sometimes complicated by capacity choices that must be made before demand is known. Consider an airline, printing press operator, or elective surgery clinic, each of which must schedule capacity before the respective demands for the 11:00 A.M. flight, the press run next Thursday, or elective surgeries tomorrow are known. If no revenue can be realized after scheduled delivery from empty airline seats, from underutilized printing presses, or empty surgical theatres, random customer arrivals force a firm with fixed capacity to choose between underutilizing excess capacity or imposing service denials and *stockouts* on regular customers.

The "spoilage" from unsold capacity and the "spill" of high-margin repeat customers for whom no capacity remains are serious problems that may affect the firm's financial success and indeed its survival. In Figure 14.8, a reduction in capacity from Q^{d_1} to a level just sufficient to meet mean demand at P_0 reduces the spoilage for low-demand events (Q^{d_2}) from *AB* to *CD*, but introduces spill (i.e., Spill_2) for high-demand events (Q^{d_1}). Revenue or yield management (YM) is an integrated set of managerial economics techniques designed to deal with these pricing and capacity allocation problems under fixed capacity and random demand.

[21] F. Harris and P. Peacock provide a thorough overview of YM techniques and potential industry applications in "Hold My Place Please: Yield Management Improves Capacity Allocation Guesswork," *Marketing Management* 4, no. 2 (Fall 1995), pp. 34–46.

Figure 14.8 Spill and Spoilage with Random Demand and Fixed Prices

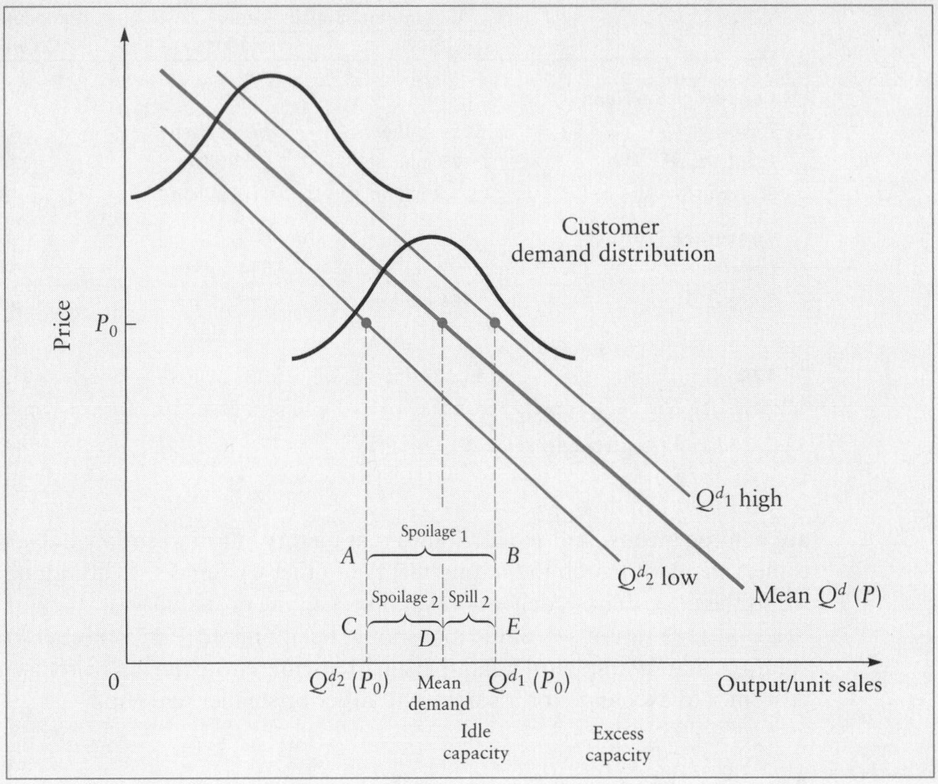

EXAMPLE

Spill and Spoilage at Sport Obermeyer[22]

The selling season in fashion retailing is short (lasting no more than several months), and customer demand at the product-line level is fickle and hard to forecast. Consequently, buyers for retail merchants like Neiman Marcus, Bloomingdale's, Saks Fifth Avenue, Rich's, and Macy's must place orders far in advance of actual sales without really knowing which fashion trends will sell well and which will sell poorly. Sport Obermeyer faces this problem with ski clothes. In a particular winter ski season, Pandora ski parkas may become a fashion statement and quickly sell out. If Pandora parkas go on backorder, creating frustrated buyers, the store will lose that customer's goodwill and future sales. In addition, the lost retail contribution margin every time Sport Obermeyer "spills" one of these customers is $15.

On the other hand, Pandora's line of ski parkas may not "catch on" this season. Instead, they may end up as spoilage (i.e., a large inventory of unsold winter clothes). The merchant would then incur losses on the unsold merchandise and forgo the

[22] Based on M. Fisher et al., "Making Supply Meet Demand in an Uncertain World," *Harvard Business Review* (May/June 1994), pp. 83–93.

opportunity to sell another Champion sweatshirt that could have occupied the ski parka's shelf space. Sport Obermeyer can use the tools of yield management to balance these costs of spill and spoilage and thereby determine how many parkas to order and what shelf space to devote to parkas versus sweatshirts.

A CROSS-FUNCTIONAL SYSTEMS MANAGEMENT PROCESS

Firms might respond to unanticipated demand fluctuations in the presence of capacity constraints by simply auctioning off their scarce product to the highest bidder or by holding massive clearance sales when faced with inventory overhang. Much to their detriment, department store retailers take a myopic marketing view of what markdown prices can accomplish. Fashion-conscious customers shop numerous stores to "win" the trendy items and do so with little repeat purchase loyalty. Everyone else has become habituated to wait for the inevitable and deep discount sales. The proportion of department store revenue earned through transactions at clearance sale prices rose from 8 percent in 1970 to 55 percent in 2001.[23] Even regular customers of leading department stores report buying at discount prices almost as often (46%) as at regular prices (54%). Not surprisingly, profitability in the department store retailing sector has collapsed, and consolidation mergers have taken some of the best known retailers out of business. What might these stores have done differently?

One alternative would be for the retail merchant's suppliers to develop flexible manufacturing systems (FMSs) so they could respond to demand fluctuations more quickly. If reorder cycles could occur several additional times within the fashion season, merchants could stockpile less inventory and yet experience fewer stockouts.

EXAMPLE

TOYOTA PLANS TO ASSEMBLE CARS WITHIN FIVE DAYS OF A CUSTOM ORDER[24]

Toyota Motor Corp. has raised the bar in delivery service for custom-ordered vehicles. Using advanced information technology, direct marketing, just-in-time logistics, and an FMS, Toyota reduced the time required to assemble a custom-ordered car to just 5 days. The industry average has fluctuated between 30 and 60 days in recent years. Production to order allows Toyota to reduce inventories 28 percent, substantially reducing costs. Whether unpredictable demand for certain types of models will overwhelm the limited surge capacity of this FMS system remains to be seen. It sounds almost too good to be true.

An FMS is often a short-sighted approach to the problem, one that attempts to use operations alone to solve a problem that is really cross-functional. Some manufacturing environments are simply inappropriate for the application of FMS technology. The economies from large production runs in textile manufacturing or metal working imply that designer jeans and refrigerator manufacturing operations should

[23] B. P. Pashigian, "Demand Uncertainty and Sales," *American Economic Review* 78, no. 5 (December 1993), pp. 936–953; and "Priced to Move," *Wall Street Journal* (August 7, 2001), p. A6.

[24] Based on "Toyota Develops a Way," *Wall Street Journal* (August 6, 1999), p. A4.

adopt transfer lines that minimize new setups in order to realize massive cost savings. A flexible manufacturing system will not provide the answer to unpredictable demand fluctuations in these types of production environments.

One alternative to resolve the problems of high-margin spill is simply to acquire more capacity. Of course, no company can afford to build unlimited additional capacity. Aggregate capacity planning incorporates a careful financial analysis of the capital budgeting problem that identifies the optimal fixed capacity for any line of business. A better alternative is to reserve some of this optimal fixed capacity for late-arriving, high-margin customers. Reserving capacity as the moment of delivery approaches should not be interpreted as "excess capacity" but rather as idle capacity that presents a sustainable revenue opportunity. This insight is one that comes out of revenue management analysis.

Revenue Management
A cross-functional order acceptance and refusal process.

Every company has some orders that it should refuse. **Revenue management** (RM), often called yield management, is fundamentally an order acceptance and refusal process that links marketing decisions about demand creation and pricing with operations decisions about scheduling and financial decisions about capacity planning. The objective is to decide which orders to accept at particular prices and which to refuse. These relationships are depicted in Figure 14.9 as a cross-functional triangle of account management, forecasting, and scheduling decisions. Practitioners of yield management believe that the sources of sustainable price premiums lie in these cross-functional systems management processes. In this view, innovative products and successful advertising campaigns are quickly reverse engineered and readily imitated. Advertising and product design cannot therefore provide sustainable

Figure 14.9 Cross-Functional Revenue Management

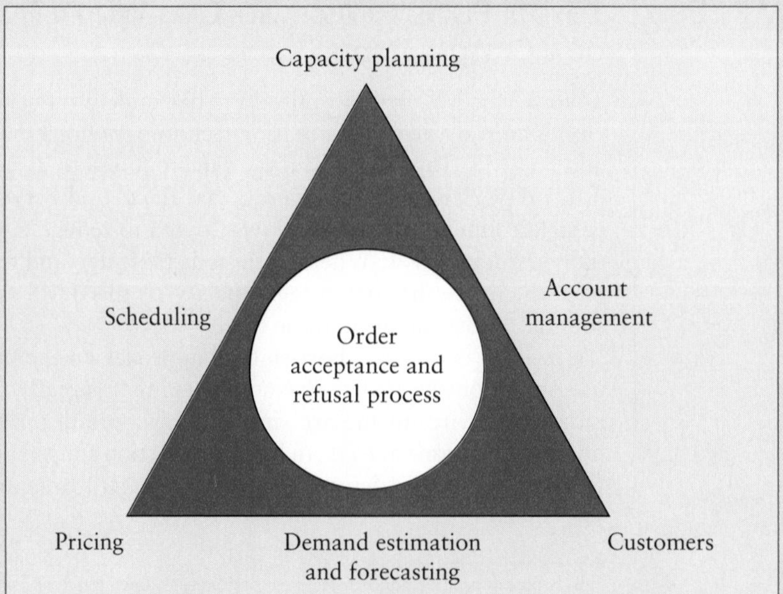

competitive advantage. Process advantages, on the other hand, prove much more difficult for competitors to imitate.

SOURCES OF SUSTAINABLE PRICE PREMIUMS

Yield management processes add conspicuous tangible value for which customers gladly pay higher prices. In most cases, the added value arises through customizing and optimizing the account and order management. In the airline industry, for example, some customers want extensive flexibility of reservations that allows frequent changes in departure and arrival times. If an airline has the operations capability and information technology to provide this service, business travelers with unconfirmed meeting schedules will offer large price premiums to secure this *change order responsiveness*. To take another example, Disney offers substantial price premiums to gift product suppliers who can deliver high quality on time as promised. When Disney order clerks submit an error-laden request that needs to be changed within the normal 30-day reorder cycle, Disney volunteers to pay even more. Such supplements to revenue go exclusively to firms that have the systems management processes that can handle extraordinary change order requests.

Firms compete on other aspects of order processing as well. Some customers want short *scheduling delays* (e.g., just-in-time retailers without warehouses). Others want high *delivery reliability* and a small probability of being denied service in the event of a stockout (e.g., business executives traveling to a stockholders' meeting). Still others value *conformance to product or service specifications*. For time-sensitive deliveries of organ transplants, for example, excellent on-time service records warrant paying high airfares. The alternative would be a much more expensive jet charter service. Manufacturers as well as service firms can establish sustainable price premiums based on these same order-processing characteristics of change order responsiveness, minimal scheduling delay, delivery reliability, and conformance to specifications.

All these sources of sustainable price premiums are prominent in airline services at "fortress hubs" where one carrier controls more than 65 percent of the seat departures. Figure 14.10 displays the major hub airports in the continental United States and provides pricing and market share data for the top two carriers. In each of these cities, the dominant firm(s) have sufficient operating capacity and systems control to provide high-quality service. At Dallas–Ft. Worth, for example, American Airlines has high schedule convenience, with departures quite close to the time preferences of a DFW-origin traveler. Similarly, at this airport American can offer high delivery reliability, schedule conformance to expectations, and change order responsiveness. Passengers, especially business travelers, will pay substantial premiums for these high service quality characteristics because of the additional value such flights create in their own business activities. YM systems reserve idle capacity to meet these high-value demands when the late arrival of such requests is forecasted. YM systems also "protect" fewer seats and release more capacity to deep discount leisure segments of the market. Overall, fares per revenue passenger mile at a fortress hub such as Atlanta (where Delta has a 70% share) are 84 percent higher than at Orlando, where Delta again is the leading carrier but has only 32 percent of the market.

REVENUE MANAGEMENT DECISIONS

Revenue management (RM) can be divided into three decisions: (1) a proactive pricing and aggregate capacity planning decision, (2) an inventory or capacity reallocation

Figure 14.10 Ratio of Business to Leisure Fares and Airline Market Shares at Hub Airports

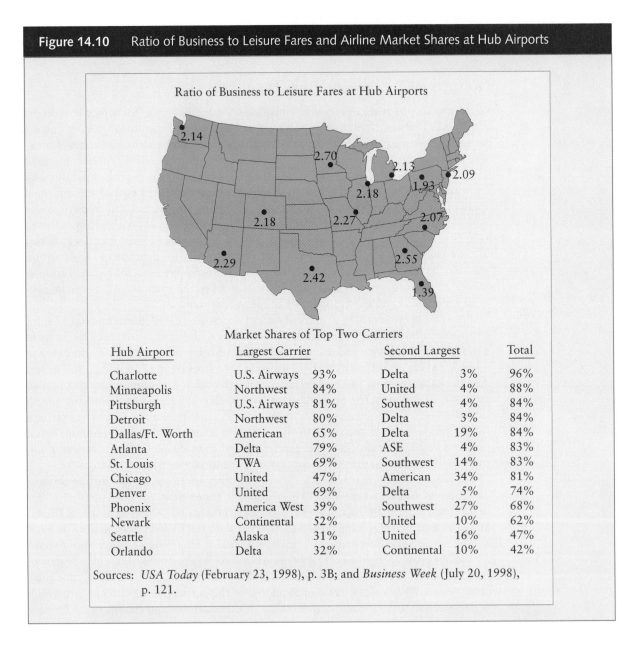

Ratio of Business to Leisure Fares at Hub Airports

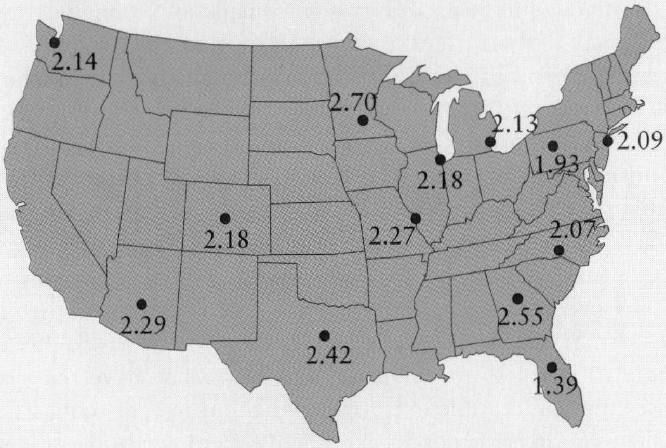

Market Shares of Top Two Carriers

Hub Airport	Largest Carrier		Second Largest		Total
Charlotte	U.S. Airways	93%	Delta	3%	96%
Minneapolis	Northwest	84%	United	4%	88%
Pittsburgh	U.S. Airways	81%	Southwest	4%	84%
Detroit	Northwest	80%	Delta	3%	84%
Dallas/Ft. Worth	American	65%	Delta	19%	84%
Atlanta	Delta	79%	ASE	4%	83%
St. Louis	TWA	69%	Southwest	14%	83%
Chicago	United	47%	American	34%	81%
Denver	United	69%	Delta	5%	74%
Phoenix	America West	39%	Southwest	27%	68%
Newark	Continental	52%	United	10%	62%
Seattle	Alaska	31%	United	16%	47%
Orlando	Delta	32%	Continental	10%	42%

Sources: *USA Today* (February 23, 1998), p. 3B; and *Business Week* (July 20, 1998), p. 121.

decision, and (3) an overbooking decision. Figure 14.11 places these decisions in a RM conceptual framework, showing a flow chart of the components of a revenue management process. What all three decisions have in common is a tactical focus that depends on anticipated rival responses; a systems management philosophy that integrates marketing, operations, and finance; and finally a multiproduct orientation that continuously reconfigures the firm's product offerings. We now address the managerial economics of each RM decision.

Proactive Price Discrimination *Proactive price discrimination* involves maximizing profits in the light of anticipated late-arriving demand and rival firm responses. In principle, computerized decision support systems (DSS) make it possible

Figure 14.11 Revenue Management Flow Chart

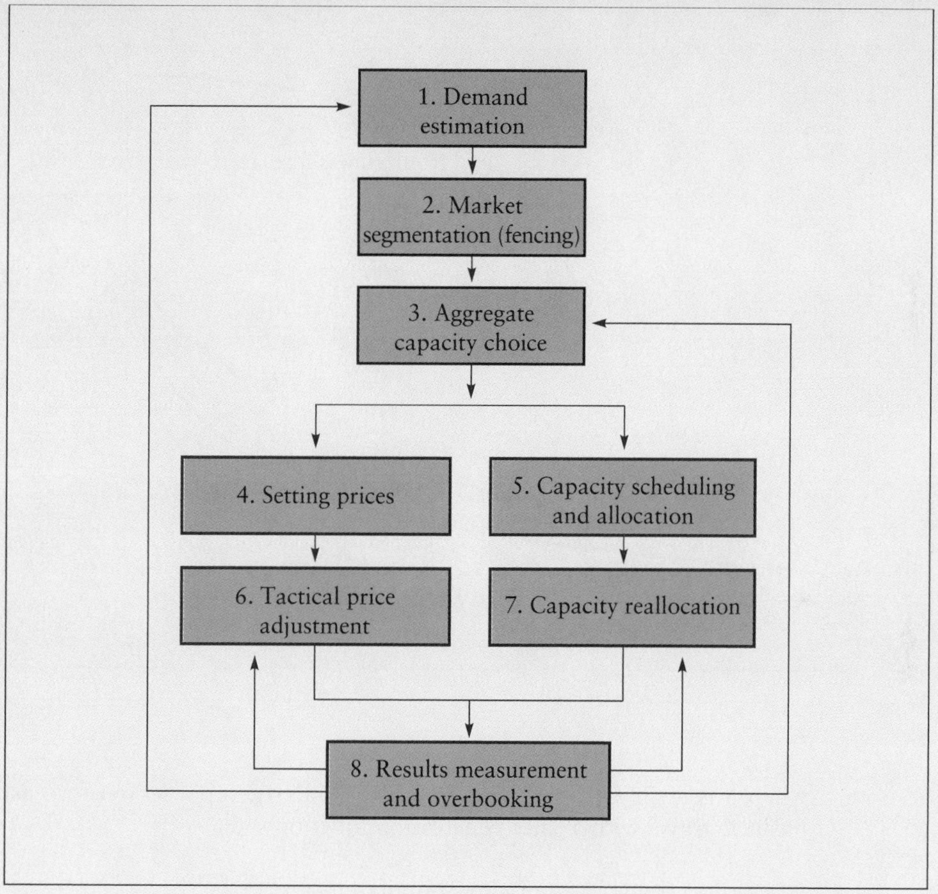

to reauction the remaining seats on a flight or the remaining runs on the printing press each time a new customer arrives on a reservation system. Conceivably, each customer would then experience first-degree price discrimination and pay a unique price that reflects time of delivery, service costs, and price elasticity. Few RM practitioners have adopted bid price systems. Instead, most set prices and initially allocate capacity with the familiar techniques of marginal analysis that we discussed earlier in the chapter for differential fares that allocate the capacity between business and nonbusiness air travelers on the 11 A.M. Thursday flight DFW to LAX.

CAPACITY REALLOCATION The second step in revenue management is to *reallocate capacity* as delivery times approach in the light of advance sales and confirmed orders. Suppose you forecasted advance sales for business class on Thursday departures from Dallas to Los Angeles in accordance with the exponential function (tickets purchased = aB^t) estimated in semilog form as

$$\ln(\text{tickets}) = \ln a + \ln B(t) = \alpha + \beta t \qquad [14.13]$$

Figure 14.12 Advance Sales Forecasts, Bookings, and Threshold Curves

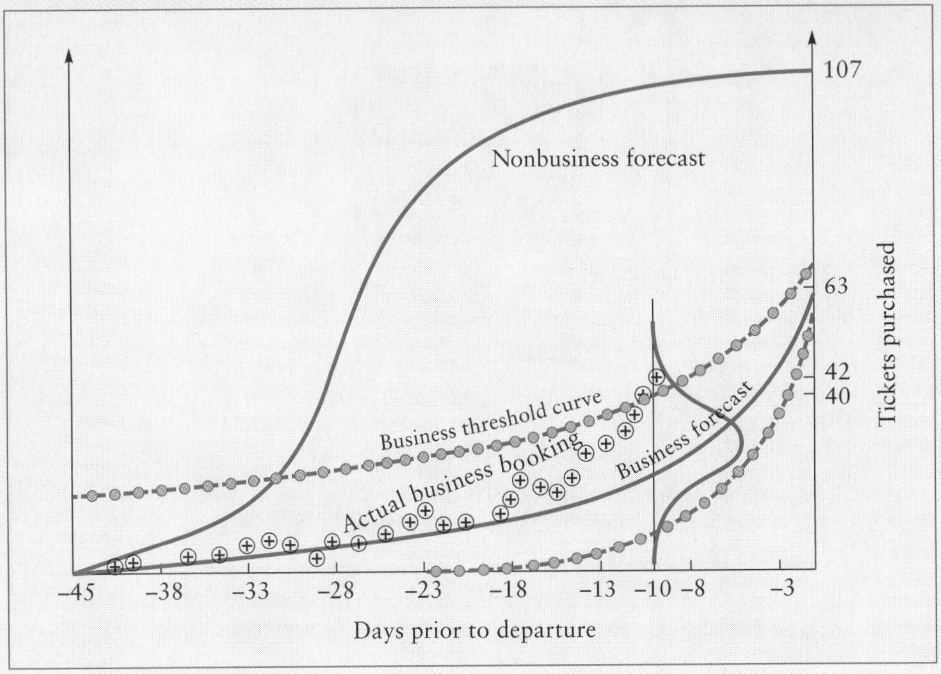

where t is a simple time trend variable. Similarly, suppose you forecasted all nonbusiness travel with a sales penetration function such as

$$\text{Tickets purchased} = e^{k_1 - k_2(1/t)} \quad [14.14]$$

estimated as

$$\ln(\text{tickets}) = k_1 - k_2(1/t) \quad [14.15]$$

where k_1 and k_2 are constants defining the rate of sales growth throughout the advance sales period. These forecasted business and nonbusiness "booking curves" are plotted in Figure 14.12. Note that the curves exhibit the early- and late-arriving characteristics of demand in the nonbusiness and business markets, respectively.

The forecasted booking curves reflect new demand arrivals and cancellations and are, in that sense, net bookings. If such bookings require substantial nonrefundable deposits on advance sales, then they reflect realized revenue rather than just potential sales.[25] For the 11:00 A.M. flight to Los Angeles, the final demand target in Figure 14.12 is 63 business and 107 nonbusiness passengers. This *initial* allocation of total capacity applies when customer reservations open 180, 120, 60, or in our case, 45 days prior to departure. It is subject to change (and in fact often is changed) by the revenue managers.

[25] In the last RM decision, we consider the effects of no-shows on authorized overbookings.

Confidence intervals based on the different demand arrival distributions are then used to determine when actual bookings deviate a given amount, which triggers an exception report. For example, business travel appears to be greater than forecasted ticket sales at day $t - 10$ by a statistically significant amount. This violation of the **threshold sales curve** raises the question of whether to stop sales in the nonbusiness class where contribution margins ($P_{\text{nonbus}} - MC = \$188 - \$130 = \$58$) are clearly lower than in the business class segment, where $P_{\text{bus}} - MC = \$261 - \$130 = \$131$.

Threshold Sales Curve

A level of advance sales that triggers reallocation of capacity.

The answer to this capacity reallocation question lies in applied statistics and in the initial profit-maximizing capacity choice. Marginal capacity expansions are justified as long as the expected incremental revenue minus marginal cost (i.e., the additional expected contribution to fixed cost) is greater than the incremental cost of additional capacity. In capacity reallocation, the cost of additional capacity in the business class is an opportunity cost, or the forgone contribution from selling one less seat in the nonbusiness class. At the margin, we would reallocate capacity as long as the expected contribution margin from allocating another seat to business travelers would exceed the lost contribution margin from a boarding denial in nonbusiness. That is,

$$(P_{\text{bus}} - MC)(\textit{Prob Shortage}_{\text{bus}}) = (P_{\text{nonbus}} - MC)$$
$$\$131\ (\textit{Prob Shortage}_{\text{bus}}) = \$58 \qquad [14.16]$$

where the *Prob Shortage*$_{\text{bus}}$ is the probability that the business class will in fact be full and, therefore, the probability that the extra business-class seat will realize its \$131 marginal contribution.[26]

The preannounced prices and resulting contribution margins of \$58 and \$131 indicated (using Equation 14.16) that high yield spill should occur 44.1 percent of the time:

$$(\textit{Prob Shortage}_{\text{bus}}) = \$58/\$131 = 0.441$$

For any business-class demand distribution (say, normally distributed with a mean of 60 seats and a standard deviation of 20 seats), we can calculate the optimal capacity choice as

$$\mu_{\text{seats}} + z_{\alpha}\sigma_{\text{seats}} = 60 + 0.148 \times 20 = 63 \text{ seats} \qquad [14.17]$$

where z_{α} is the absolute value of the standard normal critical value (z value) for one-tailed alpha from Table 1 in Appendix B. These calculations correspond to the initial situation in which business-class capacity was set at 63 seats (see Figure 14.1). On this flight, 63 seats is often referred to as the **protection level** for business-class seats. Similarly, 107 seats is the **authorization level** for nonbusiness-class seats.

Protection Level

Capacity reserved for sale in higher margin segments.

Authorization Level

Capacity authorized for sale in lower margin segments.

Now recall that at day $t - 10$ in Figure 14.12, we received an exception report: It appears that the arrival distribution for next Thursday's flight is not normally distributed with mean 60 and standard deviation 20, that is, N(60,20). Instead, the exception report may indicate mean demand has increased to N(62,20). Again, using the fact that with prices of \$261 and \$188 the optimal probability of stockout in business class is 0.441, we can use Equation 14.17 to calculate the new optimal

[26] It is quite possible to have a positive probability of stockout on both sides of Equation 14.16. Here, however, we assume an unlimited demand in the nonbusiness segment at the low fare of \$188 for Dallas–Ft. Worth–LAX. That is, the probability of stockout is assumed to be 1.0 on the right-hand side.

capacity allocation at 62 seats + 0.148(20) seats = 65 seats. This result implies that a stop-sales policy of 105 seats should apply to the bookings accepted in nonbusiness travel and two seats (107 − 105) should be reallocated to business class. Continued monitoring of bookings relative to the forecast thresholds may result in a return of these seats to nonbusiness class or a still further allocation toward business travelers.

The same questions and analyses of capacity allocation apply in assemble-to-order manufacturing when a sport apparel manufacturer or a customized paper products manufacturer must decide which orders to accept and which to refuse (i.e., how to allocate fixed total capacity). As yield management moves out of the service sector (e.g., airlines, hotels, rental cars, advertising agencies, hospitals, professional services) and into manufacturing, these managerial economics techniques become increasingly important.[27]

EXAMPLE

The Optimal Probability of a Stockout at Sport Obermeyer

Recall that Sport Obermeyer must allocate its fixed retail shelf and display rack space between Pandora parkas and Champion sweatshirts. The lost retail contribution margin every time Sport Obermeyer "spills" a Pandora parka customer is $15. The lost retail contribution margin on a Champion sweatshirt is $4. Knowing these margins and the relative sales effectiveness of particular shelf space, Sport Obermeyer can use the tools of yield management to balance the costs of spoilage and spill in order to decide the optimal incidence of stockouts in Pandora parkas. Using Equation 14.16, Sport Obermeyer calculates that Pandora parkas should stock out 27 percent of the time: $Prob\ (Shortage_{\text{parka}}) = 0.27$. With demand distribution data, Sport Obermeyer can calculate that a probability of shortage of $4/$15 = 0.27 requires stocking 85 size-8 parkas in each of its stores.

Optimal Overbooking
A marginal analysis technique for balancing the cost of idle capacity (spoilage) against the opportunity cost of unserved demand (spill).

Optimal Overbooking The third and final yield management decision is an **optimal overbooking** decision. Here the airline authorizes the reservation clerks to sell more seats than are available on each departure to combat the lost revenue from "no-shows." Of course, many tickets entail discount fares that require advance purchase, but some business-class tickets are not purchased until check-in time. This means that a confirmed sale is not realized revenue until delivery time. In some industries orders can be canceled or shipments refused. At times the air carriers experienced up to 35 percent no-shows in certain city-pair markets.

The optimal overbooking decision illustrates marginal analysis in practice. Each airline seeks to minimize the summed costs of spoilage and spill. In Figure 14.13, as expected demand of business travelers approaches planned capacity and the expected load factor approaches 100 percent, the total cost of spoilage (i.e., unsold seats × $\text{contribution}_{\text{bus}}$) declines toward zero. In contrast, as the expected load factor approaches 100 percent, the costs of high-yield spill rise for three reasons. First, oversales represent lost contributions, which might have been captured by other service offerings (e.g., later flights); that is, some customers will go to a competitor. Second, oversales necessitate out-of-pocket expenses to compensate passengers who

[27] See F. Harris and J. Pinder, "A Revenue Management Approach to Order Booking and Demand Management in Assemble-to-Order Manufacturing," *Journal of Operations Management* (December 1995), pp. 299–309.

Figure 14.13 How the Overbooking Decision Minimizes the Summed Cost of Spoilage and Spill

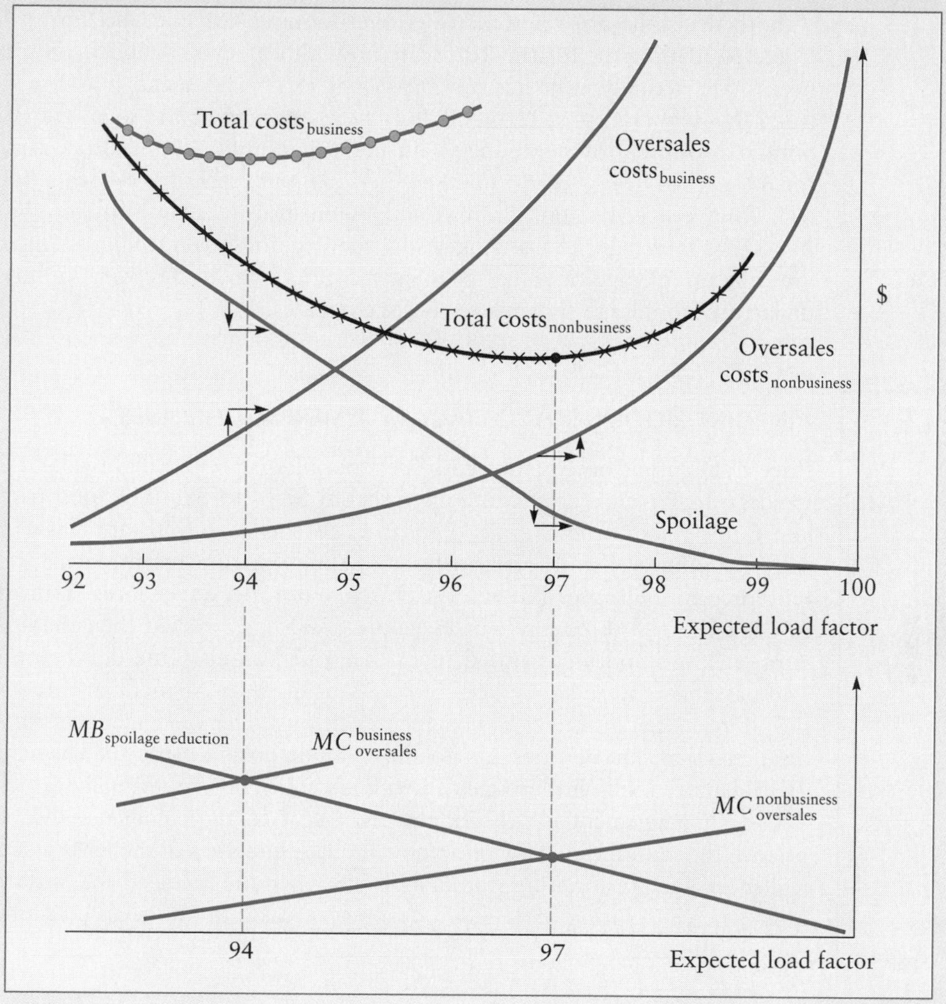

board the airplane and then volunteer to give up their seats. And third, oversales and the resulting stockouts sacrifice customer goodwill and brand loyalty, thereby causing lost future sales. These rising total costs of high-yield spill also are depicted in Figure 14.13.

Total summed costs are reduced when the load factor increases as long as the rising costs of oversales are more than offset by the falling cost of spoilage. From load factors below 92–97 percent, the declining cost of spoilage more than offsets the rising cost of oversales for nonbusiness travel. Beyond 97 percent, the rate of spoilage cost reduction is less than the rate of oversales cost increase. This relationship is shown in the lower diagram by comparing the $MC_{\text{nonbusiness oversales}}$ to the marginal benefit of reduced spoilage, $MB_{\text{spoilage reduction}}$, which is the MC of unsold seats *saved* by planning a higher load factor. For the nonbusiness class, the optimal planned load factor appears to be 97 percent. In contrast, in the business class the $MC_{\text{business oversales}}$ is so much higher as load factor increases that the optimal planned load factor is only 94 percent.

Both decisions are referred to as overbooking decisions because a 97 percent expected load factor for the 105 seats now allocated to nonbusiness travelers may necessitate actually booking not $0.97 \times 105 = 102$ seats, but rather 127 seats $[(127 \times (1 - 0.2) = 102]$ in periods when no-shows are averaging 20 percent. Similarly, optimal overbooking in business may imply confirming reservations not for 61 seats in heavy (35%) no-show periods, but rather for 94 seats ($94 \times 0.65 = 61$). On average, 102 nonbusiness and 61 business travelers enplane for the Thursday 11:00 A.M. flight to Los Angeles. Of course, these 163 total passengers expected are only an average of actual passenger counts, which may vary on any particular departure from large spoilage to severe oversales.

EXAMPLE

Pinpoint Booking Accuracy at American Airlines[28]

Price differentials on American Airlines' popular 5:30 P.M. flight (Flight 2015) from Chicago to Phoenix are huge, ranging from $238 to $1,404 round trip. American constantly adjusts the capacity allocation to each of seven fare classes as advance sales data deviate from forecast. Four weeks prior to a recent departure, American had already sold 69 of the 125 coach seats at Super Saver fares. With three weeks to departure, all three fare classes below $300 had reached their maximum authorization levels and were closed to further reservations. One day before departure, 130 passengers were booked on the 125-seat flight, but American was still authorizing up to five additional full coach reservations. The yield management computers predicted that cancellations and no-shows might go as high as 10. The next day Flight 2015 departed full with no one denied boarding. The systems management objective of yield management is "to sell the right seat to the right customer at the right price at the right time" (Sabre Solutions). Such outcomes of the RM system are a critical success factor for American in a period when the index of U.S. airfares has risen only 5 percent during 1995–2005 despite increases in all urban consumer prices of 27 percent.

Yield management continuously reallocates capacity and adjusts these overbooking authorizations as advance sales data roll in. The incremental revenues from effective yield management can be significant. For example, American Airlines recently calculated its additional revenue from attending to these problems at $467 million per year. Marriott International estimates that revenue management contributes as much as $200 million each year to its revenue stream. And the Canadian Broadcasting Corporation realized a $2 million revenue gain the first two weeks after it adopted revenue management techniques.[29]

[28] Based on "High-Tech Pricing Boosts Business Fares," *Charlotte Observer* (November 9, 1997), p. 1D; and "For U.S. Airlines, a Shakeout," *Wall Street Journal* (September 19, 2005), p. A1.

[29] As cited in R. Cross, *Revenue Management: Hardcore Tactics for Market Domination* (New York: Broadway Books, 1997).

EXAMPLE

REVENUE MANAGEMENT IN BASEBALL: THE BALTIMORE ORIOLES[30]

Recent applications of revenue management have taken the techniques out of travel services and into private-pay elective surgeries, radio and television advertising, opera and symphony concerts, law firms, consulting firms, golf courses, and now baseball. Like airlines, all these businesses have fixed capacity with perishable inventory; once the last out of the fifth inning has been called, empty seats offer no realizable value. Although season ticket holders are prominent in the planning of any professional sports franchise, single-game and three-game ticket packages remain a substantial source of revenue. And unstable demand makes prediction of sales in these more immediate segments a challenging and potentially highly profitable process to do well, especially in baseball.

Most professional teams celebrate their sellouts, but some fail to realize that spare capacity (however slight) as game time approaches is a substantial revenue opportunity. Allowing discount ticket packages and promotions to displace last-minute walk-in customers often sacrifices high-margin repeat purchase business. At the same time, overall attendance in professional baseball remains below prestrike levels of the 1980s, and many games are played in ballparks only half full. The Baltimore Orioles revenue manager attempts to balance both of these errors of understocking and of overstocking. Single-game seats purchased well in advance are available at a discount. However, a substantial capacity of well-placed seats is protected in anticipation of late-arriving, high-willingness-to-pay, game-day-only customers. Advance sales are tracked, and variances are noted relative to previous sales histories for that home stand against similar opponents. As game day approaches, authorization levels for release of discount tickets gradually adjust to reflect the probability of stockout in higher-margin segments. Ideally, on game day, perhaps 97 percent of the seats are filled with fans in a variety of different segments paying a variety of different prices, each reflecting the location, customer responsiveness, reliability, timing, and other ticketing services that particular customers prefer, thereby adding maximum value.

[30] Based on "Managing Baseball's Yield," *Barron's* (September 11, 1995), p. 50.

SUMMARY

- All pricing decisions should be proactive, systematically analytical, and value based, not reactive, ad hoc, and cost-based.
- Two conditions are required for effective differential pricing:
  1. One must be able to segment the market and prevent the transfer of the product (or service) from one segment to another.
  2. Differences in the elasticity of demand at a given price between the market segments must be discernable.
- To maximize profits using differential pricing, the firm must allocate output in such a way that marginal revenue is equal in the different market segments.
- Differential pricing is often implemented through the direct segmentation of intertemporal pricing or pricing by delivery location.
- Indirect segmentation to support differential pricing is often accomplished through two-part pricing. Optimal *two-part prices* entail a lump-sum access fee and a user charge that equals or exceeds marginal cost and varies per unit consumed.

- Couponing is another way to price discriminate while charging the same list prices to different customers, some of whom are highly price sensitive and will redeem coupons and others who will not.
- Bundling is a third pricing mechanism that indirectly segments customers who have inversely correlated demand across multiple products.
- *Price discrimination* is the act of selling the same good or service produced by a given distribution channel at different prices to different customers at the same time.
- A good's pricing strategy varies throughout the product or service's life cycle. A frequent pattern is target pricing, followed by penetration pricing, price skimming, value-based pricing, limit pricing, and finally niche pricing.
- *Full-cost pricing* and *target pricing* are inconsistent with the marginal pricing rules of economic theory. *Incremental contribution analysis* is a widely applicable method of economic analysis that can help managers achieve a more efficient and profitable level of operation.
- Pricing on the Internet suffers from anonymity and lack of reputation effects, along with search across various product qualities being especially difficult to verify prior to purchase. These complications imply distinctly different pricing approaches for commodity-like products, search goods, and experience goods.
- B2B pricing on the Internet requires a two-step process of multi-attribute matching to qualify for consideration as a supplier and then a dynamic pricing scheme to trade off additional features and functions as sources of value-in-use against lower price point alternatives.
- Yield management (YM) or revenue management (RM) consists of pricing and capacity allocation techniques for fixed-capacity manufacturers or service firms with perishable inventory and random demand.
- Flexible manufacturing systems and production-to-order with just-in-time delivery can seldom fully resolve the problem posed by RM.
- RM provides an optimal order acceptance and refusal process with cross-functional resolution of account management, demand forecasting, and scheduling decisions.
- Proactive price discrimination equates the marginal revenue from different segments of the target market. It does so with differential value-based prices that reflect delivery reliability, change order responsiveness, scheduling convenience, conformance to expectations, and the value of these service quality characteristics to the particular class of customers (i.e., third-degree price discrimination).
- RM reallocates inventory or service capacity in accordance with the condition $(P - MC)_a(Prob\ Shortage)_a = (P - MC)_b$. This procedure identifies optimal protection levels for high-margin segments, accounts, and customers and an optimal authorization level for release of capacity to lower-margin segments, accounts, and customers.
- The optimal overbooking decision equates the declining marginal cost of spoilage as load factor or capacity utilization increases with the rising marginal cost of spill (i.e., oversales).

Exercises

Answers to the exercises in blue can be found in Appendix C at the back of the book.

1. The price elasticity of demand for a textbook sold in the United States is estimated to be −2.0, whereas the price elasticity of demand for books sold overseas is −3.0. The U.S. market requires hardcover books with a marginal cost of \$40; the overseas market is normally served with softcover texts on newsprint, having a marginal cost of only \$15. Calculate the profit-maximizing price in each market.

$$\left[\textit{Hint}\text{: Remember that } MR = P\left(1 + \frac{1}{E_D}\right)\right]$$

2. The price elasticity of demand for air travel differs radically from first-class (−0.3) to unrestricted coach (−0.4) to restricted discount coach (−0.9). What do these elasticities mean for optimal prices (fares) on a cross-country trip with incremental variable costs (marginal costs) equal to \$120?
3. American Export-Import Shipping Company operates a general cargo carrier service between New York and several Western European ports. It hauls two major categories of freight: manufactured items and semimanufactured raw materials. The demand functions for these two classes of goods are

$$P_1 = 100 - 2Q_1$$
$$P_2 = 80 - Q_2$$

where Q_i = tons of freight moved. The total cost function for American is

$$TC = 20 + 4(Q_1 + Q_2)$$

a. Determine the firm's total profit function.
b. What are the profit-maximizing levels of price and output for the two freight categories?
c. At these levels of output, calculate the marginal revenue in each market.
d. What are American's total profits if it is effectively able to charge different prices in the two markets?
e. If American is required by law to charge the same per-ton rate to all users, calculate the new profit-maximizing level of price and output. What are the profits in this situation?
f. Explain the difference in profit levels between the differential pricing and uniform pricing cases. *Hint:* First calculate the point price elasticity of demand under the uniform price-output solution.

4. DVDs and DVD players are no longer niche products; 31 million players have been sold in the United States. Sony sells both DVD players and DVDs. What should be Sony's approach to pricing? What difference will it make to Sony pricing if customers have now become dissimilar?
5. Phillips Industries manufactures a certain product that can be sold directly to retail outlets or to the Superior Company for further processing and eventual sale as a completely different product. The demand function for each of these markets is

$$\text{Retail Outlets: } P_1 = 60 - 2Q_1$$
$$\text{Superior Company: } P_2 = 40 - Q_2$$

where P_1 and P_2 are the prices charged and Q_1 and Q_2 are the quantities sold in the respective markets. Phillips's total cost function for the manufacture of this product is

$$TC = 10 + 8(Q_1 + Q_2)$$

a. Determine Phillips's total profit function.
b. What are the profit-maximizing price and output levels for the product in the two markets?
c. At these levels of output, calculate the marginal revenue in each market.
d. What are Phillips's total profits if the firm is effectively able to charge different prices in the two markets?
e. Calculate the profit-maximizing level of price and output if Phillips is required to charge the same price per unit in each market. What are Phillips's profits under this condition?

6. In the face of stable (or declining) enrollments and increasing costs, many colleges and universities, both public and private, find themselves in progressively tighter financial dilemmas that require basic reexamination of the pricing schemes used by institutions of higher learning. One proposal advocated by the Committee for Economic Development (CED) and others has been the use of more nearly full-cost pricing of higher education, combined with the government provision of sufficient loan funds to students who would not otherwise have access to reasonable loan terms in private markets. Advocates of such proposals argue that the private rate of return to student investors is sufficiently high to stimulate socially optimal levels of demand for education, even with the higher tuition rates. Others argue against the existence of significant external benefits to undergraduate education to warrant the current high levels of public support.

As with current university pricing schemes, proponents of full-cost pricing generally argue for a standard fee (albeit higher than at present) for all students. Standard-fee proposals ignore relative cost and demand differences among activities in the university.

a. Discuss several possible rationales for charging different prices for different courses of study.

b. What are the income-distribution effects of a pricing scheme that charges the same fee to all students?

c. If universities adopted a system of full-cost (or marginal cost) pricing for various courses, what would you expect the impact on the efficiency of resource allocations within the university to be?

d. Would you complain less about large lecture sections taught by graduate students if these were priced significantly lower than small seminars taught by outstanding scholars?

e. What problems could you see arising from a university that adopted such a pricing scheme?

7. General Medical makes disposable syringes for hospitals and doctor supply companies. The company uses cost-plus pricing and currently charges 150 percent of average variable costs. General Medical learned of an opportunity to sell 300,000 syringes to the Department of Defense if they can be delivered within three months at a price not in excess of \$1 each. General Medical normally sells its syringes for \$1.20 each.

If General Medical accepts the Defense Department order, it will have to forgo sales of 100,000 syringes to its regular customers over this time period, although this loss of sales is not expected to affect future sales.

a. Should General Medical accept the Defense Department order?

b. If sales for the balance of the year are expected to be 50,000 units less because of some lost customers who do not return, should the order be accepted? (Ignore any effects beyond one year.)

8. The Pear Computer Company just developed a totally revolutionary new personal computer. It estimates that it will take competitors at least two years to produce equivalent products. The demand function for the computer is estimated to be

$$P = 2{,}500 - 0.0005Q$$

The marginal (and average variable) cost of producing the computer is \$900.

a. Compute the profit-maximizing price and output levels assuming Pear acts as a monopolist for its product.

b. Determine the total contribution to profits and fixed costs from the solution generated in Part (a).

Pear Computer is considering an alternative pricing strategy of price skimming. It plans to set the following schedule of prices over the coming two years:

Time Period	Price	Quantity Sold
1	\$2,400	200,000
2	2,200	200,000
3	2,000	200,000
4	1,800	200,000
5	1,700	200,000
6	1,600	200,000
7	1,500	200,000
8	1,400	200,000
9	1,300	200,000
10	1,200	200,000

c. Calculate the contribution to profit and overhead for each of the 10 time periods and prices.

d. Compare your results in Part (c) with your answers in Part (b).

e. Explain the major advantages and disadvantages of price skimming as a pricing strategy.

9. Explain the effect on capacity reallocations of advance sales data indicating mean demand of 55 rather than 60 during a slow travel week for business class, using the information in Figures 14.1, Table 14.2, and Equation 14.17.

10. Suppose the frequent-flyer program raised the cost of high-yield spill twofold because business customers who are denied boarding now take their business to other carriers for several future trips, not just the current one. Reanalyze the overbooking decision in Figure 14.13 under these circumstances. Will overbooking of business-class service increase or decrease?

11. An aircraft with 100 seats serves passengers through two types of fares: full ($505) and discount ($105). Extra passengers have $5 marginal cost. Demand for discount tickets is unlimited, while demand for full-fare tickets is evenly distributed between 11 and 30 seats. How many seats should be protected for full-fare passengers?

12. What criteria should correlate with price premiums in capacity-constrained service businesses such as accounting firms and advertising agencies?

13. Why is a long-haul trucking company not a good candidate for yield management techniques?

CASE EXERCISE

CONGESTION PRICING LIBRARY RESEARCH

During times of peak usage of network resources such as highways, mainframe computers, and power transmission lines, providing access to an additional user imposes costs on all other users. Congestion pricing or peak-load pricing systems at least partially internalize these external costs of congestion. How can congestion pricing be made more viable? Analyze the OBU project underway for truck congestion tolls on the European roadways and read the abstract *Congestion Pricing for Congestion Avoidance.* Outline an application of this approach to a congested service facility in your own community.

PART V

Organizational Architecture and Regulation

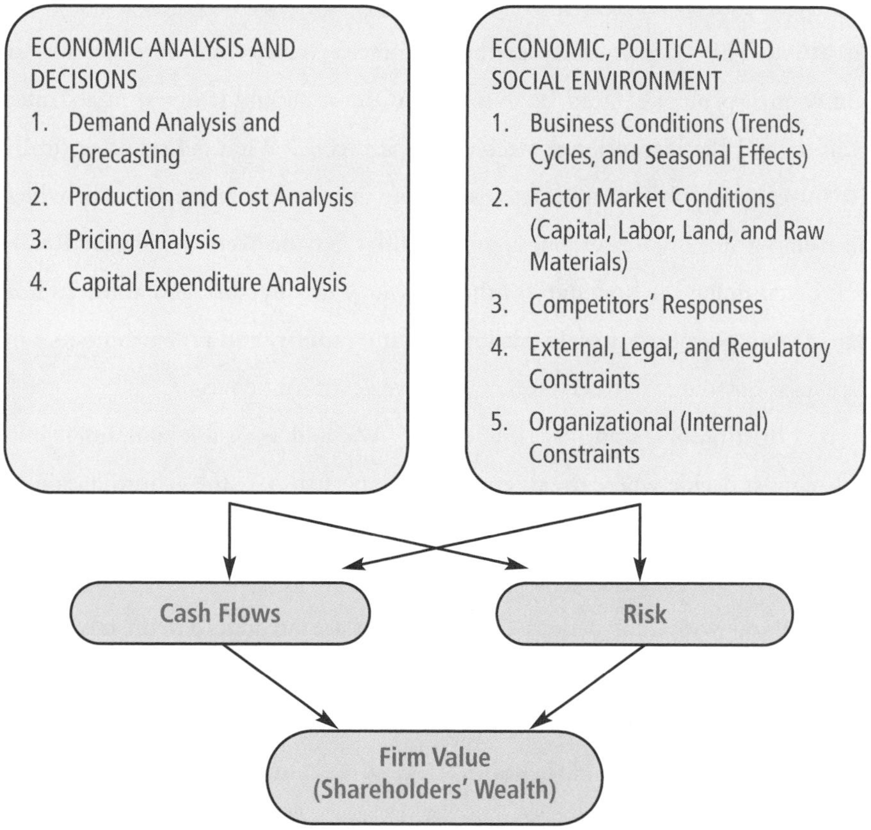

Part V addresses the new institutional economics of organizational architecture as well as the regulation of business. Major themes include incentive contracting, the choice of organizational form (e.g., vertically integrating to redraw the boundaries of the firm), and the regulation/deregulation debate. Chapter 15 discusses the theory of business contracting, managerial incentive contracts, the principal-agent problem, corporate governance, licensing of trade secrets, the dissolution of partnerships, and vertical integration. Appendix 15A explores optimal mechanism design in auctions and incentive compatibility for joint ventures. Chapter 16 then addresses the economic regulation of business, including antitrust, patenting, and licensing, as well as regulatory and private market approaches for controlling externalities. Chapter 17 discusses capital budgeting techniques used in acquisition, merger and spin-off activities to change the organizational boundaries of the firm.

CHAPTER

15

CONTRACTING, GOVERNANCE, AND ORGANIZATIONAL FORM

CHAPTER PREVIEW This chapter explores the coordination and control problems faced by every business organization and the institutional mechanisms designed to solve these problems in a least-cost manner. The most important organizational architecture decision is determining the boundary of the firm (i.e., the span of hierarchical control). In dealing with external suppliers, outsource partners, internal divisions, authorized distributors, franchisees, and licensees, every firm must decide where the internal organization stops and where market transactions take over. Contracts between business organizations provide an *ex ante* framework that defines these relationships, but all contracts are purposefully incomplete. Consequently, every firm must address the potential for postcontractual opportunistic behavior by business partners and then design governance mechanisms to reduce these contractual hazards.

Should Dell make or buy subassembly components for their PCs? Should Kodak license its digital camera technology for Internet distribution by AOL, or should it invest in a strategic partnership with AOL? What if Kodak vertically integrated by buying an Internet service provider as Microsoft did in buying WebTV? Should Red Hat adopt open source architecture and allow its licensees to duplicate, modify, and redistribute its Linux-based software without charge?

We address these questions initially from the perspective of the coordination game between manufacturers and distributors using the game theory techniques of Chapter 13. Vertical requirements contracts are introduced in the moral hazard framework of purposefully incomplete contracts. The principal-agent problem is explained and then resolved with incentive contracting and governance mechanisms. Thereafter, we develop extensively the choice of organizational form between relational contracting, joint ventures, alliances, and vertical integration with an application to the hosiery industry.

MANAGERIAL CHALLENGE

Controlling the Vertical: Ultimate TV[1]

Enormous business opportunities loom on the horizon for companies that operate at the intersection of Web-based Internet services and the TV. Personal computers have penetrated into 70 percent of American households, but televisions are present in literally every household, with a measured

MANAGERIAL CHALLENGE

penetration now reaching 98 percent. Over the next 5–10 years, 220 million analog television sets may be replaced by $150 billion worth of television-enabled PCs and digital televisions. The lure for customers will be Internet-based interactive services and much higher digital picture quality.

Microsoft has invested heavily in digital entertainment programming for these "smart televisions" and television-enabled PCs. Their know-how and trade secret investments are largely nonredeployable and include the operating system and user interface backbone for everything from interactive museum tours to distance learning virtual courses. However, all these investments may be focused on the wrong distribution channel. WebTV Networks Inc. has perfected a system that allows consumers to surf the Internet through their low-end analog TVs.

The core of WebTV's (now MSN TV) product is a patented signal compression chip that crams the capabilities of a TV tuner, cable modem, and high-speed video modem into one $50 unit. MSN TV's technology has freed content providers of the bandwidth limitations that prevent the Net from transmitting high-speed Web images and video. It may also have freed consumers of the need to upgrade to digital TV. Most households are able to connect the device to their analog TV set and begin surfing the Internet within 15 minutes.

If twenty-first-century households will be able to cruise the Net and download video with inexpensive network PCs or old analog televisions, Microsoft's huge investment in digital entertainment will decline exponentially in value. Digital TV manufacturers quickly established partnerships with WebTV to assess the danger and take the first steps towards acquiring an equity stake in this emergent technology.

© ANGELO CAVALLI/PHOTODISC RED/GETTY IMAGES

In late 1997, Microsoft decided to vertically integrate and preemptively bought WebTV for $425 million. Microsoft intended to combine its one-way dependent and reliant digital entertainment assets with WebTV's technology to produce digital consumer products for cell phones, pagers, and handheld PCs. In addition, because cable companies appear most likely to trigger the adoption of "Ultimate TVs" through their leasing of set-top control boxes to residential customers, Microsoft sought to become a cable TV industry standard through vertical integration by investing more than $10 billion in equity ownership in AT&T, Telewest, Comcast, and three European cable firms. The ensuing transfers of equity ownership upstream to the set-top software provider represents the inception of Microsoft's vertical integration into interactive TV.

[1] Based on "Why Microsoft Is Glued to the Tube," *BusinessWeek* (September 22, 1997), p. 96; "Microsoft to Buy WebTV for $425 Million," *Wall Street Journal* (May 7, 1997), p. A8; "Microsoft's Blank Screen," *The Economist* (September 16, 2000), p. 74; and "Smart TV Gets Even Smarter," *BusinessWeek* (April 16, 2001), pp. 132–133.

INTRODUCTION

Organizational form and institutional arrangements play an extensive role in eliciting efficient behavior. Incentive contracts can motivate manager-agents to pursue the interests of owner-principals. Incentive-compatible revelation mechanisms can increase the market value of joint ventures between partners such as IBM, Siemens, and Toshiba. On another front, allowing the freewheeling of electricity from one public utility to another or privatizing Conrail, British Telecom, Japan Air Lines, Teléfonos de México, and Société Générale can improve the incentives to maximize capitalized value in these formerly bloated public monopolies. However, the role of institutions in motivating efficient behavior goes far beyond the design of incentive contracts and recent deregulation and privatization initiatives.

Institutional choices also involve the form of organization that companies adopt. For example, some manufacturers such as Volvo-GM Trucks, IBM, and Goodyear Tires develop franchise dealerships rather than engage in the vertical requirements contracting with independent retailers preferred by manufacturers such as Apple and Michelin. Other firms adopt stand-alone subsidiaries as independent divisions but centralize the production of common components (e.g., General Motors' Chevrolet, Cadillac, and Buick divisions all buy from Fisher Body Co.). Perhaps the most important application of these concepts occurs in deciding the boundary of the firm: whether to vertically integrate throughout the supply chain like Exxon or outsource like Dell.

The Role of Contracting in Cooperative Games

In Chapter 13, we saw that once a manufacturer commits to updating a product, distributors sometimes find that their best-reply response is to continue extensive selling efforts and postsale services. If so, the required coordination of manufacturer and distributor actions can be achieved by a self-enforcing reliance relationship. At other times, however, the payoffs are such that coordination requires something more than the best-reply response concept we examined. Consider again the decisions in Figure 15.1. These are the same actions and payoffs we examined earlier in the Manufacturer-Distributor II game (Figure 13.4).

Recall that in the subgame perfect equilibrium {Update, Discontinue, Advertise}, the retail distributor is better off discontinuing some selling effort, knowing full well that the manufacturer's best-reply response is to advertise anyway. See the boxed and starred outcome in Figure 15.1. This odd combination of actions dominates all other sequential patterns that meet the conditions of best-reply response for each player at each proper subgame node in the decision tree. However, sales volume would decline, so the manufacturer is clearly worse off than would have been the case had the distributor continued all selling efforts. In that event, the manufacturer would realize either \$300,000 or \$350,000, whereas updating and advertising to prevent a sales collapse from the distributors reduced selling effort results in a manufacturer's payoff of only \$280,000.

Moreover, the institutional arrangements under which defection by the retail distributor occurs regularly are not value-maximizing. The subgame perfect equilibrium strategy {Update, Discontinue, Advertise} creates total value after expenses of \$120,000 + \$280,000 = \$400,000. {Update, Continue, Not Advertise} generates \$450,000 total payoffs, and {Update, Continue, Advertise} generates \$480,000 total payoffs. One might then expect some organizational form to emerge to realize this additional value. One alternative is vertical integration. By buying the distributor firm (for something slightly more than the discounted present value of \$120,000), the manufacturer could impose the value-maximizing actions and resolve coordination and control with internal monitoring and incentive systems within the consolidated firm.

Figure 15.1 Vertical Requirements Contracting Is Required to Maximize Value

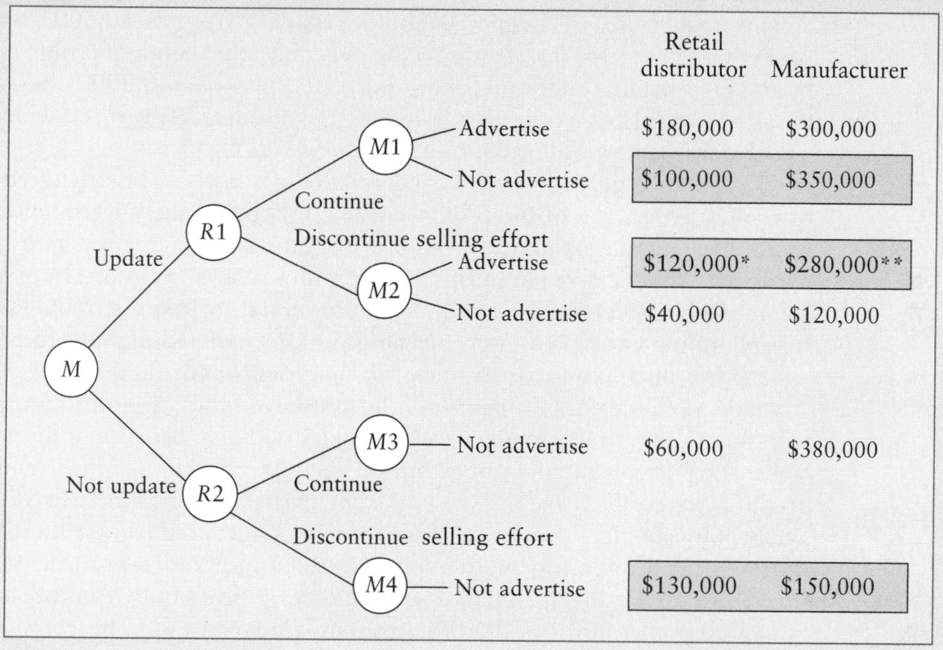

Alternatively, manufacturers might suspend shipments to retail distributors and change distributors frequently as one after another violated the expectations of the relationship and pursued the "Discontinue" strategy. Because instability in the distribution channel imposes substantial start-up costs, the manufacturer may instead enter into a *cooperative* game of credible promises and side payments (i.e., a relational contract).

VERTICAL REQUIREMENTS CONTRACTS

Contracts
Third-party enforceable agreements designed to facilitate deferred exchange.

Contracts are binding, third-party enforceable agreements designed to facilitate deferred exchange. A *promisee* undertakes some costly action (perhaps paying a consideration) in exchange for and relying upon the *promisor's* pledge of a subsequent performance. Here, the manufacturer updates the product, relying upon the retail distributor to subsequently perform presale selling efforts. The manufacturer then decides about manufacturer-sponsored advertising that requires a coordinated ad investment by the retail distributor. Of course, distributors can appear to promise one thing and then deliver another, but vertical requirements contracts are one method of establishing the credibility of such promises.

Vertical Requirements Contract
A third-party enforceable agreement between stages of production in a product's value chain.

For the contracting problem in Figure 15.1, a **vertical requirements contract** might offer the distributor \$120,000 plus one-half of the difference in total value created from cooperative versus equilibrium noncooperative actions. A cooperative surplus of \$480,000 − \$400,000 = \$80,000 is generated by the retail distributors who provide full selling services when the manufacturer updates and advertises the product. Therefore, the manufacturer might offer the distributor's *threat point* (the \$120,000 payoff from defecting) plus one-half of this increase in value from performing as promised (namely, another \$40,000). Such an agreement would yield actions that increase the manufacturer's payoff from \$280,000 to \$320,000. Assuming alternative distributors were available, this contract would be accepted by the present distributor, and both players would be \$40,000 better off than in the subgame perfect equilibrium {Update, Discontinue, Advertise}, which made no use of third-party-enforceable contracting.

The actual vertical requirements contract here is likely to be structured around an offer of a percentage of the profits. By acknowledging the uncertainty of the final product value, the manufacturer and distributor could agree to share this risk. In particular, a vertical requirements contract that offered to grant 33 percent of the summed profits (\$160,000 of \$480,000) to an authorized distributor in exchange for full selling effort and after-sale service of an updated manufacturer-advertised product would maximize the value of this business opportunity.

Again, credible commitments are the key. Given the decision timing, the manufacturer could promise to advertise but then not do so. Because of this second possibility of postcontractual opportunism, the retail distributor may require escrow accounts for cooperative advertising or the parties could stipulate a \$51,000 damage penalty should the manufacturer breach its duty to advertise after the distributor expended full effort in attempting to sell an upgraded product. In that event (in Figure 15.1), the manufacturer would have \$300,000 from advertising and \$350,000 − \$51,000 = \$299,000 from not advertising. The retail distributor would be better off continuing its selling effort (\$100,000 + \$51,000) rather than discontinuing selling effort (\$120,000). We could then anticipate a value-maximizing {Update, Continue Effort, Advertise} outcome with a maximum value of \$180,000 + \$300,000 = \$480,000 profit payoff.

Negotiating position may in the end reallocate some of the cooperative surplus back to the manufacturer in the form of franchise fees. For example, a profit-sharing franchise contract with the \$51,000 stipulated penalty clause for manufacturer breach on advertising might start by asking the distributor to pay a \$50,000 per period franchise fee. On net, then, the distributor would receive updated products, \$180,000 in operating profits minus \$50,000 in franchise fees, plus a stipulated damages agreement regarding co-op advertising funded by the manufacturer. The manufacturer would receive continued full selling effort by the distributor, \$300,000 in operating profits, plus the \$50,000 fee as franchisor.

The Function of Commercial Contracts

Forming such a contract provides a hostage beyond the mere reputational asset that prospective distributors might offer. In exchange for an agreed consideration, the promisee receives a credible promise. The promisor's commitment to perform is credible because the legal rules of contract interpretation and enforcement provide assurance that any expectations clearly spelled out by the parties will be met. Although courts seldom order recalcitrant contractors to perform specifically as was promised, they are quick to award **expectation damages** that leave the parties no worse off than was anticipated under the contract. Standard contract remedies therefore provide incentives for efficient precaution by the promisor and for no more than efficient reliance on the promise by the promisee.

Expectation Damages
A remedy for breach of contract designed to elicit efficient precaution and efficient reliance on promises.

EXAMPLE

CRANKSHAFT DELIVERY DELAY CAUSES PLANT CLOSING

The role of contract remedies as incentives is well illustrated by the historical case of *Hadley v. Baxendale,* Court of Exchequer 1854, 9 Exch 341. A mill owner ordered a replacement for a broken crankshaft from a machine shop that agreed to a standard repair and return of the mill owner's equipment. When return delivery was delayed because of poor road conditions, the mill owner sued for lost profits resulting from his extended plant closing. The court rejected this claim for extraordinary damages because the machine shop had taken the customary shipping precautions and would have been expected to do more (perhaps by arranging for an expedited delivery by express coach) only if the mill owner had stipulated the extraordinary damages that would arise from further delay.

In other words, the machine shop was entitled to expect that the mill owner would not rely excessively on the promise of a three-day repair unless informed to the contrary. If the mill owner had time-sensitive business scheduled immediately thereafter and no temporary substitute crankshaft available, it was his responsibility to disclose those potentially destructive private facts and thereby elicit a different level of precaution. Therefore, the mill owner's reliance was excessive and inefficient, not deserving of the reinforcement that would have resulted from the Court awarding lost profit.[2]

A stipulation procedure in the law of contract works exceptionally well for fully anticipated events. However, the rules of contract law that have evolved (several of which are summarized in the bottom half of Table 15.1) also reduce the transaction costs of renegotiation and settlement when *unanticipated* events occur. For example, the market price that can be realized on a Volvo-GM truck can change dramatically between making an investment at a manufacturing facility to design and produce an updated truck that only runs on ethanol and the subsequent promotion and sale of such trucks six months later. Suppose in the meantime that the market price collapses because a competitor's new and improved hybrid-fuel truck is introduced.

If the initial truck manufacturer and distributor agreed to a fixed-price contract six months earlier, the manufacturer will get the agreed-upon revenue because the distributor took that risk. On the other hand, if changes in the regulatory environment over the six months make it illegal to sell that ethanol-based model of truck, then the **frustration of purpose doctrine** of the Uniform Commercial Code (UCC) would excuse the distributor from the contractual obligation to pay.

Frustration of Purpose Doctrine

An illustration of the default rules of contract law that can result in excusal of contract promises.

Contracts facilitate deferred exchange. The rules of contract law, as embodied primarily in the common law but also codified in statutes including the UCC, provide predictable outcomes at low transaction costs. For example, the courts almost always impose a liability for *expectation damages* on parties that breach their contract promises. Because circumstances change, expectation damages are often more efficient than forcing a promisor to fulfill the contract. In these cases, the costs of the

[2] An excellent extended discussion of the role of contract remedies as incentives for efficient reliance and efficient precaution against nonperformance appears in R. Cooter and T. Ulen, *Law and Economics,* 2nd ed. (Reading, MA: Addison-Wesley, 1997), pp. 214–232.

Table 15.1 A Spectrum of Alternative Contract Environments for Manufacturers and Distributors

	Spot Market Transactions	Vertical Requirements Contract	Relational Contract
Timing	Instantaneous, one-time-only	Deferred exchange; promise of future performance for immediate consideration	Repeat business
Players	Anonymous buyers/sellers	Contract partners	Well-known dealers/agents
Enforcement	Barter or consideration for a consideration	Enforced by impartial third parties	Self-enforcing; best-reply responses
Information	Perfect (complete and certain) information + competition leads to efficient markets	Purposefully incomplete contracts embrace ambiguity; governance mechanisms	Reputation; signaling/bluffing games

Some Rules of Contract Law

Contracts facilitate deferred exchange by addressing uncertain performance outcomes (the incomplete contract problem), unobservable effort in assuring performance (the moral hazard problem), and recontracting hazards (the holdup problem)

Basic Functions of Contract	Illustrative Contract Rule
1. Providing incentives for efficient precaution and efficient reliance	1. Award of expectation damages
2. Encouraging the discovery of asymmetric information	2. Required disclosure of destructive but not constructive facts
3. Providing risk allocation mechanisms	3. Frustration of purpose doctrine
4. Reducing transaction costs	4. Nonexcusal in forward sales contracts

expectations damages are often less than the costs of taking the actions specified in the contract.

In some cases, contract promises are excused altogether. These excusals fall into two categories: exceedingly rare *formation excusals* and more frequent *performance excusals*. If I sell you a damaged Learjet without disclosing the damage, you (the buyer) can ask to be excused. On the other hand, an astute buyer of a damaged jet who recognizes the potential for enhancing the value through inexpensive repair can profit from his or her asymmetric information without concern about whether the Court might later set aside the sales contract and restore the plane to its original owner. Contract law rules of formation excusal support this delicate balance of requiring the disclosure of *destructive facts* without reducing the incentive to develop asymmetric information that enhances value (i.e., *constructive facts*).

EXAMPLE

THE ENFORCEMENT AND EXCUSAL OF CONTRACT PROMISES: THE EXTRAORDINARY CASE OF 9/11[3]

In a typical *performance excuse*, contingent events like a change in regulatory constraints may, as we have seen, frustrate the purpose of a contract.

Contracts are also excused because of unforeseen natural disasters or acts of war. On the morning of September 11, 2001, Bank of New York was obligated to clear

[3] Based in part on "Little Changes at Bank of New York," *Wall Street Journal* (March 8, 2002), p. C11.

and provide cash settlements for about 84,000 government security transactions. The client firms such as JPMorgan Chase & Co. had invested large sums in real-time hard-wired data feeds and sophisticated telecommunications connections to Bank of New York. Yet, three of the bank's buildings in lower Manhattan were either damaged or forced to close because of the terrorist attack. At one point, Bank of New York owed Citigroup and Morgan $30 million each on settlements the bank could not authorize for final clearance because of the chaos at their business facilities.

Under other circumstances, each day said settlement was delayed could have resulted in a claim against the Bank of New York for expectation damages of approximately $(1/365) \times 5\% \times \$30$ million = $4,109 per contract per day. With razor-slim margins on these clearing and settlement operations, such damages would have quickly exhausted all profit. Today, Bank of New York would likely be expected to maintain insurance against such business interruptions. Yet, under the unforeseen circumstances of 9/11, an act of war had prevented performance of the contract, and the Bank of New York was entitled to a performance excuse.

Spot Market Transaction

An instantaneous one-time-only exchange of typically standardized goods between anonymous buyers and sellers.

Spot market transactions pose the least informational and incentive problems. For example, buying electricity off the grid at quarter until the hour for delivery on the hour avoids pricing risk and the possibility of opportunistic behavior. Complete and certain information plus competitive entry and exit in efficient markets implies that equilibrium market prices will reflect all relevant information. This makes the current price the best forecast of future prices. However, the availability of simple commodity transactions today fails to solve several issues that arise in most business contracting.

Consider the deferred exchange of a present consideration for a promise of future forward sales. Suppose, that is, the truck manufacturer and distributor entered into a forward sales contract for diesel fuel to be used as a promotion to enhance the distributor's selling effort, and subsequently the price of diesel fuel tripled, what would happen?

Forward Sales Contracts

A consensual agreement to exchange goods delivered in the future for cash today, with no possibility of performance excuse.

The default rule of the UCC for **forward sales contracts** is very explicit and subject to few, if any, excusals. If the truck manufacturer sold forward to the distributor 100,000 gallons of diesel at $2.33 per gallon in June 2006 for truck sales promotions at delivery in December 2006, and if the December spot market price rises to $4, the manufacturer took *that* risk of rising cost in fulfilling the contract. A manufacturer's plea that it would be ruinous financially to deliver as promised will fall on deaf ears; the manufacturer must either deliver the 100,000 gallons in December or face an immediate court judgment of $(\$4 - \$2.33) \times 100{,}000 = \$167{,}000$ awarded to the distributor. Every commercial contract must either stipulate the allocation of such risks or operate under these default rules that are intended to increase predictability and thereby reduce the transaction costs of forward business contracting.

Table 15.1 summarizes several other characteristic differences between spot market transactions, reputation-based relationships, and vertical requirements contracts between manufacturers and distributors (that might include forward sales agreements for the diesel gasoline promotion). Whether manufacturers and distributors will decide to employ spot market transactions, relational contracting, fixed profit-share franchise contracts, or vertically integrate depends on the relative transaction costs of coordination and control in the various contractual settings.

Incomplete Information, Incomplete Contracting, and Postcontractual Opportunism

Incomplete Information
Uncertain knowledge of payoffs, choices, etc.

Practically all exchanges, whether for products, financial claims, or labor services, are conducted under conditions of **incomplete information.** On the one hand, decision makers often face random disturbances on the outcome of their actions. This type of incomplete information is typically handled in routine ways by risk spreading in insurance markets, which pool such casualty risks and thereby reduce the loss exposure to any individual business or household. Randomly occurring injuries at a consumer electronics assembly plant seldom coincide with injuries in a firm's delivery trucks or severe weather disruptions at a firm's shipping facility. As a result, modest insurance premiums can cover the cost of the anticipated claims involving such diversifiable risk events.

Full Contingent Claims Contract
An agreement about all possible future events.

However, incomplete information as to the existence and probability of remote risks (i.e., what possible outcomes might occur) often prevent the parties at risk from writing insurance contracts. Consider the **full contingent claims contract** you and your surgeon would need to write before an organ transplant operation or two pharmaceutical companies would need before one licensed the rights to produce a pregnancy-related drug to the other. To develop all the accurate information required for an agreement about potential losses and full compensation in all possible future contingencies is simply prohibitively expensive. Consequently, few transplant patients and few business partners attempt to negotiate full contingent claims contracts. Such prohibitively expensive information costs explain why contracts are often incomplete by design.

Postcontractual Opportunistic Behavior
Actions that take advantage of a contract partner's vulnerabilities and are not specifically prohibited by the terms.

One immediate consequence of incomplete contracts is the possibility of **postcontractual opportunistic behavior** that is not specifically prohibited by the contract. Employees who receive on-the-job training (OJT) may moonlight with their new skills. Managers may reconfigure assets following a labor contract concession in ways their on-going employees did not anticipate. Baseball players may attempt a hold out at the time of contract renewals just before a World Series. Knowing this tendency, companies provide less OJT, workers agree to fewer wage concessions, and owners develop more farm team replacement players than they otherwise would. So, the incompleteness of contracts results in inefficient behavior as an inescapable consequence of costly and therefore incomplete information. To reduce these inefficiencies, companies adopt governance mechanisms such as mandatory arbitration agreements to help resolve postcontractual disputes.

Corporate Governance and the Problem of Moral Hazard

Governance Mechanisms
Processes to detect, resolve, and reduce postcontractual opportunism.

Professor Oliver Williamson emphasizes that contracts pose the *ex ante* framework but that **governance mechanisms** provide the *ex post* implementation required to maximize value:

> The parties to commercial contracts are held to be perceptive about the nature of the contractual relations of which they are a part, including an awareness of potential contractual hazards. However, because complex contracts are unavoidably

> incomplete—it being impossible or prohibitively costly to make provision for all possible contingencies *ex ante*—much of the relevant contractual action is borne by the *ex post* mechanisms of governance.[4]

Hence, because of postcontractual opportunistic behavior, any vertical requirements contract between the manufacturer and distributor in Figure 15.1 will be only the beginning of their agreement. In addition, the firms will need to resolve a pivotal coordination and control issue: the inherent unobservability of selling effort on the part of the retail distributor. Unobservable effort in fulfilling contract promises illustrates a difficult but standard business contracting problem of "moral hazard." After securing terms to their liking, all contract partners must be wary of the potential for shirking on the agreement in inconspicuous and hard-to-detect but potentially ruinous ways.

Moral Hazard Problem
A problem of postcontractual opportunism that arises from unverifiable or unobservable contract performance.

In the next section we will apply the moral hazard idea to managerial contracting, but first let's consider the commercial lender's **moral hazard problem** with eliciting unobservable borrower effort in selecting safe working capital projects. A known reliable borrower may approach a lender with a randomly occurring liquidity crisis that necessitates an extension of its bank line of credit.[5] The lender then offers terms for the loan renewal: an interest rate, principal amount, collateral requirements, and loan term. The situation is depicted in Figure 15.2. If the borrower decides to accept,

Figure 15.2 The Problem of Moral Hazard in Line-of-Credit Lending

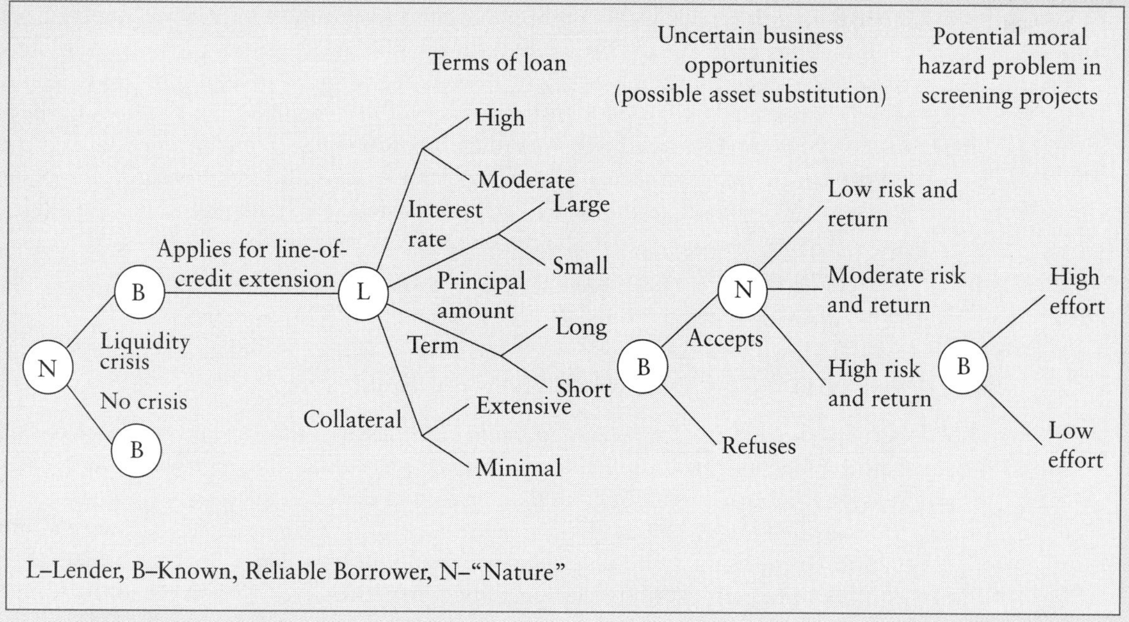

[4] Oliver Williamson, "Economics and Organization: A Primer," *California Management Review* (Winter 1996), p. 136. See also Williamson's *The Mechanisms of Governance* (New York: Oxford University Press, 1996).

[5] In the situation examined here, we abstract from the *hidden information* problem of adverse selection (by assuming that the borrowers are known customers of the lending institution) to focus attention on the *hidden action* problem of moral hazard in commercial lending.

a line of credit extension is granted. Then a random process intervenes presenting one of several uncertain business opportunities to the borrower. As in earlier chapters, we signify the role of uncertainty at a node in the decision tree with a large *N* for a choice by Nature. The possible business opportunities are a spectrum from the relatively safe investments in inventory during periods of backorders and stockouts to an extension of the company's receivables policy allowing customers to pay within 90 days rather than pay cash at the point of purchase. Because product sales may be sensitive to credit terms such as "90 days same as cash," the latter use of working capital has a higher expected return but is risky in that uncollected customer accounts may skyrocket.

The moral hazard problem for the lender is then motivated. The commercial bank wants the borrower to exercise great care, high effort, and good judgment in selecting projects on which to expend its newly granted working capital from the line-of-credit extension. However, banks must move carefully in setting the loan terms to elicit this largely hidden action. Remember, the bank does not know in advance what business opportunity the borrower will be facing. This is not a project financing situation where the commercial banker can take part in assessing the company's capital budgeting proposals and directly monitor its ROI. Instead, the bank makes the funds available and must then elicit subsequent borrower effort in appropriately screening projects that are randomly presented for possible investment.

What loan terms should the lender offer? Large loans with long repayment terms are most desired by the borrower to gain the most financial flexibility in the face of its current liquidity crisis. Having more funds and more time to straighten out a business plan that has gone awry is preferable from the point of view of the borrower, but do these terms elicit more or less effort in screening projects so as to prevent or contain a loss? Surprisingly, higher interest rates to reflect the high default risk are not the answer. A high interest rate forces reliable borrowers to seek out *riskier* working capital projects in order to secure higher expected returns and therefore be in a position to repay the loan. More moderate rates supported by extensive collateral pledges of security would seem to move the reliable borrower in the direction of more effort to find safer projects.[6]

The Need for Governance Mechanisms

Perhaps the most effective way to manage the risks of default and nonpayment may be for the lender to establish a *governance mechanism* through which it regularly reassesses a borrower's financial ratios and makes decisions about ongoing access to the extended line of credit. The more frequent, more convenient, and more audited these financial reports, the better the governance mechanism will work. In essence, the bank becomes almost a project financing partner for every major use of its funds in order to motivate the desired care, effort, and judgment from the borrower. In the

[6] In other circumstances, lenders would face an adverse selection problem of detecting whether unknown borrowers are from a fraudulent or reliable subpopulation of loan applicants, and the offered terms of the loan will then affect the acceptance and refusals that determine the proportion of the loan portfolio from each group. Moderate interest rates and high collateral are intended in that situation to allow borrowers to signal their reliable intent to repay.

end, a project-by-project financing approval process is precluded by the definition of the problem, but the closer a governance mechanism can come to this result, the less likely a default will be.

Hiring managerial talent involves a similar moral hazard problem because managerial effort is inherently unobservable. In particular, managers are paid for their creative ingenuity in proactively solving problems; they are paid to think hard about problems that haven't happened yet. As such, managers can easily shirk and instead devote their creative ingenuity to activities unrelated to their job. Because of this inability to directly observe managerial effort, we mistakenly blame managers at times for poor performance attributable really to nothing more than bad luck, and we fail to acknowledge managerial merit at times because we misassume that good performance is attributable to good luck. In the next section, we will see that "incentive contracting" with a minimum salary guarantee and a performance-based bonus (e.g., a stock option or restricted stock grant) can be an efficient solution to the moral hazard problem in managerial contracting.

There is another issue with incomplete managerial contracting, however, and that relates to contract renewals. When executives have acquired unique company-specific knowledge and skills as well as pensions and severance packages not redeployable to others, they are in a favorable position in negotiating with compensation subcommittees of the board of directors. The executive's institutional memory is at least somewhat irreplaceable. Consequently, when it comes time to renew their contracts, senior executives often engage in "holdups."

Evidence of such holdups is plentiful: massive executive "loans" are often forgiven, incentive-based compensation lost in the face of poor performance is often reinstated or replaced through golden parachutes triggered by a hostile takeover, and option strike prices are often reset to lower levels in down markets. Considerable effort to retain experienced senior managers is clearly value maximizing, but the compensation subcommittee of the board must be an independent body prepared to monitor, benchmark, and whistle-blow on these contract renewals if necessary. Beyond holdup, outright deception and fraud remain a frequent problem. For example, backdating option grants to dates when the strike price was in the money are clearly criminal events, and the SEC is treating them as such.

Table 15.2 provides a list of the implementation mechanisms of corporate governance available to address this holdup issue.

Table 15.2 Implementation Mechanisms of Corporate Governance

- **Internal monitoring by independent board of director subcommittees**
- **Internal/external monitoring by large creditors**
- **Internal/external monitoring by owners of large blocks of stock**
- **Auditing and variance analysis**
- **Internal benchmarking**
- **Corporate culture of ethical duties**
- **High employee morale supportive of whistle blowers**

WHAT WENT RIGHT • WHAT WENT WRONG

MORAL HAZARD AND HOLDUP AT ENRON AND WORLDCOM[7]

Misaccounting for short-term business expenses as long-term capital investments required a $3.8 billion restatement of lower operating profits at WorldCom in fiscal year 2000. Enron executives depleted pension reserve accounts while heralding the attractiveness of employee stock option plans for retirement planning. Business news in 2002 made it abundantly clear that governance mechanisms are needed, but still the question remains, "Why, exactly?" Why don't debt contracts of bond holders, personal loan contracts that senior executives use to relocate their often lavish households, and performance-based incentive contracts aligning owner and managerial interests prevent these abuses? Is it just that too many gratuitous payments have been extracted from compensation committees, too many executive loans have been forgiven, and too many deferred stock options have been reset to lower strike prices when stock prices fell? That is, are the incentives in all this incentive contracting just misaligned? The answer is decisively "No." The more fundamental problem is that incomplete contracts invite postcontractual opportunistic behavior, requiring vigorous corporate governance mechanisms.

[7] Based on "Taken for a Ride," *The Economist* (July 13, 2002), p. 64; and "WorldCom Aide Conceded Flaws," *Wall Street Journal* (June 16, 2002), p. A3.

THE PRINCIPAL-AGENT MODEL

Many types of owner-principals hire manager-agents to stand in and conduct their business affairs. Parent companies set up principal-agent relationships with subsidiaries. Manufacturer principals employ retail distributor and advertising agents. And most importantly, equity owners hire executives with managerial incentive contracts. The owners' objective in such principal-agent relationships is to offer incentives to managers to act in a value-maximizing manner on behalf of the principals and to forego alternative employment opportunities.

THE EFFICIENCY OF ALTERNATIVE HIRING ARRANGEMENTS

Managerial hiring contracts may take on several pure or hybrid forms, including straight salary, wage rate, or profit sharing. In straight salary contracts, the manager and firm agree on a total compensation package and specific conditions of employment. In other contexts, such as consulting, the managerial consultant may receive an hourly wage rate equal to the best alternative employment opportunity in the competitive labor market for his or her type of consulting services. In Figure 15.3, the managerial consultant is hired for, say, 50 hours per week at wage rate W_a. D_l is the firm's input demand, which is the marginal revenue product of these labor services—namely, the marginal output of additional hours times the marginal revenue from selling that additional output. Because each firm is atomistic in the labor market for these management consulting services, S_l is the perfectly elastic supply

Figure 15.3 Alternative Managerial Labor Contracts

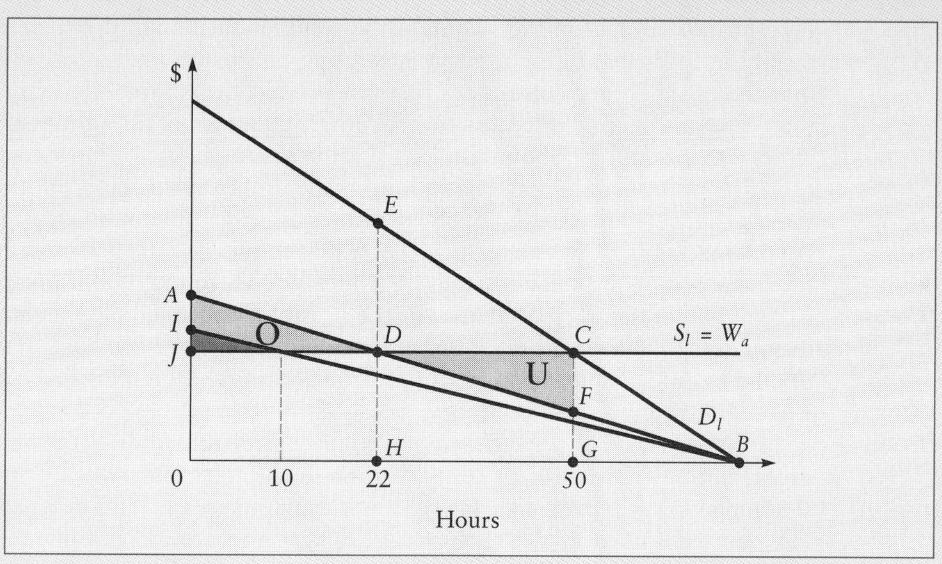

facing any given employer at the going market wage. Beyond 50 hours, the declining D_l no longer exceeds the incremental input cost along S_l.

Managers also may secure employment under a pure profit-sharing contract. Like pure commission-based salespeople or manufacturer's trade representatives, the manager may accept a percentage (say 40%) of the receipts directly attributable to his or her efforts in lieu of wage or salary income. Think of the percentage finder's fee sometimes offered for cost-saving suggestions in big corporations or the federal government. Again in Figure 15.3, we can represent this third alternative hiring arrangement as the ray *AB*, wherein the manager receives 40 percent of the owner's willingness to pay for each hour of management services. Initially, this profit share will exceed the wage rate alternative. For example, during the first 22 hours of work, the profit-sharing contract will overcompensate by area *ADJ* (shaded area **O**). Thereafter the profit share falls below the manager's market wage rate per hour.

If 40 percent proves to be an equilibrium profit share, the overcompensation (shaded area *ADJ* labeled **O**) will just equal the undercompensation for the last 28 hours of work (shaded area *DCF* labeled **U**). This level leaves both the owners and the manager indifferent between this hiring arrangement and the alternative 50-hour-per-week wage rate contract at W_a. If the profit share were reduced to, say, 35 percent (represented by the ray *IB*), the dark-shaded amount of overcompensation for the first 10 hours would fail to offset the massive undercompensation for hours 10 to 50. The manager would then reject the profit-sharing contract in favor of the wage rate offer. By raising the profit share back to 40 percent, the firm appears able to restore the attractiveness of each contract, at least for certain types of workers. In reality, as we shall now see, the situation in hiring managerial talent is often rather different.

Work Effort, Creative Ingenuity, and the Moral Hazard Problem in Managerial Contracting

Pure profit-sharing contracts contain the seeds of their own destruction. Suppose several individuals are involved in generating pharmaceutical sales, and the input that the profit sharer contributes to team production is largely unobservable. No time card can successfully monitor the input, perhaps because a measure of work effort rather than work hours is really what is required. The rational employee then considers his or her alternatives. As long as the profit-sharing compensation exceeds the alternative wage rate, he or she dedicates unobservable work effort to this job. Beyond 22 hours of work effort, however, the employee can earn more by working for someone else at the alternative wage rate W_a. Therefore, the disloyal (but rational) trade representative underworks the territory; he or she moonlights. This predictable response is another aspect of the *moral hazard problem*. Only a *moral* sense of duty to one's employer prevents this problem from becoming a real *hazard* to the business.

Predicting such behavior, the employer may decide to withdraw the offer of a pure profit-sharing contract. Let's see why. If the territory is underworked by 28 hours, the employer saves profit-sharing payments equal to area *DFGH* in Figure 15.3, but loses output valued at the much larger *ECGH* and therefore is out the net value [*ECGH* − *DFGH* − *ADJ* (the overpayment area for the first 22 hours of work), all of which is equal to area *EDC*] relative to a wage contract that just paid piece rates for 50 hours of work at an implicit wage rate of W_a per hour. The fact that work effort is largely unobservable makes the pure profit-sharing contract unattractive to the employer relative to a piece-rate contract.

This generalization is not always true. For example, in hiring attendants for parking garages, the time clock and customer complaints (e.g., horn blowing and broken parking gate barriers) monitor the required input quite well. A dismissal policy in the employment contract making time-on-task a condition of employment motivates the required input. Similar time-on-task constraints and output quotas are employed in hiring sharecroppers and retail sales clerks. In these instances, the firms and their employees have evolved ways to resolve the moral hazard problem. Nobel Laureate Ronald Coase emphasized that private voluntary bargaining between principals and agents will often find ways to contract around such problems.[8]

The problem of moral hazard arises then only when an employee's action such as work effort is directly observable only at a prohibitive cost. Consider again the pharmaceutical sales representative for whom appointment logbooks and random follow-up monitoring simply cannot detect the persuasive effort necessary to secure orders from physician customers. One could trail around after the sales representative and interview each physician after the sales calls were completed to try to detect the ingenuity and perseverance the sales rep displayed, but quite obviously, this monitoring practice would be prohibitively expensive. Instead, in the face of truly "hidden actions," the pharmaceutical company is more likely to favor some performance-based incentive contract involving benchmarking rather than the pure profit-sharing contract.

[8] See J. Farrell, "Information and the Coase Theorem," *Journal of Economic Perspectives* (Fall 1987), pp. 113–129.

Benchmarking

A comparison of performance in similar jobs, firms, plants, divisions, etc.

During a period of **benchmarking,** the employer reassigns previously low productivity sales territories to above-average trade representatives to see whether their effort can alter the success rate per sales call. If so, the employer concludes that lack of effort by prior sales representatives was responsible for the low sales. After several such benchmarkings, the employer is able to identify those sales representatives to be kept and those to be dismissed. Importantly, the "keepers" are then allowed to retain all the productive accounts they have developed.

For managerial jobs, however, the moral hazard problem is significantly harder to resolve. The input senior management contributes to team production is not time on task at the desk, but rather what we have called *creative ingenuity:* creatively formulating and solving problems that may not even have arisen as yet. Managers are paid to think, not to shuffle papers. The difficulty is in detecting when creative ingenuity is being applied to the employer's business, rather than another business for whom the manager may be mentally moonlighting. Of course, eventually the difference will show up in performance, but over how long a period and how big a difference? These questions are tough to answer satisfactorily after a senior manager has shirked his or her duties to the detriment of shareholder value and been let go.

More problematically, the shirking manager may never be let go, and the hard-working manager may never be rewarded. If random disturbances affect the company's performance, it is difficult even after the fact to separate unobservable shirking from negative random disturbances. How, then, are owners to know when to blame senior managers for downturns in company performance and when to give them credit for upturns? One governance mechanism often used to analyze these variances is the **company audit.** Managers report on the sources and uses of funds in accordance with generally accepted accounting principles (GAAP). Any period-to-period variances are then assessed and verified by independent auditors.[9] Despite dedicated efforts, auditors can seldom separate the effects of management decisions from random disturbances in company performance. That is, the moral hazard problem is much harder to solve when combined with the performance uncertainty most firms face.

Company Audit

A governance mechanism for separating random disturbances from variation in unobservable effort.

Some companies address the problem of managerial moonlighting by benchmarking one manager against another (say, in comparable plants or geographic divisions). They hope that the effects of business cycle factors and random time-series disturbances will be highly correlated across plants and divisions, and that the manager's effort and creative ingenuity will therefore correspond with the plant or division's differential performance. Unfortunately, they are usually wrong. As a result, Japanese companies rely on intense loyalty-building exercises, peer pressure, and lifetime employment contracts (following some probationary period) to reduce mental moonlighting and other forms of shirking.

In isolation, neither hidden effort (unobservability) nor performance uncertainty pose any special difficulty for owner-principals hiring manager-agents. The moral hazard resulting from the unobservability of a manager's input is, by itself, resolvable by assigning the manager lagged residual income claims (e.g., deferred stock options or restricted stock). Settling up *ex post* with a manager, after all the effects of his or her effort and ingenuity have had time to influence performance, creates more effective performance-based incentives.

[9] This audit mechanism is explored at greater length at the end of the chapter in the first Case Exercise.

EXAMPLE

Indexed Stock Options at Adobe Systems, Dell, and Cisco[10]

To align managerial incentives with equity owner interests, most companies regularly award deferred stock options to their managers. These performance-based bonuses entitle the holder to purchase company stock at a slight discount to its current value. If the firm's performance subsequently improves, capitalized value rises and both shareholders and the managers stand to gain. To exercise their options, managers often must wait three to five years, but they sometimes realize gains of 50 to 80 percent or more. By 2004, CEO compensation in *Fortune* 500 companies averaged $7 million, 57 percent of which involved options-based compensation for superior performance.

To acquire the stock for these deferred compensation programs, some companies dilute equity by issuing new shares, while others repurchase shares on the open market. To reduce the cost of these "buybacks," especially in a rising market, some companies such as Adobe Systems, Dell, and Cisco index the exercise price for their deferred options to the average stock price of their industry. When all the related companies do well, the value of the option rises, but so does the exercise price. As a result, the managers do not exercise their options at that juncture and instead are motivated to outperform their peers in related companies in both good times and bad.

Similarly, performance uncertainty taken alone creates a risk-allocation problem that may be easily resolved with insurance. Managers are somewhat less able to diversify than owners because of the specific human capital the manager often invests in a long-term relationship with his or her corporate employer. This situation results in risk-averse owners and risk-averse managers frequently structuring some sort of risk-sharing agreement, such as a guaranteed baseline salary combined with a performance-based bonus.

EXAMPLE

P&G Pays Ad Executives Based on Their Performance

Procter & Gamble places more than $3 billion per year in advertising through Saatchi & Saatchi, Leo Burnett, and other ad agencies. Traditionally, agencies earned flat-rate fees assessed as 15 percent of the ad dollars expended for the client. In the 1990s, Ford, Colgate-Palmolive, and P&G broke out of this flat-rate system and began paying a baseline fixed fee plus a performance bonus. Now, account executives at the agencies earn a fixed salary if their creative communications are less than compelling and P&G sales stay flat. On the other hand, a hugely successful ad campaign can earn multimillion dollar bonuses if P&G's sales growth can be attributed to the advertising. Both the clients, the ad agency owners, and the account execs now share in the risks of consumer whimsy, but a base salary provides a safety net should random misfortune occur.

[10] Based on "Stock Options That Don't Reward Laggards," *Wall Street Journal* (March 30, 1999), p. A26; "Corporate America Faces Declining Value of Options," *Wall Street Journal* (October 16, 2000), p. A1; "The Gravy Train Just Got Derailed," *BusinessWeek* (November 19, 2001), p. 118; and "CEO Compensation Survey," *Wall Street Journal* (April 11, 2005), p. R1.

FORMALIZING THE PRINCIPAL-AGENT PROBLEM

Principal-Agent Problem
An incentives conflict in delegating decision-making authority.

Incentive Compatibility Constraint
An assurance of incentive alignment.

Participation Constraint
An assurance of ongoing involvement.

The real difficulty for managerial contracting arises then when input unobservability and performance uncertainty occur simultaneously. The coexistence of these problems constitutes the so-called **principal-agent problem** most firms face. Settling up *ex post facto* with management teams then no longer creates the desired incentives. Some managers get unlucky and receive blame they did not deserve, and others get lucky and receive credit they did not earn.

The principal-agent problem can be formalized as an optimization problem subject to dual constraints. The principal chooses a profit-sharing rate and a manager's salary guarantee to maximize the expected utility of the risk-averse owner-principals' profit where profit depends on the manager-agent's effort, on the cost of the managerial incentives contract, and on random disturbances. An **incentive compatibility constraint** then aligns the effort chosen by the manager in response to the share and salary offer with the effort that maximizes the expected utility of the owner-principals. That is, an incentive-compatible profit share and salary elicit the managerial effort and creative ingenuity required to maximize the owner's value. Third and finally, the **participation constraint** ensures that the manager will reject his or her next best offer of alternative employment.

In the next section, we illustrate the meaning of each of these three elements with a linear optimal incentives contract, which can solve the principal-agent problem. However, understand that an optimal managerial incentives contract is easier to describe than to attain.[11] See the Case Exercise at the end of this chapter to try your hand at balancing all the competing objectives involved.

SCREENING AND SORTING MANAGERIAL TALENT WITH OPTIMAL INCENTIVES CONTRACTS

Asymmetric information arises in all hiring decisions, but it often plays an especially prominent role in managerial hiring decisions. Job applicants know all the information, but potential employers have access only to the information that applicants select for their resumés. Thus, among perhaps 19 resumé facts that the personnel department might like to know, the applicant discloses only 14. Let's see how linear share contracts can be used to sort managerial talent based on one of these undisclosed characteristics—namely, a manager's risk aversion.

Suppose a large bank has two openings for which it desires managers of different risk aversion. One position is the assistant vice president for commercial construction loans in a city with overbuilt office developments and, consequently, very high vacancy rates. The other position is an assistant vice president to manage the venture capital loan portfolio, to interact with owners of new start-up businesses, and to represent the bank at the entrepreneurship club of the city. As you might suspect, the bank has two rather different people in mind as ideal candidates for these openings. In the commercial construction area, the bank seeks an instinctively cautious and

[11] Even the solution we describe is limited to separable functions in effort and money income. The general principal-agent problem with risk-averse owners and managers has multiple solutions and requires *nonlinear* incentive contracts relating salary and profit share to company performance. See Jean Tirole, *The Theory of Industrial Organization* (Cambridge, MA: MIT Press, 1988), pp. 35–54; and David Kreps, A Course in *Microeconomic Theory* (Princeton, NJ: Princeton University Press, 1990), Chapter 16.

WHAT WENT RIGHT WHAT WENT WRONG

WHY HAVE RESTRICTED STOCK GRANTS REPLACED EXECUTIVE STOCK OPTIONS AT MICROSOFT?[12]

In 2004, Microsoft announced that it would use approximately $30 billion of its $60 billion in cash and short-term investments to buy back stock 2004–2008 and that it would join numerous other companies in granting restricted stock rather than stock options as a performance-based bonus to more than 10,000 of its 30,000 employees. Why change the Microsoft performance bonuses?

Several reasons are behind this change. First, restricted stock cannot be sold if an executive leaves the company. In contrast, once stock options vest, they are typically sold. During the heyday of the booming information economy in the late 1990s, Microsoft's options created literally thousands of multimillionaires among Microsoft's senior managers. Too many of these valuable human resources simply choose to retire early and move on to other pursuits; one former executive took up professional bowling. So, restricted stock is expected to enhance the retention of pivotal employees relative to granting options.

A second reason a board of directors prefers restricted stock is because senior managers are often able to negotiate option features that work against optimal incentive contracting. For example, few option exercise prices are indexed relative to the industry group or strategic competitors. So stock options reward mediocrity when all share prices in an industry rise together. Third, most senior executive options are "reloaded." As soon as the option contracts vest (in 2–5 years) and are exercised, senior managers negotiate the issue of new options with new exercise prices but the old expiration date (of typically 10 years). This clause allows executives to profit from induced volatility in their share prices. They have a powerful incentive to swing for the fences with high-risk projects whenever options in the money can be converted to cash at an intermediate date and then replaced with new options expiring at the original dates.

Finally, few stock option contracts restrict in any way the executive's ability to "unwind" his or her risk exposure by hedging the risks the options create. Selling short a long option position that ties the manager's wealth to that of the shareholders is hardly justifiable given that the objective of performance-based pay is the aligning of managerial incentives with shareholder interests. Restricted stock has none of these drawbacks.

[12] "Microsoft Ushers Out Era of Options," *Wall Street Journal* (July 9, 2003), p. A1; Lucian Bebchuk et al., "Managerial Power and Rent Extraction in the Design of Executive Compensation," 69 *University of Chicago Law Review*, 751 (Summer 2002); B. Hall and K. Murphy, "The Trouble with Stock Options," *Journal of Economic Perspectives* (Summer 2003); and "Finance 2.0: An Interview with Microsoft's CFO," *The McKinsey Quarterly*, no. 1 (2005).

safety-conscious manager who will take every opportunity to reduce the large default risk already present in this portion of the bank's business. Both jobs are simply listed as assistant vice president positions; no further details are given.

Two managers with the requisite training and experience apply for the bank positions. Their resumés are similar. However, unbeknownst to the bank, one drives an old Porsche, not insured against collision damage, and has skydiving as an undisclosed former hobby. Instead of skydiving, this individual (let's call him Dashing) now prefers bungee jumping, which he understandably decides would be

Figure 15.4 Sorting Managers with Linear Share Contracts

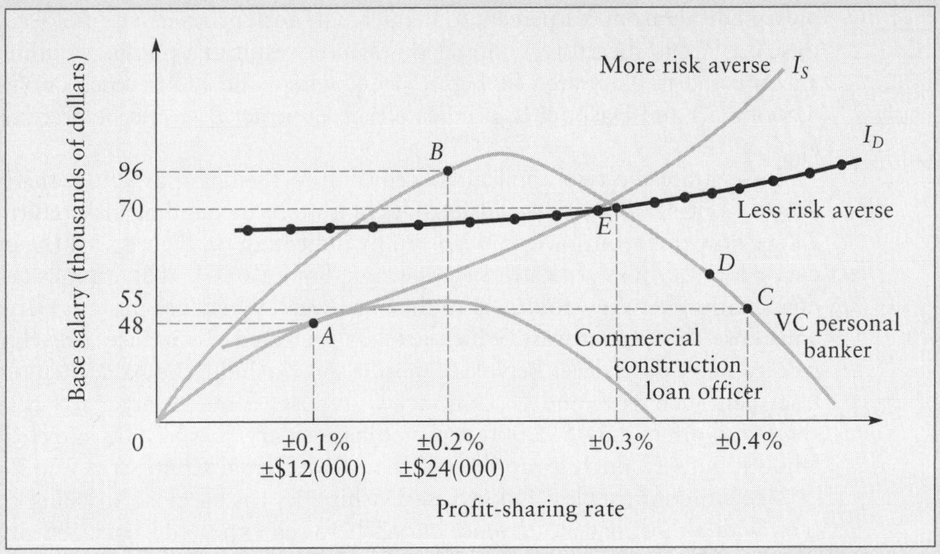

inappropriate to list as a hobby on an application for a bank job. The other individual (you guessed it, Smooth) drives a dealer-serviced Land Rover on which she carries the maximum auto insurance coverage. Despite never leaving town, Smooth keeps the Rover in four-wheel drive at all times to secure the extra traction. Once while attending a formal cocktail party with a few close friends, Smooth revealed that she spent her Christmas bonus on "more insurance, of course." Thinking none of these details to be of any real significance to the bank, she too omits that information from the job application.

Linear Incentives Contract

A linear combination of salary and profit sharing intended to align incentives.

The bank's problem is to sort these two types of individuals, both of whom are well qualified, into the jobs appropriate for their different risk aversions. In Figure 15.4, we display the guaranteed base salary and profit-sharing rate, the two components of a **linear incentives contract.** On the horizontal axis are various percentages that represent what additions to *or subtractions from* one's pay occur as a result of the profit-sharing agreement. A greater share rate initially elicits more effort and creative ingenuity and results in greater expected profit contribution from the manager's activities. Eventually, at still higher share rates the profit contribution actually declines. The two hill-shaped curves in Figure 15.4 represent expected profit-sharing payouts that would allow the firm to just break even on its incentive payments to the two managers. The lower expected profit curve corresponds to the commercial construction loans job, and the higher curve corresponds to the venture capital loans job.

Let's suppose that the company has expected sales of $100 million and a net cash flow from sales of 12 percent. Hence, expected profits available for distribution to owners and managers run $12 million. The bank first elicits responses to two tentative contract offers for their assistant vice president jobs. Contract *A* offers $48,000 salary plus or minus 0.1 percent of the net cash flow or $12,000, which implies a $36,000 to $60,000 possible range of income outcomes. Contract *B* offers $96,000 salary plus or minus 0.2 percent, or a $72,000 to $120,000 range. Contracts *A* and *B* are not equally attractive. One dominates the other in that minimum outcomes under Contract *B* exceed the maximum outcomes under Contract *A*. Because risk increases only modestly from 0.1 percent to 0.2 percent, both prospective employees are likely to select *B*, and therefore, contract *B* is said to result in a **pooling equilibrium.** Such an outcome is illustrated in Figure 15.4, where the indifference curves for both Smooth (I_S) and Dashing (I_D) indicate that Contract *B* would be preferred by both applicants.

Pooling Equilibrium
A decision setting that elicits indistinguishable behavior, etc.

To separate the two applicants according to their risk aversion, the bank withdraws Contract *B* and instead introduces a more demanding risk-return trade-off. To see how this would work, we begin by indicating on Figure 15.4 the indifference curve for the more risk-averse applicant, Smooth (I_S), that establishes a line of demarcation between contracts to the northwest, which are more preferred than *A*, and those to the southeast, which are less preferred. To induce a revelation of the risk-aversion differences between Smooth and Dashing, the bank then offers a contract pair such as *A* and *C*. Contract *C* imposes a much larger 0.4 percent profit share and offers only $55,000 expected base salary, just $7,000 above Contract *A*. Smooth finds *C* much less preferred than the original Contract *A* and immediately says so. In contrast, less risk-averse Dashing (I_D) is so close to being risk neutral (i.e., with almost flat indifference curves between expected salary and profit share), that Dashing may well prefer Contract *C*. This **separating equilibrium** in which Smooth reveals her stronger risk aversion by rejecting *C* in favor of *A*, whereas Dashing does just the reverse, attains several of the employer's objectives. First, these profit-sharing contracts are incentive-compatible contracts in that they elicit appropriate effort and creative ingenuity from both managers while maximizing the shareholders' value. Second, these profit-sharing contracts sort Dashing as the manager to head up the venture capital personal banking group and Smooth as the bank manager for the commercial construction group. The reductions in expected profit to compensate each manager would have been larger without this matching of risk aversion and job types.

Separating Equilibrium
A decision setting that elicits distinguishable behavior.

However, one aspect of an optimal incentives contract remains unaddressed. The participation constraint has not yet been satisfied. An alternative employer can offer Contract *D*, which attracts Smooth with both more expected salary and lower profit risk while retaining the separating properties of the (*A*,*C*) contract pair. As long as such improvements in both risk and return are possible, Smooth will continue to resign and move. Only with contract pair (*A*, *E*) will both the incentive compatibility and participation constraints be satisfied; Dashing selects Contract *E* while Smooth selects Contract *A*, and both remain in the bank's employ. In addition to resolving the sorting of managerial talent, if it induces the appropriate effort from both managers and prevents their being bid away to alternative employment opportunities, this linear incentives contract constitutes a solution to the principal-agent problem in managerial contracting.

Choosing the Efficient Organizational Form

Nonredeployable, Specific Assets
Assets whose replacement cost basis for value is substantially greater than their liquidation value.

Ultimately, the choice of organizational form (e.g., spot market transactions, relational contracting, franchise profit sharing, or vertical integration) depends upon what best suits the governance needs of the asset owners involved. Assets can be **nonredeployable, specific assets** with little or no value in second-best use, such as remote plants and work-in-process inventories, or they may be nonspecific investments that are fully redeployable, such as corporate jet aircraft, popular finished goods in inventory, and Treasury cash. In addition, some assets are dependent on unique complementary investments (e.g., specially designed computer hardware and closed-architecture software), while others are not (e.g., a flexible power plant designed to run on natural gas, coal, or biodiesel). One classic example of these asset-characteristic dichotomies is a hot-rolled steel-making plant belonging to companies such as Republic and U.S. Steel, which requires a blast furnace, converter, reduction furnace, and rolling mill. Because meting the ore and then the metal requires substantial energy, thermal economies of scope require locating these plants beside one another to avoid the reheating expense. However, the organization form question is not whether the operations will be physically integrated and in adjacent locations, but rather whether they will be jointly or separately owned and managed.

At one end of the spectrum, spot market recontracting is efficient for fully redeployable durable assets, not dependent upon other complementary assets. Rental cars provide a good illustration of such assets that may be allocated through spot markets with no loss of efficiency, as shown at the top left of Table 15.3. The limiting feature of this organizational form, however, is the potential for "holdup" inherent in the frequent renewal of spot market contracts. If one party has nonredeployable assets (e.g., a steel mill's blast furnace or a stadium of a sports franchise), spot market recontracting provides too many opportunities for unique engineers or star players to appropriate the surplus value in any business relationship. Owners of nonredeployable assets wish to avoid this holdup hazard by securing longer-term supply contracts.

Reliant Assets

At least partially non-redeployable durable assets.

Reliant assets are nonredeployable durable assets sold in thin markets for less than their value in first-best use. These assets are highly specific to their current use because of substantial unrecoverable sunk cost investments either in acquisition, distribution, or promotion. Specialized equipment in remote locations such as a bauxite mine is the most common reliant asset. Where reliant assets are dependent on unique complements (like an aluminum plant) in order to achieve any substantial value added, one has the maximum potential for holdup in spot market recontracting.

These dependency relations may be either one way or bilateral. Manufacturers with independent distributors are a good example of a bilateral dependent relationship involving reliant assets. Each party in a Volvo-GM Heavy Truck Corporation

Table 15.3 Efficient Organizational Form Depends on Asset Characteristics

	Fully Redeployable Durable Assets	Nonredeployable Reliant Assets
Not Dependent on Unique Complements	Spot market recontracting	Long-term supply contracts + risk management
One-Way Dependent Assets	Relational contracts (alliances)	Vertical integration
Bilateral Dependent Assets	Relational contracts (joint ventures)	Fixed profit-sharing contracts

manufacturer/distributor relationship is equally dependent on the other. In such cases, independent dealers often gravitate toward vertical requirements contracts with a fixed profit share, as shown in the bottom right corner of Table 15.3.

EXAMPLE

Schwinn and Sylvania Dealers Offered Exclusive Territories[13]

The Schwinn and Sylvania companies sold their bicycles and TVs through authorized dealers who were prohibited from reselling to unauthorized bike shops and electronics stores. Although the dealers could carry other product lines, the resale restriction allowed dealers an exclusive territory. Prosecutors in the U.S. Justice Department saw this vertical territorial restriction as anticompetitive, not as a transaction cost-reducing contractual alternative to the governance mechanisms that would otherwise be necessary to protect Schwinn and Sylvania's brand name capital.

Fortunately for Sylvania, in *Continental T.V., Inc., et al. v. GTE Sylvania Inc.*, 433 U.S. 36 (1977), the Supreme Court disagreed. In this case the Court explicitly recognized that brand capital is a specialized, nonredeployable asset that would be compromised if third-party dealers were allowed to sell the Sylvania product with unauthorized marketing plans. Exclusive territories therefore became subject to a rule of reason analysis that weighs a legitimate manufacturer interest in presale selling effort and postsale services against an illegal attempt to prevent reductions in the manufacturer's suggested retail price. Sylvania's fixed profit-sharing contracts with exclusive territories were seen as an efficient and legal organizational form.

Relational Contracts
Promissory agreements of coordinated performance among owners of highly interdependent assets.

When assets are dependent on unique complements but not reliant because of their substantial redeployability, the parties often adopt long-term performance-based **relational contracts.** Redeployable corporate jets and pilots provide a good illustration. Pilots need not own the planes nor secure fixed profit-share contracts to operate the planes. Instead, as indicated in Table 15.3, the organizational form of a jet charter company is normally one of long-term relational contracts with standby pilots who report on short notice for piecemeal assignments. This alliance works well, and both the pilots and plane owners understand that the longevity and reliability of the relationship enhances value relative to spot market recontracting.

Pepsi and Starbucks entered into an alliance to sell cold frappuccino through soft drink machines. Starbucks assets in this alliance are redeployable but one-way dependent on any of several companies with tens of thousands of drink machines. So, a Starbucks-Pepsi alliance is the appropriate organizational form. To take a related example, Genentech's biotechnology is fully redeployable but one-way dependent on marketing behemoth partners such as Pfizer or GlaxoSmithKline. As a result, Genentech has consistently entered into 10 marketing partnerships, 20 licensing agreements, and numerous product development alliances with large drugmakers.

[13] See S. Dutta, J. Heide, and M. Bergen, "Vertical Territorial Restrictions and Public Policy," *Journal of Marketing* 63 (October 1999), pp. 121–134.

EXAMPLE

KODAK AND AOL TIME WARNER FORM A DIGITAL PHOTOGRAPHY ALLIANCE

When Kodak built a fully intergrated, five-step digital photography solution of image capture, editing, processing, distribution, and storage, it clearly required a phone or cable company to complement the Web site in providing broadband services. However, just as clearly, Kodak was redeployable to more than one broadband provider. Consequently, although Kodak was dependent on broadband complements, it presented little contractual hazard of *ex post* holdup.

In addition to online delivery of digital prints from film submitted to one of its 30,000 retail developing locations, Kodak believes that it will soon be one-way dependent on an online partner as customers increasingly edit, store, share photos, and order reprints over the Internet. Of course, AOL Time Warner is fully redeployable to many other uses. Because Kodak is one-way dependent but not reliant upon AOL Time Warner, and because AOL Time Warner is neither dependent nor reliant on Kodak, a relational contract to establish a Kodak–AOL alliance to distribute digital photography online is the efficient organizational form.

In contrast, consider the bilateral dependency of a relational contract between a PC assembler and a chip supplier. Without specially designed Motorola computer chips, Apple iMacs have little value, and without Apple iMacs, these Motorola chips have little value. Yet, each manufacturer makes reliance investments that are specific to the other partner's design decisions. Hence, as indicated in the bottom left cell of Table 15.3, a joint venture is the efficient organizational form. The term *joint ventures* is often reserved for bilateral relationships that establish a separate corporate identity. Appendix 15A addresses incentive-compatible revelation mechanisms for eliciting asymmetric cost information from joint ventures partners.

Finally, when reliant assets are one-way dependent on unique complementary resources, the most efficient organizational form is vertical integration. Remote aluminum plants are one-way dependent on nearby bauxite mines. In contrast, because the bauxite can be shipped anywhere, the mine owners are not dependent on the local aluminum plant. Both assets entail substantial sunk cost investment, but only the remote aluminum plant is a nonredeployable durable asset (i.e., one with little value to other companies should the nearby bauxite source no longer be available). In this situation, upstream vertical integration by the aluminum manufacturer is required in order to prevent opportunistic holdup by the bauxite mine owners.

Sometimes capitalized value is one-way dependent on a unique *downstream* complementary firm. eBay's huge success in attracting sellers of one-of-a-kind items to their network of auction buyers necessitated an electronic payments platform. By 2002 PayPal had captured that market, signing up 12 million households and 3 million businesses (28,000 new users a day) who wished to authorize credit card charges with nothing more exchanged than an e-mail address and a charge amount. At one point, 61 percent of 30 million settlements on PayPal were transactions generated off eBay's 150 million postings. Consequently, in July 2002 eBay paid $1.4 billion to acquire PayPal and thereby vertically integrate downstream. PayPal had become a unique complement to nonredeployable eBay assets.

▲WHAT WENT RIGHT ▼WHAT WENT WRONG

CABLE ALLIES REFUSE TO ADOPT MICROSOFT'S WEBTV AS AN INDUSTRY STANDARD[14]

Demand for interactive television with Internet surfing, Web shopping, interactive sports, and e-mail has grown quickly in hotel and airport lounges but slowly elsewhere. Cable companies such as AT&T and Time Warner appear most likely to trigger the adoption of these smart TVs in households through their leasing of set-top control boxes to residential customers. After acquiring WebTV (now renamed MSN TV) for $425 million in 1997, Microsoft shifted to an alliance strategy to secure the adoption of its complex software by the cable TV operators. Microsoft's interactive WebTV product known as UltimateTV was fully redeployable across competing cable service companies, and the cable companies sought to remain fully redeployable across interactive TV software providers. Because Microsoft/WebTV was one-way dependent on cable providers, but cable had numerous other ways to generate value without Microsoft, an alliance was the efficient organizational form for these asset characteristics.

Microsoft's product offering required the cumbersome software architecture of Windows CE. Standard set-top control boxes don't have enough memory or fast enough microprocessors to support Microsoft's operating system. Consequently, Microsoft invested more than $10 billion in co-designing digital entertainment networks and new set-top control boxes with seven cable companies worldwide (AT&T: $5 billion; Telewest Comm in the U.K.: $2.6 billion; Comcast: $1 billion; and another $1.2 billion in Rogers, NTL, and UPC in Canada and Europe). In return, AT&T Broadband and its subsidiary TCI promised forward sales contracts for a total of 10 million set-top control boxes employing Microsoft CE software in a Motorola-built unit, the DCT5000. Today, the first 250,000 DCT5000s sit idly stacked in a Seattle warehouse. Microsoft's software was simply too complex, too costly, and too late.

The full installation costs for the Microsoft DCT5000 cable networks skyrocketed to $500 per household control box. Yet marketing research showed that cable subscribers would willingly add only $5 per month to their cable bills in order to secure these enhanced services. Ongoing delays induced Europe's largest cable company, UPC, to order set-top digital entertainment software from Liberate, a Microsoft rival. By March 2002, even AT&T announced that it had no plans at present to deploy interactive WebTV software and that Microsoft would build only the replacement for the scrolling online TV guide.

Had the cable companies allowed Microsoft/WebTV to become an industry standard, full-scale vertical integration would have been warranted. Microsoft's digital entertainment assets would then have been one-way dependent on cable service providers, whose assets would have been no longer redeployable. This classic case for vertical integration is shown in Table 15.3. Once when Bill Gates was presenting UltimateTV as a possible industry standard, a cable company president Brian Roberts half-jokingly suggested that Microsoft buy the entire cable industry.

[14] Based on "Microsoft's Blank Screen," *The Economist* (September 16, 2000), p. 74; and "Set-Top Setback: Microsoft Miscues," *Wall Street Journal* (June 14, 2002), p. A1.

INTERNATIONAL PERSPECTIVES

ECONOMIES OF SCALE AND INTERNATIONAL JOINT VENTURES IN CHIP MAKING[15]

Approximately one dozen large electronics companies in the United States, Europe, and Japan were once involved in producing memory chips. Up-front costs for each item were staggering. For example, the cost of developing the 64-megabit memory chip design and production technology was estimated to range from $600 million to $1 billion. Once developed, memory chips then required investment of an additional $600 million to $750 million in a "fab," a fabrication plant that produced up to 10 million chips a month.

Because of the massive scale economies available in such a cost structure, many of the semiconductor companies involved in these research and development efforts formed international joint ventures to share the huge fixed costs and risks involved. Some of these partnerships include:

U.S. Company	Foreign Partner
AT&T	NEC (Japan)
Texas Instruments	Hitachi (Japan)
Motorola	Toshiba (Japan)
IBM	Siemens (Germany)

Initially these joint ventures took various forms. For example, AT&T and NEC agreed to swap basic chip-making technologies. Texas Instruments and Hitachi agreed to develop a common design and manufacturing process and then do low-volume production together, with mass production and marketing to be done separately by each company. Motorola and Toshiba entered into a partnership to co-manufacture memory (and logic) chips. In the end, massive scale economies from production rates of millions per plant per month led to a consolidation of production in the Hitachi and Toshiba plants in Japan.

[15] Based on "The Costly Race Chipmakers Cannot Afford to Lose," *BusinessWeek* (December 10, 1990), pp. 185–187; and "Two Makers of Microchips Broaden Ties," *Wall Street Journal* (November 21, 1991), p. 84.

PROSPECT THEORY MOTIVATES FULL-LINE FORCING

At times the span of hierarchical control inside the firm is determined by the most effective marketing. Social psychologists have long noticed that people buy both lottery tickets and disability insurance. Daniel Kahneman and Amos Tversky hypothesized that people are risk-preferring at wealth levels below their current socioeconomic position and risk-averse above (as in Figure 15.5), that is, their absolute value of utility losses is perceived as greater, often much greater, than an equal-dollar-valued utility gain.[16]

Prospect Theory

A basis for hypothesizing that the satisfaction from avoiding losses exceeds the anticipation of equal-value prospective gains.

In a product category such as minivans, their observation is that a household contemplating a Caravan SE model with full options for $22,000 will perceive the decline in satisfaction from dropping down to a $17,000 base model Caravan as much greater than the increase in satisfaction associated with giving up another $5,000 to purchase a $27,000 Caravan LX or SXT model. The fact that perceived losses outweigh equal-value prospective gains reflects a theorem of **prospect theory** that has many implications for the optimal boundaries of the firm.

[16] Daniel Kahneman and Amos Tversky, "Prospect Theory: An Analysis of Decision under Risk," *Econometrica* 47, no. 2 (March 1979), pp. 263–291; and Colin Camerer, "An Experimental Test of Several Generalized Utility Theories," *Journal of Risk and Uncertainty* 2, no. 1 (April 1989), pp. 61–104.

Figure 15.5 Full-Line Forcing

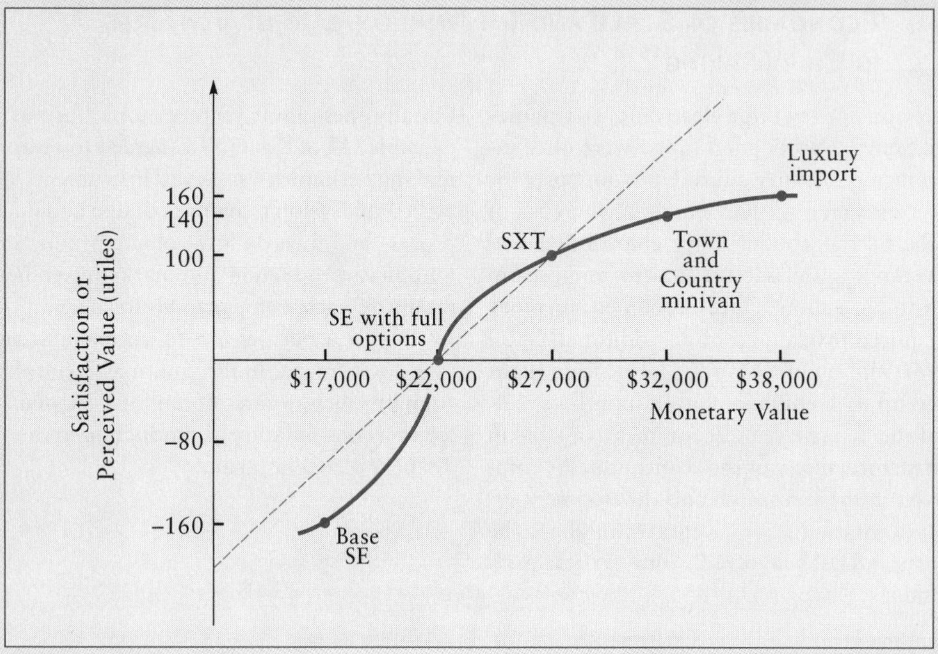

For one thing, marketers are well advised to distribute trial products ("try now, pay later") because the utility loss if the consumer contemplates returning the product and owes nothing will be greater than the utility gained by prospective additional consumption with the money saved. Second, receivables managers are well advised to ask consumers to forgo something prospective to pay for their product (i.e., a projected year-end bonus, tax refund, or frequent flyer award). Again, the payment in prospective additional consumption forgone will be perceived as less undesirable than an equivalent cash payment that means giving up current consumption.

Finally, firms with good-quality house brands should encourage premium brands in the channel, and those with premium brands should encourage the introduction of super-premium brands. If no such distribution channel arrangements can be secured, the implication is that firms selling moderately priced brands should buy premium brands. If none exist, firms are advised to develop their own and force them into the channel. Hanes Hosiery pursues a "good, better, best" product strategy with private labels, L'Eggs, and Hanes. Marriott developed its Fairfield Inns, Courtyard by Marriott, and Marriott Resorts and International Hotels. The Gap launched not only the downscale fighting brand Old Navy but also went out and acquired Banana Republic.

Let's return to Figure 15.5 to see exactly why full-line forcing works. Auto dealers face an especially difficult competitive environment with mobile customers, innumerable substitute makes and models, and Internet search engines comparing price discounts by competing dealers on a real-time basis. Moving their repeat-purchase "customers for life" up along a base-car-to-luxury-car product spectrum is one key to profitability in the auto dealership business. Another key is to avoid selling only base automobiles.

In Figure 15.5, stepping down from an SE model minivan with full options to a base model saves a customer \$5,000 but sacrifices 50 percent of the perceived value of the minivan product line (−160 out of 320 total). Spending another \$5,000 to step up to an SXT or LX luxury model garners only an additional 30 percent (+100/320) of the product line's perceived value. Although the unit sales of the dealership do not change, the mere presence of the LX and SXT model drives such a customer to justify spending \$5,000 to avoid the greater disutility of the base model while congratulating himself or herself for avoiding spending another \$5,000 for a smaller relative increase in satisfaction.

After providing high quality (and high margin) service and maintenance for the SE with full options over several years, the dealership then plans to see that same customer back in the showroom eyeing the SXT models. Again, full-line forcing can encourage the "upsell" to the \$27,000 SXT model. Saving \$5,000 by continuing to purchase SEs with options will result in a 30 percent disutility of (−100/320), whereas purchasing the \$5,000-more-expensive Town and Country model in Figure 15.5 would increase satisfaction by only 40 utiles, 12.5 percent. Again, the careful shopper, after comparing marginal benefits and marginal costs, decides to go with the SXT, and the dealership rejoices.

EXAMPLE

FULL-LINE FORCING IN PENS, ASPIRIN, AND MULTIVITAMINS AT REVCO AND ECKERD

Perhaps the most amazing aspect of prospect theory is the extent to which retail market shares can be altered by the practice of full-line forcing. Eckerd and Revco fully control the distribution channel policy in their own drug stores. In-house store brands can be sold beside national brands. Suppose Revco Aspirin at \$2.89 for 100 80-mg tablets secures a 30 percent market share against a generic aspirin product selling 100 80-mg tablets at \$1.50. Revco can allocate additional shelf space to non-store-brand painkillers and chooses between Bayer Aspirin at \$2.89 and Tylenol at \$5.29. Not surprisingly, Revco Aspirin's market share falls if the cheaper Bayer product is introduced. But what is astounding is that, in case after case, introducing the Tylenol product raises Revco Aspirin sales to a 40 percent market share, reduces generic aspirin from 70 to 40 percent, and raises Tylenol to 20 percent.

Because some people experience side effects from aspirin but not from Tylenol, a fairer comparison perhaps is to investigate the same experiment with absolutely identical multivitamins. Revco multivitamins at \$3.29 per 100 tablets might again secure 30 percent of the market relative to generic multivitamins at \$1.99 with 70 percent market share. Introducing One-A-Day brand multivitamins at \$5.19 into the channel will actually raise the market share of Revco's product. That is, with the good-better-best product strategy, market shares might distribute as follows: 40 percent generic, 40 percent Revco, and 20 percent One-A-Day. The disutility of lost perceived consumption outweighs equal-value utility gains.

VERTICAL INTEGRATION

Search, bargaining, and holdup costs are all reduced when internal transfers and the monitoring and incentive systems within the firm replace the spot market contracting and recontracting necessitated by operating at arm's length with outside suppliers and independent distributors. As we have seen, Nobel laureate Ronald Coase and Oliver Williamson argue that these factors explain why the firm emerged as an organizational form despite the diseconomies of ever-wider spans of managerial control.[17] Another motive for a manufacturer to vertically integrate upstream to suppliers or downstream to retail distributors involves the inefficiency of successive monopolization (i.e., the presence of market power over price at more than one stage of production). For example, the transfer of Disney Studio's downstream equity to Pixar (the upstream digital entertainment content provider) is a method of precommitment by Pixar to exercise upstream price restraint and not spoil the downstream market. We now illustrate these ideas further with a detailed study of vertical integration in the hosiery industry.

Consider, first, an upstream yarn supplier who operates in a competitive intermediate product market and a downstream hosiery manufacturer who enjoys the market power to mark up the wholesale price for pantyhose above its marginal cost. Figure 15.6 illustrates the situation each firm faces when the yarn inputs are

Figure 15.6 Hosiery Integration Analysis with Upstream Competitor

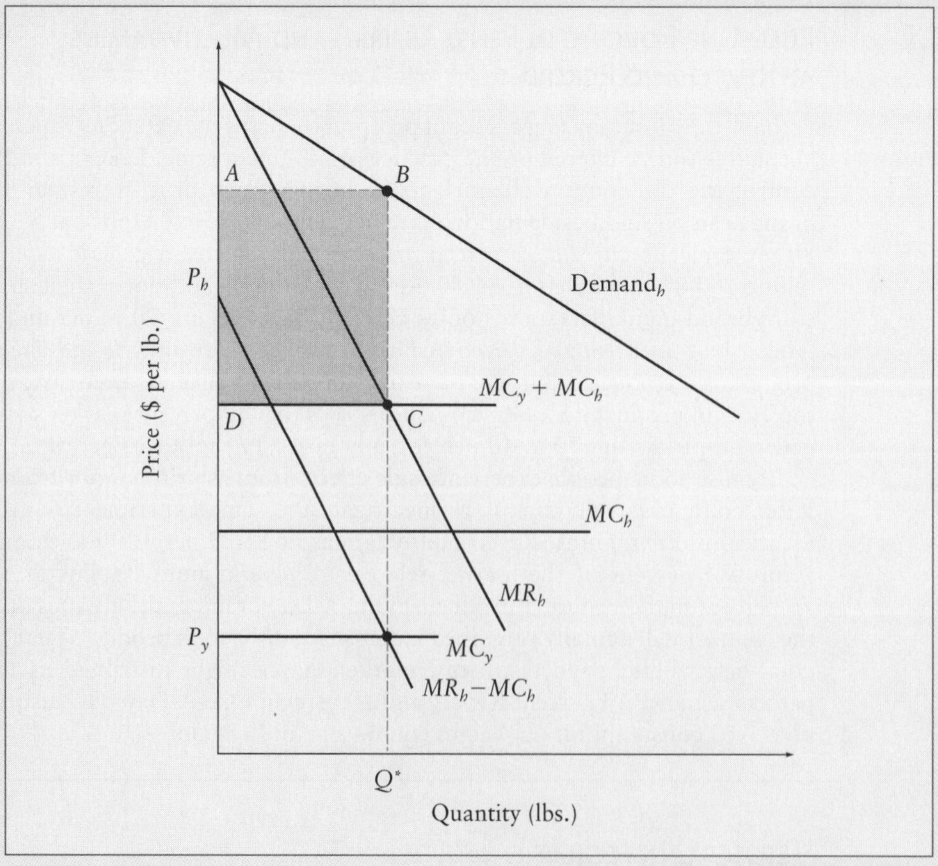

[17] For more extensive discussion of this topic, see S. Hamilton and K. Stiegert, "Vertical Coordination," *Journal of Law and Economics* (April 2000).

combined in fixed proportions with manufacturing labor and machinery to yield hosiery output. The outside demand curve and its marginal revenue capture the hosiery manufacturer's revenue opportunities in the wholesale pantyhose product market. Given the marginal cost of hosiery production (MC_h) and the competitive price of yarn ($P_y = MC_y$), the manufacturer sets summed marginal cost of hosiery production and yarn inputs ($MC_h + MC_y$) equal to hosiery marginal revenue (MR_h) at output Q^*. This joint profit-maximizing output decision maximizes hosiery profits by setting the marginal cost of yarn equal to the net marginal revenue product of the yarn supplier. So, subtracting the downstream marginal cost (MC_h) from the downstream marginal revenues (MR_h) leaves the *net* revenue opportunity available to the upstream yarn supplier—that is, $MR_h - MC_h$. Setting this derived demand for yarn inputs equal to upstream marginal costs (MC_y) identifies Q^* as the yarn supplier's preferred throughput rate as well as the hosiery manufacturer's preferred output rate. Thus, the upstream supplier who prices yarn so as to just recover marginal cost imposes no throughput constraint on downstream hosiery operations.

The hosiery manufacturer in Figure 15.6 would not change the yarn input prices, nor the wholesale output prices, nor the throughput quantity if it were to vertically integrate upstream and operate the yarn supplier. Therefore, vertical integration can only result in disadvantages associated with a wider span of managerial control. For profits *ABCD* to remain unchanged, these disadvantages would need to be offset by another factor such as reduced transaction costs. In general, in the absence of other factors, we would conclude that in Figure 15.6, the hosiery manufacturer has no profit motive for backward integration into the competitive yarn supplier's business.

In contrast, however, consider the case in which the yarn supplier has a proprietary process that is unique and therefore adds substantial value itself to the hosiery manufacturing process. In Figure 15.7, the derived demand for the yarn input is again $MR_h - MC_h$, and everything else about the hosiery operations remains the same as in Figure 15.6, except that now the upstream firm has the market power to mark up its own marginal cost (MC_y). By taking a second marginalization of the revenue, subtracting off the hosiery production cost, and setting $MMR_h - MC_h = MC_y$, the yarn supplier maximizes upstream profits *EFGH* by choosing a price P'_y at throughput Q'. If P'_y exceeds the upstream marginal cost MC_y, the summed marginal cost facing the hosiery manufacturer is now higher, and consequently, the desired output declines from Q^* to Q'. Although hosiery prices rise to P'_h, the higher costs and smaller output of hosiery operations cause the profits of the downstream firm (the manufacturer) to decline (i.e., *IJKL* in Figure 15.7 < *ABCD* in Figure 15.6). That is, the presence of profit margins upstream results in a throughput constraint that unambiguously reduces downstream profitability.[18]

Backward vertical integration by the hosiery manufacturer can squeeze out the margins upstream by simply setting an internal transfer price for yarn $P_y = MC_y$. This change will return the optimal throughput to Q^*, the profit-maximizing level for the consolidated yarn and hosiery operations. That is, even after paying the upstream profits *EFGH* to secure the control rights from the yarn company, the downstream hosiery manufacturer has higher net profits (*ABCD* − *EFGH*) than its

[18] This implication holds without qualification here because of fixed proportions production, i.e., the efficient input mix remains unchanged despite the reduction in output. Under variable proportions, vertical integration may be motivated or not, depending on the input substitutability and possible cost savings.

Figure 15.7 Hosiery Integration Analysis with Upstream Market Power

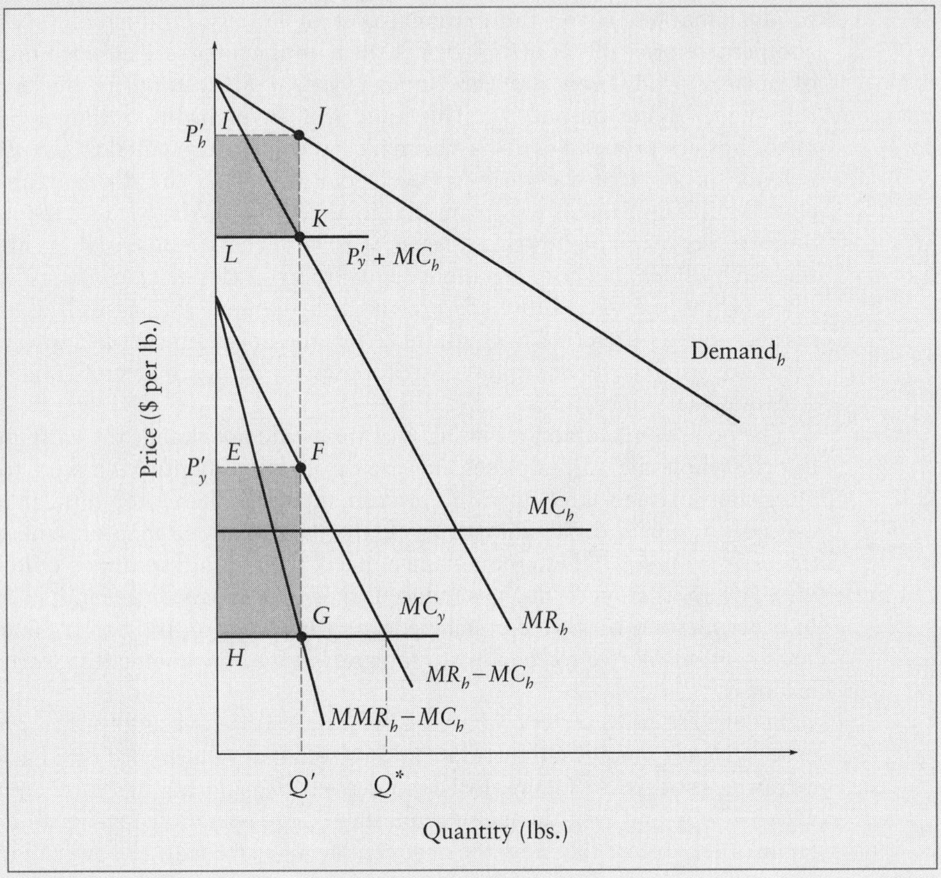

profit from independent operations *IJKL*. Consequently, we would expect these two firms to coordinate their operations either as a joint venture or as a vertically integrated firm.

The Dissolution of Assets in a Partnership

Vertical integration is the most extreme organizational form on a continuum from outsourcing with spot market transactions, through relational contracting, vertical requirements contracting, and extending to alliances and joint ventures. In Appendix 15A we will see how subtle institutional arrangements can align the interests of partners in a joint venture. But what happens when a joint venture or partnership must be dissolved?

Optimal Mechanism Design

An efficient procedure that creates incentives to motivate the desired behavioral outcome.

First, consider the simpler question of how to divide a deceased individual's personal belonging's fairly. In fair division procedures, the key to an optimal mechanism design for fair division is open communication and role reversal. This reasoning suggests letting one party divide the estate and the other choose which half he or she

WHAT WENT RIGHT • WHAT WENT WRONG

DELL REPLACES VERTICAL INTEGRATION WITH VIRTUAL INTEGRATION[19]

New developments in information technology, such as the enterprise resource planning system SAP, have widened the efficient span of hierarchical control. Rather than enabling larger vertically integrated companies, SAP enables virtual integration. Dell Inc. owns almost no PC component manufacturing operations. Instead, it outsources its requirements to several hundred supplier-partners who are tied together in a real-time monitoring, adaptation, and control system using the Internet. Its patented build-to-order business model must handle effectively an extraordinarily complex set of just-in-time component flows to support a final product assembly that ships 10,000 possible product configurations direct to a customer.

Information technology plays a key role in the governance mechanisms for this type of virtually integrated supply chain management. When this business model is successful, plant and equipment requirements decline, inventories shrink, and operating leverage rises substantially. With less fixed capital investment than a vertically integrated competitor, the return on invested capital climbs accordingly. Dell stock appreciated 300-fold in its first fifteen years of operation.

[19] Based on "Identity Crisis," *Wall Street Journal* (October 10, 2000), p. C1; "Direct Hit," *The Economist* (January 9, 1999), pp. 55–58; and J. Margretta, "The Power of Virtual Integration," *Harvard Business Review* (March/April 1998), pp. 72–85.

prefers. Under the incentives created by this procedure, the person dividing the estate will offer larger or more numerous possessions in one parcel if another parcel contains particularly valuable possessions. In short, one party "cuts the cake," and the other party gets to choose.

THE DISSOLUTION OF A DECAYING BUSINESS

The optimal mechanism design for fair division necessitates sequential game analysis when the prize is decaying with the passage of time as the players negotiate. Suppose a partnership must divide $3 million in assets. The only catch is that the assets, which the two partners must agree upon dividing, decline in value by $1 million each time either party refuses the proposed division. Perhaps the assets are perishable pharmaceuticals or intellectual property that decays in value quickly. Or alternatively, once the capital markets get wind that the partnership is fracturing, any synergistic value of the two subsets of assets quickly evaporates.

The two principals toss a coin to see who should make the first offer of how to split the $3 million. Suppose Joe wins the toss. How much should he offer to Kim to secure her acceptance of the offer and forgo her rights of first refusal? Kim gets to structure a second-round offer should this first proposed division be refused, and she will also respond to Joe's third and final offer should the second proposal be refused. Notice that the endgame to this problem happens after three rounds when the assets are gone. Think about how little Kim would be willing to accept in the third and final round. Can Kim hold out for more than

Figure 15.8 Dissolution of Assets in a Partnership

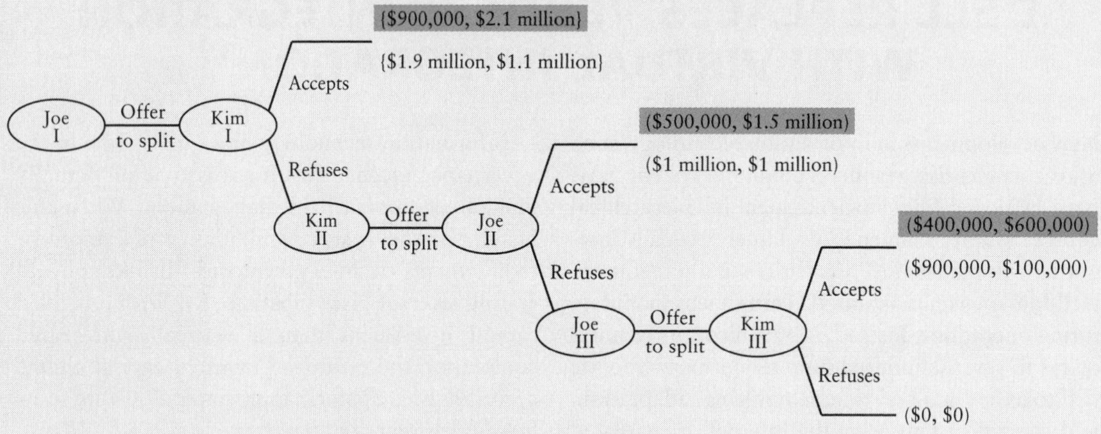

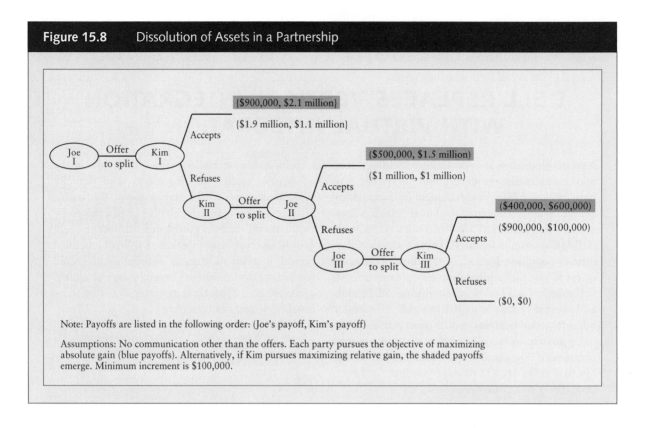

Note: Payoffs are listed in the following order: (Joe's payoff, Kim's payoff)

Assumptions: No communication other than the offers. Each party pursues the objective of maximizing absolute gain (blue payoffs). Alternatively, if Kim pursues maximizing relative gain, the shaded payoffs emerge. Minimum increment is $100,000.

this amount in the second round? What, therefore, is the maximum Joe needs to offer to trigger an acceptance in the first round? Does this game have a first-mover advantage, or is it better to play second and be the respondent in the third and final round?

These and related questions can be addressed with the sequential game techniques of Chapter 13. In Figure 15.8, Joe makes the final offer at the far right but, as you may suspect, in one sense Kim's right of refusal controls this endgame. Because $100,000 is preferable to zero, Kim's best-reply response is to accept an offer to split the final million as $900,000 for Joe and $100,000 for Kim. This analysis implies that in the preceding (second) round, Kim can offer Joe $1 million (i.e., $100,000 more than Joe's endgame outcome), and Joe's best-reply response is to accept. Stepping the backwards induction one more round back, this second-round analysis implies that if Joe offers Kim $1.1 million in the first round (i.e., $100,000 more than Kim's second round outcome), Kim will accept. Note that we are short-circuiting threats and modes of communication other than simply stating the offers. Also note that we assumed each party believes the other party is maximizing absolute gain, without regard to the relative distribution. In such circumstances, making the first *and the last* offer appears advantageous to Joe.

Mechanism design features of this problem include the rotating offer and right of refusal, the lack of communication about objectives and credible threats, and the coin toss to decide who offers first. Any of these could be changed, and it might make quite a difference. For example, suppose Kim's reputation was that she pursued relative wealth, not absolute wealth. In that event, the outcome ($0, $0) would quite literally be preferable to the alternative of her partner Joe going $800,000 up at ($900,000,

$100,000). Even splitting the last million dollars ($500,000, $500,000) would not be preferable to ($0, $0). So only an asymmetric distribution *favoring* Kim (say, $400,000, $600,000 in the shaded box) would elicit her acceptance.

In earlier rounds, Joe now knows that he must increase the unequal distribution in Kim's favor in order to secure her acceptance, and Kim knows that the same is not true of Joe. Given the $100,000 minimum increments, Kim reasons by backward induction from the ($400,000, $600,000) outcome of Round 3 that she can offer as little as ($500,000, $1.5 million) to secure Joe's acceptance in Round 2. Finally, this intermediate outcome implies by the relative gain reasoning motivating Kim that Joe must elicit her acceptance at the start of the negotiations by offering a {$900,000, $2.1 million} split in Round 1. Comparing the blue and shaded offers in Round 1, it makes $1 million of difference whether the mechanism design allows communication of Kim's motivation to maximize relative (not absolute) gain as opposed to a mechanism design with unknown silent partners responding through intermediaries. Small changes in the institutional procedures or the organization architecture often make this large a difference in tactical encounters.

SUMMARY

- Businesses make choices about organizational form that define the span of hierarchical control from the vertically integrated oil company at one extreme to the virtual manufacturer Dell, which outsources all manufacturing and assembly to supplier-partners.
- All external and internal business relationships require a solution to the twin problems of coordination and control. External business relationships can be organized through spot market transactions, long-term contracts, or reputation effects in relational contracting. These forms of organization differ in their timing, players, enforcement, and information structure.
- Long-term vertical requirements contracts provide an *ex ante* framework for resolving coordination and control problems between manufacturers, suppliers, and distributors. Because all contracts are purposefully incomplete, *ex post* opportunistic behavior requires governance mechanisms to reduce several types of contractual hazards. The *moral hazard problem* arises because of the unobservability of effort in contract performance. The *postcontractual opportunistic behavior,* called "holdup," presents another commonly occurring contractual hazard.
- Exchange under incomplete information and under asymmetric information differ. *Incomplete information* refers to the uncertainty that is pervasive in practically all transactions and motivates insurance markets. *Asymmetric information,* on the other hand, refers to private information one party possesses, that the other party cannot independently verify.
- Asymmetric information leads to the *problem of adverse selection.*
- Contracts are seldom complete because full *contingent claims contracting* is often prohibitively expensive. Intentionally incomplete contracting allows *postcontractual opportunistic behavior* and leads to holdup. Resolving the *holdup problem* in managerial contracting necessitates the use of *governance mechanisms.*
- Governance mechanisms include internal monitoring by director subcommittees and large creditors, internal/external monitoring by large block shareholders, auditing and variance analysis, benchmarking, an ethically dutiful corporate culture, and whistle-blowing.
- Managerial labor can be hired in several ways: for example, straight salary, wage rate, or profit sharing. Pure profit sharing results in moonlighting, however, because the manager's inputs (effort and creative ingenuity) are largely unobservable. Unobservable effort leads to the *moral hazard problem,* which can be resolved by setting up *ex post facto* (e.g., with deferred stock options).
- In combination, random disturbances in firm performance and unobservable managerial effort present a more difficult *principal-agent problem* to resolve. Owner-principals do not know when to blame manager-agents for weak performance or give credit for strong performance. *Optimal incentives contracts* involving some guaranteed salary and a profit-sharing bonus can, in theory, resolve the principal-agent problem.
- Linear combinations of salary and profit sharing can also be used to elicit asymmetric information about

managerial preferences, sort managers by their own personal risk aversion, and prevent adverse selection in managerial hiring. Boards of directors face a holdup problem in renewing senior executive contracts, necessitating governance mechanisms.

- What form of organization to adopt (e.g., spot market transactions, long-term vertical requirements contracts, relational contracts, or vertical integration) depends on the contractual hazards that need to be avoided. What contractual hazards arise in business relationships depends on the asset characteristics, redeployability or specificity of the fixed assets, and the relative dependence of those fixed assets on unique complementary assets.
- Perceived utility losses are often larger (in absolute value) than equivalent-value utility gains, implying a hybrid utility function suggested by prospect theory.
- Prospect theory implies sellers should distribute trial products, take prospective income in payment, and full-line force.
- Vertical integration is an optimal organizational form when the assets are one-way dependent on complementary assets and are largely nonredeployable.
- Optimal mechanism design seeks to motivate value-maximizing behavior while reducing transaction costs.
- Mechanism design features such as first offer, right of first refusal, lack of communication, and credible threats in a dissolution of assets in a partnership can be analyzed as a sequential game.
- Small changes in the institutional procedures often make a large difference in the outcome and distribution of payoffs.

Exercises

Answers to the exercises in blue can be found in Appendix C at the back of the book.

1. Suppose an enhanced effectiveness of cooperative advertising occurs if the distributor shares its superior on-the-spot information about current trends in the marketplace with the manufacturer. Explain how each of the following would affect the information-sharing objective:
   a. All details of co-op advertising are agreed to up front in the franchise contract
   b. Advertising is pursued independently by the manufacturer and the retail distributor
   c. Cooperative advertising allowances are rebated back to the distributor out of the franchise fees
2. If contract promises were not excused because of acts of war, would the clearing and settlements clients of Bank of New York change their behavior? If so, how? What reliance behavior would be considered efficient? What reliance behavior would be considered excessive?
3. For each of the possible loan terms the commercial lender might offer, identify what choices by the lender would be the worst for combating the moral hazard problem in Figure 15.2.
4. If coal mine tonnage can be shipped elsewhere cheaply, but an adjacent coal-fired power plant is not redeployable to other uses, what organizational form would be adopted by the power plant owners? Why?
5. Would warehouse operators insist on owning their own trucking companies? Why or why not? What coordination and control problems and contractual hazards would these companies encounter?
6. What organizational form would warehouse operators and truck hauling companies adopt?
7. In benchmarking sales representatives against one another, what problems arise from continuing to reassign the above-average trade representatives to previously unproductive sales territories?
8. Explain how the optimal incentives contract would differ if the less risk-averse bank officer (Dashing in Figure 15.4) had generated the smaller expected profit (i.e., the lower hill-shaped curve).

9. In the Division of a Decaying Business game, what should you offer if the assets at the start of the game are $4 million rather than $3 million? Now is there a first-mover or second-mover advantage? Why?
10. Analyze the pure Nash equilibrium and mixed Nash equilibrium strategies in the following manufacturer-distributor coordination game. How would you recommend restructuring the game to secure higher expected profit for the manufacturer?

		Manufacturer	
		Product Update/ Higher MSRP	**No Update/ Same MSRP**
Distributor	**Discontinue Special Selling Services**	0 / $1 M	$2 M / $4 M
	Continue Special Selling Services	$6 M / $2 M	0 / 0

CASE EXERCISES

BORDERS BOOKS AND AMAZON.COM DECIDE TO DO BUSINESS TOGETHER

In 2001, Borders Books, the leading chain of bookshop retailers, entered into an agreement with Amazon.com, the online retailer, to fulfill Internet orders from the Borders.com Web site. Using Table 15.4 and the following questions, what organizational form would you predict for this business relationship?

QUESTIONS

1. Are Amazon.com's warehouses, Web pages, and one-click sales methods fully redeployable to other products? If so, name a few such products. If not, why not?
2. Are Borders' fixed assets fully redeployable? If so, suggest how. If not, why not?
3. Is Borders dependent on Amazon as a unique complement? That is, is Amazon.com the only potential company that could process Internet-based orders for Borders?
4. Is Amazon dependent on Borders for referrals, or does it have its own Internet-based order flow?
5. Is your answer consistent with the multiyear fee-for-service contract between Borders and Amazon.com whereby Amazon processes the order, ships the book, records the sales, and pays Borders a referral fee? One Borders executive described this as a "low-risk, low return" approach to online sales while retaining Borders' focus on its core mission of running bookshops.

DESIGNING A MANAGERIAL INCENTIVE CONTRACT[20]

Specific Electric Co. asks you to implement a pay-for-performance incentive contract for its new CEO. The CEO can either work hard with a personal cost of $200,000 or reduce her effort, thereby avoiding the personal cost. The CEO faces three possible outcomes: her company experiences good luck with probability 0.3, medium luck with probability 0.4, or bad luck with probability 0.3. Although the management team can distinguish the three "states" of luck as the quarter unfolds, the compensation committee of the board of directors (and the shareholders) cannot do so. Sometime thereafter, the CEO decides to expend high or low work effort, and one of the observable shareholder values then results.

	Shareholder Value		
	Good Luck (30%)	**Medium Luck (40%)**	**Bad Luck (30%)**
High CEO Effort	**$1 billion**	**$800 million**	**$500 million**
Low CEO Effort	**$800 million**	**$500 million**	**$300 million**

Assume 10 million shares and a $65 initial share price, implying a $650,000,000 initial shareholder value. Since the CEO's effort and the company's luck are unobservable to the owners and company directors, it is not possible upon observing a reduction to $50 share prices and $500,000,000 value to distinguish whether the company experienced low CEO effort and medium luck, or high CEO effort and bad luck.

Answer the following questions from the perspective of a member of the compensation committee who is aligned with shareholder interests and is deciding on bonus plans for the CEO.

QUESTIONS

1. What is the maximum amount it would be worth to shareholders to elicit high CEO effort all the time rather than low CEO effort all the time?
2. If you decide to pay 1 percent of this amount (in Question 1) as a cash bonus, what performance level (what share price or shareholder value) in the table should trigger the bonus? Suppose you decide to elicit high CEO effort when and if medium luck occurs by paying the bonus for $800 million outcomes. What criticism can you see of this incentive contract plan?
3. Suppose you decide to elicit high CEO effort when and if good luck occurs by paying the bonus for $1,000,000,000 outcomes only. What criticism can you see of this incentive contract plan?
4. Suppose you decide to elicit high CEO effort when and if bad luck occurs by paying the bonus for $500 million outcomes. What criticism can you see of this incentive contract plan?
5. In seeking to identify what share price to employ in triggering the payment of the bonus so as maximize shareholder value, how much would you, the compensation committee, be willing to pay an auditor who examines the expense

[20] An earlier version of this exercise was suggested by B. Ramy Elitzur of Tel Aviv University. An earlier version of this exercise appeared in Chapter 1. Using your deeper knowledge of the principal-agent problem, try it again.

and revenue flows in real time and delivers perfect forecast information about the "luck" the firm is experiencing? Compare value with this perfect information relative to the best choice among the incentive contract plans in Questions 2, 3, and 4.

6. Design a stock option–based incentive plan to elicit high effort. Show that this incentive contract improves shareholder value relative to the best of the cash-based incentive plans in Questions 2, 3, or 4.

7. Design a restricted stock incentive plan to elicit high effort. Show that this incentive contract improves shareholder value relative to all prior alternatives.

8. Financial audits are basically sampling procedures to verify with a predetermined accuracy the sources and uses of the company receipts and expenditures; the larger the sample, the higher is the accuracy. What's the maximum amount the compensation committee would be willing to pay for a perfect forecast if it were possible for the auditors to distinguish good from medium luck? Medium from bad luck?

THE DIVISION OF INVESTMENT BANKING FEES

You are the lead underwriter among a syndicate of five investment banks composed of yourself, the syndicate comanager, and syndicate members 3, 4, and 5. Your syndicate finds a deal worth $100 million in fees. You must submit a proposal as to how the fees should be divided, and the syndicate then votes by majority rule.

Your syndicate is rational and democratic in the sense that the division of fees will be decided based upon maximization of absolute gain in this single deal, and the members also have reputational reasons in future deals (where the lower-ranked members hope to achieve more influence and get a higher-ranked position) to abide by a majority decision.

If your proposal is rejected by vote of the syndicate, you are displaced as lead underwriter, removed altogether from the deal making, and replaced by the comanager who then makes a proposal to the remaining four. If his deal is rejected, he too is removed, and syndicate member 3 makes a proposal to the three firms remaining, and so on.

DISCUSSION QUESTION

1. What should you offer and to whom?

LIBRARY EXERCISE

VERTICAL INTEGRATION AT GM-FISHER BODY

Read the three papers by R. H. Coase, R. Freeland, and B. Klein in the April 2000 issue of the *Journal of Law and Economics*, and then explain the competing arguments as to why General Motors vertically integrated upstream to buy out Fisher Body Co.

APPENDIX

15a

AUCTION DESIGN AND INFORMATION ECONOMICS

In this appendix, we discuss optimal mechanism designs for auctions and other institutional procedures. Selling airline and concert tickets by soliciting sealed bids with purchase guaranteed for given dates (as does Priceline) versus posting ascending price offers with amendment and cancellation (as does eBay) are instances of alternative mechanism designs for auctions. Often the purpose of such mechanism design choices is to induce the revelation of asymmetric information that is needed to maximize shareholder value for the auction buyers or sellers.

Mechanism design can also address coordination and control problems in joint ventures and partnerships. Specifically, an incentive-compatible contract (IC contract) can induce partners to reveal their private proprietary information about preliminary cost projections to one another. In an IC contract, each partner will incur the net cost of his or her own information revelation on the other partner. Hence, the IC contract imposes a mechanism design for sharing profits that serves the self-interest of each partner through revealing the true and complete cost information to the other partner. This incentive-compatible revelation mechanism provides a complex example of the concept of optimal mechanism design.

QUEUE SERVICE RULES

A simple business application of the concept of optimal mechanism design is the queue service rule for filling customer orders from those waiting to purchase. The traditional first-come, first-served procedure induces an inefficient pattern of customer arrivals at, for example, a concert site. If the box office opens at 9:00 A.M., a few potential customers arrive three hours earlier or even the night before. Others stand on queue for two hours, and many more show up to wait in line at 8:00 A.M.

What customers are willing to pay for tickets is surely affected by the inconvenience of this wait. And the subpopulation of customers who have low opportunity cost of time (and are therefore willing to arrive the earliest, wait the longest, and obtain tickets with the greatest probability) may not be the subpopulation who will pay the most for tickets. For this reason, many ticket agencies have no objection to a wealthy patron paying someone with lower opportunity cost of time to stand on queue, purchase the ticket, and transfer it at face value to the higher-willingness-to-pay customer.[1] In any case, all this waiting time is time wasted; other queue service

[1] Scalpers, of course, charge higher prices still, but note that such gray markets reveal to the ticket agency what those customers who are not willing to show up at the ticket window and wait are in fact willing to pay. This information helps the ticket agency set an optimal price.

rules may be much more efficient, and as a result, more of the customer's willingness to pay may be captured by the concert promoters and sports teams.

FIRST-COME, FIRST-SERVED VERSUS LAST-COME, FIRST-SERVED

As a provisional alternative, consider last-come, first-served. Under this queue service rule, a customer has no incentive to stand on queue and wait. Indeed, any time a queue forms, all those in front of the last person to arrive have an incentive to leave and go about their other business, returning later when fewer people are likely to show up. In essence, the last-come, first-served mechanism design has removed the incentives for inefficient behavior artificially created by first-come, first-served. Customers do not inherently prefer to arrive early and peak-load their demands. Instead, it was the nonoptimal queue service rule that artificially created incentives to arrive early, stand around, and wait.

With last-come, first-served, in contrast, customers have an incentive to spread their arrivals throughout the ticket window's normal hours of operation. Once a more or less uniform distribution of customer arrivals throughout the day can be established, the ticket agency can adjust its capacity and set its service rate to deal with the steady stream of customers who arrive and purchase with no waiting.

EXAMPLE

CONTAINERIZED SHIPPING AT SEA-LAND

Historically, ocean shipping rates have been heavily regulated based on categories of cargo (e.g., paper, film, frozen fish) and shipping lanes (e.g., Rotterdam to New York, Liverpool to Jacksonville, Seoul to San Francisco). Conferences of ocean shipping companies announced common carrier shipping rates for first-come, first-served customers. More than half the world's cargo still moves under publicly mandated ocean shipping contracts at these uniform shipping rates. With no ability to adjust prices, salespeople maximized the volume of cargo. The only good ship was a full ship. Because empty slots on a container ship perish as a revenue opportunity the moment the ship sails and because a container ship such as the *Regina Maersk* has space above decks for more than 700 containers, shippers queued up large volumes of cargo in anticipation of each ship's departure. In this mechanism design, the customers' waiting time became a substantial implicit cost totaling millions of dollars a day that otherwise might have gone to the shipper as additional revenue.

Today, deregulation is fast approaching the ocean shipping industry, and a spot market auction for space in containerized ships has emerged. The immediate consequence has been the delaying of low-priority shipments such as rolls of newsprint from one voyage to the next in favor of higher-rate cargo such as perishable pharmaceuticals. In response to this new business environment, Sea-Land Service, Inc., of Charlotte, North Carolina, optimized the placement of their containers around the world. Each empty container at each freight terminal is assigned a forecasted net revenue opportunity at that location and at other potential locations along the shipping route. Shippers who offer less waiting time can charge higher rates; last-come, first-served policies may become widespread for certain high-margin cargo.

Few ticketing operations have adopted a last-come, first-served queue service rule. Under last-come, first-served, recall that any customer should leave the queue whenever a later arrival preempts his or her priority ranking as last in line. But customers will not wish to return many times to the ticket window. Again, time is money. So, customers ahead in line are likely to offer side payments to late arrivals to induce *them* to leave. Predictably those with the highest opportunity cost of time will end up bribing those with lower opportunity cost to leave and return.

The problem is that this side payment system again reduces the ticket agency's receipts because in many ways it has just replaced the inefficiency of arriving early and waiting with the inefficiency of arriving often, departing, and returning. The recipients of the side payments are no worse off because they voluntarily decide to leave and return later, but those who make the side payments now turn to the window and surely offer less than they otherwise would have paid to secure good seats. How can the ticket agency's mechanism design deal with this subtle complication?

Stratified Lotteries for Concerts

Lotteries and online auctions may hold the key to an effective mechanism design. Online sales are cheaper than phone sales because they require no operators and no toll-free line charges, if customers will accept an Internet or faxed ticket, thereby saving the ticketing agent's mailing expense. Only 1 in 10 live entertainment tickets are distributed online, but this channel is growing much faster than industry sales as a whole. Suppose rather than announcing in advance what position in the customer queue would be served first, the ticketing agency simply picked a position at random. In effect, that's exactly what a lottery for the right to purchase a ticket does. Anytime prior to the day of sale, a customer stops by an Internet Web site to pick up a lottery number.

EXAMPLE

Online Auctions and Stratified Lotteries at Ticketmaster[2]

Stratified Lottery
A randomized mechanism for allocating scarce capacity across demand segments.

Because those customers with low willingness to pay are equally likely to get the winning lottery numbers as those with high willingness to pay, Ticketmaster and other companies adopt a **stratified lottery** scheme. Rights to purchase high-price seats are distributed in one lottery, medium-price seats in another, and low-price seats in a third. At a designated date, the winning numbers are chosen at random and posted on the Web site and public-access TV channels. Only those customers holding the winning lottery numbers arrive to buy tickets, and because seat availability is assured, customers have no reason to arrive early, queue up, and wait. This lottery mechanism design does reduce waiting time while allowing the ticket agency to charge higher uniform prices for each class of seats.

Holding auctions online can present a conflict of interest with Ticketmaster's traditional business of adding a \$3 to \$5 convenience fee for computerized ticket distribution by mail and in music stores. As the exclusive ticketing agent for 70 million tickets worth \$3 billion, Ticketmaster is wary of reselling tickets above face value. The sports teams, concert halls, and promoters would then suspect Ticketmaster of underpricing the original tickets to charge convenience fees on not one but two sales.

[2] Based on "Ticket Scalpers Find a Home on the Web," *Wall Street Journal* (February 4, 1999), p. B1; "A Winning Ticket," *The Economist* (August 22, 1998), p. 52; S. Rosen and A. Rosenfeld, "Ticket Pricing," *Journal of Law and Economics* 40, no. 2 (1997), pp. 351–377; and "Don't Scalp Us. We'll Scalp You," *BusinessWeek* (April 19, 2004), p. 44.

Ticketmaster could, of course, simply defer to the arenas and promoters in setting the face value prices, but a better alternative may be available.

Ticketmaster and StubHub.com, are both conducting "official" Internet auctions for various sports teams. Last year, the New York Jets earned close to $100 million in auctioned ticket sales on behalf of season ticket holders, with most transactions occurring at about 30 percent over face value. The team takes approximately 10 percent of this "gate," and the rest goes to the season ticket holder. But what type of auction should Ticketmaster design?

AUCTIONS

TYPES OF AUCTIONS

Everything from *Monday Night Football* to mineral rights, forest land, airline tickets, used equipment, and the electromagnetic spectrum have been allocated to their highest valued use through auctions. The choices in auction design are numerous, as illustrated in Table 15A.1. Bidding can be *sequential* with rebid opportunities like most estate auctions or *simultaneous* as in the sealed-bid auctions for newly issued government debt securities. Bid prices can be *continuous* or constrained by *minimum discrete bid* improvements. The New York Stock Exchange recently switched to continuous decimalization of their auction prices from the one-eighth-tick size restrictions on minimum bid improvements. Bids may be *sealed,* revealed by *open outcry,* or *posted* anonymously as on eBay. Bidding can be *one-time only* or *dynamic,* repeated in multiple rounds with cancellation and amendment of prior bids allowed (so-called *open bidding*). Finally, owners can place a minimum reservation price (the "*reserve*"), below which the item will not sell, or allow an auction to proceed with *no minimum.*

Perhaps the most important design differences between major types of auctions are who pays, what amount, and how the winner is determined. In some auctions *all bidders pay* (e.g., on Priceline.com, credit card information must accompany all offers, and conceivably the seller could collect from all bidders if the prices were acceptable). Of course, most auctions adopt the *highest-wins-and-pays* allocation rule.

Table 15A.1 A Comparison of Auction Mechanism Design Characteristics

eBay	Priceline
Sequential	Simultaneous
Minimum bid improvement	Continuous
Posted prices	Posted offers to buy (reverse auction)
Multiple rounds	One-time-only if seller "hits"
Open bidding	Credit card immediately authorized
Reserve	No reserve
Highest wins and pays	All accepted bids pay
First (highest) price	Whatever price was bid
English ascending price	Dutch discriminatory descending price
Consolidated feedback on seller	Seller anonymous

What the winner pays (whether it is his or her own *highest bid* or, at times, the *second-highest bid*) and how the auctioneer arrives at the winning bid can differ. **English auctions** ascend to higher and higher prices with open outcry or posted bids until the last bidder to make an offer exceeding all other offers is declared the winner.

English Auction

An ascending price auction.

Dutch auctions work in the opposite direction by identifying the first bidder to register an acceptance as the auctioneer announces a succession of descending asking prices. The wholesale flower market in the Netherlands operates in this way, hence the term *Dutch auction*. In *ascending-price auctions* the winner takes all, but in *descending-price auctions* the winner is often given the opportunity to purchase less than the total capacity available for sale, and the auction then continues downward.

Dutch Auction

A descending price auction.

Which of these and other auction design characteristics maximize the revenue to the seller and which allocate resources to their highest-valued use are important business questions and public policy issues. One well-understood insight from mechanism design theory is that asymmetric information will lead to timid bidding in ascending price auctions because of the winner's curse. To illustrate the winner's curse, consider the following auction situation:[3] You are developing a bidding strategy for an asset whose value to the seller is a random variable distributed uniformly between \$0 and \$100. The seller observes this value and desires some profit on the transaction to cover the auction expenses, but places no minimum reservation price on the auction. You anticipate that a rational seller will refuse all offers below his or her personal value. The asset might be a baseball player's labor contract or a set of maps of the subterranean geological formations in a petroleum-rich area. Because of different complementary assets and skill, your value is certain to be 50 percent higher than the seller's personal asset value. What offer should you make?

Winner's Curse in Asymmetric Information Bidding Games

If neither party knows the true value, an expected value of \$50 plus a small premium (i.e., well below \$75) is a reasonable offer that will be accepted. However, if the seller knows the true value, consider what reasonable offers will be accepted and what reasonable offers will be refused. To simplify the analysis, suppose just three offers and three realizations of the seller's value are possible: \$0, \$55, and \$100. In Figure 15A.1, we see that should the true value be zero, only offers that overpay for the asset will be accepted. These payoffs are shown in the shaded boxes to the right of the decision tree. Should the true value be \$55, \$55 offers will be refused and again only \$100 offers that overpay (even relative to the \$75 value to the bidder) will be accepted (see the lowest boxed payoff). If the assets have the maximum possible value to the seller of \$100, offers of \$0, \$55, *and* \$100 will be refused. In short, all reasonable offers will be refused. Therefore, surprisingly, you should offer nothing at all! If you win such an auction, you are cursed with having overpaid for the asset. Welcome to the **winner's curse!**

Winner's Curse

Concern about overpaying as the highest bidder in an auction.

[3] Adapted from M. Bazeman and W. Samuelson, "I Won the Auction But Don't Want the Prize," *Journal of Conflict Resolution* (December 1983), pp. 618–634. See also R. McAfee and J. McMillan, "Auctions and Bidding," *Journal of Economic Literature* (September 1987), pp. 699–738.

Figure 15A.1 Winner's Curse in an Asymmetric Information Bidding Game

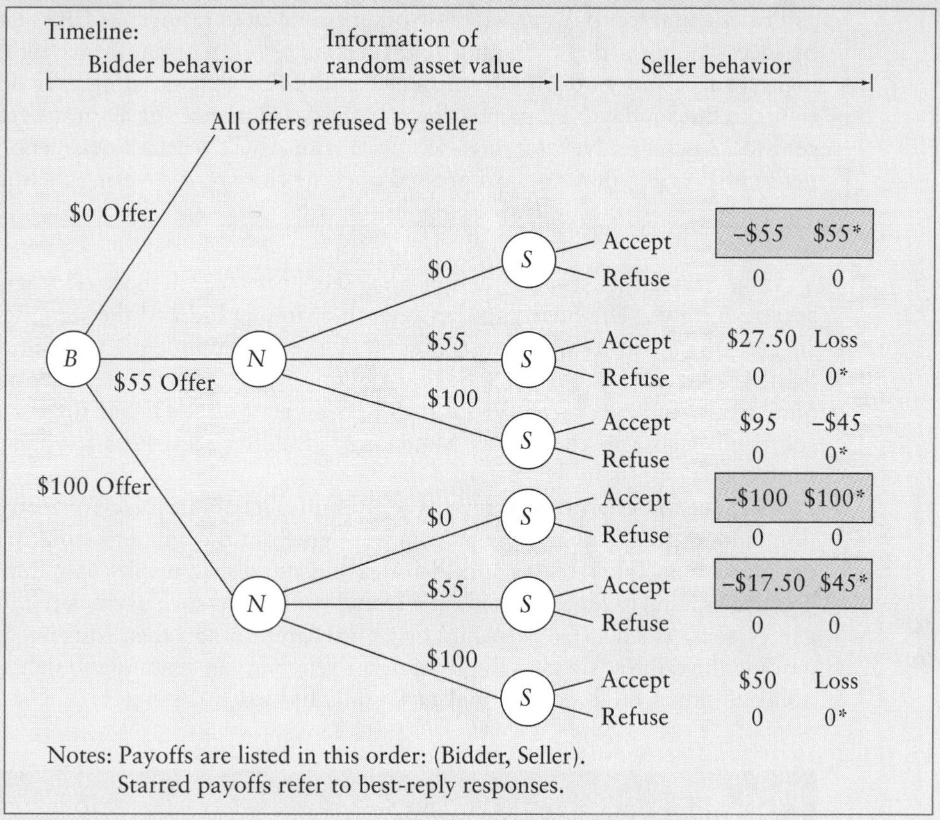

EXAMPLE

WINNER'S CURSE AT ESPN[4]

When bids for the right to televise *Monday Night Football* reached $4 billion for eight years (1998–2005), NBC decided that the winner would be cursed with losses of $150 million to $175 million per year and dropped out of the bidding. ABC continued bidding and eventually won the "prize" for $4.4 billion ($550 million per year). Because ABC had debuted this show and sold its ad slots for 30 years, they were in the best position to know its true value. Starting in the 2006 season, ESPN has agreed to pay almost twice as much ($1.1 billion per year) for the next eight years. ESPN hopes to garner sufficient revenue to break even from cable subscriber fees it charges Comcast and Time Warner as well as from the traditional advertising slots.

Viewership has tumbled 33 percent to 26 million since the peak interest in professional football in the early 1980s. Although the new television rights do allow for more TV time-outs in which to sell commercials, $50 million per three-hour game works out to eighty-four 15-second spots (28 per hour), each costing $600,000

[4] Based on "Thrown for a Loss by the NFL," *Time* (January 26, 1998), p. 52; "A Ball ESPN Couldn't Afford to Drop," *BusinessWeek* (May 2, 2005), p. 42; and "Marketers Rely on Oscar," *Wall Street Journal* (February 2), 2006, p. B3.

that will be required just to break even. By comparison, 15-second spots on the Oscars award show sell for $840,000 to reach 40 to 50 million viewers, and the Super Bowl with 90 million viewers sells for $1.25 million.

Professional football can increase other prime-time ratings, as CBS demonstrated by successfully shifting the Sunday *NFL Game of the Week* audience right into their highest-rated show *60 Minutes*. And when the Fox Broadcasting network won the rights to the Sunday NFL games, the *60 Minutes* audience share shrank from 30 percent to 22 percent. Nevertheless, we agree with ABC's recent assessment of the winner's curse. ESPN may be hard pressed to come close to recovering their investment.

Table 15A.2 lists several auction price sequences for offshore oil tracts and FCC spectrum rights. The huge gaps between the winning bid and the second highest bid suggest that a winner's curse was present. The winning bidder for offshore oil in the Santa Barbara channel paid $11.4 million more than the second highest bid. Similarly, Wireless Co. paid $12.2 million more than GTE bid for the cell phone spectrum license in the Dallas Metro area. Bidding sequences for star players in professional sports look similar.

Mechanism design theory reveals several insights about this asymmetric information bidding game. First, most bidders will figure out the winner's curse in an auction design such as Table 15A.2 and therefore bid timidly, if at all.[5] To induce more aggressive bidding in repeated, multiple-round versions of such asymmetric information games, sellers such as De Beers find they must carefully sort their rough-cut diamonds, grading them into "sights." Reputation for reliability in grading the sights more economically than the bidders could pick, cull, and resell the rejects is what brings De

Table 15A.2 Bids for Offshore Oil Contracts and FCC Spectrum Rights

Offshore Oil[a]		FCC Spectrum[b]		
Santa Barbara Channel	Alaska North Slope	Miami Metro Area	Dallas Metro Area	Bidder
$43.5	$10.5	$131.7	$84.2	Wireless Co.
32.1	5.2	126.0	72.0	GTE Inc.
18.1	2.1	125.5	68.7	Wireless Co.
10.2	1.4	119.4		
6.3	0.5	119.3		
	0.4	113.8		
		113.7		
		108.4		

[a]In millions, 1969 dollars.
[b]In millions, 1995 dollars.
Source: Adapted from Tables II and IV in R. Weber, "Making More for Less," *Journal of Economics and Management Strategy*, 6, no. 3 (Fall 1997), pp. 529–548.

[5] Notice that the same conclusion applies to a continuous-bid version of the auction, though experimental evidence suggests that most first-time players misperceive the asymmetric information nature of the seller's right of refusal and incorrectly bid $50 to $75. See C. Camerer, "Progress in Behavioral Game Theory," *Journal of Economic Perspectives* 11, no. 4 (Fall 1997), pp. 167–188.

Beers's buyers back, auction after auction. De Beers then has a minimum participation rule that insists on a certain number of bids if one wishes to be asked back.

Secondly, if the asymmetric information is discoverable by appraisals, marketing research, or other similar investments, another insight from auction design theory is that the seller should conduct a multiple-round auction with open bidding. Open bidding allows the bidders to react to asymmetric information revealed in prior rounds and therefore reduces the winner's curse. This idea was used by the Federal Communications Commission in the spectrum auctions for personal communication systems (PCS) such as cell phones, mobile fax and data service, and voice-mail pagers.

INFORMATION REVELATION IN COMMON-VALUE AUCTIONS

To illustrate this role of open bidding, consider two PCS bidders: Wireless Co., an alliance of Sprint and several large cable TV companies that spent $2.1 billion and won the rights to serve 145 million customers in 29 metropolitan service areas, and PCS PrimeCo, an alliance of three regional Bell companies that spent $1.1 billion and won the rights to serve 57 million customers in 11 metropolitan service areas. Several winning bids are listed in Table 15A.3. For example, Wireless paid $46.6 million for the Louisville, Kentucky, service area. How did Wireless decide what to bid?

Suppose that both bidders know that the net present value of the rights to transmit PCS services in Louisville is a random variable uniformly distributed from $10 million to $60 million with six discrete values possible—for example, $10 million, $20 million, $30 million, $40 million, $50 million, and $60 million. Also assume (provisionally) that both parties value the asset identically, a so-called **common-value auction.** The problem then from the bidders' point of view is to elicit sufficient information from the market environment and from the offers of other bidders to correctly identify the value and ensure a profit (i.e., not overpay for the asset). In advance, each company conducts marketing research experiments to narrow the possible outcomes and thereby better inform its own bid. Suppose Wireless Co.'s marketing research results are unable to exclude the two tails of the uniform distribution of possible values (i.e., $10 million and $60 million) but can exclude with certainty

Common-Value Auction

Auction where bidders have identical valuations when information is complete.

Table 15A.3 Winning Bids in Broadband PCS Auction

Market	Population[a]	Winner	Second Highest	Bid[b]	Price/Pop.
New York	26.4	Wireless	Alaacr	$442.7	$16.76
San Francisco	11.9	PacTel	AmerPort	$202.2	$17.00
Charlotte	9.8	BellSouth	CCI	$70.9	$7.27
Dallas	9.7	Wireless	GTE	$84.2	$8.68
Houston	5.2	PrimeCo.	Wireless	$82.7	$15.93
New Orleans	4.9	PrimeCo.	Powertel	$89.5	$18.17
Louisville	3.6	Wireless	PrimeCo.	$46.6	$13.10
Salt Lake City	2.6	Wireless	GTE	$46.2	$17.95
Jacksonville	2.3	PrimeCo.	GTE	$44.5	$19.56

[a]In millions from the 1990 census.
[b]Price paid for 30 MHz Block B spectrum rights, March 1995.
Source: P. Cramton, "The FCC Spectrum Auctions," *Journal of Economics and Management Strategy*, 6, no. 3 (Fall 1997), pp. 431–496.

\$20 million and \$30 million as well as \$50 million. Taken by itself, this information allows Wireless to narrow its probability assessments to \$10 million, \$40 million, and \$60 million.

Weighting each outcome equally yields an expected value bid of \$36.7 million as follows:

$$\frac{1}{3}(\$10 \text{ million}) + \frac{1}{3}(\$40 \text{ million}) + \frac{1}{3}(\$60 \text{ million}) = \$36.7 \text{ million}$$

Similarly, PCS PrimeCo conducts its own marketing research which, let's assume, excludes \$10 million, \$30 million, and \$50 million as possible outcomes for the Louisville service area. That is, PCS PrimeCo has access to separate information that causes it to calculate a different expected value bid:[6]

$$\frac{1}{3}(\$20 \text{ million}) + \frac{1}{3}(\$40 \text{ million}) + \frac{1}{3}(\$60 \text{ million}) = \$40 \text{ million}$$

These best estimates of the common value are based on the asymmetric information available to the two firms. Consequently, in a simultaneous sealed-bid auction, the most a seller could hope to realize is \$40 million. With sealed bids, no information is conveyed to the competitor, and an optimal bidding strategy is therefore simply to shade your bid slightly below the Bayesian expected value based on your own information set. PCS PrimeCo would therefore bid something just under \$40 (\$39.6) million and win the spectrum rights for the Louisville service area.

Bayesian Strategy with Open Bidding Design

Notice, however, from the seller's point of view *ex post facto* (after receiving the sealed bids) that the joint information set of the two parties suggests PCS PrimeCo has underpaid. To review, the union of the two sets of marketing research outcomes excludes \$10 million, \$20 million, \$30 million, and \$50 million. Said another way, the *combined* marketing research results have narrowed the possible outcomes for the value of the Louisville service area to \$40 million and \$60 million. Neither firm has access to this much information. Each simply knows a subset of all the marketing research available. But as a seller in such a setting, the FCC wishes to elicit full revelation of *all* asymmetric information because it affects the winning bid.

[6] The equally weighted probabilities of 1/3 are actually Bayesian probabilities of each possible remaining value based on a perfectly accurate forecast that \$10 million, \$30 million, and \$50 million (the prime numbers in the set of possible asset values) have been ruled out. It is helpful if we think of the marketing research as identifying Prime and Not Prime numbers between 1 and 6 multiplied by 1 million. Then, the Bayesian probability (\$20 million/Perfect Forecast of Not Prime) $= (0.167 \times 1.0)/[0.167 + (0.833 \times 0.4)] = 0.33$ where 0.167 is the prior probability before the marketing research is conducted that \$20 million will be the realized asset value. The number 1.0 is the accuracy of the forecasting instrument; for example, the conditional probability that when \$20 million is the true value, the conclusion from the marketing research will be that the value is Not Prime, meaning "not a prime number between 1 and 6." The number 0.833 is the prior probability that the asset value will be something other than \$20 million. And finally, the number 0.4 is the probability that when something other than \$20 million is the true asset value, the perfectly accurate forecasting instrument will still say Not Prime. That happens with \$40 million and \$60 million (i.e., twice in five possibilities).

The analysis here is easily modified to incorporate less than perfect forecasts from the marketing research, which is helpful because imperfect forecasts are the reality of business. See E. Rasmussen, *Games and Information*, 3rd ed. (Cambridge: Basil Blackwell, 2001), Chapter 13, Section 5.

If \$40 million and \$60 million are equally likely, and the bidders can somehow discern this information, the Louisville service area is worth just under \$50 million, not PCS PrimeCo's bid of just under \$40 million.

One way to bring all the asymmetric information into play is to adopt a sequential open-bidding auction design in which each company is chosen at random to post its bid (in one round, then the random order of posting procedure is redone for Round 2, Round 3, etc.).[7] Then, whichever company bids first, the other company will deduce the first bidder's additional marketing research results and proceed to increase its bid in light of the more complete information available. For example, if PCS PrimeCo bids first, and bids \$40 million based on its own asymmetric information, Wireless Co. will then be in a position to deduce that PCS PrimeCo's marketing research excluded \$10 million, \$30 million, and \$50 million as possible values. That's the only information that would be consistent with a bid of \$40 million in a simultaneous sealed-bid auction over an asset with a uniform distribution from \$10 million to \$60 million with only these six possible outcomes. Knowing from its own marketing research that \$20 million, \$30 million, and \$50 million have also been ruled out, Wireless will immediately place a winning bid of just under \$50 million:

$$\frac{1}{2}(\$40 \text{ million}) + \frac{1}{2}(\$60 \text{ million}) = \$50 \text{ million}$$

With many more than these two bidders and other service areas in which Wireless Co. would be required to bid first and in which PCS PrimeCo had a turn playing the fast second, this sequential open-bidding auction design would work well. Winning bids would rise to the Bayesian expected asset values reflecting all available information, and highest-value users would receive the assets.

EXAMPLE

Open Bidding Simultaneous Auction of PCS Spectrum Rights[8]

Thirty firms ultimately participated in the broadband spectrum auctions. The FCC specified two 30-MHz blocks for each of 51 metropolitan service areas. A special feature of these metropolitan service areas was strong interdependencies in providing service in contiguous service areas. Bidders were encouraged therefore to assemble and reassemble efficient bundles of licenses as the auction progressed. Consequently, the FCC adopted multiple-round simultaneous auctions with open bidding to allocate spectrum rights. Each bidder was told there would be several rounds of bidding, all bids in each round were announced, and each bidder was allowed to cancel or amend bids from round to round. All bids in every metro area remained open as long as any bidding activity continued in any service area. The auction lasted 112 rounds over a four-month period. Using this auction design, the FCC raised \$7.7 billion. AT&T paid \$49.3 million and Wireless Co. paid \$46.6 million for the A block and B block spectrum rights in Louisville.

[7] Open bidding with a nonrandom, structured sequence of role reversals on multiple auctions allows bidders to signal and punish one another (tit for tat) and therefore increases the likelihood of tacit collusion.

[8] Based on "Market Design and the Spectrum Auctions," *Journal of Economics and Management Strategy* 6, no. 3 (Fall 1997); and "Sale of Wireless Frequencies," *Wall Street Journal* (March 25, 1998), p. A3.

STRATEGIC UNDERBIDDING IN PRIVATE-VALUE AUCTIONS[9]

Private-Value Auction
Auction where the bidders have different valuations when information is complete.

One serious drawback of English open outcry auctions is the strategic reticence (tendency to underbid) that bidders exhibit. If the bidders have common information but different valuations (i.e., a so-called **private-value auction**), those with high willingness to pay have an incentive to refrain from aggressive bidding in an attempt to just exceed the bid of the player with the second highest valuation. For example, in the FCC's spectrum auctions, the cellular phone incumbents already established in a metropolitan area had higher valuation than other bidders. In the early rounds of any such open bidding auction over private values, eventual high bidders hold back. Analysis of the FCC data suggests only 53 percent of the eventual winners were the high bidders after the early rounds. Sellers worry that this strategic reticence dampens the overall level of bidding throughout the auction and may well reduce final revenue.

Suppose two bidders each value a service or asset between \$0 million and \$10 million. No information about the actual net present values is known. That is, no common-value information, asymmetric or otherwise, is available. In this purely private-value auction that lasts only one round, the bids are sealed, and the highest bid wins. Your valuation is \$6 million. What should you bid?

With two bidders present, each must assume that the other will offer something less than his or her private value, say $k \times v$ where k is a proportion and v is the private value.[10] Any bids by Alice (P_a) that are greater than k times Bob's value (v_b) will win. That is, anytime $P_a/k > v_b$, Alice wins the auction and realizes a profit of $v_a - P_a$. With uniform density, the probability that Bob's value is any given number between \$0 and \$10 million is 1/10 million. Again, Alice wins when this value is between \$0 and P_a/k dollars. Therefore, Alice's cumulative probability of winning is P_a/k events, each of which has a marginal probability of 1/10 million; that is, Alice's cumulative probability of winning is $P_a/(k \times (10 \text{ million})$. Alice's expected profit from the auction may therefore be written as follows:

$$\text{E}(\text{Profit}_a) = (v_a - P_a)\frac{P_a}{k \cdot 10{,}000{,}000} \qquad [15\text{A}.1]$$

Differentiating Equation 15A.1 with respect to P_a and setting the derivative equal to zero, Alice's expected profit from the auction is maximized when

$$(v_a - 2P_a)\frac{1}{k \cdot 10{,}000{,}000} = 0 \qquad [15\text{A}.2]$$

that is, when $P_a = v_a/2$. Alice maximizes her expected profit from participating in the auction, conditional on Bob's choosing a kv_b bidding rule, by choosing to reduce her own private value by 1/2. Because Alice and Bob are symmetrically situated in this bidding game, Bob too should reduce his private value by 1/2. With $k = 1/2$, the players are in a Nash equilibrium. Each maximizes self-interest, conditional on the other player's bidding $v/2$, by bidding half of his or her own private value. In a two-player, simultaneous, highest-price-wins-and-pays sealed-bid auction, the rational underbidding is fully 50 percent!

[9] Two excellent elaborations of this and the next topic are J. McMillan, "Bidding in Competition," *Games, Strategies, and Managers* (New York: Oxford University Press, 1992), Chapter 11; and E. Rasmussen, "Auctions," *Games and Information*, 2nd ed. (Cambridge, MA: Basil Blackwell, 1993), Chapter 12.

[10] This example relies on McMillan, *op. cit.*, pp. 138, 208–209.

Figure 15A.2 Strategic Underbidding Declines and Seller Revenue Rises with Bidder Entry in Private-Value Auctions

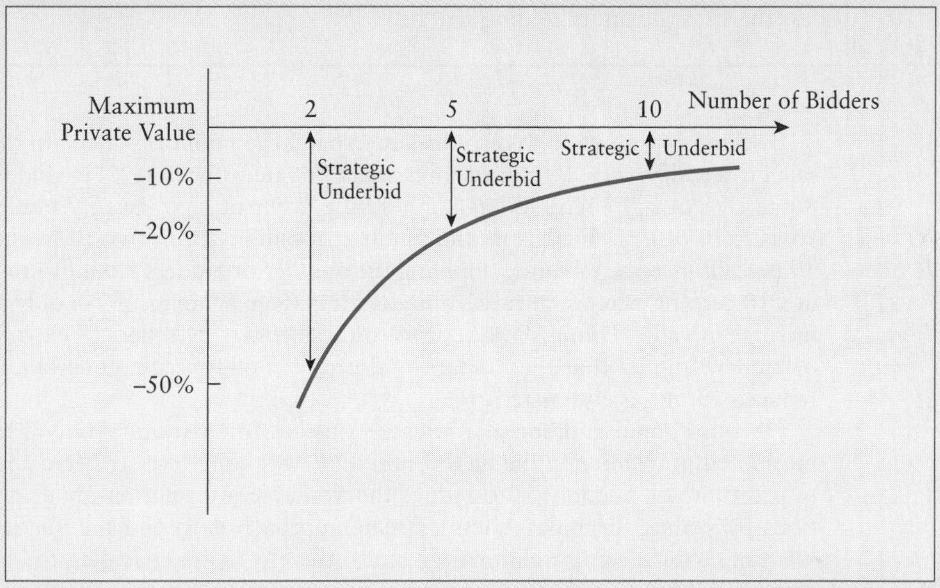

In the case of five bidders, it is easy to show that a rational bidder should reduce true private value by 1/5, and if *n* bidders, by 1/*n*.[11] Quite intuitively, therefore, the more bidders, the smaller is the rational underbidding. See Figure 15A.2. Sellers understand this reasoning and therefore provide sorting services (in De Beers's case) and handsome catalogs and live exhibitions (in Christie's case) to draw bidders into the auction process. Paul Klemperer of Oxford University describes how this fundamental insight determined many of the auction design decisions for the British spectrum auctions. Thirteen different companies entered the bidding, resulting in the highest per-capita revenue raised by all the European and Asian 3G auctions.

EXAMPLE

EXPONENTIAL VALLEY INC. AUCTIONS A CHIP PATENT[12]

Exponential Valley Inc., a Silicon Valley microprocessor start-up, decided to auction its portfolio of 45 issued and pending patents rather than move into production. The computer chip patents include features that would allow a competitor to match forthcoming chip products from industry leader Intel Corp. Intel regularly sues companies who make clones of their chips and has been effective in deterring entry with this strategy. The Exponential Valley patents appear to offer an opportunity

[11] See Rasmussen, *op. cit.*, p. 296; and Paul Klemperer, "Spectrum Auctions," *European Economic Review* 46 (2002), pp. 829–845.

[12] Based on "An Auction of Chip Patents May Ignite Bidding War," *Wall Street Journal* (August 1, 1997), p. B5.

to provide protection from Intel's patent infringement suits. At considerable expense, Exponential developed a large prospectus of technical and bidding information that it targeted to possible bidders: AMD, Chromatic Research Inc., and Texas Instruments. Exponential Valley did so because the larger the number of bidders, the less the strategic underbidding will be.

If sellers expend enough resources to expand the pool of bidders, in the limit the seller can realize $(n - 1)/n$ of the maximum private value (v_{max}). Five bidders implies 80 percent of v_{max}. Ten bidders implies 90 percent of v_{max}. Twenty bidders implies 95 percent of v_{max}. Increasing the number of bidders from two to five results in a 30 percent increase in value, doubling the number of bidders from five to ten results in a 10 percent increase in value, and doubling them again results in only a 5 percent increase in value. Diminishing returns to these efforts by sellers to expand the pool of bidders implies that the fundamental problem of strategic underbidding will be reduced but never eliminated.

Of course, underbidding in a private-value auction is rational only if bidders can be assured of winning in the final round. One way to reduce strategic underbidding in private-value auctions is to reduce the available information about other valuations by sealing the bids. A less extreme approach is to end the auction without warning, after several preliminary rounds, thereby in effect sealing the bids unpredictably. Of course, as we saw in the previous section, it can be in the seller's interest to induce the revelation of all asymmetric information. In fact, sellers often have an incentive to preannounce expert appraisals of value (as Christie's and Sotheby's auction houses do) in order to reduce the winner's curse.

This concern is important in auction design, but not always controlling. The reason is that some asymmetrically held information can, if revealed, lower the rational bid (see the first Case Exercise at the end of this appendix). So, sealing bids is a design alternative that becomes more attractive the greater the variation in private values and the more symmetric the information pertaining to valuation among the bidders. Obviously, open bidding or preannouncing appraisals is more attractive whenever favorable information is known to the seller. However, even when the seller is in the dark, open bidding has a positive expected value for the seller because the exchange of common-value information always reduces the winner's curse.

Second-Highest Sealed-Bid Auctions: A Revelation Mechanism

Incentive-Compatible Revelation Mechanism

A procedure for eliciting true revelation of privately-held information from agents with competing interests.

Strategic underbidding is especially troubling, of course, if the seller is collecting bid revenue from all participants in the auction. A "seller" may be attempting to assess whether buyer willingness to pay justifies investment in a new facility (e.g., a ballpark, a pool, a set of tennis courts, or a clubhouse). Each potential user is asked what he or she would pay for access. If sufficient demand exists, the facility manager then builds the facility and collects the highly divergent, discriminatory prices from each "bidder." The key to such an assessment is designing an **incentive-compatible revelation mechanism.** The same thing is true in designing a private-value auction. If, as an auction designer, one could remove the incentive to underbid and at the same time prevent a winner's curse, one could align incentives with true revelation of value. Think through the following illustration of an ingenious incentive-compatible auction mechanism that won William Vickery the Nobel prize![13]

Following Vickery, rather than requiring the winning bidder to pay the high bid, what if the auction mechanism design specified in advance that the highest bid wins but that the winner would pay the second-highest bid? Notice that the winner's curse is no longer present. By definition, under the rules of a highest-pays-second-highest sealed-bid auction, the payment triggered by bidding one's true private value cannot exceed the next best alternative selling price. This use of a verifiable second opinion and exit option to shore up the bidder's protection from suffering a winner's curse was the key insight of William Vickery's incentive-compatible mechanism design. True revelation of maximum willingness to pay proves compatible, through an ingenious mechanism design, with the bidder's desire to avoid the winner's curse.

Vickery Auction

An incentive-compatible revelation mechanism for drawing out sealed bids equal to private value.

To sum up, no bidder in a **Vickery auction** has any incentive to underbid. Reducing your bid below your private value has no effect on the payment due should you win. Instead, underbidding in a second-highest sealed-bid auction when you are the highest-willingness-to-pay participant simply increases the probability of losing an auction asset that it would have been possible to acquire for less than it is worth to you. And if someone else values the asset more than you, no payment is triggered by bidding up to your own private value. Therefore, for all possible cases, true revelation of private value dominates underbidding as a bidding strategy. And because bids are sealed and the auction lasts only one round, no strategic bidding, false carding, or signaling can have any effect on other participants in the auction. Therefore, No Underbidding is a dominant strategy equilibrium for all bidders.[14] Of course, realized revenue is still reduced by the full difference between highest and second-highest valuations, but at least the seller learns the true value of the auctioned asset.

EXAMPLE

SECOND-HIGHEST SEALED-BID AUCTION: U.S. TREASURY BILLS[15]

Auction design decisions in security markets focus (appropriately) on which auction mechanisms raise the most revenue for the issuers. On this question, debate currently rages about the optimal design of Treasury bill new-issue security auctions. Denmark and Sweden adopted diametrically opposed designs. The Swedes sell government bills and bonds at discriminatory Dutch auction prices; the Danes sell at a uniform second-highest sealed-bid price. Given this diversity of expert opinion and practice, the U.S. Federal Reserve authorized the New York Federal Reserve Bank to experiment with both designs for two-year and five-year notes. Most Treasury auctions in the United States (and indeed around the world) are discriminatory descending-price (Dutch) auctions; buyers pay whatever they bid for quantities of

[13] Every game theory and mechanism design theory book describes the Vickery auction, also known as the second-highest sealed-bid auction, or the uniform price auction. Vickery's original article is also revealing and insightful; see W. Vickery, "Counterspeculation, Auctions, and Competitive Sealed Tenders," *Journal of Finance* 16, no. 8 (1961), p. 37.

[14] The bidder's degree of risk aversion has no bearing on this result. However, more risk-averse bidders do ensure against losing in winner-take-all first-price sealed-bid auctions by increasing their bid relative to the seller revenue from a second-highest sealed-bid auction. We discuss the role of risk aversion further in the next section.

[15] Based on "Bidding Up Debt Auctions," *BusinessWeek* (September 8, 1997), p. 26; and S. Nandi, "Treasury Auctions: What Do the Recent Models and Results Tell Us?" *Federal Reserve Bank of Atlanta Economic Review* (Fourth Quarter 1997).

T-bonds along a demand schedule submitted by each bidder. If the market-clearing price implies a yield of 5.03 percent, a typical bidder may get $5 million worth of T-bonds at her highest submitted price yielding 5.00 percent, $7 million worth of T-bonds at a lower price yielding 5.02 percent, and perhaps another $10 million at the market-clearing (lowest) price yielding 5.03 percent.

Uniform price second-highest sealed-bid auctions are different. Every bidder in this Vickery auction might pay the uniform-slightly-higher price associated with a yield of 5.02 percent, and the Treasury's marginal cost of raising debt capital will decline from 5.03 percent to 5.02 percent. However, some still higher-priced transactions no longer take place, and other lower-price transactions also no longer take place. Therefore it is unclear analytically what will happen to Treasury revenue; it depends on the interest rate elasticity of T-bill demand. The recent Vickery auction experiments have raised nearly identical revenue to the traditional Treasury auction methods.

This result highlights the insight that the principal advantages of second-highest sealed-bid Vickery auctions are not to raise seller revenue, but rather to minimize strategic underbidding, reveal true private valuations, and reduce bidder collusion among small numbers of bidders. In contrast, security markets are highly efficient, with numerous potential buyers willing to pay a common value for these T-bond and T-bill assets. Therefore, second-highest sealed-bid mechanism design is more appropriate for the private placement IPO market employed in the Google IPO. In sum, combining managerial insight about auction design with a careful analysis of the particulars of the business setting is important.

Revenue Equivalence of Alternative Auction Types[16]

Under particular circumstances, the four simplest types of auctions (English ascending price, Dutch descending uniform price, first-price sealed-bid, and highest pays second-highest sealed bid) yield equivalent revenue to the seller-auctioneer. For example, both first-price sealed-bid auction participants and Dutch descending uniform price auction participants must pay whatever they bid if their bids prove to be the winning market-clearing bids. In addition, participants in both types have no access to information about bidders with lesser valuations than themselves. Consequently, the optimal bidding strategy in a Dutch or first-price sealed-bid auction is identical, and thus the winning bids will be identical (see Table 15A.4).

Similarly, for private-value auctions, as English auction participants learn more and more in the course of the bidding about the independent valuations of other bidders, the person with the highest valuation will ultimately offer an amount just in excess of the second highest bidder. Second-highest sealed bid auctions induce, as we have seen, true revelation of value from all bidders, but the winner also pays an amount just equal to the second highest bidder. Hence, an English ascending price auction and a second-highest sealed bid auction yield essentially the same expected revenue to the seller in private-value auctions. Indeed, it turns out that with risk-neutral bidders and private values, all four simple auction types result in the same expected revenue (i.e., an amount just equal to the highest value minus the full

[16] For a more extensive discussion of this topic, see A. Dixit and S. Skeath, *Games of Strategy* (New York: Norton, 1999), Chapter 15; and E. Rasmussen, *op. cit.*, Chapter 12.

Table 15A.4 Seller Expected Revenue from Auction Types

	Private-Value Auctions (Patent License, Sales Territory, Estate Antiques)			
Risk-Neutral Bidders	Dutch = Uniform Price	First-Price = Sealed-Bid	English =	Second-Highest Sealed-Bid
Risk-Averse Bidders	Dutch = Uniform Price	First-Price > Sealed-Bid	English =	Second-Highest Sealed-Bid
	Common-Value Auctions (Mineral Lease, Logging Rights, Aircraft)			
Risk-Neutral Bidders	English >	Second-Highest > Sealed-Bid	Dutch = Uniform Price	First-Price Sealed-Bid
Risk-Averse Bidders	English >	Second-Highest ≷ Sealed-Bid	Dutch = Uniform Price	First-Price Sealed-Bid

difference to the next highest bid). From a seller's perspective this revenue equivalence theorem (RET) is a depressing result; one would hope to do better.

In several instances, one auction type does raise more expected revenue than another. These optimal mechanism design differences depend upon the risk preference of the bidders and upon the common-value or private-value nature of the item being auctioned. Continuing first with the private-value auctions, if bidders are risk averse and they are operating under the lack of information of a Dutch or first-place sealed-bid design, they will seek to reduce the probability of losing the item when their valuation is highest. Consequently, relative to the situation in an English or second-highest sealed-bid auction in which the winning bidder pays essentially the second highest bid, risk-averse Dutch or first-price sealed-bid auction participants raise their bids in order to reduce the probability of being outbid by a close second valuation. Strategic underbidding to avoid the winner's curse is still present but it is mitigated by risk aversion. So, a seller-auctioneer can raise more revenue on average when the bidders are risk averse and the values are independent and private by conducting a Dutch or first-price sealed-bid auction. These results for private-value auctions for items such as patent licenses, sales territories, antiques, and fine art are summarized in the top section of Table 15A.4.

As to common-value auctions for items that have thick resale markets such as crude oil, mineral leases, forest logging rights, equity and debt securities, and easily redeployable surplus equipment such as commercial aircraft, the source of uncertainty in the valuation is an estimation risk. Every bidder knows that the true value at resale is identical across all auction participants; it's just that this true value is an unknown while the oil is still in the ground, the logs still in the forest, the IPOs yet unissued, and so on. Each bidder must therefore assess this true value from his or her own forecast information in a Dutch uniform price or first-price sealed-bid auction and from any additional information that can be gleaned from the sequence of bids in the English auction. The Bayesian updating of the initial estimates (the "priors") in the sequential process of an English auction will tend to result in a pooling of the bidders' information; therefore, winning bids in the English auction will tend toward the mean estimate of the population of forecasts. Mechanisms which facilitate the learning of this best unbiased estimate of what the harvestable common value of the resource truly is reduce strategic underbidding to avoid the winner's curse.

Hence, as shown in the bottom section of Table 15A.4, a seller-auctioneer can raise the most revenue with an English common-value auction. And as we saw in the previous section, second-highest sealed-bid designs can also substantially reduce the winner's curse in these common-value auctions, raising the seller's projected revenue. For common-value auctions, these results go through whether bidders are risk neutral or not.[17]

EXAMPLE

Internet Auction Design Becomes a Big E-Business Debate: eBay Versus Priceline[18]

Online auctions experienced a truly explosive rate of Internet site development and attracted tremendous investor interest. Eight sites existed in July 1998; 400 existed in July 1999, and more than 3,000 sites existed in July 2000. Some of the sites issued public shares and realized massive equity market value. By 2005, eBay Inc. reached 150 million listings. Shortly after its initial public offering in 2000, Priceline exceeded the *combined* market value of the major airlines (American, Delta, United) whose unsold last-minute tickets it offered to liquidate.

In the information economy, online auctions are a key business model that may displace the two traditional price-setting processes: (1) one-on-one negotiation (haggling) and (2) a menu of fixed price quotes provided by the seller. Business-to-business (B2B) transactions may continue to require one-on-one negotiation over the time, quality, availability, and delivery dimensions of the "deal," but in business-to-consumer transactions, auction prices themselves establish most of what is needed for a "deal."

Between 2000 and 2002, however, Priceline's share price fell 90 percent. For one thing, Priceline failed to secure a broad patent for its reverse auction design. Public commentary suggests Priceline's patents will not protect the company from subsequent imitators. Priceline employs an ascending-posted-price highest-wins-and-pays auction mechanism design. Bids are listed anonymously to reduce collusion and posted continuously to mitigate the strategic underbidding that accompanies any private-value auction (i.e., the winner's curse). Bid payments must be guaranteed with a credit card at the time the buyers' offers are placed; subsequently, bids cannot be cancelled and are executed automatically if the offer is accepted.

eBay has a more transparent ascending-price auction design with posted-prices and highest-wins-and-pays rules for declaring a winner. Rather than allowing sellers to remain anonymous until they decide to "hit" a Priceline buyer's posted offer, eBay consolidates feedback on the seller's past performance and hot-links it to the bidding site. Also unlike Priceline, eBay allows open bidding (i.e., offers are repeated in multiple rounds, and prior offers may be cancelled or amended). If open bidding proves to be optimal for auctioning airline tickets, automobiles, and machinery, eBay rather than Priceline will thrive.

[17] Risk aversion introduces the same complication into the analysis as earlier; that is, Dutch uniform price and first-price sealed-bid participants raise their bids to reduce the probability of losing an item to a close second competitor. Still, the benefits of information pooling tend to favor English or second-highest sealed-bid designs for common-value auctions.

[18] Based on "The Heyday of the Auction," *The Economist* (July 24, 1999), pp. 67–68; "Redesigning Business: Priceline," *Harvard Business Review* (November/December 1999), pp. 19–21; "Dotty about dot.commerce?" *The Economist* (February 26, 2000), p. 24; "Going, Going, Gone, Sucker!" *BusinessWeek* (March 20, 2000), pp. 124–125; and "Inside: Is Priceline Vulnerable?" *Harvard Business Review* (December 3, 1999), pp. 19–21.

A still larger auction design issue is whether to continue the traditional ascending-price (English) auction or adopt descending-price (Dutch) auction procedures. Basement.com and OutletZoo.com start prices high and drop them in increments until all the units for sale have been demanded. Clearly, sellers can realize more revenue in discriminatory Dutch auctions by charging differentially higher prices to the early bidders than can be realized in uniform-price Dutch or English auctions that identify a market-clearing price. Of course, sophisticated institutional and industrial buyers understand this concept as well, and this segment may well prefer a traditional nonauction Web site such as Grainger.com where sellers post initial best offers and then focus on availability, delivery, installation, technical support, and other after-sale services. Establishing the value-in-use of these extras in the "total offering" may prove as critical as seller warranties and replacement guarantees to B2B customers.[19]

Contractual Approaches to Asymmetric Information in Online Auctions

In some ways Priceline.com is like couponing without the brand name as a guarantee of redemption security. Priceline's mechanism design does provide a way to price discriminate to the price-sensitive customer segments without degrading one's brand identity. Perhaps this explains why Delta Air Lines took a substantial equity stake in Priceline; Delta could liquidate its inventory without cannibalizing higher fare sales. But anonymous sellers offering unverifiable product or service claims on Priceline must credibly commit to higher quality products if they hope to attract anything more than rock-bottom prices. As we have seen, hostage or bonding mechanisms are the key to credible commitments.

Appraisal
An estimate of value by an independent expert.

First, sellers can invest in and disseminate **appraisals** to try to distinguish their auction offerings from fraudulently advertised products. Independent certified appraisals, such as buy-back guarantees, place a floor under the value of the product offered for sale. Perhaps a tract of development land or the intellectual property in a patent lease is up for bids; the seller can pay for an appraisal about the range of values typically paid in resale markets for land or intellectual property assets with similar characteristics. Two drawbacks prevent the widespread adoption of this approach, however. Certified appraisals are expensive, and appraisals seldom establish maximum or unique asset value.

The second contractual approach sellers can adopt to establish credibility for their auction claims is to signal their respective quality by offering *warranties and replacement guarantees*. These signaling features of the product offering are observable to the buyer at the point of sale and are highly correlated with the unobservable product or service quality at issue. Automobile tire manufacturers who take shortcuts vulcanizing the tire casings that embed steel wire belts in their tire treads will make shorter treadware warranties and provide guarantees against fewer blowout hazards. The buyer can therefore pay more for warranted tires and feel confident that the tire quality is above that offered by nonwarranted suppliers. Encouraging buyers to screen alternate suppliers in this way therefore achieves a separating equilibrium to the asymmetric information exchange that would be more costly for sellers to secure through independent appraisal of each potential tire.

[19] See Ajit Kambil and Eric van Heck, *Making Markets* (Boston: HBS Press, 2002); James Anderson and James Narus, *Business Market Management* (New York: Prentice Hall, 1999); and R. Oliva, "Sold on Reverse Auctions," *Marketing Management* (March/April 2003), p. 45.

Another way for sellers to credibly commit to the delivery of a high-quality durable product is to offer to lease rather than sell the product and then to accept *lease terms with a high residual value.* This feature of leasing offers a net advantage over buying in that sellers with informational advantages will credibly commit to forward value through the take-back provisions of the lease. If one seller says you can lease with a 60 percent residual at the end of 4 years and another quotes a 40 percent residual at the end of 4 years, all other things the same, the lease payments will recover depreciation only two thirds as great in the 60 percent residual lease. In that case, buyers may well be willing to lease a higher quality/higher priced product. Of course, such an approach to establishing credibility will not be adopted if sellers foresee substantial obsolescence risk. Therefore, high residuals seldom occur alone; usually other lease terms (e.g., financing charges, initial asset prices, or lease closing fees) adjust upward to "price in" the extra seller risk when residuals increase.

Contingent Payments
A fee schedule conditional on the outcome of uncertain future events.

Finally, sellers can agree to accept **contingent payments**—that is, seller revenue dependent on the performance the buyer experiences. Suppose the due diligence required to establish clear value in an asset sale is prohibitively expensive. If a tract of development land has buried fuel tanks that are unknown to the seller but that necessitate substantial environmental remediation, the land seller can agree *ex ante* to pay for the restoration of the land. If timberland sales or oil field leases prove particularly productive, the buyer and seller can agree to larger money payments than if the actual harvested timber and oil pumped prove disappointing.

These contingent payment contracts can be arranged as progress payments, so that the buyer and seller take small and continuous steps away from one another while money remains owed. Sometimes corporations employ contingent payments while exchanging hostages in an asset sale by requiring the seller to take a financial stake (perhaps 15 percent of the cash flow to equity owners) in the buyer's subsidiary spun off to manage the new assets. Given the low priority of an equity owner should the spin-off declare bankruptcy and need to liquidate, contingency payments increase the seller's incentives to reveal hidden features that determine the true cash flows realizable from the asset.

Incentive-Compatible Revelation Mechanisms

Perhaps the most powerful mechanism design tool for drawing out privately held asymmetric information is William Vickery's self-enforcing revelation mechanism. Later, Edward Clarke and Ted Groves added the idea of multiple agents in group decision making such that the mechanism design objective became demand or cost revelation in a partnership that had to be compatible with the incentives of all the parties: an incentive-compatible (IC) revelation mechanism.

EXAMPLE

Intel and Analog Inc. Form Partnership to Develop DSP Chip[20]

Intel Corp. has dominated the manufacture of semiconductor chips for computer microprocessors for more than a decade. With AMD and Siemens beginning to pose some threat in this traditional market, Intel formed a joint venture in 1999 with Analog Devices Inc. to move into the chip market for communications devices such

[20] Based on Intel Corporation and Analog Design Inc. joint press releases (February 3, 1999); and "TI Lays Out DSP Plans Until 2010," *Hardware Reviews and News* on the The-View.com (December 6, 1999).

as cell phones, pagers, and wireless videophones. Intel and Analog jointly developed a new line of digital signal processor (DSP) chips. DSP chips take analog signals like voice, photo images, and video and convert them to digital signals to be transmitted over wireless systems. Given the enormous growth in wireless communications, new signal compression and encryption capabilities of the Intel-Analog chip are expected to compete well against rival DSP suppliers Texas Instruments (TI) and Lucent Technologies. DSP chips also appear to have application in modems and other networking devices that provide high-speed access to the Internet. Speech recognition systems for machine-controlled applications are a complementary value-adding technology. By 2010, DSP chips will provide the functionality of a laptop computer on a thumbtack that fits into wristwatch-size devices. DSP chip sales growth has recently approached 30 percent per year, reaching total sales of $5.7 billion.

Groups of Intel and Analog engineers will collaborate on designing the core architecture of the chip, and the two companies will then separately develop and sell products based on the design. The contingent payoffs to each firm are therefore based in part on their cooperative design success and in part on their separate product development and marketing efforts. This joint venture contract provides incentives for continuing cooperation far beyond those generated by a simple profit-sharing agreement, yet it preserves each company's option to pursue some business plans privately.

COST REVELATION IN JOINT VENTURES AND PARTNERSHIPS

When pivotal information in such partnerships is privately held and verification by third parties is infeasible or undesirable, the partners seek to adopt procedures to assure true revelation of this asymmetric information. Consider a joint venture to develop several new personal computer products between a PC designer-manufacturer, such as Apple Computer, and Motorola, a leading supplier of computer chips.[21] The Apple operating system depends on the capabilities of the Motorola chips, and the chips are produced in anticipation of the future requirements of the operating system. The partners believe they can better sustain a competitive advantage in this fast-moving technology by jointly developing new products. After the joint venture covers development and production costs, they agree to split the profits equally.

Each partner in the joint venture has private information about cost to which the other partner does not have access. For example, as it develops the Power PC, Apple knows its operating system development costs, and Motorola knows its computer chip design and production costs. Although neither can independently verify the other partner's asymmetric information, the success of a joint venture often depends on each partner's ability to generate enough operating profits to recover development costs. Determining profit potential requires an accurate revelation of true costs. Let's see why and what can be done to achieve this goal.

[21] The general structure of this section relies on A. Dixit and B. Nalebuff, *Thinking Strategically* (New York: Norton, 1991), pp. 306–319. The illustration here is based on "Apple Wants Other PC Makers to Build Computers to Use Macintosh Software," *Wall Street Journal* (January 28, 1994), p. B5; and "IBM, Apple in PC Design Accord," *Wall Street Journal* (November 8, 1994), p. B5.

The study of incentive-compatible revelation mechanisms can provide some answers. Each partner faces random disturbances in its cost factors.[22] Sometimes software development is delayed by inconspicuous but debilitating bugs in the programming, which increase the cost from, say, \$80 to \$120 million. Similarly, sometimes chip development and production necessitates redesign (e.g., Intel's problems with the Pentium chip), increasing that cost from, say, \$50 to \$70 million. Neither partner can hope to discover and rectify all such problems in advance. However, each can detect early warning signals of cost overruns and, if need be, cancel that particular one of their several joint projects.

Cost Overruns with Simple Profit-Sharing Partnerships

When both cost overruns happen simultaneously, the product development joint venture should shut down, because the variable costs of proceeding to full-scale production (\$120 million + \$70 million) will exceed the projected revenue available, say, \$180 million. These projected operating profits and losses appear in Table 15A.5. If Apple experiences \$120 million cost (the column labeled High Costs), the partnership will cancel the project whenever Motorola also experiences high cost of \$70 million (the row labeled High Costs) because proceeding would result in a \$10-million operating loss. By the same token, when only one partner or neither partner experiences high costs, the joint venture project should go forward and realize profits of \$30 million, \$10 million, and \$50 million, respectively. Only with correct operate and shutdown decisions can the joint venture generate its maximum value.

The incentive problem is that initially each partner has an incentive to overstate true costs in order to be overcompensated from the joint venture revenues. For example, in Table 15A.5, if Apple reveals true costs of \$80 million and Motorola claims costs of \$70 million when in fact its true costs are \$50 million, Motorola's joint profit share declines by \$10 million from one half of \$50 million (top left cell) to one half of \$30 million (lower left cell). But with \$20 million extra reimbursement from overstating its cost, Motorola ends up with (1/2) \$30 million + \$20 million, which exceeds one half of \$50 million by \$10 million. Similarly, if Apple overstates its costs, the Apple profit share falls from \$25 million to \$5 million, but this decline is more than offset by the \$40 million extra reimbursement for overstating its \$80 million actual cost to \$120 million.

Table 15A.5 Joint Profits (in Millions) from a Simple Profit-Sharing Partnership with \$180 Million in Revenue

		Apple	
		Low Costs (\$80)	High Costs (\$120)
Motorola	Low Costs (\$50)	\$50	\$10
	High Costs (\$70)	\$30	−\$10

[22] Similar arguments can be made about asymmetric information regarding random disturbances in demand.

If low cost and cost overruns are equally likely at Motorola and if the probability of a cost overrun at Apple is 0.3, then expected costs are \$60 million at Motorola and \$92 million at Apple. With true revelation of costs, expected net profit from the joint venture is then (0.5 × 0.7) \$50 million + (0.5 × 0.3) \$10 million + (0.5 × 0.7) \$30 million + (0.5 × 0.3) \$0 = \$29.5 million, or \$14.75 million for each partner.[23] However, if one or both partners overstate costs, the projects with mixed costs in the southwest and northeast cells of Table 15A.5 will also be canceled, and the expected net profit from the joint venture then declines. For example, if Apple falsely reveals \$120 million when low costs of \$80 million are present, the joint development project is canceled whenever Motorola experiences \$70 million cost. This cancellation results in the partners forgoing the \$30 million profit on the mixed cost project in the southwest cell and reduces the expected value of the joint venture to \$19 million (i.e., \$9.5 million per partner).[24] Value-maximizing managers facing asymmetric information seek some revelation mechanism that will provide appropriate incentives to induce the revelation of true costs, thereby preserving and capturing the full \$14.75-million-per-partner expected value of both the low cost and the mixed cost projects.

CLARKE-GROVES INCENTIVE-COMPATIBLE REVELATION MECHANISM

One such revelation mechanism is known as the Clarke tax mechanism.[25] Edward Clarke's path-breaking idea was that to create appropriate incentives for asymmetric cost (or demand) revelation in a partnership, each party's revelation should trigger an imposition of the expected costs on (and the forgone profit opportunity losses suffered by) the other partners. In this way, the maximizing incentives of each of the asymmetrically informed partners could be made compatible. For our PC product development example, Table 15A.6 indicates the revenue shares each partner would

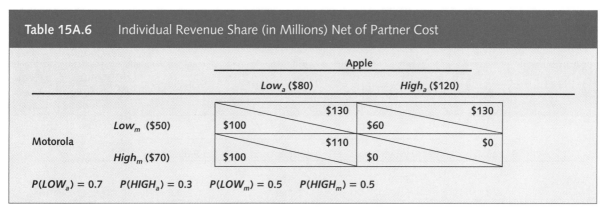

Table 15A.6 Individual Revenue Share (in Millions) Net of Partner Cost

		Apple	
		Low$_a$ (\$80)	*High$_a$* (\$120)
Motorola	*Low$_m$* (\$50)	\$100 / \$130	\$60 / \$130
	High$_m$ (\$70)	\$100 / \$110	\$0 / \$0

P(LOW$_a$) = 0.7   *P(HIGH$_a$)* = 0.3   *P(LOW$_m$)* = 0.5   *P(HIGH$_m$)* = 0.5

Note: Column-player payoffs are above diagonal. Row-player payoffs are below diagonal.

[23] Note that the project in the southeast cell of Table 15A.5 is canceled because of mutual early warnings of high cost and therefore a projected operating loss.

[24] This expected value is calculated as (0.5 × 0.7) \$50 million + (0.5 × 0.3) \$10 million = \$19 million.

[25] This revelation mechanism is also referred to as the Clarke-Groves revelation mechanism after Ted Groves, who formalized the concept, thereby showing a different connection to William Vickery's earlier work on incentive-compatible auction design.

receive under a Clarke tax mechanism. The row player Motorola gets the below-diagonal payoffs in each cell, and the column player Apple gets the above-diagonal payoffs in each cell.

After the other party's expected costs are covered, each partner's payoff is then recalculated as the residual or net revenue share from all noncanceled projects triggered by its own cost revelations. To illustrate, if Motorola reveals Low_m cost, the current project will proceed independent of Apple's cost, and Motorola will realize \$88 million, which is \$180 million total partnership revenue minus the \$92 million expected cost of Apple:

$$\begin{aligned}&\text{Expected Net Revenue Share (Low for Motorola)}\\&= \$180 \text{ million} - (0.7 \times \$80 \text{ million}) + (0.3 \times \$120 \text{ million})\\&= \$88 \text{ million}\end{aligned}$$

This figure appears in the third column of Table 15A.7. However, if Motorola announces $High_m$ cost, the project is canceled whenever Apple detects early warning signs that its own cost is $High_a$. Consequently, should Motorola decide to reveal high cost when low cost is present, its net revenue would fall from \$88 million to 0.7 (\$180 million − \$80 million) + 0.0 (\$180 million − \$120 million) = \$70 million, also listed in the third (Net Revenue Shares) column of Table 15A.7. Motorola's net revenue share declines because of a zero probability of realizing the \$60 million revenue share in the northeast cell of Table 15A.6. The false overstatement of cost by Motorola results in that project being canceled, and everyone loses. Under a Clarke tax mechanism, not just actions but information revelations themselves have consequences. And, as we shall see, these consequences can induce the true revelation of partnership costs.

The importance of the discovery of such incentive-compatible revelation mechanisms can hardly be overemphasized; they have led to many path-breaking private sector and public policy applications. Clarke first developed the concept in the context of the true demand revelations needed in consumption partnerships to

Table 15A.7 Expected Net Profit Shares (in Millions) with True Cost Revelation Under an Optimal Incentives Contract

		Apple		
	Probability	Net Revenue Shares	Expected Costs	Net Profit Shares
Low_a	0.7	\$120	\$80	\$28
$High_a$	0.3	\$ 65	\$60	\$ 1.5
		\$103.5	\$74	\$29.5

		Motorola		
	Probability	Net Revenue Shares	Expected Costs	Net Profit Shares
Low_m	0.5	\$88	\$50	\$19
$High_m$	0.5	\$70	\$49	\$10.5
		\$79	\$49.5	\$29.5

INTERNATIONAL PERSPECTIVES

JOINT VENTURE IN MEMORY CHIPS: IBM, SIEMENS, AND TOSHIBA[26]

IBM once entered into an agreement with Siemens and Toshiba to coproduce computer memory chips. At the same time, AMD and Intel announced similar joint ventures to develop flash memory chips with Fujitsu and Sharp, respectively. Flash chips retain the information needed to restart computer operating systems when the power is interrupted. In all three cases, the Japanese firm will contribute its superior manufacturing capability, and the American and German firms will contribute their design and innovative research capabilities.

The key question in such joint ventures is whether the Western companies will simply give away their technological knowledge while their Japanese partners deliver little asymmetric information in exchange. To ensure an evenly balanced partnership, the manufacturing know-how of the Japanese will be dissected as production cost information under various market conditions to be revealed and analyzed by the joint venture partners.

[26] Based on "Pragmatism Wins as Rivals Start to Cooperate on Memory Chips," *Wall Street Journal* (July 14, 1993), p. B1.

finance a jointly consumed park, pool, or playground.[27] The demand revelation problem in assessing an optimal tax share in a consumption partnership is analogous to the cost revelation problem in assessing an optimal profit share in a business partnership.

AN OPTIMAL INCENTIVES CONTRACT

Optimal Incentives Contract
An agreement about payoffs and penalties that creates appropriate incentives.

Self-Enforcing Reliance Relationship
A noncontractual, mutually beneficial agreement.

To organize a joint venture or partnership around a Clarke-Groves revelation mechanism usually involves the implementation of a so-called **optimal incentives contract.** Each party agrees in advance to a set of partnership net revenue shares associated with the expected payoffs from a revelation mechanism (see the third column of Table 15A.7). The important thing to appreciate is that the problem of independently verifying asymmetric information has not gone away. A third party attempting to enforce the contract (e.g., a U.S. district court) would still have just as much trouble verifying the claims for cost reimbursement arising under this contract as the parties had in trying to verify their own partner's cost. Entering into a partnership incentives contract does not define away the asymmetric information problem. Instead, the revelation mechanism creates incentives for a **self-enforcing reliance relationship** between the partners, not unlike the incentive-compatibility constraint we described in Chapter 15 as characterizing the optimal incentives contract between owner-principals and manager-agents.

[27] To build the appropriate size urban park or swimming pool requires private information about use value and willingness to pay. However, if one asks potential demanders who assume their answer will determine their tax share, the respondents will understate their willingness to pay. See Edward Clarke, *Demand Revelation and the Provision of Public Goods* (Boston: Ballinger, 1980). For more on the applications of revelation mechanisms, see R. Cornes and T. Sandler, "Clarke's Demand-Revealing Mechanism," *Theory of Externalities, Public Goods, and Club Goods* (New York: Cambridge University Press, 1986), pp. 105–108; Hal Varian, *Intermediate Microeconomics* (New York: Norton, 1999), pp. 622–627.

The structure of incentives underlying Table 15A.7 is fully capable of inducing the partners to reveal their true costs; each would be worse off not doing so. We have already seen how Motorola would be worse off overstating its cost. Similarly, if Apple were to overstate its cost, profitable projects in the southwest cell of Table 15A.6 would be canceled. Rather than realizing 0.5 ($130 million) + 0.5 ($110 million) = $120 million from the good fortune of incurring Low_a cost, Apple would instead realize only 0.5 ($130 million) = $65 million, which fails to cover its own low-cost realization of $80 million. In addition, this false overstatement of cost and the cancellation of the profitable project in the southwest cell reduces Apple's expected receipts from the partnership to just (0.5 × 0.7) $130 million + (0.5 × 0.3) $130 million = $65 million, whereas with true revelation it realizes $103.5 million: (0.5 × 0.7) $130 million + (0.5 × 0.7) $110 million + (0.5 × 0.3) $130 million = 0.7 ($120 million) + 0.3 ($65 million) = $103.5 million. Truth-telling dominates false revelation for both partners.

We can now also explain why both Apple and Motorola would adopt an optimal incentives contract that credibly commits each partner to a true revelation of asymmetric cost information. Apple realizes an expected net profit with true revelation of $103.5 million expected receipts minus expected costs of $74 million (i.e., $29.5 million), shown in the last column of Table 15A.7. And similarly, Motorola realizes an expected net profit of $79 million expected receipts minus $49.5 million expected costs (i.e., $29.5 million). Each of these amounts equals the $29.5 million joint profits potentially available in the original simple profit-sharing contract of Table 15A.5. However, recall that each party knows in advance that the other party will have private information about cost overruns. Each could therefore predict that the simple profit-sharing partnership would lead to cost overstatement, cancellation of the mixed cost projects, and loss of value. This proactive reasoning implies that only the mutual low-cost outcome in Table 15A.5 will escape cancellation and actually generate profit. Therefore, only a much smaller expected profit—that is, just 0.5 × 0.7 ($50 million) = $17.5 million—is assured by the simple profit-sharing contract. This smaller amount from simple profit sharing is what rational parties choosing among partnership contracts would compare to the $29.5 million expected net profit from an optimal incentives contract.

The application of incentive-compatible revelation mechanisms and optimal incentives contracts has led to many exciting new types of asymmetric information partnerships. The same principles also underlie support the concept of an efficient breach of contract in the economics of contract law. When one partner breaches a contractual relationship, the legal remedies take into account the opportunities forgone and expectation damage costs imposed on the partner who does not breach.[28] These concepts have become a key for achieving partnership or joint venture success in both small firms and large corporations under asymmetric information.

Implementation of IC Contracts

Incentive-compatible contracts are implemented with contingent claims contracting, a standard form instrument for sophisticated business attorneys. The parties agree on the projected probabilities for the various levels of cost, the likely auditable joint operating profit for the partnership, and the unobservable reimbursable cost to each

[28] A good supplemental reading on efficient breach of contracts is R. Cooter and T. Ulen, *Law and Economics, 4th ed.* (Glenview, IL: Pearson Addison-Wesley, 2003).

INTERNATIONAL PERSPECTIVES

WHIRLPOOL'S JOINT VENTURE IN APPLIANCES IMPROVES UPON MAYTAG'S OUTRIGHT PURCHASE OF HOOVER[29]

Sometimes joint ventures are designed to increase the value of assets sold through a phased partnership rather than an immediate sale. As a potential buyer of Philips' European appliance division, Whirlpool sought access to more private information than due diligence by its merger and acquisition attorneys could uncover. Philips had a consumer franchise of nine appliance brands and a pan-European network of retail dealers who were second only to Electrolux in market share. But like other intangible assets (e.g., pivotal human resources and technical know-how), brands and distribution relationships are notoriously hard to value. In a new corporate organization and culture, could the Philips brands be redeployed without Philips' extremely strong reputation in European electronics? Would the fragmented network of independent dealers remain loyal once Whirlpool's name was substituted for Philips? And most important, what cost savings could be realized by sourcing all of the design, procurement, and production of Whirlpool and Philips components globally to achieve economies of scale?

These questions were best answered by a joint venture in which Philips retained a 47 percent ownership stake, and Whirlpool immediately assumed management control in exchange for $381 million. After both parties shared cost and demand information for three years and fully assessed potential value, the remainder of the business was sold to Whirlpool for $610 million.

In contrast, Maytag satisfied its strategic plan to enter the European market by purchasing outright Chicago Pacific Corporation, whose Hoover Appliance division had a substantial retail dealer network in Britain. However, Maytag knew little about the growing retail power of superstore chains near British shopping malls and still less about the marketing research on British households. Consequently, Maytag stumbled from one promotional blunder to another and eventually sold the Hoover European subsidiary at a $130 million loss. Again, with carefully designed incentives, a joint venture could have elicited the revelation of valuable asymmetric information for greater success of Maytag's European initiative.

[29] Based on A. Nanda and P. Williamson, "Use Joint Ventures to Ease the Pain of Restructuring," *Harvard Business Review* (November/December 1995), pp. 119–128.

party in each contingency. These agreements form the contract expectations and define the contract damages should unforeseen events induce either party to breach the contract.

The information revelation leads to cancellation or go-ahead decisions. More generally, of course, consequences other than project cancellation versus go-ahead can result from the information revelation of one partner. The information revealed can cause an expansion or contraction of the efforts (R&D efforts, prototype development efforts, marketing research efforts, etc.) of the other partner. And a revelation of misinformation fails to maximize what both can agree in advance would be the optimal course of action in each contingent state. It is those losses that the Clarke tax mechanism then deducts from joint profits to find IC contract receipts. This process, of course, can prove quite a bit more complicated than the preceding example suggests; it presents a big challenge for the negotiating team of corporate attorneys.

In addition, you may have already noticed one further issue. The sum of the individual net revenue shares in every cell of Table 15A.7 where the project goes ahead is greater than $180 million, the projected operating profit from the partnership. Thus, IC revelation mechanisms generally "break the budget." Specifically, if both parties declare high cost, each is entitled to an IC payout ($100 million in the case of Motorola and $130 million in the case of Apple) that together break the budget. To emphasize the generality of this result, the particular example has been constructed to exhibit "budget breaking" in each contingent event, except cancellation. More typically, some cells would exhibit surplus, and others would exhibit deficit. Still, the deficit cells may arise first. What is the partnership to do? What implementation procedure can handle this deficit budgeting problem?

Recall that both partners have substantially greater net profit shares under the IC contract ($29.5 million) than the expected profit from a simple profit-sharing agreement ($17.5 million). Eliciting true information revelation really does have value, and both parties therefore would be willing to make *ex ante* commitments to cover such a deficit. Examining the third column of Table 15A.7 shows that Apple's expected net revenue share is $103.5 million, while Motorola's is $79 million. Consequently, $182.5 − $180 = $2.5 million per period (perhaps 2.5/0.05 = $50 million as a capital sum to cover the perpetual expected deficit) must be posted as a bond to implement the procedure. Each partner would be asked to establish credible commitment to the IC contract partnership by investing $25 million *ex ante* to achieve an increase in expected profit of $12 million ($29.5 − $17.5) per period.[30] Although complicated, these IC contracts clearly make sense for value-maximizing managers.

[30] Technically, the investment to cover projected deficits will change an individual household's behavior unless we impose the restriction of quasi-linear preferences. In company settings, this assumption is plausible; see Varian, *op.cit.*, pp. 274–277.

SUMMARY

- First-come, first-served is a mechanism design for servicing a queue that reduces seller revenue because of predictable congestions and expected waiting time. Last-come, first-served introduces leave-and-return transaction costs and therefore also reduces seller revenue.
- Stratified lotteries and auctions can relieve congestion and reduce transaction costs in the queue, raising seller revenue.
- Auction design choices are multifaceted but at the simplest level always include who pays, what amount, and how the winner is determined. Simple auction types are English ascending price auctions, Dutch descending price auctions, first-price sealed-bid auctions, and second-highest sealed-bid auctions.
- Auctions also differ in the resale opportunities available to the participants. Common-value auctions have thick resale markets where the items can be easily resold at a consensual fair market value. Private-value auction items have no common resale value and instead involve assets with differing valuations to the auction participants.
- The winner's curse implies that strategic underbidding is rational when the seller or other buyers have asymmetrically advantaged information about a common-value auction.
- Open bidding is a procedure for posting the offers in multiple rounds with cancellation and modification privileges to induce auction participants to pool their information about estimates of value. Open bidding reduces the winner's curse and raises expected auction revenue in common-value auctions.
- What simple auction types raise the greatest expected revenue for the seller-auctioneer depends upon the common-value or private-value nature of the item being auctioned and on the auction participants' risk aversion.
- Dutch auctions and first-price sealed-bid auctions have identical information structures and identical bidding strategies, and therefore they generate identical expected revenue to the seller.

- Relative to Dutch or first-price sealed-bid auctions, English ascending price and second-highest sealed-bid auctions raise the seller's expected revenue in common-value auctions for items such as crude oil, forest logging rights, and aircraft because they encourage the most pooling of bidder information. In private-value auctions, bidders who are risk averse offer higher bids and therefore generate more auctioneer-seller revenue in Dutch and first-price sealed-bid auctions.
- To escape adverse selection and elicit high-quality auction goods necessitates some sort of bonding mechanism to induce *self-enforcing reliance relationships* between buyers and sellers. Warranties, independent appraisals, leases with a high residual, collateral, irrevocable money-back guarantees, contingent payments, and brand names all provide assurance to buyers that the seller will not misrepresent the product quality. Such hostage mechanisms support asymmetric information exchange.
- Joint ventures and partnerships face an asymmetric information problem in reimbursing each member for privately known costs that are unverifiable. In both demand revelation problems for funding public goods and *cost revelation problems* for partnerships, each member has an initial incentive to falsely reveal (overstate) his or her private (cost) information.
- Both understatement of demand and overstatement of cost result in the cancellation of profitable partnership projects. Yet, each individual member may be better off with exaggerated cost reimbursement than with a simple profit share. Preserving the maximum value of the partnership requires an *incentive-compatible revelation mechanism.*
- Under an incentive-compatible (IC) mechanism, cost revelations incur the expected costs imposed on and opportunities forgone by the other partners. Each partner agrees that not just actions, but information revelations themselves, have consequences for profit-share payout. Such a governance mechanism must be self-enforcing, however, because the asymmetric information problem has not disappeared. A court would have just as much trouble verifying the claims for reimbursement under this incentives contract as it would under the initial simple profit-sharing contract.
- Incentive-compatible revelation mechanisms do motivate partners to reveal their true projections of costs.
- IC revelation mechanisms are implemented through contingent claims contracts and often require *ex ante* posting of a bond to solve the breaking-of-the-budget problem. Quasi-linear preferences are then required to assure a unique Clarke-Groves revelation mechanism solution for individual households. Business firms would, however, meet this condition without quasi-linear preferences.

Exercises

Answers to the exercises in blue can be found in Appendix C at the back of the book.

1. What auction design features reduce the winner's curse and therefore reduce strategic underbidding?
2. Why don't airlines and hotel chains worry about self-destructive cannibalization of their own higher-priced live sales when they list seats and rooms for sale in the virtual marketplace on Priceline.com?
3. What advantage does eBay's open bidding provide to sellers? Why?
4. Which two of the following are most clearly common-value auction items: Viper sports cars, electricity, patent licenses, T-bills, antiques, or fine art?
5. If some auction participants for crude oil field leases have estimates that the oil in the ground is worth \$1.2 million, \$1.3 million, or \$1.5 million with certainty; and other auction participants have estimates that the same oil field lease is worth \$1.1 million, \$1.3 million, or \$1.5 million with certainty; and a third group of auction participants have estimates that the same oil field lease is worth \$1.1 million, \$1.2 million, or \$1.3 million, and all three forecasts contain the true common value, what is that value? How would you as auctioneer-seller design an auction to reduce strategic underbidding and realize this true value?
6. Distinguish common-value and private-value auctions; provide examples of each. Distinguish descending price (Dutch) auctions and ascending price (English) auctions; provide examples of each.
7. You are developing a bidding strategy for an ascending price sealed-bid auction of a crude oil field worth between \$1 million and \$51 million to the seller. Because your extraction costs are lower, your value is 20 percent greater than the seller's value. The

seller faces transaction costs of conducting the sale and therefore will not accept an offer unless it exceeds her personal value. How much should you bid?

8. How can a second-highest sealed-bid ascending price auction design diminish the "winner's curse" and reduce the strategic underbidding that arises in highest-wins-and-pays typical ascending price auctions with sealed bids?
9. Some newly issued T-bills are auctioned by discriminatory pricing in Dutch auctions, whereas other newly issued T-bills are auctioned by uniform prices second-highest sealed-bid ascending price auctions. Which auction design is more like private placement of corporate newly issued bonds and IPO stock? Which auction design is more likely to increase seller revenue?
10. Fast Second and Speedo are trying to decide what to bid for a license in a cellular phone auction where the possible values of the new license are \$10 million, \$20 million, \$30 million, \$40 million, \$50 million, and \$60 million, each equally likely. The auction is single-round sequential, both parties have exactly the same value for the asset but neither knows its true value from the possible distribution (i.e., a so-called common-value auction), and Fast Second gets to bid after Speedo.

    Each company has invested in marketing research about the value of the license, which can come out one of two ways: possible values of \$20, \$30, or \$50 million, or possible values of \$20, \$40, or \$60 million. Whichever result arises is known to be 100 percent accurate (i.e., the license is worth one of the three identified amounts with certainty). Speedo proceeds with a bid of \$33 million. Fast Second has marketing research saying that the value of the license is \$20, \$40, or \$60. How much should Fast Second bid?

    Set up the Bayesian probability rule for Fast Second of BAYES PROB (\$40 million value/Forecast of \$33 million bid by Speedo).
11. Show that not just overstatement but also understatement of cost is dominated by truth-telling in the joint venture of Motorola and Apple.
12. What payoffs would be required under an optimal incentives contract, similar to Table 15A.7, if the cost overruns at Apple became as likely as those at Motorola?

Discussion Question

1. In this appendix we have assumed bidder's valuations are independent, but suppose they are affiliated. That is, suppose on eBay you wish to learn more about what a particular item is worth (a Beatles album) or you wish to affiliate with those who think Beatles albums are valuable, and that affects your own personal valuation. How will this change from independent to affiliated valuations affect bidding strategy on eBay? Do you observe such behavior on the site?

Case Exercises

Spectrum Auction

Continuing the analysis of broadband spectrum auctions from the appendix, suppose that two bidders know that the net present value of the rights to transmit PCS services in Louisville is a random variable uniformly distributed from \$10 million to \$60 million with six discrete values possible: \$10 million, \$20 million, \$30 million, \$40 million, \$50 million, and \$60 million. Also assume that both parties value the asset identically, making it a common-value auction. In advance, each company conducts marketing research experiments to narrow the possible outcomes and thereby better inform its own bid. Suppose Wireless Co.'s marketing research results exclude the two tails of the uniform distribution of possible values (i.e., \$10 million and \$60 million) as well as \$40 million. Similarly, PCS PrimeCo conducts its own marketing research that excludes \$10 million, \$30 million, and \$50 million as possible outcomes for the Louisville service area.

QUESTIONS

1. What should Wireless Co. bid in a single-round sealed-bid common-value auction? What should PCS PrimeCo bid in this same auction?
2. If Wireless goes first in a sequential posted price auction with multiple rounds to follow, what should PCS PrimeCo respond in Round 2? In Round 3, will Wireless then wish to amend its earlier bid? Why or why not?
3. What auction design would be in the seller's best interest: single-round sealed-bid or multiple-round open bidding?
4. Identify other factors that could affect the optimal auction design.

DEBUGGING COMPUTER SOFTWARE: INTEL[31]

Debugging has been a way of life in the computer industry from its inception. Indeed, the origin of the term *debugging* derives from the daily process of removing dead moths from the thousands of electronic tubes in the ENIAC, the first electronic computer. Every piece of computer hardware or software ever shipped has likely had logic faults. Indeed, most popular software programs contained thousands of known "bugs" in their first-generation products. In 1994, incomplete debugging of the floating point division calculator in the Pentium I computer chip caused a massive product recall that cost Intel \$475 million dollars.

Why do computer component manufacturers release products with known bugs? One obvious answer is that delayed release may allow competitors to preempt the market with new technologies that render your product obsolete. Another important answer is a central insight of managerial economics that everything worth doing is not necessarily worth doing well. Computer design and manufacturing firms face a rising marginal cost of correcting thousands of bugs detected by their beta testing process. At some point, each firm must balance the lost sales and replacement costs from product recalls against the ever-increasing cost of design perfection from continuously more debugging.

A somewhat surprising third answer may, however, hold the key; fixing bugs in subsequent generations of software sells upgrades. Early Microsoft Windows products had a nasty bug that caused the program to crash with the finality of a hopeless error message—"unrecoverable application error." Microsoft fixed the bug and proceeded to sell millions of copies of the upgrade. Bugs in programs limit their durability, and in technology businesses the selling of upgrades is a part of the business plan.

QUESTION

1. Discuss the practice of selling upgrades (sometimes called "versioning") as a mechanism design. What objective is being served? How well will this approach work, in the long run?

[31] Based on "It's Not a Bug, It's a Feature," *Forbes* (February 13, 1995), p. 192.

CHAPTER 16

Government Regulation

CHAPTER PREVIEW Managerial decisions designed to maximize shareholder wealth face many constraints. Some of these constraints arise from a business's moral social responsibilities. Other constraints take the form of laws or other legal obligations. A wide array of government regulations are constraining (e.g., prohibiting collusion) but in other cases enabling (e.g., protecting trade secrets). To make value-maximizing decisions, managers must fully understand the regulatory aspects of their environment. This chapter explores several types of regulatory issues: antitrust, business permits, licensing and patents, and a market-based approach to environmental regulation.

MANAGERIAL CHALLENGE

Deregulation and the Coase Theorem

Professor Ronald Coase from the University of Chicago Law School received the Nobel Prize in Economics for his work on the relationship among property rights, transaction costs, and the role of government. Coase challenged the prevailing view that economic externalities, such as water, air, and noise pollution, could only be resolved through governmental action. Coase argued that externalities should often not be viewed as one party inflicting harm on another. For example, a factory might use the surrounding buildings to absorb noise from its production process. The owners of a nearby amusement park might desire less noise so that they could attract more tourists.

Coase claimed that such reciprocal externalities could be resolved without government intervention if the transaction costs of arriving at a private voluntary bargaining solution were kept low. He argued the issue was one of the appropriate specification and assignment of property rights. For example, planes landing at Logan airport in Boston might need to avoid violating a sensible decibel level entitlement assigned to property owners in Winthrop and Revere surrounding the airport. Otherwise, damage claims would arise, and monetary compensation or other noise proofing settlements would be awarded.

In air pollution control, this Coasian approach to allocating "rights to pollute" has been adopted

MANAGERIAL CHALLENGE

on a widespread basis. Under the conditions of the Clean Air Act, the Environmental Protection Agency (EPA) grants allowances for about 50 percent of the sulfur dioxide emissions from electric utility plants. Congress then gave polluters the right to trade these pollution allowances among themselves. For example, if one firm already has emission levels at its plants that are within EPA bounds, it can sell its excess allowances. Other firms that do not meet the emissions standards can choose either to buy the pollution rights at a market price, or to install the needed pollution control equipment—whichever is cheaper. The Chicago Board of Trade quickly created a market on which these pollution allowances are actively traded. Take a look at the auction prices for sulfur dioxide allowances (a component of acid rain) at http://www.epa.gov/airmarkets.

The view of government regulation of business is changing. Interest in allowing market forces to operate in a constrained environment rather than relying on detailed regulatory commands continues to grow. Deregulation of most aspects of the transportation industries is complete; natural gas pipelines and telephone companies have been greatly deregulated; and the electric utility industry is moving toward deregulation. Greater deregulation will open new opportunities for future managers and confront them with new challenges.

THE REGULATION OF MARKET STRUCTURE AND CONDUCT

Antitrust regulation is designed to increase competition by eliminating attempts to monopolize an industry, as well as by attacking certain patterns of anticompetitive conduct, such as price fixing and exclusionary contracts, that are believed to have harmful effects on markets.

MARKET PERFORMANCE

Ultimately what society would like from the producers of goods and services is a multidimensional performance concept that includes these elements:

1. Resources should be allocated in an *efficient* manner, sometimes labeled static efficiency.
2. Producers should be *technologically progressive;* that is, they should attempt to develop and quickly adopt new techniques that will result in lower costs, improved quality, or a greater diversity of better products.
3. Producers should operate in a manner that encourages *full employment* of productive resources, including human capital.

MARKET CONDUCT

A structure-conduct-performance model of the factors that influence market performance is illustrated in Figure 16.1. Market performance is dependent on the conduct of firms in their

1. *Pricing behavior*
2. *Product policy*
3. *Sales promotion and advertising policy*
4. *Research, development, and innovation strategies*

Figure 16.1 A Conceptual Market Structure-Conduct-Performance Model

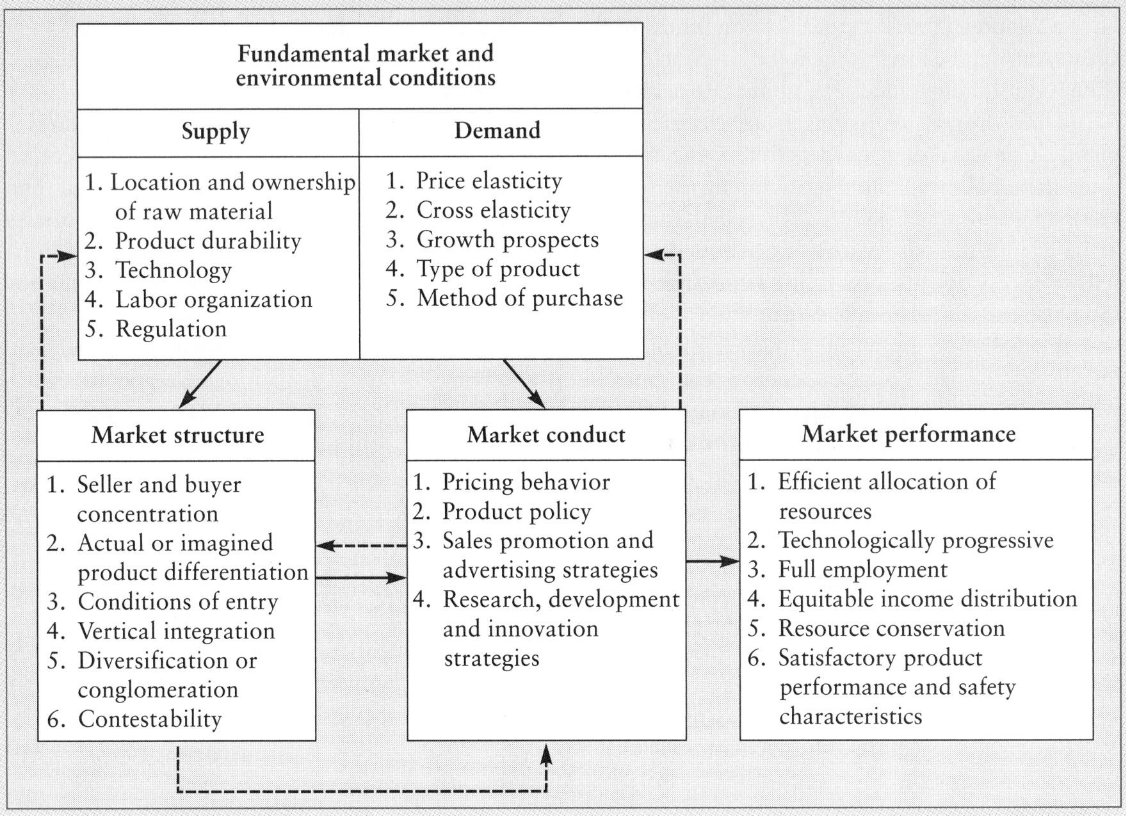

Market Structure

Both market performance and market conduct depend on the structure of the particular market. The concept of market structure refers to three main characteristics of buyers and sellers:

1. The degree of *seller and buyer concentration* in the market, as well as the size distribution of these sellers or buyers: On the seller side, concentration determines whether an industry is classified as monopoly, oligopoly, pure competition, or some variant thereof. Buyer concentration is also important because the bargaining power of buyers affects the gross margin sellers can earn.
2. The degree of objective or perceived *differentiation* between the products or services of competing producers: When buyers perceive the product of one firm to be different from that of another, these buyer preferences will impart a degree of market power to the seller that ultimately affects that seller's market conduct and performance.
3. The *conditions surrounding entry* into and exit from the market: When significant barriers to entry exist, competition may cease to become a disciplining

force on existing firms, making performance less than the competitive ideal. Exit barriers diminish the competitive discipline imposed by potential (as opposed to actual) competitors.

THREAT OF ENTRY

Entry barriers allow established sellers to raise prices above the minimum average cost of production and distribution without motivating new sellers to enter the industry. Barriers to entry may be classified into four types: product differentiation, absolute cost advantage, economies of scale, and limited access to distribution. These general types of entry barriers and how they arise are summarized in Table 16.1; the consequences of the entry barriers on new competitors are also listed.

CONTESTABLE MARKETS AND THE STRUCTURE-PERFORMANCE RELATIONSHIP

A theory of *contestable markets,* developed by William Baumol, J. C. Panzar, and R. D. Willig' provides additional useful insights into the structure-conduct-performance

Table 16.1 Type and Consequences of Barriers to Entry

Type	Consequences for New Entrants
A. Product differentiation barriers arise from 1. Buyer preferences, conditioned by advertising, for established brand names 2. Patent control of superior product designs by existing firms 3. Ownership or control of favored distribution systems (e.g., exclusive auto dealerships)	A. 1. New entrants cannot sell their products for as high a price as existing firms can 2. Sales promotion costs for new entrants may be prohibitive 3. New entrants may be unable to raise sufficient capital to establish a competitive distribution system
B. Absolute cost advantages of established firm's production and distribution arise from 1. Control of superior production techniques by patent or secrecy 2. Exclusive ownership of superior natural resource deposits 3. Inability of new firms to acquire necessary factors of production (management, labor, equipment) 4. Superior access to financial resources at lower costs	B. 1. Costs of new entrants are higher than for existing firms, so even though existing firms may charge a price that results in above-normal profits, new entrants may be unable to make even a normal profit at that price
C. Economies of large-scale production and distribution (or sales promotion) arise from 1. Capital-intensive nature of industry production processes 2. High initial start-up costs	C. 1. The entry of a new firm at a sufficient scale will result in an industry price reduction and a disappearance of the profits anticipated by the new entrants 2. New firms may be unable to acquire a sufficient market share to sustain efficient operations
D. Limited access to distribution channel	D. Closed shelf-space or Internet portals will necessitate massive slot-in investments and may prohibit certain business models

Source: Joseph Bain, *Industrial Organization,* pp. 237–265.

relationship.[1] Contestable markets yield perfectly competitive performance in a market structure characterized by only a few firms.

A perfectly contestable market is easily accessible to potential entrants and easy to escape because capital investments are redeployable (trucks, patented inventions, information). The potential competitors use the incumbent firms' pre-entry price to evaluate whether entry would be profitable. With freedom of entry and exit and fully redeployable assets, potential competitors are not worried about incumbents' pricing reactions. If profit potential disappears after initial entry, new entrants can simply leave the industry. The possibility of hit-and-run profits by potential entrants will cause even a dominant incumbent firm to set prices equal to average cost, because any higher price leaves opportunity for profitable entry.

The theory of contestable markets shifts the focus of attention in market structure, conduct, and performance relationships to the conditions of exit. The lower the barriers to entry *and exit,* the more nearly a market structure fits the perfectly contestable market model, and consequently, the more likely are prices and outputs to meet the perfectly competitive market norm of price equal to long-run average total cost.

EXAMPLE

Why City-Pair Airlines Are Not Contestable Markets

Aircraft, of course, seem to be the classic redeployable asset. Put an aircraft on the resale market, and within several weeks, one should be able to realize close to the replacement value of the asset. However, several features of the airline business do not meet the conditions of contestable markets. First, hub investments are sunk costs often not redeployable into other airline route structures. Second, costs of switching from one airline to another are often raised by frequent flyer programs, flight schedules, and ticket promotions that restrict interline transfers. Finally, airline incumbents change prices two or three times a day, adjusting to competitive threats much more quickly than hit-and-run entrants can move in and out of city pair markets. So, think of trucking (not airlines) as an example of contestable markets.

Antitrust Regulation Statutes and their Enforcement

Antitrust Laws

A series of laws passed since 1890 to limit monopoly power and to maintain competition in most American industries.

Since 1890, a number of federal laws have been passed with the intent of preventing monopoly and of maintaining competition in U.S. industry. The ultimate objective of these laws is to protect the public from the abuses and inefficiencies of monopoly power. These laws, known as **antitrust laws**, were initially directed at the large stockholder trusts such as Standard Oil, American Tobacco, and several coal and railroad trusts. Under a trust agreement, the voting rights to the stock of a number of directly competitive firms were conveyed to a legal trust. The trust then managed the firms collectively, thereby maximizing profits. Although extremely successful on the bottom line of the income statement, high prices and restricted outputs resulted. In this section we summarize the most important of these antitrust laws and their effects on business decisions.

[1] William J. Baumol, J. C. Panzar, and R. D. Willig, *Contestable Markets and the Theory of Industry Structure* (New York: Harcourt Brace Jovanovich, 1982).

THE SHERMAN ACT (1890)

The Sherman Act was the first federal-level antitrust law designed to regulate monopoly and the use of monopoly power. Its important provisions are brief, but they are wide ranging. First, it declares illegal

> every contract, combination in the form of a trust or otherwise, or conspiracy in restraint of commerce among the several States, or with foreign nations . . .

It further declares that

> every person who shall monopolize, or attempt to monopolize, or combine or conspire with any other person or persons, to monopolize any part of the trade or commerce among the several States, or with foreign nations, shall be deemed guilty of a misdemeanor.

THE CLAYTON ACT (1914)

The Clayton Act prohibited four anticompetitive business practices:

1. *Price discrimination* between purchasers of commodities was illegal, except to the extent that it was based on differences in grade, quality, and quantity of the product sold. Lower prices were permitted only where they made "due allowances for differences in the cost of selling or transportation" and where they were offered "in good faith to meet competition." To discriminate otherwise in wholesale pricing was illegal if the effect was to substantially lessen competition or tend to create a monopoly.
2. Section 3 prohibited sellers from leasing or making "a sale or contract for the sale of . . . commodities . . . on the condition that the lessee or purchaser thereof shall not use or deal in the . . . commodity . . . of a competitor." This prohibition against "exclusive dealing and *tying contracts*" was not absolute, but only applied to the extent that the practice substantially lessened competition or tended to create a monopoly.

EXAMPLE

WHY MILLER BEER IS SO HARD TO FIND IN MEXICO[2]

Mexico is the world's eighth largest beer market. Since the 1994 NAFTA agreement, Corona and Modelo beer exports grew fivefold to account for 11 percent of the U.S. market. Budweiser owns a 50 percent noncontrolling stake of the Modelo brewer. The Miller Brewing Co. attempted the same sort of penetration into the Mexican domestic market without any real success. Modelo and its rival FEMSA have 99 percent of the market. For one thing, FEMSA owns large convenience store channels in Mexico, and Miller is not stocked on their shelves. In other cases, bars are paid to deal exclusively with Modelo. As a consequence, a six-pack of Modelo Especial costs $4.60 in Mexico versus $1.80 for the best-seller in Brazil and $2.20 for the best-seller in Chile. Such exclusive dealing contracts that foreclose the Modelo customers from doing business with a competitor would be prohibited in the United States.

[2] Based on "Why Corona Is Big Here," *Wall Street Journal* (January 17, 2003), p. B1.

3. Section 7, the *antimerger* section, barred any corporation engaged in commerce from acquiring the shares of a competing firm or from purchasing the stocks of two or more competing firms, where substantial damage to competition could be proven or where it tended to create a monopoly. Later, the Celler-Kefauver amendments extended this antimerger policy to include asset acquisitions.
4. *Interlocking directorates,* defined as a case where the same person is on the board of directors of two or more firms, were declared illegal in Section 8 under these circumstances: (a) if the corporations competed with one another; (b) if any one had capital, surplus, and undivided profits in excess of $1 million; and (c) if "the elimination of competition . . . between them would constitute a violation of any of the provisions of the antitrust laws."

THE FEDERAL TRADE COMMISSION ACT (1914)

The Federal Trade Commission (FTC) Act was passed as a supplement to the Clayton Act. Its major antitrust provision, found in Section 5, merely states "that unfair methods of competition in commerce are hereby declared illegal." The Clayton Act established the Federal Trade Commission as an independent government antitrust agency.

THE ROBINSON-PATMAN ACT (1936)

The Robinson-Patman Act can be discussed both as antitrust legislation aimed at controlling the pricing aspects of market conduct and as an expression of a government policy aimed at restricting certain forms of price competition, thereby benefiting a special group of sellers. The act's provisions are summarized here:

1. Section 2(a) makes it illegal to discriminate in price when selling goods of "like grade and quality" where the effect may be to "substantially lessen competition or tend to create a monopoly" or "to injure, destroy, or prevent competition."

   A seller who is charged with price discrimination has two legal defenses enumerated in Section 2(b): First, the "cost defense" permits differentials in price that "make only due allowance for differences in the cost of manufacture, sale, or delivery." Second, the "good faith defense" permits a lower price to be charged to meet "an equally low price of a competitor."
2. Sections 2(d) and 2(e) prohibit the seller from allowing discounts to a buyer for merchandising services rendered the seller by the buyer, unless similar discounts are offered to all buyers. Secret rebates were prohibited; advertising or promotional allowances, for example, must be made available to all buyers, not just a few selected large firms.

THE HART-SCOTT-RODINO ANTITRUST IMPROVEMENT ACT (1976)

The Hart-Scott-Rodino Act requires larger companies (i.e., those with assets and sales over $100 million and $10 million, respectively) that are planning to merge to provide notification and information concerning the proposed merger to the Antitrust Division of the Department of Justice and to the Federal Trade Commission. After notification of the proposed merger, a waiting period of 30 days ensues during which these government antitrust enforcement agencies review the information submitted by the companies and examine the competitive effects of the merger proposal. The initial waiting period often is extended by enforcement officials in order to seek additional documents from the companies. After reviewing the information submitted, the government can either challenge the proposed merger in federal court or allow the merger to be completed, possibly with some modifications. Companies can appeal rulings by the FTC, and private complainants can bring antitrust suits to the federal courts. State attorneys general can also initiate federal antitrust suits.

EXAMPLE

California's Class Action Suit Against Microsoft Settled for $1.1 Billion

In January 2003, a U.S. district court in Washington found Microsoft guilty of maintaining a 92 percent monopoly of desktop operating system software by using anticompetitive practices. Two and a half years later in 2005, the defendant settled a class action lawsuit filed by the California Attorney General on behalf of 13 million California individuals and businesses. Microsoft agreed to pay $5 to $29 vouchers for each California buyer who licensed either Windows 95 or Windows 98 between 1995 and 2001 as compensation for the alleged overcharges. The vouchers could be used for laptop, desktop, or tablet computers and for software from any computer company. If all 51 million vouchers are submitted, Microsoft stands to lose $1.1 billion. Although this figure seems enormous, Microsoft in 2005 had almost $60 billion in cash and short-term investments.

Government agencies can use various methods to enforce the antitrust laws. Most antitrust cases are settled with *consent decrees* negotiated between the company and enforcement officials. Under a consent decree, a company agrees to take certain actions (or not engage in other actions) in return for the government agreeing not to seek additional penalties in the courts. In cases filed by antitrust agencies against a company, the courts may issue an *injunction* requiring (or prohibiting) certain actions by the company. The courts may also impose *fines* and, in certain instances, *prison sentences* if the defendants are found guilty of violating the antitrust laws. In cases involving charges of monopolization, the courts may require *divestiture* of certain assets by the company. Finally, in antitrust cases filed by private individuals and companies, the party filing the suit may be entitled to *treble damages* if the defendant is found guilty.

Antitrust Prohibition of Selected Business Decisions

Collusion: Price Fixing

Explicit agreements among competitors to fix prices along with other overt forms of collusion, such as market-sharing agreements, are per se illegal under the Sherman Act. The courts generally declared such agreements illegal, regardless of whether they cause injury to competitors. The legality of other less explicit forms of collusion is not as clear-cut. For example, price leadership practiced in some industries normally is not prosecuted under the antitrust laws. In a few cases, such as the sugar and ocean shipping industry, firms have been legislatively exempted from the antitrust laws and are legally permitted to jointly set prices and allocate output.

Mergers That Substantially Lessen Competition

Market Concentration Ratio

The percentage of total industry output produced by the 4, 8, 20, or 50 largest firms.

When industry sales, assets, or contributions to value added are concentrated in a few hands, market conduct and performance are less likely to be competitive in nature. One widely used index of market concentration is the **market** (or *industry*) **concentration ratio.** It may be defined as the percentage of total industry output (measured in terms of sales, employment, value added, or value of shipments) attributable to the 4, 8, 20, or 50 largest companies.

Data on market concentration ratios are regularly made available from the Census Bureau, based on the *Census of Manufacturers*. The Census Bureau defines industries in terms of SIC product categories. The SIC system consists of up to a seven-digit category code, indicating increasing specificity of industry and product as the number of digits increases. All manufacturing, for example, is specified by the first digit, food and kindred products by a two-digit category, candy and other confectionary products by a four-digit category, and sugar- or chocolate-coated nuts by a five-digit category.

Table 16.2 provides concentration ratios for selected industries. Some industries have become highly concentrated, such as breakfast cereals, turbine generators, aluminum, and lightbulbs. Some industries, such as hosiery, concrete block and brick, as well as sporting goods, are highly fragmented at the national level. One hypothesis of the structure-conduct-performance paradigm is that performance will be more competitive in the lower concentration markets. This hypothesis does not always hold; occasionally very concentrated industries such as PC desktop microprocessors are highly competitive.

Table 16.2 Concentration Ratios and Herfindahl-Hirschman Index for Selected Industries

		Share of Value Added Accounted for by the 4, 8, and 20 Largest Companies in Each Manufacturing Industry			
SIC	Industry Name	4-Firm Ratio	8-Firm Ratio	20-Firm Ratio	Herfindahl-Hirschman Index
31123	Breakfast cereals	82	93	100	3000
311511	Fluid milk	46	57	71	1012
31511	Hosiery and socks	35	45	64	318
32561	Soap and detergents	49	62	72	949
32411	Petroleum refining	47	67	92	809
32721	Flat glass	76	98	100	1677
327331	Concrete block and brick	24	32	44	206
331315	Aluminum sheet, plate, and foil	75	89	98	2286
333611	Turbine and turbine generator sets	88	91	96	2403
33511	Electric lamp bulbs	90	94	98	2848
32992	Sporting and athletic goods	24	32	46	199
33991	Jewelry and silverware	18	26	39	142

Source: 2002 *Census of Manufacturers*, U.S. Department of Commerce.

Figure 16.2 Market Share Dynamics in Microprocessors for Desktop PCs

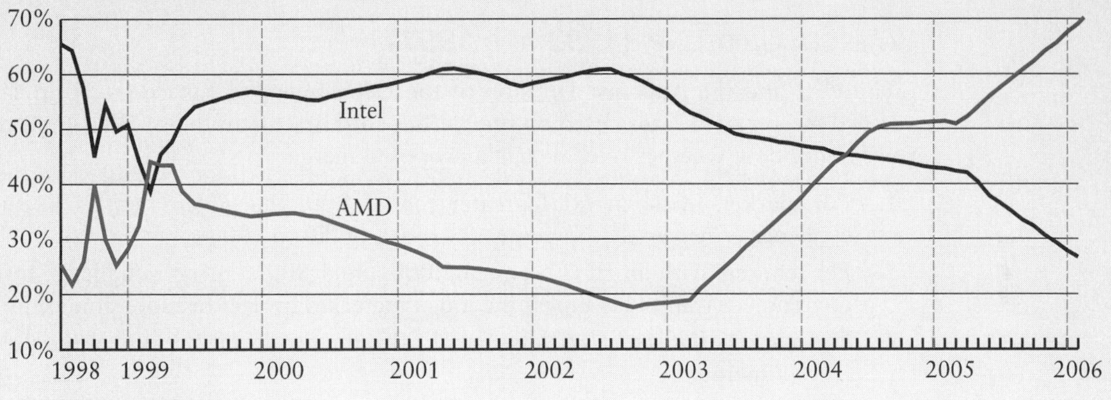

Source: ZD InfoBeads.

EXAMPLE

INTEL AND AMD FIGHT IT OUT IN DESKTOP MICROPROCESSORS

Intel has acquired most of its rivals, but two remaining firms compete vigorously. Figure 16.2 shows the dynamics of market share for Intel and AMD, who together control more than 90 percent of the chip production for microprocessors in desktop PCs, where margins are very slim. In general, Intel technology has an advantage in notebook computers but starting in 2004 lost its dominant role in lower end desktop machines. Consolidation mergers to reduce excess capacity in such an industry occur regularly. However, efficiency gains from further consolidation in already concentrated industries such as microprocessors are typically tiny. Because of sizable premiums paid to target-firm shareholders, risk-adjusted cumulative returns to acquiring-firm shareholders are consistently negative.[3] For these reasons, mergers between firms such as AMD and Intel are seldom approved by the antitrust authorities.

Herfindahl-Hirschman Index

A measure of market concentration equal to the sum of the squares of the market shares of the firms in a given industry.

Another important measure of market concentration is the **Herfindahl-Hirschman Index,** or *HHI*:

$$HHI = \sum_{i=1}^{N} S_i^2$$

where S_i is the market share of the *i*th firm and N is the number of firms in the industry. For example, in a relevant market consisting of just three firms, such as baby food (where Gerber has 70%, Beech-Nut has 16%, and Heinz has 14% market share), the *HHI* is $70^2 + 16^2 + 14^2$, which is equal to 5,352. *HHI* has a maximum value of 10,000 and decreases as the number of firms (N) increases. The *HHI* measures of market concentration, but accentuates the potential influence of leading

[3] See Robert Bruner, "Does M & A Pay?" *Journal of Applied Finance* (Spring/Summer 2002), pp. 45–68.

firms with asymmetrically large market shares. *HHI* values for selected industries are also shown in Table 16.2. Microsoft's 92 percent market share makes the *HHI* in software operating systems 8,526.

Merger Guidelines (1992 and 1997)

The FTC and the Antitrust Division of the Department of Justice (DOJ) in 1992 issued merger guidelines based on the Herfindahl-Hirschman Index (*HHI*) that they use in deciding whether to challenge a proposed merger:

1. For markets with an *HHI* greater than 1,800, the government is likely to challenge a merger that increases the index by 50 to 100 points, or more.
2. For markets with an *HHI* between 1,000 and 1,800, a merger challenge by the government is unlikely unless the index increases by 100 or more points.
3. For markets with an *HHI* less than 1,000, the government is unlikely to challenge a merger.

A merger increases the *HHI* by 2 times the product of the market shares of the candidate firms. So when Beech-Nut and Heinz's baby food division wished to merge, the merger was challenged because the 5,352 point *HHI* changed as follows:

$$\begin{aligned}
HHI \text{ before} &= S^2_{\text{Gerber}} + S^2_{\text{Beech-Nut}} + S^2_{\text{Heinz}} = 5{,}352 \\
HHI \text{ after} &= S^2_{\text{Gerber}} + (S_{\text{Beech-Nut}} + S_{\text{Heinz}})^2 \\
&= S^2_{\text{Gerber}} + (S^2_{\text{Beech-Nut}} + S^2_{\text{Heinz}} + 2S_{\text{Beech-Nut}}S_{\text{Heinz}}) \\
&= 70^2 + (16^2 + 14^2 + 2 \cdot 16 \cdot 14) \\
&= 5{,}352 + \Delta HHI \\
&= 5{,}352 + 448 = 5{,}800
\end{aligned}$$

The merger guidelines also list other factors that are considered in the analysis, including the ease with which competitors can enter the industry, likely failure of the to-be-acquired firm without the merger, and possible gains in efficiency for the (combined) firm.

In addition to defining the relevant product market, the geographical market is also important in determining market control or power. Is the market local, regional, national, or international? Generally, a narrower definition of the market will heighten the measure of potential monopoly power and raise the probability of a merger substantially lessening competition. If the FTC or Antitrust Division comes to this conclusion, they will seek an injunction in federal court to stop the proposed merger.

EXAMPLE

Trustbusters Reappear: DISH Network-DIRECTV Merger Disapproved[4]

European antitrust authorities blocked the $41 billion merger of General Electric and Honeywell on market concentration grounds. Honeywell and GE exhausted all appeals in December 2005. The two companies dominate the regional and corporate jet engine markets. Higher concentration in a two- or three-firm industry appears prohibited.

[4] Based on "Is the FTC Defending Goliath?" *BusinessWeek* (December 18, 2000), pp. 160–162; and "Murdoch Wins DIRECTV," *Wall Street Journal* (April 10, 2003), p. B1.

Similarly, the FTC blocked a proposed merger between Heinz and Beech-Nut with 16 percent and 14 percent, respectively, of the baby food market. The rationale was that the Herfindahl-Hirschman index (*HHI*) for baby foods measured 5,352, relative to the 1,800-point presumptive benchmark that causes concern. But, in this case, the reason concentration is so enormous in baby food is that the behemoth Gerber has 70 percent of the market and is itself responsible for 4,900 of the 5,352 *HHI* points. The FTC did not accept the Heinz and Beech-Nut argument that together their two firms could realize scale economies, lower distribution and R&D costs, and thereby compete more effectively against the dominant firm.

Finally, Charlie Ergen's privately held EchoStar (DISH Network) launched a $26 billion bid for Hughes Electronics' subsidiary DIRECTV. DISH Network and DIRECTV were the top two satellite TV providers in the United States. Ergen argued that the relevant market included cable TV systems, with a combined industry share distribution as follows:

Comcast	33%
DIRECTV	17%
Time Warner	17%
DISH Network	13%
Charter Comm.	10%
Cox Comm.	10%
HHI	2,036

The FTC and the Antitrust Division disagreed, defined the relevant market narrowly as satellite TV, and prohibited the merger. Even under the broader definition, ΔHHI for the proposed merger was 442 points, well beyond the 50-points safe harbor of the merger guidelines for an industry with *HHI* already in excess of 1,800. Ergen's case, therefore, rested on potential efficiencies from the removal of duplicate satellite transmissions, freeing bandwidth for additional channels.

Rather than filing a lawsuit to prevent a merger between large competing firms, antitrust enforcement agencies sometimes negotiate a consent decree that permits a merger to take place provided certain conditions are met to minimize the anticompetitive effects of the merger. For example, in the case of AT&T's $12.6 billion acquisition of McCaw Cellular (the largest U.S. cellular telephone company), the consent decree contained provisions requiring AT&T to operate McCaw as a separate subsidiary and allowing McCaw customers to pick any long-distance carrier to handle long-distance calls made on their cellular telephones. In another instance, the antitrust commission of the European Union insisted that British Airways divest itself of 353 landing slots at London's Heathrow Airport if BA and American Airlines wished to merge. Rather than lose that many of its prized assets, BA decided to continue competing with American.

MONOPOLIZATION

As we saw earlier, firms engaged in overt forms of collusion with other companies can be successfully prosecuted under the Sherman Act. Companies acting alone also can be charged under the act with illegally attempting to monopolize a market or engaging in monopolistic practices. However, proving such alleged violations of the laws often is quite difficult. Before the Microsoft case in 1998, the last large monopolization case brought by the antitrust enforcement officials resulted in the breakup of AT&T back in 1982.

EXAMPLE

Potentially Anticompetitive Practices: Microsoft's Tying Arrangements[5]

Netscape alleged that dominant software maker Microsoft used its leading position in the market for computer operating systems to gain an anticompetitive advantage in the market for applications software such as Microsoft's Internet Explorer and Media Player. Netscape complained that Microsoft illegally tied its Internet access software (Microsoft Explorer) to sales of Windows 95, which provided the operating system for 92 percent of the personal computers in the United States. Microsoft distributed Explorer free with every sale of Windows 95 to Compaq and Dell computers, priced Windows 95 without Explorer much higher, and threatened to remove the Windows 95 license if any Web browser other than Microsoft Explorer was preinstalled on the PCs Compaq shipped. Over four quarters in late 1996 and 1997, Microsoft's share of the Web browser market grew from 20 percent to 39 percent. By 1999, Netscape's share had fallen from a high of 84 percent to 47 percent, and Microsoft's product accompanied by the allegedly anticompetitive practices had resulted in a 53 percent share. Today Netscape has about 8 percent of a market that Internet Explorer dominates. Was this evidence of "substantial harm to competition," or just substantial harm to a particular competitor?

Tying arrangements that extend the monopoly power of a dominant firm in one market to another distinct product and relevant market are illegal per se. Because Microsoft's sales practices precluded Netscape from selling its Web browser, Microsoft was required under a consent decree to unbundle the two products and change its pricing practices. Nevertheless, in May 1998, the Justice Department and 20 state attorneys general filed suit, alleging illegal tying arrangements and other anticompetitive practices. Microsoft was found guilty of the alleged violations.

In 2004, the European Court of Justice ruled against Microsoft in a complaint first filed by Sun Microsystems that Microsoft illegally bundled their Media Player product with Windows. Windows without Media Player was priced much higher. Because Microsoft has a dominant firm monopoly in PC operating systems, with market share that grew between 1997 and 2005 from 86 percent to 93 percent, the Court ruled that Microsoft must unbundle its Media Player and offer the diminished capability version of Windows cheaper than the expanded capability version. The Court levied a $625 million fine, and seeks much higher penalties should Microsoft not comply.

[5] Based on "Browse This," *U.S. News & World Report* (December 5, 1997), p. 59; "U.S. Sues Microsoft Over PC Browser," *Wall Street Journal* (October 21, 1997), p. A3; "Knowing the ABCs of the Antitrust Case Against Microsoft," *Wall Street Journal* (October 30, 1997), p. B1; "Microsoft's Browser: A Bundle of Trouble," *The Economist* (October 25, 1997), p. 74; "Microsoft on Trial," *Wall Street Journal* (April 4, 2000), p. A16; and "Microsoft Is Dealt Blow by EU Judge," *Wall Street Journal* (December 23, 2004), p. A3.

WHOLESALE PRICE DISCRIMINATION

A large company that operates as a manufacturer or distributor in two (or more) different geographic (or product) markets and cuts wholesale prices in one market and not in the other market can be accused under the Robinson-Patman Act of engaging in illegal price discrimination. Differential pricing directly to final product customers is allowed (and often based on "what the market will bear") but not so in pricing to intermediate product resellers (wholesalers, distributors, etc.). For example, the publisher Penguin Books paid a large judgment to independent booksellers after it was proved that Penguin offered Barnes & Noble and Borders large-volume discounts and other trade promotions that were unrelated to the cost of serving those accounts. Similarly, six vending machine companies sued Philip Morris, alleging that other distributors and retail merchants received rebates, buybacks, and promotional allowances intended to lower costs and allow the favored distributors to drive the complainants out of business. The Robinson-Patman Act was designed to prohibit this kind of favoritism in wholesale trade.

REFUSALS TO DEAL

In general, a manufacturer can refuse to deal with any retail distributor who fails to follow company policies that are based on legitimate business justifications. However, this authority is subject to three limitations. First, the orders of a renegade discounter can be refused if and only if the manufacturer acts independently of compliant dealers whose sales at higher price points are suffering because of the increased competition (*United States v. GM,* 1966). Second, an explicit well-justified policy must be in place in advance; the manufacturer cannot pressure individual dealers, threaten suspension of shipments of new "hot" products, or offer to reinstate if the offending discounters agree to raise their prices (*FTC v. Stride Rite,* 1996). Finally, manufacturers cannot lock in buyers of durable products by refusing to supply parts to independent service organizations (ISOs), especially if the ISO prices are far below the manufacturer's service prices. In *Eastman Kodak v. Image Technical Services* (1992), the Supreme Court argued that customers should be able to select independent service and nonwarranty repair well after the sale. Kodak's defense that ISO maintenance and repair failed to meet Kodak's quality standards was disproved by the evidence.

COMMAND AND CONTROL REGULATORY CONSTRAINTS: AN ECONOMIC ANALYSIS

Federal, state, and local governments are involved in the regulation of business enterprises. Table 16.3 contains a partial listing of the federal government agencies and departments. In addition to the Federal Trade Commission and Antitrust Division of the Department of Justice discussed earlier, many other agencies regulate business decisions. State regulations encompass a wide range of activities, including regulation of public utility companies and licensing of various businesses, such as health care facilities, and numerous professions, such as law and accounting. Local governments frequently set and enforce zoning laws and building codes. Regulatory constraints can be imposed in non-discriminatory ways on any set of similar business. For example, the European Union prohibits direct-to-consumer advertising of prescription drugs. These constraints can affect a firm's operating costs (both fixed and variable), capital costs, and revenues.

Table 16.3 Partial Listing of Federal Government Regulatory Agencies

Department/Agency	Purpose
Environmental Protection Agency (EPA)	Regulates pollution of air, water, and land
Consumer Product Safety Commission (CPSC)	Protects against unreasonable risks of injury associated with consumer products
Equal Employment Opportunity Commission (EEOC)	Enforces laws on employment discrimination based on race, religion, and sex
Labor: Employment Standards Administration	Enforces minimum wage and overtime laws
Labor: Occupational Safety and Health Administration (OSHA)	Regulates safety and health conditions in the workplace
Labor: National Labor Relations Board (NLRB)	Regulates labor relations between employers and employees (and their unions)
Interstate Commerce Commission (ICC)	Regulates interstate surface transportation
Nuclear Regulatory Commission (NRC)	Regulates civilian use of nuclear energy
Securities and Exchange Commission (SEC)	Regulates issuance of new securities and trading of existing securities
Federal Communications Commission (FCC)	Regulates radio and television broadcasting and interstate telephone service
Federal Reserve System	Regulates commercial banks and bank holding companies
Agriculture: Food Safety and Inspection Service	Regulates meat and poultry industry for safety and accurate labeling
Health and Human Services: Food and Drug Administration (FDA)	Regulates safety of food, drugs, and cosmetics
Energy: Federal Energy Regulatory Commission (FERC)	Regulates interstate rates for transportation and sale of natural gas and transmission and sale of electricity
Transportation: Federal Aviation Administration (FAA)	Regulates safety of airplanes, airports, and airline operations
Transportation: National Highway Traffic Safety Administration (NHTSA)	Regulates safety of motor vehicles and tires
Labor: Mine Safety and Health Administration	Regulates safety and health in mines
Treasury: Office of Comptroller of the Currency	Regulates national banks
Treasury: Bureau of Alcohol, Tobacco, and Firearms (BATF)	Regulates manufacture and sale of alcoholic beverages, tobacco, explosives, and firearms

The Deregulation Movement

Beginning in the late 1970s and continuing through the 2000s, the business environment moved toward relying less on government regulation and more on the marketplace to achieve desired economic objectives. For example, the Ocean Shipping Reform Act of 1998 deregulated freight rates for the 40-foot containers that ship apparel, consumer electronics, autos, and ores from Asia to the United States and ship computer software, forest products, and grain back to Asia. The one-way cost of $3,500 for a 6,000-garment container has declined to $1,500.

Deregulation of electric power generation and transmission companies increased competition and provided more power supply options to wholesale customers. For example, energy merchant Duke Power sells electricity throughout the nation, with new generating plants in New England, Mississippi, and California.

THE REGULATION OF EXTERNALITIES

In the normal course of business, every firm faces decisions that impose spillover costs upon third parties. Both managers and the public have a keen interest in least-cost implementation of the kinds of remedies society mandates for controlling externalities.

EXTERNALITIES DEFINED

Externality

A spillover of benefits or costs from one production or utility function to another.

Externalities exist when a third party receives benefits or bears costs from consumption or production activities for which the market system does not enable them to receive full payment. Pollution by-products of trucking deliveries, for example, combine with certain atmospheric conditions and cause smog. In places such as Los Angeles this smog may impose significant costs on asthmatic residents and some businesses such as the Pasadena Sightseeing Company. In short, externalities arise with any interdependency of household utility or firm production functions that is not reflected in market prices.

Only externalities that are not conveyed through the price system result in inefficiencies. Thus when mad cow disease causes preference for meat to shift from beef to chicken, the price of beef will fall and that of chicken will rise, making beef producers and chicken consumers worse off, and chicken producers and beef consumers better off, because of the price change. But all of these so-called **pecuniary externalities** have operated through the market price system, and they therefore pose no inefficiency.

Pecuniary Externality

A spillover that is reflected in prices and therefore results in no inefficiency.

The legal doctrine of "coming to the nuisance" in *Spur Industries v. Del Webb Development,* S.C. Arizona, 1972 (108 Ariz. 178, 494 P.2d 700) illustrates why pecuniary externalities result in no inefficiency. If the land you purchase for an eventual subdivision development is located next to a cattle feedlot, the price you pay per acre will reflect the stench. The reduced price of the land will internalize the spillover effects. Later, if residents of the subdivision complain about the stench and the feedlot is declared a pubic nuisance, you, the developer, may have to pay to relocate the cattle feeding business. Again, when external effects *are* reflected in prices, all affected parties directly participate in the transaction, and there is no inefficiency.

When non-pecuniary externalities are present, however, resources are likely to be misallocated. Producers or consumers are less likely to engage in an action that contributes to society's well-being if they are not fully compensated for all benefits generated. Similarly in the case of negative externalities, a producer or consumer will likely overallocate resources to some production or consumption activity if part of the cost is shifted to others.

In general an external cost should be reduced to the point where the marginal spillover costs saved by any further reduction just equal the marginal lost profits from the externality-generating activity. Similarly, an action that generates external benefits should be expanded to the point where the marginal benefits to all of society from such an expansion just equal the marginal costs.

COASIAN BARGAINING FOR RECIPROCAL EXTERNALITIES

Reciprocal Externality

A spillover that results from competing incompatible uses.

In many cases, externalities arise because of incompatible uses of air, land, or water resources. For example, late-night takeoffs and landings by FedEx jets may disturb sleep in houses around the airport. Feeding of thousands of animals in a small enclosed feedlot create offensive odors in adjacent subdivisions. Agricultural land runoff of nutrient-rich water may adversely affect downstream intake by a bottled water plant. No adverse consequences would occur if either party were absent.

Ronald Coase's famous paper "The Problem of Social Cost," illustrates a reciprocal externality between a spark-throwing railroad and a farmer with adjacent flammable fields. Coase's ingenious and intriguing claim was that under certain conditions involving full information and low transaction costs, the answer to the question, "Who's liable and therefore who should pay damages?" had no effect on the resource allocation decisions of these parties. In particular, if the railroad had the property right to throw sparks along its right-of-way, the trains scheduled down this track and the acreage planted along it would be exactly the same as if the railroad had the liability for all spark-induced damages along its tracks.

EXAMPLE

Coase's Railroad

To see how this remarkable result arises through Coasian bargaining, consider the payoffs in Table 16.4. If the railroad has the property right (i.e., Panel a), the farmer incurs $600 worth of crop destruction per train per 10 acres planted along the tracks. Initially, the railroad ignores these external spillover costs and chooses an activity level of trains that maximizes its own profits (i.e., two trains in the bottom row of Panel a). The farmer would plant 10 rather than 20 acres along the tracks in order to earn $300 and avoid losing $800 (in the extreme southeast cell). If substantial impediments to bargaining were present, no further action would take place in an unregulated market environment. And yet, a mutually beneficial private voluntary bargaining opportunity would exist.

In particular, if the railroad were to cut back to one train, the farmer's profit would rise from $300 to $900, while the railroad's profit would decline by $500 (from $1,500 to $1,000). Accordingly, $501 is a minimally sufficient bribe to elicit

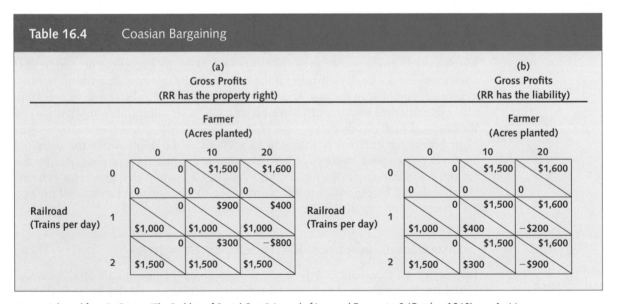

Table 16.4 Coasian Bargaining

(a) Gross Profits (RR has the property right)

Railroad (Trains per day)	Farmer (Acres planted): 0	10	20
0	0 0	$1,500 0	$1,600 0
1	0 $1,000	$900 $1,000	$400 $1,000
2	0 $1,500	$300 $1,500	−$800 $1,500

(b) Gross Profits (RR has the liability)

Railroad (Trains per day)	Farmer (Acres planted): 0	10	20
0	0 0	$1,500 0	$1,600 0
1	0 $1,000	$1,500 $400	$1,600 −$200
2	0 $1,500	$1,500 $300	$1,600 −$900

Source: Adapted from R. Coase, "The Problem of Social Cost," *Journal of Law and Economics* 2 (October 1960), pp. 1–44.

the lower train-activity level, and $600 is the savings in fewer crops burned. Thus, Coase predicted that if the parties have few impediments to bargaining, the farmer would offer a side payment sufficient to abate the incremental (second) train and its spark hazard, because the second train is worth less (to the railroad) than the incremental agricultural losses cost the farmer. Just how much the farmer will pay and how little the railroad will accept is not addressed, but one thing is clear: Potential gains from trade do motivate a bargain to reduce railroad activity from two trains to one and acreage planted from 20 to 10.

Now, consider the case in which the railroad has the liability for spark-induced crop damages. Initially, the farmer prepares to plant 20 acres along the tracks as this activity level maximizes his or her independent profit (at $1,600). However, no trains are profitable with this much acreage in production because $600 in damages per train per 10 acres (i.e., $1,200 altogether) is owed when the railroad has $1,000 gross profit with one train, and $2,400 in damages is owed when the railroad offers to compensate the farmer for not only crop damages, but also lost profit if the farmer would plant fewer acres. In particular, the railroad can offer the farmer $101 to plant 10 acres rather than 20 acres since the farmer's gross profit differs by only $100 (i.e., $1,500 versus $1,600). If the railroad then also compensates the farmer $600 for one train's crop damage on 10 acres, the railroad owes $701 and earns a gross profit of $1,000.

Table 16.4, Panel b, displays the gross profits before crop damages have been compensated. Shown in the middle row of Panel b, the railroad offers the farmer compensation in excess of $100 (perhaps, $101) to scale back the acreage planted from 20 acres, where farmer gross profit is $1,600, to 10 acres, where farmer gross profit is $1,500. This reallocation of activities is worth $600 in damage savings to the railroad. Again, Coasian bargaining leads the parties to agree upon one train and 10 acres.

Coase Theorem
A prediction about the emergence of private voluntary bargaining in reciprocal externalities with low transaction costs.

The **Coase theorem** states that reciprocal externality generators and recipients will choose efficient activity levels whatever the initial liability assignment. It makes no claim about the distributional consequences of reversing the direction of a liability assignment. Quite obviously, making the railroad liable in one instance, instead of asking the farmer to cover his or her own crop losses from burned fields in the other, results in quite different net profit outcomes. However, what the Coase theorem does assert is that in reciprocal externality settings with small numbers of affected parties, resource allocation as to the externality-generating and externality-receiving activity levels will be unchanged independent of the initial liability assignment; one train will be scheduled, and 10 acres will be planted.

QUALIFICATIONS OF THE COASE THEOREM

Some qualifications are in order, many of which Coase himself recognized. First, technical transaction costs of searching for and identifying the responsible owners and affected parties, of detecting violations of one's property rights, and of internally negotiating the side payments within a group of claimants must all remain low and be unaffected if liability assignment is reversed. Second, neither party can operate in a purely competitive market, for then the net profits required for side payments would be nonexistent. And, third, and perhaps most important, one party quickly makes an offer the other is just willing to accept only when the information regarding the payoffs in Table 16.4, Panels (a) and (b) is complete, certain, and known to both parties.

When information is incomplete, private voluntary bargaining doesn't necessarily lead to resource allocation that won't vary with the direction of liability assignment. This qualification of the Coase theorem holds even if property rights are fully specified, completely assigned, and enforced at little or no cost. In all incompatible use situations involving asymmetrically known cost information, the precautionary actions of the plaintiff and the defendant have some bearing on the assignment of liability. For example, the parties in Coase's railroad example would avoid liability in part by employing spark arresters or land setbacks as long as the benefit in crop-loss savings exceeded the cost. However, the problem posed by asymmetric information is that some aspects of precaution are inherently unobservable or unverifiable (e.g., attentiveness to subtle signals of impending hazard) while others are observable but affect accident avoidance in a nondeterministic way (e.g., good brakes may lock up on rain-slickened roads when less effective brakes would not). Recall that unobservability and random disturbances together result in the problem of moral hazard, which we discussed in Chapter 15.

No incentive-compatible mechanism can both preserve the voluntary nature of the Coasian bargaining and also elicit true revelation of the unobservable damages. Therefore, contrary to the traditional understanding of the Coase theorem, disputants in reciprocal externality conflicts might be expected not to engage in private voluntary bargaining alone, but rather to delegate the question of damage assessment and recovery to third-party court systems.[6] Civil procedural rules in an impartial court system can be seen as credible commitment mechanisms. Through these mechanisms potential disputants submit to liability assignments and wealth transfer remedies that motivate efficient accident avoidance despite frequently asymmetric information. So, the implication of the Coase theorem holds: Parties that are disputing over incompatible uses will contract their way to an efficient allocation of resources unless high transaction costs discourage the required bargaining.

Impediments to Bargaining

Regulation will continue to have a role because of impediments to bargaining. Several impediments are recognized in the legal system. Prohibitive notification and search costs (to identify absentee owners and notify all the affected parties) are the justification for certifying **class action suits** in the case of oil spills and other large-scale externalities affecting many claimants. Voluntary private bargaining about incompatible uses may also be impeded by the need for continuous monitoring of an unverifiable bargain, such as an agreement to restrain one's catch to the maximum sustainable rate of harvest of a deep sea fishery.

Class Action Suits
A legal procedure for reducing the search and notification costs of filing a complaint.

Finally, the most significant impediment to bargaining in large-numbers externality cases is the strategic holdout or free rider. When a court grants an injunction against a polluter's operation, relief from the injunction may require that the polluter obtain a unanimous waiver from all the affected parties. If many claimants are

[6] See F. Harris, "Economic Negligence, Moral Hazard, and the Coase Theorem," *Southern Economic Journal* 56, no. 3 (January 1990), pp. 698–704.

Strategic Holdout
A negotiator who makes unreasonable demands at the end of a unanimous consent process.

certified as possessing such a right of waiver, each claimant has an incentive to hold out for more compensation than would be required to cover his or her damages. The predictable presence of **strategic holdouts** short-circuits Coase's private voluntary bargaining hypothesis. In such cases, the courts therefore adopt other mechanisms that assign liability for payment of permanent damages.

EXAMPLE

BOOMER V. ATLANTIC CEMENT CO., INC., 26 N.Y. 2D 219, COURT OF APPEALS, NY

A large cement plant valued at almost $200 million spewed cement dust regularly across a neighborhood of Albany, New York. Some of the affected households were unable to continue their laundry operations; small airborne particulates required frequent washing and repainting of cars and homes. Asthmatics suffered more health problems. The Atlantic Cement plant was declared a public nuisance, and the court chose among three types of injunctions: (1) an order to cease operations until the air pollution could be abated, (2) an order to cease operations until a waiver could be obtained from each household in the affected neighborhood, or (3) an order declaring the cement plant liable for $740,000 in permanent damages and requiring a cessation of operations until these court-specified damages were paid.

Because the first injunction hinged on undeveloped technology and the second created strategic holdouts, the New York Court of Appeals in effect licensed the ongoing nuisance for a one-time fee of $740,000 in 2006 dollars. No private voluntary bargain to reduce the cement dust could have overcome the strategic free-rider/strategic holdout problem. And, as result of having to pay court-mandated damages, the plant's owners did begin to internalize the social cost of cement production when establishing new plants.

SOLUTION BY REGULATORY DIRECTIVE

One simplistic approach to solving externality problems is to prohibit the action that generates the external effects. In most cases, however, this approach is suboptimal and frequently impractical. Auto emissions could be cut to zero if autos were banned, but the economic effects of such a move, at least in the short run, would be disastrous for all developed economies. Moreover, seldom does an optimal solution require that externalities be completely eliminated; a strict zero-pollution policy often entails excessive pollution-abatement costs.

EXAMPLE

MANDATORY AUTO INSPECTIONS

Auto inspections are a good example of a solution by regulatory directive. Recognizing that significant external benefits are to be gained from reducing serious automotive accidents caused by poorly maintained equipment, no state government gives the consumer the choice of regular inspection and maintenance of brakes, lights, and other safety equipment; it simply mandates inspection and repair for all vehicles. Cancer-causing lead additives in gasoline and ozone shield-depleting chlorofluorocarbon (CFC) refrigeration gases have also been massively reduced by such regulatory directives (see Figure 16.3).

Figure 16.3 CFC Production

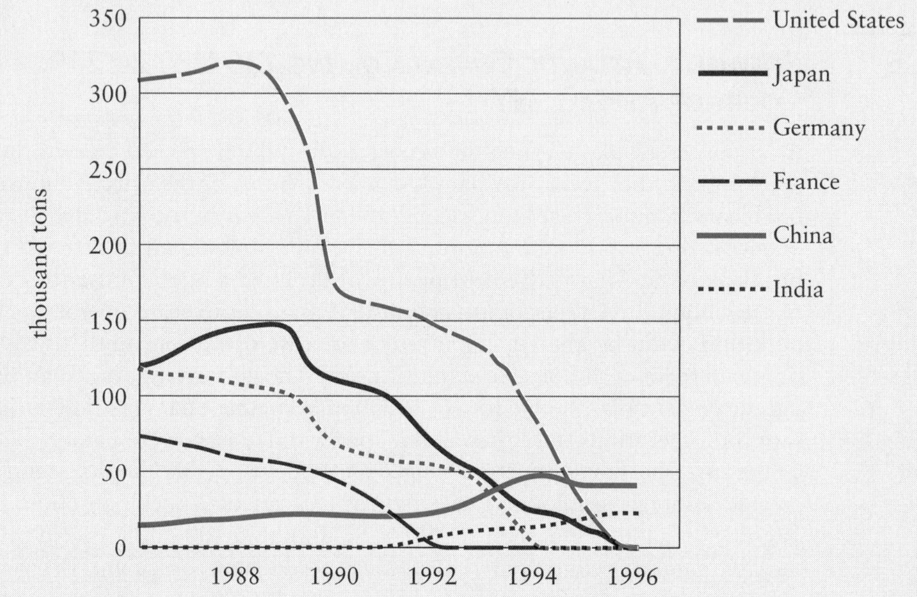

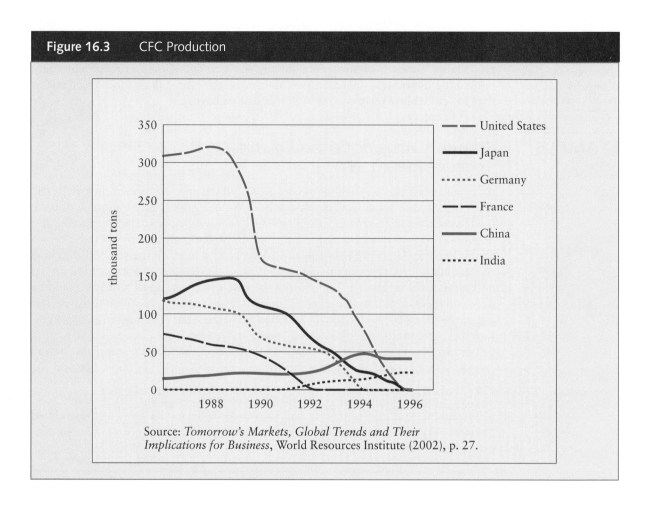

Source: *Tomorrow's Markets, Global Trends and Their Implications for Business*, World Resources Institute (2002), p. 27.

One problem with this approach to setting an overall emissions standard arises when multiple sources of pollution are present, as in the acidification of rain along the Eastern forests from coal-fired power plants in the Midwest. Under regulatory edict, each of the polluting entities (each point source) must be directed as to how it should act. A simple proportionate distribution of "pollution rights" to each plant would not take into account the dramatic difference in the cost of abatement from one plant to another. Instead, optimality would equalize the marginal effectiveness of the last dollar spent on pollution abatement by each polluter. So, a low-cost point source's regulatory permit should require more abatement than a permit for a high-cost point source. Yet, this sort of detailed point-source regulation is seldom achieved.

Solution by Taxes and Subsidies

Another potentially efficient solution to externality problems is to provide subsidies (either in the form of cash or tax relief) to those whose activities generate significant external benefits and to tax those whose activities create external costs. Such a tax and subsidy scheme, however, requires a tremendous amount of information to administer the program effectively.

Consider the analysis required for a per-unit pollution tax T^* in Figure 16.4. Demand per truck is the private willingness to pay (WTP) for trucking deliveries

Figure 16.4 Optimal Per Unit Pollution Tax

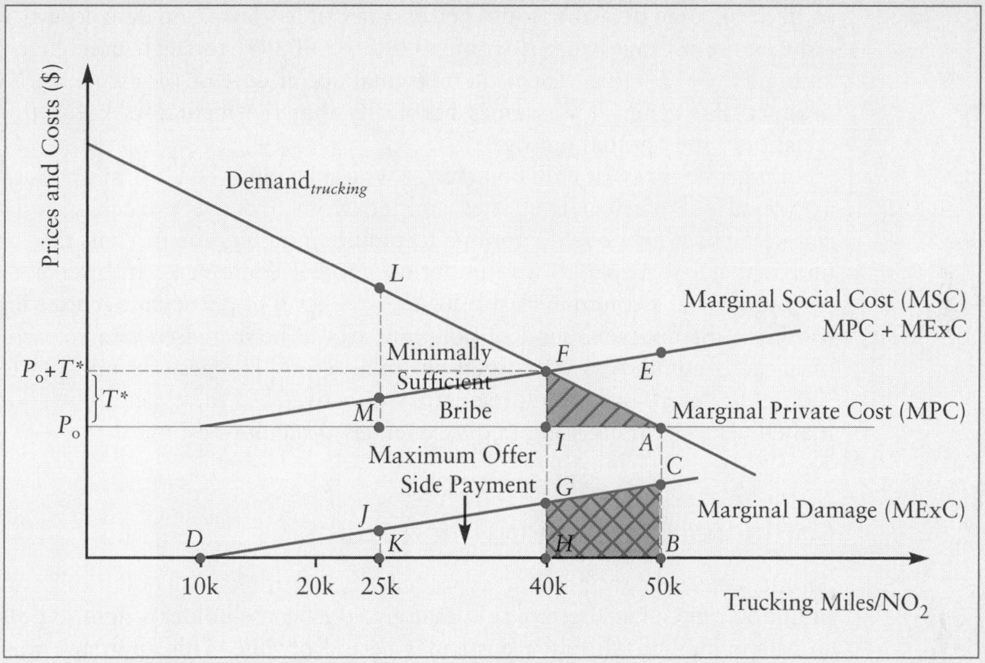

throughout the Los Angeles area. Setting marginal private cost (MPC) equal to private WTP, the trucking company will put 50,000 miles a year on its typical delivery truck. Still more delivery miles are avoided by the managers because the price additional customers are willing to pay for deliveries is less than the MPC of operating the truck. The problem is that trucking mileage generates the by-product nitrous oxide (NO_2), which causes smog. Through careful environmental science, businesses such as the Pasadena Sightseeing Co. and asthmatic citizens of Los Angeles estimate that the air pollution causes damages from lost tourist business as well as eyes, nose, and throat irritants of area BCD. Consequently, although marginal benefit (P_o) equals MPC at the private market equilibrium Point *A*, additional costs attributable to the NO_2 externality—namely, CB at 50,000 miles—suggest that full costs are substantially higher: at Point *E*, MPC (*AB*) + MExC (*CB*) > P_o.

When private plus external costs exceed marginal benefits to the delivery truck's customers at 50,000 miles, the joint product trucking mileage/NO_2 is produced in excess of its optimal level. Fifty thousand miles per year is too much trucking. However, the question, as always, comes down to *how much less* trucking and associated pollution abatement is optimal.

In Figure 16.4, the reduction in mileage at which marginal social cost (MSC), which is the sum of MPC + MExC, just equals marginal willingness to pay for trucking is 40,000 miles at Point *F*. Clearly, the smog victims have damages (area *GHBC*) great enough to compensate the trucking company for its lost profits (area *FIA*) associated with a 10,000-mile reduction in mileage. And the maximum side payment smog victims would offer for the next 10,000-mile reduction from 40K to 30K (area *JKHG*) is smaller than the minimally sufficient bribe (area LMIF) that the trucking company would accept. But zeroing in on 40,000 miles as the optimal mileage (not 35K, 38K, 42K, or 45K) is difficult because accurate marginal external cost information is so hard to come by. An optimal per-unit tax of T^* levied on delivery truck mileage reduces the mileage chosen from 50,000 to 40,000 through user charges in the amount $P_0 + T^*$ that reflect the marginal social cost of the (trucking/NO_2) joint product. But again, T^* assumes heroically that the regulators know that 40,000 constitutes the optimal mileage.

In practice, a tax or emission charge would be placed on a firm's pollutants, such as pounds of particulate matter emitted from a delivery truck or power plant smokestack. A firm could continue to pollute if it pays the per-unit tax, or it could find that it is cheaper to buy pollution control equipment. If, after a reasonable period of time, a community still believes the level of particulate matter in the air is too high, the tax per pound of pollutant would be increased in a stepwise fashion until the community was satisfied with the result. The per-unit tax solution avoids the rigidity of all-or-nothing regulatory directives but the exact amount of an optimal effluent tax or emission tax is extremely difficult to estimate.

Solution by Sale of Pollution Rights

Another increasingly popular approach to the problem of pollution is the sale of pollution rights. Licenses are sold that give the license holder a right to pollute up to some specific limit during a particular period of time. This approach was adopted under the 1990 Clean Air Act. The U.S. Environmental Protection Agency (EPA) sets a maximum level of some pollutant that may be safely emitted in an area. The federal government then sells, at auction, licenses to individual firms giving them the right to pollute up to that specified amount. The licenses can be freely traded, which permits their price to fluctuate with market demands and innovations in abatement technology. Because it is essentially market oriented, this approach causes pollution costs to be internally recognized in all the price and production decisions of individual firms.

EXAMPLE

Plant Expansion Requires Purchase of Open-Market Pollution Rights: Times Mirror Co.

The United States and the European Union have active markets for sulfur dioxide and nitrous oxide pollution rights (credits). These markets allow electric utilities, trucking companies, and manufacturing firms to buy and sell pollution credits in continuous auctions. Also, a private placement market exists in which brokers, as well as some states, arrange customized contracts for pollution credits between companies that have excess credits to sell and companies that need credits to comply with environmental regulations. For example, the Times Mirror Company was able to complete a $120-million expansion of a paper-making plant near Portland, Oregon, after buying the right to emit 150 tons of additional hydrocarbons into the air annually. The pollution credits were acquired for $50,000 from the owners of two businesses that held surplus credits: a chemical plant that had gone out of business and a dry-cleaning firm that adopted a pollution-free cleaning fluid.

GOVERNMENTAL PROTECTION OF BUSINESS

In addition to regulating business enterprises, numerous government programs and policies protect businesses by restricting the entry of competitors.

LICENSING AND PERMITTING

When the government requires and issues a license permitting someone to practice a particular business, profession, or trade, it is by definition restricting the entry of some potential new competitors into that practice. Licensing is generally used to protect the public from fraud or incompetence in those cases where the potential for harm is quite large. Nevertheless, by restricting output, government licensure presents monopoly rents to license or permit holders.

Recently, Mecklenburg County, North Carolina, which surrounds Charlotte, learned that its role as a ground transportation hub was threatened because the smog permits authorized by the EPA. North Carolina regulatory agencies foreclosed the construction of additional freight trucking terminals until some other dust-generating facility was closed. No additional permits will be authorized making those businesses with preexisting permits more valuable.

PATENTS

Patent
A legal government grant of monopoly power that prevents others from manufacturing or selling a patented article.

Patents are by definition a legal government grant of monopoly power. A patent holder may prevent others from manufacturing or selling a patented product or from using some patented process. The patent holder may grant a license permitting others to make limited use of the patent in exchange for royalty payments. The monopoly granted by a patent is not, however, an absolute one. First, it is limited to a 17-year period, and few renewals are permitted. It is possible that a shorter patent monopoly period would provide sufficient incentives to encourage a high level of inventive activity. Serious proposals suggest shortening the patent period to just four years for computer software, for example. Second, competing firms are not prohibited from engineering around an existing patent and bringing out a closely competing, alternative design. Third, many patents are successfully challenged by competitors, especially in the European Union, where patent applications are not kept secret.

THE OPTIMAL DEPLOYMENT DECISION: TO LICENSE OR SECURE CAPTIVE USE

Finally, we discuss the decision as to whether to license patents and trade secrets to competitors. Think of Apple's source code for the graphical user interface, Pfizer's automated drug discovery technology, and Disney's films and characters. Fifty years ago, 78 percent of the assets of U.S. nonfinancial corporations were tangible assets (real estate, inventories, and plant and equipment). Today that figure is just 53 percent; intangible assets such as patents, copyrights, and goodwill have grown to nearly dominate the account books. In addition, as the information economy comes center stage, intellectual property has become an all-important source of competitive advantage.

WHAT WENT RIGHT / WHAT WENT WRONG

AVENTIS[7]

The following list shows the top 10 patented drugs in 2000 and 2006. The instability on this list is striking. Once a drug goes off patent (e.g., Prozac in 2001 and Zocor in 2004), the sales evaporate quickly. Generic drugs have become 42 percent of the U.S. prescription drug market. Generics usually enter the market at a 60–75 percent discount and eventually sell for as little as 20 percent of the original patented drug's price.

When Eli Lilly's patent on Prozac ended, the firm lost 70 percent of its sales to generic rivals *within one month*. To prevent such disruptive shocks to the recovery of enormous fixed R&D costs, some pharmaceutical companies routinely file frivolous patent extensions that change simply the coating or the delivery system (tablet to liquid, for example). The White House proposed in late 2002 a 30-month extension on patents challenged by a generic substitute to reduce frivolous patenting. Of equal concern, Aventis (a Franco-German drug group headquartered in Strasbourg, France) is accused of bribing the American generic drug producer Andrix \$90 million to delay the introduction of its cheaper substitute heart attack drug. Such sums suggest just how extensive the monopoly markup on patented pharmaceuticals must be.

[7] Based on "Don't Look Down," *The Economist* (January 6, 2001), p. 62; "Bloom and Blight," *The Economist* (October 26, 2002), p. 60; "Protection Racket," *The Economist* (May 19, 2001), p. 58; and www.imshealth.com (accessed September 2006).

Best-Selling Patented Drugs, 2000

Drug	Patent Owner	Treatment	Drug	Patent Owner	Treatment
1. Losec	AstraZeneca	ulcers	6. Prozac	Eli Lilly	depression
2. Lipitor	Pfizer	cholesterol	7. Celebrex	Pfizer	arthritis
3. Zocor	Merck	cholesterol	8. Seroxat	GlaxoSmithKline	depression
4. Norvasc	Pfizer	high blood pressure	9. Claritin	Schering-Plough	allergies
5. Orgastro	Abbott Labs	ulcers	10. Zyprexa	Eli Lilly	schizophrenia

Best-Selling Patented Drugs, 2006

Drug	Patent Owner	Treatment	Drug	Patent Owner	Treatment
1. Lipitor	Pfizer	cholesterol	6. Enbel	Angen Wyeth	arthritis
2. Nexium	AstraZeneca	acid reflux	7. Effexor	Wyeth	depression
3. Plavix	Sanofi	platelet aggregation	8. Orgastro	Abbott Labs	ulcers
4. Serentide	GlaxoSmithKline	allergies	9. Zyprexa	Eli Lilly	schizophrenia
5. Norvasc	Pfizer	high blood pressure	10. Singulair	Schein	allergies

In 2005, 10 firms passed Thomas Edison's record of 1,093 patents acquired (see Table 16.5). IBM acquired 2,972 patents, Canon acquired 1,837, and Hewlett-Packard acquired 1,801. IBM Corporation was seeking patent protection at the astounding rate of 10 patent applications per working day.[8] Some of this activity is

[8] "The Knowledge Monopolies," *The Economist* (April 8, 2000), pp. 75–78; "Business Methods Patents," *Wall Street Journal* (October 3, 2000), p. B14; "Mind Over Matter," *Wall Street Journal* (April 4, 2002), p. A1; and "Innovation." *Forbes* (July 5, 2004), pp. 142–146.

Table 16.5 Top 10 Firms with Patents Granted in 2005

IBM	2,972
Canon	1,837
Hewlett-Packard	1,801
Matsushita	1,701
Samsung	1,645
Micron Technology	1,561
Intel	1,551
Hitachi	1,293
Toshiba	1,149
General Electric	906

strategic patenting of technology portfolios where companies do not wish to make a new device immediately, but they can plausibly describe how they would make it, what the device is used for, and the novelty of the idea. These evidentiary requirements are part of obtaining a patent.

Not just electronic devices, genetic engineering, and computer software, but also business process methods are "hot" current areas of patenting activity. Dell received a patent on the direct-to-the-consumer business model, and Walker Digital (parent of Priceline.com) received a patent on the Internet-based reverse auction in which buyers post prices that sellers can then "hit" to execute a sale. Patent attorneys believe the ATM machine, frequent flyer programs, and even credit cards could be patented as business processes if they were invented today.

Table 16.6 shows that the financial markets are definitely capitalizing this "knowledge capital" into the equity market value of companies with patents, trade secrets, and proprietary know-how. Almost half of the $22 billion market value of

Table 16.6 Knowledge Capital, 1998 ($ Billions)

	Sales	Book Value	Total Market Value	Market Value of Intangibles*
Merck	23.6	12.6	139.9	48.0
Bristol-Myers Squibb	16.7	7.2	107.0	30.5
Johnson & Johnson	22.6	12.4	92.9	29.7
DuPont	39.9	11.3	87.0	26.4
Dow Chemical	20.1	7.7	21.8	10.2
Monsanto	7.5	4.1	33.2	6.0

Business Method Patents

Patent Number	Date Issued	Device/Process	Inventors	Affiliate
5,797,127	8/18/98	Reverse auctions	Jay Walker et al.	Priceline.com
5,960,411	9/28/99	One-click buying	Jeff Bezos et al.	Amazon.com

*Estimated market value attributable to intangible, nonfinancial assets.

Source: Baruch Lev, *CFO* (February 1999); and *The Economist* (June 12, 1999), p. 62.

▲WHAT WENT RIGHT ▼WHAT WENT WRONG

TECHNOLOGY LICENSES COST PALM ITS LEAD IN PDAs[9]

In 1996, Palm single-handedly created the personal digital assistant (PDA) craze. Like Apple, Palm builds its own software and hardware. Worldwide, Palm operating systems run three quarters of all handheld devices that are capable of surfing the Internet. Unlike Apple, Palm decided to license its OS technology to competing manufacturers Handspring and Sony. Within two short years, Handspring surpassed Palm in manufacturing sales of PDAs by offering expansion slots and peripheral equipment such as phones and music players.

Licensing always entails such risks, but Palm really had little choice in the matter. Cell phone giant Nokia had licensed its Series 60 mobile-phone software to Siemens and Matsushita. The three firms together control 47 percent of the global cell phone market. Series 60 technology enables a cell phone to send and receive digital camera pictures, e-mail, and, most importantly, to browse a stripped-down version of the Net. If either Nokia or Palm succeeds in getting its OS adopted as an industry standard for handheld Web surfing, it will set in motion a virtuous circle of increasing returns. Recently, Palm and Handspring merged into palmOne to achieve a larger installed base.

[9] "Matsushita to Use Nokia's Cellphone Software," *Wall Street Journal* (December 20, 2000), p. B10; and "One Palm Flapping," *The Economist* (June 2, 2001), p. 65.

Dow Chemical and more than a third of the $140 billion market value of Merck are discounted cash flow from intangible assets, mostly intellectual property. Much of Amazon.com's $11 billion market value arises from licensing fees on their business methods patents. Between 1994 and 1999, IBM boosted its annual revenues from licensing its intellectual property by more than 200 percent from $500 million to $1.6 billion. In consumer products too, Reebok recently paid $250 million in royalties to obtain a 10-year exclusive license to market National Football League-branded uniforms, hats, and equipment and to have its trademark on the players' apparel of all NFL teams. So, substantial revenue is available from licensing, but of course licensing better enables one's competitors to compete for a firm's own regular customers.

Pros and Cons of Patent Protection

Much debate continues about whether patent and trade secret protection motivates first-mover companies to innovate or stifles technological research by fast-second companies. Imitators often substantially advance some aspect of a new technology, but they must license the original patents or run the risk of defending themselves against patent infringement lawsuits. Jeff Bezos of Amazon.com proposed that 20-year patent protection for computer software and business methods be reduced to only 3–5 years. Patent protection outside the United States is already diminished. In Europe, patent applications invite legal challenge, and a majority of initial patents have been overturned. The EU has also decided not to issue patents for either computer software or business methods. In this environment, trade secrets, proprietary know-how, and internal business practices take on added importance.

Whether to "bury" the trade secrets or to acknowledge openly their existence and license them to competitors is a significant strategic decision about the firm's contracting and governance mechanisms. No less important is the decision as to whether to develop know-how in-house or to license proprietary know-how from competitors. Many executives believe that manufacturing managers and R&D experts should interact on an ongoing basis in order to develop a reservoir of noncodifiable tacit knowledge.

EXAMPLE

COMPETING BUSINESS PLANS AT CELERA GENOMICS AND HUMAN GENOME SCIENCES

Genomics has revolutionized drug discovery and development, with some respected industry analysts predicting that "all drug discovery efforts will soon be genomics-based."[10] Celera Genomics, the company that finished reading the human genome sequence in 2000, expects to sell information, in effect to license its genome database, for as much as $90 million a year. It is hoped that comparing which genes are expressed and which remain recessive in various diseases will lead drug scientists to new blockbuster therapies and early detection of harmful side effects. However, an in-depth understanding of the biology of therapeutic mechanisms at the molecular level will also be key. Human Genome Sciences (HGS) has decided therefore to position itself as a drug maker, attempting to patent drug processes, not simply license genetic information to traditional drug companies. HGS's first product, a wound healer, is in clinical trials.

In Table 16.7, Motorola and Lucent Technologies (the spin-off of Bell Labs from AT&T) are trying to decide whether to develop in-house or license proprietary trade secrets in telecommunications engineering and software. Because of Lucent's long-term experience in this arena, if Motorola develops and patents the process and devices, Lucent expects to be successful as an imitator earning $9 billion. Should licensing of some proprietary know-how prove necessary, Lucent believes an inexpensive limited

Table 16.7 To License or Develop Expertise In-House?

		Motorola	
		Develop/Patent	Imitate/License
Lucent	Develop/Patent	$1 billion $5 billion	$3 billion $4 billion
	Imitate/License	−$1 billion $9 billion	0 0

[10] *BusinessWeek* (January 8, 2001), p. 113.

WHAT WENT RIGHT ▼ WHAT WENT WRONG

MOTOROLA: WHAT THEY DIDN'T KNOW HURT THEM[11]

Motorola, Inc., was a pioneer in communications engineering with many of the early analog devices in radio, television, and military signal processing to its credit. More recently Motorola developed and successfully launched the first handheld cell phones and also took the lead in satellite-based wireless communications with Iridium, a global cellular network project. Ambitious future projects include a satellite-based, high-speed, high-security video conferencing network for corporate customers and a satellite-based transcontinental and transoceanic connection for land-based cell phone companies.

Network reliability problems began to arise, however, when Motorola insisted on slowly developing its own digital wireless proprietary know-how rather than licensing the needed trade secrets and patents from Lucent or QUALCOMM Incorporated. Motorola had little expertise in digital switches, computing equipment, and communications software. Yet, proprietary knowledge in these areas proved critical in attempting to integrate Motorola's satellite system with land-based cell phone networks. At one point, Motorola launched a cell phone system whose software essentially blocked any other user from simultaneously connecting through the same cell tower and receiving station. In effect, this device crashed the local cell network anytime it was in use.

Consequently, during a period in 1998 when QUALCOMM cell phones sold by the hundreds of thousands, Motorola was late to market with a competing product launch and even then announced a series of further delays. The operations problems were exacerbated by Motorola's lack of a common platform for its product configurations. Rather than mixing and matching standard components like Dell's operations strategy for assembling PCs, Motorola assembles cell phones from 10 different platforms with few interchangeable components.

Perhaps it is not surprising that QUALCOMM and Lucent, a former division of AT&T, experienced less trouble adding know-how in wireless technology to their long-standing expertise in wire-based telecommunications networks than Motorola experienced trying to add know-how in digital switches and communications software to their long-standing expertise in analog wireless hardware. Motorola should have licensed the proprietary know-how rather than attempt to develop it in-house.

[11] Based on "Unsold State: Motorola Struggles to Regain Its Footing," *Wall Street Journal* (April 22, 1998), p. A1; and "How Motorola Roamed Astray," *Wall Street Journal* (October 26, 2000), p. B12.

license will be sufficient. Consequently, Motorola will be unable (in that circumstance) to recover its fully allocated research and development costs and will therefore lose money (i.e., the −\$1 billion payoff in the southeast cell). In contrast, if Lucent develops and patents the needed process, its first-mover advantage would bring in substantial license fees from Motorola, who would need the proprietary knowledge gained through the trade secret license. Hence, the payoffs describing this situation are \$4 billion/\$3 billion in the northeast cell.

To complete the description of the payoff matrix, if neither firm develops the process, no profits accrue to either party. And if they compete head to head in a patent race, we assume the development costs will rise such that total profits fall from $7 billion to $6 billion, divided $5 to $1 between the technology leader Lucent and follower Motorola. What should Lucent do?

If Lucent could be sure Motorola was proceeding, Lucent would most prefer to wait and play "fast second." $9 billion in the southwest cell is certainly attractive relative to $5 billion in the northwest cell. However, Motorola can be expected to avoid the development expense and attempt itself to wait, imitate, and license as required to fill in the gaps in its own trade secrets and proprietary know-how. Indeed, Motorola has a dominant strategy to wait, imitate, and license. Consequently, Lucent anticipates that the payoff ($4 billion/$3 billion) in the northeast cell will emerge as an iterated dominant equilibrium. Recall that an iterated dominant equilibrium strategy is a self-interest maximizing action by Lucent that is consistent with dominant-strategy responses of Motorola. At the northeast cell ($4 billion/$3 billion), neither party wishes to deviate to another action; therefore {$\text{Develop}_{\text{Lucent}}$, $\text{License}_{\text{Motorola}}$} is a Nash equilibrium strategy, and the only Nash equilibrium in Table 16.7.

Although the numbers in Table 16.7 are only illustrative, thinking through the game theory analysis can often provide insight in predicting rival reaction to company moves and countermoves. In this case, an analysis such as Table 16.7 clearly indicates the advantages of the licensing alternative rather than the in-house development Motorola actually pursued.

CONCLUSION ON LICENSING

The decision to license depends in part on the availability of increasing returns and the competitive advantage offered by cost reductions. In Europe, where few industry standards have emerged for information technology products and where patents are often successfully challenged, first-mover firms have licensed to competitors rather than simply watch their trade secrets and proprietary know-how be steadily eroded by imitators. The result is increased competition, lower prices for consumers, and a faster rate of technological adoption. For example, prices for some digital TV components (e.g., digital video broadcasting chips) keep dropping, and the digital technology is quickly being incorporated into related products such as cell phones, pagers, and secure video business networks for corporate meetings.

In the United States, Red Hat uses a general public license to penetrate as quickly as possible into the operating system market with its Linux-based software that is intended to compete with Windows NT and eventually with Windows itself. Red Hat allows its suppliers and customers to copy, modify, and redistribute Red Hat software at no charge as long as they do so without charge. This open-source software strategy is an attempt to achieve the inflection point for increasing returns that Microsoft's competitors, including Apple, never reached.

A final tactical advantage of licensing comes from reducing recontracting hazards. In purchasing high-end Alpha chips from Digital Equipment Corporation (now a division of Hewlett-Packard), many workstation manufacturers worry about the postcontractual opportunism. At contract renewal, once their designs are optimized for the Alpha technology, the manufacturers are vulnerable to major price increases for these sole-source-supplied chips. Digital can credibly commit to more stable prices and thereby increase the rate of adoption for its product by licensing to both AMD and Intel. By allowing customers to dual source the Alpha chip technology, Digital credibly commits to renew its supply contracts without price gouging.

Intel employed this licensing strategy itself while trying to establish the Pentium series of chips as an industry standard in PCs. IBM also licensed its operating system technology to Microsoft to speed the rate of adoption of DOS-based equipment. Apple Computers pursued the opposite nonlicensing strategy, thereby effectively slowing the rate of adoption of Macs, and lost to IBM and Microsoft in attempting to establish an industry standard once those companies reached the level of product acceptance that set off increasing returns.

SUMMARY

- *Market performance* refers to the efficiency of resource allocation within and among firms, the technological progressiveness of firms, the tendency of firms to fully employ resources, and the impact on the equitable distribution of resources.
- *Market conduct* refers to the pricing behavior; the product policy; the sales promotion and advertising policy; the research, development, and innovation strategies; and the legal tactics employed by a firm or group of firms.
- *Market structure* refers to the degree of seller and buyer concentration in a market, the degree of actual or imagined product differentiation between products or services of competing producers, and the conditions surrounding entry into the market.
- Contestable markets are assumed to have freedom of entry and exit for potential competitors, slow-reaching incumbents, and low switching costs for consumers. In a perfectly contestable market, the resulting set of prices and outputs approaches those expected under perfect competition.
- Measures of market concentration include:
  - the market concentration ratio, defined as the percentage of total industry output attributable to the 4, 8, 20, or 50 largest companies.
  - the Herfindahl-Hirschman Index (HHI), which is equal to the sum of the squares of the market shares of all firms in an industry.
- A group of antitrust laws has been passed to prevent monopoly and to encourage competition in U.S. industry. The most important of these acts are the Sherman Act of 1890, the FTC and Clayton Acts of 1914, the Robinson-Patman Act of 1936, the Celler-Kefauver Antimerger Act of 1950, the Hart-Scott-Rodino Antitrust Improvement Act of 1976, and Merger Guidelines of 1992 and 1997.
- Federal, state, and local governments all impose regulations on business enterprises. Regulatory constraints can affect a firm's operating costs (both fixed and variable), capital costs, and revenues.
- The current political and economic environment favors a significant reduction in the amount of government regulation and interference in the operation of the private sector of the economy. Recent deregulation includes banking, transportation, natural gas pipeline, electric utility, and telecommunications industries.
- A number of regulatory policies, such as licensing and issuing patents, are designed to restrict competition.
- Externalities exist when a third party receives benefits or bears costs arising from an economic transaction in which he or she is not a direct participant. The impact of externalities is felt outside of (external to) the normal market pricing and resource-allocation mechanism.
- Pecuniary externalities, in which spillover effects are reflected in the market pricing mechanism, result in no inefficiencies.
- Ronald Coase has shown that an efficient allocation of resources can generally be achieved in the case of small-numbers externalities by contractual bargaining between the creator and recipient of the externality.
- Impediments to private voluntary bargaining include prohibitive search and notification costs, internal negotiation costs among large numbers of affected parties, prohibitive monitoring costs, and an absence of the surpluses required for making side payments.
- Many possible solutions to problems of externalities exist and include solution by voluntary side payment, governmental prohibition, regulatory directive, imposition of pollution taxes or subsidies, a sale of rights to create the externality, and merger.
- Whether to develop and license or wait and imitate is an organizational form decision about the protection afforded by patents, the relative importance of proprietary know-how, the availability of industry standards, technological lock-in, value-enhancing complements, and other sources of increasing returns.

Exercises

Answers to the exercises in blue can be found in Appendix C at the back of the book.

1. If Apple iPod only played iTunes, and iTunes only could be heard on the Apple iPod, could Apple price the technologically integrated bundle any way they wanted? If other electronic music can play on an iPod, what determines whether there are any limitations on the bundled pricing of iPods and iTunes? What are those limitations?
2. An industry is composed of Firm 1, which controls 70 percent of the market, Firm 2 with 15 percent of the market, and Firm 3 with 5 percent of the market. About 20 firms of approximately equal size divide the remaining 10 percent of the market. Calculate the Herfindahl-Hirschman Index before and after the merger of Firm 2 and Firm 3 (assume that the combined market share after the merger is 20 percent). Would you view a merger of Firm 2 with Firm 3 as procompetitive or anticompetitive? Explain.
3. How can you justify the existence of government-granted monopolies for public utilities such as natural gas distribution and electricity in the light of the traditional economic argument that the more competition there is, the more likely it is that an efficient allocation of resources will occur?
4. Suppose an industry is composed of eight firms with the following market shares:

A	30%	E	8%
B	25	F	5
C	15	G	4
D	10	H	3

Based on the (revised 1997) merger guidelines, would the Antitrust Division likely challenge a proposed merger between

a. Firms C and D (assume the combined market share is 25 percent)?

b. Firms F and G (assume the combined market share is 9 percent)?

Explain your answer.

5. What economic arguments can be made in favor of mandatory seat-belt usage laws in automobiles and mandatory helmet laws for motorcycles?
6. What are the incentives to innovate for a monopoly firm as compared with a firm in a competitive market if patent protection is not available?
7. Would you consider the fractional ownership jet taxi industry (NetJets, FlexJets, etc.) to be a contestable market? Why or why not?
8. The industry demand function for bulk plastics is represented by the following equation:

$$P = 800 - 20Q$$

where Q represents millions of pounds of plastic.

The total cost function for the industry, exclusive of a required return on invested capital, is

$$TC = 300 + 500Q + 10Q^2$$

where Q represents millions of pounds of plastic.

a. If this industry acts like a monopolist in the determination of price and output, compute the profit-maximizing level of price and output.

b. What are total profits at this price and output level?

c. Assume that this industry is composed of many (500) small firms, such that the demand function facing any individual firm is

$$P = \$620$$

Compute the profit-maximizing level of price and output under these conditions (the industry's total cost function remains unchanged).

d. What are total profits, given your answer to Part (c)?

e. Because of the risk of this industry, investors require a 15 percent rate of return on investment. Total industry investment amounts to \$2 billion. If the monopoly solution prevails, as calculated in Parts (a) and (b), how would you describe the profits of the industry?

f. If the competitive solution most accurately describes the industry, is the industry operating under equilibrium conditions? Why or why not? What would you expect to happen?

g. The Clean Water Coalition proposed pollution control standards for the industry that would change the industry cost curve to the following:

$$TC = 400 + 560Q + 10Q^2$$

What is the impact of this change on price, output, and total profits under the monopoly solution?

h. Assume these standards are being proposed only in the state of Texas, which has 50 of the 500 producers. What impact would you expect the new standards to have on Texas firms? The rest of the industry?

9. A product you produce has the following annual demand function:

$$P = 90 - 0.003Q$$

The marginal cost of producing the product is \$30. If the firm pays a fee of \$50,000 to the General Drug Research Council, it can have its product's effectiveness certified. The demand function for a certified product is expected to be

$$P = 100 - 0.003Q$$

a. Calculate the price, output, and profit contribution if the product is not certified.

b. Calculate the price, output, and profit contribution if the product is certified.

c. Should the firm undergo the certification process?

10. Discuss the problems of aircraft noise around an airport from an externality perspective and propose a possible solution if (a) housing existed in the airport area before the airport was built and (b) housing was built adjacent to the airport after the airport was built.

11. A sheep rancher leased the mineral rights beneath her grazing land to an oil company. She fears that discharges from the oil wells will pollute her underground water resources. Consequently, the contract for the sale of mineral rights requires that the rancher and the oil company reach a mutually agreeable solution to the water contamination problem should it occur. If this bargaining fails to reach a conclusion acceptable to both sides, the mineral rights lease will be terminated automatically, and the rancher will be required to return a portion of the lease proceeds to the oil company. The portion that must be returned to the oil company is to be determined through a process of binding arbitration. Discuss likely outcomes should this problem arise.

12. Branding Iron Products, a specialty steel fabricator, operates a plant in the town of West Star, Texas. The town has grown rapidly because of recent discoveries of oil and gas in the area. Many of the new residents have expressed concern at the amount of pollution (primarily particulate matter in the air and waste water in the town's river) emitted by Branding Iron. Three proposals have been made to remedy the problem:

a. Impose a tax on the amount of particulate matter and the amount of waste water emitted by the firm.

b. Prohibit pollution by the firm.

c. Offer tax incentives to the firm to clean up its production processes.

Evaluate each of these alternatives from the perspectives of economic efficiency, equity, and the likely long-term impact on the firm.

13. An industry produces its product, Scruffs, at a constant marginal cost of $50. The market demand for Scruffs is equal to

$$Q = 75{,}000 - 600P$$

a. What is the value to a monopolist who is able to develop a patented process for producing Scruffs at a cost of only $45?

b. If the industry producing Scruffs is purely competitive, what is the maximum benefit that an inventor of a process that will reduce the cost of producing Scruffs by $5 per unit can expect to receive by licensing her invention to the firms in the industry?

14. If the decision to develop and license or wait and imitate in Table 16.7 is a simultaneous-play repeated game between Lucent and Motorola for each new generation of technology, what happens if the Motorola payoff in the southwest cell is positive $2 billion? How should Motorola "play" in this modified licensing game? How should Lucent play?

CASE EXERCISES

PRICE FIXING OF AUCTION HOUSE COMMISSIONS

Go to www.usdoj.gov/atr/public/press_releases/2000/6639.htm. Read the case on *U.S. v. Sotheby's Holdings Inc.* and the accompanying article regarding auction house collusion. What parallels do you see to the sellers on eBay and airline Web sites?

MICROSOFT TYING ARRANGEMENTS

1. Which of the following is a violation of the antitrust laws in the United States and why? (a) Microsoft monopolizes the market in PC operating systems with a 92 percent market share; (b) Microsoft attempts to monopolize the market in Internet portals with a pattern of anticompetitive tactics (tying arrangements, refusals to deal, etc.); (c) Microsoft sells Windows plus Microsoft Internet Explorer for less than Windows without Internet Explorer installed as the default browser; (d) Microsoft gives Internet Explorer away free to individual adopters with variable cost estimated at $0.0067; (e) Microsoft threatens to delicense Compaq and Dell, who would then be unable to preinstall Windows on PCs they ship unless Compaq and Dell exclude Netscape's Internet browser from the user interface.

2. What difference does it make to the tying arrangement issues if Internet Explorer is a functionally integrated component of Windows? What if it's more like a radio in an automobile than a steering post interlock device?

3. How should Microsoft market long-distance telephone services in the new wireless telecommunications devices that also include Internet portals?

Music Recording Industry Blocked from Consolidating

Given the following market share distributions, the U.S. Antitrust Division blocked a merger of BMG and EMI in 2001, and the European Commission blocked a merger of Time Warner's music division and EMI in 2000. Analyze these decisions and present arguments both pro and con.

U.S. Market Shares		World Market Share	
Vivendi Universal	20%	Vivendi Universal	21%
Sony	20%	Sony	19%
BMG	15%	EMI	13%
Time Warner	13%	Time Warner	12%
EMI	11%	BMG	12%

What else should be involved in such merger policies?

CHAPTER

17

LONG-TERM INVESTMENT ANALYSIS

CHAPTER PREVIEW Investment analysis (capital budgeting) is the process of planning for the purchases of assets whose returns (cash flows) are expected to continue beyond one year. When making capital budgeting decisions, the firm's managers commit resources to the expansion of its productive capacity, improvement of its cost efficiency, or diversification of its asset base. Each of these decisions affects future cash flows the firm expects to generate and the risk of those cash flows. Capital expenditures are a bridge between short-term price and output decisions and longer-term strategic decisions that wealth-maximizing managers must make to remain competitive. Public sector managers use cost-benefit analysis and cost-effectiveness analysis when considering many long-term resource allocation decisions. These techniques also are presented in this chapter.

MANAGERIAL CHALLENGE

Multigenerational Effects of Ozone Depletion and Greenhouse Gases[1]

The long-term effects of ozone depletion from chlorofluorocarbon (CFC) emissions and of CO_2 and other greenhouse gases from the burning of fossil fuels are controversial. Some scientists insist that the release of CFCs has opened a gaping hole in the ozone shield that provides protection from UV rays and that the increasing concentration of greenhouse gases has raised global temperatures. What is less controversial is that these environmental events have massive consequences for human health and wealth. Increasing incidence of skin cancers, melting polar icecaps, and a rising sea level imply tangible losses of catastrophic proportions—perhaps many billions of dollars annually. Some of these losses are immediate, but others are perhaps 100 years off. Benefit-cost analysis normally considers projects no more than 20 to 30 years long and employs discount rates of 2 percent to 7 percent. How should one discount such an uncertain and distant future as is involved in ozone depletion and greenhouse gases?

Assuming a constant discount rate equal to the rate of return on long-term government bonds (5.3 percent), the discount factor that should be applied to find the present value of projected benefits or losses avoided in year 100 would be $(1/1.053^{100})$ = .00572 or $5,717 present value per million dollars of future losses avoided. Notice what happens, however, if uncertainty about the appropriate discount rate varies from 2 percent to 7 percent. The discount factor at 100 years would then vary from $(1/1.02^{100})$ = .13803 or $138,033 per million dollars for 2 percent, to as little as $(1/1.07^{100})$ = .00115, or 1,152 per million dollars for 7 percent.

The possibility of lower discount rates implies that $13.8 billion dollars should be spent today to avoid the projected $100 billion in delayed damage 100 years from now! Of course, the higher 7 percent

MANAGERIAL CHALLENGE

rate implies spending just $115.2 million to avoid the $100-billion future loss. This range of present value estimates from $115 million to $13.8 billion is beyond what any analyst can work with in doing sensitivity analysis. What should a benefit-cost analyst conclude? And what should businesses whose cash flows are dependent on "fun in the sun" recreation like Hilton Head and Wet-N-Wild or physical assets built near sea level like the Shanghai business district and Miami Beach hotels conclude about the justifiable capital expenditure to slow down or reverse global warming?

One insight is that it's not the average discount rate between 2 and 7 percent (4.5 percent) that matters in such circumstances, just as the average depth of a pool does not determine the hazard to someone who cannot swim. Instead, the lowest applicable discount rate largely determines the present value of very distant cash flow streams because higher discount rate scenarios inevitably reduce present values to essentially zero (less than a penny per dollar) at 100 years.

Martin Weitzman has calculated what discount rate is implied by assuming the discount rate begins at 4 percent and then follows a random path with equi-probable higher and lower rates and a standard deviation of 3 percent. The results led him to recommend a constant sliding scale discount rate of 2 percent for 25- to 75-year cash flows, *and only 1 percent for 76- to 300-year cash flows.* The fact that higher and lower discount rates have such dramatically nonsymmetric effects on present value when very distant benefits are involved means that value of reducing CO_2 emissions and other greenhouse gases may be much higher than previously thought.

[1] Based on Richard Newell and William Pizer, "Discounting the Benefits of Climate Change Mitigation," Resources for the Future (December 2001); and Martin Weitzman, "Gamma Discounting," *American Economic Review* (March 2001).

THE NATURE OF CAPITAL EXPENDITURE DECISIONS

Previous chapters were mostly concerned with analytical tools and decision models that help managers make the most efficient use of existing resources. This chapter considers decisions to replace or expand the capital resource base.

Decisions to replace assets may change the technology employed by a firm, which alters the relevant production and cost functions. Most replacement decisions are based on managers' expectations that a sufficiently lower cost function will justify the required outlays for the replacement.

Decisions to expand a firm's asset base also increase the scale or size of the productive facilities. Expansion decisions rely on forecasts of future demand and costs after the expansion. If quantity demanded is suitably high or costs sufficiently low, the resulting profits may justify the expansion decision.

Capital Expenditure
A cash outlay designed to generate a flow of future cash benefits over a period of time extending beyond one year.

Capital Budgeting
The process of planning for and evaluating capital expenditures.

A **capital expenditure** is a cash outlay that is expected to generate a flow of future cash benefits lasting longer than one year. It is distinguished from a normal operating expenditure, which is expected to result in cash benefits during the coming one-year period. (The choice of a one-year period is arbitrary, but it does serve as a useful guideline.) **Capital budgeting** is the process of planning for and evaluating capital expenditures. In addition to asset replacement and expansion decisions, other types of decisions that can be analyzed using capital budgeting techniques include research and development expenditures, investments in employee education and training, lease-versus-buy decisions, and mergers and acquisitions.

Current capital outlays, by definition, have a long-range impact by determining products that will be produced, markets to be entered, the location of plants and facilities, and the type of technology (with its associated costs) to be used. Capital expenditures require careful analysis because they are costly to make and often more costly to reverse.

A Basic Framework for Capital Budgeting

Recall from earlier chapters that economic theory indicates that a firm should operate at the point where the marginal cost of an additional unit of output just equals the marginal revenue derived from that output. Following this rule will lead to profit maximization by a firm. As we saw in the Sara Lee example in Chapter 2, this principle may be applied to the capital budgeting decisions of the firm. In the context of capital budgeting, the marginal revenue may be thought of as the rates of return earned on successive investments. Marginal cost may be interpreted as the firm's weighted marginal cost of capital—that is, the cost of successive increments of capital acquired by the firm, weighted by the proportions of their use in the firm's capital structure.

EXAMPLE

Capital Budgeting Decision: Clark Candy Company

This basic capital budgeting decision-making framework for the Clark Candy Company is illustrated in Figure 17.1. The company has nine investment projects under consideration, labeled *A*, *B*, *C*, . . . , *I*. The model assumes that all projects have the same risk. This schedule of projects often is called the *investment opportunity curve.* The projects are indicated by lettered bars on the graph. For example, Project *A* requires an investment of $2 million and is expected to generate a 24 percent rate of return. Project *B* will cost $1 million ($3 million minus $2 million on the horizontal axis) and generate a 22 percent rate of return, and so on. Graphically, the projects are arranged in descending order by their rates of return, indicating that no firm has a limitless number of possible investment projects that all generate high rates of return. As new products are produced, new markets entered, and cost-saving technologies adopted, the number of highly profitable investment opportunities tends to decline. The *marginal cost of capital curve* represents the marginal cost of capital to the firm; that is, the cost of each additional dollar raised in the capital markets.

Using this basic model, the firm should undertake Projects *A*, *B*, *C*, *D*, and *E*, because their returns exceed the firm's marginal cost of capital. Although implementing this conceptual model involves some practical difficulties, it offers a guideline for optimal decision making.

Figure 17.1 A Simplified Capital Budgeting Model

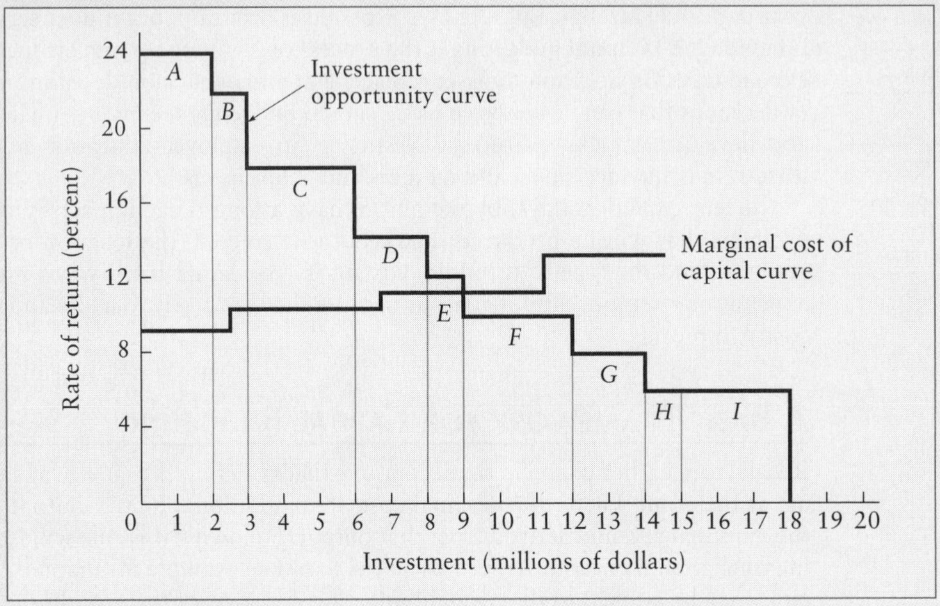

The Capital Budgeting Process

The process of selecting capital investment projects consists of the following important steps:

1. Generate alternative capital investment project proposals.
2. Estimate cash flows for the project proposals.
3. Evaluate and choose, from the alternatives available, those investment projects to implement.
4. Review the investment projects after they have been implemented.

Generating Capital Investment Projects

Ideas for new capital investments can come from many sources both inside and outside the firm. Proposals can originate at all levels in the organization, from factory workers all the way up to the board of directors. Most medium- and large-sized firms have departments whose responsibilities include searching for and analyzing capital expenditure projects. These departments include cost accounting, industrial engineering, marketing research, research and development, and corporate planning personnel.

Capital expenditure projects can be classified into various categories, depending on the benefits expected. One category includes projects that are designed to *reduce costs*. Like products that become obsolete, technological progress also renders plants, equipment, and production processes obsolete. Normal wear and tear make older plants and equipment more costly to operate due to more downtime and higher maintenance costs. Obsolescence and deterioration require replacement of older facilities with new, more efficient plants and equipment.

A second category of capital expenditures includes projects designed to *improve a firm's demand curve,* or to respond to changes in that curve. If increased demand for a product line is forecast, and if existing manufacturing and distribution facilities are inadequate to meet this demand, then the firm must develop proposals for expanding capacity. A firm also may make investments in advertising/product promotion campaigns to influence the demand for its products. Although often not thought of as traditional capital expenditures, these promotional outlays have all the characteristics of capital investments and can be analyzed in the same way.

A third category of capital expenditure projects includes those that create *future growth options* for the firm. For example, investing in research and development (R&D) can be viewed as a capital expenditure that creates future growth options for the firm. Any particular R&D project will be difficult to justify using traditional capital expenditure analysis procedures, because those procedures normally do not consider the option value created by R&D outlays. These outlays give the firm the "option," but not the obligation, to make further outlays that are needed to bring a new product to market. Without the initial R&D outlays, the firm would not possess the option to make the second-phase expenditures and to reap the associated rewards.[2]

A fourth type of capital expenditure includes projects designed to *meet legal requirements and health and safety standards,* such as proposals for pollution control outlays, ventilation, employee safety, and fire-protection equipment. At first glance it may seem that these outlays are "simply required" and thus no analysis is needed. However, managers can choose not to make these outlays and just shut down a plant. The decision depends on whether the remaining cash flows in a project are sufficiently large to justify the additional outlays necessary to keep the plant operating.

EXAMPLE

CAPITAL EXPENDITURES AT CHRYSLER: THE GRAND CHEROKEE[3]

In early 1992 Chrysler Corporation introduced its new Grand Cherokee sport utility vehicle. The vehicle was developed using an unusual (for Chrysler) "platform team" approach. Instead of developing this new vehicle sequentially, passing it from market research to design to engineering to manufacturing, Chrysler assembled a team of 700 to 800 engineering, marketing research, and design personnel and told them to develop the new vehicle as a team. As a result, the new Cherokee was developed and brought to the market more quickly and at a lower cost than had been typical for other American auto companies. The new Grand Cherokee was developed and a new plant built in Detroit to produce it, all for about $1.1 billion. In comparison, in the early 1980s, General Motors spent $1 billion each just on the plants it built, before factoring in new-product development costs. Chrysler planned to sell up to 175,000 of these vehicles each year, realizing a profit of $5,500 per unit.

---

[2] See Nalin Kulatilaka and Alan Marcus, "Project Valuation under Uncertainty: When Does DCF Fail?" *Journal of Applied Corporate Finance* (Fall 1992), pp. 92–100; and Lenos Trigeorgis, "Real Options and Interactions with Financial Flexibility," *Financial Management* (Autumn 1993), pp. 202–224, for discussion of real options in capital budgeting.

[3] Based largely on "Iacocca's Last Stand at Chrysler," *Fortune* (April 20, 1992), p. 63ff.

The Grand Cherokee capital expenditures contain elements of both demand curve management and cost reduction. Chrysler saw sales of its older, smaller Jeep Cherokee decline from a peak of nearly 200,000 units per year to about 125,000, primarily because of stiff competition from the Ford-built Explorer. Chrysler hoped to regain much of this lost market share. In addition, the decision to build the Grand Cherokee in an efficient new plant in Detroit rather than in its older underutilized plant in Toledo reflected a commitment to hold costs of production at a minimum. Finally, it was Chrysler's intention to cut the price of its old Jeep Cherokee and market it aggressively as a low-cost, sporty utility vehicle alternative. Chrysler hoped that this strategy would permit it to expand export sales in Europe. Thus Chrysler created for itself the option either to retain the older model if it sold well at a lower price, or to phase out the older model and close the Toledo plant. The evaluation process of this and many other major capital expenditure projects contains elements of cost reduction, demand management, and creation of strategic options.

EXAMPLE

SARA LEE: CREATING STRATEGIC OPTIONS IN EASTERN EUROPE[4]

Sara Lee Corporation is a large, U.S.-based multinational manufacturer and marketer of branded high-quality consumer products. Among other items it produces and sells, Sara Lee is a major producer and marketer of coffee products in Holland, Belgium, Spain, France, and Denmark. During the 1990s, Sara Lee made a number of strategic acquisitions designed to enhance its long-term international position. With the opening of the economies of the former Soviet satellite states in Eastern Europe, Sara Lee embarked on a strategy designed to give it the needed "options" to expand into the Eastern European market. It acquired a 51 percent interest in Compack Trading and Packing Company, Hungary's largest coffee business. This acquisition gave Sara Lee an opportunity to develop experience operating a firm in the emerging, and somewhat peculiar, business climate of Eastern Europe. Although the acquisition of Compack was unlikely to provide immediate, positive returns to Sara Lee, it gave Sara Lee the expertise needed for considering other acquisitions and expansions in the Eastern European markets. On the basis of traditional capital investment criteria this acquisition was probably difficult to justify, but when the value of the strategic options it would create for making future investments in the region were considered, Sara Lee found it to be an attractive acquisition.

EXAMPLE

ALTERNATIVE INVESTMENTS FOR CLEAN AIR[5]

The 1990 Clean Air Act placed strict new standards on air pollution. A California program provides polluting firms with a new investment alternative to meet the standards of the act. Prior to the implementation of the new market-based program in California, a polluting firm had two (legal) options: close the plant or make the

[4] Based on Sara Lee Corporation, *1991 Annual Report.*

[5] Based on "Cold Cash for Old Clunkers," *Newsweek* (April 6, 1992), p. 61.

capital investments needed to bring the plant up to acceptable emission standard levels. The California plan created a market for pollution rights. For example, suppose a factory must reduce its nitrogen oxide emissions by 130,000 pounds per year at a cost of $1 million to install the necessary equipment. Under the California plan, the firm could buy 1,000 older cars, which emit an average of 130 pounds of nitrogen oxide a year, for a price of $700 per year each. The cars would be scrapped, removing them permanently from the roads, thereby reducing harmful emissions by the required 130,000 pounds. The company would save $300,000. In 1990, Unocal bought 8,376 pre-1971 cars for $700 each. These cars accounted for 13 million pounds of emissions per year, as much as the hydrocarbon emissions from 250,000 new cars or one large oil refinery. As this market-based approach spreads, financial managers will have one more investment alternative available when considering investments to meet pollution standards.

ESTIMATING CASH FLOWS

One of the most important and difficult steps in the selection process is estimating the cash flows associated with investment projects. Because the cash flows occur in the future, their value is *uncertain*. We assume the decision maker is able to estimate cash flows with sufficient accuracy to use these estimates in deciding whether to undertake the capital investment decisions. An intentional or unintentional introduction of *bias* in cash-flow estimates also causes difficulties. Individuals who have a vested interest in the project often struggle with making objective cash-flow estimates. The natural tendency is to be overly optimistic through underestimating the costs and overestimating the benefits of an investment project. Therefore, a review of the estimates by someone outside the department or division proposing the expenditure is helpful.

Certain basic guidelines are helpful when analyzing investment alternatives. First, cash flows should be measured on an *incremental* basis. In other words, the cash-flow stream for the project should represent the difference between the cash-flow streams to the firm with and without acceptance of the investment project. Second, cash flows should be measured on an *after-tax* basis, using the firm's marginal tax rate. Third, all the *indirect effects* of the project throughout the firm should be included in the cash-flow calculations. If a department or division of the firm is contemplating a capital investment that will alter the revenues or costs of other departments or divisions, then these external effects should be incorporated into the cash-flow estimates. Fourth, *sunk costs* should not be considered when evaluating the project. A sunk cost is an outlay that has been made (or committed to be made). Because sunk costs cannot be recovered, they should not be considered in the decision to accept or reject a project. Fifth, the value of resources used in the project should be measured in terms of their *opportunity costs*. Recall from Chapter 8 that opportunity cost is the value of a resource in its next best alternative use. In the context of capital budgeting, opportunity costs of resources (assets) are the cash flows that these resources can generate if they are not used in the project under consideration.

For a typical investment project, an initial investment is made in year 0, which generates a series of yearly net cash flows over the life of the project (n). The net investment ($NINV$) of a project is defined as the initial net cash outlay in year 0.

It includes the acquisition cost of any new assets plus installation and shipping costs and tax effects.[6]

The incremental, after-tax net cash flows (*NCFs*) of a particular investment project are equal to cash inflows minus cash outflows. For any year during the life of the project, these may be defined as the difference in net income after tax ($\Delta NIAT$) with and without the project plus the difference in depreciation (ΔD):

$$NCF = \Delta NIAT + \Delta D \quad [17.1]$$

$\Delta NIAT$ is equal to the difference in net income before tax ($\Delta NIBT$) times $(1 - t)$, where t is the corporate (marginal) income tax rate:

$$\Delta NIAT = \Delta NIBT(1 - t) \quad [17.2]$$

$\Delta NIBT$ is defined as the difference in revenues (ΔR) minus the differences in operating costs (ΔC) and depreciation (ΔD):

$$\Delta NIBT = \Delta R - \Delta C - \Delta D \quad [17.3]$$

Substituting Equation 17.3 into Equation 17.2 yields

$$\Delta NIAT = (\Delta R - \Delta C - \Delta D)(1 - t) \quad [17.4]$$

Substituting this equation into Equation 17.1 yields the following definition of net cash flow:

$$NCF = (\Delta R - \Delta C - \Delta D)(1 - t) + \Delta D \quad [17.5]$$

EXAMPLE

Cash-Flow Estimation: Hamilton Beach/Proctor-Silex, Inc.

To illustrate the cash-flow calculations, consider the following example. Suppose that Hamilton Beach/Proctor-Silex, a manufacturer of small electric appliances, has been offered a contract to supply a regional merchandising company with a line of food blenders to be sold under the retail company's private brand name. Hamilton Beach/Proctor-Silex's treasurer estimates that the initial investment in new equipment required to produce the blenders would be $1 million. The equipment would be depreciated (using the straight-line method)[7] over five years with a zero (0) estimated salvage value at the end of the five-year contract period. Based on the contract specifications, the treasurer estimates that incremental revenues (additional sales) would be $800,000 per year. The incremental costs if the contract is accepted will be $450,000 per year. These include cash outlays for direct labor and materials, transportation, utilities, building rent, and *additional* overhead. The firm's marginal income tax rate is 40 percent.

[6] When the new asset is replacing an existing asset, one must also include in the net investment calculation the net proceeds from the sale of the existing asset and the taxes associated with its sale. See R. Charles Moyer, James R. McGuigan, and William J. Kretlow, *Contemporary Financial Management,* 10th ed. (Cincinnati: South-Western, 2006), pp. 312–315, for a discussion of the cash flow calculations for replacement decisions.

[7] This depreciation method is just one of several possible methods that can be used. See Moyer, McGuigan, and Kretlow, *op. cit.*, pp. 326–330, for a discussion of the various depreciation methods.

Based on the information, *NINV* and *NCF* can be calculated for the project. The net investment (*NINV*) is equal to the $1 million initial outlay for the new equipment. The difference in revenues (ΔR) with and without the project is equal to $800,000 per year and the difference in operating costs (ΔC) is equal to $450,000 per year. The difference in depreciation (ΔD) is equal to the initial outlay ($1 million) divided by 5, or $200,000 per year. Substituting these values, along with $t = 0.40$, into Equation 17.5 yields the following:

$$NCF = (\$800{,}000 - \$450{,}000 - \$200{,}000)(1 - 0.40) + \$200{,}000$$
$$= \$290{,}000$$

Hamilton Beach/Proctor-Silex must decide whether it wants to invest $1 million now to receive $290,000 per year in net cash flows over the next five years. The next section illustrates two of the criteria used in evaluating investment proposals.

EVALUATING AND CHOOSING THE INVESTMENT PROJECTS TO IMPLEMENT

Once a capital expenditure project has been identified and the cash flows have been estimated, a decision to accept or reject the project is required. Acceptance of the project results in a cash-flow stream to the firm; that is, a series of either cash inflows or outflows for a number of years into the future. Typically, a project will result in an initial (first-year) outflow (investment) followed by a series of cash inflows (returns) over a number of succeeding years. To compare and choose among alternative projects with their associated cash-flow streams, the desirability of each project must be measured. The basic problem in measuring and comparing the desirability of investment projects is assessing the value of cash flows that occur at different points in time.

Various criteria are used to assess the desirability of investment projects. This section focuses on two widely used discounted cash-flow methods:[8]

- Internal rate of return (r)
- Net present value (NPV)

Internal Rate of Return (IRR)

The discount rate that equates the present value of the stream of net cash flows from a project with the project's net investment.

INTERNAL RATE OF RETURN The **internal rate of return (IRR)** is defined as the discount rate that equates the present value of the net cash flows from the project with the net investment. The following equation is used to find the internal rate of return:

$$\sum_{t=1}^{n} \frac{NCF_t}{(1 + r)^t} = NINV \qquad [17.6]$$

where n is the life of the investment and r is the internal rate of return.

An investment project should be accepted if the internal rate of return is greater than or equal to the firm's required rate of return (cost of capital); if not, the project should be rejected.

[8] For those not familiar with discounting (present value) techniques, Appendix A at the end of this book provides a review of these concepts.

EXAMPLE

Calculation of Internal Rate of Return: Hamilton Beach/Proctor-Silex

The internal rate of return for the Hamilton Beach/Proctor-Silex investment project is calculated as follows:

$$\sum_{t=1}^{5} \frac{290{,}000}{(1+r)^t} = 1{,}000{,}000$$

$$\sum_{t=1}^{5} \frac{1}{(1+r)^t} = \frac{1{,}000{,}000}{290{,}000} = 3.4483$$

The term $[\sum_{t=1}^{5} 1/(1+r)^t]$ represents the present value of a \$1 annuity for five years discounted at r percent and is equal to 3.4483. The value 3.4483 in the *Period 05* row of Table 5 in Appendix B falls between 3.5172 and 3.4331, which corresponds to discount rates of 13 and 14 percent, respectively. Interpolating between these values yields an internal rate of return of

$$\begin{aligned} r &= 0.13 + \frac{3.5172 - 3.4483}{3.5172 - 3.4331}(0.14 - 0.13) \\ &= 0.1382 \end{aligned}$$

or 13.8 percent.

If Hamilton Beach/Proctor-Silex requires a rate of return of 12 percent on projects of this type, then the project should be accepted because the expected return (13.8 percent) exceeds the required return (12 percent). Later in this chapter we consider how to determine the required return (i.e., the firm's cost of capital).

Net Present Value (NPV)

The present value of the stream of net cash flows resulting from a project, discounted at the required rate of return (cost of capital), minus the project's net investment.

Net Present Value The **net present value (NPV)** of an investment is defined as the present value, discounted at the firm's required rate of return (cost of capital), of the stream of net cash flows from the project minus the project's net investment. Algebraically, the net present value is equal to

$$NPV = \sum_{t=1}^{n} \frac{NCF_t}{(1+k)^t} - NINV \qquad [17.7]$$

where n is the expected life of the project and k is the firm's required rate of return (cost of capital).

An investment project should be accepted if the net present value is greater than or equal to zero and rejected if its net present value is less than zero. This is so because a positive net present value translates directly into increases in stock prices and increases in shareholder wealth.

EXAMPLE

Net Present Value Calculation: Hershey Foods

Hershey Foods is considering an investment in a new wrapping machine for its "Kiss" candies. The machine has an initial cost (net investment) of \$2.5 million. It is expected to produce cost savings from reduced labor and to generate additional revenues because of its increased reliability and productivity. Over its anticipated economic life of five years, the new "Kiss" wrapping machine is expected to generate the following stream of net cash flows (NCF_t).

Year (t)	Net Cash Flow (NCF_t)
1	\$600,000
2	800,000
3	800,000
4	600,000
5	250,000

If Hershey requires a return (k) of 15 percent on a project of this type, should it make the investment?

Hershey can solve this problem by computing the net present value of the cash flows from this project (using Equation 17.7) as follows:

Year (1)	Cash Flow (2)	Present Value Interest Factor at 15%* (3)	Present Value (4) = (2) × (3)
0	(\$2,500,000)	1.00000	(\$2,500,000)
1	600,000	0.86957	521,742
2	800,000	0.75614	604,912
3	800,000	0.65752	526,016
4	600,000	0.57175	343,050
5	250,000	0.49718	124,295
			(\$379,985)

*Table 4, Appendix B.

Because this project has a negative net present value, it does not contribute to the goal of maximizing shareholder wealth. Therefore, it should be rejected.

NET PRESENT VALUE VERSUS INTERNAL RATE OF RETURN Both the net present value and the internal rate of return methods result in identical decisions to either accept or reject individual projects. Net present value is greater than (less than) zero if and only if the internal rate of return is greater than (less than) the required rate of return k. In the case of *mutually exclusive* projects—that is, projects where the acceptance of one alternative precludes the acceptance of one or more other alternatives—the two methods may yield contradictory results; one project may have a *higher* internal rate of return than another and, at the same time, a *lower* net present value.

Consider, for example, mutually exclusive projects X and Y shown in Table 17.1. Both require a net investment of \$1,000. Based on the internal rate of return, Project X is preferred, with a rate of 21.5 percent compared with Project Y's rate of 18.3 percent. Based on the net present value with a discount rate of 5 percent, Project Y (\$270) is preferred to Project X (\$240). Thus it is necessary to determine which of the two criteria is the correct one to use in this situation. The outcome depends on

Table 17.1 Net Present Value Versus Internal Rate of Return for Mutually Exclusive Investment Projects

	Project *X*	Project *Y*
Net investment	$1,000	$1,000
Net cash flows		
Year 1	667	0
Year 2	667	1,400
Net present value at 5%	$240	$270
Internal rate of return	21.5%	18.3%

what *assumptions* the decision maker chooses to make about the *implied reinvestment rate* for the net cash flows generated from each project. The net present value method assumes that cash flows are *reinvested at the firm's cost of capital,* whereas the internal rate of return method assumes that these cash flows are *reinvested at the computed internal rate of return.*[9] Generally, the cost of capital is considered to be a more realistic reinvestment rate than the computed internal rate of return because it is the rate the next (marginal) investment project can be assumed to earn. In Figure 17.1, the last project invested in, Project *E*, offers a rate of return nearly equal to the firm's marginal cost of capital. Consequently, the net present value approach is normally superior to the internal rate of return when choosing among mutually exclusive investments. Table 17.2 summarizes the two techniques.

Table 17.2 Summary of the Capital Budgeting Decision Criteria

Criterion	Project Acceptance Decision Rule	Benefits	Weaknesses
Net present value (NPV) method	Accept project if project has a positive or zero NPV; that is, if the present value of net cash flows, evaluated at the firm's cost of capital, equals or exceeds the net investment required	Considers the timing of cash flows Provides an objective, return-based criterion for acceptance or rejection; most conceptually accurate approach	Difficulty in interpreting the meaning of the NPV computation
Internal rate of return (IRR) method	Accept project if IRR equals or exceeds the firm's cost of capital	Easy to interpret the meaning of IRR Considers the timing of cash flows Provides an objective, return-based criterion for acceptance or rejection	Sometimes gives decision that conflicts with NPV; multiple rates of return problem*

*See Moyer, McGuigan, and Kretlow, *Contemporary Financial Management*, 9th ed., p. 315, for a discussion of the multiple internal rates of return problem.

[9] A more thorough discussion of this problem and the underlying assumptions is found in J. Hirshleifer, "On the Theory of the Optimal Investment Decision," *Journal of Political Economy* 66 (August 1958), pp. 95–103; and James H. Lorie and Leonard J. Savage, "Three Problems in Rationing Capital," *Journal of Business* 23 (October 1955), pp. 229–239.

REVIEWING INVESTMENT PROJECTS AFTER IMPLEMENTATION

An important but often neglected step in the selection process is the review of investment projects *after* they have been implemented. This review provides information on the effectiveness of the selection process. In the review, the actual cash flows from an accepted project are compared with the estimated cash flows at the time the project was proposed. This type of analysis requires the firm to keep accounting records that associate specific costs and revenues with various investment projects. Because estimating future cash inflows and outflows is uncertain, actual values usually don't agree perfectly with the estimated values. The analysis should check for any large or systematic discrepancies in the cash flow estimates by individual departments, plants, or divisions, and then find the reasons for these discrepancies. Such analysis enables decision makers to better evaluate investment proposals in the future.

ESTIMATING THE FIRM'S COST OF CAPITAL

A firm's cost of capital is an important input in the capital budgeting analysis procedure. The theory and measurement of a firm's cost of capital is a complex topic that is more appropriately dealt with at length in financial management texts. The purpose of this section is to provide an introduction to the topic and to summarize some of its most important elements.

Cost of Capital
The cost of funds that are supplied to a firm. The cost of capital is the minimum rate of return that must be earned on new investments undertaken by a firm.

The **cost of capital** is concerned with what a firm has to pay for the capital (i.e., the debt, preferred stock, retained earnings, and common stock) it uses to finance new investments. It also can be thought of as the rate of return required by investors in the firm's securities. As such, the firm's cost of capital is determined in the capital markets and is closely related to the degree of risk associated with new investments, existing assets, and the firm's capital structure. In general, the greater the risk of a firm as perceived by investors, the greater the return investors will require and the greater will be the cost of capital.

The cost of capital also can be thought of as the minimum rate of return required on new investments.[10] If a new investment earns an internal rate of return that is greater than the cost of capital, the value of the firm increases. Correspondingly, if a new investment earns a return less than the firm's cost of capital, the firm's value decreases.

The following discussion focuses on the two major sources of funds for most firms: debt and common equity. Each of these sources of funds has a cost. The cost of each of the various component sources of capital is an important input in the calculation of a firm's overall cost of capital.

COST OF DEBT CAPITAL

The pretax cost of debt capital to the firm is the rate of return required by investors. For a debt issue, this rate of return k_d equates the present value of all expected future

[10] Technically, this statement assumes that the risk of the new investments is equal to the risk of the firm's existing assets. Also, when used in this context, the cost of capital refers to a weighted cost of the various sources of capital used by the firm. The computation of the weighted cost of capital is considered in this chapter.

receipts—interest I and principal repayment M—with the offering price V_0 of the debt security:

$$V_0 = \sum_{t=1}^{n} \frac{I}{(1 + k_d)^t} + \frac{M}{(1 + k_d)^n} \quad [17.8]$$

The cost of debt k_d can be found by using the methods for finding the discount rate (that is, yield to maturity) discussed in Appendix A.

Most *new* long-term debt (in the form of bonds) issued by companies is sold at or close to par value (normally \$1,000 per bond), and the coupon interest rate is set at the rate required by investors. When debt is issued at par value, the pretax cost of debt, k_d, is equal to the coupon interest rate. Interest payments made to investors, however, are deductible from the firm's taxable income. Therefore, the *after-tax* cost of debt is computed by multiplying the pretax cost by 1 minus the firm's marginal tax rate t:

$$k_i = k_d(1 - t) \quad [17.9]$$

EXAMPLE

Cost of Debt Capital: AT&T

To illustrate the cost of debt computation, suppose that AT&T sells \$100 million of 8.5 percent first-mortgage bonds at par. Assuming a corporate marginal tax rate of 40 percent, the after-tax cost of debt is computed as

$$\begin{aligned} k_i &= k_d(1 - t) \\ &= 8.5(1 - 0.40) = 5.1\% \end{aligned}$$

Cost of Internal Equity Capital

Like the cost of debt capital, the cost of equity capital to the firm is the equilibrium rate of return required by the firm's common stock investors.

Firms raise equity capital in two ways: (1) *internally,* through retained earnings, and (2) *externally,* through the sale of new common stock. The cost of internal equity to the firm is less than the cost of new common stock because the sale of new stock requires the payment of flotation costs.

The concept of the cost of internal equity (or simply *equity,* as it is commonly called) can be developed using several different approaches, including the *dividend valuation model* and the *capital asset pricing model.*

Dividend Valuation Model

A model (or formula) stating that the value of a firm (i.e., shareholder wealth) is equal to the present value of the firm's future dividend payments, discounted at the shareholder's required rate of return. It provides one method of estimating a firm's cost of equity capital.

Dividend Valuation Model Recall from Chapter 1 that shareholder wealth was defined as the present value, discounted at the shareholder's required rate of return k_e, of the expected future returns generated by a firm (see Equation 1.1). For the typical firm, these future returns can take two forms: the payment of dividends to the shareholder or an increase in the market value of the firm's stock (capital gain). For the shareholder who plans to hold the stock indefinitely, the value of the firm (shareholder wealth, according to the **dividend valuation model**) is

$$V_0 = \sum_{t=1}^{\infty} \frac{D_t}{(1 + k_e)^t} \quad [17.10]$$

where D_t is the dividend paid by the firm in period t.[11] If the shareholder chooses to sell the stock after n years, his or her wealth (V_0) is

$$V_0 = \sum_{t=1}^{n} \frac{D_t}{(1 + k_e)^t} + \frac{V_n}{(1 + k_e)^n} \tag{17.11}$$

where V_n is the market value of the shareholder's holdings in period n. Equation 17.11 is identical to 17.10, because the value of the firm in period n is based on the future returns (dividends) of the firm in periods $n + 1, n + 2, \ldots$[12]

If the dividends of the firm are expected to grow *perpetually* at a *constant compound rate* of g per year, then the value of the firm (Equation 17.10) can be expressed as[13]

$$V_0 = \frac{D_1}{k_e - g} \tag{17.12}$$

where D_1 is the dividend expected to be paid in period 1 and V_0 is the market value of the firm. If D_1 is the dividend *per share* (rather than total dividends) paid in period 1, then V_0 represents the market price *per share* of common stock. Solving Equation 17.12 for k_e yields

$$k_e = \frac{D_1}{V_0} + g \tag{17.13}$$

The following example illustrates how Equation 17.13 can be applied in estimating the cost of equity capital.

EXAMPLE

COST OF INTERNAL EQUITY CAPITAL: FRESNO COMPANY

Suppose the current price of the common stock of Fresno Company (V_0) is \$32. The dividend per share of the firm next year, D_1, is expected to be \$2.14. Dividends have been growing at an average compound annual rate of 7 percent over the past 10 years, and this growth rate is expected to be maintained for the foreseeable future. Based on this information, the cost of equity capital is estimated as

$$k_e = \frac{2.14}{32} + 0.07 = 0.137$$

or 13.7 percent.

[11] A profitable firm that reinvests all its earnings and never distributes any dividends would still have a positive value to stockholders, because its market value would be increasing, and shareholders could sell their stock and obtain a capital gain on their investment in the firm.

[12] The value of the firm in period n is

$$V_n = \sum_{t=n+1}^{\infty} \frac{D_t}{(1 + k_e)^{t-n}}$$

When this expression is substituted in Equation 17.11, Equation 17.10 is obtained.

[13] Equation 17.12 is often referred to as the *Gordon model,* for Myron J. Gordon, who pioneered its use. See Myron J. Gordon, *The Investment, Financing, and Valuation of the Corporation* (Homewood, IL: Irwin, 1962). More complicated forms of Equations 17.12 and 17.13 must be used if the constant growth assumption does not apply.

Figure 17.2 The Security Market Line (SML)

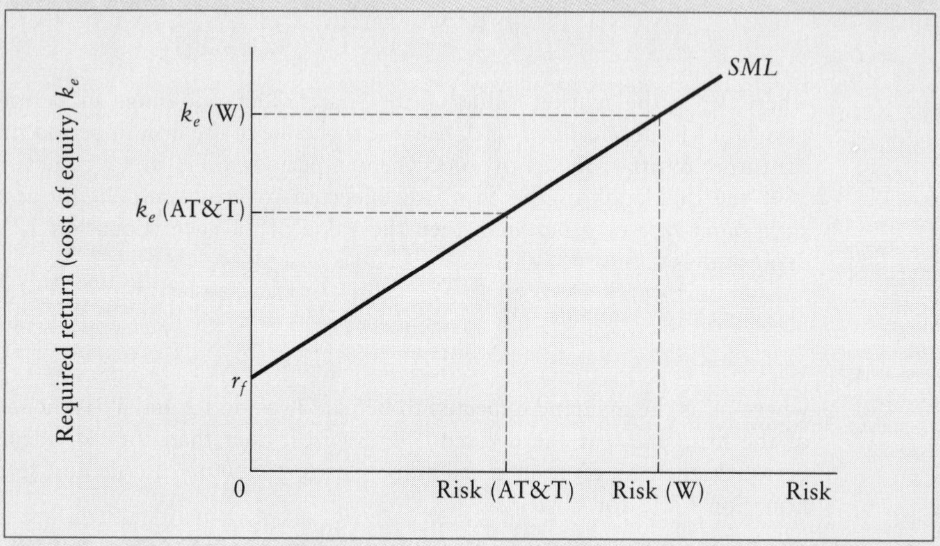

Capital Asset Pricing Model (CAPM)

A theory that formally describes the nature of the risk-required return trade-off. It provides one method of estimating a firm's cost of equity capital.

Capital Asset Pricing Model Another technique that can be used to estimate the cost of equity capital is the **capital asset pricing model (CAPM).** The CAPM is a theory that formally describes the risk-required return trade-off for securities. According to the CAPM theory, the rate of return required by investors consists of a risk-free return r_f plus a premium compensating the investor for bearing the risk. The risk premium varies from stock to stock.

Obviously less risk is associated with an investment in a stable stock, such as AT&T, than in the stock of a small, wildcat oil drilling firm W. As a result, an investor in the drilling stock requires a higher return than the AT&T investor. Figure 17.2 illustrates the difference between required rates of return (or the cost of internal equity) for the two securities. The relationship illustrated in this figure is called the *security market line* (SML). The SML depicts the risk-return relationship in the market for all securities.

The cost of equity capital can be quantified using the CAPM. The CAPM assumes that a single risk-free rate exists, and the risk-required return trade-off for stocks is characterized by a straight line sloping upward from the risk-free rate. The required return can be obtained by calculating the risk associated with a stock.

Risk is defined as the variability of outcomes (e.g., returns). The variability of returns for individual stocks is closely related to the variability of stock prices. In the context of the CAPM and the SML, *total* variability of returns is not considered to be the relevant measure of risk, however. Instead, total variability can be divided into two components:

- *Unsystematic risk:* The variability of returns that is *unique* to a security includes return variability caused by such factors as differing management skills, strikes, natural disasters, effects of new competition, and so on.

- *Systematic* or *nondiversifiable risk*: The variability of returns that affects *all* securities is measured by the co-movement or covariation of a security's returns with the returns of the overall market. The overall market movement is usually measured by some broad market index such as the S&P 500 stock index. Systematic variability is caused by factors such as changes in the level of interest rates, the impact of recessions or business expansions, and so on.

If an investor holds a well-diversified portfolio of individual securities, the variability of returns arising from unique factors affecting individual securities can possibly be diversified away, leaving only systematic risk.

To use the SML to estimate the cost of equity, one must estimate the systematic risk of individual securities. One measure of the systematic risk of a stock is the stock's *beta*, β. (Beta is estimated as the slope of a regression line between an individual security's returns and the returns for a market index.)[14]

The stock market as a whole has a beta of 1.0; stocks whose prices fluctuate less than the market as a whole have betas of less than 1.0; and stocks with price fluctuations greater than the market have betas greater than 1.0. For example, if a stock has a beta equal to 1.0, a 5 percent increase (or decrease) in the returns on the market index would be expected to be associated with a 5 percent increase (or decrease) in that security's returns. If a stock has a beta of 2.0, a 5 percent increase (or decrease) in market returns would be expected to be associated with a 10 percent increase (or decrease) in that security's returns. Finally, a beta of 0.5 implies that a 5 percent increase (or decrease) in market returns would be expected to be associated with a 2.5 percent increase (or decrease) in that security's returns.

Thus, according to the CAPM, the cost of equity calculation can be illustrated as

$$k_e = r_f + \beta(k_m - r_f) \tag{17.14}$$

where k_m is the expected return on the market as a whole. This equation shows that the risk premium portion of a firm's cost of equity is proportional to its beta.

EXAMPLE

COST OF INTERNAL EQUITY CAPITAL: MIDWESTERN POWER COMPANY

To illustrate the k_e calculation using the CAPM, suppose that the Midwestern Power Company common stock has a beta (β) of 0.8, and the present risk-free rate (r_f) is 7 percent. If the expected return on the market (k_m) is 13 percent, substituting these values into Equation 17.14 yields

$$\begin{aligned} k_e &= 7.0 + 0.8(13.0 - 7.0) \\ &= 11.8\% \end{aligned}$$

[14] See Moyer, McGuigan, and Kretlow, *Contemporary Financial Management,* 10th ed., Chapters 6 and 12, for a more detailed discussion of the CAPM theory and its use in calculating the cost of equity capital.

Cost of External Equity Capital

The cost of external equity is greater than the cost of internal equity for the following reasons:

- Flotation costs associated with new shares are usually high enough that they cannot realistically be ignored.
- The selling price of the new shares to the public must be less than the market price of the stock before announcement of the new issue, or the shares may not sell. Before any announcement, the current market price of a stock usually represents an equilibrium between supply and demand. If supply is increased (all other things being equal), the new equilibrium price will be lower.

When a firm's future dividend payments are expected to grow forever at a constant per-period rate of g, the cost of external equity k_e' is defined as

$$k_e' = \frac{D_1}{V_{net}} + g \qquad [17.15]$$

where V_{net} is the net proceeds to the firm on a per-share basis.

EXAMPLE

Cost of External Equity Capital: Fresno Company

To illustrate, consider the Fresno Company example used in the cost of internal equity discussion, where $V_0 = \$32$, $D_1 = \$2.14$, $g = 0.07$, and $k_e = 13.7$ percent. Assuming that new common stock can be sold at \$31 to net the company \$30 a share after flotation costs, k_e' is calculated using Equation 17.15 as follows:

$$k_e' = \frac{2.14}{30} + 0.07$$
$$= 0.141 \text{ or } 14.1\%$$

Because of the relatively high cost of newly issued equity, many companies try to avoid this means of raising capital. The question of whether a firm should raise capital with newly issued common stock depends on the firm's investment opportunities.

Weighted Cost of Capital

Firms calculate their cost of capital to determine a discount rate to use when evaluating proposed capital expenditure projects. Recall that the purpose of capital expenditure analysis is to determine which *proposed* projects the firm should *actually* undertake. Therefore, it is logical that *the capital whose cost is measured and compared with the expected benefits from these proposed projects should be the next or marginal capital the firm raises.* Typically, companies estimate the cost of each capital component as the cost they expect to have to pay on these funds during the coming year.[15]

[15] Stated another way, the cost of the capital acquired by the firm in earlier periods (the *historical* cost of capital) is *not* used as the discount rate in determining next year's capital expenditures.

In addition, as a firm evaluates proposed capital expenditure projects, it normally does not specify the proportions of debt and equity financing for each individual project. Instead, each project is presumed to be financed with the same proportion of debt and equity contained in the company's target capital structure.

Thus the appropriate cost of capital figure to be used in capital budgeting is not only based on the next capital to be raised but also weighted by the proportions of the capital components in the firm's long-range target capital structure. This figure is called the *weighted,* or *overall, cost of capital.*

The general expression for calculating the weighted cost of capital k_a is as follows:

$$k_a = \begin{bmatrix} \text{equity} \\ \text{fraction} \\ \text{of capital} \\ \text{structure} \end{bmatrix} \begin{bmatrix} \textit{cost} \\ \textit{of} \\ \textit{equity} \end{bmatrix} + \begin{bmatrix} \text{debt} \\ \text{fraction} \\ \text{of capital} \\ \text{structure} \end{bmatrix} \begin{bmatrix} \textit{cost} \\ \textit{of} \\ \textit{debt} \end{bmatrix}$$

$$= \left[\frac{E}{D+E}\right](k_e) + \left[\frac{D}{D+E}\right](k_i) \qquad [17.16]$$

where D is the amount of debt and E the amount of equity in the target capital structure.[16]

EXAMPLE

WEIGHTED COST OF CAPITAL: COLUMBIA GAS COMPANY

To illustrate, suppose that Columbia Gas has a current (and target) capital structure of 75 percent equity and 25 percent debt. (The proportions of debt and equity should be the proportions in which the firm intends to raise funds in the future.) For a firm that is not planning a change in its target capital structure, these proportions should be based on the current *market value weights* of the individual components (debt and common equity). The company plans to finance next year's budget with \$75 million of retained earnings ($k_e = 12\%$) and \$25 million of long-term debt ($k_d = 8\%$). Assume a 40 percent marginal tax rate. Using these figures, the weighted cost of capital being raised to finance next year's capital budget is calculated using Equation 17.16 as

$$\begin{aligned} k_a &= 0.75 \times 12.0 + 0.25 \times 8.0 \times (1 - 0.40) \\ &= 10.2\% \end{aligned}$$

This discount rate should be used to evaluate projects of average risk.

[16] If the target capital structure contains preferred stock, a preferred stock term is added to Equation 17.16. In this case Equation 17.16 becomes

$$k_a = \left(\frac{E}{E+D+P}\right)(k_e) + \left(\frac{D}{E+D+P}\right)(k_i) + \left(\frac{P}{E+D+P}\right)(k_p)$$

where P is the amount of preferred stock in the target capital structure and k_p is the component cost of preferred stock.

Cost-Benefit Analysis

The remainder of this chapter is devoted to some techniques of analysis that may be used to assist in public and not-for-profit sector resource allocation decisions. The primary analytical model examined is cost-benefit analysis, although cost-effectiveness studies are also discussed.

Cost-Benefit Analysis
A resource allocation model that can be used by public and not-for-profit sector organizations to evaluate programs or investments on the basis of the magnitude of the discounted benefits and costs.

Cost-benefit analysis is used to evaluate programs and investments based on a comparison of their benefits and costs. Cost-benefit analysis is the logical public sector counterpart to the capital budgeting techniques discussed earlier. The following sections of this chapter focus on the additional problems that arise in allocating resources and making other economic decisions in public and not-for-profit sector organizations, including the measurement of benefits and costs, the determination of an appropriate discount rate, and the uses and limitations of the model.

Uses of Cost-Benefit Analysis

In general, cost-benefit analysis is a method that assesses the desirability of projects through both a long and a wide view of a particular program expenditure or policy change. As in private sector capital budgeting, cost-benefit analysis often is used when the economic consequences of a project or a policy change are likely to extend beyond one year. Unlike capital budgeting, however, cost-benefit analysis seeks to measure all economic impacts of the project, that is, side effects as well as direct effects.

Accept-Reject Decisions

Cost-benefit analysis may be used for a number of purposes, depending on the nature of the project, the constraints of public policy, and the requirements of the information user or decision maker. One use is to determine whether a specific expenditure is economically justifiable. For instance, one might examine a program designed to eradicate tuberculosis, considering the current costs of the disease that could be averted by a specific expenditure of funds. Benefits (averted costs) may be divided into four categories:

1. Expenditures on medical care, including physician and nurse fees, drug costs, and hospital and equipment charges
2. Loss of gross earnings during the disease
3. Reduction in gross earnings after the disease because of decreased employment opportunities resulting from the social stigma attached to the illness
4. The pain and discomfort associated with having the disease

Social Discount Rate
The discount rate to be used when evaluating benefits and costs from public sector investments.

Suppose a particular program to eradicate tuberculosis requires a one-time outlay of $250 million (Table 17.3). Assume that the total benefits (averted disease costs) of this one-year program are expected to accrue for a period of five years. If one accepts, for the moment, that an appropriate **social discount rate** is 15 percent, the program may be evaluated in the net present-value analysis framework developed in the capital budgeting discussion. The decision rule is to accept the project if the (discounted) benefits are greater than or equal to the (discounted) costs.

Table 17.3 Net Cost-Benefit Analysis

End of Year (1)	Actual Dollar Benefit (Cost) (2)	Present Value Interest Factor at 15 Percent* (3)	Discounted Benefits and Costs ($ Million) (4) = (2) × (3)
0	($250,000,000)	1.000	($250.00)
1	150,000,000	0.870	130.50
2	125,000,000	0.756	94.50
3	100,000,000	0.658	65.80
4	50,000,000	0.572	28.60
5	25,000,000	0.497	12.43
			Net benefits = $81.83

*Appendix B, Table 4.

Because the program has a positive calculated net discounted benefit, in this case $81.83 million, it is an acceptable project.

Alternative decision-making criteria include the internal rate of return and the benefit-cost ratio. According to the internal rate of return criterion, a project is acceptable if the IRR is greater than or equal to the appropriate social discount rate. In the case of the tuberculosis eradication program, the IRR for the benefits and costs shown in Table 17.3 is 32.4 percent. Because this exceeds the social discount rate of 15 percent, the project is acceptable. According to the benefit-cost ratio criterion, a project is acceptable if the benefit-cost ratio is greater than or equal to 1.0, where the **benefit-cost ratio** is equal to the present value of the benefits (discounted at the social discount rate) divided by the present value of the costs (similarly discounted). For the tuberculosis eradication program, the benefit-cost ratio is equal to

Benefit-Cost Ratio

The ratio of the present value of the benefits from a project or program (discounted at the social discount rate) to the present value of the costs (similarly discounted).

$$\text{Benefit-cost ratio} = \frac{130.50 + 94.50 + 65.80 + 28.60 + 12.43}{250}$$

$$= 1.33$$

Because this ratio exceeds 1.0, the project is acceptable according to this criterion. All three decision criteria give identical decisions to accept or reject individual projects.

PROGRAM-LEVEL ANALYSIS

In addition to being used to evaluate whether an entire program is economically justifiable, cost-benefit analysis can also determine whether the size of an existing program should be increased (or reduced) and, if so, by what amount. This determination may be made using traditional marginal analysis as developed earlier in the text.

Returning again to the tuberculosis control program, assume that, because of strong lobbying from the AMA, a number of expenditure levels beyond the originally proposed $250 million are being considered. Table 17.4 summarizes these

Table 17.4 Schedule of Program Benefits for Various Cost Levels

Program Cost ($ Millions)	Discounted Program Benefits ($ Millions)	Net Program Benefits ($ Millions)
$250	$331.83	$ 81.83
300	496.00	196.00
350	540.00	190.00
400	565.00	165.00

Table 17.5 Marginal Analysis of Benefits and Costs

Program Cost ($ Millions)	Marginal Cost ($ Millions)	Discounted Marginal Benefits ($ Millions)
$ 0	—	—
250	$250	$331.83
300	50	164.17
350	50	44.00
400	50	25.00

proposed programs and their expected benefits. An analysis that looked at only one of these proposed program expenditure levels would have concluded that any of the program levels was worthwhile because each proposal generates positive expected net program benefits.

When analyzed as a group, however, these program levels clearly show a limit to the economically justifiable expenditure of funds for tuberculosis control. The required analysis is summarized in Table 17.5. A level of expenditure of $300 million is best because it generates an additional (marginal) $164.17 million in benefits, but the marginal program cost (in comparison to the $250 million program level) is only $50 million. To increase the program to $350 million would be counterproductive, because only $44 million in benefits are generated for the additional $50 million outlay (marginal costs exceed marginal benefits).

Steps in Cost-Benefit Analysis

The general principles of cost-benefit analysis may be summarized by answering the following set of questions:[17]

1. What is the objective function to be maximized?
2. What are the constraints placed on the analysis?
3. What costs and benefits are to be included, and how may they be valued?

[17] The next two sections of this chapter draw heavily on the review article by A. R. Prest and R. Turvey, "Cost-Benefit Analysis: A Survey," *Economic Journal* (December 1965), p. 683.

4. What investment evaluation criterion should be used?
5. What is the appropriate discount rate?

The decision-making process in cost-benefit analysis may be traced in the flowchart presentation of Figure 17.3. Program objectives are set by the public through their political representatives. Alternatives are enumerated, explored, and

Figure 17.3 Schematic of the Cost-Benefit Analysis Process

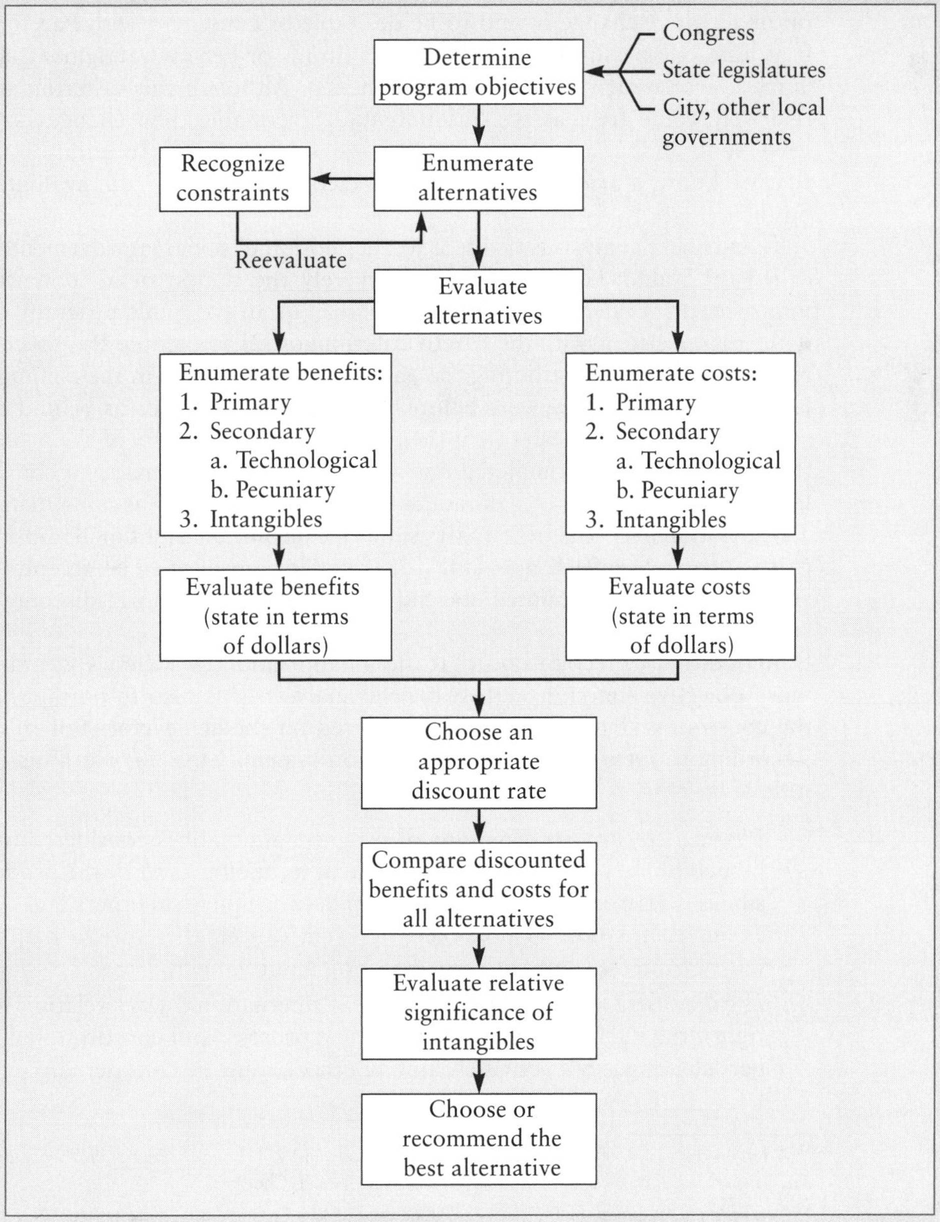

revised in the light of constraints that may be operative in the system. These alternatives are then compared by enumerating and evaluating program benefits and costs in a present-value framework. Discounted benefits are compared with discounted costs, and intangibles are considered so a recommendation may be made about the merits of one or more alternative programs.

Objectives and Constraints in Cost-Benefit Analysis

Cost-benefit analysis is merely an application of resource allocation theory. As such, we need to examine it in the light of several criteria proposed by welfare economists as important for evaluating alternatives. One such criterion is Pareto optimality.[18] A change is said to be desirable or consistent with Pareto optimality if at least one person is made better off (in his or her own judgment) and no one is made worse off (in their own judgments). Although this criterion seems to be relatively value free, as well as potentially verifiable, few changes are likely to leave some individuals better off and *no one* worse off. In addition, it assumes that we know, *a priori,* how people affected by a program will evaluate its effects on them.

Cost-benefit analysis is tied to a weaker notion of social improvement, sometimes called the Kaldor-Hicks criterion, or merely the notion of a "potential" Pareto improvement. Under this criterion, a change (or an economic program) is desirable if (1) it is consistent with the Pareto criterion, or (2) a potential Pareto improvement may be made by redistributing the gains so that all people in the community are at least as well off as they were before the change. This notion is behind cost-benefit analysis. A project is desirable if the benefits exceed the costs of the project because the project could be completed and the gainers *could* be made to compensate the losers. The fact that gainers do not in fact compensate losers is not a matter of direct consideration in cost-benefit analysis, but the income distributional impacts of a program are an extremely important side issue. For a project to be acceptable requires simply that total discounted societal benefits exceed the total discounted societal costs.

In addition to recognizing that the maximization of society's wealth is the primary objective function in cost-benefit analysis, it is also important to establish the constraints that may exist or be placed on the achievement of this objective. According to Otto Eckstein's classification system,[19] these constraints include the following:

1. *Physical constraints.* The type of program alternatives considered is ultimately limited by the currently available state of technology and by the production possibilities derived from the relationship between physical inputs and outputs. For example, it is not yet possible to prevent cancer; therefore, a major emphasis must be directed toward early detection and treatment.
2. *Legal constraints.* Domestic as well as international laws relating to property rights, the right of eminent domain, due process, and constitutional limits on a particular agency's activities, among others, must be considered.

---

[18] A further discussion of the Pareto criterion is provided in W. J. Baumol, *Economic Theory and Operations Analysis,* 4th ed. (Englewood Cliffs, NJ: Prentice Hall, 1977), Chapter 21.

[19] Otto Eckstein, "A Survey of the Theory of Public Expenditure Criteria," in *Public Finances: Needs, Sources and Utilization,* ed. James M. Buchanan (Princeton, NJ: Princeton University Press, 1961).

3. *Administrative constraints.* Effective programs require that individuals are available or can be hired and trained to carry out the program objectives. Even the best-conceived program is worthless unless individuals with the proper mix of technical and administrative skills are available.
4. *Distributional constraints.* Programs affect different groups in different ways because gainers are rarely the same as losers. When distributional impacts are of concern, the objective of cost-benefit analysis might be presented in terms of maximizing total benefits less total costs, subject to the constraint that benefits-less-costs for a particular group reach a prespecified level.
5. *Political constraints.* What may be optimal may not be feasible because of the slowness and inefficiency of the political process. Many times what is *best* is tempered by what is *possible,* given the existence of strong competing interest groups as well as an often cumbersome political mechanism.
6. *Financial or budget constraints.* More often than not, agencies work within the bounds of a predetermined budget. In other words, the objective function must be altered to the suboptimizing form of maximizing benefits given a fixed budget. Virtually all programs have some absolute financial ceiling above which the program may not be expanded, in spite of the magnitude of social benefits.
7. *Social and religious constraints.* It is futile to tell Indian Hindus to eat sacred cattle to solve their nutritional problems. This example is just one of the social and religious constraints that may limit the range of feasible program alternatives.

ANALYSIS AND VALUATION OF BENEFITS AND COSTS

Cost-benefit analysis is quite similar to traditional private sector profit-and-loss accounting. In the private sector the firm is guided by the criterion that private revenues must equal or exceed private costs over the long run for the firm to survive. In contrast, in cost-benefit analysis the economist asks whether society as a whole will be better off by the adoption or nonadoption of a specific project or by the acceptance of one project to the exclusion of alternatives. As Ezra Mishan points out:

> . . . For the more precise concept of the revenue of the private concern, the economist substitutes the less precise, yet meaningful, concept of the social benefit. For the costs of the private concern, the economist will substitute the concept of opportunity cost . . . or social value forgone elsewhere in moving factors into a projected economic activity.[20]

The starting point for evaluating benefits and costs of a project is the observable market valuations. It requires that the following conditions be met (or at least approximately met):

- Consumers equate the value of the marginal unit of each commodity consumed to the value of forgone alternatives.
- Producers operate so that each commodity is produced in a manner that sacrifices the lowest value of forgone alternatives.

[20] Ezra J. Mishan, *Cost-Benefit Analysis: An Introduction* (New York: Praeger, 1971), pp. 7–8.

These conditions are present in a competitive economy. With this assumption in mind, benefits may be measured by the market price of the outputs from a public program or by the price consumers would be *willing* to pay if they were charged. Similarly, costs are measured as the monetary expenditures necessary to undertake a project. When the assumed conditions of competition do not exist (e.g., when externalities or economies of scale are present), then the estimate of benefits and costs must be modified to take account of this situation.

Direct Benefits

Benefits and costs may be categorized in a number of ways. *Primary* or *direct* benefits of a project consist of the value of goods or services produced if the project is undertaken compared to conditions without the project. The primary benefit of an irrigation project is the value of the additional crops produced on the irrigated land less the cost of seeds, labor, and equipment required to produce the crops. The primary benefits attributable to a college education might be considered as the increase in gross earnings of the graduate over what would have been earned without a college degree. In sum, the value of primary or direct benefits of a project may be taken as the total amount users pay (assuming pure competition) or would be willing to pay (total revenue if a charge is made, plus the consumers' surplus when pure competition does not prevail). Although this principle of evaluating direct benefits may be reasonably straightforward for irrigation projects, the estimation of direct benefits in the valuation of human life, as in accident prevention[21] programs, poses serious conceptual problems.

Direct Costs

Direct or *primary costs* are generally easier to measure than direct benefits. They include the capital costs necessary to undertake the project, operating and maintenance costs incurred over the life of the project, and personnel expenses. Once again the estimation of these costs is generally much easier for investments in physical assets such as dams, canals, and so on, than it is for human resource investments. Remember that the costs being measured are opportunity costs, or the social value forgone elsewhere because factors of production in an alternate area of activity. If a proposed project will draw 20 percent of the required labor from the ranks of the unemployed, the market cost (wage payments) of these workers' services will overstate the true social cost.[22] A similar conclusion applies for the use of idle land. With *no* alternative use, the opportunity cost of the use of this land is zero (for as long as no productive alternative uses exist), no matter what the government happens to actually pay its owner in compensation. Such compensation to the owner only affects the *distribution* of the benefits derived from land usage.

---

[21] For a summary of this problem, see Ezra J. Mishan, "Evaluation of Life and Limb: A Theoretical Approach," *Journal of Political Economy* (July/August 1971), pp. 687–705. See also *Journal of Risk and Uncertainty* 8, no. 1 (January 1994), for a series of articles dealing with cost-benefit analyses of health and safety regulations and the valuation of human life.

[22] A discussion of this issue is provided by Robert Haveman, "Evaluating Public Expenditures under Conditions of Unemployment," in *Public Expenditures and Policy Analysis,* eds. Robert Haveman and Julius Margolis (Chicago: Markham, 1970).

INDIRECT COSTS AND BENEFITS

In addition to the primary impacts of a project, government investment invariably creates *secondary* or *indirect* effects. Secondary costs and benefits may be of two types: *real* or *technological* effects, and *pecuniary* effects. Real secondary benefits may include reductions in necessary outlays for other government projects, for example when an early glaucoma-detection campaign reduces the number of people who go blind, thereby reducing future government disability transfer payments. Similarly, an irrigation dam may reduce flooding and create a recreational area. These secondary benefits should be counted in a cost-benefit study. The same argument applies in accounting for secondary costs. For example, the Wallisville Dam Project in Texas was alleged to cause in excess of $500,000 in damages annually to saltwater fishing because of its impacts on the tidal marshlands. This real secondary cost should have been counted in the cost-benefit analysis of the Wallisville Project.

Pecuniary benefits should generally not be included in the enumeration of "countable" benefits in a study. They generally arise in the form of lower input costs, increased volumes of business, or changes in land values resulting from a project. For example, an improved highway may lead to greater business volume and profitability of gas stations, souvenir shops, and restaurants along that road, as well as higher land values and consequently higher rents to the landlords. Many of these benefits are purely distributional in nature because some business will be drawn from firms along other roads once the new road is completed.

If the economy is operating under conditions of full employment, secondary impacts of the multiplier effect and induced investment that may occur as a result of a particular government investment also should not be counted. Under full employment, these benefits must be presumed to occur whether the expenditure of funds is public or private. The objective of a regional project may be to stimulate local investment, generate multiplier effects, and reduce regional unemployment. Under special circumstances it may be appropriate to include some of these secondary effects in the analysis.

INTANGIBLES

A final group of program benefits and costs is intangibles. For these recognizable impacts of a project, it is either extremely difficult or impossible to calculate a dollar value. Intangibles may include such notions as quality of life, aesthetic contributions (or detriments), and balance-of-payments impacts. Intangibles may be merely listed reasonable dollar estimates of benefits, and costs cannot be determined. Alternatively, they may be analyzed by making trade-offs against tangibles in such a manner that the cost of additional increments of intangible improvement, for instance, may be compared with the forgone tangible benefits of a project. An example of this sort of trade-off analysis can be seen in the U.S. Maritime program. One objective of the U.S. Maritime subsidies is to reduce the U.S. balance-of-payments deficit. A comparison of real program costs with balance-of-payments impacts can provide the basis for a choice among the commitment of various levels of real resources to gain foreign exchange savings. As one study of this matter concludes, "It is scarcely credible . . . that the Nation would have been willing to spend $1 to save $1 of foreign exchange."[23]

[23] Gerald R. Jantscher, "Federal Aids to the Maritime Industries," *The Economics of Federal Subsidy Programs*, Joint Economic Committee (Washington, DC: U.S. Government Printing Office, February 26, 1973).

The Appropriate Rate of Discount

Social Discount Rate

The discount rate to be used when evaluating benefits and costs from public sector investments.

When the benefits or costs of a program extend beyond a one-year time limit, they must be discounted back to some common point in time for purposes of comparison. Most people prefer current consumption to future consumption, so the **social discount rate** is used to adjust for this preference.[24] The choice of the appropriate discount rate to evaluate public investments is critical to the conclusions of any cost-benefit analysis. Projects that may appear to be justified at a low discount rate, say 5 percent, may seem to be a gross misallocation of resources at a higher rate, such as 15 percent. The choice of a discount rate is likely to have a profound impact on the type of projects to be accepted. A low rate favors investments with long lives, most of which will be of the durable "bricks and mortar" variety, whereas a high rate favors those whose benefits become available soon after the initial investment. When urgent public needs are apparent, a high rate will tend to be more appropriate. To take an extreme example, when deaths from automobile accidents are rising at an alarming rate, it does little good to invest in a dam, even though at a low rate of discount this may appear to be a better alternative than investing to reduce the automobile accident rate.

A higher rate may completely switch investment priorities. In spite of the fact that the choice of a discount rate may completely alter the outcome of a careful cost-benefit analysis, it is given little attention in many studies. In some cases the researcher may select a rate merely because it has been used in the past (probably with equally little justification). Other studies merely select some arbitrary rate, or rates, and perform the analysis, letting the reader decide which is best.[25]

The literature on the social discount rate is extensive and, in many cases, contradictory. Rather than attempt to synthesize and summarize the many points of view that have been expressed, the following discussion focuses on the opportunity cost criterion for estimating the social discount rate. This approach has been most clearly explained by Baumol.[26] Baumol's discussion is based on a recognition of the fact that resources invested in a particular manner in one sector could be withdrawn from that sector and invested elsewhere to yield either a higher or a lower rate of return.

The discount rate performs the function of allocating resources between the public and private sectors; and appropriate discount rate should be chosen to properly indicate when resources should be transferred from one sector to another. Simply then, if resources can earn 20 percent in the private sector, they should not be transferred to the public sector unless they can earn something greater than 20 percent on the invested resources. As Baumol explains:

> The correct discount rate for the evaluation of a government project is the percentage rate of return that the resources utilized would otherwise provide in the private sector.[27]

---

[24] A review of discounting and present-value concepts is provided in Appendix A.

[25] Weisbrod, for example, used both 10 percent to represent the opportunity cost of capital in the private sector and 4 percent to represent the cost of government borrowing to perform his analysis. See Burton A. Weisbrod, *Economics of Public Health: Measuring the Economic Impact of Diseases* (Philadelphia: University of Pennsylvania Press, 1960).

[26] William J. Baumol, "On the Social Rate of Discount," *American Economic Review* (September 1968), pp. 788–802; "On the Discount Rate for Public Projects," in *Public Expenditures and Policy Analysis*, eds. Robert Haveman and Julius Margolis (Chicago: Markham, 1970), pp. 272–290; and "On the Appropriate Discount Rate for Evaluation of Public Projects," statement in *The Planning-Programming-Budgeting System: Progress and Potentials*, Subcommittee on Economy in Government, Joint Economic Committee, 90th Congress, 1st Session (Washington, DC: U.S. Government Printing Office, 1967).

[27] Baumol, *op. cit.*, "On the Discount Rate for Public Projects," p. 274.

In calculating the opportunity cost of funds withdrawn from the private sector, one should recognize that funds withdrawn from corporate investment will generally incur a higher opportunity rate than funds taken from consumption. If funds used by a firm generally yield a 20 percent rate of return *before taxes*,[28] then this rate represents the opportunity cost of these funds to society. The cost of funds withdrawn from consumption may be estimated by reference to the rate of return on risk-free bonds, such as U.S. government securities. Consumers investing in such securities that pay, say, a 10 percent rate of interest, are actually indicating their preference between current consumption and future consumption. Those consumers who do not invest in these risk-free securities are indicating that they place a higher implied personal opportunity value on current consumption than the risk-free security rate. For nonbondholders, one must conclude that the opportunity cost of present consumption to them is at least as high, if not higher, than that of investors in risk-free securities.

We conclude, as does Baumol, that

> the correct discount rate for a project will be a weighted average of the opportunity cost rate for the various sectors from which the project would draw its resources, and the weight for each such sector in this average is the proportion of the total resources that would come from that sector.[29]

EXAMPLE

COSTS AND BENEFITS OF A TOYOTA AUTOMOBILE PLANT IN KENTUCKY

Toyota built an assembly plant near Lexington, Kentucky, that is able to produce 200,000 automobiles annually. To get Toyota to locate the plant in Kentucky, the state agreed to invest approximately $325 million over a 20-year period. These expenditures include the following:

• Land and site preparation	$ 33 million
• Local highway construction	47 million
• Employee training center and education of workers	65 million
• Education of Japanese workers and families	5 million
• Interest on economic development bonds	167 million

The returns to the state over the 20-year period are estimated at $632 million in income, sales, and payroll taxes from Toyota, its suppliers, and related businesses.

These numbers yield an internal rate of return of 25 percent, according to a University of Kentucky research team. Because the state's economic resources are limited, one must consider whether these resources should have been invested in other projects that would have generated even higher rates of return. However, as Brinton Milward, director of the university's center for business and economic

---

[28] The opportunity cost of funds withdrawn from corporate investment must be on a before-tax basis, because that is the true rate of return these resources generate. The fact that the corporate income tax may transfer up to 35 percent of this amount directly to the government is a distributional matter and not an efficiency consideration.

[29] Baumol, *op. cit.*, "On the Discount Rate for Public Projects," p. 279. Baumol raises a number of other important issues in his development of an appropriate social discount rate, such as the role of risk in public versus private investments, the problem of externalities not accounted for in both the public and private sectors, and income distribution issues. None of these, however, alters the fundamental arguments presented here.

research, explains, "Could you have put these funds into improvements in education and transportation and come up with a better benefit-cost ratio? My guess is no. Manufacturing has a pretty high multiplier" (in terms of the repeated turnover of money in the form of jobs and sales).

Cost-Effectiveness Analysis

Although cost-benefit analysis may be applied in a wide range of areas, in many types of government activity it is simply not feasible because of the problems of measuring the value of program outputs. For instance, program analyses in the fields of national security, health and safety, and income redistribution are more frequently conducted using the cost-effectiveness framework than the cost-benefit one. Cost-benefit analysis asks the questions: "What is the dollar value of program costs and benefits, and do the benefits exceed the costs by a sufficient amount, given the timing of these outcomes, to justify undertaking the program?" In contrast, the question asked by **cost-effectiveness analysis** is: "Given that some prespecified objective is to be attained, what are the costs associated with various alternative means for reaching that objective?" In essence, cost-effectiveness analysis *begins* with the premise that some identified program outputs are useful, and it proceeds to explore (1) how these outputs may be most efficiently achieved *or* (2) what the costs are of achieving various levels of the prespecified output.

Cost-Effectiveness Analysis
An analytical tool designed to assist public decision makers in their resource allocation decisions when benefits cannot be easily measured in dollar terms, but costs can be monetarily quantified.

In many governmental programs, the outputs can be specified and measured, but difficulty in evaluating these outputs in dollar terms precludes the use of cost-benefit analysis. For example, it is easy to measure or prespecify the number of families placed in adequate housing as a result of low-income housing programs. But it is far more difficult to evaluate the societal benefits accruing from this program because its major impacts are income redistribution. Cost-effectiveness analysis is widely applied in Department of Defense program studies. The benefits of most defense activities may be thought of as providing levels of deterrence. But for any specific program, such as the strategic nuclear bomber force, it is virtually impossible to quantify and evaluate benefits in dollar terms. In such cases, cost-effectiveness analysis may be useful.

Constant-Cost Studies

With these general remarks about cost-effectiveness analysis in mind, three more specific types of these studies are examined. *Constant-cost studies* attempt to specify the output that may be achieved from a number of alternative programs, assuming all are funded at the same level (costs are constant between alternatives). In essence, constant-cost studies measure what may be acquired for a specific outlay of funds. Constant-cost studies differ from cost-benefit studies because no attempt is made to place dollar values on the outputs of alternative programs. The greatest use of constant-cost studies is in cases where program outputs have multiple dimensions (potential income distribution effects, aesthetic effects, or impacts on future economic development), such as the case in many urban renewal programs. Decision makers may examine several alternatives for land provided by urban renewal. They might choose on the basis of what uses—industrial, commercial, or residential—offer the greatest potential profitability. Alternatively, an explicit attempt may be made to provide for planned development considering the aesthetics of development, the impacts of current development on surrounding areas and future development potential, and the desire to provide a mix of different cultures and income groups within the city. For projects such as these, all one can do is attempt to spell out all the impacts of several alternative, equal-cost schemes, which is likely to be a monumental task in itself. With impacts clearly identified, it becomes the decision maker's responsibility to weigh (subjectively) the outputs of each alternative and to make a choice.

LEAST-COST STUDIES

The second type of cost-effectiveness analysis is *least-cost studies.*[30] As might be expected, the emphasis of these studies is to identify the least expensive way of generating some quantity of an output. For instance, a city might decide that it wishes to reduce by 20 percent the number of burglaries occurring each year within its jurisdictional limits. One approach could be to expand the size of the police force, increase the number of foot patrol officers, and increase the number of squad cars on the streets at any one time. Another possibility might be to require builders to install security bars on the windows of all new homes and to provide cash or tax incentives for current homeowners to improve their personal security systems. A third alternative might be a community drive supporting Operation Identification, where individuals place permanent identifying marks on their belongings to make "fencing" of this merchandise more difficult. If it is recognized that drug addicts are responsible for many burglaries, a drug rehabilitation program may be considered. Combinations of these programs are also possible. Each of these alternatives is evaluated in terms of the expenditure required to achieve the desired objective: a 20 percent reduction in burglaries.

OBJECTIVE-LEVEL STUDIES

A third type of cost-effectiveness analysis is *objective-level studies*. These studies attempt to estimate the costs of achieving several alternative performance levels of the same objective. This approach may be illustrated with the case of reducing automobile emission levels. Table 17.6 provides some hypothetical data relating to various emission-control standards.

In addition to the increased fuel and maintenance costs and the added new-car costs, other effects of a program to reduce auto emissions must be considered. For example, what is the relative impact of such a program on various income groups? In areas where the automobile is a necessity, a program that substantially increases the cost of driving without simultaneously providing feasible alternative means of transportation could be disastrous. Given the current domestic energy situation, one must examine the effects of increased fuel consumption by less efficient engines on the balance of payments. Finally, in performing objective-level studies, we must be aware of the state-of-technology assumptions that are being made. Although the

[30] The discussion of both constant-cost and least-cost studies is based largely on Neil M. Singer, *Public Microeconomics* (Boston: Little, Brown & Co., 1972), Chapter 12.

Table 17.6 Hypothetical Data Relating to the Cost of Achieving Various Levels of Auto Emission Reductions

Percentage of 1998 Emission Levels	Costs ($ Millions—Including Fuel Consumption, More Frequent Maintenance, and Added New-Car Costs)
90	$ 200
70	250
40	500
20	2,500
10	7,500
5	38,000
1	140,000

estimates in Table 17.6 may be realistic for the reciprocating engine, they may far overstate actual costs if alternative technology were assumed. Table 17.6 *does* illustrate that as the level of objective achievement increases, the associated costs frequently increase at a much more rapid rate. Objective-level studies do not directly measure program benefits, but they do measure intermediate program outputs or objectives. This information may help the decision maker to reach more rational decisions. For example, the $2.5 billion expenditure needed to reduce emissions to 20 percent of their 1998 levels may be reasonable. What is less clear is whether an additional 19 percent (from 20% to 1%) emissions reduction is worth the required incremental expenditure of $137.5 billion ($140 billion less $2.5 billion).

Thus, in comparison to cost-benefit analyses, cost-effectiveness analyses provide less positive inputs on which economic decisions can be made. They furnish decision makers with disciplined studies relating program costs with some measurable but unvalued estimates of program outputs.

Summary

- A *capital expenditure* is a current outlay of funds that is expected to provide a flow of future cash benefits.
- The capital expenditure decision process should consist of the following steps: generating alternative investment proposals, estimating cash flows, evaluating and choosing the projects to undertake, and reviewing the projects after implementation.
- The *internal rate of return (IRR)* is the discount rate that equates the present value of the net cash flows from the project with the net investment. An investment project should be accepted (rejected) if its internal rate of return is greater than or equal to (less than) the firm's required rate of return (i.e., cost of capital).
- The *net present value (NPV)* of an investment is the present value of the net cash flows from the project, discounted at the firm's required rate of return (i.e., cost of capital), minus the project's net investment. An investment project should be accepted (rejected) if its net present value is greater than or equal to (less than) zero.
- The *cost of capital* is the cost of funds that are supplied to the firm. It is influenced by the riskiness of the firm, both in terms of its capital structure and its investment strategy.
- The after-tax cost of debt (issued at par) is equal to the coupon rate multiplied by 1 minus the firm's marginal tax rate.

- The cost of equity can be estimated using a number of different approaches, including the dividend valuation model and the capital asset pricing model.
- The weighted cost of capital is calculated by weighting the costs of specific sources of funds, such as debt and equity, by the proportions of each of the capital components in the firm's long-range target capital structure.
- *Cost-benefit analysis* is the public sector counterpart of capital budgeting techniques used for resource allocation decisions.
- Cost-benefit analysis involves the following steps:
  1. Determining the program objectives
  2. Enumerating the alternative means of achieving the objectives, subject to the legal, political, technological, budgetary, and other constraints that limit the scope of action
  3. Evaluating all primary, secondary, and intangible benefits and costs associated with each alternative
  4. Discounting the benefits and costs using a social discount rate to arrive at an overall measure of the desirability of each alternative (e.g., benefit-cost ratio)
  5. Choosing (or recommending) the best alternative based on the overall measure of desirability and the relative magnitude of the unquantifiable intangibles
- Because of the measurement problems arising from the intangible impacts and economic externalities of many public programs, cost-benefit analysis is most useful in comparing projects with similar objectives and similar magnitudes of intangibles and externalities.
- In cases where it is not feasible to place dollar values on final program outputs, *cost-effectiveness analysis* may be used. Cost-effectiveness analysis assumes *a priori* that the program objectives are worth achieving and focuses on the least-cost method of achieving them.

Exercises

Answers to the exercises in blue can be found in Appendix C at the back of the book.

1. A firm has the opportunity to invest in a project having an initial outlay of $20,000. Net cash inflows (before depreciation and taxes) are expected to be $5,000 per year for five years. The firm uses the straight-line depreciation method with a zero salvage value and has a (marginal) income-tax rate of 40 percent. The firm's cost of capital is 12 percent.
   a. Compute the internal rate of return and the net present value.
   b. Should the firm accept or reject the project?
2. A machine that costs $12,000 is expected to operate for 10 years. The estimated salvage value at the end of 10 years is $0. The machine is expected to save the company $2,331 per year before taxes and depreciation. The company depreciates its assets on a straight-line basis and has a marginal tax rate of 40 percent. The firm's cost of capital is 14 percent. Based on the internal rate of return criterion, should this machine be purchased?
3. A company is planning to invest $75,000 (before taxes) in a personnel training program. The $75,000 outlay will be charged off as an expense by the firm this year (Year 0). The returns estimated from the program in the form of greater productivity and a reduction in employee turnover are as follows (on an after-tax basis):

   Years 1–10: $7,500 per year
   Years 11–20: $22,500 per year

   The company has estimated its cost of capital to be 15 percent. Assume that the entire $75,000 is paid at time zero (the beginning of the project). The marginal tax rate for the firm is 40 percent.

   Based on the net present value criterion, should the firm undertake the training program?
4. Alliance Manufacturing Company is considering the purchase of a new automated drill press to replace an older one. The machine now in operation has a book value of zero and a salvage value of zero. However, it is in good working condition with an expected life of 10 additional years. The new drill press is more efficient than the existing one and, if installed, will provide an estimated cost savings (in labor, materials, and maintenance) of $6,000 per year. The new machine costs $25,000 delivered and installed. It has an estimated useful life of 10 years, and a salvage value of $1,000 at the end of this

period. The firm's cost of capital is 14 percent and its marginal income tax rate is 40 percent. The firm uses the straight-line depreciation method.

a. What is the net cash flow in year zero (that is, initial outlay)?

b. What are the net cash flows after taxes in each of the next 10 years?

c. What is the net present value of the investment?

d. Should Alliance replace its existing drill press?

5. Sam's Cleaners is considering opening a new store. The store will be owned by Sam and will cost $200,000 to build. It will be located on a piece of land that will be leased at a rate of $2,000 per year, payable at the end of each year. For planning purposes, the store is expected to have a maximum 20-year life. Cleaning equipment for the new store will cost an additional $40,000 and have an economic life of 20 years. The equipment will be depreciated on a straight-line basis to an estimated salvage value of $0 at the end of 20 years. The building will be depreciated on a straight-line basis to an estimated salvage value of $40,000.

Operating revenues are expected to be $60,000 per year during the first 10 years. These revenues are expected to equal $100,000 per year for years 11–20. Cash operating costs, exclusive of lease payments, are expected to be $20,000 per year during the first 10 years of operation and to increase to $26,000 per year for years 11–20. The firm's marginal tax rate is 40 percent.

a. Compute the net investment for the new cleaning store.

b. Compute the annual net cash flows for the new cleaning store.

c. Compute the project's net present value assuming a 12 percent cost of capital (required rate of return).

d. Should Sam's Cleaners open the new store?

6. The Charlotte Bobcats, a recent expansion basketball team, has been offered the opportunity to purchase the contract of an aging superstar basketball player from another team. The general manager of the Bobcats wants to analyze the offer as a capital budgeting problem. The Bobcats would have to pay the other team $800,000 to obtain the superstar. Being somewhat old, the basketball player is expected to be able to play for only four more years. The general manager figures that attendance, and hence revenues, would increase substantially if the Bobcats obtained the superstar. He estimates that *incremental* returns (additional ticket revenues less the superstar's salary) would be as follows over the four-year period:

Year	Incremental Returns
1	$450,000
2	350,000
3	275,000
4	200,000

The general manager has been told by the owners of the team that any capital expenditures must yield at least 12 percent after taxes. The firm's (marginal) income tax rate is 40 percent. Furthermore, a check of the tax regulations indicates that the team can depreciate the $800,000 initial expenditure over the four-year period.

a. Calculate the internal rate of return and the net present value to determine the desirability of this investment.

b. Should the Bobcats sign the superstar?

7. An acre planted with walnut trees is estimated to be worth $15,000 in 25 years. If you want to realize a 12 percent rate of return on your investment, how much can you afford to invest per acre? (Ignore all taxes and assume that annual cash outlays to maintain your stand of walnut trees are nil.)

8. Panhandle Industries, Inc., currently pays an annual common stock dividend of \$2.20 per share. The company's dividend has grown steadily over the past 10 years at 8 percent per year; this growth trend is expected to continue for the foreseeable future. The company's present dividend payout ratio, also expected to continue, is 40 percent. In addition, the stock presently sells at eight times current earnings; that is, its "multiple" is 8.

   Calculate the company's cost of equity capital using the dividend capitalization model approach.

9. Panhandle Industries, Inc. (see Exercise 8), stock has a beta, β, of 1.15 as computed by a leading investment service. The present risk-free rate is 7 percent, and the expected return on the stock market is 13 percent. Compute the company's cost of equity capital using the capital asset pricing model. How does this value compare with the one determined in Exercise 8 using the dividend capitalization model?

10. The Gordon Company currently pays an annual common stock dividend of \$4.00 per share. Its dividend payments have been growing at a steady rate of 6 percent per year, and this rate of growth is expected to continue for the foreseeable future. Gordon's common stock is currently selling for \$65.25 per share. The company can sell additional shares of common stock after flotation costs at a net price of \$60.50 per share.

    Based on the dividend capitalization model, determine the cost of

    a. Internal equity (retained earnings)

    b. External equity (new common stock)

11. Baker Manufacturing Company has a beta, β, estimated at 1.10. The risk-free rate is 6 percent and the expected market return is 12 percent. Compute the company's cost of equity capital.

12. The Williams Company has a present capital structure (that it considers optimal) consisting of 30 percent long-term debt and 70 percent common equity. The company plans to finance next year's capital budget with additional long-term debt and retained earnings. New debt can be issued at a coupon interest rate of 10 percent. The cost of retained earnings (internal equity) is estimated at 15 percent. The company's marginal tax rate is 40 percent.

    Calculate the company's weighted cost of capital for the coming year.

13. Several studies report low private and social rates of return on an investment in securing (providing) graduate education in many disciplines. In spite of this evidence, an increasing number of schools have been offering advanced-level degrees. (Surprisingly, in spite of normative prescriptions of economic theory, economics falls into the category of these low-return disciplines.)

    a. How can you explain this seeming contradiction to an efficient allocation of societal resources?

    b. Can you suggest some alternatives that could help direct more resources away from low-return educational programs toward higher-return alternatives?

14. The state of Glottamora has \$100 million remaining in its budget for the current year. One alternative is to give Glottamorans a one-time tax rebate. Alternatively, two proposals have been made for state expenditures of these funds.

    The first proposed project is to invest in a new power plant, costing \$100 million and having an expected useful life of 20 years. Projected benefits accruing from this project are as follows:

Years	Benefits Per Year (\$ Millions)
1–5	\$ 0
6–20	20

The second alternative is to undertake a job retraining program, also costing $100 million and generating the following benefits:

Years	Benefits Per Year ($ Millions)
1–5	$20
6–10	14
11–20	4

The state Power Department argues that a 5 percent discount factor should be used in evaluating the projects, because that is the government's borrowing rate. The Human Resources Department suggests using a 12 percent rate, because that more nearly equals society's true opportunity rate.

a. What is implied by the various departments' desires to use different discount rates?
b. Evaluate the projects using both the 5 percent and the 12 percent rates.
c. What rate do you believe to be more appropriate?
d. Make a choice between the projects and the tax-refund alternative. Why did you choose the alternative you did?

15. The Department of Transportation wishes to choose between two alternative accident prevention programs. It has identified three benefits to be gained from such programs:

- Reduced property damage, both to the vehicles involved in an accident and to other property (e.g., real estate that may be damaged at the scene of an accident)
- Reduced injuries
- Reduced fatalities

The department's experts are willing to provide dollar estimates of property damage savings that are expected to accrue from any program, but they will only estimate the number of injuries and fatalities that may be averted.

The first program is relatively moderate in its costs and will be concentrated in a large city. It involves upgrading traffic signals, improving road markers, and repaving some potholed streets. Because of the concentration and value of property in the city, savings from reduced property damage are expected to be substantial. Likewise, a moderate number of traffic-related deaths and injuries could be avoided.

The second program is more ambitious. It involves straightening long sections of dangerous rural roads and installing improved guardrails. Although the property damage savings are expected to be small in relation to total cost, the reduction in traffic-related deaths and injuries should be substantial.

The following table summarizes the expected costs and payoffs of the two programs:

Year	1	2	3	4	Total
Alternative #1					
Cost ($000)	200	200	100	50	550
Reduced property damage ($000)	50	100	250	100	500
Lives saved	60	40	35	25	160
Injuries prevented	500	425	300	150	1,375
Alternative #2					
Cost ($000)	700	1,800	1,100	700	4,300
Reduced property damage ($000)	150	225	475	300	1,150
Lives saved	50	75	100	125	350
Injuries prevented	800	850	900	900	3,450

Assume that a 10 percent discount rate is appropriate for evaluating government programs:

a. Calculate the net present costs of the two programs.

b. Generate any other tables that you may find useful in choosing between the programs.

c. Can you arrive at any unambiguous choice between the two alternatives? What factors are likely to weigh on the ultimate choice made?

16. One study completed for the American Enterprise Institute estimated the cost per life saved in several programs supported or mandated by the government. The following results were reported:

Estimates of cost per life saved	
Recommended for cost-benefit analysis by the National Safety Council for traffic safety	$37,500
Kidney dialysis at home	$99,000
Instructions to military pilots on when to crash-land airplanes	$270,000
Consumer Product Safety Commission's proposed lawn mower safety standards	$240,000 to $1,920,000
OSHA-proposed acrylonitrile exposure standard	$1,963,000 to $624,976,000
OSHA coke-oven emission standard	$4,500,000 to $158,000,000

Other analyses indicated that a proposed plan to further reduce carbon monoxide auto emissions would cost $1 billion in increased costs of production and costs to the consumer and that the plan would prolong two lives in 20 years. This ratio could be compared with the $200 it would cost to prevent each of 24,000 premature deaths per year by installing cardiac care units in ambulances.

Some studies of the value of a human life computed an implicit value in the range of $200,000 to $700,000. These studies examined wage differentials for hazardous jobs and provided estimates of what people are willing to pay for a small decrease in risk.

a. Given these estimates of the value of a human life, which of the programs discussed do you think should be pursued?

b. How can you explain the actions of a mine operator who may spend $5 million to free a trapped miner?

CASE EXERCISES

COST-BENEFIT ANALYSIS[31]

The Michigan State Fairgrounds is centrally located in the Detroit Standard Metropolitan Statistical Area (SMSA), which consists of Wayne, Oakland, and Macomb counties. The population within the SMSA numbered 4,197,931 persons in 2000, more than 47 percent of the state's total population. More than 59 percent and 75 percent of the state's population reside within 60 and 100 miles, respectively, of the fairground site. The site is located near an efficient freeway system that connects many areas of the state. The State Fairgrounds is operated by the Agriculture

[31] Adapted from an unpublished paper by Eric Hartshom of Wayne State University, "Cost-Benefit Analysis Concerning the Proposed Redevelopment Program for the Michigan State Fairgrounds."

Department and is in a deplorable state of disrepair. Costs have exceeded revenues by a substantial margin every year in the recent past. A redevelopment program has been proposed for the fairgrounds that would serve several purposes:

1. Revitalization of the fairgrounds would prevent further economic deterioration of the existing facilities, increase attendance and consequently revenues, and perhaps make the fairgrounds an economically viable entity.
2. A further benefit to be realized would be an economic stimulus to the area resulting from increased employment from the initial construction program, as well as increased revenues realized from the additional business that the proposed new facilities would generate.
3. Finally, aesthetic value could be realized from the upgrading and redevelopment of what is currently a marginal area of the city.

The redevelopment program would consist of the overall rehabilitation of the grounds and buildings as well as the construction of several income-producing buildings, including a hotel and convention facility and a dog track (providing dog racing is legalized in Michigan and the fairgrounds can obtain the necessary license). Either a new coliseum would be constructed or the present one redesigned and refurbished. The cost of the redevelopment program would be $20 million. Construction would take three years with 50 percent of the cost incurred in year 0, 30 percent in year 1, and 20 percent in year 2. The redevelopment program would require funding by the state and federal governments. The following estimated benefits would be derived from the project:

1. *Initial construction benefits.* Previous studies showed that 38 worker-years of employment are derived from each $1 million in construction. Assuming an hourly rate of $6, 40 hours per week, and 50 weeks per year, and relating this calculation to the $20 million cost of the redevelopment program, results in $9,120,000 of economic benefit to be derived through increased employment. Like the construction costs, these benefits would be spread over three years ($4.560 million in year 0, $2.736 million in year 1, and $1.824 million in year 2).
2. *Coliseum.* An appropriate coliseum facility could generate an additional $500,000 annually (years 3–20) from shows and events not currently available in the Detroit area.
3. *Increased state fair attendance.* With improved facilities (such as those planned in the redevelopment program), annual attendance at the state fair is expected to increase from 700,000 presently to 1,000,000 people. Assuming present per capita expenditures ($3.33) at the Michigan State Fair, the increased attendance would result in an additional $1 million in revenue annually (years 3–20).
4. *Convention and hotel facility.* It is estimated that a 200-room hotel, convention, and dining facility located at the fairgrounds would generate nearly $1.5 million in additional revenue annually (years 3–20).
5. *Dog-racing track.* It is estimated that an average dog-racing facility will produce $1.5 million in revenue annually. However, it must be realized that dog racing is similar to horse racing, and it is expected that a portion of the revenues generated by a dog track would be realized owing to a transfer of funds from local horse-racing facilities. Because this transfer of funds should not be considered in the analysis, it would be assumed that one-third of the dog-racing revenues will result from the redistribution of funds from local horse-racing tracks.

Consequently only $1 million in annual revenues (years 3–20) will be attributed to the proposed dog-racing track.

Type of Cost or Benefit	Year(s)	Annual Benefit (+) or Cost (−) ($ Million)
Construction outlay	0	$−10.000
Construction outlay	1	−6.000
Construction outlay	2	−4.000
Increased employment	0	+4.560
Increased employment	1	+2.736
Increased employment	2	+1.824
Coliseum	3–20	+0.500
State Fair attendance	3–20	+1.000
Convention and hotel facility	3–20	+1.500
Dog-racing track	3–20	+1.000

The costs and benefits of the proposed redevelopment are summarized in the table. Assume that a 10 percent interest rate is appropriate for discounting the costs and benefits of the proposed project.

QUESTIONS

1. Determine the benefit-cost ratio (defined as the ratio of discounted benefits to costs) for the proposed fairground development.
2. Based on this analysis, should the redevelopment program be undertaken?
3. List some of the secondary benefits and costs, as well as intangibles, associated with the project.

   In calculating the benefits of the fairground redevelopment program, increased employment opportunities were included.
4. What assumption about employment in the Detroit area must be made in associating these benefits with the project?
5. Recalculate the benefit-cost ratio, assuming that these benefits are not included in the analysis. How does this result affect the desirability of the project?

   In calculating the benefits of the fairground redevelopment project, it was assumed that $1.5 million in additional annual revenue would be generated from the convention and hotel facility.
6. What assumption is being made about the effects of this facility on other hotel and convention facilities? Is this assumption realistic?
7. Suppose that only $500,000 of the facility's annual revenues can be attributed to "new" convention and hotel business. Recalculate the benefit-cost ratio under this assumption (also exclude employment benefits). How does this calculation affect the desirability of the project?
8. Suppose that the fairground is unable to obtain a license to operate a dog-racing track. Assume that construction costs are reduced by 15 percent if a dog-racing track is not built. Recompute the benefit-cost ratio under this assumption (also exclude employment and convention facility benefits). How does this calculation affect the desirability of the proposed redevelopment project?

Industrial Development Tax Relief and Incentives

Tax relief competition between states seeking high-paying industrial jobs threatens to overpay for any conceivable net benefits. In 1993, Alabama paid more than $300 million in highway, rail, sewer, and other infrastructure investments to obtain a $300 million Mercedes plant with 1,500 jobs. In 1998, North Carolina agreed to build a new runway for $130 million and provide job training and tax breaks worth another $142.3 million to obtain a $300 million FedEx hub.

Questions

1. Assess the likely benefits of such a plant or hub and how one should go about analyzing them.
2. What form might a report to the Industrial Development Commission take? Outline the requisite components.

APPENDIX A

The Time Value of Money

Introduction

Many economic decisions involve benefits and costs that are expected to occur at different future points in time. For example, the construction of a new office complex requires an immediate outlay of cash and results in a stream of expected cash inflows (benefits) over many future years. To determine if the expected future cash inflows are sufficient to justify the initial outlay, we must have a way to compare cash flows occurring at different points in time. Also, recall from Chapter 1 that the value of a firm is equal to the discounted (or present) value of all expected returns. These future returns are discounted at a rate of return that is consistent with the risk of the expected future returns. When future returns are more certain, the discount rate used is lower, resulting in a higher present value of the firm, *all other things being equal.* Conversely, when future returns are riskier or more uncertain, they are discounted at a higher rate, resulting in a lower present value of the firm, *all other things being equal.*

An explicit solution to the problem of comparing the benefits and costs of economic transactions that occur at different points in time requires answers to the following kinds of questions: Is \$1 to be received one year from today worth less than \$1 in hand today? If so, why is it worth less? How much less is it worth?

The answers to these questions depend on the alternative uses available for the dollar between today and one year from today. Suppose the dollar can be invested in a guaranteed savings account paying a 6-percent annual rate of return (interest rate). The \$1 invested today will return \$1(1.06) = \$1.06 one year from today. To receive exactly \$1 one year from today, only \$1/(1.06) = \$0.943 would have to be invested in the account today. Given the opportunity to invest at a 6-percent rate of return, we see that \$1 to be received one year from today is indeed worth less than \$1 in hand today, its worth being only \$0.943. Thus, the existence of opportunities to invest the dollar at positive rates of return makes \$1 to be received at any future point in time worth less than \$1 in hand today.[1] This is what is meant by the *time value of money.* The investor's required rate of return is called the *discount rate.*

Present Value of a Single Payment

We can generalize this result for any future series of cash flows and any interest rate. Assume that the opportunity exists to invest at a compound rate of r percent per annum. Then the *present value* (value today) of \$1 to be received at the end of year n, discounted at r percent, is

$$PV_0 = \frac{1}{(1 + r)^n} \qquad \text{[A.1]}$$

[1] In this analysis we are abstracting from price level considerations. Changes in the level of prices (the value of the dollar in terms of the quantity of goods and services it will buy) can also affect the worth of the dollar. In theory, future price increases (or decreases) that are *anticipated* by the market will be reflected in the interest rate.

The term $1/(1 + r)^n$ is often called a Present Value Interest Factor, or $PVIF_{r,n}$. Table 4 in Appendix B contains PVIF values for various interest rates, r, and periods in the future, n.

EXAMPLE

Present Value

If an opportunity exists to invest at a compound rate of return of 12 percent, then the present value of \$1 to be received four years ($n = 4$) from today is

$$PV_0 = \frac{1}{(1 + .12)^4} = (PVIF_{12\%,4})$$
$$= \$1\,(0.6355)$$
$$= \$0.6355$$

As we see in Table A.1, investing \$0.6355 today at an interest rate of 12 percent per annum will give \$1 at the end of four years.

Alternatively, the PVIF factors from Table 4 in Appendix B could be used to find the present value of \$1 expected to be received in four years ($n = 4$), assuming an interest rate of 12 percent ($r = 12\%$), as follows:

$$PV_0 = \$1(PVIF_{12\%,4})$$
$$= \$1(0.63552)$$
$$= \$0.6355$$

Table A.1 Present Value of \$1 to Be Received at the End of Four Years

Year	Return Received at End of Year	Value of Investment at End of Year	
0 (present)	—	\$.6355	← Initial amount invested
1	.6355(.12) = \$.0762	.6355 + .0762 = .7117	
2	.7117(.12) = .0854	.7117 + .0854 = .7971	
3	.7971(.12) = .0957	.7971 + .0957 = .8928	
4	.8928(.12) = .1072	.8928 + .1072 = 1.000	

EXAMPLE

Present Value of a Deferred Bequest

What is the present value of an expected bequest of \$2 million to your university if the expected remaining life span of the donor is eight years and the university uses an interest rate of 9 percent to evaluate gifts of this type?

$$PV_0 = \$2{,}000{,}000(PVIF_{9\%,8})$$
$$= \$2{,}000{,}000(0.50187)$$
$$= \$1{,}003{,}740$$

Your university would be indifferent between receiving \$1,003,740 today or \$2 million in eight years.

Solving for the Interest or Growth Rate

Present value interest factors (*PVIF*) can also be used to solve for interest rates. For example, suppose you wish to borrow \$5,000 today from an associate. The associate is willing to loan you the money if you promise to pay back \$6,802 four years from today. The compound interest rate your associate is charging can be determined as follows:

$$PV_0 = \$6{,}802(PVIF_{r,4})$$

$$\$5{,}000 = \$6{,}802(PVIF_{r,4})$$

$$PVIF_{r,4} = \frac{\$5{,}000}{\$6{,}802}$$

$$= 0.735$$

Reading across the Period 04 row in Table B.4, 0.735 (rounded to three places for simplicity) is found in the 8% column. Thus, the effective interest rate on the loan is 8 percent per year, compounded annually.

EXAMPLE

Calculation of Earnings Growth Rates for Hanamaker Paper

Another common application of the use of *PVIF* factors from Table B.4 is the calculation of the compound rate of growth of an earnings or dividend stream. For example, Hanamaker Paper Company had earnings per share of \$2.56 in 2001. Security analysts have forecasted 2006 earnings per share to be \$6.37. What is the expected compound annual rate of growth in Hanamaker Paper Company's earnings per share? We can use the *PVIF* factors from Table B.4 to solve this problem, as follows:

$$\$2.56 = \$6.37(PVIF_{r,5})$$

$$PVIF_{r,5} = 0.40188$$

Looking across the Period 5 row in Table B.4 we find a *PVIF* equal to 0.40188 under the 20% column. Thus the compound annual growth rate of earnings for Hanamaker Paper Company is 20 percent. (Interpolation can be used for *PVIF* values between the values found in the tables. In practice, financial calculators are normally used for these types of calculations.)

Present Value of a Series of Equal Payments (Annuity)

The present value of a series of *equal* \$1 payments to be received at the end of each of the next n years (an *annuity*), discounted at a rate of r percent, is

$$PV_0 = \frac{1}{(1+r)^1} + \frac{1}{(1+r)^2} + \ldots + \frac{1}{(1+r)^n}$$

$$PV_0 = \sum_{t=1}^{n} \frac{1}{(1+r)^t} \quad \text{[A.2]}$$

Table A.2 Present Value of $1 to Be Received at the End of Each of the Next Four Years

Year	Return Received at End of Year	Amount Withdrawn at End of Year	Value of Investment at End of Year	
0 (present)	—	—	$3.0374	← initial amount invested
1	$3.0374(.12) = $.3645	$1.00	$3.0374 + .3645 − 1.00 = 2.4019	
2	2.4019(.12) = .2882	1.00	2.4019 + .2882 − 1.00 = 1.6901	
3	1.6901(.12) = .2028	1.00	1.6901 + .2028 − 1.00 = .8929	
4	.8929(.12) = .1071	1.00	.8929 + .1071 − 1.00 = .0000	

For example, the present value of $1 to be received at the end of each of the next four years, discounted at 12 percent, is

$$PV_0 = \sum_{t=1}^{4} \frac{1}{(1+.12)^t}$$

$$= \frac{1}{(1+.12)^1} + \frac{1}{(1+.12)^2} + \frac{1}{(1+.12)^3} + \frac{1}{(1+.12)^4}$$

$$= 0.89286 + 0.79719 + 0.71178 + 0.63552 = \$3.0374$$

As shown in Table A.2, investing $3.0374 today at 12 percent will return exactly $1 at the end of each of the next four years, with nothing remaining in the account at the end of the fourth year. Again, rather than perform the present value calculations (Equation A.2), we can use a table to look up the values we need. Table B.5 in Appendix B contains the present values at various interest rates of $1 to be received at the end of each year for various periods of time. The values in Table B.5 are called Present Value Interest Factors for Annuities, or $PVIFA_{r,n}$, where r is the interest rate per period and n is the number of periods (normally years).

Using the $PVIFA$ factors from Table B.5, the present value of an annuity ($PVAN_0$) can be computed as

$$PVAN_0 = PMT(PVIFA_{r,n}) \qquad \text{[A.3]}$$

where PMT = the annuity amount to be received each period.

EXAMPLE

Present Value of an Annuity

You have recently purchased the winning ticket in the Florida lottery and have won $30 million, to be paid in equal $3 million increments ($PMT$) at the end of each of the next ten years. What are your winnings worth to you today using an interest rate of 8 percent? The $PVIFA$ factors from Table B.5 can be used to solve this problem as follows:

$$PVAN_0 = \$3{,}000{,}000(PVIFA_{8\%,10})$$
$$= \$3{,}000{,}000(6.7101)$$
$$= \$20{,}130{,}300$$

Thus, your $30-million winnings are worth only $20,130,300 to you today.

Solving for the Interest Rate

Present Value of an Annuity interest factors also can be used to solve for the rate of return expected from an investment. This rate of return is often referred to as the internal rate of return from an investment. Suppose the Big Spring Tool Company purchases a machine for $100,000. This machine is expected to generate annual cash flows of $23,740 to the firm over the next five years. What is the expected rate of return from this investment?

Using Equation A.3 we can determine the expected rate of return in this example as follows:

$$PVAN_0 = PMT(PVIFA_{r,5})$$
$$\$100{,}000 = \$23{,}740(PVIFA_{r,5})$$
$$PVIFA_{r,5} = 4.2123$$

From the Period 05 row in Table B.5, we see that a *PVIFA* of 4.2123 occurs in the 6% column. Hence, this investment offers a 6-percent expected (internal) rate of return.

Present Value of a Series of Unequal Payments

The present value of a series of *unequal* payments (PMT_t, $t = 1, \ldots, n$) to be received at the end of each of the next n years, discounted at a rate of r percent, is

$$PV_0 = \sum_{t=1}^{n} \frac{PMT_t}{(1 + r)^t}$$
$$= \sum_{t=1}^{n} PMT_t(PVIF_{r,t}) \qquad [A.4]$$

The $PVIF_{r,t}$ values are the interest factors from Table B.4. Thus, the present value of a series of unequal payments is equal to the sum of the present value of the individual payments.

EXAMPLE

Project Evaluation for Intel

Intel Corporation is evaluating an investment in a new chip-manufacturing facility. The facility is expected to have a useful life of five years and yield the following cash flow stream after the initial investment outlay:

End of Year t	Cash Flow PMT_t
1	+ $1,000,000
2	+ 1,500,000
3	− 500,000
4	+ 2,000,000
5	+ 1,000,000

The negative cash flow in Year 3 arises because of the expected need to install pollution control equipment during that year. The present value of this series of unequal payments can be computed using *PVIF* factors from Table B.4 and assuming a 10-percent interest (required) rate on the investment:

$$\begin{aligned} PV &= \$1{,}000{,}000(PVIF_{10\%,1}) + \$1{,}500{,}000(PVIF_{10\%,2}) \\ &\quad - \$500{,}000(PVIF_{10\%,3}) + \$2{,}000{,}000(PVIF_{10\%,4}) \\ &\quad + \$1{,}000{,}000(PVIF_{10\%,5}) \\ &= \$1{,}000{,}000(0.90909) + \$1{,}500{,}000(0.82645) \\ &\quad - \$500{,}000(0.75131) + \$2{,}000{,}000(0.68301) \\ &\quad + \$1{,}000{,}000(0.62092) \\ &= \$3{,}760{,}050 \end{aligned}$$

The present value of these cash flows ($3,760,050) should be compared to the required initial cash outlay to determine whether to invest in the new manufacturing facility.

TABLES

Table B.1*

Values of the Standard Normal Distribution Function

Z	0	1	2	3	4	5	6	7	8	9
−3.	.0013	.0010	.0007	.0005	.0003	.0002	.0002	.0001	.0001	.0000
−2.9	.0019	.0018	.0017	.0017	.0016	.0016	.0015	.0015	.0014	.0014
−2.8	.0026	.0025	.0024	.0023	.0023	.0022	.0021	.0021	.0020	.0019
−2.7	.0035	.0034	.0033	.0032	.0031	.0030	.0029	.0028	.0027	.0026
−2.6	.0047	.0045	.0044	.0043	.0041	.0040	.0039	.0038	.0037	.0036
−2.5	.0062	.0060	.0059	.0057	.0055	.0054	.0052	.0051	.0049	.0048
−2.4	.0082	.0080	.0078	.0075	.0073	.0071	.0069	.0068	.0066	.0064
−2.3	.0107	.0104	.0102	.0099	.0096	.0094	.0091	.0089	.0087	.0084
−2.2	.0139	.0136	.0132	.0129	.0126	.0122	.0119	.0116	.0113	.0110
−2.1	.0179	.0174	.0170	.0166	.0162	.0158	.0154	.0150	.0146	.0143
−2.0	.0228	.0222	.0217	.0212	.0207	.0202	.0197	.0192	.0188	.0183
−1.9	.0287	.0281	.0274	.0268	.0262	.0256	.0250	.0244	.0238	.0233
−1.8	.0359	.0352	.0344	.0336	.0329	.0322	.0314	.0307	.0300	.0294
−1.7	.0446	.0436	.0427	.0418	.0409	.0401	.0392	.0384	.0375	.0367
−1.6	.0548	.0537	.0526	.0516	.0505	.0495	.0485	.0475	.0465	.0455
−1.5	.0668	.0655	.0643	.0630	.0618	.0606	.0594	.0582	.0570	.0559
−1.4	.0808	.0793	.0778	.0764	.0749	.0735	.0722	.0708	.0694	.0681
−1.3	.0988	.0951	.0934	.0918	.0901	.0885	.0869	.0853	.0838	.0823
−1.2	.1151	.1131	.1112	.1093	.1075	.1056	.1038	.1020	.1003	.0985
−1.1	.1357	.1335	.1314	.1292	.1271	.1251	.1230	.1210	.1190	.1170
−1.0	.1587	.1562	.1539	.1515	.1492	.1469	.1446	.1423	.1401	.1379
− .9	.1841	.1814	.1788	.1762	.1736	.1711	.1685	.1660	.1635	.1611
− .8	.2119	.2090	.2061	.2033	.2005	.1977	.1949	.1922	.1894	.1867
− .7	.2420	.2389	.2358	.2327	.2297	.2266	.2236	.2206	.2177	.2148
− .6	.2743	.2709	.2676	.2643	.2611	.2578	.2546	.2514	.2483	.2451
− .5	.3085	.3050	.3015	.2981	.2946	.2912	.2877	.2843	.2810	.2776
− .4	.3446	.3409	.3372	.3336	.3300	.3264	.3228	.3192	.3156	.3121
− .3	.3821	.3783	.3745	.3707	.3669	.3632	.3594	.3557	.3520	.3483
− .2	.4207	.4168	.4129	.4090	.4052	.4013	.3974	.3936	.3897	.3859
− .1	.4602	.4562	.4522	.4483	.4443	.4404	.4364	.4325	.4286	.4247
− .0	.5000	.4960	.4920	.4880	.4840	.4801	.4761	.4721	.4681	.4641

*Note: Table values give the probability of a value occurring which is *less than Z* standard deviations from the mean.

Note 1: If a random variable X is not "standard," its values must be "standardized": $Z = (X - \mu)/\sigma$. That is:

$$P(X \leq x) = N\left(\frac{x - \mu}{\sigma}\right)$$

Note 2: For $z \leq -4$, $N(z) = 0$ to 4 decimal places; for $z \geq 4$, $N(z) = 1$ to 4 decimal places.

Table B.1

Values of the Standard Normal Distribution Function (continued)

Z	0	1	2	3	4	5	6	7	8	9
.0	.5000	.5040	.5080	.5120	.5160	.5199	.5239	.5279	.5319	.5359
.1	.5398	.5438	.5478	.5517	.5557	.5596	.5636	.5675	.5714	.5753
.2	.5793	.5832	.5871	.5910	.5948	.5987	.6026	.6064	.6103	.6141
.3	.6179	.6217	.6255	.6293	.6331	.6368	.6406	.6443	.6480	.6517
.4	.6554	.6591	.6628	.6664	.6700	.6736	.6772	.6808	.6844	.6879
.5	.6915	.6950	.6985	.7019	.7054	.7088	.7123	.7157	.7190	.7224
.6	.7257	.7291	.7324	.7357	.7389	.7422	.7454	.7486	.7517	.7549
.7	.7580	.7611	.7642	.7673	.7703	.7734	.7764	.7794	.7823	.7852
.8	.7881	.7910	.7939	.7967	.7995	.8023	.8051	.8078	.8106	.8133
.9	.8159	.8186	.8212	.8238	.8264	.8289	.8315	.8340	.8365	.8389
1.0	.8413	.8438	.8461	.8485	.8508	.8531	.8554	.8577	.8599	.8621
1.1	.8643	.8665	.8686	.8708	.8729	.8749	.8770	.8790	.8810	.8830
1.2	.8849	.8869	.8888	.8907	.8925	.8944	.8962	.8980	.8997	.9015
1.3	.9032	.9049	.9066	.9082	.9099	.9115	.9131	.9147	.9162	.9177
1.4	.9192	.9207	.9222	.9236	.9251	.9265	.9278	.9292	.9306	.9319
1.5	.9332	.9345	.9357	.9370	.9382	.9394	.9406	.9418	.9430	.9441
1.6	.9452	.9463	.9474	.9484	.9495	.9505	.9515	.9525	.9535	.9545
1.7	.9554	.9564	.9573	.9582	.9591	.9599	.9608	.9616	.9625	.9633
1.8	.9641	.9648	.9656	.9664	.9671	.9678	.9686	.9693	.9700	.9706
1.9	.9713	.9719	.9726	.9732	.9738	.9744	.9750	.9756	.9762	.9767
2.0	.9772	.9778	.9783	.9788	.9793	.9798	.9803	.9808	.9812	.9817
2.1	.9821	.9826	.9830	.9834	.9838	.9842	.9846	.9850	.9854	.9857
2.2	.9861	.9864	.9868	.9871	.9874	.9878	.9881	.9884	.9887	.9890
2.3	.9893	.9896	.9898	.9901	.9904	.9906	.9909	.9911	.9913	.9916
2.4	.9918	.9920	.9922	.9925	.9927	.9929	.9931	.9932	.9934	.9936
2.5	.9938	.9940	.9941	.9943	.9945	.9946	.9948	.9949	.9951	.9952
2.6	.9953	.9955	.9956	.9957	.9959	.9960	.9961	.9962	.9963	.9964
2.7	.9965	.9966	.9967	.9968	.9969	.9970	.9971	.9972	.9973	.9974
2.8	.9974	.9975	.9976	.9977	.9977	.9978	.9979	.9979	.9980	.9981
2.9	.9981	.9982	.9982	.9983	.9984	.9984	.9985	.9985	.9986	.9986
3.	.9987	.9990	.9993	.9995	.9997	.9998	.9998	.9999	.9999	1.0000

Source: *Statistical Analysis: With Business and Economic Applications,* by Ya-lun Chou.

Table B.2* Table of "Students" Distribution—Value of t

Degrees of Freedom	Probability												
	0.9	0.8	0.7	0.6	0.5	0.4	0.3	0.2	0.1	0.05	0.02	0.01	0.001
1	0.158	0.325	0.510	0.727	1.000	1.376	1.963	3.078	6.314	12.706	31.821	63.657	636.619
2	0.142	0.289	0.445	0.617	0.816	1.061	1.386	1.886	2.920	4.303	6.965	9.925	31.598
3	0.137	0.277	0.424	0.584	0.765	0.978	1.250	1.638	2.353	3.182	4.541	5.841	12.924
4	0.134	0.271	0.414	0.569	0.741	0.941	1.190	1.533	2.132	2.776	3.747	4.604	8.610
5	0.132	0.267	0.408	0.559	0.727	0.920	1.156	1.476	2.015	2.571	3.365	4.032	6.869
6	0.131	0.265	0.404	0.553	0.718	0.906	1.134	1.440	1.943	2.447	3.143	3.707	5.959
7	0.130	0.263	0.402	0.549	0.711	0.896	1.119	1.415	1.895	2.365	2.998	3.499	5.408
8	0.130	0.262	0.399	0.546	0.706	0.889	1.108	1.397	1.860	2.306	2.896	3.355	5.041
9	0.129	0.261	0.398	0.543	0.703	0.883	1.100	1.383	1.833	2.262	2.821	3.250	4.781
10	0.129	0.260	0.397	0.542	0.700	0.879	1.093	1.372	1.812	2.228	2.764	3.169	4.587
11	0.129	0.260	0.396	0.540	0.697	0.876	1.088	1.363	1.796	2.201	2.718	3.106	4.437
12	0.128	0.259	0.395	0.539	0.695	0.873	1.083	1.356	1.782	2.179	2.681	3.055	4.318
13	0.128	0.259	0.394	0.538	0.694	0.870	1.079	1.350	1.771	2.160	2.650	3.012	4.221
14	0.128	0.258	0.393	0.537	0.692	0.868	1.076	1.345	1.761	2.145	2.624	2.977	4.140
15	0.128	0.258	0.393	0.536	0.691	0.866	1.074	1.341	1.753	2.131	2.602	2.947	4.073
16	0.128	0.258	0.392	0.535	0.690	0.865	1.071	1.337	1.746	2.120	2.583	2.921	4.015
17	0.128	0.257	0.392	0.534	0.689	0.863	1.069	1.333	1.740	2.110	2.567	2.898	3.965
18	0.127	0.257	0.392	0.534	0.688	0.862	1.067	1.330	1.734	2.101	2.552	2.878	3.922
19	0.127	0.257	0.391	0.533	0.688	0.861	1.066	1.328	1.729	2.093	2.539	2.861	3.883
20	0.127	0.257	0.391	0.533	0.687	0.860	1.064	1.325	1.725	2.086	2.528	2.845	3.850
21	0.127	0.257	0.391	0.532	0.686	0.859	1.063	1.323	1.721	2.080	2.518	2.831	3.819
22	0.127	0.256	0.390	0.532	0.686	0.858	1.061	1.321	1.717	2.074	2.508	2.819	3.792
23	0.127	0.256	0.390	0.532	0.685	0.858	1.060	1.319	1.714	2.069	2.500	2.807	3.767
24	0.127	0.256	0.390	0.531	0.685	0.857	1.059	1.318	1.711	2.064	2.492	2.797	3.745
25	0.127	0.256	0.390	0.531	0.684	0.856	1.058	1.316	1.708	2.060	2.485	2.787	3.725
26	0.127	0.256	0.390	0.531	0.684	0.856	1.058	1.315	1.706	2.056	2.479	2.779	3.707
27	0.127	0.256	0.389	0.531	0.684	0.855	1.057	1.314	1.703	2.052	2.473	2.771	3.690
28	0.127	0.256	0.389	0.530	0.683	0.855	1.056	1.313	1.701	2.048	2.467	2.763	3.674
29	0.127	0.256	0.389	0.530	0.683	0.854	1.055	1.311	1.699	2.045	2.462	2.756	3.659
30	0.127	0.256	0.389	0.530	0.683	0.854	1.055	1.310	1.697	2.042	2.457	2.750	3.646
40	0.126	0.255	0.388	0.529	0.681	0.851	1.050	1.303	1.684	2.021	2.423	2.704	3.551
60	0.126	0.254	0.387	0.527	0.679	0.848	1.046	1.296	1.671	2.000	2.390	2.660	3.460
120	0.126	0.254	0.386	0.526	0.677	0.845	1.041	1.289	1.658	1.980	2.358	2.617	3.373
∞	0.126	0.253	0.385	0.524	0.674	0.842	1.036	1.282	1.645	1.960	2.326	2.576	3.291

*Note: Probabilities given are for two-tailed tests. For example, a probability of 0.05 allows for 0.025 in one tail of the distribution and 0.025 in the other.

Table 2 is taken from Table III of Fisher and Yates: *Statistical Tables for Biological, Agricultural and Medical Research,* published by Longman Group, Ltd., London (previously published by Oliver and Boyd, Edinburgh), and by permission of the authors and publishers.

Table B.3 The *F*-Distribution—Upper 5 Percent Points

δ_2 \ δ_1	1	2	3	4	5	6	7	8	9	10	12	15	20	24	30	40	60	120	∞
1	161.4	199.5	215.7	224.6	230.2	234.0	236.8	238.9	240.5	241.9	243.9	245.9	248.0	249.1	250.1	251.1	252.2	253.3	254.3
2	18.57	19.00	19.16	19.25	19.30	19.33	19.35	19.37	19.38	19.40	19.41	19.43	19.45	19.45	19.46	19.47	19.48	19.49	19.50
3	10.13	9.55	9.28	9.12	9.01	8.94	8.89	8.85	8.81	8.79	8.74	8.70	8.66	8.64	8.62	8.59	8.57	8.55	8.53
4	7.71	6.94	6.59	6.39	6.26	6.16	6.09	6.04	6.00	5.96	5.91	5.86	5.80	5.77	5.75	5.72	5.69	5.66	5.63
5	6.61	5.79	5.41	5.19	5.05	4.95	4.88	4.82	4.77	4.74	4.68	4.62	4.56	4.53	4.50	4.46	4.43	4.40	4.36
6	5.99	5.14	4.76	4.53	4.39	4.28	4.21	4.15	4.10	4.06	4.00	3.94	3.87	3.84	3.81	3.77	3.74	3.70	3.67
7	5.59	4.74	4.35	4.12	3.97	3.87	3.79	3.73	3.68	3.64	3.57	3.51	3.44	3.41	3.38	3.34	3.30	3.27	3.23
8	5.32	4.46	4.07	3.84	3.69	3.58	3.50	3.44	3.39	3.35	3.28	3.22	3.15	3.12	3.08	3.04	3.01	2.97	2.93
9	5.12	4.26	3.86	3.63	3.48	3.37	3.29	3.23	3.18	3.14	3.07	3.01	2.94	2.90	2.86	2.83	2.79	2.75	2.71
10	4.96	4.10	3.71	3.48	3.33	3.22	3.14	3.07	3.02	2.98	2.91	2.85	2.77	2.74	2.70	2.66	2.62	2.58	2.54
11	4.84	3.98	3.59	3.36	3.20	3.09	3.01	2.95	2.90	2.85	2.79	2.72	2.65	2.61	2.57	2.53	2.49	2.45	2.40
12	4.75	3.89	3.49	3.26	3.11	3.00	2.91	2.85	2.80	2.75	2.69	2.62	2.54	2.51	2.47	2.43	2.38	2.34	2.30
13	4.67	3.81	3.41	3.18	3.03	2.92	2.83	2.77	2.71	2.67	2.60	2.53	2.46	2.42	2.38	2.34	2.30	2.25	2.21
14	4.60	3.74	3.34	3.11	2.96	2.85	2.76	2.70	2.65	2.60	2.53	2.46	2.39	2.35	2.31	2.27	2.22	2.18	2.13
15	4.54	3.68	3.29	3.06	2.90	2.79	2.71	2.64	2.59	2.54	2.48	2.40	2.33	2.29	2.25	2.20	2.16	2.11	2.07
16	4.49	3.63	3.24	3.01	2.85	2.74	2.66	2.59	2.54	2.49	2.42	2.35	2.28	2.24	2.19	2.15	2.11	2.06	2.01
17	4.45	3.59	3.20	2.96	2.81	2.70	2.61	2.55	2.49	2.45	2.38	2.31	2.23	2.19	2.15	2.10	2.06	2.01	1.96
18	4.41	3.55	3.16	2.93	2.77	2.66	2.58	2.51	2.46	2.41	2.34	2.27	2.19	2.15	2.11	2.06	2.02	1.97	1.92
19	4.38	3.52	3.13	2.90	2.74	2.63	2.54	2.48	2.42	2.38	2.31	2.23	2.16	2.11	2.07	2.03	1.98	1.93	1.88
20	4.35	3.49	3.10	2.87	2.71	2.60	2.51	2.45	2.39	2.35	2.28	2.20	2.12	2.08	2.04	1.99	1.95	1.90	1.84
21	4.32	3.47	3.07	2.84	2.68	2.57	2.49	2.42	2.37	2.32	2.25	2.18	2.10	2.05	2.01	1.96	1.92	1.87	1.81
22	4.30	3.44	3.05	2.82	2.66	2.55	2.46	2.40	2.34	2.30	2.23	2.15	2.07	2.03	1.98	1.94	1.89	1.84	1.78
23	4.28	3.42	3.03	2.80	2.64	2.53	2.44	2.37	2.32	2.27	2.20	2.13	2.05	2.01	1.96	1.91	1.86	1.81	1.76
24	4.26	3.40	3.01	2.78	2.62	2.51	2.42	2.36	2.30	2.25	2.18	2.11	2.03	1.98	1.94	1.89	1.84	1.79	1.73
25	4.24	3.39	2.99	2.76	2.60	2.49	2.40	2.34	2.28	2.24	2.16	2.09	2.01	1.96	1.92	1.87	1.82	1.77	1.71
26	4.23	3.37	2.98	2.74	2.59	2.47	2.39	2.32	2.27	2.22	2.15	2.07	1.99	1.95	1.90	1.85	1.80	1.75	1.69
27	4.21	3.35	2.96	2.73	2.57	2.46	2.37	2.31	2.25	2.20	2.13	2.06	1.97	1.93	1.88	1.84	1.79	1.73	1.67
28	4.20	3.34	2.95	2.71	2.56	2.45	2.36	2.29	2.24	2.19	2.12	2.04	1.96	1.91	1.87	1.82	1.77	1.71	1.65
29	4.18	3.33	2.93	2.70	2.55	2.43	2.35	2.28	2.22	2.18	2.10	2.03	1.94	1.90	1.85	1.81	1.75	1.70	1.64
30	4.17	3.32	2.92	2.69	2.53	2.42	2.33	2.27	2.21	2.16	2.09	2.01	1.93	1.89	1.84	1.79	1.74	1.68	1.62
40	4.08	3.23	2.84	2.61	2.45	2.34	2.25	2.18	2.12	2.08	2.00	1.92	1.84	1.79	1.74	1.69	1.64	1.58	1.51
60	4.00	3.15	2.76	2.53	2.37	2.25	2.17	2.10	2.04	1.99	1.92	1.84	1.75	1.70	1.65	1.59	1.53	1.47	1.39
120	3.92	3.07	2.68	2.45	2.29	2.17	2.09	2.02	1.96	1.91	1.83	1.75	1.66	1.61	1.55	1.50	1.43	1.35	1.25
∞	3.84	3.00	2.60	2.37	2.21	2.10	2.01	1.94	1.88	1.83	1.75	1.67	1.57	1.52	1.46	1.39	1.32	1.22	1.00

Table B.3 The *F*-Distribution—Upper 1 Percent Points (continued)

δ_2 \ δ_1	1	2	3	4	5	6	7	8	9	10	12	15	20	24	30	40	60	120	∞
1	4052	4999.5	5403	5625	5764	5859	5928	5982	6022	6056	6106	6157	6209	6235	6261	6287	6313	6339	6366
2	98.50	99.00	99.17	99.25	99.30	99.33	99.36	99.37	99.39	99.40	99.42	99.43	99.45	99.46	99.47	99.47	99.48	99.49	99.50
3	34.12	30.82	29.46	28.71	28.24	27.91	27.67	27.49	27.35	27.23	27.05	26.87	26.69	26.60	26.50	26.41	26.32	26.22	26.13
4	21.20	18.00	16.69	15.98	15.52	15.21	14.98	14.80	14.66	14.55	14.37	14.20	14.02	13.93	13.84	13.75	13.65	13.56	13.46
5	16.26	13.27	12.06	11.39	10.97	10.67	10.46	10.29	10.16	10.05	9.89	9.72	9.55	9.47	9.38	9.29	9.20	9.11	9.02
6	13.75	10.92	9.78	9.15	8.75	8.47	8.26	8.10	7.98	7.87	7.72	7.56	7.40	7.31	7.23	7.14	7.06	6.97	6.88
7	12.25	9.55	8.45	7.85	7.46	7.19	6.99	6.84	6.72	6.62	6.47	6.31	6.16	6.07	5.99	5.91	5.82	5.74	5.65
8	11.26	8.65	7.59	7.01	6.63	6.37	6.18	6.03	5.91	5.81	5.67	5.52	5.36	5.28	5.20	5.12	5.03	4.95	4.86
9	10.56	8.02	6.99	6.42	6.06	5.80	5.61	5.47	5.35	5.26	5.11	4.96	4.81	4.73	4.65	4.57	4.48	4.40	4.31
10	10.04	7.56	6.55	5.99	5.64	5.39	5.20	5.06	4.94	4.85	4.71	4.56	4.41	4.33	4.25	4.17	4.08	4.00	3.91
11	9.65	7.21	6.22	5.67	5.32	5.07	4.89	4.74	4.63	4.54	4.40	4.25	4.10	4.02	3.94	3.86	3.78	3.69	3.60
12	9.33	6.93	5.95	5.41	5.06	4.82	4.64	4.50	4.39	4.30	4.16	4.01	3.86	3.78	3.70	3.62	3.54	3.45	3.36
13	9.07	6.70	5.74	5.21	4.86	4.62	4.44	4.30	4.19	4.10	3.96	3.82	3.66	3.59	3.51	3.43	3.34	3.25	3.17
14	8.86	6.51	5.56	5.04	4.69	4.46	4.28	4.14	4.03	3.94	3.80	3.66	3.51	3.43	3.35	3.27	3.18	3.09	3.00
15	8.68	6.36	5.42	4.89	4.56	4.32	4.14	4.00	3.89	3.80	3.67	3.52	3.37	3.29	3.21	3.13	3.05	2.96	2.87
16	8.53	6.23	5.29	4.77	4.44	4.20	4.03	3.89	3.78	3.69	3.55	3.41	3.26	3.18	3.10	3.02	2.93	2.84	2.75
17	8.40	6.11	5.18	4.67	4.34	4.10	3.93	3.79	3.68	3.59	3.46	3.31	3.16	3.08	3.00	2.92	2.83	2.75	2.65
18	8.29	6.01	5.09	4.58	4.25	4.01	3.84	3.71	3.60	3.51	3.37	3.23	3.08	3.00	2.92	2.84	2.75	2.66	2.57
19	8.18	5.93	5.01	4.50	4.17	3.94	3.77	3.63	3.52	3.43	3.30	3.15	3.00	2.92	2.84	2.76	2.67	2.58	2.49
20	8.10	5.85	4.94	4.43	4.10	3.87	3.70	3.56	3.46	3.37	3.23	3.09	2.94	2.86	2.78	2.69	2.61	2.52	2.42
21	8.02	5.78	4.87	4.37	4.04	3.81	3.64	3.51	3.40	3.31	3.17	3.03	2.88	2.80	2.72	2.64	2.55	2.46	2.36
22	7.95	5.72	4.82	4.31	3.99	3.76	3.59	3.45	3.35	3.26	3.12	2.98	2.83	2.75	2.67	2.58	2.50	2.40	2.31
23	7.88	5.66	4.76	4.26	3.94	3.71	3.54	3.41	3.30	3.21	3.07	2.93	2.78	2.70	2.62	2.54	2.45	2.35	2.26
24	7.82	5.61	4.72	4.22	3.90	3.67	3.50	3.36	3.26	3.17	3.03	2.89	2.74	2.66	2.58	2.49	2.40	2.31	2.21
25	7.77	5.57	4.68	4.18	3.85	3.63	3.46	3.32	3.22	3.13	2.99	2.85	2.70	2.62	2.54	2.45	2.36	2.27	2.17
26	7.72	5.53	4.64	4.14	3.82	3.59	3.42	3.29	3.18	3.09	2.96	2.81	2.66	2.58	2.50	2.42	2.33	2.23	2.13
27	7.68	5.49	4.60	4.11	3.78	3.56	3.39	3.26	3.15	3.06	2.93	2.78	2.63	2.55	2.47	2.38	2.29	2.20	2.10
28	7.64	5.45	4.57	4.07	3.75	3.53	3.36	3.23	3.12	3.03	2.90	2.75	2.60	2.52	2.44	2.35	2.26	2.17	2.06
29	7.60	5.42	4.54	4.04	3.73	3.50	3.33	3.20	3.09	3.00	2.87	2.73	2.57	2.49	2.41	2.33	2.23	2.14	2.03
30	7.56	5.39	4.51	4.02	3.70	3.47	3.30	3.17	3.07	2.98	2.84	2.70	2.55	2.47	2.39	2.30	2.21	2.11	2.01
40	7.31	5.18	4.31	3.83	3.51	3.29	3.12	2.99	2.89	2.80	2.66	2.52	2.37	2.29	2.20	2.11	2.02	1.92	1.80
60	7.08	4.98	4.13	3.65	3.34	3.12	2.95	2.82	2.72	2.63	2.50	2.35	2.20	2.12	2.03	1.94	1.84	1.73	1.60
120	6.85	4.79	3.95	3.48	3.17	2.96	2.79	2.66	2.56	2.47	2.34	2.19	2.03	1.95	1.86	1.76	1.66	1.53	1.38
∞	6.63	4.61	3.78	3.32	3.02	2.80	2.64	2.51	2.41	2.32	2.18	2.04	1.88	1.79	1.70	1.59	1.47	1.32	1.00

Source: E. S. Pearson and H. O. Hartley, *Biometrika Tables for Statisticians*, Vol. 1, Table 18 with permission.

Table B.4 Present Value of $1 (*PVIF*)

Period	1%	2%	3%	4%	5%	6%	7%	8%	9%	10%	Period
01	.99010	.98039	.97007	.96154	.95233	.94340	.93458	.92593	.91743	.90909	01
02	.98030	.96117	.94260	.92456	.90703	.89000	.87344	.85734	.84168	.82645	02
03	.97059	.94232	.91514	.88900	.86384	.83962	.81639	.79383	.77228	.75131	03
04	.96098	.92385	.88849	.85480	.82270	.79209	.76290	.73503	.70883	.68301	04
05	.95147	.90573	.86261	.82193	.78353	.74726	.71299	.68058	.64993	.62092	05
06	.94204	.88797	.83748	.79031	.74622	.70496	.66634	.63017	.59627	.56447	06
07	.93272	.87056	.81309	.75992	.71063	.66506	.62275	.58349	.54705	.51316	07
08	.92348	.85349	.78941	.73069	.67684	.62741	.58201	.54027	.50189	.46651	08
09	.91434	.83675	.76642	.70259	.64461	.59190	.54393	.50025	.46043	.42410	09
10	.90529	.82035	.74409	.67556	.61391	.55839	.50835	.46319	.42241	.38554	10
11	.89632	.80426	.72242	.64958	.58468	.52679	.47509	.42888	.38753	.35049	11
12	.88745	.78849	.70138	.62460	.55684	.49697	.44401	.39711	.35553	.31683	12
13	.87866	.77303	.68095	.60057	.53032	.46884	.41496	.36770	.32618	.28966	13
14	.86996	.75787	.66112	.57747	.50507	.44230	.38782	.34046	.29925	.26333	14
15	.86135	.74301	.64186	.55526	.48102	.41726	.36245	.31524	.27454	.23939	15
16	.85282	.72845	.62317	.53391	.45811	.39365	.33873	.29189	.25187	.21763	16
17	.84436	.71416	.60502	.51337	.43630	.37136	.31657	.27027	.23107	.19784	17
18	.83602	.70016	.58739	.49363	.41552	.35034	.29586	.25025	.21199	.17986	18
19	.82774	.68643	.57029	.47464	.39573	.33051	.27651	.23171	.19449	.16354	19
20	.81954	.67297	.55367	.45639	.37689	.31180	.25842	.21455	.17843	.14864	20
21	.81143	.65978	.53755	.44883	.35894	.29415	.24151	.19866	.16370	.13513	21
22	.80340	.64684	.52189	.42195	.34185	.27750	.22571	.18394	.15018	.12285	22
23	.79544	.63414	.50669	.40573	.32557	.26180	.21095	.17031	.13778	.11168	23
24	.78757	.62172	.49193	.39012	.31007	.24698	.19715	.15770	.12640	.10153	24
25	.77977	.60953	.47760	.37512	.29530	.23300	.18425	.14602	.11597	.09230	25

Table B.4 Present Value of $1 (*PVIF*) (continued)

Period	11%	12%	13%	14%	15%	16%	17%	18%	19%	20%	Period
01	.90090	.89286	.88496	.87719	.86957	.86207	.85470	.84746	.84043	.83333	01
02	.81162	.79719	.78315	.76947	.75614	.74316	.73051	.71818	.70616	.69444	02
03	.73119	.71178	.69305	.67497	.65752	.64066	.62437	.60863	.59342	.57870	03
04	.65873	.63552	.61332	.59208	.57175	.55229	.53365	.51579	.49867	.48225	04
05	.59345	.56743	.54276	.51937	.49718	.47611	.45611	.43711	.41905	.40188	05
06	.53464	.50663	.48032	.45559	.43233	.41044	.38984	.37043	.35214	.33490	06
07	.48166	.45235	.42506	.39964	.37594	.35383	.33320	.31392	.29592	.27908	07
08	.43393	.40388	.37616	.35056	.32690	.30503	.28478	.26604	.24867	.23257	08
09	.39092	.36061	.33288	.30751	.28426	.26295	.24340	.22546	.20897	.19381	09
10	.35218	.32197	.29459	.26974	.24718	.22668	.20804	.19106	.17560	.16151	10
11	.31728	.28748	.26070	.23662	.21494	.19542	.17781	.16192	.14756	.13459	11
12	.28584	.25667	.23071	.20756	.18691	.16846	.15197	.13722	.12400	.11216	12
13	.25751	.22917	.20416	.18207	.16253	.14523	.12989	.11629	.10420	.09346	13
14	.23199	.20462	.18068	.15971	.14133	.12520	.11102	.09855	.08757	.07789	14
15	.20900	.18270	.15989	.14010	.12289	.10793	.09489	.08352	.07359	.06491	15
16	.18829	.16312	.14150	.12289	.10686	.09304	.08110	.07073	.06184	.05409	16
17	.16963	.14564	.12522	.10780	.09293	.08021	.06932	.05998	.05196	.04507	17
18	.15282	.13004	.11081	.09456	.08080	.06914	.05925	.05083	.04367	.03756	18
19	.13768	.11611	.09806	.08295	.07026	.05961	.05064	.04308	.03669	.03130	19
20	.12403	.10367	.08678	.07276	.06110	.05139	.04328	.03651	.03084	.02608	20
21	.11174	.09256	.07680	.06383	.05313	.04430	.03699	.03094	.02591	.02174	21
22	.10067	.08264	.06796	.05599	.04620	.03819	.03162	.02622	.02178	.01811	22
23	.09069	.07379	.06014	.04911	.04017	.03292	.02702	.02222	.01830	.01509	23
24	.08170	.06588	.05322	.04308	.03493	.02838	.02310	.01883	.01538	.01258	24
25	.07361	.05882	.04710	.03779	.03038	.02447	.01974	.01596	.01292	.01048	25

Table B.5 Present Value of an Annuity of $1 (*PVIFA*)

Period	1%	2%	3%	4%	5%	6%	7%	8%	9%	10%	Period
01	.9901	.9804	.9709	.9615	.9524	.9434	.9346	.9259	.9174	.9091	01
02	1.9704	1.9416	1.9135	1.8861	1.8594	1.8334	1.8080	1.7833	1.7591	1.7355	02
03	2.9410	2.8839	2.8286	2.7751	2.7233	2.6730	2.6243	2.5771	2.5313	2.4868	03
04	3.9020	3.8077	3.7171	3.6299	3.5459	3.4651	3.3872	3.3121	3.2397	3.1699	04
05	4.8535	4.7134	4.5797	4.4518	4.3295	4.2123	4.1002	3.9927	3.8896	3.7908	05
06	5.7955	5.6014	5.4172	5.2421	5.0757	4.9173	4.7665	4.6229	4.4859	4.3553	06
07	6.7282	6.4720	6.2302	6.0020	5.7863	5.5824	5.3893	5.2064	5.0329	4.8684	07
08	7.6517	7.3254	7.0196	6.7327	6.4632	6.2093	5.9713	5.7466	5.5348	5.3349	08
09	8.5661	8.1622	7.7861	7.4353	7.1078	6.8017	6.5152	6.2469	5.9852	5.7590	09
10	9.4714	8.9825	8.7302	8.1109	7.7217	7.3601	7.0236	6.7101	6.4176	6.1446	10
11	10.3677	9.7868	9.2526	8.7604	8.3064	7.8868	7.4987	7.1389	6.8052	6.4951	11
12	11.2552	10.5753	9.9589	9.3850	8.8632	8.3838	7.9427	7.5361	7.1601	6.8137	12
13	12.1338	11.3483	10.6349	9.9856	9.3935	8.8527	8.3576	7.9038	7.4869	7.1034	13
14	13.0088	12.1062	11.2960	10.5631	9.8986	9.2950	8.7454	8.2442	7.7860	7.3667	14
15	13.8651	12.8492	11.9379	11.1183	10.3796	9.7122	9.1079	8.5595	8.0607	7.6061	15
16	14.7180	13.5777	12.5610	11.6522	10.8377	10.1059	9.4466	8.8514	8.3126	7.8237	16
17	15.5624	14.2918	13.1660	12.1656	11.2740	10.4772	9.7632	9.1216	8.5435	8.0215	17
18	16.3984	14.9920	13.7534	12.6592	11.6895	10.8276	10.0591	9.3719	8.7556	8.2014	18
19	17.2201	15.2684	14.3237	13.1339	12.0853	11.1581	10.3356	9.6036	8.9501	8.3649	19
20	18.0457	16.3514	14.8774	13.5903	12.4622	11.4699	10.5940	9.8181	9.1285	8.5136	20
21	18.8571	17.0111	15.4149	14.0291	12.8211	11.7640	10.8355	10.0168	9.2922	8.6487	21
22	19.6605	17.6581	15.9368	14.4511	13.1630	12.0416	11.0612	10.2007	9.4424	8.7715	22
23	20.4559	18.2921	16.4435	14.8568	13.4885	12.3033	11.2722	10.3710	9.5802	8.8832	23
24	21.2435	18.9139	16.9355	15.2469	13.7986	12.5503	11.4693	10.5287	9.7066	8.9847	24
25	22.0233	19.5234	17.4181	15.6220	14.9039	12.7833	11.6536	10.6748	9.8226	9.0770	25

Table B.5 Present Value of an Annuity of $1 (*PVIFA*) (continued)

Period	11%	12%	13%	14%	15%	16%	17%	18%	19%	20%	Period
01	.9009	.8929	.8850	.8772	.8696	.8621	.8547	.8475	.8403	.8333	01
02	1.7125	1.6901	1.6681	1.6467	1.6257	1.6052	1.5852	1.5656	1.5465	1.5278	02
03	2.4437	2.4018	2.3612	2.3216	2.2832	2.2459	2.2096	2.1743	2.1399	2.1065	03
04	3.1024	3.0373	2.9745	2.9137	2.8550	2.7982	2.7432	2.6901	2.6386	2.5887	04
05	3.6959	3.6048	3.5172	3.4331	3.3522	3.2743	3.1993	3.1272	3.0576	2.9906	05
06	4.2305	4.1114	3.9976	3.8887	3.7845	3.6847	3.5892	3.4976	3.4098	3.3255	06
07	4.7122	4.5638	4.4226	4.2883	4.1604	4.0386	3.9224	3.8115	3.7057	3.6046	07
08	5.1461	4.9676	4.7988	4.6389	4.4873	4.3436	4.2072	4.0776	3.9544	3.8372	08
09	5.5370	5.3282	5.1317	4.9464	4.7716	4.6065	4.4506	4.3030	4.1633	4.0310	09
10	5.8892	5.6502	5.4262	5.2161	5.0188	4.8332	4.6586	4.4941	4.3389	4.1925	10
11	6.2065	5.9377	5.6869	5.4527	5.2337	5.0286	4.8364	4.6560	4.4865	4.3271	11
12	6.4924	6.1944	5.9176	5.6603	5.4206	5.1971	4.9884	4.7932	4.6105	4.4392	12
13	6.7499	6.4235	6.1218	5.8424	5.5831	5.3423	5.1183	4.9095	4.7147	4.5327	13
14	6.9819	6.6282	6.3025	6.0021	5.7245	5.4675	5.2293	5.0081	4.8023	4.6106	14
15	7.1909	6.8109	6.4624	6.1422	5.8474	5.5755	5.3242	5.0916	4.8759	4.6755	15
16	7.3792	6.9740	6.6039	6.2651	5.9542	5.6685	5.4053	5.1624	4.9377	4.7296	16
17	7.5488	7.1196	6.7291	6.3729	6.0472	5.7487	5.4746	5.2223	4.9897	4.7746	17
18	7.7016	7.2497	6.8389	6.4674	6.1280	5.8178	5.5339	5.2732	5.0333	4.8122	18
19	7.8393	7.3650	6.9380	6.5504	6.1982	5.8775	5.5845	5.3176	5.0700	4.8435	19
20	7.9633	7.4694	7.0248	6.6231	6.2593	5.9288	5.6278	5.3527	5.1009	4.8696	20
21	8.0751	7.5620	7.1016	6.6870	6.3125	5.9731	5.6648	5.3837	5.1268	4.8913	21
22	8.1757	7.6446	7.1695	6.7429	6.3587	6.0113	5.6964	5.4099	5.1486	4.9094	22
23	8.2664	7.7184	7.2297	6.7921	6.3988	6.0442	5.7234	5.4321	5.1668	4.9245	23
24	8.3481	7.7843	7.2829	6.8351	6.4338	6.0726	5.7465	5.4509	5.1822	4.9371	24
25	8.4217	7.8431	7.3300	6.8729	6.4641	6.0971	5.7662	5.4669	5.1951	4.9476	25

Table B.6 Durbin-Watson Statistic for 2.5% Significance (One-Tail) or 5.0% Significance (Two-Tail)

	$m = 1$		$m = 2$		$m = 3$		$m = 4$		$m = 5$	
n	d_L	d_U	d_L	d_U	d_L	d_U	d_L	d_U	d_L	d_U
15	0.95	1.23	0.83	1.40	0.71	1.61	0.59	1.84	0.48	2.09
16	0.98	1.24	0.86	1.40	0.75	1.59	0.64	1.80	0.53	2.03
17	1.01	1.25	0.90	1.40	0.79	1.58	0.68	1.77	0.57	1.98
18	1.03	1.26	0.93	1.40	0.82	1.56	0.72	1.74	0.62	1.93
19	1.06	1.28	0.96	1.41	0.86	1.55	0.76	1.73	0.66	1.90
20	1.08	1.28	0.99	1.41	0.89	1.55	0.79	1.72	0.70	1.87
21	1.10	1.30	1.01	1.41	0.92	1.54	0.83	1.69	0.73	1.84
22	1.12	1.31	1.04	1.42	0.95	1.54	0.86	1.68	0.77	1.82
23	1.14	1.32	1.06	1.42	0.97	1.54	0.89	1.67	0.80	1.80
24	1.16	1.33	1.08	1.43	1.00	1.54	0.91	1.66	0.83	1.79
25	1.18	1.34	1.10	1.43	1.02	1.54	0.94	1.65	0.86	1.77
26	1.19	1.35	1.12	1.44	1.04	1.54	0.96	1.65	0.88	1.76
27	1.21	1.36	1.13	1.44	1.06	1.54	0.99	1.64	0.91	1.75
28	1.22	1.37	1.15	1.45	1.08	1.54	1.01	1.64	0.93	1.74
29	1.24	1.38	1.17	1.45	1.10	1.54	1.03	1.63	0.96	1.73
30	1.25	1.38	1.18	1.46	1.12	1.54	1.05	1.63	0.98	1.73
31	1.26	1.39	1.20	1.47	1.13	1.55	1.07	1.63	1.00	1.72
32	1.27	1.40	1.21	1.47	1.15	1.55	1.08	1.63	1.02	1.71
33	1.28	1.41	1.22	1.48	1.16	1.55	1.10	1.63	1.04	1.71
34	1.29	1.41	1.24	1.48	1.17	1.55	1.12	1.63	1.06	1.70
35	1.30	1.42	1.25	1.48	1.19	1.55	1.13	1.63	1.07	1.70
36	1.31	1.43	1.26	1.49	1.20	1.56	1.15	1.63	1.09	1.70
37	1.32	1.43	1.27	1.49	1.21	1.56	1.16	1.62	1.10	1.70
38	1.33	1.44	1.28	1.50	1.23	1.56	1.17	1.62	1.12	1.70
39	1.34	1.44	1.29	1.50	1.24	1.56	1.19	1.63	1.13	1.69
40	1.35	1.45	1.30	1.51	1.25	1.57	1.20	1.63	1.15	1.69
45	1.39	1.48	1.34	1.53	1.30	1.58	1.25	1.63	1.21	1.69
50	1.42	1.50	1.38	1.54	1.34	1.59	1.30	1.64	1.26	1.69
55	1.45	1.52	1.41	1.56	1.37	1.60	1.33	1.64	1.30	1.69
60	1.47	1.54	1.44	1.57	1.40	1.61	1.37	1.65	1.33	1.69
65	1.49	1.55	1.46	1.59	1.43	1.63	1.40	1.66	1.36	1.69
70	1.51	1.57	1.48	1.60	1.45	1.63	1.42	1.66	1.39	1.70
75	1.53	1.58	1.50	1.61	1.47	1.64	1.45	1.67	1.42	1.70
80	1.54	1.59	1.52	1.63	1.49	1.65	1.47	1.67	1.44	1.70
85	1.56	1.60	1.53	1.63	1.51	1.66	1.49	1.68	1.46	1.71
90	1.57	1.61	1.55	1.64	1.53	1.66	1.50	1.69	1.48	1.71
95	1.58	1.62	1.56	1.65	1.54	1.67	1.52	1.69	1.50	1.71
100	1.59	1.63	1.57	1.65	1.55	1.67	1.53	1.70	1.51	1.72

m = number of independent variables
n = number of observations
Source: From J. Durbin and G. S. Watson, "Testing for Serial Correlation in Least-Squares Regression," *Biometrika,* Vol. 38 (1951); 159–177. With the permission of the authors and the Trustees of *Biometrika.*

Table B.7

Critical Values for the Dickey-Fuller Test

	Sample Size			
	25	**50**	**100**	∞
F ratio	7.24	6.73	6.49	6.25
AR(1) model	2.16	2.08	2.03	2.00
AR(1) model with constant	0.72	0.66	0.63	0.60
AR(1) model with constant and time trend	−0.15	−0.15	−0.28	−0.33

D. Dickey and W. Fuller, "Likelihood Ratio Tests for Autoregressive Time Series with A Unit Root," *Econometrica*, 49, 1981.

APPENDIX C

CHECK ANSWERS TO SELECTED END-OF-CHAPTER EXERCISES

CHAPTER 1

CASE EXERCISE

5. \$1,200,000

CHAPTER 2

1. Budget = \$875 million
2. c. $v = 0.067$
4. a. 0.0062

APPENDIX 2A

1. d. $Q^* = 8$ ($MR = MC = 20$)
3. a. $100 - 12Q + 1.5Q^2$
5. b. $Q^* = 5$
8. a. 25 units newspaper advertising

CHAPTER 3

2. 44%
5. Chow: 11.528 million
7. $P = \$90$
8. a. $E_D = -0.45$
11. a. −3%
12. a. $E_D = -4.01$
16. a. $E_X = 1.34$. Close substitutes.
19. $Q_{2006} = 5{,}169$, $Q_{2007} = 3{,}953$

CHAPTER 4

2. c. $Y = 11.148 + 1.492X$
4. d. $R^2 = 0.885$
5. a. Income coefficient = 5.9492
8. b. $E_A = 0.98$
14. a. $Y' = -14.7351 + 3.9214$ Size $+ 3.5851$ Rooms -0.1181 Age -2.8317 Garage

CASE EXERCISE—DEMAND ESTIMATION

2. $E_D = -3.38$

APPENDIX 4A

3. a. $Y' = 1.210 + 0.838$ Selling Expenses, $R^2 = 0.93$
5. a. $S' = 247.644 + 0.3926\text{Advertising} - 0.7339\text{Price}$
   $\text{Log}(S') = 2.4482 + 0.7296\text{LogAdvertising} - 0.2406\text{LogPrice}$

CHAPTER 5

3. b. Sum(Actual/Forecast)/6 = 636.6%/6 = 106.1%, thus +6%
4. b. $GNP = C + I + G = 635 + 120 + 200 = 955$
8. b. $Y'_{2007} = 259.03$
9. a. December 2005 = 468
11. a. $Q = 10{,}200(000)$

CHAPTER 6

1. Both increase
3. Outsource abroad and buy foreign assets
6. 50% decline. Relative purchasing power parity

CHAPTER 7

3. b. 10 or 11 men
5. c. $AP_x = 6X - 0.4X^2$
9. a. 4.88%

CASE EXERCISE

4. $E_K = 0.415$

APPENDIX 7A

1. d. $Q^* = 43.231$

CHAPTER 8

3. a. \$10,000
8. a. $TC = 150 + 200Q - 9Q^2 + 0.25Q^3$

CASE EXERCISE

1. \$4.55

APPENDIX 8A

1. a. $L^* = 2.5$ units
3. a. \$10

CHAPTER 9

2. a. $Q^* = \$574.08$ (million)
6. a. \$30,000,000

CASE EXERCISE—COST FUNCTIONS

5. $Q^* = 1{,}675$

CASE EXERCISE—CHARTER AIRLINE

3. 23,900

APPENDIX 9A

1. c. $C = \$803.51$

CHAPTER 10

5. a. $P = \$8$
8. b. $P^* = \$1{,}220$
10. b. \$900,000 on advertising

CHAPTER 11

3. c. $Q^* = 125$
5. e. $\pi^* = \$263{,}625$
6. b. $P^* = \$60$
11. a. ROI = 14.2%
12. a. ROI = 12.98%

CHAPTER 12

2. a. $P^* = \$145$, $Q_A^* = 30$
5. a. $P^* = \$9{,}666.70$
6. c. $P^* = \$125$

CHAPTER 13

3. b. Dominant strategy for AMC is to "Not Abide"

5. {$150, Match}, No
6. Least should pass
8. {Late, Late} is one of two pure Nash equilibria.

Chapter 14

1. $P_{US} = \$12$
3. a. $\pi = -20 + 96Q_1 + 76Q_2 - 2Q_1^2 - Q_2^2$
11. 26 seats

Chapter 15

3. High interest rates, large principal, long term, unsecured
4. Vertical integration if power plant dependent on this type of coal. Otherwise, long-term supply contracts.

Case Exercise—Incentive Contract

5. $1,200,000

Case Exercise—Division of Investment Banking Fees

1. Lead underwriter = $97 million
   Syndicate Comanager = 0
   Syndicate Member 3 = $1 million
   Syndicate Member 4 = 0
   Syndicate Member 5 = $2 million

Chapter 15A

4. Electricity, T bills
5. $1.3 million.
   Use open bidding, multiple-rounds, highest-wins-and-pays
11. Apple's expected profit is $1.5 million less from understatement.

Chapter 16

4. a. HHI before = 1,964
8. b. $\pi^* = \$450$ million
14. Coordinate on Nash equilibrium (Lucent Imitate, Motorola Develop) in joint venture with compensation of at least $1 billion to Motorola.

Chapter 17

2. IRR = 9.1%
4. b. $NCF_{10} = \$5,560$
6. a. i. IRR = 14.94%
8. $k_e = 13.4\%$
10. b. $k'_e = 13\%$
12. $k_a = 12.3\%$
14. b. Power plant: $NPV_{@12\%} = -\$22.71$ million

Case Exercise

1. B/C ratio = 1.90

INDEX

N

Q

R

Notes

Notes

Notes

Notes

Notes

Notes

Chapter 16: Government Regulation

Chapter 17: Long-Term Investment Analysis

Appendix A: The Time Value of Money

🌐 This symbol denotes an International Perspectives example.